Music Library Association
Index and Bibliography Series

Mark Palkovic, Series Editor

1. *An Alphabetical Index to Claudio Monteverdi Tutte Le Opere,* edited by the Bibliography Committee of the New York Chapter, MLA, 1964.
2. *An Alphabetical Index to Hector Berlioz Werke,* edited by the Bibliography Committee of the New York Chapter, MLA, 1964.
3. *A Checklist of Music Bibliographies and Indexes in Progress and Unpublished,* compiled by the MLA Publications Committee, Walter Gerboth, chair; Shirley Branner; and James B. Coover; 1965; 2nd ed. by James Pruett, 1969; 3rd ed. by Linda Solow, 1974; 4th ed. by Dee Baily, 1982.
4. *A Concordance of the Thematic Indexes to the Instrumental Works of Antonio Vivaldi,* by Lenore Coral, 1965; 2nd ed., 1972.
5. *An Alphabetical Index to Tomás Luis de Victoria Opera Omnia,* edited by the Bibliography Committee of the New York Chapter, MLA, 1966.
6. *An Alphabetical Index to Robert Schumann Werke: Schumann Index, Part 1,* compiled by Michael Ochs, 1967.
7. *An Alphabetical Index to the Solo Songs of Robert Schumann: Schumann Index, Part 2,* compiled by William J. Weichlein, 1967.
8. *An Index to Maurice Frost's "English & Scottish Psalm & Hymn Tunes,"* by Kirby Rogers, 1967.
9. *Speculum: An Index of Musically Related Articles and Book Reviews,* compiled by Arthur S. Wolff, 1970; 2nd ed., 1981.
10. *An Index to "Das Chorwerk," Vols. 1–110,* compiled by Michael Ochs, 1970.
11. *Bach Aria Index,* compiled by Miriam Whaples, 1971.
12. *Annotated Bibliography of Writing about Music in Puerto Rico,* compiled by Annie Figueroa Thompson, 1975.
13. *Analyses of Twentieth-Century Music, 1940–1970,* compiled by Arthur Wenk, 1975.
14. *Analyses of Twentieth-Century Music, 1970–1975,* compiled by Arthur Wenk, 1976; 2nd ed., 1984.
15. *Analyses of Nineteenth-Century Music: 1940–1975,* compiled by Arthur Wenk, 1976; 2nd ed., *1940–1980*, 1984.
16. *Writings on Contemporary Music Notation,* compiled by Gerald Warfield, 1976.
17. *Literature for Voices in Combination with Electronic and Tape Music: An Annotated Bibliography,* compiled by J. Michele Edwards, 1977.
18. *Johannes Brahms: A Guide to His Autographs in Facsimile,* by Peter Dedel, 1978.
19. *Source: Music of the Avant Garde; Annotated List of Contents and Cumulative Indices,* by Michael D. Williams, 1978.
20. *Eighteenth-Century American Secular Music Manuscripts: An Inventory,* compiled by James J. Fuld and Mary Wallace Davidson, 1980.
21. *Popular Secular Music in America through 1800: A Checklist of Manuscripts in North American Collections,* compiled by Kate Van Winkle Keller, 1980.
22. *Palestrina: An Index to the Casimiri, Kalmus, and Haberl Editions,* by Allison Hall, 1980.
23. *E. H. Fellowes: An Index to The English Madrigalists and The English School of Lutenist Song Writers,* by Allison Hall, 1984.
24. *Music in New York during the American Revolution: An Inventory of Musical References in "Rivington's New York Gazette,"* by Gillian B. Anderson with editorial assistance by Neil Ratliff, 1987.
25. *Analyses of Nineteenth- and Twentieth-Century Music, 1940–1985,* by Arthur B. Wenk, 1987.
26. *Opera Performances in Video Format: A Checklist of Commercially Released Performances,* by Charles Croissant, 1991.
27. *A Thematic Catalog of the Works of Robert Valentine,* by J. Bradford Young, 1994.
28. *Pro-Musica: Patronage, Performance, and a Periodical—An Index to the Quarterlies,* by Paula Elliot, 1997.
29. *Musical Memorials for Musicians: A Guide to Selected Compositions,* by R. Michael Fling, 2001.
30. *Music Inspired by Art: A Guide to Recordings,* by Gary Evans, 2002.
31. *An Index to Music Published in* The Etude *Magazine, 1883–1957,* by E. Douglas Bomberger, 2004.
32. *Bibliographic Control of Music, 1897–2000,* by Richard P. Smiraglia, compiled and edited with J. Bradford Young, 2006.
33. *Grawemeyer Award for Music Composition: The First Twenty Years,* by Karen R. Little and Julia Graepel, 2007.

Grawemeyer Award for Music Composition

The First Twenty Years

Karen R. Little
Julia Graepel
with assistance from
R. Scott Adams

Music Library Association
Index and Bibliography Series, No. 33

THE SCARECROW PRESS, INC.
Lanham, Maryland • Toronto • Plymouth, UK
And
MUSIC LIBRARY ASSOCIATION, INC.
2007

SCARECROW PRESS, INC.

Published in the United States of America
by Scarecrow Press, Inc.
A wholly owned subsidiary of
The Rowman & Littlefield Publishing Group, Inc.
4501 Forbes Boulevard, Suite 200, Lanham, Maryland 20706
www.scarecrowpress.com

Estover Road
Plymouth PL6 7PY
United Kingdom

British Library Cataloguing in Publication Information Available

Library of Congress Cataloging-in-Publication Data

Little, Karen R.
Grawemeyer award for music composition : the first twenty years / Karen R. Little, Julia Graepel.
p. cm. — (Music Library Association index and bibliography series ; no. 33)
Includes bibliographical references and index.
ISBN-13: 978-0-8108-5694-3 (hardcover : alk. paper)
ISBN-10: 0-8108-5694-8 (hardcover : alk. paper)
1. Grawemeyer Collection of Contemporary Music—Catalogs. 2. Music—20th century—Bibliography—Catalogs. 3. Music—21st century—Bibliography—Catalogs. 4. Dwight Anderson Music Library—Catalogs. I. Graepel, Julia, 1978– II. Title.
ML136.L85L57 2007
016.7809'04—dc22

2006025310

Printed in the United States of America

∞™ The paper used in this publication meets the minimum requirements of American National Standard for Information Sciences—Permanence of Paper for Printed Library Materials, ANSI/NISO Z39.48-1992.
Manufactured in the United States of America.

Contents

Acknowledgments

Many people deserve appreciation for their roles, both large and small, in compiling this catalog. The first, Dr. Christopher Doane, dean of the School of Music at the University of Louisville, deserves thanks for his gentle suggestion that the time was right for such a work and for his thoughtful follow-through of support in the form of a graduate assistantship loaned to the music library from the Music Theory and Composition Division of the School of Music. Dr. Steve Rouse, head of that division at the school, was responsible for recruiting a wonderful graduate assistant to do the bulk of the editorial work on the catalog. R. Scott Adams worked tirelessly as this graduate assistant. More than "just" a graduate assistant, Scott enthusiastically tackled all tasks related to the compilation of the catalog—both large and small, boring and exciting. Likewise, Dr. Paul Brink, professor of theory and composition and former coordinator of Grawemeyer Award for Music Composition provided feedback on the content of the Introduction portion of the catalog.

We would be remiss if we did not also recognize the untiring work of Anderson Music Library staff members Carolyn Gettler and Rachel Hodge, who helped transform brief cataloging records to the full cataloging records that comprise the main section of this catalog. In addition, the staff of the University of Louisville Libraries, Office of Libraries Technology, headed by Weiling Liu, provided invaluable assistance. Mark Paul, assistant director of that division, provided unending technical support as he implemented the move of the individual bibliographic records from our online catalog to the printed page. Without all of these individuals, this catalog would not have been possible and the authors extend their thanks to them.

Introduction

The University of Louisville's annual Grawemeyer Award for Music Composition is the largest monetary award offered in its field. The prize's objective can best be summarized using the description from the official website:

> The University of Louisville offers an international prize in recognition of outstanding achievement by a living composer in a large musical genre: choral, orchestral, chamber, electronic, song-cycle, dance, opera, musical theater, extended solo work and more.

The award was first offered in 1985 thanks to the grand and generous vision of H. Charles Grawemeyer and his establishment of a $9 million endowment fund at the University of Louisville in Louisville, Kentucky. Initially, the monetary award to the winner was $150,000. In recent years, the award amount has risen to $200,000. From its first year to the present, the number of submissions, consisting of a score and a professional-quality recording, has ranged from 95 to 210 entries annually. Entry rules stipulate that each submission have had its premiere in a five-year period prior to the year of submission and that the work be submitted not by the composer but rather by a music professional such as a conductor, performer, school, or publisher. One of the hallmarks of the award, felt critically important by Mr. Grawemeyer, is the high priority placed on the opinions of laypersons in the final selection of the winners.

The Dwight Anderson Memorial Music Library at the University of Louisville houses these submitted scores, forming one of the largest new music collections in North America. Although the collection is most regularly used by students and faculty at the University of Louisville, it is accessible to any interested persons for use within the library.

The huge majority of the collection consists of scores and recordings that are currently unpublished or unavailable for purchase. Therefore, it is a particularly valuable resource for those who are interested in studying contemporary compositions or for those who simply wish to stay current on the progression and development of contemporary art music. And as an international award, each award year can be seen as an inclusive snapshot of that year's trends and advancements in contemporary art music across the world.

The following catalog seeks to accurately detail the score holdings of the collection. The catalog contains a listing of all the scores entered from award year 1985 through 2005 alphabetized by composer. Each entry includes composer name, including birth and death dates when available, title, publication information if published, a physical description of the score, duration, when available, instrumentation, commissioning information, and the entry's call number. When a composition is submitted in more than one award year, the original entry's call number is followed by the statement, "Re-entered as" followed by its new call number.

Two appendixes, one listing the winning composer and work by year and one listing all composers' names submitting entries by year, are included. The work concludes with an index listing names and genres. The names listed in the index are those who had secondary roles in the production of the composition, such as poets, librettists, and commissioning agents for the new work.

A couple of anomalies exist in the catalog. One concerns an entry policy in place during the early years of the award. When the award was initiated in 1985, the long-term significance of an archive of submissions was not immediately recognized so composers were given the option of having their submitted materials returned to them. As a result, during the first few years of the award, a number of composers did request their scores be returned and the archive is missing those materials. After a couple of years, when the concept of maintaining an archive was adopted, that policy changed and subsequently composers were required to allow the University of Louisville to retain all submitted materials. Although the library has retained the vast majority of the entries, the library does not hold some materials from those early years. This is noted in the catalog with the statement, after the brief bibliographic entry, "No materials available."

Another anomaly relates to the two years that the prize was not awarded. The first of the two years is 1988, when the final panel of judges decided not to declare a winner. Although there was no winner announced from this group of composers, all entries are archived and the catalog lists all of the 118 submissions from that year. The second anomaly affects award year 1999. This is the year the date of the award announcement was postponed; therefore, no scores were called for during the subsequent year and the recipient was announced as the 2000 award winner. The collection reflects this change by grouping that year's archives under the year 2000.

The Grawemeyer Award in Music Composition is one of the world's most important honors in new music; therefore, the archived collection of entries housed at the University of Louisville's Dwight Anderson Music Library must be made available to all. Not only are the winners of great consequence to recent music history but the totality of the entered compositions and their composers, as they represent every major region in the world, demonstrate the development of contemporary art music. By compiling all of the information relevant to the collection into one comprehensive source, it is hoped that awareness of and access to this significant collection will increase.

Catalog

1. Aaronson, Peter, 1954– The beast within beauty. N.p.: Peter Aaronson, 1997.
1 score (156 p.); 28 cm.
English words by Lori Walters.
Original work by Lori Walters and Carolyne Haycraft.
Opera.
Composed for: voices, orchestra, specifics unclear.
Call no.: **2001/001**

2. Abbado, Marcello, 1926– Ottavo ricercare: per violino e orchestra. Partitura. Milano: Edizioni Curci, 1997.
1 score (54 p.); 30 cm.
Composed for: violin, 2 flutes, 2 oboes, 2 clarinets, 2 bassoons, 2 horns, 2 trumpets, timpani, violin I, violin II, viola, violoncello, double bass.
Call no.: **1998/001**

3. Abrams, Arthur, 1936– The open gate: a new musical. New York, NY: n.p., 2003.
1 score (various pagings); 28 cm.
English words by David Willinger.
Based on the novel The manor by Isaac Bashevis Singer.
Composed for: voices, SATB chorus, violin, clarinet, synthesizer, piano, double bass, percussion.
Call no.: **2004/001**
Also available:
Call no.: **2004/001 libretto**

4. Adamo, Mark, 1962– Little women: opera in two acts. New York, NY: G. Schirmer, 1998 (1/9/02 printing).
1 score (2 v. [543 p.]); 43 cm.
Words by Mark Adamo.
Original work by Louisa May Alcott.
Duration: 2:00:00.
Composer's note and synopsis.
Composed for: 3 sopranos, 2 mezzo-sopranos, mezzo-soprano/contralto, tenor, baritone, 2 bass-baritones, quartet of female voices, flute (also piccolo, alto flute), oboe (also English horn), clarinet in A (also bass clarinet), bassoon (also contrabassoon), horn, percussion, piano (also celesta, synthesizer), harp, violin I, violin II, viola, violoncello, double bass.
Commissioned by: Houston Grand Opera.
Call no.: **2003/001**
Also available:
Call no.: **2003/001 libretto**

5. Adamo, Mark, 1962– Little women: opera in two acts. New York, NY: G. Schirmer, 2002 (1/22/03 printing).
1 score (2 v. (543 p.)); 36 cm.
Words by Mark Adamo.
Original work by Louisa May Alcott.
"Corrected 05/02"—p. 1.
Duration: 2:00:00.
Composer's note and synopsis.
Composed for: 3 sopranos, 2 mezzo-sopranos, mezzo-soprano/contralto, tenor, baritone, 2 bass-baritones, quartet of female voices, flute (also piccolo, alto flute), oboe (also English horn), clarinet in A (also bass clarinet), bassoon (also contrabassoon), horn, percussion, piano (also celesta, synthesizer), harp, violin I, violin II, viola, violoncello, double bass.
Commissioned by: Houston Grand Opera.
Call no.: **2004/002**

6. Adams, John, 1947– Chamber symphony. New York, NY: Hendon Music: Boosey & Hawkes, 1993.
1 score (106 p.); 36 cm.
At end of score: "Berkeley, CA: December 29, 1992."
Contents: Mongrel airs—Aria with walking bass—Roadrunner.
Composed for: flute (also piccolo), oboe, clarinet in

E♭ (also clarinet), clarinet (also bass clarinet), bassoon, contrabassoon, horn, trumpet, trombone, percussion (cowbell, hi-hat, woodblock, snare drum, pedal bass drum, roto-toms, 2 bongos, tambourine, timbal, claves), synthesizer, violin, viola, violoncello, double bass.
Call no.: **1994/001**

7. Adams, John, 1947– Harmonielehre. Pennsauken, NJ: G. Schirmer/Associated Music, 1985.
1 score (159 p.); 46 cm.
For orchestra.
Reproduced from manuscript.
Contents: Pt. 1—Pt. 2. The Anfortas wound—Pt. 3. Meister Eckhardt and Quackie.
Composed for: 4 flutes (2nd–4th also piccolo), 3 oboes (3rd also English horn), 4 clarinets (all also clarinet in A, 3rd–4th also bass clarinet), 3 bassoons (3rd also contrabassoon), 4 horns, 4 trumpets, 3 trombones, 2 tubas, timpani, percussion (tubular bells, 2 marimbas, 2 glockenspiels, 2 triangles, xylophone, crotales, high cymbal, bell tree, 3 suspended cymbals, bass drum, tam-tams, sizzle cymbal, vibraphone, gong), 2 harps, piano, celesta, violin I, violin II, viola, violoncello, double bass.
Call no.: **1986/001**

8. Adams, John, 1947– Violin concerto. N.p.: Hendon Music, 1993.
1 score (188 p.); 32 cm.
At end: Berkeley, CA, November 1, 1993.
1995 Grawemeyer Award winning work.
Composed for: violin, 2 flutes (both also piccolo, 2nd also alto flute), 2 oboes (2nd also English horn), 2 clarinets (2nd also bass clarinet), 2 bassoons, 2 horns, trumpet, percussion (marimba, 5 roto-toms, tubular bells, 2 bongo drums, 2 conga drums, bass drum, suspended cymbal, tambourine, 3 timbales, guiro, timpani, vibraphone, claves, high cowbell), 2 synthesizers, violin I, violin II, viola, violoncello, double bass.
Call no.: **1995/001**

9. Adams, John Luther, 1953– Clouds of forgetting, clouds of unknowing. Fairbanks, AK: Taiga Press, 1995.
1 score (149 p.); 36 cm.
For chamber orchestra.
Duration: ca. 1:02:00.
Includes program notes, performance instructions, and biographical information.
Composed for: 2 flutes (both also piccolo), 2 clarinets (both also bass clarinet), 2 horns, trumpet, bass trombone, percussion (marimba, vibraphone, chimes, glockenspiel, bass drum), celesta, piano, violin I, violin II, viola, violoncello, double bass.
Call no.: **1998/002**

10. Adams, John Luther, 1953– Forest without leaves. N.p.: n.p., 1984.
1 score (165 p.); 30 cm.
Words by John Haines.
For mixed choir and orchestra.
Reproduced from holograph.
Duration: ca. 1:10:00.
Composed for: flute (also piccolo, alto flute), oboe (also English horn), 2 clarinets (both also clarinets in E♭ and A, 1st also bass clarinet, 2nd also contrabass clarinet), bassoon, 2 horns, trumpet, trombone, tuba, percussion (chimes, vibraphone, anvils, sizzle cymbal, tam-tam, timpani, suspended cymbal, crash cymbals, tenor drum, bass drum, snare drum, crotales), harp, violin I, violin II, viola, violoncello, double bass.
Call no.: **1985/001**

11. Adams, John Luther, 1953– In the white silence. Fairbanks, AK: Taiga Press, 1998.
1 score (146 p.); 33 cm.
For celesta, harp, string quartet, 2 vibraphones, and string quintet or orchestra.
Biographical information on p. 3 of cover.
Composed for: percussion (2 vibraphones, glockenspiel), celesta, harp, violin I, violin II, viola, violoncello, double bass.
Call no.: **2001/002**

12. Adès, Thomas, 1971– Asyla: for orchestra (1997). Full score. London: Faber Music, 1997.
1 score (106 p.); 42 cm.
Duration: ca. 25:00.
2000 Grawemeyer Award winning work.
Composed for: 3 flutes (2nd–3rd also piccolo, 3rd also bass flute), 3 oboes (2nd–3rd also English horn; 3rd also bass oboe), 3 clarinets (1st–2nd also clarinet in A, 2nd also bass clarinet, 3rd also contrabass clarinet), 3 bassoons (3rd also contrabassoon), 4 horns, 3 trumpets (3rd also piccolo trumpet), 2 trombones, bass trombone, tuba, percussion (timpani, 4 roto-toms, 4 small tuned finger drums, 2 bell plates, tuned cowbells, 6 tubular bells, Chinese cymbal, hi-hat, 3 tins, geophone, water gong, large fixed ratchet, fixed washboard, tam-tam, bass drum, 4 tuned gongs, 4 suspended cymbals, small choke cymbal, side drum, sandpaper blocks, bag full of metal knives and forks, washboard, glockenspiel, crash cymbals, small ratchet, large gong, 6 other gongs, crotales, pedal bass drum, sizzle cymbal), 2 pianos (1st also upright piano; 2nd also upright piano

tuned 1/4 step down and celesta), harp, violin I, violin II, viola, violoncello, double bass.
Commissioned by: John Feeney Charitable Trust.
Call no.: **1998/003**
Re-entered as: **2000/002**

13. Adès, Thomas, 1971– Powder her face: opera in two acts. Full score. London: Faber Music, 1995.
1 score (2 v., 680 p.); 30 cm.
Words by Philip Hensher.
Reproduced from holograph.
Composed for: voices, clarinet (also bass clarinet, soprano saxophone, bass saxophone), 2 clarinets in A (both also bass clarinet, contrabass clarinet, swanee whistle), horn, trumpet, trombone, tuba, percussion (tubular bells, snare drum, flat bass drum, pedal bass drum, small bongo, 2 timbales, roto-tom, clash cymbals, 2 suspended cymbals, sizzle cymbal, hi-hat, 3 temple blocks, 3 brake drums, tambourine, triangle, tam-tam, vibraslap, washboard, cabasa, large fishing reel, whip, lion's roar, popgun, rattle, scrap metal, electric bell), harp (also electric bell, fishing reel), accordion (also electric bell, fishing reel), piano (also fishing reel), 2 violins, viola, violoncello, double bass (also fishing reel).
Commissioned by: Almeida Opera.
Call no.: **1997/001**
Also available:
Call no.: **1997/001 libretto**
Call no.: **1997/001 vocal score**

14. Adler, James, 1950– Memento mori: an AIDS requiem: for soprano, mezzo-soprano, baritone, men's chorus (T.T.B.B.) and orchestra. Full score. N.p.: James Adler, 1995.
1 score (163 p.); 28 cm.
Traditional Latin, Hebrew, or English texts with words by Quentin Crisp, Justin Smith, Denise Stokes, and Bill Weaver.
Duration: ca. 1:15:00.
Composed for: soprano, mezzo-soprano, tenor, baritone, TTBB men's chorus, flute (also piccolo, alto flute), oboe (also English horn), clarinet (also bass clarinet), bassoon, 2 horns, trumpet, trombone, tuba, percussion (bass drum, glockenspiel, snare drum, tam-tam, suspended cymbal, temple blocks, timpani, triangle, tubular bells, woodblock, xylophone), harp, piano (also organ), violin I, violin II, viola, violoncello, double bass.
Call no.: **1998/004**

15. Adler, Samuel, 1928– Concerto: for 'cello and orchestra. Full score. Bryn Mawr, PA: T. Presser Co., 1995.
1 score (93 p.); 44 cm.
Solo part edited by Stephen Geber.
Composed for: violoncello, piccolo, 2 flutes, 2 oboes, English horn, 2 clarinets, bass clarinet, 2 bassoons, contrabassoon, 4 horns, 3 trumpets, 2 trombones, bass trombone, tuba, timpani, percussion (glockenspiel, marimba, tam-tam, cymbals, bass drum, 3 triangles, 3 bongos, tom-toms, 3 woodblocks, xylophone, 3 temple blocks, timbales, suspended cymbals, snare drum, claves), celesta, piano, violin I, violin II, viola, violoncello, double bass.
Commissioned by: Eastman School of Music.
Call no.: **2000/001**

16. Adler, Samuel, 1928– Concerto: for piano and orchestra. Full score. N.p.: n.p., 1983.
1 miniature score (108 p.); 28 cm.
Reproduced from manuscript.
Composed for: piano, piccolo, 2 flutes, 2 oboes, 2 clarinets, 2 bassoons, 4 horns, 3 trumpets, 3 trombones, tuba, timpani, percussion (xylophone, vibraphone, glockenspiel, marimba, bass drum, snare drum, tenor drum, gongs, tom-toms, triangle, suspended cymbal, sizzle cymbal), violin I, violin II, viola, violoncello, double bass.
Commissioned by: Bradford Gowans.
Call no.: **1986/002**

17. Adler, Samuel, 1928– Concerto for viola and orchestra. King of Prussia, PA: T. Presser Co., 200-?.
1 score (116 p.); 43 cm.
Composed for: viola, piccolo, 2 flutes, 2 oboes, English horn, 2 clarinets, bass clarinet, 2 bassoons, 4 horns, 3 trumpets, 2 trombones, bass trombone, tuba, timpani, percussion (triangle, xylophone, vibraphone, 5 woodblocks, 5 temple blocks, tam-tam, cymbals, 3 tom-toms, marimba, bell tree, glockenspiel, bass drum), violin I, violin II, viola, violoncello, double bass.
Commissioned by: Pittsburgh Symphony Orchestra.
Call no.: **2002/001**

18. Adler, Samuel, 1928– Lux perpetua: a poem for organ and orchestra. Bryn Mawr, PA: Theodore Presser, 1998.
1 score (85 p.); 36 cm.
Composed for: piccolo, 2 flutes, 2 oboes, English horn, 2 clarinets, bass clarinet, 2 bassoons, 4 horns, 3 trumpets, 2 trombones, bass trombone, tuba, timpani, percussion, organ, violin I, violin II, viola, violoncello, double bass.
Commissioned by: Dallas Symphony Orchestra.
Call no.: **2001/003**

19. Adler, Samuel, 1928– Time in tempest everywhere: for soprano, oboe, piano and chamber orchestra. Bryn Mawr, PA: Theodore Presser Co., 1993.
1 score (93 p.); 39 cm.
English words by W. H. Auden.
Contents: No time—Another time—Poet, oracle, and wit—Our bias—If I could tell you.
Composed for: soprano, oboe, piano, 2 flutes, 2 clarinets, 2 bassoons, 2 horns, 2 trumpets, percussion (xylophone, glockenspiel, suspended cymbal, marimba, woodblock, bass drum, snare drum, cymbals, chimes), violin I, violin II, viola, violoncello, double bass.
Commissioned by: Plymouth Trio and Cleveland Chamber Symphony.
Call no.: **1997/002**

20. Agudelo, Graciela, 1945– Meditaciones sobre Abya-Yala. N.p.: n.p., 1995.
11 leaves of music; 45 cm.
Contents: Adiós—Curare—Visión—Tacuabé—Guanacos—Tambor.
Composed for: flute (also voice).
Commissioned by: Universidad Nacional Autónoma de México.
Call no.: **2000/003**

21. Agudelo, Graciela, 1945– Parajes de la memoria: la selva: para orquesta. N.p.: n.p., 1993.
1 score (42 p.); 35 cm.
Includes performance instructions in Spanish and English.
Composed for: piccolo, 2 flutes, alto flute, 3 oboes, English horn, clarinet in E♭, 2 clarinets, bass clarinet, 3 bassoons, contrabassoon, 8 horns, 2 trumpets, 2 trombones, bass trombone, tuba, percussion (timpani, woodblock, medium ratchet, temple blocks, sleigh bells, tam-tam, cymbals, snare drum, 2 congas, metal chimes, medium thundersheet, bass drum, crash cymbals, woodblock, xylophone, vibraphone, rain stick, bamboo chimes, 2 vainas, claves, bongos, tenabris, maracas, guiro, 3 tom-toms, whip), 2 harps, celesta, violin I, violin II, viola, violoncello, double bass.
Call no.: **1996/107**

22. Aguila, Miguel del, 1957– Wind quintet no. 2: op. 46. New York, NY: Peer-Southern Concert Music, 1994.
1 score (49 p.); 28 cm.
Reproduced from manuscript.
Duration: ca. 30:00.
Contents: Back in time—In heaven—Under the earth—Far away.
Composed for: flute, oboe, clarinet, bassoon, horn.
Commissioned by: Bach Camerata.
Call no.: **1996/036**

23. Aho, Kalevi, 1949– Symphony no. 11: for six percussionist[s] and orchestra (1997–98). Finland: Warner/Chappell Music, 1998.
1 score (181 p.); 42 cm.
Reproduced from manuscript.
Duration: ca. 34:00.
Composed for: 2 flutes (2nd also alto flute), 2 oboes, heckelphone, 2 clarinets in A (2nd also bass clarinet), 2 bassoons, 2 trumpets, 3 horns, baritone, 2 trombones, tuba, percussion (suspended cymbals, sleigh bells, tenor drum, castanets, 3 timpani, 2 antique cymbals in F, 2 triangles, glass wind chimes, 2 stones, kantele, medium tam-tam, bass drum, large triangle, slapstick, castanets, 2 congas, 2 maracas, tenor drum, 2 antique cymbals in B, chimes, vibraphone, small triangle, piccolo snare drum, snare drum, Arabian hand drum, 2 antique cymbals in A, 2 bongos, cowbells, 2 antique cymbals in E, 6 Japanese temple bells, tam-tam, bell tree, anvil, djembe, crash cymbals), violin I, violin II, viola, violoncello, double bass.
Commissioned by: Lahti Symphony Orchestra.
Call no.: **2002/002**

24. Aigmüller, Andreas, 1952– Konzert: für Fagott und Orchester, op. 69. Brühl: AMA-Musikverlag, 1995.
1 score (74 p.); 30 cm.
Reproduced from manuscript.
Composed for: bassoon, 2 flutes (both also piccolo), 2 oboes (both also English horn), 2 clarinets (both also bass clarinet), 2 bassoons (both also contrabassoon), 4 horns, 3 trumpets, 3 trombones, tuba, timpani, percussion (vibraphone, xylophone, glockenspiel, side drum, triangle, cymbals, bass drum, tam-tam), harp, violin I, violin II, viola, violoncello, double bass.
Call no.: **2001/004**

25. Aikman, James, 1959– Piano quintet: in four movements, 1997. Ann Arbor, MI: J. Aikman, 1997.
1 score (58 p.); 28 cm.
Duration: 25:00.
Includes program notes by the composer in English.
Composed for: violin, viola, violoncello, double bass, piano.
Commissioned by: Cathedral Arts.
Call no.: **2004/003**

26. Ain, Noa, 1942– Trio.
Call no.: **1985/002**
No materials available.

27. Aitken, Hugh, 1924– Symphony (1998). N.p.: n.p., 1998.
1 score (162 p.); 37 cm.
Composed for: piccolo, 2 flutes, 2 oboes, English horn, 2 clarinets, bass clarinet, 3 bassoons, 4 horns, 3 trumpets, 3 trombones, tuba, timpani, percussion, violin I, violin II, viola, violoncello, double bass.
Commissioned by: Seattle Symphony.
Call no.: **2004/004**

28. Aitken, Hugh, 1924– Symphony I (1998). N.p.: n.p., 1998.
1 score (162 p.); 44 cm.
Composed for: piccolo, 2 flutes, 2 oboes, English horn, 2 clarinets, bass clarinet, 3 bassoons, 4 horns, 3 trumpets, 3 trombones, tuba, timpani, percussion, violin I, violin II, viola, violoncello, double bass.
Commissioned by: Seattle Symphony.
Call no.: **2001/005**

29. Aĭzenshtadt, A. M., 1954– Concert: for flute and string quartet. N.p.: n.p., 1992.
1 score (various pagings); 42 cm.
Composed for: flute, 2 violins, viola, violoncello.
Call no.: **1994/038**

30. Aĭzenshtadt, A. M., 1954– Navazhdenie: misticheskai͡a opera v 5-ti kartinakh. Moskva: n.p., 1994.
1 score (15, 403 leaves); 30 cm.
Russian words (Cyrillic) by A. Aĭzenshtadt; also printed as text.
Composed for: 3 sopranos, boy alto, bass-baritone, flute, oboe, clarinet, bassoon, horn, 2 harps, percussion (vibraphone, glockenspiel), piano, organ, violin I, violin II, viola, violoncello, double bass.
Call no.: **1997/043**
Also available:
Call no.: **1997/043 libretto**

31. Aĭzenshtadt, A. M., 1954– Seans magii: monoopera v odnom akte (vos′mi ėpizodakh). Moskva: n.p., 1998.
1 score (1 v.); 30 cm.
Russian words by A. Aĭzenshtadt; also printed as text.
For voice and orchestra.
Composed for: voice, oboe (also English horn), bowed glass, harpsichord (also celesta), piano, percussion (marimba, 2 tam-tams, wind chimes, bells), violin I, violin II, viola, violoncello, double bass.
Call no.: **2002/052**

32. Albert, Stephen, 1941–1992. Concerto for violoncello and orchestra (1990). New York, NY: G. Schirmer, 1990.
1 score (142 p.); 36 cm.
"Revised 7/90"—p. 1.
Reproduced from manuscript.
Composed for: violoncello, 3 flutes (3rd also piccolo), 2 oboes, 2 clarinets in A, 2 bassoons, contrabassoon, 4 horns, 2 trumpets, timpani, percussion (cymbals, bass drum, gong, vibraphone, triangle, xylophone, woodblock, glockenspiel, tambourine), harp, piano, violin I, violin II, viola, violoncello, double bass.
Commissioned by: Baltimore Symphony Orchestra.
Call no.: **1991/001**

33. Albert, Stephen, 1941–1992. Concerto for violoncello and orchestra, 1990. Chester, NY: G. Schirmer Rental Library, 1990.
1 score (140 p.); 36 cm.
Reproduced from manuscript.
"Unrevised. For perusal only."
Composed for: violoncello, 3 flutes (3rd also piccolo), 2 oboes, 2 clarinets in A, 2 bassoons, contrabassoon, 4 horns, 2 trumpets, timpani, percussion (cymbals, bass drum, gong, vibraphone, triangle, xylophone, woodblock, glockenspiel, tambourine), harp, piano, violin I, violin II, viola, violoncello, double bass.
Commissioned by: Baltimore Symphony Orchestra.
Call no.: **1992/001**

34. Albert, Stephen, 1941–1992. Flower of the mountain. New York, NY: G. Schirmer, 1986.
1 score (48 p.); 36 cm.
Words by James Joyce.
For soprano and orchestra.
Composed for: soprano, 2 flutes (2nd also piccolo), 2 oboes (2nd also English horn), 2 clarinets, 2 bassoons, 2 horns, 2 trumpets, timpani, percussion (vibraphone, triangle, xylophone, glockenspiel), harp, piano, violin I, violin II, viola, violoncello, double bass.
Call no.: **1987/001**

35. Albert, Stephen, 1941–1992. Into eclipse. New York, NY: G. Schirmer, 1989.
1 score (105 p.); 52 cm.
English words.
For tenor and orchestra.
Text from Ted Hughes's adaptation of Seneca's Oedipus.
"Rev. 1/89"—p. 1.
Reproduced from manuscript.
Contents: Prologue and riddle song—Oedipus 1—A quiet fate—Ghosts—Oedipus 2.
Composed for: tenor, 2 flutes (2nd also piccolo, alto flute), 2 oboes (2nd also English horn), 2 clarinets (2nd also bass clarinet), 2 bassoons, contrabassoon, 4 horns, 2 trumpets, 3 trombones, tuba, percussion (glockenspiel, 2

vibraphones, 2 sets of chimes, antique cymbal, marimba, bass drum, timpani, xylophone, triangle, roto-toms, claves, snare drum, cymbals, gong), harp, piano, celesta, violin I, violin II, viola, violoncello, double bass.
Call no.: **1990/001**

36. Albert, Stephen, 1941–1992. Symphony: RiverRun. Chester, NY: G. Schirmer, 1985.
1 score (125 p.); 52 cm.
Reproduced from manuscript.
"Revised Dec. 1985."
Contents: Rain music—Leafy speafing—Beside the rivering waters—Rivers end.
Composed for: 3 flutes (2nd also alto flute, 3rd also piccolo), 2 oboes, English horn, clarinet (also clarinet in E♭), clarinet in A, bass clarinet, alto saxophone, 2 bassoons, contrabassoon, 4 horns, 3 trumpets, 3 trombones, tuba, timpani, percussion (2 vibraphones, chimes, bass drum, large gong, glockenspiel, xylophone), 2 harps, piano, violin I, violin II, viola, violoncello, double bass.
Commissioned by: National Symphony Orchestra.
Call no.: **1986/003**
Re-entered as: **1988/001** and **1989/001**

37. Albert, Thomas, 1948– Thirteen ways: for flute (piccolo, alto flute), clarinet (bass clarinet), violin (viola), cello, percussion and piano. N.p.: Thomas Albert, 1997.
1 score (71 p.); 28 cm.
"Inspired by 'Thirteen ways of looking at a blackbird' by Wallace Stevens."
Composed for: flute (also piccolo, alto flute), clarinet (also bass clarinet), violin (also viola), violoncello, percussion, piano.
Commissioned by: Eighth Blackbird.
Call no.: **2003/002**

38. Albright, William, 1944–1998. Chasm: symphonic fragment, 1985–89. N.p.: n.p., 1989.
1 score (56 p.); 44 cm.
"Part III of Spaces."
Duration: 13:00.
Reproduced from manuscript.
Composed for: 3 flutes (3rd also piccolo), 2 oboes, English horn, 2 clarinets, bass clarinet, alto saxophone, 2 bassoons, contrabassoon, 4 horns, trumpet in D, 3 trumpets, 2 trombones, bass trombone, tuba, timpani, percussion (organ, vibraphone, crotales, 2 castanets, 2 log drums, snare drum, marimba, maracas, 2 woodblocks, whip, anvil, 3 suspended cymbals, 2 tam-tams, 3 tom-toms, 2 bass drums, wind machine, glockenspiel, 3 triangles, 5 temple blocks, flexatone), harp, piano (also celesta), violin I, violin II, viola, violoncello, double bass.
Call no.: **1991/002**
Also available:
Call no.: **1991/002 miniature score**

39. Albright, William, 1944–1998. Concerto for harpsichord and string orchestra (1991). N.p.: W. Albright, 1991.
1 score (81 p.); 28 cm.
Reproduced from holograph.
Contents: Largo maestoso; Allegro semplice—Marcia funebre—Incantation and hoopla.
Composed for: harpsichord, violin I, violin II, viola, violoncello, double bass.
Commissioned by: Musart Society.
Call no.: **1993/001**

40. Albright, William, 1944–1998. Flights of fancy: ballet for organ (1991–2). New York, NY: C. F. Peters, 1993.
55 p. of music; 22 x 29 cm.
Duration: ca. 32:00.
Contents: Curtain raiser—Valse triste—Tango fantastico—Pas de deux—Ragtime lullabye—Shimmy—Hymn—Alla marcia: the A.G.O. fight song.
Composed for: organ.
Commissioned by: American Guild of Organists.
Call no.: **1997/003**

41. Albright, William, 1944–1998. Rustles of spring: for flute, alto saxophone or clarinet in A, violin, violoncello, pianoforte, 1994. N.p.: C. F. Peters, 1994.
1 score (76 p.); 22 x 28 cm.
Duration: 19:00.
Includes program note in English by the composer.
Contents: Vernal equinox—The wedding dance (after Brueghel)—Solar eclipse (in memoriam FSA).
Composed for: flute, alto saxophone, or clarinet in A; violin, violoncello, piano.
Commissioned by: MidAmerican Center for Contemporary Music, Contemporary Ensemble (Rice University), California E.A.R. Unit.
Call no.: **1996/001**
Re-entered as: **1998/005**

42. Alexander, Josef, 1907–1989. Threesome: for two clarinets (B♭) and piano. N.p.: n.p., 198-?.
1 score (34 p.); 36 cm.
Reproduced from manuscript.
Composed for: 2 clarinets, piano.
Commissioned by: American Chamber Ensemble.
Call no.: **1987/002**

43. Allanbrook, Douglas, 1921– Ethan Frome: lyric opera in 3 acts and an epilogue. N.p.: n.p., 199-?.
1 score (3 v.); 44 cm.
English words by John Hunt.
Original work by Edith Wharton.
Reproduced from manuscript.
Composed for: piccolo, 2 flutes, 2 oboes, 2 clarinets, 2 bassoons, 4 horns, 2 trumpets, 3 trombones, harp, violin I, violin II, viola, violoncello, double bass, offstage ensemble (clarinet, 2 violins, tuba).
Call no.: **2001/006**

44. Allanbrook, Douglas, 1921– Moon songs: children's chorus and orchestra. N.p.: n.p., 1986.
1 score (60 p.); 32 cm.
English words.
Text from poems by Wordsworth, Shelley, and Jonson.
Reproduced from manuscript.
Composed for: children's chorus, 2 flutes (2nd also piccolo), 2 oboes, clarinet, bass clarinet, 2 bassoons, 2 horns, trumpet, percussion (slapstick, woodblocks, glockenspiel, snare drum, bongos), harp, violin I, violin II, viola, violoncello, double bass.
Commissioned by: Glen Ellyn Children's Chorus and New Philharmonic.
Call no.: **1988/002**

45. Alvear, Maria de, 1960– As far as we know. N.p.: n.p., 2001.
1 score (51 p.); 42 cm.
Spanish words.
For voice and orchestra.
Composed for: voice, 3 flutes, 3 oboes, 3 clarinets, bassoon, 2 horns, 2 trumpets, 2 trombones, tuba, percussion, piano, violin I, violin II, viola, piano.
Call no.: **2004/030**

46. Ambrosi, Angela, 1967– Minimal music. N.p.: n.p., 1988.
2 p., 11 leaves of music; 30 cm.
Reproduced from holograph.
Composed for: piano.
Call no.: **1989/002**

47. Amram, David, 1930– Giants of the night: a concerto for flute and orchestra. New York, NY: C. F. Peters, 1999.
1 score (202 p.); 44 cm.
Duration: ca. 38:00.
Contents: Allegro con brio (for Charlie Parker)—Andante cantabile (for Jack Kerouac)—Rondo giocoso (for Dizzy Gillespie).
Composed for: flute, oboe, English horn, 2 clarinets, 2 bassoons, 2 horns, 2 trumpets, 2 trombones, timpani, percussion, harp, violin I, violin II, viola, violoncello, double bass.
Commissioned by: James Galway.
Call no.: **2004/005**

48. Amram, David, 1930– Kokopelli: a symphony in three movements. New York, NY: C. F. Peters, 1997.
1 score (132 p.); 36 cm.
Reproduced from manuscript.
Contents: Lene tawi (flute song)—Mizmor kakddum (song of antiquity)—Danza del mundo (dance of the world).
Composed for: 2 flutes (2nd also piccolo), oboe, English horn, 2 clarinets, 2 bassoons, 4 horns, 3 trumpets, 3 trombones, tuba, timpani, percussion (rattle, frame drum, bass drum, tam-tam, sleigh bells, snare drum, triangle, tom-toms, tambourine, crotales, maracas, crash cymbals, glockenspiel, timbales, woodblocks, xylophone, congas, bongos, suspended cymbal, Chinese gong, cowbell), harp, violin I, violin II, viola, violoncello, double bass.
Commissioned by: Nashville Symphony.
Call no.: **1998/006**

49. Ancarola, Francesca, 1968– Loop$_2$: para guitarra acustica amplificada y reverberada y cinta digital. N.p.: n.p., 1992.
1 score (7 leaves); 26 cm.
Reproduced from manuscript.
Duration: 7:25.
Composed for: amplified guitar, tape.
Call no.: **1993/120**

50. Anderson, Beth, 1950– Piano concerto. N.p.: Beth Anderson, 1997.
1 score (107 p.); 28 cm.
For piano and string orchestra with percussion.
Duration: 13:00.
Composed for: piano, violin I, violin II, viola, violoncello, double bass, percussion (marimba, hi-hat, suspended cymbal, triangle, snare drum, bass drum).
Call no.: **2002/003**

51. Anderson, Julian, 1967– Symphony: for orchestra (2003). London: Faber Music, 2003.
1 miniature score (103 p.); 30 cm.
Reproduced from holograph.
Duration: ca. 18:00.
Composed for: 3 flutes (also alto flute, piccolo, extra flute tuned 1/4-tone flat), 3 oboes (also English horn), 3 clarinets (also clarinets in A and E♭, bass clarinet,

extra clarinet tuned 1/4-tone flat), bass clarinet (also contrabass clarinet), 3 bassoons (also contrabassoon), 4 horns, 3 trumpets (also trumpet in D), 3 trombones, tuba, timpani, percussion (2 side drums, large tam-tam, glockenspiel, whip, bass drum, large triangle, 2 suspended cymbals, tuned cowbells, marimba, vibraphone, guiro, large military drum with snares, tubular bells, 2 low tom-toms), harp, piano (also extra piano or keyboard sampler tuned 1/4-tone flat), violin I, violin II, viola, violoncello, double bass.
Commissioned by: City of Birmingham Symphony Orchestra.
Call no.: **2005/001**

52. Andersson, Magnus F., 1953– Under bron, under tiden. Stockholm: Svensk Music, 1991.
1 score (66 p.); 43 cm.
For winds and percussion.
Reproduced from manuscript.
At end of score: "FineParis9111272205MFA."
Composed for: 4 flutes, 3 oboes, 3 clarinets, bass clarinet, 2 bassoons, contrabassoon, trumpet, 4 horns, 2 trombones, bass trombone, euphonium, tuba, percussion (6 cymbals, large tam-tam, 2 woodblocks, 2 temple blocks, 2 large wood drums, hi-hat, 2 wood drums, timbal, glockenspiel, tubular bells, large tom-tom, bass drum).
Call no.: **1994/002**

53. Andriessen, Louis, 1939– Hadewijch: de materie, part II: soprano, 8 voices, and large ensemble, 1988. Amsterdam: Donemus, 1989.
1 score (89 p.); 41 cm.
Dutch words.
Reproduced from holograph.
Duration: ca. 25:00.
Composed for: soprano, vocal octet, 3 flutes, 2 oboes, 2 English horns, 5 clarinets, 2 bass clarinets, contrabass clarinet, 4 horns, 4 trumpets, 4 trombones, tuba, percussion (glockenspiel, vibraphone, 7 gongs, snare drum, guiro, string drum, rattle, slapstick, bell tree, tam-tam), 2 guitars, bass guitar, 2 pianos, 2 synthesizers, harp, violin I, violin II, viola, violoncello, double bass.
Call no.: **1992/002 no.2**

54. Andriessen, Louis, 1939– Hadewijch: de materie, part II: soprano, 8 voices, and large ensemble, 1988. London; New York, NY: Boosey & Hawkes, 1992.
1 score (89 p.); 36 cm.
Dutch words.
Reproduced from holograph.
Duration: ca. 25:00.
Composed for: soprano, vocal octet, 3 flutes, 2 oboes, 2 English horns, 5 clarinets, 2 bass clarinets, contrabass clarinet, 4 horns, 4 trumpets, 4 trombones, tuba, percussion (glockenspiel, vibraphone, 7 gongs, snare drum, guiro, string drum, rattle, slapstick, bell tree, tam-tam), 2 guitars, bass guitar, 2 pianos, 2 synthesizers, harp, violin I, violin II, viola, violoncello, double bass.
Call no.: **1994/003**

55. Andriessen, Louis, 1939– The last day (revised version 1996). Full score. London: Boosey & Hawkes, 1996.
1 score (107 p.); 36 cm.
Dutch words.
For solo voices (TTBarBar), child's voice, and orchestra.
Words by Lucebert and from a folksong.
Composed for: 2 tenors, 2 baritones, child's voice, 3 flutes (1st–2nd also piccolo), 2 oboes (2nd also English horn), 2 clarinets, bass clarinet, contrabass clarinet, contrabassoon, 2 horns, 2 trumpets, 2 trombones, percussion (xylophone, glockenspiel, vibraphone, marimba, chimes, 2 large triangles, 2 rattles, 4 woodblocks, large tom-tom, log drum, 2 snare drums, large bass drum, timpani, 2 suspended cymbals, large tam-tam, gong, anvil, large whip, police whistle), harp, 2 pianos, 2 synthesizers, 2 electric guitars, bass guitar, violin I, violin II, viola, violoncello, double bass.
Commissioned by: Co-producers of Ensemble Parade (Donemus, Stichting Gaudeamus, De Ijsbreker, Het Concertgebouw NV, NPS-Radio, Asko Ensemble, Schoenberg Ensemble, Nederlands Blazers Ensemble, Nieuw Ensemble, and Holland Festival).
Call no.: **1998/007**

56. Andriessen, Louis, 1939– De materie, part I: tenor, 8 voices, and large ensemble, 1988. Amsterdam: Donemus, 1989.
1 score (94 p.); 41 cm.
Dutch words.
Reproduced from holograph.
Duration: ca. 25:00.
Composed for: tenor, vocal octet, 3 flutes, 2 English horns, 5 clarinets, 3 bass clarinets, 4 horns, 4 trumpets, 4 trombones, tuba, percussion (2 marimbas, bass marimba, glockenspiel, vibraphone, snare drum, 2 bass drums, log drum, 2 metal boxes with hammers, tam-tam, timpani, 8 tom-toms, metal chimes), 2 guitars, bass guitar, 2 pianos, 2 synthesizers, violin I, violin II, viola, violoncello, double bass.
Call no.: **1992/002 no.1**

57. Andriessen, Louis, 1939– De materie, part IV: female speaking voice, 8 voices, and large ensemble, 1988. Amsterdam: Donemus, 1989.
1 score (28 p.); 41 cm.
Text in Dutch and French; French also printed as text with Dutch translation.
Reproduced from holograph.
Duration: ca. 25:00.
Composed for: female speaker, vocal octet, 3 flutes, 4 oboes, 5 clarinets, 2 bass clarinets, contrabass clarinet, 4 horns, 4 trumpets, 4 trombones, tuba, percussion (glockenspiel, vibraphone, 11 gongs, snare drum, bass drum, string drum, rattle, 3 cowbells, bell tree, tam-tam, timpani, 2 bell plates), 2 guitars, bass guitar, 2 pianos, 2 synthesizers, harp, celesta, violin I, violin II, viola, violoncello, double bass.
Call no.: **1992/002 no.4**

58. Andriessen, Louis, 1939– De stijl: de materie, part III: 4 women voices and large ensemble 1985. Amsterdam: Donemus, 1989.
1 score (154 p.); 41 cm.
Dutch words.
Reproduced from holograph.
Duration: 25:00.
Composed for: 2 sopranos, 2 altos, 3 flutes, 2 alto saxophones (both also baritone saxophone), 2 tenor saxophones, baritone saxophone, 4 trumpets, 4 trombones, percussion (2 drum sets [hi-hat, cymbals, boobams, snare drum, bass drum], vibraphone, 4–5 gongs, metal), 3 pianos, synthesizer, upright piano, 2 guitars, bass guitar, optional double bass.
Call no.: **1992/002 no.3**

59. Andriessen, Louis, 1939– De stijl: for large ensemble, 1985. Amsterdam: Donemus, 1985.
1 score (iii, 154 p.); 42 cm.
Dutch words with English translation.
For 4 women's voices with instrumental ensemble.
Duration: 25:00.
Composed for: 4 female voices, 3 flutes (1st also piccolo), 2 alto saxophones (one also baritone saxophone), 2 tenor saxophones, baritone saxophone, 4 trumpets, 4 trombones, percussion (2 drum sets [hi-hat, cymbals, 8 boobams, snare drum, bass drum], vibraphone, 5 gongs, metal), piano, electric piano, synthesizer, upright piano, 2 guitars, bass guitar, double bass.
Commissioned by: Fonds voor de Scheppende Toonkunst.
Call no.: **1988/003**

60. Andriessen, Louis, 1939– Writing to Vermeer: 6 scenes. Score. London: Boosey & Hawkes, 1998.
1 score (2 v.); 42 cm.
English words by Peter Greenaway.
Opera.
Duration: ca. 1:30:00.
Composed for: 2 sopranos (2nd also harpsichord), mezzo-soprano, 2 children's voices, women's chorus, 3 flutes (also piccolo, alto flute), 2 oboes (also English horn), bass clarinet, contrabass clarinet (also bass clarinet), 2 horns, 2 trumpets (also bass trumpet), 2 pianos, 2 harps, 2 electric guitars, cimbalom, percussion (celesta, glockenspiel, gongs, vibraphone, bell tree, bass drum, guiro, 2 large triangles, chimes, breaking glass, tambourine, 2 pairs of bongos, 2 large cymbals, heavy object thrown in water, xylophone, 2 woodblocks, 2 small tom-toms, castanets, tam-tam, large sizzle cymbal, timpani, large gong, large tom-toms, old clock, anare drum, small bongo, hard metal, hard high metal, large rattle, loud log drum, large woodblock, low metal tube), violin I, violin II, viola, violoncello, double bass (with C-string).
Call no.: **2005/002**

61. Andriessen, Louis, 1939– Writing to Vermeer: opera in 6 scenes. London: Boosey & Hawkes, 1998.
1 score (285 p.); 30 cm.
English words by Peter Greenaway.
Duration: ca. 1:30:00.
Composed for: 2 sopranos (2nd also harpsichord), mezzo-soprano, 2 children's voices, women's chorus, 3 flutes (also piccolo, alto flute), 2 oboes (also English horn), bass clarinet, contrabass clarinet (also bass clarinet), 2 horns, 2 trumpets (also bass trumpet), 2 pianos, 2 harps, 2 electric guitars, cimbalom, percussion (celesta, glockenspiel, gongs, vibraphone, bell tree, bass drum, guiro, 2 large triangles, chimes, breaking glass, tambourine, 2 pairs of bongos, 2 large cymbals, heavy object thrown in water, xylophone, 2 woodblocks, 2 small tom-toms, castanets, tam-tam, large sizzle cymbal, timpani, large gong, large tom-toms, old clock, anare drum, small bongo, hard metal, hard high metal, large rattle, loud log drum, large woodblock, low metal tube), violin I, violin II, viola, violoncello, double bass (with C-string).
Call no.: **2001/007**

62. Androsch, Peter, 1963– Bellum docet omnia: die Implosion der Werte. N.p.: Peter Androsch, 1993.
1 score (5 p.); 21 x 30 cm.
German or Hungarian words.
For SATB chorus.
Reproduced from manuscript.
Composed for: 6 sopranos, 6 mezzo-sopranos, 6 altos, 8 tenors, 10 baritones, 20 basses.

Commissioned by: Kulturverein KANAL Schwertberg.
Call no.: **1996/002**

63. Angius, Fulvio, 1936– La victoire de Notre Dame: leggenda medioevale per soli, coro e strumenti. N.p.: n.p., 198-?.
1 score (373 p.); 38 cm.
French words by S. Benati and F. Macciantelli.
Original work by Rutebeuf.
Reproduced from manuscript.
Composed for: contralto, tenor, 2 baritones, SATB chorus, soprano recorder, alto recorder, flute, oboe, horn, trumpet, piano, viola d'amore, lute, percussion (xylorimba, triangle, snare drum, suspended cymbal, maraca, drum, tam-tam, tambourine, bell).
Call no.: **1989/003**

64. Anichini, Antonio, 1962– Drei geometrische Etüden = Three geometrical studies: for 2 pianos (1993–94). Score. N.p.: n.p., 1994.
1 score (156 p.); 21 x 30 cm.
Program notes in English precede score (translated by Diane Marie Friedl).
Composed for: 2 pianos.
Call no.: **1996/003**

65. Anichini, Antonio, 1962– Flötenkonzert: per flauto e orchestra (1996/7). Partitura. N.p.: n.p., 1997.
1 score (56 p.); 30 cm.
Reproduced from holograph.
Composed for: flute, 2 flutes (both also piccolo), 2 oboes, 2 clarinets, 2 bassoons, contrabassoon, 4 horns, 3 trumpets, 2 trombones, 2 sets of timpani, violin I, violin II, viola, violoncello, double bass.
Call no.: **1998/008**

66. Antoniou, Theodore, 1935– The bacchae: opera in two acts. N.p.: n.p., 1992.
1 score (16, A–N p.); 43 cm.
English words by Keith Bothsford.
Original work by Euripides.
Score not complete.
Reproduced from manuscript.
Composed for: voices, SATB chorus, flute (also piccolo), 2 clarinets, horn, trumpet, trombone, percussion (crotales, timpani, snare drum, vibraphone, bass drum, temple blocks, crash cymbals, chimes), piano, synthesizer, violin I, violin II, viola, violoncello, double bass.
Call no.: **1993/002**

67. Antoniou, Theodore, 1935– Oedipus at Colonus. N.p.: n.p., 1998.
1 score (v, 85 p.); 37 cm.
Ancient and contemporary Greek words by Yorgos Michaelidis.
Opera in one act.
Composed for: mezzo-soprano, 2 tenors, baritone, bass, men's chorus, 2 flutes (2nd also piccolo), 2 oboes, 2 clarinets (2nd also bass clarinet), 2 bassoons (2nd also contrabassoon), 4 horns, 2 trumpets, 3 trombones, tuba, timpani, percussion (marimba, vibraphone, glockenspiel, large tam-tam, snare drum, suspended cymbals, low woodblock, Chinese theater gong, thundersheet, daoli, double bass bow, triangle beater, tubular chimes, wind machine, 5 tom-toms, crash cymbals, low bass drum), harp, piano, violin I, violin II, viola, violoncello, double bass.
Commissioned by: Orchestra of Sudwest Funk.
Call no.: **2000/004.**
Re-entered as: **2001/008**
Also available:
Call no.: **2000/004 libretto**
Re-entered as: **2001/008 libretto**

68. Antoniou, Theodore, 1935– Skolion: for orchestra, 1986. N.p.: n.p., 1986.
1 score (51 p.); 44 cm.
Reproduced from manuscript.
Duration: ca. 16:00.
Composed for: 3 flutes (3rd also piccolo), 3 oboes (3rd also English horn), 3 clarinets (3rd also bass clarinet), 3 bassoons, 4 horns, 3 trumpets, 3 trombones, tuba, percussion (chimes, suspended cymbal, timpani, xylophone, flexatone, antique cymbals, vibraphone, triangle, sleigh bells, whip, tam-tam, flexatone, glockenspiel, marimba, bongos, wind machine, crash cymbals, temple blocks), harp, piano, violin I, violin II, viola, violoncello, double bass.
Call no.: **1987/003**

69. Antunes, Jorge, 1942– Cantata dos dez povos: para quarteto vocal solista (soprano, contralto, tenor e baixo), 11 declamadores, coro misto, orquestra sinfônica ae fita magnética, 1998/1999. N.p.: n.p., 1999.
1 score (131 p.); 42 cm.
Portuguese words.
Reproduced from manuscript.
Composed for: soprano, alto, tenor, bass, 11 narrators, SATB chorus, piccolo, 2 flutes, 2 oboes, English horn, 2 clarinets, bass clarinet, 2 bassoons, contrabassoon, 5 horns, 4 trumpets, 4 trombones, tuba, percussion, 2 harps, violin I, violin II, viola, violoncello, double bass, tape.
Commissioned by: Universidade de Brasilia.
Call no.: **2001/009**

Re-entered as: **2002/004**

70. Antunes, Jorge, 1942– Idiosynchronie: pour ensemble instrumental, 1991. Milano: Edizioni Suvini Zerboni, 1991.
1 score (A–E, 70 p.); 50 cm.
Reproduced from manuscript.
Includes performance instructions in French.
Composed for: 2 piccolos, 2 flutes, 2 clarinets, bass clarinet, bassoon, contrabassoon, 4 horns, 4 trombones, tuba, percussion (steel pan with glass beads, water gong, 2 water glasses, 2 wine glasses, 2 jingle bells, whip, woodblock, bottle, 4 cowbells, suspended cymbal, triangle, box of glass beads, box of nuts and bolts, box of plastic beads, ratchet, 2 maracas, 3 zinc cymbals, temple block, tam-tam, musical saw, 2 bass drums, oil drum, 4 bows), 2 violoncellos, 2 double basses.
Commissioned by: Ministère de la Culture Française.
Call no.: **1994/004**

71. Antunes, Jorge, 1942– Klarinettenquintett: (quintetto KarlOS), per clarinetto in si bemolle e quartetto d'archi. Brasília, Brasil: Sistrum, 1996.
1 score (107 p.); 33 cm.
Composed for: clarinet, 2 violins, viola, violoncello.
Commissioned by: Karl Schlechta.
Call no.: **2000/005**

72. Antunes, Jorge, 1942– Rimbaudiannisia MCMXCV: pour enfants solistes, choeur d'enfants, masques, lumières et ensemble instrumental. Brasilia, Brasil: Sistrum, 1995.
1 score (113 p.); 30 cm.
French words.
Duration: 23:13.
Contents: Expiation pour Cumiqoh—Voyelles—Dithyrambus.
Composed for: children's voices, children's chorus, flute, oboe, English horn, clarinet, bass clarinet, bassoon, trombone, percussion (whip, timpani, 4 bongos, maracas, vibraphone, 4 crotales, anvil), violin, viola, violoncello, double bass.
Commissioned by: Radio France.
Call no.: **1997/004**

73. Applebaum, Edward, 1937– Symphony no. 2. St. Louis, MO: Magnamusic-Baton, 1984.
1 score (36 p.); 32 cm.
Duration: ca. 17:00.
Composed for: 3 flutes (all also piccolo, 2nd also alto flute, 3rd also bass flute), 3 oboes (3rd also English horn), 3 clarinets (1st also clarinet in E♭), bass clarinet, 3 bassoons (3rd also contrabassoon), 4 horns, 4 trumpets, 3 trombones, bass trombone, tuba, percussion (vibraphone, chimes, tam-tam, bells, crotales, timpani, suspended cymbal, marimba, bass drum, triangle, xylophone, wind chimes), harp, piano (also celesta), violin I, violin II, viola, violoncello, double bass.
Commissioned by: National Endowment for the Arts.
Call no.: **1985/004**

74. Applebaum, Edward, 1937– Symphony no. 4: orchestra (1995). Score. Saint Louis, MO: MMB Music, 1997.
1 score (54 p.); 44 cm.
Duration: 25:00.
Composed for: 3 flutes (2nd also piccolo and alto flute, 3rd also piccolo), 3 oboes (3rd also English horn), soprano saxophone (also tenor and baritone saxophones), 3 clarinets (3rd also bass clarinet), 3 bassoons (3rd also contrabassoon), 4 horns, 3 trumpets, 3 trombones (3rd also bass trombone), tuba, timpani, percussion (vibraphone, 5 tom-toms, 3 triangles, 2 suspended cymbals, finger cymbals, bass drum, large tenor drum, gong, bongos, 5 temple blocks, chimes, crotales, marimba, wind chimes), piano (also celesta), harp, violin I, violin II, viola, violoncello, double bass.
Call no.: **2000/006**

75. Arad, Atar, 1945– String quartet. N.p.: n.p., 1998.
1 score (57 p.); 33 cm.
Composed for: 2 violins, viola, violoncello.
Call no.: **2001/010**
Re-entered as: **2003/003**

76. Arcà, Paolo, 1953– Angelica e la luna: opera in un atto. Milano: Edizioni Suvini Zerboni, 1985.
1 score (ii, 203 p.); 30 cm.
Italian words by Giovanni Carli Ballola.
Reproduced from manuscript.
Duration: ca. 55:00.
Composed for: 4 sopranos, 3 tenors, flute (also piccolo), clarinet (also bass clarinet), horn, piano (also celesta), harp, 2 violins, viola, violoncello.
Call no.: **1986/005**

77. Archer, Violet, 1913–2000. The meal: a one-act opera. N.p.: n.p., 1983.
1 score (232 p.); 38 cm.
English words by Rowland Holt Wilson.
Reproduced from manuscript.
Composed for: tenor, baritone, flute (also piccolo), oboe, clarinet (also bass clarinet), bassoon, horn, trumpet, trombone, timpani, percussion (snare drum, glockenspiel, xylophone, gong, cymbals, slapstick, bass

drum), piano (also celesta), violin I, violin II, viola, violoncello, double bass.
Call no.: **1986/006**

78. Argento, Dominick, 1927– Casa Guidi.
Commissioned by: Minnesota Orchestra.
Call no.: **1985/005**
No materials available.

79. Argento, Dominick, 1927– Casanova's homecoming.
Call no.: **1986/007**
No materials available.

80. Argento, Dominick, 1927– Walden pond: nocturnes and barcaroles for mixed chorus, three violoncellos and harp. Full score. New York, NY: Boosey & Hawkes, 1996.
1 score (v, 96 p.); 28 cm.
English words; also printed as text.
Contents: The pond—Angling—Observing—Extolling—Walden revisited.
Composed for: SATB chorus, 3 violoncellos, harp.
Commissioned by: Dale Warland and Dale Warland Singers.
Call no.: **1997/005**
Re-entered as: **1998/009**

81. Argersinger, Charles, 1951– Dream sequence: (suite for piano): for solo piano. Pullman, WA: Charles Argersinger, 1997.
37 p. of music; 28 cm.
Contents: Chess and the art of war (ca. 5:00)—Seduction (ca. 6:30)—Escherrondo (ca. 3:30).
Composed for: piano.
Commissioned by: Washington State Music Teachers Association and Music Teachers National Association.
Call no.: **2000/007**

82. Armer, Elinor, 1939– The great instrument of the Geggerets: uses of music in uttermost parts, III. N.p.: n.p., 1989.
1 score (59 p.); 28 cm.
Words by Ursula K. Le Guin.
For narrator and orchestra.
First performed Mar. 11, 1989 by Ursula Le Guin, narrator; with the Philharmonic, JoAnn Falletta, conductor, in San Francisco, CA.
At end: Berkeley, Ca, Nov. 26, 1988.
Composed for: narrator, piccolo, 2 flutes, 2 oboes, 2 clarinets, bass clarinet, 2 bassoons, contrabassoon, 2 horns, 2 trumpets, trombone, tuba, percussion (harmonica, slapstick, timpani, bass drum, 2 bongos, 3 tom-toms, xylophone, ratchet, crash cymbals, marimba, glockenspiel, bicycle wheel, sand blocks, cowbell, temple blocks, triangle, 2 suspended cymbals, sizzle cymbal, Renaissance drum, tambourine, gym whistle, ratchet, 3 woodblocks, snare drum, castanets, bicycle wheel), piano, violin I, violin II, viola, violoncello, double bass.
Commissioned by: Bay Area Women's Philharmonic.
Call no.: **1990/002**

83. Armer, Elinor, 1939– Island Earth. Saint Louis, MO: MMB Music, 1996.
1 score (84 p.); 44 cm.
English words by Ursula K. Le Guin.
For chorus (SATB) and orchestra.
"First proof."
Annotated with corrections.
Composed for: SATB chorus, 3 flutes (3rd also piccolo), 2 oboes, 2 clarinets (2nd also bass clarinet), 2 bassoons (2nd also contrabassoon), 4 horns, 2 trumpets, 3 trombones, tuba, percussion (2 gongs, 3 suspended cymbals, sizzle cymbal, rain stick, vibraphone, 3 woodblocks, snare drum, 4 tom-toms, 2 bongos, glockenspiel, crotales, maracas, lion's roar, whip, timpani, bass drum, tam-tam, chimes, sand blocks, bell tree, castanets, triangle), harp, piano, violin I, violin II, viola, violoncello, double bass.
Commissioned by: Women's Philharmonic and San Francisco Boys Chorus.
Call no.: **1996/004**

84. Armer, Elinor, 1939– Lockerbones/airbones: five songs for mezzo-soprano, flute, violin, piano, and percussion. N.p.: n.p., 1985.
1 score (various pagings); 42 cm.
Words by Ursula K. Le Guin.
Reproduced from holograph.
At end of score: "Elinor Armer, MacDowell, Berkeley, 1983."
Contents: The anger—The child on the shore—Footnote—Hard words—For Katya.
Composed for: mezzo-soprano, flute, violin, piano, percussion (4 timbales, 2 bongos, 2 brake drums, 3 gongs, 2 suspended cymbals, vibraphone, breakable wood lathe, 4 tom-toms, glockenspiel, 4 woodblocks, 5 temple blocks, tambourine, maracas, tam-tam, triangle, castanets, wind chimes, sand blocks, water gong, 2 pipes, guiro, 2 cowbells).
Call no.: **1985/006**

85. Armer, Elinor, 1939– String quartet, 1983. N.p.: n.p., 1983.
1 score (19 p.); 40 cm.
Reproduced from holograph.
At end: Elinor Armer, May 1983.
Contents: Grievance—Four soliloquies—A joyful noise.

Composed for: 2 violins, viola, violoncello.
Call no.: **1985/007**

86. Armer, Elinor, 1939– String quartet, 1983. N.p.: J.B. Elkus & Son; Osterville: Overland Music Distributors, 1987.
1 score (20 p.); 28 cm.
Duration: 14:00.
Contents: Grievance—Four soliloquies—A joyful noise.
Composed for: 2 violins, viola, violoncello.
Call no.: **1988/004**

87. Arnold, Malcolm, 1921– Symphony 9, opus 128. N.p.: Novello, 1990.
1 score (208 p.); 41 cm.
Reproduced from holograph.
Duration: 51:41.
Composed for: piccolo, 2 flutes, 2 oboes, 2 clarinets, 2 bassoons, 4 horns, 3 trumpets, 3 trombones, tuba, timpani, percussion (glockenspiel, cymbals, bass drum, xylophone), harp, violin I, violin II, viola, violoncello, double bass.
Call no.: **1995/002**

88. Arrigo, Girolamo, 1930– O notte, o dolce tempo: (1988). Palermo: n.p., 1988.
1 score (80 p.); 37 cm.
Italian words by Michelangelo Buonarroti; also printed as text.
For 12 voices and orchestra.
Reproduced from manuscript.
Duration: ca. 22:00.
Composed for: 3 sopranos, 3 mezzo-sopranos, 3 tenors, 3 basses, 2 flutes, 2 oboes, 2 bassoons, 2 horns, violin I, violin II, viola, violoncello, double bass.
Commissioned by: Ministère de la Culture Française.
Call no.: **1991/003**

89. Artemov, Vi͡acheslav, 1940– Na nopoge svetlogo mira = On the threshold of [a] bright world: a symphony for large orchestra. N.p.: n.p., 1990.
1 score (127 p.); 40 cm.
Reproduced from manuscript.
Duration: ca. 42:00.
Annotated for performance.
Composed for: 4 flutes (3rd–4th also piccolo), 3 oboes, English horn, 4 clarinets (4th also bass clarinet), 4 bassoons (4th also contrabassoon), 6 horns, 4 trumpets, 3 trombones, tuba, percussion (2 gongs, 2 suspended cymbals, chimes, tam-tam, glockenspiel, 2 gongs, vibraphone, crash cymbals, drum, timpani, bass drum), 2 harps, piano, celesta, organ, violin I, violin II, viola, violoncello, double bass.
Commissioned by: National Symphony Orchestra (Washington, DC).
Call no.: **1992/003**

90. Artemov, Vi͡acheslav, 1940– Requiem. N.p.: n.p., 198-?.
1 score (251 p.); 43 cm.
Latin words.
Reproduced from holograph.
Duration: ca. 1:20:00.
Composed for: 4 flutes (3rd–4th also piccolo), 2 oboes, English horn, 4 clarinets (3rd also clarinet in E♭), 2 bassoons, contrabassoon, 4 horns, 4 trumpets, 3 trombones, tuba, percussion (2 glockenspiels, bass drum, 2 flexatones, timpani, triangle, vibraphone, tambourine, suspended cymbal, chimes, whip, crash cymbals, church bell, tam-tam, maracas, crotales, guiro, woodblock, ratchet), 2 harps, piano, organ, celesta, violin I, violin II, viola, violoncello, double bass.
Call no.: **1990/003**

91. Asch, Glenn, 1955– Concerto in F for violin + chamber orchestra. N.p.: n.p., 198-?.
1 score (157 p.); 34 cm.
Reproduced from manuscript.
Composed for: violin, 2 flutes, 2 oboes, clarinet, clarinet in A, 2 bassoons (2nd also contrabassoon), 2 horns, percussion (trap set, woodblock, glockenspiel, temple blocks), violin I, violin II, viola, violoncello, double bass.
Commissioned by: Denver Chamber Orchestra.
Call no.: **1989/004**

92. Asia, Daniel, 1953– Black light. N.p.: D. Asia Music, 1990.
1 score (55 p.); 44 cm.
"Revised 9/91."
Reproduced from holograph.
Composed for: piccolo, 2 flutes, 2 oboes, English horn, 2 clarinets, bass clarinet, 2 bassoons, contrabassoon, 4 horns, 3 trumpets, 3 trombones, tuba, timpani, percussion (marimba, xylophone, vibraphone, glockenspiel, 4 cymbals, sizzle cymbal, 3 tam-tams, triangle, 7 drums, 2 bass drums, 4 woodblocks, 4 temple blocks, slapstick), harp, piano, violin I, violin II, viola, violoncello, double bass.
Commissioned by: American Composers Orchestra.
Call no.: **1992/004**

93. Asia, Daniel, 1953– Cello concerto. N.p.: D. Asia, 1997.
1 score (62 p.); 28 cm.
Composed for: violoncello, 2 flutes (2nd also piccolo), 2

oboes (2nd also English horn), 2 clarinets, 2 bassoons (2nd also contrabassoon), 4 horns, 2 trumpets, 2 trombones, timpani, percussion (medium suspended cymbal, bass drum, glockenspiel, snare drum, woodblock, xylophone, large tam-tam, medium tom-tom, small triangle), harp, violin I, violin II, viola, violoncello, double bass.
Commissioned by: consortium of orchestras and Carter Brey.
Call no.: **2000/008**

94. Asia, Daniel, 1953– Piano concerto (1994). N.p.: Dan Asia, 1994.
1 score (138 p.); 43 cm.
Duration: 32:00.
Composed for: piano, 3 flutes (3rd also piccolo), 3 oboes (3rd also English horn), 3 clarinets (3rd also bass clarinet), 3 bassoons (3rd also contrabassoon), 4 horns, 3 trumpets, 2 trombones, bass trombone, tuba, timpani, percussion (tenor drum, bass drum, snare drum, 2 woodblocks, marimba, 3 triangles, xylophone, temple blocks, glockenspiel, timbales, vibraphone, 2 suspended cymbals, 2 tom-toms, tam-tam, low sizzle cymbal, crotales, high bongo, tambourine), harp, violin I, violin II, viola, violoncello, double bass.
Commissioned by: André-Michel Schub and Phoenix Symphony, Jacksonville Symphony, Chattanooga Symphony, Grand Rapids Symphony, Milwaukee Symphony, New Jersey Symphony, and North Carolina Symphony.
Call no.: **1996/005**

95. Asia, Daniel, 1953– Piano trio. Bryn Mawr, PA: Merion Music: Theodore Presser, 1996.
1 score (64 p.); 28 cm.
Duration: 28:00.
Composed for: violin, violoncello, piano.
Commissioned by: Philip Vance.
Call no.: **1998/010**

96. Asia, Daniel, 1953– Scherzo sonata. N.p.: Dan Asia, 1987.
48 leaves of music; 30 cm.
Reproduced from manuscript.
Composed for: piano.
Commissioned by: Jonathan Shames.
Call no.: **1989/005**

97. Asia, Daniel, 1953– Songs from The page of swords: for bass-baritone, oboe, and chamber ensemble. Ensemble version. N.p.: Daniel Asia, 1992.
1 score (60 p.); 44 cm.
English words by Paul Pines, also printed as text.
Duration: ca. 25:00.
Contents: Glyph/the messenger—My Egyptian sister—Mein Bruder—Reincarnation—New Year's, 1979, ending the decade—Glyph/the message.
Composed for: bass-baritone, oboe, flute, 2 clarinets (2nd also bass clarinet), bassoon, horn, percussion (marimba, glockenspiel, crotales), piano, 2 violins, viola, violoncello, double bass.
Commissioned by: Paul Fromm Music Foundation.
Call no.: **1990/004**

98. Asia, Daniel, 1953– String quartet II. King of Prussia, PA: Merion Music: T. Presser Co., 1992.
1 score (66 p.); 36 cm.
Composed for: 2 violins, viola, violoncello.
Call no.: **2004/006**

99. Asia, Daniel, 1953– Symphony 1: for orchestra. N.p.: n.p., 1987.
1 score (108 p.); 44 cm.
Reproduced from holograph.
Duration: ca. 20:00.
At end: Dec. 9, 1987, London.
Composed for: 3 flutes (3rd also piccolo), 3 oboes (3rd also English horn), 3 clarinets (3rd also bass clarinet), 3 bassoons (3rd also contrabassoon), 4 horns, 3 trumpets, 3 trombones, tuba, timpani, percussion (marimba, 2 xylophones, crotales, vibraphone, 2 glockenspiels, 3 cymbals, sizzle cymbal, 3 tam-tams, large gong, 4 triangles, 2 timbales, 2 tom-toms, snare drum, bass drum, log drum, 2 woodblocks, 5 temple blocks, claves, slapstick), harp, piano (also celesta), violin I, violin II, viola, violoncello, double bass.
Commissioned by: American Composers Orchestra.
Call no.: **1991/004**

100. Asia, Daniel, 1953– Symphony II: celebration symphony. N.p.: D. Asia Music, 1990.
1 score (119 p.); 44 cm.
Duration: 26:00.
Contents: Ma tovu—Ashrenu—L'kha dodi—Hine El yeshuati—Halleluyah.
Composed for: 3 flutes (3rd also piccolo), 3 oboes (3rd also English horn), 3 clarinets (3rd also bass clarinet), 3 bassoons (3rd also contrabassoon), 4 horns, 3 trumpets, 3 trombones, tuba, timpani, percussion (marimba, xylophone, vibraphone, 2 glockenspiels, 4 cymbals, 2 tam-tams, 2 triangles, 2 timbales, 2 tom-toms, snare drum, 2 bass drums, 2 woodblocks, chimes), harp, piano (also celesta, synthesizer), violin I, violin II, viola, violoncello, double bass.
Call no.: **1993/003**

101. Asia, Daniel, 1953– Symphony no. 3. N.p.: n.p., 1992.
1 score (230 p.); 44 cm.
Reproduced from manuscript.
Composed for: 4 flutes (also 2 piccolos), 2 oboes, English horn, 3 clarinets, bass clarinet, 2 bassoons, contrabassoon, 6 horns, 4 trumpets, 3 trombones, bass trombone, tuba, percussion (bass drum, tam-tam, suspended cymbal, crotales, 3 triangles, vibraphone, glockenspiel, temple blocks, 4 woodblocks, log drum), timpani, piano, 2 harps, violin I, violin II, viola, violoncello, double bass.
Commissioned by: Phoenix Symphony and Meet the Composer.
Call no.: **1994/005**

102. Asia, Daniel, 1953– Symphony no. 4 (1993). Bryn Mawr, PA: Merion Music: T. Presser Co., 1993.
1 score (137, 23, 18 p.); 44 cm.
Composed for: 2 flutes, 2 oboes, 2 clarinets, 2 bassoons, 4 horns, 2 trumpets, 2 trombones, percussion (large triangle, small triangle, bass drum, woodblocks, low cymbal, crotales, timbales, large suspended cymbal, claves, tam-tam, chimes, vibraphone, marimba, glockenspiel, snare drum), timpani, harp, piano, celesta, violin I, violin II, viola, violoncello, double bass.
Commissioned by: Phoenix Symphony.
Call no.: **1995/003**

103. Asia, Daniel, 1953– Woodwind quintet. Bryn Mawr, PA: Theodore Presser, 1998.
1 score (28 p.); 36 cm.
Duration: ca. 14:00.
Composed for: flute, oboe, clarinet, horn, bassoon.
Commissioned by: Dorian Woodwind Quintet and National Endowment for the Arts.
Call no.: **2002/005**

104. Atehortuá, Blas Emilio, 1933– Musica d'orchestra per Bela Bartok, op. 135 = Musica de orquesta para Bela Bartok, op. 135. N.p.: n.p., 1985.
1 score (80 p.); 42 cm.
Reproduced from holograph.
At end of score: "Abril de 1985."
Duration: 16:00.
Contents: Quasi improvvisata—Intermezzo—Cadenza—In memoriam—Toccata.
Composed for: piccolo, 2 flutes, 2 oboes, English horn, 2 clarinets, bass clarinet, 2 bassoons, contrabassoon, 4 horns, 3 trumpets, 2 trombones, bass trombone, tuba, timpani, percussion (xylophone, snare drum, suspended cymbal, crash cymbals, tambourine, tubular bells, gong, bass drum, whip, 3 temple blocks), harp, celesta, violin I, violin II, viola, violoncello, double bass.
Call no.: **1986/008**

105. Atehortúa, Blas Emilio, 1933– Piano concerto no. 2, op. 155 (1992). N.p.: n.p., 1992.
1 score (69 p.); 49 cm.
Reproduced from holograph.
At end of score: "Blas Atehortúa / Pittsburgh, Pennsylvania, April 1st 1992."
Composed for: piano, piccolo, 2 flutes, 2 oboes, English horn, 2 clarinets, 2 bassoons, contrabassoon, 4 horns, 3 trumpets, 3 trombones, tuba, timpani, percussion (snare drum, tam-tam, 2 bongos, vibraphone, xylophone, suspended cymbal, tambourine, whip, glockenspiel, tubular bells, bass drum, 3 temple blocks, crash cymbals, triangle, bow), harp, celesta, violin I, violin II, viola, violoncello, double bass.
Call no.: **1994/006**

106. Auerbach, Lera, 1974– 24 preludes for piano. N.p.: Lera Auerbach, 1999.
57 p. of music; 30 cm.
Composed for: piano.
Commissioned by: Tom and Vivian Waldeck.
Call no.: **2003/004**

107. Auerbach, Lera, 1974– Concerto #2: for piano and orchestra: requiem for the millennium part I. 2nd ed. N.p.: Lera Auerbach, 1997.
1 score (56 p.); 36 cm.
Composed for: piano, 3 flutes (also piccolo), 2 oboes, English horn, 3 clarinets, 2 bassoons, contrabassoon, 4 horns, 3 trumpets, 3 trombones, tuba, timpani, percussion, harp, violin I, violin II, viola, violoncello, double bass.
Call no.: **2001/011**

108. Austin, Dorothea, 1922– Analogy: for viola, cello and piano. N.p.: Dorothea Austin, 1985.
1 score (19 p.); 36 cm.
Reproduced from manuscript.
Composed for: viola, violoncello, piano.
Call no.: **1988/005b**

109. Austin, Dorothea, 1922– Metamorphosis. N.p.: Dorothea Austin, 1986.
1 score (18 leaves); 32 cm.
Reproduced from holograph.
Composed for: violoncello, piano.
Call no.: **1988/005c**

110. Austin, Dorothea, 1922– Syndetos: for piano. N.p.: Dorothea Austin, 1984.

10 p. of music; 29 cm.
Reproduced from holograph.
Composed for: piano.
Call no.: **1988/005a**

111. Austin, Elizabeth R., 1938– Rose sonata: for piano solo and reciter (2002). N.p.: Elizabeth R. Austin, 2002.
21 p. of music; 22 x 37 cm.
Principally German and some English words; also printed as text with English and German translation.
Texts by Ingeborg Bachman, Rainer Maria Rilke, William Carlos Williams, and Johann Wolfgang von Goethe.
Duration: ca. 26:00.
Composed for: narrator, piano.
Commissioned by: Jane Meredith Roche.
Call no.: **2005/003**

112. Austin, Elizabeth R., 1938– Wilderness symphony: for narrators and orchestra. N.p.: n.p., 1987.
1 score (iii, 52 p.); 42 cm.
Words by Carl Sandburg; also printed as text.
Reproduced from holograph.
Duration: ca. 19:00.
Composed for: 2 narrators (male, female), 2 flutes (2nd also piccolo), 2 oboes (2nd also English horn), 2 clarinets, alto saxophone, 2 bassoons (2nd also contrabassoon), 4 horns, 2 trumpets, 2 tenor trombones, bass trombone, tuba, timpani, percussion (glockenspiel, xylophone, chimes, finger cymbals, triangles, crash cymbals, bamboo wind chimes, claves, guiro, 5 temple blocks, snare drum, vibraphone, 4 cowbells, hi-hat, ride cymbals, large maracas, castanets, vibraslap, woodblocks, whip, tambourine, 2 suspended cymbals, tam-tam, 2 bongos, bass drum), banjo, harp, piano (also celesta), violin I, violin II, viola, violoncello, double bass.
Call no.: **2001/012**
Re-entered as: **2002/006**

113. Aviram, Eilon, 1960– Six and a half (years old). N.p.: n.p., 199-?.
1 score (50 p.); 28 cm.
For orchestra.
Duration: ca. 11:00.
Composed for: 2 piccolos, 2 flutes, 2 oboes, 2 English horns, 4 clarinets (3rd–4th also bass clarinet), 2 bassoons, 3 horns, 2 trumpets, 2 trombones, bass trombone, tuba, timpani, percussion (bass drum, snare drum, triangle, tambourine, mark tree, glockenspiel, tam-tam, celesta), harp, piano, violin I, violin II, viola, violoncello, double bass.
Call no.: **1997/006**

114. Avni, Tzvi, 1927– Se questo è un uomo = If this is man: five songs for soprano and orchestra, on poems by Primo Levi (1998). Tel Aviv: Israel Music Institute, 1998.
1 score (74 p.); 37 cm.
Italian words by Primo Levi; also printed as text.
Notes by the composer in Hebrew and English.
Composed for: soprano, 2 flutes (2nd also piccolo), 2 oboes (2nd also English horn), 2 clarinets (2nd also bass clarinet), 2 bassoons, 4 horns, 2 trumpets, 3 trombones, tuba, timpani, percussion (triangle, small gong, suspended cymbal, maracas, snare drum, glockenspiel, vibraphone, temple blocks, whip, ratchet, tambourine, tom-toms, guiro, gong, cowbell, wind chimes, tam-tam), harp, violin I, violin II, viola, violoncello, double bass.
Call no.: **2001/013**

115. Azevedo, Sérgio, 1968– Concerto for 2 pianos: para two pianos and large ensemble, or orchestra. Score. N.p.: n.p., 2001.
1 score (33, 20, 7, 62 p.); 42 cm.
Duration: ca. 22:00–23:00.
Composed for: 2 pianos, 2 flutes (also 2 piccolos), oboe, 3 clarinets in A (also bass clarinet), bassoon, 2 horns, trumpet, trombone, tuba, percussion (pedal bass drum, 3 toms, snare drum, 3 bongos, cowbell, woodblock, guero, hi-hat cymbal, sizzle cymbal, claves, rattle, glass chimes, xylophone, vibraphone, glockenspiel, tam-tam, bass drum, whip, triangle, large cardbox, 4 balloons with sharp pin), timpani, celesta, harp, violin I, violin II, viola I, viola II, violoncello I, violoncello II, double bass.
Commissioned by: Music Department of the Calouste Gulbenkain Foundation (Lisbon).
Call no.: **2005/004**

116. Babbitt, Milton, 1916– Concerto for piano and orchestra, 1985. New York, NY: C. F. Peters Corp., 1986.
1 score (242 p.); 34 cm.
Reproduced from holograph.
At end: 9/7/85.
Composed for: piano, 2 flutes (2nd also piccolo), 2 oboes (2nd also English horn), 3 clarinets (2nd also clarinet in E♭, 3rd also bass clarinet), 2 bassoons (2nd also contrabassoon), 3 horns, 2 trumpets, 2 trombones (2nd also bass trombone), tuba, percussion (2 tom-toms, tenor drum, snare drum, field drum, tambourine, tam-tam, 2 suspended cymbals, 3 woodblocks), harp, vibraphone, marimba, celesta, violin I, violin II, viola, violoncello, double bass.

Commissioned by: American Composers Orchestra.
Call no.: **1987/004**

117. Babcock, David, 1956– 5. Symphonie, op. 58. N. p.: n.p., 2001.
1 score (106 p.); 30 cm.
Reproduced from manuscript.
Duration: ca. 32:00.
Composed for: 2 flutes, 2 oboes, 2 clarinets, bass clarinet, 2 bassoons, 4 horns, 3 trumpets, 3 trombones, tuba, timpani, percussion (snare drum, xylophone, cymbals, tubular bells, glockenspiel, woodblock, triangle, 2 tom-toms, whip), harp, violin I, violin II, viola, violoncello, double bass.
Call no.: **2005/005**

118. Bach, Jan, 1937– Anachronisms: (string quartet no. 2), 1991. N.p.: n.p., 1991.
1 score (64 p.); 29 cm.
Program notes by the composer.
Contents: Sonatina—Song without words—In moto perpetuo—Dueling cadenzas—Broadway boogie woogie.
Composed for: 2 violins, viola, violoncello.
Commissioned by: WFMT Fine Arts Radio (Chicago) and Vermeer String Quartet.
Call no.: **1993/004**

119. Bach, Jan, 1937– Harp concerto, 1986. N.p.: n.p., 1986.
1 score (105 p.); 28 cm.
Composed for: harp, flute, oboe, 2 clarinets, bass clarinet, 2 bassoons, 2 horns, trumpet, trombone, timpani, percussion (vibraphone, xylophone, marimba, glockenspiel, suspended cymbal, splash cymbal, tam-tam, triangle, claves, 3 woodblocks, 2 temple blocks, slapstick, flexatone, 4 tom-toms, bass drum, roto-tom, snare drum, 2 drums), violin I, violin II, viola, violoncello, double bass.
Commissioned by: Diane Evans.
Call no.: **1990/005**

120. Bach, Jan, 1937– Horn concerto. N.p.: n.p., 1982.
1 score (161 p.); 39 cm.
Reproduced from holograph.
Duration: ca. 35:00.
At end of score: "Score completed January 9, 1983. DeKalb IL."
Composed for: horn, 2 flutes, 2 oboes, 2 clarinets in A, bass clarinet, 2 bassoons, contrabassoon, 4 horns, 3 trumpets, 3 trombones, tuba, timpani, percussion (vibraphone, xylophone, glockenspiel, tam-tam, suspended cymbal, hi-hat, crash cymbals, triangle, 2 cowbells, slapstick, 4 tom-toms, bass drum, snare drum, 3 drums, 4 temple blocks, woodblock), harp, violin I, violin II, viola, violoncello, double bass.
Commissioned by: Betty Bootjer Butler and Jonathan Boen.
Call no.: **1985/008**

121. Bach, Jan, 1937– The last flower: a parable in music. N.p.: n.p., 1995.
1 score (52 p.); 28 cm.
English words by James Thurber.
Duration: ca. 15:00.
Composed for: violoncello, clarinet, harp, percussion (chimes, tam-tam, siren, 3 tom-toms, Chinese gong, suspended cymbal, ratchet, small mouth siren, vibraphone, police whistle, snare drum, timpani, sandpaper blocks, 3 triangles, mouth bird whistle, crotales, guiro, scraper, bongo, cowbells, temple blocks); narrators.
Commissioned by: Ronen Chamber Ensemble.
Call no.: **1997/007**

122. Bach, Jan, 1937– Songs of the streetwise: for SATB choir and steel band: settings of nine poems selected from the Streetwise collection "From hard times to hope." N.p.: n.p., 2000.
1 vocal score (48 p.); 28 cm.
English words; also printed as text.
Duration: ca. 25:00.
Composed for: SATB chorus, steel band.
Commissioned by: South Bend Chamber Singers.
Call no.: **2003/005**

123. Bäcker, Horst-Hans, 1959– Rapsodia Mallorquina: für Orchester = pour orchestre = for orchestra (2002). Bonn: Hillbrecht-Verlag, 2002.
1 score (61 p.); 30 cm.
Duration: ca. 13:00.
Composed for: piccolo, flute, oboe, English horn, 2 clarinets, 2 bassoons, contrabassoon, 2 horns, 2 trumpets, piccolo snare drum, tambourine, violin I, violin II, viola, violoncello, double bass.
Call no.: **2005/006**

124. Bacon, Ernst, 1898–1990. Trio II.
Commissioned by: Louise Davies and Judy Wilbur.
Call no.: **1988/006**
No materials available.

125. Badian, Maya, 1954– Holocaust in memoriam: symphony. Ottawa, ON: Lucian Badian Editions, 1998.
1 score (51 p.); 28 cm.
Duration: 20:00.
Composed for: 3 flutes (3rd also piccolo), 2 oboes, English horn, 2 clarinets, bass clarinet, 3 bassoons (3rd

also contrabassoon), 4 horns, 3 trumpets, 3 trombones, tuba, percussion (timpani, triangle, 2 woodblocks, 2 crotales, tubular bells, xylophone, 3 temple blocks, 3 bongos, tam-tam, vibraphone, 3 tom-toms, glockenspiel, bass drum), celesta, piano, violin I, violin II, viola, violoncello, double bass.
Call no.: **2000/010**

126. Bailey, Keith McDonald, 1952– Danse grazioso: composed for piano. N.p.: n.p., 1991.
3 leaves of music; 30 cm.
Reproduced from manuscript.
Corrected version submitted by the composer in 1991.
Composed for: piano.
Call no.: **1989/006**

127. Bainbridge, Simon, 1952– Ad ora incerta: four orchestral songs from Primo Levi: 1994. London: Novello, 1994.
1 score (109 p.); 43 cm.
Italian words by Primo Levi; also printed as text with English translations.
For mezzo-soprano, solo bassoon, and orchestra.
Reproduced from holograph.
Duration: 30:00.
Contents: Il canto del corvo—Lunedi—Il tramonto di Fossoli—Buna.
1997 Grawemeyer Award winning work.
Composed for: mezzo-soprano, bassoon, 2 piccolos, 2 flutes (2nd also alto flute, piccolo), 2 oboes, English horn, 4 clarinets (3rd–4th also bass clarinet), contrabassoon, 4 horns, 4 trumpets, 3 trombones, timpani, percussion (marimba, glockenspiel, tubular bells, medium tam-tam, sizzle cymbal, high suspended cymbal, snare drum, flexatone, police whistle, 2 crystal wine glasses, 2 crotales, xylophone, large tam-tam, medium suspended cymbals, bell tree, claves, triangle, large suspended cymbal, bass drum, cabasa, large maracas), harp, violin I, violin II, viola, violoncello, double bass.
Commissioned by: BBC.
Call no.: **1996/006**
Re-entered as: **1997/008**

128. Baiocchi, Regina A. Harris, 1956– Foster pet: for mezzo, oboe, percussion, piano. N.p.: Regina A. Harris Baiocchi, 1991.
1 score (9 p.); 29 cm.
English words by the composer.
Reproduced from manuscript.
Composed for: mezzo-soprano, oboe, piano, percussion (glockenspiel, cabasa).
Commissioned by: Mostly Music.
Call no.: **1992/005**

129. Baiocchi, Regina A. Harris, 1956– Orchestral suite: for orchestra. N.p.: n.p., 1992.
1 score (25 p.); 22 x 30 cm.
Reproduced from manuscript.
Duration: 12:00.
Contents: Against the O.D.S.—Mother to Nique—Thunder!
Composed for: 2 flutes (2nd also piccolo), oboe, clarinet, bassoon, 3 trumpets, 3 horns, 3 trombones, tuba, percussion (crash cymbals, snare drum, tom-tom, bass drum, slapstick, thundersheet, timpani), violin I, violin II, viola, violoncello, double bass.
Call no.: **1994/007**

130. Bajoras, Feliksas Romualdas, 1934– Exodus II. N.p.: n.p., 1996.
1 score (124 p.); 30 cm.
For orchestra.
Reproduced from holograph.
Composed for: 3 flutes (3rd also piccolo), 3 oboes (3rd also English horn), 3 clarinets (3rd also bass clarinet), 3 bassoons (3rd also contrabassoon), 4 horns, 3 trumpets, 3 trombones, tuba, percussion (timpani, claves, cowbell, triangle, 2 woodblocks, whip, bells, tubular bells, marimba, xylophone, crash cymbals, castanet, crotales, gong, snare drum, vibraphone, bongos, 2 tom-toms, tambourine, bass drum, maraca, glockenspiel, tam-tam, temple block, conga, cabasa, suspended cymbal, agogo bell, trap set), piano, violin I, violin II, viola, violoncello, double bass.
Call no.: **1997/009**

131. Bajoras, Feliksas Romualdas, 1934– Koncertas smuikui: ir simfoniniam orkestrui = Concerto for violin and symphony orchestra. N.p.: n.p., 2000.
1 score (333 [i.e., 321] p.); 29 cm.
Reproduced from manuscript.
Composed for: violin, 2 flutes (2nd also piccolo), alto flute (also piccolo), 2 oboes, English horn, 3 clarinets (2nd also clarinet in E♭, 3rd also bass clarinet), 3 bassoons (3rd also contrabassoon), 2 horns, 2 trumpets, 3 trombones, tuba, percussion (glockenspiel, triangle, bongos, tom-tom, slapstick, steel drum, gong, maraca or chocalho, tambourine, 2 drumsticks, metal frame, marimba, small bell, vibraslap, claves, castanets, woodblock, agogo bell, brake drum, talking drum, cymbals, tam-tam, vibraphone, military snare drum, cowbell, temple blocks, suspended cymbals, hi-hat, bass drum, rimshot, wire brush), violin I, violin II, viola, violoncello, double bass.
Call no.: **2003/006**

132. Bajoras, Feliksas Romualdas, 1934– Missa in musica. N.p.: n.p., 199-?.
1 score (144 p.); 30 cm.
Latin words.
Reproduced from manuscript.
Includes performance instructions (p.142–44).
Composed for: voice, trombone, double bass, piano.
Call no.: **1994/008**

133. Bajoras, Feliksas Romualdas, 1934– Suokos: styginių kvartetui, 1998. N.p.: n.p., 1998.
1 score (72 p.); 30 cm.
For string quartet.
Reproduced from manuscript.
Composed for: 2 violins, viola, violoncello.
Call no.: **2001/014**

134. Baker, Claude, 1948– Awaking the winds: for orchestra (1992–93). St. Louis, MO: MMB Music, 1993.
1 score (54 p.); 46 cm.
Reproduced from manuscript.
Duration: ca. 15:00.
Composed for: 3 flutes (2nd–3rd also piccolo), 3 oboes, 3 clarinets (also bass clarinet), 3 bassoons, 4 horns, 3 trumpets, 3 trombones, harp, celesta, piano, violin I, violin II, viola, violoncello, double bass.
Call no.: **1994/009**

135. Baker, Claude, 1948– Shadows: four dirge-nocturnes for orchestra (1990). Score. St. Louis, MO: MMB Music, 1990.
1 score (58 p.); 46 cm.
Reproduced from holograph.
Duration: ca. 17:00.
Performance notes and preface by the composer.
Composed for: 3 flutes (2nd–3rd also piccolo), 3 oboes, 2 clarinets, bass clarinet, 3 bassoons, 4 horns, 3 trumpets, 2 trombones, bass trombone, tuba, timpani (also 5 temple cup gongs, 10 crotales), percussion (marimba, vibraphone, crotales, tam-tam, bell tree, maracas, bells, chimes, bongos, suspended cymbal, Chinese temple gong, 2 woodblocks, guiro, roto-tom, bass drum, 2 tom-toms, 2 tambourines, bamboo wind chimes, glass wind chimes), harp, piano (also celesta), violin I, violin II, viola, violoncello, double bass.
Commissioned by: Saint Louis Symphony Orchestra.
Call no.: **1991/005**

136. Baker, Claude, 1948– Whispers and echoes: for orchestra (1994–1995). St. Louis, MO: MMB Music, 1995.
1 score (79 p.); 36 cm.
Duration: ca. 18:00.
Composed for: 3 flutes (2nd–3rd also piccolo), 3 oboes (3rd also English horn), 2 clarinets, bass clarinet, 3 bassoons, 4 horns, 3 trumpets, 2 trombones, bass trombone, tuba, 4 timpani (also 4 suspended cymbals), percussion (vibraphone, crotales, 5 temple blocks, xylophone, Chinese temple gong, 3 woodblocks, glockenspiel, marimba, 2 tam-tams), harp, piano, violin I, violin II, viola, violoncello, double bass.
Call no.: **1996/007**

137. Baksa, Andreas, 1950– Monarchia—Monarchia: Ballett in 2 Akten. N.p.: n.p., 1994.
1 score (139 p.); 37 cm.
For soprano and orchestra.
Reproduced from holograph.
Duration: ca. 29:00.
Composed for: soprano, 3 flutes (3rd also piccolo), 3 oboes, 3 clarinets, bass clarinet, bassoon, contrabassoon, 4 horns, 3 trumpets, 2 trombones, tuba, soprano saxophone, percussion (glockenspiel, congas, tam-tam, xylophone, triangle, cymbals, drum set, tambourine, side drum, large drum, bass drum, metal guiro, ratchet, flexatone, synthetic drum, bamboo chimes, bell tree, Chinese cymbal, gong, woodblock), harp, piano, organ, harpsichord, celesta, accordion, timpani, electric bass, didgeridoo, violin I, violin II, viola, violoncello, double bass.
Call no.: **1995/004**

138. Balada, Leonardo, 1933– Cristobal Colon: opera en dos actos (noviemb. 1986). Partitura. Pittsburgh, PA: Beteca Music, 1990.
1 score (2 v.); 44 cm.
Spanish words by Antonio Gala.
Corrected July 1989, Febr. 1990.
Duration: ca. 2:10:00.
Composed for: soprano, mezzo-soprano, 2 tenors, 6 baritones, 3 bass-baritones, 4 basses, SATB chorus, 2 flutes (2nd also piccolo), 2 oboes (2nd also English horn), 2 clarinets (2nd also bass clarinet), 2 bassoons (2nd also contrabassoon), 3 horns, 3 trumpets, 2 trombones, bass trombone, tuba, percussion (timpani, bongos, bass drum, 3 tom-toms, 2 tambourines, temple blocks, claves, woodblock, snare drum, 4 castanets, brake drum, whip, musical saw, ratchet, penny whistle, sleigh bells, cencerro, triangle, 3 suspended cymbals, crash cymbals, tam-tam, crotales, glockenspiel, vibraphone, 2 chimes, thundersheet), harp, harpsichord, violin I, violin II, viola, violoncello, double bass.
Call no.: **1992/006**

139. Balada, Leonardo, 1933– Music for oboe and orchestra: (lament from the cradle of the earth). N.p.: Beteca Music, 1993.
1 score (112 p.); 36 cm.
"Corrected: Aug. 1993, Nov. 1993"—p. 2 of cover.
Duration: ca. 24:00.
Composed for: oboe, 2 flutes, 2 oboes, English horn, 2 clarinets, bass clarinet, 2 bassoons, contrabassoon, 4 horns, 3 trumpets, 3 trombones, tuba, timpani, percussion (xylophone, vibraphone, tubular bells, temple blocks, snare drum, glockenspiel, marimba, tam-tam, suspended cymbals, bass drum, 3 triangles, 3 bongos, tom-toms, 3 woodblocks), harp, piano, celesta, violin I, violin II, viola, violoncello, double bass.
Commissioned by: Lorin Maazel and Pittsburgh Symphony Society.
Call no.: **1994/010**

140. Balada, Leonardo, 1933– Music for oboe and orchestra: (lament from the cradle of the earth). N.p.: Beteca Music, 1996.
1 score (104 p.); 28 cm.
"Corrected: Aug. 1993, Nov. 1993, April 1996"—p. 2 of cover.
Duration: ca. 21:00.
Composed for: oboe, 2 flutes, 2 oboes, English horn, 2 clarinets, bass clarinet, 2 bassoons, contrabassoon, 4 horns, 3 trumpets, 3 trombones, tuba, timpani, percussion (xylophone, vibraphone, tubular bells, temple blocks, snare drum, glockenspiel, marimba, tam-tam, suspended cymbals, bass drum, 3 triangles, 3 bongos, tom-toms, 3 woodblocks), harp, piano, celesta, violin I, violin II, viola, violoncello, double bass.
Commissioned by: Lorin Maazel and Pittsburgh Symphony Society.
Call no.: **1997/010**

141. Balada, Leonardo, 1933– No-res (nothing/nada): tragifonia en dos partes para voz-declamada, coro y orquesta = a symphonic tragedy in two parts for voice-narrated, chorus and orchestra. Rev. orchestra score. New York, NY: G. Schirmer, 1978.
1 score (95 p.); 35 cm.
Words by Jean Paris.
Duration: ca. 40:00.
"Revised version April 1997."
"Corrected December 1997."
"In part I the text of the voice and chorus is in several universal languages. In part II the voice narrates in the language of the place where the work is performed, while the chorus sings in English"—Title page verso.
Composed for: narrator, SATB chorus, 3 flutes (2nd also piccolo, 3rd is optional), 3 oboes (3rd is optional), 3 clarinets (3rd also bass clarinet), 2 bassoons, contrabassoon, 4 horns, 3 trumpets (4th optional), 2 trombones, bass trombone, tuba, percussion (2 hand cymbals, 4 suspended cymbals, tam-tam, 3 timpani, 3 tom-tom, 3 snare drums, bass drum, whip, temple blocks, glockenspiel, xylophone, vibraphone, chimes), piano (also amplified cembalo), electric organ (also accordion), electronic tape, voice, mixed chorus, violin I, violin II, viola, violoncello, double bass.
Commissioned by: Fund. J. March of Madrid.
Call no.: **2003/007**

142. Balakauskas, Osvaldas, 1935– Opera strumentale. Vilnius: n.p., 1987.
1 score (189 p.); 41 cm.
For orchestra.
Reproduced from manuscript.
Contents: Sinfonia—Cavatina—Duetti—Aria—Coro I: motet—Quartetti—Recitativo—Rituale—Coro II: fuga.
Composed for: 3 flutes (1st also alto flute, 3rd also piccolo), 3 oboes (3rd also English horn), 3 clarinets (3rd also bass clarinet), 3 bassoons (3rd also contrabassoon), 4 horns, 3 trumpets, 3 trombones, tuba, timpani, percussion (triangle, snare drum, tom-tom, tam-tam, bass drum, flexatone, woodblocks, cowbells, glockenspiel, vibraphone, xylophone, marimba, chimes), harp, piano (also celesta), violin I, violin II, viola, violoncello, double bass.
Call no.: **1990/006**

143. Balassa, Sándor, 1935– A day-dreamer's diary: for chamber orchestra (or orchestra) = Egy álmodozó naplója: kamarazenekarra (vagy zenekarra), op. 35. Partitura. Budapest: Editio Musica, 1984.
1 score (115 p.); 42 cm.
Reproduced from holograph.
At end of score: "28, January, 1983, Budakeszl."
Composed for: 3 flutes (2nd also piccolo, 3rd also alto flute), 2 oboes (2nd also English horn), 3 clarinets (2nd also clarinet in E♭, 3rd also bass clarinet), 2 bassoons, 2 horns, 2 trumpets, harp, celesta, violin I, violin II, viola, violoncello, double bass.
Commissioned by: Elizabeth Sprague Coolidge Foundation.
Call no.: **1985/009**

144. Baldissera, Marino, 1969– Jánas 3: per orchestra. N.p.: n.p., 1997.
1 score (15 leaves); 42 cm.
Reproduced from manuscript.
Composed for: 2 flutes (2nd also piccolo), 2 oboes (2nd also English horn), 2 clarinets (2nd also bass clarinet),

2 bassoons, 4 horns, 2 trumpets, 3 trombones (3rd also bass trombone), tuba, percussion (timpani, snare drum, vibraphone, 2 suspended cymbals, 3 Chinese blocks, 3 tom-toms, xylophone, glockenspiel, medium tam-tam, gong, maracas, crash cymbal, 2 bongos, 2 congas, bass drum), harp, celesta, violin I, violin II, viola, violoncello, double bass.
Call no.: **2000/011**

145. Ballard, Louis W., 1931– Fantasy aborigine no. 6 (Niagara): the maid of the mist and the thunderbeings, 1993. Santa Fe, NM: New S.W. Music Publications, 1993.
1 score (286 p.); 36 cm.
Suite for symphony orchestra.
Composed for: piccolo, 2 flutes, alto flute, 2 oboes, English horn, 2 clarinets, bass clarinet, 2 bassoons, contrabassoon, 4 horns, 3 trumpets, 2 trombones, tuba, timpani, percussion (Iroquois bark rattle, 2 turtle-shell rattles, 8 horn rattles, 2 deer-hoof rattles, 2 peach-stone dice bowls, Seneca flute, 2 water drums, rain sticks, gourd rattles, tom-tom, seashell rattles, bass drum, snare drum, bongos, cowbells, bass bongo, drum set [4 toms, 4 cymbals, pedal bass, snare drum, 2 hi-hats, tree chimes, tambourine], suspended cymbal, crash cymbals, gongs, flexatone, claves, guiro, sand paper, woodblocks, temple blocks, afuche, cabasa, tubular bells, triangles, xylophone, marimba), piano, celesta, synthesizer, violin I, violin II, viola, violoncello, double bass.
Commissioned by: Cabrillo Music Festival Symphony Orchestra.
Call no.: **1994/011**

146. Balliana, Franco, 1954– Oltre: per violino solo. N.p.: n.p., 1984.
1 v. of music; 37 cm.
In 5 movements.
Reproduced from holograph.
Composed for: violin.
Call no.: **1985/010**

147. Ballif, Claude, 1924–2004. Dracoula: drame nocturne en deux parties de Viorel Stéphane, op. 58. N. p.: n.p., 1984.
1 score (435 p.); 39 cm.
French words.
Reproduced from manuscript.
Composed for: 3 sopranos, mezzo-soprano, tenor, baritone, various mixed voices, flute (also piccolo), oboe (also English horn), sopranino saxophone (also alto and baritone saxophones), horn, trumpet (also cornet), trombone (also bass trombone), percussion (crotales, studded cymbal, 3 tam-tams, snare drum, 2 Turkish cymbals, military drum, glockenspiel, vibraphone, antique cymbals, gongs, bass drum, xylophone, marimba, glass chimes, guiro, 3 triangles, tom-toms, 3 congas, claves, timpani, 2 bongos, mark tree, small rin), harp, accordion, 2 violins, viola, violoncello, double bass.
Commissioned by: État français.
Call no.: **1988/007**

148. Ballif, Claude, 1924–2004. Haut les rêves! concert symphonique no 2. N.p.: n.p., 1984.
1 score (119 leaves); 30 cm.
Concerto for violin and orchestra.
Reproduced from holograph.
At end of score: "9 juillet–22 nov. 84."
Duration: 26:00.
Composed for: violin, 2 flutes (both also piccolo), 2 oboes, clarinet in A, bassoon, 2 horns, violin I, violin II, viola, violoncello, double bass.
Call no.: **1989/007**

149. Ballif, Claude, 1924–2004. Un moment de printemps, op. 60. N.p.: n.p., 1987.
1 score (27 p.); 29 cm.
Reproduced from holograph.
Composed for: flute, violin, clarinet, violoncello, piano.
Call no.: **1990/007**

150. Baltakas, Vykintas, 1972– Poussla: für solistisches Ensemble und Orchester (2002). Studienpartitur. Vienna; New York, NY: Universal Edition, 2002.
1 miniature score (53 p.); 30 cm.
Duration: ca. 12:00.
Composed for: ensemble (oboe, clarinet in E♭, soprano saxophone, violin, accordion, piano, tuba), 2 flutes, 2 oboes, 2 clarinets, bass clarinet, 2 bassoons, contrabassoon, 4 horns, 2 trumpets, 2 trombones, tuba, percussion (temple blocks, cowbell, snare drum, tom-tom, bass drum, 2 timpani, slapper), violin, viola, violoncello, double bass.
Commissioned by: WDR.
Call no.: **2004/007**

151. Bank, Jacques, 1943– De Bijlmer opera. Amsterdam: Donemus, 1999.
1 score (142 p.); 42 cm.
Dutch words by Fer Bank.
Opera in 17 scenes.
Reproduced from manuscript.
Duration: ca. 1:15:00.
Composed for: mezzo-soprano, baritone, SATB chorus, flute (also piccolo), soprano saxophone (also baritone

saxophone), alto saxophone, tenor saxophone (also soprano saxophone), horn, 3 trumpets, 2 trombones, bass trombones, percussion (flexatone, 3 cymbals, 4 woodblocks, tam-tam, marimba, celesta, 3 bongos, 3 tom-toms, xylophone, vibraphone, bass drum, 4 cowbells, 3 crotales), 4 timpani, piano, double bass.
Call no.: **2002/007**

152. Bank, Jacques, 1943– Episodes de la vie d'un artiste: for baritone, mezzo soprano, tenor, boys' choir, mixed choir and orchestra: 1992/93. Amsterdam: Donemus, 1994.
1 score (v, 136 p.); 42 cm.
French or English words; also printed as text; principally from the memoirs and letters of Hector Berlioz.
Reproduced from manuscript.
Duration: ca. 65:00.
Composed for: mezzo-soprano, tenor, baritone, boys' chorus, SATB chorus, piccolo, 2 flutes (2nd also piccolo), 2 oboes, English horn, 2 clarinets (1st also clarinet in E♭), bass clarinet, 2 bassoons, contrabassoon, 4 horns, trumpet in D, 2 trumpets, 2 trombones, bass trombone, tuba, timpani, percussion (xylophone, celesta, 4 cymbals, large anvil, snare drum, bass drum, vibraphone, tambourine, 3 bongos, 3 tom-toms, marimba, 3 tam-tams, triangle, 5 woodblocks), 2 harps, piano, 2 accordions, violin I, violin II, viola, violoncello, double bass.
Commissioned by: Kees Hillen and Rotterdam Philharmonic.
Call no.: **1997/011**

153. Bank, Jacques, 1943– Requiem voor een levende: (1985): voor spreekstem, gemengd koor, 4 saxofoons, 9 akkordeons, 3 contrabassen, slagwerk. Amsterdam: Donemus, 1986.
1 score (115 p.); 42 cm.
Latin or French words; also printed as text.
Reproduced from holograph.
Contents: Libera me—Requiem aeternam—Dies irae—Sis mortuus.
Composed for: narrator, SATB chorus, soprano saxophone, alto saxophone, tenor saxophone, baritone saxophone, percussion (xylophone, marimba, vibraphone, bass drum, bongo, tom-tom, woodblock, piano, tam-tam, snare drum, 4 cymbals, wind machine, timpani, large sheet of zinc), 9 accordions, 3 double basses.
Call no.: **1991/006**

154. Barab, Seymour, 1921– Cantata: rest eternal grant them, o cosmos: for soprano, tenor, baritone and orchestra. New York, NY: Seesaw Music, 1995.
1 score (84 p.); 39 x 44 cm.
English words by Kurt Vonnegut.
Reproduced from manuscript.
Composed for: soprano, tenor, baritone, flute, oboe, clarinets, bassoon, 4 horns, trumpet, trombone, violin I, violin II, viola, violoncello, double bass.
Call no.: **1998/011**

155. Baratello, Marino, 1951– Aria: per soprano e orchestra. N.p.: n.p., 1988.
1 score (28 p.); 48 cm.
Italian words from "Canti orfici" by Dino Campana.
Reproduced from holograph.
Duration: 8:30.
Composed for: soprano, 4 flutes, 2 oboes, English horn, clarinet in E♭, 2 clarinets, 2 bassoons, contrabassoon, 4 horns, 4 trumpets, 2 trombones, tuba, percussion (tambourine, maracas, gong, tam-tam, medium cymbal, timpani), harp, celesta, violin I, violin II, viola, violoncello, double bass.
Call no.: **1989/008**

156. Barati, George, 1913–1996. Violin concerto, 1986. N.p.: n.p., 1986.
1 score (84 p.); 29 cm.
Reproduced from manuscript.
Composed for: violin, 2 flutes (2nd also piccolo), 2 oboes, 2 clarinets, 2 bassoons, 4 horns, 2 trumpets, 3 trombones, timpani, percussion (triangle, cymbals, woodblocks, snare drum, crash cymbals, tambourine, tam-tam, xylophone, glockenspiel, bass drum), harp, violin I, violin II, viola, violoncello, double bass.
Call no.: **1987/005**

157. Barnes, Milton, 1931–2001. Concerto for viola & full orchestra. N.p.: n.p., 1977.
1 score (150 p.); 39 cm.
Variations on the traditional medieval Hebrew tune "Chad Gadyo."
Reproduced from manuscript.
Duration: 27:30.
Composed for: viola, 2 flutes, 2 oboes, 2 clarinets, 2 bassoons, 2 horns, 2 trumpets, 3 trombones, tuba, timpani, percussion (snare drum, bass drum, 3 tom-toms, triangle, tambourine, xylophone), violin I, violin II, viola, violoncello, double bass.
Commissioned by: Blue Mountain Summer School of Music, Collingwood, Ontario.
Call no.: **1994/012**

158. Barnes, Milton, 1931–2001. Papageno variations: after The magic flute by W.A. Mozart: for double bass & piano. N.p.: Milton Barnes, 1988.
1 score (20 p.) + 1 part (13 p.); 32 cm.

Reproduced from manuscript.
Composed for: double bass, piano.
Commissioned by: Rick Murrin.
Call no.: **1992/007**

159. Barnett, Carol, 1949– Meeting at Seneca Falls. N.p.: n.p., 1998.
1 score (152 p.); 36 cm.
Words by Marisha Chamberlain.
For solo voices, narrator, and chamber orchestra.
Duration: ca. 24:00.
Composed for: narrator, 3 sopranos, 3 altos, 3 baritones, flute, clarinet, bassoon, horn, percussion (suspended cymbal, maracas, triangle, snare drum, small woodblock, 4 tom-toms, slapstick, glockenspiel, castanets, claves, bass drum, timpani, marimba), piano (also electric celesta), violin, viola, violoncello, double bass.
Commissioned by: Upper Midwest Women's History Center.
Call no.: **2000/012**

160. Barrett, Richard, 1959– Opening of the mouth: for two vocalists, eleven instrumentalists and electronics. London: United Music Publishers, 1999.
1 score (154 p.); 31 cm.
German words by Paul Celan; also printed as text with English translation.
Contents: Engführung (I)—Largo—Schneebett—Zungenentwurzeln—Tenebrae—Engführung (II).
Composed for: soprano, mezzo-soprano, flute (also piccolo, alto flute), bass clarinet (also bass recorder, clarinet in C, contrabass clarinet), percussion (vibraphone, Thai gong, flexatone, crotales, steel drum, 2 pebbles, 2 claves, Mexican bean, vibraslap, tambourine, metal chimes, glass chimes, wood chimes, bamboo chimes, shell chimes, rain stick, chains, sandpaper blocks, snare drum, tam-tam, thundersheet, pedal bass drum, large suspended wooden board, tabla, tubular bell, slit drum, vibraphone plate, temple block, xylophone plate, cowbell, roto-tom, triangle, 2 guiros, 3 suspended cymbals, Chinese cymbal, wind gong), mandolin (also mandola), 12-string guitar (also electric guitar), koto (also bass koto), violin (also viola, hardanger fiddle), violoncello, sampling keyboard (also signal processing).
Commissioned by: Festival of Perth, Western Australia.
Call no.: **2001/015**
Re-entered as: **2003/008**

161. Barrett, Richard, 1959– Vanity: for orchestra. London: United Music Publishers, 1997.
1 miniature score (78 p.); 34 cm.
Duration: ca. 27:00.
Reproduced from manuscript.
Composed for: 3 piccolos, 3 oboes (2nd also oboe d'amore, 3rd also English horn), 3 clarinets in E♭ (1st also clarinet, 3rd also bass clarinet), 3 bassoons (2nd–3rd also contrabassoon), soprano saxophone (also tenor saxophone), alto saxophone (also baritone saxophone), 6 horns, 2 trombones, bass trombone, 2 bass tubas, percussion (3 triangles, small tam-tam, glass chimes, sleigh bells, crotales, thundersheet, 2 small timbales, wood chimes, 2 log drums, marimba, bell plate, 2 medium roto-toms, 2 woodblocks, maracas, large guiro, sandpaper blocks, Chinese cymbal, 2 tom-toms, 2 wood plate drums, cimbalom, 2 bongos, 3 congas, shell chimes, 6 temple blocks, ratchet, vibraslap, slapstick, small suspended cymbal, Japanese woodblock, high noh theater drum, large tenor drum, large bass drum, pedal bass drum), 2 pianos, 2 electric bass guitars, violin I, violin II, viola, violoncello, double bass.
Commissioned by: Rex Foundation.
Call no.: **1998/012**

162. Barroso, Sergio, 1946– Concerto: for viola and orchestra. N.p.: Sergio Barroso, 1996.
1 score (69 p.); 28 cm.
Reproduced from manuscript.
Small orchestra and electronics version.
Composed for: viola, 2 flutes (2nd also piccolo), oboe, English horn, clarinet, bass clarinet, bassoon, contrabassoon, 2 horns, 2 trumpets, trombone, tuba, timpani, percussion (large bass drum, tenor drum, Cuban bongos, small tom-tom, large gong, 2 suspended cymbals, marimba, 2 temple blocks, woodblock, claves, 3 maracas, guiro, small ratchet, vibraslap, whip), harp, midi keyboard controller, violin I, violin II, viola, violoncello, double bass.
Call no.: **2001/016 small orch.**

163. Barroso, Sergio, 1946– Concerto: for viola and orchestra. N.p.: Sergio Barroso, 1999.
1 score (72 p.); 28 cm.
Reproduced from manuscript.
Full orchestra version.
Composed for: viola, 3 flutes (3rd also piccolo, alto flute), 2 oboes, English horn, 2 clarinets, bass clarinet, 2 bassoons, contrabassoon, 4 horns, 3 trumpets, 2 trombones, bass trombone, tuba, timpani, percussion (large bass drum, tenor drum, Cuban bongos, small tom-tom, large gong, 3 suspended cymbals, hi-hat, marimba, 2 temple blocks, woodblock, claves, 4 maracas, guiro, small ratchet, vibraslap, whip), harp, piano, violin I, violin II, viola, violoncello, double bass.
Call no.: **2001/016 full orch.**

164. Barry, Gerald, 1952– Wiener Blut. Oxford: Oxford University Press, 2001.
1 score (91 p.); 30 cm.
"Corrected October 2001"—Pref.
Reproduced from manuscript.
Composed for: flute, oboe, clarinet, bass clarinet, bassoon, 2 horns, trumpet, 2 violins, viola, violoncello, double bass.
Commissioned by: Birmingham Contemporary Music Group.
Call no.: **2004/008**

165. Barsom, Paul, 1961– Seventy thousand Assyrians. N.p.: n.p., 1999.
1 score (43 p.); 44 cm.
For concert band.
Composed for: 4 flutes (1st–2nd also piccolo), 3 oboes, clarinet in E♭, 3 clarinets, bass clarinet, 3 bassoons, contrabassoon, alto saxophone, tenor saxophone, baritone saxophone, 8 horns, 4 trumpets, 3 trombones, euphonium, 4 tubas, timpani, percussion (glockenspiel, tambourine, chimes, woodblock, lion's roar, splash cymbal, large suspended cymbal, vibraslap, xylophone, ratchet, triangle, metal plate, tam-tam, slapstick, anvil, maracas, medium suspended cymbal, Chinese cymbal, claves, 2 brake drums, cowbell, 2 bass drums, sandpaper blocks, small tambourine, glass or metal wind chimes, 4 tom-toms, vibraphone, large and small woodblocks, bongos, slapstick, slit drum, marimba, sizzle cymbal, snare drum, bell tree).
Commissioned by: Pennsylvania State University Symphonic Wind Ensemble.
Call no.: **2002/008**

166. Bartholomée, Pierre, 1937– Fredons et tarabusts: sérénade: pour grand orchestre. Bruxelles: CeBeDeM, 1997.
1 score (174 p.); 31 cm.
Reproduced from holograph.
Duration: ca. 42:00.
Composed for: 4 flutes (3rd also piccolo, 4th also alto flute), 4 oboes (4th also English horn), 4 clarinets (4th also bass clarinet), 4 bassoons (4th also contrabassoon), 4 horns, 4 trumpets (3rd also piccolo trumpet), 2 trombones, bass trombone, tuba, percussion (bass drum, snare drum, large cymbal, gong, 2 maracas, 3 tom-toms, vibraphone, re-re, tumba, temple blocks, 2 tam-tams, whip, timbales, triangle, suspended cymbal, marimba, large bongo, tubular bells, cog rattle, cowbells, switch), harp, piano (also celesta), violin I, violin II, viola, violoncello, double bass.
Commissioned by: Crédit Communal de Belgique.
Call no.: **1998/013**

167. Bartholomée, Pierre, 1937– Œdipe sur la route: opéra en quatre actes. N.p.: Musica Scripta-Éditions, 2002.
1 score (2 v.); 31 cm.
French words by Henry Bauchau.
Commissioned by: Théâtre Royal de la Monnaie.
Call no.: **2005/007** (v. 2 only)

168. Bassett, Leslie, 1923– Concerto for orchestra. New York, NY: C. F. Peters, 1991.
1 score (85 p.); 39 cm.
Reproduced from holograph.
Duration: ca. 28:00.
Composed for: 3 flutes (3rd also piccolo), 3 oboes (3rd also English horn), 3 clarinets (3rd also bass clarinet), 3 bassoons (3rd also contrabassoon), 4 horns, 3 trumpets, 2 trombones, bass trombone, tuba, percussion (timpani, cymbals, triangle, bell tree, tam-tam, suspended cymbal, vibraphone, tom-toms, temple blocks, glass wind chimes, crotales, bass drum, xylophone, slapstick, chimes, sizzle cymbal, glockenspiel, marimba, snare drum, tenor drum), harp, piano, celesta, violin I, violin II, viola, violoncello, double bass.
Commissioned by: Serge Koussevitsky Music Foundation in the Library of Congress, Koussevitsky Music Foundation, and Detroit Symphony Orchestra.
Call no.: **1993/005**

169. Bassett, Leslie, 1923– Thoughts that sing, breathe and burn: music for orchestra. New York, NY: C. F. Peters, 1997.
1 score (42 p.); 44 cm.
Composed for: piccolo, 2 flutes, 3 oboes (3rd also English horn), 3 clarinets (3rd also bass clarinet), 3 bassoons (3rd also contrabassoon), 4 horns, 3 trumpets, 3 trombones, tuba, percussion (4 timpani, suspended cymbal, 5 temple blocks, bell tree, xylophone, snare drum, vibraphone, 5 bongos, slapstick, tam-tam, glockenspiel, chimes, bass drum, triangle, sizzle cymbal), piano, celesta, harp, violin I, violin II, viola, violoncello, double bass.
Call no.: **2002/009**

170. Bates, Augusta Cecconi, 1933– Ship of the world.
Call no.: **1985/010a**
No materials available.

171. Batik, Roland, 1951– Konzert: für Klavier und Orchester Nr. 1, 1993. Partitur. Wien: Doblinger, 1994.
1 score (130 p.); 35 cm.
Duration: ca. 28:00.
Composed for: piano, alto flute, 2 oboes, 2 clarinets, 2 bassoons, 2 horns, timpani, percussion (triangle, snare

drum, crash cymbal), jazz bass, violin I, violin II, viola, violoncello, double bass.
Call no.: **1995/005**

172. Battistelli, Giorgio, 1953– Prova d'orchestra: 6 scene musicali di fine secolo (1994–1995). Partitura. N.p.: Ricordi, 1995.
1 score (356 p.); 41 cm.
Italian or French words by Giorgio Battistelli, liberally adapted from Federico Fellini.
Musical theater.
Reproduced from holograph.
"Edizione provvisoria"—p. 1 of cover.
Composed for: 3 sopranos, 3 contraltos, 3 tenors, baritone, 2 basses, SATB chorus, 2 flutes (2nd also piccolo), 2 oboes, 2 clarinets, bass clarinet, 2 bassoons (2nd also contrabassoon), 4 horns, 3 trumpets, 3 trombones, tuba, percussion (marimba, tubular bells, snare drum, thundersheet, high maracas, 3 bongos, crotales, bass drum, timpani, low tam-tam, guiro, flexatone, mother of pearl wind chimes, 2 woodblocks, ratchet, crank siren, bar chimes, 4 tom-toms, glockenspiel, crash cymbals, chocalho, lion's roar, water gong, wind machine, police whistle, vibraphone, 5 temple blocks, whip, thundersheet, tubular bells), synthesizer, harp, accordion, violin I, violin II, viola, violoncello, double bass.
Call no.: **1997/012**

173. Bauer, Ross, 1951– Icons: bassoon solo and orchestra. New York, NY: C. F. Peters, 1997.
1 score (99 p.); 44 cm.
Duration: ca. 20:00.
Composed for: bassoon, 2 flutes (2nd also piccolo, alto flute), 2 oboes, English horn, 2 clarinets, bass clarinet, 2 bassoons, contrabassoon, 4 horns, 2 trumpets, 2 trombones, bass trombone, timpani, percussion (glockenspiel, vibraphone, 3 suspended cymbals, medium triangle, medium gong, large tam-tam, xylophone, marimba, temple blocks, claves, snare drum, 2 bongos, 4 tom-toms, tenor drum, bass drum), piano, harp, violin I, violin II, viola, violoncello, double bass.
Commissioned by: Berkeley Symphony.
Call no.: **2002/010**

174. Bauer, Ross, 1951– Icons: for bassoon and orchestra. New York, NY: C. F. Peters, 1997.
1 score (99 p.); 44 cm.
Composed for: bassoon, 2 flutes (2nd also piccolo, alto flute), 2 oboes, English horn, 2 clarinets, bass clarinet, 2 bassoons, contrabassoon, 4 horns, 2 trumpets, 2 trombones, bass trombone, timpani, percussion (glockenspiel, vibraphone, 3 suspended cymbals, medium triangle, medium gong, large tam-tam, xylophone, marimba, temple blocks, claves, snare drum, 2 bongos, 4 tom-toms, tenor drum, bass drum), piano, harp, violin I, violin II, viola, violoncello, double bass.
Commissioned by: Berkeley Symphony.
Call no.: **2000/013**

175. Bauer, Ross, 1951– Ritual fragments: soprano, flute (piccolo, alto), clarinet (bass clarinet), violin, violoncello, percussion, and piano. New York, NY: C. F. Peters, 1996.
1 score (44 p.); 28 cm.
English words from The magic world: American Indian songs and poems (ed. William Brandon); also printed as text.
Duration: ca. 13:00.
Contents: Paiute: ghost dance song—Ojibwa: spring song—Omaha: the rock (fragment of a ritual)—Quechuan fragment—Pima: a dancing song—Dakota: song—Osage: from a legend—Navaho: from the night chant—Mescalero Apache: dawn song (from the gotal ceremony).
Composed for: soprano, flute (also alto flute, piccolo), clarinet (also bass clarinet), piano, violin, violoncello, percussion (glockenspiel, vibraphone, 3 suspended cymbals, small triangle, large tam-tam, marimba, 5 temple blocks, 2 bongos, 4 tom-toms, snare drum).
Commissioned by: Fromm Music Foundation at Harvard University.
Call no.: **1997/013**

176. Bauman, Jon W., 1939– Dialogues: an opera in five scenes, 1986. N.p.: Jon Bauman, 1986.
1 score (116 p.); 36 cm.
English words by Sister Maura, S.S.N.D., and from Psalm 52.
Duration: ca. 55:00.
Composed for: mezzo-soprano, tenor, baritone, bass, violin I, violin II, viola, violoncello, double bass.
Call no.: **1992/008**

177. Baumgartner, Roland, 1955– Missa pacis: the mass of peace. N.p.: n.p., 198-?.
1 score (276 p. in various pagings); 42 cm.
Latin words.
Special texts by Jochen Bauer.
Reproduced from manuscript.
Composed for: soprano, alto, tenor, bass, SATB chorus, 2 flutes, 2 oboes, 2 clarinets, 2 bassoons, 3 horns, 3 trumpets, 3 trombones, tuba, timpani, percussion (cymbals, triangle, xylophone, glockenspiel, gongs, marimba, large bell, African drums, bells, steel drums), organ, guitar, electric bass guitar, synthesizer, jazz drums, violin I, violin II, viola, violoncello, double bass.
Call no.: **1988/008**

178. Baur, John, 1947– String quartet no. 3: requiem (1998/9). N.p.: n.p., 1999.
1 score (56 p.); 28 cm.
Composed for: 2 violins, viola, violoncello.
Commissioned by: Ceruti Quartet.
Call no.: **2002/011**

179. Bawden, Rupert, 1958– Le livre de Fauvel. N.p.: n.p., 1986.
1 score (82 p.); 36 cm.
Latin or French words.
For soprano, mezzo-soprano, and orchestra.
Reproduced from holograph.
Duration: ca. 14:00.
Composed for: soprano, mezzo-soprano, piccolo (also alto flute), heckelphone, bass clarinet (also clarinet in E♭, soprano saxophone), contrabassoon, horn, piccolo trumpet, alto trombone, percussion (side drum, tenor drum, bass drum, 2 temple blocks, tam-tam, maracas, bell tree, 2 suspended cymbals, vibraphone), harp, piano (also celesta), 2 violins, 2 violas, 2 violoncellos, double bass.
Commissioned by: Aldeburgh Festival Foundation.
Call no.: **1987/006**

180. Beadell, Robert, 1925– Symphony II. N.p.: n.p., 1986.
1 score (171 p.); 44 cm.
English words.
For mezzo-soprano, baritone, SATB chorus, and orchestra.
Text from works by Carl Sandburg.
Reproduced from holograph.
At end of score: "Robert Beadell 10/4/86 Lincoln, Nebraska."
Contents: Prologue—Vox populi—Eclogue—Metropole—Aria—...of the Apocalypse—Epilogue.
Composed for: mezzo-soprano, baritone, SATB chorus, piccolo, 2 flutes, 2 oboes, 2 clarinets, alto saxophone, 2 bassoons, 4 horns, 3 trumpets, 3 trombones, tuba, percussion (timpani, snare drum, tom-toms, bongos, bass drum, crash cymbals, suspended cymbals, triangle, anvil, glass wind chimes, bells, crotales, chimes, xylophone, vibraphone, marimba), harp, violin I, violin II, viola, violoncello, double bass.
Call no.: **1988/009**

181. Beall, John, 1942– Ethan Frome: opera in two acts, 1994–97. N.p.: J. Held and J. Beall, 1997.
1 score (2 v.); 44 cm.
English words by Jack Held.
Original work by Edith Wharton.
Composed for: voices, 2 flutes, 2 oboes, 2 clarinets, 2 bassoons, 4 horns, 2 trumpets, 3 trombones, tuba, timpani, percussion (glockenspiel, tam-tam, suspended cymbal, woodblock, snare drum, crash cymbals, sleigh bells, bass drum, triangle), harp, violin I, violin II, viola, violoncello, double bass.
Call no.: **2000/014**

182. Beall, John, 1942– Symphony no. 2: Spruce Knob. N.p.: n.p., 2001.
1 score (41 p.); 44 cm.
Composed for: piccolo, 2 flutes, 2 oboes, 2 clarinets, bass clarinet, 3 bassoons (also contrabassoon), 4 horns, 3 trumpets, 3 trombones, tuba, timpani, percussion, harp, violin I, violin II, viola, violoncello, double bass.
Commissioned by: West Virginia Symphony Orchestra.
Call no.: **2005/008**

183. Beamish, Sally, 1956– Concerto: for violin and orchestra. N.p.: n.p., 1994.
1 score (146 p.); 30 cm.
Reproduced from manuscript.
Duration: 28:00.
Composed for: violin, 2 flutes (2nd also piccolo), 2 oboes (2nd also English horn), 2 clarinets (2nd also clarinet in E♭), 2 bassoons, 4 horns, 3 trumpets, 2 trombones, bass trombone, tuba, timpani, percussion (cymbals, suspended cymbal, cimbalom, side drum, marimba, mark tree, maracas, bass drum, 3 temple blocks, piccolo side drum, 5 tom-toms, 3 tuned temple bells, tam-tam, xylophone, vibraphone, ratchet, crotales, tubular bells), violin I, violin II, viola, violoncello, double bass.
Commissioned by: BBC.
Call no.: **1996/008**

184. Beamish, Sally, 1956– Concerto for viola and orchestra. N.p.: Sally Beamish, 1998.
1 score (96 p.); 30 cm.
"Revised 1998"—p. 1.
Composed for: viola, 2 flutes (2nd also piccolo), 2 oboes, 2 clarinets (2nd also bass clarinet), 2 bassoons, 2 horns, 2 trumpets, timpani, percussion (snare drum, piccolo snare drum, 6 tom-toms, 5 temple blocks, suspended cymbal, glockenspiel, whip), violin I, violin II, viola, violoncello, double bass.
Commissioned by: Phillip Dukes.
Call no.: **2001/017**

185. Beamish, Sally, 1956– Concerto no. 2 for viola and orchestra: "The seafarer." N.p.: Scottish Music Information Centre, 2001.
1 score (114 p.); 37 cm.
Composed for: viola, 2 flutes (2nd also piccolo), 2 oboes,

2 clarinets (2nd also bass clarinet), 2 bassoons (2nd also contrabassoon), 2 horns, 2 trumpets, timpani, percussion, violin I, violin II, viola, violoncello, double bass.
Commissioned by: Swedish Chamber Orchestra and Scottish Chamber Orchestra.
Call no.: **2004/009**

186. Beamish, Sally, 1956– Concerto no. 2 for viola and orchestra: "The seafarer." Glasgow, Scotland: Scottish Music Centre, 2001.
1 score (114 p.); 30 cm.
Composed for: viola, 2 flutes (2nd also piccolo), 2 oboes, 2 clarinets (2nd also bass clarinet), 2 bassoons (2nd also contrabassoon), 2 horns, 2 trumpets, timpani, percussion, violin I, violin II, viola, violoncello, double bass.
Commissioned by: Swedish Chamber Orchestra and Scottish Chamber Orchestra.
Call no.: **2005/009**

187. Beamish, Sally, 1956– The imagined sound of sun on stone: for saxophone and orchestra. N.p.: Sally Beamish, 1999.
1 score (102 p.); 30 cm.
Edited by John Harle.
Duration: 20:00.
Composed for: saxophone, 2 flutes (2nd also piccolo), 2 oboes, 2 clarinets (2nd also bass clarinet), 2 bassoons (2nd also contrabassoon), 2 horns, 2 trumpets, timpani, percussion (crotales, suspended cymbal, tubular bells, 5 tom-toms, chocalho (Mexican bean shaker), rain stick, bamboos, frame drum (bodhran), snare drum, bass drum, heavy wind chimes), violin I, violin II, viola, violoncello, double bass.
Commissioned by: St. Magnus Festival and Swedish Chamber Orchestra.
Call no.: **2002/012**

188. Beamish, Sally, 1956– Knotgrass elegy. Glasgow: Scottish Music Information Centre, 2001.
1 score (x, 91 p.); 42 cm.
English words by Donald Goodbrand Saunders; also printed as text.
Oratorio for soprano, countertenor, baritone, saxophone, dance band, children's choir, SATB chorus, and orchestra.
Inspired by Graham Harvey's book The killing of the countryside.
Composed for: soprano, countertenor, baritone, saxophone, SATB chorus, children's chorus, 2 flutes, piccolo, 2 oboes, English horn, 2 clarinets, bass clarinet, 2 bassoons, contrabassoon, 4 horns, 3 trumpets, 2 trombones, bass trombone, tuba, onstage dance band (clarinet, trumpet, trombone, jazz kit, piano, violin, double bass), timpani, percussion, violin I, violin II, viola, violoncello, double bass.
Commissioned by: BBC.
Call no.: **2003/009**

189. Beaser, Robert, 1954– Concerto for piano and orchestra. N.p.: Helicon Music; European American Music Distributors, 1990.
1 score (176 p.); 44 cm.
Reproduced from manuscript.
Duration: ca. 30:00.
Composed for: piano, piccolo, 2 flutes, 2 oboes, English horn, 2 clarinets, bass clarinet, 2 bassoons, contrabassoon, 4 horns, 3 trumpets, 2 trombones, bass trombone, tuba, timpani, percussion (vibraphone, glockenspiel, xylophone, marimba, crotales, tubular bells, 2 steel pipes, snare drum, militrary drum, 2 bongos, 2 timbales, conga, 3 tom-toms, bass drum, Mexican bean shaker, vibraslap, whip, 4 suspended cymbals, hi-hat, Chinese cymbal, crash cymbals, 2 tam-tams, tambourine, ratchet, guiro), harp, celesta, violin I, violin II, viola, violoncello, double bass.
Commissioned by: Pamela Mia Paul.
Call no.: **1992/009**

190. Beaser, Robert, 1954– The food of love: opera in one act. N.p.: Helicon Music; Valley Forge, PA: European American Music Distributors, 1999.
1 score (216 p.); 44 cm.
English words by Terrence McNally.
Reproduced from holograph.
Duration: ca. 45:00.
Composed for: 3 sopranos, child soprano, 2 mezzo-sopranos, 4 tenors, 3 baritones, 2 bass-baritones, 2 flutes (both also piccolo), 2 oboes (both also English horn), 2 clarinets (both also clarinet in E♭, bass clarinet), 2 bassoons (both also contrabassoon), 2 trumpets, 4 horns, 2 trombones, bass trombone, timpani, percussion (vibraphone, glockenspiel, xylophone, crotales, chimes, snare drum, field drum, 2 bongos, 2 timbales, low conga, low tom, bass drum, 2 steel pipes, 2 temple blocks, maracas, Mexican bean shaker, sandpaper blocks, frusta, cabassa, LP gourd guiro, vibraslap, tambourine, crash cymbal, suspended cymbals, sizzle cymbal, low tam-tam, medium gong, trap set, triangle, lion's roar), piano (also celesta), harp, violin I, violin II, viola, violoncello, double bass.
Commissioned by: WNET/Great Performances, Glimmerglass Opera, and New York City Opera.
Call no.: **2001/018**
Re-entered as: **2002/013**

191. Beaser, Robert, 1954– The seven deadly sins.
Call no.: **1985/011**
No materials available.

192. Beck, Jeremy, 1960– Black water: for soprano and piano. N.p.: J. Beck, 1995.
1 score (81 p.); 28 cm.
English words; also printed as text.
Original work by Joyce Carol Oates.
Composed for: soprano, piano.
Call no.: **2000/015**

193. Beck, Jeremy, 1960– Death of a little girl with doves: a symphonic rhapsody for soprano and orchestra. 2nd ed. N.p.: Jeremy Beck, 1999.
1 score (104 p.); 36 cm.
English words by Jeremy Beck; also printed as text.
Based on the life and letters of Camille Claudel.
Duration: ca. 35:00.
Composed for: soprano, piccolo, 2 flutes, 2 oboes, 2 clarinets, bass clarinet, 2 bassoons, contrabassoon, 4 horns, 3 trumpets, 3 trombones, tuba, timpani, percussion (crotales, chimes, glockenspiel, xylophone, marimba, crash cymbals, triangle, snare drum, claves, tam-tam, bass drum, suspended cymbal, vibraphone, wind chimes), harp, piano, violin I, violin II, viola, violoncello, double bass.
Commissioned by: Waterloo/Cedar Falls Symphony Orchestra.
Call no.: **2001/019**

194. Beckel, Jim, 1948– The glass bead game: concerto for horn and wind ensemble, after Hermann Hesse. Full score. N.p.: James A. Beckel, 1997.
1 score (122 p.); 40 cm.
Accompaniment originally for orchestra.
Duration: 20:00.
Contents: The call & awakening—Father Jacobus—Magister Ludi coronation and march.
Composed for: horn, piccolo, 2 flutes, oboe, 2 bassoons, clarinet in E♭, 3 clarinets, bass clarinet, alto saxophone, tenor saxophone, baritone saxophone, 3 trumpets, 4 horns, 2 trombones, bass trombones, baritone, tuba, timpani, percussion (xylophone, vibraphone, chimes, glockenspiel, suspended cymbal, Chinese gong, triangle, small splash cymbal, snare drum, crotales, bell tree, mark tree, bass drum, wind chimes).
Commissioned by: Kent L. Leslie.
Call no.: **2002/014**

195. Beerman, Burton, 1943– Jesus' daughter: an intermedia dance-opera, 1995. N.p.: Burton Beerman, 1995.
1 score (50 p.); 28 x 31 cm.
English words; also printed as text.
Composed for: mezzo-soprano, electric clarinet, interactive virtual music, video computers, percussion (timpani, 3 tom-toms, 3 triangles, marimba, vibraphone, chimes), dancer.
Call no.: **1997/014**

196. Beerman, Burton, 1943– Womin: for chorus, dancer, [keyboard] and interactive video. N.p.: Burton Beerman, 1989.
1 score (42 p.); 28 cm.
English words by Brent Beerman; also printed as text.
Composed for: SATB chorus, keyboard, dancer.
Call no.: **1995/006**

197. Bell, Elizabeth, 1928– Duovarios: for two pianos. N.p.: n.p., 1987.
1 score (33 p.); 28 cm.
Duration: ca. 13:00.
Composed for: 2 pianos.
Call no.: **1992/010**

198. Bell, Elizabeth, 1928– Les neiges d'antan: sonata for violin and piano, 1998. N.p.: Elizabeth Bell, 1999.
1 score (72 p.); 28 cm.
Duration: ca. 20:00.
Composed for: violin, piano.
Call no.: **2003/010**

199. Bell, Larry, 1952– Reminiscences and reflections: twelve preludes and fugues for piano. Boston, MA: Casa Rustica Publications, 1998.
88 p. of music; 28 cm.
Duration: ca. 1:00:00.
Composed for: piano.
Call no.: **2002/015**

200. Bellisario, Angelo, 1932– Orione: oratorio per voce recitante, tenore, baritono, coro di voci bianche, coro misto e orchestra. N.p.: n.p., 1992.
1 score (167 p.); 50 cm.
Italian words by Gino Viziano.
Reproduced from manuscript.
Composed for: narrator, tenor, baritone, SATB chorus, boys' chorus, flute, oboe, English horn, clarinet, bassoon, 3 horns, trombone, harp, organ, celesta, timpani, percussion (suspended cymbal, triangle, xylophone, bass drum, temple block, snare drum), violin I, violin II, viola, violoncello, double bass.
Call no.: **1994/013**
Also available:
Call no.: **1994/013 libretto**

201. Bello, Joakin, 1935– Tawantinsuyu mosoq p'unchay anqosa = Ofrenda de los andes por la paz. N.p.: n.p., 1986.
1 score (vii, 47 leaves); 28 cm.
Quechua words; also printed as text with English translation.
Reproduced from manuscript.
Composed for: soprano, tenor, SATB chorus, Andean instruments (zampoña, kenas, charango, guitar, tiple, cuatro, trutruca, cultrún), piano, synthesizer, percussion (timbales, chimes, tape), violin I, violin II, viola, violoncello, double bass.
Call no.: **1994/014**

202. Bellucci, Giacomo, 1928– Quartetto 8, 1982. N.p.: G. Bellucci, 1981.
1 score (ii, 24 p.); 34 cm.
For English horn and string quartet.
Reproduced from holograph.
Composed for: English horn, 2 violins, viola, violoncello.
Call no.: **1987/007**

203. Benjamin, George, 1960– Palimpsests. Score. Harlow, Essex, England: Faber Music, 2002.
1 miniature score (57 p.); 30 cm.
For orchestra.
Duration: 8:00; ca. 13:00.
Reproduced from holograph.
Contents: Palimpsest I (2000)—Palimpsest II (2002).
Composed for: 4 flutes (also piccolo, alto flute), 4 clarinets (also bass clarinet), contrabassoon, 3 horns, 4 trumpets (also piccolo trumpet), bass trumpet, tenor trombone (also bass trombone), bass trombone, tuba, percussion (xylophone, medium side drum, whip, 3 side drums, bass drum), piano (also celesta), 2 harps, 5 violins, 3 violas, 8 double basses.
Commissioned by: London Symphony Orchestra, Konzerthaus Wien, Kölner Philharmonie, Carnegie Hall, Société Philharmonique de Bruxelles and Bruxelles 2000, Salzburger Festspiele, Musikfestwochen Luxern, and Edinburgh International Festival.
Call no.: **2005/010**

204. Bentoiu, Pascal, 1927– Simfonia a 8-a: (imagini), op. 30 (1987). N.p.: n.p., 1992.
1 score (231 p.); 35 cm.
Romanian words by Mihai Eminescu (5th mvt.); French translation follows score.
For orchestra with soprano (5th mvt.).
Reproduced from holograph.
Composed for: soprano, piccolo, 2 flutes, 2 oboes, English horn, 2 clarinets, bass clarinet, 2 bassoons, contrabassoon, 4 horns, 2 trumpets, 2 trombones, bass trombone, tuba, percussion (glockenspiel, triangle, tam-tam, gong, vibraphone, marimba, xylophone, 3 suspended cymbals, bass drum, claves, bongos, woodblock, 2 tom-toms, 3 temple blocks, tam-tam, gong), harpsichord, organ, celesta, violin I, violin II, viola, violoncello, double bass.
Call no.: **1993/006**

205. Benzecry, Esteban, 1970– El compendio de la vida: fantasia sinfonica: "Cuatro impresiones pictoricas," 1993. N.p.: n.p., 1993.
1 score (156 p.); 42 cm.
Reproduced from holograph.
Duration: ca. 23:00.
Contents: El compendio de la vida—La guerra—La paz—El compendio de las culturas.
Composed for: piccolo, 2 flutes, 2 oboes, 2 clarinets, 2 bassoons, 4 horns, 3 trumpets, 3 trombones, tuba, timpani, percussion (bass drum, cymbals, suspended cymbals, triangle, glockenspiel, xylophone, snare drum), harp, piano, celesta, violin I, violin II, viola, violoncello, double bass.
Call no.: **1998/014**

206. Berger, Jonathan, 1954– Concerto for viola and orchestra, 1992. N.p.: Maor Music, 1992.
1 score (68 p.); 43 cm.
Composed for: viola, 3 flutes, 3 oboes, 3 clarinets (3rd also bass clarinet), 2 bassoons, 4 horns, 3 trumpets, 2 trombones, bass trombone, tuba, percussion (timpani, crotales, tam-tam, large gong, tubular chimes, snare drum, tenor drum, 4 tom-toms, tambourine, glockenspiel, xylophone, marimba), violin I, violin II, viola, violoncello, double bass.
Call no.: **1998/015**

207. Berio, Luciano, 1925–2003. Continuo: for orchestra. Wien: Universal Edition, 1991.
1 score (91 p.); 60 cm.
Reproduced from manuscript.
Composed for: piccolo, 2 flutes, alto flute, 2 oboes, English horn, clarinet in E♭, 3 clarinets, bass clarinet, alto saxophone, tenor saxophone, 2 bassoons, contrabassoon, 4 trumpets, 6 horns, 4 trombones, 2 tubas, 2 harps, celesta, piano, electric organ, marimba, vibraphone, violin I, violin II, viola, violoncello, double bass.
Call no.: **1993/007**

208. Berio, Luciano, 1925–2003. Continuo: for orchestra. Partitur. Wien: Universal Edition, 1991.
1 score (84 p.); 59 cm.

Reproduced from holograph.
Composed for: piccolo, 2 flutes, alto flute, 2 oboes, English horn, clarinet in E♭, 3 clarinets, bass clarinet, alto saxophone, tenor saxophone, 2 bassoons, contrabassoon, 4 trumpets, 6 horns, 4 trombones, 2 tubas, 2 harps, celesta, piano, electric organ, marimba, vibraphone, violin I, violin II, viola, violoncello, double bass.
Call no.: **1994/015**

209. Berio, Luciano, 1925–2003. Ekphrasis: (continuo II): per orchestra (1996). Partitura. Wien: Universal Edition, 1996.
1 score (95 p.); 59 cm.
"Edizione provvisoria (1a) 4.12.1996."
Reproduced from manuscript.
Duration: ca. 20:00.
Composed for: piccolo, 2 flutes, alto flute, 2 oboes, clarinet in E♭, 3 clarinets, bass clarinet, alto saxophone, tenor saxophone, 2 bassoons, contrabassoon, 6 horns, 4 trumpets (2nd also piccolo trumpet), 4 trombones, 2 bass tubas, harp, piano, celesta, violin I, violin II, viola, violoncello, double bass, marimba, accordion.
Call no.: **1998/016**

210. Berio, Luciano, 1925–2003. Formazioni: per orchestra (1985–1987). Partitur. Wien: Universal Edition, 1987.
1 score (91 p.); 48 cm.
Reproduced from manuscript.
"Korr.X/87"—p. 1.
Composed for: 4 flutes (also 2 piccolos), 2 oboes, English horn, clarinet in E♭, 3 clarinets, bass clarinet, alto saxophone, tenor saxophone, 2 bassoons, contrabassoon, 6 horns, 4 trumpets, 4 trombones, 2 tubas, percussion (timpani, glockenspiel, tam-tam, slide whistle), 2 harps, celesta (also electric organ), violin I, violin II, viola, violoncello, double bass.
Commissioned by: Concertgebouw Orchestra.
Call no.: **1989/009**

211. Berio, Luciano, 1925–2003. Notturno: per orchestra d'archi (1995). Partitur. Wien: Universal Edition, 1995.
1 score (76 p.); 36 cm.
Reproduced from manuscript.
"Provisorische Ausgabe 5.7.1995."
Composed for: violin I, violin II, viola, violoncello, double bass.
Call no.: **1996/009**

212. Berio, Luciano, 1925–2003. Notturno (quartetto III). Partitura. Wien: Universal Edition, 1993.
1 score (51 p.); 30 cm.
Composed for: 2 violins, viola, violoncello.
Commissioned by: Internationale Musikforschungsgesellschaft, Konzerthaus Wien, and South Bank Centre London.
Call no.: **1995/007**

213. Berio, Luciano, 1925–2003. Solo: for trombone and orchestra (1999). Wien: Universal Edition, 1999.
1 score (63 p.); 30 cm.
Reproduced from holograph.
Duration: ca. 22:00.
Composed for: trombone, piccolo, 3 flutes, alto flute, oboe, clarinet in E♭, 3 clarinets, bass clarinet, alto saxophone, tenor saxophone, bassoon, 4 trumpets, 4 horns, 3 trombones, tuba, 12 violins, 8 violas, 8 violoncellos, 6 double basses.
Call no.: **2001/020**

214. Berkeley, Michael, 1948– Baa-baa black sheep. Full score. Oxford: Oxford University Press, 1995.
1 score (428 p.); 42 cm.
Words by David Malouf.
Opera in 3 acts.
Based on Rudyard Kipling's Baa baa black sheep and The jungle book.
Reproduced from manuscript.
Composed for: voices, SATB chorus, piccolo, flute (also alto flute), oboe, clarinet, bassoon (also contrabassoon), 2 horns, 2 trumpets, 2 trombones, bass trombone, tuba, percussion (temple blocks, marimba, vibraphone, suspended cymbals, roto-toms, wood chimes, maracas, 2 tom-toms, medium tam-tam, Chinese gongs, bass drum, cimbalom, snare drum, bongo, tubular bells, gong, crotales, log drums, sizzle cymbal, medium woodblocks, guiro, triangle, tambourine, timpani), harp, piano, violin I, violin II, viola, violoncello, double bass.
Commissioned by: Cheltenham International Festival.
Call no.: **1996/010**

215. Berkeley, Michael, 1948– For the savage Messiah. N.p.: n.p., 1985.
1 score (33 p.); 30 cm.
Reproduced from manuscript.
Composed for: violin, viola, violoncello, double bass, piano.
Commissioned by: Schubert Ensemble.
Call no.: **1986/009**

216. Berkeley, Michael, 1948– The garden of earthly delights. Oxford: Oxford University Press, 1998.
1 score (101 p.); 30 cm.

For orchestra.
Duration: ca. 18:00.
Composed for: violin (also claves, rattle, small tam-tam), soprano saxophone (also claves, rattle, medium tam-tam), tenor trombone (also claves, rattle, medium-large tam-tam), piccolo, 3 flutes (3rd also piccolo), 4 oboes (4th also English horn), 4 clarinets (3rd also clarinet in E♭, 4th also bass clarinet), 3 bassoons, contrabassoon, 6 horns, 4 trumpets, 3 trombones, 2 tubas, timpani, percussion (suspended cymbal, castanets, crotales, tam-tam, rattle, lion's roar, sizzle cymbal, 3 tom-toms, 2 woodblocks, bass drum, cowbells, whip, vibraphone, claves, guiro, snare drum, maracas, cabasa, tuned gongs, Chinese gong, Javanese or Thai gongs, crash cymbals, marimba, glockenspiel, triangle, flexatone), 2 harps, violin I, violin II, viola, violoncello, double bass.
Commissioned by: BBC.
Call no.: **2001/021**

217. Berkeley, Michael, 1948– Or shall we die?
Call no.: **1985/012**
No materials available.

218. Bermel, Derek, 1967– Voices: for solo clarinet and orchestra. New York, NY: Peermusic Classical, 1997.
1 score (98 p.); 44 cm.
Duration: 17:00–18:00.
Performance instructions in English.
Composed for: clarinet, piccolo, 2 flutes, 2 oboes, English horn, 2 clarinets (1st also clarinet in E♭, 2nd also bass clarinet), alto saxophone, 2 bassoons, contrabassoon, 4 horns, 3 trumpets, 2 trombones, bass trombone, tuba, piano, harp, electric guitar, electric bass, timpani, percussion (glockenspiel, flexatone, anvil, tambourine, afuxe, sleigh bells, ratchet, button gong, tuned gongs, lion's roar, marimba, large bass drum, suspended cymbal, cuíca, cowbell, agogo bell, claves, slapstick, police whistle, xylophone, drum set (snare drum, pedal bass drum, tom-tom, hi-hat, ride cymbal), castanets, vibraslap), violin I, violin II, viola, violoncello, double bass.
Commissioned by: American Composers Orchestra.
Call no.: **2004/010**

219. Bernstein, Charles Harold, 1917– Ararat suite: for flute and trumpet, 1986. N.p.: n.p., 1987.
1 score (18 p.); 34 cm.
Reproduced from manuscript.
Contents: Unknown creatures—Modes of being—Strange modes of being—Strange—Being.
Composed for: flute, trumpet.
Call no.: **1992/011**

220. Bernstein, Charles Harold, 1917– Dimensions: six pieces for English horn and percussion. N.p.: n.p., 1988.
1 score (22 p.); 34 cm.
Reproduced from manuscript.
Composed for: English horn, percussion (tam-tam, tambourine, temple bowls, snare drum, 4 triangles, wine glass, wind chimes, vibraphone, suspended cymbals, hi-hat, timpani).
Call no.: **1989/010**

221. Bernstein, Charles Harold, 1917– Leda; Songs without words. N.p.: n.p., 1989.
1 score (14 p.); 33 cm.
English words (1st work).
Reproduced from holograph.
Composed for: soprano, violin.
Call no.: **1995/008**

222. Bernstein, Charles Harold, 1917– Strawberry creek concerto: for flute and bassoon. N.p.: n.p., 1987.
1 score (23 p.); 52 cm.
Reproduced from holograph.
At end of score: "Charles Harold Bernstein July 3, 1987 Paris, France 12/87."
Composed for: flute, bassoon, 2 flutes, 2 oboes, 2 clarinets, 2 bassoons, 2 horns, 2 trumpets, percussion (timpani, wind chimes), violin I, violin II, viola, violoncello, double bass.
Call no.: **1988/010**

223. Bernstein, Seymour, 1927– Song of nature: for SATB choir, narrator and organ or piano. N.p.: Seymour Bernstein, 1997.
1 score (28 leaves); 28 cm.
English words by Ralph Waldo Emerson.
Composed for: narrator, SATB chorus, organ (or piano).
Call no.: **1998/017**
Also available:
Call no.: **1998/017 arr.**

224. Beveridge, Thomas, 1938– Symphony of peace. Washington, DC: Yizkor Press, 2002.
1 score (11, 24, 6, 10, 11 p.); 43 cm.
English words from the Bible.
Cantata for large chorus with soloists and orchestra.
Duration: 1:00:00–1:05:00.
Composed for: soprano, tenor, bass-baritone, SATB chorus, flugelhorn, alto saxophone, electric bass, celesta, harp, piano, organ (or tape), 2 flutes (also piccolo), 2 oboes, English horn, 2 clarinets, bass clarinet, 2 bassoons, contrabassoon, 3 trumpets, 4 horns, 3 trombones,

tuba, violin I, violin II, viola, violoncello, double bass, timpani, percussion (cowbells, sheep bells, chimes, glockenspiel, cymbals, suspended cymbal, hi-hat, triangle, crotales, large tam-tam, tambourine, slap-stick, snare drum, bass drum, 2 brake drums, anvil).
Call no.: **2005/011**
Also available:
Call no.: **2005/011 vocal score**

225. Bianchi Alarcon, Vicente, 1929– Triptico sinfonico. Partitura. N.p.: n.p., 1990.
1 score (27 p.); 33 cm.
For orchestra.
"Obra instrumental basada en las 3 tonadas chilenas creadas por Pablo Neruda y Vicente Bianchi inspiradas en los proceres de la independencia de Chile con el titulo 'Musica para la historia de Chile.'"
Reproduced from holograph.
Composed for: piccolo, 2 flutes, 2 oboes, English horn, 2 clarinets, 2 bassoons, 4 horns, 3 trumpets, 2 trombones, percussion (timpani, cymbals, drum), violin I, violin II, viola, violoncello, double bass.
Call no.: **1992/012**

226. Bianchi, Frederick W., 1954– The Rauschenberg variations, 1988. N.p.: F. Bianchi, 1988.
1 score (39 p.); 44 cm.
For orchestra.
Reproduced from manuscript.
"A perusal score only and not suggested for performance"—cover.
Duration: ca. 10:00.
Composed for: 2 flutes, 2 oboes, English horn, clarinet in E♭, 2 clarinets, bass clarinet, 2 bassoons, 4 horns, 3 trumpets, 3 trombones, tuba, timpani, percussion (2 bongos, 2 timbales, bass drum, 3 roto-toms, 3 tom-toms, timpani, tenor drum, gong), harp, piano, violin I, violin II, viola, violoncello, double bass.
Call no.: **1991/007**

227. Bibalo, Antonio, 1922– Macbeth: 1985. Oslo version. N.p.: n.p., 1989.
1 score (2 v.); 43 cm.
English words.
Opera in 3 acts.
Reproduced from manuscript.
Composed for: soprano, 2 mezzo-sopranos, 2 contraltos, 5 tenors, 5 baritones, 3 basses, SATB chorus, 2 flutes (both also piccolo), 2 oboes (2nd also English horn), 2 clarinets, bass clarinet, 2 bassoons, contrabassoon, 4 horns, 3 trumpets, 3 trombones, tuba, timpani, harp, piano, percussion (suspended cymbal, 2 tam-tams, military drum, bass drum, xylophone, vibraphone), violin I, violin II, viola, violoncello, double bass.
Call no.: **1994/016**

228. Biggin, Tony, 1952– The gates of Greenham. N.p.: n.p., 1985.
1 score (2 v. [456 p.]); 37 cm.
English words.
Reproduced from manuscript.
"This score is uncorrected in the accidentals etc."—p. 2 of cover.
Composed for: soprano, alto, tenor, baritone, women's semi-chorus, SATB chorus, 3 flutes (3rd also piccolo), 2 oboes, English horn, 2 clarinets, bass clarinet, 2 bassoons, contrabassoon, 4 horns, 3 trumpets, 2 trombones, bass trombone, tuba, timpani, percussion (side drum, bass drum, cymbals, triangle, suspended cymbal, whip, guiro, funeral bell, glockenspiel, xylophone, drum kit [snare drum, bass drum, 3 floor tom-toms, hi-hat, 2 ride cymbals]), electric guitar, bass guitar, violin I, violin II, viola, violoncello, double bass.
Call no.: **1986/010**

229. Biggs, Hayes, 1957– Ochila laeil: mixed chorus, horn and organ (1999). New York, NY: C. F. Peters, 2000.
1 score (21 p.); 28 cm.
Hebrew words (romanized).
Organ part edited by Walter Hilse.
Composed for: SATB chorus, horn, organ.
Commissioned by: Florilegium Chamber Orchestra.
Call no.: **2002/016**

230. Biggs, John, 1932– Concerto for cello and chamber orchestra. Ventura, CA: Consort Press, 1996.
1 score (42 p.); 36 cm.
Duration: 22:30.
Composed for: violoncello, 2 oboes, 2 bassoons, 2 horns, violin I, violin II, viola, violoncello, double bass.
Commissioned by: New West Symphony.
Call no.: **2001/022**

231. Biggs, John, 1932– Fantasy: for wind octet. Santa Barbara, CA: Consort Press, 1986.
1 score (40 p.); 36 cm.
Reproduced from manuscript.
Duration: ca. 16:00.
Composed for: 2 oboes, 2 clarinets, 2 horns, 2 bassoons.
Call no.: **1987/008**

232. Biggs, John, 1932– Hobson's choice: an opera in three acts. Full score. Ojai, CA: Consort Press, 2000.
1 score (207 p.); 36 cm.
English words.

Original work by Harol Brighouse.
Composed for: soprano, 2 mezzo-sopranos, contralto, 2 tenors, 2 baritones, bass, flute, clarinet, bassoon, piano, violin, viola, violoncello, double bass.
Call no.: **2002/017**
Re-entered as: **2005/012**

233. Biggs, John, 1932– Japanese fables: for chorus, narrator & small orchestra. Santa Barbara, CA: Consort Press, 1984.
1 score (44 p.); 28 cm.
Reproduced from holograph.
"The text is drawn from stones of the Zen Buddhists, and from haiku by Basho, Buson, Chora, Hokushi, Issa, Joso, Kikusha-Ni, Ryota, Shiki, and Sokan."
At end: Temecula, CA May 6, 1984.
Duration: ca. 20:00.
Contents: Meditation on the value of time and emptiness—Dance of the frog—Dance of the toad—Dance of the baby turtle—Trio—Meditation on the moon—The riddle—Epilogue.
Composed for: narrator, SATB chorus, 6 flutes, 2 oboes, English horn, 2 clarinets, bass clarinet, 2 bassoons, percussion (glass wind chimes, suspended cymbal, large gong, glockenspiel, slapstick, sandpaper, xylophone, timpani, guiro, bass drum, bell tree), double bass.
Commissioned by: Olympic Program Committee of California State University at Los Angeles.
Call no.: **1985/013**

234. Biggs, John, 1932– Songs of laughter, love and tears.
Call no.: **1986/011**
No materials available.

235. Bilucaglia, Claudio, 1946– Otto poesie da un soldo: per tenore e orchestra. N.p.: n.p., 1982.
1 score (47 p.); 47 cm.
English words; also printed as text with Italian translation.
Reproduced from manuscript.
8 poems from Joyce's Pomes penyeach.
Duration: 18:30.
Contents: Watching the needleboats at San Sabba—A flower given to my daughter—She weeps over Rahoon—Tutto è sciolto—On the beach at Fontana—Simples—Flood—Nightpiece.
Composed for: tenor, 3 flutes (3rd also piccolo), 3 oboes (3rd also English horn), 3 clarinets (3rd also bass clarinet), 3 bassoons (3rd also contrabassoon), 4 horns, 3 trumpets, 3 trombones, tuba, percussion (timpani, bass drum, suspended cymbal, vibraphone), harp, violin I, violin II, viola, violoncello, double bass.
Call no.: **1985/014**

236. Bimstein, Phillip Kent, 1947– Dark winds rising: [for] string quartet and tape. Springdale, UT: Frankling Stark Music, 1992.
1 score (64 leaves); 28 cm.
English words.
Composed for: tape, 2 violins, viola, violoncello.
Call no.: **1993/008**

237. Bingham, Judith, 1952– Chartres: for orchestra. N.p.: Maecenas Music, 1991.
1 score (98 p.); 35 cm.
Orchestral work about Chartres Cathedral.
Reproduced from manuscript.
Duration: 38:00.
Composed for: 2 flutes (1st also piccolo), 2 oboes (1st also English horn), 2 clarinets, bass clarinet, 2 bassoons, contrabassoon, 4 horns, 3 trumpets, 2 trombones, bass trombone, tuba, timpani, percussion (handbells, tubular bells, 2 bowl gongs, vibraphone, keyboard glockenspiel, cimbalom, bell tree, triangle, steel drum, castanets, 3 tenor drums, bass drum, whip, woodblocks, 2 metronomes, wind machine), 2 harps, piano, organ, violin I, violin II, viola I, viola II, violoncello I, violoncello II, double bass I, double bass II.
Call no.: **1996/011**

238. Bingham, Judith, 1952– Otherworld: for SATB chorus, semi-chorus, orchestra & organ (2000). Kenley, Surrey, UK: Maecenas Music, 2000.
1 score (89 p.); 43 cm.
English words from various sources.
Duration: ca. 40:00.
Contents: [Untitled]—Orion the hunter—God is one and alone—Movement 5.
Composed for: SATB chorus (on stage), SATB semi-chorus (off stage), piccolo, 2 flutes, 2 oboes, clarinet in E♭, 2 clarinets, bassoon, contrabassoon, 4 horns, 2 trumpets, 2 trombones, bass trombone, tuba, timpani, percussion, organ, violin I, violin II, viola, violoncello, double bass.
Commissioned by: Plymouth Music Series and Three Choirs Festival of Hereford, England.
Call no.: **2003/011**

239. Binkerd, Gordon, 1916–2003. Piano sonata #3. N.p.: n.p., 1985.
25 p. of music; 35 cm.
Reproduced from manuscript.
Duration: ca. 20:00.
Composed for: piano.
Call no.: **1986/012**

240. Bird, Hubert, 1939– Legacy: a concert narrative in commemoration of John F. Kennedy. N.p.: Hubert C. Bird, 1994.
1 score (129 p.); 36 cm.
English words; some also printed as text with corresponding music.
For narrator, soprano, chorus, and chamber orchestra.
Contents: Prelude (narration): now close the windows / Robert Frost—Introduction—Watch long enough, and you will see the leaf / Conrad Aiken—Chorus: let us now praise famous men / Ecclesiasticus—Solo: the illusion of eternity / Richard Eberhart—(Recorded narration): from President Kennedy's inaugural address—Chorus (chorale): since then have passed—Narration: we in this country / John F. Kennedy—Chorus: and we are the true spirit—Solo with chorus: the master-songs are ended / Edwin Arlington Robinson—Narration: the departure / William Vaughn Moody—Solo: from me to thee glad serenades—Narration: requiem / Robert Hillyer—Solo flute: contemplation—Solo: is it the aster? / Robert Hillyer—Narration: President John Fitzgerald Kennedy—Chorus: the light that is the spirit.
Composed for: narrator, soprano, SATB chorus, 2 flutes, oboes, clarinet, 2 bassoons, horn, euphonium, trombone, timpani, percussion (snare drum, triangle, suspended cymbal, crash cymbals, vibraphone, chimes, bells), piano, double bass.
Commissioned by: Keene Pops Choir, New Hampshire.
Call no.: **1995/009**

241. Biriotti, León, 1929– Sinfonia da requiem (8th): soprano, coro y orquesta (por las víctimas del Holocausto). N.p.: n.p., 1998.
1 score (106 p.); 37 cm.
Spanish words from the Bible; also printed as text.
Reproduced from holograph.
Includes corrections (p. 106).
Composed for: soprano, SATB chorus, piccolo, 2 flutes, 2 oboes, English horn, 2 clarinets, bass clarinet, 2 bassoons, contrabassoon, 4 horns, 2 trumpets, 3 trombones, tuba, piano, timpani, percussion (snare drum, low bass drum, low tam-tam, crash cymbals, suspended cymbal), violin I, violin II, viola, violoncello, double bass.
Commissioned by: Newton Symphony Orchestra and Boston's Chorus Pro Musica.
Call no.: **2001/023**

242. Birtwistle, Harrison, 1934– The mask of Orpheus. London: Universal Edition, 1986.
1 score (3 v.); 62 cm.
English words.
Opera in 3 acts.
Libretto by Peter Zinovieff.
Reproduced from manuscript.
1987 Grawemeyer Award winning work.
Composed for: 2 sopranos, 3 mezzo-sopranos, alto, 3 tenors, 3 baritones, bass-baritone, bass, 3 piccolos, 4 flutes, 3 alto flutes, bass flute, 4 oboes, oboe d'amore, 2 English horns, bass oboe, 2 clarinets in E♭, 4 clarinets, 3 bass clarinets, contrabass clarinet, 3 soprano saxophones, 4 bassoons, 3 contrabassoons, 4 horns, 4 trumpets, 6 trombones, bass trombone, 2 tubas, 3 harps, electric mandolin, electric guitar, electric bass, percussion (2 guiros, marimba, 2 vibraphones, 2 maracas, 4 bass drums, 3 conches, 7 bongos, 3 tambourines, 2 crotales, 3 bamboo pipes, 17 cowbells, 3 congas, claves, 7 drums, 17 temple blocks, 8 log drums, 3 glockenspiels, 5 tam-tams, 3 ratchets, 7 metal tubes, 3 xylophones, 7 suspended cymbals, glass chimes, bell tree, 3 whips, 4 hi-hats, afuche, noh harp) tape.
Call no.: **1987/009**
Also available:
Call no.: **1987/009 libretto**
Call no.: **1987/009 vocal score**

243. Birtwistle, Harrison, 1934– Secret theatre: [for fourteen players]. London: Universal Edition, 1984.
1 score (84 p.); 43 cm.
Duration: 28:00.
Reproduced from holograph.
Composed for: flute, oboe, clarinet, contrabassoon, horn, trumpet (also piccolo trumpet), trombone, percussion (vibraphone, xylophone, 3 tom-toms, 3 suspended Turkish cymbals, tam-tams, 3 sizzle cymbals, crotales), piano, 2 violins, viola, violoncello, double bass.
Call no.: **1985/015**

244. Biscarini, Marco, 1965– Da lontano . . . adagio. N.p.: n.p., 2001.
1 score (27 p.); 36 cm.
For accordion and orchestra.
Duration: 10:00.
Composed for: accordion, 2 flutes, 2 oboes, 2 clarinets, 2 bassoons, 2 horns, 3 trumpets, 2 trombones, tuba, percussion (tom-tom, chimes, snare drum, crotales, cymbals, ride cymbal, crash cymbals, tam-tam, tubular bells), 5 timpani, violin I, violin II, viola, violoncello, double bass.
Call no.: **2003/012**

245. Bisceglia, Stefano, 1955– Trotterellata misteriosa: rondó per pianoforte, schiocco di lingua, battiti di mani e voci recitanti: op. 16 n. 1. N.p.: n.p., 19-?.
1 score (33 p.); 37 cm.
Italian words.

Reproduced from holograph.
Composed for: reciting voices (also hand claps), piano.
Call no.: **1985/016**

246. Bischof, Rainer, 1947– Sinfonia, op. 40, 1994. Wien: Doblinger, 1995.
1 score (22 p.); 42 cm.
Reproduced from manuscript.
Composed for: flute, oboe, clarinet, bassoon, 2 horns, violin I, violin II, viola, violoncello, double bass.
Call no.: **2001/024**

247. Bjerno, Erling D., 1929– Sonoris IV: for marimba solo, opus 205. Odense N, Denmark: MarimPercussion, 1995.
10 p. of music; 30 cm.
Composed for: marimba.
Call no.: **1997/015**

248. Bjerno, Erling D., 1929– Symfoni: nr. 6, op. 191. N.p.: n.p., 19-?.
1 score (99 leaves); 43 cm.
Danish words; also printed as text following score.
For orchestra and solo soprano or alto.
Text by Arne Bøgh Larsen.
Reproduced from holograph.
Duration: 30:00.
Composed for: soprano (or alto), 2 flutes (2nd also piccolo), 2 oboes (2nd also English horn), 2 clarinets, 2 bassoons, 4 horns, 3 trumpets, 3 trombones, tuba, timpani, percussion (triangle, snare drum, cymbals, tam-tam, vibraphone, chimes), celesta, violin I, violin II, viola, violoncello, double bass.
Call no.: **1993/009**

249. Blackford, Richard, 1954– Voices of exile: a cantata: for mezzo-soprano, tenor and baritone soloists, SATB chorus, children's chorus, instrumental ensemble and tape. London: Novello, 2001.
1 score (144 p.); 42 cm.
Principally English words from various sources; also printed as text.
Duration: 55:00.
Includes notes by the composer.
Composed for: mezzo-soprano, tenor, baritone, SATB chorus, children's chorus, 2 flutes (both also piccolo), 2 clarinets (both also bass clarinet), 2 horns, 2 trumpets, trombone, tuba, percussion (bass drum, marimba, suspended cymbal, snare drum, bongos, crash cymbals, chromatic crotales, tam-tam, congas, claves, 4 timpani, Chinese cymbal, triangle, cowbell), 3 synthesizers (1st also piano), violin, tape.
Commissioned by: Bournemouth Symphony Chorus and Poole Arts Centre.
Call no.: **2003/013**

250. Blackwood, Easley, 1933– Fifth symphony, op. 34. Chicago, IL: Blackwood Enterprises, 1991.
1 score (121 p.); 27 cm.
Reproduced from manuscript.
Duration: 26:00.
Composed for: 3 flutes, 2 oboes, English horn, 2 clarinets in A, bass clarinet, 2 bassoons, contrabassoon, 4 horns, 3 trumpets, 3 trombones, tuba, timpani, percussion (cymbals, bass drum, triangle, snare drum, tam tam), violin I, violin II, viola, violoncello, double bass.
Commissioned by: Chicago Symphony Orchestra.
Call no.: **1993/010**

251. Blaha, Joseph Leon, 1951– Concerto for piano and wind ensemble. N.p.: Joseph L. Blaha, 1991.
1 score (153 p.); 28 cm.
Includes performance instructions.
Composed for: piano, piccolo, 2 flutes, 2 oboes, English horn, clarinet in E♭, 6 clarinets, alto clarinet, bass clarinet, contrabass clarinet, 2 alto saxophones, tenor saxophone, baritone saxophone, 2 bassoons, contrabassoon, 3 cornets, 2 trumpets, 4 horns, 2 trombones, bass trombone, baritone, tuba, timpani (also sizzle cymbal), percussion (bells, chimes, suspended cymbal, hi-hat, triangle, anvil, mounted cowbell, tam-tam, mounted woodblock, claves, vibraslap, ratchet, slapstick, snare drum, field drum, 4 tom-toms, bongos, tambourine, vibraphone, cymbals, 2 triangles, metal wind chimes, bass drum, xylophone, sleigh bells, 5 temple blocks).
Call no.: **1993/011**

252. Blaha, Joseph Leon, 1951– Sonata for horn and piano. N.p.: Joseph Blaha, 1984.
1 score (54 p.) + 1 part; 28 cm.
Contents: Soliloquies—Fantasies—Songs—Dances.
Composed for: horn, piano.
Commissioned by: Willard Zirk.
Call no.: **1988/011**

253. Blake, Christopher, 1949– Clairmont triptych: a painter's appassionata: for wind quintet & piano. N.p.: Christopher Blake, 1988.
1 score (80 p.); 30 cm.
Reproduced from holograph.
Composed for: flute, oboe, clarinet, horn, bassoon, piano.
Commissioned by: Music Federation of New Zealand.
Call no.: **1989/011**

254. Blake, Christopher, 1949– The coming of Tanemahuta: concerto for piano & orchestra. N.p.: Christopher Blake, 1987.
1 score (148 p.); 37 cm.
Reproduced from holograph.
Contents: The coming of existence—The coming of life—The coming of death.
Includes program note in English.
Composed for: piano, 2 flutes (both also piccolo), 2 oboes (2nd also English horn), 2 clarinets (2nd also bass clarinet), 2 bassoons, 4 horns, 2 trumpets, timpani, percussion (vibraphone, xylophone, marimba, glockenspiel, 2 flexatones, 2 suspended cymbals, 3 temple blocks, tam-tam, triangle, bass drum, 4 roto-toms, 2 snare drums, 2 tom-toms, 2 bongos, 2 congas), violin I, violin II, viola, violoncello, double bass.
Commissioned by: Auckland Philharmonia Orchestra.
Call no.: **1991/008**

255. Blake, Christopher, 1949– Night walking with the great salter. N.p.: n.p., 1989.
1 score (75 p.); 37 cm.
For orchestra.
Reproduced from holograph.
Composed for: 2 flutes (both also piccolo), 2 oboes (2nd also English horn), 2 clarinets (2nd also bass clarinet), 2 bassoons (2nd also contrabassoon), 4 horns, 3 trumpets, 3 trombones, tuba, percussion (3 tom-toms, timpani, xylophone, slapstick, bass drum, tam-tam, 3 sets of claves, 2 congas, 4 bongos, 2 snare drums, sandpaper blocks, guiro, maracas, woodblock, 2 temple blocks), violin I, violin II, viola, violoncello, double bass.
Call no.: **1992/013**

256. Blake, Christopher, 1949– Symphony the islands. N.p.: Christopher Blake, 1994.
1 score (261 p.); 30 p.
Program notes and poems by Charles Brasch.
Reproduced from manuscript.
Composed for: 3 flutes (3rd also piccolo), 3 oboes (3rd also English horn), 3 clarinets (2nd–3rd also bass clarinet, 2nd also clarinet in E♭), 3 bassoons (3rd also contrabassoon), 4 horns, 4 trumpets (1st–2nd also piccolo trumpet), 2 trombones, bass trombone, tuba, timpani, percussion (glockenspiel, vibraphone, bass drum, 4 suspended cymbals, 2 temple blocks, xylophone, 3 tam-tams, 3 roto-toms, 2 Chinese cymbals, 2 crash cymbals), harp, piano, synthesizer, violin I, violin II, viola, violoncello, double bass.
Commissioned by: New Zealand Symphony Orchestra.
Call no.: **1998/018**

257. Blake, Christopher, 1949– Till human voice wake us: music for symphony orchestra and tenor. N.p.: Christopher Blake, 1986.
1 score (70 p.); 37 cm.
Primarily English with some French words; also printed as text.
Text from foreword to We will not cease by Archibald Baxter and Philippians 4:7.
Reproduced from holograph.
Composed for: tenor, 2 flutes (both also piccolo), 2 oboes (2nd also English horn), 2 clarinets (both also bass clarinet, 1st also clarinet in E♭), 2 bassoons (2nd also contrabassoon), 4 horns, 3 trumpets (1st also cornet), 3 trombones, tuba, timpani, percussion (vibraphone, glockenspiel, snare drum, suspended cymbal, tam-tam, xylophone, crash cymbals, triangle, bass drum, sleigh bells, brass chimes), harp, piano, violin I, violin II, viola, violoncello, double bass.
Commissioned by: Radio New Zealand and New Zealand Symphony Orchestra.
Call no.: **1990/008**

258. Blake, David, 1936– Rise dove: for bass and orchestra, 1983. London: Novello, 1983.
1 score (ix, 155 p.); 43 cm.
English or French words; also printed as text.
Text from Cahier d'un retour au pays natal by Aimé Césaire, translated into English by David Blake.
Duration: ca. 33:00.
Includes performance instructions.
Composed for: bass, 3 flutes (2nd also alto flute, 3rd also piccolo), 2 oboes (2nd also English horn), 3 clarinets (2nd also clarinet in E♭, 3rd also bass clarinet), alto saxophone, baritone saxophone, 2 bassoons (2nd also contrabassoon), 4 horns, 3 trumpets, 3 trombones, tuba, timpani, percussion (boobams, xylophone, marimba, 2 bongos, side drum, bass drum, 3 congas, 3 suspended cymbals, tambourine, maracas, chocalho, whip, tenor drum, claves, guiro, sand blocks, tam-tam, 3 tom-toms, 3 woodblocks, triangle, crash cymbals, 5 crotales, Trinidad steel drum), harp, piano, celesta, violin I, violin II, viola, violoncello, double bass.
Commissioned by: BBC.
Call no.: **1985/017**

259. Blank, William, 1957– Cris: pour piano et ensemble. Driae, Suisse: Editions Papillon, 2000.
1 score (98 p.); 30 cm.
Reproduced from manuscript.
Duration: 27:00.
Composed for: piano, bass flute (also alto flute), English horn, bass clarinet, contrabass clarinet (also clarinet), trumpet, horn, trombone, percussion (marimba, tubu-

lar bells, crotales, tam-tam, Chinese cymbal), viola, violoncello, double bass.
Commissioned by: Fondation Nicati-de Luze.
Call no.: **2002/018**

260. Blauvelt, Peter, 1956– Interna: sixth string quartet, with soprano (1993–95). N.p.: Peter Blauvelt, 1995.
1 score (21 p.); 28 cm.
English words by Peter Blauvelt.
Reproduced from manuscript.
Duration: 20:00.
Composed for: soprano, 2 violins, viola, violoncello.
Call no.: **1998/019**

261. Blauvelt, Peter, 1956– Monuments: for wind octet, 1996–97. N.p.: n.p., 1997.
1 score (19 leaves); 28 cm.
Reproduced from manuscript.
Duration: 20:30.
Composed for: 2 flutes, 2 clarinets, 2 horns, 2 bassoons.
Call no.: **2001/025**

262. Blauvelt, Peter, 1956– Piano quartet, 1998–99. N. p.: Peter Blauvelt, 2000.
1 score (21 leaves); 28 cm.
Reproduced from manuscript.
Duration: 24:15.
Composed for: violin, viola, violoncello, piano.
Call no.: **2002/019**

263. Blechinger, Alexander, 1956– Die böse 7: Therese Krones und ihr Galan. N.p.: n.p., 1991.
1 score (421 p.); 31 cm.
German words by Roman Rocek.
Opera.
Composed for: voices, SATB chorus, flute, oboe, clarinet, bassoon, contrabassoon, horn, trumpet, trombone, tuba, piano, cembalo, percussion (timpani, cymbals, claves, chimes, thundersheet, military drum, slapstick, glockenspiel, maracas, snare drum, bass drum), violin I, violin II, viola, violoncello, double bass.
Call no.: **1994/017**

264. Blechinger, Alexander, 1956– Orpheus jetzt: Ballett in 10 Bildern. Partitur. N.p.: n.p., 1990.
1 score (294 p.); 30 cm.
German words by Roman Rocek.
Contents: Sonnenuntergang—Rushhour—Pas de deux—Auf der Couch—Untergrundbahn—In den Kanälen—Disco down town—Im Treppenhaus—Danach—Finale.
Composed for: narrator, 2 flutes (both also piccolo), 2 oboes (2nd also English horn), 2 clarinets (2nd also bass clarinet), 2 tenor saxophones (1st also soprano and sopranino saxophones, 2nd also alto saxophone), 2 bassoons (2nd also contrabassoon), 2 horns (1st also horn in B♭), 2 trumpets, 3 trombones, bass trombone, percussion (chimes, maracas, timpani, xylophone, glockenspiel, pea whistle, pistol, cymbals, slot machine, drum set [crash cymbal, ride cymbal, hi-hat, 4 tom-toms, snare drum, bass drum, claves, bells, tambourine]), harp, piano, guitar, violin I, violin II, viola, violoncello, double bass.
Call no.: **1992/014**

265. Blechinger, Alexander, 1956– Song of constitution, op. 34. N.p.: Filmkunst-Musikverlag, 1987.
1 score (214 p.); 34 cm.
English words.
Reproduced from holograph.
Composed for: SATB chorus, 2 flutes (both also piccolo), 2 oboes, 3 clarinets (3rd also tenor saxophone), 2 bassoons, contrabassoon, 4 horns, 3 trumpets, 2 trombones, bass trombone, percussion (timpani, triangle, jazz set [2 cymbals, 3 tom-toms, woodblock, trap set], tam-tam, vibraphone, xylophone, tambourine, wood hammer, crash cymbals, washboard), harp, violin I, violin II, viola, violoncello, double bass.
Call no.: **1988/012**

266. Blockeel, Dirk, 1955– Aan snaren opgehangen kruisweg: strijkkwartet (1992–1993). N.p.: n.p., 1993.
1 score (38 leaves); 30 cm.
Reproduced from manuscript.
"Verlucht met fragmenten uit houtsneden van Geert Monteyne."
Composed for: 2 violins, viola, violoncello.
Call no.: **1996/012**

267. Blum, Yaakov, 1947– Trio en 5 mouvements. N.p.: n.p., 1990.
1 score (44 leaves); 31 cm.
Composed for: violin, violoncello, piano.
Call no.: **1991/009**

268. Blumenfeld, Harold, 1923– Seasons in hell: the lives of Arthur Rimbaud. St. Louis, MO: MMB Music, 1994.
1 score (292 p.); 36 cm.
Words by Charles Kondenk.
Opera in 2 acts.
Reproduced from holograph.
At end: first draft, 15 January 1992 to 20 July 1993, Cassis and St. Louis; revision and orchestral score, 21 November 1993 to 22 April 1994, St. Louis.
Duration: 2:00:00.

Composed for: 5 sopranos, mezzo-soprano, 2 contraltos, 7 tenors, 2 baritone, 3 basses, SATB chorus, TB men's chorus, 3 flutes (all also piccolo, 1st also alto flute), oboe (also English horn), 2 clarinets (1st also clarinet in E♭, 2nd also bass clarinet), soprano saxophone, alto saxophone (also clarinet), 2 bassoons (2nd also contrabassoon), 3 horns, trumpet, trombone, tuba, percussion (2 xylophones, vibraphone, glockenspiel, 6 cymbals, 3 large tam-tams, 6 whitehall bells, 3 tom-toms, snare drum, bongos, tambourines, 5 woodblocks, bamboo chimes, maracas, chimes, large thundersheet, dobaci, 3 very large tam-tams, anvil, timpani, bass drum, ratchet, 2 triangles, maracas, metal shaker, whip, marimba, bongos, tenor drum, 5 temple blocks), harp, piano (also celesta and autoharp), 2 tapes, violin I, violin II, viola, violoncello, double bass.
Call no.: **1997/016**
Re-entered as: **1998/020**
Also available:
Call no.: **1997/016 libretto**
Call no.: **1997/016 vocal score**

269. Bo, Sonia, 1960– Da una lettura di Husserl.
Call no.: **1986/013**
No materials available.

270. Bo, Sonia, 1960– Polittico: cinque liriche per soprano e piccolo organico strumentale. Partitura. Milano: Ricordi, 1992.
1 score (184 p.); 31 x 36 cm.
Italian words; also printed as text preceding each section.
Texts by Giambattista Marino, Ugo Foscolo, Teofilo Folengo, Ludovico Ariosto, and Torquato Tasso.
Composed for: soprano, violin, piano, percussion (tom-toms, bongos, vibraphone, crotales, metal wind chimes, glockenspiel, sleigh bells, cymbals, tsiang, woodblocks, temple blocks, maracas).
Call no.: **1993/012**

271. Bodorová, Sylvie, 1954– Terezín ghetto requiem: per baritono e quartetto d'archi, 1997. N.p.: n.p., 1997.
1 score (36 p.); 30 cm.
Latin and Hebrew (romanized) words; also printed as text.
Jewish and Catholic religious texts.
Reproduced from manuscript.
Composed for: baritone, 2 violins, viola, violoncello.
Commissioned by: Warwick Arts Foundation.
Call no.: **2001/026**

272. Body, Jack, 1944– Melodies for orchestra: (1982). N.p.: n.p., 1982.
1 score (69 leaves); 37 cm.
Reproduced from holograph.
At end of score: December 31, 1982, Wellington.
Composed for: piccolo, 2 flutes (2nd also alto flute), 2 oboes, 2 clarinets, 2 bassoons, 4 horns, trumpet, trumpet in D, 2 trombones, bass trombone, tuba, percussion (xylophone, glockenspiel, tenor drum, bass drum), harp, piano, violin I, violin II, viola, violoncello, double bass.
Commissioned by: New Zealand Symphony Orchestra.
Call no.: **1985/018**

273. Boer, Ed de, 1957– Symfonie no. 1: (uit het dagboek van Etty Hillesum): voor groot orkest, 1987–'89. Baxtel, The Netherlands: Ed de Boer, 1989.
1 score (131 p.); 42 cm.
Reproduced from manuscript.
Duration: ca. 40:00.
Commentary by the composer in Dutch, with English translation by Hilary Reynolds.
Contents: Ruïnes—Systemen—Epiloog.
Composed for: piccolo, 3 flutes (3rd also piccolo), 3 oboes, English horn, 3 clarinets (all also clarinet in A, 2nd–3rd also clarinet in E♭), 2 bass clarinets (2nd also clarinet), 3 bassoons, contrabassoon, 6 horns, piccolo trumpet, 4 trumpets (1st also piccolo trumpet, 4th also flugelhorn), flugelhorn, 2 trombones (1st also alto trombone), bass trombone, 2 Wagner tubas, 2 tubas, timpani, percussion (triangle, castanets, 2 woodblocks, sand blocks, maracas, guiro, vibraslap, bongo, 3 snare drums, 4 cymbals, tenor drum, tom-tom, bass drum, 2 tam-tams, chimes, xylophone, vibraphone), 2 harps, organ, celesta, violin I, violin II, viola, violoncello, double bass.
Commissioned by: Dutch Broadcasting Company N.C.R.V.
Call no.: **1991/026**

274. Bokser, Zelman, 1951– The woman who dared.
Call no.: **1985/019**
No materials available.

275. Bolcom, William, 1938– Fifth symphony, 1989. N. p.: Bolcom/Marks/Presser, 1989.
1 score (113 p.); 34 cm.
"Uncorrected score"—p. 2.
Reproduced from manuscript.
Contents: Pensive/active—Scherzo mortele—Hymne à l'amour—Machine.
Composed for: 3 flutes (3rd also piccolo), 2 oboes, English horn, 2 clarinets (1st also clarinet in E♭, 2nd also clarinet in A), bass clarinet, 2 bassoons, contrabassoon, 4 horns, 3 trumpets, 2 trombones, bass trombone, tuba,

4 timpani, percussion (button gongs, crotales, bass marimba, sizzle cymbal, suspended cymbals, snare drum, tenor drum, piccolo snare drums, bass drums, tam-tam, glockenspiel), harp, violin I, violin II, viola, violoncello, double bass.
Commissioned by: Philadelphia Orchestra.
Call no.: **1991/010**

276. Bolcom, William, 1938– Fourth symphony. Full score. Bryn Mawr, PA: Theodore Presser, 1986.
1 score (186 p.); 46 cm.
English words from poem by Theodore Roethke.
Reproduced from manuscript.
Contents: Soundscape—The rose (Theodore Roethke): with solo mezzo-soprano.
Composed for: mezzo-soprano, piccolo, 2 flutes, 2 oboes, English horn, 2 clarinets (1st also clarinet in E♭), bass clarinet, 2 bassoons, contrabassoon, 4 horns, 4 trumpets, 2 trombones, 2 bass trombones, tuba, timpani, percussion (3 snare drums, marimba, glockenspiel, crotales, 3 suspended cymbals, 4 tom-toms, tam-tam, triangle, chimes, bass drum), harp, piano (also celesta), violin I, violin II, viola, violoncello, double bass.
Commissioned by: Saint Louis Symphony.
Call no.: **1988/013**

277. Bolcom, William, 1938– Gaea. N.p.: E.B. Marks: Bolcom Music, 1996.
1 score (124 p.); 33 cm.
Concerto 3 consists of Concertos 1 and 2 played simultaneously.
Duration: ca. 19:00.
Contents: Concerto 1 for piano left hand and chamber orchestra (orchestra I)—Concerto 2 for piano left hand and chamber orchestra (orchestra II)—Concerto 3 for two pianos left hand and full orchestra (orchestra III).
Composed for: 2 pianos (left hand), 3 flutes (3rd also piccolo), 2 oboes, English horn, 3 clarinets (1st also clarinet in E♭, 3rd also bass clarinet), 2 bassoons, contrabassoon, 4 horns, 3 trumpets, 2 trombones, bass trombone, tuba, percussion (7 Thai gongs, crotales, small snare drum, tambourine, chimes, cymbals, glockenspiel, tenor drum, bass drum), celesta, violin I, violin II, viola, violoncello, double bass.
Commissioned by: Meet the Composer/Reader's Digest Commissioning Program.
Call no.: **1997/017**

278. Bolcom, William, 1938– McTeague: an opera in two acts. Full score. N.p.: Marks Music, 1992.
1 score (2 v. [505 p.]); 34 cm.
English words by Arnold Weinstein and Robert Altman; based on the novel by Frank Norris.
Composed for: soprano, boy soprano, 2 mezzo-sopranos, tenor, 3 baritones, 2 basses, men's quartet (2 tenors, baritone, bass), small SATB chorus, 3 flutes (1st also alto flute, 3rd also piccolo), 3 oboes (3rd also English horn), 3 clarinets (1st also clarinet in E♭, 2nd also clarinet in A, 3rd also bass clarinet), 3 bassoons (3rd also contrabassoon), 4 horns, 3 trumpets (1st also flugelhorn and piccolo trumpet), 2 trombones, bass trombone, tuba, timpani, percussion (crotales, slapstick, woodblock, 3 tom-toms, 2 crash cymbals, tam-tam, choke cymbals, jawbone, snare drum, bass drum, 2 suspended cymbals, ratchet, tambourine, clock bell, marimba), harp, piano sampler, violin I, violin II, viola, violoncello, double bass.
Commissioned by: Lyric Opera of Chicago.
Call no.: **1993/013**
Also available:
Call no.: **1993/013 vocal score**

279. Bolcom, William, 1938– Sixth symphony (1996–7). N.p.: E.B. Marks Music Corp.; Bryn Mawr, PA: T. Presser, 1998.
1 score (124 p.); 44 cm.
Duration: ca. 25:00.
Composed for: 3 flutes (3rd also piccolo), 3 oboes (3rd also English horn), English horn, 3 clarinets (1st also clarinet in E♭, 2nd also clarinet in E♭ and alto saxophone, 3rd also bass saxophone), 3 bassoons (3rd also contrabassoon), 4 horns, 3 trumpets (3rd also flugelhorn), 3 trombones, tuba, timpani, percussion (glockenspiel, crotales, large suspended cymbal, large bass drum, triangle, bongos, 2 woodblocks, ratchet, tambourine, tenor drum, trap set), harp, piano, violin I, violin II, viola, violoncello, double bass.
Commissioned by: National Symphony Orchestra of Washington, D.C.
Call no.: **2000/016**

280. Bolcom, William, 1938– Songs of innocence and of experience: 1956–1981 (orchestration 1981–82). New York, NY: E.B. Marks Music, 1982.
1 score (3 v. [473 p.]); 62 cm.
Words by William Blake.
Reproduced from holograph.
Contents: Songs of innocence—Songs of experience.
Composed for: SATB chorus, 3 flutes (2nd also alto flute, 1st and 3rd also piccolo), 3 oboes (3rd also English horn), 3 clarinets (2nd also clarinet in E♭, 3rd also bass clarinet), 3 bassoons (3rd also contrabassoon), 2 alto saxophones (both also tenor saxophone, 2nd also baritone saxophone), 6 horns, 3 trumpets (2nd also cornet, 1st also piccolo trumpet), 2 flugelhorns, 3 trombones, 2 bass trombones, euphonium, 2 tubas, percussion,

harp, piano (also celesta, electric piano, harmonium), organ, electric guitar, electric bass, 2 electric violins (1st also mandolin, 2nd also fiddle), violin I, violin II, viola, violoncello, double bass.
Call no.: **1985/020**

281. Bolcom, William, 1938– A view from the bridge: an opera in two acts, based on the play View from the bridge by Arthur Miller. Full score. New York, NY: E.B. Marks: Bolcom Music, 2002.
1 score (2 v. [653 p.]); 43 cm.
English words by Arnold Weinstein and Arthur Miller.
Composed for: 3 sopranos, alto, 3 tenors, 2 baritones, bass-baritone, 2 basses, SATB chorus, 3 flutes (3rd also piccolo), 3 oboes (3rd also English horn), 2 clarinets (1st also A clarinet), bass clarinet (also clarinet in E♭), 2 bassoons, contrabassoon, 4 horns, 3 trumpets (1st also optional piccolo trumpet), 2 trombones, bass trombone, tuba, percussion (glockenspiel, crotales, optional xylophone, marimba, triangle, crash cymbals, 3 suspended cymbals, optional Thai gongs, castanets, 2 woodblocks, slapstick, tambourine, snare drum, tenor drum, 3 tom-toms, bass drum), timpani, harp, keyboard, violin I, violin II, viola, violoncello, double bass.
Commissioned by: Lyric Opera of Chicago.
Call no.: **2003/015**
Also available:
Call no.: **2003/015 vocal score**

282. Bolcom, William, 1938– A Whitman triptych. N.p.: E.B. Marks Music Co.: Bolcom Music, 1995.
1 score (121 p.); 44 cm.
Words by Walt Whitman.
For voice and orchestra.
Contents: Come up from the fields father—Scented herbage of my breast—Years of the modern.
Composed for: voice, 3 flutes (3rd also piccolo), 3 oboes (3rd also English horn), 3 clarinets (3rd also bass clarinet), 3 bassoons (3rd also contrabassoon), 4 horns, 3 trumpets, 2 trombones, bass trombone, tuba, timpani, percussion (glockenspiel, crotales, 2 suspended cymbals, 2 Thai gongs, tenor drum, small bass drum, tambourine), harp, piano (also celesta), violin I, violin II, viola, violoncello, double bass.
Commissioned by: San Francisco Opera Orchestra.
Call no.: **1996/013**

283. Bolle, James, 1931– Piano concert. N.p.: James Bolle, 1999.
1 score (37 p.); 36 cm.
Composed for: piano, flute, oboe, English horn, clarinet, bass clarinet, bassoon, horn, 2 trumpets, trombone, percussion, violin I, violin II, viola, violoncello, double bass.
Call no.: **2001/027**

284. Bon, André, 1946– La jeune fille au livre. Paris: Durand, 1995.
1 score (353 p.); 30 cm.
Principally French with some English and German words.
Film opera.
Libretto by Michel Beretti.
Reproduced from manuscript.
Composed for: 3 sopranos, mezzo-soprano, 3 tenors, 4 baritones, bass, SATB chorus, 2 flutes (also piccolo), 2 oboes, 2 clarinets, 2 bassoons, 3 horns, 2 trumpets, 2 trombones, tuba, percussion (vibraphone, marimba, glockenspiel, tubular bells, 2 spring coils, 2 triangles, crash cymbals, suspended cymbal, medium tam-tam, low tam-tam, bass drum, snare drum, tenor drum, timbales, maracas), piano, violin I, violin II, viola, violoncello, double bass.
Commissioned by: Ministère de la Culture Française, Foundation Beaumarchais, and Foundation Henry Clews à La Napoule.
Call no.: **1995/010**
Re-entered as: **2000/017**

285. Bond, Victoria, 1950– Ancient keys. N.p.: n.p., 2003.
1 score (85 p.); 28 cm.
For solo piano with chamber orchestra.
Composed for: piano, 2 flutes (also piccolo), 2 oboes (also English horn), 2 clarinets (also bass clarinet), 2 bassoons, 2 horns, 2 trumpets, bass trombone, timpani, percussion (bass drum, snare drum, suspended cymbals, tam-tam, celesta, glockenspiel, tubular bells), violin I, violin II, viola, violoncello, double bass.
Commissioned by: Paul Barnes and Indianapolis Chamber Orchestra.
Call no.: **2005/013**

286. Bond, Victoria, 1950– Molly Manybloom: for soprano and string quartet. N.p.: n.p., 1990.
1 score (50 p.); 28 cm.
English words from Ulysses by James Joyce.
Reproduced from holograph.
At end: July 11, 1990, Greenwich Village, NYC.
Composed for: soprano, 2 violins, viola, violoncello.
Commissioned by: Ida Faiella and l'Ensemble, Albany, NY.
Call no.: **1991/011**
Re-entered as: **1992/015**

287. Bond, Victoria, 1950– Travels. Full score. N.p.: Subito Music, 1995.
1 score (2 v.); 34 cm.
English words by Ann Goette.
Opera in 2 acts.
Composed for: voices, SATB chorus, flute (also piccolo), oboe, clarinet (also bass clarinet), bassoon, 2 horns, trumpet, timpani, percussion (suspended cymbal, bass drum, triangle, glockenspiel, snare drum, cowbell, claves, guiro, tambourine, castanets, 4 tom-toms, hi-hat, crash cymbals), piano, violin I, violin II, viola, violoncello, double bass.
Call no.: **1996/014**

288. Bond, Victoria, 1950– Variations on a theme of Brahms: for orchestra. N.p.: Subito Music, 1998.
1 score (71 p.); 28 cm.
Composed for: piccolo, 2 flutes, 2 oboes (2nd also English horn), 2 clarinets, 2 bassoons, contrabassoon, 4 horns, 3 trumpets, 3 trombones, tuba, timpani, percussion (5 tuned roto-toms, tubular chimes, tambourine, tenor drum, glockenspiel, triangle, bass drum, snare drum, 3 tam-tams, xylophone), violin I, violin II, viola I, viola II, violoncello I, violoncello II, double bass.
Call no.: **2001/028**

289. Bond, Victoria, 1950– What's the point of counterpoint?
Composed for: 2 flutes, 2 oboes, 2 clarinets, 2 bassoons, 4 horns, 3 trumpets, 3 trombones, tuba, percussion, timpani, harp, violin I, violin II, viola, violoncello, double bass.
Commissioned by: Empire Institute for Performing Arts.
Call no.: **1986/014**
No materials available.

290. Bonneau, Paul G., 1962– Latin mass: for choir, orchestra, soprano and mezzo-soprano soloists (2002). Conductor's score. N.p.: n.p., 2002.
1 score (96 p.); 44 cm.
Latin and English words.
Composed for: soprano, mezzo-soprano, SATB chorus, 2 flutes, 2 oboes, 2 clarinets, bass clarinet, 2 bassoons, 2 horns, 2 trumpets, trombone, bass trombone, tuba, percussion (2 timpani, vibraphone, crash cymbals, suspended cymbal, snare drum, bass drum, triangle, claves), violin I, violin II, viola, violoncello, double bass.
Call no.: **2005/014**

291. Borkowski, Marian, 1934– De profundis: na chór mieszany i orkiestrę = for mixed choir and orchestra. Partytura = Score. Warsawa: ZAiKS, 1998.
1 score (17 p.); 30 cm.
Latin words.
Duration: ca. 13:00.
Composed for: SATB chorus, 3 flutes, 3 clarinets, 4 trumpets, 4 horns, 4 trombones, percussion (timpani, tam-tam, tubular bells, bass drum), violin I, violin II, violin III, viola, violoncello, double bass.
Call no.: **2002/020**

292. Börtz, Daniel, 1943– En gycklares berättelser: konsert för blockflöjt och orkester (1999–2000). Partitur. Stockholm: Gehrmans Musikförlag, 2000.
1 score (60 p.); 42 cm.
For recorder and orchestra.
Duration: ca. 22:00.
Composed for: recorder (sopranino, alto, tenor), 2 flutes (2nd also piccolo), 2 oboes (2nd also English horn), 2 clarinets (2nd also clarinet in E♭), bass clarinet, 2 bassoons, 2 trumpets, 2 horns, 2 trombones, tuba, percussion (timpani, piccolo snare drum, 4 bongos, 4 tom-toms, bass drum, crotales, xylophone, vibraphone, sizzle cymbal, 3 suspended cymbals, 2 tam-tams, 3 gongs, claves), violin I, violin II, viola, violoncello, double bass.
Call no.: **2003/014**

293. Borwick, Doug, 1952– The voice of the Lord: for orchestra. N.p.: D. Borwick, 1984.
1 score (69 p.); 36 cm.
Reproduced from holograph.
Duration: ca. 12:00.
Composed for: piccolo, 2 flutes, 2 oboes, English horn, 2 clarinets, bass clarinet, 2 bassoons, contrabassoon, 4 horns, 3 trumpets, 2 trombones, bass trombone, tuba, percussion (timpani, xylophone, sizzle cymbal, bass drum, suspended cymbal, crash cymbals, 3 tom-toms, tam-tam, snare drum), violin I, violin II, viola, violoncello, double bass.
Call no.: **1985/021**

294. Borzova, Alla, 1961– Majnun songs: cantata: for tenor, flute, riq (Egyptian tambourine), rain stick, string quartet, and tape. Full score. N.p.: Borzova & Dmitriev Music, 1996.
1 score (79 p.); 36 cm.
Russian words with English translation; translation also printed as text.
Original texts by Manjun; translated by Mickael Kurgantzev and Ann Michael.
Reproduced from manuscript.
Duration: ca. 24:00.
Composed for: tenor, flute, riq (Egyptian tambourine), rain stick, 2 violins, viola, violoncello, tape.
Call no.: **2004/011**

295. Bose, Hans-Jürgen von, 1953– 63, dream palace: opera based on a novel by James Purdy = Traumpalast '63: Oper nach einer Novelle von James Purdy (1989–90). Full score = Partitur. Mainz: Ars Viva Verlag, 1990.
1 score (495 p.); 46 cm.
English and German words by Hans-Jürgen von Bose.
Reproduced from holograph.
Composed for: 2 sopranos, treble soprano, mezzo-sopranos, countertenor, tenor, baritone, bass, flute (also piccolo, alto flute and bass flute), oboe (also English horn), 2 clarinets (1st also clarinet in E♭ and bass clarinet; 2nd also soprano and alto saxophones and bass clarinet), soprano saxophone (also sopranino, alto, and baritone saxophones), 2 trumpets, trombone, tuba, percussion (claves, maraca, woodblock, rattle, whip, guiro, chocalho, hyoshige, shell chimes, metal chimes, whisper chimes, bird calls, pea whistle, cukoo call, klaxon, spoon, flexatone, friction drum, slide whistle, congas, bongos, snare drum, tom-toms, bass drum, triangle, cymbals, sizzle cymbal, hi-hat, cowbell, Chinese gong, tam-tams, glockenspiel, tubular bells, mouth organ, xylophone, vibraphone, marimba, castanets, jew's harp, timpani), electric guitar (also tenor banjo), accordion, piano (also celesta, electric piano, prepared piano, toy piano, electric organ), 4 violins, viola, violoncello, 2 double basses.
Commissioned by: Stadt München.
Call no.: **1992/142**

296. Bose, Hans-Jürgen von, 1953– . . . im Wind gesprochen: geistliche Musik für Sopran-Solo, 2 Sprecher, gem. Chor, Orgel und Kammerorchester auf Texte der Bibel, Fragmente des Messe-Textes, von Giordano Bruno, Sophokles/Hölderlin, Nicolas Born, Cristoph Meckel, Rolf Dieter Brinkmann und Hans Magnus Enzensberger, 1984/85. Partitur. Mainz: B. Schott's Söhne, 1985.
1 score (81 p.); 45 cm.
German and Latin words.
Duration: ca. 22:00.
Composed for: 2 narrators, soprano, SATB chorus, flute (also piccolo), 2 oboes, English horn, clarinet (also clarinet in E♭), bass clarinet (also clarinet), 3 trumpets, 3 trombones, timpani, percussion (hammer, bass drum, chimes, military drum, suspended cymbals, crash cymbals, xylophone, woodblock, tam-tam, marimba, snare drum, hi-hat, tam-tam, sizzle cymbals), harp, 4 violas, 3 violoncellos, 3 double basses.
Call no.: **1986/117**
Also available:
Call no.: **1986/117 vocal score**

297. Botti, Susan, 1962– EchoTempo: soprano, percussion & orchestra. N.p.: S. Botti/SUBO Music, 2001.
1 score (60 p.); 44 cm.
English words; also printed as text.
Texts: American Indian poetry.
Contents: Spring is opening—Neither spirit nor bird—War god's horse song II—In the great night.
Composed for: soprano, percussion (marimba, bells, chimes, keys, coco rattles, crotales, maracas, mounted frame drum, suspended cymbals, small gong, 5 hand drums, suspended metal bell plates, cowbells, small gongs, brake drums), 3 flutes (2nd also alto flute, 3rd also piccolo), 2 oboes, English horn, 2 clarinets, bass clarinet, 2 bassoons, contrabassoon, 4 horns, 3 trumpets, 2 trombones, bass trombone, tuba, percussion (vibraphone, 4 brake drums, slapstick, shaker, suspended cymbals, small metal scraper, woodblock, afuché, puilis, bass drum, 3 tom-toms, rainstick, sandpaper blocks, large tam-tam), harp, violin I, violin II, viola, violoncello, double bass.
Commissioned by: New York Philharmonic.
Call no.: **2003/016**

298. Boudreau, Walter, 1947– Berliner Momente: pour orchestre. Quebec: Centre de Musique Canadienne, 1988.
1 score (59 p.); 44 cm.
Reproduced from holograph.
Composed for: 2 flutes (both also piccolo), oboe, English horn, clarinet, bass clarinet, bassoon, contrabassoon, 4 horns, 2 trumpets, 2 trombones, bass trombone, contrabass tuba, timpani, percussion (glockenspiel, vibraphone, mark tree, 3 suspended cymbals, water phone, tam-tam, 5 brake drums, bass drum with mounted cymbal, snare drum, 2 tubular bells, crotales, whip, 3 tom-toms), violin I, violin II, viola, violoncello, double bass.
Commissioned by: Société Radio-Canada.
Call no.: **1992/016**

299. Boulez, Pierre, 1925– Sur incises: pour trois pianos, trois harpes et trois percussions-claviers (1996/1998). Partition. Wien: Universal Edition, 1999.
1 score (221 p.); 30 cm.
"Édition 17.11.1999."
Duration: 40:00.
2001 Grawemeyer Award winning work.
Composed for: 3 pianos, 3 harps, percussion (vibraphone, steel drums, crotales, glockenspiel, timbales, marimba, tubular bells).
Call no.: **2001/029**

300. Bouliane, Denys, 1955– Qualia sui: trio pour violon, violoncelle et piano (2001). Köln; Montréal:

Studio Silène, 2001.
1 score (83 p.); 22 x 28 cm.
Duration: ca. 28:00.
Composed for: violin, violoncello, piano.
Commissioned by: Trio Fibonacci.
Call no.: **2005/015**

301. Boyce, Cary, 1955– Dreams within a dream. Bloomington, IN: Aguavá New Music Studio, 2003.
1 score (176 p.); 36 cm.
Principally English words; also printed as text.
Oratorio for soprano solo, chorus, and chamber orchestra.
Texts by John Keats, Linda McKay Feldmann, Kenneth Patchen, William Butler Yeats, Edgar Allan Poe, Francis William Bourdillon, Louise Bogan, St. John of the Cross, Calderón de la Barca, and from the Mass for the dead.
Duration: ca. 40:00.
Composed for: soprano, SATB chorus, 2 flutes, 2 oboes, 2 clarinets, 2 bassoons (also contrabassoon), horn, trumpet, trombone, percussion (bell, vibes, chimes, crotales, mark tree, wood wind chimes, stone or glass wind chimes, anvil/iron pipe/brake drum, medium-large chain or sleigh bells, large suspended cymbal, large tam-tam, 4 roto-toms, bass drum), harp, piano, violin I, violin II, viola, violoncello, double bass.
Commissioned by: Bloomington Chamber Singers and Gerald Sousa.
Call no.: **2005/016**

302. Boykan, Martin, 1931– Elegy, for soprano and six instruments, 1982. N.p.: n.p., 1982.
1 score (6, 98 p.); 39 cm.
English, German, and Italian words; English translation printed as text.
Duration: ca. 35:00–40:00.
Contents: Ist alles denn verloren / Goethe—A sè stesso / Leopardi—Agonia / Ungaretti—Der Spinnerin Lied / Brentano—The winters are so short / Dickinson—Im Mitternacht / Goethe—A bronze immortal takes leave of Han / Li Ho; tr. by A.C. Graham.
Composed for: soprano, flute (also piccolo), clarinet (also bass clarinet), violin, violoncello, double bass, piano.
Call no.: **1985/022**

303. Boykan, Martin, 1931– String quartet no. 3. New York, NY: C. F. Peters, 1998.
1 score (31 p.); 35 cm.
Reproduced from manuscript.
Composed for: 2 violins, viola, violoncello.
Call no.: **2000/018**

304. Bradić, Srećko, 1963– Credo. N.p.: n.p., 1994.
1 score (60 p.); 42 cm.
Latin words.
For solo soprano, solo tenor, SATB chorus, orchestra, and organ.
Reproduced from holograph.
Composed for: soprano, tenor, SATB chorus, 3 flutes (3rd also piccolo), 2 oboes, 2 clarinets, 2 bassoons, 4 horns, 3 trumpets, 3 trombones, tuba, timpani, percussion (snare drum, tenor drum, 5 tom-toms, tambourine, 3 suspended cymbals, crash cymbals, triangle, bells, celesta, tubular bells, large gong, bass drum, tam-tam), organ, violin I, violin II, viola, violoncello, double bass.
Call no.: **1998/021**

305. Bradić, Srećko, 1963– Koncert za violu i violončelo. N.p.: n.p., 2002.
1 score (38 p.); 42 cm.
Reproduced from manuscript.
Composed for: violin, violoncello, piccolo flute, 2 flutes, 2 oboes, 2 clarinets, bass clarinet, 2 bassoons, 6 horns, 3 trumpets, 3 trombones, timpani, percussion (snare drum, tambourine, suspended cymbals, crash cymbals, triangle, celesta, glockenspiel, chimes, bass drum, tam-tam, gong), harp, violin I, violin II, viola, violoncello, double bass.
Call no.: **2004/012**

306. Bradić, Srećko, 1963– Penetration: za klavir i dugaćki orkestar. N.p.: n.p., 1993.
1 score (84 p.); 43 cm.
For piano and string orchestra.
Reproduced from manuscript.
Composed for: piano, 30 violins, 10 violas, 10 violoncellos, 8 double basses.
Call no.: **1997/018**

307. Brady, Tim, 1956– Strange attractions: six études for solo electric guitar, live electronics and tape (1992–1996). N.p.: T. Brady, 1997.
1 score (ca. 71 p.); 29 cm.
Program notes.
Contents: Linear projection in a jump-cut world—Collapsing possibility wave—Difference engine no. 1–3—Pandemonium architecture—Minimal surface—Memory riot.
Composed for: electric guitar, live electronics, tape.
Call no.: **2000/019**

308. Brant, Henry, 1913– 500: hidden hemisphere: a spatial quadruple compendium. New York, NY: Carl Fischer, 1992.

1 score (210 p.); 36 cm.
For three concert bands and an ensemble of Caribbean steel drums (each with its own conductor).
Duration: 1:00:00.
Reproduced from manuscript.
Includes performance instructions.
Composed for: Caribbean steel drum ensemble: 3 trebles, 2 altos, 2 tenors, 2 guitars, 2 violoncellos, baritone; band I: 3 flutes (all also piccolo), 2 oboes, clarinet in E♭, 4 clarinets, bass clarinet, contrabass clarinet, bassoon, contrabassoon, 4 horns, 2 alto saxophones (1st also soprano and tenor saxophones), 2 tenor saxophones (1st also alto saxophone, both also baritone saxophone), 5 trumpets (1st also piccolo trumpet), 4 trombones, 2 euphoniums, 2 tubas, percussion (3 sets of chimes, tambourine, crash cymbals, 2 Chinese blocks, cowbell, 3 triangles, glockenspiel, drum set [2 suspended cymbals, snare drum, hi-hat cymbal set, bass drum, 2 tom-toms]); band II: 4 flutes (all also piccolo), 2 oboes (2nd also English horn), clarinet in E♭, 10 clarinets, bass clarinet, contrabass clarinet, bassoon, contrabassoon, 5 horns, 2 alto saxophones (1st also soprano saxophone), 2 tenor saxophones (2nd also baritone saxophone), 6 trumpets (all also flugelhorn), 4 trombones, 2 euphoniums, 4 tubas, percussion (3 sets of timpani, tambourine, 2 crash cymbals, woodblock, 2 triangles, gong, bass drum, glockenspiel, xylophone, drum set [2 suspended cymbals, snare drum, hi-hat cymbal set, bass drum, 2 tom-toms]); band III: 4 flutes (all also piccolo), 2 oboes (2nd also English horn), clarinet in E♭, 12 clarinets, bass clarinet, contrabass clarinet, bassoon, contrabassoon, 5 horns, 2 alto saxophones, 2 tenor saxophones (2nd also baritone saxophone), 7 trumpets (all also flugelhorn, 1st also piccolo trumpet), 5 trombones, 2 euphoniums, 3 tubas, percussion (3 glockenspiels, crash cymbals, maracas, cowbell, 2 triangles, 3 gongs, xylophone, drum set [2 suspended cymbals, snare drum, hi-hat cymbal set, bass drum, 2 tom-toms]).
Commissioned by: Lincoln Center Out-of-Doors.
Call no.: **1993/014**

309. Brant, Henry, 1913– Crystal antiphonies: for alternating symphony orchestra (on stage) and concert band (at back of hall) each with its own conductor, 2000. Complete score. New York, NY: Carl Fischer, 2000.
1 score (103 p.); 44 cm.
Composed for: orchestra: 3 flutes (2nd–3rd also piccolo), 3 oboes (3rd also English horn), 3 clarinets, 3 bassoons (3rd also contrabassoon), 4 horns, 3 trumpets, 3 trombones, 8 timpani, percussion (5 Chinese blocks, 5 cowbells, marimba), piano, violin I, violin II, viola, violoncello, double bass; concert band: 6 piccolos, 12 clarinets, 2 alto saxophones, 2 tenor saxophones, 4 horns, 6 trumpets, 6 trombones, 7 flugelhorns, 2 euphoniums, 2 tenor tubas, 4 bass tubas, harp, piano, celesta, percussion (timpani, 5 tom-toms, 3 bass drums, 2 pairs of cymbals, 2 gongs, glockenspiel, xylophone, vibraphone, chimes).
Commissioned by: Swarovski Musik Wattens.
Call no.: **2002/021**

310. Brant, Henry, 1913– Dormant craters: spatial events for sixteen percussionists, 1995. New York, NY: Carl Fischer, 1995.
1 score (86 p.); 36 cm.
Reproduced from manuscript.
Annotated for performance.
Composed for: percussion (timpani, chimes, snare drum, vibraphone, xylophone, glockenspiel, 4 small Chinese gongs, 4 high Chinese gongs, jazz drumset, 4 suspended cymbals, hi-hats, 3 large Chinese gongs, 5 Chinese blocks, tam-tams, cowbells, pan-covers pair, large slapstick, 3 large bass drums, 4 tom-toms, 2 pedal bass drums, 3 large triangles, 3 large knob gongs, 4 small knob gongs, 3 small triangles, bass steel drum, crash cymbals).
Commissioned by: Lincoln Center for the Performing Arts.
Call no.: **1996/015**

311. Brant, Henry, 1913– Four score: 4 spatial quartets for a string quartet of equal gamut, 1993. New York: Carl Fischer, 1993.
1 score (4 v.); 36 cm. + 1 part; 28 cm.
Each instrument is placed in a corner of the hall, with distant mezzo-violin obbligato.
Part for obbligato mezzo-violin.
Reproduced from manuscript.
Composed for: mezzo-violin (small viola tuned as violin), violin, viola, "tenor-cello," violoncello.
Call no.: **1994/018**

312. Brant, Henry, 1913– Ghosts & gargoyles: spatial soliloquies: for solo flute with flute octet & jazz drummer (2001). New York, NY: Carl Fischer, 2001.
1 score (64 p.); 44 cm.
Reproduced from manuscript.
Composed for: flute (also piccolo and bass flute), 2 piccolos (also flutes), 2 flutes (also piccolos), 2 alto flutes, 2 bass flutes, percussion (snare drum, suspended cymbal, large tom-tom, hi-hat).
Commissioned by: New Music Concerts.
Call no.: **2004/013**

313. Brant, Henry, 1913– Plowshares & swords: spatial announcements for 74 solo musicians. New York, NY: C. Fischer, 1995.
1 score (a–h, 45 p.); 36 cm.
For orchestra.
Reproduced from holograph.
Includes performance instructions.
Composed for: 3 flutes, 3 oboes, 3 clarinets, 3 bassoons, 4 horns, 3 trumpets (also flugelhorns), 3 trombones (also euphoniums), tuba, percussion (snare drum, cymbal pair, hi-hat, 4 small gongs, vibraphone, xylophone, 4 tom-toms, 2 jazz pedal bass drums, treble steel drum, 2 bass steel drums, glockenspiel, 3 large gongs, chimes, low marimba, timpani, 3 bass drums), 2 pianos, celesta, 24 violins, violas, 8 violoncellos, 6 double basses.
Commissioned by: American Composers Orchestra.
Call no.: **1998/022**

314. Brant, Henry, 1913– Plowshares & swords: spatial announcements for 74 solo musicians. New York, NY: C. Fischer, 1995.
1 score (a–g, 45 p.); 38 cm.
For orchestra.
Reproduced from holograph.
Includes performance instructions in English.
Composed for: 3 flutes, 3 oboes, 3 clarinets, 3 bassoons, 4 horns, 3 trumpets (also flugelhorns), 3 trombones (also euphoniums), tuba, percussion (snare drum, cymbal pair, hi-hat, 4 small gongs, vibraphone, xylophone, 4 tom-toms, 2 jazz pedal bass drums, treble steel drum, 2 bass steel drums, glockenspiel, 3 large gongs, chimes, low marimba, timpani, 3 bass drums), 2 pianos, celesta, 24 violins, violas, 8 violoncellos, 6 double basses.
Commissioned by: American Composers Orchestra.
Call no.: **2000/020**

315. Brant, Henry, 1913– Western springs.
Call no.: **1985/023**
No materials available.

316. Brauns, Martins, 1951– We shall live again once more: a dream about Riga = Sapnis par Rīgu. N.p.: n.p., 200-?.
1 score (54 p.); 42 cm.
Latvian words.
For 7 solo voices, choir, and large orchestra.
Composed for: 7 voices, SATB chorus, 3 flutes (also piccolo), 3 oboes, 3 clarinets (also bass clarinet), soprano saxophone, alto saxophone, tenor saxophone, 3 bassoons (also contrabassoon), 4 horns, 3 trumpets, 3 trombones, tuba, timpani, percussion (drum kit, cymbals, side drum, snare drum, marimba), electric guitar, bass guitar, keyboards (minimum 3), ethnic instruments, violin I, violin II, viola, violoncello, double bass.
Call no.: **2005/017**

317. Bresnick, Martin, 1946– For the sexes: the gates of paradise: for piano solo. N.p.: Carl Fischer, 2001.
24 p. of music; 28 x 37 cm.
Composed for: piano.
Call no.: **2005/018**

318. Bresnick, Martin, 1946– String quartet no. 2: "Bucephalus."
Composed for: 2 violins, viola, violoncello.
Call no.: **1985/024**
No materials available.

319. Breznikar, Joseph, 1950– Cascade: a rhapsody for guitar and chamber orchestra. N.p.: J. Breznikar, 1997.
1 score (107 p.); 28 cm.
Composed for: guitar, alto saxophone, horn, trumpet, percussion (timpani, marimba, suspended cymbal, tom-tom, temple blocks, congas, glockenspiel), violin I, violin II, viola, violoncello, double bass.
Call no.: **2000/021**

320. Breznikar, Joseph, 1950– Twelve American etudes: for guitar. Carbondale, IL: Sterling Sounds Music, 1991.
72 p. of music; 28 cm.
Contents: Electric energy—On a swing—Free-form fugue—Restless activity—Meditative connections—Latin affects [sic]—Blue improvisations—Reflective repetitions—Piano accordance—Reminiscent overtones—Shimmering streams—Jaz-ical-blu-roc.
Composed for: guitar.
Call no.: **1992/017**

321. Brief, Todd, 1953– Idols. Score. Wien: Universal Edition, 1989.
1 score (vii, 57 p.); 47 cm.
"Korr. 2/89."
Reproduced from manuscript.
Duration: ca. 15:00.
Performance instructions in English and German.
Composed for: flute (also piccolo and alto flute), clarinet (also bass clarinet), percussion (marimba, vibraphone, glockenspiel, crotales, 2 bongos, 4 tom-toms, woodblock, 4 cymbals, 2 tam-tams, 4 finger cymbals, 2 maracas, 2 triangles, mark tree, set of glass chimes, bamboo chimes), piano, violin, violoncello.

Commissioned by: Serge Koussevitzky Music Foundation.
Call no.: **1990/009**

322. Brief, Todd, 1953– Idols: for chamber ensemble. Score. Vienna: Universal Edition, 1987.
1 score (iv, 57 p.); 41 cm.
Reproduced from manuscript.
Duration: ca. 15:00.
Performance instructions in English.
Composed for: flute (also piccolo and alto flute), clarinet (also bass clarinet), percussion (marimba, vibraphone, glockenspiel, crotales, 2 bongos, 4 tom-toms, woodblock, 4 cymbals, 2 tam-tams, 4 finger cymbals, 2 maracas, 2 triangles, mark tree, set of glass chimes, bamboo chimes), piano, violin, violoncello.
Commissioned by: Serge Koussevitzky Music Foundation.
Call no.: **1991/012**

323. Brief, Todd, 1953– Idols: for chamber ensemble. Score. Wien: Universal Edition, 1988.
1 score (58 p.); 35 cm.
Duration: ca. 15:00.
Composed for: flute (also piccolo and alto flute), clarinet (also bass clarinet), percussion (marimba, vibraphone, glockenspiel, crotales, 2 bongos, 4 tom-toms, woodblock, 4 cymbals, 2 tam-tams, 4 finger cymbals, 2 maracas, 2 triangles, mark tree, set of glass chimes, bamboo chimes), piano, violin, violoncello.
Commissioned by: Serge Koussevitzky Music Foundation.
Call no.: **1992/018**
Re-entered as: **1993/015**

324. Brief, Todd, 1953– Idols: for ensemble. Score. Wien: Universal Edition, 1988 (6/88 printing).
1 score (vii, 57 p.); 47 cm.
Reproduced from manuscript.
Duration: ca. 15:00.
Performance instructions in English and German.
Composed for: flute (also piccolo and alto flute), clarinet (also bass clarinet), percussion (marimba, vibraphone, glockenspiel, crotales, 2 bongos, 4 tom-toms, woodblock, 4 cymbals, 2 tam-tams, 4 finger cymbals, 2 maracas, 2 triangles, mark tree, set of glass chimes, bamboo chimes), piano, violin, violoncello.
Commissioned by: Serge Koussevitzky Music Foundation.
Call no.: **1989/012**

325. Brief, Todd, 1953– Jeweled light: for soprano and chamber ensemble. N.p.: Todd Brief, 1990.
1 score (70 p.); 44 cm.
Italian words; also printed as text with English translation.
Duration: 10:00.
Contents: In the morning you always come back / Cesare Pavese, translated by Alan Williamson—Se pure osi = Jeweled light / Mario Luzi, translated by I. L. Salomon.
Composed for: soprano, flute (also alto flute), clarinet, harp, piano, percussion (vibraphone, crotales, mark tree, triangle, woodblock, 3 cymbals, low sizzle cymbal, 2 bongos, tam-tam), violin, viola.
Call no.: **1994/019**

326. Brief, Todd, 1953– Slow lament: for soprano and piano. New York, NY: American Composers Alliance, 1984.
1 score (iv, 41 p.); 35 x 41 cm.
Spanish words; also printed as text with English translation.
Text by Pablo Neruda.
Reproduced from holograph.
At end: Bellagio, New York, West Berlin, 1984.
Duration: 16:00.
Composed for: soprano, piano.
Commissioned by: Fromm Music Foundation.
Call no.: **1986/015**

327. Brisman, Heskel, 1923– Sinfonia sacra: for mezzo-soprano & orchestra. Bryn Mawr, PA: T. Presser, 1996.
1 score (58 p.); 36 cm.
English words.
Text: Psalms 13, 148, and 94.
Composed for: mezzo-soprano, 3 flutes (3rd also piccolo), 3 oboes (3rd also English horn), 3 clarinets (3rd also bass clarinet), 3 bassoons (3rd also contrabassoon), 4 horns, 3 trumpets, 2 trombones, bass trombone, tuba, timpani, percussion (suspended cymbal, tenor drum, anvil, large triangle, large Chinese gong, tambourine), harp, violin I, violin II, viola, violoncello, double bass.
Call no.: **2000/022**

328. Brizzi, Aldo, 1960– De la trasmutatione de metalli IV: per sola percussione, 1988. N.p.: n.p., 1988.
1 score (11 p.); 36 cm.
Reproduced from holograph.
Composed for: timpani, 3 bongos, 3 tom-toms, bass drum, pedal bass drum.
Call no.: **1989/013**

329. Brizzi, Aldo, 1960– Kammerkonzert N. 2: per 10

archi solisti. N.p.: n.p., 1989.
1 score (15 p.); 36 cm.
Reproduced from manuscript.
Composed for: 6 violins, 2 violas, violoncello, double bass.
Commissioned by: Fondation Sophia Antipolis.
Call no.: **1990/010**

330. Brizzi, Aldo, 1960– The labyrinth trial: for viola and tape. N.p.: n.p., 1996.
1 score (18 p.); 37 cm.
Includes commentary by the composer and performance instructions.
Composed for: viola, tape.
Commissioned by: Ministère de la Culture Française.
Call no.: **1998/023**

331. Brizzi, Aldo, 1960– Il libro dell'interrogazione poetica: per 6 percussionisti e gruppo di 9 strumenti, 1983–84. N.p.: n.p., 1984.
1 score (ii, 50 p.); 42 cm.
Reproduced from holograph.
Duration: 16:00.
Composed for: percussion (6 tom-toms, bass drum, timpani, 2 Chinese drums, 4 bronze sheets, anvil, 2 Javanese gongs, 9 tam-tams, large cymbal, 8 stones), clarinet, bass clarinet, contrabassoon, horn, 2 violins, viola, violoncello, double bass.
Call no.: **1986/015**

332. Broadstock, Brenton, 1952– Dark side: for orchestra. N.p.: n.p., 1999.
1 score (various pagings); 30 cm.
"Symphony no. 5"—Program notes.
Composed for: piccolo, 2 flutes, 2 oboes, English horn, 2 clarinets, bass clarinet, 2 bassoons, contrabassoon, 4 horns, 2 trumpets, 3 trombones, tuba, percussion (timpani, bass drum, 3 tom-toms, bell tree, suspended cymbal, snare drum, tam-tam, marimba, chimes, glockenspiel), violin I, violin II, viola, violoncello, double bass.
Commissioned by: Krasnoyarsk Academic Symphony Orchestra.
Call no.: **2002/022**

333. Broadstock, Brenton, 1952– Stars in a dark night: symphony #2 (1989): for orchestra. Box Hill North, Australia: Australia Music, 1989.
1 score (96 p.); 30 cm.
Duration: ca. 23:00.
Includes program note by the composer in English.
Composed for: piccolo, flute, oboe, English horn, clarinet, bass clarinet, bassoon, contrabassoon, 4 horns, 3 trumpets, 3 trombones, tuba, harp, piano (also celesta), percussion (suspended cymbal, lion's roar, crotales, bell tree, vibraphone, gong, 2 timbales, triangle, tam-tam, snare drum, bass drum, glockenspiel, tambourine, 2 tom-toms, slapstick, tenor drum, chimes, Chinese cymbal, 3 bongos, timpani), violin I, violin II, viola, violoncello, double bass.
Commissioned by: Melbourne Symphony Orchestra.
Call no.: **1991/013**

334. Broadstock, Brenton, 1952– Stars in a dark night: symphony #2 (1989): for orchestra. Sydney: G. Schirmer (Australia), 1989.
1 score (96 p.); 30 cm.
Duration: ca. 23:00.
Includes program note by the composer in English.
Composed for: piccolo, flute, oboe, English horn, clarinet, bass clarinet, bassoon, contrabassoon, 4 horns, 3 trumpets, 3 trombones, tuba, harp, piano (also celesta), percussion (suspended cymbal, lion's roar, crotales, bell tree, vibraphone, gong, 2 timbales, triangle, tam-tam, snare drum, bass drum, glockenspiel, tambourine, 2 tom-toms, slapstick, tenor drum, chimes, Chinese cymbal, 3 bongos, timpani), violin I, violin II, viola, violoncello, double bass.
Commissioned by: Melbourne Symphony Orchestra.
Call no.: **1992/019**

335. Broadstock, Brenton, 1952– Voices from the fire: symphony #3, 1991: for orchestra. Sydney: G. Schirmer (Australia), 1992.
1 score (93 p.); 30 cm.
Duration: ca. 23:00.
Includes program note by the composer.
Composed for: piccolo, 2 flutes (2nd also alto flute), 2 oboes, English horn, 2 clarinets, bass clarinet, 2 bassoons, 4 horns, 3 trumpets, 2 trombones, bass trombone, tuba, timpani, percussion (2 tom-toms, slapstick, glockenspiel, bell tree, gong, tam-tam, suspended cymbal, 2 timbales, vibraphone, bass drum, triangle), piano (also celesta), violin I, violin II, viola, violoncello, double bass.
Commissioned by: Australian Broadcasting Corporation.
Call no.: **1993/016**

336. Bröder, Alois, 1961– Îsôt als blansche Mains: für grosses Orchester mit Frauenchor, 1989/90. N.p.: n.p., 1990.
1 miniature score (43 p.); 30 cm.
Women's voices are treated like instrumental voices.
Reproduced from holograph.
Duration: ca. 15:00.
Composed for: women's chorus, 3 flutes (3rd also pic-

colo), 3 oboes (3rd also English horn), 3 clarinets (2nd also clarinet in E♭, 3rd also bass clarinet), 3 bassoons (3rd also contrabassoon), 4 horns, 3 trumpets, 3 trombones, tuba, percussion (thundersheet, shell chimes, 3 woodblocks, 2 bongos, bass drum, vibraphone, 2 tam-tams, Chinese cymbal, snare drum, 3 tom-toms, timpani, marimba, 3 suspended cymbals, 2 congas, tenor drum, xylophone), 2 harps, piano (also celesta), violin I, violin II, viola, violoncello, double bass.
Call no.: **1996/016**

337. Brody, Jeffrey, 1950– Concerto for organ and orchestra. N.p.: Ashbrook Music, 1995.
1 score (324 p.); 36 cm.
Reproduced from manuscript.
Duration: 50:00–1:02:00.
Composed for: organ, 3 flutes (3rd also picccolo), 3 oboes (3rd also English horn), 3 clarinets (3rd also bass clarinet), 3 bassoons (3rd also contrabassoon), 4 horns, 3 trumpets, 2 trombones, bass trombone, tuba, timpani, percussion (bass drum, snare drum, cymbals, xylophone, tambourine, triangle, hammer, glockenspiel), 2 harps, celesta, violin I, violin II, viola, violoncello, double bass.
Call no.: **1996/017**

338. Brody, Jeffrey, 1950– Concerto for organ and orchestra. N.p.: Ashbrook Music, 1995.
1 score (240 p.); 36 cm.
Reproduced from manuscript.
Duration: 41:30.
Composed for: organ, 3 flutes (3rd also piccolo), 3 oboes (3rd also English horn), 3 clarinets (3rd also bass clarinet), 3 bassoons (3rd also contrabassoon), 4 horns, 3 trumpets, 2 trombones, bass trombone, tuba, timpani, percussion (bass drum, snare drum, cymbals, xylophone, tambourine, triangle, hammer, glockenspiel), 2 harps, celesta, violin I, violin II, viola, violoncello, double bass.
Call no.: **1998/024**

339. Brody, Jeffrey, 1950– Jabberwocky: duet for two tenors and chamber orchestra. N.p.: Jeff Brody, 1984.
1 score (33, 2 p.); 44 cm.
English words by Lewis Carroll; also printed as text.
Originally for two tenors and two pianos.
Reproduced from holograph.
Duration: ca. 11:00.
Composed for: 2 tenors, 2 flutes (both also piccolo), 2 clarinets, 2 bassoons, 2 horns, 2 trumpets, trombone, bass trombone, timpani, percussion (cymbals, bass drum, tam-tam, triangle, glockenspiel), harp, celesta, violin I, violin II, viola, violoncello, double bass.
Call no.: **1985/025**

340. Brody, Jeffrey, 1950– Passacaglia: für Orchester. N.p.: Ashbrook Music, 1996.
1 score (63 p.); 36 cm.
Reproduced from manuscript.
Duration: 15:00.
Composed for: 3 flutes (3rd also piccolo), 3 oboes (3rd also English horn), 3 clarinets (3rd also bass clarinet), 3 bassoons (3rd also contrabassoon), 4 horns, 3 trumpets, 2 trombones, bass trombone, tuba, timpani, percussion (glockenspiel, tam-tam, crash cymbals, bass drum, snare drum, triangle, celesta), harp, violin I, violin II, viola, violoncello, double bass.
Call no.: **2000/023**

341. Brophy, Gerard, 1953– Yo yai pakebi, man mai yapobi: for percussion and large orchestra (1999). N.p.: n.p., 1999.
1 score (90 p.); 42 cm.
Composed for: 4 flutes (2nd–3rd also alto flute, 4th also piccolo), 4 oboes (4th also English horn), 4 clarinets (3rd–4th also bass clarinet), 4 bassoons (3rd–4th also contrabassoon), alto saxophone, 2 tenor saxophones, baritone saxophone, 8 horns, 4 trumpets, 4 trombones, tuba, piano (also synthesizer), percussion (djembe, marimba, mbungbung, tjoll, feng gong, rain stick, sange, gorong, mark tree, calabash, gankogui, 4 cymbals, chizumana, fromtomfrom, ganza, drum kit [high, medium, and low suspended cymbals, hi-hat, snare, kick drum], timpani, ferre, breqete, tjoll, vibraphone, surdo, 2 basket rattles, debindha, doundoun, bell), violin I, violin II, viola, violoncello, double bass.
Commissioned by: Het Residentie Orkest.
Call no.: **2003/017**

342. Brouwer, Margaret, 1940– Light: for soprano, harpsichord, flute, clarinet, violin, violoncello, and percussion. New York, NY: Carl Fischer, 2001.
1 score (38 p.); 43 cm.
English words.
Texts from Hildegard of Bingen's Mystical writings and a lecture by Richard Feynman.
Contents: The fiery power: a vision of Hildegard von Bingen—Nederlandse Licht—Atoms.
Composed for: soprano, harpsichord, flute, clarinet, violin, violoncello, percussion.
Commissioned by: Cleveland Museum of Art.
Call no.: **2003/018**

343. Brouwer, Margaret, 1940– Remembrances: for orchestra. New York, NY: Carl Fisher, 1996.
1 score (54 p.); 36 cm.
Duration: 14:00.
Composed for: 2 flutes (2nd also piccolo), 2 oboes, Eng-

lish horn, 2 clarinets, 2 bassoons (2nd also contrabassoon), 4 horns, 3 trumpets, 3 trombones, tuba, timpani, percussion (glockenspiel, xylophone, vibraphone, tam-tam, suspended cymbal), harp, violin I, violin II, viola, violoncello, double bass.
Commissioned by: Roanoke Symphony.
Call no.: **1997/019**

344. Bruce, Neely, 1944– Americana.
Call no.: **1986/016**
No materials available.

345. Bruce, Neely, 1944– Convergence: some parades for Charlie's dad. N.p.: Neely Bruce, 2000.
1 score (4 v.); 28 cm.
English words.
A multi-media composition.
For 6 or more marching bands, 12 or more choruses, multiple organs, symphony orchestra, West African drums, Javanese gamelan, steel drums, chamber orchestra, corps of fifers, pipers, etc., and hundreds of bells.
Contents: The black notebook: performance notes and various music—Historical and phantom marches: band music—Editions and arrangements: choral music—Preludes and paraphrases: organ music.
Commissioned by: American Composers Forum.
Call no.: **2002/023**

346. Bruce, Neely, 1944– Geographical preludes: new piano music, March 1999–July 2001. N.p.: Chamberlain Hill Publications, 2003.
94 p. of music; 28 cm.
Composed for: piano.
Call no.: **2005/019**

347. Bryant, Curtis, 1949– Prelude and fugue. N.p.: n.p., 1986.
1 score (47 p.); 28 cm.
For orchestra.
Composed for: piccolo, 2 flutes, oboe, English horn, 2 clarinets, bass clarinet, alto saxophone, 2 bassoons, 4 horns, 3 trumpets, 2 trombones, bass trombone, tuba, timpani, percussion (triangle, marimba, tambourine, snare drum, tubular bells, crash cymbals, bass drum, glockenspiel, tam-tam, roto-toms, xylophone, crotales, woodblock), harp, violin I, violin II, viola, violoncello, double bass.
Commissioned by: Macon Symphony Orchestra.
Call no.: **1987/010**

348. Bryant, Curtis, 1949– Sextet for piano, winds and strings. N.p.: n.p., 1983.
1 manuscript score (20 leaves); 28 cm.
Reproduced from holograph.
Duration: 16:10.
Composed for: flute, clarinet, violin, viola, violoncello, piano.
Commissioned by: Atlanta Chamber Players.
Call no.: **1985/026**

349. Bryant, Curtis, 1949– Zabette: an opera in three acts. Union City, GA: Curtis Bryant Music, 1999.
1 score (iii, 456 p.); 28 cm.
English words by Mary R. Bullard.
Includes program notes and synopsis.
Composed for: voices, SATB chorus, 2 flutes (2nd also piccolo), 2 oboes (2nd also English horn), 2 clarinets (2nd also bass clarinet), 2 bassoons, 2 horns, 2 trumpets, trombone, bass trombone, tuba, percussion (3 timpani, vibraphone, tubular bells, snare drum, field drum, bass drum, crash cymbals, suspended cymbal, tam-tam, tambourine, triangle, African djun djun, cabasa, or shekere, 2–3 guiros), violin I, violin II, viola, violoncello, double bass.
Call no.: **2001/030**

350. Buelow, William Lee, 1941– Sonata for violin and piano. Marietta, OH: W.L. Buelow Publ., 1997.
1 score (33 p.); 36 cm. + 1 part; 28 cm.
Composed for: violin, piano.
Commissioned by: Duo Grishman-Chiu.
Call no.: **2000/024**

351. Buhr, Glenn, 1954– Beren and Lúthien: after the mythical tale by J. R. R. Tolkien: for orchestra. N.p.: n.p., 1984.
1 miniature score (83 p.); 28 cm.
Reproduced from manuscript.
Duration: ca. 21:00.
At end of score: "25 Feb. 1984 Ann Arbor."
Contents: Beren Erchamion—Tinúviel—The lay of Leithian.
Composed for: 3 flutes (3rd also piccolo), 3 oboes (3rd also English horn), 3 clarinets in A (3rd also clarinet in E♭), bass clarinet, 2 bassoons, contrabassoon, 4 horns, 3 trumpets, 2 trombones, bass trombone, tuba, timpani, percussion (marimba, glockenspiel, tam-tam, tubular bells, wind chimes, crash cymbals, suspended cymbal, finger cymbals, bell tree, crotales, vibraphone, xylophone, triangle, field drum, bass drum, 4 tom-toms), harp, piano (also celesta), violin I, violin II, viola, violoncello, double bass.
Call no.: **1986/017**

352. Buhr, Glenn, 1954– Lure of the fallen Seraphim: for orchestra. N.p.: Glenn Buhr, 1987.

1 score (261 p.); 28 cm.
Reproduced from manuscript.
Duration: ca. 30:00.
Composed for: 3 flutes (3rd also piccolo), 3 oboes (3rd also English horn), 3 clarinets (all also clarinet in A, 3rd also clarinet in E♭), bass clarinet, 2 bassoons, contrabassoon, 4 horns, 3 trumpets (1st also piccolo trumpet), 2 trombones, bass trombone, tuba, timpani, percussion (marimba, vibraphone, glockenspiel, triangle, finger cymbals, suspended cymbal, crash cymbals, snare drum, temple blocks, tam-tam, bass drum, tambourine, floor tom-tom, bongo, xylophone, crotales, wind chimes, 4 tom-toms, field drum), harp, piano (also celesta), violin I, violin II, viola, violoncello, double bass.
Commissioned by: Toronto Symphony.
Call no.: **1989/014**

353. Bukowski, Mirosław, 1936– Recueillement: na sopran i orkiestrę, do stów Wincenteego Korab-Brzozowskiego = for soprano and orchestra to words by Wincenty Korab-Brzozowski, 1998–2000. Partytura. N.p.: n.p., 2000.
1 score (55 p.); 30 cm.
French words; printed also as text following score.
Reproduced from manuscript.
Composed for: soprano, 2 flutes (2nd also piccolo), 2 oboes (2nd also English horn), 2 clarinets, 2 bassoons, 2 horns, trumpet, trombone, timpani, percussion (2 triangles, chimes, tam-tam), violin I, violin II, viola, violoncello, double bass.
Call no.: **2002/024**

354. Buller, John, 1927– Bakxai = (The Bacchae). Oxford: Oxford University Press, 1992.
1 score (237 p.); 42 cm.
Greek and English words.
Opera.
Libretto by the composer after Euripides.
Composed for: mezzo-soprano, 3 tenors, 3 baritones, bass, small female chorus (6 sopranos, 3 mezzo-sopranos), 3 flutes (3rd also piccolo), 3 oboes (3rd also English horn), 3 clarinets, 2 bassoons, contrabassoon, 4 horns, 3 trumpets, 2 trombones, bass trombone, percussion (timpani, 3 roto-toms, snare drum, congas, tam-tam, bongos, 3 woodblocks, 5 temple blocks, jingle bells, maracas, castanets, tambourine, 5 tom-toms, timbales, xylophone, glockenspiel, tubular bells, tenor drum, bass drum, crotales, jingle bells, vibraphone, 3 suspended cymbals), harp, celesta, violin I, violin II, viola, violoncello, double bass.
Commissioned by: English National Opera.
Call no.: **1993/017**

355. Buller, John, 1927– Of three Shakespeare sonnets. Oxford: Oxford University Press, 1985.
1 score (28 p.); 41 cm.
English words.
For soprano and instrumental ensemble.
Reproduced from manuscript.
Composed for: mezzo-soprano, flute, clarinet, harp, 2 violins, viola, violoncello.
Commissioned by: Nash Ensemble.
Call no.: **1986/018**

356. Bulow, Harry, 1951– Sonata for piano: (1995). N.p.: n.p., 1995.
38 p. of music; 28 cm.
Composed for: piano.
Call no.: **2000/025**

357. Buren, John van, 1952– Fünf Gesänge nach Catull: für Mezzosopran und Ensemble. Hamburg: Peer Musikverlag, 1985.
1 score (61 p.); 30 cm.
Latin words; also printed as text with German or English translations.
Reproduced from manuscript.
Contents: Iam ver egelidos—Vivamus—Troia—Furi et Aureli—Paene insularum.
Composed for: mezzo-soprano, flute, violoncello, harpsichord, percussion (vibraphone, cymbals, slit drum, tam-tam, cabasa, 2 bongos, conga).
Call no.: **1986/115**

358. Burghardt, Benedikt, 1960– Mimaamakim: salmo 130: per coro misto a cappella. Grossrosseln: Musikverlag Hayo, 2002.
1 score (29 p.); 30 cm.
Hebrew words (romanized); also printed as text with German, Italian, French, and English translations following score.
Composed for: SATB chorus.
Call no.: **2005/020**

359. Burghardt, Benedikt, 1960– Wie leicht wird Erde sein: für Sopran, B-Klarinette, Streichorchester und Schlagzeug. N.p.: B. Burghardt, 1995.
1 score (36 p.); 34 cm.
German words; also printed as text.
Poem by Nelly Sachs.
Reproduced from manuscript.
Duration: ca. 13:00.
Composed for: soprano, clarinet, percussion (bass kettle drum, timpani, triangle, 2 large cymbals, snare drum, tubular bells), violin I, violin II, viola, violoncello, double bass.

Call no.: **1998/025**

360. Burghardt, Daryl, 1968– Te deum: for wind ensemble and chorus. N.p.: D.A. Burghardt, 1999.
1 score (38 p.); 43 cm.
Latin words; also printed as text with English translation.
Composed for: SATB chorus, piccolo, 2 flutes, 2 oboes, English horn, clarinet in E♭, 3 clarinets, bass clarinet, 2 bassoons, contrabassoon, 2 alto saxophones, tenor saxophone, baritone saxophone, 3 trumpets, 4 horns, 3 trombones, bass trombone, euphonium, tuba, 3 double basses, organ, celesta, harp, marimba, percussion, timpani.
Commissioned by: Bands of Michigan State University.
Call no.: **2001/031**

361. Burgstahler, Elton, 1924– Dorian Gray: opera in three acts. N.p.: n.p., 198-?.
1 score (483 p.); 29 cm.
Words in English.
Reproduced from holograph.
Composed for: voices, piccolo, 2 flutes, 2 oboes, 2 clarinets, bass clarinet, 2 bassoons, 4 horns, 2 trumpets, 3 trombones, tuba, timpani, percussion (bass drum, snare drum, tam-tam, gong, cymbals, xylophone, chimes, bell tree), violin I, violin II, viola, violoncello, double bass.
Call no.: **1985/027**

362. Burrell, Diana, 1948– Symphonies of flocks, herds, and shoals: for orchestra. London: United Music Publishers, 1997.
1 score (135 p.); 34 cm.
Includes biographical sketch of composer and program notes.
Composed for: piccolo, 3 flutes (3rd also piccolo), 3 oboes (3rd also English horn), English horn, 3 clarinets, 3 bassoons (3rd also contrabassoon), contrabassoon, 6 horns, 3 trumpets, 2 trombones, bass trombone, tuba, 2 descant recorders, timpani (also stones and flexatone), percussion (2 vibraphones, crotales, xylophone, 4 tom-toms, 4 roto-toms, whip, 2 woodblocks, claves, maracas, tambourine, geophone, mark tree, whistle, 3 suspended cymbals, rainmaker, bamboo chimes, 2 triangles, bass drum, 5 pairs of stones, tam-tam, Chinese bell tree, 3 flexatones, guiro), harp, piano, violin I, violin II, viola, violoncello, double bass.
Commissioned by: BBC.
Call no.: **1998/026**

363. Burrs, Leslie Savoy, 1952– The Geron fantasy. N.p.: Compermutation Pub., 1992.
1 score (153 p.); 36 cm.
For orchestra.
Composed for: 2 flutes, 2 oboes, 2 clarinets, 2 bassoons, 2 horns, 2 trumpets, 2 trombones, timpani, harp, violin I, violin II, viola, violoncello, double bass.
Commissioned by: Charleston Symphony Orchestra.
Call no.: **1993/018**

364. Burrs, Leslie Savoy, 1952– Vanqui. Full score. N.p.: Leslie Savoy Burrs, 1996.
1 score (2 v.); 43 cm.
English words by John A. Williams.
Opera.
Composed for: voices, SATB chorus, 2 flutes, 2 oboes, 2 clarinets, 2 bassoons, 4 horns, 2 trumpets, 2 trombones, piano, chakaba, percussion, harp, violin I, violin II, viola, violoncello, double bass.
Commissioned by: Opera/Columbus.
Call no.: **2001/032**

365. Bush, Alan Dudley, 1900–1996. The earth in shadow: for mixed chorus and symphony orchestra, op. 102. Full score. N.p.: n.p., 198-?.
1 score (57 p.); 38 cm.
English words.
Text by Nancy Bush.
Reproduced from manuscript.
Composed for: SATB chorus, piccolo, 2 flutes, 2 oboes, English horn, 2 clarinets, bass clarinet, 2 bassoons, contrabassoon, 4 horns, 3 trumpets, 2 trombones, bass trombone, timpani, percussion (tambourine, side drum, crash cymbals, bass drum, bass triangle), piano, violin I, violin II, viola, violoncello, double bass.
Call no.: **1987/011**

366. Buss, Howard J., 1951– Modern times: for narrator, flute/piccolo and 4 percussion. Lakeland, FL: Brixton Publications, 1996.
1 score (v, 35 p.); 28 cm.
English words by the composer; also printed as text.
Reproduced from manuscript.
Includes program notes, performance instructions, and biographical information.
Contents: Info glut—Night tide—The hunt—Five question interlude—The asphalt blanket—To a neglected child—Giggles!—Modern times.
Composed for: flute (also piccolo), percussion (xylophone, lion's roar, tam-tam, vibraslap, suspended cymbals, bell tree, bongos, marimba, snare drum, bass drum, anvils, glass jug or jars, conga, wind chimes, triangle, vibraphone, roto-toms, tambourine, police whistle, shaker, duck call, glockenspiel, timpani, agogo bells, hi-hat, woodblock, frog croak, boing box effect, guiro).
Call no.: **2001/033**

367. Bussotti, Sylvano, 1931– Le bal miró: prima suite antologie per orchestra. Partitura. Milano: G. Ricordi, 1986.
1 score (71 p.); 46 cm.
Bussottioperaballet.
Reproduced from manuscript.
Contents: Verde—Sardana—Prestissimo—Masse—Tutti.
Composed for: piccolo, 3 flutes (3rd also alto flute and 2nd also piccolo), 2 oboes, English horn, clarinet in E♭, 2 clarinets, bass clarinet, 2 bassoons, contrabassoon, 4 horns, 3 trumpets, 3 trombones, tuba, percussion (glockenspiel, xylophone, xylorimba, marimba, vibraphone, chimes, timpani, triangle, crash cymbals, 4 suspended cymbals, sizzle cymbal, hi-hat, 4 tam-tams, bass drum, 4 tom-toms, guiro, 2 bongos, 2 congas, 2 woodblocks, military drum, whip, tambourine, maracas, 5 temple blocks, large gong, 10 cowbells, tamburo coperto), harp, piano, celesta, violin I, violin II, viola, violoncello, double bass.
Call no.: **1988/014**

368. Bussotti, Sylvano, 1931– Il catalogo è questo: per orchestra, con flauto, violino e viola obbligati. Partitura. Milano: G. Ricordi, 1984.
1 score (76 p.); 43 cm.
Bussottioperaballet.
Reproduced from manuscript.
At end of score: "Torino, 10 gennaio 1984."
Composed for: flute, violin, viola, piccolo, 2 flutes (both also alto flute), 2 oboes, English horn, 2 clarinets, bass clarinet, 2 bassoons, contrabassoon, 4 horns, 3 trumpets, 2 trombones, tuba, percussion (glockenspiel, crash cymbals, gong, triangle, hi-hat, vibraphone, 4 suspended cymbals, 3 tam-tams, studded cymbal, marimba, bass drum, 2 plastic garbage pails, bells, 4 tom-toms, 2 maracas, military drum, timpani, African wood drum, 2 bongos), harp, piano, celesta, violin I, violin II, viola, violoncello, double bass.
Call no.: **1986/019**

369. Bussotti, Sylvano, 1931– L'inspizatione: melodramma in tre atti. Partitura. Milano: Ricordi, 1986.
1 score (111 p.); 39 cm.
Italian words by the composer.
Bussottioperaballet.
Reproduced from manuscript.
Composed for: 2 sopranos, 2 tenors, baritone, 2 basses, piccolo, 2 flutes, 2 oboes, crumhorn, English horn, 2 clarinets, bass clarinet, alto saxophone, 2 bassoons, contrabassoon, 4 horns, 3 trumpets, 2 trombones, tuba, percussion (timpani, covered drum, 3 whips, 3 tam-tams, bass drum, wind machine, military drum, plastic garbage pails, hi-hat, bass drum, cymbals, glockenspiel, vibraphone, marimba, chimes, 4 suspended cymbals, 4 tom-toms, triangle, 2 gongs, sleigh bells, 5 cowbells, crash cymbals, 2 bongos, xylomarimba, 2 maracas, 2 slit drums), harp, piano, celesta, harpsichord, violin I, violin II, viola, violoncello, double bass.
Call no.: **1990/011**

370. Bussotti, Sylvano, 1931– Madrelingua: rappresentazione sinfonica, per coro maschile, arpa obbligata e orchestra (1994). N.p.: Edizioni Bussottioperaballet, 1995.
1 score (30 p.); 30 cm.
Italian words.
Reproduced from manuscript.
Composed for: harp, men's chorus, 3 flutes (3rd also piccolo), 2 oboes, 2 clarinets, bass clarinet, 2 bassoons, contrabassoon, 4 horns, 3 trumpets (3rd also piccolo trumpet), 2 trombones, tuba, celesta, percussion (timpani, glockenspiel, vibraphone, 2 gongs, hi-hat, 3 tam-tams, tambourine, castanets, vibraslap, agogo bells, bass drum, roto-toms, triangle, 2 suspended cymbals, steel drum, wind machine, bells, rain stick, woodblock, large Japanese temple bell, switch, metal tube shaker, xylorimba, lujons, tamorra, triccheballacche, 3 cut demijohns, bin zasara), violin I, violin II, viola, violoncello, double bass.
Commissioned by: Gestione autonoma dei concerti dell'Accademia Nazionale di Santa Cecilia, Roma.
Call no.: **2000/026**

371. Butler, Martin, 1960– A better place: chamber opera in one act. Oxford: Oxford University Press, 1999.
1 score (173 p.); 30 cm.
English words by Cindy Oswin.
Duration: ca. 50:00.
Composed for: soprano, mezzo-soprano, tenor, baritone, flute (also piccolo), oboe, 2 clarinets (2nd also bass clarinet), bassoon, 2 horns, percussion (tam-tam, marimba, glockenspiel, 2 log drums, temple blocks, triangle, vibraphone, snare drum, small suspended cymbal, cabasa, tambourine, scaffold bar), piano, harp, violin, 2 violas, violoncello, double bass.
Commissioned by: English National Opera Studio.
Call no.: **2004/014**

372. Butsch, John Austin, 1951– Fantasy in Indigo. N.p.: n.p., 198-?.
53 leaves of music; 31 cm.
Reproduced from manuscript.
Composed for: piano.
Call no.: **1986/020**

373. Butt, James, 1929– Iter infinitus: the unbounded journey. N.p.: Sphemusations, 1991.
1 miniature score (28 p.); 30 cm.
Contents: Overture—Fugue.
Composed for: 2 flutes, 2 oboes, 2 clarinets, 2 bassoons, 4 horns, 2 trumpets, 3 trombones, tuba, timpani, percussion (triangle, snare drum, cymbals, xylophone, bass drum), violin I, violin II, viola, violoncello, double bass.
Call no.: **1993/019**

374. Butterley, Nigel, 1935– Spell of creation: for soprano and baritone solos, semichorus, double choir and orchestra. N.p.: n.p., 2000.
1 score (123 p.); 42 cm.
English and Latin words; also printed as text with English translation.
Texts by Kathleen Raine, Hildegard of Bingen, Henry Vaughan, Julian of Norwich, from the Book of Baal, and the Taittiriya Brahmana.
Duration: 44:00.
Composed for: soprano, baritone, SATB chorus, 2 flutes (also piccolos), alto flute (also piccolo), 2 oboes, English horn, 2 clarinets (2nd also bass clarinet), bassoon, contrabassoon, 4 horns, 4 trumpets, 2 trombones, bass trombone, tuba, percussion (9 tuned gongs, glockenspiel, large gong, crashed cymbals, medium suspended cymbal, medium triangle, tambourine, 2 temple blocks, 3 woodblocks, maracas, crotales, tam-tam, sleigh bells, sistrum, bass drum, 5 tom-toms, wind chimes, vibraphone, tubular bells, large suspended cymbal, bell tree, small triangle, Chinese drum, whip), harp, violin I, violin II, viola, violoncello, double bass.
Call no.: **2003/019**

375. Bužarovski, Dimitrije, 1952– Radomir's Psalms. Skopje, Macedonia: Dimitrije Buzarovski, 1999.
1 score (196 leaves); 29 x 43 cm.
Macedonian words (romanized); also printed as text (Cyrillic) with English translation.
Oratorio for 2 sopranos, tenor, bass, children's choir, choir, and orchestra.
Composed for: 2 sopranos, tenor, bass, SATB chorus, children's chorus, piccolo, 2 flutes, 2 oboes, English horn, 2 clarinets, bass clarinet, 2 bassoons, contrabassoon, 4 horns, 2 trumpets, 3 trombones, tuba, timpani, percussion, violin I, violin II, viola, violoncello, double bass.
Call no.: **2004/015**

376. Cacioppo, Curt, 1951– A distant voice calling: N'iłch'i dine'é: for string quartet (2001). Score. N.p.: Orenda Press, 2001.
1 score (54 p.); 28 cm.
Composed for: 2 violins, viola, violoncello.
Commissioned by: Arizona Friends of Chamber Music.
Call no.: **2004/016**

377. Cacioppo, Curt, 1951– Nayénĕzgąni: (slayer of monsters), 1995. N.p.: n.p., 1995.
1 score (80 p.); 28 cm.
For string quartet.
"Version 5/18/95"—p. 1.
Notes by the composer follow score.
Composed for: 2 violins, viola, violoncello.
Commissioned by: Philadelphia Chamber Music Society and Pew Charitable Trusts.
Call no.: **1998/027**
Re-entered as: **2000/027**

378. Cacioppo, Curt, 1951– Wolf: for soprano, violoncello, and piano. N.p.: n.p., 1990.
1 score (28 p.); 28 x 43 cm.
Reproduced from holograph.
Words by Peter Blue Cloud; also printed as text.
Composed for: soprano, violoncello, piano.
Commissioned by: Samuel S. Fels Fund.
Call no.: **1992/020**
Re-entered as: **1993/020** and **1996/018**

379. Caggiano, Felice, 1956– Dall' ampia ara dell' alba, 1989. N.p.: n.p., 1989.
1 score (12 leaves); 40 x 51 cm.
Reproduced from manuscript.
Duration: 11:36.
Composed for: flute, oboe, clarinet, bassoon, 2 violins, viola, violoncello.
Call no.: **1990/012**

380. Calabro, Louis, 1926– Double concerto: for viola and cello and orchestra. N.p.: n.p., 1986.
1 score (141 p.); 47 cm.
Reproduced from manuscript.
Composed for: viola, violoncello, piccolo, 2 flutes, 2 oboes, 2 clarinets, 2 bassoons, 4 horns, 3 trumpets, 2 trombones, bass trombone, tuba, timpani, percussion (bass drum, snare drum, crash cymbals, suspended cymbals, 2 tom-toms, gong, guiro, tambourine), violin I, violin II, viola, violoncello, double bass.
Call no.: **1987/012**

381. Callahan, James P., 1942– Tetraptych. N.p.: James P. Callahan, 1985.
1 score (152 p.); 44 cm.
English words.
"A symphony in 4 scenes"—title page verso.

For SATB choir, SSA choir, tenor, bass-baritone, soprano, and orchestra.
Texts from Psalm 24 and 47, John 17, Catherine de Vinck's A Passion Play, and Revelation 5, 11, 15, and 19.
Reproduced from manuscript.
Composed for: soprano, tenor, bass-baritone, SATB chorus, SSA chorus, 2 flutes (1st also piccolo), 2 oboes, 2 clarinets, bass clarinet, 2 bassoons, 4 horns, 6 trumpets, 4 trombones, 2 tubas, percussion (timpani, chimes, anvil, crash cymbals, suspended cymbal, gong, glockenspiel, xylophone, bass drum, side drum, marimba, whip, vibraphone), harp, bells, violin I, violin II, viola, violoncello, double bass.
Commissioned by: College of Saint Thomas.
Call no.: **1987/013**

382. Callaway, Ann, 1949– Concerto for bass clarinet and chamber orchestra, (1985–1987). Study score. N.p.: Laureate Music, 1991.
1 score (78 p.); 36 cm.
Contents: Moonrise soliloquy—Meteor showers—Journey on a summer night.
Composed for: bass clarinet, flute (also piccolo), oboe, 2 clarinets, bassoon, 2 horns, trumpet, trombone, bass trombone, celesta, percussion (triangle, brass wind chimes, 3 suspended cymbals, crash cymbals, gong, tam-tam, glockenspiel, sandpaper blocks, claves, guiro, snare drum, 3 tom-toms, timpani), violin I, violin II, viola, violoncello, double bass.
Call no.: **1991/014**

383. Calo, Paolo Ferdinando. Dance: for flute and piano, op. 13. N.p.: n.p., 198-?.
1 score (5 p.); 33 cm.
Composed for: flute, piano.
Call no.: **1987/014**

384. Caltabiano, Ronald, 1959– Marrying the hangman: chamber opera in one act. Bryn Mawr, PA: Merion Music: Theodore Presser, 1999.
1 score (98 p.); 43 cm.
English words by Margaret Atwood; adapted by Ben Twist and Ronald Caltabiano; also printed as text.
Text based on poem by Margaret Atwood, from Eating fire.
Composed for: 3 mezzo-sopranos, flute (also piccolo and alto flute), clarinet (also clarinet in E♭ and bass clarinet), alto saxophone (also tenor saxophone), percussion, prepared piano, violin, violoncello.
Call no.: **2001/034**

385. Caltabiano, Ronald, 1959– Preludes, fanfares, and toccatas: for orchestra. Bryn Mawr, PA: Merion Music: Theodore Presser, 1995.
1 score (83 p.); 44 cm.
Duration: ca. 17:00.
Composed for: piccolo, 2 flutes, 2 oboes, English horn, clarinet in E♭, clarinet, bass clarinet, 2 bassoons, contrabassoon, 4 horns, 3 trumpets, 2 trombones, bass trombone, tuba, timpani, percussion (bass drum, crotales, flexatone, marimba, suspended cymbals, tam-tam, xylophone, vibraphone, whip), piano, violin I, violin II, viola, violoncello, double bass.
Commissioned by: Dallas Symphony Orchestra.
Call no.: **1996/019**

386. Campana, Jose Luis, 1949– Timing.
Call no.: **1985/028**
No materials available.

387. Campbell, Ramón, 1917– Sinfonia de invierno = (Winter's symphony). Chile: n.p., 1984.
1 miniature score (26 p.); 34 cm.
Reproduced from holograph.
Duration: ca 15:00.
Composed for: piccolo, 2 flutes, 2 oboes, English horn, 2 clarinets, 2 bassoons, contrabassoon, 4 horns, 2 trumpets, 2 trombones, tuba, timpani, percussion (cymbals, triangle, tambourine, bass drum), harp, violin I, violin II, viola, violoncello, double bass.
Call no.: **1985/029**

388. Camps, Pompeyo, 1924– Marathon: metáfora lírica en uno o dos actos y veintidós escenas. Partitura. N.p.: n.p., 1989.
1 miniature score (432 p.); 28 cm.
Spanish words by Ricardo Monti.
"Según propuesta escénica de Jaime Kogan."
Reproduced from manuscript.
Duration: ca. 2:20:00.
Composed for: 3 sopranos, 2 mezzo-sopranos, contralto, 3 tenors, 3 baritones, 2 basses, SATB chorus, jazz band (soprano saxophone, 2 alto saxophones, 3 trumpets, trombone, tuba, banjo, 3 violins, 3 bandoneons, double bass, piano, percussion [cymbals, woodblock, tom-tom, snare drum, bombo]), piccolo, flute, oboe, English horn, clarinet in E♭, clarinet, bass clarinet, bassoon, contrabassoon, 4 horns, 4 trumpets, 3 trombones, tuba, timpani, percussion (suspended cymbal, 2 cymbals, tam-tam, snare drum, military drum, tumbadora, bass drum, woodblock, guiro, glockenspiel, xylophone, vibraphone, matraca, gourd rattle), harp, celesta, violin I, violin II, viola, violoncello, double bass.
Commissioned by: Teatro Colón de Buenos Aires.
Call no.: **1991/015**

389. Canepa, Louise P., 1933– Sicilians of Monterey: opera. N.p.: n.p., 1994.
1 score (2 v.); 28 cm.
English words.
In 2 acts.
Composed for: voices, SATB chorus, piano, violin, viola, violoncello.
Call no.: **1996/020**

390. Cantón, Edgardo, 1934– Música en espera de su imagen. N.p.: n.p., 1994.
1 score (43 leaves); 44 cm.
For orchestra.
Composed for: piccolo, 2 flutes, 2 oboes, English horn, 2 clarinets, bass clarinet, 2 bassoons, contrabassoon, 4 horns, 3 trumpets, 3 trombones, bass trombone, tuba, percussion (3 timbales, tam-tam, bass drum, timpani, tom-toms, temple blocks, cymbals, tambourine, maraca, triangle, chimes, bells, xylophone, vibraphone, glockenspiel), piano, celesta, violin I, violin II, viola, violoncello, double bass.
Call no.: **1996/021**

391. Capanna, Robert, 1952– Day: a secular cantata for chorus and chamber orchestra on an original text, 1998. N.p.: Robert Capanna, 1998.
1 score (183 p.); 36 cm.
English words by the composer; also printed as text.
Composed for: SATB chorus, flute (also piccolo and alto flute), oboe (also English horn), clarinet (also bass clarinet), bassoon, horn, harp, percussion (vibraphone, marimba, glockenspiel, tambourine, tubular bells, suspended cymbals, woodblock, bongos, timbales, tom-toms), violin I, violin II, violin III, viola, violoncello, double bass.
Commissioned by: Philadelphia Singers.
Call no.: **2001/035**

392. Capister, Loris, 1966– Elegia per un angelo: per coro e orchestra, liberamente tratto de un testo di O.V. de Milosz. N.p.: n.p., 1999.
1 score (30 p.); 30 cm.
Italian words; also printed as text.
Duration: ca. 8:30.
Reproduced from holograph.
Composed for: SATB chorus, 2 flutes (2nd piccolo), 2 oboes (2nd also English horn), 2 clarinets (2nd also bass clarinet), 2 bassoons (2nd also contrabassoon), 2 horns, 2 trumpets, timpani, percussion (bass drum, tam-tam, snare drum, suspended cymbal, triangle, claves, tubular bells), violin I, violin II, viola, violoncello, double bass.
Call no.: **2002/025**

393. Carlson, David, 1952– Dreamkeepers: opera in two acts. Orchestra score. N.p.: Theodore Presser Co., 1996.
1 score (352 p.); 28 cm.
English words by Aden Ross.
Composed for: soprano, contralto, tenor, baritone, SATB chorus, piccolo, 2 flutes, oboe, English horn, 2 clarinets in A, bassoon, contrabassoon, 4 horns, trumpet in D, 2 trumpets, 2 trombones, bass trombone, tuba, timpani (also roto-toms), percussion (xylophone, vibraphone, marimba, 3 tam-tams, pedal bass drum, basler drum, snare drum, triangle, glockenspiel, thundersheet, 2 brake drums, ratchet, crash cymbal, suspended cymbal, tambourine, whip, crash box, lion's roar, crotales, tubular bells, bell plate, tuned gongs, 4 amplified ute drums, ute rasp), 2 harps, celesta, tape, offstage instruments (ute drum, harp, celesta, glockenspiel), violin I, violin II, viola, violoncello, double bass.
Commissioned by: Utah Opera Company.
Call no.: **1997/020**

394. Carnota, Raul, 1947– La Salamanca. N.p.: n.p., 1991.
1 score (v, 61 leaves); 36 cm.
Spanish words.
For soloists, chorus, and orchestra.
Composer's note in Spanish on cover.
Composed for: voices, SATBarB chorus, oboe, clarinet, percussion (3 congas, bongo, claves, cabasa, bass drum, timbales, bells, cowbell, cuíca, slapstick, marimba), piano, synthesizer, guitar, electric guitar, violin I, violin II, viola, violoncello, double bass.
Call no.: **1994/020**

395. Carpenter, Gary, 1951– Satie: variations for orchestra. London: Camden Music, 1997.
1 score (85 p.); 30 cm.
Duration: 20:00.
Includes program note in English by the composer.
Composed for: 3 flutes (also piccolo), 3 oboes (also English horn), 3 clarinets (also clarinet in E♭ and bass clarinet with C extension), 3 bassoons (also contrabassoon), 4 horns, 3 trumpets, 3 trombones, tuba, celesta, harp, offstage piano (out-of-tune and in state of disrepair), percussion (snare drum, tenor drum, 3 suspended cymbals, sizzle cymbal, crash cymbals, hi-hat cymbal, vibraphone, tam-tam, 2 cowbells, guiro, cabasa, triangle, woodblock, old-fashioned typewriter, shortwave radio, bass drum, medium gong, crotales, 5 temple blocks, glockenspiel, tubular bells, tambourine, 3 tom-toms, xylophone, maraca, medium gong, low gong, 2 anvils), timpani (also whip), violin I, violin II, viola, violoncello, double bass.
Call no.: **2005/021**

396. Carr, Edwin, 1926– Symphony no. 2. N.p.: n.p., 1984.
1 score (2 v.); 37 cm.
Reproduced from holograph.
At end of score: "E.J.N.C. 10.8.84; Sydney, Auckland, Taupo."
Composed for: 3 flutes (3rd also piccolo), 3 oboes (3rd also English horn), 3 clarinets, bass clarinet, 3 bassoons, contrabassoon, 4 horns, 3 trumpets, 3 trombones, tuba, timpani, percussion (bass drum, military drum, tambourine, triangle, suspended cymbal, chimes, glockenspiel, tam-tam), harp, piano, violin I, violin II, viola, violoncello, double bass.
Call no.: **1985/030**

397. Carrabré, Thomas Patrick, 1958– Inuit games: for Katajak singers and orchestra. N.p.: T. Patrick Carrabré, 2002.
1 score (31 p.); 36 cm.
Composed for: katajak singers, 2 flutes (also piccolo), 2 oboes, 2 clarinets in A, 2 bassoons, 4 horns, 3 trumpets, 2 trombones, bass trombone, tuba, timpani, percussion, violin I, violin II, viola violoncello, double bass.
Commissioned by: CBC and Winnipeg Symphony Orchestra.
Call no.: **2005/022**

398. Carter, Elliott, 1908– Adagio tenebroso: for orchestra (1994). New York, NY: Hendon Music, 1995.
1 score (61 p.); 34 cm.
Duration: ca. 20:00.
Composed for: 3 flutes (2nd–3rd also piccolo), 2 oboes, English horn, 2 clarinets (2nd also clarinet in E♭), bass clarinet, 2 bassoons, contrabassoon, 4 horns, 3 trumpets, 2 trombones, bass trombone, tuba, timpani, percussion (xylophone, glockenspiel, snare drum, 2 metal blocks, 2 cowbells, 2 suspended cymbals, 2 woodblocks, temple blocks, wood drum, vibraphone, 4 bongos, 2 tom-toms, bass drum, marimba, tam-tam), piano, violin I, violin II, viola, violoncello, double bass.
Commissioned by: BBC.
Call no.: **1996/022**

399. Carter, Elliott, 1908– Boston concerto. 2nd ed. 4/2003. N.p.: Hendon Music: Boosey & Hawkes, 2003.
1 score (67 p.); 36 cm.
For orchestra.
Duration: ca. 15:00.
Composed for: piccolo, 3 flutes (also piccolo), 2 oboes, English horn, 3 clarinets (also bass clarinet), 3 bassoons (also contrabassoon), 4 horns, 3 trumpets, 3 trombones, tuba, harp, piano, percussion (xylophone, vibraphone, log drum, 4 bongos, high snare drum, suspended cymbal, wood chime, marimba, low snare drum, 4 temple blocks, 2 cowbells, bass drum, tom-tom, 4 woodblocks, guiro, maracas, medium snare drum), violin I, violin II, viola, violoncello, double bass.
Commissioned by: Boston Symphony Orchestra.
Call no.: **2005/023**

400. Carter, Elliott, 1908– Cello concerto (2001). New York, NY: Hendon Music, 2001.
1 score (101 p.); 36 cm.
Duration: ca. 20:00.
Composed for: violoncello, 3 flutes (3rd also piccolo), 2 oboes, English horn, 2 clarinets (2nd also bass clarinet), bass clarinet (also contrabass clarinet), 2 bassoons, contrabassoon, 4 horns, 3 trumpets, 3 trombones, tuba, percussion (glockenspiel, xylophone, marimba, temple blocks, log drums, woodblocks, cowbells, vibraphone, snare drums, tom-toms, bongos, bass drum, guiro, cymbals), timpani, harp, violin I, violin II, viola, violoncello, double bass.
Commissioned by: Chicago Symphony Orchestra.
Call no.: **2003/020**

401. Carter, Elliott, 1908– Clarinet concerto (1996). 3rd ed. Nov. 1997. Full score. New York, NY: Hendon Music, 1997.
1 score (124 p.); 28 cm.
Duration: ca. 18:00.
Composed for: clarinet, flute, 2 oboes (2nd also English horn), bassoon, horn, trumpet, trombone, tuba, percussion (glockenspiel, 2 gavels, bongos, 2 tom-toms, medium suspended cymbal, large wood drum, tam-tam, medium snare drum, metal blocks, temple blocks, large woodblock, large snare drum, large suspended cymbal, small woodblock, cencerros, small suspended cymbal, small snare drum, bass drum, whip), harp, piano, violin I, violin II, viola, violoncello, double bass.
Commissioned by: Ensemble Intercontemporain.
Call no.: **1998/028**

402. Carter, Elliott, 1908– Oboe concerto.
Call no.: **1989/015**
No materials available.

403. Carter, Elliott, 1908– Partita. N.p.: Hendon Music, 1994.
1 score (105 p.); 33 cm.
For orchestra.
Duration: ca. 18:00.
Composed for: piccolo, 2 flutes (2nd also piccolo), 2 oboes, English horn, 2 clarinets (2nd also clarinet in E♭), bass clarinet, 2 bassoons, contrabassoon, 4 horns, 3 trumpets, 3 trombones, tuba, timpani, percussion

(snare drum, tom-tom, guiro, 2 metal blocks, 2 cowbells, 2 suspended cymbals, 2 woodblocks, 4 temple blocks, wood drum, 4 bongos, 2 tom-toms, bass drum, marimba, vibraphone, glockenspiel, gavel), harp, piano, violin I, violin II, viola, violoncello, double bass.
Commissioned by: Chicago Symphony Orchestra.
Call no.: **1995/011**

404. Carter, Elliott, 1908– Penthode.
Call no.: **1986/021**
No materials available.

405. Carter, Elliott, 1908– Quintet for piano and winds, 1991. N.p.: Hendon Music, 1992.
1 score (84 p.); 28 cm.
"2nd draft Jan. 31, 1992."
Reproduced from holograph.
Composed for: oboe, clarinet, bassoon, horn, piano.
Call no.: **1993/021**

406. Carter, Elliott, 1908– String quartet no. 4 (1986). New York, NY: Hendon Music; Boosey & Hawkes, 1986.
1 score (60 p.); 29 cm.
Reproduced from manuscript.
Composed for: 2 violins, viola, violoncello.
Commissioned by: Composers String Quartet, Sequoia Quartet, and Thouvenel Quartet.
Call no.: **1987/015**

407. Carter, Elliott, 1908– String quartet no. 5. Full score. New York, NY: Hendon Music: Boosey & Hawkes, 1995.
1 score (42 p.); 28 cm.
Duration: 20:00.
Composed for: 2 violins, viola, violoncello.
Commissioned by: Antwerp, City of Culture, 1993.
Call no.: **1997/021**

408. Carter, Elliott, 1908– Symphonia: sum fluxae pretium spei: for orchestra. N.p.: Hendon Music: Boosey & Hawkes, 1997.
1 score (various pagings); 36 cm.
Contents: Partita—Adagio tenebroso—Allegro scorrevole.
Composed for: piccolo, 2 flutes (2nd also piccolo), 2 oboes, English horn, 2 clarinets (2nd also clarinet in E♭), bass clarinet, 2 bassoons, contrabassoon, 4 horns, 3 trumpets, 2 trombones, bass trombone, tuba, timpani, percussion (xylophone, glockenspiel, snare drum, tom-toms, woodblocks, guiro, metal blocks, cowbells, marimba, tam-tam, suspended cymbals, temple blocks, log drum, vibraphone, bongos, gavel, bass drum), harp, piano, violin I, violin II, viola, violoncello, double bass.
Commissioned by: Daniel Barenboim and Chicago Symphony, BBC, and Cleveland Orchestra.
Call no.: **2000/028**

409. Carter, Elliott, 1908– Triple duo.
Call no.: **1985/031**
No materials available.

410. Carter, Elliott, 1908– Violin concerto (1990). N.p.: Hendon Music: Boosey & Hawkes, 1990.
1 miniature score (75 p.); 36 cm.
Reproduced from holograph.
"4th draft, May 7, 1990."
Composed for: violin, piccolo, 2 flutes (2nd also piccolo), 2 oboes, English horn, 2 clarinets (2nd also clarinet in E♭ and bass clarinet), bass clarinet, 2 bassoons, contrabassoon, 4 horns, 3 trumpets, 2 trombones, bass trombone, tuba, timpani, percussion (glockenspiel, crotales, vibraphone, timpani, 2 suspended cymbals, 2 snare drums, tam-tam, bass drum), harp, piano, celesta, violin I, violin II, viola, violoncello, double bass.
Commissioned by: San Francisco Symphony and Ole Böhn.
Call no.: **1991/016**

411. Carter, Elliott, 1908– What next? an opera in one act. N.p.: Hendon Music; Boosey & Hawkes, 1999.
1 score (281 p.); 36 cm.
English words by Paul Griffiths.
"5/99"—Cover.
Composed for: 2 sopranos, boy alto, contralto, tenor, baritone, 2 flutes (piccolo), 2 oboes (English horn), 2 clarinets (bass clarinet), 2 bassoons (contrabassoon), 2 horns, trumpet, trombone, tuba, percussion (snare drums, 6 brake drums, cowbell, marimba, xylophone, slapstick, mounted tambourine, 5 cowbells, 3 metal pipes, large washboard, vibraphone, wood chimes, medium nipple gong, tam-tam, hammer, lion's roar, gong, small and large suspended trash cans, guiro, temple blocks, glockenspiel, log drum, bass drum, 2 tom-toms, cymbals, sizzle cymbal, 4 woodblocks, thundersheet, 2 bongos), onstage percussion (cymbals, 2 snare drums, 4 temple blocks, 2 cowbells, 2 brake drums, 3 metal pipes, flexatone, bongo, guiro, gong, 4 woodblocks, 2 suspended cymbals, slapstick, flexatone), piano, harp, violin I, violin II, viola, violoncello, double bass.
Call no.: **2001/036**
Also available:
Call no.: **2001/036 vocal score**

412. Carter, Elliott, 1908– What next? an opera in one act. 3rd ed. N.p.: Hendon Music; Boosey & Hawkes, 1999.
1 score (281 p.); 36 cm.
English words by Paul Griffiths.
"3rd ed. 9/99"—p. 1.
Composed for: 2 sopranos, boy alto, contralto, tenor, baritone, 2 flutes (piccolo), 2 oboes (English horn), 2 clarinets (bass clarinet), 2 bassoons (contrabassoon), 2 horns, trumpet, trombone, tuba, percussion (snare drums, 6 brake drums, marimba, xylophone, slapstick, mounted tambourine, 6 cowbells, 3 metal pipes, large washboard, vibraphone, wood chimes, medium nipple gong, tam-tam, hammer, lion's roar, gong, small and large suspended trash cans, guiro, temple blocks, glockenspiel, log drum, bass drum, 2 tom-toms, cymbals, sizzle cymbal, 4 woodblocks, thundersheet, 2 bongos), onstage percussion (cymbals, 2 snare drums, 4 temple blocks, 2 cowbells, 2 brake drums, 3 metal pipes, flexatone, bongo, guiro, gong, 4 woodblocks, 2 suspended cymbals, slapstick, flexatone), piano, harp, violin I, violin II, viola, violoncello, double bass.
Call no.: **2002/026**
Also available:
Call no.: **2002/026 vocal score**

413. Cassils, Craig, 1950– Clowns. N.p.: n.p., 1986.
1 score (1 v.) ports.; 29 cm.
English words.
Musical for young voices.
Includes libretto (15 leaves) and performance instructions.
Composed for: voices, SATB chorus, piano.
Call no.: **1988/015**

414. Cassils, Craig, 1950– Clowns: a musical for young voices. Carol Stream, IL: Somerset Press, 1988.
1 score (56 p.); 31 cm.
English words.
Includes performance instructions.
Composed for: voices, SATB chorus, piano.
Call no.: **1989/016**

415. Castiglioni, Niccolo, 1932–1996. Mottetto.
Call no.: **1989/017**
No materials available.

416. Catán, Daniel, 1949– Florencia en el Amazonas: opera en dos actos. New York, NY: Boosey & Hawkes, 1996.
1 score (3 v. [630 p.]); 36 cm.
Spanish words by Marcela Fuentes-Berain.
Composed for: 2 sopranos, mezzo-sopranos, tenor, 2 baritones, bass, SATB chorus, piccolo, flute, 2 oboes, 2 clarinets, bass clarinet, bassoon, contrabassoon, 3 horns, 2 trumpets, 2 trombones, tuba, marimba, piano, harp, timpani, percussion (steel pan, djembe, tambourine, bass drum, side drum, suspended cymbal, cymbals, gong, tubular bells, wind machine), violin I, violin II, viola, violoncello, double bass.
Commissioned by: Houston Grand Opera.
Call no.: **2002/027**

417. Causton, Richard, 1971– Millennium scenes: music for large orchestra in two parts. Oxford: Oxford University Press, 2001.
1 score (77 p.); 37 cm.
Reproduced from holograph.
Duration: ca. 15:00.
At end of score: London 19-2-99; revised Bologna, 7-8-01.
Composed for: 3 flutes (all also piccolo), 3 oboes (2nd–3rd also English horn), 3 clarinets (3rd also clarinet in E♭), 3 bassoons (3rd also contrabassoon), 4 horns, 4 trumpets, 2 trombones, bass trombone, tuba, timpani, percussion (apito, tam-tam, glockenspiel, log drum, gong, Japanese woodblock, pedal bass drum, tenor drum, car horn, suspended cymbal, cowbells, thundersheet, bongos, vibraphone, tom-toms, 2 bass drums, roto-toms, sandpaper blocks), piano, violin I, violin II, viola, violoncello, double bass.
Commissioned by: BBC.
Call no.: **2004/017**

418. Cavanna, Bernard, 1951– Concerto pour violon et orchestre. Paris: Editions Musicales Européennes, 1988.
1 score (98 p.); 32 cm.
Duration: 22:00.
Composed for: violin, 2 flutes (2nd also piccolo), 2 oboes (2nd also English horn), clarinet in E♭, clarinet, bass clarinet, soprano saxophone, 2 bassoons, 4 horns, 2 trumpets, trombone, bass trombone, percussion (xylophone, vibraphone, chimes, bass drum, snare drum, small tom-tom, crash cymbals, tam-tam, marimba, xylorimba, glockenspiel, bass drum with cymbals, 2 suspended cymbals), timpani, harp, accordion, violin I, violin II, viola, violoncello, double bass.
Commissioned by: Radio France.
Call no.: **2004/018**

419. Cecconi, Monic, 1936– Il signait . . . Vincent. N.p.: n.p., 199-?.
1 score (3 v.); 38 cm.
French words by Jacques Unal.
Opera-passion.

Reproduced from manuscript.
Composed for: 2 sopranos, mezzo-soprano, 2 tenors, 2 baritones, bass, SATB chorus, 2 flutes (1st also alto flute), 2 oboes (2nd also English horn), 2 clarinets, 2 bassoons, 2 horns, 2 trumpets, 2 trombones, tuba, percussion (tubular bells, marimba, 2 snare drums, 4 tom-toms, tambourine, whip, guiro, 3 cymbals, crash cymbals, 3 tam-tams, vibraphone, timbales, ratchet, glass chimes, xylophone, bass drum, 4 bongos, 4 temple blocks, Chinese cymbal, castanets, sleigh bells), tape, violin I, violin II, viola, violoncello, double bass.
Call no.: **1992/021**
Also available:
Call no.: **1992/021 libretto**

420. Cerha, Friedrich, 1926– Acht Sätze nach Hölderlin-Fragmenten: für Streichsextett (1995). Partitur. Wien: Universal Edition, 1998.
1 score (55 p.); 30 cm.
Contents: Schönes Leben!—Doch ist uns gegeben—Es kommen Stunden—Wie wenn die alten Wasser in andrem Zorn—Die Linien des Lebens sind verschieden—Und unstet wehn und irren—Weh mir—Das Herz ist wieder wach.
Composed for: 2 violins, 2 violas, 2 violoncellos.
Commissioned by: Kölner Philharmonie.
Call no.: **2000/029**

421. Cerha, Friedrich, 1926– Hymnus: für Orchester (2000). Studienpartitur. Wien: Universal Edition, 2001.
1 miniature score (54 p.); 42 cm.
"Provisorische Ausgabe (UA); 26.11.2001."
Reproduced from holograph.
Duration: ca. 24:00.
Composed for: 4 flutes (also piccolo), 4 oboes, 5 clarinets in A (also bass clarinet), 4 bassoons, 6 horns, 4 trumpets, 4 trombones, tuba, timpani, percussion (tubular bells, thick suspended cymbals, bass drum, very large bass drum, very large tam-tam), 15 violins, 6 violas, 5 violoncellos, 4 double basses.
Commissioned by: Konzerthaus Berlin.
Call no.: **2005/024**

422. Cerha, Friedrich, 1926– "Im Namen der Liebe": für Bariton und Orchester (1999). Wien: Universal Edition, 2000.
1 vocal score (48 p.); 30 cm.
German words by Peter Turrini; also printed as text.
Keyboard reduction by Helmut Schmidinger.
"Provisorische Ausgabe (UA) 30.10.2000."
Duration: ca. 26:00.
Composed for: baritone, piano (orchestral reduction).
Commissioned by: Festivals de Música de Canarias.
Call no.: **2003/021**

423. Cerha, Friedrich, 1926– Impulse: für grosses Orchester (1992–1993). Studienpartitur. Wien: Universal Edition, 1996.
1 miniature score (86 p.); 30 cm.
"Korrigierte Ausgabe 26.2.1996."
Reproduced from holograph.
Duration: ca. 23:00.
Composed for: 3 flutes (2nd–3rd also piccolo, 3rd also alto flute), 3 oboes (3rd also English horn), 3 clarinets in A (3rd also bass clarinet), 2 bassoons, contrabassoon, 5 horns, 3 trumpets, 4 trombones, contrabass tuba, percussion (crotales, claves, whip, 4 bongos, glockenspiel, timpani, 3 temple blocks, 5 tom-toms, vibraphone, 3 woodblocks, 3 timbales, marimba, tamtam, xylorimba, tubular bells, 3 suspended cymbals, bass drum), harp, violin I, violin II, viola, violoncello, double bass.
Commissioned by: Wiener Philharmoniker.
Call no.: **1997/022**

424. Cerha, Friedrich, 1926– Jahrlang ins Ungewisse hinab: für Kammerorchester (1995–1996). Studienpartitur. Wien: Universal Edition, 1997.
1 score (97 p.); 30 cm.
"Provisorische Ausgabe (ua) 21.1.1997."
Reproduced from manuscript.
Duration: ca. 27:00.
Composed for: soprano, flute, clarinet in A, bass clarinet, bassoon (also contrabassoon), 2 horns, 2 trumpets, 2 trombones, percussion (xylorimba, vibraphone, 5 timpani, tenor drum, 3 gongs, lion's roar, 5 tom-toms, crotales, tubular bells, maracas, claves, 5 temple blocks, 3 suspended cymbals, thundersheet, large tamtam, glockenspiel, 4 woodblocks, 4 bongos, large bass drum), harp, piano, accordion, organ, violin I, violin II, viola, violoncello, double bass.
Call no.: **1998/029**

425. Cerha, Friedrich, 1926– Langegger Nachtmusik Nr. 3: für Orchester (1991). Partitur. Wien: Universal Edition, 1991.
1 score (92 p.); 30 cm.
Reproduced from manuscript.
Duration: ca. 23:00.
Composed for: 2 flutes (2nd also piccolo and alto flute), 2 oboes (2nd also English horn), 2 clarinets in A (2nd also clarinet in E♭), bass clarinet, 2 bassoons, contrabassoon, 3 horns, 3 trumpets, 3 trombones, timpani, percussion (tam-tam, 2 hanging cymbals, 3 flat Chinese

gongs, tubular bells, marimba, xylorimba, bass drum, 4 roto-toms, 4 tom-toms, 2 bongos, tambourine, small temple block, woodblock, high claves), harp, violin I, violin II, viola, violoncello, double bass, concertino (accordion, organ, soprano saxophone [also alto saxophone], vibraphone, guitar), offstage ensemble (trumpet, 2 horns, tuba, percussion (xylorimba, bass drum, 2 congas, crotales, glockenspiel, woodblock, claves), regal, celesta, 2 violins, viola, violoncello, double bass).
Commissioned by: Rundfunk-Sinfonieorchester Berlin.
Call no.: **1994/021**
Re-entered as: **1995/012**

426. Cerha, Friedrich, 1926– Der Rattenfänger. Partitur. Wien: Universal Edition, 1987.
1 score (2 v.); 49 cm.
German words.
Opera.
Reproduced from manuscript.
Composed for: 2 sopranos, mezzo-soprano, alto, 6 tenors, 4 baritones, 3 basses, 2 flutes (2nd also piccolo and alto flute), 2 oboes, English horn, 3 clarinets in A (2nd also clarinet in E♭, 3rd also bass clarinet), soprano saxophone (also alto saxophone), 2 bassoons, contrabassoon, 4 horns, 3 trumpets, 3 trombones, baritone, percussion (vibraphone, snare drum, tambourine, field drum, maracas, guiro, 3 temple blocks, tissue paper, xylorimba, chimes, cabasa, sizzle cymbals, tam-tam, cardboard, wrapping paper, 2 bongos, 2 tom-toms, bass drum, 2 cymbals, aluminum foil, glass paper, newspaper, 2 congas, slapstick, suspended cymbals, crash cymbals, timpani, crotales, 2 woodblocks, Chinese gong), harp, organ, guitar (also bass guitar), violin I, violin II, viola, violoncello, double bass.
Commissioned by: Steirischer Herbst.
Call no.: **1992/022**

427. Chaĭkovskiĭ, Aleksandr, 1946– Kontsert no 2: dlia fortepiano s orkestrom. Partitura. N.p.: n.p., 1989.
1 score (88 p.); 39 cm.
Reproduced from holograph.
Composed for: piano, triangle, violin I, violin II, viola, violoncello, double bass.
Call no.: **1994/146**

428. Chalaev, Shirvani, 1936– Quater-poems: for baritone end [sic] orcherstra [sic]. Dagestan: n.p., 1996.
1 score (19 p.); 41 cm.
Lak words.
Reproduced from holograph.
Composed for: baritone, 2 flutes, 2 oboes, 2 clarinets, 2 bassoons (2nd also contrabassoon), 4 horns, 3 trumpets, 3 trombones, tuba, timpani, percussion (cymbals, snare drum, tam-tam, suspended cymbals, triangle, timpani, xylophone, celesta), harp, violin I, violin II, viola, violoncello, double bass.
Call no.: **1998/160**

429. Challulau, Tristan Patrice, 1959– Et le vent . . . : concerto pour orchestra op 61 (avec récitant). Aix-en-Provence: L'Ecrit, 199-?.
1 score (iii, 62 p.); 30 cm.
French words by Alfred Sapin; also printed as text.
"Ces poèmes pourront être lus par un récitant ou simplement être insérés dans le programme"—p. iii.
Duration: 19:00.
Composed for: optional narrator, 2 flutes (1st also piccolo), 2 oboes, 2 clarinets (2nd also bass clarinet), 2 bassoons, 2 horns, 2 trumpets, percussion (tubular bells, large triangle, large tam-tam, timbales, Tibetan bell), violin I, violin II, viola, violoncello, double bass.
Call no.: **1997/023**

430. Challulau, Tristan Patrice, 1959– La hermosa alejandra: 6° concerto: 1° concerto pour guitare et orchestre, 1992. Aix-en-Pce., France: Ecrit, 1992.
1 score (52 p.); 30 cm.
Reproduced from manuscript.
Duration: ca. 15:00.
Composed for: guitar, flute, oboe, clarinet, bassoon, horn, trumpet, trombone, tuba, harp, percussion (2 timbales, bongo, chimes, tam-tam, triangle, maracas, guiro, rideau de verre), violin I, violin II, viola, violoncello, double bass.
Call no.: **1994/022**

431. Challulau, Tristan Patrice, 1959– Ne la citta dolente, . . . Marina: 9 images d'après l'enfer de dante: quatrième concerto pour piano et orchestre. N.p.: n.p., 1991.
1 score (70 p.); 30 cm.
Reproduced from manuscript.
Duration: ca. 15:00.
Composed for: piano, 2 flutes (2nd also piccolo), 2 oboes, English horn, 2 clarinets, 2 bassoons (2nd also contrabassoon), 2 horns, 2 trumpets, 2 trombones, percussion (timpani, tam-tam, vibraphone, bells, 3 tom-toms), violin I, violin II, viola, violoncello, double bass.
Call no.: **1992/023**

432. Challulau, Tristan Patrice, 1959– Requiem: op. 55, 1993/1998. Aix-en-Pce., France: l'Écrit, 1998.
1 score (120 p.); 30 cm.
Latin words; also printed as text following score.
For soloists, choir, and orchestra.
Composed for: soprano, baritone, SATB chorus, trombone, percussion (timbales, bongos, 2 galets, tubular

bells), organ, violin I, violin II, viola, violoncello, double bass.
Commissioned by: État français.
Call no.: **2000/030**

433. Challulau, Tristan Patrice, 1959– Requiem; [Requiem pour une mère]. Aix-en-Pce., France: l'Écrit, 1995.
1 score (131 p.); 30 cm.
First work: Latin words; also printed as text. Second work: French words; also printed as text following score.
First work for soloists, choir, and orchestra; 2nd work for female voices.
Text of 2nd work from poems by Albertine Benedetto.
Composed for: soprano, baritone, SATB chorus, trombone, percussion (timbales, bongos, 2 galets, tubular bells), organ, violin I, violin II, viola, violoncello, double bass.
Commissioned by: État français.
Call no.: **1996/023**

434. Chambers, Wendy Mae, 1953– A mass for mass trombones. N.p.: n.p., 1993.
1 score (various leavings); 44 cm.
For solo trombone and 76 trombones.
Reproduced from manuscript.
Composed for: trombone, 58 trombones, 18 bass trombones.
Call no.: **1994/023**
Re-entered as: **1997/024**

435. Chambers, Wendy Mae, 1953– Twelve squared: a voodoo tone poem: for percussion ensemble. N.p.: Whole Sum Productions, 1994.
1 score (ca. 102 p.); 22 x 36 cm.
Contents: Snake dancer—Dance (mental minuet)—Snake of deep waters—Hoodoo root doctor—Wild ride—The barons—Shangó (master of magick)—Manman Brigitte—The sun—A priest—Fire-breathing serpent.
Composed for: 9 tom-toms, sleigh bells, 2 pairs of cricket callers, 3 bass drums, 2 tambourines, 6 maracas, vibraslap, 6-toned marimbula, 6 pairs of claves, 2-toned log drums, 5 pentatonic temple blocks, 3 glockenspiels, 5 pitched gongs, 4 suspended cymbals, 3 triangles, 3 Chinese gongs, 3 tam-tams, 3 lion's roars, 3 thundersheets, 4 double bass bows, water gong, 2 sets of bongos, theremin, 2 congas, 3 rain sticks, bamboo wind chimes, clapstick rattle, ratchet, 6 tin cans, jumbo tambourine, wind tube, pipe length, 3 sets of crotales, marine bell, tubular chimes, 2 anvils, 4 brake drums, crank siren, buzzer, 3 mark trees, 6 cowbells.
Call no.: **2000/031**

436. Chan, Ka Nin, 1949– Revelation.
Call no.: **1985/032**
No materials available.

437. Chance, Nancy Laird, 1931– Odysseus: a song cycle for solo voice, percussion, and orchestra. Bryn Mawr, PA: Theodore Presser, 1981.
1 score (115 p.); 38 cm.
Greek words from Homer's Odyssey, transliterated into the international phonetic alphabet; Greek text with English translation printed as text.
Composed for: baritone, 3 flutes (3rd also piccolo), 2 oboes, English horn, 2 clarinets, bass clarinet, 2 bassoons, contrabassoon, 4 horns, 3 trumpets, 2 trombones, bass trombone, tuba, percussion (timpani, tenor drum, bass drum, 2 flexatones, 2 sets of glass wind chimes, claves, vibraphone, xylophone, gong, tubular bells, woodblocks, tambourine, mounted sleigh bells, snare drum, sizzle cymbal, triangle, cabasa, tam-tam, guiro, bongos, brass wind chimes, castanets, ratchet, suspended cymbal, glockenspiel), harp, violin I, violin II, viola, violoncello, double bass.
Call no.: **1988/016**
Re-entered as: **1989/018**

438. Chandler, Stephan, 1947– Symphony II: at Badwater. N.p.: Stephan Chandler, 1992.
1 score (77 p.); 36 cm.
Contents: Golden Canyon sunup—Noon on the salt flats—Skidoo, October 1912.
Composed for: 2 flutes (1st also piccolo), 2 oboes, 2 clarinets (1st also clarinet in E♭), 2 bassoons, 4 horns, 2 trumpets, trombone, bass trombone, timpani, percussion (snare drum, field drum, bass drum, crash cymbals, suspended cymbal, triangle, woodblock, whip, ratchet, bells, piano), violin I, violin II, viola, violoncello, double bass.
Call no.: **1994/024**

439. Charloff, Aaron, 1941– A child's world: suite for orchestra (1986). Tel Aviv: Israel Music Institute, 1989.
1 score (47 p.); 36 cm.
Duration: 13:10.
Contents: Little march—The hurdy gurdy—A bad dream—Naughty boy—The see saw—Lullaby.
Composed for: 2 flutes (2nd also piccolo), 2 oboes, 2 clarinets, 2 bassoons, 2 horns, 2 trumpets, timpani, percussion (triangle, suspended cymbal, woodblocks, snare drum, bass drum), harp, celesta, violin I, violin II, viola, violoncello, double bass.
Call no.: **1991/050**

440. Charloff, Aaron, 1941– Concerto: for clarinet and symphony orchestra (1996). Tel Aviv: Israel Music Institute, 1997.
1 score (118 p.); 42 cm.
Duration: ca. 18:00.
Composed for: clarinet, 2 flutes (2nd also piccolo), 2 oboes (2nd also English horn), clarinet (also bass clarinet), 2 bassoons, 2 horns, 2 trumpets, timpani, percussion (glockenspiel, xylophone, triangle, suspended cymbals, crash cymbals, tam-tam, woodblocks, temple blocks, snare drum, bass drum, tambourine, castanets, maracas, xylophone, timbales), piano (also celesta), violin I, violin II, viola, violoncello, double bass.
Call no.: **2001/068**

441. Charloff, Aaron, 1941– The divine image: for soprano, mezzo-soprano, baritone, mixed choir and symphony orchestra (1999). Score. Tel Aviv: Israel Music Institute, 1999.
1 score (84 p.); 42 cm.
English words; also printed as text.
Texts by William Blake, from Isaiah 35:5–10, and Psalms 100 and 148.
Duration: ca. 20:00.
Contents: Song of experience—Song of innocence.
Composed for: soprano, mezzo-soprano, baritone, SATB chorus, piccolo, 2 flutes, 2 oboes, English horn, 2 clarinets, bass clarinet, 2 bassoons, contrabassoon, 4 horns, 3 trumpets, 2 trombones, bass trombone, tuba, timpani, percussion (glockenspiel, xylophone, maracas, triangle, suspended cymbal, crash cymbals, anvil, tambourine, timbales, side drums, bass drum, tam-tam), celesta, harp, piano (also organ), violin I, violin II, viola, violoncello, double bass.
Call no.: **2004/051**
Also available:
Call no.: **2004/051 vocal score**

442. Charloff, Aaron, 1941– L'oiseau de la guerre = The bird of war: symphony no. 2 (1992). Tel Aviv: Israel Music Institute, 1992.
1 score (157 p.); 37 cm.
Hebrew words (with romanization); also printed as text with English translation.
For orchestra and soprano (4th mvt.).
Text in 4th mvt. from Genesis and Isaiah.
Reproduced from manuscript.
Composed for: soprano, 2 flutes (2nd also piccolo), 2 oboes (2nd also English horn), 2 clarinets (2nd also bass clarinet), 2 bassoons, 4 horns, 2 trumpets, 3 trombones, tuba, timpani, percussion (glockenspiel, xylophone, bells, triangle, 3 woodblocks, maracas, castanets, crash cymbals, suspended cymbal, 3 bongos, tambourine, snare drum, bass drum, tam-tam), harp, piano, violin I, violin II, viola, violoncello, double bass.
Call no.: **1995/041**
Also available:
Call no.: **1995/041 mvt. 4 vocal score**

443. Charloff, Aaron, 1941– L'oiseau de la guerre = The bird of war: symphony no. 2 (1992). Tel Aviv: Israel Music Institute, 1992.
1 score (157 p.); 42 cm.
Hebrew words (with romanization); also printed as text with English translation.
For orchestra and soprano (4th mvt.).
Text in 4th mvt. from Genesis and Isaiah.
Reproduced from manuscript.
Composed for: soprano, 2 flutes (2nd also piccolo), 2 oboes (2nd also English horn), 2 clarinets (2nd also bass clarinet), 2 bassoons, 4 horns, 2 trumpets, 3 trombones, tuba, timpani, percussion (glockenspiel, xylophone, bells, triangle, 3 woodblocks, maracas, castanets, crash cymbals, suspended cymbal, 3 bongos, tambourine, snare drum, bass drum, tam-tam), harp, piano, violin I, violin II, viola, violoncello, double bass.
Call no.: **1998/064**

444. Charloff, Aaron, 1941– Symphonic dances: for symphony orchestra (1989). Tel Aviv: Israel Music Institute, 1989.
1 score (77 p.); 36 cm.
Duration: 8:45.
Composed for: piccolo, 2 flutes, 2 oboes, English horn, 3 clarinets, bass clarinet, 2 bassoons, contrabassoon, 4 horns, 3 trumpets, 3 trombones, tuba, timpani, percussion (xylophone, vibraphone, bass drum, cymbals, side drum, maracas, tam-tam, triangle, Chinese tom-tom, tambourine), harp, piano, celesta, violin I, violin II, viola, violoncello, double bass.
Call no.: **1990/043**

445. Charpentier De Castro, Eduardo, 1927– Concierto: para oboe y orquesta. N.p.: Eduardo Charpentier De Castro, 1986.
1 score (26 p.); 44 cm.
Reproduced from manuscript.
Contents: Opus amigo—Pastorale—Mejorana.
Composed for: oboe, piccolo, 2 flutes, 2 oboes, 2 clarinets, 2 bassoons, 4 horns, 4 trumpets, 3 trombones, tuba, timpani, percussion (snare drum, bass drum, cymbals, suspended cymbal, glockenspiel, gong, woodblock), harp, violin I, violin II, viola, violoncello, double bass.
Commissioned by: Gabriel Galindo.
Call no.: **1988/017**

446. Charpentier, Jacques, 1933– Symphonie no. 7: Acropolis.
Call no.: **1986/022**
No materials available.

447. Chasalow, Eric, 1955– Dream songs: for orchestra and tape (2000–01). N.p.: Eric Chasalow, 2001.
1 score (59 p.); 44 cm.
English words (tape); also printed as text.
At the end: March 11, 2001.
"Corrected 6/4/01"—p. 59.
Composed for: 2 flutes (2nd also piccolo), 2 oboes, 2 clarinets, 2 bassoons, 2 horns, 2 trumpets, 2 trombones, tuba, percussion (triangle, suspended cymbal, crotales, marimba, tambourine, tom-toms, bass drum, hi-hat, vibraphone, woodblock, bongos, tam-tam), piano, violin I, violin II, viola, violoncello, double bass, tape.
Commissioned by: Boston Modern Orchestra Project and Gil Rose.
Call no.: **2003/022**
Re-entered as: **2005/025**

448. Chasalow, Eric, 1955– First quartet (1990). N.p.: Eric Chasalow, 1990.
1 score (44 p.); 28 cm.
Reproduced from holograph.
Composed for: 2 violins, viola, violoncello.
Call no.: **1994/025**

449. Chen, Qigang, 1951– [Wu xing] = Wu xing = Les cinq éléments: pour orchestre. Paris: G. Billaudot, 2001.
1 score (32 p.); 42 cm.
Duration: ca. 10:00.
Editorial and performance notes in English and French.
Contents: Shui = L'eau = Water—Mu = Le bois = Wood—Huo = Le feu = fire—Tu = La terre = Earth—Jin = Le métal = Metal.
Composed for: 3 flutes (also piccolo), 3 oboes (also English horn), 3 clarinets (also clarinet in E♭ and bass clarinet), 3 bassoons (also contrabassoon), 4 horns, trumpet, 2 trumpets, 3 trombones, tuba, percussion (vibraphone, xylophone, 6 temple-blocks, bass drum, log drum, bass marimba, tubular bells, triangle, 6 woodblocks, medium suspended cymbal, glockenspiel, large tam-tam, metal chimes, bamboo chimes) harp, piano (also celesta) 30 violins, 12 violas, 10 violoncellos, 8 double basses.
Commissioned by: Radio France 1998.
Call no.: **2005/026**

450. Chen, Yi, 1953– Chinese myths cantata: for chorus & orchestra, 1996. Bryn Mawr, PA: T. Presser, 1996.
1 score (105 p.); 44 cm.
Words in Chinese; also printed as text with English translation.
Composed for: SATB chorus, 2 flutes (both also piccolo), 2 oboes, 2 clarinets (both also clarinet in E♭ and bass clarinet), 2 bassoons (2nd also contrabassoon), 4 horns, 2 trumpets, 2 trombones, bass trombone, percussion (timpani, 2 suspended cymbals, bamboo tree, crotales, woodblock, tambourine, ratchet, glockenspiel, bongo, small bell, cymbals, thundersheet, sound tree, small Chinese cymbals, bass drum, tam-tam, tom-tom, clapper), violin I, violin II, viola, violoncello, double bass, 4 Chinese traditional instruments (erhu, yanqin, pipa, zheng).
Commissioned by: Women's Philharmonic and Chanticleer.
Call no.: **1997/025**

451. Chen, Yi, 1953– Dunhuang fantasy: for organ and wind ensemble. King of Prussia, PA: Theodore Presser, 1999.
1 miniature score (48 p.); 22 x 28 cm.
Program notes in English and Chinese.
Composed for: organ, flute, oboe, clarinet, bass clarinet, contrabassoon, horn, trumpet, trombone, percussion (mark tree, 2 bongos, snare drum, suspended cymbal, 2 tom-toms, bass drum, tam-tam).
Commissioned by: American Guild of Organists.
Call no.: **2002/028**

452. Chen, Yi, 1953– Eleanor's gift: concerto for cello and orchestra, 1998. Bryn Mawr, PA: Theodore Presser, 1998.
1 score (57 p.); 44 cm.
Duration: ca. 15:00.
Program notes included.
Composed for: violoncello, 2 flutes, 2 oboes, 2 clarinets, 2 bassoons, 2 horns, 2 trumpets, trombone, percussion (4 timpani, temple blocks, tambourine, mark tree, Japanese high woodblock, vibraphone, tam-tam, suspended cymbal, bass drum), violin I, violin II, viola, violoncello, double bass.
Call no.: **2000/205**

453. Chen, Yi, 1953– Golden flute: concerto for flute and orchestra. Bryn Mawr, PA: Theodore Presser, 1997.
1 score (69 p.); 37 cm.
Program notes in English.
Duration: ca. 15:00.
Composed for: flute, 2 flutes (both also piccolo), 2 oboes, 2 clarinets, bass clarinet, 2 bassoons, 4 horns, 2 trumpets, 3 trombones, timpani (also cymbal and triangle),

percussion (vibraphone, 5 temple blocks, 5 gongs, Japanese woodblock, glockenspiel, tam-tam, crotales, small bell, bass drum), harp, violin I, violin II, viola, violoncello, double bass.
Call no.: **1998/030**

454. Chen, Yi, 1953– Percussion concerto, 1998. Score. King of Prussia, PA: Theodore Presser, 1998.
1 score (113 p.); 44 cm.
Chinese words (romanized); English translation printed as text.
2nd movement includes vocals performed by the soloist.
Text by Su Shi.
Program and biographical information included.
Contents: The night deepens—Prelude to water tune—Speedy wind.
Composed for: percussion (vibraphone, xylophone, marimba, mark-tree, bowl chime, Chinese cymbals, 6 Peking gongs, medium gong, large gong, tam-tam, high Japanese woodblock, 5 temple blocks, 5 Chinese tom-toms, dagu), 3 flutes (also piccolo), 3 oboes, 3 clarinets (also bass clarinet), 2 bassoons, contrabassoon, 4 horns, 3 trumpets, 3 trombones, tuba, percussion (bow, timpani, high suspended cymbal, Chinese cymbals, 2 fingerbells, crash cymbals, gongs, 5 woodblocks, snare drum, 3 tom-toms, 2 Peking gongs, crotales, tam-tam, 3 temple blocks, claves, bass drum), violin I, violin II, viola, violoncello, double bass.
Commissioned by: Evelyn Glennie and Singapore Symphony Orchestra.
Call no.: **2005/157**

455. Chen, Yi, 1953– Percussion concerto: for percussion and orchestra. Full score. King of Prussia, PA: Theodore Presser, 1998.
1 score (108 p.); 44 cm.
"Unrevised score for perusal only."
Contents: The night deepens—Prelude to water tune—Speedy wind.
Composed for: percussion, 3 flutes, 3 oboes, 3 clarinets, 2 bassoons, contrabassoon, 4 horns, 3 trumpets, 3 trombones, tuba, percussion, violin I, violin II, viola, violoncello, double bass.
Call no.: **2003/146**

456. Chen, Yi, 1953– Piano concerto, 1992. Bryn Mawr, PA: Theodore Presser Co., 1992.
1 score (132 p.); 44 cm.
Duration: 17:00.
Composed for: piano, 3 flutes (all also piccolo), 2 oboes, English horn, 2 clarinets, bass clarinet, 2 bassoons, contrabassoon, 4 horns, 3 trumpets, 3 trombones, tuba, timpani, percussion (vibraphone, tubular bells, crotales, suspended cymbal, crash cymbals, tam-tam, xylophone, bell tree, 5 temple blocks, 3 woodblocks, large Beijing gong, triangle, snare drum, small Beijing gong, 3 nipple gongs, bass drum), violin I, violin II, viola, violoncello, double bass.
Commissioned by: Brooklyn Philharmonic Orchestra.
Call no.: **1995/013**

457. Chen, Yi, 1953– Symphony no. 2: 1993. Bryn Mawr, PA: Theodore Presser, 1993.
1 score (45 p.); 44 cm.
Duration: 18:00.
Composed for: 3 flutes, 2 oboes, English horn, 2 clarinets, bass clarinet, 2 bassoons, contrabassoon, 4 horns, 3 trumpets, 3 trombones, tuba, timpani (also suspended cymbal, Chinese cymbals, glockenspiel), percussion (3 temple blocks, snare drum, small bell, wind chimes, tam-tam, tubular chimes, large bongo, handbell, triangle, bass drum, tubular chimes, vibraphone, Chinese cymbals, small Beijing gong), harp (also suspended cymbal and triangle), violin I, violin II, viola, violoncello, double bass.
Commissioned by: Women's Philharmonic San Francisco.
Call no.: **1996/024**

458. Chernishev, Igor, 1936– America: [muzyka i aranzhirovka]. N.p.: n.p., 199-?.
1 manuscript score (22 p.); 31 cm.
For jazz band.
In ink.
Composed for: 2 alto saxophones, 2 tenor saxophones, baritone saxophone, 5 trumpets, 4 trombones, drums, synthesizer, electric piano, double bass.
Call no.: **1994/026**

459. Chesne, Steven, 1960– Symphony no. 4: the air, the ether and the music of the mind.
Call no.: **1988/018**
No materials available.

460. Chiaramello, Giancarlo, 1939– Orfeo: azione scenica per voci, danzatori e suoni. N.p.: n.p., 1982.
1 score (197 leaves); 42 cm.
Words in Italian by Luciano Damiani.
Reproduced from holograph.
At end of score: Rome 18.2.82.
Composed for: voices, 2 piccolos, 4 flutes, alto flute, bass flute, 2 oboes, English horn, clarinet in E♭, 3 clarinets, bass clarinet, 4 bassoons, contrabassoon, 8 horns, piccolo trumpet, 4 trumpets, 4 trombones, tuba, percussion (piano, marimba, timpani, bass drum, 6 tom-toms,

2 tumbas, 2 bongos, 5 temple blocks, 5 suspended cymbals, tam-tam, gong, snare drum, 3 metal plates, 12 steel plates, claves, triangle, maracas, sleigh bells, tambourine, vibraslap, flexatone, cowbells), violin I, violin II, viola, violoncello, double bass.
Call no.: **1985/033**

461. Chiarappa, Richard, 1948– Hoop! a new musical for high school. West Hartford, CT: Hoop Productions, 1986.
1 condensed score (109 p.); 29 cm.
English words by Martha and Richard Chiarappa.
Arranged by Frank Hunter.
Reproduced from manuscript.
Composed for: 2 flutes, oboe, 2 clarinets, alto saxophone, tenor saxophone, baritone saxophone, horn, 2 trumpets, 2 trombones, tuba, percussion (drums, vibraphone), harp, piano, violin I, violin II, violin III, viola, violoncello, double bass.
Call no.: **1988/019**
Also available:
Call no.: **1988/019 libretto**

462. Chihara, Paul, 1938– Forever Escher: (double quartet) for saxophone quartet and string quartet. New York, NY: Edition Peters, 1994.
1 score (40 p.); 28 cm.
Composed for: soprano saxophone, alto saxophone, tenor saxophone, baritone saxophone, 2 violins, viola, violoncello.
Commissioned by: Amherst Saxophone Quartet.
Call no.: **2001/037**

463. Child, Peter, 1953– Estrella: the assassination of Augusto César Sandino. N.p.: n.p., 1988.
1 score (94 p.); 28 cm.
"From the poetry of Ernesto Cardenal, Pablo Antonio Cuadra and Pablo Neruda; English translation by Bridget Aldaraca, Edward Baker, Ileana Rodriguez and Marc Zimmerman."
Reproduced from holograph.
Composed for: mezzo-soprano, baritone, SATB chorus, 2 flutes (2nd also piccolo), 2 oboes (2nd also English horn), 2 bassoons (2nd also contrabassoon), 2 trumpets, 2 trombones, percussion (tam-tam, bass drum, timpani, maracas, suspended cymbal, chimes), piano, violin I, violin II, viola, violoncello, double bass.
Commissioned by: Cantata Singers.
Call no.: **1990/013**

464. Child, Peter, 1953– Reckoning time: a song of Walt Whitman: a dramatic oratorio in five parts. Cambridge, MA: n.p., 199-?.
1 score (168 p.); 36 cm.
English words by Alan Brody.
For baritone, actor, chorus, and orchestra.
Composed for: actor, baritone, SATB chorus, 2 flutes (2nd also piccolo and alto flute), 2 oboes (2nd also English horn), 2 clarinets (2nd also bass clarinet), 2 bassoons (2nd also contrabassoon), 2 horns, 2 trumpets, 2 trombones, timpani, percussion (glockenspiel, xylophone, vibraphone, chimes, antique cymbal, suspended cymbals, bass drum, triangle, maracas, snare drum, crash cymbal, large tam-tam, woodblock), harp, piano (and celesta), violin I, violin II, viola, violoncello, double bass.
Call no.: **1997/026**

465. Childs, William, 1957– A day in the forest of dreams: for woodwind quintet and piano. N.p.: Lunacy Music, 1999.
1 score (68 p.); 22 x 36 cm.
Contents: First glimpses of sunlight—Afternoon dance.
Composed for: flute, oboe, clarinet, horn, bassoon, piano.
Commissioned by: Dorian Woodwind Quintet.
Call no.: **2001/038**

466. Childs, William, 1957– Just like Job. N.p.: William Childs, 1997.
1 score (130 p.); 44 cm.
English words by Maya Angelou.
Cantata for tenor, choruses, and orchestra.
Composed for: tenor, 2 SATB choruses, piccolo, 3 flutes, 3 oboes, English horn, 3 clarinets, bass clarinet, 2 bassoons, contrabassoon, 4 horns, piccolo trumpet, 3 trumpets, 2 trombones, bass trombone, tuba, timpani, percussion (gong, cymbals, suspended cymbal, glockenspiel, bass drum, chimes, bell tree, snare drum, xylophone, slapstick, vibraslap, wind chimes, anvil, bell tree, triangle), harp, piano, violin I, violin II, viola, violoncello, double bass.
Commissioned by: Akron Symphony Orchestra.
Call no.: **1998/031**

467. Childs, William, 1957– Tone poem for Holly. N.p.: n.p., 1993.
1 score (67 leaves); 43 cm.
For orchestra.
Reproduced from holograph.
At end: 3/10/93, 3:00 A.M., Brooklyn.
Composed for: 2 flutes, 2 oboes (2nd also English horn), 2 clarinets, bass clarinet, 2 bassoons, 2 horns, 2 trumpets, 2 trombones, tuba, timpani, percussion (glockenspiel, bell tree, triangle, xylophone, vibraphone, chimes, snare drum), harp, piano (also celesta), violin

I, violin II, viola, violoncello, double bass.
Commissioned by: Los Angeles Philharmonic.
Call no.: **1997/027**

468. Chin, Unsuk, 1961– I. Konzert: für Klavier und Orchester, 1996/97. London: Boosey & Hawkes, 1998.
1 score (137 p.); 30 cm.
Reproduced from holograph.
Composed for: piano, 2 flutes (2nd also piccolo), 2 oboes (2nd also English horn), 2 clarinets, 2 bassoons, 2 horns, 2 trumpets, 2 trombones, tuba, timpani, percussion (xylophone, glockenspiel, marimba, vibraphone, 2 tam-tams, bass drum, 2 triangles, 4 bongos, 2 tom-toms, 4 woodblocks, antique cymbal, maracas, crash cymbals, tambourine, 3 small snare drums, tenor drum, lithophone, suspended cymbal, whip, tubular bells, Glasplättchen, bell plates), celesta, harp, mandolin, violin I, violin II, viola, violoncello, double bass.
Commissioned by: BBC.
Call no.: **2000/032**

469. Chin, Unsuk, 1961– Kālá: für 2 Solisten, gemischtes [sic] Chor und Orchester. London: Boosey & Hawkes, 2000.
1 score (90 p.); 30 cm.
Principally Danish, German, French, and Finnish words; also printed as text with German.
Texts by Gerhard Rühm, Inger Christensen, Unica Zürn, Gunnar Ekelöf, Arthur Rimbaud, and Paavo Haavikko.
Reproduced from holograph.
Duration: ca. 30:00.
Composed for: soprano, bass, SATB chorus, 3 flutes (3rd also piccolo), 3 oboes (3rd also English horn), 3 clarinets (3rd also bass clarinet), 2 bassoons, contrabassoon, 4 horns, 4 trumpets, 2 trombones, tuba, celesta, harp, harmonium, piano, percussion (glockenspiel, vibraphone, marimba, antique cymbals, chimes, 6 cowbells, Alpine herd cowbell, small triangle, 4 cymbals, 4 tam-tam, 3 thundersheets, nipple gongs, tambourine, 3 snare drums, 2 timpani, bass drum, sistrum, glass chimes, sleigh bells bunched together, guiro, 3 temple bowls, metal rattles, maracas, 2 temple blocks), violin I, violin II, viola, violoncello, double bass.
Commissioned by: Gothenburg Symphony Orchestra–National Orchestra of Sweden, Danish National Radio Symphony Orchestra, and Oslo Philharmonic Orchestra.
Call no.: **2003/023**

470. Chin, Unsuk, 1961– Konzert: für Violine und Orchester (2001). London: Boosey & Hawkes, 2001.
1 score (116 p.); 36 cm.
Reproduced from holograph.
Duration: ca. 24:00.
2004 Grawemeyer Award winning work.
Composed for: violin, 2 flutes, 2 oboes, 2 clarinets, 2 bassoons, contrabassoon, 4 horns, 4 trumpets, 2 trombones, tuba, celesta (also cembalo), 2 harps, percussion (glockenspiel, 2 vibraphones, xylophone, 2 marimbas, lithophone, crotales, tubular bells, cowbells, small triangle, very small pair of cymbals, 3 cymbals with stand, 3 tam-tams, large thunder machine, metal block, Javanese gong, 3 timpani, bass drum, small tambourine, 2 snare drums, gong drum, zanza, guiro, claves), violin I, violin II, viola, violoncello, double bass.
Commissioned by: Deutsches Symphonie–Orchester Berlin.
Call no.: **2004/019**

471. Chou, Wen-Chung, 1923– Echoes from the gorge: a quartet for percussion. New York, NY: C. F. Peters Corp., 1989.
1 score (v, 47 p.); 28 x 43 cm.
Reproduced from manuscript.
Duration: ca. 20:00.
Includes performance instructions in English.
Contents: Prelude: exploring the odes—Raindrops on bamboo leaves—Echoes from the gorge: resonant and free—Autumn pond—Clear moon—Shadows in the ravine—Old tree by the cold spring—Sonorous stones—Droplets down the rocks—Drifting clouds—Rolling pearls—Peaks & cascades—Falling rocks & flying spray.
Composed for: castanets, claves, 4 cowbells, 2 bongos, 2 congas, snare drum, metal chimes, sizzle cymbal, finger bells, gongs, Chinese cymbal, crash cymbals, tam-tams, Chinese tom-tom, 2 timbales, bass drum, parade drum, ride cymbal, 4 woodblocks, 4 tom-toms, 2 sets of bamboo chimes, cymbals, metal sheet, 4 temple blocks, 2 tenor drums, string drum.
Call no.: **1990/131**

472. Chou, Wen-Chung, 1923– String quartet: Clouds. New York: C. F. Peters, 1997.
1 score (41 p.); 28 cm.
Duration: ca. 35:00.
Includes program and performance notes by the composer in English.
Composed for: 2 violins, viola, violoncello.
Commissioned by: Barlow Endowment for Music Composition at Bringham Young University.
Call no.: **2002/029**

473. Chung, Sundo, 1969– Dong chang yi: für Soprano, 2 Becken & Live-Elektronik. N.p.: n.p., 1998.

1 score (14 p.); 36 cm.
Language undetermined.
Composed for: soprano, Turkish cymbal, Chinese cymbal, live electronics.
Call no.: **2000/033**

474. Cikker, Ján, 1911– Ode to joy.
Call no.: **1985/034**
No materials available.

475. Clarke, James, 1957– Kammersymphonie: (2001). London: G. Ricordi & Co., 2001.
1 score (22, 17, 17, 15 p.); 30 x 43 cm.
Reproduced from manuscript.
Duration: 26:00.
Contents: Delirium—Delmenhorst—Delos—Night.
Composed for: flute (also bass flute), oboe (also English horn), clarinet (also bass clarinet), piano, percussion (sizzle cymbal, 2 Chinese cymbals, metal chains, log drum, tubular bells, 4 bell plates, large tam-tam, 4 gongs, vibraphone), 2 violins, viola, violoncello, double bass.
Call no.: **2004/020**

476. Clarke, Rosemary, 1920– A canticle of praise: Psalms 150, 121, 23: for mixed choir, piano, organ, and trumpets. Full score. Hollywood, CA: Judy Green Music, 1984.
1 score (34 p.); 28 cm.
Reproduced from manuscript.
Duration: ca. 9:00.
Composed for: SATB chorus, piano, organ, trumpets.
Commissioned by: R. Eustice Klein.
Call no.: **1989/019**

477. Clausen, René, 1953– A new creation. N.p.: Mark Foster Music, 1990.
1 score (110 p.); 34 cm.
English and Latin words.
For soloists (SATB), chorus (SATB), orchestra, and organ.
Reproduced from manuscript.
Duration: 50:00.
Composed for: soprano, alto, tenor, bass, SATB chorus, 2 flutes, oboe, bassoon, timpani, organ, harp, violin I, violin II, viola, violoncello, double bass.
Call no.: **1991/017**

478. Clay, Carleton, 1942– At midnight on the 31st of March: a theater piece, with music. N.p.: n.p., 2002.
1 score (213 p.); 29 cm.
English words by Carleton Clay.
Original work by Josephine Young Case.
Reproduced from holograph.
Composed for: voices, SATB chorus, synthesizer, violoncello, viola, flute, clarinet, horn.
Call no.: **2005/027**
Also available:
Call no.: **2005/027 libretto**

479. Clay, Carleton, 1942– A Frost diary. N.p.: n.p., 1992.
1 score (64 leaves); 28 cm.
English words; also printed as text.
Text from poems by Carol Frost.
Duration: ca. 30:00.
Contents: Prayer for my son—Acorns—Harriet Street—Ode to the horseshoe crab—Advice to an infatuee—Unfinished song.
Composed for: soprano, flute (also alto flute and piccolo), clarinet (also clarinet in E♭ and bass clarinet), alto saxophone (also soprano saxophone), trumpet, percussion (tom-tom, woodblocks, wind drum, vibraphone, timpani, bell), violoncello.
Commissioned by: Catskill Conservatory.
Call no.: **1993/022**

480. Clay, Carleton, 1942– A Frost diary: for flute, clarinet, saxophone, trumpet, voice, percussion and violoncello. N.p.: n.p., 1992.
1 score (54 leaves); 28 cm.
English words by Carol Frost.
Duration: ca. 30:00.
Contents: Prayer for my son—Acorns—Harriet Street—Ode to the horseshoe crab—Advice to an infatuee—Unfinished song.
Composed for: voice, flute (also alto flute and piccolo), clarinet (also clarinet in E♭ and bass clarinet), alto saxophone (also soprano saxophone), trumpet, percussion (tom-tom, woodblocks, wind drum, vibraphone, timpani, bell), violoncello.
Commissioned by: Catskill Conservatory.
Call no.: **1994/027**

481. Clayton, Laura, 1943– Terra lucida: rondo for orchestra. New York, NY: C. F. Peters, 1989.
1 score (73 p.); 34 cm.
Duration: ca. 14:00.
Composed for: piccolo, 2 flutes, 2 oboes, 2 clarinets, 2 bassoons, contrabassoon, 4 horns, 2 trumpets, 2 trombones, tuba, timpani, percussion (2 timbales, 3 woodblocks, tam-tams, triangle, glockenspiel, 3 Chinese tom-toms, bass drum, 3 suspended cymbals, castanets, xylophone, marimba), harp, piano, violin I, violin II, viola, violoncello, double bass.
Commissioned by: American Composers Orchestra.
Call no.: **1990/014**

482. Clearfield, Andrea, 1960– Women of valor: oratorio for soprano, mezzo-soprano, narrator and orchestra (2000). N.p.: n.p., 2000.
1 score (252 p.); 44 cm.
English words from various sources.
Duration: 1:00:00.
Composed for: narrator, soprano, mezzo-soprano, 2 flutes (2nd also piccolo and alto flute), 2 oboes (2nd also English horn), 2 clarinets, bass clarinet, 2 bassoons, 4 horns, 3 trumpets, 2 trombones, tuba, percussion (3 timpani, temple blocks, dumbek, 2 bongos, crotales, vibraphone, marimba, xylophone, glockenspiel, 2 pairs of finger cymbals, 3 riqs, cabasa, medium frame drum, 3 tom-toms, snare drum, bass drum, suspended cymbal, triangle, mark tree, chimes, guiro, claves, sistrum), harp, piano (also celesta), violin I, violin II, viola, violoncello, double bass.
Call no.: **2002/030**

483. Cleary, David, 1954– Crosscultural variations. N.p.: n.p., 2002.
1 score (52 p.); 28 cm.
Composed for: violin, viola, violoncello, double bass, piano.
Commissioned by: Palmer Museum of Art.
Call no.: **2004/021**

484. Cleary, David, 1954– The deeper magic. N.p.: n.p., 1996.
1 score (19 p.); 28 cm.
Reproduced from holograph.
Includes performance notes.
Composed for: violin, viola.
Commissioned by: Duo Renard (Mark Miller, Ute Miller).
Call no.: **2002/031**

485. Cleary, David, 1954– Fanfares for Teddy Roosevelt: for orchestra. N.p.: D. Cleary, 1995.
1 score (47 p.); 28 cm.
Composed for: 2 flutes (2nd also piccolo), 2 oboes, 2 clarinets in A, 2 bassoons, 4 horns, 2 trumpets, 3 trombones, tuba, timpani, percussion (glockenspiel, tam-tams, triangles, crash cymbals, suspended cymbal, bass drum, snare drum), harp, violin I, violin II, viola, violoncello, double bass.
Commissioned by: Boston Chamber Ensemble.
Call no.: **2000/034**

486. Cleary, David, 1954– Fourteen movie characters: for solo piano. N.p.: n.p., 1997.
31 p. of music; 28 cm.
Reproduced from manuscript.
Composed for: piano.
Commissioned by: Kathryn Rosenbach and American Composers Forum–Boston Area Chapter.
Call no.: **2001/039**

487. Cleary, David, 1954– Harriet Zinnes songs: for high soprano, contrabass and piano. N.p.: David Cleary, 1991.
1 score (50 p.); 28 cm.
English words.
Reproduced from manuscript.
Contents: Just wait—Colors—She dances—Time machines—Helicopter: how.
Composed for: soprano, double bass, piano.
Call no.: **1998/032**

488. Cleary, David, 1954– String quartet no. 2: Artaria. N.p.: n.p., 1992.
1 score (86 p.); 28 cm.
Reproduced from manuscript.
Composed for: 2 violins, viola, violoncello.
Commissioned by: Artaria String Quartet.
Call no.: **1997/028**

489. Coates, Gloria, 1938– Chiaroscuro. N.p.: Gloria Coates, 1990.
1 score (60 p.); 43 cm.
For orchestra.
Reproduced from manuscript.
Duration: 27:00.
Contents: Illumination—Mystical plosives—Dream sequence.
Composed for: piccolo, flute (also alto flute), 2 oboes (2nd also English horn), 2 clarinets (2nd also bass clarinet), bassoon, contrabassoon, 4 horns, 3 trumpets, 2 trombones, bass trombone, tuba, timpani, percussion (bass drum, rattle, marimba, 2 gongs, vibraphone, xylophone, bells, flexatone, cymbals, triangle, glockenspiel, snare drum, Chinese temple blocks, field drum, bongo, suspended cymbal, woodblocks), harp, violin I, violin II, viola, violoncello, double bass.
Commissioned by: Stuttgarter Philharmonie.
Call no.: **1993/023**

490. Coble, William, 1959– Chamber symphony (2003). Chicago, IL: William Coble, 2003.
1 score (38 p.); 28 x 44 cm.
Final revision of Chamber symphony (2000).
Duration: ca. 16:30.
Includes composer's note in English.
Composed for: flute (also piccolo), oboe, clarinet (also clarinet in E♭), horn, trumpet, trombone, harp (or piano), piano, percussion (claves, sizzle cymbal, low

"clunky" snare drum, high snare drum, xylophone, vibraphone, marimba, tam-tam, 2 woodblocks, bass drum, triangle, 2 congas, bongos, glockenspiel, 4 timpani, brass wind chimes, 4 temple-blocks, chimes, ratchet, small brake drum), violin I, violin II, viola, violoncello, double bass.
Call no.: **2005/028**

491. Coelho de Souza, Rodolfo Nogueira, 1952– Concerto for computer and orchestra. N.p.: n.p., 1999.
1 score (78 p.); 44 cm.
Duration: ca. 17:30.
Composed for: computer, piccolo, 2 flutes, 2 oboes, English horn, 2 clarinets, bass clarinet, 2 bassoons, 4 horns, 3 trumpets, 2 trombones, bass trombone, tuba, percussion (4 timpani, snare drum, tubular bells, bass drum, xylophone, suspended cymbal, 4 woodblocks, triangle, glass wind chimes, glockenspiel, tam-tam, 4 temple blocks, wood wind chimes, crotales or antique cymbals, whistle, claves, agogo bells or 2 cowbells, vibraphone, suspended metal sheet, 4 tom-toms, 2 maracas, metal wind chimes, guiro, 2 bongos, 3 gongs, shell wind chimes), celesta, violin I, violin II, viola, violoncello, double bass.
Call no.: **2002/040**

492. Coenen, Carl, 1971– I belong to you. N.p.: n.p., 1994.
2 leaves of music; 30 cm.
English words by A. Hidding.
Melody with chord symbols.
Composed for: voice, unspecified accompaniment.
Call no.: **1996/025**

493. Cogan, Robert, 1930– Portrait of Celan: for soprano voice and piano. Cambridge, MA: Publication Contact International, 2001.
1 score (24 p.); 28 cm.
English words; also printed as text.
Text translated into English by John Felstiner.
Contents: Pour the wasteland—Below a painting—Nocturne—The poles—The numbers—With all my thoughts—Pour the wasteland: Epilogue.
Reproduced from manuscript.
Composed for: soprano, piano.
Call no.: **2004/022**

494. Cogan, Robert, 1930– String quartet "America is": a folio with texts by William Carlos Williams. Sample performance version. Cambridge, MA: Publication Contact International, 1995.
1 score (ca. 48 p.); 22 x 36 cm. + 1 sample performance version (ca. 30 p.; 22 x 36 cm).
English worlds; also printed as text.
Includes performance instructions.
Composed for: 2 violins, viola, violoncello.
Call no.: **1997/029**

495. Cohan, John Alan, 1947– Canticles to the bridegroom: for high voice and piano. N.p.: n.p., 1985.
1 score (52 leaves); 33 cm.
English words by St. John of the Cross.
Song cycle.
Reproduced from manuscript.
Contents: O living flame of love—The one I most desire—Upon a night of darkness—Send no messingers to me—Beneath the apple tree.
Composed for: high voice, piano.
Call no.: **1986/023**

496. Cohan, John Alan, 1947– World of dreams: for soprano and piano. N.p.: n.p., 198-?.
1 score (30 leaves); 31 cm.
Words in English by George Crabbe.
Reproduced from holograph.
Composed for: soprano, piano.
Call no.: **1985/035**

497. Cohen, Allen, 1951– Duo-partita: for violoncello and guitar. N.p.: n.p., 2001.
1 score (27 p.); 28 cm.
Duration: ca. 16:00.
Composed for: violoncello, guitar.
Commissioned by: Claremont Duo.
Call no.: **2004/023**

498. Cohen, Howard A., 1955– Tönebiegung = The bends, 1989. N.p.: n.p., 1989.
1 score (3 leaves); 30 cm.
Reproduced from manuscript.
Duration: ca. 10:00.
Performance instructions by the composer in English.
Composed for: flute, 2 tuners.
Call no.: **1993/024**

499. Cohen, Shimon, 1937– Concerto: for trombone, tenor, and orchestra (1995). N.p.: n.p., 1995.
1 score (101 p.); 37 cm.
Composed for: trombone, 2 flutes, 2 oboes, 2 clarinets, bass clarinet, 2 bassoons, 4 horns, 3 trumpets, 3 trombones, tuba, timpani, percussion, harp, celesta, violin I, violin II, viola, violoncello, double bass.
Call no.: **2001/040**

500. Cohen, Shimon, 1937– Festive dances. Full score. N.p.: n.p., 1982.

1 score (67 p.); 42 cm.
Reproduced from holograph.
Composed for: piccolo, 2 flutes, descant recorder, 2 oboes, English horn, 2 clarinets, piccolo clarinet, bass clarinet, 2 bassoons, contrabassoon, 4 horns, 4 trumpets, 3 trombones, tuba, timpani, percussion (bells, bass drum, glockenspiel, tambourine, snare drum, xylophone, crash cymbals, suspended cymbals, woodblock, maracas, tam-tam), harp, piano, celesta, violin I, violin II, viola, violoncello, double bass.
Call no.: **1986/024**

501. Cohn, James, 1928– Concerto for clarinet and string orchestra, op. 62. N.p.: James Cohn, 1986.
1 score (31 p.); 29 cm.
Reproduced from manuscript.
Duration: 12:34.
Composed for: clarinet, violin I, violin II, viola, violoncello, double bass.
Call no.: **2001/041**

502. Coleman, Linda Robbins, 1954– For a beautiful land: a symphonic poem: for orchestra. Des Moines, IA: Linda Robbins Coleman, 1996.
1 score (65 p.); 36 cm.
Duration: ca. 11:00.
Includes program notes and biographical information.
Composed for: 2 flutes (2nd also piccolo), 2 oboes, 2 clarinets, 2 bassoons, 2 horns, timpani, percussion (2 pairs of crash cymbals, suspended cymbals, snare drum, glockenspiel, gong), violin I, violin II, viola, violoncello, double bass.
Commissioned by: Cedar Rapids Orchestra.
Call no.: **1997/030**

503. Coleman, Linda Robbins, 1954– Hibernia suite: for string orchestra. Des Moines, IA: Coleman Creative Services, 1999.
1 score (40 p.); 28 cm.
"Perusal score."
Duration: ca.16:20.
Contents: Land of youth = Tir na nÓg—The lover = Leannán—Dancing = Dahmsa.
Composed for: violin I, violin II, viola, violoncello, double bass.
Commissioned by: Wartburg Community Symphony.
Call no.: **2000/035**

504. Coleman, Linda Robbins, 1954– Journeys: a symphonic poem for orchestra. N.p.: Linda Robbins Coleman, 1992.
1 score (71 p.); 35 cm.
Duration: ca. 10:00.
Includes program notes and biographical information.
Composed for: 2 flutes (2nd also piccolo), 2 oboes, 2 clarinets, 2 bassoons, 4 horns, 3 trumpets, 3 trombones, tuba, timpani, percussion (suspended cymbals, finger cymbals, crash cymbals, snare drum, bass drum, glockenspiel, chimes, castanets, tambourine, gong), harp, piano, violin I, violin II, viola, violoncello, double bass.
Commissioned by: Wartburg Community Symphony.
Call no.: **1996/026**

505. Coleman, Randolph, 1937– The crowns of Nineveh: for amplified orchestra and electronic tape. N.p.: n.p., 1985.
1 score (39 p.); 47 x 47 cm.
Reproduced from manuscript.
Composed for: 3 flutes (3rd also piccolo), 2 oboes (both also English horn), contrabass clarinet (also bass clarinet), bassoon (also contrabassoon), 4 horns, 3 trumpets, 3 trombones, tuba, percussion (timpani, bell tree, sand blocks, snare drum, sizzle cymbal, whip, 2 triangles, cowbells, glockenspiel, truck brake drum, tam-tam, tambourine, 3 wind chimes, marimba, crotales, 2 suspended cymbals, maracas, vibraphone, guiro, triangle, bass drum, 5 temple blocks, 3 woodblocks, 5 drums), piano, organ, violin I, violin II, viola, violoncello, double bass, electronic tape.
Commissioned by: Oberlin College.
Call no.: **1986/025**

506. Coleman, Randolph, 1937– The great lalula. N.p.: n.p., 1988.
1 score (82 p.); 44 cm.
For voice and large amplified chamber ensemble.
Nonsense words by Christian Morgenstern.
Reproduced from holograph.
Composed for: voice, alto flute, oboe, bass clarinet, horn, trumpet, euphonium, 2 pianos (2nd also celesta), percussion, 2 violins, viola, 2 violoncellos, electric bass.
Commissioned by: Oberlin Contemporary Ensemble.
Call no.: **1989/020**

507. Colgrass, Michael, 1932– Arctic dreams: for symphonic wind ensemble, 1991. N.p.: Colgrass Music, 1991.
1 score (128 p.); 44 cm.
Tone poem.
Reproduced from manuscript.
Duration: ca. 27:00.
Contents: Inuit landscape—Throat-singing with laughter—The whispering voices of the spirits who ride with the lights in the sky—Polar night—Spring light: ice floating in the sun—The hunt—Drum dancer.

Composed for: 6 flutes (all also piccolo, 4th–6th also alto flute), 3 oboes, clarinet in E♭, 6 clarinets, bass clarinet, contrabass clarinet, 3 bassoons, contrabassoon, soprano saxophone, alto saxophone, baritone saxophone, 6 trumpets, 6 horns, 4 trombones, 2 bass trombones, 2 euphoniums, 2 tubas, piano (also celesta), harp, 2 double basses, percussion (timpani, bongos, 2 congas, 2 snare drums, 2 piccolo snare drums, 2 field drums, 2 bass drums, 3 large cymbals, medium gong, large gong, 2 water gongs, 2 triangles, string of free-hanging bells, 2 sets of sleigh bells, medium alarm bell, reco-reco, sandpaper blocks, lion's roar, crotales, glockenspiel, Parsifal bells, vibraphone, 2 sets of chimes, 2 xylophones).
Commissioned by: James Keene.
Call no.: **1996/027**

508. Colgrass, Michael, 1932– Arias: for clarinet & orchestra, 1992. N.p.: Colgrass Music, 1992.
1 score (115 p.); 44 cm.
Reproduced from manuscript.
Duration: ca. 30:00.
Includes program notes by the composer.
Composed for: clarinet, 2 flutes (1st also alto flute, 2nd also piccolo), oboe, English horn, bass clarinet, bassoon, contrabassoon, 4 horns, 2 trumpets, 2 trombones, tuba, timpani, percussion (2 snare drums, 2 tenor drums, bass drum, 3 triangles, suspended cymbal, 2 suspended cymbals, gong, glockenspiel, crotales, marimba, xylophone, vibraphone, chimes, 6 cowbells, trap set, 4 ghetto blasters), harp, piano (celesta and ghetto blaster), violin I, violin II, viola, violoncello, double bass.
Commissioned by: Toronto Symphony.
Call no.: **1993/025**

509. Colgrass, Michael, 1932– Chaconne: for viola and orchestra. N.p.: Colgrass Music, 1984.
1 score (88 p.); 32 cm.
Duration: 30:00.
Includes program and performance notes.
Composed for: viola, 3 flutes (2nd also piccolo), 2 oboes, 2 clarinets, bass clarinet, contrabassoon, 4 horns, 3 trumpets, 3 trombones, tuba, timpani, percussion (glockenspiel, vibraphone, chimes, marimba, crotales, 2 triangles, ratchet, 3 woodblocks, 3 cowbells, 2 tambourines, bongos, timbales, field drum, sizzle cymbal, large cymbal, gong, bass drum), harp, piano (also celesta), violin I, violin II, viola, violoncello, double bass.
Commissioned by: Toronto Symphony.
Call no.: **1985/036**
Re-entered as: **1988/020**

510. Colgrass, Michael, 1932– Crossworlds: for flute, piano & orchestra. N.p.: Colgrass Music, 2002.
1 score (81 p.); 43 cm.
Concerto for flute and piano with orchestra.
Duration: ca. 33:30.
Program note by the composer in English.
Composed for: flute, piano, piccolo, 2 oboes (also English horn), clarinet in E♭, clarinet, bass clarinet, bassoon, contrabassoon, 2 trumpets, 4 horns, trombone, bass trombone, celesta, harp, timpani, percussion (glockenspiel, xylophone, crotales, vibraphone, marimba, chimes, tambourine, bongos, 2 darbuka, tenor drum, field drum, bass drum, 3 cowbells, 4 suspended cymbals, 4 small button gongs, tam-tam), violin I, violin II, viola, violoncello, double bass.
Commissioned by: Boston Symphony Orchestra.
Call no.: **2004/024**
Re-entered as: **2005/029**

511. Colgrass, Michael, 1932– The Schubert birds, 1989. N.p.: Colgrass Music, 1989.
1 score (84 p.); 44 cm.
Concerto for orchestra.
Reproduced from manuscript.
Duration: ca. 17:00.
Based on Schubert's Kupelwieser waltz.
Includes program notes in English by the composer.
Composed for: 2 flutes (2nd also piccolo), 2 oboes (2nd also English horn), 2 clarinets (1st also clarinet in A and clarinet in E♭, 2nd also bass clarinet), bassoon, contrabassoon, 2 horns, 2 trumpets, percussion (timpani, timbales, large sizzle cymbal, glockenspiel, crotales, chimes, vibraphone, marimba), violin I, violin II, viola, violoncello, double bass.
Commissioned by: Canadian National Arts Centre Orchestra.
Call no.: **1991/018**

512. Colgrass, Michael, 1932– The Schubert birds: for orchestra: 1989. Toronto, ON: Colgrass Music Co.; New York, NY: C. Fischer, 1989.
1 score (84 p.); 31 cm.
For orchestra.
Reproduced from holograph.
At end: Toronto 9 Nov. 1989.
Duration: ca. 17:00.
Based on Schubert's Kupelwieser waltz.
Composed for: 2 flutes (2nd also piccolo), 2 oboes (2nd also English horn), 2 clarinets (1st also clarinet in A and clarinet in E♭, 2nd also bass clarinet), bassoon, contrabassoon, 2 horns, 2 trumpets, percussion (timpani, timbales, large sizzle cymbal, glockenspiel, crotales, chimes, vibraphone, marimba), violin I, violin II,

viola, violoncello, double bass.
Commissioned by: Canadian National Arts Centre Orchestra.
Call no.: **1994/028**

513. Colgrass, Michael, 1932– Snow walker: for organ and orchestra, 1990. N.p.: Colgrass Music; New York, NY: Carl Fischer, 1990.
1 score (86 p.); 28 cm.
Reproduced from manuscript.
Preface and program notes by the composer.
Contents: Polar landscape—Throat-singing, with laughter—The whispering voices of the spirits who ride with the lights in the sky—Ice and light—Snow walker.
Composed for: organ, 2 flutes (2nd also piccolo), 2 oboes, English horn, 2 clarinets (1st also clarinet in E♭, 2nd also bass clarinet), 2 bassoons (2nd also contrabassoon), 2 horns, 2 trumpets, trombone, bass trombone, tuba, timpani, percussion (glockenspiel, vibraphone, chimes, 2 tenor drums, 2 congas, 2 bongos, timbal, bass drum, 2 crash cymbals, 2 tam-tams, 4 suspended cymbals, reco-reco, triangle, sleigh bells, strings of free-hanging bells), harp, piano (also celesta), violin I, violin II, viola, violoncello, double bass.
Commissioned by: Calgary International Organ Festival.
Call no.: **1992/024**

514. Colgrass, Michael, 1932– Urban requiem: for four saxophones and wind orchestra, 1995. N.p.: Colgrass Music, 1995.
1 score (100 p.); 43 cm.
Includes performance and program notes.
Reproduced from manuscript.
Duration: ca. 27:00–28:00.
Composed for: soprano saxophone, alto saxophone, tenor saxophone, baritone saxophone, piccolo, flute, alto flute, 2 oboes, English horn, clarinet in E♭, clarinet, bass clarinet, 2 bassoons, contrabassoon, 4 horns, 3 trumpets, 2 trombones, bass trombone, tuba, synthesizer, harp, 2 double basses, timpani, percussion (xylophone, glockenspiel, crotales, vibraphone, chimes, marimba, 2 tam-tams, cymbals, bass drum, bongos, 2 African drums, 2 African log drums, 2 tenor pans, timbales, 2 cowbells, tambourine, sleigh bells, snare drum, small tom-tom, floor tom-tom, 3 cymbals, 2 large sizzle cymbals, 4 large suspended cymbals, medium suspended cymbal, tiny crash cymbals).
Commissioned by: University of Miami Wind Ensemble.
Call no.: **1997/031**
Re-entered as: **1998/033** and **2000/036**

515. Colgrass, Michael, 1932– Winds of Nagual: a musical fable for wind ensemble on the writings of Carlos Castaneda, 1985. N.p.: Colgrass Music, 1985.
1 score (100 p.); 44 cm.
Duration: 25:00.
Composed for: 6 flutes (2nd also alto flute, 6th also piccolo), contrabassoon, clarinet in E♭, 6 clarinets, bass clarinet, alto clarinet, contrabass clarinet, soprano saxophone, alto saxophone, 6 horns, 6 trumpets (2nd also cornet), flugelhorn, 6 trombones, 2 euphoniums, 2 tubas, percussion (Parsifal bells, vibraphone, crotales, chimes, xylophone, marimba, bass drum, 3 gongs, 4 suspended cymbals, 4 crash cymbals, 5 cowbells, temple blocks, bongos, timbales, snare drum, tenor drum, field drum, timpani), piano (also celesta), harp, 2 double basses.
Commissioned by: New England Conservatory Wind Ensemble.
Call no.: **1986/026**
Re-entered as: **1989/021**

516. Collier, Graham, 1937– Bread & circuses = (Panem et circenses). N.p.: Graham Collier, 2001.
6 leaves of music; 30 cm.
Composed for: unspecified.
Call no.: **2003/024**

517. Consoli, Marc-Antonio, 1941– Afterimages.
Call no.: **1985/037**
No materials available.

518. Consoli, Marc-Antonio, 1941– String quartet.
Composed for: 2 violins, viola, violoncello.
Call no.: **1985/038**
No materials available.

519. Constant, Marius, 1925–2004. 103 regards dans l'eau: pour violon et 12 instruments. Paris: Editions Salabert, 1984.
1 score (124 p.); 36 cm.
Reproduced from holograph.
Duration: 35:00.
Composed for: violin, flute, clarinet, bass clarinet, horn, percussion (timpani, vibraphone, 3 cymbals, thin cymbal, tam-tam), piano, harp, 2 violins, viola, violoncello, double bass.
Call no.: **1985/039**

520. Constant, Marius, 1925–2004. Des droits de l'homme: oratorio drammatique. Paris: Editions Salabert, 1989.
1 score (176 p.); 41 cm.
English, French, and Latin words.
For soprano, narrators, chorus, tape, and orchestra.

Texts by Yves Jamiaque, Lou Bruder, Marius Constant, and Gustave Flaubert.
Historical texts from the Magna Carta, Premier pacte de la confédération suisse, Habeas corpus, Bill of Rights, Constitution of the United States, Initiation maçonnique, La Fayette, Voltaire, Cahier des doléances, Mirabeau, Rabaut St. Etienne, Marat, Gaultier de Biauzat, Psaume Protestant, "Schema Israel," Déclaration des droits de l'homme (1789).
Reproduced from manuscript.
Duration: ca. 1:12:00.
Contents: Des origines—Initiation—Versailles—Doléances—Déclaration—Final.
Composed for: 5–6 narrators, soprano, SATB chorus, tape, 3 flutes (2nd–3rd also piccolo), 3 oboes (3rd also English horn), clarinet in E♭, 2 clarinets, bass clarinet, 2 bassoons, contrabassoon, 4 horns, 3 trumpets, 3 trombones, tuba, 2 sets of timpani, percussion (vibraphone, xylophone, chimes, 2 military drums, 2 tom-toms, 2 bongos, 2 congas, bass drum, 2 suspended cymbals, Chinese cymbal, 2 tam-tams, 2 cowbells, 2 temple blocks, woodblock, maracas, wind machine, 2 claves, glockenspiel, snare drum, 4 castanets, thundersheet, temple blocks), 2 harps, piano (also celesta), violin I, violin II, viola, violoncello, double bass.
Call no.: **1993/026**
Also available:
Call no.: **1993/026 vocal score**

521. Constant, Marius, 1925–2004. Sade-Teresa: mélodrame fantastique en 4 tableaux. Partition d'orchestre. Paris: Editions Salabert, 1996.
1 score (179 p.); 42 cm.
French words by Pierre Bourgeade.
Opera.
Duration: 1:40:00.
Composed for: mezzo-soprano, countertenor, 2 baritones, bass, oboe (also English horn), clarinet (also bass clarinet and contrabass clarinet), synthesizer, electronic organ, percussion (bongos, bass drum, wind machine, marimba, large tam-tam, timbales, vibraphone, bells, metal chimes, timpani, glockenspiel, 2 tom-toms, tambourine, cencerros, metal plate, whip, large cymbal, temple blocks, cymbals), viola, 3 violoncellos.
Call no.: **1998/034**
Also available:
Call no.: **1998/034 libretto**

522. Constantinides, Dinos, 1929– Symphony no. 2. N. p.: n.p., 1983.
1 score (92 p.); 28 cm.
Reproduced from holograph.
Duration: 23:00.
Contents: Images—Idyll—Insights—Identity.
Composed for: piccolo, 2 flutes, 2 oboes, English horn, 2 clarinets, bass clarinet, 2 bassoons, contrabassoon, 4 horns, 3 trumpets, 3 trombones, tuba, timpani, percussion (xylophone, suspended cymbal, vibraphone, snare drum, chimes, crash cymbals, triangle, vibraphone, gong, bass drum, cowbell), harp, synthesizer (also piano), violin I, violin II, viola, violoncello, double bass.
Commissioned by: Baton Rouge Symphony Orchestra.
Call no.: **1985/040**

523. Conyngham, Barry, 1944– Fly. N.p.: Universal Edition, 1984.
1 score (402 p. in various pagings); 30 cm.
English words by Murray Copland.
Opera.
Reproduced from holograph.
Duration 1:30:00.
Composed for: 3 flutes (1st–2nd also alto flute, 3rd also piccolo), 3 oboes (3rd also English horn), 3 clarinets (3rd also bass clarinet), 2 bassoons, contrabassoon, 4 horns, 3 trumpets, 3 trombones, bass trombone, tuba, timpani, percussion (suspended cymbals, 2 tam-tams, vibraphone, bass drum, antique cymbals, glockenspiel, marimba, chimes, snare drum, 4 gongs, maracas, flexatone, tom-toms, xylophone, 5 wood drums, crash cymbals), harp, piano (also celesta and harpsichord), violin I, violin II, viola, violoncello, double bass.
Commissioned by: Victoria State Opera.
Call no.: **1985/041**

524. Conyngham, Barry, 1944– Monuments: for piano and orchestra: (1989). N.p.: Universal Edition, 1989.
1 score (130 p.); 31 cm.
Contents: "Uluru" the rock: Sydney Opera House—The Barrier Reef: the snowy scheme—The apostles: cityscape.
Composed for: piano, 3 flutes (all also piccolo and alto flute), 3 oboes (3rd also English horn), 2 clarinets, bass clarinet, 2 bassoons, contrabassoon, 4 horns, 3 trumpets, 2 trombones, bass trombone, tuba, timpani, percussion (anvil, 2 suspended cymbals, bass drum, claves, tam-tam, chimes, crotales, vibraphone, 3 gongs, maracas, temple blocks, woodblocks, 4 tom-toms, xylophone, snare drum), harp, celesta, violin I, violin II, viola, violoncello, double bass.
Commissioned by: Albany Symphony Orchestra.
Call no.: **1992/025**

525. Cooney, Cheryl, 1953– Nacht lieder: a song cycle. N.p.: C. Cooney, 1982.

1 score (28 leaves); 28 cm.
German words; also printed as text with English translation.
Poems by Arnim, Eichendorf, Brentano, Tieck, Kurz, Goethe, and Hesse.
Reproduced from holograph.
Contents: Sterne—Schweigt der Menschen—Mondnacht—Abendständchen—Liebe dankt in süssen Tönen—Bedrängnis—Willst du immer weiter schweifen?—Im Nebel—Der stille Grund.
Composed for: voice, piano.
Call no.: **1985/042**

526. Cooper, Paul, 1926–1996. Last call: arias and recitatives on poems of C.E. Cooper. New York, NY: Edition Wilhelm Hansen / Chester Music New York, 1990.
1 score (55 p.); 28 cm.
English words; also printed as text.
Contents: The hour between dawn and sunrise—Tomorrow is the day—The pain is in the hooded wounded eyes—It kills pell mell—Each day he stands—When indifferent nature—The humming birds have not returned.
Composed for: soprano, flute, clarinet, piano, violin, viola, violoncello.
Commissioned by: Da Camera Society.
Call no.: **1991/019**

527. Cooper, Paul, 1926–1996. Symphony in two movements.
Commissioned by: Houston Symphony Orchestra.
Call no.: **1985/043**
No materials available.

528. Cooper, Rose Marie, 1937– The purple dress: a musical drama. N.p.: n.p., 1985.
1 vocal score (ii, 32 p.); 28 cm.
English words by Rose Marie Cooper and Evalyn P. Gill.
Chamber opera in 8 scenes, based on O. Henry's short story.
Composed for: narrator, voices, piano.
Call no.: **1986/027**

529. Cooper, Rose Marie, 1937– Sonata. N.p.: n.p., 198-?.
20 leaves of music; 28 cm.
Reproduced from holograph.
Composed for: piano.
Call no.: **1987/016**
Also available:
Call no.: **1987/016 sketches**

530. Cooper, Rose Marie, 1937– Sonata. N.p.: n.p., 198-?.
21 leaves of music; 28 cm.
For piano.
Reproduced from holograph.
Composed for: piano.
Call no.: **1989/022**
Re-entered as: **1990/015**

531. Copley, Evan, 1930– Piano concerto number three. Greenley, CO: Evan Copley, 1985.
1 score (110 p.); 39 cm.
Reproduced from manuscript.
Composed for: piano, 2 flutes (2nd also piccolo), 2 oboes, 2 clarinets, 2 bassoons, contrabassoon, 4 horns, 3 trumpets, 3 trombones, tuba, percussion (timpani, suspended cymbal, bass drum, xylophone), violin I, violin II, viola, violoncello, double bass.
Call no.: **1989/023**

532. Coral, Giampaolo, 1944– Tout à coup et comme par jeu: pour flûte et orchestre. Partitura. Milano: Casa musicale Sonzogno, 1983.
1 score (37 p.); 39 cm.
Reproduced from holograph.
Duration ca. 14:00.
Includes French poem by Stéphane Mallarmé.
Composed for: flute, piccolo, 2 flutes, 2 oboes, English horn, 2 clarinets, bass clarinet, 2 bassoons, contrabassoon, 4 horns, 3 trumpets, 3 trombones, tuba, timpani, percussion (xylophone, bells, glockenspiel, military drum, snare drum, 4 tom-toms, triangle, cymbals, 4 temple blocks), harp, piano, celesta, violin I, violin II, viola, violoncello, double bass.
Call no.: **1985/044**

533. Cordero, Roque, 1917– Cuarta sinfonia: (Panameńa). N.p.: n.p., 1986.
1 score (181 p.); 45 cm.
Reproduced from manuscript.
Composed for: piccolo, 2 flutes, 2 oboes, English horn, 2 clarinets, bass clarinet, 2 bassoons, 4 horns, 3 trumpets, 3 trombones, tuba, timpani, percussion (snare drum, tom-toms, guiro, triangle, bass drum, cymbals, chimes, 3 suspended cymbals), violin I, violin II, viola, violoncello, double bass.
Call no.: **1988/021**

534. Cordero, Roque, 1917– Four messages: for flutes and piano. N.p.: Roque Cordero, 1992.
1 score (33 p.); 28 cm.
Reproduced from manuscript.
Composed for: flute, alto flute, piccolo, piano.
Call no.: **1996/028**

535. Corghi, Azio, 1937– Blimunda: opera lirica in tre atti: da Memorial do convento di José Saramago. Partitura. Milano: Ricordi, 1989.
1 score (311 p.); 42 cm.
Italian words by Rita Desti, Carmen M. Radulet, Azio Corghi, and José Saramago.
Reproduced from manuscript.
Composed for: mezzo-soprano, contralto, tenor, baritone, vocal octet (2 sopranos, 2 altos, 2 tenors, 2 basses), SATB chorus, piccolo, 2 flutes (2nd also alto flute), 2 oboes, English horn, clarinet in E♭, 2 clarinets, bass clarinet, 2 bassoons, contrabassoon, 4 horns, 4 trumpets, 3 trombones, tuba, timpani, percussion (snare drum, 3 tom-toms, log drum, tambourine, bass drum, woodblock, temple blocks, wood and bamboo wind chimes, maracas, whip, xylophone, marimba, suspended cymbals, crash cymbals, 2 tam-tams, Thai gong, triangle, glockenspiel, crotales, chimes, flexatone, 2 steel drums), 2 harps, tape, violin I, violin II, viola, violoncello, double bass.
Call no.: **1991/020**
Also available:
Call no.: **1991/020 libretto**

536. Corghi, Azio, 1937– La cetra appesa: cantata su temi popolari verdiani: per soprano, voce recitante, coro (coro popolare, banda) e orchestra. Partitura. Milano: Ricordi, 1994.
1 score (x, 139 p.); 42 cm.
Italian words; also printed as text.
Texts by Attilio Bertolucci, Salvatore Quasimodo, Temistocle Solera, and from Bible psalms.
Composed for: narrator, soprano, SATB chorus, piccolo, 2 flutes, alto flute, 2 oboes, oboe d'amore, English horn, clarinet in E♭, 2 clarinets, bass clarinet, 3 bassoons, contrabassoon, 6 horns, 4 trumpets, 3 trombones, tuba, timpani, percussion (snare drum, military drum, bass drum, triangle, crotales, 3 suspended cymbals, crash cymbals, 3 gongs, 3 tam-tams, claves, 2 woodblocks, wood drums, xylorimba, celesta, vibraphone, tubular bells, piano, wind machine, thundersheet), 3 harps, violin I, violin II, viola, violoncello, double bass.
Commissioned by: Orchestra Sinfonica "Arturo Toscanini."
Call no.: **1996/029**

537. Corghi, Azio, 1937– Divara, Wasser und Blut: dramma musicale in tre atti dal dramma teatrale In nomine Dei di José Saramago. Partitura. Milano: Ricordi, 1993.
1 score (412 p.); 39 cm.
Italian words by Azio Corghi and José Saramago; Italian translation by Giulia Lanciani.
Duration: 1:45:00.
Composed for: 2 sopranos, mezzo-soprano, contralto, tenor, baritone, bass, SATB chorus, piccolo, 2 flutes (2nd also alto flute), 2 oboes, English horn, 2 clarinets (2nd also clarinet in E♭), bass clarinet, 2 bassoons, contrabassoon, 5 horns, 3 trumpets, cornet, 3 trombones, tuba, timpani, harp, organ, percussion (friction drum, ratchet, 2 woodblocks, log drum, tambourine, military drum, snare drum, bass drum, triangle, suspended cymbals, crash cymbals, large tam-tam, flexatone, Japanese temple bell, Thai gong, chimes, church bells, xylophone, marimba), violin I, violin II, viola, violoncello, double bass.
Commissioned by: Städtische Bühnen Münster.
Call no.: **1994/029**
Also available:
Call no.: **1994/029 libretto**

538. Corghi, Azio, 1937– . . . Fero dolore: cantata drammatica dal Pianto della Madonna sopra Il lamento d'Arianna di Claudio Monteverdi: per voce femminile, oboe d'amore, percussione, archi. Partitura. Milano: Ricordi, 1994.
1 score (viii, 48 p.); 31 cm.
Italian words; also printed as text.
Includes performance notes in English and Italian.
Duration: ca. 30:00.
Composed for: soprano, oboe d'amore, percussion (whip, tom-tom, steel drum), violin I, violin II, viola, violoncello, double bass.
Commissioned by: Festival Pianistico Internazionale di Brescia e Bergamo e da Ferrara Musica.
Call no.: **1998/035**

539. Corghi, Azio, 1937– Gargantua: opera lirica in due atti. Milano: Edizioni Suvini Zerboni, 1983.
1 score (2 v.); 42 cm.
Italian words by Augusto Frassineti.
Original work by François Rabelais.
Reproduced from manuscript.
Includes performance instructions in Italian.
Composed for: 2 sopranos, mezzo-soprano, contralto, tenor, baritone, 2 basses, SATB chorus, SATB madrigal chorus, women's chorus, onstage ensemble (ratchet, bagpipe, galoubet, 2 tambourines, cymbals), electronics, tape, piccolo (also ocarina), 2 flutes, 2 oboes, English horn, clarinet in E♭, 2 clarinets, bass clarinet, alto saxophone, 2 bassoons, contrabassoon, 4 horns, 4 trumpets, 3 trombones, tuba, percussion (timpani, 5 roto-toms, xylophone, xylorimba, glockenspiel, vibraphone, tubular bells, 4 mounted tubular bells, 3 cowbells, flexatone, 2 woodblocks, 5 temple blocks, cymbals, suspended cymbal, hi-hat, triangle, 2 tam-

tams, snare drum, military drum, tom-tom, bass drum, lion's roar, tambourine, whip, wooden ratchet, Jew's harp), 2 harps, harmonium, violin I, violin II, viola, violoncello, double bass.
Commissioned by: Teatro Regio di Torino.
Call no.: **1988/022**

540. Corghi, Azio, 1937– La morte di Lazzaro: cantata drammatica per voce recitante, coro misto, coro di voci bianche, ottoni e percussioni. Partitura. Milano: Ricordi, 1995.
1 score (viii, 80 p.); 41 cm.
Italian words by José Saramago; also printed as text.
"Partitura ad esclusivo uso promozionale da non usare per l'esecuzione"—p. 1 of cover.
Composed for: narrator, SATB chorus, children's chorus, 3 trumpets, 3 trombones, timpani (also suspended cymbal), percussion (snare drum, 5 tom-toms, bass drum, bongos, congas, dumbuk, Chinese tom-tom, friction drum, 2 woodblocks, 2 wood drums, xylophone, xylorimba, marimba, flexatone, cymbals, large tam-tam, thundersheet, crotales, glockenspiel, celesta, steel drum, vibraphone, tubular bells, bell plate, Thai gong).
Call no.: **1997/032**

541. Corghi, Azio, 1937– Un petit train de plaisir: balletto per 2 pianoforte e percussioni su musiche di Gioachino Rossini. Partitura. Milano: Ricordi, 1992.
1 score (xx, 325 p.); 36 cm.
Duration: ca. 54:00.
Includes program notes and performance instructions in Italian.
Composed for: 2 pianos, percussion (mouth organ, bull-roarer, boobams, bass drum, Neopolitan friction drum, 2 church bells, 3 Chinese tom-toms, cuckoo call, claves, cricket call, dobachi, glockenspiel, handbell, crash cymbals, Chinese gong, harmonium, iron chains, metal sheet, timpani, 8 log drums, lion's roar, train whistle, marimba, nightingale call, 3 bell plates, pop bottle, ratchet, 7 roto-toms, signal whistle, sandpaper blocks, snare drum, 3 suspended cymbals, sistrum, soprano steel drum, sizzle cymbal, tam-tam, 5 temple blocks, tambourine, triangle, 2 woodblocks, chocalho, whip, friction drum, xylophone, sceta vajasse, bass marimba, congas, vibraphone, celesta, darbuka, musical saw, flexatone, tubular bells, kalungu, musical glasses, bronze bells, Thai gong, antique cymbals, bongos, mark tree, brake drums, tablas).
Call no.: **1993/027**

542. Corigliano, John, 1938– Fantasia on an ostinato. N.p.: Schirmer, 1986.
1 miniature score (52 p.); 36 cm.
For orchestra.
Based on a repetitive passage from Beethoven's Symphony no. 7 (2nd movement, Allegretto).
"2nd proofs; 77% reduced; 9/2/86."
Composed for: 3 flutes (3rd also piccolo), 3 oboes, 3 clarinets, 3 bassoons (3rd also contrabassoon), 4 horns, piccolo trumpet in D, 3 trumpets, 3 trombones, tuba, timpani, percussion (xylophone, glockenspiel, brake drum, suspended cymbals, bass drum, vibraphone, tubular bells, tambourine, tam-tam, whip, roto-toms, crotales, 3 temple blocks, triangle, tenor drum, snare drum, ratchet), harp, piano, violin I, violin II, viola, violoncello, double bass.
Call no.: **1987/017**

543. Corigliano, John, 1938– Symphony no. 1 (1988–9). New York, NY: G. Schirmer, 1990.
1 score (131 p.); 36 cm.
"Un-revised copy; for examination only"—Cover.
Duration: ca. 40:00.
Contents: Apologue: of rage and remembrance—Tarantella—Chaconne: Giulio's song—Epilogue.
1991 Grawemeyer Award winning work.
Composed for: 4 flutes (2nd–4th also piccolo), 3 oboes, English horn, 3 clarinets (3rd also clarinet in E♭ and contrabass clarinet), bass clarinet, 3 bassoons, contrabassoon, 6 horns, 5 trumpets (1st also trumpet in A), 2 trombones, 2 bass trombones, 2 tubas, percussion (xylophone, anvils, brake drum, timpani, 2 bass drums, vibraphone, suspended cymbal, tam-tam, glockenspiel, triangle, snare drum, 3 tom-toms, temple blocks, tenor drum, whip, crotales, marimba, tambourine, police whistle, ratchet, cymbals, flexatone, finger cymbals, roto-toms, tenor drum, chimes, hammer on metal plate, field drum), harp, piano, celesta, violin I, violin II, viola, violoncello, double bass.
Commissioned by: Chicago Symphony.
Call no.: **1991/021**

544. Corozine, Vince, 1935– Tribute. N.p.: n.p., 198-?.
1 score (134 leaves); 29 x 35 cm.
For orchestra.
Reproduced from manuscript.
Composed for: piccolo, 4 flutes, oboe, English horn, 3 clarinets, bass clarinet, soprano saxophone, alto saxophone, tenor saxophone, baritone saxophone, 2 bassoons, 3 horns, 3 trumpets (also 2 flugelhorns), 3 trombones, tuba, timpani, percussion (trap set, 2 marimbas, xylophone, congas, tambourine, woodblock, bongos, triangle, cowbell, cabasa, guiro, snare drum, timbales, gong, castanets, finger cymbals, wind chimes, bell plate, bell tree, suspended cymbal), 2 harps, piano, electric piano, celesta, synthesizer, harpsichord, guitar,

electric bass, 9 violins, 6 violoncellos, double bass.
Call no.: **1989/024**

545. Correggia, Enrico, 1933– Duna. Paris: Editions Salabert, 1986.
1 score (27 p.); 46 cm.
Reproduced from holograph.
Composed for: bass flute, guitar, piano, 4 violins, 2 violas, 2 violoncellos, double bass.
Commissioned by: France Ministère de la Culture.
Call no.: **1987/018**

546. Correggia, Enrico, 1933– Musik für das Ende der Tage: Requiem: per soprano, baritono, coro e orchestra. N.p.: n.p., 2003.
1 score (121 p.); 43 cm.
English words from Vision and prayer by Dylan Thomas; also printed as text with Italian translation.
Composed for: soprano, baritone, SATB chorus, 2 flutes, 2 oboe, 2 clarinets, 2 bassoons, 4 horns, 4 trumpets, 2 trombones, tuba, percussion (2 timpani, 3 suspended cymbals, 3 tom-toms, tam-tam, 3 wood-blocks, 3 temple-blocks), violin I, violin II, violin III, violin IV, viola I, viola II, violoncello I, violoncello II, double bass I, double bass II.
Call no.: **2005/030**

547. Correggia, Enrico, 1933– Narcissus et Eco: pour deux voix solistes d'enfants, maîtrise [et] ensemble. Torino: Edizioni Antidogma Musica, 1997.
1 score (64 p.); 35 cm.
Latin words; also printed as text with Italian translation.
For 2 children's voices, choir, and 13 instruments.
Reproduced from holograph.
Composed for: 2 children's voices, flute, clarinet, oboe d'amore, 2 horns, percussion (vibraphone, 2 cymbals, Burma bell, 2 cymbals, gong, 2 tam-tams, bell tree, 2 tom-toms, conga, 3 woodblocks), piano, guitar, 2 violins, viola, violoncello.
Commissioned by: Radio France.
Call no.: **1998/036**

548. Correggia, Enrico, 1933– Vox: pour violoncelle et orchestre. Roma: BMG Ariola, 1993.
1 score (72 p.); 37 cm.
Reproduced from holograph.
Composed for: violoncello, 2 flutes, 2 oboes, 2 clarinets, 2 bassoons, 2 horns, 2 trumpets, 2 trombones, percussion (2 tam-tams, 3 cymbals, 3 timbales, 3 temple blocks, vibraphone, 3 woodblocks), 10 violins, 4 violas, 3 violoncellos, 2 double basses.
Commissioned by: Radio France.
Call no.: **1995/014**

549. Cotel, Morris Moshe, 1943– Dreyfus: opera in two acts. N.p.: M.M. Cotel & Mordecai Newman, 1982.
1 score (2 v. [448 p.]); 58 cm.
English words by Mordecai Newman.
Reproduced from manuscript.
Duration: ca. 2:15:00.
Composed for: mezzo-soprano, 6 tenors, 2 baritones, 7 basses, SATB chorus, flute (also piccolo), oboe, clarinet, soprano saxophone, bassoon, horn, harp, piano, vibraphone (also xylophone), marimba, percussion (snare drum, tenor drum, bass drum, tambourine, triangle, 2 suspended cymbals, guiro, maracas, 3 tam-tams, 3 antique cymbals, 6 tom-toms, ratchet, woodblock, whip, hand cymbal, 2 antique cymbals), 2 violins, 2 violas, violoncello, double bass.
Call no.: **1986/028**
Re-entered as: **1990/016**
Also available:
Call no.: **1990/016 libretto**

550. Cotel, Morris Moshe, 1943– Haftarah: fantasy for piano. N.p.: M.M. Cotel, 1986.
18 p. of music; 30 x 40 cm.
Reproduced from manuscript.
Duration: ca. 25:00.
Composed for: piano.
Call no.: **1991/022**

551. Cotel, Morris Moshe, 1943– Variations with a little help: piano solo for the left hand alone. N.p.: M.M. Cotel, 1991.
41 p. of music; 28 cm.
Composed for: piano (left hand).
Call no.: **1996/030**

552. Cotton, Jeffery, 1957– Concerto for clarinet, strings and harp (2002). N.p.: Jeffery Cotton, 2002.
1 score (92 p.); 36 cm.
Duration: ca. 27:00.
Includes composer's note in English.
Composed for: clarinet in A, harp, violin I, violin II, viola, violoncello, double bass.
Commissioned by: Metamorphosen Chamber Orchestra.
Call no.: **2005/031**

553. Cotton, Jeffery, 1957– Suite from "Pyramus and Thisbe": for string orchestra (2002). N.p.: n.p., 2002.
1 score (vi, 149 p.); 28 cm.
Ballet suite for string orchestra.
Duration: ca. 30:00.
Program notes by the composer in English.
Composed for: violin I, violin II, viola, violoncello, double bass.

Commissioned by: Metamorphosen Chamber Orchestra.
Call no.: **2004/025**

554. Cowie, Edward, 1943– Gaia: 24 voices, chamber orchestra (2001–2). Full score. N.p.: United Music Publishers, 2003.
1 score (2 v. [426 p.]); 30 cm.
English words by the composer.
Duration: ca. 1:05:00.
Contents: Towards big bang—The formation of Gaia—Voices from the sea—The voices of insects—The voices of birds—The voices of mammals—The voices of homo—The voices of Gaia.
Composed for: 6 sopranos, 6 altos, 6 tenors, 6 basses, flute (also piccolo, alto flute, and bass flute), oboe (also English horn), clarinet (also clarinet in A, clarinet in E♭, bass clarinet, contrabass clarinet), saxophone (soprano and alto), bassoon, horn, trumpet (also trumpet in C and trumpet in D), trombone, tuba, percussion, timpani, harp, piano (also celesta), violin I, violin II, viola, violoncello, double bass.
Commissioned by: BBC.
Call no.: **2005/032**

555. Cox, Alan, 1953– Illuminations. N.p.: n.p., 1987.
1 score (190 leaves); 28 cm.
French words by Arthur Rimbaud.
Reproduced from manuscript.
Contents: A une raison—Après la deluge—Bottom—Mystique—Vies—Enfance—Démocratie—Barbare—Jeunesse.
Composed for: voice, piccolo, flute, oboe, clarinet, bassoon, horn, trumpet, percussion (xylophone, vibraphone, side drum, suspended cymbal, 2 tam-tams, bass drum, triangle, glockenspiel, crotales, chimes, anvil, maracas, woodblock, guiro, tom-tom, crash cymbals, woodblock, snare drum), harp, celesta, violin I, violin II, viola, violoncello, double bass.
Call no.: **1992/026**

556. Cox, Alan, 1953– Six orchestral images: after Magritte, 1990. N.p.: n.p., 1990.
1 score (136 p.); 43 cm.
Reproduced from manuscript.
Contents: L'empire des lumières = The empire of light—La durée poignardée = Time transfixed—Un peu de l'âme des bandits = A little of the bandit's soul—Le blanc-seing: (carte blanche) = Blank signature—Le faux miroir = The false mirror—Le jockey perdu 1926 = The lost jockey 1926.
Composed for: 3 flutes (3rd also piccolo), 2 oboes, English horn, 2 clarinets, bass clarinet, 2 bassoons, contrabassoon, 4 horns, 2 trumpets, 2 trombones, bass trombone, tuba, timpani, harp, celesta, percussion (glockenspiel, crotales, triangle, bass drum, 2 tam-tams, suspended cymbal, vibraphone, anvil, snare drum, chimes, woodblocks, crash cymbals, snare drum), violin I, violin II, viola, violoncello, double bass.
Commissioned by: Berkeley Symphony.
Call no.: **1994/030**

557. Cresswell, Lyell, 1944– Concerto for 'cello and orchestra. N.p.: n.p., 198-?.
1 score (90 p.); 43 cm.
Reproduced from manuscript.
Duration: ca. 30:00.
Composed for: violoncello, piccolo, 2 flutes, 3 oboes (3rd also English horn), 2 clarinets, bass clarinet, 3 bassoons (3rd also contrabassoon), 4 horns, 3 trumpets, 3 trombones, tuba, timpani, percussion (glockenspiel, tubular bells, 2 suspended cymbals, xylophone, temple blocks, snare drum, bass drum), harp, violin I, violin II, viola, violoncello, double bass.
Commissioned by: Scottish National Orchestra.
Call no.: **1985/045**

558. Cresswell, Lyell, 1944– A modern ecstacy. N.p.: n.p., 1986.
1 miniature score (126 p.); 37 cm.
English words by Patrick Maguire, also printed as text.
For mezzo-soprano, baritone, and orchestra.
Reproduced from manuscript.
Duration: ca. 45:00.
Contents: The creation—Shove's law—Declaration of war—Prayer to Amar—The lunacy—The war—Amar's lament.
Composed for: mezzo-soprano, baritone, piccolo, flute, 2 oboes (2nd also English horn), 2 clarinets (2nd also bass clarinet), 2 bassoons, 4 horns, 3 trumpets, 3 trombones, tuba, timpani, percussion (3 suspended cymbals, castanets, snare drum, bass drum, tubular bells, xylophone, cimbalom), violin I, violin II, viola, violoncello, double bass.
Commissioned by: anonymous donor.
Call no.: **1990/017**

559. Crivelli, Carlo, 1953– Iride. N.p.: n.p., 1986.
1 score (39 p.); 21 x 30 cm.
Reproduced from holograph.
At end of score: "5 juglio – 15 agosto '86."
Duration: 14:30.
Composed for: violin, flute, guitar, clarinet, vibraphone, tam-tam, bassoon, double bass.
Call no.: **1987/019**

560. Crouser, Jennifer Jean, 1965– Messe in D-Dur = Mass in D-major: for choir (S.A.T.B.), soloists and orchestra. N.p.: Jennifer Jean Crouser, 1987.
1 score (119 p.); 34 cm.
German words.
Reproduced from manuscript.
Composed for: SATB chorus, soprano, alto, tenor, baritone, bass, 2 flutes, clarinet, horn, trumpet, violin I, violin II, viola, violoncello, double bass.
Call no.: **1989/025**
Also available:
Call no.: **1989/025 parts**
Call no.: **1989/025 vocal score**

561. Crumb, David, 1962– Quartet: for piano and strings. N.p.: n.p., 200-?.
1 score (81 p.); 28 cm.
"Score for first performance"—cover.
Composed for: violin, viola, violoncello, piano.
Call no.: **2003/025**

562. Crumb, George, 1929– Quest: guitar, soprano saxophone, harp, contrabass and percussion (two players). Score. New York, NY: C. F. Peters, 1996.
1 score (25 p.); 31 x 41 cm.
"Facsimile printing from the manuscript by the composer."
"Revised version February 1994"—p. 25.
Duration: ca. 25:00.
Program and performance notes in English and German.
Contents: Refrain 1—Dark paths—Fugitive sounds—Refrain 2—Forgotten dirges—Fugitive sounds—Refrain 3—Nocturnal.
Composed for: guitar, soprano saxophone, harp, double bass, percussion (Appalachian hammered dulcimer, 2 high maracas, African talking drum, crotales, 2 sleigh bells, 5 tam-tams, 3 suspended cymbals, Chinese temple gong, claves, marimba, African log drum, glass wind chimes, rute, flexatone, vibraphone, large timpani with detached large cymbal, Chinese cymbal, bamboo wood chimes, metal wind chimes, 4 Japanese temple bells, Mexican rain stick, Thai wooden buffalo bell, 5 Chinese temple blocks, conga, African gourd rattle, guiro, bell tree).
Call no.: **1998/037**

563. Crumb, George, 1929– Unto the hills: Appalachian songs of sadness, yearning and innocence for singer, percussion quartet and amplified piano. N.p.: n.p., 2002.
1 score (23 p.); 28 x 43 cm.
English words; also printed as text.
Reproduced from manuscript.
Contents: Poor wayfaring stranger—All the pretty little horses—Ten thousand miles—Appalachian epiphany: sunset and nightfall—Black, black, black is the color—The riddle—Poor wayfaring stranger (echo).
Composed for: voice, piano, percussion (vibraphone, glockenspiel, bamboo wind chimes, Indian ankle bells, finger cymbals, Vietnamese wooden "frog" voice, Thai wooden buffalo bell, medium Chinese cymbal, 2 maracas, large Chinese temple gong, small Chinese temple gong, 5 cowbells, Tibetan prayer stones, mounted tambourine, unmounted tambourine, soprano recorder, very small triangle, large Chinese cymbal, medium cymbal, large spring drum, tiny Japanese bell, wind machine, African log drum, bell tree, sleigh bells, conga, guiro, glass wind chimes, claves, two mounted castanets, xylophone, flexatone, large timpani, medium bass drum, cello bow, marimba, large bass drum, small tam-tam, medium tam-tam, 4 Japanese temple bells, 2 bongos, 3 tom-toms, sandpaper blocks, rute, tubular bells, cuíca, crotales, large cymbal, large tam-tam, very large tam-tam, small bass drum, 5 temple blocks, 2 Chinese woodblocks, African thumb piano, large spring drum, Indian ankle bells).
Call no.: **2004/026**

564. Crumb, George, 1929– Unto the hills: songs of sadness, yearning and innocence: a cycle of Appalachian folk songs for voice, percussion quartet and amplified piano (American songbook III). New York, NY: C. F. Peters Corp., 2002.
1 score (25 leaves); 28 x 40 cm.
English words; also printed as text.
Reproduced from manuscript.
Includes program note by the composer in English.
Contents: Poor wayfaring stranger—All the pretty little horses: an Appalachian lullaby—Ten thousand miles—Appalachian epiphany: a psalm for sunset and dusk (instrumental interlude)—Ev'ry night when the sun goes in—Black, black, black is the color—The riddle—Poor wayfaring stranger (echo).
Composed for: voice, piano, percussion (vibraphone, glockenspiel, bamboo wind chimes, Indian ankle bells, finger cymbals, Vietnamese wooden "frog" voice, Thai wooden buffalo bell, medium Chinese cymbal, 2 maracas, large Chinese temple gong, small Chinese temple gong, 5 cowbells, Tibetan prayer stones, mounted tambourine, unmounted tambourine, soprano recorder, very small triangle, large Chinese cymbal, medium cymbal, large spring drum, tiny Japanese bell, wind machine, African log drum, bell tree, sleigh bells, conga, guiro, glass wind chimes, claves, two mounted castanets, xylophone, flexatone, large timpani, medium bass drum, cello bow, marimba, large bass drum,

small tam-tam, medium tam-tam, 4 Japanese temple bells, 2 bongos, 3 tom-toms, sandpaper blocks, rute, tubular bells, cuíca, crotales, large cymbal, large tam-tam, very large tam-tam, small bass drum, 5 temple blocks, 2 Chinese woodblocks, African thumb piano, large spring drum, Indian ankle bells).
Call no.: **2005/033**

565. Cumming, Richard, 1928– Jubilate: in memoriam John Browning: for orchestra. N.p.: n.p., 2003.
1 score (63 p.); 36 cm.
Reproduced from manuscript.
Duration: ca. 25:00.
Contents: Entrances and introductions—Reflections—Fun and games—Memory and desire—Summer afternoons—Departures and farewell.
Composed for: 2 flutes (also piccolo), 2 oboes (also English horn), 2 clarinets, 2 bassoons, 2 horns, 2 trumpets, 2 trombones, timpani, percussion (snare drum, bass drum, crash cymbals, suspended cymbal, woodblock, 2 gourds, triangle, tom-tom, whip, glockenspiel, vibraphone), harp, violin I, violin I, viola, violoncello, double bass.
Call no.: **2005/034**

566. Cummings, Robert, 1939– Concerto for oboe. N.p.: n.p., 198-?.
1 score (28 p.); 35 cm.
Reproduced from manuscript.
Composed for: oboe, 2 flutes, violin I, violin II, viola, violoncello, double bass.
Call no.: **1989/026**

567. Cunningham, Karen, 1954– All aboard: a piano, synthesizer and multimedia work. Albuquerque, NM: Karen Cunningham, 1999.
1 score (various pagings); 28 cm.
Includes chart of timings.
Contents: Here come the trains!—The gandy dancers—All aboard!—Hobo waltz.
Composed for: piano, synthesizer, recorded sounds, recorded voices.
Commissioned by: MTNA Foundation 1999.
Call no.: **2002/032**

568. Curran, Alvin S., 1938– Crystal psalms. N.p.: n.p., 1988.
1 score (12 leaves); 23 x 30 cm. + 1 score (7 leaves); 31 cm. + performance notes (3 leaves; 30 cm.)
Primarily Yiddish and Hebrew words.
Radio concert for 7 choruses, 6 instrumental quartets, percussion, accordions, and magnetic tape.
Large score for groups 1–6, other score for group 7.
Written to commemorate the 50th anniversary of Kristallnacht.
Reproduced from manuscript.
Includes performance notes in English.
Composed for: 7 SATB choruses, 6 instrumental groups (group 1: 4 bass flutes, percussion, accordion; group 2: 2 tubas, 2 saxophones, percussion, accordion; group 3: 4 bass trombones, percussion, accordion; group 4: 4 violoncellos, percussion, accordion; group 5: 4 violas, percussion, accordion; group 6: 4 bass clarinets, percussion, accordion), tape.
Call no.: **1990/018**
Also available:
Call no.: **1990/018 Group I (Roma)**

569. Curran, Alvin S., 1938– Inner cities. 2–11. N.p.: n.p., 2003.
1 v. of music; 28 cm.
Composed for: piano (also toy piano).
Call no.: **2005/035**

570. Curtis-Smith, Curtis, 1941– Christopher the Christ-bearer: 1992. N.p.: n.p., 1992.
1 score (xix, 174 p.); 36 cm.
Primarily English words, also printed as text.
A cantata/melodrama for soprano, baritone, and chamber group.
Libretto by C. Curtis-Smith, based on Columbus's Log, the Libro de las profecías, Hernando Cortés, Catholic Mass excerpts, the Navajo night chant, a Hawaiian prayer, and poems by Linda Hogan.
Reproduced from manuscript.
"There are revisions in this score which differ from the recorded performance (DaCamera, Houston, December 5, 1992), especially in I, III, and X. In VII (This blessed gold) the spoken soprano text has been changed"—p. xix.
Duration: ca. 50:00.
Contents: They sing from earth and sky—In the name of our Lord—In first light—The naming aria—You can smell the flowers—2 January, 1493—This blessed gold—They have the softest and gentlest voices (credo)—Buffalo; O Lord, our Lord, praised be Thy name—Navajo night chant.
Composed for: soprano, baritone, flute (also piccolo and alto flute), clarinet in A, trumpet, percussion (glockenspiel, orchestra bells, vibraphone, marimba, chimes, tam-tam, small snare drum, tambourine, bass drum), guitar, piano, violin, violoncello, double bass.
Commissioned by: DaCamera, Houston, Texas.
Call no.: **1994/031**

571. Curtis-Smith, Curtis, 1941– Concerto: for left

hand and orchestra (1990). N.p.: n.p., 1994.
1 score (149 p.); 40 cm.
At end of score: revised 1994.
Reproduced from manuscript.
Duration: ca. 30:00.
Composed for: piano (left hand), piccolo, 2 flutes, 2 oboes, English horn, 2 clarinets, bass clarinet, 2 bassoons, contrabassoon, 4 horns, 3 trumpets, 2 trombones, bass trombone, tuba, timpani, percussion (orchestra bells, xylophone, vibraphone, marimba, chimes, triangle, 2 suspended cymbals, large tam-tam, bass drum), harp, violin I, violin II, viola, violoncello, double bass.
Commissioned by: Irving S. Gilmore International Keyboard Festival.
Call no.: **1996/031**

572. Curtis-Smith, Curtis, 1941– A farewell . . . = Les adieux: music for horn, string quartet, and piano (2001). N.p.: n.p., 2001.
1 score (58 p.); 28 cm.
Duration: 22:27.
Program notes in English by the composer.
Contents: Horn calls and lament—Bursts of light—Shadows—Consolation—Danse macabre: Dies irae.
Composed for: horn, 2 violins, viola, violoncello, piano.
Commissioned by: Barlow Endowment for Music Composition at Brigham Young University.
Call no.: **2003/026**

573. Curtis-Smith, Curtis, 1941– Second piano trio: ("The secret heart of sound") (1992–93). N.p.: n.p., 1993.
1 score (42 p.); 36 cm.
Reproduced from manuscript.
Composed for: violin, violoncello, piano.
Commissioned by: Merling Trio.
Call no.: **1995/015**
Re-entered as: **1997/033**

574. Curtis-Smith, Curtis, 1941– Twelve etudes: for piano (2000). N.p.: n.p., 2000.
47 p. of music; 36 cm.
Suite of 12 movements.
Duration: 40:08.
Program notes by the composer in English.
Composed for: piano.
Call no.: **2002/033**

575. Curtis-Smith, Curtis, 1941– Twelve etudes: for piano (2000). N.p.: n.p., 2002.
51 p. of music; 36 cm.
Suite of 12 or 13 movements.
Duration: ca. 40:00.
Includes 13th etude, which "may be substituted for Etude X, or may be performed along with the other etudes"—p. 48.
Composed for: piano.
Call no.: **2004/027**

576. Curtis-Smith, Curtis, 1941– Violin concerto. N.p.: E.B. Marks Music; Bryn Mawr, PA: Theodore Presser, 1998.
1 score (118 p.); 36 cm.
Duration: 20:00.
Composed for: violin, 2 flutes (2nd also piccolo), 2 oboes, 2 clarinets (both also clarinet in A), 2 bassoons, 2 horns, 2 trumpets, timpani, percussion (marimba, vibraphone, orchestra bells, chimes), soprano saxophone (also alto saxophone), violin I, violin II, viola, violoncello, double bass.
Commissioned by: Pro Musica Chamber Orchestra of Columbus, OH.
Call no.: **2001/042**

577. Custer, Beth, 1958– My grandmother. N.p.: Beth Custer, 2002.
1 score (114 leaves); 22 x 28 cm.
Music for the silent film My grandmother (= Moya babushak, chemi bebia).
Composed for: clarinet, trumpet, piano, violin, violoncello, electric guitar, electric bass, drums.
Call no.: **2005/036**

578. Cyr, Gordon, 1925– Symphony no. 2. N.p.: n.p., 1990.
1 score (97 p.); 43 cm.
Reproduced from holograph.
For orchestra.
At end: Aug. 2, 1990 Baltimore.
Duration: ca. 14:30.
Composed for: piccolo, 2 flutes, 2 oboes, English horn, 2 clarinets, bass clarinet, 3 bassoons, contrabassoon, 4 horns, 3 trumpets, 3 trombones, tuba, percussion (crash cymbals, suspended cymbal, 2 tam-tams, triangle, temple blocks, chimes, xylophone, vibraphone, glockenspiel, snare drum, 4 low tom-toms, timpani), harp, piano, violin I, violin II, viola, violoncello, double bass.
Call no.: **1995/016**
Re-entered as: **1996/032**

579. Czarnecki, Sławomir Stanisław, 1949– Hombark-concerto: per violino e archi. N.p.: n.p., 1997.
1 score (49 p.); 30 cm.
Reproduced from manuscript.

Duration: ca. 15:00.
Composed for: violin, violin I, violin II, viola, violoncello, double bass.
Call no.: **2001/043**

580. Czernowin, Chaya, 1957– Pnima . . . ins Innere: (inward) 1998–1999. N.p.: n.p., 1999.
1 score (180 p.); 28 cm.
Nonsense syllables.
Composed for: soprano, alto, 2 basses/baritones, clarinet (also bass clarinet and soprano clarinet), saxophone (also alto saxophone and sopranino), trombone, singing saw, viola, violoncello, percussion (bass drum, marimba, vibraphone, 2 wood boxes, hi-hat, cymbals, large low guiro, high guiro, friction drum, lion's roar, bowed tam-tam, finger cymbal, medium plastic bottle, cardboard, glass bottle or metal bowl, wire rack, pair of stones, fixated pair of cans, metal beater, plastic bag filled with large cans, plastic bag filled with small cans, timpani, thundersheet, 2 large maracas, 2 sets of sea urchins, chimes, large rain stick, bongos, pair of cans, tuned bottles), 10 violins, 6 violas, 4 violoncellos, 6 double basses.
Commissioned by: Stadt München.
Call no.: **2002/034**

581. D'Alessio, Greg, 1963– Smoke and mirrors: for 17 players and tape. N.p.: n.p., 1998.
1 score (131 p.); 36 cm.
Duration: 16:00.
Composed for: tape, flute (also piccolo), clarinet, bass clarinet, horn, trumpet, trombone, 2 violins, viola, 2 violoncellos, double bass, harp, piano, percussion (ratchet, sand block, castanets, claves, pitched gongs, marimba, crotales, tambourine, vibraphone, temple blocks, woodblock, Chinese cymbal, timpani, snare drum, sizzle cymbal, bongos, bowed suspended cymbal, large tam-tam, orchestral cymbals, floor tom-tom, pitched gongs).
Call no.: **2000/037**

582. Dal Porto, Mark, 1955– Song of the night: three nocturnes for oboe, voice, & piano. N.p.: Mark Dal Porto, 2003.
1 score (49 p.); 28 cm.
English words; also printed as text.
Text by Friedrich Nietzsche, Mevlana Rumi, and Friedrich Rückert.
Contents: Midnight song—Night and sleep—At midnight.
Composed for: oboe, voice, piano.
Call no.: **2005/037**

583. Dalbavie, Marc-André, 1961– Color: pour orchestre. Partition d'orchestre. Paris: Gérard Billaudot, 2002.
1 miniature score (42 p.); 42 cm.
Duration: 17:00.
Composed for: 3 flutes, 2 oboes, English horn, 3 clarinets, 2 bassoons, contrabassoon, 4 horns, 3 trumpets, 2 trombones, bass trombone, tuba, percussion (tubular bells, marimba, vibraphone, 2 bongos, 2 tom-toms, tumba, side drum, crash cymbals, suspended cymbal, bass drum, triangle, 4 large gongs, tam-tam), timpani, piano, harp, 22 violins, 8 violas, 6 violoncellos, 6 double basses.
Call no.: **2005/038**

584. Dalbavie, Marc-André, 1961– Concertate il suono. Paris: Gérard Billaudot, 2002.
1 score (70 p.); 43 cm.
Duration: 25:00.
Composed for: 4 trumpets, 3 trombones, tuba, percussion, harp, violin I, violin II, viola, violoncello, double bass; group A: 2 violins, viola, violoncello, flute, oboe, bass clarinet; group B: 2 violins, viola, violoncello, vibraphone, flute, oboe, bass clarinet; group C: 2 violins, viola, violoncello, harp, flute, oboe, clarinet, 2 horns, group D: 2 violins, viola, violoncello, celesta, alto flute, oboe (also English horn), clarinet, horn.
Commissioned by: Cleveland Orchestra and Chicago Symphony Orchestra.
Call no.: **2002/035**

585. Dalbavie, Marc-André, 1961– Concerto pour orchestre. Partition d'orchestre. Paris: G. Billaudot, 1999.
1 score (91 p.); 60 cm.
Reproduced from holograph.
Duration: 22:55.
Composed for: 4 trumpets, 3 trombones, tuba, piano, percussion (gongs, xylophone, whip, cymbals, tubular bells, bass drum, glockenspiel, tom-toms), timpani, violin I, violin II, viola, violoncello, double bass, offstage ensemble (4 flutes, 3 oboes, English horn, 4 clarinets, 4 horns, harp, vibraphone, 4 violins, 2 violas, 2 violoncellos).
Commissioned by: Minnesota Orchestra.
Call no.: **2001/044**

586. Dalbavie, Marc-André, 1961– Concerto pour violon et orchestre. Paris: G. Billaudot, 1996.
1 miniature score (64 p.); 42 cm.
Includes performance and program notes.
Duration: 24:00.
Composed for: violin, 3 flutes, 2 oboes, 3 clarinets, 2 bas-

soons, 3 trumpets, 3 trombones, bass trombone, tuba, timpani, percussion (vibraphone, bells, suspended cymbals, glockenspiel, tam-tam, bass drum), piano, synthesizer, violin I, violin II, viola, violoncello, double bass.
Commissioned by: Radio France.
Call no.: **2000/038**

587. Dalbavie, Marc-André, 1961– Seuils. Paris: Editions Jobert, 1992.
1 score (3 v.); 32–45 cm.
French words.
For soprano, orchestra, and electronics.
Reproduced from manuscript.
Composed for: soprano, electronics, 2 flutes (1st also piccolo), 2 oboes, 2 clarinets, bass clarinet, 2 bassoons (2nd also contrabassoon), 2 horns, 2 trumpets, 2 trombones, tuba, percussion (vibraphone, marimba, chimes, bongos, glockenspiel, gongs, timbales, 3 tom-toms, xylophone, cymbals, bass drum), piano, celesta, synthesizer, harp, violin I, violin II, viola, violoncello, double bass.
Call no.: **1993/028**

588. Damnianovitch, Alexandre, 1958– Nativite: pour chœur à voix égales. N.p.: n.p., 2001.
1 score (15 p.); 30 cm.
Serbian words (Cyrillic and romanized); also printed as text with French and English translations.
Seven orthodox-Serbian Christmas songs.
Reproduced from manuscript.
Duration: ca. 15:00.
Composed for: chorus (equal voices).
Commissioned by: Commande de l'Etat.
Call no.: **2005/039**

589. Dan, Ikuma, 1924–2001. Symphony no. 6: Hiroshima. N.p.: n.p., 1985.
1 score (221 p.); 37 cm.
Reproduced from manuscript.
Composed for: 2 piccolos, 4 flutes, 2 oboes, 2 clarinets, bass clarinet, clarinet in E♭, 2 bassoons, 6 horns, 3 trumpets, 3 trombones, tuba, timpani, percussion (triangle, cymbals, tam-tam, bass drum, snare drum, chimes), harp, 2 Japanese bamboo flutes, violin I, violin II, viola, violoncello, double bass.
Call no.: **1986/029**

590. Dănceanu, Liviu, 1954– Sapte zile: pentru trombon si orchestra = Seven days: trombone concerto, op. 56. N.p.: n.p., 1992.
1 score (60 p.); 39 cm.
Reproduced from manuscript.
Composed for: trombone, 2 flutes, 2 oboes, 2 clarinets, 3 horns, 2 trombones, percussion (2 gongs, timpani, metal chimes, tam-tam, 3 tom-toms, simantra, glass chimes, cymbals), Korg synthesizer, violin I, violin II, viola, violoncello, double bass.
Call no.: **1997/034**

591. Danielpour, Richard, 1956– An American requiem: for chorus, orchestra, and soloists (2001). New York, NY: Associated Music Publishers, 2001 (1/14/02 printing).
1 score (204 p.); 36 cm.
Latin and English words from various sources; also printed as text with English translation.
"To the memory of those who died in the wake of the tragic events of September 11, 2001; and in tribute to the American soldier—past, present, and future"—caption.
Duration: ca. 60:00.
Composed for: mezzo-soprano, tenor, baritone, SATB chorus, 3 flutes (2nd also alto flute, 3rd also piccolo), 3 oboes (3rd also English horn), 3 clarinets (3rd also bass clarinet), 3 bassoons (3rd also contrabassoon), 4 horns (all also Wagner tuba), 3 trumpets, 2 trombones, bass trombone, tuba, 6 offstage trombones, timpani, percussion, piano (also celesta), harp, violin I, violin II, viola, violoncello, double bass.
Commissioned by: Pacific Symphony Orchestra.
Call no.: **2003/027**

592. Danielpour, Richard, 1956– An American requiem: for chorus, orchestra, and soloists (2001). New York, NY: Associated Music Publishers, 2001 (1/22/03 printing).
1 score (204 p.); 36 cm.
Latin and English words from various sources; also printed as text with English translation.
"To the memory of those who died in the wake of the tragic events of September 11, 2001; and in tribute to the American soldier—past, present, and future"—caption.
Duration: ca. 60:00.
Composed for: mezzo-soprano, tenor, baritone, SATB chorus, 3 flutes (2nd also alto flute, 3rd also piccolo), 3 oboes (3rd also English horn), 3 clarinets (3rd also bass clarinet), 3 bassoons (3rd also contrabassoon), 4 horns (all also Wagner tuba), 3 trumpets, 2 trombones, bass trombone, tuba, 6 offstage trombones, timpani, percussion, piano (also celesta), harp, violin I, violin II, viola, violoncello, double bass.
Commissioned by: Pacific Symphony Orchestra.
Call no.: **2004/028**

593. Danielpour, Richard, 1956– An American requiem: for chorus, orchestra, and soloists (2001). New York, NY: Associated Music Publishers, 2002 (1/24/03 printing).
1 score (204 p.); 36 cm.
Latin and English words from various sources; also printed as text with English translation.
"Corrected 6/02"—p. 1.
"To the memory of those who died in the wake of the tragic events of September 11, 2001; and in tribute to the American soldier—past, present, and future"—caption.
Duration: ca. 60:00.
Composed for: mezzo-soprano, tenor, baritone, SATB chorus, 3 flutes (2nd also alto flute, 3rd also piccolo), 3 oboes (3rd also English horn), 3 clarinets (3rd also bass clarinet), 3 bassoons (3rd also contrabassoon), 4 horns (all also Wagner tuba), 3 trumpets, 2 trombones, bass trombone, tuba, 6 offstage trombones, timpani, percussion, piano (also celesta), harp, violin I, violin II, viola, violoncello, double bass.
Commissioned by: Pacific Symphony Orchestra.
Call no.: **2005/040**

594. Danielpour, Richard, 1956– The awakened heart: a symphonic triptych for orchestra, 1990. New York, NY: Associated Music Publishers, 1990.
1 score (168 p.); 36 cm.
Reproduced from holograph.
Duration: ca. 19:00.
Contents: Into the world's night—Epiphany—My hero bares his nerves.
Composed for: 3 flutes (3rd also piccolo), 2 oboes (2nd also English horn), 3 clarinets (3rd also bass clarinet), 3 bassoons (3rd also contrabassoon), 4 horns, 3 trumpets, 3 trombones, tuba, timpani, percussion (xylophone, glockenspiel, tubular bells, tambourine, suspended cymbal, vibraphone, mounted castanets, bass drum, suspended crash cymbals, Chinese cymbal, 2 snare drums, ratchet, triangle, guiro, Chinese cowbell, timbales, 4 roto-toms, floor tom-tom, tom-tom, 3 gongs, brake drum, crotales, marimba), harp, piano, violin I, violin II, viola, violoncello, double bass.
Commissioned by: Baltimore Symphony.
Call no.: **1991/023**

595. Danielpour, Richard, 1956– Concerto for cello and orchestra (1994). New York, NY: Associated Music Publishers, 1994.
1 score (152 p.); 43 cm.
In 1 movement.
"Rev. 11/94"—p. 1.
Duration: ca. 20:00.
Composed for: violoncello, 3 flutes (3rd also piccolo), 2 oboes, English horn, 3 clarinets (3rd also bass clarinet), 3 bassoons (3rd also contrabassoon), 4 horns, 3 trumpets, 3 trombones, timpani, percussion (anvil, bass drum, bongos, brake drum, chimes, cowbell, glockenspiel, 2 gongs, mounted guiro, 2 marimbas, ratchet, roto-toms, snare drum, suspended cymbal, tam-tam, tenor drum, Tibetan bowls, floor tom-tom, vibraphone, xylophone), harp, piano (also celesta), violin I, violin II, viola, violoncello, double bass.
Commissioned by: San Francisco Symphony.
Call no.: **1996/033**

596. Danielpour, Richard, 1956– Concerto for cello and orchestra (1994). New York, NY: Associated Music Publishers, 1994.
1 miniature score (152 p.); 28 cm.
In 1 movement.
"Rev. 11/94"—p. 1.
Duration: ca. 20:00.
Composed for: violoncello, 3 flutes (3rd also piccolo), 2 oboes, English horn, 3 clarinets (3rd also bass clarinet), 3 bassoons (3rd also contrabassoon), 4 horns, 3 trumpets, 3 trombones, timpani, percussion (anvil, bass drum, bongos, brake drum, chimes, cowbell, glockenspiel, 2 gongs, mounted guiro, 2 marimbas, ratchet, roto-toms, snare drum, suspended cymbal, tam-tam, tenor drum, Tibetan bowls, floor tom-tom, vibraphone, xylophone), harp, piano (also celesta), violin I, violin II, viola, violoncello, double bass.
Commissioned by: San Francisco Symphony.
Call no.: **1997/035**

597. Danielpour, Richard, 1956– Concerto for cello and orchestra, 1994: in one movement. New York, NY: Associated Music Publishers, 1994.
1 score (152 p.); 36 cm.
Composed for: violoncello, 3 flutes (3rd also piccolo), 2 oboes, English horn, 3 clarinets (3rd also bass clarinet), 3 bassoons (3rd also contrabassoon), 4 horns, 3 trumpets, 3 trombones, timpani, percussion (anvil, bass drum, bongos, brake drum, chimes, cowbell, glockenspiel, 2 gongs, mounted guiro, 2 marimbas, ratchet, roto-toms, snare drum, suspended cymbal, tam-tam, tenor drum, Tibetan bowls, floor tom-tom, vibraphone, xylophone), harp, piano (also celesta), violin I, violin II, viola, violoncello, double bass.
Commissioned by: San Francisco Symphony.
Call no.: **1995/017**

598. Danielpour, Richard, 1956– Concerto for orchestra: (Zoroastrian riddles). New York, NY: Associated Music Publishers, 1996.

1 score (185 p.); 44 cm.
"Corr. 5/21/96"—p. 1.
Composed for: 3 flutes (2nd–3rd also piccolo), 2 oboes, English horn, 3 clarinets (3rd also bass clarinet), 3 bassoons (3rd also contrabassoon), 4 horns, 3 trumpets, 3 trombones, tuba, timpani, percussion (2 tam-tams, bass drum, xylophone, vibraphone, brake drums, floor tom-toms, snare drum, guiro, bongos, 2 cowbells, glockenspiel, vibraslap, crotales, castanets, tambourine, slapstick, roto-toms, ratchet, suspended cymbals, 2 water gongs, marimba, chimes, switch, timbales, woodblock, metal plate, 2 tom-toms, sandpaper blocks), harp, piano (also celesta), violin I, violin II, viola, violoncello, double bass.
Call no.: **1998/038**

599. Danielpour, Richard, 1956– Elegies. New York, NY: Associated Music, 1999.
1 score (106 p.); 43 cm.
English words by Kim Vaeth; also printed as text.
For mezzo-soprano and baritone with orchestra.
Duration: 33:00.
Contents: Vigil—Lacrimosa—Benediction—Litany—In paradisum.
Composed for: mezzo-soprano, baritone, 3 flutes (3rd also piccolo), 2 oboes (2nd also English horn), 3 clarinets (3rd also bass drum), 2 bassoons, 4 horns, 3 trumpets, 2 trombones, bass trombone, tuba, timpani, percussion (glockenspiel, vibraphone, chimes, floor tom-tom, suspended cymbal, cowbell, brake drum, xylophone, guiro, castanets, ratchet, tam-tam, rute, slapstick, 2 tom-toms), piano (also celesta), violin I, violin II, viola, violoncello, double bass.
Commissioned by: Jacksonville Symphony Association.
Call no.: **2000/039**

600. Danielpour, Richard, 1956– Quintet for piano and strings (1988). N.p.: Associated Music Publishers, 1989.
1 score (94 p.); 28 cm.
Composed for: 2 violins, viola, violoncello, piano.
Commissioned by: Chamber Music Society.
Call no.: **1990/019**

601. Danielpour, Richard, 1956– Sonnets to Orpheus: for soprano and chamber ensemble. Full score. New York, NY: Associated Music Publishers, 1992.
1 score (174 p.); 28 cm.
English words by Rilke, translated into English by Stephen Mitchell.
"Corrected 8/92"—p. 1.
Duration: ca. 28:00.
Contents: Prologue—Dance the orange—Elegy—Tarantella—Anthem—Epilogue.
Composed for: soprano, flute, clarinet, horn, percussion (glockenspiel, vibraphone, tubular bells, triangle), piano (also celesta), violin I, violin II, viola, violoncello, double bass.
Commissioned by: Chamber Music Society of Lincoln Center.
Call no.: **1993/029**

602. Danielpour, Richard, 1956– Sonnets to Orpheus: for soprano and chamber ensemble. Full score. New York, NY: Associated Music Publishers, 1993.
1 score (162 p.); 28 cm.
English words by Rilke, translated into English by Stephen Mitchell; also printed as text.
"Correct as of 12/9/93; not final"—p. 1.
Duration: ca. 28:00.
Contents: Prologue—Dance the orange—Elegy—Tarantella—Anthem—Epilogue.
Composed for: soprano, flute, clarinet, horn, percussion (glockenspiel, vibraphone, tubular bells, triangle), piano (also celesta), violin I, violin II, viola, violoncello, double bass.
Commissioned by: Chamber Music Society of Lincoln Center.
Call no.: **1994/032**

603. Danielpour, Richard, 1956– Urban dances: for brass quintet. New York, NY: Associated Music, 1989.
1 score (66 p.); 36 cm.
Reproduced from manuscript.
Contents: Riddle dance—Burlesque—Shadow dance: dirge—Peripetia.
Composed for: 2 trumpets, horn, trombone, tuba.
Commissioned by: Saturday Brass Quintet and Chamber Music America.
Call no.: **1992/027**

604. Danielpour, Richard, 1956– Violin concerto: a fool's paradise (1999). New York, NY: Associated Music Publishers, 2000.
1 score (180 p.); 36 cm.
Duration: 30:00.
Composed for: violin, 3 flutes (3rd also piccolo), 3 oboes (3rd also English horn), 3 clarinets (2nd also A clarinet and bass clarinet), 4 horns, 3 trumpets, 2 trombones, bass trombone, tuba, timpani, percussion (water gong, crotales, mounted castanets, bass drums, claves, crash cymbals, tom-toms, slapstick, xylophone, vibraslap, chimes, marimba, vibraphone, mounted guiro, suspended cymbal, hi-hat, tam-tam, rute, floor tom-tom, snare drum, unmounted guiro, tambourine), piano

(also celesta), harp, violin I, violin II, viola, violoncello, double bass.
Commissioned by: Saratoga Performing Arts Center and Philadelphia Orchestra.
Call no.: **2002/036**

605. Daniels, Melvin L., 1931– One of the pretty ones: an opera in six scenes. N.p.: n.p., 1984.
1 condensed score (55 p.); 28 cm.
Words by A. C. Greene and M. L. Daniels.
Story by A. C. Greene.
Reproduced from manuscript.
Duration: 45:00.
Composed for: soprano, 3 mezzo-sopranos, 3 altos, 2 tenors, 2 baritones, 2 basses, SATB chorus, orchestra.
Call no.: **1985/046**

606. Dapelo, Riccardo, 1962– Rêve d'un papillon. N.p.: n.p., 1992.
1 score (55 p.); 30 cm.
For orchestra.
Duration: ca. 16:00.
Performance instructions in Italian.
Composed for: flute, clarinet, bass clarinet, trumpet, bass trombone, percussion (3 woodblocks, 3 temple blocks, 2 bongos, 3 tom-toms, snare drum, claves, vibraphone, large tam-tam, large gong, 2 bell plates, 2 small crotales, whip, 3 suspended cymbals), harpsichord, harp, marimba, violin I, violin II, viola, violoncello, double bass.
Call no.: **1994/033**

607. Daugherty, Michael, 1954– MotorCity triptych: for orchestra. New York, NY: Peermusic, 2001.
1 score (225 p.); 36 cm.
Duration: ca. 30:00.
Includes biographical information and program notes by the composer in English.
Contents: Motown Mondays—Pedal to the metal—Rosa Parks Boulevard.
Composed for: piccolo, 3 flutes, 2 oboes, English horn, clarinet in E♭, clarinet, bass clarinet, 2 bassoons, contrabassoon, 4 horns, 4 trumpets, 2 trombones, bass trombone, tuba, timpani, percussion (claves, ride cymbal, djembe, Middle Eastern tambourine, Cameroon pod rattles on string, ratchet, vibraphone, suspended cymbal, glockenspiel, xylophone, tam-tam, whip, finger cymbals, brake drum, chimes, Chinese gong, 3 splash cymbals, bass drum, vibraslap, mechanical siren, Indian temple bells, woodblocks, 3 triangles, ride cymbal, 4 tom-toms), harp, violin I, violin II, viola, violoncello, double bass.
Commissioned by: Detroit Symphony Orchestra.
Call no.: **2003/028**

608. Davidovsky, Mario, 1934– Concertante: for string quartet & orchestra (1989). New York, NY: C. F. Peters Corp., 1990.
1 score (73 p.); 44 cm.
Reproduced from manuscript.
Composed for: 2 violins, viola, violoncello, 3 flutes (all also piccolo and alto flute), oboe, English horn, 2 clarinets (2nd also bass clarinet), contrabass clarinet, bassoon, 4 horns, 3 trumpets, 3 trombones, tuba, percussion (timpani, tambourine, vibraphone, 2 tam-tams, castanet, glockenspiel, ratchet, claves, hi-hat, 5 tom-toms, bongo, 5 temple blocks, guiro, cymbals, tubular bells, crotales, 3 cowbells, 2 triangles, bass drum, timbales, snare drum, 2 sizzle cymbals, 3 woodblocks,), harp, piano, violin I, violin II, viola, violoncello, double bass.
Commissioned by: Philadelphia Orchestra.
Call no.: **1991/024**

609. Davidovsky, Mario, 1934– Shulamit's dream: for soprano and orchestra. New York, NY: C. F. Peters, 1993.
1 score (47 p.); 44 cm.
English words; also printed as text.
Reproduced from manuscript.
Composed for: soprano, 3 flutes (3rd also piccolo and alto flute), oboe, English horn, 2 clarinets, bass clarinet, bassoon, contrabassoon, 4 horns, 3 trumpets, 3 trombones, tuba, timpani, percussion (2 sizzle cymbals, 2 triangles, medium suspended cymbal, 5 tam-tams, 2 tambourines, ratchet, 2 sets of claves, 5 tom-toms, bongo, vibraphone, 3 woodblocks, 2 maracas, castanets, timbales, bass drum, tubular bells, marimba, glockenspiel, 5 temple blocks, 3 cowbells), harp, piano, violin I, violin II, viola, violoncello, double bass.
Commissioned by: San Francisco Symphony.
Call no.: **1994/034**

610. Davidson, Tina, 1952– They come dancing: for full orchestra. N.p.: T. Davidson, 1996.
1 score (95 p.); 36 cm.
"8/96"—p. 1.
Composed for: piccolo, 2 flutes, 2 oboes, English horn, 2 clarinets, bass clarinet, 2 bassoons, contrabassoon, 4 horns, 3 trumpets, 2 trombones, tuba, percussion (vibraphone, glockenspiel, temple blocks, tenor drums, large cymbal, snare drum, cowbells, bass drum, timpani, marimba, tam-tam, glockenspiel, tom-toms), piano, violin I, violin II, viola, violoncello, double bass.
Commissioned by: Meet the Composer/Reader's Digest Commissioning Program, Women's Philharmonic, Westmoreland Symphony Orchestra, New Orchestra

of Westchester, and Roanoke Symphony.
Call no.: **2000/040**

611. Davies, Peter Maxwell, 1934– Antarctic symphony: (Symphony no. 8). Full score. N.p.: Boosey & Hawkes, 2002.
1 score (126 p.); 31 cm.
Duration: 40:00.
Composer's program notes in English, German, and French.
Composed for: piccolo, 2 flutes, 2 oboes, English horn, 2 clarinets in A, bass clarinet, 2 bassoons, double bassoon, 4 horns, 3 trumpets, 3 trombones, tuba, timpani (with Japanese temple gong and 2 cymbals), percussion (xylophone, glockenspiel, marimba, crotales, tubular bells, bell tree, very small high woodblock, tambourine, side drum, 2 bass drums [small, very large], Chinese cymbals, crash cymbals, 4 suspended cymbals [very small, small, medium, large], nipple gong, tam-tam [with plastic soapdish], 5 tuned brandy glasses [with water], 2 small pebbles, football rattle, biscuit tin [filled with broken glass], 2 lengths builders' scaffolding [small, medium, large]), celesta, harp, violin I, violin II, viola, cello, double bass.
Commissioned by: Philharmonia Orchestra.
Call no.: **2004/029**

612. Davies, Peter Maxwell, 1934– Caroline Mathilde: a ballet in two acts. London: Chester Music; Bury St. Edmunds, Suffolk: Music Sales, 1990.
1 score (2 v.); 30 cm.
Original work by Flemming Flindt.
Reproduced from manuscript.
Duration: ca. 2:25:00.
Composed for: 2 flutes (2nd also piccolo and alto flute), 2 oboes (2nd also English horn), 2 clarinets (both also clarinet in A, 2nd also bass clarinet), 2 bassoons (2nd also contrabassoon), 2 horns, 2 trumpets, 2 trombones, timpani, percussion (glockenspiel, marimba, crotales, 2 tambourines, bass drum, side drum, 4 suspended cymbals, crash cymbals, tenor drum, flexatone, thundersheet, sandpaper, lion's roar, guiro, jingling johnny, claves, tam-tam, 2 roto-toms, 2 woodblocks, 3 temple blocks, tabor, anvil), violin I, violin II, viola, violoncello, double bass.
Commissioned by: Det Kongelige Teater.
Call no.: **1992/028**

613. Davies, Peter Maxwell, 1934– Symphony no. 3. N.p.: Boosey & Hawkes, 1985.
1 score (242 p.); 30 cm.
Composed for: 3 flutes, alto flute, 2 oboes, English horn, 2 clarinets, bass clarinet, 2 bassoons, contrabassoon, 4 horns, 3 trumpets, 2 trombones, bass trombone, tuba, timpani, violin I, violin II, viola, violoncello, double bass.
Call no.: **1986/030**

614. Davis, Anthony, 1951– Amistad. New York, NY: G. Schirmer, 1997 (11/7/97 printing).
1 score (2 v. [650 p.]); 44 cm.
Words by Thulani Davis.
Opera.
Composed for: voices, SATB chorus, piccolo, 2 flutes, 2 oboes, English horn, 2 clarinets, bass clarinet, 2 bassoons, contrabassoon, 4 horns, 3 trumpets, 3 trombones, tuba, timpani, percussion (chimes, vibraphone, marimba, glockenspiel, 2 African bells, tom-tom, conga, bass drum, snare drum, trap set, xylophone), celesta, harp, violin I, violin II, viola, violoncello, double bass.
Commissioned by: Lyric Opera of Chicago.
Call no.: **1998/039**

615. Davis, Anthony, 1951– Amistad. New York, NY: G. Schirmer, 1998 (12/29/98 printing).
1 score (2 v. (650 p.)); 44 cm.
Words by Thulani Davis.
Opera.
Composed for: voices, SATB chorus, piccolo, 2 flutes, 2 oboes, English horn, 2 clarinets, bass clarinet, 2 bassoons, contrabassoon, 4 horns, 3 trumpets, 3 trombones, tuba, timpani, percussion (chimes, vibraphone, marimba, glockenspiel, 2 African bells, tom-tom, conga, bass drum, snare drum, trap set, xylophone), celesta, harp, violin I, violin II, viola, violoncello, double bass.
Commissioned by: Lyric Opera of Chicago.
Call no.: **2000/041**
Also available:
Call no.: **2000/041 libretto**

616. Davis, Anthony, 1951– Esu variations. New York, NY: G. Schirmer, 1995.
1 score (72 p.); 44 cm.
For orchestra.
Composed for: 4 flutes (2nd also piccolo), 4 oboes, 4 clarinets, 4 bassoons (4th also contrabassoon), 4 horns, 4 trumpets, 2 trombones, bass trombone, tuba, timpani, percussion (vibraphone, glockenspiel, chimes, bells, marimba, drum set), violin I, violin II, viola, violoncello, double bass.
Commissioned by: Atlanta Committee for the Olympic Games Cultural Olympiad.
Call no.: **1996/034**

617. Davis, Anthony, 1951– Esu variations. New York, NY: G. Schirmer, 1995.
1 score (72 p.); 36 cm.
For orchestra.
Composed for: 4 flutes (2nd also piccolo), 4 oboes, 4 clarinets, 4 bassoons (4th also contrabassoon), 4 horns, 4 trumpets, 2 trombones, bass trombone, tuba, timpani, percussion (vibraphone, glockenspiel, chimes, bells, marimba, drum set), violin I, violin II, viola, violoncello, double bass.
Commissioned by: Atlanta Committee for the Olympic Games Cultural Olympiad.
Call no.: **1997/036**

618. Davis, Anthony, 1951– Tania. New York, NY: G. Schirmer, 1992.
1 score (2 v.); 22 cm.
English words.
Opera.
Libretto by Michael-John LaChiusa.
Reproduced from manuscript.
Composed for: soprano saxophone, alto saxophone, tenor saxophone, flute, clarinet, bass clarinet, bassoon, violin, violoncello, piano, celesta, synthesizer, electronic tape, percussion (trap set, vibraphone, marimba, timpani).
Commissioned by: American Music Theater Festival.
Call no.: **1994/035**

619. Davis, Anthony, 1951– Voyage through death to life upon these shores. New York, NY: G. Schirmer, 1991.
1 score (62 p.); 29 cm.
English words by Robert Hayden.
Reproduced from manuscript.
Composed for: soprano, alto, tenor, bass, SATB chorus.
Call no.: **1993/030**
Re-entered as: **1995/018**

620. Davis, Anthony, 1951– X: the life and times of Malcolm X. Chester, NY: G. Schirmer Rental Library, 1987.
1 score (3 v.); 36 cm.
Words by Thulani Davis.
Story by Christopher Davis with assistance from Rhonda Levine.
Opera.
Composed for: 5 sopranos, 5 mezzo-sopranos, 10 tenors, 4 baritones, bass-baritone, bass, 2 flutes (2nd also alto flute), oboe, 3 clarinets (1st also contrabass clarinet, 2nd also bass clarinet), soprano saxophone, alto saxophone, tenor saxophone, bassoon, contrabassoon, 2 horns, 2 trumpets, 2 trombones, bass trombone, timpani, percussion (vibraphone, marimba, trap set), piano, celesta, harp, electric bass, violin I, violin II, viola, violoncello, double bass.
Call no.: **1988/023**
Re-entered as: **1989/027** and **1990/021**
Also available:
Call no.: **1990/021 libretto**

621. Davis, William Mac, 1953– The city of light. TX: n.p., 1989.
1 score (84 leaves); 44 cm.
English words.
For tenor, baritone and soprano solo, narrator, mixed chorus, and orchestra.
Reproduced from holograph.
Contents: Prologue and adoration—Tribulation and judgement—Revelation and triumph.
Composed for: narrator, tenor, baritone, soprano, SATB chorus, 3 flutes (3rd also piccolo), 2 oboes, 2 clarinets, bass clarinet, 2 bassoons, 4 horns, 3 trumpets, 3 trombones, tuba, timpani, percussion (4 tom-toms, bass drum, suspended cymbal, tenor drum, tam-tam, vibraphone, orchestra bells, xylophone, cymbals, chimes, wind chimes, triangle, snare drum), harp, piano, violin I, violin II, viola, violoncello, double bass.
Call no.: **1990/020**

622. Davye, John J., 1929– Four days from my life: ballet in five scenes. N.p.: John J. Davye, 1990.
1 score (34 p.); 43 cm.
For instrumental ensemble.
Reproduced from manuscript.
Contents: Funeral—The party—The wedding—Married life—Funeral: concluded.
Composed for: flute (also alto flute), clarinet (also bass clarinet), trumpet, trombone, percussion (bass drum, 4 tom-toms, claves, 5 temple blocks, tam-tam, suspended cymbal, chimes, drum set [ride cymbal, snare drum, bass drum, hi-hat], ratchet, slide whistle, duck call), organ, 2 violins, viola, violoncello.
Call no.: **1991/025**

623. Dawson, Sarah, 1952– Divinity dwells under seal: song cycle for soprano & orchestra. Boulder, CO: Sarah Dawson, 1991.
1 score (44 p.); 44 cm.
English words by Emily Dickinson; also printed as text.
Reproduced from manuscript.
Duration: ca. 18:00.
Composed for: soprano, 2 flutes, 2 oboes, 2 clarinets (2nd also bass clarinet), 2 bassoons (2nd also contrabassoon), 2 horns, 2 trumpets, trombone, 3 timpani (also sizzle cymbal), harp, violin I, violin II, viola, violon-

cello, double bass.
Commissioned by: Women's Philharmonic.
Call no.: **1992/029**

624. Dawson, Sarah, 1952– Kernos. New York, NY: Sarah Dawson, 1998.
55 p. of music; 28 cm.
Reproduced from holograph.
Composed for: piano.
Call no.: **2003/029**

625. Dayer, Xavier, 1972– Le marin: opéra de chambre d'après le texte de Fernando Pessoa. Drize, Suisse: Editions Papillon, 1999.
1 score (235 p.); 30 cm.
French words.
Reproduced from manuscript.
Composed for: 3 sopranos, onstage clarinet, onstage alto saxophone, onstage violoncello, flute (also alto flute and piccolo), oboe (also English horn), clarinet (also bass clarinet and clarinet in E♭), bassoon (also contrabassoon), horn, trumpet, trombone (also bass trombone), percussion (2 suspended cymbals, crotales, 6 gongs, vibraphone, tam-tam, 3 Chinese cup gongs, snare drum, large newspaper, rain stick, large pane of glass set on a metal basin, 2 triangles, tubular bells, marimba, 2 bongos, 2 tom-toms, maracas, bass drum), piano (also celesta), 2 violins, viola, violoncello, double bass.
Commissioned by: Festival Amadeus (Meinier / Genève).
Call no.: **2002/037**

626. De Rossi Re, Fabrizio, 1960– Concerto: per arpa e orchestra (1998). Partitura. Milano: Casa Musicale Sonzogno di Piero Ostali, 1998.
1 score (46 p.); 30 cm.
Reproduced from holograph.
Composed for: harp, 2 flutes (1st also piccolo), 2 oboes, 2 clarinets, 2 bassoons, 2 horns, 2 trumpets, 2 trombones, percussion, celesta, violin I, violin II, viola, violoncello, double bass.
Commissioned by: Orchestra Regionale del Lazio.
Call no.: **2004/031**

627. De Sutter, Rudy, 1955– Requiem. N.p.: n.p., 1986.
1 score (1 v.); 30 cm.
Latin words.
Reproduced from manuscript.
Composed for: voice, SATB chorus, synthesizers, samplers, computer, percussion.
Call no.: **1991/029**

628. Deak, John, 1943– Jack and the beanstalk: concerto for contrabass and orchestra. N.p.: Jon Deak, 1991.
1 score (155 p.); 44 cm.
English words.
Includes speaking parts for the instrumentalists.
Based on the fairy tale, adapted by the composer.
Reproduced from manuscript.
Composed for: double bass, piccolo, 2 flutes, 2 oboes, 2 clarinets (2nd also bass clarinet), 2 bassoons (2nd also contrabassoon), 4 horns, 2 trumpets, 2 trombones, tuba, timpani, percussion (bass drum, glockenspiel, tubular chimes, woodblocks, duck call, cowbells, hammer on wood, police whistle, tam-tam, sandpaper blocks, snare drum, cymbals, suspended cymbal, temple blocks, claves, slide whistle, tom-toms, acme siren, train whistle, ratchet, bicycle horn, hi-hat, Chinese opera gong, warbling whistle, goose call, slapstick, tambourine, guiro, dog bark), harp, violin I, violin II, viola, violoncello, double bass.
Commissioned by: National Symphony Orchestra.
Call no.: **1992/030**

629. Dean, Brett, 1961– Beggars and angels: for orchestra, 1999. Berlin: Boosey & Hawkes/Bote & Bock, 2004.
1 score (75 p.); 42 cm.
"Rev. 01/04"—caption.
Duration: ca. 20:00.
Includes biographical information and program notes in English and German.
Composed for: 4 flutes (also piccolo and alto flute), 3 oboes (also English horn), 3 clarinets (also clarinet in E♭ and bass clarinet), bass clarinet, 3 bassoons (also contrabassoon), 6 horns, 4 trumpets, 3 trombones (also bass trombone), tuba, timpani, percussion (vibraphone, xylophone, glockenspiel, roto-toms, sizzle cymbal, rain stick, ratchet, 2 bongos, snare drum, drum kit, tubular bells, cymbals, 3 Chinese cymbals, tambourine, 3 tam-tams, tom-toms, 5 suspended cymbals, whip, tenor drum, 3 woodblocks, cabasa, marimba, 3 triangles, crotales, large bass drum, 2 metal lids, 5 tuned metal plates), harp, piano (also celesta), violin I, violin II, viola, violoncello, double bass.
Commissioned by: Symphony Australia.
Call no.: **2005/041**

630. Dean, Brett, 1961– Carlo: music for strings, sampler & tape (1997). Partitur. Berlin: Boosey & Hawkes: Bote & Bock, 2000.
1 score (65 p.); 31 cm.
Prerecorded tape includes excerpts from madrigal Moro lasso by C. Gesualdo.

Duration: ca. 21:00.
Preface in English and German.
Composed for: 8 violins, 3 violas, 3 violoncellos, double bass, sampler, tape.
Commissioned by: Australian Chamber Orchestra.
Call no.: **2002/041**

631. Dean, Brett, 1961– Carlo: music for strings, sampler, and tape (1997). Full score. Berlin: Boosey & Hawkes: Bote & Bock, 2000.
1 score (71 p.); 31 cm.
Prerecorded tape includes excerpts from madrigal Moro lasso by C. Gesualdo.
Duration: ca. 20:00.
Preface in English and German.
Composed for: 8 violins, 3 violas, 3 violoncellos, double bass, sampler, tape.
Commissioned by: Australian Chamber Orchestra.
Call no.: **2003/031**

632. Deane, Raymond, 1953– The wall of cloud: chamber opera in prologue and three acts, 1997. Dublin: Contemporary Music Centre, 1997.
1 score (235 p.); 30 cm.
English words; libretto by the composer.
Based on the 8th century Chinese play Ch'ien's soul leaves her body.
Reproduced from manuscript.
Composed for: 2 sopranos, mezzo-soprano, tenor, flute (also alto flute, piccolo, small ocarina, descant recorder, auxiliary percussion), clarinet (also bass clarinet and auxiliary percussion), percussion (bongos, bodhran, log drum, woodblocks, glockenspiel, gong, suspended cymbal, rin [Korean prayer bowls], wood chimes, metal chimes), harp, violin (also auxiliary percussion), violoncello (also auxiliary percussion), double bass.
Commissioned by: Opera Theatre Company.
Call no.: **2001/045**
Also available:
Call no.: **2001/045 vocal score**

633. Decker, Pamela, 1955– Nightsong and ostinato dances: for organ. Boston, MA: Wayne Leupold, 1994.
31 p. of music; 31 cm.
Composed for: organ.
Call no.: **1996/035**

634. DeGaetano, Robert, 1952– The Challenger: for piano solo. N.p.: R. DeGaetano, 1987.
85 leaves of music; 28 cm.
Reproduced from holograph.
Contents: Maestoso (Challenger theme)—Militaire (Mike Smith)—Broad, lyrical & serious (Ellison Onizuka)—Moderato (Christa McAuliffe)—Fast & accurate (Gregory Jarvis)—Slow & deliberate (Dick Scobee)—Espressivo (Ronald McNair)—Driven (Judith Resnik).
Composed for: piano.
Commissioned by: Alice Tully.
Call no.: **1988/024**

635. Del Tredici, David, 1937– Child Alice: part II.
Call no.: **1985/047a**
No materials available.

636. Del Tredici, David, 1937– Dracula: for soprano and thirteen instruments. New York, NY: Boosey & Hawkes, 1999.
1 score (156 p.); 31 cm.
English words by Alfred Corn; also printed as text.
Duration: ca. 20:00.
Includes program notes.
Composed for: amplified soprano-narrator, flute (also piccolo), clarinet (also bass clarinet), trumpet, horn, percussion (xylophone, tubular bells, bar chimes, glass wind chimes, guiro, 2 bongo drums, crash cymbals, 2 woodblocks, 2 timpani, bass drum, triangle, 2 suspended cymbals, 2 tam-tams, snare drum, tenor drum, low conga, hi-hat, 5 temple blocks, ratchet, tambourine, high siren, large anvil, large wind machine), theremin, piano (also celesta), violin I, violin II, viola, violoncello, double bass.
Commissioned by: Eos Orchestra.
Call no.: **2002/042**

637. Del Tredici, David, 1937– Gay life: a cycle of six songs: for amplified baritone and orchestra, 2000. 1st ed., uncorrected. New York: Boosey & Hawkes, 2000.
1 score (170 p.); 36 cm.
English words; also printed as text.
Texts by Michael D. Calhoun, W. H. Kidde, Allen Ginsberg, Paul Monette, and Thom Gunn.
Composed for: amplified baritone, 3 flutes (2nd–3rd also piccolo), 3 oboes (3rd also English horn), 3 clarinets (3rd also clarinet in E♭), bass clarinet, 3 bassoons (3rd also contrabassoon), 4 horns, 3 trumpets, 3 trombones, tuba, timpani, percussion (xylophone, vibraphone, marimba, tubular bells, glockenspiel, crotales, crash cymbals, large and small suspended cymbals, large and small tam-tams, triangle, tambourine, cowbell, ratchet, whip, castanets, guiro, glass wind chimes, 2 woodblocks, 5 temple blocks, bass drum, snare drum, tenor drum, 2 bongo drums, siren, large wind ma-

chine), celesta, harpsichord, harp, violin I, violin II, viola, violoncello, double bass.
Commissioned by: San Francisco Symphony and Michael Tilson Thomas.
Call no.: **2003/032**

638. Del Tredici, David, 1937– Grand trio: for violin, cello and piano. N.p.: n.p., 2001.
1 score (67 p.); 28 cm.
Composed for: violin, violoncello, piano.
Commissioned by: Clarice Smith Performing Arts Center at University of Maryland.
Call no.: **2004/032**

639. Del Tredici, David, 1937– The spider and the fly: for high soprano, high baritone and orchestra. New York, NY: Boosey & Hawkes, 1998.
1 score (290 p.); 36 cm.
English words by Mary Howitt; also printed as text.
Composed for: soprano, baritone, 3 flutes (2nd–3rd also piccolo), 3 oboes (3rd also English horn), 4 clarinets (3rd also clarinet in E♭, 4th also bass clarinet), 3 bassoons (3rd also contrabassoon), 4 horns, 3 trumpets, 3 trombones, tuba, timpani, percussion (glockenspiel, vibraphone, tambourine, glass wind chimes, ratchet, claves, large whip, tenor drum, 2 timbales, 3 tom-toms, snare drum, large wind machine, bell tree, 5 temple blocks, castanets, marimba, large tam-tam, 2 suspended cymbals, crash cymbals, bass drum, triangle, 2 bongos, 2 woodblocks, xylophone, tubular bells, guiro, 2 cowbells, anvil), celesta, harp, violin I, violin II, viola, violoncello, double bass.
Commissioned by: Philharmonic-Symphony Society of New York.
Call no.: **2000/042**
Re-entered as: **2001/046**

640. Del Tredici, David, 1937– Steps: for orchestra (1990). New York, NY: Boosey & Hawkes, 1990.
1 miniature score (200 p.); 36 cm.
Reproduced from manuscript.
Contents: Giant steps—Giant giant steps—Stepping down.
Composed for: 4 flutes (3rd–4th also piccolo), 3 oboes (3rd also English horn), 3 clarinets (3rd also clarinet in E♭), bass clarinet, 3 bassoons (3rd also contrabassoon), 4 horns, 4 trumpets, 4 trombones, tuba, timpani, percussion (snare drum, 2 timbales, 2 bongos, 2 congas, tenor drum, bass drum, 2 suspended cymbals, tam-tam, crash cymbals, tambourine, rachet, anvil, guiro, maracas, whip, siren, wind machine, glass wind chimes, triangle, 2 cowbells, 2 woodblocks, 2 temple blocks, xylophone, glockenspiel, vibraphone, marimba, tubular bells), harp, celesta, violin I, violin II, viola, violoncello, double bass.
Commissioned by: New York Philharmonic and Meet the Composer Orchestra Residencies Program.
Call no.: **1991/027**

641. Delz, Christoph, 1950–1993. Im Dschungel: Ehrung für Rousseau den Zöllner = In the jungle: homage to Rousseau the customs officer. 3rd ed. Partitur. Binningen, Switzerland: Christoph Delz, 1984.
1 score (72 p.); 42 cm.
Reproduced from holograph.
Includes performance instructions in German and English.
Contents: Im Dschungel—Yadwigha: Der Traum.
Composed for: 5 flutes (2nd also alto flute, 1st and 3rd–5th also piccolo), 3 oboes (3rd also oboe d'amore), English horn, 3 clarinets (2nd–3rd also clarinet in E♭), bass clarinet, soprano saxophone, alto saxophone, tenor saxophone, 2 bassoons, contrabassoon, 6 horns (3rd–6th also Wagner tuba), 3 trumpets, bass trumpet, 3 trombones, contrabass tuba, percussion (timpani, 2 bass drums, 2 side drums, congas, 2 tom-toms, bongos, African slit drum, lion's roar, 2 tambourines, xylophone, 2 temple blocks, woodblock, crash cymbals, suspended cymbal, 4 tam-tams, thundersheet, anvil, 2 hammers, wood, 3 sistrums, 4 maracas, 2 slapsticks, 8 finger cymbals, mounted rattle, 2 cowbells, referee whistle, circular saw), harp, violin I, violin II, viola, violoncello, double bass.
Commissioned by: Staatliche Musikkredit-Kommission Basel.
Call no.: **1985/048**

642. Dembski, Stephen, 1949– Sonata for violin and piano. N.p.: n.p., 1988.
1 score (95 p.); 28 cm.
Reproduced from holograph.
Composed for: violin, piano.
Commissioned by: James Buswell, Ronald Copes, and Gregory Fulkerson.
Call no.: **1989/028**
Re-entered as: **1990/022**

643. Dembski, Stephen, 1949– Spectra. N.p.: n.p., 1985.
1 score (101 p.); 28 cm.
For chamber orchestra.
"Written for the chamber orchestra PRISM, and first performed on April 3, 1985."
Reproduced from holograph.
Composed for: flute, oboe, clarinet, bassoon, horn, trumpet, percussion (vibraphone, cymbals), violin I, violin

II, viola, violoncello, double bass.
Commissioned by: PRISM Camber Orchestra.
Call no.: **1986/031**

644. Demos, Nick, 1962– New world sketches: for traditional Greek folk instruments & string orchestra. Study score. N.p.: Nick J. Demos, 2000.
1 miniature score (65 p.); 28 cm.
Duration: 28:22.
Program notes by the composer.
Contents: Ellis Island, 1917—Lullaby for Louis—Promised land—Songs for my fathers.
Composed for: clarinet, violin, bouzouki, dumbek, violin I, violin II, viola, violoncello, double bass.
Call no.: **2003/033**

645. Dench, Chris, 1953– Afterimages: for 21 instrumentalists. Grosvenor Place, NSW: Australian Music Centre, 1987.
1 score (various pagings); 37 cm.
Reproduced from holograph.
Duration: ca. 12:30.
Includes performance instructions.
Composed for: flute (also piccolo and alto flute), 2 oboes (1st also English horn and bass oboe, 2nd also English horn and oboe d'amore), clarinet in E♭ (also clarinet in A and bass clarinet), clarinet (also alto clarinet), alto clarinet (also contrabass clarinet), 2 baritone saxophones (1st also soprano and tenor saxophones, 2nd also alto saxophone), trumpet (also piccolo trumpet and flugelhorn), alto trombone, 2 bass trombones (1st also trombone), percussion (bass drum, tenor drum, 2 cowbells, 2 woodblocks, 2 gongs, 2 cymbals, sizzle cymbal, tubular bells, lion's roar, 4 tam-tams, bongo, timbal, conga, snare drum, bongo, crotales), 2 violins, viola, 2 violoncellos, double bass.
Commissioned by: BBC.
Call no.: **1992/032**

646. Dench, Chris, 1953– Dé/ployé: for piccolo. London: United Music Publishers Ltd., 1990.
13 p. of music; 30 x 43 cm.
Composed for: piccolo.
Commissioned by: Laura Chislett.
Call no.: **1990/023 no.2**

647. Dench, Chris, 1953– Sulle scale della fenice: for flute. London: United Music Publishers Ltd., 1989.
18 p. of music; 30 x 43 cm.
Reproduced from manuscript.
Duration: 10:00.
Composed for: flute.
Call no.: **1990/023 no.3**

648. Dench, Chris, 1953– Vier darmstädter Aphorismen: for solo flutist. London: United Music Publishers Ltd., 1990.
20 p. of music; 30 x 43 cm.
Contents: Venezia: flute—Dark neumes. Piccolo fragment: piccolo—Artaud: bass flute—Gelb: violett: alto flute.
Composed for: flute (also piccolo, alto flute, bass flute).
Call no.: **1990/023 no.1**

649. Denev, Ljubomir, 1951– Homo ludens: symphonic variations for violoncello and orchestra. Full score. Sofia, Bulgaria: Musicautor, 1996.
1 score (80 p.); 43 cm.
Duration: 22:20.
Program note by the composer.
Contents: The sprite's hunter—The magic string—Forest sprites' dance—Storm and finale.
Composed for: violoncello, 2 flutes (2nd also piccolo), 2 oboes, 2 clarinets (2nd also bass clarinet), 2 bassoons, 3 horns, 2 trumpets, trombone, timpani, percussion, harp, piano (also celesta), violin I, violin II, viola, violoncello, double bass.
Commissioned by: Bulgarian National Radio.
Call no.: **2003/034**

650. Depraz, Raymond, 1915– Twilight symphony.
Call no.: **1985/049**
No materials available

651. Derfler, Carl, 1950– Symphony: no. 1. N.p.: n.p., 199-?.
1 score (127 p.); 28 cm.
Composed for: 2 flutes, 2 oboes, 2 clarinets, 2 bassoons, 4 horns, 3 trumpets, 3 trombones, tuba, timpani, percussion (orchestral bells, glockenspiel, celesta, suspended cymbal, bass drum, triangle, snare drum, chimes, tambourine, woodblock, xylophone, tubular bells), violin I, violin II, viola, violoncello, double bass.
Call no.: **1998/040**

652. Deussen, Nancy Bloomer, 1931– Concerto for clarinet and small orchestra. N.p.: Brazinmusikanta Publications, 1995.
1 score (39 p.); 36 cm.
Duration: 24:22.
Composed for: clarinet, harp, violin I, violin II, viola, violoncello, double bass, timpani, percussion (triangle, glockenspiel, xylophone, suspended cymbal, tenor drum, woodblock, crash cymbals, gong).
Commissioned by: Richard Nunemaker.
Call no.: **2002/043**

653. Deutsch, Bernd Richard, 1977– Musik zu einem imaginären Drama: für Kammerorchester (Nr. 5, 1999). Partitur. Wien: Doblinger, 2000.
1 score (118 p.); 42 cm.
Reproduced from manuscript.
Duration: ca. 17:00.
Composed for: 2 flutes (1st also piccolo, 2nd also alto flute), 2 oboes (2nd also English horn), 2 clarinets (2nd also bass clarinet), 2 bassoons (2nd also contrabassoon), 2 trumpets, 2 horns, percussion (timpani, tambourine, maracas, guiro, 4 woodblocks, 4 bongos, 4 tom-toms, gongs, xylophone, marimba, chimes, glockenspiel, bass drum, snare drum, tam-tam, 4 temple blocks, triangle, flexatone, metal chimes, switch, vibraphone), piano, celesta, violin I, violin II, viola, violoncello, double bass.
Commissioned by: Österreichische Kammersymphoniker.
Call no.: **2002/044**

654. Deutsch, Herbert A., 1932– The new Jerusalem: an homage to Charles Ives. N.p.: n.p., 1988.
1 score (32 p.); 44 cm.
English words.
For chorus, offstage brass quartet, and symphonic band.
"Originally Fantasia II on the fugueing [sic] tune New Jerusalem."
"Revised July–October 1988."
Reproduced from holograph.
Composed for: SATB chorus, offstage brass quartet (2 trumpets, 2 trombones), piccolo, 2 flutes, oboe, bassoon, 3 clarinets, bass clarinet, 2 alto saxophones, tenor saxophone, baritone saxophone, 2 horns, 3 trumpets, 2 trombones, euphonium, tuba, timpani, synthesizer, percussion (xylophone, vibraphone, snare drum, bass drum, glockenspiel, Chinese woodblock, triangle, crash cymbals, field drum, chime).
Call no.: **1991/030**

655. Deutsch, Herbert A., 1932– TRANSCENDance: symphony in one movement: for symphonic wind ensemble. N.p.: n.p., 1991.
1 score (61 p.); 44 cm.
Reproduced from holograph.
Composed for: piccolo, 2 flutes, oboe, clarinet in E♭, 3 clarinets, alto clarinet, bassoon, 2 alto saxophones (1st also soprano saxophone), tenor saxophone, baritone saxophone, 3 cornets, flugelhorn, 2 horns, bass trombone, baritone, double bass, electric bass, timpani (also timbales), percussion (glockenspiel, vibraphone, sleigh bells, suspended cymbal, temple blocks, crash cymbals, snare drum, bass drum, hi-hat, gong, woodblocks, wind chimes, bell tree, sizzle cymbal, bongos, cowbell, claves, mounted tambourine).
Commissioned by: Hofstra University Wind Ensemble.
Call no.: **1993/031**

656. Di Vittorio, Salvatore, 1967– Sinfonia no. 2: "Lost innocence," 1997. N.p.: Salvatore Di Vittorio, 1997.
1 score (39 p.); 44 cm.
Reproduced from manuscript.
Duration: ca. 12:00.
Contents: Requiem for a child; March, on lost innocence—Dance of tears—Child-heart, song of truth; Revelation: the abandoned cradle—Elegy, for man.
Composed for: 2 flutes (2nd also piccolo), 2 oboes, 2 clarinets, 2 bassoons, 4 horns, 2 trumpets, 3 trombones, tuba, timpani, percussion (glockenspiel, finger cymbals, chimes, antique cymbals, hand cymbals, xylophone, snare drum, tam-tam, bass drum), harp, piano (also celesta), violin I, violin II, viola, violoncello, double bass.
Call no.: **1998/041**

657. Diaconoff, Ted, 1928– Concerto for cello and chamber orchestra (1985). N.p.: T. Diaconoff, 1985.
1 score (109 p.); 28 cm.
Reproduced from manuscript.
Duration: 22:00.
Composed for: violoncello, 2 flutes, 2 oboes, 2 clarinets, 2 bassoons, 2 horns, violin I, violin II, viola, violoncello, double bass.
Call no.: **1986/032**

658. Diamond, David, 1915–2005. Symphony no. 9: for large orchestra and bass-baritone soloist (1984–'85). N.p.: n.p., 1985.
1 miniature score (158 p.); 34 cm.
English words.
Reproduced from holograph.
At end of score: "25 March, 1984–28 July, 1985; Rochester, N.Y."
Duration: ca. 40:00.
Composed for: bass-baritone, piccolo, 2 flutes (2nd also alto flute), 2 oboes, English horn, clarinet in E♭, 2 clarinets, bass clarinet, 2 bassoons, contrabassoon, 6 horns, piccolo trumpet, 3 trumpets, 3 trombones, tuba, timpani, percussion (snare drum, tenor drum, bass drum, woodblock, large cymbal, large gong, triangle, tambourine, xylophone, glockenspiel, anvil), harp, piano, violin I, violin II, viola, violoncello, double bass.
Call no.: **1986/033**

659. Diamond, David, 1915–2005. Symphony no. ten: (1987; 2000). N.p.: n.p., 2000.
1 score (398 p.); 44 cm.

Reproduced from holograph.
Composed for: piccolo, 2 flutes, 2 oboes, English horn, clarinet in E♭, 2 clarinets, bass clarinet, 2 bassoons, contrabassoon, 4 horns, piccolo trumpet, 3 trumpets, bass trumpet, 2 trombones, bass trombone, tuba, timpani, percussion (tenor drum, snare drum, bass drum, large cymbals, large gong, guiro, triangle, glockenspiel, xylophone, tubular bells), organ, piano, harp, violin I, violin II, viola, violoncello, double bass.
Call no.: **2002/045**

660. Dick, Robert, 1950– Concerto: for flute/bass flute, strings and percussion (1990). N.p.: n.p., 1990.
1 score (36 p.); 43 cm.
Composed for: flute (also bass flute), percussion (timpani, steel drum, vibraphone, 3 suspended cymbals, hi-hat, tam-tam, snare drum, 3 tom-toms, 4 roto-toms, 2 bongos, bass drum, 5 woodblocks, 5 temple blocks, 2 maracas, tambourine), violin I, violin II, viola, violoncello, double bass.
Commissioned by: National Endowment for the Arts.
Call no.: **1991/031**

661. Dick, Robert, 1950– A new prehistory: for mixed sextet: flute (piccolo), B♭ clarinet (bass clarinet), violin, 'cello, piano, percussion, 2001. N.p.: Multiple Breath Music, 2002.
1 score (10 leaves); 22 x 28 cm.
Duration: ca. 15:00.
Composer's notes in English.
Composed for: flute (also piccolo), clarinet (also bass clarinet), violin, violoncello, piano, percussion.
Commissioned by: Koussevitsky Foundation.
Call no.: **2005/042**

662. DiDomenica, Robert, 1927– Jean Genet's The balcony: an opera in two acts: 1972. Score. Newton Centre, MA: Margun Music, 1985.
1 score (a–b, 416 p.); 28 cm.
English words by Bernard Frechtman.
Reproduced from holograph.
Composed for: 2 sopranos, 2 mezzo-sopranos, 2 contraltos, 2 tenors, 2 baritones, 2 basses, SATB chorus, offstage ensemble (trumpet, trombone, chimes), English horn, clarinet in E♭, bass clarinet, soprano saxophone, alto saxophone, tenor saxophone, baritone saxophone, bassoon, contrabassoon, 3 horns, 3 trumpets, 3 trombones, timpani, percussion (snare drum, tenor drum, bass drum, triangle, 3 suspended cymbals, gong, glockenspiel, xylophone, vibraphone, chimes), harp, guitar, violin I, violin II, viola, violoncello, double bass.
Call no.: **1993/032**

663. Diemer, Emma Lou, 1927– Variations for piano, four hands: Homage to Ravel, Schoenberg, and May Aufderheide. Ft. Lauderdale, FL: Plymouth Music Co., 1989.
1 score (44 p.); 31 cm.
Prefatory material by the composer.
Composed for: piano (4 hands).
Call no.: **1991/032**

664. Dijk, Rudi Martinus van, 1932– Concerto for violin and orchestra, 1983/1984. Amsterdam: Donemus, 1991.
1 score (160 p.); 41 cm.
Reproduced from holograph.
Duration: ca. 30:00.
Composed for: violin, 3 flutes (both also alto flute, 3rd also piccolo), 2 oboes, clarinet in E♭, 2 clarinets, 2 bassoons, 4 horns, 2 trumpets, 3 trombones, tuba, timpani, percussion (snare drum, tenor drum, bass drum, triangle, guiro, temple blocks, woodblock, tam-tam, suspended cymbal, crash cymbals, celesta, suspended sizzle cymbal, tubular bells, wind machine), harp, piano, violin I, violin II, viola, violoncello, double bass.
Call no.: **1993/145**

665. Dillon, James, 1950– Blitzschlag: flute and orchestra: 1989–96. London: Edition Peters, 1996.
1 score (58 p.); 43 cm.
Reproduced from manuscript.
Composed for: flute, 2 flutes (1st also piccolo), 2 oboes (2nd also English horn), clarinet in E♭, clarinet, bass clarinet, 2 bassoons, contrabassoon, 3 horns, 2 trumpets, 2 trombones, tuba, timpani, percussion (triangle, tubular bells, crotales, thundersheet, glockenspiel, temple blocks, metal sheet, 2 spring coils, xylorimba, sizzle cymbal, sleigh bells, gongs, cowbells, crotales, vibraphone, cymbals, waterphone, bongos, bass drum, mark tree, 2 tam-tams), violin I, violin II, viola, violoncello, double bass.
Commissioned by: Radio France.
Call no.: **2000/043**

666. Dillon, James, 1950– Helle Nacht: orchestra. Full score. London; New York, NY: Edition Peters, 1988.
1 score (85 p.); 42 cm.
Duration: 28:00.
Composed for: 3 flutes (all also piccolo, 3rd also alto flute), 3 oboes (3rd also English horn), 3 clarinets (3rd also bass clarinet and contrabass clarinet), 3 bassoons (3rd also contrabassoon), 4 horns, 3 trumpets, 3 trombones (3rd also bass trombone), tuba, percussion (timpani, tambourine, triangle, tam-tam, glockenspiel, snare drum, 2 gongs, mark tree, tubular bells, 3 cow-

bells, sleigh bells, crotales, 2 bongos, anvil, 2 suspended cymbals, suspended bell, maracas, marimba, bass drum, gong, ratchet, 4 tom-toms), harp, piano, violin I, violin II, viola, violoncello, double bass.
Commissioned by: BBC.
Call no.: **1990/024**

667. Dillon, James, 1950– Ignis noster: orchestra, 1991–92. London; New York, NY: Edition Peters, 1992.
1 score (80 p.); 42 cm.
Reproduced from manuscript.
Composed for: 4 flutes (2nd also piccolo), 4 oboes (4th also English horn), 4 clarinets (4th also bass clarinet), 4 bassoons (4th also contrabassoon), 6 horns, 5 trumpets, 4 trombones, tuba, 2 sets of timpani, percussion (tubular bells, glockenspiel, Javanese gongs, Caribbean steel drums, 3 spring coils, Chinese cymbal, whip, tubular bass bells, vibraphone, 2 triangles, military snare drum, tambourine, lion's roar, xylophone, 3 cowbells, 3 tam-tams, snare drum, 4 tom-toms, bass drum, crotales, 2 suspended cymbals, 2 bongos, 2 congas, woodblock), piano (also celesta, harmonium), harp, violin I, violin II, viola, violoncello, double bass.
Commissioned by: BBC Promenade Concerts.
Call no.: **1995/020**

668. Dillon, James, 1950– String quartet, 1983. London; New York, NY: Edition Peters, 1984.
1 miniature score (36 p.); 30 cm.
Reproduced from manuscript.
Composed for: 2 violins, viola, violoncello.
Commissioned by: Huddersfield Contemporary Musical Festival.
Call no.: **1985/050**

669. Dillon, James, 1950– Überschreiten: chamber orchestra. Score. London; New York, NY: Edition Peters, 1986.
1 score (111 p.); 31 cm.
Includes instructions for performance in English.
Composed for: flute (also piccolo and alto flute), oboe, clarinet, bass clarinet, bassoon (also contrabassoon), horn, trumpet, trombone (also bass trombone), tuba, percussion (tubular bells, crotales, suspended bell, 8 gongs, glockenspiel, suspended cymbal, tam-tam, anvil, metal sheet, triangle, snare drum, 5 tom-toms, bass drum), piano (also Hammond organ), 2 violins, viola, violoncello, double bass.
Commissioned by: London Sinfonietta.
Call no.: **1988/025**

670. Dillon, James, 1950– Violin concerto. Full score. London; New York, NY: Edition Peters, 2000.
1 score (51 p.); 42 cm.
Composed for: violin, piccolo, flute, alto flute, 2 oboes, English horn, 2 clarinets, bass clarinet, 2 bassoons, contrabassoon, 4 horns, 3 trumpets, 2 trombones, bass trombone, tuba, timpani, percussion (sand block, sleigh bells, bodhran, tam-tam, temple block, sizzle cymbal, tambourine, bongos, 3 triangles, xylophone, metal chimes, glockenspiel, gong, crotales, lion's roar, bass drum), harp, piano, violin I, violin II, viola, violoncello, double bass.
Commissioned by: BBC.
Call no.: **2002/046**

671. Dillon, Lawrence, 1959– Appendage: for soprano, violin, viola, cello, clarinet in B♭, tenor saxophone and piano, 1993. New York, NY: American Composers Editions, 1993.
1 score (108 p.); 28 cm.
English and French words; words of "Last lullabye" also printed as text.
Contents: Appendage—Tes yeux—Warm eyes—Appendage—Recognition—Last lullabye.
Composed for: soprano, violin, viola, violoncello, clarinet, tenor saxophone, piano.
Call no.: **2000/044**

672. Dillon, Lawrence, 1959– Furies and muses: for bassoon and string quartet (1997). New York, NY: American Composers Alliance, 1997.
1 score (67 p.); 28 cm.
Duration: ca. 26:00.
Biographical information follows score.
Composed for: bassoon, 2 violins, viola, violoncello.
Call no.: **2003/035**

673. Dillon, Lawrence, 1959– String quartet no. 1 in D/E♭: jests and tenderness (1998). New York, NY: American Composers Editions, 1998.
1 score (63 p.); 28 cm.
Composed for: 2 violins, viola, violoncello.
Call no.: **2002/047**

674. Dillon, Lawrence, 1959– Symphony no. 1: appearance, disappearance, reflection (1998). New York, NY: American Composers Edition, 1998.
1 score (119 p.); 28 cm.
Duration: 30:00.
Composed for: flute (also piccolo), 2 oboes (2nd also English horn), 2 bassoons (2nd also contrabassoon), 2 horns, violin I, violin II, viola, violoncello, double bass.
Commissioned by: Carolina Chamber Symphony.
Call no.: **2001/047**

675. Dinescu, Violeta, 1953– 35. Mai. N.p.: n.p., 198-?.
1 score (2 v.); 30 cm.
German words.
Children's opera in 7 scenes.
Libretto by the composer after the book by Erich Kästner.
Reproduced from manuscript.
Composed for: voices, flute, oboe, clarinet, bassoon, horn, trumpet, trombone, percussion (xylophone, triangle, vibraphone, tambourine, cymbals, timpani, ratchet, flexatone, bongos, glockenspiel, antique cymbals, chimes, Chinese cymbals, 2 tam-tams, wind chimes, bass drum, marimba, tom-toms), harp, organ, celesta, piano, harpsichord, violin I, violin II, viola, violoncello, double bass.
Call no.: **1988/026**

676. Dinescu, Violeta, 1953– Akrostichon: Klangstück für Orchester. Partitur. Berlin: Astoria Verlag, 1983.
1 score (56 p.); 29 cm.
Reproduced from holograph.
Composed for: 2 flutes (1st also piccolo), 2 oboes (2nd also English horn), 2 clarinets, 2 bassoons, 2 horns, 2 trumpets, trombone, percussion (2 cymbals, 2 tam-tams, timpani, triangle, flexatone, vibraphone, marimba, chimes, 3 bongos, 3 tom-toms), violin I, violin II, viola, violoncello, double bass.
Call no.: **1985/051**

677. Dinescu, Violeta, 1953– Der Kreisel: Ballett nach Mörikes Märchen "Die Historie von der schönen Lau." Partitur. Berlin: Astoria, 1984.
1 score (176 p.); 35 cm.
Words by Olaf Göück, Tina Schneider, and Gunther Volz.
Composed for: voices, 2 flutes, 2 oboes, 2 clarinets, 2 bassoons, 4 horns, 2 trumpets, trombone, percussion (cymbals, bells, vibraphone, xylophone, marimba, 2 snare drums, bass drum, 3 bongos, 3 tam-tams, 3 woodblocks, hi-hat, flexatone, timpani, whip, flexatone, 3 triangles), harp, piano (also celesta), organ, violin I, violin II, viola, violoncello, double bass.
Call no.: **1986/034**

678. Distler, Jed, 1956– The death of Lottie Shapiro: a song cycle for four sopranos and piano. N.p.: n.p., 1985.
1 score (various pagings); 34 cm.
English words.
Reproduced from manuscript.
Composed for: 4 sopranos, piano.
Call no.: **1989/029**

679. Dobbins, Lori, 1958– Vision: for chamber orchestra. Newton Centre, MA: GunMar Music, 1997.
1 score (111 p.); 36 cm.
Composed for: 2 flutes (1st also piccolo, 2nd also alto flute), 2 oboes, 2 clarinets (2nd also bass clarinet), 2 bassoons (2nd also contrabassoon), 2 horns, 2 trumpets, percussion (marimba, vibraphone, sizzle cymbal, 2 suspended cymbals, hi-hat, 2 triangles, glass wind chimes, 3 tom-toms, snare drum, small bass drum, glockenspiel, tam-tam, 2 woodblocks, 3 temple blocks, 4 bongos, tambourine, rain stick), violin I, violin II, viola, violoncello, double bass.
Commissioned by: Pro Arte Chamber Orchestra of Boston.
Call no.: **2002/048**

680. Dobrowolny, Miro, 1959– Masken: Annäherung an Pirandello: für Orchester. N.p.: n.p., 1995.
1 score (28 p.); 30 cm.
Based on the play by Pirandello; excerpt printed as text in German.
Reproduced from manuscript.
Composed for: 2 flutes (2nd also piccolo), 2 oboes, 2 clarinets, 2 bassoons (2nd also contrabassoon), 2 horns, 2 trumpets, 2 trombones, timpani, percussion (bass drum, tam-tam, tenor drum, marimba, glockenspiel, cymbals), violin I, violin II, viola, violoncello, double bass.
Call no.: **1996/037**

681. Doherty, Sue, 1956– Present passage: an electronic work for dance. N.p.: n.p., 1988.
1 score (i, 30 leaves); 44 cm.
"Combination of percussion and musique concrete"—leaf i.
Reproduced from manuscript.
Includes performance instructions (leaf 1).
Composed for: electronic sounds.
Call no.: **1990/025**

682. Dolden, Paul, 1956– Entropic twilights. N.p.: n.p., 2000.
1 score (A–F, 140 p.); 36 cm.
For multitrack tape and computer.
Reproduced from manuscript.
Duration: 42:00.
Program notes by the composer and performance instructions (p. A–F).
Contents: Twilight's nomadic desire—Twilight's sleep—Twilight's ritual incantations.
Composed for: tape (piccolo, flute, oboe, English horn, bassoon, contrabassoon, clarinet, bass clarinet, soprano saxophone, alto saxophone, tenor saxophone, baritone

saxophone, trumpet, trombone, bass trombone, horn, tuba, violin, viola, violoncello, double bass, acoustic guitar, electric guitar, sitar, vibraphone, marimba, timpani, piano, gamelan pots, gamelan tams, electric bass, drum kit [kick drum, snare drum, hi-hat, mounted toms, floor tom-toms, various cymbals], soprano recorder, alto recorder, tenor recorder, dulcimer, banjo, plucked piano, soprano, alto, tenor, bass, wine glasses filled with different amounts of water producing desiring pitches, finger snaps, piano harmonics, gamelan vibes, boy soprano, timpani, large bass drum, nipple gongs, gold plates, bells, low poles, bowls, wheel rims, saucepans, bender gongs, tubular bells).
Commissioned by: ACREQ ("Twilight's Nomadic Dance"), New Adventures in Sound ("Twilight's Sleep"), and RESEAUX ("Twilight's Ritual Incantations").
Call no.: **2002/049**

683. Donatoni, Franco, 1927–2000. Cloches: per due pianoforti, otto strumenti a fiato e due percussioni: (1988–89). Partitura. Milano: Ricordi, 1989.
1 score (151 p.); 42 cm.
Composed for: 2 pianos, piccolo, flute, oboe, English horn, clarinet, bass clarinet, bassoon, contrabassoon, percussion (vibraphone, crotales, chimes, 3 tom-toms, 5 temple blocks, marimba, glockenspiel, 3 gongs, 4 bongos).
Commissioned by: "Musica '89" di Strasbourg.
Call no.: **1990/026**

684. Donatoni, Franco, 1927–2000. Hot: per sassofono sopranino e tenore e sei strumentisti (1989). Partitura. Milano: Ricordi, 1989.
1 score (155 p.); 41 cm.
Reproduced from holograph.
Composed for: soprano saxophone (also tenor saxophone), clarinet in E♭ (also clarinet), trumpet, bass trombone, percussion (vibraphone, marimba, 5 rototoms, 4 bongos, 2 suspended cymbals), piano, double bass.
Commissioned by: Association des Saxophonistes de France.
Call no.: **1991/033**

685. Donatoni, Franco, 1927–2000. In cauda. Partitura. Milano: Ricordi, 1982.
1 score (81 p.); 69 cm.
Italian words by Brandolino Brandolini d'Adda; also printed as text.
Composed for: SATB chorus, piccolo, 2 flutes, 2 oboes, English horn, 2 clarinets, bass clarinet, 2 bassoons, contrabassoon, 4 horns, 3 trumpets, 3 bass trombones, contrabass tuba, timpani, percussion (tam-tam, bass drum, suspended cymbal, tambourine, 4 temple blocks, triangle, gong, 4 bongos, chimes), violin I, violin II, viola, violoncello, double bass.
Commissioned by: Süddeutscher Rundfunk.
Call no.: **1985/052**

686. Donatoni, Franco, 1927–2000. In cauda II: per orchestra (1993–94). Partitura. Milano: Ricordi, 1994.
1 score (93 p.); 38 cm.
Reproduced from holograph.
Instrumentation and performance notes in Italian, English, and German.
Composed for: piccolo, 2 flutes, 2 oboes, English horn, 2 clarinets, bass clarinet, 2 bassoons, contrabassoon, 4 horns, 3 trumpets, 3 trombones, contrabass tuba, timpani, percussion (large tam-tam, large suspended cymbal, 4 temple blocks, large bass drum, large drum, large triangle, large gong, 4 bongos), violin I, violin II, viola, violoncello, double bass.
Commissioned by: Süddeutscher Rundfunk Stuttgart.
Call no.: **1998/042**

687. Donatoni, Franco, 1927–2000. Ronda: per violino, viola, violoncello e pianoforte (1984). Milano: Ricordi, 1984.
1 score (33 p.); 35 cm.
Reproduced from holograph.
Duration: ca. 13:30.
Composed for: violin, viola, violoncello, piano.
Commissioned by: Ministero della Cultura Francana.
Call no.: **1985/053**

688. Donatoni, Franco, 1927–2000. Sweet basil: per trombone e big band (1993). Milano: Ricordi, 1993.
1 score (121 p.); 40 cm.
Duration: ca. 8:30.
Reproduced from holograph.
Includes performance instructions and program note in Italian.
Composed for: trombone, 2 alto saxophones (1st also clarinet in E♭, 2nd also clarinet and piccolo flute), tenor saxophone (also flute), baritone saxophone (also clarinet and bass clarinet), 3 trumpets, horn, 2 bass trombones, contrabass trombone, contrabass tuba, double bass, guitar, piano, percussion (bass drum, tom-toms, suspended cymbals, snare drum, bongos, hi-hat, temple blocks).
Commissioned by: Ministere de la Culture et de la Communication, Italia.
Call no.: **1996/038**

689. Dong, Kui, 1967– Shui diao ge to & song: for a

mixed chorus, percussion and piano. N.p.: Kui dong, 2003.
1 score (61 p.); 36 cm.
Chinese and English words; also printed as text with English translation.
Text by Su Shui and Denise Newman.
Includes notes by Newman and the composer.
Composed for: SATB chorus, piano, percussion (vibraphone, 38" timpani, triangle, handheld small Peking opera gong, Tibetan finger cymbals, 2 woodblocks, tam-tam, vibraslap, 2 string bows, 9 crotales, 5 temple blocks, 3 Chinese tom-toms, bass drum, Chinese cymbals, Tibetan bowl, suspended cymbal).
Commissioned by: Dale Warland Singers.
Call no.: **2005/043**

690. Dorman, Avner, 1975– Variations without a theme. N.p.: Avner Dorman, 2003.
1 score (70 p.); 44 cm.
For orchestra.
Duration: 14:30.
Program note in English.
Composed for: 4 flutes (also piccolo and alto flute), 3 oboes (also English horn), 3 clarinets (also clarinet in E♭ and bass clarinet), 3 bassoons (also contrabassoon), 4 horns, 3 trumpets, 3 trombones, tuba, harp, piano (also celesta), timpani, percussion (cymbals, 2 glockenspiels, triangle, crotales, sleigh bells, wind chimes, bell tree, vibraphone, flexatone, woodblocks, chimes, snare drum, tambourine, metal plate/brake drum, drum set [hi-hat, bass drum, crash cymbals, cowbell, ride cymbal]), violin I, violin II, viola, violoncello, double bass.
Call no.: **2005/044**

691. Dosaj, Dev, 1959– Requiem. Full score. Los Angeles, CA: Dev Dosaj, 1999.
1 score (184 p.); 28 cm.
Latin words; also printed as text with English translation.
Duration: 35:00–40:00.
Composed for: SATB chorus, 2 flutes, oboe, 2 clarinets, horn, optional trumpet, timpani, optional percussion (tambourine, gong, cymbals), violin I, violin II, viola, violoncello, double bass.
Call no.: **2004/033**

692. Downes, Andrew, 1950– Ballads for Christmas. West Hagley, West Midlands, England: Lynwood Music, 1992.
1 score (iv, 53 p.); 30 cm.
English words; also printed as text.
For soprano and alto voices with piano or harp.
Texts: "poems from around the world as well as traditional English words and poems from other areas"—p. i.
Composed for: women's chorus, harp (or piano).
Commissioned by: Midland Chamber Players.
Call no.: **1994/036**

693. Downes, Andrew, 1950– Centenary firedances: opus 43. West Hagley, West Midlands: Lynwood Music, 1988.
1 score (56 p.); 37 cm.
For orchestra.
Includes program notes and reviews.
Reproduced from manuscript.
Composed for: 3 flutes (3rd also piccolo), 2 oboes, 2 clarinets, 2 bassoons, contrabassoon, 4 horns, 3 trumpets in D, trumpet, 2 trombones, bass trombone, tuba, timpani, percussion (xylophone, tubular bells, 2 marimbas, gong, bass drum, cowbells, side drum, glockenspiel, suspended cymbal, tom-toms, Chinese blocks), violin I, violin II, viola, violoncello, double bass.
Commissioned by: City of Birmingham in association with Dragonfire, Ltd.
Call no.: **1993/033**

694. Downes, Andrew, 1950– Concert overture: "Towards a new age": scored for symphony orchestra. West Hagley, West Midland: Lynwood Music, 1996.
1 score (37 p.); 30 cm.
Program note in English.
Composed for: 3 flutes (3rd also piccolo), 2 oboes, 2 clarinets, 2 bassoons, contrabassoon, 4 horns, 2 trumpets, 2 trombones, bass trombone, tuba, timpani, percussion (glockenspiel, marimba, snare drum, tubular bells, cymbals, bass drum), violin I, violin II, viola, violoncello, double bass.
Commissioned by: Institution of Mechanical Engineers.
Call no.: **2000/045**

695. Downes, Andrew, 1950– Concerto for 4 solo horns and symphony orchestra, opus 77. Stourbridge: Lynwood Music, 2002.
1 score (113 p.); 30 cm.
Duration: 25:00.
Composed for: 4 horns, 3 flutes (also piccolo), 2 oboes, 2 clarinets, bass clarinet, 2 bassoons, contrabassoon, 2 horns, 2 trumpets, 2 trombones, bass trombones, tuba, timpani, percussion, violin I, violin II, viola, violoncello, double bass.
Call no.: **2005/045**

696. Downes, Andrew, 1950– The marshes of Glynn: cantata for tenor solo, choir, and orchestra. West

Hagley, West Midlands: Lynwood Music Photo-Editions, 1985.
1 score (102 p.); 39 cm.
Words in English by Sidney Lanier.
Composed for: tenor, SATB chorus, 3 flutes (2nd–3rd also piccolo), 2 oboes (2nd also English horn), 2 clarinets, 2 clarinets in A, bass clarinet, 2 bassoons, contrabassoon, 4 horns, 3 trumpets, 2 trumpets, 2 trombones, bass trombone, tuba, timpani, percussion (gong, suspended cymbal, crotales, glockenspiel, vibraphone, woodblock, bass drum, side drum, triangle), celesta, violin I, violin II, viola, violoncello, double bass.
Commissioned by: Birmingham School of Music.
Call no.: **1988/027**

697. Downes, Andrew, 1950– Sonata: for eight flutes or flute choir (op. 58). West Hagley, West Midlands, England: Lynwood Music, 1996.
1 score (72 p.); 30 cm.
Composed for: 5 flutes (2nd also piccolo), 2 alto flutes, bass flute.
Commissioned by: friends of Albert Cooper, flutemaker.
Call no.: **1998/043**

698. Downes, Andrew, 1950– Sonata: for violin and piano. West Hagley, West Midlands: Lynwood Music, 1994.
1 score (25 p.) + 1 part (10 p.); 30 cm.
Composed for: violin, piano.
Call no.: **1996/039**

699. Downes, Andrew, 1950– Sonata for eight horns, opus 53. West Hagley, West Midlands: Lynwood Music, 1994.
1 score (ii, 44 p.); 30 cm.
Duration: 26:00.
Composed for: 8 horns.
Commissioned by: Jim Lowe, Janice Lee Sperling, and British Horn Trio.
Call no.: **1997/037**

700. Downes, Andrew, 1950– Sonata for two pianos: "The Lord will be a refuge for the oppressed; a refuge in times of trouble" (Ps. 9, v. 9.): opus 40. West Hagley, West Midlands: Lynwood Music Photo-Editions, 1987.
1 score (63 p.); 30 cm.
Includes program notes and Psalm text.
Reproduced from holograph.
Composed for: 2 pianos.
Commissioned by: Interdenominational Society for Russian Jewry.
Call no.: **1992/033**

701. Downes, Andrew, 1950– Symphony no. 3. West Midlands: Lynwood Music, 1992.
1 score (72 p.); 39 cm.
Reproduced from manuscript.
Composed for: 3 flutes (3rd also piccolo), 2 oboes, 3 clarinets, 2 bassoons, contrabassoon, 4 horns, 3 trumpets, 2 trombones, bass trombone, tuba, timpani, percussion (crotales, 2 glockenspiels, xylophone, 3 marimbas, agogo bell, 3 cowbells, Chinese blocks, whip, woodblock, suspended cymbal, cymbals, gong, tubular bells, tom-toms, frame drums, large bongos, side drum, bass drum, drum kit, 6 unpitched drums), violin I, violin II, viola, violoncello, double bass.
Call no.: **1995/021**

702. Downey, John W., 1927–2004. Concerto for doublebass and orchestra. N.p.: Theodore Presser Co., 1987.
1 score (various pagings); 37 cm.
Reproduced from manuscript.
Composed for: double bass, piccolo, 2 flutes, 2 oboes, English horn, 2 clarinets (both also clarinet in A), bass clarinet, 2 bassoons, contrabassoon, 4 horns, 2 trumpets, 2 trombones, bass trombone, tuba, timpani, percussion (chimes, 5 tom-toms, glockenspiel, crash cymbals, tambourine, bass drum, gong, suspended cymbal, 4 bongos, vibraphone, xylophone, crotales, snare drum, triangle, marimba), harp, celesta, violin I, violin II, viola, violoncello, double bass.
Call no.: **1988/028**

703. Downey, John W., 1927–2004. Discourse: for oboe, harpsichord, and string orch., 1984. N.p.: n.p., 1984.
1 score (52 p.); 36 cm.
Reproduced from holograph.
Composed for: oboe, harpsichord, violin I, violin II, viola, violoncello, double bass.
Call no.: **1991/034**

704. Downey, John W., 1927–2004. For those who suffered: yad vashem—an impression: for chamber orchestra. N.p.: John Downey, 1994.
1 score (117 p.); 36 cm.
Composed for: flute (also piccolo), oboe (also English horn), clarinet, horn, trumpet, percussion (tambourine, bass drum, maracas, suspended cymbal, vibraphone, ratchet, low siren, deep tenor drum, crash cymbals, large tam-tam, 4 sets of wind chimes, woodblock, 3 tom-toms, snare drum, cowbell, 2 anvils, xylophone, triangle, chimes, orchestra bells, crotales), piano, accordion, violin I, violin II, viola, violoncello, double bass.
Call no.: **1997/038**

705. Downey, John W., 1927–2004. Piano trio. Shorewood, WI: n.p., 1984.
1 score (40 p.); 37 cm.
At end of score: "With thanks to God, John Downey Shorewood, Wis. Nov. 6, 1984."
Reproduced from holograph.
Composed for: violin, violoncello, piano.
Commissioned by: MacDowell Club of Milwaukee.
Call no.: **1985/054**

706. Dran, Tatiana Grecic, 1965– Woman and a dragon: an original composition for string quartet. Pembroke, Bermuda: Tatiana G. Dran, 2001.
1 score (15 leaves); 28 cm.
Composed for: 2 violins, viola, violoncello.
Call no.: **2003/036**

707. Drew, James, 1929– The book of lights: for clarinet, viola, cello, and piano. Orange City, FL: Artistry Press, 1993.
1 score (37 p.); 28 cm.
Duration: ca. 30:00.
Contents: Vox spiritus—The resonance of memory—The sounds of stars by candlelight—Of sublime truths grey wolf sings—Vox transfiguratus.
Composed for: clarinet, viola, violoncello, piano.
Call no.: **1994/037**

708. Drew, James, 1929– Piano concerto: (the celestial cabaret). N.p.: James Drew, 1991.
1 score (4 p.); 36 x 46 cm. + 1 part (8 p.); 29 x 44 cm.
Composed for: piano, trumpet, 2 trombones, percussion (timpani, chimes, glockenspiel, snare drum, 3 drums, vibraphone, gong, bass drum, suspended cymbal), 2 violins, violoncello.
Commissioned by: Summerfaire International Festival.
Call no.: **1992/034**

709. Dreznin, Sergei, 1955– Requiem for victims of Nazism: for soloists, choir and orchestra. N.p.: n.p., 1986.
1 score (135 p.); 42 cm.
Latin, Russian, French, German, and English words.
Reproduced from manuscript.
Composed for: 2 flutes (2nd also piccolo), 2 oboes, 2 clarinets in A (2nd also alto saxophone), 2 bassoons (2nd also contrabassoon), 4 horns, 3 trumpets, 3 trombones, tuba, vibraphone, xylophone, timpani, percussion (snare drum, 4 tom-toms, suspended cymbal, bass drum, 3 bongos, triangle, woodblock, tam-tam, slapstick), harp, piano, cembalo, celesta, organ, violin I, violin II, viola, violoncello, double bass.
Call no.: **1988/029**

710. Druckman, Jacob, 1928–1996. Brangle: for orchestra. Full score. New York, NY: Boosey & Hawkes, 1991.
1 score (93 p.); 34 cm.
Reproduced from holograph.
Duration: 22:00.
Composed for: 3 flutes (2nd also piccolo, 3rd also alto flute), 2 oboes, English horn, 2 clarinets, bass clarinet, 2 bassoons, 4 horns, 3 trumpets, 2 trombones, bass trombone, tuba, timpani, percussion (vibraphone, marimba, glockenspiel, tubular chimes, 3 suspended cymbals, sizzle cymbal, 2 tam-tams, 2 timbales, 2 congas, 5 tom-toms, bass drum, tambourine, triangle, cowbell, sleigh bells, maracas, vibraslap), harp, piano, violin I, violin II, viola, violoncello, double bass.
Commissioned by: Chicago Symphony Orchestra.
Call no.: **1992/035**

711. Druckman, Jacob, 1928–1996. Come round: for six players. N.p.: Boosey & Hawkes, 1992.
1 score (79 p.); 28 cm.
Duration: 25:00.
Composed for: flute (also alto flute), clarinet (also bass clarinet), violin, violoncello, piano, percussion (cymbals, 4 tom-toms, bass drum, tam-tam).
Commissioned by: Saratoga Performing Arts Center, Santa Fe Music Festival, and Ravinia Festival.
Call no.: **1993/034**

712. Druckman, Jacob, 1928–1996. Counterpoise: for soprano and orchestra. Uncorrected score. New York: Boosey & Hawkes, 1994.
1 score (91 p.); 36 cm.
English words by Emily Dickinson and French words by Guillaume Apollinaire.
Contents: "Nature" is what we see / Dickinson—Salomé / Apollinaire—La blanche neige / Apollinaire—I taste a liquor never brewed / Dickinson.
Composed for: soprano, 2 flutes (2nd also piccolo), alto flute, 2 oboes, English horn, 2 clarinets, bass clarinet, 2 bassoons, 4 horns, 3 trumpets, 2 trombones, bass trombone, tuba, timpani, percussion (vibraphone, marimba, glockenspiel, tubular chimes, 2 suspended cymbals, sizzle cymbal, crash cymbals, tambourine, tam-tam, 4 tom-toms, snare drum, bass drum, triangle, finger cymbals, sleigh bells, cowbell), harp, piano (also celesta), violin I, violin II, viola, violoncello, double bass.
Commissioned by: Philadelphia Orchestra.
Call no.: **1995/022**
Re-entered as: **1996/040**

713. Druckman, Jacob, 1928–1996. Vox humana.

Call no.: **1985/055**
Re-entered as: **1988/030**
No materials available.

714. Drummond, Dean, 1949– Congressional record. Upper Nyack, NY: Hypersound, 1999.
1 score (109 p.); 29 cm.
English words excerpted from the United States Congressional record.
Includes instruments invented by Harry Partch.
Reproduced from holograph.
Composed for: baritone, synthesizer (Yamaha WX5 wind controller MIDI'd to a microtonally programmed Yamaha DX7II synthesizer), adapted guitar, chromelodeon, 2 harmonic canons, diamond marimba, zoomoozophone, boo/juststrokerods.
Commissioned by: Newband.
Call no.: **2001/048**

715. Drummond, Dean, 1949– The last laugh. Upper Nyack, NY: Hypersound, 1996.
1 score (v, 463 p.); 28 cm.
Based on the film The last laugh = Der letzte Mann by F. W. Murnau.
Silent film music for 10 players.
Includes instruments invented by Harry Partch.
Reproduced from holograph.
Composed for: flute (also alto flute), trumpet, violoncello, synthesizer (also chromelodeon), 2 harmonic canon players, kithara II (also bass marimba, rhythm boat, 2 Balinese angklungs), zoomoozophone I (also bongos), zoomoozophone II (also spoils of war, medium Chinese tom-tom, steel bowl, Peking opera gong, two Chinese cymbals and sleigh bells), diamond marimba (also boo, bloboy, juststrokerods, hi-hat).
Commissioned by: Meet the Composer/Reader's Digest Commissioning Program in partnership with National Endowment for the Arts and Lila Wallace-Reader's Digest Fund.
Call no.: **1997/039**

716. Du, Mingxin, 1928– Concerto: spirit of spring: for piano and orchestra. N.p.: n.p., 198-?.
1 score (100 p.); 40 cm.
Reproduced from manuscript.
Composed for: piano, piccolo, 2 flutes, 2 oboes, 2 clarinets, 2 bassoons, 4 horns, 3 trumpets, 3 trombones, tuba, timpani, percussion (triangle, cymbals, piccolo snare drum), harp, celesta, violin I, violin II, viola, violoncello, double bass.
Call no.: **1992/036**

717. Dubedout, Bertrand, 1958– Episodes transparents: pour choeur à 32 voix et bande magnétique. N.p.: n.p., 198-?.
1 score (98 p.); 42 cm.
Words in multiple languages.
Reproduced from manuscript.
Duration: 27:00.
Composed for: 32 SATB voices, tape.
Commissioned by: État français.
Call no.: **1989/030**

718. Dubrovay, László, 1943– II Konzert: für Klavier und Orchester. Budapest: Editio Musica Budapest, 1988.
1 score (174 p.); 41 cm.
Reproduced from manuscript.
Duration: ca. 32:00.
Composed for: piano, 3 flutes (3rd also piccolo), 2 oboes, English horn, 2 clarinets, bass clarinet, 2 bassoons, contrabassoon, 4 horns, 4 trumpets, 3 trombones, tuba, timpani, percussion (snare drum, tambourine, bass drum, suspended cymbal, cymbals, tam-tam, triangle, chimes, bells, crotales), 2 harps, celesta, violin I, violin II, viola, violoncello, double bass.
Call no.: **1988/031**

719. Dubrovay, László, 1943– Concerto: magyar népihangszerekre, 4 szólistúra és zenekarra = Concerto: for Hungarian folksinstruments [sic] and orchestra. N.p.: n.p., 1999.
1 score (103 p.); 42 cm.
Reproduced from manuscript.
Duration: ca. 24:00.
Composed for: tilinkó flute, Transylvanian flute, bagpipe, Jew's harp, hurdy-gurdy, dulcimer, piccolo, 2 flutes, 2 oboes, English horn, 2 clarinets, bass clarinet, 2 bassoons, contrabassoon, 4 horns, 4 trumpets, 3 trombones, tuba, percussion (2 timpani, triangle, snare drum, 5 bongos, 5 tom-toms, bass drum, suspended cymbal, tam-tam, glockenspiel), celesta, violin I, violin II, viola, violoncello, double bass.
Call no.: **2003/037**

720. Dubrovay, László, 1943– Faust, az elkárhozott: III. [i.e. IV] szvit nagyzenekarra = Faust, the damned: III. [i.e. IV] suite for orchestra. N.p.: n.p., 1998.
1 score (102 p.); 42 cm.
Fourth orchestral suite from the ballet.
Reproduced from manuscript.
Composed for: piccolo, 2 flutes, 2 oboes, English horn, 2 clarinets, bass clarinet, 2 bassoons, contrabassoon, 4 horns, 4 trumpets, 3 trombones, bass trombone, tuba, timpani, percussion (2 small tambourines, claves, 5 bongos, 5 temple blocks, 4 tom-toms, bells, crotales,

vibraphone, gong, suspended cymbal, crash cymbals, tambourine, tam-tam, bass drum, ratchet, triangle), piano, organ, celesta, violin I, violin II, viola, violoncello, double bass.
Call no.: **1998/044**

721. Dubrovay, László, 1943– Faust, az elkárhozott = Faust, the damned. N.p.: n.p., 1998.
1 score (4 v.); 42 cm.
Four orchestral suites from the ballet.
Reproduced from manuscript.
Composed for: piccolo, 2 flutes, 2 oboes, English horn, 2 clarinets, bass clarinet, 2 bassoons, contrabassoon, 4 horns, 4 trumpets, 3 trombones, bass trombone, tuba, timpani, percussion (2 small tambourines, claves, 5 bongos, 5 temple blocks, 4 tom-toms, bells, crotales, vibraphone, gong, suspended cymbal, crash cymbals, tambourine, tam-tam, bass drum, ratchet, triangle), piano, organ, celesta, violin I, violin II, viola, violoncello, double bass.
Call no.: **2000/046**

722. Dubrovay, László, 1943– A képfaragó: egyfelvonásos táncjáték, Gáli József szinopszisa alapján. Budapest: n.p., 1993.
1 score (189 p.); 35 cm.
Ballet in one act.
At end of score: "Budapest 1993 oktober 20-án."
Duration: ca. 39:00.
Reproduced from manuscript.
Composed for: 2 piccolos, 2 flutes, 3 oboes, English horn, clarinet in E♭, 2 clarinets, bass clarinet, 3 bassoons, contrabassoon, 4 horns, 4 trumpets, 3 trombones, tuba, timpani, percussion (4 bongos, 2 piccolo drums, 4 tom-toms, 2 bass drums, 4 suspended cymbals, crash cymbals, gong, tam-tam, triangle, crotales, xylophone, vibraphone, bells, handbells), harp, celesta, violin I, violin II, viola, violoncello, double bass.
Call no.: **1995/023**

723. Duckworth, William, 1943– Southern harmony. Book one[–book four]: SSAATTBB chorus. New York, NY: Monroe Street Music, 1993.
1 score (4 v.); 23 x 32 cm.
Based on hymns from: Southern harmony / William Walker. 1854.
Contents: Book 1. Consolation; Wondrous love; Hebrew children; Solemn thought; Rock of ages—Book 2. Cheerful; War department; Condescension; Holy manna; Bozrah—Book 3. The mouldering vine; Mear; Leander; Sardina; Windham—Book 4. Distress; Nashville; The turtle dove; Primrose; Social band.
Composed for: SATB chorus.
Commissioned by: Wesleyan Singers.
Call no.: **1995/024**

724. Durkó, Zsolt, 1934–1997. Piano concerto.
Call no.: **1985/056**
No materials available.

725. Dusapin, Pascal, 1955– Niobe: (ou Le rocher de Sipyle). N.p.: n.p., 1982.
1 score (73 p.); 28 x 37 cm.
French words.
Reproduced from holograph.
Composed for: soprano, 12 mixed voices, oboe, English horn, 2 clarinets (2nd also bass clarinet), 2 bassoons (2nd also contrabassoon), trumpet, 2 trombones.
Call no.: **1985/057**

726. Dutilleux, Henri, 1916– L'arbre des songes: concerto pour violon et orchestre, 1983/85. Partition. Mainz; New York, NY: Schott, 1985.
1 score (116 p.); 50 cm.
Reproduced from manuscript.
Duration: ca. 25:00.
Composed for: violin, piccolo, 2 flutes (2nd also piccolo), 3 oboes (1st also oboe d'amore), clarinet in E♭, 2 clarinets in A, bass clarinet, 2 bassoons, contrabassoon, 3 horns, 3 trumpets, 3 trombones, tuba, timpani, percussion (cimbalom, 2 suspended cymbals, 2 tam-tams, crotales, tubular bells, vibraphone, 3 bongos, 3 tom-toms, snare drum, glockenspiel), harp, piano (also celesta), violin I, violin II, viola, violoncello, double bass.
Commissioned by: Radio France.
Call no.: **1988/032**

727. Dutton, Brent, 1950– A moon rising white: cantata for bass-baritone, choir, trumpet, and percussion quartet. N.p.: Brent Dutton, 1991.
1 score (41 leaves); 28 cm.
English words by Shih Ching.
Reproduced from manuscript.
Composed for: bass-baritone, SATB chorus, trumpet, percussion.
Call no.: **1992/037**

728. Dzubay, David, 1964– Dancesing in a green bay: soprano & mixed sextet (fl., cl., vn., vc., pn., pc.) (1999). Bloomington, IN: Pro Nova Music, 1999.
1 score (46 p.); 36 cm.
English words by E. E. Cummings; also printed as text.
Duration: 20:00.
Contents: between green/ mountains—the/ sky/ was—grEEn's d—All in green went my love riding—six—

(sitting in a tree-)—in the rain-.
Composed for: soprano, flute, clarinet, violin, violoncello, piano, percussion.
Commissioned by: Voices of Change.
Call no.: **2004/034**

729. Dzubay, David, 1964– Sun moon stars rain: for orchestra (1997). Bloomington, IN: Pro Nova Music, 2000.
1 score (96 p.); 36 cm.
"Rev. 2000."
Duration: 18:00.
Contents: Summer—Autumn—Winter—Spring.
Composed for: 3 flutes (all doubling piccolo), 2 oboes, English horn, 2 clarinets, bass clarinet (also contrabass clarinet), 2 bassoons, contrabassoon, 4 horns, 3 trumpets, 2 trombones, bass trombone, tuba, timpani, percussion (glockenspiel, medium suspended cymbal, 3 gongs, tam-tam, marimba, vibraphone, bell tree, splash cymbals, roto-toms, 3 triangles, 2 suspended cymbals, bamboo wind chimes, wood wind chimes, 5 temple blocks, 4 tom-toms, crotales, cowbell, xylophone, glass wind chimes, 3 woodblocks, bass drum), harp, celesta, piano, violin I, violin II, viola, violoncello, double bass.
Commissioned by: Barlow Endowment for Music Composition at Brigham Young University.
Call no.: **2002/050**

730. Dzubay, David, 1964– Symphony no. 1 (1996). Saint Louis, MO: MMB Music, 1996.
1 score (152 p.); 41 cm.
Duration: 33:00.
Includes program notes by the composer.
Contents: Rage, rage . . . — . . . they dance their glories into shadow— . . . as filaments of memory spin . . . .
Composed for: 3 flutes (2nd–3rd also piccolo), 2 oboes, English horn, 2 clarinets, bass clarinet, 2 bassoons, contrabassoon, 4 horns, 3 trumpets, 2 trombones, bass trombone, tuba, timpani (also cymbal), percussion (glockenspiel, small suspended cymbal, mark tree, 2 cowbells, large tam-tam, marimba, wood wind chimes, bongos, 6 tom-toms, vibraphone, triangle, large suspended cymbal, bell tree, glass wind chimes, lion's roar, small bass drum, medium suspended cymbal, metal wind chimes, 3 Japanese temple bowls, 2 woodblocks, 5 temple blocks, snare drum, bass drum), harp, piano, violin I, violin II, viola, violoncello, double bass.
Commissioned by: Meet the Composer/Reader's Digest Commissioning Program in partnership with National Endowment for the Arts and Lila Wallace-Reader's Digest Fund.
Call no.: **1997/040**

731. Earnest, John David, 1940– Only in the dream.
Call no.: **1985/058**
No materials available.

732. Eaton, John, 1935– Antigone. N.p.: n.p., 2003.
1 score (583 p.); 28 cm.
English words by Nicholas Rudall.
Original work by Sophocles.
Composed for: soprano, jazz singer, mezzo-soprano, tenor, baritone, flute (also piccolo, alto flute, and bass flute), clarinet (also bass clarinet), piano, percussion, violin, violoncello, electronics.
Call no.: **2005/046**

733. Eaton, John, 1935– Ars poetica. N.p.: n.p., 1986.
1 score (15 p.); 49 cm.
English words; also printed as text.
Song cycle.
Text based on poems by William Butler Yeats.
Reproduced from manuscript.
Composed for: mezzo-soprano, flute, harp, violoncello.
Call no.: **1987/020**

734. Eaton, John, 1935– Golk. N.p.: n.p., 1995.
1 score (134 p.); 34 cm.
English words by Richard Stern, based on his novel.
Opera in one act.
Reproduced from holograph.
Composed for: soprano, mezzo-soprano, tenor, baritone, flute (also piccolo, alto flute, and bass flute), clarinet (also bass clarinet), percussion (xylophone, temple blocks, ratchet, woodblocks, snare drum, tenor drum, suspended cymbal, sizzle cymbal, trap set, tambourine, triangle, crotales, vibraphone, sandpaper blocks, tam-tam), piano, synthesizer, violin (also electric violin), amplified violoncello.
Call no.: **1997/041**

735. Eaton, John, 1935– Mass: for soprano soloist, soprano II, alto, tenor, baritone, bass and clarinet, piano, two percussionists and optional electronics. N.p.: n.p., 1997.
1 score (139 p.); 28 cm.
English and Latin words.
Composed for: 2 sopranos, alto, tenor, baritone, bass, clarinet, piano, percussion, optional electronics.
Commissioned by: Indiana University Contemporary Vocal Ensemble.
Call no.: **2000/047**
Re-entered as: **2001/049** and **2004/035**

736. Eaton, John, 1935– Peer Gynt. N.p.: n.p., 1992.
1 score (74 p.); 36 cm.
Collection of dramatic pieces.
Reproduced from manuscript.
Includes performance instructions.
Composed for: flute (also piccolo, alto, and bass flutes), clarinet (also bass and contrabass clarinets), violin, violoncello, piano, percussion (temple blocks, antlers, Tibetan bowl, 3 suspended cymbals, sizzle cymbal, 2 sets of chimes, glockenspiel, crotales, xylophone, marimba, 2 triangles, sleigh bells, 3 water gongs, large jug, anvil, thundersheet, woodblocks, jawbone, ratchet, 4 tambourines, bass tambourine, snare drum, tenor drum, 2 bongos, bass drum).
Commissioned by: New York New Music Ensemble.
Call no.: **1993/036**

737. Eaton, John, 1935– Songs of desperation and comfort. N.p.: n.p., 1993.
1 score (xii, 75 p.); 44 cm.
English words; also printed as text.
Song cycle for mezzo-soprano and chamber orchestra.
Includes program notes and performance instructions.
Contents: Holy Sonnet no. XIV / John Donne—Lullaby for Estela / Patrick Creagh—Lear on the Heath / William Shakespeare—To old Roscoff; Blind man's cry / Tristan Corbière; translated by Patrick Creagh.
Composed for: mezzo-soprano, 2 flutes (both also piccolo, 1st also bass flute, 2nd also alto flute), 2 oboes (also English horn), 2 clarinets (1st also contrabass clarinet, 2nd also bass clarinet), 2 bassoons (both also contrabassoons), 2 horns, 2 trumpets, 2 trombones, percussion (snare drum, tenor drum, bass drum, tambourine, drum, 7 roto-toms, cymbals, sizzle cymbal, 3 gongs, tuned gongs, chimes, marimba, vibraphone, anvil, wind machine, flexatone, timpani, 2 tom-toms, suspended cymbal, glockenspiel, crotales, ratchet, whirlagag, thundersheet), harp, piano, violin I, violin II, viola, violoncello, double bass.
Call no.: **1995/025**

738. Eaton, John, 1935– The tempest. Full score. Pennsauken, NJ: G. Schirmer, 1985.
1 score (3 v.); 49 cm.
English words.
Opera.
Libretto adapted from Shakespeare by Andrew Porter.
Reproduced from manuscript.
At end of score: "finished 2/21/85."
Composed for: 2 sopranos, 2 mezzo-sopranos, contralto, 6 tenors, 5 baritones, 3 basses, jazz singer, SATB chorus, Renaissance ensemble (recorder, shawm, lute), jazz trio (alto saxophone, guitar, electric bass), tape, 2 flutes (both also piccolo), 2 oboes, English horn, 2 clarinets, bass clarinet, 2 bassoons, contrabassoon, 4 horns, 3 trumpets, 2 trombones, bass trombone, tuba, timpani, percussion (3 gongs, bass drum, chimes, cymbals, vibraphone, marimba, triangles, wind machine, bongos, sizzle cymbal, timbales, 2 anvils, thundersheet, temple blocks, woodblocks, sandpaper blocks, snare drum, tom-toms, suspended cymbals, ratchet, tam-tam, tambourine, flexatone, tenor drum, slapstick, glockenspiel, lion's roar, water bottle), 2 harps, 2 pianos, violin I, violin II, viola, violoncello, double bass.
Commissioned by: Santa Fe Opera.
Call no.: **1986/035**
Re-entered as: **1989/032**
Also available:
Call no.: **1989/032 vocal score**

739. Eben, Petr, 1929– Four Biblical dances: for organ. London: United Music Publishers, 1993.
60 p. of music; 31 cm.
Includes program notes in English and German by the composer.
Contents: The dance of David before the Ark of the Covenant—The dance of the Shulammite—The dance of Jephtha's daughter—The wedding in Cana.
Composed for: organ.
Call no.: **1997/042**

740. Eben, Petr, 1929– Jeremias. Partitura. N.p.: n.p., 1997.
1 score (255 p.); 34 cm.
German words by Stefan Zweig.
Church opera.
Reproduced from holograph.
Composed for: voices, SATB chorus, flute, oboe, clarinet, bassoon, horn, trumpet, trombone, percussion (tom-tom, gong, triangle, cymbals), organ, violin I, violin II, viola, violoncello, double bass.
Call no.: **1998/045**

741. Ebenhöh, Horst, 1930– Konvokation: für Kammerorchester, op. 62/2. Wien: H. Ebenhöh, 198-?.
1 score (123 p.); 30 cm.
Composed for: oboe, horn, percussion (cymbals, snare drum, bongos, temple blocks), piano, violin I, violin II, viola, violoncello, double bass.
Call no.: **1988/033**
Re-entered as: **1989/033**

742. Eberhard, Dennis, 1943– To catch the light: songs of grieving children: for soprano solo, treble solo, boy choir and orchestra, 1995. N.p.: Dennis Eberhard, 1995.

1 score (189 p.); 36 cm.
English words; also printed as text.
Texts by Ann Burrell, Pavel Friedmann, Patti Logston, and the composer.
Reproduced from manuscript.
Duration: ca. 45:00.
Includes notes by the composer.
Composed for: soprano, boy soprano, boys' chorus, 2 flutes (2nd also piccolo, alto flute), 2 oboes (2nd also English horn), 2 clarinets (2nd also bass clarinet), 2 bassoons (2nd also contrabassoon), 2 horns, trumpet, trombone, timpani, percussion (crotales, orchestra bells, tubular chimes, vibraphone, 3 suspended cymbals, 3 tam-tams, 5 tom-toms, bass drum), piano (also celesta), harp, violin I, violin II, viola, violoncello, double bass.
Call no.: **2003/038**

743. Eder, Helmut, 1916– Episoden: Konzert für Klavier und Orchester, opus 110. Partitur. Wien: Doblinger, 1998.
1 score (51 p.); 35 cm.
Reproduced from manuscript.
Duration: ca. 22:00.
Composed for: piano, flute (also piccolo), oboe, clarinet (also bass clarinet), bassoon, 2 horns, trumpet, percussion (glockenspiel, xylophone, vibraphone, marimba, 3 gongs, 2 cowbells, 3 woodblocks, 4 temple blocks, tambourine, 3 suspended cymbals, 3 bongos, 3 tom-toms, snare drum, bass drum), violin I, violin II, viola, violoncello, double bass.
Call no.: **2002/051**

744. Eder, Helmut, 1916– Haffner-Konzert: für Flöte und Orchester, op. 82. Wien: Musikverlag Doblinger, 1984.
1 score (45 p.); 30 cm.
Reproduced from holograph.
Duration: ca. 20:00.
Composed for: flute, piccolo, 2 oboes, 3 clarinets, 2 bassoons, 3 horns, 2 trumpets, 2 trombones, tuba, timpani, percussion (xylophone, glockenspiel, vibraphone, chimes, bell plate, 2 crash cymbals, 3 triangles, tambourine, castanets, 2 temple blocks, 2 snare drums, whip, 2 bongos, 2 congas, bass drum, 4 gongs, tam-tam), 26 violins, 8 violas, 7 violoncellos, 6 double basses.
Commissioned by: Internationale Stiftung Mozarteum.
Call no.: **1989/034**

745. Edwards, Ross, 1943– Maninyas: concerto for violin and orchestra. N.p.: Universal Edition, 1990.
1 score (99 p.); 31 cm.
Reproduced from holograph.
Duration: ca. 25:00.
Composed for: violin, piccolo, 2 flutes, 2 oboes, English horn, clarinet in E♭, 2 clarinets in A, bass clarinet, 2 bassoons, contrabassoon, 3 horns, 2 trumpets, 2 trombones, bass trombone, timpani, percussion (vibraphone, marimba, 2 congas, bass drum, xylophone, glockenspiel, 2 tom-toms), harp, piano, violin I, violin II, viola, violoncello, double bass.
Commissioned by: Australian Broadcasting Corporation.
Call no.: **1992/038**

746. Einaudi, Ludovico, 1955– Rondó: per soprano e orchestra. Partitura. Milano: G. Ricordi & C. Editori, 1982.
1 score (70 p.); 47 cm.
Italian words by C. Pavese; also printed as text.
Reproduced from holograph.
Duration: ca. 13:00.
Composed for: soprano, 3 flutes (2nd–3rd also piccolo), 2 oboes (2nd also English horn), clarinet in E♭, 2 clarinets, 2 bassoons, 2 horns, 3 trumpets, 2 trombones, percussion (tam-tam, maracas, snare drum, guiro, 2 woodblocks, 2 temple blocks, ratchet, bass drum, sizzle cymbal, tambourine, marimba, 2 bongos, 4 cowbells), harp, violin I, violin II, viola, violoncello, double bass.
Call no.: **1985/059**

747. Einem, Gottfried von, 1918–1996. Alchemistenspiegel: op. 90. Partitur. Wien: Musikverlag Doblinger, 1990.
1 score (30 p.); 30 x 42 cm.
German words.
Poem by Lotte Ingrisch.
Reproduced from manuscript.
Composed for: medium voice, 2 clarinets, 2 bassoons, 2 horns, bass trombone, timpani, percussion (tenor drum, military drum, bass drum, triangle, medium bell, cymbals), violin I, violin II, viola, violoncello, double bass.
Call no.: **1991/139**

748. Ekizian, Michelle, 1956– Beyond the reach of wind and fire: for orchestra (with mezzo-soprano at epilogue). N.p.: n.p., 1989.
1 score (xv, 183 p.); 28 cm.
English words by Theodore Roethke; also printed as text.
Duration: ca. 21:25.
Composed for: mezzo-soprano, 2 flutes (2nd also piccolo), 2 oboes (2nd also English horn), 2 clarinets (1st also clarinet in E♭), 2 bassoons, 4 horns, 2 trum-

pets, 2 trombones, bass trombone, tuba, timpani (also crotales), percussion (triangle, vibraphone, tubular chimes, 4 suspended cymbals, snare drum, 5 tom-toms, glockenspiel, xylophone, marimba, 2 sizzle cymbals, tambourine, tenor drum, suspended crotales, 3 cowbells, 3 woodblocks, 3 tam-tams, bass drum), violin I, violin II, viola, violoncello, double bass.
Commissioned by: American Composers Orchestra and Jerome Foundation.
Call no.: **1990/027**
Re-entered as: **1991/035** and **1992/039**

749. Ekizian, Michelle, 1956– Octoéchos: for double string quartet and soprano. N.p.: n.p., 1986.
1 manuscript score (iii, 193 p.); 28 cm.
English words by Theodore Roethke; printed also as text (p. 128).
Reproduced from manuscript.
Soprano performs only in the optional "Epilogue."
Duration: 14:30 (Octoéchos); 10:00 (Epilogue).
Composed for: soprano, 4 violins, 2 violas, 2 violoncellos.
Call no.: **1988/034**

750. Ekizian, Michelle, 1956– Red harvest: concerto for violin and orchestra. N.p.: M. Ekizian, 1997.
1 score (viii, 223 p.); 36 cm.
Composed for: violin, 2 flutes (2nd also piccolo), 2 oboes (2nd also English horn), 2 clarinets, 2 bassoons, 4 horns, 3 trumpets, 2 trombones, 4 timpani, harp, violin I, violin II, viola, violoncello, double bass.
Commissioned by: Mary Flagler Cary Charitable Trust, Interfaith Committee of Remembrance, and Jerry Jacobs.
Call no.: **2000/048**
Re-entered as: **2001/050**

751. Ekizian, Michelle, 1956– Saber dances: for orchestra. N.p.: Michelle Ekizian, 1992.
1 score (xv, 98 p.); 36 cm.
Duration: ca. 15:00.
Contents: The earth is within me—And now my dance has measure.
Composed for: piccolo, 2 flutes, 2 oboes, English horn, 2 clarinets (1st also clarinet in E♭), bass clarinet, 2 bassoons, contrabassoon, 4 horns, 3 trumpets (1st also trumpet in D), 2 trombones, bass trombone, tuba, timpani (also sandpaper blocks and crotales), percussion (vibraphone, glockenspiel, hi-hat, 2 sizzle cymbals, 3 suspended cowbells, 3 suspended woodblocks, 2–4 maracas, snare drum, 5 tom-toms, xylophone, crotales, 2 suspended triangles, 3 suspended cymbals, crash cymbals, slapstick, tenor drum, 2 tam-tams, tambourine, guiro, bass drum), violin I, violin II, viola, violoncello, double bass.
Commissioned by: Fromm Music Foundation at Harvard University and Barlow Endowment at Brigham Young University.
Call no.: **1993/037**

752. Ekizian, Michelle, 1956– Symphony no. 1: when light divided: for orchestra with mezzo-soprano and baritone soloists. N.p.: Michelle Ekizian, 1994.
1 score (vii, 134 p.); 36 cm.
English and Armenian words; also printed as text.
Texts by Theodore Roethke and Gregory of Narek.
Duration: ca. 25:00.
Includes performance instructions by the composer.
Composed for: mezzo-soprano, baritone, 2 flutes (2nd also piccolo), 2 oboes, 2 clarinets, 2 bassoons, 2 horns, 2 trumpets, trombone, bass trombone, timpani (also bell tree, medium triangle, sandpaper blocks), percussion (vibraphone, crotales, sleigh bells, hi-hat, large sizzle cymbal, maracas, medium snare drum, large tam-tam, marimba, glockenspiel, suspended cowbell, large suspended cymbal, medium tambourine, large guiro, medium tenor drum, large bass drum), violin I, violin II, viola, violoncello, double bass.
Call no.: **1995/026**
Re-entered as: **1996/041**

753. Elias, Brian, 1948– Five songs to poems by Irina Ratushinskaya: for mezzo soprano & orchestra. London: Chester Music, 1989.
1 score (128 p.); 31 cm.
Russian words (with romanization) and texts in Cyrillic printed separately with English translation.
Reproduced from holograph.
"Perusal score."
Duration: ca. 25:00.
Composer's note and performance instructions.
Contents: It seemed to you that it was night—And I undid the old shawl—No, I'm not afraid—Pencil letter—Mermaids, and stars with rays.
Composed for: mezzo-soprano, 4 flutes (1st–2nd also alto flute, 3rd–4th also piccolo), 2 oboes, English horn, 2 clarinets (2nd also clarinet in E♭), bass clarinet, 2 bassoons, contrabassoon, 4 horns, 3 trumpets (1st also flugelhorn), 2 trombones, bass trombone, tuba, timpani, percussion (vibraphone, 4 gongs, glockenspiel, tubular bells, bass drum, crotales, side drum, 4 tam-tams, 5 bell plates, tambourine, 3 triangles, suspended cymbals, 4 Japanese temple bells, handbell), 2 harps, celesta, violin I, violin II, viola, violoncello, double bass.

Commissioned by: BBC.
Call no.: **1990/028**
Re-entered as: **1991/036**

754. Elias, Brian, 1948– Laments: for mezzo soprano, small chorus & orchestra. London: Chester Music, 1998.
1 score (111 p.); 37 cm.
Grico words; also printed as text with English translation.
Texts from Canti di pianto e d'amore dall'antico Salento.
"Revised 7/98"—p. 1.
Reproduced from manuscript.
Duration: ca. 22:00.
Contents: Ce su, cardiá cameni, clafse, clafse—Icha ammés to coráfimmu—Mila, mila dòdeca.
Composed for: mezzo-soprano, small SATB chorus, 3 flutes (3rd also piccolo and alto flute), 2 oboes, English horn, 2 clarinets (2nd also clarinet in E♭), bass clarinet, contrabassoon, 4 horns, 3 trumpets, 2 trombones, bass trombone, tuba, timpani, percussion (vibraphone, triangle, crotales, 2 gongs, tenor drum, 3 suspended cymbals, bass drum, tam-tam, snare drum, tambourine), celesta, harp, violin I, violin II, viola, violoncello, double bass.
Commissioned by: BBC.
Call no.: **2000/049**

755. Elias, Brian, 1948– Laments: for mezzo soprano, small chorus & orchestra. London: Chester Music, 1998.
1 score (111 p.); 42 cm.
Grico words; also printed as text with English translation.
Texts from Canti di pianto e d'amore dall'antico Salento.
"Revised 7/98"—p. 1.
Reproduced from manuscript.
Duration: ca. 22:00.
Contents: Ce su, cardiá cameni, clafse, clafse—Icha ammés to coráfimmu—Mila, mila dòdeca.
Composed for: mezzo-soprano, small SATB chorus, 3 flutes (3rd also piccolo and alto flute), 2 oboes, English horn, 2 clarinets (2nd also clarinet in E♭), bass clarinet, contrabassoon, 4 horns, 3 trumpets, 2 trombones, bass trombone, tuba, timpani, percussion (vibraphone, triangle, crotales, 2 gongs, tenor drum, 3 suspended cymbals, bass drum, tam-tam, snare drum, tambourine), celesta, harp, violin I, violin II, viola, violoncello, double bass.
Commissioned by: BBC.
Call no.: **2002/053**

756. Eliasson, Anders, 1947– Breathing room: July: for mixed choir a cappella.
Composed for: SATB chorus.
Call no.: **1985/060**
No materials available.

757. Eliasson, Anders, 1947– Concerto: (sette passaggie), per clarinetto ed orchestra. N.p.: AB Nordiska Musikförlaget, 1993.
1 score (109 p.); 42 cm.
Reproduced from manuscript.
Composed for: clarinet, 2 flutes (2nd also piccolo), 2 oboes (2nd also English horn), 2 clarinets (2nd also bass clarinet), 2 bassoons, 3 horns, 2 trumpets, 2 trombones, violin I, violin II, viola, violoncello, double bass.
Call no.: **1998/046**

758. Eliasson, Anders, 1947– Concerto per trombone. Partitura. N.p.: Warner/Chappell Music Scandinavia AB, 2000.
1 score (106 p.); 30 cm.
Duration: ca. 23:00.
Composed for: trombone, 3 flutes (3rd also piccolo), 2 oboes, English horn, 3 clarinets, 3 bassoons (3rd also contrabassoon), 4 horns, 3 trumpets, 3 trombones, tuba, timpani, percussion (glockenspiel, claves, 6 tom-toms, snare drum, tambourine, suspended cymbal, tambourine, bass drum), violin I, violin II, viola, violoncello, double bass.
Commissioned by: Rikskonserter Stockholm.
Call no.: **2002/054**

759. Englund, Einar, 1916–1999. Concerto: per clarinetto in B♭ ed orchestra, 1991. Helsinki: Einar Englund: Finnish Music Information Center, 1991.
1 score (102 p.); 36 cm.
Reproduced from holograph.
Composed for: clarinet, 2 flutes, 2 oboes, 2 clarinets, 2 bassoons, 4 horns, 2 trumpets, 3 trombones, timpani, percussion (piccolo snare drum, tambourine, woodblock, tom-toms, cymbals, bass drum, orchestra bells, vibraphone, marimba), harp, celesta, violin I, violin II, viola, violoncello, double bass.
Commissioned by: Helsinki Music Festival.
Call no.: **1994/039**

760. Eötvös, Peter, 1944– Chinese opera: (1986). Paris: Éditions Salabert, 1986.
1 score (78 p.); 42 cm.
For instrumental ensemble.
Reproduced from manuscript.
Duration: ca. 35:00.

Composed for: 2 flutes (both also piccolo and alto flute), 2 oboes (both also English horn), 3 clarinets (1st–2nd also clarinet in E♭, 3rd also bass clarinet), 2 bassoons, 2 horns, 2 trumpets (both also piccolo trumpet), 2 trombones, tuba (also sousaphone), percussion (timpani, bass drum, Chinese bass drum, 4 Chinese opera gongs, tam-tam, Chinese crash cymbals, 8 crotales, 2 temple blocks, 2 ratchets, Chinese drum, low cymbal, whisper chimes), harp, synthesizer, violin I, violin II, viola, violoncello, double bass.
Call no.: **1990/029**

761. Eötvös, Peter, 1944– ZeroPoints: for orchestra (1999). Partitur. Mainz; New York, NY: Schott, 2000.
1 score (66 p.); 42 cm.
Reproduced from holograph.
Composed for: 2 piccolos, 2 flutes, 2 oboes, English horn, clarinet, clarinet in A, clarinet in E♭, bass clarinet, 2 bassoons, contrabassoon, soprano saxophone, tenor saxophone, 4 horns, 2 trumpets, piccolo trumpet, 2 trombones, bass trombone, tuba, percussion (bass drum, vibraphone, cymbals, tam-tam, metal chimes, steel drum, triangle, timpani, tubular bells, steel drum, 2 sleigh bells, marimba, glockenspiel, crotales, string drum), 2 harps, piano (also celesta), violin I, violin II, viola, violoncello, double bass.
Commissioned by: London Symphony Orchestra.
Call no.: **2002/055**

762. Erb, Donald, 1927– Concerto: for violin and orchestra. Bryn Mawr, PA: Merion Music: Theodore Presser, 1992.
1 score (112 p.); 46 cm.
Composed for: violin, 3 flutes (2nd also alto flute and telephone bell, 3rd also piccolo), 2 oboes, English horn, 2 clarinets, bass clarinet, 2 bassoons (2nd also telephone bell), contrabassoon, 4 horns (4th also telephone bell), 3 trumpets, 2 trombones, bass trombone, tuba, timpani, percussion (2 stem glasses, glockenspiel, chimes, 3 tam-tams, 3 bass drums, nipple gong, 4 tuned drums, small triangle, sizzle cymbal, crotales, marimba, 2 harmonicas, large suspended cymbal, snare drum, vibraphone, gong, xylophone, 2 bongos, 2 timbales, gallon glass jug), harp, piano, synthesizer, violin I, violin II, viola, violoncello, double bass.
Commissioned by: Grand Rapids Symphony.
Call no.: **1994/040**

763. Erb, Donald, 1927– Concerto for brass and orchestra. Bryn Mawr, PA: Merion Music: T. Presser, 1989.
1 score (90 p.); 31 cm.
Composed for: 3 flutes (3rd also piccolo and alto flute), 2 oboes, English horn, 2 clarinets, bass clarinet, 2 bassoons, contrabassoon, 4 horns, 3 trumpets, 2 trombones, bass trombone, tuba, timpani, percussion (chimes, vibraphone, marimba, crotales, bass drum, tam-tam, 5 tuned drums, gallon jug, mounted wine glass, suspended cymbal, snare drum, glockenspiel, roto-toms, 2 harmonicas, xylophone, nipple gong, tom-toms), harp, piano (also celesta and synthesizer), violin I, violin II, viola, violoncello, double bass.
Commissioned by: Chicago Symphony Orchestra.
Call no.: **1991/037**

764. Erb, Donald, 1927– Concerto for brass and orchestra: (1986). Bryn Mawr, PA: Theodore Presser, 1986.
1 score (90 p.); 56 cm.
Duration: ca. 15:00.
Composed for: 3 flutes (3rd also piccolo and alto flute), 2 oboes, English horn, 2 clarinets, bass clarinet, 2 bassoons, contrabassoon, 4 horns, 3 trumpets, 2 trombones, bass trombone, tuba, timpani, percussion (chimes, vibraphone, marimba, crotales, bass drum, tam-tam, 5 tuned drums, gallon jug, mounted wine glass, suspended cymbal, snare drum, glockenspiel, roto-toms, 2 harmonicas, xylophone, nipple gong, tom-toms), harp, piano (also celesta and synthesizer), violin I, violin II, viola, violoncello, double bass.
Commissioned by: Chicago Symphony Orchestra.
Call no.: **1988/035**
Re-entered as: **1989/035**

765. Erb, Donald, 1927– Concerto for orchestra.
Commissioned by: Atlanta Symphony Orchestra.
Call no.: **1986/036**
No materials available.

766. Erb, Donald, 1927– Evensong. Kansas City, MO: D.E. Ramsey, 1993.
1 score (73 p.); 44 cm.
For orchestra.
Contents: Laus amicorum—Elegy for Marcel Dick—Old Badman.
Composed for: 2 flutes (3rd also piccolo and alto flute), 2 oboes, English horn, 2 clarinets, bass clarinet, 2 bassoons, contrabassoon, 4 horns, 3 trumpets, 2 trombones, bass trombone, tuba, timpani, percussion (C harmonica, glockenspiel, marimba, finger cymbal, medium bass drum, large suspended cymbal, slide whistle, bongos, timbales, chimes, vibraphone, large bass drum, 2 tam-tams, medium suspended cymbal, tuned drums, C gong, small bass drum, snare drum, small suspended cymbal, xylophone, nipple gong, 6 roto-toms), harp, piano (also synthesizer), violin I, violin II, viola, violoncello, double bass.

Commissioned by: Cleveland Orchestra.
Call no.: **1995/027**

767. Erb, Donald, 1927– Evensong. Bryn Mawr, PA: Merion Music: T. Presser Co., 1998.
1 miniature score (75 p.); 28 cm.
For orchestra.
Duration: ca. 21:00.
Program note by the composer.
Contents: Laus amicorum—Elegy for Marcel Dick—Old Badman.
Composed for: 2 flutes (3rd also piccolo and alto flute), 2 oboes, English horn, 2 clarinets, bass clarinet, 2 bassoons, contrabassoon, 4 horns, 3 trumpets, 2 trombones, bass trombone, tuba, timpani, percussion (C harmonica, glockenspiel, marimba, finger cymbal, medium bass drum, large suspended cymbal, slide whistle, bongos, timbales, chimes, vibraphone, large bass drum, 2 tam-tams, medium suspended cymbal, tuned drums, C gong, small bass drum, snare drum, small suspended cymbal, xylophone, nipple gong, 6 roto-toms), harp, piano (also synthesizer), violin I, violin II, viola, violoncello, double bass.
Commissioned by: Cleveland Orchestra.
Call no.: **2000/050**

768. Erb, Donald, 1927– Ritual observances. Bryn Mawr, PA: Merion Music: T. Presser, 1992.
1 score (130 p.); 43 cm.
For orchestra.
Composed for: 3 flutes (3rd also piccolo), 2 oboes, English horn, 3 clarinets (3rd also clarinet in E♭), bass clarinet, 2 bassoons (both also telephone bells), contrabassoon (also telephone bells), 4 horns, 3 trumpets, 2 trombones, bass trombone, tuba, timpani, percussion (gong, 2 harmonicas, crotales, xylophone, bass drum, roto-tom, nipple gong, tam-tam, suspended cymbal, slide whistle, metal wind chimes, chromatic harmonica, chimes, vibraphone, mark tree, 2 bongos, 2 timbales, marimba, glockenspiel, snare drum, 4 tuned drums), harp, piano (also synthesizer), violin I, violin II, viola, violoncello, double bass.
Commissioned by: St. Louis Symphony.
Call no.: **1993/038**

769. Erić, Zoran, 1950– Oberon concerto: for flute and instrumental ensemble. Belgrade: Quatrico, 1998.
1 score (133 p.); 30 cm.
Composed for: flute, clarinet, bass clarinet, 4 trombones, percussion (bongos, congas, tom-toms, steel drums, gongs, triangles, woodblocks, African shaker, glockenspiel, marimba), 8 violins, 4 violas, 4 violoncellos, 4 double basses, 4 female voices (amplified and processed, a piacere).
Commissioned by: BEMUS Festival.
Call no.: **2001/051**

770. Ermirio, Federico, 1950– Lumina: per 15 esecutori (1989). N.p.: n.p., 1989.
1 score (38 p.); 31 cm.
Reproduced from manuscript.
Duration: ca. 11:00.
Composed for: flute (also alto flute), oboe, clarinet (also bass clarinet), horn, trumpet, trombone, percussion (marimba, snare drum, drum, tam-tam, vibraphone, 2 suspended cymbals, 4 tom-toms, low drum), harp, piano, 2 violins, viola, violoncello, double bass.
Call no.: **1990/030**

771. Eröd, Iván, 1936– Vox lucis: Kantate für Bariton, Oboe-Solo und Orchester, op. 56. Partitur. Wien: Doblinger, 1989.
1 score (95 p.); 35 cm.
English, French, German, Hungarian, Italian, and Russian words; also printed as text with German translation.
Texts by T.S. Eliot, Paul Claudel, Ossip Mandelstam, Rainer Maria Rilke, Giuseppe Ungaretti, and Sándor Weöres.
Reproduced from manuscript.
Duration: ca. 30:00.
Composed for: baritone, oboe, 2 flutes (2nd also piccolo), alto flute, 2 clarinets in A, bass clarinet, 2 bassoons, 2 horns, tuba, timpani, percussion (glockenspiel, 2 sets of chimes, vibraphone), harp, celesta, violin I, violin II, viola, violoncello, double bass.
Commissioned by: Musikverein für Steiermark.
Call no.: **1991/038**

772. Errázuriz, Sebastián, 1975– Estudio sinfónico no 1: op. 6. N.p.: n.p., 1999.
1 score (53 p.); 33 cm.
Duration: 8:00.
Composed for: 3 flutes (3rd also piccolo), 2 oboes, 2 clarinets, bass clarinet, 2 bassoons, 4 horns, 3 trumpets, 2 trombones, bass trombone, tuba, harp, 2 timpani, percussion (glockenspiel, snare drum, cymbals, bass drum), violin I, violin II, viola, violoncello, double bass.
Call no.: **2002/056**

773. Esbrí, Alejandro, 1959– In 5 and 7 assembly kit: for Korg M-1 solo synthesizer: (sequenced electronic work) = En 5 y 7 modelo para armar: para sintetizador Korg M-1, solo: (obra electrónica secuenciada) 1991. Partitura. N.p.: Alejandro Esbrí, 1991.
37 leaves of music; 22 x 29 cm.

Reproduced from manuscript.
Composed for: synthesizer.
Call no.: **1992/040**

774. Escobar, Roberto, 1926– Tower of the winds. N.p.: n.p., 1992.
1 score (10 p.); 36 cm.
For string quartet.
Reproduced from manuscript.
Duration: 10:00.
Composed for: 2 violins, viola, violoncello.
Call no.: **1996/042**

775. Escot, Pozzi, 1933– Aria. Cambridge, MA: Publication Contact International, 1998.
1 score (5 p.); 29 cm.
Vocalize.
Duration: 3:15.
Composed for: voice, flute, clarinet, alto saxophone.
Commissioned by: William Malone.
Call no.: **2003/039a**

776. Escot, Pozzi, 1933– Aria II: for soprano or soprano and electronics. Cambridge, MA: Publication Contact International, 2001.
1 leaf of music; 28 cm.
"Textual singing either using vowels, consonants, vowels/consonants, words, or combination"—preface.
Duration: ca. 3:00.
Composed for: soprano, electronics.
Commissioned by: Patrice Pastore.
Call no.: **2003/039b**

777. Escot, Pozzi, 1933– Cristhos: trilogy for the six million, #2. Revised (1993). Cambridge, MA: Publication Contact International, 1993.
1 score (19 p.); 22 x 29 cm.
Composed for: flute, bassoon, 3 violins, percussion (4 bass drums, 3 tom-toms, 2 snare drums, anvil, 3 woodblocks, whip, small gong, 3 tam-tams).
Call no.: **1995/028**

778. Escot, Pozzi, 1933– Jubilation. Cambridge, MA: Publication Contact International, 1991.
1 score (11 p.); 28 cm.
For string quartet.
Duration: 4:00.
Composed for: 2 violins, viola, violoncello.
Commissioned by: New England Conservatory.
Call no.: **1993/039**

779. Escot, Pozzi, 1933– Mirabilis III: for voice, three flutes, three violins. Cambridge, MA: Publication Contact International, 1995.
1 score (19 p.); 22 x 29 cm.
Latin words.
Text: O virtus quam mirabilis.
Duration: 3:00.
Composed for: voice, 3 flutes, 3 violins.
Call no.: **1997/044**

780. Escot, Pozzi, 1933– Sarabande for Lillian. Cambridge, MA: Publication Contact International, 1999.
1 score (24 p.); 22 x 29 cm.
"In some instances other woodwinds may be used and registers changed"—title page verso.
Composed for: 5 flutes, 2 violoncellos, snare drum.
Call no.: **2002/057**

781. Escot, Pozzi, 1933– Violin concerto: for solo violin and orchestra (2002–03). Cambridge, MA: Publication Contact Internat., 2003.
1 score (22 p.); 28 cm.
Composed for: violin, flute, oboe, clarinet, bassoon, horn, trumpet, trombone, violin II, violin II, viola, violoncello, double bass.
Call no.: **2005/047**

782. Escot, Pozzi, 1933– Violin concerto (Mvt. I): for solo violin and orchestra. Cambridge, MA: Publication Contact International, 2002.
1 score (8 p.); 28 cm.
Duration: 1:00.
Composed for: violin, flute, oboe, clarinet, bassoon, horn, trumpet, trombone, violin I, violin II, viola, violoncello, double bass.
Call no.: **2004/036**

783. Escot, Pozzi, 1933– Visione 97: for eight singers or mixed chorus. Cambridge, MA: Publication Contact International, 1997.
1 score (17 p.); 22 x 28 cm.
"The original 'Okotechos Ensemble' VISIONE97 commission was for eight solo singers and did not include alto parts. Thus, the alto parts are only to be sung when VISIONE97 is performed by a mixed chorus"—verso.
Composed for: 2 sopranos, 2 altos, 2 tenors, 2 baritones, 2 basses (or mixed chorus).
Commissioned by: Oktoechos Ensemble.
Call no.: **2001/052**

784. Ėshpaĭ, Andreĭ I͡Akovlevich, 1925– 4th concerto for violin and orchestra. Score. N.p.: n.p., 1994.
1 score (119 p.); 40 cm.
Reproduced from manuscript.

Composed for: violin, piccolo, 2 flutes, 2 oboes, 2 clarinets, 2 bassoons, contrabassoon, 4 horns, 3 trumpets, 3 trombones, tuba, timpani, percussion (triangle, tambourine, whip, cymbals, bass drum), harp, violin I, violin II, viola, violoncello, double bass.
Call no.: **1995/029**

785. Ėshpaĭ, Andreĭ I͡Akovlevich, 1925– VIth Symphony: (Liturgy). N.p.: n.p., 1988.
1 score (93 p.); 41 cm.
Russian words (Cyrillic).
For chorus and orchestra.
Reproduced from manuscript.
Composed for: SATB chorus, 3 flutes (3rd also piccolo), 2 clarinets, 2 oboes, 2 bassoons, contrabassoon, 4 horns, 3 trumpets, 3 trombones, tuba, timpani, percussion (cymbals, drum, tam-tam, chimes), harp, piano, celesta, violin I, violin II, viola, violoncello, double bass.
Call no.: **1994/041**

786. Ėshpaĭ, Andreĭ I͡Akovlevich, 1925– Concerto for double bass, bassoon and string orchestra. N.p.: n.p., 1994.
1 score (32 p.); 40 cm.
Reproduced from holograph.
Composed for: double bass, bassoon, violin I, violin II, viola, violoncello, double bass.
Call no.: **2000/051**

787. Ėshpaĭ, Andreĭ I͡Akovlevich, 1925– Concordia discordans. N.p.: n.p., 1996.
1 score (36 p.); 40 cm.
For string quartet.
Reproduced from manuscript.
Composed for: 2 violins, viola, violoncello.
Call no.: **1997/045**

788. Ėshpaĭ, Andreĭ I͡Akovlevich, 1925– Kont͡sert dli͡a al'ta s orkestrom. Partytura. N.p.: n.p., 1987.
1 score (105 p.); 40 cm.
Concerto for violin and orchestra.
Reproduced from manuscript.
Composed for: viola, piccolo, 2 flutes, 2 oboes, 2 clarinets, 2 bassoons, 4 horns, 3 trumpets, 2 trombones, bass trombone, tuba, timpani, 2 harps, violin I, violin II, viola, violoncello, double bass.
Call no.: **1989/036**

789. Estacio, John, 1966– Filumena: an opera in two acts. N.p.: n.p., 2003.
1 score (470 p.); 44 cm.
English words by John Murrell.
Composed for: soprano, 2 mezzo-sopranos, 3 tenors, 2 baritones, SATB chorus, 2 flutes (also piccolo), 2 oboes (also English horn), 2 clarinets (also bass clarinet), 2 bassoons, 4 horns, 2 trumpets, 2 trombones, bass trombone, tuba, timpani, percussion, piano (also ragtime piano), accordion, guitar (also mandolin), bagpipes, harp, band (optional: 2 trumpets, 3 trombones, tuba, percussion), violin I, violin I, viola, violoncello, double bass.
Commissioned by: Calgary Opera and Banff Centre.
Call no.: **2005/048**

790. Estévez, Milton, 1947– Apuntes con refran, 1982. N.p.: n.p., 1987.
1 score (7, 61 leaves); 30 cm.
For orchestra and tape.
Reproduced from manuscript.
Includes performance instructions.
Composed for: 2 flutes (1st also piccolo), alto flute, bass flute, 2 oboes, English horn, 3 clarinets (3rd also bass clarinet), 2 bassoons, 4 horns, 3 trumpets, 3 trombones, tuba, percussion (2 suspended cymbals, snare drum, pedal bass drum, tubular bells, xylophone, marimba, 3 tom-toms, timpani, Chinese woodblocks, 2 tam-tams, triangle, suspended bass drum), harp, tape, violin I, violin II, viola, violoncello, double bass.
Call no.: **1988/036**

791. Estévez, Milton, 1947– Cinco desencuentros con episodio cualquiera: para orquesta y cinta magnética, 1986. N.p.: n.p., 1986.
1 score (vii, 39 p.); 36 cm.
For orchestra and magnetic tape.
Reproduced from manuscript.
Includes performance instructions in Spanish.
Composed for: 2 flutes (1st also piccolo), alto flute, bass flute, 2 oboes, 3 clarinets (3rd also bass clarinet), 2 bassoons, 4 horns, 2 trumpets, 2 trombones, percussion (triangle, crotales, 2 suspended cymbals, 2 tam-tams, 2 cowbells, guiro, Chinese blocks, 2 woodblocks, 2 bongos, snare drum, 2 congas, 3 tom-toms, timpani, pedal bass drum, vibraphone, glockenspiel, tubular bells, xylophone, maracas, whip, bass drum), synthesizer, violin I, violin II, viola, violoncello, double bass.
Call no.: **1987/021**

792. Estrada, Julio, 1943– Eolo'oolin: pour 6 percussions (1981–1983). N.p.: n.p., 1988.
1 score (various pagings); 30 x 42 cm.
"(E.17 1981–84, revision 1988)"—p. 2.
Reproduced from manuscript.
Includes introduction and performance instructions in English.

Composed for: 17 roto-toms, 6 parchment drums, 2 big drums (one with pedal), 5 cuícas, 3 stew pots with handle and 180 marble balls, 6 anvils with 6 metal hammers, 20 suspended cymbals, 6 tam-tams, 6 gongs, 10 thick sheets of metal, hand saw, rattle, 12 pairs of maracas, 4 pairs of tenabaris, set of suspended bamboo bells, 6 pairs of claves, 6 pairs of woodblocks, 19 Chinese woodblocks, 2 teponaztlis, 12 pieces of smooth wood, 2 rasps, 6 cricket balls, 6 Aztec whistles of the dead, 8 stones, 4 pieces of rough mosaic, 12 continuum sticks, 12 super-ball sticks, 3 smooth rib sticks.
Call no.: **2003/040**

793. Eyerly, Scott, 1958– Variations on a theme by Honegger: for orchestra. New York, NY: Henmar Press, 1988.
1 score (155 p.); 34 cm.
Reproduced from manuscript.
Duration: ca. 30:00.
Composed for: 3 flutes (3rd also piccolo), 2 oboes, English horn, 3 clarinets in A (3rd also bass clarinet), 3 bassoons (3rd also contrabassoon), 4 horns, 3 trumpets, 2 trombones, bass trombone, tuba, percussion (timpani, xylophone, 2 glockenspiels, 8 tom-toms, snare drum, bongos, tambourine, 3 tam-tams, 3 brake drums, 8 suspended cymbals, crash cymbals, 3 woodblocks, glass wind chimes, triangle), harp, violin I, violin II, viola, violoncello, double bass.
Call no.: **1990/031**

794. Faiman, Jonathan, 1969– Conversations: with piano and orchestra. Full score. N.p.: n.p., 2002.
1 score (57 p.); 36 cm.
Duration: 15:00.
Composed for: piano, piccolo, 2 flutes, 2 oboes (2nd also English horn), 2 clarinets (2nd also bass clarinet), 2 bassoons (2nd also contrabassoon), 2 horns, 2 trumpets, 2 trombones, tuba, timpani (also suspended cymbals and tam-tam), percussion (snare drum, 3 roto-toms, glockenspiel), violin I, violin II, viola, violoncello, double bass.
Commissioned by: Ian Hobson.
Call no.: **2004/037**

795. Faith, Richard, 1926– Trio for violin, cello (or horn) and piano. N.p.: n.p., 198-?.
1 score (65 p.); 36 cm.
Reproduced from holograph.
Composed for: violin, violoncello (or horn), piano.
Call no.: **1985/061**

796. Falik, I͡Uriĭ Aleksandrovich, 1936– Mass: for soloists, mixed chorus and chamber ensemble. N.p.: n.p., 1996.
1 score (62 p.); 36 cm.
Latin words.
Reproduced from manuscript.
Composed for: voices, SATB chorus, 2 oboes, 2 bassoons, bells, 2 violas, violoncello, double bass.
Call no.: **2000/052**

797. Falik, I͡Uriĭ Aleksandrovich, 1936– Symphony n 2: Kaddish. N.p.: n.p., 1993.
1 score (55 p.); 35 cm.
Reproduced from manuscript.
Composed for: 4 flutes (4th also piccolo), 3 clarinets (also clarinet in E♭), bass clarinet, 4 horns, 4 trumpets, 3 trombones, tuba, timpani, percussion (piccolo drum, bass drum, tam-tam, vibraphone, bells), celesta, violin I, violin II, viola, violoncello, double bass.
Call no.: **1995/030**

798. Fanticini, Fabrizio, 1955– Di retro al sol: per orchestra. Partitura. Milano: Ricordi, 1986.
1 score (21 p.); 83 cm.
Reproduced from holograph.
Duration: ca. 9:00.
Composed for: piccolo, flute, alto flute, oboe, English horn, 2 clarinets, bass clarinet, bassoon, contrabassoon, 4 horns, 2 trumpets, 2 trombones, bass tuba, percussion (vibraphone, chimes, glockenspiel, crotales, flexatone, timpani), harp, celesta, violin I, violin II, violin III, violin IV, viola I, viola II, viola III, violoncello I, violoncello II, double bass I, double bass II.
Call no.: **1989/037**
Re-entered as: **1990/032**

799. Farago, Pierre, 1969– La pleurante des rues de Prague: pièce pour 17 instruments à cordes solistes: d'aprés La pleurante des rues de Prague de Sylvie Germain, 1999. N.p.: n.p., 1999.
1 score (118 p.); 36 cm.
Composed for: 9 violins, 3 violas, 3 violoncellos, 2 double basses.
Call no.: **2001/053**

800. Farquhar, David, 1928– Symphony no. 2. N.p.: D. Farquhar, 1984.
1 score (115 leaves); 39 cm.
Reproduced from holograph.
Duration: ca. 29:00.
Composed for: 3 flutes (3rd also piccolo), 2 oboes, 2 clarinets, 2 bassoons, 4 horns, 3 trumpets, 3 trombones, tuba, timpani, percussion (cymbals, side drum, tambourine, suspended cymbal, triangle), piano, violin

I, violin II, viola, violoncello, double bass.
Commissioned by: NZ Symphony Orchestra.
Call no.: **1985/062**

801. Faulconer, Bruce, 1951– Sonata for flute and piano, 1986. Dallas, TX: Bruce L. Faulconer, 1986.
1 score (28 p.) + 1 part (14 p.); 28 x 44 cm.
Composed for: flute, piano.
Call no.: **1992/041**

802. Faulconer, Bruce, 1951– Washington-on-the-Brazos: a symphonic poem. Dallas, TX: Bruce L. Faulconer, 1986.
1 score (130 p.); 44 cm.
Reproduced from manuscript.
Composed for: 3 flutes (3rd also piccolo), 3 oboes, 3 clarinets, 3 bassoons, 4 horns, 3 trumpets, 3 trombones, tuba, timpani, percussion (bass drum, xylophone, snare drum, cymbals, chimes, triangle, crotales, glockenspiel), harp, celesta, violin I, violin II, viola, violoncello, double bass.
Commissioned by: McLean-Paris Foundation.
Call no.: **1987/022**

803. Fedele, Ivan, 1953– Concerto: per pf. e orchestra (1993). Milano: Edizioni Suvini Zerboni, 1993.
1 score (135 p.); 63 cm.
Reproduced from holograph.
Duration: ca. 22:00.
Composed for: piano, 2 flutes, 2 oboes, 2 clarinets, 2 bassoons, 2 horns, 2 trumpets, 2 trombones, timpani (also bass drum and suspended cymbals), percussion (bell plates, tuned gongs, glockenspiel, vibraphone, tubular bells, marimba, 3 suspended cymbals), harp, violin I, violin II, viola, violoncello, double bass.
Commissioned by: Radio France.
Call no.: **1996/043**

804. Felciano, Richard, 1930– An American Decameron: songs from the interviews of Studs Terkel, for soprano and chamber ensemble. N.p.: Richard Felciano, 2001.
1 score (114 p.); 36 cm.
English words; also printed as text.
Duration: 1:00:00.
Composed for: soprano, flute (also piccolo and alto flute), clarinet (also soprano and bass clarinets), violin, violoncello, piano (also celesta), percussion (2 bongos, 2 tom-toms, tenor drum, snare drum, 2 timpani, vibraphone, marimba, xylophone, glockenspiel, tubular chimes, 5 temple blocks, 3 woodblocks, 2 suspended cymbals, triangle, whip, maracas, crotales, mounted ratchet, very large tam-tam).
Commissioned by: Serge and Natalie Koussevitzky Foundation.
Call no.: **2003/041**

805. Feld, Jindřich, 1925– III. Symfonie: pro symfonický orchestr: "Fin de siècle." Partitura. Prahae: Editio Bärenreiter, 1998.
1 score (112 p.); 32 cm.
Reproduced from manuscript.
At end of score: Praha 24.12.1998.
Duration: ca. 30:00.
Composed for: 3 flutes (3rd also piccolo), 3 oboes (3rd also English horn), 3 clarinets (3rd also bass clarinet), 3 bassoons (3rd also contrabassoon), 4 horns, 3 trumpets, 3 trombones, tuba, harp, percussion (xylophone, glockenspiel, chimes, 3 bongos, woodblocks, snare drum, bass drum, triangle, suspended cymbals, crash cymbals, gong), timpani, violin I, violin II, viola, violoncello, double bass.
Call no.: **2004/039**

806. Feld, Jindřich, 1925– VI. smyčcový kvartet (1993). Partitura. Praha: Bärenreiter Editio Supraphon, 1996.
1 score (32 p.); 27 x 34 cm.
Duration: ca. 27:00.
Reproduced from manuscript.
Composed for: 2 violins, viola, violoncello.
Call no.: **1997/046**

807. Felder, David, 1953– In between: for solo percussionist and chamber orchestra (1999–2000). Bryn Mawr, PA: Theodore Presser, 1999.
1 score (61 p.); 44 cm.
Originally for percussionist and electronics.
Composed for: percussion (marimba, vibraphone, crotales, KAT controller with Akai S-3000 sampler, musical saw, temple bowls, medium bass drum or kick drum, 2 large bass drums, wood/log drum), 2 flutes (all also piccolo and alto flute), 2 oboes (2nd also English horn), 2 clarinets (1st also clarinet in E♭, 2nd also bass and contrabass clarinets), bassoon, contrabassoon, 2 horns, 2 trumpets, trombone, bass trombone, tuba, timpani, percussion (marimba, vibraphone, glockenspiel, crotales, cymbals, opera gong, medium gong, large gong, tam-tams, small bass drum, log drums, claves, small shakers, small flexatone, several small triangles, bells, wind chimes and other light ringing metal, splash cymbal, cymbals, bass drum, woodblocks, small shakers, vibraslap, 2 medium tom-toms, 2 large tom-toms, kick drum), electric guitar, electric bass guitar, piano (also celesta), violin I, violin II, viola, violoncello, double bass.

Commissioned by: June in Buffalo, 2000.
Call no.: **2002/058**

808. Felder, David, 1953– A pressure triggering dreams. Bryn Mawr, PA: Merion Music: Theodore Presser, 1996.
1 score (72 p.); 44 cm.
For orchestra.
"Updated 8/96."
Composed for: 3 flutes (1st also bass flute, 2nd also alto flute, 3rd also piccolo), 3 oboes (3rd also English horn), 2 clarinets (2nd also clarinet in E♭), bass clarinet (also contrabass clarinet), 2 bassoons, contrabassoon, 4 horns, 3 trumpets, 2 trombones, bass trombone, tuba, percussion (marimba, vibraphone, crotales, tuned temple bowls, opera gong, small sizzle cymbal, claves, bongos, 3 high roto-toms, low tuned gong, 2 tam-tams, xylophone, medium sizzle cymbal, log drum, 3 woodblocks, 4 tom-toms, 2 bass drums, KAT with s-1000 sampler and disk samples, medium tuned gong, 6 tin cans, glockenspiel), harp, electronics, electric bass, keyboard player (piano and Kurzweil K-2000), violin I, violin II, viola, violoncello, double bass.
Commissioned by: American Composers Orchestra.
Call no.: **1998/047**

809. Felder, David, 1953– Six poems from Neruda's "Alturas . . .": for orchestra (1992). Bryn Mawr, PA: Merion Music: T. Presser, 1994.
1 score (86 p.); 43 cm.
"Updated 2/94."
Composed for: orchestra: 3 flutes (also alto flute and piccolo), 2 oboes (also English horn), 2 clarinets (1st also clarinet in E♭), 2 bassoons, contrabassoon, 4 horns, 3 trumpets, 3 trombones, tuba, timpani, percussion (vibraphone, glockenspiel, crotales, splash cymbal, sizzle cymbal, 6 tuned skins, large gong, tam-tam, large bass drum, rain stick, marimba, suspended cymbal, chimes, 6 tuned metal, metal bar, medium bass drum), harp, piano, celesta, violin I, violin II, viola, violoncello, double bass.
Commissioned by: Buffalo Philharmonic.
Call no.: **1995/031**

810. Felder, David, 1953– Three pieces for orchestra (1996). Bryn Mawr, PA: Merion Music: Theodore Presser, 1996.
1 score (62 p.); 44 cm.
"Updated 5/96."
Contents: Zack attack—For two shades of the seventh light—Preface for Ark.
Composed for: 3 flutes (2nd also alto flute, 3rd also piccolo), 3 oboes (3rd also English horn), 3 clarinets (2nd also clarinet in E♭, 3rd also bass clarinet), 2 bassoons, contrabassoon, 4 horns, 3 trumpets (1st also piccolo trumpet, 3rd also trumpet in D), 2 trombones, bass trombone, tuba, timpani, percussion (2 marimbas, vibraphone, electronics, crotales, 2 tam-tams, xylophone, glockenspiel, kick drum, 3 tom-toms, 3 bass drums, claves, 3 woodblocks, gong), harp, keyboard, electric bass, violin I, violin II, violin III, viola I, viola II, violoncello I, violoncello II, double bass.
Commissioned by: Buffalo Philharmonic.
Call no.: **1997/047**

811. Feldmann, Francine Greshler, 1949– The secret of the webbing purple: (a musical fantasy). N.p.: Blue Dalmatian Productions, 1995.
1 score (41 leaves); 28 cm.
English words by the composer.
Songs.
Contents: My cat named Mike—The mole-house waltz—Beee nice to me—This world's a beauty 'cause of me—I am the webbing purple—If I could fly—I'm Tamara's tomato—She's got a beauty—Let's go—I think you should have it.
Composed for: unspecified.
Call no.: **2001/054**
Also available:
Call no.: **2001/054 text**

812. Fennelly, Brian, 1937– A sprig of andromeda: (from a Thoreau symphony): for orchestra. Milano: G. Ricordi & C., 1992.
1 score (78 p.); 28 cm.
Duration: ca. 13:00.
Composed for: piccolo, 2 flutes, 2 oboes, English horn, 2 clarinets, bass clarinet, 2 bassoons, contrabassoon, 4 horns, 3 trumpets, 3 trombones, tuba, timpani, percussion (xylophone, vibraphone, chimes, tambourine, temple blocks, snare drum, glockenspiel, marimba, tam-tam, 2 bongos, woodblock), harp, piano, celesta, violin I, violin II, viola, violoncello, double bass.
Call no.: **1995/032**

813. Ferber, Sharon, 1968– The third mother. N.p.: n.p., 2002.
1 score (11 p.); 28 cm.
Hebrew words (romanized) by Nathan Alterman; English translation printed as text.
Composed for: SATB chorus.
Call no.: **2004/038**

814. Ferko, Frank, 1950– Stabat mater: for SATB chorus (divisi) unaccompanied, with five additional pieces for optional interpolation for soprano solo,

SATB chorus (divisi) unaccompanied. Boston, MA: E.C. Schirmer, 2000.
1 score (111 p.); 28 cm.
Latin words, with interpolated texts in English; also printed as text with English translation.
"Pre-publication copy."
Piano accompaniment for rehearsal only.
Includes performance note and commentary by the composer.
Contents: Interpolated texts: Introduction / prophecy of Simeon—Andromache's lament / Euripides, tr. Richmond Lattimore—The mother / Padraic H. Pearse—From "The death cycle machine" / Charlotte Mayerson—Elegy / Sally M. Gall.
Composed for: soprano, SATB chorus.
Commissioned by: His Majestie's Clerkes.
Call no.: **2001/055**

815. Ferko, Frank, 1950– Stabat mater: for SATB chorus (divisi) unaccompanied, with five additional pieces for optional interpolation for soprano solo, SATB chorus (divisi) unaccompanied. Boston, MA: E.C. Schirmer Music Co.: a division of ECS Pub., 2000.
1 score (111 p.); 28 cm.
Latin words, with interpolated texts in English; also printed as text with English translation.
Piano accompaniment for rehearsal only.
Includes performance note and commentary by the composer.
Contents: Interpolated texts: Introduction / prophecy of Simeon—Andromache's lament / Euripides, tr. Richmond Lattimore—The mother / Padraic H. Pearse—From "The death cycle machine" / Charlotte Mayerson—Elegy / Sally M. Gall.
Composed for: soprano, SATB chorus.
Commissioned by: His Majestie's Clerkes.
Call no.: **2004/040**

816. Fermani, Simone, 1954– Strong as death is love: cantata for soprano, choir and organ. N.p.: n.p., 1984.
1 score (47 p.); 34 cm.
Latin words from the Bible's Canticum canticorum; also printed as text.
Reproduced from holograph.
Includes performance instructions.
Composed for: soprano, SATB chorus, organ.
Call no.: **1985/063**

817. Ferneyhough, Brian, 1943– Carceri d'invenzione I: chamber orchestra. London; New York, NY: Edition Peters, 1983.
1 score (38 p.); 31 cm.
Duration: 12:00–13:00.
Composed for: flute (also piccolo), oboe (also English horn and triangle), clarinet, bass clarinet, bassoon (also contrabassoon), horn (also triangle), trumpet (also triangle), tenor/bass trombone, tenor tuba (also euphonium), percussion (glockenspiel, 5 woodblocks, 5 drums [2 timbales, 3 tom-toms], large bass drum), piano, 2 violins, viola, violoncello, double bass.
Commissioned by: London Sinfonietta.
Call no.: **1987/023 no.2**

818. Ferneyhough, Brian, 1943– Carceri d'invenzione IIa: solo flute and chamber orchestra. London: Hinrichsen Edition: Peters Edition, 1985.
1 score (55 leaves); 30 cm.
Duration: 12:00–13:00.
Composed for: flute, 2 oboes (2nd also English horn), 2 clarinets (1st also clarinet in E♭; 2nd also bass clarinet), bassoon, 2 horns, 8 violins, 2 violas, 2 violoncellos, double bass.
Commissioned by: Roberto Fabbriciani.
Call no.: **1987/023 no.4**

819. Ferneyhough, Brian, 1943– Carceri d'invenzione III. London; New York, NY: Peters Edition, 1986.
1 score (36 p.); 30 cm.
Duration: ca. 10:30.
Instructions for performance.
Composed for: 2 flutes, 2 oboes, 2 clarinets, bass clarinet, bassoon, 2 horns, 2 trumpets, 2 trombones, bass tuba, percussion.
Commissioned by: Südwestfunk Baden-Baden.
Call no.: **1987/023 no.6**

820. Ferneyhough, Brian, 1943– Etudes transcendantales. London: Edition Peters; Hinrichsen Edition, 1985.
1 score (52 p.); 22 x 30 cm.
German words.
Settings of poems by Ernst Meister and Alrun Moll.
Duration: ca. 25:00.
Includes performance instructions.
Composed for: mezzo-soprano (also claves), flute (also piccolo and alto flute), oboe (also English horn), violoncello, harpsichord.
Commissioned by: Ministère de la Culture Française.
Call no.: **1986/037**

821. Ferneyhough, Brian, 1943– Etudes transcendantales: 1982–85. London: Edition Peters, 1985.
1 score (54 p.); 21 x 30 cm.
German words.
Settings of poems by Ernst Meister and Alrun Moll.
Duration: ca. 27:00.

Composed for: mezzo-soprano (claves), flute (piccolo, alto flute), oboe (English horn), harpsichord, violoncello.
Commissioned by: Ministère de la Culture Française.
Call no.: **1987/023 no.5**

822. Ferneyhough, Brian, 1943– Fourth string quartet. London; New York, NY: Edition Peters, 1990.
1 score (29p.); 29 cm.
Italian words.
For soprano and string quartet.
Errata sheets included.
Composed for: soprano, 2 violins, viola, violoncello.
Commissioned by: Chamber Music Society of Basel.
Call no.: **1991/039**

823. Ferneyhough, Brian, 1943– Intermedio alla ciaccona: violine solo. London: Peters Edition, 1986.
8 p. of music; 30 cm.
Composed for: violin.
Commissioned by: Südwestdeutscher Rundfunk.
Call no.: **1987/023 no.3**

824. Ferneyhough, Brian, 1943– Mnemosyne, 1986. London: Peters Edition, 1986.
10 p. of music; 21 x 30 cm.
"This score does not contain tape-materials."
Composed for: bass flute, tape.
Commissioned by: Südwestdeutscher Rundfunk.
Call no.: **1987/023 no.7**

825. Ferneyhough, Brian, 1943– String trio. Score. London; New York, NY: Edition Peters, 1995.
1 score (50 p.); 21 x 30 cm.
Composed for: violin, viola, violoncello.
Commissioned by: Paris Autumn Festival.
Call no.: **2000/053**

826. Ferneyhough, Brian, 1943– Superscriptio: solo piccolo. London; New York, NY: Edition Peters, 1982.
8 p. of music; 31 cm.
Duration: ca. 5:30.
Composed for: piccolo.
Call no.: **1987/023 no.1**

827. Ferneyhough, Brian, 1943– Third string quartet. Score. London; New York, NY: Edition Peters, 1987.
1 score (25 p.); 30 cm.
Reproduced from holograph.
Duration: ca. 18:00.
Composed for: 2 violins, viola, violoncello.
Commissioned by: Arditti String Quartet.
Call no.: **1988/037**

828. Ferneyhough, Brian, 1943– Third string quartet. London; New York, NY: Edition Peters, 1988.
1 score (28 p.); 31 cm.
Reproduced from holograph.
Duration: ca. 18:00.
Composed for: 2 violins, viola, violoncello.
Commissioned by: Arditti String Quartet.
Call no.: **1990/033**

829. Ferrero, Lorenzo, 1951– Salvatore Giuliano: opera in un atto, 1985. Partitura. Milano: Ricordi, 1985.
1 score (281 p.); 60 cm.
Italian words by Giuseppe di Leva.
Composed for: soprano, mezzo-soprano, 2 tenors, 2 baritones, bass-baritone, 2 basses, SATB chorus, piccolo, 2 flutes, 2 oboes, English horn, clarinet in E♭, 2 clarinets, bass clarinet, alto saxophone, baritone saxophone, 2 bassoons, contrabassoon, 4 horns, 3 trumpets, 2 trombones, bass trombone, tuba, percussion (timpani, crash cymbals, 5 tom-toms, 2 bongos, tambourine, 3 triangles, tam-tam, military drum, vibraphone, roto-toms, metal plate, maracas, bass drum, suspended cymbal, snare drum), harp, electric piano, electric guitar, electric bass guitar, violin I, violin II, viola, violoncello, double bass.
Commissioned by: Teatro dell'Opera di Roma.
Call no.: **1987/024**

830. Ferreyra, Beatriz, 1937– Ríos del sueño. N.p.: n.p., 2000.
3 leaves of music; 21 x 30 cm.
Contents: Río de los pájaros—Río de los pájaros azules—Río de los pájaros escondidos.
Composed for: computer.
Commissioned by: INA-GRM and Bregman Studio, Dartsmouth College.
Call no.: **2003/042**

831. Ferris, William, 1937–2000. Acclamations for organ and orchestra.
Call no.: **1985/064**
No materials available.

832. Festinger, Richard, 1948– Smokin' with cocuswood: for oboe, string quartet and piano. N.p.: n.p., 1992.
1 score (89 p.); 28 cm.
Composed for: oboe, 2 violins, viola, violoncello, piano.
Commissioned by: San Francisco Contemporary Music Players.
Call no.: **1994/042**

833. Fields, Matthew H., 1961– Crossroads: for high

voice and seven players. N.p.: Matthew H. Fields, 1994.
1 score (128 p.); 28 cm.
English words by A. J. Cannaday; also printed as text.
Composed for: high voice, tenor recorder, harpsichord, guitar, 2 violins, viola, violoncello.
Call no.: **2000/054**

834. Fikejz, Daniel, 1954– Eva: music for ballet: performed by symphonic orchestra & soprano, samplers & virtual synthesizers. N.p.: n.p., 2002.
1 score (various pagings); 30 cm.
Nonsense words.
Composed for: soprano, samplers, virtual synthesizers, percussion, 2 bassoons, 2 oboes, English horn, alto saxophone, piano, harp, violin I, violin II, viola, violoncello, double bass, 2 flutes, 2 trumpets, horn, 2 clarinets, trombone, SATB chorus, bass clarinet, acoustic guitar acoustic bass, timpani, hammond organ.
Call no.: **2005/049**

835. Fink, Myron S., 1932– Chinchilla. N.p.: M. Fink, 1982.
1 score (3 v.); 56 cm.
English words by Donald Moreland.
Opera in 3 acts.
Reproduced from manuscript.
Composed for: 2 flutes (2nd also piccolo), 2 oboes, English horn, 2 clarinets (all also clarinet in A, 2nd also bass clarinet), saxophone in C, tenor saxophone (also baritone saxophone), 2 bassoons, 2 horns, trumpet, trombone, tuba, timpani, percussion (cymbals, 2 tom-toms, snare drum, bass drum, hi-hat, xylophone, woodblock, triangle, cowbell, marimba, gong), banjo, harp, piano, guitar, violin I, violin II, viola, violoncello, double bass.
Commissioned by: Tri-Cities Opera.
Call no.: **1988/038**

836. Fink, Myron S., 1932– The conquistador. N.p.: Myron S. Fink, 1993.
1 score (3 v., [343 p.]); 44 cm.
English words by Donald Moreland.
Opera in 3 acts.
Reproduced from manuscript.
Duration: 2:43:46.
Composed for: 2 flutes (2nd also piccolo), 2 oboes (2nd also English horn), 2 clarinets in A (1st also clarinet in E♭, 2nd also bass and contrabass clarinets), 2 bassoons (2nd also contrabassoon), 4 horns, 2 trumpets, 3 trombones, tuba, timpani, percussion (roto-toms, woodblocks, snare drum, cymbals, triangle, rattle, gong, xylophone, marimba, glockenspiel, chimes, bell), harp, celesta, violin I, violin II, viola, violoncello, double bass.
Call no.: **2001/056**

837. Finsterer, Mary, 1962– Ruisselant. Partitura. Milan: Ricordi, 1993.
1 score (xv, 77 p.); 42 cm.
For chamber orchestra.
Reproduced from manuscript.
Duration: ca. 13:00.
Includes instructions for performance.
Composed for: piccolo (also flute), oboe, clarinet, bass clarinet, contrabassoon, horn, trumpet, bass trombone, percussion (woodblock, temple block, snare drum, 2 tom-toms, bass drum, suspended cymbal, tubular bells, glockenspiel, xylophone, vibraphone), piano (also celesta), violin I, violin II, viola, violoncello, double bass.
Call no.: **1995/033**

838. Firsova, Elena, 1950– Augury = [Prorit͡sanie]: for large symphony orchestra and mixed chorus, op. 38. N.p.: n.p., 1988.
1 score (60 p.); 30 cm.
Russian words (Cyrillic) by Dmitri Smirnov; original English text by William Blake printed as text.
Composed for: SATB chorus, piccolo, 2 flutes, 2 oboes, English horn, 2 clarinets, bass clarinet, 2 bassoons, contrabassoon, 4 horns, 3 trumpets, 3 trombones, tuba, timpani, percussion (triangle, suspended cymbal, gong, bass drum, tam-tam, glockenspiel, vibraphone, marimba, bells), harp, celesta, violin I, violin II, viola, violoncello, double bass.
Commissioned by: BBC Proms.
Call no.: **1996/044**

839. Fišer, Luboš, 1935– Sonata: per viola solo e quartetto d'archi. Partitura. N.p.: n.p., 1991.
1 score (14 p.); 39 cm.
Reproduced from manuscript.
Composed for: viola, 2 violins, viola, violoncello.
Call no.: **1996/045**

840. Flagello, Nicolas, 1928–1994. Concerto sinfonico. N.p.: n.p., 1985.
1 score (94 p.); 57 cm.
For saxophone quartet and orchestra.
Reproduced from manuscript.
Composed for: soprano saxophone, alto saxophone, tenor saxophone, baritone saxophone, piccolo, 2 flutes, 2 oboes, English horn, 2 clarinets, bass clarinet, 2 bassoons, contrabassoon, 4 horns, 3 trumpets, 2 trombones, bass trombone, tuba, timpani, percussion

(suspended cymbal, bass drum, crash cymbals, rolled cymbal, tenor drum, marimba, vibraphone, glockenspiel, gong, snare drum, tubular bells, bell tree), harp, celesta, violin I, violin II, viola, violoncello, double bass.
Call no.: **1986/038**

841. Flagello, Nicolas, 1928–1994. Credendum: for violin and orchestra. N.p.: n.p., 1985.
1 score (57 p.); 44 cm.
Reproduced from manuscript.
Composed for: violin, 3 flutes (2nd also piccolo), 2 oboes, English horn, 2 clarinets, bass clarinet, 2 bassoons, contrabassoon, 4 horns, 3 trumpets, 2 trombones, bass trombone, tuba, timpani, percussion (gong, suspended cymbal, crash cymbals, tenor drum, bass drum), harp, celesta, violin I, violin II, viola, violoncello, double bass.
Call no.: **1989/038**

842. Flagello, Nicolas, 1928–1994. Quattro amori.
Call no.: **1985/065**
No materials available.

843. Flammer, Ernst Helmuth, 1949– Das erschwiegene Wort! . . . ausgeweitet . . . : für Solo-Percussion und grosses Orchester (1993/94). N.p.: E.H. Flammer-Eigenverlag, 1994.
1 score (35 p.); 42 cm.
Composed for: percussion (3 snare drums, vibraphone, marimba, 4 Chinese gongs, 3 bongos, 3 congas, crotales, 2 small tam-tams, large tam-tam, timpani, Chinese cymbals, bell cymbals, 2 rins, water gong, guiro, 5 temple blocks, steel drum), 2 flutes (2nd also piccolo), oboe, English horn, clarinet, bass clarinet, bassoon, contrabassoon, 3 horns, 2 trumpets, 2 trombones, contrabass tuba, timpani, percussion (Chinese cymbals, crotales, bamboo chimes, brass chimes, 3 snare drums, crash cymbals, thundersheet, bass drum, flexatone, rain stick, xylophone, wooden board, bamboo rasp, 3 woodblocks, 3 slit drums, 3 tam-tams), harp, celesta, violin I, violin II, viola, violoncello, double bass.
Commissioned by: Japanische Staatsregierung.
Call no.: **1997/048**

844. Fleischer, Tsippi, 1946– 1992: an oratorio (1991): for mixed choir, guitars and mandolas ensemble and symphony orchestra: commemorating the 500th anniversary of the expulsion of Jews from Spain. Tel Aviv, Israel: Israel Music Institute, 1991.
1 score (94 p.); 42 cm.
Medieval Hebrew, Arabic, and Spanish words; also printed as text with English translation and with phonetic transcription (p. 4–8).
In commemoration of the expulsion of Jews from Spain.
Reproduced from manuscript.
Includes program notes in English and Hebrew (p. 2–3).
Composed for: SATB chorus, 6 guitars, 6 mandolas, 3 flutes (1st also piccolo), 2 oboes (2nd also English horn), 2 clarinets (2nd also bass clarinet), 2 bassoons, 4 horns, 2 trumpets, 3 trombones, tuba, timpani, percussion (xylophone, vibraphone, chimes, metallophone, triangle, castanets, maracas, bongos, glockenspiel, marimba, 2 suspended cymbals, tom-tom, tambourine), harp, violin I, violin II, viola, violoncello, double bass.
Call no.: **1996/046**

845. Fleischer, Tsippi, 1946– Medea: a new vision of the myth: opera in 7 scenes for mezzo-soprano and 4 acting instrumentalists. N.p.: Tsippi Fleischer, 1995.
1 score (47 p.); 30 x 42 cm.
Principally English with some Hebrew words by Rivka Kashtan.
Reproduced from manuscript.
Composed for: mezzo-soprano, recorder (also flute, piccolo, and alto flute), violoncello (must be a woman), clarinet (also bass clarinet and alto saxophone), percussion (xylophone, glockenspiel, sleigh bells, cowbells, cymbals, medium gong, bongos, tam-tam, woodblock, triangle).
Call no.: **2000/055**

846. Floyd, Carlisle, 1926– Cold sassy tree. Full score. New York, NY: Boosey & Hawkes, 2000.
1 score (2 v.); 44 cm.
English words.
Opera in 3 acts.
Based on the novel by Olive Ann Burns.
"2nd ed, 11/00"—cover of vol. 1, in red ink.
Composed for: voices, piccolo, 2 flutes, 2 oboes (2nd also English horn), 2 clarinets, 2 bassoons, 4 horns, 2 trumpets, 2 trombones, tuba, timpani, percussion, piano (also celesta), harp, violin I, violin II, viola, violoncello, double bass.
Commissioned by: Houston Grand Opera and San Diego Opera.
Call no.: **2002/059**

847. Floyd, Carlisle, 1926– A time to dance: reflections on mortality: for chorus, bass-baritone, and orchestra. New York, NY: Boosey & Hawkes, 1992.
1 score (120 p.); 36 cm.
English words by Lucretius (Dryden), Webster, Twain, Donne, Herrick, Hughes, Amis, Auslander, Ellis, and Day-Lewis.

Composed for: bass-baritone, SATB chorus, 2 flutes (2nd also piccolo), 2 oboes (2nd also English horn), 2 clarinets (2nd also bass clarinet), 2 bassoons, 4 horns, 2 trumpets, 2 trombones, tuba, timpani, percussion (xylophone, suspended cymbal, snare drum, vibraphone, glockenspiel, antique cymbals, wind chimes, tenor drum, gong, bell tree, anvil, chimes), harp, piano (also celesta), violin I, violin II, viola, violoncello, double bass.
Commissioned by: American Choral Directors Association.
Call no.: **1996/047**
Also available:
Call no.: **1996/047 vocal score**

848. Flynn, George, 1937– Kanal: for piano. Mount Vernon, NY: Imprimis Music, 1976.
61 p. of music; 34 cm.
Reproduced from manuscript.
Composed for: piano.
Call no.: **1986/040**

849. Flynn, George, 1937– A reign of love: for speaker and orchestra. N.p.: George Flynn, 1992.
1 score (ii, 67 p.); 44 cm.
English words adapted from the poetry of William Shakespeare; also printed as text.
Composed for: narrator, 3 flutes (3rd also piccolo), 3 oboes (3rd also English horn), 3 clarinets (3rd also bass clarinet), 2 bassoons, 4 horns, 3 trumpets, 2 trombones, bass trombone, tuba, percussion (triangle, 3 cymbals, 3 bongos, 5 tom-toms, timbales, bass drum, glockenspiel, xylophone, vibraphone, marimba, chimes), piano, violin I, violin II, viola, violoncello, double bass.
Commissioned by: Yakima Symphony Orchestra.
Call no.: **1994/043**

850. Foison, Tristan, 1961– Comme un ciel déchiré = Like a sky split asunder: concerto for violin and orchestra. N.p.: n.p., 1996.
1 score (88 leaves); 43 cm.
Composed for: violin, 2 flutes, 2 oboes, 2 clarinets, 2 bassoons, 4 horns, 2 trumpets, 3 trombones, tuba, percussion (snare drum, 2 tam-tams, cymbals, wind chimes, triangle, bass drum, timbales, vibraphone, temple block, tambourine), harp, celesta, violin I, violin II, viola, violoncello, double bass.
Commissioned by: Atlanta Music Club.
Call no.: **1997/049**

851. Foley, John B., 1939– Like winter waiting. Director's edition/full score. Portland, OR: OCP Publications, 2000.
1 score (168 p.); 28 cm.
English words.
Advent concert or musical play for SATB choir and piano, with optional instrumental ensemble.
Performance instructions in English.
Composed for: soprano, alto, baritone, SATB chorus, children's chorus, flute, oboe, horn, violin, double bass, timpani, percussion, piano.
Call no.: **2004/041**
Also available:
Call no.: **2004/041 vocal score**

852. Forsyth, Malcolm, 1936– Concerto for: trumpet & orchestra, 1987. N.p.: n.p., 1988.
1 score (86 p.); 39 cm.
Reproduced from holograph.
Duration: ca. 19:00.
Composed for: trumpet, 2 flutes (2nd also piccolo), 2 oboes, 2 clarinets, 2 bassoons, 2 horns, 3 trombones, timpani, percussion (xylophone, vibraphone, hand cymbals, suspended cymbals), violin I, violin II, viola, violoncello, double bass.
Commissioned by: Canadian Broadcasting Corporation.
Call no.: **1992/042**

853. Forsyth, Malcolm, 1936– Electra rising: Concerto for violoncello and chamber orchestra. N.p.: Malcolm Forsyth, 1995.
1 score (109 p.); 44 cm.
Reproduced from manuscript.
Duration: 30:00.
Composed for: violoncello, 2 flutes (2nd also piccolo), 2 oboes, 2 clarinets (both also clarinet in A), 2 bassoons, 2 horns, 2 trumpets, timpani (also suspended cymbal and large Mexican rain stick), percussion (glass wind chimes, xylophone, vibraphone, small Peruvian rain stick, glockenspiel, 5 temple blocks, 2 bongos, 2 small tom-toms, bass drum), harp, violin I, violin II, viola, violoncello, double bass.
Commissioned by: Canadian Broadcasting Corporation and Calgary Philharmonic Society.
Call no.: **1998/048**

854. Foss, Lukas, 1922– Celebration: for brass quintet and orchestra, 1998. Full score. N.p.: Lucas Foss, 1999.
1 score (93 p.); 36 cm.
Composed for: 2 trumpets, horn, trombone, tuba, flute, oboe, clarinet, bassoon, 2 horns, percussion, timpani, violin I, violin II, viola, violoncello, double bass.
Call no.: **2001/057**

855. Foss, Lukas, 1922– Exeunt: 1982. New York, NY: C. Fischer, 1982.

1 score (34 p.); 46 cm.
For orchestra.
Composed for: 2 flutes (2nd also piccolo), 2 oboes, 2 clarinets, 2 bassoons, 4 horns, 3 trumpets, 3 trombones, tuba, timpani, percussion (chimes, vibraphone, xylophone, anvil, bass drum, cymbals, gong, snare drum), harp, piano, electric guitar, violin I, violin II, viola, violoncello, double bass.
Commissioned by: N.E.A. Consortium.
Call no.: **1988/039**

856. Foss, Lukas, 1922– Guitar concerto: "American landscapes": 1989. New York, NY: Carl Fischer, 1989.
1 score (66 p.); 36 cm.
For guitar and chamber orchestra.
Reproduced from manuscript.
Composed for: guitar, flute (also piccolo), oboe, clarinet, bassoon, horn, trumpet, trombone, percussion (Jew's harp, small bowl, timpani, vibraphone, snare drum, military drum, bass drum, chimes, cymbals, bongos, timbales, sandpaper blocks, xylophone), harp, piano, violin I, violin II, viola, violoncello, double bass.
Call no.: **1990/034**

857. Foss, Lukas, 1922– Piano concerto for the left hand. New York, NY: Carl Fischer Rental Library, 1994.
1 score (106 p.); 36 cm.
Duration: ca 24:00
Composed for: piano (left hand), 2 flutes, 2 oboes, 2 clarinets, 2 bassoons, 2 horns, 2 trumpets, 2 trombones, timpani, percussion (2 woodblocks, temple blocks, cymbals, snare drum, tenor drum, side drum, bass drum, gong, 2 tom-toms, cowbell, vibraphone, xylophone, tambourine, chimes, whip, anvil, timbales), harp, celesta, violin I, violin II, viola, violoncello, double bass.
Commissioned by: Boston Symphony Orchestra.
Call no.: **1995/034**

858. Foss, Lukas, 1922– Renaissance concerto: for flute and orchestra. Full score. N.p.: n.p., 1985.
1 score (75 p.); 37 cm.
Reproduced from manuscript.
Contents: Intrada—Baroque interlude (after Rameau)—Recitative (after Monteverdi)—Jouissance.
Composed for: flute, flute (also piccolo), oboe, clarinet, bassoon, horn, 2 trumpets, trombone, timpani, percussion (chimes, tambourine, glockenspiel, triangle, Renaissance drum), harp, harpsichord, violin I, violin II, viola, violoncello, double bass.
Commissioned by: Barlow Endowment for Music Composition at Brigham Young University and Buffalo Philharmonic Orchestra.
Call no.: **1987/025**

859. Foss, Lukas, 1922– String quartet no. 4. N.p.: n.p., 1998.
1 score (21 p.); 28 cm.
Composed for: 2 violins, viola, violoncello.
Commissioned by: Buffalo Chamber Music Society.
Call no.: **2000/056**

860. Foss, Lukas, 1922– String quartet no. 4. Full score. New York, NY: Pembroke Music Co., 2000.
1 score (23 p.); 31 cm.
Composed for: 2 violins, viola, violoncello.
Commissioned by: Buffalo Chamber Music Society.
Call no.: **2003/043**

861. Foss, Lukas, 1922– String quartet no. 5. N.p.: Lukas Foss, 2000.
1 score (33 p.); 33 cm.
Composed for: 2 violins, viola, violoncello.
Call no.: **2004/042**

862. Foss, Lukas, 1922– Symphonic fantasy: in two movements. Full score. N.p.: n.p., 2001.
1 score (75 p.); 44 cm.
For orchestra.
Composed for: piccolo, 2 flutes, 2 oboes, English horn, 2 clarinets, bass clarinet, 2 bassoons, contrabassoon, 2 horns, 3 trumpets, 3 trombones, tuba, timpani, percussion (xylophone, snare drum, tom-tom, bass drum, cymbals, gong, triangle), harp, piano (also celesta), violin I, violin II, viola, violoncello, double bass.
Commissioned by: Boston University.
Call no.: **2005/050**

863. Foss, Lukas, 1922– Symphony no. 3: "symphony of sorrows." N.p.: Lukas Foss, 1991.
1 score (100 p.); 36 cm.
Contents: Fugue: of strife and struggle—Elegy for Anne Frank—Wasteland—Prayer.
Composed for: piccolo, 2 flutes, 2 oboes, English horn, 2 clarinets, bass clarinet, 2 bassoons, contrabassoon, 4 horns, 3 trumpets, 4 trombones, tuba, timpani, percussion (vibraphone, 2 snare drums, military drum, whip, 4 cymbals, marimba, chimes, anvil, tenor drum, bass drum, xylophone, gong, tam-tam), harp, organ, piano (also celesta), violin I, violin II, viola, violoncello, double bass.
Call no.: **1993/040**
Re-entered as: **1994/044**

864. Foss, Lukas, 1922– Symphony no. 4: "Window to the past." N.p.: n.p., 1994.
1 score (204 p.); 37 cm.
Duration: ca. 35:00.
Annotated for performance (world premiere).
Composed for: 2 flutes (2nd also piccolo), 2 oboes, 2 clarinets, 2 bassoons, 4 horns, 3 trumpets, 2 trombones, bass trombone, tuba, timpani, percussion (vibraphone, tom-toms, triangle, cymbals, 2 drums, chimes, xylophone, bass drum, Japanese temple bowl, marimba, tambourine, glass chimes, antique cymbals, bongos, 2 woodblocks, Jew's harp, 2 gongs, snare drum, cowbells, flexatone, suspended cymbal, tenor drum, whip), harp, piano (also celesta), harmonica or accordion (optional), violin I, violin II, viola, violoncello, double bass.
Commissioned by: City College of New York.
Call no.: **1998/049**

865. Fouad, Ashraf, 1958– Ithaca: for chorus, soloists, piano and orchestra. N.p.: n.p., 199-?.
1 score (133 p.); 30 cm.
English words; also printed as text.
Poems by C. P. Cavafy, translated into English by Rae Dalven.
Reproduced from manuscript.
Composed for: voices, SATB chorus, 2 flutes, 2 oboes, 2 clarinets, bassoon, 2 horns, 2 trumpets, 2 trombones, 4 timpani, celesta, piano, violin I, violin II, viola, violoncello, double bass.
Commissioned by: American University in Cairo.
Call no.: **2000/057**

866. Francesconi, Luca, 1956– Ballata: opera in due atti (1996–99). Partitura. Milano: Ricordi, 2002.
1 score (691 p.); 41 cm.
Italian and English words.
Reproduced from holograph.
Composed for: soprano, mezzo-soprano, 3 tenors, 3 baritones, violin, clarinet, accordion, cimbalom, double bass, trumpet, percussion, women's chorus, men's chorus, 2 piccolos, 2 flutes, 2 oboes, English horn, clarinet in E♭, 2 clarinets, bass clarinet, 2 bassoons, contrabassoon, 4 horns, 3 trumpets (also piccolo trumpet), 3 trombones (also bass trombone), tuba, harp, piano (also celesta), electronics, percussion, violin I, violin II, viola, violoncello, double bass.
Call no.: **2005/051**

867. Francesconi, Luca, 1956– Passacaglia.
Call no.: **1985/066**
No materials available.

868. Frank, Lawrence E., 1937– The battle of Blenheim: cantata for solo tenor, chorus and chamber orchestra. Rancho Palos Verdes, CA: L.E. Frank, 1997.
1 score (61 p.); 28 cm.
English words by Robert Southey.
"Work originally written 1965 and rewritten in 1997."
Composed for: tenor, SATB chorus, flute, oboe, clarinet, bassoon, horn, trumpet, percussion (tenor drum, snare drum, woodblock, cymbals), violin I, violin II, viola, violoncello, double bass.
Call no.: **1998/050**

869. Franzén, Olov, 1946– The vacuum state: for big symphony orchestra, 1981–83. Stockholm: Svensk Musik, 1983.
1 score (115 p.); 57 cm.
Reproduced from manuscript.
Duration: ca. 20:00.
Composed for: 4 flutes (3rd–4th also piccolo), 2 oboes, English horn, clarinet in E♭, 2 clarinets, bass clarinet, 2 bassoons, contrabassoon, 4 horns, 4 trumpets, 3 trombones, tuba, percussion (timpani, crotales, glockenspiel, tubular bells, vibraphone, tambourine, guiro, 8 tom-toms, bass drum, 3 triangles, sleigh bells, sistrum, crash cymbals, 5 suspended cymbals, tam-tam, 15 tuned Thai gongs), harp, violin I, violin II, viola, violoncello, double bass.
Call no.: **1990/035**

870. Frazelle, Kenneth, 1955– Concerto for chamber orchestra. Full score. N.p.: Subito Music Publishing, 2002.
1 score (166 p.); 28 cm.
Composed for: 2 flutes, 2 oboes, 2 clarinets, 2 bassoons, 2 horns, 2 trumpets, timpani, percussion, piano, violin I, violin II, viola, violoncello, double bass.
Commissioned by: Los Angeles Chamber Orchestra, Boston Modern Orchestra Project, National Chamber Orchestra, and Orchestra X.
Call no.: **2005/052**

871. Frazelle, Kenneth, 1955– The motion of stone. N.p.: n.p., 1998.
1 score (178 leaves); 36 cm.
English words by A. R. Ammons.
For chorus and chamber orchestra.
Reproduced from manuscript.
Composed for: soprano, alto, tenor, baritone, SATB chorus, flute, oboe, English horn, clarinet, 2 horns, trumpet, timpani, percussion (glockenspiel, bass drum, triangle, bongos, suspended cymbal, crash cymbals, guiro, maracas, sand block, chisel, snare drum, claves, tambourine), harp, piano, viola, violoncello, double bass.

Commissioned by: Gardner Museum.
Call no.: **2000/058**

872. Freedman, Harry, 1922– Borealis: for orchestra, children's choir, 3 choirs SATB. N.p.: Harry Freedman, 1997.
1 score (38 p.); 44 cm.
Undetermined language and some English words.
Duration: ca. 16:00.
Composed for: 3 SATB choruses, children's chorus, 2 flutes (2nd also piccolo), oboe, English horn, 2 clarinets, bass clarinet, 2 trumpets, 2 horns, 2 trombones, percussion (marimba, tom-toms, glockenspiel, xylophone, vibraphone, bongos, 4 log drums, suspended cymbals, small bass drum, small metal wind chimes), harp, violin I, violin II, viola, violoncello, double bass.
Commissioned by: Canadian Broadcasting Corporation.
Call no.: **2002/060**

873. Freidlin, Jan, 1944– Concerto: for cello, string orchestra & vibrafone [sic]. N.p.: n.p., 1994.
1 score (30 p.); 39 cm.
Reproduced from holograph.
Composed for: violoncello, vibraphone, violin I, violin II, viola, violoncello, double bass.
Call no.: **1996/048**

874. Freund, Don, 1947– Madame Bovary: ballet after the novel by Gustave Flaubert (1995). St. Louis, MO: MMB Music, 1995.
1 score (2 v. [282 p.]); 32 cm.
"To choreographic scenario by Jacques Cesbron."
For orchestra.
Duration: ca. 1:00:00.
Composed for: piccolo, 2 flutes (2nd also alto flute), 2 oboes (2nd also English horn), 2 clarinets (2nd also clarinet in E♭), bass clarinet, alto saxophone, 2 bassoons (2nd also contrabassoon), 4 horns, 3 trumpets, 2 trombones, bass trombone, tuba, harp, piano, violin I, violin II, viola, violoncello, double bass.
Call no.: **1997/050**

875. Freund, Don, 1947– Passion with tropes. N.p.: D. Freund, 1983.
1 miniature score (417 p.); 28 cm.
English words.
Theatre-oratorio in 2 parts.
For soloists, chorus, orchestra, chamber groups, and jazz ensemble.
Composed for: 2 sopranos, 2 mezzo-sopranos, 2 tenors, baritone, bass, chant chorus, jazz ensemble (drum set, electric bass, electric piano, electric guitar, 2 trumpets, 2 trombones, alto saxophone, tenor saxophone), woodwind quintet (flute, oboe, clarinet, horn, bassoon), brass quintet (2 trumpets, trombone, horn, tuba), string quintet (2 violins, viola, violoncello, double bass), chamber percussion (4 tom-toms, wood drum, roto-toms, vibraphone), piccolo, 2 flutes (2nd also alto flute), oboe, 2 clarinets (1st also clarinet in E♭), bass clarinet (also contrabass clarinet), alto saxophone (also soprano, tenor, and baritone saxophones), bassoon (also contrabassoon), 3 horns, 2 trumpets, 2 trombones, percussion (vibraphone, glockenspiel, bass drum, 2 tam-tams, marimba, temple blocks, bongos, timbales, 2 suspended cymbals, triangle, 3 cowbells, 2 brake drums, bells, 2 lead pipes, gong, chimes, tom-toms, snare drum, lion's roar, crotales, metal plates), piano, celesta, guitar, violin I, violin II, viola, violoncello, double bass.
Call no.: **1985/067**
Re-entered as: **1989/039**
Also available:
Call no.: **1985/067 libretto**
Re-entered as: **1989/039 libretto**

876. Friedman, David, 1950– King Island Christmas: a new Christmas oratorio. N.p.: n.p., 1997.
1 score (403 p.); 28 cm.
English words by Deborah Baley Brevoort.
Original work by Jean Rogers.
Composed for: SATB chorus, piano.
Call no.: **1998/051**

877. Friedman, Stan, 1951– Hypatia: an opera, 1991. N. p.: n.p., 1991.
1 score (2 v. [360 leaves]); 22 x 28 cm.
English words by Stanley Friedman, Joy Tanks, and Julia Millen.
Reproduced from holograph.
Duration: 2:15:00.
Composed for: soprano, mezzo-soprano, tenor, baritone, bass-baritone, bass, SATB chorus, men's chorus, actors, dancers, 3 flutes (3rd also piccolo), 2 oboes, 2 clarinets, bassoon, 2 horns, 2 trumpets, 2 trombones, timpani, percussion (vibraphone, glockenspiel, crash cymbals, suspended cymbal, tambourine, tam-tam, bass drum, snare drum, xylophone), harp, violin I, violin II, viola, violoncello, double bass.
Call no.: **1997/051**
Also available:
Call no.: **1997/051 libretto**
Call no.: **1997/051 suite**

878. Friedman, Stan, 1951– Moravian cantata: parodie VI, 1984–85. N.p.: n.p., 1985.

1 score (68 p.); 33 cm.
English words.
For high voice and 12-part trombone ensemble.
"Based on the chorale Faulkner (11, A) by Antes When my love to Christ grows weak."
Reproduced from manuscript.
At end of score: "1st draft: 16 Dec. 1984; revision: 9 Nov. 1985."
Duration: ca. 24:00.
Composed for: voice, trombone choir I (soprano trombone, alto trombone, trombone, bass trombone), trombone choir II (soprano trombone, alto trombone, trombone, bass trombone), trombone choir III (soprano trombone, alto trombone, trombone, bass trombone).
Commissioned by: Moravian Trombone Choir of Downey, CA.
Call no.: **1986/041**

879. Funicelli, Stanley A., 1948– Sonata no. 1: for unaccompanied violin. N.p.: n.p., 1994.
8 leaves of music; 28 cm.
Reproduced from holograph.
Duration: ca. 12:40.
Composed for: violin.
Call no.: **2000/059**

880. Funk, Eric, 1949– Concert, op. 71: piano. N.p.: n.p., 1996.
1 score (39 p.); 35 cm.
Reproduced from manuscript.
Composed for: piano, 2 flutes, 2 oboes, 2 clarinets, 2 bassoons, 4 horns, 2 trumpets, 3 trombones, tuba, violin I, violin II, viola, violoncello, double bass.
Call no.: **2004/043**

881. Funk, Eric, 1949– Concerto: for horn, violin, violincello [sic], & piano, op. 53, 1990. N.p.: n.p., 1990.
1 score (30 p.); 28 cm.
Reproduced from holograph.
Duration: 21:00.
Composed for: horn, violin, violoncello, piano.
Commissioned by: IHS.
Call no.: **1994/045**

882. Funk, Eric, 1949– Concerto, op. 55, 1991. N.p.: n.p., 1991.
1 score (25 p.); 28 cm.
Reproduced from manuscript.
Composed for: violoncello, violin I, violin II, viola, violoncello, double bass.
Call no.: **1993/041**

883. Funk, Eric, 1949– Symphony no. 3: "Hradčany." N.p.: n.p., 1995.
1 score (34 leaves); 52 x 60 cm.
Reproduced from holograph.
Composed for: clarinet, piccolo, 2 flutes, 2 oboes, 2 clarinets, bass clarinet, 2 bassoons, 4 horns, 4 trumpets, 3 trombones, timpani, percussion (tam-tam, snare drum, bass drum, suspended cymbal), violin I, violin II, viola, violoncello, double bass.
Call no.: **1996/049**

884. Furman, James, 1937– String quartet, 1986. N. p.: n.p., 1986.
1 score (44 p.); 28 cm.
Reproduced from manuscript.
Composed for: 2 violins, viola, violoncello.
Commissioned by: Manhattan String Quartet.
Call no.: **1988/040**

885. Furrer, Beat, 1954– Aria: für Sopran und Ensemble (1999). Partitur. Basel; New York, NY: Bärenreiter, 1999.
1 score (95 p.); 30 x 42 cm.
German words.
"Provisorisches Informationsmaterial."
Reproduced from manuscript.
Composed for: soprano, clarinet, percussion, piano, violin, viola, violoncello.
Call no.: **2002/061**

886. Furrer, Beat, 1954– Narcissus: Oper in sechs Szenen, nach Ovids Metamorphosen (1992–1994). Partitur. Wien: Universal Edition, 1994.
1 score (2 v. [330 p.]); 30 cm.
German and Latin words.
Reproduced from manuscript.
Composed for: mezzo-soprano, SSAATTBB chorus, 2 flutes (both also alto flute, 1st also bass flute), 2 clarinets (both also bass clarinet), tenor saxophone (also alto saxophone), bassoon (also contrabassoon), 2 horns, 2 trumpets, 2 trombones, tuba, percussion (marimba, tubular bells, claves, maracas, crotales, spring coil, 2 cymbals, 2 tam-tams, tom-toms, bass drum, metal block, cowbells, vibraphone, glockenspiel, temple blocks, 3 woodblocks, suspended cymbals, 3 triangles, 3 bongos, 2 timpani), harp, piano, violin I, violin II, viola, violoncello, double bass.
Call no.: **1997/052**

887. Fussell, Charles, 1938– Wilde: symphony in three movements for baritone and orchestra. N.p.: n.p., 1990.
1 score (various pagings); 44 cm.

English words by Will Graham.
"Corrections: July 9 '90, July 19 '90 (3rd mov.), Nov. '90."
Reproduced from manuscript.
Contents: London—In the South—Paris.
Composed for: baritone, 3 flutes (3rd also piccolo), 2 oboes, English horn, 2 clarinets, bass clarinet, 2 bassoons, contrabassoon, 6 horns, 3 trumpets, 2 trombones, bass trombone, tuba, timpani, percussion (vibraphone, xylophone, glockenspiel, chimes, 3 suspended cymbals, tenor drum, snare drum, triangle, bass drum, crash cymbals, 3 gongs), piano, violin I, violin II, viola, violoncello, double bass.
Commissioned by: Newton Symphony Orchestra.
Call no.: **1993/042**

888. Gabay Vigil, Marcos, 1954– Frost svaner. N.p.: n.p., 1995.
1 score (37 p.); 28 cm.
Latin words.
For baritone and chamber orchestra.
Composed for: baritone, piccolo, flute, horn, percussion (tubular bells, finger cymbals, bell tree), mandolin, violin I, violin II, viola, violoncello, double bass.
Call no.: **1998/052**

889. Gabeli, Katia, 1981– Memories of my childhood's dreams: ballet. N.p.: n.p., 1990.
7 p. of music; 32 cm.
Reproduced from manuscript.
Contents: Fragment of broken blue glass—In love with violin—A voice in a forest—Web of autumn branches—Fearful dream.
Composed for: violin.
Commissioned by: Yevgeny Panifilov.
Call no.: **1994/046**

890. Gaburo, Kenneth, 1926–1993. Antiphony VIII: revolution: for one percussionist and tape.
Composed for: percussion, tape.
Commissioned by: Steve Schick.
Call no.: **1985/068**
No materials available.

891. Gaburo, Kenneth, 1926–1993. Antiphony IX (a dot.).
Duration: 21:40.
Call no.: **1986/042**
No materials available.

892. Gaburo, Kenneth, 1926–1993. Enough! —(not enough)—. N.p.: n.p., 1988.
1 score (11 p.); 28 x 44 cm. + 1 booklet (19 p.; 28 cm.)
English words.
"For 40 or more voices, percussion, and conductor; on a text by Benjamin Franklin."
Graphic notation.
Booklet contains performance notes in English.
Composed for: 40 voices, percussion.
Commissioned by: CSU-Fresno.
Call no.: **1989/040**

893. Gagneux, Renaud, 1948– Orphee: opéra en 5 actes et 1 prologue. Paris: Durand S.A., 1990.
1 score (2 v.); 58 cm.
Words in French, German, romanized Greek, Italian, and Latin.
Includes texts by Euripides, Homer, Schikaneder, Striggio, and Virgil.
Reproduced from holograph.
Duration: ca. 1:45:00.
Composed for: 2 sopranos, mezzo-sopranos, contralto, tenor, baritone, bass, SATB chorus, 4 flutes (all also piccolo), 4 oboes (also 2 English horns), 4 clarinets (also 2 bass clarinets), 4 bassoons (also 2 contrabassoons), 6 horns (also 2 natural horns), 4 trumpets, 4 trombones, 2 bass trombones, 2 tubas, timpani, percussion (wood chimes, vibraphone, maracas, woodblock, 5 temple blocks, claves, metal chimes, xylorimba, crotales, glockenspiel, castanets, 3 tam-tams, guiro, ratchet, whip, chimes, train whistle, geophone, wind machine, lion's roar, shell chimes, triangle, tambourine, Chinese cymbal, 3 suspended cymbals, 3 gongs, bass drum, hand cymbals, bird whistle), 2 harps, piano, celesta, violin I, violin II, viola, violoncello, double bass.
Commissioned by: René Terrasson and Opéra du Rhin.
Call no.: **1992/043**

894. Galli, Hervé, 1957– Piece for piano no. 1 bis.: theme & variations. N.p.: n.p., 1988.
91 p. of music; 28 cm.
Composed for: piano.
Call no.: **1989/041**

895. Gamberini, Leopoldo, 1922– Christopher Columbo: 12 10 1492: cantata scenica. N.p.: n.p., 1988.
1 score (184 p.); 36 cm.
Italian words.
Stage cantata for baritone, chorus, and orchestra.
Text based on Columbus's logbook by Gamberini and C. Cormagi.
Reproduced from holograph.
Duration: ca. 50:00.
Composed for: baritone, SATB chorus, 2 flutes (2nd also piccolo), 2 oboes (2nd also English horn), 2 clarinets,

2 bassoons, 4 horns, 4 trumpets, 3 trombones, tuba, timpani, harp, violin I, violin II, viola, violoncello, double bass.
Call no.: **1991/040**

896. Gamstorp, Göran, 1957– Growings: 1989–91. N. p.: n.p., 1991.
1 score (155 p.); 42 cm.
For orchestra and tape.
Duration: ca. 55:00.
Composed for: piccolo, 3 flutes, 3 oboes, English horn, 3 clarinets, bass clarinet, 3 bassoons, contrabassoon, 6 horns, 4 trumpets, 4 trombones, 2 tubas, 6 timpani, percussion (2 suspended cymbals, 3 gongs, 4 low tom-toms, tam-tam, 4 bongos, bass drum), tape, violin I, violin II, viola, violoncello, double bass.
Call no.: **2002/062**

897. Gandy, G. Patrick, 1962– The beast. N.p.: n.p., 199-?.
1 score (66 p.); 49 cm.
For orchestra.
Reproduced from holograph.
Composed for: piccolo, flute, oboe, 2 clarinets, bassoon, 4 horns, 3 trumpets, 3 trombones, tuba, harp, percussion (triangle, bass drum, timpani, cymbals), piano, celesta, violin I, violin II, viola, violoncello, double bass.
Call no.: **1998/053**

898. García, Orlando Jacinto, 1954– Auschwitz: nunca se olvidaran. N.p.: n.p., 1993.
1 score (65 leaves); 36 cm.
Spanish words.
For chorus (SATB) and orchestra.
Duration: ca. 18:00.
Composed for: SATB chorus, flute, oboe, clarinet, 2 horns, trumpet, trombone, percussion (vibraphone, chimes, timpani, tam-tam, gong, snare drum, glockenspiel, marimba, suspended cymbal, bass drum), piano, violin I, violin II, viola, violoncello, double bass.
Commissioned by: Miami Master Chorale and New World Symphony.
Call no.: **1996/050**

899. García, Orlando Jacinto, 1954– Sombras iluminadas: for full orchestra. N.p.: n.p., 1997.
1 score (84 p.); 36 cm.
Duration: 18:00.
Composed for: piccolo, 2 flutes, 2 oboes, English horn, 2 clarinets, bass clarinet, 2 bassoons, contrabassoon, 4 horns, 3 trumpets, 3 trombones, tuba, percussion, harp, violin I, violin II, viola, violoncello, double bass.
Commissioned by: Center for the Diffusion of Contemporary Music, Spain (CDMC).
Call no.: **2003/044**

900. García, Orlando Jacinto, 1954– Treno para las Americas = Threnody for the Americas: a work for chamber orchestra and soprano. N.p.: n.p., 1988.
1 score (ii, 72 leaves); 36 cm.
Spanish words; also printed as text with English translation.
Reproduced from holograph.
At end: 7/88, Miami, FL.
Duration: ca. 21:00.
Composed for: soprano, flute (also piccolo), oboe (also English horn), clarinet, bassoon, percussion (vibraphone, guiro, timbales, 3 suspended cymbals, orchestra bells, maracas, marimba, 3 suspended gourds, crotales, claves, bongos, tam-tam, chimes, bass drum), 2 pianos (1st also celesta), violin I, violin II, viola I, viola II, violoncello I, violoncello II, double bass.
Commissioned by: New Music America 1988 Festival.
Call no.: **1992/044**

901. García, Orlando Jacinto, 1954– Voces celestiales = Celestial voices. N.p.: n.p., 1993.
1 score (75 p.); 36 cm.
For 2 solo double basses with orchestra.
Duration: ca. 18:00.
Composed for: 2 double basses, 2 flutes, 2 oboes, 2 clarinets, 2 bassoons, 4 horns, 2 trumpets, 2 trombones, percussion (chimes, timpani, vibraphone, bass drum, marimba, glass wind chimes, guiro, snare drum, 3 triangles, temple block, brake drum, glockenspiel, tenor drum, 3 suspended cymbals), violin I, violin II, viola, violoncello, double bass.
Call no.: **1995/035**

902. Gardner, Maurice, 1909– Unicinium: concerto for string quartet and chamber orchestra. Full score. Ft. Lauderdale, FL: Staff Music Publ. Co., 1997.
1 score (72 p.); 29 cm.
Composed for: 2 violins, viola, violoncello, 2 flutes, 2 oboes, 2 clarinets, 2 bassoons, 2 horns, 2 trumpets, trombone, percussion (vibraphone, crash cymbals, snare drum, timpani, xylophone, medium roto-tom, triangle, temple blocks, bells, woodblock), violin I, violin II, viola, violoncello, double bass.
Commissioned by: Miami Quartet.
Call no.: **1998/054**

903. Garton, Graham, 1929– Millennium symphony. Full score. Bermuda: Graham Garton, 1999.
1 score (2 v.); 28 cm.

"One" in 37 languages and English words; also printed as text.
For contralto (or mezzo-soprano) solo, mixed chorus, and symphony orchestra.
Duration: 1:42:00.
Contents: March of the years—Mental flight: Millennium poem by Ben Okri.
Composed for: contralto (or mezzo-soprano), SATB chorus, 2 flutes, piccolo, 2 oboes, 2 clarinets, 2 bassoons, 4 horns, 3 trumpets, 2 trombones, bass trombone, tuba, 4 timpani, percussion (xylophone, vibraphone, glockenspiel, side drum, woodblock, bass drum, cymbals, triangle, tambourine, gong, temple blocks, rattle, coconut shells ad lib.), violin I, violin II, viola, violoncello, double bass.
Call no.: **2002/063**

904. Garuti, Mario, 1957– Il giardino delle esperidi: fantasia per violino (1983–1984). Milano: G. Ricordi, 1986.
4 leaves of music; 32 x 39 cm.
Reproduced from holograph.
Composed for: violin.
Call no.: **1985/069**

905. Garwood, Margaret, 1927– Rappaccini's daughter: an opera in 2. N.p.: n.p., 198-?.
1 vocal score (214 p.); 33 cm.
English words by the composer.
Original work by Nathaniel Hawthorne.
Reproduced from holograph.
Duration: ca. 1:40:00.
Composed for: soprano, mezzo-soprano, tenor, baritone, bass-baritone, orchestra (specifics unclear).
Call no.: **1985/070**

906. Gaslini, Giorgio, 1929– Sprint: balletto in 6 scene. Partitura. N.p.: n.p., 1998.
1 score (373 p.); 43 cm.
"Due tempi."
Reproduced from holograph.
Duration: ca. 1:00:00.
Composed for: 2 flutes (1st also piccolo), oboe (also English horn), clarinet (also bass clarinet), bassoon, 2 horns, 3 trumpets, 2 trombones, tuba, alto saxophone (also soprano saxophone), percussion (timpani, 3 tom-toms, bass drum, triangle, woodblock, xylophone, chimes, suspended cymbal, maracas, bicycle bell, temple block, 2 tambourines, ratchet, gong, bells, 2 tumbas), harp, piano (also accordion), mandolin, violin I, violin II, viola, violoncello, double bass.
Commissioned by: Teatro Sociale di Rovigo.
Call no.: **2000/060**
Also available:
Call no.: **2000/060 piano score**

907. Gates, Crawford, 1921– Music to the New Hill Cumorah Pageant: op. 75. N.p.: n.p., 198-?.
1 score (378 p. in various pagings); 28 cm.
English words.
For orchestra, mixed chorus and children's chorus.
Reproduced from manuscript.
Composed for: SATB chorus, children's chorus, 3 flutes (3rd also piccolo), 2 oboes, English horn, 2 clarinets, bass clarinet, 2 bassoons, contrabassoon, 4 horns, 4 trumpets, 3 trombones, tuba, timpani, percussion (2 snare drums, field drum, tenor drum, suspended cymbals, vibraphone, tambourine, cymbals, slapstick, glockenspiel, 2 bongos, 2 timbales, chimes, 5 tom-toms, bass drum, xylophone, anvil, bell tree, 5 roto-toms, crotales, gong, marimba, ratchet, temple blocks, hisser, crash cymbals, 4 triangles, mark tree, gourd), harp, piano (also celesta), organ, violin I, violin II, viola, violoncello, double bass.
Commissioned by: Church of Jesus Christ of Latter-day Saints.
Call no.: **1989/042**

908. Gates, Crawford, 1921– Visions of eternity: an oratorio for mixed chorus, orchestra, a quartet of soloists, op. 87. N.p.: n.p., 1992.
1 score (various pagings); 44 cm.
English words from Section 76 of the Doctrine and Covenants.
Composed for: soprano, alto, tenor, bass, SATB chorus, 3 flutes (3rd also piccolo), 2 oboes, English horn, 2 clarinets (both also clarinet in A), bass clarinet, 2 bassoons, contrabassoon, 4 horns, 4 trumpets, 2 trombones, bass trombone, tuba, timpani, percussion (cymbals, 4 triangles, snare drum, 4 suspended cymbals, tenor drum, 5 tom-toms, glockenspiel, 2 bongos, tambourine, bass drum, xylophone, gong, bell tree, vibraphone, chimes), 2 harps, piano (also celesta), organ, violin I, violin II, viola, violoncello, double bass.
Commissioned by: Ricks College.
Call no.: **1994/047**

909. Gellman, Steven, 1947– Universe symphony. N.p.: S. Gellman, 1986.
1 score (iii, 125 p.); 44 cm.
Reproduced from holograph
"For full orchestra and polyphonic synthesizers"—p. i.
First performed Jan. 8, 1986, Roy Thompson Hall, Toronto.
Composed for: 4 flutes (2nd–3rd also piccolo, 4th also alto flute), 3 oboes, English horn, 3 clarinets (3rd also clari-

net in E♭), bass clarinet, 3 bassoons, contrabassoon, 4 horns, 4 trumpets (1st–2nd also piccolo trumpet), 2 trombones, bass trombone, tuba, timpani, percussion (snare drum, bass drum, crash cymbals, suspended cymbal, sizzle cymbal, 3 tam-tams, 4 tuned gongs, crotales, vibraphone, xylophone, celesta), harp, violin I, violin II, viola, violoncello, double bass, synthesizers.
Commissioned by: Andrew Davis and Toronto Symphony.
Call no.: **1987/026**
Re-entered as: **1988/041** and **1989/043**

910. Gentile, Ada, 1947– Come dal nulla: per clarinetto in si bemolle. Milano: G. Ricordi, 1984.
5 p. of music; 35 x 48 cm.
Composed for: clarinet.
Call no.: **1985/071**

911. Gentile, Ada, 1947– Concertante per flauto, chitarra e orchestra. Partitura. Milano: Ricordi, 1989.
1 score (69 p.); 42 cm.
Reproduced from holograph.
Duration: ca. 15:00.
Composed for: flute, guitar, 2 oboes, 2 clarinets, 2 bassoons, contrabassoon, 4 horns, 3 trumpets, 3 trombones, tuba, percussion (timpani, vibraphone, xylorimba, bass drum, string drum, snare drum, 3 bongos, 5 tom-toms, tam-tam, 3 suspended cymbals, woodblock, gong, glockenspiel), harp, piano, celesta, violin I, violin II, viola, violoncello, double bass.
Commissioned by: Accademia Nazionale di S. Cecilia di Roma.
Call no.: **1992/045**

912. Gerber, Steven R., 1948– Duo in three movements: for violin and piano.
Composed for: violin, piano.
Call no.: **1985/072**
No materials available.

913. Gerber, Steven R., 1948– Spirituals: for clarinet and string quartet (2000). N.p.: Stephen R. Gerber, 2000.
1 score (56 p.); 28 cm.
Duration: ca. 18:00.
Contents: Melody over a drone I—Minimalist tendencies—Amazing grace notes: homage to John Harbison—Call and response—Two pentatonic fragments—Minor and major—Melody over a drone II—Canons and chorus—Six-bar blues-tango in 3/4 time—Major blues—Homage to Ravel.
Composed for: clarinet, 2 violins, viola, violoncello.
Commissioned by: Concertante Chamber Players.
Call no.: **2004/044**
Re-entered as: **2005/053**

914. Gerber, Steven R., 1948– Symphony no. 1 (1988–89). N.p.: Steven R. Gerber, 1991.
1 score (93 leaves); 28 cm.
Reproduced from manuscript.
Duration: 21:00.
Composed for: 2 flutes (2nd also piccolo), 2 oboes, 2 clarinets (2nd also clarinet in E♭), 2 bassoons, 4 horns, 2 trumpets, 3 trombones, tuba, timpani, harp, violin I, violin II, viola, violoncello, double bass.
Call no.: **1992/046**
Re-entered as: **1993/043**

915. Gerber, Steven R., 1948– Symphony no. 1 (1988–89). N.p.: Steven R. Gerber, 1991.
1 score (93 p.); 28 cm.
Reproduced from manuscript.
Duration: 21:00.
Composed for: 2 flutes (2nd also piccolo), 2 oboes, 2 clarinets (2nd also clarinet in E♭), 2 bassoons, 4 horns, 2 trumpets, 3 trombones, tuba, timpani, harp, violin I, violin II, viola, violoncello, double bass.
Call no.: **1994/048**

916. Gerber, Steven R., 1948– Viola concerto (1996). N.p.: S.R. Gerber, 1996.
1 score (57 p.); 28 cm.
Duration: 19:00–20:00.
Composed for: viola, 2 flutes, 2 oboes, 2 clarinets, 2 bassoons, 2 horns, 2 trumpets, timpani, percussion (tam-tam, suspended cymbal, snare drum, glockenspiel, tambourine, triangle), harp, piano, violin I, violin II, viola, violoncello, double bass.
Call no.: **1998/055**
Re-entered as: **2000/061**, **2001/058**, **2002/064**, and **2003/045**

917. Gerber, Steven R., 1948– Violin concerto (1993). N.p.: S.R. Gerber, 1993.
1 score (73 p.); 37 cm.
Reproduced from manuscript.
Duration: ca. 21:00.
Composed for: violin, 2 flutes, 2 oboes, 2 clarinets in A, 2 bassoons, 2 horns, 2 trumpets, timpani, percussion (suspended cymbal, bass drum), violin I, violin II, viola, violoncello, double bass.
Call no.: **1995/036**
Re-entered as **1996/051** and **1997/053**

918. Gerulewicz, Gerardo Américo, 1966– Poema de sombra y fuego: poema sinfónico sobre textos de Vi-

cente Gerbasi. Caracas, Venezuela: Fundación Vicente Emilio Sogo, 1998.
1 miniature score (59 p.); 37 cm.
Includes performance and program notes.
Composed for: 3 flutes (3rd also piccolo), 3 oboes (3rd also English horn), 2 clarinets, bass clarinet, 2 bassoons, contrabassoon, 4 horns, 2 trumpets, 3 trombones, tuba, timpani, percussion (triangle, 3 temple blocks, claves, slapstick, guiro, maracas, drum, bongos, 3 tom-toms, 3 suspended cymbals, bass drum, tam-tam, glockenspiel, vibraphone, xylophone, marimba, chimes), celesta, 2 harps, violin I, violin II, viola, violoncello, double bass.
Call no.: **2003/046**

919. Ghosn, Rita, 1963– Poém symphonique: pour mezzo-soprano et orchestre. N.p.: n.p., 198-?.
1 score (52 p.); 35 cm.
French words; also printed as text with English translation.
Text from Khalil Gibran's Prophète, translated by Camille Aboussouan.
Reproduced from manuscript.
Composed for: mezzo-soprano, 2 flutes, 2 oboes, 2 clarinets, 2 bassoons, 3 horns, trumpet, trombone, percussion (snare drum, suspended cymbal, tambourine, triangle, timpani), harp, piano, violin I, violin II, viola, violoncello, double bass.
Call no.: **1989/044**

920. Giannotti, Stefano, 1963– La città sonora = ("The city of sounds"). N.p.: S.I.A.E., 2000.
1 score (64 p.) ports. (col.); 26 x 37 cm.
Program notes in English.
Contents: Senza titolo: parte I: for tape or person walking—Armonie urbane: for a large ensemble—Megaphono: for electric guitar, trombone, pop group (live or on tape), tapes and electronics—Senza titolo: parte II: for tape and four cellos.
Composed for: part I: tape or person walking; part II: oboe, alto saxophone, bass tuba, violoncello, contemporary music male singer, blues male singer, pop orchestra (2 flutes, accordion, harmonium, 5 electric guitars, bass guitar, keyboards, drums, rap singer), jazz wind ensemble (saxophone consort or brass consort: nine instruments); part III: trombone, electric guitar, pop orchestra (live or on tape), tapes, live electronics; part IV: tape (prerecorded female voice), 4 violoncellos.
Call no.: **2002/065**

921. Gielen, Michael, 1927– Streichquartett: un vieux souvenir. Studienpartitur. Frankfurt; New York, NY: H. Litolff's Verlag/C. F. Peters, 1987.
1 score (v, 30 p.); 31 cm.
Duration: 36:00–38:00.
Includes instructions for performance in English.
Composed for: 2 violins, viola, violoncello.
Commissioned by: WGUC (public radio station of the University of Cincinnati).
Call no.: **1988/042**

922. Gillingham, David, 1947– Heroes, lost and fallen: a Vietnam memorial. Full score. Milwaukee, WI: Composers' Editions: distributed by H. Leonard, 1991.
1 score (76 p.); 31 cm.
"Tone poem for symphonic band"—cover.
Includes program notes.
Composed for: piccolo, 2 flutes, 2 oboes, bassoon, contrabassoon, 3 clarinets, bass clarinet, 2 alto saxophones, tenor saxophone, baritone saxophone, 4 horns, 3 trumpets, 3 trombones, euphonium, tuba, timpani, piano, percussion (vibraphone, marimba, chimes, xylophone, crotales, bells, snare drum, bass drum, tam-tam, 4 tom-toms, suspended cymbal, crash cymbals).
Commissioned by: Dan and Linda Wagner.
Call no.: **1992/047**

923. Gillingham, David, 1947– Waking angels: wind ensemble. Greensboro, NC: C. Alan Publications, 1997.
1 score (40 p.); 43 cm.
Composed for: piccolo, flute, oboe, clarinet, bass clarinet, bassoon, 2 trumpets, 2 horns, trombone, tuba, harp, piano, double bass, timpani, percussion (bells, xylophone, vibraphone, large suspended cymbal, crash cymbals, metal police whistle, large tam-tam, crotales, chimes, medium tam-tam, 5 hanging metal plates, marimba, 4 bass drums, bass marimba, 4 metal brake drums, snare drum).
Commissioned by: University of Georgia Bands.
Call no.: **2000/062**

924. Gillingham, David, 1947– When speaks the signal-trumpet tone: concertino for solo trumpet and wind orchestra. Greensboro, NC: C. Alan Publications, 1999.
1 score (70 p.); 44 cm.
Includes program notes.
Composed for: trumpet, 2 flutes (both also piccolo), 2 oboes, 2 clarinets, bass clarinet, 2 bassoons, 3 trumpets, 4 horns, 2 trombones, bass trombone, tuba, string bass, piano, timpani, percussion (crotales, xylophone, medium brake drum, marimba, vibraphone, bells, tambourine, large brake drum, chimes, medium tom-tom, crash cymbal, hi-hat, bass drum, large tam-tam, snare drum).

Commissioned by: University of Georgia Bands.
Call no.: **2002/066**

925. Glass, Paul, 1934– Lamento dell'acqua. Bern: Müller + Schade, 1990.
1 score (90 p.); 43 cm.
Theme and variations for orchestra.
Reproduced from manuscript.
Duration: ca. 24:00.
Composed for: 2 flutes (2nd also piccolo and alto flute), 2 oboes (2nd also English horn), 2 clarinets (2nd also bass clarinet and clarinet in E♭), 2 bassoons (2nd also contrabassoon), 2 horns, 2 trumpets, percussion (timpani, chimes, glockenspiel, bass drum, marimba, crash cymbals, 3 suspended cymbals, xylophone, 3 drums, 3 tam-tams, 5 tom-toms, 3 triangles, vibraphone, 3 woodblocks), piano, violin I, violin II, viola, violoncello, double bass.
Commissioned by: Settimane Musicali di Ascona.
Call no.: **1991/041**

926. Glass, Paul, 1934– Sinfonia n. 3. N.p.: n.p., 1986.
1 score (95 p.); 42 cm.
Reproduced from manuscript.
Duration: ca. 18:30.
Composed for: 2 flutes (2nd also piccolo), 2 oboes (2nd also English horn), alto saxophone, 2 clarinets (2nd also bass clarinet), 2 bassoons (2nd also contrabassoon), 2 horns, 2 trumpets, trombone, percussion (timpani, 4 triangles, chimes, orchestra bells, crash cymbals, xylophone, 5 tom-toms, vibraphone, bass drum, marimba, 3 snare drums, 3 woodblocks, 3 suspended cymbals, 2 tam-tams), harp, violin I, violin II, viola, violoncello, double bass.
Call no.: **1988/043**
Re-entered as: **1989/045**

927. Glass, Philip, 1937– Orphée: an opera in two acts. New York, NY: Dunvagen, 1991.
1 score (2 v.); 36 cm.
French words; stage directions in English.
Based on the film by Jean Cocteau; adaptation by Philip Glass; edited by Robert Brustein.
Composed for: 2 sopranos, mezzo-sopranos, 4 tenors, 2 baritones, bass-baritone, 2 basses, flute (also piccolo), clarinet, bassoon, horn, trumpet, trombone, percussion (cymbals, tambourine, maracas, bass drum, snare drum, tenor drum, woodblock, triangle, hi-hat, glockenspiel, chimes, tam-tam, castanets), harp, synthesizer, violin I, violin II, viola, violoncello, double bass.
Call no.: **1994/049**

928. Glick, Andrew J., 1948– Solstitium. N.p.: n.p., 198-?.
1 score (17 p.); 28 cm.
Latin words.
For organ and SATB choir.
Text by the composer in English with Latin translation by Jeffrey Henderson.
Composed for: SATB chorus, organ.
Commissioned by: Cambridge Singers.
Call no.: **1989/046**

929. Glickman, Sylvia, 1932– Am I a murderer? A cantata for bass voice, flute, piccolo, clarinet, bass clarinet, violin, viola, cello and piano. N.p.: Sylvia Glickman, 1997.
1 score (42 p.); 28 cm.
English words by Frank Fox, with adaptations of poetry by Wladyslaw Salengel, Menachem Gebirtig, and J. Papesnikov.
Text based on: Czy ja jestem mordercą? by Calel Perechodnik.
Composed for: bass, piccolo, clarinet, bass clarinet, violin, viola, violoncello, piano.
Call no.: **1998/056**

930. Glickman, Sylvia, 1932– The walls are quiet now. N.p.: Hildegard Pub. Co., 1993.
1 score (78 p.); 28 cm.
Originally for chamber orchestra; revised and reorchestrated for full orchestra.
"Reflects the emotions evoked by the memorial wall outside the Gruenwald S-Bahn station in Berlin, Germany. The wall honors the memory of the Jews of the city, transported to concentration camps."
Contents: Fear, foreboding—Fright—Frenzy—Lest we forget.
Composed for: piccolo, 2 flutes, 2 oboes, 2 clarinets, 2 bassoons, 4 horns, 2 trumpets, 2 trombones, tuba, timpani, percussion (snare drum, triangle, xylophone, marimba, woodblock, glockenspiel, roto-toms, tam-tam, chimes), violin I, violin II, viola, violoncello, double bass.
Commissioned by: Lehigh Valley Chamber Orchestra.
Call no.: **1994/050**

931. Glinsky, Albert, 1952– Throne of the third heaven. N.p.: Albert Glinsky, 1989.
1 score (134 p.); 29 cm.
For orchestra.
Duration: ca. 25:00.
Composed for: 3 flutes (3rd also piccolo), 3 oboes (3rd English horn), 3 clarinets (3rd also bass clarinet), 3 bassoons (3rd also contrabassoon), 4 horns, 3 trumpets, 2 trombones, bass trombone, tuba, timpani, percussion (2 tenor drums, low drum, bass drum, tam-

bourine, crash cymbals, suspended cymbal, triangle, xylophone, vibraphone, glockenspiel, chimes), harp, piano, celesta, violin I, violin II, viola, violoncello, double bass.
Commissioned by: Erie Philharmonic Orchestra.
Call no.: **1990/036**

932. Glise, Anthony, 1956– Noah!. St. Joseph, MO: Aevia Publications, 1995.
1 score (146 p.); 28 cm.
Ballet.
Composed for: flute, oboe, horn, percussion (cymbals, snare drum, anvil, 2 drums), timpani, guitar, violin I, violin II, viola, violoncello, double bass.
Commissioned by: Pointe Station Ballet Company.
Call no.: **2000/063**

933. Glise, Anthony, 1956– Sonata for violin and guitar, op. 12: the secession. London: BMI-Aevia Publications, 1995.
1 score (22 p.) + 1 part (12 p.); 28 cm.
Biographical information in English, German, French, and Italian.
Composed for: violin, guitar.
Commissioned by: Ken Sugita.
Call no.: **1998/057**

934. Glise, Anthony, 1956– Trio for violin, viola and 'cello: "The canonization," op. 19. Kansas City, MO: Aevia Publications; Cincinnati, OH: Willis Music, 1999.
1 score (14 p.); 28 cm.
Biography of composer in English, German, French, Italian, and Dutch.
Composed for: violin, viola, violoncello.
Commissioned by: Trio Parnasse.
Call no.: **2002/067**

935. Globokar, Vinko, 1934– L'armonia drammatica: pour sept solistes vocaux, choeur mixte, orchestre, bande/son. Partitura. Paris: Editions Ricordi, 1993.
1 score (271, 62 p.); 72 cm.
Primarily Italian words by Edoardo Sanguineti.
Musical drama.
Reproduced from holograph.
Composed for: soprano, mezzo-soprano, contralto, child's voice, tenor, baritone, bass, SATB chorus, tenor saxophone, piccolo, flute, alto flute, oboe, English horn, clarinet in E♭, clarinet in A, bass clarinet, bassoon, contrabassoon, 4 horns, piccolo trumpet, trumpet, trombone, bass trombone, tuba, percussion (4 tom-toms, crash cymbals, medium pedal cymbal, wind machine, whistle, crank siren, small friction drum, flexatone, 2 woodblocks, maracas, bass drum, bongos, 2 Chinese gongs, large pedal cymbal, claves, sleigh bells, temple blocks, cog rattle, triangle, sandpaper block, snare drum, large tam-tam, 2 crotales, small pedal cymbal, log drum, whip, large friction drum, thundersheet, fog horn, guiro, wood hammer), synthesizer, electric guitar, bass guitar, tenor saxophone, violin I, violin II, violin III, viola, violoncello, double bass.
Call no.: **1996/052**

936. Globokar, Vinko, 1934– Labour: pour orchestre. Partition d'orchestre. Paris: Ricordi, 1992.
1 score (53 p.); 58 cm.
Reproduced from holograph.
Duration: ca. 27:00.
Composed for: piccolo, 2 flutes, alto flute, 3 oboes, English horn, clarinet, clarinet in E♭, bass clarinet, contrabass clarinet, 3 bassoons, contrabassoon, 4 horns, piccolo trumpet, 2 trumpets, bugle, 2 trombones, bass trombone, contrabass trombone, tuba, timpani, percussion (marimba, 3 roto-toms, temple blocks, 3 cymbals, wood chimes, 3 tam-tams, vibraphone, 2 woodblocks, Chinese gong, glass chimes, bass drum, tubular bells, side drum, timbales, African wood drum, metal chimes, bucket of water, flexatone, bongos, wind machine, guiro, 2 thundersheets, sleigh bells, jazz flute, tambourine, 2 maracas, 2 finger cymbals, friction drum), harp, piano, synthesizer, violin I, violin II, viola, violoncello, double bass.
Commissioned by: WDR Köln.
Call no.: **1994/051**

937. Ġlonti, P'elik's, 1927– Marianbad elegy: symphony concerto (for cello and orchestra). N.p.: n.p., 199-?.
1 score (99 p.); 41 cm.
Reproduced from manuscript.
Composed for: violoncello, 3 flutes (3rd also piccolo), alto flute, 3 oboes, English horn, clarinet in E♭, 2 clarinets, bass clarinet, 3 bassoons (3rd also contrabassoon), 4 horns, 4 trumpets, 3 trombones, tuba, percussion (timpani, xylophone, slapstick, 2 tom-toms, 3 bongos, 2 gongs, vibraphone, tam-tam, military snare drum, tambourine, snare drum, crash cymbals, 3 suspended cymbals, bass drum, tubular bells), celesta, 2 harps, violin I, violin II, viola, violoncello, double bass.
Call no.: **2002/068b**

938. Ġlonti, P'elik's, 1927– Marienbadische Elegie: simfonii͡a-kont͡sert: dli͡a bol′shogo simfonicheskogo orkestra = symphony-concerto: for full symphony or-

chestra. Partitura. N.p.: Georgian Music Fund, 199-?.
1 score (103 p.); 34 cm.
Reproduced from manuscript.
Composed for: violoncello, 3 flutes (3rd also piccolo), alto flute, 3 oboes, English horn, clarinet in E♭, 2 clarinets, bass clarinet, 3 bassoons (3rd also contrabassoon), 4 horns, 4 trumpets, 3 trombones, tuba, percussion (timpani, xylophone, slapstick, 2 tom-toms, 3 bongos, 2 gongs, vibraphone, tam-tam, military snare drum, tambourine, snare drum, crash cymbals, 3 suspended cymbals, bass drum, tubular bells), celesta, 2 harps, violin I, violin II, viola, violoncello, double bass.
Call no.: **2002/068a**

939. Godfrey, Daniel, 1949– String quartet no. 3. New York, NY: Carl Fischer, 2002.
1 score (71 p.); 28 cm.
Composed for: 2 violins, viola, violoncello.
Commissioned by: Cassatt String Quartet and Serge Koussevitzky Music Foundation.
Call no.: **2004/045**

940. Godfrey, Daniel, 1949– Symphony in minor. N.p.: Daniel S. Godfrey, 1999.
1 score (152 p.); 36 cm.
Composed for: 2 flutes (2nd also piccolo), 2 oboes (2nd also English horn), 2 clarinets (2nd also bass clarinet), 2 bassoons, 2 horns, 2 trumpets, percussion (timpani, tom-toms, field drums, suspended cymbals, vibraphone, marimba, wind chimes, bell tree, brake drums, temple blocks, cowbells, timbales), violin I, violin II, viola, violoncello, double bass.
Commissioned by: Jack and Linda Hoeschler.
Call no.: **2001/059**

941. Goehr, Alexander, 1932– Behold the sun. Mainz; New York, NY: Schott, 1984.
1 score (5 v.); 42 cm.
English and German words by John McGrath and the composer.
Opera in 3 acts.
Reproduced from manuscript.
Composed for: 3 sopranos, mezzo-soprano, 4 tenors, 5 baritones, bass, SATB chorus, offstage band (2 piccolos, cornet, tuba, cymbals, drum), stage band (2 piccolos, clarinet in E♭, cornet, tuba, violin, double bass, cymbals, drum), 3 flutes (2nd–3rd also piccolo), 2 oboes, English horn, 3 clarinets (2nd also clarinet in E♭, 3rd also bass clarinet), alto saxophone, 2 bassoons, contrabassoon, 4 horns, 4 trumpets (3rd also bass trumpet, 4th also cornet), 3 trombones, timpani, percussion (vibraphone, triangle, side drum, suspended cymbals, 4 tom-toms, finger cymbals, xylophone, wood drum, Chinese gong, bass drum, crash cymbals, tam-tam, maracas, small cymbal, siren, tambourine, military drum, tenor drum, crotales, gun shots, temple blocks, guiro, tubular bells, 2 congas, 2 gongs, Indian bells, low bell, cowbells, glockenspiel, whip, snare drum), piano, violin I, violin II, viola, violoncello, double bass.
Commissioned by: Deutsche Oper am Rhein Düsseldorf-Duisburg.
Call no.: **1986/043**
Also available:
Call no.: **1986/043 vocal score**

942. Goldstaub, Paul R., 1947– Variation sonata: journey through prisms (1984). N.p.: n.p., 1984.
47 leaves of music; 32 cm.
Reproduced from holograph.
Composed for: piano.
Call no.: **1985/073**

943. Gołembiowski, Jarosław, 1958– 2nd string quartet op. 92. 1st ed. Chicago, IL: Jaroslaw Golembiowski Music Productions, 2003.
1 score (48 p.); 28 cm.
Duration: 15:00.
Composed for: 2 violins, viola, violoncello.
Commissioned by: Polish National Alliance.
Call no.: **2005/054**

944. Goleminov, Marin, 1908–2000. Lamento: pour grand orchestre symphonique. Partition. N.p.: n.p., 1992.
1 score (14 p.); 43 cm.
Reproduced from manuscript.
Composed for: piccolo, 2 flutes, 2 oboes, English horn, 2 clarinets, bass clarinet, 2 bassoons, contrabassoon, 4 horns, 3 trumpets, 3 trombones, tuba, timpani, percussion (bass drum, tam-tam, triangle, snare drum, cymbals), violin I, violin II, viola, violoncello, double bass.
Call no.: **1996/053**

945. Golijov, Osvaldo, 1960– The dreams and prayers of Isaac the Blind: for klezmer clarinet and string quartet. N.p.: Osvaldo Golijov, 1994.
1 score (63 p.); 21 x 28 cm.
Composed for: klezmer clarinet, 2 violins, viola, violoncello.
Commissioned by: Schleswig-Holstein Musik Festival, Musical Society of University of Michigan, and Chamber Series at University of Kansas.
Call no.: **2000/064**

946. Golijov, Osvaldo, 1960– La pasion: según San Marcos. N.p.: Universal Edition, 2000.
1 score (various pagings); 28 cm.
Spanish and Aramaic words.
For instrumental and vocal soloists with orchestra.
Composed for: soprano, SATB chorus, 2 trumpets, 2 trombones, accordion, guitar, tres, beriembau, piano, percussion (caxixi, maracas, bass drum, okonkolo, itotele, iya, bongos, congas, timbales, cajon, udu, bells, wind chimes, shakers, 5 sticks [kitiplas], whistle, agogo, gua gua, cuíca, quinto), 6 violins, 6 violoncellos, 3 double basses.
Commissioned by: Internationale Bachakademie Stuttgart.
Call no.: **2002/069**

947. Golijov, Osvaldo, 1960– La pasion: según San Marcos. N.p.: Universal Edition, 2000.
1 score (various pagings); 36 cm.
Spanish and Aramaic words; also printed as text following score.
For instrumental and vocal soloists, choir, and orchestra.
Conversation between Osvaldo Golijov and David Harrington in English follows score.
Composed for: soprano, SATB chorus, 2 trumpets, 2 trombones, accordion, guitar, tres, beriembau, piano, percussion (caxixi, maracas, bass drum, okonkolo, itotele, iya, bongos, congas, timbales, cajon, udu, bells, wind chimes, shakers, 5 sticks [kitiplas], whistle, agogo, gua gua, cuíca, quinto), 6 violins, 6 violoncellos, 3 double basses.
Commissioned by: Internationale Bachakademie Stuttgart.
Call no.: **2004/046**

948. Gomez, Alice, 1960– Homenaje a Cesar Chavez: (1927–1993). Conductor's score. N.p.: n.p., 1996.
1 score (62 p.); 36 cm.
For orchestra.
Duration: 12:05.
Composed for: 3 flutes, 2 oboes, English horn, 2 bassoons, contrabassoon, 4 horns, 2 trumpets, 3 trombones, timpani, percussion (glockenspiel, congas, gong, chimes, suspended cymbal, brake drum), piano, violin I, violin II, viola, violoncello, double bass.
Commissioned by: San Antonio Symphony.
Call no.: **1997/054**

949. Gomez, Alice, 1960– Primitive echoes: concerto for timpani and orchestra. N.p.: Alice Gomez, 1992.
1 score (41 p.); 30 cm.
Duration: 14:00.
Contents: Spirit dance—Ancient whispers—Mountain chant.
Composed for: timpani, 2 flutes, 2 oboes, 2 clarinets, 2 bassoons, 2 horns, 2 trumpets, violin I, violin II, viola, violoncello, double bass.
Call no.: **1993/044**

950. Gondai, Atsuhiko, 1965– The beginning of the end/after the end: for chamber orchestra. Tokyo: Schott Japan, 2003.
1 score (40 p.); 44 cm.
Duration: 17:00.
Composed for: flute (also piccolo), oboe, clarinet (also bass clarinet), bassoon, horn, trumpet, trombone, harp, piano, percussion (tubular bells, vibraphone, glockenspiel, bass drum, piccolo woodblock), 7 violins, 2 violas, 2 violoncellos, double bass.
Commissioned by: Izumi Hall, Kioi Hall, and Shirakawa Hall.
Call no.: **2005/055**

951. Gonzalez, Luis Jorge, 1936– Inti-raymi: suite for orchestra. N.p.: n.p., 1990.
1 score (62 p.); 28 cm.
Contents: Convocation and processional—Morning prayer—Sacrificial dance.
Composed for: 2 flutes (2nd also piccolo), 2 oboes (2nd also English horn), 2 clarinets (1st also clarinet in E♭, 2nd also bass clarinet), 2 bassoons, 2 horns, 2 trumpets, percussion (timpani, bass drum, medium gong, triangle, cymbals, 4 tom-toms, glockenspiel, guiro, snare drum), harp, piano (also celesta), violin I, violin II, viola, violoncello, double bass.
Call no.: **1993/045**

952. Gonzalez, Luis Jorge, 1936– Retablo de navidad: para soprano, coro y orquesta. N.p.: n.p., 1985.
1 score (93 p.); 28 cm.
Spanish words.
Cantata.
Texts by Gustavo Carrizo and the composer.
Reproduced from manuscript.
Composed for: soprano, SATB chorus, piccolo, 2 flutes, 2 oboes, 2 clarinets, 2 bassoons, 4 horns, 2 trumpets, 3 trombones, tuba, timpani, percussion (suspended cymbal, chimes, triangle, 4 tom-toms, bass drum, snare drum, gong, celesta), violin I, violin II, viola, violoncello, double bass.
Call no.: **1986/044**

953. Goode, Daniel, 1936– Tunnel-funnel: for fifteen instruments. N.p.: n.p., 1985.
1 score (217 p.); 36 cm.
Reproduced from manuscript.
Composed for: 4 flutes (2nd–4th also alto flute, 4th

also bass flute), 3 trombones, bass trombone, percussion (marimba, vibraphone, glockenspiel, xylophone), piano, 2 violins, viola, violoncello, double bass.
Call no.: **1990/037**
Re-entered as: **1991/042**

954. Gordon, Jerold James, 1962– Calaveras: imaginary ballet in one act (three tableaux) for symphony orchestra after engravings by J.G. Posada. N.p.: Alfred Lengnick, 1991.
1 score (62 p.); 30 cm.
Duration: ca. 19:00.
Program notes by the composer in English.
Composed for: 3 flutes (1st also alto flute, 3rd also piccolo), 3 oboes (3rd also English horn), 3 clarinets (3rd also bass clarinet), 3 bassoons (3rd also contrabassoon), 4 horns, 3 trumpets (1st–2nd also trumpet in D), 3 trombones, tuba, timpani, percussion (bombo, side drum, whip, claves, 2 gongs, suspended cymbals, triangle, raspador, 3 bongos, 2 tom-toms, 3 congas, maraca, tenor drum, woodblock, marimba, xylophone, vibraphone, glockenspiel, crotales, bells), harp, violin I, violin II, viola, violoncello, double bass.
Commissioned by: BBC Welsh Symphony Orchestra.
Call no.: **1993/046**

955. Gordon, Jerold James, 1962– Kantate Nr. 1: Hiob: für Sopran, Bariton und Kammerorchester = Cantata no. 1: Job: for soprano, baritone and chamber orchestra. N.p.: Jerold James Gordon, 1989.
1 score (51 p.); 42 cm.
German words; also printed as text with English translation.
"Gedichtzyklus von Hans-Jörg Modlmayr; Konzeption und Zusammenstellung der Rezitative aus dem biblischen Buch Hiob von Hildegard Modlmayr-Heimath."
Reproduced from manuscript.
Duration: ca. 40:00.
Composed for: soprano, baritone, flute (also piccolo), oboe, English horn, clarinet, bass clarinet, bassoon, horn, 3 violins, 2 violas, 2 violoncellos.
Commissioned by: Bernhard Volkenhoff.
Call no.: **1992/048**

956. Górecki, Henryk Mikołaj, 1933– Kleines Requiem für eine Polka: für Klavier und 13 Instrumente: opus 66. Study score. London; New York, NY: Boosey & Hawkes, 1993.
1 score (48 p.); 30 cm.
Reproduced from manuscript.
Composed for: piano, flute, oboe, clarinet, bassoon, horn, trumpet, trombone, chimes, 2 violins, viola, violoncello, double bass.
Commissioned by: Holland Festival.
Call no.: **1994/052**

957. Górecki, Henryk Mikołaj, 1933– Quasi una fantasia: II. qwartet smyczkowy: op. 64, 1990–1991. N.p.: Boosey & Hawkes, 1991.
1 score (46 leaves); 30 cm.
For string quartet.
Duration: ca. 12:30.
Composed for: 2 violins, viola, violoncello.
Commissioned by: Kosciuszko Foundation, Beigler Trust, and Lincoln Center for the Performing Arts.
Call no.: **1992/049**

958. Gorelli, Olga, 1920– I forgive: a short cantata for soprano, oboe, bassoon, and piano. N.p.: n.p., 1986.
1 score (31 leaves); 28 cm.
Reproduced from manuscript.
Duration: ca. 11:00.
Composed for: soprano, oboe, bassoon, piano.
Call no.: **1988/044**

959. Gorelli, Olga, 1920– The river: a suite for flute and piano. N.p.: n.p., 1988.
1 score (16 leaves) + 1 part (5 leaves); 28 cm.
Contents: The river is born—The river flows to the sea—Man abuses the river—The river has run dry.
Composed for: flute, piano.
Call no.: **1990/038**

960. Gould, Morton, 1913–1996. Classical variations: on colonial themes: for orchestra, 1985. New York, NY: G. Schirmer/Associated Music, 1985.
1 score (44 p.); 47 cm.
Reproduced from holograph.
Duration: 14:00.
Composed for: 2 flutes (both also piccolo), 2 oboes, 2 clarinets, 2 bassoons, 4 horns, 2 trumpets, 2 trombones, timpani, percussion (chimes, snare drum, cymbals, bass drum, tambourine), harp, violin I, violin II, viola, violoncello, double bass.
Call no.: **1987/027**

961. Gould, Morton, 1913–1996. Concerto: for flute and orchestra, 1983–84. Pennsauken, NJ: G. Schirmer/Associated Music, 1984.
1 score (101 p.); 56 cm.
Reproduced from holograph.
At end of score: "Completed May 19, 1984."
Duration: ca. 34:00.
Contents: Rhapsodic—Elegiac variations—Intermezzo—Rondo (finale).

Composed for: flute, 2 piccolos, 3 oboes, 3 clarinets, 3 bassoons (3rd also contrabassoon), 4 horns, 3 trumpets, 3 trombones, tuba, timpani, percussion (bass drum, xylophone, snare drum, bongos, tenor drum, chimes, crash cymbals, triangle, finger cymbals), harp, celesta, violin I, violin II, viola, violoncello, double bass.
Commissioned by: Katherine Lewis.
Call no.: **1986/045**
Re-entered as: **1989/047**

962. Gould, Morton, 1913–1996. Ghost waltzes: for piano. New York, NY: G. Schirmer; Milwaukee, WI: H. Leonard, 1992.
20 p. of music; 31 cm.
Duration: ca. 11:00.
Composed for: piano.
Commissioned by: Lewis F. Kornfeld, Jr.
Call no.: **1994/053**

963. Gould, Morton, 1913–1996. Quotations: for double chorus and orchestra (wind ensemble). New York, NY: G. Schirmer, 1983.
1 score (various pagings); 57 cm.
English words.
Reproduced from manuscript.
Duration: ca. 20:00.
Contents: Hallelujah—Hosanna amen—Walkin' on air—The early bird—A bird in hand—Ballads—Sermon—Postscript.
Composed for: double SATB chorus, 2 flutes, 2 oboes, 2 clarinets, 2 bassoons, 4 horns, 3 trumpets, 3 trombones, tuba, harp, piano, 2 double basses, percussion (timpani, chimes, temple blocks, steel plate, trolley bell, sandpaper blocks, 3 tom-toms, xylophone, crash cymbals, gong, 2 tam-tams, suspended cymbal, vibraphone, triangle, bass drum, maracas, snare drum, finger cymbals, tambourine, bongos, castanets).
Commissioned by: L. Anthony Fisher.
Call no.: **1985/074**

964. Gould, Morton, 1913–1996. Stringmusic (1993). New York, NY: G. Schirmer, 1994.
1 score (63 p.); 36 cm.
Duration: ca. 30:00.
Contents: Prelude—Tango—Dirge—Ballad—Strum: perpetual motion.
Composed for: violin I, violin II, viola, violoncello, double bass.
Commissioned by: Hechinger Foundation.
Call no.: **1995/037**

965. Gould, Morton, 1913–1996. Stringmusic: for string orchestra. Full score. New York, NY: G. Schirmer; Milwaukee, WI: Distributed by H. Leonard, 1995.
1 score (52 p.); 31 cm.
Duration: ca. 30:00.
Contents: Prelude—Tango—Dirge—Ballad—Strum: perpetual motion.
Composed for: violin I, violin II, viola, violoncello, double bass.
Commissioned by: Hechinger Foundation.
Call no.: **1996/054**

966. Grantham, Donald, 1947– The boor: an opera in one act after Chekhov. N.p.: n.p., 1988.
1 vocal score (250 p.); 29 cm.
English words by the composer.
Reproduced from manuscript.
Duration: ca. 1:00:00.
Composed for: soprano, mezzo-soprano, tenor, baritone, flute (also piccolo), oboe (also English horn), clarinet in A (also bass clarinet), bassoon (also contrabassoon), horn, trumpet, bass trombone, percussion, harp, piano, 2 violins, viola, violoncello, double bass.
Call no.: **1991/043**

967. Grantham, Donald, 1947– Hymn to the earth. Austin, TX: Piquant Press, 2001.
1 score (61 p.); 44 cm.
English words translated by Charles Boer from original text by Homer; also printed as text.
For orchestra and women's chorus.
Duration: 14:00.
Program note and biographical information in English.
Composed for: soprano, women's chorus, 3 flutes (3rd also piccolo), 3 oboes, 3 clarinets (3rd also bass clarinet), 2 bassoons, contrabassoon, 4 horns, 4 trumpets, 3 trombones, tuba, timpani, percussion (crotales, 4 tom-toms, xylophone, tam-tam, suspended cymbal, tambourine, triangle, bass drum, crash cymbals, mark tree), piano (also celesta), harp, violin I, violin II, viola, violoncello, double bass.
Commissioned by: New Texas Music Works.
Call no.: **2004/047**

968. Greenbaum, Matthew, 1950– Psalter. N.p.: n.p., 1991.
1 score (90 p.); 28 cm.
German words from Psalm 104.
Contents: Aria sopra passacaglia—Hocquetus I—Aria sopra bordone—Hocquetus II.
Composed for: mezzo-soprano, alto flute, English horn, violin, viola, violoncello, harp, piano.
Commissioned by: Network for New Music.
Call no.: **1993/047**

969. Greenberg, Robert M., 1954– In shape: concerto in three movements for two pianos and marimba. Berkeley, CA: Fallen Leaf Press, 1991.
1 score (73 p.); 43 cm.
Duration: ca. 21:00.
Composed for: 2 pianos, marimba.
Call no.: **1992/050**

970. Greenberg, Robert M., 1954– On trial: concerto for vibraphone and chamber ensemble (1994). N.p.: Robert M. Greenberg, 1994.
1 score (131 p.); 22 x 36 cm.
Duration: ca. 27:10.
Composed for: vibraphone, flute, clarinet, bassoon, piano, violin, viola, violoncello.
Call no.: **1996/055**

971. Greenleaf, Robert B., 1946– Under the arbor: an opera in two acts. N.p.: Robert B. Greenleaf, 1992.
1 score (2 v.); 44 cm.
English words by Marian Motley Carcache.
Composed for: 4 sopranos, 4 mezzo-sopranos, 2 tenors, 3 baritones, bass, SATB chorus, 2 flutes, 2 oboes, 2 clarinets, 2 bassoons, 2 horns, 3 trumpets, 2 trombones, timpani, percussion (chimes, low triangle), violin I, violin II, viola, violoncello, double bass.
Call no.: **1996/056**

972. Grisey, Gérard, 1946–1998. Epilogue. Partitura. N.p.: Ricordi, 1985.
1 score (23 p.); 76 cm.
For orchestra.
Reproduced from manuscript.
Composed for: 4 flutes, 4 oboes, 4 clarinets, contrabass clarinet, bassoon, contrabassoon, 2 saxophones, 4 trumpets, 4 horns, 3 trombones, tuba, harp, accordion, piano, electric guitar, percussion, violin I, violin II, viola, violoncello, and double bass.
Commissioned by: Biennale di Venezia.
Call no.: **1986/046a**

973. Grisey, Gérard, 1946–1998. L'icône paradoxale: (hommage à Piero della Francesca): pour deux voix de femmes et grand orchestre divisé en deux groupes. Partitura. Paris: Editions Ricordi, 1994.
1 score (46 p.); 72 cm.
Italian words.
Reproduced from manuscript.
Composed for: soprano, mezzo-soprano, 4 flutes (all also piccolo, 1st–2nd also alto flute), 2 oboes (both also English horn), 4 clarinets (1st–2nd also clarinet in A, 2nd also bass clarinet), bass clarinet, baritone saxophone (also tenor saxophone), 2 bassoons, 2 contrabassoons, 4 horns, 4 trumpets, trombone, 2 bass trombones, tuba, contrabass tuba, percussion (tubular bells, large bass drum, 3 congas, 3 boobams, 3 large bongos, 3 tam-tams, medium Chinese cymbal, cymbals, marimba, 5 tom-toms, Balinese gong, 5 small Thai gongs, crotales, large wood drum, medium timbales, thundersheet, xylophone, large timbales, temple block, medium gong, tuned gongs, vibraphone, 2 sandpaper blocks, 3 guiros, small triangle, glockenspiel, small bongo, small pellet bell), piano (also celesta), violin I, violin II, viola, violoncello, double bass.
Commissioned by: Los Angeles Philharmonic Association and Teatro alla Scala.
Call no.: **1997/055**

974. Grisey, Gérard, 1946–1998. Le noir de l'étoile: spectacle pour six percussionistes, bande magnétique et retransmission in situ de signaux astronomiques. Partitura. Paris: Ricordi, 1990.
1 score (138 p.); 35 cm.
Reproduced from manuscript.
Composed for: tape, percussion (6 bongos, 5 tom-toms, snare drum, bass drums, wood drum, log drum, 2 tam-tams, 2 gong, 2 Chinese cymbal, 2 sizzle cymbals, spring coil, guiro, 2 maracas, friction drum, romble, 5 Chinese drums, 9 roto-toms, Balinese gong, cymbale tournante, polystyrene tablet, sandpaper tablet, friction drum, 5 congas, 2 cabasa, 6 boobams, timpani, geophone, African drum).
Commissioned by: Ministero della Cultura Francese and Percussionisti de Strasburgo.
Call no.: **1992/051**

975. Grisey, Gérard, 1946–1998. Talea: per flauto, clarinetto, violino, violoncello e pianoforte. Partitura. Paris: Ricordi, 1986.
1 score (70 p.); 31 x 47 cm.
Includes performance instructions and program notes in Italian, French, English, and German.
Duration: ca. 15:00.
Reproduced from holograph.
At end: 1985–1986, Paris, Berkeley, Bruxelles.
Composed for: flute (also piccolo, alto, and bass flutes), clarinet (also clarinet in A and bass clarinet), violin, violoncello, piano.
Commissioned by: Radio France.
Call no.: **1989/048**

976. Grisey, Gérard, 1946–1998. Le temps et l'écume. Partitura. N.p.: Ricordi, 1989.
1 score (71 p.); 68 cm.
For orchestra.
Reproduced from manuscript.

Includes performance instructions in French.
Composed for: piccolo, 2 flutes (both also piccolo and alto flute), 2 oboes (both also English horn), 2 clarinets (both also clarinet in A and clarinet in E♭), bass clarinet (also contrabass clarinet), 2 bassoons (2nd also contrabassoon), 2 horns, 2 trumpets, 2 trombones, percussion (xylorimba, glockenspiel, tubular bells, 5 cencerros, 2 bell plates, 2 bass drums, 3 Chinese drums, 3 maracas, 2 friction drums, vibraphone, 2 gongs, timpani, 3 slit drums, 9 woodblocks, guiro, 4 congas, snare drum, 4 bongos, 9 mokubios, 4 temple blocks, xylophone, crotales, 2 bell plates, tam-tam, 3 log drums), 2 synthesizers, violin I, violin II, viola, violoncello, double bass.
Commissioned by: Radio France.
Call no.: **1991/044**

977. Grisey, Gérard, 1946–1998. Transitoires. Partitura. Paris: Sté. Ame. des Editions Ricordi, 1981.
1 score (47 p.); 60 cm.
For orchestra.
Composed for: 4 flutes (all also piccolo, 3rd–4th also alto flute), 4 oboes (3rd–4th also English horn), 2 clarinets, 2 clarinets in A (2nd also clarinet), bass clarinet (also contrabass clarinet), alto saxophone (also soprano saxophone), tenor saxophone (also alto and soprano saxophones), 2 bassoons (2nd also contrabassoon), 4 horns, 4 trumpets, 3 bass trombones, tuba (also contrabass tuba), percussion (tubular bells, bass drum, 6 bongos, vibraphone, marimba, crotales, gong, tumba, tom-tom, crash cymbals, steel drum, glockenspiel, cymbals, wood drum, timbal, string drum, snare drum, 6 woodblocks, 3 tam-tams, wind machine), harp, accordion, electric organ, electric guitar, violin I, violin II, viola, violoncello, double bass.
Commissioned by: Comune di Palermo.
Call no.: **1986/046**

978. Grisey, Gérard, 1946–1998. Vortex temporum: I, II, III: pour piano et cinq instruments (1994–1996). Partition. Paris: Ricordi, 1996.
1 score (141 p.); 40 x 50 cm.
Composed for: piano, violin, viola, violoncello, flute (also piccolo, alto and bass flutes), clarinet (also clarinet in A and bass clarinet).
Commissioned by: Deutsches Kultusministerium, Ministerium für Kunst Baden-Württemberg, and Westdeutscher Rundfunk Köln.
Call no.: **1998/058**

979. Grové, Stefans, 1922– Afrika hymnus. Pretoria: University of South Africa, 1996.
44 p. of music; 21 x 30 cm.
Includes biographical and program notes in Afrikaans and English.
Composed for: organ.
Commissioned by: Foundation for the Creative Arts.
Call no.: **1997/056**

980. Grové, Stefans, 1922– Afrika hymnus II: fünf Tonbilder aus dem ländlichen Afrika für Orgel (1997). N.p.: n.p., 1997.
59 p. of music; 42 cm.
Reproduced from manuscript.
Composed for: organ.
Call no.: **2003/047**

981. Grové, Stefans, 1922– Raka: a symphonic poem in the form of a concerto for piano and orchestra, 1997. N.p.: n.p., 1997.
1 score (103 p.); 30 cm.
Reproduced from manuscript.
Duration: 25:00.
Composed for: piano, piccolo, 2 flutes, 2 oboes, English horn, 2 clarinets, bass clarinet, 2 bassoons, contrabassoon, 4 horns, 3 trumpets, 2 trombones, bass trombone, tuba, harp, percussion (marimba, xylophone, timpani, guiro, woodblock, tom-tom, tenor drum, bass drum, gong), violin I, violin II, viola, violoncello, double bass.
Commissioned by: SAMRO Endowment for the National Arts.
Call no.: **2002/070**

982. Grové, Stefans, 1922– Raka: a symphonic poem in the form of a concerto for piano and orchestra, 1997. N.p.: n.p., 1997.
1 score (103 p.); 42 cm.
Reproduced from manuscript.
Duration: 25:00.
Composed for: piano, piccolo, 2 flutes, 2 oboes, English horn, 2 clarinets, bass clarinet, 2 bassoons, contrabassoon, 4 horns, 3 trumpets, 2 trombones, bass trombone, tuba, harp, percussion (marimba, xylophone, timpani, guiro, woodblock, tom-tom, tenor drum, bass drum, gong), violin I, violin II, viola, violoncello, double bass.
Commissioned by: SAMRO Endowment for the National Arts.
Call no.: **2005/056**

983. Gruber, Heinz Karl, 1943– Aerial: concerto for trumpet and orchestra. Full score. London: Boosey & Hawkes, 1999.
1 score (83 p.); 36 cm.
Contents: Done with the compass, done with the chart!—Gone dancing.

Composed for: trumpet, 3 flutes (2nd–3rd also piccolo), 2 oboes, 4 clarinets (3rd also clarinet in E♭, 4th also bass clarinet), alto saxophone (also soprano saxophone), tenor saxophone (also soprano saxophone), 2 bassoons, contrabassoon, 4 horns, 3 trumpets, 3 trombones, tuba, timpani, percussion (crotales, Chinese tam-tam, bass drum with foot pedal, large bass drum, side drum, bongos, tom-toms, hi-hat, suspended Chinese cymbal, cowbell, suspended tambourine, glockenspiel, vibraphone, xylorimba, marimba), piano, violin I, violin II, viola, violoncello, double bass.
Commissioned by: British Broadcasting Corporation.
Call no.: **2001/060**

984. Gruber, Heinz Karl, 1943– Cello concerto.
Composed for: violoncello, orchestra.
Call no.: **1992/052**
No materials available.

985. Gruber, Heinz Karl, 1943– Dancing in the dark: concert piece for large orchestra. Full score. London: Boosey & Hawkes, 2002.
1 score (72 p.); 42 cm.
Composed for: 3 flutes (also piccolo), 3 oboes (also English horn), 4 clarinets (also clarinets in A and E♭ and bass clarinet), 2 bassoons, contrabassoon, 6 horns (also Wagner tubas in F and B♭), 4 trumpets, 3 trombones (also tenor horn), tuba, timpani, percussion (drum kit with 3 cowbells, 2 woodblocks, tambourine, 2 bongos, 2 tom-toms, side drum, floor tom-tom, bass drum, splash cymbal, sizzle cymbal, hi-hat, Chinese cymbal, 2 suspended cymbals, large bass drum, 2 large rutes, 2 Chinese tam-tams, glockenspiel, crotales, xylorimba, vibraphone, marimba, crash cymbals), harp, piano, violin I, violin II, viola, violoncello, double bass.
Commissioned by: Vienna Philharmonic Orchestra.
Call no.: **2005/057**

986. Gruhn, Oliver, 1968– Vier Lieder für Sopran und Orchester. N.p.: Oliver Gruhn, 1994.
1 score (61 p.); 30 cm.
German words.
Texts by John Keats and Herman Hesse.
Contents: Grille und Heimchen—Weisse Rose in der Dämmerung—Jahrestag—Wie eine Welle.
Composed for: soprano, 2 flutes, 2 oboes, heckelphone, 2 clarinets, bass clarinet, 2 bassoons, contrabassoon, 4 horns, 3 trumpets, 3 trombones, tuba, timpani, harp, violin I, violin II, viola, violoncello, double bass.
Call no.: **1998/059**

987. Gubaĭdulina, Sof'i͡a Asgatovna, 1931– Alleluja: für Chor, Knabensopran und Orchester (Farbenklavier ad lib.) = for choir, boy's soprano and orchestra (colour organ ad. lib.). Hamburg: Musikverlag Hans Sikorski, 1990.
1 score (181 p.); 42 cm.
Russian words; English and German translations printed as text.
Reproduced from manuscript.
Performance instructions in English and German.
Composed for: boy soprano, SATB chorus, piccolo, 2 flutes, 2 oboes, clarinet in E♭, 2 clarinets, bass clarinet, 2 bassoons, contrabassoon, 4 horns, 3 trumpets, 3 trombones, tuba, percussion (timpani, 2 suspended cymbals, marimba, cymbals, 3 tom-toms, vibraphone, 3 bass drums, tam-tam, chimes), 2 harps, piano, celesta, cembalo, organ, violin I, violin II, viola, violoncello, double bass.
Call no.: **1994/054**

988. Gubaĭdulina, Sof'i͡a Asgatovna, 1931– Concerto for viola and orchestra. New York, NY: G. Schirmer, 1997.
1 score (85 p.); 36 cm.
"Revised 6/97"—p. 1.
Duration: 20:00–30:00.
Reproduced from holograph.
Composed for: viola, piccolo, 2 flutes, alto flute (also piccolo), bass flute, 2 oboes, 2 clarinets, 2 bassoons, 3 horns (also Wagner tubas), 3 trumpets, 2 trombones, bass trombone, tuba imperiale (contrabass tuba), percussion (timpani, bass drum, cymbals, tam-tam, vibraphone, marimba, xylophone, bells, glockenspiel, triangle), piano, celesta, cembalo, string quartet (violin, viola, violoncello, double bass), violin I, violin II, viola, violoncello, double bass.
Commissioned by: Mrs. H. C. Smith Commissioning Fund.
Call no.: **1998/060**

989. Gubaĭdulina, Sof'i͡a Asgatovna, 1931– Concerto for viola and orchestra. New York, NY: G. Schirmer, 1998.
1 score (85 p.); 43 cm.
"Revised 7/98"—p. 1.
Duration: 34:00.
Reproduced from holograph.
Composed for: viola, piccolo, 2 flutes, alto flute (also piccolo), bass flute, 2 oboes, 2 clarinets, 2 bassoons, 3 horns (also Wagner tubas), 3 trumpets, 2 trombones, bass trombone, tuba imperiale (contrabass tuba), percussion (timpani, bass drum, cymbals, tam-tam, vibraphone, marimba, xylophone, bells, glockenspiel, triangle), piano, celesta, cembalo, string quartet (violin, viola, violoncello, double bass), violin I, violin II, viola, violoncello, double bass.

Commissioned by: Mrs. H. C. Smith Commissioning Fund.
Call no.: **2000/065**

990. Gubaĭdulina, Sof'ia Asgatovna, 1931– Kontsert dlia al'ta s orkestrom. New York, NY: G. Schirmer, 1996.
1 score (85 p.); 42 cm.
Concerto for viola and orchestra.
Duration: 20:00–30:00.
Reproduced from holograph.
Composed for: viola, piccolo, 2 flutes, alto flute (also piccolo), bass flute, 2 oboes, 2 clarinets, 2 bassoons, 3 horns (also Wagner tubas), 3 trumpets, 2 trombones, bass trombone, tuba imperiale (contrabass tuba), percussion (timpani, bass drum, cymbals, tam-tam, vibraphone, marimba, xylophone, bells, glockenspiel, triangle), piano, celesta, cembalo, string quartet (violin, viola, violoncello, double bass), violin I, violin II, viola, violoncello, double bass.
Commissioned by: Mrs. H. C. Smith Commissioning Fund.
Call no.: **2001/061**

991. Gubaĭdulina, Sof'ia Asgatovna, 1931– The light of the end: for large orchestra. New York, NY: G. Schirmer, 2003.
1 score (108 p.); 36 cm.
Duration: 20:00.
Composed for: 4 flutes (also piccolo and alto flute), oboe, English horn, heckelphone, 2 clarinets, bass clarinet, 2 bassoons, contrabassoon, 4 horns, 3 trumpets, trombone, bass trombone (also tenor trombone in F), contrabass trombone, tuba, percussion (timpani, vibraphone, marimba, 2 sets of chimes, bar chimes, glockenspiel, crotales, antique cymbals, 5 suspended cymbals, crash cymbals, large tam-tam, bass drum, bell plates), harp, violin I (20 minimum), violin II (18 minimum), viola (14 minimum), violoncello (14 minimum), double bass (12 minimum).
Commissioned by: Boston Symphony Orchestra.
Call no.: **2005/058**

992. Gubaĭdulina, Sof'ia Asgatovna, 1931– Pro et contra: dlia bol'shogo simfonicheskogo orkestra, 1989. Chester, NY: G. Schirmer, 1989.
1 score (38 p., 28 leaves); 44 cm.
"4th movement added by composer for 1990 performance, Louisville Orchestra"—leaf 1, in pencil.
Reproduced from manuscript.
Composed for: piccolo, 2 flutes, alto flute, 2 oboes, clarinet in E♭, 2 clarinets, bass clarinet, 2 bassoons, contrabassoon, 4 horns, 3 trumpets, 3 trombones, tuba, percussion (timpani, tam-tam, 2 bass drums, vibraphone, tom-tom, 5 suspended cymbals, 2 cymbals, orchestra bells, chimes, marimba, xylophone, crotales), 2 harps, piano, celesta, cembalo, violin I, violin II, viola, violoncello, double bass.
Commissioned by: Louisville Orchestra.
Call no.: **1990/039**

993. Gubaĭdulina, Sof'ia Asgatovna, 1931– Stimmen . . . Verstummen . . . : Sinfonie in 12 Sätzen. Hamburg: H. Sikorski, 1986.
1 score (203 p.); 42 cm.
Includes performance note by the composer in German and English.
Composed for: 4 flutes (3rd also piccolo, 4th also alto flute), 2 oboes, 3 clarinets (2nd also tenor saxophone, 3rd also alto saxophone), bass clarinet, 3 bassoons, contrabassoon, 4 horns, 3 trumpets, 4 trombones, tuba, percussion (timpani, triangle, 2 snare drums, alto drum, tenor drum, tom-toms, 10 suspended cymbals, 4 tam-tams, bass drum, xylophone, 3 chimes, 3 vibraphones, 3 marimbas, 3 tubular bells), harp, celesta, organ, violin I, violin II, viola I, violin II, violoncello I, violoncello II, double bass I, double bass II.
Commissioned by: Berliner Festwochen, 1986.
Call no.: **1987/028**
Re-entered as: **1988/045**

994. Gubaĭdulina, Sof'ia Asgatovna, 1931– Two paths: (dedication to Mary and Martha): music for two solo violas and symphony orchestra. New York, NY: G. Schirmer, 1999.
1 score (59 p.); 29 cm.
"Final proofs of publication 12–99"—p. 1.
Composed for: 2 violas, piccolo, 2 flutes (2nd also bass flute), 2 oboes, clarinet in E♭, 2 clarinets, bass clarinet, 2 bassoons, contrabassoon, 4 horns, 3 trumpets, 2 trombones, bass trombone, contrabass trombone, tuba, timpani, percussion (vibraphone, marimba, crotales, bell plate, bar chimes, snare drum, glockenspiel, tam-tam, 3 gongs), celesta, piano, violin I, violin II, viola, violoncello, double bass.
Commissioned by: New York Philharmonic.
Call no.: **2002/071**

995. Guinjoan, Joan, 1931– Concerto no. 1: para violín y orchesta. Madrid: EMEC, 1986.
1 score (92 p.); 43 cm.
Reproduced from manuscript.
Composed for: violin, 2 flutes (2nd also piccolo), 2 oboes, 2 clarinets (2nd also bass clarinet), 2 bassoons, 4 horns, 2 trumpets, 2 trombones, percussion (timpani, 4 temple blocks, 4 cowbells, tambourine,

triangle, crotales, xylophone, 4 bongos, 4 tom-toms, tam-tam, gong, vibraphone, glockenspiel, snare drum, bass drum, 4 cymbals), harp, violin I, violin II, viola, violoncello, double bass.
Call no.: **1990/040**

996. Gustafson, Dwight, 1930– Songs of the kings: a string quartet. N.p.: n.p., 1993.
1 score (54 p.); 28 cm.
Reproduced from holograph.
Composed for: 2 violins, viola, violoncello.
Call no.: **1996/057**

997. Guy, Barry, 1947– After the rain = Nach dem Regen. London: Novello, 1992.
1 miniature score (57 p.); 30 cm.
For string orchestra (24 strings).
Includes program note by the composer.
Contents: Refrain—Chorale—Antiphon—Refrain—Chanson—Canon—Antiphon—Motet—Antiphon—Refrain.
Duration: 25:30.
Composed for: violin I, violin II, viola, violoncello, double bass.
Commissioned by: Richard Hickox and City of London Sinfonia.
Call no.: **1993/048**

998. Guy, Barry, 1947– Bird gong game: written for an absent soloist (until the concert day). Griffinstown, CO; Kilkenny, Ireland: Maya Recordings, 1992.
1 score (2 leaves); 56 x 66 cm. and 73 x 91 cm.
Chance composition for improvising soloist (various instruments), flute, oboe, clarinet/bass clarinet, trumpet, and percussion.
Graphic and conventional notation with colored symbols.
Includes performance instructions.
Limited edition screen print prepared by Advanced Graphics, London.
Composed for: flute, oboe, clarinet (also bass clarinet), trumpet, percussion.
Commissioned by: Alan Davie.
Call no.: **1994/055**

999. Guy, Barry, 1947– Ceremony: for violin and tape. N.p.: Barry Guy, 1995.
1 score (2 leaves); 30 x 43 cm.
Includes program note by the composer.
Reproduced from holograph.
Composed for: Baroque violin, tape.
Commissioned by: Maya Hornburger.
Call no.: **2000/066**

1000. Guy, Barry, 1947– Concerto for orchestra: "Falling water." London: Novello; Bury St. Edmunds, Suffolk: Music Sales Ltd., 1996.
1 score (80 p.); 42 cm.
Composed for: 2 flutes (1st also alto flute), 2 oboes (1st also English horn), 2 clarinets (2nd also bass clarinet), 2 bassoons (2nd also contrabassoon), 2 horns, 2 trumpets (1st also trumpet in D), percussion (timpani, anvil, crotales, 2 bass drums, small tam-tams, 5 tuned gongs, vibraslap, metal, glass chimes), 14 violins, 4 violas, 4 violoncellos, 2 double basses.
Commissioned by: City of London Sinfonietta.
Call no.: **1997/057**
Re-entered as: **2001/062**

1001. Guy, Barry, 1947– Un coup de dés. London: Novello, 1994.
1 leaf of music; 45 x 64 cm. folded to 23 x 26 cm. + 1 performance guide (8 leaves: ill.; 30 cm.).
French words; also printed as text with English translation.
For vocal quartet.
Words and phrases from Stéphane Mallarmé's Un coup de dés jamais n'abolira le hasard.
Graphic notation.
Duration: ca. 10:00.
Performance guide in English.
Composed for: countertenor, 2 tenors, bass.
Call no.: **1998/061**

1002. Guy, Barry, 1947– The eye of silence. London: Novello, 1988.
1 score (37 p.); 51 cm.
For violin and orchestra.
Reproduced from holograph.
Duration: ca. 17:00.
Composed for: violin, 2 flutes, violin I, violin II, violin III, violin IV, violin V, violin VI, violin VII, violin VIII, viola I, viola II, violoncello I, violoncello II, double bass.
Commissioned by: John Lubbock and Orchestra of St. John.
Call no.: **1992/053**

1003. Guy, Barry, 1947– Folio: (2002). London: Novello; Bury St. Edmunds, Suffolk: Music Sales Ltd, 2002.
1 score (3 v.); 30–42 cm.
For violin, Baroque violin, double bass, and strings.
Vol. 1 and 3 reproduced from holograph.
Contents: Bass improvisation—Prelude—Ortiz I—Postlude—Bass improvisation—Folio five (with commentaries)—Memory (solo violins in duo)—Ortiz II.

Composed for: violin, Baroque violin, double bass, violin I, violin II, viola, violoncello, double bass.
Commissioned by: Free Radiccals Festival Glasgow.
Call no.: **2004/048**

1004. Guy, Barry, 1947– Inachis: violin solo, 2002. N. p.: n.p., 2002.
6 leaves of music; 39 cm.
Reproduced from holograph.
Notes by the composer in English.
Composed for: violin.
Commissioned by: Maya Homburger.
Call no.: **2005/059**

1005. Guy, Barry, 1947– Nasca lines. N.p.: n.p., 2001.
1 score (various foliations); 45 cm.
English and nonsense words by Alan Davie.
For orchestra (23 players).
Graphic notation.
Composer's notes and performance instructions in English.
Composed for: voice, flute, oboe, clarinet, trumpet, bassoon, voice, percussion (5 woodblocks, 3 roto-toms, 3 gongs, 3 cymbals, tam-tam, bass drum, crotales, marimba), piano (also synthesizer), 2 violins, viola, violoncello, double bass, harp (also accordion and synthesizer), electric guitar, soprano saxophone, alto saxophone, tenor saxophone, baritone saxophone, bass clarinet, electric bass.
Commissioned by: Upstream Ensemble.
Call no.: **2003/048**

1006. Guy, Barry, 1947– Redshift: 1998. London: Novello Publishing, 1998.
1 score (4 p.); 30 cm.
Duration: 10:00.
Composed for: 2 violoncellos.
Call no.: **2002/072**

1007. Guy, Barry, 1947– Theoria. N.p.: n.p., 1991.
1 score (46 p.); 22 x 30 cm.
For piano with instrumental ensemble.
Reproduced from holograph.
Composed for: piano, 3 trumpets, 3 soprano saxophones, 2 trombones, tuba, 3 double basses, percussion.
Call no.: **1995/038**

1008. Guyard, Christophe, 1951– 3e sonate pour piano. Paris: G. Billaudot, 1987.
17 p. of music; 31 cm.
Duration: 11:30.
Preface by the composer in French.
Composed for: piano.
Call no.: **1988/046**

1009. Guyot, Vincent, 1964– Concerto pour clarinette basse et orchestre. N.p.: n.p., 1996.
1 score (80 p.); 35 cm.
Reproduced from manuscript.
Duration: 16:10.
Composed for: bass clarinet, 2 flutes (2nd also piccolo), 2 clarinets, 2 bassoons, 2 horns, 2 trumpets, trombone, percussion (timpani, bass drum, side drum, temple blocks, guiro, tam-tam, tubular bells), harp, violin I, violin II, viola, violoncello, double bass.
Call no.: **2001/063**

1010. Gwiazda, Henry, 1952– ThepOeticsOfimmersiOn. N.p.: n.p., 1995.
1 score (2 leaves); 28 cm.
Consists of instruction notes by the composer.
Both works created using Focal Point 3D Audio by Bo Gehring. 1st work is a headphone work; 2nd work is for speakers alone.
Contents: ThefLuteintheworLdthefLuteistheworLd—Buzzingreynold'sdreamland.
Composed for: flute, electronic sounds.
Commissioned by: Barlow Endowment (thefLuteintheworLdthefLuteistheworLd only).
Call no.: **2000/067**

1011. Gyulai-Gaál, János, 1924– Hegedűverseny. Partitúra. Kissvábhegy: n.p., 1997.
1 score (145 p.); 35 cm.
For violin and orchestra.
Duration: ca. 28:00.
Composed for: violin, 2 flutes, piccolo, 2 oboes (2nd also English horn), 2 clarinets, 2 bassoons, 4 horns, 3 trumpets, 3 trombones, harp, celesta, percussion (glockenspiel, piccolo snare drum, cymbals, triangle, tambourine), timpani, violin I, violin II, viola, violoncello, double bass.
Call no.: **2002/073**
Also available:
Call no.: **2002/073 piano reduction**

1012. Haas, Georg Friedrich, 1953– In vain: für 24 Instrumente (2000). Studienpartitur. Wien: Universal Edition, 2000.
1 score (216 p.); 42 cm.
Duration: ca. 1:10:00.
Composed for: 2 flutes (1st also piccolo, 2nd also piccolo, bass flute), oboe, 2 clarinets (2nd also bass clarinet), soprano saxophone (also tenor saxophone), bassoon, 2 horns, 2 trombones, percussion (marimba, crotales, glockenspiel, bell plate, cymbals, tam-tam, vibraphone, Chinese cymbal), accordion, harp, piano, 3 violins, 2 violas, 2 violoncellos, double bass.

Commissioned by: WDR.
Call no.: **2002/074**
Re-entered as: **2005/060**

1013. Haas, Georg Friedrich, 1953– Nacht: Kammeroper (1995/96). Partitur. Wien: Universal Edition, 1996.
1 score (235 p.); 30 cm.
German words by the composer after texts by Friedrich Hölderlin.
Reproduced from manuscript.
Duration: ca. 1:15:00.
Composed for: soprano, mezzo-soprano, tenor, baritone, bass, flute (also piccolo and bass flute), 2 clarinets (both also bass clarinet), bassoon (also contrabassoon), 3 trombones, 2 tubas, percussion (timpani, tubular bells, glockenspiel, tuned gongs, cymbals, 2 triangles, maracas, guiros, woodblocks, 2 tom-toms, bass drum, crotales, castanets, vibraphone, ratchet, 2 bongos, tam-tam, 2 temple blocks), accordion, tape, 2 violins, viola, 4 violoncellos, 3 double basses.
Commissioned by: Bregenzer Festspiele 1996.
Call no.: **1997/058**

1014. Haas, Georg Friedrich, 1953– Violinkonzert (1998). Studienpartitur. Wien: Universal Edition, 1998.
1 miniature score (31 p.); 42 cm.
Reproduced from manuscript.
Composed for: violin, 3 flutes (3rd also piccolo), 2 oboes, English horn, 3 clarinets (3rd also clarinet in E♭), bass clarinet, 3 bassoons (3rd also contrabassoon), 4 horns, 3 trumpets, 3 trombones (3rd also bass trombone), tuba, percussion (30 gongs, timpani, temple block, ratchet, tam-tam, bass drum, xylophone, crotales, whip, woodblock, small snare drum, lion's roar, glockenspiel), accordion, violin I, violin II, viola, violoncello, double bass.
Commissioned by: ORF.
Call no.: **2000/068**

1015. Haflidi, Hallgrimsson, 1941– Crucifixion: op. 24: for orchestra, 1996–1997. London: Chester Music, 1997.
1 score (104 p.); 42 cm.
"Corrected 3/9/97"—p. 1.
Reproduced from holograph.
Duration: ca. 33:00.
Composed for: 3 flutes (all also piccolo), 3 oboes (3rd also oboe d'amore), 3 clarinets (3rd also bass clarinet), 3 bassoons (3rd also contrabassoon), 4 horns, 3 trumpets, 3 trombones (3rd also bass trombone), tuba, timpani (also small tam-tam), percussion (xylophone, glockenspiel, marimba, snare drum, bass drum, 2 suspended cymbals, large tam-tam, triangle), piano, violin I, violin II, viola, violoncello, double bass.
Commissioned by: Royal Philharmonic Orchestra.
Call no.: **1998/063**

1016. Haflidi, Hallgrimsson, 1941– Ombra: for viola and string orchestra, op. 27. Bury St. Edmunds, Suffolk, England: Chester Music, 1999.
1 score (69 p.); 30 cm.
"Revised version 1999."
"Perusal score."
Reproduced from holograph.
Composed for: viola, violin I, violin II, viola, violoncello, double bass.
Commissioned by: Icelandic State Broadcasting Corporation.
Call no.: **2002/076**

1017. Haflidi, Hallgrimsson, 1941– Passía: op. 28: tenor, mezzo-soprano, kór, orgel, hljómsveit. N.p.: n.p., 2002.
1 score (174 p.); 42 cm.
Icelandic words; also printed as text.
Texts by Baldur Óskarsson, Hannes Pétursson, Hallgrímur Pétursson, Matthías Jóhannessen, and Steinn Steinarr.
Reproduced from holograph.
Composed for: tenor, mezzo-soprano, SATB chorus, flute, piccolo, oboe, English horn, clarinet, bass clarinet, bassoon, contrabassoon, horn, trumpet, trombone, bass trombone, harp, timpani, percussion (bass drum, tubular bells, suspended cymbal, 2 marimbas, vibraphone, large tam-tam, snare drum, basler drum, glockenspiel, triangle, mark tree), 2 organs, violin I, violin II, viola, violoncello, double bass.
Commissioned by: Motet Choir of Hallgrimskirkja.
Call no.: **2004/049**
Re-entered as: **2005/062**

1018. Hagen, Daron, 1961– Seven last words: concerto for piano left hand & orchestra. Partitura. New York, NY: Carl Fischer, 2001.
1 score (137 p.); 28 cm.
Duration: ca. 26:00.
Composed for: piano (left hand), 2 flutes (both also piccolo), 2 oboes, 2 clarinets, 2 bassoons, 2 horns, 2 trumpets, 2 trombones, tuba, timpani, percussion (2 bass drums, tam-tam, glockenspiel, 4 pitched roto-toms, anvil, woodblock, suspended cymbal, vibraphone, marimba, snare drum, tubular bells), violin I, violin II, viola, violoncello, double bass.
Commissioned by: New Mexico Symphony Orchestra.
Call no.: **2003/049**

1019. Haigh, Howard, 1959– Saeta: for chorus and chamber orchestra. N.p.: H. Haigh, 1991.
1 miniature score (50 p.); 30 cm.
"Revised 1991."
Reproduced from holograph.
Composed for: SATB chorus, 2 flutes (1st also piccolo), oboe, clarinet, bassoon, percussion (sizzle cymbal, medium cymbal, maracas, woodblocks, tom-tom, marimba, tam-tam, bass drum, bongos, cowbells, xylophone, vibraphone, glockenspiel, tambourine, 2 small cymbals), piano, violin I, violin II, viola, violoncello, double bass.
Commissioned by: Crouch End Festival Chorus.
Call no.: **1992/054**

1020. Haines, Margaret E., 1941– The Revelation of Jesus Christ!: "Revelation" in music. Budd Lake, NJ: Haines Productions, 1988.
1 score (174 p.); 28 cm.
English words.
"For choir and soloists or ensemble; piano accompaniment, synthesizer to narration; suggestions for light drama, organ."
Composed for: voices, SATB chorus, piano, organ (or synthesizer), trumpet, timpani, cymbals.
Call no.: **1990/041**

1021. Hakim, Naji, 1955– Les noces de l'agneau: trois tableaux symphoniques pour orchestre. London: United Music Publishers, 1997.
1 score (152 p.); 31 cm.
Includes biographical note on the composer and preface in English and French.
Contents: Une fête de feu—Le bien-aimé drapé de pourpre—L'Espirit et l'épouse.
Composed for: 2 flutes (1st also piccolo), 2 oboes (2nd also English horn), 2 clarinets (2nd also bass clarinet), 2 bassoons (2nd also contrabassoon), 2 horns, 2 trumpets, timpani, percussion (bass drum, cymbals, triangle, tambourine, castanets, drum, side drum, tam-tam, xylophone, crotales), violin I, violin II, viola, violoncello, double bass.
Call no.: **2001/064**

1022. Hakim, Naji, 1955– Seattle concerto: for organ & orchestra. London: United Music Publishers, 1999.
1 score (160 p.); 42 cm.
Preface in English and French.
Composed for: organ, 3 flutes (3rd also piccolo), 3 oboes (3rd also English horn), 2 clarinets, bass clarinet, 2 bassoons, contrabassoon, 4 horns, 4 trumpets, 3 trombones, tuba, timpani, percussion (tambourine, tenor drum, suspended cymbal, bass drum, triangle, xylophone, woodblocks, glockenspiel, snare drum, tom-toms, bongos, tam-tam, side drum, guiro), 2 harps, piano, violin I, violin II, viola, violoncello, double bass.
Commissioned by: American Guild of Organists.
Call no.: **2002/075**

1023. Hakola, Kimmo, 1958– Clarinet concerto (2001). Score. Helsinki, Finland: Warner Chappell; Fennica Gehrman, 2001.
1 score (174 p.); 30 cm.
Composed for: clarinet, 2 flutes, 2 oboes, 2 clarinets (also clarinet in E♭ and bass clarinet), 2 bassoons, 2 horns, 2 trumpets, 2 trombones, tuba, timpani, percussion, harp, violin I, violin II, viola, violoncello, double bass.
Call no.: **2005/061**

1024. Halffter, Cristóbal, 1930– Concierto a cuatro para cuarteto de saxofones y orquesta. Partitur. Wien: Universal Edition, 1990.
1 score (38 p.); 30 cm.
Reproduced from holograph.
Duration: 22:00–24:00.
Performance instructions include multiphonics.
Composed for: soprano saxophone, alto saxophone, tenor saxophone, baritone saxophone, 3 flutes (3rd also piccolo), 3 oboes, 3 clarinets, 3 bassoons (3rd also contrabassoon), 4 horns, 3 trumpets, 3 trombones, bass trombone, percussion (xylophone, woodblock, tubular bells, crotales, sleigh bells, bass drum, glockenspiel, vibraphone, 2 tom-toms, tam-tam, thundersheet, marimba, 2 temple blocks, suspended cymbal, claves, glass wind chimes, 2 bongos, gong, timpani), violin I, violin II, viola, violoncello, double bass.
Commissioned by: Südwestfunk Baden-Baden.
Call no.: **1991/045**

1025. Halffter, Cristóbal, 1930– Concierto para piano y orquesta. Partitur. Wien: Universal Edition, 1988.
1 score (54 p.); 61 cm.
"Korr. VIII/88"—cover.
Reproduced from holograph.
Duration: ca. 30:00.
Composed for: piano, 4 flutes (3rd–4th also piccolo), 4 oboes, 4 clarinets, 3 bassoons, contrabassoon, 6 horns, 4 trumpets, 3 trombones, bass trombone, percussion (bell plates, Javanese gong, xylophone, Cuban timbales, bass drum, vibraphone, 3 bongos, timpani, suspended cymbal, tam-tam, glockenspiel, marimba, 3 tom-toms, tubular bells, 2 congas, gong), harp, celesta, violin I, violin II, viola, violoncello, double bass.
Call no.: **1989/049**

1026. Halffter, Cristóbal, 1930– La del alba seria . . . : Fragmente aus der Oper "Don Quijote" für Soli, Chor und Orchester (1997). Studienpartitur. Wien: Universal Editon, 1998.
1 condensed score (59 p.); 42 cm.
Spanish words by Andrés Amorós from Miguel de Cervantes and other Spanish poets; also printed as text.
"Korrigierte Ausgabe, 10.07.1998."
Duration: ca. 40:00.
Composed for: 2 sopranos, baritone, SATB chorus, 2 piccolos, 2 flutes (2nd also alto flute), 3 oboes, English horn, 4 clarinets (3rd also clarinet in E♭, 4th also bass clarinet), 4 bassoons (4th also contrabassoon), 6 horns, 4 trumpets (1st also piccolo trumpet), 4 trombones (4th also bass trombone), tuba, percussion (vibraphone, flexatone, plate bells, timpani, claves, glass wind chimes, timbales, glockenspiel, crotales, suspended cymbal, gong, snare drum, conga drums, bass drum, marimba, tubular bells, wood wind chimes, tam-tam, tom-toms, xylophone, thundersheet, sand block, bongos), onstage percussion (log drum, bass drums), harp, clavicembalo (also electric piano), violin I, violin II, viola, violoncello, double bass.
Call no.: **2001/065**

1027. Halffter, Cristóbal, 1930– . . . No queda mas que el silencio . . . : concierto no. 2: para violoncello y orquesta. Partitur. Wien: Universal Edition, 1986.
1 score (48 p.); 59 cm.
Reproduced from holograph.
Duration: ca. 39:00.
Composed for: violoncello, 4 flutes (2nd also alto flute, 3rd–4th also piccolo), 4 oboes (4th also English horn), 4 clarinets (4th also bass clarinet), 4 bassoons (4th also contrabassoon), 6 horns, 4 trumpets, 3 trombones, bass trombone, percussion (2 bell plates, marimba, tam-tam, chimes, vibraphone, timpani with suspended cymbal, Javanese gong, bass drum, xylophone, anvil, gong, 2 congas, crotales), celesta, violin I, violin II, viola, violoncello, double bass.
Commissioned by: Südwestfunk Baden-Baden.
Call no.: **1987/029**

1028. Halffter, Cristóbal, 1930– Odradek: hommage à Franz Kafka: für Orchester (1996). Partitur. Wien: Universal Edition, 1996.
1 score (39 p.); 59 cm.
"Provisorische Ausgabe (ua) 18.11.1996."
Reproduced from holograph.
Duration: ca. 23:00.
Composed for: 2 piccolos, 2 flutes, 3 oboes (3rd also English horn), 3 clarinets (3rd also bass clarinet), 4 bassoons (4th also contrabassoon), 4 horns, 4 trumpets, 3 trombones, bass trombone, contrabass tuba, percussion (marimba, glockenspiel, tubular bells, 4 tom-toms, bass drum, xylophone, bell plates, timpani, 2 crotales, vibraphone, claves, thundersheet, large gong, 4 Cuban timbales, glockenspiel, whip, tam-tam, 4 bongos), harp, violin I, violin II, viola, violoncello, double bass.
Commissioned by: Czech Philharmonic, Prague.
Call no.: **1998/062**

1029. Halffter, Cristóbal, 1930– Preludio para Madrid—92: para coro mixto y orquesta. N.p.: Universal Edition, 1992.
1 score (34 leaves); 41 cm.
Spanish words.
Reproduced from holograph.
Duration: 10:50.
Composed for: SATB chorus, 2 piccolos, 2 flutes, 3 oboes, 4 clarinets, 4 bassoons, 6 horns, 4 trumpets, 3 trombones, bass trombone, tuba, timpani, percussion (xylophone, castanets, marimba, crotales, cymbals, glockenspiel, snare drum, tambourine, chimes, bass drum, 2 bongos), harpsichord, violin I, violin II, viola, violoncello, double bass.
Call no.: **1993/049**

1030. Halffter, Cristóbal, 1930– Siete cantos de España: para soprano, baritono y orquesta. Partitura. Wien: Universal Edition, 1993.
1 score (73 p.); 60 cm.
Words in Ladino, Old Spanish, and Spanish; also printed as text with some German translations.
Texts by Josef al-Katib, Gutierre de Cetina, Jorge Manrique, Abraham Ibn Ezra, Francisco de Quevedo, Yehuda Ibn Giyat, Yosef Ibn Saddiq, Pedro Manuel Ximenez de Urrea, and other anonymous poets.
Reproduced from manuscript.
Duration: ca. 50:00.
Contents: Tant' amare—Madrigal—Tres morillas—Mote = Wahlspruch—Gar ke fareyo—Amor constante más allá de la muerte—Ensalada.
Composed for: soprano, baritone, 4 flutes (3rd–4th also piccolo), 4 oboes, 4 clarinets, 4 bassoons (4th also contrabassoon), 6 horns, 4 trumpets, 4 trombones, 2 harps, electric piano, celesta, harpsichord, percussion (xylophone, tubular bells, Javanese gongs, timpani, 2 suspended cymbals, 3 woodblocks, bow, vibraphone, tam-tam, large bells, Cuban timbales, thundersheet, bow, glockenspiel, marimba, gong, 2 tom-toms, sand block, vibraphone, 2 crotales, bass drum, 2 wood drums, 4 temple blocks), violin I, violin II, viola, violoncello, double bass.
Call no.: **1994/056**
Re-entered as: **1995/039**

1031. Halffter, Cristóbal, 1930– Sinfonia ricercata: concierto para organo y orquesta. Partitur. Wien: Universal Edition, 1982.
1 score (35 p.); 56 cm.
Reproduced from holograph.
Includes performance instructions.
Composed for: organ, 3 flutes (2nd also piccolo), 3 oboes, 3 clarinets (2nd also clarinet in E♭, 3rd also bass clarinet), 4 bassoons (4th also contrabassoon), 4 horns, 4 trumpets, 4 trombones, viola I, viola II, viola III, violoncello I, violoncello II, violoncello III, double bass I, double bass II.
Commissioned by: Sinfonieorchester des Österreichischen Rundfunks, Wien.
Call no.: **1985/075**

1032. Halffter, Cristóbal, 1930– Versus: para orquesta, 1983. Wien: Universal Edition, 1983.
1 score (51 p.); 70 cm.
Reproduced from holograph.
Contents: Thesis—Antithesis—Synthesis.
Composed for: 4 flutes (3rd–4th also piccolo), 4 oboes (4th also English horn), 4 clarinets (3rd also clarinet in E♭, 4th also bass clarinet), 4 bassoons (4th also contrabassoon), 4 horns, 4 trumpets, 4 trombones, percussion (vibraphone, bass drum, 2 woodblocks, tam-tam, marimba, 2 timbales, 2 bell plates, tom-tom, tubular bells, xylophone, suspended cymbal), violin I, violin II, viola, violoncello, double bass.
Commissioned by: Tonhalle Orchester Zürich.
Call no.: **1986/047**

1033. Hall, Charles J., 1925– The city in the sea. N.p.: n.p., 1970.
1 miniature score (33 leaves); 28 cm.
English words adapted from the Bible and Edgar Allen Poe.
For narrator, solo voice, chorus, and orchestra.
Reproduced from manuscript.
Composed for: narrator, voice, SATB chorus, 2 piccolos, 3 flutes, 3 oboes, 3 clarinets, bass clarinet, 2 bassoons, contrabassoon, 4 horns, 4 trumpets, 4 trombones, 2 tubas, timpani, percussion (suspended cymbal, tam-tam, bass drum, vibraphone, bells, maracas, tambourine, castanets), harp, violin I, violin II, viola, violoncello, double bass.
Call no.: **1985/076**

1034. Hall, Juliana, 1958– Night dances: soprano and piano, 1987. N.p.: n.p., 1987.
1 score (1 v.); 29 cm.
English words; also printed as text.
Texts from Emily Dickinson (1st and 6th songs), Sylvia Plath (2nd song), Emily Brönte (3rd–4th songs), Edna St. Vincent Millay (5th song), and Elizabeth Bishop (7th song).
Reproduced from manuscript.
Contents: The crickets sang—The night dances—Song—Sleep, mourner, sleep!—Some things are dark—A spider sewed at night—Sonnet.
Composed for: soprano, piano.
Commissioned by: Schubert Club of Saint Paul, Minnesota.
Call no.: **1991/046**

1035. Hallberg, Bengt, 1932– Glädjens dansande sträng . . . = The dancing string of joy . . . : concert piece for male chorus, folk musicians, piano solo and symphony orchestra, 1988. Stockholm: Svensk Musik, 1988.
1 score (57 p.); 36 cm.
Swedish words by E. A. Karlfeldt.
Reproduced from manuscript.
Composed for: male chorus, folk musicians (violins, cow horn), piano, piccolo, 2 flutes, 2 oboes, English horn, 2 clarinets, bass clarinet, 2 bassoons, contrabassoon, 4 horns, 3 trumpets, 3 trombones, tuba, percussion (xylophone, suspended cymbals, tambourine, glockenspiel, string of small bells, snare drum, triangle, timpani, bass drum), harp, violin I, violin II, viola, violoncello, double bass.
Commissioned by: Gothenburg Symphony Orchestra.
Call no.: **1991/047**

1036. Hamilton, Iain, 1922– Concerto no. II: for piano and orchestra, 1987–1988. Full score. Bryn Mawr, PA: Theodore Presser, 1988.
1 score (193 p.); 42 cm.
Reproduced from manuscript.
Duration: 30:00.
Composed for: piano, 2 flutes, 2 oboes (2nd also English horn), 2 clarinets, 2 bassoons, 4 horns, 3 trumpets, 2 trombones, bass trombone, tuba, timpani, percussion (bells, glockenspiel, crotales, tam-tam, bass drum, side drum, 3 cymbals), harp, celesta, violin I, violin II, viola, violoncello, double bass.
Call no.: **1993/050**

1037. Hammerth, Johan, 1922– Pianokonsert. Stockholm: Swedish Music Information Center, 1990.
1 score (211 p.); 49 cm.
Duration: 37:00.
Composed for: piano, 2 flutes (1st also piccolo), 2 oboes, 2 clarinets (2nd also bass clarinet), 2 bassoons (2nd also contrabassoon), 4 horns, 2 trumpets, 2 trombones, bass trombone, tuba, timpani, percussion (vibraphone, chimes, crotales, marimba, bass drum, military drum,

2 bongos, 2 cymbals, orchestra bells, xylophone, 2 tam-tams, 3 tom-toms, snare drum, military drum), harp, piano, violin I, violin II, viola, violoncello, double bass.
Call no.: **1993/051**

1038. Hanger, Howard, 1944– Symphony for Barbara. Full score. N.p.: n.p., 198-?.
1 miniature score (59, 30, 48); 29 cm.
Reproduced from manuscript.
Composed for: jazz combo (trap set, bass, piano, flugelhorn, violin), piccolo, 2 flutes, 2 oboes, 2 clarinets, bass clarinet, 2 bassoons, 4 horns, 3 trumpets, 3 trombones, tuba, percussion (xylophone, timpani, snare drum, cymbals, bass drum, triangle, tambourine), violin I, violin II, viola, violoncello, double bass.
Commissioned by: NC Arts Council.
Call no.: **1985/077**

1039. Hankinson, Ann Shrewsbury, 1944– Chamber symphony. N.p.: n.p., 1986.
1 score (55 leaves); 31 cm.
For chamber orchestra.
Reproduced from holograph.
Duration: ca. 12:00.
Contents: Autumn—Winter—Spring—Summer.
Composed for: 2 flutes, 2 oboes, 2 clarinets, 2 bassoons, 2 horns, 2 trumpets, percussion (vibraphone, cymbals, marimba), violin I, violin II, viola, violoncello, double bass.
Commissioned by: Madeline Fern Schatz.
Call no.: **1987/030**

1040. Hanks, N. Lincoln, 1969– Tota pulchra: for mixed choir (SSSAAATTTBBB). N.p.: N. Lincoln Hanks, 1997.
1 score (38 p.); 22 x 28 cm.
Latin words; also printed as text with English translation.
Duration: ca: 10:00.
Composed for: SATB chorus.
Commissioned by: Dale Warland Singers.
Call no.: **2001/066**

1041. Hannah, Ronald, 1945– Suite of orchestral dances: ". . . The common air that bathes the globe." N.p.: n.p., 1996.
1 score (139 p.); 28 cm.
Program notes in English by the composer.
Contents: Croatian melody—Ivory Coast melody—Balinese lullaby—Australian melody—North American melody—Venezuelan melody.
Composed for: 2 flutes (2nd also piccolo), 2 oboes (2nd also English horn), 2 clarinets (2nd also bass clarinet), 2 bassoons, 4 horns, 2 trumpets, 2 trombones, bass trombone, tuba, percussion (xylophone, tambourine, snare drum, cymbals, triangle, gong, woodblocks, sleigh bells, maracas, guiro, bongos, vibraphone, bell tree, claves, snare drum sticks, rattle, wind chimes, temple blocks), timpani, violin I, violin II, viola, violoncello, double bass.
Commissioned by: Edmonton Symphony Orchestra.
Call no.: **2002/077**

1042. Hannay, Roger, 1930– Symphony 5: in five movements. N.p.: Hrothgar Music, 1988.
1 score (160 p.); 28 cm.
For orchestra.
Reproduced from holograph.
Composed for: piccolo, 2 flutes, 2 oboes, English horn, 2 bassoons, 4 horns, 3 trumpets, 2 trombones, bass trombone, tuba, timpani, percussion (suspended cymbal, vibraphone, xylophone, triangle, snare drum, tenor drum, woodblock, 4 tom-toms, glockenspiel), harp, violin I, violin II, viola, violoncello, double bass.
Call no.: **1991/048**

1043. Hanson, Geoffrey, 1939– Sinfonia amoris. N.p.: n.p., 1981.
1 score (4 v.); 42 cm.
English and Latin words.
For narrator, soloists, chorus and orchestra.
Texts by Rabindrinath Tagore, St. John of the Cross, and from the Stabat mater, the Bible, and the Buddhist Jataka tales.
Reproduced from manuscript.
Contents: Storge: a canticle of mother love for counter tenor and mezzo soprano soloists, chorus and orchestra—Eros: a canticle of erotic love for soprano and tenor soloists and instrumental ensemble with optional ballet—Philia: a canticle of friendship for narrator (baritone), counter tenor, tenor, bass, chorus and orchestra—Agape: a canticle of compassion for counter tenor, tenor, bass/baritone soloists, chorus and orchestra.
Composed for: narrator, mezzo-soprano, countertenor, SATB chorus, piccolo, flute, 2 oboes, English horn, clarinet, bassoon, contrabassoon, 2 horns, 2 trumpets, 3 trombones, timpani, percussion (cymbals, bass drum, woodblock, triangle, bell, whip, tam-tam, tambourine, snare drum, small drum, small handbells, celesta, xylophone, wind machine, antique cymbals, vibraphone), harp, piano, sitar, organ, violin I, violin II, viola, violoncello, double bass.
Call no.: **1985/078**

1044. Hanson, Geoffrey, 1939– War! Cry war!: for soprano, mezzo soprano and baritone soloists, speaker, chorus, male semi chorus, orchestra and prepared tape. N.p.: Geoffrey Hanson, 1986.
1 score (244 p.); 30 cm.
English and Latin words.
Reproduced from holograph.
Composed for: narrator, soprano, mezzo-soprano, baritone, SATB chorus, men's chorus, flute (also piccolo and alto flute), oboe (also English horn), clarinet, bassoon, 2 horns, 2 trumpets, 3 trombones, tuba, timpani, percussion (snare drum, cymbals, bass drum, whip, xylophone, tam-tam, suspended cymbal, triangle, woodblock), harp, piano, organ, tape, violin I, violin II, viola, violoncello, double bass.
Commissioned by: Tring Choral Society.
Call no.: **1990/042**

1045. Hanuš, Jan, 1915– Concerto-fantasia: per violoncello solo e orchestra, (1991), opus 117. Partitura. Prague: Panton, 1995.
1 score (71 p.); 40 cm.
Duration: ca. 18:00.
Composed for: violoncello, 2 flutes (2nd also piccolo), 2 oboes (2nd also English horn), 2 clarinets (2nd also bass clarinet), alto saxophone, 2 bassoons, 4 horns, 3 trumpets, 2 trombones, bass trombone, tuba, percussion (timpani, snare drum, 4 tom-toms, 4 temple blocks, bass drum, triangle, medium gong, crash cymbals, 3 suspended cymbals), harp, vibraphone, electric guitar, violin I, violin II, viola, violoncello, double bass.
Call no.: **1996/058**

1046. Harbison, John, 1938– Cello concerto. New York, NY: Associated Music, 1994.
1 score (114 p.); 46 cm.
Duration: ca. 21:00.
Composed for: violoncello, 3 flutes (2nd also alto flute, 3rd also piccolo), 3 oboes, 2 clarinets (also clarinet in E♭), bass clarinet, 3 bassoons (3rd also contrabassoon), 4 horns, 2 trumpets, 3 trombones, timpani, percussion (3 gongs, bass drum, glockenspiel, 2 log drums, 2 triangles, claves, cuíca, 2 bongos, xylophone, 3 crotales, 2 suspended cymbals, tambourine, 5 temple blocks, 3 tam-tams, 4 tom-toms, vibraphone, Japanese temple bell, crash cymbals, marimba, tubular bells, snare drum, guiro), harp, piano (also celesta), violin I, violin II, viola, violoncello, double bass.
Commissioned by: Boston Symphony Orchestra and Chicago Symphony Orchestra.
Call no.: **1995/040**

1047. Harbison, John, 1938– Four psalms for vocal soloists, chorus, and orchestra (1999). Full score. New York, NY: Associated Music Publishers, 1999.
1 score (157 p.); 43 cm.
Text in English and Hebrew (romanized).
Composed for: soprano, mezzo-soprano, tenor, bass, SATB chorus, 2 flutes (2nd also piccolo), 2 oboes (2nd also English horn), 2 clarinets (2nd also bass clarinet), 2 bassoons (2nd also contrabassoon), 4 horns, 2 trumpets, 2 trombones, timpani, percussion, harp, piano, violin I, violin II, viola, violoncello, double bass.
Commissioned by: Israeli Consulate of Chicago.
Call no.: **2001/067**

1048. Harbison, John, 1938– The great Gatsby: opera in two acts. New York, NY: Associated Music, 1999.
1 score (4 v.); 36 cm.
English words by the composer, Murray Horwitz, and F. Scott Fitzgerald.
Original work by F. Scott Fitzgerald.
Duration: ca. 2:30:00.
Composed for: soprano, 3 mezzo-sopranos, 3 tenors, 2 baritones, bass-baritone, 2 basses, SATB chorus, 3 flutes (3rd also piccolo), 2 oboes, English horn, 3 clarinets (2nd also clarinet in E♭, 3rd also soprano saxophone), bass clarinet, 2 bassoons, contrabassoon, 4 horns, 3 trumpets, 3 trombones, tuba, timpani, percussion (marimba, glockenspiel, flexatone, bass drum, brake drum, cowbells, triangle, wood drum, tam-tam, auto horn, xylophone, vibraphone, steel drums, suspended cymbals, snare drum, castanets, claves, chimes, crotales, telephone bell [or triangle], siren, crash cymbals, temple blocks, slapstick, maracas), piano, harp, banjo, violin I, violin II, viola, violoncello, double bass, onstage band (clarinet [also soprano saxophone], trumpet, trombone, tuba, trap set [bass drum, tom-tom, castanets, cowbells, woodblock, snare drum, hi-hat, ride cymbal], piano, banjo, violin).
Commissioned by: Metropolitan Opera.
Call no.: **2004/050**

1049. Harbison, John, 1938– The great Gatsby: opera in two acts (lyric opera of Chicago version). New York, NY: Associated Music, 1999.
1 score (4 v.); 44 cm.
English words by the composer, Murray Horwitz, and F. Scott Fitzgerald.
Original work by F. Scott Fitzgerald.
Duration: ca. 2:30:00.
Composed for: soprano, 3 mezzo-sopranos, 3 tenors, 2 baritones, bass-baritone, 2 basses, SATB chorus, 3 flutes (3rd also piccolo), 2 oboes, English horn, 3 clarinets (2nd also clarinet in E♭, 3rd also soprano

saxophone), bass clarinet, 2 bassoons, contrabassoon, 4 horns, 3 trumpets, 3 trombones, tuba, timpani, percussion (marimba, glockenspiel, flexatone, bass drum, brake drum, cowbells, triangle, wood drum, tam-tam, auto horn, xylophone, vibraphone, steel drums, suspended cymbals, snare drum, castanets, claves, chimes, crotales, telephone bell [or triangle], siren, crash cymbals, temple blocks, slapstick, maracas), piano, harp, banjo, violin I, violin II, viola, violoncello, double bass, onstage band (clarinet [also soprano saxophone], trumpet, trombone, tuba, trap set [bass drum, tom-tom, castanets, cowbells, woodblock, snare drum, hi-hat, ride cymbal], piano, banjo, violin).
Commissioned by: Metropolitan Opera.
Call no.: **2003/050**

1050. Harbison, John, 1938– Mottetti di Montale. New York, NY: Associated Music Publishers, 1999.
1 score (3 v.); 31–36 cm.
Italian words; also partially printed as text with English translation.
Text: Le Occasioni by Eugenio Montale.
Contents: La Primavera di Sottoripa—Il saliscendi bianco—Due libri.
Composed for: mezzo-soprano, flute (also piccolo), oboe (also English horn), clarinet (also bass clarinet), horn, harpsichord (also organ, celesta), violin, viola, violoncello, double bass.
Call no.: **2002/078**

1051. Harbison, John, 1938– Oboe concerto. New York, NY: Associated Music Pub.; Chester, NY: G. Schirmer Rental Library, 1992.
1 score (90 p.); 28 cm.
"11/12/92."
Composed for: oboe, 2 flutes (2nd also piccolo), 2 clarinets, alto saxophone (also bass clarinet), 3 bassoons (3rd also contrabassoon), 2 horns, 2 trumpets, 2 trombones, tuba, timpani, percussion (tubular bells, xylophone, tam-tam, suspended cymbal, crash cymbal, gong, glockenspiel, vibraphone, snare drum, triangle, 3 woodblocks, temple blocks, marimba), harp, violin I, violin II, viola, violoncello, double bass.
Commissioned by: San Francisco Symphony.
Call no.: **1994/057**

1052. Harbison, John, 1938– Requiem. Full score. New York, NY: Associated Music Publishers, 2003.
1 score (290 p.); 36 cm.
For chorus (SATB) with solo voices and orchestra.
Duration: ca. 1:00:00.
Composed for: soprano, mezzo-soprano, tenor, baritone, SATB chorus, 2 flutes, 2 oboes, 2 clarinets, 2 bassoons (also contrabassoon), 2 horns, 2 trumpets, 3 trombones, timpani, percussion, piano (also celesta), harp, violin I, violin II, viola, violoncello, double bass.
Commissioned by: Boston Symphony Orchestra.
Call no.: **2005/063**

1053. Harbison, John, 1938– String quartet no. 2. New York, NY: Associated Music Publishers, 1987.
1 score (64 p.); 28 cm.
Duration: 26:00.
Composed for: 2 violins, viola, violoncello.
Commissioned by: Harvard Musical Association.
Call no.: **1989/050**

1054. Harbison, John, 1938– Symphony no. 2. Corrected score April 8, '87. New York, NY: Associated Music, 1987.
1 score (98 p.); 36 cm.
Reproduced from holograph.
Duration: ca. 20:00.
Composed for: 3 flutes (3rd also piccolo), 2 oboes, English horn, clarinet in E♭, 2 clarinets, bass clarinet, 3 bassoons (3rd also contrabassoon), 4 horns, 4 trumpets (1st and 3rd also piccolo trumpet), 2 trombones, bass trombone, tuba, timpani, percussion (glockenspiel, vibraphone, crotales, triangle, snare drum, suspended cymbals, sizzle cymbal, crash cymbals, tam-tam, gong, 3 tom-toms, side drum, bass drum, temple blocks, castanets, thundersheet, lion's roar), harp, piano (also celesta), violin I, violin II, viola, violoncello, double bass.
Commissioned by: San Francisco Symphony.
Call no.: **1988/047**
Re-entered as: **1991/049**

1055. Harbison, John, 1938– Symphony no. 3, 1990. New York, NY: G. Schirmer, 1991.
1 miniature score (122 p.); 36 cm.
Reproduced from manuscript.
Duration: 21:00.
Composed for: 3 flutes (3rd also piccolo), 3 oboes (3rd also English horn), 3 clarinets (3rd also bass clarinet), 3 bassoons (3rd also contrabassoon), 4 horns, 3 trumpets, 3 trombones, tuba, timpani, percussion (4 suspended cymbals, triangle, 4 tom-toms, bell, chimes, crotales, xylophone, tambourine, timbales, lujon, temple blocks, marimba, tenor drum, snare drum, brake drums, vibraphone, cowbell, bass drum, woodblock, log drum, tam-tam, glockenspiel), piano, violin I, violin II, viola, violoncello, double bass.
Commissioned by: Baltimore Symphony Orchestra.
Call no.: **1992/055**

1056. Harbison, John, 1938– Ulysses' bow. N.p.: Associated Music Publishers, 1984.
1 score (108 p.); 49 cm.
Ballet for orchestra.
Reproduced from holograph.
"Score corrected May 15 84."
Composed for: 3 flutes (3rd also piccolo), 3 oboes (3rd also English horn), 3 clarinets (1st also soprano saxophone, 2nd also alto saxophone, 3rd also bass clarinet), 2 bassoons, contrabassoon, 4 horns, 2 trumpets, 2 trombones, bass trombone, tuba, timpani, percussion (snare drum, tenor drum, bass drum, 4 suspended cymbals, crash cymbals, 2 gongs, temple blocks, tubular bells, triangle, tambourine, vibraphone, glockenspiel, xylophone, marimba, slapstick), harp, piano (also celesta), violin I, violin II, viola, violoncello, double bass.
Call no.: **1985/079**

1057. Harman, Chris Paul, 1970– Uta: for viola and orchestra (2000). N.p.: Chris Paul Harman, 2000.
1 score (42 p.); 28 cm.
Duration: ca. 16:00.
Composed for: viola, 2 flutes, 2 oboes, 2 clarinets, 2 bassoons, 2 horns, 2 trumpets, percussion (crotales, tubular bells, marimba, tam-tam, timpani, vibraphone, 4 woodblocks), piano, harp, violin I, violin II, viola, violoncello, double bass.
Commissioned by: MusicCanadaMusique 2000 Festival.
Call no.: **2003/051**

1058. Harmon, John, 1935– Earth Day portrait: for symphony orchestra and narrators. Fish Creek, WI: Alliance Publications, 2001.
1 score (75 p.); 36 cm.
English words; also printed as text.
Texts by John Muir, Aldo Leopold, and Gaylord Nelson; assembled with connecting text by Jon Becker.
Pre-publication draft.
Duration: ca. 21:15.
Contents: Fanfare for our common earth—Invocation—Music for the earth—Words for the earth—Pledge for our common earth.
Composed for: narrator, piccolo, 2 flutes, 2 oboes, English horn, 2 clarinets, bass clarinet, 2 bassoons, 4 horns, 3 trumpets, 2 trombones, bass trombone, tuba, harp, timpani, percussion (orchestra bells, xylophone, chimes, suspended cymbal, crash cymbals, triangle, snare drum, wind chimes, bass drum), violin I, violin II, viola, violoncello, double bass.
Commissioned by: Earth/Art.
Call no.: **2003/052**

1059. Harper, Edward, 1941– Hedda Gabler. N.p.: n.p., 1985.
1 vocal score (308 p. in various pagings); 30 cm.
English words.
Opera in 3 acts.
Based on Henrik Ibsen's Hedda Gabler.
"Corrections up to 28-2-85."
Reproduced from manuscript.
Call no.: **1986/048**

1060. Harper, William, 1949– Dead birds. N.p.: n.p., 198-?.
1 score (various pagings); 28 cm. + synopsis (4 leaves; 28 cm.)
English words by Armand Schwerner.
Hybrid of opera, dance, and theater.
Reproduced from manuscript and typescript.
Synopsis includes some performance instructions.
Composed for: 3 voices, SATB chorus, unspecified instruments/electronics, 3 dancers, 5 children.
Call no.: **1985/080**

1061. Harris, Ross, 1945– Waituhi: the life of the village. N.p.: n.p., 1984.
1 score (221 leaves); 42 cm.
English and Maori words by Witi Ihimaera, based on his novel Whanau.
New Zealand opera with a Maori setting in 4 acts.
Reproduced from holograph.
Composed for: voices, tape, flute, oboe, clarinet, bassoon, horn, trumpet, trombone, percussion (dry leaves, bass drum, suspended cymbals, timpani, claves, wooden gong, sticks, bell, snare drum), guitar, organ, violin I, violin II, viola, violoncello, double bass.
Call no.: **1985/081**

1062. Harrison, Charles A., 1966– Reflection: for orchestra. N.p.: n.p., 1991.
1 score (81 p.); 36 cm.
For orchestra.
Thesis (M. Mus.)—Northwestern University, 1991.
Composed for: 4 flutes (1st and 3rd also piccolo), 2 oboes, English horn, 4 clarinets, bass clarinet, 4 bassoons, contrabassoon, 4 horns, 4 trumpets, 3 trombones, bass trombone, tuba, timpani, percussion (bass drum, snare drum, tam-tam, gong, suspended cymbal, cabasa, tambourine), harp, celesta, violin I, violin II, viola, violoncello, double bass.
Call no.: **1993/052**

1063. Harrison, Lou, 1917–2003. Piano concerto: with selected orchestra. New York, NY: C. F. Peters, 1985.
1 score (89 p.); 44 cm.

Reproduced from holograph.
Composed for: piano, 3 trombones, 2 harps, percussion (bass drum, side drum, bongo, 4 drums, glockenspiel), violin I, violin II, viola, violoncello, double bass.
Call no.: **1986/049**
Re-entered as: **1990/044**

1064. Harrison, Lou, 1917–2003. Rhymes with silver. N.p.: Hermes Beard Press, 1996.
1 score (75 leaves); 28 cm.
Contents: Prelude—Allegro—Scherzo—Ductia—Gigue and musette—Chromatic rhapsody—Romantic waltz—Fox trot—Threnody—In honor of Prince Kantemir—5-tone kit—Round dance.
Composed for: violin, viola, violoncello, piano, percussion.
Commissioned by: Mark Morris.
Call no.: **2003/053**

1065. Harrison, Lou, 1917–2003. Symphony no. 3.
Call no.: **1985/082**
No materials available.

1066. Hartke, Stephen Paul, 1952– Concerto for clarinet and orchestra: "Landscapes with blues": (2001). Glendale, CA: S. Hartke, 2001.
1 score (158 p.); 36 cm.
"Score in C"—caption.
Duration: ca. 28:00.
Contents: Senegambia—Delta nights—Philamayork.
Composed for: clarinet, 2 flutes (2nd also piccolo), 2 oboes (2nd also English horn), 2 clarinets, bassoon, contrabassoon, 4 horns, 2 trumpets, percussion (2 bongos, 2 suspended cymbals, splash cymbal, woodblock, pedal bass drum, shaker, slapstick, vibraslap, goat herd bells, xylophone, marimba), piano, harp, violin I, violin II, viola, violoncello, double bass.
Commissioned by: Iris.
Call no.: **2003/054**

1067. Hartke, Stephen Paul, 1952– Pacific rim: for orchestra. St. Louis, MO: Norruth Music, 1988.
1 score (55 p.); 46 cm.
Reproduced from holograph.
Duration: ca. 10:00.
Composed for: 2 piccolos (1st also flute), 2 oboes, clarinet in E♭, clarinet, 2 bassoons, 2 horns, 2 trumpets, 2 trombones, percussion (water chime, vibraslap, agogo bells, 4 tom-toms, 2 crotales, bass drum, pedal bass drum, 2 woodblocks, gong), violin I, violin II, viola, violoncello, double bass.
Commissioned by: Los Angeles Chamber Orchestra and National Endowment for the Arts.
Call no.: **1989/051**

1068. Hartke, Stephen Paul, 1952– Symphony no. 2: orchestra (1990). St. Louis, MO: Norruth Music; MMB Music, 1991.
1 score (105 p.); 45 cm.
Duration: 25:00–28:00.
Reproduced from holograph.
At end: Glendale, California June 1990–January 1991.
Composed for: 2 flutes, 2 oboes (2nd also English horn), 2 clarinets (1st also clarinet in E♭, 2nd also bass clarinet), 2 bassoons (2nd also contrabassoon), 2 horns, 2 piccolo trumpets (both also trumpet), percussion (4 suspended bells, handbell, 6 wooden slit drums, steel drum), harp, harpsichord, violin I, violin II, viola, violoncello, double bass.
Commissioned by: Los Angeles Chamber Orchestra.
Call no.: **1992/056**

1069. Hartke, Stephen Paul, 1952– Symphony no. 3: for countertenor, two tenor and baritone soli, with orchestra (2003). New York, NY: 21C Media Group, 2003.
1 score (108 p.); 44 cm.
English words; also printed as text.
Text by anonymous Anglo-Saxon poet (8th–9th century AD), translated and adapted by the composer.
Duration: ca. 25:00.
Composed for: countertenor, 2 tenors, baritone, 3 flutes (also piccolo), 2 oboes, English horn, 2 clarinets, bass clarinet, 3 bassoons (also contrabassoon), 4 horns, 4 trumpets, 4 trombones, tuba, timpani, percussion (bass drum, Chinese opera cymbals, Noah bells, vibraphone, medium crash cymbals, marimba, large crash cymbals), piano (also celesta), harp, violin I, violin II, viola, violoncello, double bass.
Commissioned by: New York Philharmonic.
Call no.: **2005/064**

1070. Harvey, Jonathan, 1939– Cello concerto. Full score. London: Faber, 1990.
1 score (85 p.); 42 cm.
Duration: 19:00.
Reproduced from holograph.
Composed for: violoncello, concertante group (glockenspiel, crotales, small suspended triangle, electric keyboard, large celesta, harp, vibraphone), 3 flutes (2nd–3rd also piccolo), 3 oboes (3rd also English horn), 3 clarinets (3rd also bass clarinet), 3 bassoons (3rd also contrabassoon), 4 horns, 4 trumpets, 3 trombones, tuba, percussion (2 small woodblocks, temple block, 2 triangles, mark tree, tubular bells, tam-tam, guiro, 4 cowbells, Japanese temple bell, 4 suspended cymbals, 2 bongos, bass drum, gong), violin I, violin II, viola, violoncello, double bass.

Commissioned by: Orchestra Sinfonica dell'Emiglia Romagna "Arturo Toscanini."
Call no.: **1994/058**

1071. Harvey, Jonathan, 1939– Death of light/light of death: for chamber ensemble after Grünewald's "Crucifixion" in the Issenheim altarpiece (1998). London: Faber Music, 1998.
1 score (52 p.); 30 cm.
Reproduced from holograph.
Duration: ca. 17:00.
Composed for: oboe (also English horn), harp (also tam-tam), violin, viola, violoncello.
Commissioned by: Musée d'Unterlinden, Colmar (France), and Ensemble Intercontemporain.
Call no.: **2001/069**

1072. Harvey, Jonathan, 1939– Madonna of winter and spring: for orchestra, synthesizers & electronics. Full score. London: Faber Music, 1986.
1 score (135 p.); 42 cm.
Reproduced from manuscript.
Composed for: 4 flutes (3rd–4th also piccolo, 1st also alto flute), 3 oboes (3rd also English horn), 3 clarinets (3rd also bass clarinet), 3 bassoons (3rd also contrabassoon), 4 horns, 4 trumpets (4th also piccolo trumpet), 3 trombones, tuba, percussion (vibraphone, snare drum, 2 tam-tams, xylophone, suspended cymbal, 2 gongs, claves, whip, glockenspiel, woodblock, maracas, bass drum, 2 bongos, 5 temple blocks, 2 cowbells, 2 crash cymbals, triangle, tubular bells, Indian bells), harp, piano, violin I, violin II, viola, violoncello, double bass, synthesizers, electronics.
Commissioned by: BBC.
Call no.: **1987/031**

1073. Harvey, Jonathan, 1939– White as jasmine: for soprano and orchestra (1999). London: Faber Music, 2000.
1 miniature score (62 p.); 30 cm.
English words by Mahadevi and Allama Prabhu; also printed as text.
Reproduced from manuscript.
Duration: ca. 14:00.
Composed for: soprano, 3 flutes (also piccolo and alto flute), 3 oboes (also English horn), 3 clarinets (also bass clarinet), 3 bassoons (also contrabassoon), 4 horns, 3 trumpets, 3 trombones, tuba, piano, SY77 synthesizer, celesta, harp, percussion (tubular bells, snare drum, 2 congas, Tibetan finger cymbals, vibraphone, cowbells, temple bowl with small marble, crotales, 2 suspended cymbals, claves, slide whistle, bass drum, 2 high bongos, 5 temple blocks, large tam-tam, 2 triangles, set of boobams), violin I, violin II, viola, violoncello, double bass.
Commissioned by: Wiener Konzerthaus-Gesellschaft.
Call no.: **2005/065**

1074. Hatzis, Christos, 1953– Confessional. N.p.: n.p., 1997.
1 score (93 p.); 36 cm.
For violoncello and orchestra.
"Based on the chant I behold your bridal chamber my Lord, and I wear not the proper vestments to enter, sung in Greek Orthodox churches on the eve of Palm Sunday"—program notes.
Reproduced from manuscript.
Includes program notes and performance instructions.
Composed for: violoncello, 2 flutes, 2 oboes (2nd also English horn), 2 clarinets (1st also clarinet in E♭), 2 bassoons, 4 horns, 2 trumpets, 2 trombones, tuba, percussion (celesta, marimba, vibraphone, 2 timpani, bass drum, orchestra cymbals, suspended cymbals, gong, tam-tam, temple blocks), harp, violin I, violin II, viola, violoncello, double bass.
Commissioned by: Shauna Rolston.
Call no.: **2000/069**

1075. Hatzis, Christos, 1953– Constantinople. N.p.: Christos Hatzis, 2000.
1 score (various pagings); 36 cm.
Greek, Latin, Arabic, and Serbian words; also printed as text with English translation.
Texts from various sources, including the Koran, the Roman Catholic Mass, and Greek and Serbian Orthodox chants.
Composer's note in English.
Composed for: soprano, alto, violin, violoncello, piano, electroacoustics, visual media.
Call no.: **2003/055**

1076. Hatzis, Christos, 1953– String quartet no. 2: the gathering. N.p.: n.p., 1999.
1 score (116 p.); 36 cm.
Includes program notes and performance instructions in English.
Composed for: 2 violins, viola, violoncello.
Commissioned by: St. Lawrence Quartet.
Call no.: **2001/070**

1077. Haubenstock-Ramati, Roman, 1919–1994. Amerika; eine Oper in 2 Teilen nach dem gleichnamigen Roman von Franz Kafka und der Bühnenbearbeitung von Max Brod. Revidierte Fassung. Wien: Universal Edition, 1970.
Words by the composer.

1 score (286 p.); 41 cm.
Universal Edition, Nr. 14774
Reproduced from holograph.
In part graphic notation.
Composed for: sopranos, mezzo-soprano, alto, tenor, bass-baritone, 2 basses, SATB chorus, 3 flutes (all also piccolo), 2 oboes, 3 clarinets, 2 bassoons, 4 horns, 4 trumpets, 3 trombones, tuba, percussion (timpani, 3 tom-toms, conga, bass drum, 5 cencerros, 3 suspended cymbals, tam-tam, sleigh bells, 3 snare drums, 2 bongos, 5 temple blocks, suspended metal sheet, field drum, 5 woodblocks, 2 gongs, 5 steel drums), piano, celesta, harmonium (also vibraphone), xylophone (also marimba), xylorimba (also mandolin), violin I, violin II, viola, violoncello, double bass.
Call no.: **1993/053**

1078. Haubenstock-Ramati, Roman, 1919–1994. Miroirs = Mirrors: Mobile für 16 Klaviere. Wien: Universal Edition, 1984.
5 p., 60 leaves of music; 21 x 30 cm.
Reproduced from holograph.
Performance instructions in English.
Composed for: 16 pianos.
Call no.: **1986/050**

1079. Haubenstock-Ramati, Roman, 1919–1994. Nocturnes 3. Partitur. Wien: Universal Edition, 1985.
1 score (74 p.); 36 cm.
For orchestra.
Reproduced from manuscript.
Duration: ca. 22:00.
Composed for: 4 flutes, 4 trombones, percussion (vibraphone, 2 cymbals, 5 cowbells, tam-tam, marimba, chimes, 3 tom-toms, tenor drum, 2 gongs, claves, metal chimes, bass drum), harpsichord, harp, piano, celesta, violin I, violin II, viola, violoncello, double bass.
Commissioned by: Wiener Konzerthaus Gesellschaft.
Call no.: **1989/052 no.3**

1080. Haubenstock-Ramati, Roman, 1919–1994. Nocturnes I. Partitura. Wien: Universal Edition, 1981.
1 score (73 p.); 25 cm.
For orchestra.
Composed for: 4 flutes, 4 trombones, percussion (vibraphone, 2 cymbals, 5 cowbells, tam-tam, marimba, chimes, 3 tom-toms, tenor drum, 2 gongs, claves, metal chimes, bass drum), harpsichord, harp, piano, celesta, violin I, violin II, viola, violoncello, double bass.
Commissioned by: ORF-Graz.
Call no.: **1989/052 no.1**

1081. Haubenstock-Ramati, Roman, 1919–1994. Nocturnes II. Partitura. Wien: Universal Edition, 1982.
1 score (159 p.); 25 cm.
For orchestra.
Duration: ca. 29:00.
Composed for: 4 flutes, 4 trombones, percussion (vibraphone, 2 cymbals, 5 cowbells, tam-tam, marimba, chimes, 3 tom-toms, tenor drum, 2 gongs, claves, metal chimes, bass drum), harpsichord, harp, piano, celesta, violin I, violin II, viola, violoncello, double bass.
Commissioned by: ORF-Graz.
Call no.: **1989/052 no.2**

1082. Havelka, Svatopluk, 1925– Poggii Florentini ad Leonardum Aretinum epistola de Magistri Hieronymi de Praga supplicio (Jeroným Pražský) = List Poggia Braccioliniho Leonardu Brunimu z Arezza o odsouzení mistra Jeronýma z Prahy (Jeroným Pražský), 1984. N.p.: n.p., 1984.
1 score (96 p.); 40 cm.
Latin words.
For 4 soloists (SATB), madrigal chorus, children's chorus, mixed chorus, orchestra, and organ.
Duration: ca. 1:15:00.
Contents: Poggius salutem dicit Leonardo Aretino et de defensione M. Hieronymi—De pluribus martyribus—De laudatione M. Joannis Hus—De morte M. Hieronymi et epilogus.
Composed for: soprano, alto, tenor, bass, small SATB chorus, children's chorus, 4 flutes (2nd and 4th also piccolo, 3rd also alto flute), 4 oboes (4th also English horn), clarinet in E♭, 2 clarinets, bass clarinet, 3 bassoons, contrabassoon, 6 horns, 4 trumpets, 4 trombones, tuba, timpani, percussion (5 temple blocks, chimes, suspended cymbal, sleigh bells, 3 woodblocks, crotales, 4 bongos, 4 cowbells, maracas, 3 tom-toms, 2 gongs, tam-tam, claves, bass drum, 4 Javanese gongs, tambourine, glockenspiel, marimba, vibraphone), harp, electric piano, celesta, organ, electric bass guitar, violin I, violin II, viola, violoncello, double bass.
Call no.: **1988/048**

1083. Hazon, Roberto, 1930– I promessi sposi: balletto. Partitura. Milano: Casa Musicale Sonzogno di Piero Ostali, 1985.
1 score (2 v.); 39 cm.
In 2 acts.
Reproduced from holograph.
Composed for: piccolo, 2 flutes, 2 oboes, English horn, 2 clarinets, bass clarinet, 2 bassoons, contrabassoon, 4 horns, 3 trumpets, 3 trombones, tuba, timpani, percussion (vibraphone, cymbals, triangle, glockenspiel, chimes, tambourine, 2 snare drums, xylophone, sleigh

bells, whip, piccolo snare drum, bass drum, tam-tam, suspended cymbals, ratchet), harp, piano, celesta, violin I, violin II, viola, violoncello, double bass.
Call no.: **1986/051**

1084. He, Xuntian, 1953– Four dreams: for orchestra and erhu, op. 14. N.p.: n.p., 1987.
1 score (43 p.); 32 cm.
Reproduced from manuscript.
Composed for: erhu, 4 horns, 4 trumpets, 4 trombones, piano, celesta, percussion (glockenspiel, tubaphone, chimes, triangle, tam-tam, timpani, bass drum), violin I, violin II, violin III, violin IV, viola I, viola II, violoncello I, violoncello II, violoncello III, violoncello IV, double bass I, double bass II.
Call no.: **1991/051**

1085. He, Xuntian, 1953– Phonism: for ten performers. N.p.: n.p., 1991.
1 score (46 p.); 22 x 30 cm.
Reproduced from manuscript.
Composed for: flute, oboe, clarinet, mandolin, guitar, harp, violin, viola, violoncello, percussion (3 cymbals, tam-tam, bass drum).
Call no.: **1995/042**

1086. He, Xuntian, 1953– Sounds of nature: for seven performers. Score. N.p.: n.p., 198-?.
1 score (8 leaves); 30 x 42 cm.
Reproduced from manuscript.
Composed for: 7 performers (unspecified).
Call no.: **1988/049**
Re-entered as: **1989/053**

1087. Healey, Derek, 1936– Solana grove: a set of variations for wind quintet: op. 63. N.p.: D. Healey, 1982.
1 score (36 p.); 36 cm.
Reproduction of holograph.
Includes performance notes.
At end: Eugene, OR, August 26, 1982.
Duration: ca. 23:00.
Composed for: flute, oboe, clarinet, horn, bassoon.
Call no.: **1986/052**

1088. Heggie, Jake, 1961– Dead man walking: an opera in two acts. N.p.: Bent Pen Music, 2000.
1 score (2 v.); 44 cm.
English words by Terrence McNally.
Original work by Sister Helen Prejean, CSJ.
Composed for: 3 sopranos, 6 mezzo-sopranos, 4 tenors, 5 baritones, bass-baritone, children's chorus, men's chorus, women's chorus, 3 flutes (3rd also piccolo and alto flute), 2 oboes, English horn, 2 clarinets, bass clarinet, 3 bassoons (3rd also contrabassoon), 4 horns, 3 trumpets, 2 trombones, bass trombone, harp, piano, timpani, percussion (snare drum, tom-toms, temple blocks, bass drum, tambourine, triangle, crash cymbals, suspended cymbal, tam-tam, siren, glockenspiel, vibraphone, xylophone), violin I, violin II, viola, violoncello, double bass.
Commissioned by: San Francisco Opera.
Call no.: **2002/079**

1089. Heinrichs, William, 1954– Dream sequence: for orchestra (1993). N.p.: William Heinrichs, 1995.
1 score (44 p.); 44 cm.
Duration: ca. 10:40.
Composed for: piccolo, 2 flutes, 2 oboes, 2 clarinets, bass clarinet, 2 bassoons, 4 horns, 3 trumpets, 3 trombones, tuba, timpani, percussion (suspended cymbal, low tom-tom, large tam-tam, crotales), harp, piano, violin I, violin II, viola, violoncello, double bass, string quartet (2 violins, viola, violoncello).
Call no.: **1996/059**

1090. Heisinger, Brent, 1937– Concerto for piano, winds and percussion. N.p.: n.p., 1984.
1 score (67 p.); 22 x 28 cm.
Reproduced from holograph.
Contents: Prelude—Toccata and fugue—Scherzo.
Composed for: piano, piccolo, 2 flutes, 2 oboes, 2 bassoons, clarinet in E♭, 3 clarinets, alto clarinet, bass clarinet, contrabass clarinet, 2 alto saxophones, tenor saxophone, baritone saxophone, 4 horns, 3 trumpets, 3 trombones, 2 baritones, 2 tubas, celesta, percussion (orchestral bells, snare drums, xylophone, tuned drums, vibraphone, marimba, chimes, temple blocks, bongos, timbales, timpani, gong, woodblocks, roto-toms, tom-toms, bass drum).
Call no.: **1985/083**

1091. Hellawell, Piers, 1956– Inside story: violin & viola soli and orchestra (1999). Kenley, Surrey: Maecenas Music, 1999.
1 miniature score (87 p.); 30 cm.
Duration: 22:00.
Composed for: violin, viola, 2 flutes (2nd also piccolo), 2 oboes, 2 clarinets (1st also clarinet in E♭, 2nd also bass clarinet), 2 bassoons, contrabassoon, 4 horns, 2 trumpets, flugelhorn, 2 trombones, bass trombone, tuba, percussion (marimba, vibraphone, cowbell, glockenspiel, 3 blocks, snare drum, steel drum, stirred bowl of chickpeas, tubular bells, tam-tam, bath chimes, bell tree, triangle, suspended cymbal, crash cymbals, 3 tom-toms, tambourine, rain stick, toy trumpet, chick-

pea rattle, mark tree, crotales, bass drum, guiro), harp, violin I, violin II, viola, violoncello, double bass.
Commissioned by: BBC Promenade Concerts.
Call no.: **2002/080**

1092. Heller, Duane, 1951– Orpheus and Eurydice: concerto for viola and chamber orchestra. N.p.: n.p., 1980.
1 score (71 p.); 36 cm.
Reproduced from manuscript.
Composed for: viola, 2 flutes (1st also piccolo, 2nd also alto flute), 2 clarinets (2nd also bass clarinet), 2 horns, percussion (chimes, orchestra bells), harp, celesta, 6 violins, 3 violas, 3 violoncellos, 2 double basses.
Commissioned by: College of Liberal Arts at Oregon State University.
Call no.: **1991/052**

1093. Helms, Marjan, 1951– Rip van Winkle. N.p.: n.p., 1993.
1 score (323 p.); 28 x 44 cm.
English words.
Opera in 2 acts; based on characters from Washington Irving.
Score includes only a skeleton of the vocal parts.
Composed for: flute, oboe, clarinet, 2 horns, piano, synthesizer, harpsichord, timpani, percussion (vibraphone, cymbals, snare drum, bells), violin I, violin II, viola, violoncello, double bass.
Call no.: **1994/059**
Also available:
Call no.: **1994/059 vocal score**

1094. Hendricks, W. Newell, 1943– Ascona. N.p.: n.p., 1988.
1 score (325 p.); 36 cm.
English words by Karen S. Henry.
Opera.
Reproduced from manuscript.
Composed for: 3 sopranos, mezzo-soprano, 2 tenors, 2 baritones, 2 basses, flute, clarinet (also bass clarinet), bassoon, trumpet, trombone, percussion (cymbals, bass drum, sizzle cymbal, snare drum, woodblock, temple blocks, tom-toms, congas, bongos), violin I, violin II, viola, violoncello, double bass.
Call no.: **1994/060**

1095. Hennig, Michael, 1958– Music for an exhibition: after paintings by Moje Menhardt. Vienna: Michael Hennig, 1990.
1 score (iv leaves, 70 p.); 30 x 43 cm.
Includes time diagrams.
Composed for: synthesized instruments.
Call no.: **1995/043**

1096. Henshall, Dalwyn, 1957– Concerto: for percussion (1989/90). N.p.: n.p., 1992.
1 score (89 p.); 30 cm.
Composed for: percussion (timpani, vibraphone, xylorimba), violin I, violin II, viola, violoncello, double bass.
Commissioned by: Swansea Festival.
Call no.: **1997/059**

1097. Henze, Hans Werner, 1926– Il ritorno di Ulisse in patria.
Call no.: **1986/053**
No materials available.

1098. Henze, Hans Werner, 1926– Scorribanda sinfonica: (2001). London: Chester Music, 2001.
1 score (75 p.); 30 cm.
For large orchestra.
Based on music from the composer's dance drama Maratona.
"Perusal score."
Duration: ca. 15:00.
Includes composer's note.
Composed for: 4 flutes (2nd–4th also piccolo, 4th also alto flute), 4 clarinets (3rd–4th also bass clarinet), 2 oboes, oboe d'amore, English horn, 4 bassoons (4th also contrabassoon), 4 horns, 3 trumpets, 3 trombones, Wagner tuba (also bass tuba), timpani, percussion (3 tam-tams, Chinese gongs, side drum, maracas, castanets, 3 tom-toms, pitched tom-toms, guiro, crotales, ratchet, claves, sizzle cymbal, bass drum with cymbal, 3 suspended cymbals, glockenspiel, 3 bongos, vibraphone, 2 sistrum, tambourine, marimba, 3 bongos, temple blocks), harp, celesta, piano, violin I, violin II, viola, violoncello, double bass.
Commissioned by: Norddeutscher Rundfunk.
Call no.: **2003/056**

1099. Henze, Hans Werner, 1926– Sieben Liebeslieder: für Violoncello und Orchester (1984/85). Mainz; New York, NY: Schott, 1986.
1 score (108 p.); 50 cm.
Partita.
Duration: ca. 30:00.
Composed for: violoncello, 2 flutes (2nd also piccolo), alto flute (also piccolo), 2 oboes, English horn, 2 clarinets, bass clarinet, 3 bassoons (3rd also contrabassoon), 4 horns, 3 trumpets, 2 trombones, bass trombone, tuba, timpani, percussion (antique cymbals, Chinese gongs, tam-tam, 2 maracas, guiro, snare drum, military drum, 3 tom-toms, bass drum, cymbals, switch, sistrum, vibraphone), harp, piano, celesta, violin I, violin II, viola, violoncello, double bass.

Commissioned by: Westdeutscher Rundfunk Köln.
Call no.: **1987/032**
Re-entered as: **1990/045**

1100. Henze, Hans Werner, 1926– Symphonie Nr. 7 (1983/84). Studien- und Dirigierpartitur. Mainz; New York, NY: Schott, 1984.
1 score (142 p.); 42 cm.
Musik unserer Zeit = Music of our time.
Duration: ca. 46:00.
Composed for: 4 flutes (2nd–3rd also piccolo, 4th also alto flute), 2 oboes, English horn, heckelphone, 4 clarinets (4th also bass clarinet), contrabass clarinet, 4 bassoons (4th also contrabassoon), 6 horns, 2 trumpets in D, 4 trumpets, 3 trombones, bass trombone, contrabass trombone, tuba, percussion (timpani, 2 bongos, 6 tom-toms, maracas, chimes, glockenspiel, bass drum, snare drum, Chinese gong, marimba, 3 suspended cymbals, 3 tam-tams, crotales, tambourine, guiro, whip, vibraphone), harp, piano, celesta, violin I, violin II, viola, violoncello, double bass.
Commissioned by: Berlin Philharmonic Orchestra.
Call no.: **1988/050**
Re-entered as: **1989/054**

1101. Henze, Hans Werner, 1926– L'Ūpupa: und der Triumph der Sohnesliebe: ein deutsches Lustspiel, elf Tableaux aus dem Arabischen. Orchesterpartitur. London: Chester Music, 2003.
1 score (2 v.); 30 cm.
German words by the composer.
Duration: 140:00.
Composed for: soprano, alto, countertenor, tenor, baritone, bass, vocal ensemble (2 sopranos, 2 altos, 2 tenors, 2 basses), 3 flutes (also alto flute and piccolo), 3 clarinets (also bass clarinet), oboe, oboe d'amore, English horn, 3 bassoons (also contrabassoon), 4 horns (also Wagner tuba), 3 trumpets, 3 trombones (also alto and bass trombones), tuba, percussion (marimba, 5 Japanese woodblocks, mokushu, 3 small Chinese hand cymbals, 2 pairs of mounted castanets (alto and bass), glockenspiel, 3 suspended cymbals, woodblock, hyoshigi, 3 bongos, side drum, alto ratchet, crotales, 2 gongs, 12 chromatic temple blocks, binsasara, chocalho, tambourine, sistrum, 6 tom-toms, tam-tam, large log drum, soprano ratchet, flexatone, 2 Thai gliss gongs, bass drum with cymbals, 2 gliss gongs, guiro, bass ratchet, 2 pairs of unmounted castanets, deep gong), timpani, 2 harps, piano (4 hands, both also celesta), violin I, violin II, viola, violoncello, double bass, tape.
Commissioned by: Salzburg Festival.
Call no.: **2005/066**

1102. Henze, Hans Werner, 1926– Das verratene Meer: Musikdrama (1987–89). Partitur. Mainz; New York, NY: Schott, 1990.
1 score (437 p.); 59 cm.
German words by Hans-Ulrich Treichel.
Based on Gogo no eikō = The treacherous ocean by Yukio Mishima.
Composed for: soprano, countertenor, 2 tenors, 2 baritones, 2 basses, 3 flutes (2nd also piccolo, 3rd also alto flute), oboe, oboe d'amore, English horn, 2 clarinets (2nd also bass clarinet), bass clarinet (also contrabass clarinet), soprano saxophone, 3 bassoons (3rd also contrabassoon), 4 horns, 3 trumpets, alto trombone, trombone, bass trombone, contrabass trombone, timpani, percussion (3 suspended cymbals, tam-tam, 2 gongs, antique cymbals, 6 handbells, 4 Chinese gongs, Trinidad steel drum, tambourine, 6 tom-toms, snare drum, tenor drum, military drum, bass drum with cymbal, woodblock, temple blocks, castanets, maracas, odaiko, guiro, whip, aluminum foil, friction drum, ratchet, flexatone, siren, vibraphone, marimba), 2 harps, piano, celesta, tape, violin I, violin II, viola, violoncello, double bass.
Commissioned by: Deutsche Oper Berlin.
Call no.: **1991/053**

1103. Herrmann, Peter, 1941– Meschki-Agascher: für Violoncello und Klavier (1999). Leipzig: Ebert Musik Verlag, 2000.
1 score (11 p.) + 1 part (4 p.); 30 cm.
Duration: 8:00–10:00.
Composed for: violoncello, piano.
Call no.: **2001/071**

1104. Herrmann, Peter, 1941– Tape symphony: für Violoncello, Klavier und Tonband, 1999. Studienpartitur. Leipzig: Ebert Musik Verlag, 2000.
1 score (30 p.); 30 cm.
Reproduced from holograph.
Composed for: violoncello, piano, tape.
Call no.: **2002/081**

1105. Herrmann, Peter, 1941– Ten-Symphony (2001): für Oboe, Klarinette, Trompete, Posaune, Klavier, 2 Violen, 2 Violoncelli und Kontrabass. Leipzig: Ebert Musik Verlag, 2001.
1 miniature score (121 p.); 30 cm.
Contents: Kontraste—Pulsation—Adagio; Finale.
Composed for: oboe, clarinet, trumpet, trombone, piano, 2 violas, 2 violoncellos, double bass.
Call no.: **2004/052**

1106. Herrmann, Peter, 1941– Vierte Sinfonie: "Sinfonietta." Studienpartitur. Leipzig: Ebert Musik Verlag, 1996.

1 miniature score (62 p.); 30 cm.
Composed for: 2 flutes, 2 oboes, 2 clarinets, 2 bassoons, 4 horns, 2 trumpets, 3 trombones, timpani, violin I, violin II, viola, violoncello, double bass.
Call no.: **2000/070**

1107. Herrmann, Peter, 1941–Violoncello-Konzert (2002). Studienpartitur. Leipzig: Ebert Musik Verlag, 2002.
1 score (73 p.); 30 cm.
Reproduced from manuscript.
Includes biographical information.
Composed for: violoncello, oboe, clarinet, bass clarinet, bassoon, horn, piano, violin, viola, violoncello, double bass.
Call no.: **2005/067**

1108. Hersch, Michael Nathaniel, 1971– Piano concerto. N.p.: Hersch, 2002.
1 score (128 p.); 44 cm.
Composed for: piano, piccolo, 2 flutes, 2 oboes, 2 clarinets, bass clarinet, 2 bassoons, contrabassoon, 4 horns, 2 trumpets, 2 trombones, bass trombone, tuba, timpani, percussion (large chimes, glockenspiel, large suspended cymbal, large crash cymbals, large tam-tam, military snare drum, xylophone, tambourine, bass drum, large tom-tom, marimba), harp, offstage piano, violin I, violin II, viola, violoncello, double bass.
Commissioned by: Hans Vonk and St. Louis Symphony Orchestra, James DePreist and Oregon Symphony Orchestra, Mariss Jansons and Pittsburg Symphony Orchestra, and Garrick Ohlsson.
Call no.: **2005/068**

1109. Hertig, Godi, 1926– Missa 98: Messe für Chor, Sopran-Solo, Orgel und Instrumentalensemble, WV 46. Partitur. N.p.: n.p., 1998.
1 score (82 p.); 30 cm.
Latin words.
Duration: 25:00.
Composed for: soprano, SATB chorus, oboe, trumpet, timpani, 2 violins, violoncello, organ.
Call no.: **2002/082**

1110. Hespos, Hans-Joachim, 1938– Prestunissimo.
Call no.: **1985/084**
No materials available.

1111. Hespos, Hans-Joachim, 1938– Seiltanz: ein szenisches Abenteuer.
Call no.: **1985/085**
No materials available.

1112. Hespos, Hans-Joachim, 1938– Taff: Zeitwinde für Orchester. Delmenhorst: Hespos, 1986.
1 score (26 [i.e. 52] p.); 43 cm.
For bass with orchestra.
German words.
In part graphic notation.
Duration: ca. 29:00.
Reproduced from holograph.
Instructions for performance (7 leaves; 30 cm.) inserted.
Composed for: bass, piccolo, 2 flutes (2nd also piccolo), 2 oboes, English horn, heckelphone, 2 clarinets (2nd also clarinet in A), bass clarinet, alto saxophone (also tenor saxophone), 2 bassoons, contrabassoon, 4 horns, piccolo trumpet in D, 2 trumpets, flugelhorn, alto trombone, tenor trombones, bass trombone, tuba, percussion (timpani, tom-tom, 2 snare drums, xylophone, tam-tam, flexatone, chicken clucker, bass drum, plastic barrel, military drum), harp, piano, 16 violins, 10 violas, 8 violoncellos, 8 double basses.
Commissioned by: Sender Freies Berlin.
Call no.: **1990/046**

1113. Hespos, Hans-Joachim, 1938– Zá khani.
Call no.: **1986/054**
No materials available.

1114. Hespos, Hans-Joachim, 1938– Zerango: für Bajan (Akkordeon), Violine, Violoncello. Delmenhorst: Hespos, 1985.
1 score (5 p.); 43 cm.
Performance instructions (5 leaves; 28 cm.) inserted.
Duration: 8:32.
Reproduced from holograph.
Composed for: accordion, violin, violoncello.
Commissioned by: Deutscher Akkordeonlehrer-Verband.
Call no.: **1988/051**

1115. Hétu, Jacques, 1938– Images de la Révolution: opus 44, 1988. Québec: Centre de Musique Canadienne, 1989.
1 score (55 p.); 46 cm.
For orchestra.
Duration: ca. 19:00.
Contents: Le serment du Jeu de Paume—La prise de la Bastille—Le convoi de la royauté—Marat assassiné—La fête de l'Être Suprême.
Composed for: 4 flutes (3rd–4th also piccolo), 3 oboes (3rd also English horn), 3 clarinets (3rd also bass clarinet), 3 bassoons (3rd also contrabassoon), 4 horns, 3 trumpets, 3 trombones, tuba, timpani, percussion (triangle, cymbals, suspended cymbal, snare drum, tenor drum, bass drum, tam-tam, tubular bells, orchestra bells), violin I,

violin II, viola, violoncello, double bass.
Call no.: **1990/047**

1116. Hétu, Jacques, 1938– Messe: Missa pro trecentesimo anno: pour chœur mixte et orchestre (orgue ad libitum): opus 38. Montréal: Centre de musique canadienne au Québec, 1985.
1 score (63 p.); 46 cm.
Latin words.
Reproduced from manuscript.
Duration: ca. 30:00.
Composed for: SATB chorus, 2 flutes (2nd also piccolo), 2 oboes (2nd also English horn), 2 clarinets (2nd also bass clarinet), 2 bassoons (2nd also contrabassoon), 4 horns, 3 trumpets, 3 trombones, tuba, timpani, percussion (triangle, cymbals, suspended cymbal, tam-tam, bass drum, tubular bells), violin I, violin II, viola, violoncello, double bass, organ (ad lib.).
Commissioned by: Société Radio-Canada.
Call no.: **1989/055**
Also available:
Call no.: **1989/055 interludes**

1117. Heucke, Stefan, 1959– Der selbstsüchtige Riese: Märchen für Sprecher und Orchester nach Oscar Wilde, op. 20 = The selfish giant: fairytale for reciter and orchestra after Oscar Wilde, op. 20. Mainz; New York, NY: Schott, 1997.
1 score (163 p.); 42 cm.
Composed for: narrator, 2 flutes (2nd also piccolo), 2 oboes (2nd also English horn), 2 clarinets, 2 bassoons, 2 horns, 2 trumpets, 2 trombones, bass trombone, timpani, percussion (marimba, glockenspiel, snare drum, bass drum, cymbals, tam-tam, slapstick, triangle), piano, violin I, violin II, viola, violoncello, double bass.
Commissioned by: City of Kamen.
Call no.: **2001/072**

1118. Higdon, Jennifer, 1962– Blue cathedral. Philadelphia, PA: Lawdon Press, 1999.
1 score (32 p.); 43 cm.
For orchestra.
Duration: ca. 11:00.
Composed for: 2 flutes (2nd also piccolo), oboe, English horn, 2 clarinets, 2 bassoons, 4 horns, 3 trumpets, 2 tenor trombones, bass trombone, tuba, timpani, percussion (crotales, marimba, tam-tam, vibraphone, glockenspiel, bell tree, sizzle cymbal, suspended cymbal, chimes, small triangle, large triangle, bass drum, large tom-tom), violin I, violin II, viola, violoncello, double bass, 8 crystal glasses, 60–70 Chinese bells.
Commissioned by: Curtis Institute of Music.
Call no.: **2002/083**

1119. Higdon, Jennifer, 1962– City scape. N.p.: Lawdon Press, 2002.
1 score (107 p.); 44 cm.
For orchestra.
Duration: ca. 30:00.
Contents: Skyline—River sings a song to trees—Peachtree Street.
Composed for: 2 flutes, piccolo, 2 oboes, English horn, 2 clarinets, bass clarinet, 2 bassoons, contrabassoon, 4 horns, 3 trumpets, 2 trombones, bass trombone, tuba, harp, timpani (also crotales), percussion (brake drum, snare drum, 2 bongos, crash cymbals, marimba, glockenspiel, vibraphone, supended cymbal, tam-tam, bass drum, floor tom-tom, Chinese cymbal, woodblock, xylophone, crotales, 2 triangles, water gong, 5 temple blocks, tambourine, supended cymbal, guiro, sizzle cymbal), violin I, violin II, viola, violoncello, double bass.
Commissioned by: Atlanta Symphony Orchestra.
Call no.: **2005/069**

1120. Higdon, Jennifer, 1962– Concerto for orchestra. Philadelphia, PA: Lawdon Press, 2002.
1 score (118 p.); 44 cm.
Duration: ca. 32:00–35:00.
Composed for: 3 flutes (3rd also piccolo), 3 oboes, 2 clarinets, bass clarinet, 2 bassoons, contrabassoon, 4 horns, 3 trumpets, 2 trombones, bass trombone, tuba, harp, piano (also celesta), timpani, percussion (chimes, crotales, suspended cymbal, snare drum, 5 temple blocks, small triangle, sandpaper blocks, flexatone, 3 tom-toms, glockenspiel, vibraphone, tam-tam, Chinese cymbal, 3 woodblocks, maracas, 2 bongos, medium roto-tom, marimba, large triangle, bass drum, sizzle cymbal, vibraslap, castanets, guiro, floor tom-tom, slapstick), violin I, violin II, viola, violoncello, double bass.
Commissioned by: Philadelphia Orchestra.
Call no.: **2004/053**

1121. Hill, Jackson, 1941– Songs of wind, rain, and liquid fire (1984). Lewisburg, PA: J. Hill, 1984.
1 score (40 p.); 28 cm.
English words by John S. Wheatcroft.
At end: "16 Sept 1984."
Contents: Magnolia blooms (Dedication)—Lady of laurel—Littoral—Anathema: for the bombers of lambs—Sea rite.
Reproduced from manuscript.
Composed for: high voice, flute, violoncello, piano.
Commissioned by: Huntington Trio.
Call no.: **1985/086**

1122. Hill, William R., 1954– String quartet #1. N.p.: n.p., 2000.

1 score (60 p.); 34 cm.
Reproduced from holograph.
Duration: ca. 30:00.
At end of score: "William R. Hill 7/13/2000."
Composed for: 2 violins, viola, violoncello.
Call no.: **2002/084**

1123. Hillborg, Anders, 1954– Violinkonsert (1991–1992). N.p.: n.p., 1992.
1 score (88 p.); 43 cm.
Duration: ca. 23:00.
Composed for: violin, 3 flutes (all also piccolo), 3 oboes, 3 clarinets, bass clarinet, 2 contrabassoons, 2 horns, 2 trumpets, 2 trombones, tuba, violin I, violin II, viola, violoncello, double bass.
Call no.: **1997/060**

1124. Hirabe, Yayoi, 1959– Art 1907–1931: for violin, marimba, electrone (electric org.). N.p.: n.p., 1993.
1 score (19 p.); 26 x 37 cm.
Reproduced from manuscript.
Contents: Cubism—Ecole de Paris—Dada, Bauhouce—Surrealism.
Composed for: violin, marimba, electric organ.
Call no.: **1995/044**

1125. Hirt, James A., 1956– Time spirals: for orchestra, 1988. Cincinnati, OH: James Alan Hirt, 1989.
1 score (iii, 60 p.); 44 cm.
"Edited 11/89"—p. ii.
Reproduced from manuscript.
Duration: 12:00.
Composed for: 2 flutes (2nd also piccolo), 2 oboes, 2 clarinets, bass clarinet, 2 bassoons, 4 horns, 3 trumpets, 2 trombones, bass trombone, tuba, percussion (5 tom-toms, vibraphone, snare drum, crotales, timpani, wind machine, marimba, xylophone, 2 bass drums), piano, violin I, violin II, viola, violoncello, double bass.
Commissioned by: WGUC 90.9FM Cincinnati.
Call no.: **1991/054**

1126. Ho, Fred Wei-han, 1957– Journey beyond the West: the new adventures of monkey. N.p.: Transformation Art Publisher, 1995.
1 score (177 p.); 22 x 36 cm.
Chinese words by Cindy Wang.
Based on a character from the 16th century Chinese epic fantasy-adventure novel by Wu Cheng'en.
Reproduced from manuscript.
Contents: Uproar in heaven—The journey begins—Monkey meets the spider siren vampires—The journey home: the struggle for heaven on earth!
Composed for: Chinese soprano, chromodal saxophone, erhu, pipa, sona, 2 soprano saxophones (1st also alto saxophone, piccolo, flute, bass clarinet; 2nd also tenor saxophone, flute, bass clarinet), baritone saxophone (also flute), trombone (also bass trombone), percussion (trap set, bells, tom-toms, Chinese opera percussion), double bass.
Commissioned by: In Concert.
Call no.: **1997/061**

1127. Hobbs, Allen, 1937– A trilogy of psalms = Trilogie de psaumes. N.p.: Allen Hobbs, 1991.
1 score (93 p.); 36 cm.
Latin words.
For boy soprano, chorus, and instrumental ensemble.
Reproduced from holograph.
Contents: Psalmus 1: Beatus vir—Psalmus 50 [i.e. 51]: Miserere—Psalmus 148: Laudate Dominum.
Composed for: boy soprano, SATB chorus, 4 horns, piano, organ, percussion (xylophone, marimba, timpani, 5 temple blocks, chimes).
Call no.: **1992/057**

1128. Hodkinson, Sydney, 1934– Chaconne in B♭: jazz reflexion for four trios. Bryn Mawr, PA: Merion Music, 1998.
1 score (59 p.); 44 cm.
Reproduced from manuscript.
Duration 14:00.
Composed for: trio I: flute (also piccolo), clarinet (also clarinet in E♭), bass clarinet (also tenor saxophone); trio II: horn, trumpet, trombone; trio III: jazz drum set, vibraphone (also marimba), piano; trio IV: violin, violoncello, double bass.
Call no.: **2001/073**

1129. Hodkinson, Sydney, 1934– Epitaphion: lament for symphony orchestra. Bryn Mawr, PA: Merion Music: Theodore Presser, 1990.
1 score (42 p.); 44 cm.
Reproduced from the holograph.
Duration: ca. 13:30.
Includes program note by the composer.
Composed for: 3 flutes (2nd–3rd also piccolo), 3 oboes (3rd also English horn), 3 clarinets (3rd also bass clarinet), 2 bassoons, contrabassoon, 4 horns, 3 trumpets, 2 trombones, bass trombone, tuba, timpani, percussion (glockenspiel, snare drum, tenor drum, vibraphone, 2 suspended cymbals, 2 tom-toms, gong, tubular chimes, bass drum, thundersheet, crotales), harp, piano (also celesta), violin I, violin II, viola, violoncello, double bass.
Call no.: **1992/058**

1130. Hody, Jean, 1935– Hipparque: ou l'arpenteur des etoiles, 1989. N.p.: n.p., 1989.
1 score (20 p.); 30 cm.
Reproduced from manuscript.
Contents: La création—La vie—Satellisation—Au delà du cosmos.
Composed for: panpipes, guitar, piano, alto saxophone, organ.
Call no.: **1990/048**

1131. Hoffman, Joel, 1953– Double concerto.
Call no.: **1985/087**
No materials available.

1132. Hoffmann, Tom, 1947– Tree of life. N.p.: n.p., 1980.
1 score (42 leaves) + 4 parts; 28 cm.
Contents: Voices of an ancient land—Perfect passage—Zaragato night dance.
Composed for: guitar, violin, viola, violoncello.
Commissioned by: Boccherini Ensemble.
Call no.: **1992/059**

1133. Hofmeyr, Hendrik, 1957– Strykkwartet. N.p.: Hendrik Hofmeyr, 1998.
1 score (50 p.); 29 cm.
Duration: ca. 27:00.
Contents: Canone—Marcia—Notturno—Rondo.
Composed for: 2 violins, viola, violoncello.
Commissioned by: South East Music Schemes.
Call no.: **2004/054**

1134. Holab, William, 1958– Ode to a nightingale: for tenor and orchestra. N.p.: n.p., 1985.
1 score (49 p.); 44 cm.
English words by John Keats; also printed as text.
Reproduced from holograph.
Composed for: tenor, 2 flutes (2nd also piccolo), 2 oboes (2nd also English horn), 3 clarinets (1st also clarinet in A, 2nd also clarinet in E♭, 3rd also bass clarinet), 2 bassoons (2nd also contrabassoon), 4 horns, 2 trumpets, 2 trombones, bass trombone, tuba, percussion (glockenspiel, antique cymbals, tenor drum, suspended cymbal, vibraphone, tubular bells, timbales, tom-tom, bass drum, 2 triangles, xylophone, snare drum, bongos, tam-tam, bell tree, glass wind chimes, timpani, tambourine), harp, celesta (also glockenspiel), violin I, violin II, viola, violoncello, double bass.
Call no.: **1990/049**

1135. Holewa, Hans, 1905–1991. Symfoni no. 6, 1985–1986. N.p.: n.p., 1986.
1 score (89 p.); 56 cm.
Duration: ca. 30:00.
Composed for: 4 flutes (3rd also piccolo), 4 oboes (3rd also English horn), 4 clarinets (3rd also clarinet in E♭, 4th also bass clarinet), 4 bassoons (4th also contrabassoon), 4 horns, 3 trumpets, 3 trombones, tuba, timpani, percussion (xylophone, vibraphone, military drum, marimba, glockenspiel, triangle, crash cymbals, claves, tambourine, temple block, Chinese woodblock, temple block, 3 tom-toms, tabor, bass drum, tam-tam, gong, 3 snare drums, congas, 3 bongos, castanets, tenor drum, slit drum), violin I, violin II, viola, violoncello, double bass.
Commissioned by: Konserthusstiftelsen.
Call no.: **1990/050**

1136. Holland, Anthony G., 1955– B-R-A-H-M-S piano quartet. N.p.: n.p., 2000.
1 score (92 p.); 28 cm.
Contents: Barcarole buffo—Rondo remenyi—Animierlokale—Hamburg hoquetus—Musical cabala—Scherzo schumannia.
Composed for: violin, viola, violoncello, piano.
Commissioned by: Philadelphia Piano Quartet.
Call no.: **2003/057**

1137. Holland, Anthony G., 1955– Concerto: for violin and orchestra. N.p.: n.p., 1995.
1 score (112 p.); 28 cm.
Duration: ca. 18:00.
Composed for: violin, 3 flutes (3rd also piccolo), 2 clarinets in A, 2 bassoons (2nd also contrabassoon), 4 horns, 2 trumpets, 2 trombones, bass trombone, tuba, percussion (timpani, crash cymbals, suspended cymbals, crotales, triangle, tubular bells, glockenspiel, snare drum, bass drum), harp, piano, violin I, violin II, viola, violoncello, double bass.
Call no.: **1998/065**

1138. Holland, Anthony G., 1955– Concerto for organ and orchestra. N.p.: n.p., 200-?.
1 score (163 p.); 36 cm.
Duration: ca. 25:00.
Composed for: organ, 3 flutes (3rd also piccolo), 2 oboes, 2 clarinets, 2 bassoons, 4 horns, 3 trumpets, 3 trombones (3rd also bass trombone), tuba, percussion (triangle, finger cymbals, suspended cymbals, bass drum, glockenspiel, snare drum, tam-tam, crash cymbals, tambourine, tubular bells, sleigh bells, timpani), violin I, violin II, viola, violoncello, double bass.
Call no.: **2004/055**

1139. Holland, Anthony G., 1955– The Tesla tower: for symphonic wind ensemble. N.p.: n.p., 1999.

1 score (44 p.); 36 cm.
Duration: ca. 10:00.
Composed for: piccolo, 2 flutes, 2 oboes, clarinet in E♭, 3 clarinets, alto clarinet, bass clarinet, contralto clarinet, 2 bassoons, contrabassoon, 2 alto saxophones, tenor saxophone, baritone saxophone, 4 horns, 6 trumpets, 4 trombones, euphonium, tuba, percussion (glockenspiel, crash cymbal, triangle, finger cymbals, large and small tam-tams, xylophone, anvil, tubular bells, vibraphone, ratchet, suspended cymbal, tambourine, snare drum, 6 tom-toms, metal chime tree, bell tree, bass drum, temple blocks, snare timpani), piano, celesta, harp, double bass.
Commissioned by: Baldwin-Wallace Symphonic Wind Ensemble.
Call no.: **2002/085**

1140. Holler, York, 1944– Piano concerto.
Commissioned by: BBC.
Call no.: **1990/051**
No materials available.

1141. Höller, York, 1944– Aura: für grosses Orchester. London: Boosey & Hawkes, 1997.
1 score (82 p.); 30 cm.
Composer's note in German with English and French translations.
Duration: 21:00.
Composed for: 4 flutes (3rd–4th also piccolo), 3 oboes (3rd also English horn), 3 clarinets (3rd also bass clarinet), 3 bassoons (3rd also contrabassoon), 4 horns, 3 trumpets, 3 trombones, tuba, percussion (crotales, glockenspiel, xylophone, marimba, vibraphone, tubular bells, pellet bells, maracas, large woodblock, snare drum, tambourine, large tom-tom, tenor drum, bass drum, timpani, 5 cymbals, 4 gongs, 3 tam-tams), harp, piano, celesta, synthesizer, violin I, violin II, viola, violoncello, double bass.
Commissioned by: Chicago Symphony Orchestra.
Call no.: **1998/066**

1142. Höller, York, 1944– Aura: für grosses Orchester, 1991/92. London: Boosey & Hawkes, 1993.
1 score (94 p.); 31 cm.
Reproduced from manuscript.
Duration: ca. 20:00.
Composed for: 4 flutes (3rd–4th also piccolo), 3 oboes (3rd also English horn), 3 clarinets (3rd also bass clarinet), 3 bassoons (3rd also contrabassoon), 4 horns, 3 trumpets, 3 trombones, tuba, timpani, percussion (crotales, glockenspiel, xylophone, marimba, vibraphone, tubular bells, pellet bells, maracas, large woodblock, snare drum, tambourine, large tom-tom, tenor drum, bass drum, timpani, 5 cymbals, 4 gongs, 3 tam-tams), harp, 2 keyboard players (piano, celesta, synthesizer), violin I, violin II, viola, violoncello, double bass.
Commissioned by: Chicago Symphony Orchestra.
Call no.: **1996/060**

1143. Höller, York, 1944– Fanal: für Trompete und Orchester (1989/90). Partitur. N.p.: n.p., 1991.
1 score (78 p.); 43 cm.
Reproduced from holograph.
Duration: ca. 20:00.
Composed for: trumpet, 2 flutes, 2 oboes (2nd also English horn), 2 clarinets (2nd also bass clarinet), 2 bassoons (2nd also contrabassoon), 2 horns, 2 trombones, tuba, percussion (glockenspiel, vibraphone, xylorimba, chimes, 2 tam-tams, 5 cymbals, 3 wood drums, 5 tom-toms, snare drum, field drum, bass drum), harp, piano, synthesizer, violin I, violin II, viola, violoncello, double bass.
Commissioned by: Ensemble Intercontemporain.
Call no.: **1992/060**

1144. Höller, York, 1944– Pensées: Requiem für Klavier, grosses Orchester und Elektronik. London: Boosey & Hawkes, 1993.
1 miniature score (84 p.); 30 cm.
Reproduced from manuscript.
Duration: 25:00.
Composed for: piano, piccolo (also alto flute), 2 flutes, 2 oboes, English horn, 2 clarinets, bass clarinet, 2 bassoons, contrabassoon, 4 horns, 3 trumpets, 3 trombones, tuba, percussion (xylophone, marimba, crotales, glockenspiel, vibraphone, chimes, gongs, 6 cymbals, 3 tam-tams, 2 snare drums, tenor drum, tom-toms, bass drum, woodblock, maracas, timpani, sleigh bells), synthesizer, harp, violin I, violin II, viola, violoncello, double bass.
Commissioned by: Westdeutscher Rundfunk Köln.
Call no.: **1994/061**

1145. Holliger, Heinz, 1939– Scardanelli-Zyklus.
Call no.: **1986/055**
No materials available.

1146. Holloway, Robin, 1943– Clarissa.
Call no.: **1991/055**
Re-entered as: **1992/061**
No materials available.

1147. Holloway, Robin, 1943– Scenes from Antwerp: streets: clouds: docks: domes: symphonic images for orchestra, op. 85. Full score. London: Boosey & Hawkes, 1998.

1 score (87 p.); 30 cm.
Reproduced from manuscript.
Composed for: 3 flutes (3rd also piccolo), 2 oboes, English horn, 3 clarinets (2nd also contrabass, 3rd also bass clarinet), 2 bassoons, contrabassoon, 2 soprano saxophones (1st also alto saxophone, 2nd also baritone saxophone), 4 horns, 3 trumpets, 3 trombones, tuba, percussion (glockenspiel, vibraphone, marimba, crotales, tubular bells, triangle, bass drum, suspended cymbal, tam-tam), harp, violin I, violin II, viola, violoncello, double bass.
Commissioned by: Royal Flanders Philharmonic Orchestra.
Call no.: **2000/071**

1148. Holloway, Robin, 1943– Symphony: op. 88. Full score. London: Boosey & Hawkes, 1999.
1 score (149 p.); 42 cm.
Reproduced from manuscript.
Composed for: 4 flutes (3rd–4th also piccolo, 4th also alto flute), 2 oboes, English horn, 3 clarinets (3rd also clarinet in E♭), bass clarinet, contrabass clarinet, 3 bassoons (3rd also contrabassoon), 2 soprano saxophones (1st also sopranino saxophone, 2nd also alto saxophone), 2 alto saxophones (2nd also tenor saxophone), 6 horns, 4 trumpets (3rd also piccolo trumpet), 4 trombones, tuba, timpani, percussion (xylophone, glockenspiel, vibraphone, marimba, bells, 4 triangles, jingles, crotales, bell tree, woodblock, Chinese blocks, claves, maracas, ratchet, whip, tambourine, side drum, tenor drum, bass drum, clashed cymbals, 3 suspended cymbals, sizzle cymbal, tam-tam, gong, 6 anvils), harp, celesta, piano, violin I, violin II, viola, violoncello, double bass.
Commissioned by: BBC.
Call no.: **2002/086**

1149. Holloway, Robin, 1943– Third concerto for orchestra: op. 80, 1981–94. London: Boosey & Hawkes, 1995.
1 score (98 p.); 42 cm.
Reproduced from manuscript.
Composed for: 3 flutes (all also piccolo), 2 oboes, English horn, clarinet, clarinet in E♭, bass clarinet, contrabass clarinet, 2 bassoons, contrabassoon, 4 horns, 3 trumpets, piccolo trumpet, 3 trombones, tuba, timpani, percussion (bass drum, tam-tam, large suspended cymbal, snare drum, claves, woodblock, crotales, marimba, jingle bells, vibraphone, glockenspiel, maracas, xylophone, bells, 2 triangles, 2 anvils, crash cymbals), harp, piano, celesta, violin I, violin II, viola, violoncello, double bass.
Commissioned by: London Symphony Orchestra.
Call no.: **1997/062**
Re-entered as: **2001/074**

1150. Holloway, Robin, 1943– Violin concerto: op. 70. N.p.: n.p., 1990.
1 minature score (123 p.); 30 cm.
"Cadenza unrevised."
Reproduced from manuscript.
Composed for: violin, 3 flutes (2nd–3rd also piccolo, 3rd also alto flute), 2 oboes (2nd also English horn), 2 clarinets in A (1st also clarinet in E♭), 2 bassoons, 2 horns, 2 trumpets, trombone, tuba, percussion (triangle, suspended cymbal, tam-tam, timpani, crotales, glockenspiel, tambourine, maracas, vibraphone, xylophone, tubular bells, crash cymbals, jingle bells, 2 Chinese blocks, marimba), harp, piano, celesta, violin I, violin II, viola, violoncello, double bass.
Call no.: **1993/054**

1151. Holmboe, Vagn, 1909–1996. Hominis dies.
Call no.: **1986/056**
No materials available.

1152. Holsinger, David R., 1945– The deathtree: a passionwork for winds, percussion, and baritone voice. N.p.: n.p., 1986.
1 score (83 p.); 28 cm.
English words.
Composed for: baritone, piccolo, flute, oboe, 2 bassoons, clarinet in E♭, 3 clarinets, alto clarinet, bass clarinet, 2 alto saxophones, tenor saxophone, baritone saxophone, 3 cornets, 4 horns, 2 trumpets, baritone, 3 trombones, tuba, piano, percussion (vibraphone, wind chimes, 3 triangles, marimba, jingle bells, temple blocks, sizzle cymbal, gong, bass drum, snare drum, suspended cymbal, xylophone, bells, chimes, tambourine, tubular chimes, large woodblock).
Commissioned by: United States Marine Historical Foundation.
Call no.: **1990/052**

1153. Holsinger, David R., 1945– The Easter symphony: for wind symphony, percussion, baritone vocal soloist, and SSATB chorus. Full score. N.p.: n.p., 1994.
1 score (301 p.); 36 cm.
English words.
Contents: Kings—The deathtree—Symphonia ressurectus.
Composed for: baritone, SSATB chorus, piccolo, flute, oboe, clarinet in E♭, 3 clarinets, alto clarinet, bass clarinet, 2 bassoons, 2 alto saxophones, tenor saxophone, baritone saxophone, 3 cornets, 3 trumpets, 4 horns, baritone, 3 trombones, tuba, piano, timpani,

percussion (xylophone, glockenspiel, triangle, 3–4 field drums, finger cymbals, camel bells, timbales, bell tree, 4 tom-toms, jingle bells, bass drum, snare drum, temple blocks, suspended cymbals, crash cymbals, cowbell, afro-crasher, vibraphone, marimba, gong, sizzle cymbal, chimes, bells, tubular chimes, field drum).
Call no.: **1996/061**

1154. Hölszky, Adriana, 1953– Bremer Freiheit: Singwerk auf ein Frauenleben. Partitur. Berlin: Astoria Verlag, 1988.
1 score (279 p.); 77 cm.
German words by Thomas Körner.
Original work by Rainer Werner Fassbinder.
Opera for voices and instrumental ensemble.
Reproduced from manuscript.
Composed for: soprano (also castanets, ahnklung, frying pan, nightingale call, conga, jingles, cowbells, frame drum with chain, newspaper, trough, bamboo flute, modal chimes, friction drum, glass bowl), mezzo-soprano (also caxixi, frame drum with chain, snake charmer's horn, star chimes, bamboo flute), alto I (also donkey rattle, harmonica, frying pan, conga, frame drum with chain, newspaper, trough, bamboo flute, modal chimes, glass bowl), alto II (also ahnklung, tambourine, flexatone, tubular chime, temple block, conga, frame drum with chain, newspaper, bamboo flute, glass bowl, trough, frying pan), tenor I (also toy lyre, glass bowl, conga), tenor II (also ahnklung, flexatone, conga, frame drum with chain, newspaper, bamboo flute, trough, frying pan, maracas, cowbells, ratchet, rakatak, chinka-baum), tenor III (also harmonica, frying pan, conga, frame drum with chain, newspaper, trough, glass bowl, cowbells, caxixi, tubular chime, auto horn, slide whistle, sleigh bells), baritone I (also frying pan, frame drum with chain, newspaper, trough, bamboo flute, glass bowl, flexatone, cowbells, whip, copper bell, button gong), baritone II (also frying pan, trough, glass bowl, Indian sleigh bells, wood chime, toy trumpet, cuckoo bird call, bells, tam-tam, castanets, parade drum), bass I (also donkey rattle, frying pan, bass conga, newspaper, chimes, glass bowl, suspended Indian cowbells, siren, cowbells, tam-tam), bass II (also glass bowl, sistrum, harmonica, glass pipes, musical saw, frame drum with chain, ahnklung), flute (also piccolo, alto, and bass flutes, guiro, Chinese cymbals, harmonica, wood chimes), oboe (also English horn, guiro, Turkish cymbals, harmonica, wood chime, triangle), clarinet (also clarinet in E♭, bass clarinet, contrabass clarinet, guiro, Chinese cymbals, harmonica, wood chime, friction drum), bassoon (also contrabassoon, guiro, Turkish cymbals, harmonica, wood chime, trumpet (also piccolo trumpet in D, flugelhorn, antique cymbal, castanets), 2 bass trombones (also chime, tom-tom, antique cymbal, triangle), 2 violins (also cabasa, woodblock, metal rattle, guiro), 2 violoncellos (also maracas, sleigh bells), double bass (also sistrum, tam-tam, 2 antique cymbals), cymbal (also dulcimer, piano, star chime, bass drum), accordion (also piano, 2 cymbals, modal chime, gong, glockenspiel), percussion (2 woodblocks, snare drum, tom-tom, bass drum, triangle, Turkish cymbals, 2 temple blocks, slit drum, bongos, tam-tam, gong, chimes, 2 antique cymbals, timpani with cymbal, xylophone, marimba, vibraphone).
Commissioned by: City of Munich.
Call no.: **1989/056**

1155. Hölszky, Adriana, 1953– Lichtflug für Violine, Flöte und Orchester, (1989/90). Wiesbaden: Breitkopf & Härtel, 1990.
1 score (65 leaves); 108 cm.
Composed for: violin, flute; group I: flute (also piccolo), oboe, clarinet (also clarinet in E♭), bassoon, horn, trumpet, bass trombone; group II: flute (also piccolo), oboe, clarinet, bassoon, horn, trumpet, bass trombone, tuba; group III: flute (also piccolo), oboe, clarinet (also bass clarinet), bassoon (also contrabassoon), horn, trumpet, bass trombone; group IV: percussion (snare drum, bongos, tom-tom, bass drum, woodblock, small cymbal, large Chinese block, antique cymbal, triangle, glass bowl, chime, Thai gong, tam-tam).
Call no.: **1993/055**

1156. Holt, Simon, 1958– The nightingale's to blame: opera in a prologue and three scenes. Full score. London: Chester Music, 1998.
1 score (2 v., [308 p.]); 42 cm.
English words adapted and translated by David Johnston.
"Adapted from the play The love of Don Perlimplin for Belisa in the garden by Federico Garcia Lorca."
Reproduced from manuscript.
Duration: ca. 1:20:00.
Composed for: 3 sopranos, 2 mezzo-sopranos, baritone, 2 flutes (1st–2nd also alto flute and piccolo), oboe, clarinet in A, bass clarinet, horn, trumpet, percussion (pedal bass drum, 2 log drums, 2 temple blocks, large tam-tam, Chinese suspended cymbal, tambourine, castanets, guiro, lion's roar, 3 axatse, whip, glockenspiel, tubular bells, crotales, 7 tuned gongs), harp, 3 violas, 2 violoncellos, 2 double basses.
Commissioned by: Huddersfield Contemporary Music Festival and City of Munich.
Call no.: **2000/072**

1157. Holt, Simon, 1958– Sunrise's yellow noise: for solo soprano and orchestra (1999). London: Chester Music, 1999.
1 miniature score (36 p.); 30 cm.
English words, also printed as text.
Poem by Emily Dickinson.
Reproduced from holograph.
Duration: ca. 12:00.
Composed for: soprano, 3 flutes (1st–2nd also alto flute, 3rd also piccolo), 2 oboes, English horn, 3 clarinets in A (all also clarinet in E♭, 3rd also bass clarinet), contrabass clarinet, bassoon, contrabassoon, horn, 2 trumpets, 2 trombones, tuba, percussion (large bass drum, 2 Chinese suspended cymbals, large tam-tam, 2 whips, 2 woodblocks, vibraphone, 8 tuned gongs, 4 crotales, 6 handbells, tubular bells, piccolo timpani), harp, violin I, violin II, double bass.
Commissioned by: City of Birmingham Symphony Orchestra and Royal Festival Hall.
Call no.: **2002/087**

1158. Holt, Simon, 1958– Syrensong. London: Universal Edition, 1987.
1 score (44 p.); 41 cm.
For orchestra.
Reproduced from holograph.
Duration: ca. 13:00.
Composed for: 3 flutes (all also piccolo), 2 oboes (2nd also English horn), clarinet in E♭, clarinet in A, bass clarinet, bassoon, contrabassoon, 4 horns, 3 trumpets, 2 trombones, tuba, percussion (2 log drums, tam-tam, bass drum, suspended cymbal, cowbells, tubular bell, woodblock), 2 harps, piano, violin I, violin II, viola, violoncello, double bass.
Commissioned by: BBC.
Call no.: **1989/057**

1159. Holt, Simon, 1958– Walking with the river's roar: for viola solo & orchestra. Score. London: Universal Edition, 1993.
1 score (44 p.); 30 x 43 cm.
"11/93"—cover.
Reproduced from holograph.
Composed for: viola, flute, alto flute, piccolo, 2 oboes, clarinet in A, alto clarinet, bass clarinet, contrabassoon, 2 horns, 2 trumpets, bass trumpet, tuba, percussion (log drums, cowbells, suspended cymbals, bass drum, low temple blocks, Burmese gongs, large tam-tam, tubular bells, slapstick), harp, viola, violoncello, double bass.
Commissioned by: BBC Philharmonic Orchestra.
Call no.: **1994/062**

1160. Hoover, Jeffrey, 1959– My city. Washington, IL: Jeffrey Hoover, 2002.
1 score (20 p.); 28 cm.
"Piano performance score."
Duration: ca. 12:00.
Includes program note and biographical information in English.
Composed for: piano, tape, video painting.
Call no.: **2004/056**

1161. Hoover, Katherine, 1937– Night skies: tone poem: for orchestra: 1993. New York, NY: Papagena Press, 1993.
1 score (80 p.); 28 cm.
Reproduced from holograph.
Composed for: 4 flutes (2nd also shakuhachi, 3rd–4th also piccolo), 3 oboes, 3 clarinets (1st also clarinet in E♭, 3rd also bass clarinet), 3 bassoons, 6 horns, 4 trumpets, 2 trombones, 2 bass trombones, timpani, percussion (4 bongos, 4 congas, tenor drum, snare drum, castanets, slapstick, glockenspiel, tam-tam, cymbals, vibraphone, chimes, triangle, finger cymbal, bell tree, wind machine), harp, violin I, violin II, viola, violoncello, double bass.
Call no.: **2000/073**

1162. Hopkins, James, 1939– From the realm of the sea: SATB chorus and orchestra. Boston, MA: ECS Publishing, 1997.
1 score (122 p.); 36 cm.
English words.
Texts by Rabindranath Tagore, Matthew Arnold, Margaret Cavendish, James Joyce, Lord Tennyson, and from the Bible.
Duration: ca. 38:00.
Contents: Prologue: what language is thine, O sea?—The sea is calm tonight—The thunder of mighty waters—The sea-goddess—All day I hear the noise of waters—Come and rejoice—Crossing the bar—Winds of May.
Composed for: SATB chorus, 3 flutes (2nd also piccolo, 3rd also alto flute), 2 oboes, English horn, 2 clarinets, bass clarinet, 3 bassoons, 4 horns, 3 trumpets, 3 trombones, tuba, percussion (suspended cymbal, vibraphone, triangle, metal wind chimes, mark tree, marimba, glockenspiel, chimes, tam-tam, tom-toms, bass drum, xylophone, tambourine), 2 harps, celesta (also piano), violin I, violin II, viola, violoncello, double bass.
Commissioned by: Pacific Chorale.
Call no.: **2001/075**
Also available:
Call no.: **2001/075 vocal score**

1163. Hopkins, James, 1939– Songs of eternity: for chorus and orchestra. N.p.: James F. Hopkins, 1993.
1 score (61 p.); 36 cm.
English words by Rabindranath Tagore.
Duration: ca. 20:00.
Contents: My song—When death comes—Peace, my heart.
Composed for: SATB chorus, 2 flutes (2nd also piccolo), oboe, English horn, 2 clarinets (2nd also bass clarinet), 2 bassoons, contrabassoon, 4 horns, 3 trumpets, 2 trombones, bass trombone, tuba, percussion (timpani, trap set, triangle, mark tree, xylophone, vibraphone, marimba, tam-tam), harp, piano (also celesta), violin I, violin II, viola, violoncello, double bass.
Commissioned by: Orange County Philharmonic Society.
Call no.: **1997/063**

1164. Hopkins, James, 1939– Symphony no. 6: for wind orchestra.
Call no.: **1985/088**
No materials available.

1165. Horvath, Josef Maria, 1931– Requiem: für gemischten Chor a cappella, 1990. Partitur. Wien: Doblinger, 1991.
1 score (82 p.); 30 cm.
Latin words.
Reproduced from holograph.
Composed for: SATB chorus.
Commissioned by: Süddeutscher Rundfunk.
Call no.: **1992/062**

1166. Horvath-Thomas, Istvan, 1938– Kreuzweg: für Orgel, 2 Trompeten, 2 Hörner, Posaune und Chor. Partitur und Stimmen. Lottstetten/Waldshut: Kunzelmann, 1986.
1 score (20 p.); 30 cm.
Photocopy of edition published by Kunzelmann.
Composed for: SATB chorus, organ, 2 trumpets, 2 horns, 2 trombones.
Call no.: **1993/056**

1167. Hosokawa, Toshio, 1955– Ceremonial dance: for string orchestra. Japan: Schott Japan, 2000.
1 score (22 p.); 42 cm.
Duration: 15:00.
Composed for: violin I, violin II, viola, violoncello, double bass.
Commissioned by: Nippon Steel Arts Foundation.
Call no.: **2002/088**

1168. Hosokawa, Toshio, 1955– Hiroshima requiem: for speakers (3), soloists (4 or 8), chorus, children's chorus, tape and orchestra. Tokyo: Schott Japan, 1989.
1 score (30, 25 p.); 43 cm.
Japanese and Latin words.
Text: Children of the A-Bomb by Dr. Arada Osada.
Reproduced from holograph.
Contents: Preludio: night—Death and resurrection.
Composed for: 3 narrators, soprano, alto, tenor, bass, SATB chorus, children's chorus, tape, 3 flutes (2nd–3rd also piccolo, 2nd also alto flute), 3 oboes, 2 clarinets, bass clarinet, 2 bassoons, contrabassoon, 6 horns, 5 trumpets, 5 trombones, tuba, percussion (bass drum, chimes, triangle, 4 suspended cymbals, whip, snare drum, ratchet, glockenspiel, woodblock, maracas, marimba, antique cymbal, iron chains, vibraphone, low gong, guiro, lion's roar, claves, 4 tom-toms), harp, piano (also celesta), violin I, violin II, viola, violoncello, double bass.
Commissioned by: New Symphony Orchestra.
Call no.: **1990/053**

1169. Hosokawa, Toshio, 1955– Vision of Lear: opera in two acts. Mainz: Schott Musik International, 1998.
1 score (235 p.); 42 cm.
English words adapted from William Shakespeare by Tadashi Suzuki.
Composed for: 2 sopranos, alto, 3 tenors, 4 baritones, bass, flute (also piccolo, alto, and bass flutes), clarinet (also bass clarinet), percussion (large bass drum, large tam-tam, 3 suspended cymbals, 4 bongos, antique cymbals, 3 triangles, 4 tom-toms, snare drum, 4 woodblocks, lion's roar, timpani, xylophone, maracas, vibraphone, glockenspiel, tubular bells, 2 gongs, whip), harp, violin I, violin II, viola, violoncello, double bass.
Commissioned by: Landeshauptstadt München.
Call no.: **2000/074**

1170. Hosokawa, Toshio, 1955– Weihnachtskantate: for soprano, alto, chorus and orchestra. Tokyo: Schott Japan, 2002.
1 score (55 p.); 43 cm.
German words; also printed as text.
Duration: ca. 20:00.
Composed for: soprano, alto, 2 SATB choruses, 3 trumpets, 3 trombones, percussion (2 bass drums, 2 tam-tams, 4 Japanese wind chimes, 2 sets of antique cymbals, 4 rins on timpani, tubular bells), 20 violins, 8 violas, 6 violoncellos, 4 double basses.
Commissioned by: Bayerischer Rundfunk.
Call no.: **2005/070**

1171. Hove, Luc van, 1957– Symphony II: opus 34. N. p.: n.p., 1996.

1 score (124 p.); 48 cm.
Reproduced from holograph.
Duration: ca. 30:00.
Composed for: 4 flutes (3rd also alto flute, 4th also piccolo), 4 oboes (3rd also oboe d'amore, 4th also English horn), 4 clarinets (3rd also clarinet in E♭, 4th also bass clarinet), 3 bassoons, contrabassoon, 4 horns, 4 trumpets, 3 trombones, tuba, percussion (timpani, timbales, orchestra bells, xylophone, marimba, 2 tam-tams, 2 gongs, small Chinese cymbal, vibraphone, 3 suspended cymbals, small triangle, 2 bongos, snare drum, tubular bells, bass drum, 4 tom-toms, wood drums), 2 harps, violin I, violin II, viola, violoncello, double bass.
Commissioned by: Konniklÿt Filharmonisch Orkest van Vlaanderen.
Call no.: **1998/164**

1172. Hovhaness, Alan, 1911–2000. Symphony No. 50: "Mount Saint Helens."
Call no.: **1985/089**
No materials available.

1173. Howard, Dean C., 1918– Turnabout: a one act opera. Orchestral score. N.p.: n.p., 1983.
1 score (a–g, 179 p.); 22 x 28 cm.
English words.
Reproduced from holograph.
Composed for: soprano, alto, tenor, baritone, bass, flute, oboe, clarinet, bassoon, horn, trumpet, trombone, tuba, percussion (snare drum, suspended cymbal, timpani, tom-toms, triangle), violin I, violin II, viola, violoncello, double bass.
Call no.: **1985/090**

1174. Howard, Robert Charles, 1943– Sonata: for violin and piano. N.p.: Robert Charles Howard, 1985.
1 score (24 p.); 28 cm.
Reproduced from manuscript.
Composed for: violin, piano.
Call no.: **1986/057**

1175. Howrani, Waleed, 1948– Alma mater: for piano, August, 1998. N.p.: Waleed Howrani, 2001.
22 p. of music; 28 cm.
"Variations on the University of Beirut anthem"—p. 2.
Composed for: piano.
Call no.: **2003/058**

1176. Hsu, Wen-ying, 1909– Cello concerto. N.p.: Hsu, 1978.
1 miniature score (79 leaves); 28 cm.
Reproduced from manuscript.
Composed for: violoncello, 2 flutes, 2 oboes, 2 clarinets, 2 bassoons, 2 horns, trumpet, trombone, timpani, percussion (Chinese bells, 2 cymbals, 3 gongs, Chinese drum), harp, violin I, violin II, viola, violoncello, double bass.
Call no.: **1986/058**

1177. Huang, Joan, 1957– Yang-guan songs: for string quartet. Van Nuys, CA: New Music West, 1993.
1 score (53 p.); 28 cm.
Reproduced from holograph.
Contents: Morning drizzle—Golden heron pagoda—A stream of endless sorrow—Dancing fireflies lantern—Frond on the dark pond—Weeping willow, evergreen fragrance—Prancing sunbeam, gentle breeze—Silver lunar shadows—Foreboding wood.
Composed for: 2 violins, viola, violoncello.
Call no.: **1994/063**

1178. Huang, Tian, 1946– The Yi-mountain: fantasy suite. N.p.: n.p., 1990.
1 score (various pagings); 39 cm.
For orchestra.
Reproduced from manuscript.
Contents: Axi jump for moon—Girl of picking tea—Hunt in forest—The Yi-mountains—Torch festival.
Composed for: piccolo, 2 flutes, 2 oboes, 2 clarinets, 2 bassoons, 4 horns, 2 trumpets, 3 trombones, tuba, timpani, percussion (triangle, tambourine, snare drum, cymbals, vibraphone), harp, piano, violin I, violin II, viola, violoncello, double bass.
Call no.: **1991/056**

1179. Huber, Nicolaus A., 1939– Nocturnes.
Call no.: **1986/059**
No materials available.

1180. Hummel, Bertold, 1925–2002. 3. Sinfonie, op. 100 (1996): Jeremia = Yirmeyah. Partitur. Mainz; New York, NY: Schott, 1997.
1 score (157 p.); 43 cm.
Composed for: 3 flutes (3rd also piccolo), 2 oboes, English horn, 2 clarinets, bass clarinet, 2 bassoons, contrabassoon, 4 horns, 3 trumpets, 3 trombones, tuba, timpani, percussion (triangle, 4 suspended cymbals, fixed cymbal, crash cymbals, tam-tam, gong, glissando gong, anvil, chain, 2 bongos, 2 tom-toms, tambourine, snare drum, tenor drum, bass drum, 2 slit drums, 4 African slit drums, 5 temple blocks, 2 claves, guiro, vibraslap, ratchet, glockenspiel, xylophone, vibraphone, tubular bells), harp, violin I, violin II, viola, violoncello, double bass.
Call no.: **2000/075**

1181. Hundemer, Thomas, 1954– Despujol portraits. N.p.: Thomas H. Hundemer, 1986.
1 score (36 p.); 35 cm.
For orchestra.
Reproduced from manuscript.
Contents: Prologue—Les petites congäis du bon Dieu—Christmas at home—Dans la forêt profonde du Bokkor—Warum nicht!—A maiden wants to take the veil—Farewell to Mabel.
Composed for: flute (also piccolo), oboe, clarinet, bassoon, 2 horns, trumpet, timpani, percussion (bass drum, suspended cymbal, tam-tam, claves, triangle), violin I, violin II, viola, violoncello, double bass.
Call no.: **1989/058**
Re-entered as: **1990/054**

1182. Hundemer, Thomas, 1954– Spring rains. N.p.: n.p., 1991.
1 score (92 p.); 36 cm.
Latin words (last movement only).
For orchestra and soprano (last movement only).
Contents: Spring rains—Intermezzo—Night music—Agnus dei.
Composed for: soprano, flute (also piccolo), oboe, clarinet, bassoon, timpani (also vibraphone), violin I, violin II, viola, violoncello, double bass.
Commissioned by: anonymous patron of Shreveport Symphony Orchestra.
Call no.: **1993/057**

1183. Hus, Walter, 1959– "Francesco's paradox": a song-cycle for counter-tenor and piano. Brussels: Pausa Publishing, 1996.
1 score (57 p.); 30 cm. + 1 booklet (11 leaves; 13 x 24 cm.)
Dutch words; also printed as text with English and French translations in booklet.
"On the cycle of poems Francesco's paradox by Stefan Hertmans."
Composed for: countertenor, piano.
Call no.: **1998/067**

1184. Hus, Walter, 1959– Le miroir: for string quartet. N.p.: Pausa Publishing, 1995.
1 score (39 p.); 30 cm.
Composed for: 2 violins, viola, violoncello.
Commissioned by: Smith Quartet.
Call no.: **2000/076**

1185. Husa, Karel, 1921– Concerto: for violoncello and orchestra (1988). N.p.: Karel Husa, 1988.
1 score (112 p.); 49 cm.
Reproduced from manuscript.
1993 Grawemeyer Award winning work.
Composed for: violoncello, 3 flutes (3rd also piccolo), 3 oboes (3rd also English horn), 2 clarinets, bass clarinet, 2 bassoons, contrabassoon, 4 horns, 3 trumpets, 3 trombones, tuba, timpani, percussion (vibraphone, marimba, xylophone, glockenspiel, chimes, 2 suspended cymbals, 2 crash cymbals, large gong, bass drum, snare drum, tom-toms, temple blocks, woodblocks), 2 harps, violin I, violin II, viola, violoncello, double bass.
Commissioned by: School of Music of University of Southern California.
Call no.: **1992/063**
Re-entered as: **1993/058**

1186. Husa, Karel, 1921– Concerto for orchestra (1986). N.p.: K. Husa, 1986.
1 score (122 p.); 49 cm.
Contents: Cadence—Interlude I—Fantasy—In memoriam—Interlude II—Game.
Composed for: 3 flutes (1st also bass flute, 2nd–3rd also piccolo), 2 oboes, English horn, 2 clarinets, bass clarinet, 3 bassoons (3rd also contrabassoon), 5 horns, 4 trumpets, 3 trombones, tuba, timpani, percussion (vibraphone, marimba, xylophone, glockenspiel, antique cymbal, 2 handbells, 5 tom-toms, temple blocks, snare drum, bass drum, 2 cymbals, 2 suspended cymbals, Gamelan-Javanese gong, gong), 2 harps, piano, violin I, violin II, viola, violoncello, double bass.
Commissioned by: Philharmonic-Symphony Society of New York.
Call no.: **1987/034**
Re-entered as: **1988/052** and **1991/057**

1187. Husa, Karel, 1921– Concerto for trumpet and orchestra. N.p.: Karel Husa, 1987.
1 score (84 p.); 28 cm.
Reproduced from manuscript.
Composed for: trumpet, 2 flutes (2nd also piccolo), 2 oboes, 2 clarinets in A (2nd also bass clarinet), 2 bassoons (2nd also contrabassoon), 2 horns, 2 trumpets, timpani, percussion (vibraphone, xylophone, glockenspiel, chimes, suspended cymbal, gong, temple blocks, snare drum, bass drum), 2 harps, violin I, violin II, viola, violoncello, double bass.
Commissioned by: Chicago Symphony Orchestra.
Call no.: **1989/059**

1188. Hush, David, 1956– Sonata for violin solo. N.p.: David Hush, 1996.
7 p. of music; 28 cm.
Duration: 16:07.
Composed for: violin.
Call no.: **1997/064**
Re-entered as: **1998/187**

1189. Hutcheson, Jere T., 1938– Caricatures: for wind symphony. N.p.: n.p., 1997.
1 score (85 p.); 44 cm.
Duration: 22:00.
Program notes by the composer.
Composed for: 3 flutes, 2 oboes, English horn, clarinet in E♭, 3 clarinets, bass clarinet, contrabass clarinet, 2 bassoons, contrabassoon, soprano saxophone, alto saxophone, tenor saxophone, baritone saxophone, bass saxophone, 3 trumpets, 4 horns, 3 trombones, euphonium, tuba, piano, percussion (xylophone, crotales, amplified log drum, tambourine, marimba, snare drum, triangle, vibraphone, hi-hat, bass drum, 2 floor tom-toms, 2 amplified congas, 2 suspended cymbals, metal plate, slapstick, Jew's harp, prize fight bell, pistol, temple blocks, siren, timpani, tam-tam, crash cymbals).
Commissioned by: Michigan State University Wind Symphony.
Call no.: **1998/068**

1190. Hutcheson, Jere T., 1938– Concerto for piano and wind orchestra. N.p.: J. Hutcheson, 1981.
1 score (156 p.); 48 cm.
Reproduced from manuscript.
Duration: ca. 27:00.
Composed for: piano, 3 flutes (3rd also piccolo), 2 oboes, English horn, clarinet in E♭, 3 clarinets, bass clarinet, soprano saxophone, alto saxophone, tenor saxophone, baritone saxophone, 2 bassoons, 4 horns, 3 trumpets, 2 trombones, bass trombone, tuba, percussion (timpani, cymbal on timpani, crotales, suspended cymbal, xylophone, orchestra bells).
Call no.: **1985/091**

1191. Hutcheson, Jere T., 1938– Dance of time: for large orchestra. N.p.: Jere Hutcheson, 1995.
1 score (vi, 223 p.); 44 cm.
Duration: 55:00.
"Inspired by the poetry of John Calvin Gore"—p. i.
Includes program notes by the composer, with poetry by John Calvin Gore.
Composed for: 4 flutes (3rd–4th also piccolo), alto flute, 4 oboes, English horn, clarinet in E♭, 3 clarinets, bass clarinet, 4 bassoons, contrabassoon, 6 horns, 6 trumpets, 2 trombones, 2 bass trombones, 2 tubas, timpani, percussion (glockenspiel, xylophone, vibraphone, chimes, temple blocks, hi-hat, triangle, siren whistle, tam-tam, 2 anvils, 3 suspended cymbals), piano, violin I, violin II, viola, violoncello, double bass.
Call no.: **1996/062**

1192. Hyla, Lee, 1952– Lives of the saints. N.p.: n.p., 2000.
1 score (2 v.); 37 cm.
English and Italian words.
Songs for mezzo-soprano with chamber ensemble.
Reproduced from holograph.
Texts by Dante, St. Jerome, St. Teresa of Avila, and from the Golden legend.
Composed for: mezzo-soprano, flute (also bass flute), clarinet (also bass clarinet), violin, viola, violoncello, piano, percussion (bongos, congas, pedal bass drum, suspended cymbal, hi-hat, 5 roto-toms, hammered dulcimer, crotales).
Commissioned by: Barlow Foundation.
Call no.: **2002/089**

1193. Hyla, Lee, 1952– Violin concerto (2001). N.p.: n.p., 2001.
1 score (92 p.); 36 cm.
Duration: ca. 21:00.
Composed for: violin, 2 flutes (1st also piccolo), 2 oboes, 2 clarinets (1st also bass clarinet), 2 bassoons (1st also contrabassoon), 2 horns, 2 trumpets, trombone, percussion (bongos, congas, talking drum, pedal bass drum, woodblocks, tambourine, large suspended cymbal, ride cymbal, hi-hat cymbal, gong, 6 roto-toms, 7 crotales, hammered dulcimer, xylophone, marimba), harp, piano, violin I, violin II, viola, violoncello, double bass.
Call no.: **2005/071**

1194. Iannaccone, Anthony, 1943– Night rivers: symphony no. 3. Bryn Mawr, PA: Tenuto Publications: T. Presser Co., 1992.
1 score (101 p.); 28 cm.
"Perusal score."
Duration: 18:30.
Composed for: 3 flutes (3rd also piccolo), 2 oboes, 2 clarinets, bass clarinet, 2 bassoons, 4 horns, 3 trumpets, 3 trombones, tuba, timpani, percussion (marimba, xylophone, small triangle, large tam-tam, suspended cymbal), harp, piano, celesta, violin I, violin II, viola, violoncello, double bass.
Commissioned by: Michigan Council for the Arts.
Call no.: **1994/064**

1195. Iannaccone, Anthony, 1943– String quartet no. 3. N.p.: Tenuto Publications; Bryn Mawr, PA: T. Presser, 1999.
1 score (60 p.); 28 cm.
Includes biographical note about composer.
Duration: ca. 30:00.
Composed for: 2 violins, viola, violoncello.
Commissioned by: Michigan Council for Arts and Cultural Affairs and Eastern Michigan University.
Call no.: **2002/090**

1196. Iannaccone, Anthony, 1943– Two-piano inventions. N.p.: Henmar Press; New York, NY: C. F. Peters, 1990.
1 score (62 p.); 36 cm.
Duration: ca. 20:00.
"Inter-American Music Awards, published by C. F. Peters Corporation under the sponsorship of Sigma Alpha Iota."—cover.
Contents: Shadows and reflections—Currents.
Composed for: 2 pianos.
Commissioned by: Lyric Chamber Ensemble.
Call no.: **1991/058**

1197. Ichiba, Kōsuke, 1910– Symphony. Tokyo: n.p., 1982.
1 score (63 p.); 30 cm. + 43 parts; 32 cm.
Reproduced from holograph.
Duration: ca. 23:00.
English and Japanese notes.
Composed for: 2 flutes (2nd also piccolo), 2 oboes (2nd also English horn), 2 clarinets, 2 bassoons, 4 horns, 2 trumpets, 3 trombones, tuba, timpani, percussion (cymbals, triangle, xylophone, tom-toms, 2 bongos, side drum, tam-tam, bass drum), violin I, violin II, viola, violoncello, double bass.
Call no.: **1985/092**

1198. Ichiba, Kōsuke, 1910– Symphony. Tokyo, Japan: Japan Federation of Composers, 1984.
1 score (63 p.); 31 cm.
Biographical and historical notes in English and Japanese.
Reproduced from holograph.
Composed for: 2 flutes (2nd also piccolo), 2 oboes (2nd also English horn), 2 clarinets, 2 bassoons, 4 horns, 2 trumpets, 3 trombones, tuba, timpani, percussion (cymbals, triangle, xylophone, tom-toms, 2 bongos, side drum, tam-tam, bass drum), violin I, violin II, viola, violoncello, double bass.
Call no.: **1985/092a**

1199. Ichikawa, Toshiharu, 1912–1998. Piano concerto: theme and five developments in ryo-mode. Tokyo, Japan: Kyogei Music Publishers, 198-?.
1 score (99 p.); 36 cm.
Includes historical information in English.
Composed for: piano, 3 flutes (3rd also piccolo), 2 oboes (2nd also English horn), 2 clarinets (2nd also clarinet in E♭), 2 bassoons, 4 horns, 3 trumpets, 2 trombones, tuba, timpani, percussion (snare drum, tenor drum, bass drum, cymbals, tam-tam, glockenspiel), violin I, violin II, viola, violoncello, double bass, piano.
Call no.: **1985/093**

1200. Ichikawa, Toshiharu, 1912–1998. Symphonic movement: Gyō-no-shō. Tokyo: Kyogei Music, 1978.
1 score (112 p.); 36 cm.
For orchestra.
Composed for: piccolo, 3 flutes, 2 oboes, English horn, 2 clarinets, bass clarinet, 2 bassoons, contrabassoon, 4 horns, 3 trumpets, 3 trombones, tuba, timpani, percussion (snare drum, tenor drum, bass drum, 3 tom-toms, triangle, cymbals, glockenspiel), 2 harps, piano, violin I, violin II, viola, violoncello, double bass.
Call no.: **1994/065**

1201. Ichikawa, Toshiharu, 1912–1998. Violin concerto. N.p.: Kyogei Music Publishers, 198-?.
1 score (136 p.); 37 cm.
Composed for: violin, 3 flutes (3rd also piccolo), 3 oboes (3rd also English horn), 2 clarinets (2nd also bass clarinet), 2 bassoons, 4 horns, 2 trumpets, 2 trombones, tuba, timpani, percussion (snare drum, tenor drum, bass drum, cymbals, 3 tom-toms, tam-tam, triangle, tambourine, vibraphone), 2 harps, celesta, violin I, violin II, viola, violoncello, double bass.
Commissioned by: NHK FM Radio.
Call no.: **1986/060**

1202. Igoa, Enrique, 1958– Sueños fluviales: (cuarteto no. 1): para cuaarteto de cuerda, op. 30. Madrid: n.p., 1996.
1 score (36 p.); 30 cm.
For string quartet.
Duration: ca. 24:00.
Composed for: 2 violins, viola, violoncello.
Commissioned by: Centro para la Difusión de la Música Contemporánea.
Call no.: **1998/069**

1203. Ikramova, Anna, 1966– Ein Lied mit Folgen: szenisches Streichquartett mit Sprecher und Lautsprechern (1994–1996). Saarbrücken: PFAU-Verlag, 1998.
1 score (ca. 62 leaves); 21 x 30 cm.
German words.
Composed for: 2 violins, viola, violoncello, narrator, loudspeakers.
Call no.: **2001/076**

1204. Imbrie, Andrew, 1921– Dream sequence. N.p.: n.p., 1986.
1 score (61 p.); 28 cm.
Reproduced from holograph.
At end: Berkeley, June 17, 1986.
Duration: ca. 17:00.
Composed for: flute (also piccolo), oboe (also English

horn), clarinet (also bass clarinet), violin, viola, violoncello, piano, percussion (vibraphone, marimba, 7 drums, suspended cymbal, tam-tam).
Commissioned by: Frank Taplin.
Call no.: **1987/035**

1205. Imbrie, Andrew, 1921– Requiem. N.p.: n.p., 1984.
1 score (187 p.); 44 cm.
English and Latin words.
Reproduced from holograph.
Composed for: soprano, SATB chorus, 3 flutes (3rd also piccolo), 2 oboes, English horn, 2 clarinets, bass clarinet, 3 bassoons (3rd also contrabassoon), 4 horns, 3 trumpets, 3 trombones, tuba, timpani, percussion (glockenspiel, marimba, xylophone, timpani, crotales, 7 drums, tambourine, bass drum, tam-tam, 3 cymbals), harp, celesta, mandolin, violin I, violin II, viola, violoncello, double bass.
Commissioned by: San Francisco Symphony.
Call no.: **1988/053**
Re-entered as: **1989/060**

1206. Ince, Kamran, 1960– Fest: for new music ensemble and orchestra. Paoli, PA: European American Music, 1998.
1 score (107 p.); 36 cm.
Composed for: alto saxophone (also air raid siren), tenor saxophone (also clarinet), synthesizer, electric guitar, electric bass guitar, amplified violin, amplified violoncello, percussion (bass drum, 2 crotales, mini splash cymbal, glockenspiel, marimba, timpani, tam-tam), 2 flutes (2nd also piccolo), 2 oboes, 2 clarinets (1st also clarinet in E♭, 2nd also bass clarinet), 2 bassoons, 4 horns, 2 trumpets, trombone, bass trombone, violin I, violin II, viola, violoncello, double bass.
Commissioned by: Meet-the-Composer/Reader's Digest.
Call no.: **2000/077**

1207. Ince, Kamran, 1960– Symphony no. 3: siege of Vienna. N.p.: n.p., 1995.
1 score (119 p.); 36 cm.
For orchestra with synthesizer and electric bass.
Duration: ca. 28:00.
Composed for: 3 flutes (2nd–3rd also piccolo), 2 oboes, English horn, 2 clarinets (both also clarinet in E♭), clarinet in A, bass clarinet (also tenor saxophone), 3 bassoons (3rd also contrabassoon), 4 horns (all also tenor Wagner tubas), 3 trumpets (3rd also piccolo trumpet), 2 trombones, bass trombone, tuba, percussion (bass drum, vibraphone, glockenspiel, xylophone, marimba, suspended metal plate, high triangle, 3 tom-toms, medium bongo, snare drum, high bongo, low tom-tom, timpani, 2 brake drums, tenor drum), piano, synthesizer, electric bass, violin I, violin II, viola, violoncello, double bass.
Commissioned by: Albany Symphony Orchestra.
Call no.: **1998/070**

1208. Isopp, Werner, 1967– Jugendmesse: für grossen Chor und Instrumental, op. 112. Klagenfurt: Werner Isopp, 1996.
1 score (115 p. in various pagings); 30 cm.
Primarily German words.
Composed for: SATB chorus, flute, soprano saxophone, alto saxophone, piano, double bass (also electric bass), drums.
Call no.: **1997/065**

1209. Ivey, Jean Eichelberger, 1923– Forms in motion: a symphony in 3 movements. N.p.: n.p., 1972.
1 score (107 p.); 44 cm.
Reproduced from manuscript.
Duration: ca. 25:00.
Composed for: 2 flutes, alto flute (also piccolo), 2 oboes, English horn, 2 clarinets, bass clarinet, 3 bassoons (also contrabassoon), 4 horns, 3 trumpets, 2 trombones, bass trombone, tuba, timpani, percussion (xylophone, tubular bells, 3 temple blocks, snare drum, glockenspiel, tam-tam, suspended cymbal, bass drum, triangle), harp, piano (also celesta), violin I, violin II, viola, violoncello, double bass.
Call no.: **1995/045**

1210. Ivey, Jean Eichelberger, 1923– Notes toward time: mezzo-soprano, flute/alto flute, harp. N.p.: n.p., 1984.
1 score (27 p.); 37 cm.
Words by Josephine Jacobsen; also printed as text.
At end: January, 1984 New York City.
Reproduced from holograph.
Contents: The clock—The night watchman—It is the season.
Composed for: mezzo-soprano, flute (also alto flute), harp.
Commissioned by: Chamber Music Society of Baltimore.
Call no.: **1985/094**

1211. Ivey, Jean Eichelberger, 1923– Voyager: for solo cello and orchestra. New York, NY: C. Fischer, 1987.
1 score (133 p.); 47 cm.
Reproduced from holograph.
At end: July 3, 1987, New York City.
Duration: ca. 25:00.
"Supported by fellowships from the National Endow-

ment for the Arts and the John Simon Guggenheim Memorial Foundation."
Composed for: violoncello, piccolo, 2 flutes, 2 oboes, English horn, 2 clarinets, bass clarinet, 2 bassoons, contrabassoon, 4 horns, timpani, percussion (glockenspiel, tubular bells, bass drum, woodblock, glass chimes, tam-tam), 2 harps, celesta, violin I, violin II, viola, violoncello, double bass.
Call no.: **1992/064**
Re-entered as: **1994/066**

1212. Jacobs, Kenneth Allan, 1948– Passage to honor house: [for] computer synthesized tape. N.p.: n.p., 1988.
1 v. (various pagings); 28 cm.
"Digital synthesized sounds are coupled with 320 artwork projections that are exhibited synchronously with the music, controlled by an inaudible tape track"—Title page verso.
Nonstandard notation.
Duration: 1:05:00.
Contents: Choices—Age of innocence—Little ones—Obstacles—Labyrinth—Through the cracks—The road ahead—Darkness—In search of wisdom—The battle within—Despair—A vision—Time machine—Transformation.
Composed for: prerecorded tape.
Call no.: **1991/059**

1213. Jacobs, Lawrence A., 1969– Multitudinous seas incarnadine: the Macbeth overture. N.p.: Lawrence A. Jacobs, 1991.
1 score (49 p.); 36 cm.
For orchestra.
Composed for: 2 flutes, horn, breath organ, zing, brass (unspecified), timpani, percussion (bass drum, snare drum, chimes), synthesizer, strings (unspecified).
Call no.: **1992/065**

1214. Jaffe, Stephen, 1954– Concerto: for violin and orchestra. King of Prussia, PA: Merion Music: Theodore Presser, 1999.
1 score (166 p.); 43 cm.
"Corrected 12/99"—p. 3.
Reproduced from manuscript.
Duration: ca. 35:00.
Composed for: violin, 3 flutes (3rd also piccolo), 2 oboes (2nd also English horn), 2 clarinets (2nd also bass clarinet), 2 bassoons, 4 horns, 2 trumpets, trombone, bass trombone, harp, piano (also celesta), percussion (marimba, Jamaican steel drums, 2 suspended cymbals, maracas, temple blocks, bass drum, cowbell, tubular bells, gong, tam-tam, 3 tom-toms, log drum, lujan, finger cymbals, small snare drum, xylophone, glockenspiel, 3 brake drums, tabla, cabasa, triangle, 6 crotales), violin I, violin II, viola, violoncello, double bass.
Call no.: **2002/091**
Re-entered as: **2005/072**

1215. Jaffe, Stephen, 1954– Songs of turning: cantata for soprano and baritone soloists, chorus, and chamber orchestra. Full score. N.p.: S. Jaffe, 1996.
1 score (9, 136 p.); 44 cm.
English words; also printed as text.
Duration: 25:10.
Composed for: soprano, baritone, SATB chorus, flute, oboe, 3 clarinets (3rd also bass clarinet), horn, percussion (marimba, vibraphone, glockenspiel, small gong, maracas, crotales, ting sha), harp, violin I, violin II, viola, violoncello, double bass.
Commissioned by: Fromm Music Foundation, Harvard University, and Oregon Bach Festival.
Call no.: **1997/066**

1216. Jager, Robert E., 1939– Lysistrata: a musical/theater piece. N.p.: n.p., 1991.
1 score (330 p.); 44 cm.
English words by the composer.
Original work by Aristophanes.
Reproduced from manuscript.
Composed for: soprano, boy soprano, 2 mezzo-sopranos, contralto, tenor, 2 baritones, bass-baritone, SATB chorus, flute, oboe, clarinet, bassoon, horn, trumpet, trombone, electric bass guitar, 2 synthesizers, percussion (suspended cymbal, snare drum, tambourine, triangle, hi-hat, woodblock, bell tree, bass drum, xylophone, timpani, tam-tam, tom-toms, brake drum).
Call no.: **1993/059**

1217. Jankowski, Loretta, 1950– Paterson songs. N.p.: n.p., 1984.
1 score (65 p.); 28 cm.
"Text from William Carlos Williams' Paterson."
At end: January 1984.
Reproduced from holograph.
Duration: ca. 35:00.
Contents: It is dangerous—In old age—Sing me a song—Joslted—We sit and talk—Peer of the gods—The descent.
Composed for: tenor, flute, clarinet, violin, violoncello, piano.
Commissioned by: New Jersey Chamber Music Society.
Call no.: **1985/095**

1218. Jarrell, Michael, 1958– Cassandre. [French]. Paris: Editions Henry Lemoine, 1993.

1 score (187 p.); 30 cm.
French words.
Monodrama for actress (narrator), chamber orchestra, and electronics.
Text based on book by Christa Wolf.
Composed for: narrator, keyboard sampler, flute, oboe, clarinet, bass clarinet, bassoon, 2 horns, trumpet, trombone, percussion (3 tam-tams, 3 cymbals, 2 spring coils, Chinese cymbal, bass drum, 5 tom-toms, 4 bongos, marimba, tubular bells, crotales, vibraphone, small triangle, mark tree, Japanese rin, 3 woodblocks, 4 maracas, 4 bongos, 4 temple blocks, snare drum, gongs, timbales), piano, violin I, violin II, viola, violoncello, double bass.
Commissioned by: Fondation Pro Helvetia and Théatre du Chatelet.
Call no.: **1997/067 French**

1219. Jarrell, Michael, 1958– Kassandra: Monodram. Paris: Editions Henry Lemoine, 1996.
1 score (187 p.); 30 cm.
German words.
For actress (narrator), chamber orchestra, and electronics.
Text based on book by Christa Wolf.
Composed for: narrator, keyboard sampler, flute, oboe, clarinet, bass clarinet, bassoon, 2 horns, trumpet, trombone, percussion (3 tam-tams, 3 cymbals, 2 spring coils, Chinese cymbal, bass drum, 5 tom-toms, 4 bongos, marimba, tubular bells, crotales, vibraphone, small triangle, mark tree, Japanese rin, 3 woodblocks, 4 maracas, 4 bongos, 4 temple blocks, snare drum, gongs, timbales), piano, violin I, violin II, viola, violoncello, double bass.
Commissioned by: Fondation Pro Helvetia and Théatre du Chatelet.
Call no.: **1997/067 German**

1220. Jarrett, Jack Marius, 1934– Offering/pooja. N.p.: n.p., 1998.
1 score (56 p.); 28 cm.
Contents: Nectar = Panchamrutham—Mystical fire = Karpooram—Parting gift = Phamboolam.
Composed for: violin, oboe, piano, percussion (suspended cymbal, cabasa, woodblock), 2 violins, viola, violoncello, bamboo flute, mridanram, ghatham.
Commissioned by: Patricia Gray and National Musical Arts.
Call no.: **2000/078**

1221. Jeney, Zoltán, 1943– Halotti szertartás = Funeral rite. Partitura. N.p.: n.p., 2000.
1 score (3 v.); 43 cm.
Principally Latin, some Hungarian words.
For soli, mixed chorus, and orchestra.
Contents: Commendatio animæ—Vesperæ mortuorum—Vigilia defunctorum.
Composed for: mezzo-soprano, contralto, tenor, baritone, bass, SATB chorus, 4 flutes (2nd and 4th also alto flute, 2nd–3rd also piccolo, 4th also bass flute), 4 oboes (4th also English horn), 5 clarinets (2nd also basset clarinet, 3rd also clarinet in E♭, 4th–5th also bass clarinet), soprano saxophone, alto saxophone, tenor saxophone, bass saxophone, 3 bassoons, contrabassoon, 6 horns, 4 trumpets, bass trumpet, 3 trombones (all also bass trombone), tuba, timpani, percussion (12 tom-toms, 5 claves, 5 crotales, 9 gongs, 2 tam-tam, bells, vibraphone, 8 marble slabs, 8 woodblocks, 8 temple blocks, 8 maracas, 8 cowbells, 8 triangles, 8 temple gongs, 4 suspended cymbals, 2 marimbas, bass marimba, 2 ratchets, piccolo snare drum, 2 thundersheets), celesta, harp, cimbalom, piano, violin I, violin II, viola, violoncello, double bass.
Call no.: **2002/092**

1222. Jenkins, Joseph Willcox, 1928– A shabbat service: opus 168. N.p.: n.p., 1994?.
1 score (90 p.); 28 cm.
Hebrew words (romanized).
Reproduced from manuscript.
Contents: Prelude—Opening anthem: schachar avakeshcha—Sim shalom I—Sim shalom II—Interlude: meditation—Yi h′yu l′ratzon—Ein kamocha: av harachamim—L′cha adonai—Hodo al eretz—Eta chayim: hashiveinu—Adon olam.
Composed for: SATB chorus, organ, flute (also piccolo), 2 violins, viola, violoncello.
Commissioned by: Rodef Shalom Congregation, Pittsburgh, PA.
Call no.: **1996/063**

1223. Jevtic, Ivan, 1947– Concerto pour violoncelle.
Call no.: **1985/096**
No materials available.

1224. Jin, Xiang, 1935– Opera: savage land. N.p.: n.p., 1990.
1 score (314 p.); 28 cm.
Chinese words by Wan Fang.
Reproduced from manuscript.
Composed for: voices, piccolo, 2 flutes, 2 oboes, 2 clarinets, 2 bassoons, 4 horns, 2 trumpets, 3 trombones, percussion (timpani, cymbals, snare drum, bass drum, triangle, bell, tam-tam, chimes, vibraphone), harp, piano, violin I, violin II, viola, violoncello, double bass.
Call no.: **1992/066**

1225. Jin, Xiang, 1935– Opera "savage land." N.p.: n.p., 198-?.
1 score (4 v. [314 leaves]); 27 cm.
Chinese words by Wan Fang.
Reproduced from manuscript.
Composed for: voices, piccolo, 2 flutes, 2 oboes, 2 clarinets, 2 bassoons, 4 horns, 2 trumpets, 3 trombones, percussion (timpani, cymbals, snare drum, bass drum, triangle, bell, tam-tam, chimes, vibraphone), harp, piano, violin I, violin II, viola, violoncello, double bass.
Call no.: **1988/054**
Re-entered as: **1989/061**
Also available:
Call no.: **1989/061 libretto**

1226. Jirásek, Jan, 1955– Missa propria: "renaissance of humanity." Eslohe: Erdenklang Musikverlag, 1994.
1 score (51 leaves); 30 cm.
Latin words.
Composed for: SATB chorus or boys' chorus.
Call no.: **1995/046**

1227. Johnson, Tom, 1939– Bonhoeffer Oratorium. Paris: Editions 75, 1992.
1 score (3 v.); 42 cm.
German words by Dietrich Bonhoeffer.
For 4 soloists, 2 choirs, and orchestra.
Reproduced from manuscript.
Contents: Frühe Predigten—Ein Jahr (1933–34)—Die nachfolgenden Jahre—Letzte Worte.
Composed for: soprano, mezzo-soprano, tenor, baritone, 2 SATB choruses, 2 flutes, 2 oboes, 2 alto saxophones, tenor saxophone, baritone saxophone, 2 trumpets, 2 trombones, percussion (cymbals, claves, tom-tom, bass drum, triangle, xylophone, timpani, chimes, suspended cymbal, bongos, snare drum), violin I, violin II, viola, violoncello, double bass.
Call no.: **2000/079**
Re-entered as: **2001/077**

1228. Johnston, Ben, 1926– String quartet no. 9. N.p.: Smith Publications, 1988.
1 score (31 leaves); 28 cm.
Reproduced from manuscript.
Composed for: 2 violins, viola, violoncello.
Commissioned by: Friends of Stanford String Quartet.
Call no.: **1989/062**

1229. Jones, Robert W., 1932– Concerto: for viola and orchestra. N.p.: n.p., 1984.
1 score (73 p.); 28 cm.
Reproduced from holograph.
Composed for: viola, piccolo, 2 flutes, 2 oboes, 2 clarinets, bass clarinet, 2 bassoons, 4 horns, 2 trumpets, timpani, percussion (orchestra bells, suspended cymbal, vibraphone, glockenspiel, xylophone, wind chimes, triangle, tambourine, snare drum, siren, whip, cymbals), 2 harps, celesta, violin I, violin II, viola, violoncello, double bass.
Call no.: **1990/055**

1230. Jones, Samuel, 1935– Symphony no. 3: Palo Duro Canyon: for symphony orchestra. Study score. N.p.: Campanile Music; New York, NY: Carl Fischer, 1992.
1 score (98 p.); 36 cm.
Duration: 23:00.
Composed for: 3 flutes (3rd also piccolo), 3 oboes (3rd also English horn), 3 clarinets (3rd also bass clarinet), 2 bassoons, contrabassoon, 4 horns, 3 trumpets, 2 trombones, bass trombone, tuba, timpani, percussion (2 snare drums, bass drum, chimes, bells, xylophone, cymbals, suspended cymbal, 2 gongs, tambourine, triangle, bundle of sticks, tom-tom, claves, wind [prerecorded], celesta), harp, violin I, violin II, viola, violoncello, double bass.
Commissioned by: Amarillo Symphony Orchestra.
Call no.: **1994/067**

1231. Jones, Samuel, 1935– The temptation of Jesus: an oratorio. Study score. New York, NY: Campanile Music Press: Carl Fischer, 1995.
1 score (256 p.); 36 cm.
English words.
"Text taken from the Holy Scriptures and from writings of Thomas Merton."
Duration: 1:13:00.
Composed for: bass, SATB chorus, children's chorus, 2 flutes (2nd also piccolo), 2 oboes (2nd also English horn), 2 clarinets (2nd also bass clarinet), 2 bassoons, 2 horns, 2 trumpets, 2 trombones, bass trombone, timpani, percussion, celesta, harp, violin I, violin II, viola, violoncello, double bass.
Commissioned by: Second Presbyterian Church of Richmond, VA.
Call no.: **1996/064**
Also available:
Call no.: **1996/064 libretto**

1232. Jong, Hans de, 1957– Kurban bayrami: trombone—4. N.p.: n.p., 1989.
1 score (ii, 11 leaves); 42 cm.
"Turks offerfeest"—leaf ii.
Duration: 8:30.
Composed for: 4 trombones.
Call no.: **1995/019**

1233. Joseph, David, 1954– Concerto: for solo piano and orchestra, 1996. N.p.: n.p., 1996.
1 score (169 p.); 30 cm.
Reproduced from manuscript.
Composed for: piano, 3 flutes (2nd–3rd also piccolo), 3 oboes (3rd also English horn), 3 clarinets (3rd also bass clarinet), 3 bassoons (3rd also contrabassoon), 4 horns, 3 trumpets (1st also piccolo trumpet in D), 2 trombones, bass trombone, tuba, timpani, percussion (2 vibraphones, large suspended cymbal, triangle, glockenspiel, tam-tam, bass drum, cymbals), harp, violin I, violin II, viola, violoncello, double bass.
Call no.: **1998/071**

1234. Joseph, David, 1954– Rhapsody: for piano solo. N.p.: n.p., 1997.
59 p. of music; 30 cm.
Reproduced from manuscript.
Composed for: piano.
Call no.: **2000/080**

1235. Kaczynski, Adam, 1933– Shape: in 10 parts for two pianos. N.p.: n.p., 1989.
1 score (43 leaves); 30 x 42 cm.
Reproduced from holograph.
Composed for: 2 pianos.
Call no.: **1990/056**

1236. Kagel, Mauricio, 1931– . . . den 24. xii. 1931: Verstümmelte Nachrichten: für Bariton und Instrumente, 1988–91. Partitur. Frankfurt; New York, NY: Litolff/Peters, 1991.
1 score (iv, 142 p.); 35 cm.
German words from newspaper reports of Dec. 24, 1931, assembled by the composer; also printed as text.
Performance instructions in German.
String parts may be expanded.
Duration: ca. 24:00.
Composed for: baritone, violin, viola, violoncello, double bass, piano (4 hands), percussion (pipes, chimes, sizzle cymbal, sack with broken glass, wooden box, uchiwa-daiko, hi-hat, 5 temple blocks, marimba, police siren, 2 Chinese opera gongs, 3 triangles, 7 tom-toms, kakko drum, 2 snare drums, 2 bass drums, tambourine, 2 ship's bells, iron chains, pocket metronome, whistle, iron arrow, pea whistle, t'ao ku, tou ku, 2 boots, pair of shoes, crank siren, lightning, 4 cowbells, 2 Chinese cymbals, tam-tam, 3 temple blocks, 2 gongs).
Commissioned by: Südwestfunk Baden-Baden.
Call no.: **1993/060**

1237. Kagel, Mauricio, 1931– III. Streichquartet: in vier Sätzen, 1986–87. Partitur. Frankfurt; New York, NY: Litoff/Peters, 1988.
1 score (80 p.); 34 cm.
Reproduced from manuscript.
Duration: ca. 25:30.
Composed for: 2 violins, viola, violoncello.
Commissioned by: Henie-Onstad Stiftung.
Call no.: **1989/063**

1238. Kagel, Mauricio, 1931– Ein Brief: Konzertszene für Mezzosopran und Orchester, 1985–86. Partitur. Frankfurt; New York, NY: H. Litolff's Verlag/C. F. Peters, 1986.
1 score (28 p.); 34 cm.
German words.
Reproduced from holograph.
Duration: ca. 7:45.
Composed for: mezzo-soprano, alto flute, oboe d'amore, 2 clarinets, bass clarinet, 4 horns, timpani, percussion (vibraphone, bass drum, 2 crash cymbals, wood hammer, 4 tom-toms, sheet of paper), 2 pianos, violin I, violin II, viola I, viola II, violoncello I, violoncello II, double bass I, double bass II.
Commissioned by: Philharmonisches Staatsorchester Hamburg.
Call no.: **1987/036**

1239. Kagel, Mauricio, 1931– Entführung im Konzertsaal: musikalischer Bericht eines Vorfalls, 1998/99. Partitur. Frankfurt/M.; New York, NY: Henry Litolff's Verlag/C. F. Peters, 2000.
1 score (232 p.); 41 cm.
German words.
Concert opera for solo tenor, mixed choir, orchestra, and loudspeaker playback.
Duration: ca. 52:00.
Performance instructions in German and English.
Composed for: tenor, SATB chorus, 2 flutes (both also piccolo and alto flute), 2 clarinets (2nd also clarinet in E♭), bass clarinet, soprano saxophone (also alto, tenor and baritone saxophones), 2 horns, 2 trumpets, 2 trombones, tuba, percussion (bass drum, tambourine, mounted tambourine, marimba, 3 cymbals, 2 tam-tams, 2 guiros, 2 pairs of bongos, 2 pairs of timbales, tubular bells, 2 hand cymbals, whip, Indian bells, brass container, empty glass, telephone bell, vibraphone, 6 woodblocks, hi-hat, sizzle cymbal, side drum, 4 timpani, celesta, 2 vibraslap, 2 congas, chest and three large wooden balls, large sheet of paper), harp, piano, loudspeaker playback, 4 violins, 3 violoncellos, 2 double basses.
Commissioned by: European Concert Hall Organisation (ECHO).
Call no.: **2004/057**

1240. Kagel, Mauricio, 1931– Études für grosses Orchester Nr. 1, 2, 3. Partitur. Frankfurt; New York, NY: Henry Litolff's Verlag/C. F. Peters, 1993.
1 score (166 p.); 31 cm.
Duration: 26:30.
Composed for: 4 flutes (all also piccolo and alto flute), 3 oboes, English horn, 3 clarinets, bass clarinet, 3 bassoons, contrabassoon (also bassoon), 4 horns, 4 trumpets, 3 trombones, tuba, timpani, percussion (tambourine, snare drums, 5 woodblocks, 3 triangles, 13 antique cymbals, large sizzle cymbal, Chinese cymbal, vibraslaps, 2 maracas, marimba, tubular bells, 2 claves, tenor drum, large suspended cymbal, 2 congas, 3 suspended cymbals, vibraphone, 2 gongs, large cymbal pair, 2 castanets, glockenspiel, 5 tom-toms, 2 tam-tams, 2 sandpaper blocks, sleigh bells), harp, piano, celesta, violin I, violin II, viola, violoncello, double bass.
Call no.: **1998/072**

1241. Kagel, Mauricio, 1931– Das Konzert: für Soloflöte, Harfe, Schlagzeug und Streicher. Frankfurt/M.; New York, NY: Henry Litolff's Verlag/C. F. Peters, 2004.
1 score (152 p.); 33 cm.
"11/2003; mit Korr 12/2003; 1/2004."
Composed for: flute (also piccolo and alto flute), harp, percussion (2 congas, 5 temple blocks, vibraphone, 4 triangles, marimba, 3 low gongs (or tam-tams), suspended Chinese cymbal), violin I, violin II, viola, violoncello, double bass.
Commissioned by: Kunststifung NRW.
Call no.: **2005/073**

1242. Kagel, Mauricio, 1931– Der mündliche Verrat = La trahison orale: ein Musikepos über den Teufel, 1981–1983. Pariser Fassung. Partitur. Frankfurt; New York, NY: Henry Litolff's Verlag: Peters, 1983?.
1 score (449 p.); 34 cm.
German words.
A "musical epic" for 3 speakers/actors and 7 instrumentalists.
Libretto by the composer after Les Evangiles du Diable, selon la croyance populaire, ed. by Claude Seignolla.
Reproduced from manuscript.
Duration: ca. 1:30:00.
Composed for: 3 narrators, violin (also viola and cymbals), double bass (also maracas), tuba (also cow horn and tubo), piano (also electric organ), percussion (cymbals, 13 antique cymbals, box with glass shards, hunting horn, marimba, 2 ratchets, cabasa, xylophone, tam-tam, balloon, friction drum, 2 congas, 8 cowbells, bass drum, gong, woodblock, 2 coconut halves, electric bell, bull roarer, 3 iron chains, guiro, church bell, thundersheet, 2 hand cymbals, chimes, tubo, glockenspiel, wind machine, tom-tom, musical saw, anvil, toy lyre, suspended cymbals, claves).
Commissioned by: Festival d'Automne, Paris.
Call no.: **1988/055**

1243. Kagel, Mauricio, 1931– Orchestrion-Straat: für Kammerensemble. Partitur. Frankfurt/M.; New York, NY: H. Litolff's Verlag/C. F. Peters, 1996.
1 score (161 p.); 30 cm.
"Aufführungsmaterial"—p. 1 of cover.
Duration: ca. 23:00.
Composed for: 2 flutes (both also piccolo), 2 clarinets, alto saxophone, 2 trumpets, 2 tubas, percussion (xylophone, snare drum, sleigh bells, hi-hat, vibraphone, bass drum, brass collection box), accordion, piano, 2 violins, 2 violoncellos, 2 double basses.
Commissioned by: Holland Festival.
Call no.: **1997/068**

1244. Kagel, Mauricio, 1931– Schwarzes Madrigal: für Chorstimmen und Instrumente. Partitur. Frankfurt/M.; New York, NY: H. Litolff's Verlag/C. F. Peters, 2000.
1 score (132 p.); 31 cm.
German words, consisting largely of African placenames; also printed as text.
For SATB chorus, trumpet, tuba, and percussion.
Duration: ca. 22:00.
Preface and performance instructions in German and English.
Composed for: SATB chorus, trumpet, tuba, percussion (2 log drums, 6 tom-toms, 3 pairs of agogo bells, 2 sanzas, cabasa, 2 maracas, 2 guiros, sizzle cymbal, bass drum, 2 halves of a coconut, 3 congas, vibraslap, marimba, 2 sistras, Chinese cymbal).
Commissioned by: Rundfunkchor Berlin.
Call no.: **2002/093**

1245. Kaipainen, Jouni, 1956– Quartetto III, op. 25: per archi. Score. København: Edition Wilhelm Hansen, 1984.
1 score (59 p.); 35 cm.
Reproduced from holograph.
Duration: 21:30.
Composed for: 2 violins, viola, violoncello.
Call no.: **1989/064**

1246. Kalmanoff, Martin, 1920– The insect comedy: opera in three acts, prologue & epiloge. New York, NY: Operation Opera, 1964.
1 score (3 v.); 36 cm.
English words by Lewis Allan.

Original work by Karel and Josef Capek.
Composed for: voices, 2 flutes (2nd also piccolo), 2 oboes, English horn, clarinet, bass clarinet, bassoon, contrabassoon, 4 horns, 2 trumpets, 2 trombones, bass trombone, tuba, timpani, percussion (snare drum, bass drum, suspended cymbal, clash cymbal, xylophone, glockenspiel, triangle, woodblock, tambourine, ratchet, vibraphone, tubular bells, wind machine, temple blocks, tam-tam), harp, piano, celesta, harpsichord, organ, violin I, violin II, viola, violoncello, double bass.
Call no.: **1994/068**
Also available:
Call no.: **1994/068 libretto**

1247. Kaminski, Stephen, 1966– The fallen. N.p.: n.p., 1992.
1 miniature score (13 leaves); 28 cm.
For orchestra.
Duration: 6:00.
Composed for: 2 flutes, 2 oboes, 2 clarinets, 2 bassoons, 4 horns, trumpet, timpani, percussion (suspended cymbal, snare drum), violin I, violin II, viola, violoncello, double bass.
Call no.: **1993/061**

1248. Kanding, Ejnar, 1965– Corazón de aire: 2002. Copenhagen: Kanding Edition, 2002.
1 score (32 p.); 30 cm.
Nonsense syllables.
Duration: 13:00.
Composed for: mezzo-soprano, flute (piccolo, alto, and bass flutes), tenor trombone, double bass, computer (Max/MSP), video sampler.
Commissioned by: Nordic Music Committee (NOMUS).
Call no.: **2005/074**

1249. Kanding, Ejnar, 1965– Winter darkness: [for] classical accordion, 1992. N.p.: Ejnar Kanding, 1992.
20 p. of music; 34 cm.
Duration: ca. 14:00.
Composed for: accordion.
Call no.: **1993/062**

1250. Kandov, Alexander, 1949– Music for orchestra. N.p.: n.p., 1985.
1 score (93 p.); 51 cm.
Composed for: 4 flutes (4th also piccolo), 4 oboes, 4 clarinets (4th also bass clarinet), 4 bassoons (4th also contrabassoon), 6 horns, 4 trumpets, 3 trombones, tuba, percussion (timpani, chimes, marimba, vibraphone, bass drum, tam-tam, 3 tom-toms, cymbals), harp, piano, organ, violin I, violin II, viola, violoncello, double bass.
Call no.: **1986/061**

1251. Kang, Sukhi, 1934– Concerto pour piano et orchestre. Paris: M. Eschig, 1998.
1 score (91 p.); 42 cm.
Composed for: piano, piccolo, flute, 2 oboes, 2 clarinets (2nd also bass clarinet), 2 bassoons (2nd also contrabassoon), 2 horns, 2 trumpets, 2 trombones, tuba, percussion (chimes, 3 timbales, 3 bongos, 3 cowbells, xylophone, 3 tom-toms, slit drum, 2 suspended cymbals, 2 triangles, marimba, crash cymbals, large tam-tam, 2 woodblocks, 3 gongs, snare drum, vibraphone, bass drum, 3 temple blocks, glockenspiel, whip), harp, celesta, violin I, violin II, viola, violoncello, double bass.
Commissioned by: Kun Woo Paik.
Call no.: **2000/081**

1252. Kantušer, Božidar, 1921– Fifth and sixth string quartet.
Call no.: **1985/097**
No materials available.

1253. Kaplan, Aaron, 1949– Reflections: Kaplan's piano concerto #1. N.p.: n.p., 1999.
1 score (22 leaves); 28 cm.
Duration: 15:30.
Composed for: piano, flute, oboe (also English horn), clarinet, bassoon, 2 horns, 2 trumpets, percussion (vibraphone, timpani, crash cymbals), violin I, violin II, viola, violoncello, double bass.
Call no.: **2002/094**

1254. Kaplan, Amelia S., 1963– Rituals & revelations: a cantata for Rosh Hashana: for 8 solo voices and chamber orchestra. N.p.: n.p., 1997.
1 score (97 p.); 28 cm.
Transliterated Hebrew and altered Hebrew words; also printed as text with English translation.
"Based on the musaf amidah verses Malchuyot, Zichronot & Shofarot."
Includes pronunciation guide and performance instructions.
Composed for: 2 sopranos, 2 mezzo-sopranos, 2 tenors, baritone, bass, 2 flutes (2nd also piccolo), oboe, clarinet (also clarinet in E♭), clarinet in A (also bass clarinet), bassoon, 2 horns, 2 trumpets, trombone, harp, piano, percussion (timpani, chimes, crotales, vibraphone, tambourine, woodblock, suspended cymbal, gongs, tam-tams, conga drums, timbales, tom-toms), violin I, violin II, viola, violoncello, double bass.

Commissioned by: Rabbi Daniel Leifer.
Call no.: **2001/078**

1255. Kapsomenos, Dimitris, 1937– Suite popolare: for oboe and guitar. N.p.: n.p., 1990.
1 score (30 p.); 30 cm.
Contents: Syrtos—Risitiko—Pentosali—Syrtos B—Kastrinos-pithiktos.
Composed for: oboe, guitar.
Call no.: **1991/060**

1256. Karchin, Louis, 1951– American visions: (two songs on poems of Yevgeny Yevtushenko): baritone voice and chamber ensemble. New York, NY: C. F. Peters, 1999.
1 score (iv, 74 p.); 28 cm.
Words in English (translated from Russian); also printed as text.
Duration: ca. 25:00.
Includes performance notes.
Contents: Who are you, Grand Canyon?—Requiem for Challenger.
Composed for: baritone, flute (also piccolo), clarinet (also bass clarinet), violin, violoncello, piano, percussion (marimba, vibraphone, glockenspiel, timpani, suspended cymbals, temple blocks, triangle, sizzle drum, bass drum, tam-tam).
Call no.: **2001/079**

1257. Karchin, Louis, 1951– American visions: two songs on poems of Yevgeny Yevtushenko, 1998: for baritone voice and chamber ensemble. N.p.: n.p., 1998.
1 score (iv, 74 p.); 28 cm.
English words (translated from Russian); also printed as text.
Duration: ca. 20:00.
Contents: Who are you, Grand Canyon?—Requiem for Challenger.
Composed for: baritone, flute (also piccolo), clarinet (also bass clarinet), violin, violoncello, piano, percussion (marimba, vibraphone, glockenspiel, timpani, suspended cymbals, temple blocks, triangle, sizzle drum, bass drum, tam-tam).
Call no.: **2002/095**

1258. Karmanov, Pavel, 1970– . . . ARIAtions: for chamber ensemble. Moscow: Karmanov Editions, 1996.
1 score (82 p.); 30 cm.
Composed for: recorder, flute, oboe, keyboard, vibraphone, piano, harpsichord, violin I, violin II, viola, violoncello, double bass.
Call no.: **1997/069**

1259. Karnecki, Zbigniew, 1947– Krwawe gody = (Bodas de sandre) = (The bloodthirsty wedding). Partiture. N.p.: n.p., 1999.
1 score (151 p.); 30 cm.
Polish words, translated from Spanish by Carlos Marrodan Casas and Jerzy Ficowski.
"Original music for drama by Federico Garcia Lorca."
For 9 soloists, choruses, and orchestra.
Composed for: 2 mezzo-sopranos, 3 altos, 3 tenors, baritone, SATB chorus, flute (also alto and bass flutes), English horn, soprano saxophone, 3 trumpets, 3 trombones, percussion (jazz drums, side drum, 4 tom-toms, rain stick, 2 bongos, 2 congas, bass drum, claves, castanets, sleigh bells, triangle, snare drum, woodblock, hi-hat), harp, 3 guitars, violin I, violin II, viola, violoncello, bass guitar, synthetic sounds.
Commissioned by: Polski Theatre in Wroclaw.
Call no.: **2002/096**

1260. Käser, Mischa, 1959– Ordouble: fünf Charakterstücke für Orchester, obligate Solovioline und Solovioloncello. N.p.: n.p., 1996.
1 score (71 leaves); 30 cm.
"Ordoublé (1. Fassung)"—caption.
Contents: Quintendynastie—Ground—Allegro furioso-adagio vuoto—Ouverture emplumée—Sarabande domestique (Totenfeier).
Composed for: violin, violoncello, 2 flutes (2nd also alto flute and piccolo), 2 oboes (2nd also English horn), 2 clarinets (both also bass clarinet), 2 bassoons (2nd also contrabassoon), 4 horns, 2 trumpets, percussion (timpani, antique cymbals, gongs, vibraphone, celesta, guiro, woodblock, xylorimba, snare drum, triangle, claves, flexatone, whip, water gong, tambourine, sizzle cymbal, castanets, temple block, slit drum, hi-hat, tam-tam, crash cymbals, cymbals), violin I, violin II, viola, violoncello, double bass.
Commissioned by: Musikkollegium Winterthur.
Call no.: **2000/082**

1261. Kassyanik, Uri, 1948– Kont͡sert: dli͡a fortepiano s orkestrom = Concerto: for piano and orchestra. Leningrad: n.p., 1982.
1 score (67 p.); 30 cm.
Reproduced from manuscript.
Composed for: piano, flute (also piccolo), oboe (also English horn), 2 clarinets (2nd also bass clarinet), bassoon (also contrabassoon), horn, 2 trumpets, trombone, tuba, timpani, percussion (triangle, military drum, cymbals, bass drum, xylophone), violin I, violin II, viola, violoncello, double bass.
Call no.: **1991/061**

1262. Kasteelen, Ilse van de, 1957– Los heraldos: a chamber opera for actor, five singers, and instrumental quintet. Amsterdam: Donemus, 1993.
1 score (161 p.); 39 cm.
English words by Armando Bergallo and Hector Vilche.
Duration: 1:22:00.
Composed for: actor, 2 sopranos, alto, tenor, bass, clarinet in E♭ (also bass and contrabass clarinets), soprano saxophone (also alto and bass saxophones), trumpet, violoncello, percussion (timpani, marimba, vibraphone, tubular bells, glockenspiel, 2 gongs, 2 triangles, suspended cymbal, flexatone, tam-tam, maraca, temple blocks, claves, 2 ratchets, bass drum, 6 pitched drums, thundersheet, bamboo chimes, glass chimes, snare drum, vibraslap, 2 congas, 2 bongos, guiro, cowbell, cabasa).
Commissioned by: Het Amsterdams Fonds voor de Kunst and Taller Amsterdam.
Call no.: **1996/154**

1263. Katz, Darrell, 1951– The death of Simone Weil. N.p.: n.p., 200-?.
1 score (various pagings); 28 cm.
Principally English with some French words by Armando Bergallo and Hector Vilche; also printed as text.
Improvisational jazz cantata for alto voice and jazz orchestra.
Contents: Gone now—Renault—November 1938—Saint Julien—X-ray dreams—Almost paradise.
Composed for: alto, flute (also piccolo), 2 alto saxophones, tenor saxophone, baritone saxophone, 2 trumpets, horn, 2 trombones, tuba, double bass, piano, vibraphone, guitar, drums.
Call no.: **2004/058**

1264. Kaufmann, Dieter, 1941– Volksoper, op. 36. Stockholm: Edition Reimers, 1982.
1 score (94 p.); 31 x 44 cm.
German words by the composer, based on Die Hinterhältigkeit der Windmaschinen by Gert Jonke
Composed for: 2 sopranos, 3 tenors, baritone, bass-baritone, 2 basses, SATB chorus, 3 flutes (3rd also piccolo), 3 oboes, 3 clarinets (3rd also saxophone), 3 bassoons (3rd also contrabassoon), 3 horns, 3 trumpets, 3 trombones, tuba, timpani, percussion (snare drum, tom-toms, bass drum, bongos, cymbals), piano, violin I, violin II, viola, violoncello, double bass.
Call no.: **1985/098**

1265. Kaulkin, Michael, 1967– Cycle of friends: for soprano, chorus and chamber orchestra. N.p.: Michael Kaulkin, 1996.
1 score (98 p.); 28 cm.
English words; also printed as text.
Contents: Tell everyone / Sappho (translated by Mary Barnard)—My old friend prepared a chicken with millet / Meng Hao-Jan (translated by Innes Herdan)—Are friends delight or pain? / Emily Dickinson—Blue hills over the north wall / Li Po (translated by Innes Herdan)—Friendship / Aztec.
Composed for: soprano, SATB chorus, flute (also piccolo), oboe, clarinet (also bass clarinet), bassoon, horn, trumpet, percussion (wind chimes, bell tree, mark tree, 3 tom-toms, 2 bongos, low tam-tam, triangle, crotales, bass drum, suspended cymbal, woodblock, tambourine), harp, violin I, violin II, viola, violoncello, double bass.
Commissioned by: Music Group of Philadelphia.
Call no.: **1997/070**

1266. Kazandzhiev, Vasil, 1934– Symphony no. 4: "nirvana." N.p.: n.p., 2000.
1 score (169 p.); 42 cm.
Bulgarian words; English translation follows score.
For mixed choir (last mvt.) and orchestra.
Text by Peyo K. Yavorov and from the Book of Enoch.
Duration: 54:00.
Performance instructions in Bulgarian, German, English, and French follow score.
Composed for: SATB chorus, 3 flutes (2nd also alto flute, 3rd also piccolo), 2 oboes, English horn, 2 clarinets, bass clarinet, 3 bassoons (3rd also contrabassoon), 6 horns, 4 trumpets, 4 trombones, tuba, timpani, percussion (triangle, piccolo snare drum, bass drum, cymbals, tam-tam, flexatone, gong, guiro, maracas, crotales, tambourine, sheep bells, glockenspiel, xylophone, vibraphone, 3 bongos, 2 tom-toms, tubular bells, marimba, Jew's harp, ratchet, whip, temple blocks), harp, piano (also celesta), violin I, violin II, viola, violoncello, double bass.
Call no.: **2005/075**

1267. Kechley, David, 1947– In the dragon's garden. N.p.: Pine Valley Press, 1992.
1 score (14 leaves); 43 cm.
Composed for: alto saxophone (also crotales), guitar.
Commissioned by: Frank Bongiornoand Robert Nathanson.
Call no.: **1993/063**

1268. Kechley, David, 1947– Restless birds before the dark moon. N.p.: n.p., 2000.
1 score (62 p.); 44 cm.
For solo alto saxophone and symphonic band.
Composed for: alto saxophone, piccolo, 2 flutes, 2 oboes, clarinet in E♭, 3 clarinets, alto clarinet, bass clarinet,

contrabass clarinet, bassoon, contrabassoon, 4 horns, 5 trumpets (1st–2nd also piccolo trumpet, 3rd–4th also flugelhorn), 2 trombones, bass trombone, 2 euphoniums, tuba, percussion (marimba, suspended cymbal, bongos, timbales, xylophone, 3 tom-toms, tubular bells, 2 congas, snare drum, vibraphone, bass drum, log drum, timpani, temple blocks, orchestra bells, tenor drum), piano.
Commissioned by: United States Military Academy Band.
Call no.: **2002/097**

1269. Kechley, David, 1947– Restless birds before the dark moon. N.p.: Pine Valley Press, 2001.
1 score (60 p.); 44 cm.
For solo alto saxophone and symphonic band.
At end of score: Williamstown, May 2000 (most recent correction, 10/01/01).
Program notes and biographical information about composer in English.
Composed for: alto saxophone, piccolo, 2 flutes, 2 oboes, clarinet in E♭, 3 clarinets, alto clarinet, bass clarinet, contrabass clarinet, bassoon, contrabassoon, 4 horns, 5 trumpets (1st–2nd also piccolo trumpet, 3rd–4th also flugelhorn), 2 trombones, bass trombone, 2 euphoniums, tuba, percussion (marimba, suspended cymbal, bongos, timbales, xylophone, 3 tom-toms, tubular bells, 2 congas, snare drum, vibraphone, bass drum, log drum, timpani, temple blocks, orchestra bells, tenor drum), piano.
Commissioned by: United States Military Academy Band.
Call no.: **2003/059**

1270. Kechley, David, 1947– Restless birds before the dark moon. N.p.: Pine Valley Press, 2002.
1 score (60 p.); 44 cm.
For solo alto saxophone and symphonic band.
At end of score: Williamstown, May 2000 (most recent correction, 4/01/02).
Program notes and biographical information about composer in English.
Composed for: alto saxophone, piccolo, 2 flutes, 2 oboes, clarinet in E♭, 3 clarinets, alto clarinet, bass clarinet, contrabass clarinet, bassoon, contrabassoon, 4 horns, 5 trumpets (1st–2nd also piccolo trumpet, 3rd–4th also flugelhorn), 2 trombones, bass trombone, 2 euphoniums, tuba, percussion (marimba, suspended cymbal, bongos, timbales, xylophone, 3 tom-toms, tubular bells, 2 congas, snare drum, vibraphone, bass drum, log drum, timpani, temple blocks, orchestra bells, tenor drum), piano.
Commissioned by: United States Military Academy Band.
Call no.: **2005/076**

1271. Kechley, David, 1947– The skylark sings: (soprano and orchestra with chorus). Williamstown, MA: Pine Valley Press, 199-?.
1 score (119 p.); 29 cm.
English words, also printed as text.
Contents: Skylarks—Fireflies—Starlight night—Magic mushrooms—Scarecrows—The giant tortoise—Quiet birds.
Composed for: soprano, SATB chorus, 2 flutes (1st also piccolo), 2 oboes (2nd also English horn), 2 clarinets, 2 bassoons, 4 horns, 3 trumpets, 3 trombones, tuba, percussion (tubular bells, orchestra bells, xylophone, crotales, small chime tree, temple blocks, bongos, marimba, large chime tree, 2 claves, maracas, medium suspended cymbal, vibraphone, 2 guiros, large sandpaper blocks, large suspended cymbal, log drum, timpani, tam-tam, small sandpaper blocks, bell tree, small tom-tom), harp, piano, violin I, violin II, viola, violoncello, double bass.
Commissioned by: Berkshire Symphony.
Call no.: **1996/065**

1272. Kechley, David, 1947– Transformations: an orchestral triptych. Williamstown, MA: Pine Valley Press, 1998.
1 score (83 p.); 41 cm.
Includes biographical information on composer.
Contents: Still on edge—Funeral music with dance—Past refrains.
Composed for: 3 flutes (3rd also piccolo), 3 oboes (3rd also English horn), 3 clarinets (3rd also bass clarinet), soprano saxophone, alto saxophone, 3 bassoons (3rd also contrabassoon), 4 horns, 3 trumpets, 3 trombones, tuba, harp, piano, percussion (marimba, xylophone, timpani, tom-toms, snare drum, suspended cymbal, tam-tam, bass drum, vibraphone, orchestra bells, tubular bells), violin I, violin II, viola, violoncello, double bass.
Commissioned by: New England Conservatory.
Call no.: **2000/083**
Re-entered as: **2004/059**

1273. Kechley, David, 1947– Voices from the garden: for guitar quartet. Williamstown, MA: Pine Valley Press, 1993.
1 score (25 p.); 28 cm.
Composed for: 4 guitars.
Commissioned by: Minneapolis Guitar Quartet and North Carolina Guitar Quartet.
Call no.: **1994/069**

1274. Kechley, David, 1947– Winter branches: a sonata for cello and piano. N.p.: Pine Valley Press, 1986.

1 score (41 leaves); 36 cm.
Contents: Branching out—Crystal branches—Branches in the wind.
Includes program notes and biographical information about the composer in English.
Composed for: violoncello, piano.
Commissioned by: Raleigh Chamber Music Guild.
Call no.: **1989/065**

1275. Kechley, David, 1947– Winter branches: a sonata for cello and piano. Williamstown, MA: Pine Valley Press, 1989.
1 score (30 p.); 28 cm.
Contents: Branching out—Crystal branches—Branches in the wind.
Includes program notes and biographical information about the composer in English.
Composed for: violoncello, piano.
Commissioned by: Raleigh Chamber Music Guild.
Call no.: **1992/067**

1276. Keig, Betty, 1920– A celebration of American poets. N.p.: n.p., 199-?.
1 score (6 v.); 28 cm.
English words.
Song cycle.
Contents: The investigator; Housewife / Sara Henderson Hay—Hill song / Louise McNeil—Let evening come / Jane Kenyon—Backward flight / Louise McNeil—A nosty fright / May Swenson.
Composed for: soprano, mezzo-soprano, piano.
Call no.: **1996/066**

1277. Kelemen, Milko, 1924– Animaux fantastiques: für zwei Chöre, Vokal- und Instrumentalsolisten. Partitur. Hamburg: Musikverlag Hans Sikorski, 1997.
1 score (48 p.); 42 cm.
Some German words; primarily wordless.
Reproduced from manuscript.
Duration: 11:00.
Composed for: alto, 2 SATB choruses, piccolo (also bass flute), oboe (also English horn), contrabass tuba, percussion (marimba, xylophone, timpani, 3 crotales, tubular bells, high cymbals, bass drum, lion's roar, 6 woodblocks, flexatone, whip, triangle, tam-tam, slide whistle, church bells, didgeridoo).
Commissioned by: Süddeutscher Rundfunk.
Call no.: **1998/073**

1278. Kelemen, Milko, 1924– Archtypon II für Anton: für grosses Orchester. Hamburg: Musikverlag Hans Sikorski, 1995.
1 score (109 p.); 42 cm.
Reproduced from manuscript.
Composed for: 4 flutes (all also piccolo), 3 oboes, English horn, 3 clarinets, bass clarinet, 3 bassoons, contrabassoon, 6 horns, 4 trumpets, 3 trombones, 2 contrabass tubas, 2 sets of timpani, percussion (xylophone, marimba, tubular bells, bell plates, crotales, 5 pairs of crash cymbals, almglocken, 2 cowbells, 2 temple blocks, 3 tom-toms, 5 bongos, bass drum, snare drum, glockenspiel, military drum, tenor drum, ratchet, guiro, flexatone, glass chimes, celesta, slide whistle), harp, piano, violin I, violin II, viola, violoncello, double bass.
Call no.: **1997/071**

1279. Kelemen, Milko, 1924– Drammatico: requiem for Sarajevo: für Violoncello und Orchester. Hamburg: Musikverlag Hans Sikorski, 1984.
1 score (74 p.); 42 cm.
Reproduced from manuscript.
Composed for: violoncello, 3 flutes, English horn, 3 clarinets (3rd also bass clarinet), 3 trumpets, 3 trombones, timpani, percussion (xylophone, vibraphone, marimba, tubular bells, crotales, bass drum, snare drum, military drum, tenor drum, 5 cymbals, 5 almglocken, 5 temple blocks, 5 bongos, 5 glass bottles, tam-tam, anvil, maracas, claves, flexatone, stones, guiro, glass chimes), harp, piano (also cembalo, celesta, electronic organ), violin I, violin II, viola, violoncello, double bass.
Call no.: **1995/047**
Re-entered as: **1996/067**

1280. Kelemen, Milko, 1924– Good-bye my fancy: für Violine und Klavier (nach einem Gedicht von Walt Whitman). N.p.: n.p., 1998.
1 score (23 p.); 35 cm.
Reproduced from holograph.
Duration: 15:00.
Composed for: violin, piano.
Call no.: **2000/084**

1281. Kelemen, Milko, 1924– Salut au monde. N.p.: n.p., 1996.
1 score (166 p.); 42 cm.
Principally German with some English, French, and Russian words.
Text by Walt Whitman.
For narrator (baritone), soprano, alto, tenor, bass, 2 choruses, large orchestra, and light actions.
Reproduced from holograph.
Duration: 40:00.
Annotated with English translation in red ink.
Composed for: soprano, alto, tenor, baritone, bass, 2 SATB choruses, 3 flutes (all also piccolo), 2 oboes,

English horn, 2 clarinets, bass clarinet, 4 horns, 3 trumpets, 3 trombones, tuba, piano, harp, celesta, percussion, violin I, violin II, viola, violoncello, double bass.
Commissioned by: MDR, Leipzig.
Call no.: **2001/080**

1282. Kempf, Davorin, 1947– Spectrum: for a large orchestra and electronics = za veliki orkestar i elektroniku, 1985. N.p.: n.p., 1985.
1 score (92 p.); 34 cm.
Reproduced from holograph.
Duration: ca. 17:00.
Composed for: 3 flutes (3rd also piccolo), 2 oboes, English horn, 2 clarinets, bass clarinet, 2 bassoons, contrabassoon, 4 horns, 3 trumpets, 3 trombones, tuba, timpani, percussion (triangle, snare drum, suspended cymbal, bass drum, tam-tam, orchestra bells, chimes, vibraphone), harp, celesta, violin I, violin II, viola, violoncello, double bass, electronics.
Call no.: **1989/066**

1283. Kernis, Aaron Jay, 1960– Colored field: concerto for English horn & orchestra. New York, NY: Associated Music Publishers, 1994.
1 score (175 p.); 36 cm.
Composed for: English horn, 3 flutes (2nd–3rd also piccolo), 2 oboes, 3 clarinets (1st also clarinet in A, 2nd also bass clarinet, 3rd also clarinet in E♭), 2 bassoons (2nd also contrabassoon), 4 horns, 3 trumpets (2nd–3rd also trumpet in D), 2 trombones, bass trombone, tuba, timpani, percussion (4 almglocken, 2 bass drums, 5 bell plates, 4 brake drums, castanets, chimes, 4 cowbells, crotales, glockenspiel, guiro, crash cymbals, marimba, 4 nipple gongs, ratchet, rute, sandpaper blocks, slapstick, snare drum, 4 steel pipes, 3 suspended cymbals, 4 tam-tams, tambourine, tenor drum, 2 timbales, 2 bongos, 2 tom-toms, 3 triangles, vibraphone, 2 woodblocks, wooden rattle, xylophone), harp, piano (also celesta), violin I, violin II, viola, violoncello, double bass.
Commissioned by: San Francisco Symphony.
Call no.: **1995/048**

1284. Kernis, Aaron Jay, 1960– Colored field: concerto for English horn & orchestra. New York, NY: Associated Music Publishers, 1994.
1 score (175 p.); 44 cm.
Composed for: English horn, 3 flutes (2nd–3rd also piccolo), 2 oboes, 3 clarinets (1st also clarinet in A, 2nd also bass clarinet, 3rd also clarinet in E♭), 2 bassoons (2nd also contrabassoon), 4 horns, 3 trumpets (2nd–3rd also trumpet in D), 2 trombones, bass trombone, tuba, timpani, percussion (4 almglocken, 2 bass drums, 5 bell plates, 4 brake drums, castanets, chimes, 4 cowbells, crotales, glockenspiel, guiro, crash cymbals, marimba, 4 nipple gongs, ratchet, rute, sandpaper blocks, slapstick, snare drum, 4 steel pipes, 3 suspended cymbals, 4 tam-tams, tambourine, tenor drum, 2 timbales, 2 bongos, 2 tom-toms, 3 triangles, vibraphone, 2 woodblocks, wooden rattle, xylophone), harp, piano (also celesta), violin I, violin II, viola, violoncello, double bass.
Commissioned by: San Francisco Symphony.
Call no.: **1996/068**

1285. Kernis, Aaron Jay, 1960– Colored field: concerto for violoncello & orchestra. New York, NY: Associated Music Publishers, 1999.
1 score (175 p.); 36 cm.
Contents: Colored field—Pandora dance—Hymns and tablets.
2002 Grawemeyer Award winning work.
Composed for: violoncello, 3 flutes (2nd–3rd also piccolo), 2 oboes, 3 clarinets (1st also clarinet in A, 2nd also bass clarinet, 3rd also clarinet in E♭), 2 bassoons (2nd also contrabassoon), 4 horns, 3 trumpets (2nd–3rd also trumpet in D), 2 trombones, bass trombone, tuba, timpani, percussion (4 almglocken, 2 bass drums, 5 bell plates, 4 brake drums, castanets, chimes, 4 cowbells, crotales, glockenspiel, guiro, crash cymbals, marimba, 4 nipple gongs, ratchet, rute, sandpaper blocks, slapstick, snare drum, 4 steel pipes, 3 suspended cymbals, 4 tam-tams, tambourine, tenor drum, 2 timbales, 2 bongos, 2 tom-toms, 3 triangles, vibraphone, 2 woodblocks, wooden rattle, xylophone), harp, piano (also celesta), violin I, violin II, viola, violoncello, double bass.
Commissioned by: Minnesota Orchestra and Eiji Oue.
Call no.: **2002/098**

1286. Kernis, Aaron Jay, 1960– Double concerto: for violin, guitar and orchestra. 2nd ed. New York, NY: Associated Music, 1997.
1 miniature score (163 p.); 44 cm.
"Corrected Feb. 1997"—p. 1.
Duration: 30:00.
Composed for: violin, guitar, 2 flutes (2nd also piccolo), 2 oboes (2nd also English horn), 2 clarinets (1st also clarinet in A, 2nd also bass clarinet), 2 bassoons (2nd also contrabassoon), 2 horns, 2 trumpets, percussion (splash cymbal, crash cymbal, ride cymbal, hi-hat, 2 timbalinos, snare drum, floor tom-tom, pedal bass drum, 2 pairs of bongos, 2 high timbales, 2 congas, bass drum, medium bass drum, 3 medium suspended cymbals, 2 low suspended cymbals, 3 medium gongs,

2 medium tam-tams, 2 high steel pipes, 2 high triangles, 2 cowbells, 2 woodblocks, small shaker, guiro, tambourine, timpani, chimes, vibraphone, crotales, glockenspiel, xylophone), harp, celesta (also synthesizer and honky-tonk piano),violin I, violin II, viola, violoncello, double bass.
Commissioned by: Meet the Composer/Reader's Digest Commissioning Program, National Endowment for the Arts, and Lila Wallace-Reader's Digest Fund.
Call no.: **1998/074**

1287. Kernis, Aaron Jay, 1960– Garden of light: 1999. New York, NY: Associated Music Publishers, 1999.
1 score (117 p.); 43 cm.
Words by David Simpatico and Menna Elfyn.
For solo voices (boy soprano, SMzTBar), mixed chorus (SATB), children's chorus, and orchestra.
Contents: Morning of the world—Tapestry of home.
Composed for: soprano, boy soprano, mezzo-soprano, tenor, baritone, SATB chorus, children's chorus, 4 flutes (3rd–4th also piccolo), 4 oboes (4th also English horn), 4 clarinets (3rd also clarinet in E♭, 4th also bass clarinet), 3 bassoons, contrabassoon, soprano saxophone, alto saxophone, tenor saxophone, baritone saxophone, 6 horns, 4 trumpets, 3 trombones, bass trombone, tuba, timpani, percussion, electric guitar, celesta, piano, synthesizer, harp, violin I, violin II, viola, violoncello, double bass.
Commissioned by: Walt Disney Company.
Call no.: **2001/081**

1288. Kernis, Aaron Jay, 1960– Invisible mosaic III: for orchestra (1988). New York, NY: Associated Music Publishers, 1989.
1 score (90 p.); 36 cm.
Duration: ca. 14:00.
Composed for: 3 flutes (2nd–3rd also piccolo), 3 oboes (3rd also English horn), 3 clarinets (2nd also clarinet in E♭, 3rd also bass clarinet), 3 bassoons (3rd also contrabassoon), 4 horns, 3 trumpets (1st also trumpet in D), 2 trombones, bass trombone, tuba, timpani, percussion (marimba, xylophone, glockenspiel, flexatone, pane of glass, tenor drum, Peking opera cymbals, 4 cowbells, triangle, marine band harmonica, chimes, glockenspiel, 2 woodblocks, bongos, 4 brake drums, 3 cymbals, ratchet, vibraphone, ride cymbal, medium cymbal, 2 gongs, 2 crash cymbals, 4 anvils, 4 steel pipes, 4 cowbells, snare drum, crotales, 3 gongs, 3 timbales, 3 tam-tams, 5 tom-toms, bass drum, hotel bell, castanets, 3 temple blocks, tambourine), harp, piano (also celesta), violin I, violin II, viola, violoncello, double bass.
Commissioned by: American Composers Orchestra.
Call no.: **1990/058**

1289. Kernis, Aaron Jay, 1960– Lament and prayer: (1995). New York, NY: Associated Music Publishers, 1998.
1 score (53 p.); 44 cm.
For solo violin and orchestra.
"Corrected 2/98."—p. 1.
Duration: 25:00.
Performance instructions in English.
Composed for: violin, oboe, 2 harps, percussion (crotales, medium triangles, jingle bells, shakers, sizzle cymbals, small Asian bells, chimes), violin I, violin II, viola, violoncello, double bass.
Commissioned by: Minnesota Orchestra.
Call no.: **2000/085**

1290. Kernis, Aaron Jay, 1960– Lament and prayer: for solo violin, oboe, crotales, harp and strings. New York, NY: Associated Music Publishers, 1995.
1 score (53 p.); 42 cm.
Duration: 22:00.
Performance instructions in English.
Composed for: violin, oboe, 2 harps, percussion (crotales, medium triangles, jingle bells, shakers, sizzle cymbals, small Asian bells, chimes), violin I, violin II, viola, violoncello, double bass.
Commissioned by: Minnesota Orchestra.
Call no.: **1997/072**

1291. Kernis, Aaron Jay, 1960– Love scenes: for soprano and cello. New York, NY: Northlight Music/W. Hansen, 1987.
1 score (41 p.); 35 cm.
Words by Anna Swir.
Reproduced from holograph.
Duration: ca. 25:00.
Composed for: soprano, violoncello.
Commissioned by: Andre Emelianoff.
Call no.: **1988/056**

1292. Kernis, Aaron Jay, 1960– Second symphony. New York, NY: Associated Music Publishers, 1991.
1 score (106 p.); 36 cm.
Contents: Alarm—Air/Ground—Barricade.
Duration: ca. 23:00.
Composed for: 3 flutes (3rd also piccolo), 2 oboes, English horn, 2 clarinets, clarinet in A, bass clarinet, 3 bassoons (3rd also contrabassoon), 4 horns, 4 trumpets, 4 trombones, tuba, timpani, percussion (2 snare drums, tenor drum, 2 bass drums, log drum, brake drum, bongos, congas, woodblocks, reco reco,

lead pipe, mounted handbells, cowbells, thundersheet, crotales, cabasa, high triangles, China boy cymbal, 3 cymbals, 2 crash cymbals, ride cymbal, vibraphone, xylophone, glockenspiel, marimba, chimes, 2 tam-tams, tom-toms), harp, piano, violin I, violin II, viola, violoncello, double bass.
Commissioned by: Carillon Importers.
Call no.: **1993/064**

1293. Kernis, Aaron Jay, 1960– Second symphony. New York, NY: Associated Music Publishers, 1993.
1 score (106 p.); 36 cm.
"Corrected 9/93"—p. 1.
Duration: ca. 23:00.
Reproduced from holograph.
Composed for: 3 flutes (3rd also piccolo), 2 oboes, English horn, 2 clarinets, clarinet in A, bass clarinet, 3 bassoons (3rd also contrabassoon), 4 horns, 4 trumpets, 4 trombones, tuba, timpani, percussion (2 snare drums, tenor drum, 2 bass drums, log drum, brake drum, bongos, congas, woodblocks, reco reco, lead pipe, mounted handbells, cowbells, thundersheet, crotales, cabasa, high triangles, China boy cymbal, 3 cymbals, 2 crash cymbals, ride cymbal, vibraphone, xylophone, glockenspiel, marimba, chimes, 2 tam-tams, tom-toms), harp, piano, violin I, violin II, viola, violoncello, double bass.
Commissioned by: Carillon Importers.
Call no.: **1994/070**

1294. Kernis, Aaron Jay, 1960– String quartet: musica celestis. Chester, NY: G. Schirmer/Associated Music, 1990.
1 score (76 p.); 36 cm.
Duration: 35:00.
Reproduced from holograph.
At end: "10/10/90, NYC."
"Corrected and revised Oct. 25, 1990"—p. 1.
Contents: Flowing—Musica celestis; Adagio—Scherzo; Trio semplice; Scherzo—Quasi una danza.
Composed for: 2 violins, viola, violoncello.
Commissioned by: Walter W. Naumburg Foundation.
Call no.: **1991/062**

1295. Kernis, Aaron Jay, 1960– Symphony in waves: for orchestra (1989). Chester, NY: G. Schirmer, 1991.
1 score (181 p.); 36 cm.
"Newly rev. and corr. Sept./Oct. 1991."
Duration: ca. 30:00.
Reproduced from holograph.
Composed for: flute (also piccolo), 2 oboes (2nd also English horn), clarinet (also clarinet in E♭, clarinet in A, and bass clarinet), 2 bassoons (2nd also contrabassoon), 3 horns, trumpet (also trumpet in D), percussion (timpani, chimes, glockenspiel, vibraphone, marimba, crotales, 6 bell plates, 4 cowbells, 2 steel pipes, triangle, crash cymbals, suspended cymbal, ride cymbal, tam-tam, sleigh bells, 4 tom-toms, snare drum, tambourine, woodblock), piano (also celesta), violin I, violin II, viola, violoncello, double bass.
Commissioned by: Saint Paul Chamber Orchestra.
Call no.: **1992/068**

1296. Kessner, Daniel, 1946– Icoane româneşti = (Images of Romania): for orchestra and narrator: 1996. N. p.: n.p., 1996.
1 score (75 p.); 36 cm.
Romanian and English words.
Duration: ca. 14:00.
Includes composer's notes.
Contents: Dimineaţa = Morning—Scherzo: Turturica = The turtle dove/Sus = High up—Suceviţa.
Composed for: narrator, 2 flutes, oboe, English horn, 2 clarinets, 2 bassoons, 2 horns, 2 trumpets, 2 trombones, tuba, percussion (small suspended cymbal, 3 tom-toms, large tam-tam, timpani, large suspended cymbal, bass drum), violin I, violin II, viola, violoncello, double bass.
Call no.: **1998/075**

1297. Kessner, Daniel, 1946– In the center: a chamber cantata for mezzo-soprano, strings, and piano, 2000. N.p.: Daniel Kessner, 2000.
1 score (50 p.); 28 cm.
German, English, and Spanish words; also printed as text with English translations.
"May be performed with either string quartet or string ensemble"—preface.
Texts by Angelus Silesius, Walt Whitman, and Javier Alas.
Duration: ca. 23:00.
Contents: Man weiss nicht, was man ist; Gott nichts und alles / Silesius—Song of myself / Whitman—Gott ergreift man nicht; Der Himmel ist in dir / Silesius—En el centro de Dios / Alas—Three chorales to silence. Der Weise redet wenig; Mit schweigen singt man schön; Das stillschweigende Gebet / Silesius.
Composed for: mezzo-soprano, violin I, violin II, viola, violoncello, piano.
Call no.: **2002/099**

1298. Keulen, Geert van, 1943– Tympan: pour grand orchestre, 1990. Amsterdam: Donemus, 1991.
1 score (60 p.); 42 cm.
Duration: ca. 20:00.

Composed for: 2 piccolos (both also flute), 2 flutes, alto flute, 4 oboes (3rd also baritone oboe, 4th also English horn), 3 clarinets (3rd also bass clarinet), 3 bassoons, contrabassoon, 6 horns, 5 trumpets, 5 trombones, tuba, timpani, percussion (triangle, suspended cymbal, sizzle cymbal, clash cymbals, sleigh bells, gong, Javanese gong, large tam-tam, temple block, tambourine, 3 congas, snare drum, bass drum, vibraphone), synthesizer, 2 harps, piano, celesta, violin I, violin II, viola, violoncello, double bass.
Commissioned by: Koninklijk Concertgebouworkest.
Call no.: **1995/106**

1299. Keuris, Tristan, 1946–1996. Concerto: for saxophone quartet and orchestra. N.p.: Novello, 1986.
1 score (113 p.); 42 cm.
Reproduced from manuscript.
Duration: ca. 23:00.
Composed for: soprano saxophone, alto saxophone, tenor saxophone, baritone saxophone, piccolo, 2 flutes, 2 oboes, English horn, clarinet in E♭, 2 clarinets, bass clarinet, 2 bassoons, contrabassoon, 4 horns, 3 trumpets, 3 trombones, tuba, percussion (chimes, suspended cymbal, timpani, xylophone, triangle, snare drum, tambourine), harp, celesta, violin I, violin II, viola, violoncello, double bass.
Commissioned by: Rascher Saxophone Quartet.
Call no.: **1988/057**

1300. Keuris, Tristan, 1946–1996. Double concerto: for two cellos and orchestra, 1991–1992. London: Novello, 1992.
1 score (91 p.); 30 cm.
Duration: 21:00.
Composed for: 2 violoncellos, 3 flutes (2nd also piccolo, 3rd also alto flute), alto flute, 2 oboes, English horn, clarinet in E♭, 2 clarinets, bass clarinet, 4 horns, timpani, percussion (xylophone, glockenspiel, marimba, vibraphone, triangle, suspended cymbal), harp, piano, violin I, violin II, viola, violoncello, double bass.
Commissioned by: BBC.
Call no.: **1993/065**

1301. Keuris, Tristan, 1946–1996. Laudi: a symphony for mezzo-soprano, baritone, two mixed choirs, and orchestra: 1992. London: Novello, 1993.
1 score (130 p.); 44 cm.
Italian words.
"1992–'93"—caption.
Reproduced from holograph.
Duration: ca. 40:00.
Contents: Introduzione; La sera fiesolana; L'orma—Terra, vale!—Tristezza; Implorazione—I pastori.
Composed for: mezzo-sopranos, baritone, 2 SATB choruses, 4 flutes (1st–2nd also piccolo, 3rd–4th also alto flute), 2 oboes, 2 English horns, 3 clarinets (3rd also clarinet in E♭), alto saxophone, bass clarinet, 2 bassoons, contrabassoon, 4 horns, 3 trumpets, 3 trombones, tuba, timpani, percussion (xylophone, triangle, cymbals, 2 suspended cymbals, snare drum, bass drum, glockenspiel, 2 tam-tams), harp, piano, celesta, violin I, violin II, viola, violoncello, double bass.
Call no.: **1995/049**
Re-entered as: **1996/069**

1302. Keuris, Tristan, 1946–1996. String quartet no. 2, 1985. Amsterdam: Donemus, 1985.
1 score (51 p.); 38 cm.
Reproduced from holograph.
Duration: ca. 21:00.
Composed for: 2 violins viola, violoncello.
Commissioned by: NOS (Radio).
Call no.: **1987/037**

1303. Keuris, Tristan, 1946–1996. To Brooklyn Bridge: for 24 voices and instrumental ensemble, 1987–'88. London: Novello, 1988.
1 score (95 p.); 42 cm.
English words.
Reproduced from manuscript.
Duration: ca. 27:00.
Composed for: SATB chorus, clarinet in E♭, 2 clarinets, bass clarinet, soprano saxophone, alto saxophone, tenor saxophone, baritone saxophone, 2 pianos, 2 harps, 3 double basses.
Call no.: **1991/063**

1304. Khachaturi͡an, Karėn, 1920– Ėpitafii͡a: dli͡a strunnogo orkestra. N.p.: n.p., 1986.
1 score (66 p.); 40 cm.
For string orchestra with percussion.
Reproduced from holograph.
Composed for: percussion (timpani, triangle, chimes, tam-tam), violin I, violin II, viola, violoncello, double bass.
Call no.: **1987/038**

1305. Kiefer, John, 1967– Ursa major. N.p.: John Kiefer, 2003.
1 score (27 p.); 28 cm.
For orchestra.
Duration: ca. 9:00.
Composed for: 2 flutes, 2 oboes, English horn, 2 clarinets, bass clarinet, 2 bassoons, 4 horns, 3 trumpets, trombone, bass trombone, tuba, percussion (timpani, snare drum, bass drum, wind chimes, triangle, suspended cymbal,

gong, vibraphone, glockenspiel), synthesizer keyboard, violin I, violin II, viola, violoncello, double bass.
Call no.: **2005/077**

1306. Kievman, Carson, 1949– Piano concert: piano + orchestra, 1980–81. Full score. N.p.: n.p., 1981.
1 score (197 p.); 46 cm.
Reproduced from manuscript.
Composed for: piano, 2 flutes (1st also piccolo), 2 oboes, clarinet, clarinet in A, clarinet in E♭ (also bass clarinet), bassoon (also contrabassoon), 2 horns, 2 trumpets, trombone, tuba, timpani, mounted choir bells, violin I, violin II, viola, violoncello, double bass.
Call no.: **1987/039**

1307. Kievman, Carson, 1949– Symphony #2(42). New York, NY: Intelligent Company Publ., 1991.
1 score (261 p.); 36 cm.
For orchestra with SATB chorus.
Composed for: SATB chorus, 3 flutes (3rd also piccolo and bass flute), 3 oboes (3rd also English horn), 3 clarinets (2nd also clarinet in A, 3rd also bass clarinet), 3 bassoons (3rd also contrabassoon), 4 horns, 3 trumpets, 2 trombones, bass trombone, tuba, timpani, percussion (tenor drum, 3 tom-toms, bass drum, triangle, suspended cymbal, tam-tam, 7 gongs, tubular bells, 12 choir bells, snare drum, 3 glockenspiels, vibraphone, xylophone, marimba), 2 harps, violin I, violin II, viola, violoncello, double bass.
Commissioned by: Florida Philharmonic Orchestra 1990/91.
Call no.: **1996/070**

1308. Kikuchi, Masaharu, 1938– Motion play Sarutobi-Sasuke: for percussion ensemble. N.p.: n.p., 198-?.
1 score (76 p.); 26 x 36 cm.
Reproduced from manuscript.
Composed for: percussion (2 ark shells, hard woodblock, tsukeita, 3 woodblocks, xylophone, 5 rins, jazz drum set, bird whistle, 5 wind chimes, 4–6 metal plates, gopiyantra, bin-sasara, wine goblet with bow, flexatone, hi-hat, 6 suspended cymbals, Thai suspended cymbal, maracas, banko, flexatone, 4 tom-toms, bamboo chimes, steel drum, snare drum, 4 coconut shells, bongo, 3 Chinese tom-toms, conga, vase, 3 wooden tom-toms, 3 tam-tams, slapstick, timpani, metal basin, marimba, thundersheet, vibraphone, small cymbal, 2 bass drums, rute, musical saw).
Call no.: **1985/100**

1309. Killmayer, Wilhelm, 1927– Hölderlin-Lieder: nach Gedichten aus der Spätzeit: für Tenor und Orchester, I. Zyklus, 1982–1985. Partitur. Mainz: B. Schott's Söhne, 1986.
1 score (i–xii, 67 p.); 35 cm.
German words; also printed as text.
Duration: ca. 45:00.
Composed for: tenor, 2 flutes (2nd also piccolo), 2 oboes, 2 clarinets (both also clarinet in A, 2nd also clarinet in E♭ and bass clarinet), 2 bassoons (2nd also contrabassoon), 2 horns, cornet, 2 trombones, timpani, percussion (triangle, crotales, cymbals, sleigh bells, glockenspiel, vibraphone, bass drum, lithophone), harp, celesta, violin I, violin II, viola, violoncello, double bass.
Call no.: **1987/040**

1310. Killmayer, Wilhelm, 1927– Hölderlin-Lieder: nach Gedichten aus der Spätzeit für Tenor und Orchester, 1983–87. II. Zyklus. Partitur. Mainz; New York, NY: Schott, 1987.
1 score (x, 80 p.); 34 cm.
German words; also printed as text (p. v–x).
Reproduced from manuscript.
Composed for: tenor, 2 flutes (both also piccolo, 2nd also alto flute and soprano recorder), 2 oboes (2nd also English horn), 2 clarinets (all also clarinet in A, 2nd also bass clarinet), 2 bassoons (2nd also contrabassoon), 4 horns, cornet, 2 trombones, timpani, percussion (snare drum, bass drum), harp, violin I, violin II, viola, violoncello, double bass.
Call no.: **1988/058**

1311. Killmayer, Wilhelm, 1927– Die Schönheit des Morgens: fünf Romanzen für Viola und Klavier = five romances for viola and piano, 1994. Mainz; New York, NY: Schott, 1996.
1 score (20 p.) + 1 part (6 p.); 31 cm.
Duration: ca. 14:00.
Composed for: viola, piano.
Call no.: **1998/076**

1312. Kilstofte, Mark, 1958– Sonata: for alto saxophone and piano. Greenville, SC: Newmatic Press, 1999.
1 score (37 p.); 28 cm.
Duration: 18:00.
Program and performance notes by the composer.
Composed for: alto saxophone, piano.
Commissioned by: Ambassador Duo.
Call no.: **2002/100**

1313. Kimmel, Corliss, 1953– Kodiak suite. N.p.: n.p., 1992.
1 score (139 p.); 36 cm.

For orchestra.
Contents: The Russians arrive—The Russians and the natives—Fishing boats and the sea—The island.
Composed for: piccolo, 2 flutes, 2 oboes, English horn, 2 clarinets, bass clarinet, 2 bassoons, 4 horns, 3 trumpets, 3 trombones, tuba, harp, timpani, percussion (ship's bell, 2 suspended cymbals, bells, tam-tam, chimes, crash cymbals, tambourine, tom-tom, bass drum, triangle, hammer, glass, vibraphone), violin I, violin II, viola, violoncello, double bass.
Call no.: **1993/066**

1314. Kimper, Paula M., 1956– Patience & Sarah: a pioneering love story. Brooklyn, NY: Once in a Blue Moon Music Pub. Co., 1998.
Words by Wende Persons.
Original work by Isabel Miller.
1 vocal score (v, 225 p.); 28 cm.
"Suggested by the life of the painter Mary Ann Willson."—p. ii.
Composed for: voices, piano.
Commissioned by: American Opera Projects.
Call no.: **2003/060**

1315. Kingman, Daniel, 1924– The golden gyre: for soprano, baritone and chamber ensemble. N.p.: n.p., 1991.
1 score (2 v.); 28 cm.
English words by various 19th-century writers.
"A musical evocation of that turbulent and prodigious epic, which was the California gold rush, in the words of those who lived through it."
Reproduced from manuscript.
Contents: The westward march—The quest—The return.
Composed for: soprano, baritone, flute, clarinet, violin, violoncello, piano, percussion (xylophone, vibraphone, orchestra bells, suspended cymbals, antique cymbals, triangle, tambourine, castanets, woodblock, claves, slapstick, maracas, ratchet, gong, tubular chimes, 2 bells, timpani, 6 drums, 5 temple blocks).
Commissioned by: Sacramento Metropolitan Arts Commission.
Call no.: **1994/071**

1316. Kinsella, John, 1932– Symphony no. 2 1988. Dublin: Contemporary Music Centre, 1988.
1 score (303 p.); 30 cm.
Reproduced from holograph.
Composed for: 2 flutes, 2 oboes, 2 clarinets, 2 bassoons, contrabassoon, 4 horns, 4 trumpets, 2 trombones, bass trombone, tuba, timpani, celesta, violin I, violin II, viola, violoncello, double bass.
Call no.: **1990/059**

1317. Kinsey, Richard, 1954– Robin Hood: the musical. Full score. N.p.: n.p., 1985.
1 score (various pagings); 37 cm.
English words.
Lyrics and book by Kenneth R. Johnson; music by Richard Kinsey; based on a concept by Griff and Jan Duncan.
Reproduced from manuscript.
Composed for: voices, 2 recorders, 2 flutes, 2 oboes, English horn, 2 clarinets, bassoon, 2 horns, 3 trumpets, trombone, bass trombone, tuba, timpani, percussion (triangle, glockenspiel, snare drum, bass drum, cymbals, woodblock, finger cymbals, chimes, tambourine, vibraphone), harp, auto harp, guitar, violin I, violin II, viola, violoncello, double bass.
Call no.: **1987/041**
Also available:
Call no.: **1987/041 libretto**
Call no.: **1987/041 vocal score**

1318. Kirchner, Leon, 1919– Duo no. 2 for violin and piano. New York, NY: Associated Music Publishers, 2003.
1 score (31 p.); 29 cm.
"Revised 7/2002; corrected 2/2003"—p. 1.
Composed for: violin, piano.
Commissioned by: Richard and Judith Hurtig and Richard Morse.
Call no.: **2005/078**

1319. Kirchner, Leon, 1919– Music for cello and orchestra. New York, NY: Associated Music Publishers, 1992.
1 miniature score (68 p.); 36 cm.
"Latest correction 9/1/92"—p. 1.
Composed for: violoncello, 3 flutes, 2 oboes, English horn, 2 clarinets, bass clarinet, 2 bassoons, contrabassoon, 4 horns, 3 trumpets, 3 trombones, tuba, timpani, percussion (bells, xylophone, vibraphone, glockenspiel, tambourine, antique cymbals, tubular bells, 3 woodblocks, 3 temple blocks, snare drum, tenor drum, suspended cymbals, claves, bongos, side drum), piano (also celesta), violin I, violin II, viola, violoncello, double bass.
Commissioned by: Philadelphia Orchestra Association.
Call no.: **1993/067**

1320. Kirchner, Leon, 1919– Music for cello and orchestra. New York, NY: Associated Music Publishers, 1992 (1997 printing).
1 miniature score (48 p.); 28 cm.
Composed for: violoncello, 3 flutes, 2 oboes, English horn, 2 clarinets, bass clarinet, 2 bassoons, contrabassoon, 4 horns, 3 trumpets, 3 trombones, tuba, timpani,

percussion (bells, xylophone, vibraphone, glockenspiel, tambourine, antique cymbals, tubular bells, 3 woodblocks, 3 temple blocks, snare drum, tenor drum, suspended cymbals, claves, bongos, side drum), piano (also celesta), violin I, violin II, viola, violoncello, double bass.
Commissioned by: Philadelphia Orchestra Association.
Call no.: **1997/073**

1321. Kirchner, Leon, 1919– Music for cello and orchestra. New York, NY: Associated Music Publishers, 1993.
1 score (68 p.); 36 cm.
"Latest corrected score 12/93"—p. 1.
Composed for: violoncello, 3 flutes, 2 oboes, English horn, 2 clarinets, bass clarinet, 2 bassoons, contrabassoon, 4 horns, 3 trumpets, 3 trombones, tuba, timpani, percussion (bells, xylophone, vibraphone, glockenspiel, tambourine, antique cymbals, tubular bells, 3 woodblocks, 3 temple blocks, snare drum, tenor drum, suspended cymbals, claves, bongos, side drum), piano (also celesta), violin I, violin II, viola, violoncello, double bass.
Commissioned by: Philadelphia Orchestra Association.
Call no.: **1994/072**
Re-entered as: **1995/050** and **1996/071**

1322. Kirchner, Leon, 1919– Music for twelve. Chester, NY: Associated Music, 1985.
1 score (58 p.); 36 cm.
Composed for: flute, oboe, clarinet, bassoon, trumpet, horn, trombone, piano, violin, viola, violoncello, double bass.
Commissioned by: Boston Symphony Orchestra.
Call no.: **1990/060**

1323. Kirchner, Leon, 1919– Music for twelve: 1985. N.p.: n.p., 1985.
1 score (58 leaves); 43 cm.
Reproduced from holograph.
Composed for: flute, oboe, clarinet, bassoon, trumpet, horn, trombone, piano, violin, viola, violoncello, double bass.
Commissioned by: Boston Symphony Orchestra.
Call no.: **1986/062**

1324. Kirchner, Leon, 1919– Of things exactly as they are: for soprano solo, baritone solo, chorus, and orchestra. New York, NY: Associated Music Publishers, 1997.
1 score (165 p.); 44 cm.
English words.
Texts from poems by Robinson Jeffers, Emily Dickinson, Edna St. Vincent Millay, Wallace Stevens, and Robert Lowell.
Composed for: soprano, baritone, SATB chorus, 3 flutes (3rd also piccolo), 2 oboes, English horn, 2 clarinets, bass clarinet, 2 bassoons, contrabassoon, 4 horns, 3 trumpets, 3 trombones, tuba, percussion (bass drum, tam-tam, antique cymbal, tubular bells, chimes, timpani, snare drum, woodblock, claves, xylophone, bongos, temple block, suspended cymbal, triangle, glockenspiel, tenor drum), harp, piano (also celesta), violin I, violin II, viola, violoncello, double bass.
Commissioned by: Serge Koussevitzky Music Foundation in the Library of Congress and Boston Symphony Orchestra.
Call no.: **1998/077**
Re-entered as: **2000/086**, **2001/082**, and **2003/061**

1325. Kirchner, Leon, 1919– Of things exactly as they are: for soprano solo, baritone solo, chorus, and orchestra. New York, NY: Associated Music Publishers, 1997.
1 score (165 p.); 36 cm.
English words.
Texts from poems by Robinson Jeffers, Emily Dickinson, Edna St. Vincent Millay, Wallace Stevens, and Robert Lowell.
Duration: 30:00.
Composed for: soprano, baritone, SATB chorus, 3 flutes (3rd also piccolo), 2 oboes, English horn, 2 clarinets, bass clarinet, 2 bassoons, contrabassoon, 4 horns, 3 trumpets, 3 trombones, tuba, percussion (bass drum, tam-tam, antique cymbal, tubular bells, chimes, timpani, snare drum, woodblock, claves, xylophone, bongos, temple block, suspended cymbal, triangle, glockenspiel, tenor drum), harp, piano (also celesta), violin I, violin II, viola, violoncello, double bass.
Commissioned by: Serge Koussevitzky Music Foundation in the Library of Congress and Boston Symphony Orchestra.
Call no.: **2002/101**

1326. Kirchner, Volker David, 1942– Hortus magicus: für Orchester (1994). Partitur. Mainz; New York, NY: Schott, 1994.
1 score (25 p.); 42 cm.
Duration: ca. 10:00.
Composed for: piccolo, 3 flutes, 2 oboes, English horn, 3 clarinets (3rd also bass clarinet), 2 bassoons, contrabassoon, 4 horns, 3 trumpets, 3 trombones, tuba, timpani, percussion (triangle, cymbals, tam-tam, crotales, tubular bells, side drum, bass drum, glockenspiel), harp, celesta, violin I, violin II, viola, violoncello, double bass.

Commissioned by: Deutscher Musikrat.
Call no.: **1995/051**

1327. Kirchner, Volker David, 1942– Konzert: für Horn und Orchester (1996). Partitur. Mainz; New York, NY: Schott, 1997.
1 score (55 p.); 42 cm.
Duration: ca. 18:00.
Composed for: horn, 2 flutes (2nd also piccolo), 2 oboes (2nd also English horn), 2 clarinets, 2 bassoons (2nd also contrabassoon), 3 horns, 2 trumpets, 2 trombones, percussion (triangle, antique cymbals, large cymbals, large tam-tam, snare drum, bass drum), harp, piano, violin I, violin II, viola, violoncello, double bass.
Commissioned by: Schleswig-Holstein Musik Festival.
Call no.: **1998/078**

1328. Kirchner, Volker David, 1942– Missa moguntina: für Soli, Chor und Orchester (1992/93). Partitur. Mainz; New York, NY: Schott, 1993.
1 score (93 p.); 42 cm.
Reproduced from manuscript.
Duration: ca. 55 min.
Composed for: soprano, mezzo-soprano, tenor, bass, 2 basses, SATB chorus, 3 flutes (3rd also piccolo), 3 oboes (3rd also English horn), 3 clarinets (3rd also bass clarinet), 2 bassoons, contrabassoon, 4 horns, 4 trumpets (3rd also piccolo trumpet), 3 trombones, tuba, timpani, percussion (triangle, cymbals, tam-tam, cylindrical drum, bass drum, bell plate, chimes, glockenspiel), organ, violin I, violin II, viola, violoncello, double bass.
Commissioned by: "Pro Musica Viva."
Call no.: **1994/073**

1329. Kiszko, Martin, 1958– Sea star: cantata for baritone soloist, choir (SATB) and orchestra. N.p.: Martin Kiszko, 2001.
1 score (124 p.); 42 cm.
English words by Anne Ridler.
Composed for: baritone, SATB chorus, piccolo, 2 flutes, 2 oboes, 2 clarinets, bass clarinet, 2 bassoons, 4 horns, 2 trumpets, 2 trombones, tuba, percussion (timpani, tubular bells, bell tree, suspended cymbal, glockenspiel, tam-tam, xylophone, triangle, cymbals, side drum, bass drum), 2 harps, piano, celesta, violin I, violin II, viola, violoncello, double bass.
Commissioned by: David Ogden.
Call no.: **2003/062**

1330. Kittelsen, Guttorm, 1951– Alle løper efter lykken—lykken løper efter = Each one's chasing happiness—but happiness is just behind. Oslo: Norsk Musikkinformasjon, 2000.
1 score (193 p.); 43 cm.
Ballet-ballad for orchestra.
Composed for: 3 flutes (2nd–3rd also piccolo), 2 oboes, English horn, clarinet in E♭, 2 clarinets, bass clarinet, 2 bassoons, contrabassoon, 4 horns, 3 trumpets, 2 trombones, bass trombone, tuba, piano, harp, 4 timpani, percussion (xylophone, glockenspiel, crotales, sizzle cymbals, floor tom-toms, agogo, cowbell, vibraphone, ride cymbal, crash cymbals, gong, bell tree, triangle, snare drum, congas, bass drum, marimba, hi-hat, tam-tam, suspended cymbals, vibraslap, timbales, tom-toms, kick drum), violin I, violin II, viola, violoncello, double bass.
Commissioned by: Norwegian National Opera.
Call no.: **2002/102**

1331. Kittelsen, Guttorm, 1951– Concert piece for symphonic band and percussion. Oslo: Norsk Musikkinformasjon, 1992.
1 score (55 p.); 37 cm.
"Heavily revised 22/1-92 (after Italian tour 08/92)."
Reproduced from holograph.
Duration: ca. 12:00.
Composed for: 2 piccolos, 2 flutes, 2 oboes, 2 bassoons, clarinet in E♭, 3 clarinets, bass clarinet, 2 alto saxophones, tenor saxophone, baritone saxophone, 4 horns, 3 cornets, 2 trumpets (both also piccolo trumpet), 3 trombones, baritone (also euphonium), tuba, timpani (also bass drum, crash cymbals, cabasa, sleigh bells), percussion (xylophone, snare drum, crash cymbals, bass drum, anvil, tubular bells, glockenspiel, bongos, 2 suspended cymbals, marimba, crotales, tam-tam).
Call no.: **1992/069**

1332. Kiurkchiiski, Krasimir, 1936– Visaless Schengen suite. Bojenzi, Bulgaria: n.p., 2001.
1 score (108 p.); 52 cm.
For orchestra.
Reproduced from manuscript.
Composed for: 3 flutes (3rd also piccolo), 2 oboes, English horn, 2 clarinets, bass clarinet, 3 bassoons (3rd also contrabassoon), 4 horns, 3 trumpets, 3 trombones, tuba, timpani, percussion, harp, celesta, violin I, violin II, viola, violoncello, double bass.
Call no.: **2004/065**

1333. Klatzow, Peter, 1945– From the poets: suite for piano: based on texts by South African authors. N.p.: n.p., 1992.
12 p. of music; 30 cm.
Program notes by the composer.
Contents: Gebed om die gebeente = Prayer for the bones

(D. J. Opperman)—Dae voor winter = Days preceding winter (Phil du Plessis)—The watermaid's cave ("BMR")—Impundulu (A. G. Visser).
Composed for: piano.
Commissioned by: SAMRO 1992.
Call no.: **1993/068**

1334. Klein, Immanuel, 1960– Couleurs printanières: pour orchestre, op. 3, 1983. Amsterdam: Donemus, 1983.
1 score (15 p.); 58 cm.
Reproduced from holograph.
Duration: 7:30.
Composed for: piccolo, 2 flutes, 2 oboes, 2 clarinets (2nd also clarinet in E♭), bass clarinet, 2 bassoons, contrabassoon, 4 horns, 2 trumpets, 2 trombones, bass trombone, tuba, timpani, percussion (xylophone, marimba, 2 woodblocks, bongos, congas, cymbals), harp, piano, violin I, violin II, viola, violoncello, double bass.
Call no.: **1988/059**

1335. Knapik, Eugeniusz, 1951– Up into the silence: na sopran solo, baryton solo i orkiestrę = for soprano solo, baritone solo and orchestra. Partytura = Score. Kraków: Polskie Wydawnictwo Muzyczne Sa, 2000.
1 score (2 v.); 30 cm.
English, German, and Italian words.
Texts by E. E. Cummings and Jan Fabre.
Contents: Love is more thicker . . . (E. E. Cummings); Unter den berstenden Eisspiegeln (Jan Fabre)—Now air is air and thing is thing; In a time's a noble mercy of proportion (E. E. Cummings).
Composed for: soprano, baritone, piccolo, 2 flutes, 2 oboes (2nd also English horn), clarinet, clarinet in A, bass clarinet, 2 bassoons, 4 horns, 2 trumpets, 2 trombones, tuba, percussion (timpani, chimes, glockenspiel, tom-toms, bongos, snare drum, suspended cymbal, crash cymbals, claves, bass drum, tam-tam), piano, violin I, violin II, viola, violoncello, double bass.
Commissioned by: Polskie Radio i Festiwal Kraków 2000.
Call no.: **2004/060**

1336. Knight, Edward, 1961– Night of the comets. N.p.: n.p., 2000.
1 score (2 v.); 36 cm.
English words.
Musical.
Composed for: voices, SATB chorus, 5 reeds, 2 horns, 3 trumpets, trombone, percussion, harp, digital keyboard, bass guitar, violin I, violin II, viola, violoncello, double bass.
Commissioned by: Oklahoma City University Margaret E. Petree College of Music & Performing Arts.
Call no.: **2003/063**

1337. Knussen, Oliver, 1952– Horn concerto, op. 28 (1994). London: Faber Music, 1996.
1 miniature score (53 p.); 30 cm.
"Revised October 1995"—p. 53.
Duration: ca. 13:00.
Composed for: horn, 2 flutes, 2 piccolos, 2 oboes, English horn, 2 clarinets, clarinet in E♭, bass clarinet, 2 bassoons, contrabassoon, 4 horns, 2 trumpets, 2 trombones, tuba, 2 sets of timpani, percussion (marimba, triangle, 2 large tam-tams, suspended cymbal), harp, celesta, violin I, violin II, viola, violoncello, double bass.
Commissioned by: Suntory Limited.
Call no.: **1997/074**

1338. Knussen, Oliver, 1952– Violin concerto (2002). London: Faber Music, 2002.
1 score (77 p.); 30 cm.
Duration: 17:00.
Composed for: violin, 3 flutes, oboe, English horn, 2 clarinets, bassoon, contrabassoon, 3 horns, 2 trumpets, 2 trombones, timpani (also ratchet), percussion (glockenspiel, vibraphone, tubular bells, 2 triangles, 2 pairs of suspended cymbals, side drum, tenor drum, tam-tam), piano (also celesta), harp, violin I, violin II, viola, violoncello, double bass.
Commissioned by: Pittsburgh Orchestra and Philadelphia Orchestra.
Call no.: **2004/061**

1339. Knussen, Oliver, 1952– Where the wild things are: fantasy opera in nine scenes: op. 20: 1979–83. London: Faber Music, 1979.
1 score (238 p.); 42 cm.
Words by Maurice Sendak.
Duration: ca. 40:00.
"This score may not represent the final published version of the work. No quotations from it may be made (whether music or words) without the written permission of the publishers."
Composed for: voices, 3 flutes (3rd also piccolo), oboe, English horn, 3 clarinets (3rd also clarinet in E♭), bassoon, contrabassoon, 4 horns, 3 trombones, percussion (vibraphone, 2 tubular bells, 2 triangles, suspended cymbal, 2 cowbells, whip, 3 temple blocks, wood clogs, tenor drum, 3 tom-toms, xylophone, anvil, sizzle cymbal, flexatone, 2 mounted cowbells, maracas, bass drum, balloon with pin, glockenspiel, wind machine, spring coil, tam-tam, gong, whip,

claves, vibraslap, tambourine), harp, piano (4 hands), violin I (6), violin II (6), 4 violas, 4 violoncellos, 4 double basses.
Commissioned by: Opéra National, Brussels.
Call no.: **1985/101**

1340. Ko, Fang-Long, 1947– Crying mermaid: for orchesra [sic]. N.p.: n.p., 1993.
1 score (35 p.); 36 cm.
Reproduced from manuscript.
Poem in English.
Composed for: 2 flutes, 2 oboes, 2 clarinets, 2 bassoons, 4 horns, 2 trumpets, 3 trombones, tuba, percussion (timpani, 3 cymbals, 5 temple blocks, 5 tom-toms, large Chinese tom-tom, 2 tam-tams, snare drum, triangle, gong, bass drum, slapstick), violin I, violin II, viola, violoncello, double bass.
Call no.: **1998/079**

1341. Kobialka, Daniel, 1943– Antiphony across. N.p.: Lisem Enterprises, 1984.
1 score (46 p.); 36 cm.
English words.
For solo electric violin, 2 sopranos, SATB, 2 string orchestras, 4 vibraphones, 3 organs, 2 glass harmonicas, and percussion.
Reproduced from manuscript.
Composed for: electric violin, 2 sopranos, SATB chorus, percussion (4 vibraphones, 2 glass harmonicas, roto-toms, gongs, xylophone, antique cymbals, temple bells, timpani, marimba, glockenspiel), 3 organs, violin I, violin II, viola, violoncello, double bass.
Commissioned by: California Bach Society.
Call no.: **1985/102**

1342. Koc, Marcelo, 1918– Ciclo de 5 cantos para voz y piano. N.p.: n.p., 1998.
1 score (36 p.); 36 cm.
Spanish words; also printed as text.
Texts by José Isaacson and Jorge Luis Borges.
Reproduced from manuscript.
Composed for: voice, piano.
Call no.: **2003/064**

1343. Koc, Marcelo, 1918– Concierto: para viola y orquesta, 1983. N.p.: n.p., 1983.
1 score (43 p.); 37 cm.
Reproduced from manuscript.
Duration: 13:10.
Composed for: viola, piccolo, 2 flutes, 2 oboes, 2 clarinets, 2 bassoons, 3 horns, 3 trumpets, 2 trombones, tuba, timpani, percussion (suspended cymbals, military drum, 2 claves, xylophone, vibraphone, glockenspiel), harp, violin I, violin II, viola, violoncello, double bass.
Call no.: **1985/103**

1344. Koc, Marcelo, 1918– Concierto para piano y orquesta (1993). N.p.: n.p., 1993.
1 score (44 p.); 39 cm.
Reproduced from manuscript.
Duration: 13:00.
Composed for: piano, piccolo, 2 flutes, 2 oboes, 2 clarinets, bass clarinet, 2 bassoons, contrabassoon, 3 horns, 3 trumpets, 3 trombones, tuba, timpani, percussion (xylophone, vibraphone, glockenspiel, tam-tam, suspended cymbals, triangle, bass drum, snare drum, 2 claves), harp, piano, violin I, violin II, viola, violoncello, double bass.
Call no.: **1997/075**

1345. Koc, Marcelo, 1918– Poema lirico: para flauta y orquesta. N.p.: n.p., 1998.
1 score (13 p.); 32 cm.
For flute with string orchestra.
Reproduced from manuscript.
Includes 2 poems by Jorge Luis Borges.
Composed for: flute, violin I, violin II, viola, violoncello, double bass.
Call no.: **2000/087**

1346. Koch, Frederick, 1923– Blue Monday: a cycle of songs. N.p.: n.p., 1994.
1 score (23 p.); 28 cm.
English words by Langston Hughes.
Contents: Blue Monday—Prayer meeting—Mother to son—Testimonial—Harlem night song—Life is fine—Fire—Stars—Joy.
Composed for: voice, piano.
Call no.: **1996/072**

1347. Koch, Frederick, 1923– Sonata for cello. N.p.: Frederick Koch, 1995.
1 score (18 p.); 28 cm.
Reproduced from holograph.
Composed for: violoncello, piano.
Call no.: **1997/076**

1348. Koch, Frederick, 1923– Sonata for cello & piano. Waltham, MA: F.E. Warren Music Service, 1998.
1 score (24 p.); 28 cm.
Cello part edited by Regina Mushabac.
Duration: ca. 10:00.
Includes biographical information.
Composed for: violoncello, piano.
Call no.: **2000/088**

1349. Kocsák, Tibor, 1954– Anna Karenina. N.p.: n.p., 1993.
1 score (2 v.); 30 cm.
Words by Miklós Tibor.
Opera.
"Rock színház"—cover.
Reproduced from manuscript.
Composed for: voices, flute, oboe, clarinet, 2 horns, 2 trumpets, 2 trombones, percussion, 2 synthesizers, guitar, violin I, violin II, viola, violoncello, double bass.
Call no.: **1995/052**

1350. Kohler, Leonard R., 1961– Organ works: G♭ major: for organ and synthesizor [sic]. N.p.: n.p., 1990.
1 score (6 leaves); 28 x 40 cm.
Reproduced from manuscript.
Composed for: organ, synthesizer.
Commissioned by: First English Lutheran Church of Great Falls, MT.
Call no.: **1991/064**

1351. Kohler, Leonard R., 1961– Organ works: no. 1–4. N.p.: I.A. Music, 2001.
20 p. of music; 22 x 35 cm.
Contents: G♭ major—D♭ major—E major (Sky)—C minor.
Composed for: organ.
Call no.: **2003/065**

1352. Kohler, Leonard R., 1961– String quartet no. 1: (quintet for strings and synthesizer). N.p.: n.p., 1990.
1 score (14 leaves); 30 x 44 cm.
Synthesizer doubles viola part.
Reproduced from manuscript.
Composed for: synthesizer, 2 violins, viola, violoncello.
Commissioned by: Cascade Quartet.
Call no.: **1990/061**

1353. Kohoutek, Ctirad, 1929– Jediná naděje: symfonický akvarel pro orchestr = L'unica speranza: acquarello sinfonico per orchestra = The only hope: symphonic watercolour for orchestra = Die einzige Hoffnung: symphonisches Aquarell für Orchester (1997). Partitura. N.p.: n.p., 1997.
1 score (25 p.); 39 cm.
Reproduced from manuscript.
Duration: ca. 11:30.
Composed for: 2 flutes (2nd also piccolo), 2 oboes, 2 clarinets, 2 bassoons, 4 horns, 3 trumpets, 3 trombones, tuba, harp, piano, percussion (timpani, tubular bells, 3 tom-toms, bass drum, thundersheet, 3 triangles, 3 suspended cymbals, snare drum, low tam-tam, vibraphone, temple blocks, cowbells, ratchet), violin I, violin II, viola, violoncello, double bass.
Call no.: **2004/062**
Also available:
Call no.: **2004/062 miniature score**

1354. Kolb, Barbara, 1939– All in good time: for orchestra. Full score. New York, NY: Boosey & Hawkes, 1994.
1 score (56 p.); 33 cm.
Composed for: piccolo, 2 flutes, 3 oboes, clarinet in E♭, 2 clarinets, bass clarinet, soprano saxophone, 2 bassoons, contrabassoon, 4 horns, 3 trumpets, 3 trombones, tuba, percussion (3 glockenspiels, vibraphone, temple blocks, xylophone, bass drum, woodblocks, sizzle cymbal, cowbells, bongos), violin I, violin II, viola, violoncellos, double bass.
Commissioned by: Philharmonic Symphony Society of New York.
Call no.: **1995/053**
Re-entered as: **1997/077**

1355. Kolb, Barbara, 1939– Millefoglie.
Call no.: **1986/063**
Re-entered as: **1989/067**
No materials available.

1356. Kolb, Barbara, 1939– Voyants. N.p.: Boosey & Hawkes, 1992.
1 score (75 p.); 36 cm.
For piano and chamber orchestra.
"Final revision September 1992."
Reproduced from manuscript.
Composed for: piano, flute, piccolo, oboe, clarinet, bassoon, horn, trumpet, trombone, percussion (vibraphone, high cymbal, low African wood drum, chime), violin I, violin II, viola, violoncello, double bass.
Commissioned by: Radio France.
Call no.: **1993/069**

1357. Kolb, Barbara, 1939– Voyants: for piano and chamber orchestra. N.p.: Boosey & Hawkes, 1995.
1 score (47 p.); 31 cm.
"1990–1992"—caption.
Duration: ca. 21:00.
Program note by Peter M. Wolrich.
Composed for: piano, flute, piccolo, oboe, clarinet, bassoon, horn, trumpet, trombone, percussion (vibraphone, high cymbal, low African wood drum, chime), violin I, violin II, viola, violoncello, double bass.
Commissioned by: Radio France.
Call no.: **1996/073**

1358. Komarova, Tatiana, 1968– Konzert: für Klavier und Orchester (2000/01). Partitur. Mainz: Ars Viva

Verlag, 2001.
1 score (53 p.); 42 cm.
Duration: ca. 20:00.
Composed for: piano, 2 flutes, 2 oboes, 2 clarinets, 2 bassoons, 4 horns, 2 trumpets, trombone, timpani, percussion (suspended cymbal, tam-tam, snare drum, bass drum, 3 woodblocks), violin I, violin II, viola, violoncello, double bass.
Commissioned by: Musikkollegium Winterthur.
Call no.: **2003/066**

1359. Koo, Chat-Po, 1954– The jujube tree: for orchestra and zheng. N.p.: n.p., 1991.
1 score (32 p.); 30 cm.
Reproduced from manuscript.
Duration: 10:00.
Composed for: 2 zhengs, 3 flutes (all also piccolo), 3 oboes, 3 clarinets (3rd also bass clarinet), 3 bassoons (3rd also contrabassoon), 4 horns, 3 trumpets, 3 trombones, tuba, timpani, percussion (xylophone, glockenspiel, crash cymbals, 2 woodblocks, tambourine, bass drum, gong, marimba, tubular bells, suspended cymbal, triangle, tam-tam), violin I, violin II, viola, violoncello, double bass.
Call no.: **1994/074**

1360. Kopelent, Marek, 1932– Aríijah: symfonický zpěv pro orchestr. Partitura. N.p.: n.p., 1996.
1 score (73 p.); 30 cm.
Reproduced from manuscript.
Duration: ca. 22:00.
Composed for: 3 flutes, 3 oboes, 3 clarinets, 3 bassoons, 6 horns, 6 trumpets, 3 trombones, percussion (2 gongs, 2 cowbells, suspended cymbal, 2 triangles, crotales, crash cymbals), violin I, violin II, viola, violoncello, double bass.
Commissioned by: Czech Philharmonic Orchestra.
Call no.: **1998/080**

1361. Koprowski, Peter Paul, 1947– Accordion concerto. N.p.: P.P. Koprowski, 1993.
1 score (121 p.); 37 cm.
Reproduced from manuscript.
Composed for: accordion, 2 flutes, 2 oboes, 2 clarinets, 2 bassoons, 2 horns, 2 trumpets, percussion (2 tam-tams, woodblock, suspended cymbal, sizzle cymbal, glockenspiel, xylophone, glass wind chimes, bell tree, bass drum, triangle, timpani, 2 bongos, 2 congas, ratchet, maracas), violin I, violin II, viola, violoncello, double bass.
Commissioned by: Joseph Petric and CBC Vancouver Orchestra.
Call no.: **1996/074**

1362. Koprowski, Peter Paul, 1947– Ancestral voices. N.p.: P.P. Koprowski, 1996.
1 score (42 p.); 37 cm.
For string orchestra.
Reproduced from manuscript.
Composed for: violin I, violin II, viola, violoncello I, violoncello II, violoncello III, double bass.
Commissioned by: Guelph Spring Festival Chamber Orchestra.
Call no.: **1997/078**

1363. Koprowski, Peter Paul, 1947– Sinfonia concertante. N.p.: P.P. Koprowski, 1992.
1 score (110 p.); 38 cm.
Reproduced from manuscript.
Composed for: piccolo, 2 flutes, 2 oboes, 2 clarinets, 2 bassoons, 2 horns, 2 trumpets, timpani, percussion (musical saw, vibraphone, bass drum, 2 tam-tams, castanets, xylophone, maraca, glass chimes, glockenspiel, guiro, 2 triangles), violin I, violin II, viola, violoncello, double bass.
Commissioned by: National Arts Centre Orchestra.
Call no.: **1994/075**

1364. Koprowski, Peter Paul, 1947– Woodwind quintet. N.p.: P.P. Koprowski, 1992.
1 score (46 p.); 28 x 44 cm.
Reproduced from manuscript.
Duration: ca. 25:00.
Composed for: flute, oboe, clarinet, horn, bassoon.
Commissioned by: Berlin Philharmonic Wind Quintet.
Call no.: **1995/054**

1365. Kopytman, Mark Ruvimovich, 1929– Cantus V: for viola and orchestra. Jerusalem: Israeli Music Publications, 1990.
1 score (85 p.); 37 cm.
Composed for: viola, 3 flutes (3rd also piccolo), 3 clarinets (3rd also bass clarinet), 3 trumpets, 3 trombones, percussion (triangle, castanets, chocalho, tambourine, temple blocks, 3 woodblocks, 3 bongos, 3 congas, snare drum, gong, tam-tam, orchestra bells, vibraphone, marimba, xylophone, timpani), harp, harpsichord, organ, celesta, violin I, violin II, viola, violoncello, double bass.
Call no.: **1993/070**

1366. Korndorf, Nikolaĭ, 1947–2001. Sempre tutti. N.p.: n.p., 1987.
1 score (62 p.); 41 cm.
For orchestra.
Reproduced from manuscript.
Composed for: 4 flutes (4th also piccolo), 3 oboes, 3 clarinets, 2 bassoons, contrabassoon, 8 horns, 5 trumpets, 4 trombones, 2 tubas, timpani, percussion (whip,

chimes, 7 tom-toms, glockenspiel, cymbals, suspended cymbal, 2 tam-tams, snare drum, 2 drums), bass guitar, violin I, violin II, viola, violoncello, double bass.
Call no.: **1991/065**

1367. Korneitchouk, Igor, 1956– Short circuits: duets for prepared violins. Encinitas, CA: The Studio at the Post, 1998.
1 score (40 p.); 28 cm.
Includes performance and preparation instructions.
Composed for: 2 prepared violins.
Call no.: **2002/103**

1368. Kox, Hans, 1930– Concerto no. 3 for violin and orchestra, 1993. Amsterdam: Donemus, 1993.
1 score (55 p.); 41 cm.
Duration: ca. 23:00.
Composed for: violin, flute, oboe, clarinet, bassoon, 2 horns, 2 trumpets, violin I, violin II, viola, violoncello, double bass.
Commissioned by: Fonds voor de Scheppende Toonkunst.
Call no.: **1997/079**

1369. Kraft, William, 1923– Concerto for English horn and orchestra: the grand encounter, 2002. N.p.: William Kraft, 2002.
1 score (46 p.); 36 cm.
Composed for: English horn, percussion (vibraphone, crotales, glockenspiel, 4 suspended cymbals, tuned gongs), harp, alto flute, guitar, violin, violoncello, 2 flutes (2nd also piccolo), 2 oboes, 3 clarinets (3rd also bass clarinet), 3 bassoons (3rd also contrabassoon), 4 horns, 3 trumpets, 3 trombones (1st also baritone), tuba, timpani, percussion (vibraphone, 4 suspended cymbals, tuned gongs, marimba, pedal bass drum, tenor drum, field drum, 2 snare drums, bongos, crash cymbals, bass drum, lath on leather, chimes, tam-tam, triangle), piano (also celesta), violin II, violin II, viola, violoncello, double bass.
Commissioned by: Los Angeles Philharmonic.
Call no.: **2005/079**

1370. Kraft, William, 1923– Concerto for timpani and orchestra, 1983. Van Nuys, CA: New Music West, 1983.
1 score (69 p.); 36 cm.
Reproduced from holograph.
First performed by Tom Akins, timpani, and the Indianapolis Symphony Orchestra, John Nelson, conductor, in Indianapolis, Mar. 10, 1984.
Duration: 23:00.
Composed for: timpani, 2 flutes (both also piccolo), 2 oboes (2nd also English horn), 2 clarinets, 2 bassoons, 4 horns, 3 trumpets, 3 trombones, tuba, percussion (glockenspiel, crotales, 2 temple bells, 6 graduated drums, 2 suspended cymbals, 5 temple blocks, crash cymbals, snare drum, field drum, xylophone, triangle, tam-tam, chimes, bass drum, vibraphone), harp, piano (also celesta), violin I, violin II, viola, violoncello, double bass.
Commissioned by: Indiana Percussion Projects.
Call no.: **1985/104**

1371. Kraft, William, 1923– Contextures II: the final beast. Van Nuys, CA: New Music West, 1986.
1 score (106 p.); 36 cm.
Words in English, German, romanized Greek, and Latin; also printed as text with English translation.
Composed for: soprano, tenor, SA boys' chorus, old music group (hurdy gurdy, handbells, mark tree, vielle, crumhorn, viola da gamba, harp, rebec, lute, low drum, 2 recorders, tambourine, flute), 4 flutes (3rd–4th also piccolo, 4th also alto flute), 4 oboes (4th also English horn), 4 clarinets (4th also bass clarinet, 3rd also clarinet in E♭), 4 bassoons (4th also contrabassoon), 4 horns, 4 trumpets, 3 trombones, bass trombone, tuba, timpani, percussion (vibraslap, 7 graduated drums, crotales, vibraphone, chimes, tambourine, 2 bell plates, 2 anvils, flexatone, xylophone, glockenspiel, 6 drums, sleigh bells, crash cymbals, 2 timbales, 5 brake drums, snare drum, 4 tam-tams, 6 stainless steel bowls, marimba, sleigh bells, 5 muted cowbells, bass drum, 5 roto-toms, 2 suspended cymbals, 2 tambourines), harp, piano (also celesta), violin I, violin II, viola, violoncello, double bass.
Commissioned by: Meet the Composer Orchestra Residencies Program.
Call no.: **1988/060**
Re-entered as: **1989/068**

1372. Kraft, William, 1923– Settings from Pierrot lunaire: for soprano, flute (piccolo, alto flute), clarinet (bass clarinet), violin (viola), cello, percussion, and piano. Score. Van Nuys, CA: New Music West, 1991.
1 score (5, 52 p.); 29 cm.
German words by Albert Giraud, translated by Otto Erich Hartleben; also printed as text with English translation by C. E. Cooper.
Duration: 28:00.
"The Prelude and Interludes I, II, and III may be performed separately under the title Pierrot mute"—p. 4.
Contents: Prelude—Feerie—Interlude I—Mein Bruder—Interlude II—Harlequinade—Fantasmagoria: Interlude III—Selbstmord.
Composed for: soprano, flute (also piccolo and alto

flute), clarinet in A (also clarinet and bass clarinet), violin (also viola), violoncello, piano, percussion (vibraphone, glockenspiel, crotales, 2 temple blocks, 2 woodblocks, 2 cowbells, crash cymbals, 3 suspended cymbals, 2 sets of sleigh bells, low tam-tam, vibraslap, tenor drum, field drum, snare drum, bongos, pedal bass drum, bass drum).
Commissioned by: Leonard Stein and Schoenberg Institute.
Call no.: **1994/076**

1373. Kraft, William, 1923– Veils and variations: for horn and orchestra, 1988. Van Nuys, CA: New Music West, 1988.
1 score (72 p.); 50 cm.
Reproduced from manuscript.
Duration: 27:30.
Composed for: horn, 3 flutes (3rd also piccolo and alto flute), 2 oboes, English horn, 3 clarinets (3rd also bass clarinet), 3 bassoons, 4 horns, 3 trumpets, 2 trombones, bass trombone, tuba, timpani, percussion (tam-tam, crotales, triangle, glockenspiel, 2 sleigh bells, marimba, bass drum, 2 chimes, vibraphone, vibraslap, sizzle cymbal, chimes, 4 suspended cymbals, 2 sleigh bells, 5 graduated drums, bongos), harp, piano (also celesta), violin I, violin II, viola, violoncello, double bass.
Commissioned by: Jeff von der Schmidt.
Call no.: **1990/062**

1374. Krajči, Mirko, 1968– Sinfonia da requiem. N.p.: n.p., 1994.
1 score (128 p.); 30 cm.
Latin words.
For SATB chorus and orchestra.
Reproduced from holograph.
Duration: 45:00.
Composed for: SATB chorus, 2 flutes, 2 oboes, 2 clarinets, 2 bassoons, 4 horns, 3 trumpets, 3 trombones, tuba, timpani, percussion (cymbals, suspended cymbal, tam-tam, bass drum, bells), harp, violin I, violin II, viola, violoncello, double bass.
Call no.: **1998/081**

1375. Kramer, Jonathan D., 1942–2004. About face: for orchestra. N.p.: J.D. Kramer, 1989.
1 score (94 p.); 44 cm.
"Revised 11/12/89."
Duration: 16:00.
Composed for: 3 flutes (2nd–3rd also piccolo), 3 oboes (3rd also English horn), 3 clarinets (2nd also clarinet in E♭, 3rd also bass clarinet), 3 bassoons (3rd also contrabassoon), 4 horns, 3 trumpets (1st also flugelhorn, 3rd also piccolo trumpet), 2 trombones, bass trombone, tuba, timpani, percussion (marimba, xylophone, suspended cymbal, triangle, tam-tam, snare drum, glockenspiel, bass drum, 2 tom-toms, vibraphone), harp, violin I, violin II, viola, violoncello, double bass.
Commissioned by: Cincinnati Symphony Orchestra.
Call no.: **1990/063**

1376. Kramer, Jonathan D., 1942–2004. Atlanta licks: for sextet. N.p.: J.D. Kramer, 1984.
1 score (30 p.); 44 cm.
Reproduced from manuscript.
Duration: 12:00.
"Corrected."
Composed for: flute (also piccolo and alto flute), clarinet in A (also bass clarinet), violin, viola, violoncello, piano.
Commissioned by: Atlanta Chamber Players.
Call no.: **1986/064**

1377. Kramer, Jonathan D., 1942–2004. Moments in and out of time.
Call no.: **1985/106**
No materials available.

1378. Kramer, Jonathan D., 1942–2004. No beginning, no end: for orchestra and chorus. N.p.: n.p., 1983.
1 score (55 p.); 44 cm.
English words by Peretz Markish (translated from Polish); also printed as text.
Reproduced from holograph.
For chorus (SATB) and orchestra.
Duration: 10:00.
Composed for: SATB chorus, 2 flutes (2nd also piccolo), 2 oboes (2nd also English horn), 2 clarinets, 2 bassoons, 2 horns, 2 trumpets, bass trombone, tuba, percussion (timpani, xylophone, tam-tam, suspended cymbal, snare drum, bass drum, glockenspiel), violin I, violin II, viola, violoncello, double bass.
Commissioned by: Albert Metzker.
Call no.: **1985/107**

1379. Kramer, Jonathan D., 1942–2004. Notta sonata: for two pianos and percussion. N.p.: J.D. Kramer, 1994.
1 score (63 p.); 36 cm.
"Revised 10/94."
Duration: ca. 24:00.
Composed for: 2 pianos, percussion (xylophone, marimba, vibraphone, glockenspiel, 3 snare drums, 5 tom-toms, 2 congas, bongo, bass drum, timpani, suspended cymbal, sizzle cymbal, 5 tuned gongs).

Commissioned by: Barlow Endowment for Music Composition.
Call no.: **1995/055**

1380. Kramer, Jonathan D., 1942–2004. Remembrance of a people: for string orchestra, piano and optional narrator (1996). Score. St. Louis, MO: MMB Music, 1998.
1 score (72 p.); 36 cm.
Duration: 23:00 (25:00 with narration).
Poems for narration by Roger B. Goodman.
Contents: Arbeit Macht Frei—Brief lives, endless memories—Past joys, present sorrows—Their deaths shall live.
Composed for: optional narrator, violin I, violin II, viola, violoncello, double bass, piano.
Call no.: **2002/104**

1381. Krček, Jaroslav, 1939– Mše č. 4 = Mass no 4. Partitura. N.p.: n.p., 1996.
1 score (66 p.); 30 cm.
Latin words.
Composed for: voice, SATB chorus, 2 flutes, oboe, clarinet, bassoon, 3 trumpets, 3 trombones, percussion (church bells, triangle), harp, violin I, violin II, viola, violoncello, double bass.
Call no.: **1998/082**

1382. Krček, Jaroslav, 1939– Symfonie č. 4: "Desiderata": o věcech potřebných = (O wisdom of life) 2000. Praha: ABM, 2000.
1 score (95 p.); 30 cm.
English words; also printed as text with Czech translation.
For mezzo-soprano (last mvt.) and orchestra.
Text by anonymous 17th-century author.
Contents: Radost = Joy—Spočinuti = Rest in peace—Vitalita (tanec) = Vitality (dance)—Moudrost: "Desiderata": (O věcech potřebných) = Wisdom (wisdom of life).
Composed for: mezzo-soprano, 2 flutes (also piccolo), 2 oboes, 2 clarinets, 2 bassoons, 2 horns, 2 trumpets, percussion (bongos, vibraphone, glockenspiel), violin II, violin II, viola, violoncello, double bass.
Call no.: **2005/080**

1383. Krenek, Ernst, 1900–1991. Konzert für Violoncello und Orchester II = Concerto for violoncello and orchestra: op. 236, 1982. Partitur. Kassel: Bärenreiter, 1983.
1 score (46 p.); 36 cm.
Composed for: violoncello, 2 flutes (2nd also piccolo), 2 oboes, 2 clarinets (2nd also bass clarinet), 2 bassoons, 4 horns, 2 trumpets, 2 trombones, percussion (vibraphone, xylophone, glockenspiel, bass drum, snare drum, field drum, cymbals, triangle, 4 bongos, guiro, tam-tam, woodblock), harp, violin I, violin II, viola, violoncello, double bass.
Commissioned by: ORF.
Call no.: **1988/061**

1384. Krenek, Ernst, 1900–1991. Symeon der Stylit: Oratorium, 1935–36. Partitur. Kassel; New York, NY: Bärenreiter, 1987.
1 score (135 p.); 40 cm.
German and Latin words.
For soloists (SMezTBar), narrator, and mixed chorus (SATB).
Text from Byzantinisches Christentum by Hugo Ball, alternating with texts from the Psalms in Latin.
Reproduced from manuscript.
Duration: ca. 1:00:00.
Composed for: narrator, soprano, mezzo-soprano, tenor, baritone, SATB chorus, flute (also piccolo), oboe, clarinet, bassoon, horn, trumpet, trombone, timpani, percussion (triangle, gong, tam-tam, snare drum, bass drum, cymbals, xylophone, glockenspiel, sandpaper), piano, violin I, violin II, viola, violoncello, double bass.
Call no.: **1989/069**

1385. Kreutz, Robert, 1922– Francesco: a musical biography. Complete orchestral score. Golden, CO: Willard F. Jabusch & Robert E. Kreutz, 1983.
1 score (3 v.); 28 cm.
English words by Willard F. Jabusch.
Opera in 3 acts.
Reproduced from manuscript.
Composed for: flute, oboe, clarinet, bassoon, horn, 2 trumpets, 2 trombones, harp, piano (also celesta), percussion (snare drum, triangle, cymbals, timpani), violin I, violin II, viola, violoncello, double bass.
Call no.: **1992/070**

1386. Krieger, Edino, 1928– Concerto: para dois violões e cordas = for two guitars and strings. N.p.: Edino Krieger, 1994.
1 score (77 p.); 30 cm.
Composed for: 2 guitars, violin I, violin II, viola, violoncello, double bass.
Commissioned by: GHA Records of Brussels.
Call no.: **2000/089**

1387. Kritz, Robert, 1925– Lamentations for the 21st century. N.p.: Robert Kritz, 2002.
1 score (various pagings); 28 cm.
English words by Brina Rodin.

Contents: They're marching again—Renewal—Why was it done?—The span of our lives—Across the wide abyss.
Composed for: soprano, baritone, clarinet, violin, viola, violoncello, piano.
Call no.: **2004/063**

1388. Kritz, Robert, 1925– String quintet 1946: for 2 violins, 2 violas and cello. N.p.: R. Kritz, 1997.
1 score (52 p.); 28 cm.
"Revised 8/97."
Composed for: 2 violins, 2 violas, violoncello.
Call no.: **2001/083**

1389. Krivit͡skiĭ, David Isaakovich, 1937– Kont͡sert: dli͡a violʹ d'amur i strunnogo orkestra = Concerto: for viola d'amore and string orchestra. Moscow: Sovetsky Kompozitor Publ., 1991.
1 score (67 p.); 29 cm.
Composed for: viola d'amore, 9 violins, 3 violas, 3 violoncellos, double bass.
Call no.: **1996/075**

1390. Krivit͡skiĭ, David Isaakovich, 1937– Lirit͡seskai͡a pesnʹ: poėma dli͡a simfonit͡seskogo orkestra = The lyric song: the poem for symphony orchestra. Partitura = Score. N.p.: n.p., 1993.
1 score (78 p.); 40 cm.
Reproduced from manuscript.
Duration: ca. 10:30.
Composed for: 2 piccolos, 2 flutes, 2 oboes, English horn, 2 clarinets, bass clarinet, alto saxophone, tenor saxophone, 2 bassoons, contrabassoon, 4 horns, 4 trumpets, 3 trombones, tuba, percussion (timpani, trap set, triangle, 3 tom-toms, tambourine, chimes, 2 marimbas, orchestra bells, tam-tam, vibraphone (also synthesizer), woodblock, claves, 3 temple blocks, slapstick), harp, piano, celesta, violin I, violin II, viola, violoncello, double bass.
Call no.: **1994/077**

1391. Krouse, Ian, 1956– Cantiga variations: (fractal in one movement on an ancient Spanish song): for four guitars and orchestra, op. 43. N.p.: n.p., 1995.
1 score (7, 78 p.); 28 x 36 cm.
Reproduced from holograph.
Duration: ca. 22:00.
Includes facsimiles of ancient song.
Composed for: 4 guitars, 2 flutes (2nd also piccolo), 2 oboes (2nd also English horn), 2 clarinets (2nd also bass clarinet), 2 bassoons (2nd also contrabassoon), 2 horns, 2 trumpets, trombone, bass trombone, percussion (timpani, crotales, tam-tam, glockenspiel, gongs, tom-tom, bass drum, chimes), violin I, violin II, viola, violoncello, double bass.
Call no.: **1998/083**

1392. Krouse, Ian, 1956– Concerto for bass clarinet and large orchestra. N.p.: Ian Krouse, 1988.
1 score (85 p.); 44 cm.
Duration: ca. 21:00.
Composed for: bass clarinet, 4 flutes (2nd and 4th also piccolo, 3rd also alto flute), 3 oboes, English horn, 3 clarinets (1st also clarinet in A, 2nd also bass clarinet, 3rd also clarinet in E♭), 3 bassoons, contrabassoon, 4 horns, 4 trumpets (1st also piccolo trumpet, 4th also bass trumpet), 2 trombones, bass trombone, tuba, timpani, percussion (snare drum, tenor drum, 2 suspended cymbals, crash cymbals, tambourine, bass drum, tam-tam, xylophone, hi-hat, marimba, glockenspiel, ratchet, 5 tuned gongs), harp, celesta, violin I, violin II, viola, violoncello, double bass.
Call no.: **1990/064**

1393. Kubo, Mayako, 1947– Rashomon: Oper in zwei Akten, nach der Erzählung "Im Dickicht" von Ryunosuke Akutagawa. Partitur. Wien: Ariadne, 2001.
1 score (various pagings); 42 cm.
Japanese words by the composer.
"The revised and Japanese version 2001"—p. 1.
Duration: ca. 1:30:00.
Composed for: soprano, alto, countertenor, 3 tenors, bass-baritone, bass, SATB chorus, 3 flutes (all also piccolo, 2nd also alto flute), 3 oboes (3rd also English horn), 3 clarinets (2nd also alto saxophone, 3rd also bass clarinet), 2 bassoons, contrabassoon, 4 horns, 3 trumpets (3rd also piccolo trumpet), 3 trombones, tuba (also contrabass tuba), percussion, piano (also celesta), harp, violin I, violin II, viola, violoncello, double bass.
Commissioned by: Nissay Theatre Tokyo 2001.
Call no.: **2004/064**

1394. Kuehl, William F., 1919– Miniatures. N.p.: n.p., 1988.
1 score (89 leaves); 35 cm.
For orchestra.
Reproduced from manuscript.
Contents: Day dream—Quiet scene—The chase—Lost in thought—Children at play—The return.
Composed for: 2 flutes (1st also piccolo), 2 oboes, 2 clarinets, 2 bassoons, 4 horns, 2 trumpets, trombone, timpani, percussion (snare drum, bass drum, vibraphone, tubular bells, cymbals, xylophone, woodblocks, maracas, tambourine, suspended cymbal, whip), piano, violin I, violin II, viola, violoncello, double bass.
Call no.: **1991/066**

1395. Kuerti, Anton, 1938– Concertino: for piano, flute, violin and strings (1994). N.p.: n.p., 1994.
1 score (26 p.); 36 cm.
Composed for: flute, violin, piano, violin I, violin II, viola, violoncello, double bass.
Call no.: **1996/076**

1396. Kuerti, Anton, 1938– Jupiter concerto: for wind quintet and strings, 1996. N.p.: n.p., 1996.
1 score (51 p.); 22 x 36 cm.
Composed for: flute, oboe, clarinet, horn, bassoon, violin I, violin II, viola, violoncello, double bass.
Call no.: **1998/084**

1397. Kuerti, Anton, 1938– Piano concerto.
Call no.: **1988/062**
No materials available.

1398. Kuerti, Anton, 1938– Waves of the sound: clarinet trio (1989). N.p.: n.p., 1989.
1 score (42 p.); 28 cm.
Composed for: clarinet in A, violoncello, piano.
Call no.: **1990/065**

1399. Kulenty, Hanna, 1961– 1st piano concerto: for piano and chamber orchestra, 1990. N.p.: n.p., 1990.
1 score (75 p.); 43 cm.
Reproduced from holograph.
Duration: ca. 18:00.
Composed for: piano, flute (also piccolo and alto flute), clarinet, soprano saxophone, alto saxophone, 2 horns, trumpet, 2 trombones, tuba, piano, electric guitar, electric bass guitar, percussion (2 handbells, bongo, woodblock, tam-tam, 8 gamelan gongs, chimes).
Commissioned by: Fonds voor de Schepppende Toonkunst.
Call no.: **1992/071**

1400. Kulenty, Hanna, 1961– Trumpet concerto: for trumpet solo and symphony orchestra, 2002. Amsterdam: Donemus, 2002.
1 score (82 p.); 42 cm.
Reproduced from holograph.
Duration: ca. 24:00.
Composed for: trumpet, 3 flutes, 3 oboes, 3 clarinets, 3 bassoons (also contrabassoon), 4 horns, 3 trumpets, 3 trombones, tuba, timpani, percussion (large tam tam, marimba, 2 woodblocks, snare drum, 2 tom-toms, 2 timpani, bass drum), piano, violin I (14), violin II (12), 10 violas, 8 violoncellos, 6 double basses (3 with C-string).
Commissioned by: Polish Radio Programme 2.
Call no.: **2005/081**

1401. Kulesha, Gary, 1954– Concerto: for recorder and small orchestra. N.p.: Gary Kulesha, 1991.
1 score (62 p.); 36 cm.
Reproduced from manuscript.
Duration: ca. 15:00.
Composed for: recorder, 2 oboes, bassoon, marimba, harpsichord, violin I, violin II, viola, violoncello.
Call no.: **1995/056**

1402. Kupferman, Meyer, 1926–2003. Concerto for 4 guitars (1998). Rhinebeck, NY: Soundspells Productions, 1998.
1 score (117 p.); 28 cm.
For 4 guitars and orchestra.
Reproduced from manuscript.
Duration: ca. 18:00.
Composed for: 4 guitars, flute (also piccolo), oboe (also English horn), 2 clarinets (2nd also alto saxophone and bass clarinet), bassoon (also contrabassoon), 2 horns, trumpet, bass trombone, timpani, percussion (snare drum, bass drum, tuned drums, bongos, tambourine, guiro, maracas, claves, whip, vibraslap, ratchet, cowbell, triangle, finger cymbals, bell tree, temple blocks, flexatone, brake drum, slide whistle, chimes, bells, vibraphone, xylophone, marimba, cymbals, tam-tam), piano (also celesta), violin I, violin II, viola, violoncello, double bass.
Commissioned by: Augustine Foundation.
Call no.: **2001/084**

1403. Kupferman, Meyer, 1926–2003. Jazz symphony: 1988. Rhinebeck, NY: Soundspells Productions, 1988.
1 score (218 p.); 36 cm.
For saxophone jazz soloist and mezzo-soprano jazz singer with orchestra.
Duration: ca. 35:00.
Composed for: saxophone, mezzo-soprano, 2 flutes (1st also alto flute, 2nd also piccolo), 2 oboes (2nd also English horn), 2 clarinets (2nd also bass clarinet), 2 bassoons (2nd also contrabassoon), 4 horns, 3 trumpets, 3 trombones, tuba, timpani, percussion (vibraphone, xylophone, bells, chimes, triangle, finger cymbals, antique cymbals, crash cymbals, agogo bells, cabasa, bell tree, 5 temple blocks, 5 tuned drums, squeeze drum, flexatone, slide whistle, vibraslap, brake drum, 3 suspended cymbals, trap set, snare drum, tam-tam, bongos, maracas, gourd, tambourine, bass drum), harp, piano, violin I, violin II, viola, violoncello, double bass.
Commissioned by: Imre Pallo and Hudson Valley Philharmonic.
Call no.: **1989/070**

1404. Kupferman, Meyer, 1926–2003. Symphonic odyssey: for orchestra (1990). Rhinebeck, NY: Soundspells Productions, 1990.
1 score (86 p.); 37 cm.
Duration: ca. 21:00.
Composed for: piccolo, 2 flutes, 2 oboes, English horn, 2 clarinets, bass clarinet, 2 bassoons, contrabassoon, 6 horns, 4 trumpets, 3 trombones, tuba, 4 timpani, percussion (snare drum, bass drum, bongos, 5 roto-toms, tambourine, maracas, temple blocks, cabasa, brake drum, whip, bean gourd, agogo bells, sleigh bells, finger cymbals, triangle, bell tree, 3 cymbals, tam-tam, vibraslap, flexatone, chimes, vibraphone, xylophone, marimba, bells), harp, piano, violin I, violin II, viola, violoncello, double bass.
Call no.: **1998/085**
Re-entered as: **2000/090**

1405. Kurtág, György, 1926– Meine Gefängniszelle, meine Textung: Kafka-Fragmente, op. 24. N.p.: n.p., 1985.
1 score (ca. 70 leaves); 37 cm.
Includes English translation of text (5 p.; 30 cm.)
Reproduced from manuscript.
Composed for: soprano, violin.
Call no.: **1988/063**
Re-entered as: **1989/071**

1406. Kurtág, György, 1926– . . . Quasi una fantasia . . . : für Klavier und Instrumentengruppen = for piano and groups of instruments = zongorára és hangszercsoportokra: op. 27. Budapest: Editio Musica, 1989.
1 score (28 p.); 41 cm.
"The various groups of instruments are to be seated in the room as to be separated from each other as far as possible."—p. 3.
Composed for: piano, group 1 (timpani, 4 bongos, 2 snare drums, tambourine, bass drum), group 2 (3 suspended cymbals, crash cymbals, 3 gongs, tam-tam, 2 triangles), group 3 (3 suspended cymbals, low gong, Indian bells, bamboo shakers, maracas, bicycle bells, 4 crotales, vibraphone, marimba, cimbalom, celesta, harp, harmonica), group 4 (flute (also piccolo and recorder), oboe, clarinet in E♭, bass clarinet, contrabassoon), group 5 (horn, trumpet, trombone, tuba), group 6 (2 violins, viola, violoncello, double bass).
Call no.: **1990/066**

1407. Kvam, Oddvar S., 1927– Querela pacis: per due cori e orchestra = Der Wortstreit über Frieden: für 2 Chöre und Orchestra = The dispute of peace: for 2 choirs and orchestra, op. 70. N.p.: Norsk Musikkinformasjon, 198-?.
1 score (115 p.); 36 cm.
Latin words.
Text by Desiderius Erasmus; includes German and English translation.
Reproduced from manuscript.
Duration: ca. 27:00.
Composed for: 2 SATB choruses, 3 flutes (3rd also piccolo), 3 oboes, 3 clarinets, 3 bassoons (3rd also contrabassoon), 4 horns, 3 trumpets, 3 trombones, tuba, timpani, percussion (bass drum, vibraphone, chimes, snare drum, cymbals, marimba (also bass marimba), xylophone, glockenspiel, tam-tam), harp, piano, violin I, violin II, viola, violoncello, double bass.
Call no.: **1985/105**

1408. Kyburz, Hanspeter, 1960– Noesis: für Orchester (2001). Partitur. Wiesbaden: Breitkopf, 2001.
1 score (84 p.); 56 cm.
Composed for: 4 flutes (1st–2nd also piccolo), 4 oboes (4th also English horn), 4 clarinets (1st also clarinet in E♭, 4th also bass clarinet), 4 bassoons (4th also contrabassoon), 6 horns, 4 trumpets, 4 trombones, tuba, percussion (xylophone, antique cymbals, gongs, crash cymbals, suspended cymbals, tam-tams, 2 bongos, tom-toms, bass drum, vibraphone, glockenspiel, splash cymbals, sizzle cymbals, hammer, snare drum, tambourine, 2 triangles, bass bow, 4 woodblocks, 4 temple blocks, hyoshigi, ride cymbals, guiro), timpani, 2 harps, piano (also celesta), violin I, violin II, violas, violoncellos, double bass.
Call no.: **2003/067**

1409. Kyr, Robert, 1952– On the nature of creation: a cycle of four motets for mixed chorus. Boston, MA: Ione Press, 2001.
1 score (7, 5, 124 p.); 28 cm.
English words; also printed as text.
Text by the composer and adapted from the Rig Veda and Genesis, a letter by Galileo to Johannes Kepler, the Mayan Book of Counsel (Popul Vuh), and a Seneca creation myth.
Includes piano accompaniment for rehearsal.
Program notes by the composer in English.
Contents: In the beginning—The celestial healer—The ballad of good mind—Let there be music.
Composed for: SATB chorus.
Call no.: **2005/082**

1410. La Montaine, John, 1920– Concerto II for piano and orchestra: transformations: opus 55. Hollywood, CA: Fredonia Press, 1987.
1 score (140 p.); 44 cm.
Reproduced from holograph.

Includes program notes by the composer.
Contents: Mysteries, labyrinth—Affections—Conflict—Wizardry.
Composed for: piano, piccolo, flute, oboe, English horn, clarinet in E♭, clarinet, bass clarinet, bassoon, contrabassoon, timpani, percussion (xylophone, crotales, 2 sleigh bells, maracas, woodblock, 5 temple blocks, bell wheel, 2 triangles, tambourine, whip, 3 suspended cymbals, 3 gongs, 5 drums, claves), violin I, violin II, viola, violoncello, double bass.
Commissioned by: Lucille Parrish Ward.
Call no.: **1996/077**

1411. La Montaine, John, 1920– The lessons of Advent: opus 52. Hollywood, CA: Fredonia Press, 1983.
1 score (107 p.); 28 cm.
Words from various sources.
Includes performance instructions.
Composed for: voices, double SATB chorus, narrator, trumpet, drums, handbell choir, harp, oboe, guitar, organ.
Call no.: **1985/112**

1412. La Montaine, John, 1920– The marshes of Glynn: for bass solo, chorus, and orchestra, opus 53. Full score. Hollywood, CA: Fredonia Press, 1984.
1 score (71 p.); 28 cm.
English words by Sidney Lanier; also printed as text.
Composed for: bass, SATB chorus, flute (also piccolo), oboe (also English horn), clarinet in E♭, clarinet, bassoon, horn, trumpet, percussion (marimba, crotales, temple blocks, maracas, tambourine, 3 suspended cymbals, 2 gongs), violin I, violin II, viola, violoncello, double bass.
Commissioned by: Folsom family.
Call no.: **1985/110**

1413. La Montaine, John, 1920– Symphonic variations: for piano and orchestra, opus 50. Hollywood, CA: Fredonia Press, 1982.
1 score (79 p.); 28 cm.
Composed for: piano, piccolo, flute, oboe, English horn, clarinet in E♭, clarinet, bass clarinet, bassoon, contrabassoon, 2 horns, 2 trumpets, trombone, bass trombone, timpani, percussion (xylophone, suspended cymbals, crotales, gong, tambourine, claves, whip, 3 woodblocks, triangle, maracas, temple blocks, metal bar, bass drum), violins I, violin II, viola, violoncello, double bass.
Call no.: **1985/111**

1414. Lachenmann, Helmut, 1935– II. Streichquartett: Reigen seliger Geister, 1989. Wiesbaden: Breitkopf & Härtel, 1989.
1 score (72 p.); 25 x 30 cm. + instructions (9 p.; 28 cm.).
Reproduced from holograph.
Performance instructions in German.
Composed for: 2 violins, viola, violoncello.
Commissioned by: Festival d'automne à Paris and Fondation Total pour la Musique.
Call no.: **1990/067**

1415. Lachenmann, Helmut, 1935– Ausklang: Musik für Klavier mit Orchester = music for piano with orchestra. Studienpartitur. Wiesbaden: Breitkopf & Härtel, 1986.
1 score (184 p.); 35 cm.
Partitur-Bibliothek; 5168.
Performance notes in German and English.
Duration: ca. 50:00.
Composed for: piano, piccolo, 2 flutes (both also piccolo), alto flute (also piccolo), 3 oboes, 3 clarinets, bass clarinet, 3 bassoons, contrabassoon, 4 horns, 3 trumpets, 3 trombones, tuba, timpani, percussion (timpani, 2 bongos, 6 rin, 2 suspended cymbals, tam-tam, Chinese cymbal, 4 woodblocks, 5 temple blocks, wooden rin, xylorimba, antique cymbals, snare drum, 2 tom-toms, 3 anvils, 2 styrofoam sheets, guiro, vibraphone, tubular bells, bass drum, 2 thundersheets), harp, violin I, violin II, viola, violoncello, double bass.
Call no.: **1987/042**

1416. Laderman, Ezra, 1924– Concerto for clarinet and strings. New York, NY: G. Schirmer, 1995.
1 score (102 p.); 36 cm.
Composed for: clarinet, violin I, violin II, viola I, viola II, violoncello I, violoncello II, double bass.
Call no.: **1996/078**

1417. Laderman, Ezra, 1924– Concerto for double orchestra: a play within a play, 1988. New York: G. Schirmer, 1991.
1 score (183 p.); 36 cm.
Reproduced from manuscript.
Composed for: 3 piccolos, 3 flutes, 2 oboes, English horn, 2 clarinets, bass clarinet, 2 bassoons, contrabassoon, 4 horns, 3 trumpets, 3 trombones, tuba, timpani, percussion (snare drum, side drum, tom-toms, tambourine, temple blocks, woodblocks, bass drum, xylophone, vibraphone, 2 tam-tams, glockenspiel, 3 hand cymbals, triangle, Oriental cymbals, Chinese cymbals), violin I, violin II, viola, violoncello, double bass.
Call no.: **1994/078**

1418. Laderman, Ezra, 1924– Concerto for violoncello and orchestra. Chester, NY: G. Schirmer, 1985.

1 score (105 p.); 36 cm.
Reproduced from holograph.
Composed for: violoncello, piccolo, 2 flutes, 2 oboes, English horn, 2 clarinets, 2 bassoons, 4 horns, 2 trumpets, 2 trombones, bass trombone, tuba, timpani, percussion (xylophone, cymbals, snare drum, tuned drum, vibraphone, temple blocks, woodblocks, tom-toms, crash cymbals, snare drum, rattle, bass drum, tambourine), celesta, violin I, violin II, viola, violoncello, double bass.
Call no.: **1991/067**

1419. Laderman, Ezra, 1924– A mass for Cain.
Call no.: **1985/108**
No materials available.

1420. Laderman, Ezra, 1924– Pentimento. N.p.: n.p., 1985.
1 score (82 p.); 57 cm.
Reproduced from holograph.
For orchestra.
At end: 3/14/85, Teaneck, N.J.
Duration: ca. 30:00.
Composed for: 3 flutes (all also piccolo), 2 oboes, English horn, 2 clarinets (both also clarinet in E♭), bass clarinet (also clarinet in E♭), 2 bassoons, contrabassoon, 4 horns, 3 trumpets, 2 trombones, bass trombone, tuba, timpani, percussion (xylophone, glockenspiel, vibraphone, cymbals, bass drum, snare drum, tubular bells, tom-toms, tambourine, temple blocks, woodblock, triangle, side drum, bongos, tam-tam, marimba, crash cymbals), piano (also celesta), violin I, violin II, viola, violoncello, double bass.
Commissioned by: Albany Symphony Orchestra.
Call no.: **1987/043**

1421. Laderman, Ezra, 1924– Quartet for piano and strings. New York, NY: G. Schirmer, 1996.
1 score (63 p.); 28 cm.
Composed for: violin, viola, violoncello, piano.
Call no.: **1997/080**

1422. Laderman, Ezra, 1924– Quintet for piano & string quartet. New York, NY: G. Schirmer, 1990.
1 score (61 p.); 28 cm.
Reproduced from manuscript.
Composed for: 2 violins, viola, violoncello, piano.
Call no.: **1992/072**

1423. Laderman, Ezra, 1924– Quintet for piano & string quartet. New York, NY: G. Schirmer, 1990.
1 score (63 p.); 28 cm.
"Revised version."
Reproduced from manuscript.
Composed for: piano, 2 violins, viola, violoncello.
Call no.: **1993/071**

1424. Laderman, Ezra, 1924– Sanctuary: an original theme and variations, 1986. Chester, NY: Schirmer, 1986.
1 score (49 p.); 39 cm.
For orchestra.
Reproduced from manuscript.
Composed for: 3 flutes (3rd also piccolo), 2 oboes, English horn, 2 clarinets, bass clarinet, 2 bassoons, contrabassoon, 4 horns, 3 trumpets, 2 trombones, bass trombone, tuba, timpani, percussion (xylophone, vibraphone, glockenspiel, snare drum, suspended cymbal, Chinese gong, wind chimes, bass drum, woodblock, hand cymbals, temple blocks, side drum), harp, violin I, violin II, viola, violoncello, double bass.
Call no.: **1988/064**
Re-entered as: **1989/072**

1425. Laderman, Ezra, 1924– Sonata no. 3: for piano. New York, NY: G. Schirmer, 2003 (1/21/04 printing).
48 p. of music; 31 cm.
Duration: ca. 45:00
Contents: Fantasia—Ten piano pieces—Variations.
Composed for: piano.
Call no.: **2005/083**

1426. Laderman, Ezra, 1924– String quartet no. 9. N. p.: Ezra Laderman, 1999.
1 score (54 p.); 28 cm.
Composed for: 2 violins, viola, violoncello.
Commissioned by: South Mountain Association.
Call no.: **2001/085**

1427. Laderman, Ezra, 1924– String quartet number nine. New York, NY: G. Schirmer, 1999.
1 score (54 p.); 28 cm.
Composed for: 2 violins, viola, violoncello.
Commissioned by: South Mountain Association.
Call no.: **2002/105**
Re-entered as: **2003/068** and **2004/066**

1428. Laderman, Ezra, 1924– Symphony no. 5: "Isaiah."
Call no.: **1985/109**
No materials available.

1429. Laderman, Ezra, 1924– Symphony no. 7. New York, NY: G. Schirmer, 1988.
1 score (113 p.); 38 cm.
Reproduced from holograph.

Composed for: 3 flutes (3rd also piccolo), 3 oboes (3rd also English horn), 3 clarinets (3rd also bass clarinet), 2 bassoons, contrabassoon, 4 horns, 3 trumpets, 3 trombones, tuba, timpani, percussion (xylophone, vibraphone, marimba, glockenspiel, snare drum, woodblock, temple blocks, bass drum, side drum, tam-tam, cymbals, tambourine), violin I, violin II, viola, violoncello, double bass.
Commissioned by: Dallas Symphony Orchestra.
Call no.: **1990/068**

1430. Laderman, Ezra, 1924– Symphony no. 8. New York, NY: G. Schirmer, 1992.
1 score (114 p.); 36 cm.
Reproduced from holograph.
Composed for: 3 flutes (3rd also piccolo), 3 oboes (3rd also English horn), 3 clarinets (also bass clarinet), 2 bassoons (also contrabassoon), 4 horns, 3 trumpets, 3 trombones, tuba, timpani, violin I, violin II, viola, violoncello, double bass.
Commissioned by: New Haven Symphony Orchestra.
Call no.: **1995/057**

1431. Laderman, Ezra, 1924– Yisrael. New York, NY: G. Schirmer, 1998.
1 score (151 p.); 43 cm.
For orchestra.
Composed for: 3 flutes (all also piccolo), 2 oboes, English horn, 2 clarinets (2nd also clarinet in E♭), bass clarinet, 3 bassoons, 4 horns, 3 trumpets, 3 trombones, tuba, timpani, percussion (snare drum, woodblocks, tambourine, claves, tom-toms, bass drum, triangle, suspended cymbal, crash cymbals, tenor drum, xylophone, vibraphone), violin I, violin II, viola, violoncello, double bass.
Call no.: **2000/091**

1432. Laitman, Lori, 1955– Holocaust 1944: for baritone and double bass. N.p.: Enchanted Knickers Music; Riverdale, NY: Classical Vocal Reprints, 2000.
1 score (30 p.); 28 cm.
English words by Ficowski, Vogel, Rozewicz, Gershon, and Ranasinghe, also printed as text.
Includes biographical notes.
Contents: I did not manage to save / Jerzy Ficowski—How can I see you, love / David Vogel—Both your mothers / Jerzy Ficowski—What luck; Massacre of the boys / Tadeusz Rozewicz—Race / Karen Gershon—Holocaust 1944 / Anne Ranasinghe.
Composed for: baritone, double bass.
Call no.: **2002/106**

1433. Lake, Tim, 1954– An American concerto for 5-string banjo and orchestra. N.p.: n.p., 1991.
1 score (261 p.); 28 cm.
Partially reproduced from holograph.
Includes performance instructions.
Composed for: banjo, 2 flutes, 2 oboes, English horn, 2 clarinets, 2 bassoons, contrabassoon, 4 horns, 2 trumpets, 3 trombones, tuba, timpani, percussion (tubular bells, castanets, snare drum, bass drum, cymbals, xylophone), violin I, violin II, viola, violoncello, double bass.
Call no.: **1995/058**

1434. Landowski, Marcel, 1915–2000. Montsegur: opera. Paris: Editions Salaber, 1985.
1 miniature score (223 p.); 32 cm.
French words.
Original work by Lévis-Mirepoix.
Reproduced from manuscript.
Composed for: 6 voices, SATB chorus, piccolo, 2 flutes, 2 oboes, English horn, 2 clarinets, bass clarinet, 2 bassoons, contrabassoon, 4 horns, 4 trumpets, 3 trombones, tuba, percussion (gong, xylophone, bass drum, snare drum, cymbals, vibraphone, woodblock, Chinese cymbal, tambourine, military drum, timpani, marimba, glockenspiel, bells), harp, synthesizer, guitar, violin I, violin II, viola, violoncello, double bass.
Call no.: **1986/065**

1435. Lanford, John Carrol, 1955– Iscariot, the betrayed: an oratorio of intrigue. N.p.: n.p., 1990.
1 score (145 p. in various pagings); 44 cm.
Thesis (D.M.A.)—University of South Carolina, 1990.
Composed for: baritone, bass, SATB chorus, piccolo, 2 flutes, oboe, clarinet, bassoon, horn, 3 trumpets, 2 trombones, tuba, timpani, percussion (suspended cymbal, tambourine, tubular chimes, mark tree), violin I, violin II, viola, violoncello, double bass.
Call no.: **1991/068**

1436. Lang, David A., 1957– Modern painters. Chester, NY: G. Schirmer Rental Library, 1995.
1 score (2 v. [408 p.]); 44 cm.
Words by Manuela Hoelterhoff.
Opera.
Composed for: 3 sopranos, mezzo-soprano, 6 tenors, 3 baritones, 2 basses, SATB chorus, 2 flutes (2nd also piccolo), 2 oboes (2nd also English horn), 2 clarinets (2nd also bass clarinet), 2 bassoons, 2 horns, 2 trumpets, trombone, bass trombone, percussion (vibraphone, xylophone, triangle, snare drum, bass drum, tom-tom, marimba, suspended cymbal, 2 metal pipes), harp, piano, violin I, violin II, viola, violoncello, double bass.
Commissioned by: Santa Fe Opera.
Call no.: **1996/079**

1437. Lang, David A., 1957– The passing measures. Chester, NY: G. Schirmer Rental Library, 1998.
1 score (76 p.); 28 cm.
Wordless.
Duration: ca. 45:00.
Composed for: bass clarinet, 8 (or more) altos, 4 horns, 3 trumpets, 3 trombones, tuba, percussion (4 brake drums, 4 tam-tams, timpani), 2 pianos, 8 (or more) violoncellos, 2 (or more) double basses, electric bass.
Commissioned by: Birmingham Jazz and Birmingham Contemporary Music Group.
Call no.: **2000/092**
Re-entered as: **2003/069**

1438. Láng, István, 1933– IV. Szimfónia. Partitura. Budapest: Editio Musica Budapest, 1984.
1 score (57 p.); 42 cm.
Reproduced from holograph.
Duration: ca. 20:00.
Composed for: 2 piccolos, 3 oboes, English horn, 2 clarinets, bass clarinet, alto saxophone, tenor saxophone, 2 bassoons (2nd also contrabassoon), 2 trumpets, 2 bass trombones, tuba, percussion (2 snare drums, wood drum, 5 tom-toms, 2 bass drums, guiro, 2 maracas, 3 triangles, 3 suspended cymbals, 2 tam-tams, metal block, marimba, vibraphone, chimes), 30 violins, 8 double basses.
Call no.: **1985/113**

1439. Langenhuysen, Niko, 1951– Modiano. N.p.: n.p., 1988.
1 score (11 p.); 35 cm.
Reproduced from holograph.
Composed for: 2 flutes, clarinet, 2 alto saxophones, 2 horns, trumpet, 2 trombones, tuba, piano, double bass, drum set.
Call no.: **1990/069**

1440. Lanza, Alcides, 1929– Piano concerto (1993–I): for piano and chamber orchestra. Montréal: Shelan, 1993.
1 score (iii, 18 p.); 26 x 38 cm.
Includes performance instructions.
Duration: ca. 24:00.
Composed for: piano, 2 flutes, 2 oboes, 2 clarinets, 2 bassoons, trombone, percussion (triangle, crotales, wind chimes, 5 temple blocks, 3 bongos, 3 drums, 3 suspended cymbals, 3 tam-tams, bass drum, xylophone, glockenspiel), violin I, violin II, viola, violoncello, double bass.
Commissioned by: Hugo Goldenzweig.
Call no.: **1994/079**

1441. Lanza, Alcides, 1929– Piano concerto (1993–I): for piano and chamber orchestra. Montréal: Shelan, 1993.
1 score (iv, 18 p.); 28 x 41 cm.
Includes performance instructions.
Duration: ca. 24:00.
Composed for: piano, 2 flutes, 2 oboes, 2 clarinets, 2 bassoons, trombone, percussion (triangle, crotales, wind chimes, 5 temple blocks, 3 bongos, 3 drums, 3 suspended cymbals, 3 tam-tams, bass drum, xylophone, glockenspiel), violin I, violin II, viola, violoncello, double bass.
Commissioned by: Hugo Goldenzweig.
Call no.: **1996/080**

1442. Lanza, Alcides, 1929– Sensors IV: for choir, with electronic and computer sounds. Montréal: Editions Shelan, 1984.
1 score (10 p.); 28 cm.
Duration: ca 12:00–14:00.
Includes performance instructions.
Composed for: SATB chorus, electronics, computer.
Call no.: **1989/073**

1443. LaPoint, Crystal, 1958– Five songs for five souls: a song-cycle for chorus & orchestra. N.p.: Crystal LaPoint, 1996.
1 score (106 p.); 44 cm.
English words.
Poems by John Ormond, R. S. Thomas, Philip Levine, John Crowe Ransom, and Charles Causley.
Contents: Cathedral builder—Ann Griffith—For Fran—Bells for John Whiteside's daughter—Timothy Winters.
Composed for: SATB chorus, flute (also piccolo), oboe (also English horn), clarinet (also bass clarinet), bassoon, tenor saxophone (also soprano and alto saxophones), 2 horns, trumpet, trombone, harp, piano, percussion (tubular chimes, orchestra bells, tom-tom, small metal wind chimes, timpani, vibraphone, snare drum, xylophone, suspended cymbal, crash cymbals), violin I, violin II, viola, violoncello, double bass.
Commissioned by: Syracuse Chorale.
Call no.: **2000/093**

1444. Larsen, Libby, 1950– Eric Hermannson's soul: opera in two acts. N.p.: Libby Larsen, 1998.
1 score (2 v. [465 p.]); 44 cm.
English words by Chas Rader-Shieber after the short story by Willa Cather.
Composed for: soprano, 2 mezzo-sopranos, 2 tenors, baritone, bass, vocal quartet (soprano, alto, tenor, and bass), SATB chorus, flute (also piccolo), oboe, clari-

net (also clarinet in E♭, bass clarinet), bassoon (also contrabassoon), horn, percussion (suspended cymbal, 2 triangles, 2 woodblocks, sand blocks, bass drum, snare drum, orchestra bells, low tam-tam, bamboo wind chimes, musical saw, timpani, vibraphone, brass wind chimes, marimba, tubular bells, tambourine, BB shaker, tom-tom), keyboard (also synthesizer), violin I, violin II, viola, violoncello, double bass.
Commissioned by: Opera Omaha.
Call no.: **2000/094**
Also available:
Call no.: **2000/094 vocal score**

1445. Larsen, Libby, 1950– Symphony #3: Lyric. Boston, MA: E.C. Schirmer, 1991.
1 score (97 p.); 43 cm.
Reproduced from manuscript.
Contents: Deep purple—Quiet—Since Armstrong.
Composed for: 3 flutes (3rd also piccolo), 3 oboes (3rd also English horn), 3 clarinets (3rd also bass clarinet), 2 bassoons, 4 horns, 3 trumpets, 3 trombones, tuba, timpani, percussion (vibraphone, 5 tom-toms, suspended cymbal, bell tree, sandpaper blocks, snare drum, hi-hat, marimba, orchestra bells, triangle, bass drum, large tam-tam, woodblock, chimes, sleigh bells), harp, piano, violin I, violin II, viola, violoncello, double bass.
Commissioned by: Albany Symphony Orchestra.
Call no.: **1997/081**

1446. Lasoń, Aleksander, 1951– III. symfonia "1999": na chór i orkiestrę = III. Symphony "1999": for choir and orchestra. Kraków, Poland: PWM Edition, 1997.
1 score (92 p.); 42 cm.
Greek words; also printed as text with Polish translation.
Text from the Septuagint version of the Old Testament.
Reproduced from holograph.
Duration: ca. 38:00.
Composed for: SATB chorus, 3 flutes (3rd also piccolo), 3 oboes (3rd also English horn), 4 clarinets, 4 horns, 3 trumpets, 3 trombones, timpani, percussion (whip, vibraphone, bells, large suspended cymbal, crash cymbals, 2 tam-tams, bass drum, 3 tom-toms), violin I, violin II, viola, violoncello, double bass.
Commissioned by: Polish Radio.
Call no.: **2000/095**

1447. Lateef, Yusef, 1920– African-American epic suite. N.p.: Y.A. Lateef, 199-?.
1 score (199 p.); 28 cm.
For quintet and orchestra.
Contents: The African as non-American—The middle passage and transmutation—Love for all—Freedom.
Composed for: African instruments (moan flute, bamboo flute, gimbre, clay pots, dumbek, conga, hirchiriki, conch, didgiridoo, malinke, nai, djute, tabla, duckaphone, kalango, soprano saxophone, guitar, Japanese temple flute, flugelhorn), flute, oboe, clarinet, bassoon, 2 horns, 2 trumpets, 2 trombones, tuba, percussion (timpani, tenor drum, glockenspiel, crotales, tam-tam, temple blocks, anvil, cymbals, tambourine, triangle), harp, violin I, violin II, viola, violoncello, double bass.
Commissioned by: WDR Köln.
Call no.: **2000/096**

1448. Lauber, Anne, 1943– Jesus Christus: oratorio: pour choeur, 5 solistes et orchestre. Québec: Centre de musique canadienne, 1984.
1 score (iv, 244 p.); 28 cm.
Latin words; also printed as texts with French and English translations.
Reproduced from holograph.
Duration: ca. 1:30:00.
Includes performance instructions in French with English translation.
Contents: Nativité—Béatitudes—Passion—Résurrection.
Composed for: soprano, alto, tenor, baritone, bass, SATB chorus, 2 flutes (2nd also piccolo), 2 oboes (2nd also English horn), 2 clarinets, 2 bassoons, 4 horns, 2 trumpets, trombone, bass trombone, timpani, percussion (gong, side drum, xylophone, tambourine, triangle, cowbells, bass drum, cymbals, 3 tom-toms, anvils, tam-tam, thundersheet, tubular bells, whistle, whip), violin I, violin II, viola, violoncello, double bass.
Call no.: **1987/044**

1449. Lauermann, Herbert, 1955– Verbum IV: "an die Sonne": für Orchester (1995). Partitur. Wien: Doblinger, 1996.
1 score (53 p.); 30 cm.
Reproduced from manuscript.
Duration: ca. 13:00.
Composed for: 2 flutes, 2 oboes, English horn, clarinet in E♭, clarinet, bass clarinet, 2 bassoons, contrabassoon, 2 horns, trumpet in D, trombone, percussion (xylorimba, crotales, antique cymbal, triangle, vibraphone, tam-tam, 3 suspended cymbals, snare drum, anvil), piano, violin I, violin II, viola, violoncello, double bass.
Commissioned by: Gesellschaft der Musikfreunde in Wien.
Call no.: **1998/086**

1450. Lauricella, Massimo, 1961– Cristalli di luce: for chamber orchestra. N.p.: BMG, 1993.

1 score (50 p.); 30 cm.
Duration: ca. 9:00.
Composed for: flute, oboe, clarinet, bassoon, horn, violin I, violin II, viola, violoncello, double bass.
Call no.: **1995/059**

1451. Lauricella, Massimo, 1961– Imis: per flauto, clarinetto in Si♭, quartetto d'archi e pianoforte. N.p.: n.p., 1996.
1 score (25 p.); 30 cm.
Duration: 10:00.
Composed for: flute, clarinet, 2 violins, viola, violoncello, piano.
Call no.: **1997/082**

1452. Lauricella, Massimo, 1961– Spectra: per orchestra. N.p.: n.p., 1992.
1 score (46 p.); 30 cm.
Duration: ca. 12:00.
Composed for: piccolo, 2 flutes, 2 oboes, 2 clarinets, 2 bassoons, 4 horns, 3 trumpets, 3 trombones, timpani, percussion (tam-tam, bass drum, suspended cymbal, military drum, vibraphone), harp, celesta, violin I, violin II, viola, violoncello, double bass.
Call no.: **1993/072**

1453. Lauricella, Massimo, 1961– Tremiti: per quartetto d'archi. N.p.: n.p., 1988.
1 score (16 p.); 30 cm.
Reproduced from manuscript.
Includes performance instructions in Italian.
Duration: ca. 10:00.
Composed for: 2 violins, viola, violoncello.
Call no.: **1990/070**

1454. Lauricella, Sergio, 1921– Il lamento di Dona Blanca de Bivar: per soprano e archi. Roma: Edi Pan, 198-?.
1 score (25 p.); 30 cm.
Italian words, also printed as text.
Text by Paolo Lingua, based on Les aventures du dernier Abencerage by F.-R. de Chateaubriand.
Reproduced from manuscript.
Composed for: soprano, violin I, violin II, viola, violoncello, double bass.
Call no.: **1990/071**

1455. Lauten, Elodie, 1950– Waking in New York: portrait of Allen Ginsberg: from the poetry of Allen Ginsberg. Orchestral score. New York, NY: Studio 21, 2003.
1 score (2 v.); 29 cm.
English words.
Opera.
Composed for: soprano, mezzo-soprano, baritone, flute, organ, percussion, violin I, violin II, viola, violoncello, double bass.
Call no.: **2005/084**

1456. Lavista, Mario, 1943– Missa brevis: ad consolationis Dominam nostram: para coro mixto a cappella (1994–95). N.p.: n.p., 1995.
1 score (71 p.); 28 cm.
Latin words.
Composed for: SATB chorus.
Call no.: **1997/083**

1457. Lazarof, Henri, 1932– Choral symphony (no. 3). Bryn Mawr, PA: Merion Music: Theodore Presser, 1993.
1 score (94 p.); 61 cm.
Macaronic text (Latin, Italian, French, Hebrew, English, Bulgarian, Russian, and German words) by the composer.
For alto and bass-baritone soloists, mixed chorus, and orchestra.
Reproduced from manuscript.
Composed for: alto, bass-baritone, SATB chorus, 3 flutes, 3 oboes, 3 clarinets, 3 bassoons, 4 trumpets, 6 horns, 2 trombones, bass trombone, tuba, percussion (tubular bells, tam-tam, bass drum, timpani, marimba, 3 woodblocks, 5 temple blocks, 5 tom-toms, snare drum, tenor drum, xylophone, suspended cymbal, glockenspiel, 2 bongos, 2 vibraphones), 2 harps, 2 pianos, violin I, violin II, violin III, viola, violoncello, double bass.
Commissioned by: Seattle Symphony Orchestra.
Call no.: **1995/060**

1458. Lazarof, Henri, 1932– Fifth string quartet, 1997. Bryn Mawr, PA: Merion Music: T. Presser, 1998.
1 score (22 p.) + 4 parts; 28 cm.
Duration: ca. 22:00.
Composed for: 2 violins, viola, violoncello.
Commissioned by: Borromeo String Quartet.
Call no.: **2002/107**

1459. Lazarof, Henri, 1932– In celebration: Symphony no. 4. Bryn Mawr, PA: Merion Music: T. Presser, 1998.
1 score (66 p.); 28 cm.
English words; also printed as text.
For chorus (SATB) and orchestra.
Duration: ca. 25:00.
Program and biographical notes in English.
Contents: . . . joyful song / adopted from Baron van

Swieten's text to Haydn's The Creation—from The Aeolian harp / text by Samuel Taylor Coleridge— . . . and rejoice / text adapted from Ecclesiastes 3: 1–8, 19 and from Psalm 98: 4–8.
Composed for: SATB chorus, 3 flutes (3rd also piccolo), 3 oboes, 3 clarinets (3rd also clarinet in E♭, bass clarinet), 3 bassoons (3rd also contrabassoon), 4 horns, 3 trumpets, 3 trombones, tuba, timpani, percussion (claves, vibraphone, snare drum, 3 tam-tams, 5 tom-toms, 3 suspended cymbals, tubular bells, bass drum, 2 bongos, marimba, triangle, crash cymbals), harp, piano, violin I, violin II, viola, violoncello, double bass.
Commissioned by: Seattle Symphony Orchestra.
Call no.: **2000/097**

1460. Lazarof, Henri, 1932– Second cello concerto. Bryn Mawr, PA: Merion Music: T. Presser, 1992.
1 score (55 p.); 31 cm.
Duration: ca. 25:00.
Composed for: violoncello, 3 flutes, 3 oboes, 3 clarinets (3rd also bass clarinet), 3 bassoons (3rd also contrabassoon), 4 horns, 3 trumpets, 2 trombones, bass trombone, tuba, timpani, percussion (vibraphone, glockenspiel, snare drum, tenor drum, marimba, 2 cymbals, 5 tom-toms, bass drum, 2 suspended cymbals, tubular bells, 4 bongos, xylophone, 3 gongs, tam-tam), harp, piano (also celesta), violin I, violin II, viola, violoncello, double bass.
Call no.: **1993/073**

1461. Lazarof, Henri, 1932– Tableaux: after Kandinsky: for piano and orchestra. Bryn Mawr, PA: Merion Music: T. Presser, 1989.
1 score (76 p.); 31 cm.
Duration: 26:30.
Composed for: piano, 4 flutes (4th also piccolo and alto flute), 4 oboes (4th also English horn), 4 clarinets (4th also bass clarinet), 4 bassoons (4th also contrabassoon), 6 horns, 4 trumpets, 2 trombones, bass trombone, tuba, timpani, percussion (glockenspiel, vibraphone, snare drum, 5 bongos, 3 woodblocks, bass drum, suspended cymbal, tubular bells, 5 tom-toms, tenor drum, 5 temple blocks, tambourine, 3 triangles, tam-tam, marimba), harp, piano, celesta (also harmonium), violin I, violin II, viola, violoncello, double bass.
Commissioned by: Seattle Symphony.
Call no.: **1991/069**

1462. LeBaron, Anne, 1953– Pope Joan: a dance opera: concert version (2000). N.p.: Golden Croak Music: New York, NY: Sozo Arts, 2000.
1 score (72 p.); 36 cm.
Words by Enid Shomer.
Three sections from the concert version may also be performed independently: After love (10:30), Hymn (17:00), Elegy (5:30).
Composed for: soprano, flute (also piccolo), oboe (also English horn), clarinet (also bass clarinet), piano, percussion (tablas, slapstick, tom-tom, vibraslap, tambourine, antique cymbals, triangle, woodblock, roto-toms, glockenspiel, gong, chimes, maraca, mark tree, drum set), violin, viola, violoncello.
Commissioned by: Pittsburgh New Music Ensemble and Dance Alloy.
Call no.: **2002/108**

1463. Lee, Ilse-Mari, 1962– Concerto for cello and orchestra: "Mandela." Bozeman, MT: Ilse-Mari Lee, 2002.
1 score (26 p.); 36 cm.
Contents: 1948—Lamento 1976—Jubilate 1994.
Composed for: violoncello, piccolo, 2 flutes (2nd also alto flute), 2 oboes, English horn, 2 bassoons, 4 horns, 3 trumpets, 3 trombones, tuba, timpani, percussion (bass drum, claves, congas, woodblock, rain stick, tom-toms, snare drum, tambourine, xylophone, claves), celesta, violin I, violin II, viola, violoncello, double bass.
Call no.: **2004/067**

1464. Lee, Ilse-Mari, 1962– Sacajawea: a woman's life in words and music. Bozeman, MT: I. van Wyk-Vick, 1993.
1 score (various pagings); 28 cm.
English words.
Composed for: soprano, flute, oboe, violoncello, percussion (bass drum, slit drum).
Call no.: **1994/166**

1465. Lee, Thomas Oboe, 1945– Eurydice: a tone poem for cello and orchestra, (1994–1995). Cambridge, MA: Departed Feathers Music, 1995.
1 score (118 p.); 36 cm.
Composed for: violoncello, 3 flutes (3rd also piccolo), 2 oboes, 2 clarinets, 2 bassoons, 4 horns, 2 trumpets, 3 trombones, tuba, timpani, percussion (2 cymbals, bass drum, triangle, snare drum, hi-hat, floor tom-tom), harp, violin I, violin II, viola, violoncello, double bass.
Commissioned by: Andrés Diaz and Civic Symphony Orchestra of Boston.
Call no.: **1996/081**

1466. Lee, Thomas Oboe, 1945– Harp concerto (1985). Jamaica Plain: Departed Feathers Music, 1985.

1 score (82 p.); 28 x 37 cm.
Reproduced from holograph.
Composed for: harp, flute (also piccolo), oboe, 2 clarinets, 2 horns, 2 trumpets, percussion (3 gongs, marimba, snare drum, 2 tom-toms, bass drum), violin I, violin II, viola, violoncello, double bass.
Commissioned by: Pro-Arte Chamber Orchestra and Ann Hobson-Pilot.
Call no.: **1988/065**

1467. Lee, Thomas Oboe, 1945– Harp concerto (1985). W. Somerville, MA: T.O. Lee, 1985.
1 score (80 p.); 29 x 37 cm.
Reproduced from holograph.
Composed for: harp, flute (also piccolo), oboe, 2 clarinets, 2 horns, 2 trumpets, percussion (3 gongs, marimba, snare drum, 2 tom-toms, bass drum), violin I, violin II, viola, violoncello, double bass.
Commissioned by: Pro-Arte Chamber Orchestra and Ann Hobson-Pilot.
Call no.: **1986/066**

1468. Lee, Thomas Oboe, 1945– Hylidae: the tree frogs.
Commissioned by: Collage New Music and National Endowment for the Arts.
Call no.: **1985/114**
No materials available.

1469. Lee, Thomas Oboe, 1945– —I never saw another butterfly: 1991. N.p.: n.p., 1991.
1 score (32 p.); 37 cm.
English words.
Reproduced from holograph.
Composed for: mezzo-soprano, clarinet, piano.
Commissioned by: Amnesty International USA.
Call no.: **1992/073**

1470. Lee, Thomas Oboe, 1945– Mass for the Holy Year 2000. Boston, MA: Departed Feathers Music, 2000.
1 score (3, 207 p.); 28 cm.
"In nine movements and scored for SATB chorus, chamber orchestra and organ. I set the entire Latin text from the Ordinary of the Mass. In between these sections, I added four settings of contemporary poems written in English."—program notes.
"S.D.G."
Composed for: SATB chorus, 2 flutes (2nd also piccolo), 2 oboes, 2 clarinets, 2 bassoons, 2 horns, 2 trumpets, 2 trombones, tuba, timpani, percussion (bass drum, triangle), harp, organ, violin I, violin II, viola, violoncello, double bass.
Commissioned by: Boston College.
Call no.: **2002/109**
Re-entered as: **2003/070**

1471. Lee, Thomas Oboe, 1945– Stabat Mater 2002. Cambridge, MA: Departed Feathers Music, 2002.
1 score (65 p.); 28 cm.
Latin words; also printed as text with English translation.
For SATB chorus with organ accompaniment.
Includes program notes.
Composed for: SATB chorus, organ.
Commissioned by: Music department and Jesuit community at Boston College.
Call no.: **2005/085**

1472. Lee, Thomas Oboe, 1945– String quartet on B flat (1989/90). Cambridge, MA: Departed Feathers Music, 1990.
1 score (29 leaves); 29 x 36 cm.
Reproduced from holograph.
Composed for: 2 violins, viola, violoncello.
Commissioned by: Harvard Musical Association.
Call no.: **1991/070**

1473. Lee, Thomas Oboe, 1945– String trio: (1985). N.p.: n.p., 1985.
1 score (18 p.); 28 x 36 cm.
Reproduced from holograph.
Composed for: violin, viola, violoncello.
Commissioned by: St. Paul Chamber Orchestra.
Call no.: **1987/045**

1474. Lee, Thomas Oboe, 1945– That mountain: a musical drama in seven parts (1991–1992). N.p.: n.p., 1992.
1 score (221 p.); 22 x 30 cm.
English words from the writings of Henry David Thoreau; also printed as text.
Cantata for baritone and chamber ensemble.
Composed for: baritone, flute, clarinet, violin, violoncello, piano, percussion (snare drum, cymbals, hi-hat, tam-tam, tom-tom, triangle).
Commissioned by: Thoreau Society.
Call no.: **1993/074**

1475. Leef, Yinam, 1953– Concerto: for viola and symphony orchestra (1997/98). Tel Aviv: Israel Music Institute, 1998.
1 score (77 p.); 42 cm.
Duration: ca. 21:00.
Composed for: viola, 2 flutes (2nd also piccolo), 2 oboes

(2nd also English horn), 2 clarinets (2nd also bass clarinet), 2 bassoons, 3 horns, 2 trumpets, trombone, timpani, percussion (suspended cymbal, vibraphone, bass drum, 2 woodblocks, 4 temple blocks, tambourine, marimba, low tam-tam, 3 suspended cymbals, 4 tom-toms, snare drum), piano, violin I, violin II, viola, violoncello, double bass.
Commissioned by: Jerusalem Symphony Orchestra, IBA.
Call no.: **2000/098**

1476. Leek, Stephen, 1959– Great southern spirits: for SATB a cappella choir. Towong, Qld., Australia: Morton Music, 1993.
1 score (30 p.); 30 cm.
English words; also printed as text.
Texts by Anne Fairburn, Michael Doneman, and Stephen Leek.
Reproduced from manuscript.
Contents: Wirindji—Mulga—Kondalilla—Uluru.
Composed for: SATB chorus.
Call no.: **1996/082**

1477. Lees, Benjamin, 1924– Concerto for brass and orchestra.
Commissioned by: Dallas Symphony Orchestra.
Call no.: **1985/116**
No materials available.

1478. Lees, Benjamin, 1924– Concerto for French horn and orchestra. Study score. New York, NY: Boosey & Hawkes, 1992.
1 score (101 p.); 28 cm.
Composed for: horn, 3 flutes (2nd–3rd also piccolo), 3 oboes, 3 clarinets, 3 bassoons (3rd also contrabassoon), 4 horns, 3 trumpets, 2 trombones, bass trombone, tuba, timpani, percussion (bass drum, tam-tam, glockenspiel, snare drum, chimes, crash cymbals, suspended cymbals), celesta, violin I, violin II, viola, violoncello, double bass.
Commissioned by: Pittsburgh Symphony Orchestra.
Call no.: **1996/083**
Re-entered as: **1997/084**

1479. Lees, Benjamin, 1924– Concerto for percussion and orchestra. Full score. N.p.: Boosey & Hawkes, 1999.
1 score (67 p.); 36 cm.
Composed for: 3 flutes, 3 oboes, 3 clarinets, 3 bassoons, 4 horns, 3 trumpets, 2 trombones, bass trombone, tuba, timpani, percussion (xylophone, suspended cymbals, snare drum, temple blocks, tenor drum, bass drum, maracas, tam-tam, field drums, woodblock, castanets, anvil, tubular bells, glockenspiel, bongos, triangle, finger cymbals, tom-toms, energy chimes), harp, celesta, violin I, violin II, viola, violoncello, double bass.
Commissioned by: Orchestre Philharmonique de Monte Carlo.
Call no.: **2001/087**

1480. Lees, Benjamin, 1924– Echoes of Normandy: for tenor solo, organ, tape and orchestra. Full score. New York, NY: Boosey & Hawkes, 1994.
1 score (122 p.); 33 cm.
English words.
Poems by Richard Nickson, Louis Simpson, and Henry Wadsworth Longfellow.
Composed for: tenor, organ, tape, piccolo, 2 flutes, 3 oboes, 3 clarinets, 3 bassoons, 4 horns, 3 trumpets, 3 trombones, tuba, timpani, percussion (glockenspiel, xylophone, bass drum, snare drum, tam-tam, suspended cymbal, field drums, tenor drum, temple blocks, triangle), violin I, violin II, viola, violoncello, double bass.
Commissioned by: Dallas Symphony Orchestra.
Call no.: **2000/099**

1481. Lees, Benjamin, 1924– Fantasy variations: for solo piano. N.p.: n.p., 1983.
25 p. of music; 37 cm.
Reproduced from manuscript.
Composed for: piano.
Call no.: **1985/115**
Re-entered as: **1988/066**

1482. Lees, Benjamin, 1924– Piano trio no 2: ("Silent voices"). Palm Springs, CA: Benjamin Lees, 1998.
1 score (25 p.); 28 cm.
Composed for: violin, violoncello, piano.
Call no.: **2002/110**

1483. Lees, Benjamin, 1924– String quartet: no. 4. N. p.: Boosey & Hawkes, 1990.
1 score (48 p.); 28 cm.
Reproduced from holograph.
Composed for: 2 violins, viola, violoncello.
Commissioned by: Chamber Music America.
Call no.: **1993/075**

1484. Lees, Benjamin, 1924– String quartet no. 5. N. p.: Boosey & Hawkes, 2001.
1 score (79 p.); 31 cm.
Composed for: 2 violins, viola, violoncello.
Commissioned by: Cypress String Quartet.
Call no.: **2004/068**

1485. Lees, Benjamin, 1924– Symphony no. 4: ("Memorial candles"): for mezzo-soprano, with violin solos. New York, NY: Boosey & Hawkes, 1986.
1 score (117 p.); 44 cm.
Words by Nelly.
Reproduction from holograph.
Duration: ca. 50:00.
Composed for: mezzo-soprano, violins, 3 flutes (3rd also piccolo), 3 oboes, 3 clarinets, 3 bassoons (3rd also contrabassoon), 4 horns, 3 trumpets, 2 trombones, bass trombone, tuba, timpani, percussion (bass drum, snare drum, cymbals, temple blocks, tambourine, tam-tam, glockenspiel, celesta, bells, xylophone, triangle), harp, violin I, violin II, viola, violoncello, double bass.
Commissioned by: Dallas Symphony Orchestra.
Call no.: **1986/067**

1486. LeFanu, Nicola, 1947– The wildman: opera in 2 acts. London: Novello, 1995.
1 score (2 v. [iv, 423 p.]); 30 cm.
English words by Kevin Crossley-Holland.
Composed for: 14 voices, SATB chorus, flute (also piccolo and alto flute), oboe (also English horn), clarinet (also clarinets in E♭ and A, bass clarinet), horn, trumpet, percussion (suspended cymbal, vibraphone, tom-toms, bongos, bass drum, tam-tam, water gong, waterphone, squeeze drum, log drums, ratchet, slapstick, maracas, metal tubes, rain stick, stones, flexatone, tabor, temple blocks, crash cymbals), violin I, violin II, viola, violoncello, double bass.
Commissioned by: Aldeburgh Foundation, Theatre Royal, Bury St. Edmunds, and Major Road.
Call no.: **1996/084**

1487. Lenchantín, Ana Lía, 1947– "Dialogo": symphonic poem. N.p.: n.p., 1995.
1 score (3 leaves); 22 x 26 cm.
Originally for bandeon and string orchestra; arranged for string quintet.
Reproduced from manuscript.
Composed for: 2 violins, viola, violoncello, double bass.
Call no.: **2001/088 no.1**

1488. Lenchantín, Ana Lía, 1947– "That window": symphonic poem for bandoneón and string orchestra. N.p.: n.p., 1995.
2 leaves of music; 28 cm.
"Piano version."
Reproduced from manuscript.
Composed for: piano.
Call no.: **2001/088 no.2**

1489. Lendvay, Kamilló, 1928– Concerto: per sassofono soprano, orchestra e 12 voci femminile. Budapest: Kamilló Lendvay, 1996.
1 score (59 p.); 35 cm.
Wordless.
Reproduced from holograph.
Composed for: soprano saxophone, women's chorus, piccolo, 2 flutes (1st also alto flute), 2 oboes, English horn, 2 clarinets, bass clarinet, 2 bassoons, 4 horns, 3 trumpets, 3 trombones, tuba, timpani, percussion (snare drum, tambourine, tenor drum, 3 tom-toms, 3 bongos, bass drum, suspended cymbal, crash cymbals, triangle, vibraphone, xylophone, glockenspiel, crotales, celesta, cowbell, sleigh bells), harp, violin I, violin II, viola, violoncello, double bass.
Call no.: **1998/087**

1490. Lendvay, Kamilló, 1928– Stabat mater: pour mezzo-soprano solo et coeur avec accompagnement du petit orchestre, 1991. Partition. Budapest: Edition Musica Budapest, 1991.
1 score (92 p.); 35 cm.
Latin words; also printed as text.
Reproduced from holograph.
Duration: 28:00.
At end of score: 1991.jan.9–apr.27.
Composed for: mezzo-soprano, SATB chorus, oboe, clarinet, bass clarinet, bassoon, horn, organ, violin I, violin II, viola, violoncello, double bass.
Commissioned by: ARIAM Ile-de-France and Ministère de la Culture.
Call no.: **1993/076**

1491. Lennon, John Anthony, 1950– Zingari: concerto for guitar and orchestra in five movements. N.p.: ECS Publishing, 1991.
1 score (146 p.); 36 cm.
Reproduced from manuscript.
Contents: Fortuneteller—Two thieves—Call of the maiden's name—Play of the sixes—Firefeast for St. Sara.
Composed for: guitar, 3 flutes (3rd also piccolo), 2 oboes, English horn, 2 clarinets, bass clarinet, 2 bassoons, 4 horns, 3 trumpets, trombone, percussion (timpani, glockenspiel, small suspended cymbal, bass drum, temple blocks, woodblocks, 4 triangles, tubular bells, medium cymbals, medium suspended cymbal, tom-toms, xylophone, tambourine, tom-toms), harp, piano, violin I, violin II, viola, violoncello, double bass.
Call no.: **1994/080**

1492. Lentz, Daniel, 1942– Cafe desire. N.p.: LentzMusic, 2002.
1 score (110 p.); 43 cm.

English words.
For solo male soprano, solo female baritone, solo violin, solo piano, MIDI keyboards, mixed choir, 28-member wine glass ensemble, and orchestra (or virtual orchestra).
Text based on pop songs (1960s–1980s) and excerpts from love letters.
Composed for: male soprano, female baritone, violin, piano, MIDI keyboards, wine glass ensemble, 3 flutes, alto flute, 2 oboes, English horn, 6 clarinets (5th–6th also bass clarinet), bass clarinet, 3 bassoons, contrabassoon, 6 horns, 6 trumpets, 4 trombones (4th also bass trombone), bass trombone, percussion, violin I, violin II, viola, violoncello, double bass.
Call no.: **2004/069**

1493. Lentz, Georges, 1965– Ngangkar: for orchestra (1998–2000): from "Mysterium" ("Caeli enarrant . . ." VII). Wien: Universal Edition, 2000.
1 score (16 p.); 42 cm.
Reproduced from manuscript.
Composed for: alto flute, 2 clarinets (2nd also bass clarinet), 4 horns, 3 trumpets, 3 trombones, percussion (cymbals, glockenspiel, high gongs, marimba, crotales, Thai gongs, tubular bells, vibraphone) piano, harpsichord (also celesta), harp, violin I, violin II, viola, violoncello, double bass.
Commissioned by: Symphony Australia.
Call no.: **2002/111**

1494. León, Tania, 1943– Desde . . . : for orchestra. New York, NY: Peermusic Classical, 2001.
1 score (86 p.); 44 cm.
Duration: ca. 19:00.
Composed for: 3 flutes (2nd–3rd also piccolo), 2 oboes (2nd also English horn), 2 clarinets, bass clarinet, 2 bassoons, contrabassoon, 4 horns, 3 trumpets (1st also trumpet in D), 2 trombones, bass trombone, tuba, timpani, percussion (bass drum, 3 roto-toms, 3 bongos, medium sizzle cymbal, glockenspiel, crotales, 3 tom-toms, snare drum, mounted castanets, medium cowbell, 2 maracas, vibraphone, 2 congas, 2 timbales, log drum, 2 cymbals, marimba), harp, piano (also celesta), violin I, violin II, viola, violoncello, double bass.
Call no.: **2004/070**

1495. León, Tania, 1943– Horizons: for orchestra. New York, NY: Peermusic, 1999.
1 score (53 p.); 44 cm.
Composed for: 2 flutes (2nd also piccolo), 2 oboes (2nd also English horn), 2 clarinets, bass clarinet, 2 bassoons (2nd also contrabassoon), 4 horns, 3 trumpets, trombone, bass trombone, tuba, timpani, percussion (pitched roto-toms, tom-toms, snare drum, bongos, vibraphone, marimba, timbales, suspended cymbal, tam-tam, bass drum), harp, piano, violin I, violin II, viola, violoncello, double bass.
Commissioned by: Hammoniale-Festival der Frauen 1999.
Call no.: **2001/089**

1496. León, Tania, 1943– Scourge of hyacinths: opera in twelve scenes: based on the play A scourge of hyacinths by Wole Soyinka. New York, NY: Southern Music Pub. Co.; Hamburg: Peer Musikverlag, 1994.
1 score (2 v.); 28 cm.
English words.
Duration: ca. 1:30:00.
Composed for: mezzo-soprano, 3 tenors, 3 baritones, bass, flute (also alto flute and piccolo), clarinet (also bass and alto clarinets), soprano saxophone (also tenor saxophone), horn, trumpet (also cornet), trombone, percussion (4 tom-toms, snare drum, 2 bongos, 2 clay drums, 2 shakers, talking drums, quijada, guiro, nail chimes, tam-tam, sand block, 2 cowbells, mounted tambourine, vibraslap, 2 kalimbas, spirit catcher brushes, slit drum, 4 roto-toms, marimba, tubular bells, wood chimes, maracas, 2 agogo bells, suspended cymbal, bass drum, vibraphone, military drum, pedal bass drum, bell chimes, 2 congas, glockenspiel, crotales, 2 timbales, whip, box of assorted bells), piano (also celesta), violin I, violin II, viola, violoncello, double bass.
Commissioned by: City of Munich.
Call no.: **1995/061**
Also available:
Call no.: **1995/061 libretto**

1497. León, Tania, 1943– Scourge of hyacinths: opera in twelve scenes: based on the play A scourge of hyacinths by Wole Soyinka. Full score. New York, NY: Peermusic, 1995.
1 score (2 v.); 28 cm.
English words.
Duration: ca. 1:30:00.
Composed for: mezzo-soprano, 3 tenors, 3 baritones, bass, flute (also alto flute and piccolo), clarinet (also bass and alto clarinets), soprano saxophone (also tenor saxophone), horn, trumpet (also cornet), trombone, percussion (4 tom-toms, snare drum, 2 bongos, 2 clay drums, 2 shakers, talking drums, quijada, guiro, nail chimes, tam-tam, sand block, 2 cowbells, mounted tambourine, vibraslap, 2 kalimbas, spirit catcher brushes, slit drum, 4 roto-toms, marimba, tubular bells, wood chimes, 2 agogo bells, suspended cymbal, maracas, bass drum, vibraphone, military drum, pedal

bass drum, bell chimes, 2 congas, glockenspîel, crotales, 2 timbales, whip, box of assorted bells), piano (also celesta), violin I, violin II, viola, violoncello, double bass.
Commissioned by: City of Munich.
Call no.: **1998/088**

1498. Leprai, Andrea, 1963– 24 Preludes op. 1: for piano. N.p.: n.p., 1991.
37 p. of music; 30 cm.
Reproduced from manuscript.
Composed for: piano.
Call no.: **1993/077**

1499. Leprai, Andrea, 1963– Moments of love: for piano. N.p.: n.p., 1995.
41 p. of music; 30 cm.
Reproduced from holograph.
Composed for: piano.
Call no.: **1996/085**

1500. Lerdahl, Fred, 1943– Cross-currents: for orchestra, 1987. N.p.: Fred Lerdahl, 1987.
1 miniature score (38 p.); 43 cm.
Reproduced from manuscript.
Duration: ca. 10:00.
Composed for: 3 flutes (3rd also piccolo), 3 oboes, 3 clarinets, 3 bassoons, 4 horns, 2 trumpets, 2 trombones, bass trombone, tuba, percussion (3 cymbals, tam-tam, 6 tom-toms, timpani, glockenspiel, vibraphone, xylophone, marimba, tubular bells), harp, piano, violin I, violin II, viola, violoncello, double bass.
Call no.: **1990/072**

1501. Lesemann, Frederick, 1936– Symphony no. 2. N.p.: Frederick Lesemann, 1994.
1 score (150 p.); 36 cm.
Duration: 25:45.
Composed for: 3 flutes, 3 oboes (3rd also English horn), 3 clarinets (3rd also bass clarinet), 3 bassoons, 4 horns, 3 trumpets, 3 trombones, tuba, percussion (2 tom-toms, suspended cymbal, snare drum, 3 brake drums, 2 bongos, xylophone, marimba, timbales, triangle, vibraphone, tam-tam, 2 bass drums, tubular bells, cowbells), piano, violin I, violin II, viola, violoncello, double bass.
Call no.: **1998/089**

1502. Letelier Llona, Alfonso, 1912–1994. Sinfonia: el hombre ante la ciencia. N.p.: n.p., 1985.
1 score (107 p.); 35 cm.
Spanish words; also printed as text.
For mezzo-soprano and orchestra.
Reproduced from manuscript.
Contents: Azar—Entropia—Fe.
Composed for: mezzo-soprano, 2 flutes (both also piccolo and alto flute), 2 oboes, English horn, 2 clarinets, bass clarinet, 2 bassoons, 4 horns, 2 trumpets, 3 trombones, tuba, percussion (bongos, vibraphone, bass drum, cymbals, xylophone, timpani, tambourine, woodblock, snare drum, triangle), harp, piano, celesta, violin I, violin II, viola, violoncello, double bass.
Call no.: **1990/073**

1503. Leviev, Milcho, 1937– The green house: jazz cantata for 12 voices, trap drums, bass & piano. N.p.: n.p., 1991.
1 score (46 leaves); 28 cm.
English, Latin, and Bulgarian words by Scott Guy.
Reproduced from manuscript.
Contents: Saecula saeculorum—Svoboda—The r. & b. man—Threnody of the spotted owl—The green house—Celebration—Prayer.
Composed for: 12 voices, drum set, double bass, piano.
Call no.: **1994/081**

1504. Levines, Thomas Allen, 1954– A travel journal: books I-III: [for] string quartet. Jamaica Plain, MA: Thomas A. Levines, 1988.
1 score (various pagings); 28 cm.
Reproduced from manuscript.
Composed for: 2 violins, viola, violoncello.
Call no.: **1993/078**

1505. Levinson, Gerald, 1951– Anāhata: symphony no. 1 for large orchestra. Bryn Mawr, PA: T. Presser, 1986.
1 score (104 p.); 49 cm.
Duration: ca. 32:00.
Reproduced from holograph.
Composed for: 4 flutes (3rd–4th also piccolo), 4 oboes (4th also English horn), 4 clarinets (3rd also clarinet in E♭, 4th also bass clarinet), 3 bassoons (3rd also contrabassoon), 4 horns, 4 trumpets, 2 trombones, bass trombone, tuba, percussion (crotales, glockenspiel, 2 sets of tubular chimes, vibraphone, marimba, 2 suspended cymbals, 3 knobbed gongs, 3 tam-tams, 2 triangles, timpani, bass drum), harp, piano, celesta, violin I, violin II, viola, violoncello, double bass.
Commissioned by: Northeastern Pennsylvania Philharmonic and National Symphony Orchestra.
Call no.: **1988/067**
Re-entered as: **1989/074** and **1991/071**

1506. Levinson, Gerald, 1951– At the still point of the turning world, there the dance is: for chamber en-

semble. King of Prussia, PA: Merion Music; Theodore Presser Co., 2002.
1 score (39 p.); 44 cm.
Duration: ca. 20:00.
Composed for: oboe (also English horn), clarinet (also clarinet in A), bass clarinet, baritone saxophone (also soprano saxophone), viola, violoncello, double bass, guitar, percussion (3 triangles, 5 woodblocks, 3 suspended cymbals, 4 knobbed gongs, chimes, vibraphone, marimba, glockenspiel).
Commissioned by: Network for New Music.
Call no.: **2005/086**

1507. Levinson, Gerald, 1951– Sea changes: for orchestra. Bryn Mawr, PA: Merion Music; Theodore Presser, 1992.
1 score (50 p.); 59 cm.
End of score: corrected 9/91, 12/91; revised 3/92.
Reproduced from holograph.
Duration: ca. 20:00.
Composed for: 3 flutes (2nd–3rd also piccolo), 3 oboes, clarinet in E♭, 2 clarinets, bass clarinet, 3 bassoons (3rd also contrabassoon), 4 horns, 3 trumpets, 3 trombones, tuba, percussion (crotales, glockenspiel, triangle, vibraphone, tubular chimes, marimba, sleigh bells, 3 suspended cymbals, 4 knobbed gongs, 4 tam-tams, bass drum, timpani), harp, piano (also celesta), violin I, violin II, viola, violoncello, double bass.
Commissioned by: Indianapolis Symphony Orchestra, Rochester Philharmonic Orchestra, and Aspen Music Festival.
Call no.: **1993/079**

1508. Levinson, Gerald, 1951– Symphony no. 2: for large orchestra. Bryn Mawr, PA: Merion Music: T. Presser, 1995.
1 score (111 p.); 49 cm.
"La Grave, Del Mar, San Jacinto, Swarthmore: Nov. 1, 1994; corrected Dec. 9, 1994; corrected and revised Jan. 16, 1996"—p. 111.
Composed for: 3 piccolos, 4 flutes (3rd also alto flute), 4 oboes (4th also English horn), 2 clarinets in E♭ (2nd also bass clarinet), 3 clarinets (3rd also contrabass clarinet), 3 bassoons, contrabassoon, 4 horns, 4 trumpets, 4 trombones, tuba, timpani, percussion (crotales, vibraphone, chimes, bell tree, triangle, 4 suspended cymbals, 5 knobbed gongs, glockenspiel, marimba, 4 tam-tams, bass drum), harp, piano, celesta, violin I, violin II, viola, violoncello, double bass.
Commissioned by: Serge Koussevitzky Music Foundation in the Library of Congress.
Call no.: **1996/086**

1509. Levinson, Gerald, 1951– Time and the bell . . . : for piano and chamber ensemble (1998). Bryn Mawr, PA: Merion Music: T. Presser Co., 1998.
1 score (60 p.); 41 cm.
Duration: ca. 27:00.
Composed for: piano, flute (also alto flute), oboe (also English horn), clarinet (also bass clarinet), percussion (crotales, vibraphone, marimba, tubular chimes, 2 triangles, 2 suspended cymbals, sizzle cymbal, 2 large knobbed gongs [Thai or Indonesian], medium-low tam-tam, large Japanese temple bell [dobachi], 5 temple blocks, bass drum), violin, viola, violoncello.
Commissioned by: Orchestra 2001 of Philadelphia, Syracuse Society for New Music, and Los Angeles Philharmonic New Music Group.
Call no.: **2000/100**

1510. Levinson, Gerald, 1951– Time and the bell . . . : for piano and chamber ensemble (1998). Bryn Mawr, PA: Merion Music: T. Presser Co., 1998.
1 score (61 p.); 44 cm.
Duration: ca. 27:00.
Program notes by the composer in English.
Composed for: piano, flute (also alto flute), oboe (also English horn), clarinet (also bass clarinet), percussion (crotales, vibraphone, marimba, tubular chimes, 2 triangles, 2 suspended cymbals, sizzle cymbal, 2 large knobbed gongs [Thai or Indonesian], medium-low tam-tam, large Japanese temple bell [dobachi], 5 temple blocks, bass drum), violin, viola, violoncello.
Commissioned by: Orchestra 2001 of Philadelphia, Syracuse Society for New Music, and Los Angeles Philharmonic New Music Group.
Call no.: **2002/112**

1511. Levitch, Leon, 1927– Song of dreams: a movement from Requiem patris. N.p.: Leon Levitch, 1993.
1 score (55 p.); 36 cm.
Serbian words.
Composed for: soprano, tenor, SATB chorus, piccolo, flute, 2 oboes, 2 clarinets, 2 bassoons, 4 horns, 3 trumpets, 2 trombones, tuba, percussion (xylophone, timpani, suspended cymbal, triangle, tambourine), piano, celesta, violin I, violin II, viola, violoncello, double bass.
Call no.: **1996/087**

1512. Levitch, Leon, 1927– Symphony no. 2 op. 18: the taos. N.p.: Carl Fischer, 1983.
1 score (50 p.); 51 cm.
In one movement.
Reproduced from manuscript.
Composed for: 3 flutes (1st also piccolo), 2 oboes, English

horn, 2 clarinets, bass clarinet, 2 bassoons, contrabassoon, 4 horns, 3 trumpets, 4 trombones, tuba, timpani, percussion (cymbals, xylophone, gong, woodblock, triangle, bass drum, tambourine), harp, celesta, violin I, violin II, viola, violoncello, double bass.
Call no.: **1995/062**

1513. Levowitz, Adam Blake, 1968– The pied piper: a modern dance ballet. Salt Lake City, UT: Adam B. Levowitz, 1996.
1 score (383 p.); 29 cm.
Composed for: 3 flutes, 2 oboes, 2 clarinets, 2 bassoons, 4 horns, 3 trumpets, 3 trombones, percussion (timpani, suspended cymbal, bass drum, snare drum, crash cymbals, tambourine, whip, chimes, triangle, woodblock, gong, finger cymbal, field drum, tom-tom, sleigh bells), violin I, violin II, viola, violoncello, double bass.
Call no.: **1997/085**

1514. Levy, Marvin David, 1932– Masada: oratorio for tenor, speaker, chorus and orchestra. 1987 final edition. New York, NY: Boosey & Hawkes, 1987.
1 score (162 p.); 41 cm.
English words; also printed as text (p. 159–162).
Text adapted by the composer from Chronicles of Josephus, Sabbath and Festival prayer book, excerpts from Emma Lazarus, Edward R. Murrow, Moshe Dayan, and the poem of Isaac Lamdan.
Reproduced from manuscript.
Composed for: narrator, tenor, SATB chorus, 2 flutes (2nd also piccolo), 2 oboes (2nd also English horn), 2 clarinets (2nd also bass clarinet), 2 bassoons (2nd also contrabassoon), 4 horns, 2 trumpets, 2 trombones, bass trombone, percussion (chimes, snare drum, tenor drum, crash cymbals, suspended cymbal, chromatic crotales, vibraphone, xylophone, 3 woodblocks, 5 temple blocks, guiro, marimba, 3 triangles, 3 tamtams, bass drum, tambourine, 3 bongos, 3 tom-toms, claves, 5 cowbells, flexatone, whip, timpani), harp, organ, celesta, violin I, violin II, viola, violoncello, double bass.
Commissioned by: National Symphony Orchestra.
Call no.: **1989/075**

1515. Levy, Marvin David, 1932– Mourning becomes Electra: opera in three acts. Orchestra score, standard large orchestra. New York, NY: Boosey & Hawkes, 1998.
1 score (3 v.); 44 cm.
English words by Henry Butler from the play by Eugene O'Neill.
Composed for: 3 sopranos, tenor, 2 baritones, 2 basses, piccolo, 2 flutes, 2 oboes, English horn, 2 clarinets, bass clarinet, 2 bassoons, contrabassoon, 4 horns, 3 trumpets, 2 trombones, bass trombone, tuba, timpani, percussion (tam-tam, suspended cymbal, bass drum, tenor drum, snare drum, tambourine, large triangle, temple blocks, castanets, chimes, bongos, tom-toms, small woodblock, crash cymbals, guiro, ratchet, sleigh bells, whip, sizzle cymbal, 3 roto-toms, Chinese bell tree), harp, 2 electronic keyboard samplers, violin I, violin II, viola, violoncello, double bass, banda (2 horns, trumpet, trombone, bass trombone, trap set).
Call no.: **2000/101**

1516. Lewis, Clovice A., 1956– Two poems: for solo bassoon and symphonic orchestra. Lakeport, CA: Clovis A. Lewis, 1997.
1 score (33 p.); 28 cm.
Includes notes by the composer.
Composed for: bassoon, 2 flutes, 2 oboes, 2 clarinets, 2 bassoons, 2 trumpets, 3 horns, 3 trombones, tuba, timpani, percussion (cymbals, snare drum, bass drum), violin I, violin II, viola, violoncello, double bass.
Call no.: **2001/090**

1517. Lewis, Peter Scott, 1953– Second violin concerto. Bryn Mawr, PA: T. Presser Co., 1996.
1 score (144 p.); 35 cm.
"Unrevised score"—caption.
Duration: 34:00.
Composed for: violin, 2 flutes (2nd also piccolo), 2 oboes (2nd also English horn), 2 clarinets (1st also clarinet in E♭, 2nd also bass clarinet), 2 bassoons, 4 horns, 2 trumpets, trombone, bass trombone, timpani, percussion (glockenspiel, vibraphone, marimba, chimes, suspended cymbal, tam-tam, side drum, bass drum), violin I, violin II, viola, violoncello, double bass.
Commissioned by: Rotterdam Philharmonic.
Call no.: **2001/091**

1518. Lewis, Peter Scott, 1953– Second violin concerto. Bryn Mawr, PA: T. Presser Co., 1996.
1 score (144 p.); 29 cm.
Duration: 34:00.
Composed for: violin, 2 flutes (2nd also piccolo), 2 oboes (2nd also English horn), 2 clarinets (1st also clarinet in E♭, 2nd also bass clarinet), 2 bassoons, 4 horns, 2 trumpets, trombone, bass trombone, timpani, percussion (glockenspiel, vibraphone, marimba, chimes, suspended cymbal, tam-tam, side drum, bass drum), violin I, violin II, viola, violoncello, double bass.
Commissioned by: Rotterdam Philharmonic.
Call no.: **2003/071**

1519. Lewis, Peter Scott, 1953– Where the heart is pure: for mezzo soprano and chamber orchestra: 1993. N.p.: Peter Scott Lewis, 1993.
1 score (37 p.); 28 cm.
English words; also printed as text.
Based on poems by Robert Sund.
Duration: ca. 16:00.
Contents: There is no exile where the heart is pure—Night along the Columbia, day in Blewett Pass, going home—Spring poem in the Skagit Valley.
Composed for: mezzo-soprano, flute, oboe, clarinet, violin I, violin II, viola, violoncello, double bass.
Call no.: **1996/088**

1520. Lewis, Robert Hall, 1926–1996. Invenzione: 1988. Bryn Mawr, PA: Presser, 1989.
1 score (82 p.); 44 cm.
For orchestra.
Duration: 17:00–18:00.
Composed for: 4 flutes (all also piccolo, 2nd and 4th also alto flute), 3 oboes (3rd also English horn), 3 clarinets (2nd also clarinet in E♭, 3rd also bass clarinet), 3 bassoons (3rd also contrabassoon), 4 horns, 3 trumpets, 3 trombones, tuba, timpani, percussion (antique cymbals, glockenspiel, mark tree, 5 suspended cymbals, tam-tam, whip, sleigh bells, slit drum, vibraphone, tambourine, 5 tom-toms, Chinese tom-tom, 2 maracas, water phone, 4 woodblocks, xylophone, tubular bells, 3 cowbells, 5 temple blocks, rain stick, marimba, triangle, guiro, bass drum), harp, piano, celesta, violin I, violin II, viola, violoncello, double bass.
Commissioned by: Baltimore Symphony Orchestra.
Call no.: **1991/072**

1521. Lewis, Robert Hall, 1926–1996. Symphony no. 4 (1990). Bryn Mawr, PA: T. Presser, 1991.
1 score (76 p.); 44 cm.
Reproduced from holograph.
Duration: ca. 19:00.
Composed for: 3 flutes (2nd–3rd also piccolo, 2nd also alto flute), 3 oboes (3rd also English horn), 3 clarinets (2nd also clarinet in E♭, 3rd also bass clarinet), 3 bassoons (3rd also contrabassoon), 4 horns, 3 trumpets, 3 trombones, tuba, timpani, percussion (glockenspiel, mark tree, triangle, 5 bongos, maracas, claves, antique cymbals, xylophone, sleigh bells, 5 cowbells, slit drum, suspended cymbal, 2 tam-tams, tambourine, vibraphone, 5 temple blocks, 5 woodblocks, guiro, 5 tom-toms, marimba, tubular bells, bass drum), harp, piano, celesta, violin I, violin II, viola, violoncello, double bass.
Commissioned by: American Composers Orchestra.
Call no.: **1992/074**

1522. Lewkovitch, Bernhard, 1927– Apollo's art: four English madrigals (S-A-T-B). Copenhagen: Engstrøm & Sødring, 1994.
1 score (16 p.) port.; 30 cm.
English words; also printed as text with Danish translation by Lewkovitch.
Unaccompanied; piano reduction for rehearsal only.
Anonymous poems from: English madrigal verse 1588–1632 / edited by E. H. Fellowes.
Contents: Music's art—Apollo—Philomela—All four.
Composed for: SATB chorus.
Call no.: **1995/063**

1523. Lewkovitch, Bernhard, 1927– De Lamentatione Jeremiae prophetae: for choir (S-A-T-B). Copenhagen: Engstrøm & Sødring, 1994.
1 score (10 p.) facsim., port.; 30 cm.
Latin words; also printed as text with English translation.
Unaccompanied.
Duration: ca. 9:00.
Composed for: SATB chorus.
Call no.: **1996/089**

1524. Lewkovitch, Bernhard, 1927– Lauda alla poverta: 10 cantori (3,2,2,3). N.p.: Engstrøm & Sødring, 1990.
1 score (13 p.); 31 cm.
Italian words; also printed as text with Danish translation.
For 10 singers.
Poem by Jacopone da Todi.
Duration: 9:00.
Includes historical information in Danish and English by the composer.
Composed for: 5 tenors, 5 basses.
Call no.: **1992/075**
Re-entered as: **1993/080**

1525. Li, Heping, 1957– Colloquy between God and men. N.p.: n.p., 1987.
1 score (36 p.); 42 cm.
Reproduced from manuscript.
Composed for: piccolo, oboe, bassoon, xun, sanxian, d-x-o, p.b., timpani, percussion (triangle, bells, cymbals, tam-tam, xylophone), piano, violin, viola, violoncello, double bass.
Call no.: **1992/076**

1526. Licata, Charles, 1943– Church meeting: for tympani high-hats and chimes. N.p.: n.p., 1990.
1 score (26 leaves); 28 cm.
Composed for: percussion (8 hi-hats, 7 timpani).
Call no.: **1993/081**

1527. Licata, Charles, 1943– Violin sonata: for violin and piano, op. 17. Summit, NJ: Charles Licata, 2000.
1 score (32 p.) + 1 part (5 p.); 28 cm.
Composed for: violin, piano.
Call no.: **2003/072**

1528. Liderman, Jorge, 1957– The song of songs: for soprano, tenor, female chorus and three instrumental ensembles. Berkeley, CA: n.p., 2001.
1 score (xiii, 113 p.); 28 cm.
English words, also printed as text.
Based on the new translation by Ariel Bloch and Chana Bloch.
At end: "March 3, 2001/Richmond, CA."
Composed for: soprano, tenor, women's chorus, ensemble I (flute [also piccolo], oboe, violin, trumpet, double bass), ensemble II (2 pianos, percussion [2 marimbas, 2 xylophones, 2 vibraphones]), ensemble III (2 clarinets, 2 violas, 2 horns).
Call no.: **2004/071**

1529. Liebermann, Lowell, 1961– Concerto: for flute and orchestra, opus 39 (1992). Bryn Mawr, PA: T. Presser, 1992.
1 score (136 p.); 43 cm.
"Corrected 10/92"—cover.
Reproduced from manuscript.
Duration: ca. 25:00.
Composed for: flute, piccolo, flute, oboe, English horn, clarinet, bass clarinet, bassoon, contrabassoon, 2 horns, 2 trumpets, timpani, percussion (glockenspiel, triangle, cymbals, vibraphone, small triangle, snare drum, bass drum, sleigh bells, ratchet), harp, piano, violin I, violin II, violas, violoncello, double bass.
Commissioned by: James Galway.
Call no.: **1994/082**

1530. Liebermann, Lowell, 1961– Concerto: no. 2 for piano and orchestra, opus 36 (1992). Study score. Bryn Mawr, PA: Theodore Presser, 1993.
1 score (142 p.); 31 cm.
Duration: ca. 31:00.
Composed for: piano, 3 flutes (3rd also piccolo), 2 oboes, English horn, 2 clarinets, bass clarinet, 2 bassoons, contrabassoon, 4 horns, 3 trumpets, 3 trombones, tuba, timpani, percussion (snare drum, bass drum, tambourine, cymbals, suspended cymbal, antique cymbal, 2 triangles, woodblock, castanets, ratchet, slapstick, xylophone, marimba), harp, celesta, violin I, violin II, viola, violoncello, double bass.
Commissioned by: Steinway Foundation.
Call no.: **1993/082**

1531. Liebermann, Lowell, 1961– Concerto for orchestra op. 81. King of Prussia, PA: Theodore Presser, 2002.
1 score (134 p.); 44 cm.
Composed for: piccolo, 2 flutes, 2 oboes, English horn, 2 clarinets, bass clarinet, 2 bassoons, contrabassoon, 4 horns, 3 trumpets, 3 trombones, tuba, timpani, percussion (slapstick, claves, snare drum, cymbals, bass drum, cowbell, tubular bells, marimba, xylophone, woodblock, vibraphone, glockenspiel, bongo drums, tambourine, ratchet, brake drum, triangle, vibraslap), harp, piano (also celesta), violin I, violin II, viola, violoncello, double bass.
Commissioned by: Edward H. Schmidt Musical Arts Fund of Toledo Symphony.
Call no.: **2004/072**

1532. Liebermann, Lowell, 1961– Concerto for violin and orchestra op. 74. N.p.: n.p., 2000.
1 score (106 p.); 36 cm.
Composed for: violin, piccolo, 2 flutes, 2 oboes, English horn, 3 clarinets (3rd also bass clarinet), 3 bassoons (3rd also contrabassoon), 3 trumpets, 4 horns, 3 trombones, tuba, percussion, harp, piano (also celesta), violin I, violin II, viola, violoncello, double bass.
Commissioned by: Saratoga Performing Arts Center.
Call no.: **2003/073**

1533. Liebermann, Lowell, 1961– The domain of Arnheim: op.33. N.p.: n.p., 1990.
1 score (51 p.); 37 cm.
Reproduced from holograph.
At end: N.Y.C. 8/28/90.
Duration: ca. 14:00.
Composed for: 2 flutes, 2 oboes, 2 clarinets, 2 bassoons, 2 horns, 2 trumpets, trombone, timpani, percussion (bass drum, 3 gongs, suspended cymbal, vibraphone, triangle, glockenspiel, cymbals), harp, piano, celesta, violin I, violin II, viola, violoncello, double bass.
Commissioned by: New York Chamber Symphony of 92nd Street Y.
Call no.: **1992/077**

1534. Liebermann, Lowell, 1961– Loss of breath: for orchestra. Bryn Mawr, PA: T. Presser Co., 1997.
1 score (75 p.); 36 cm.
"Op. 59"—caption.
Composed for: piccolo, 2 flutes, 2 oboes, English horn, 2 clarinets, bass clarinet, 2 bassoons, contrabassoon, 4 horns, 3 trumpets, 3 trombones, tuba, timpani, percussion (crash cymbals, suspended cymbal, snare drum, small triangle, flexatone, glockenspiel, xylophone, wooden hammer, cowbell, tubular bells, anvil, tam-

tam, ratchet, claves, bass drum, slide whistle, wind machine, slapstick), harp, piano, celesta, violin I, violin II, viola, violoncello, double bass.
Call no.: **1998/090**

1535. Liebermann, Lowell, 1961– The picture of Dorian Gray: opera in two acts. Bryn Mawr, PA: T. Presser Co., 1998.
1 vocal score (244 p.); 28 cm.
Words by the composer.
Original work by Oscar Wilde.
Includes synopsis and notes.
Composed for: 2 sopranos, 3 tenors, 3 baritones, bass, offstage violin, 3 flutes (3rd also piccolo), 2 oboes, English horn, 2 clarinets, bass clarinet, 2 bassoons, contrabassoon, 4 horns, 3 trumpets, 3 trombones, timpani, percussion (crash cymbals, bass drum, slapstick, xylophone, tambourine, large tam-tam, vibraphone, marimba, small triangle, snare drum, ratchet, suspended cymbal, glockenspiel, tubular bells, large triangle, lion's roar, large bell, anvil, woodblock), celesta, harp, offstage out-of-tune upright piano, violin I, violin II, viola, violoncello, double bass.
Commissioned by: Opéra de Monte Carlo.
Call no.: **2000/102**

1536. Liebermann, Lowell, 1961– The picture of Dorian Gray: opera in two acts, op. 45. Bryn Mawr, PA: Theodore Presser Co., 1996.
1 score (646 p.); 28 cm.
English words by the composer.
Original work by Oscar Wilde.
"7/96—uncorrected."
Composed for: 2 sopranos, 3 tenors, 3 baritones, bass, offstage violin, 3 flutes (3rd also piccolo), 2 oboes, English horn, 2 clarinets, bass clarinet, 2 bassoons, contrabassoon, 4 horns, 3 trumpets, 3 trombones, timpani, percussion (crash cymbals, bass drum, slapstick, xylophone, tambourine, large tam-tam, vibraphone, marimba, small triangle, snare drum, ratchet, suspended cymbal, glockenspiel, tubular bells, large triangle, lion's roar, large bell, anvil, woodblock), celesta, harp, offstage out-of-tune upright piano, violin I, violin II, viola, violoncello, double bass.
Commissioned by: Opéra de Monte Carlo.
Call no.: **1997/086**

1537. Liebermann, Lowell, 1961– Sonata no. 2: for violoncello and piano, opus 61 (1998). Bryn Mawr, PA: Theodore Presser, 1998.
1 score (33 p.); 28 cm.
Duration: ca. 15:00.
Composed for: violoncello, piano.
Commissioned by: Wigmore Hall.
Call no.: **2001/092**

1538. Liebermann, Lowell, 1961– Symphony no. 2: opus 67 (1999). King of Prussia, PA: Theodore Presser, 1999.
1 score (150 p.); 44 cm.
English words; based on poems by Walt Whitman.
For S.A.T.B. chorus and orchestra.
Composed for: SATB chorus, piccolo, 2 flutes, 2 oboes, English horn, 2 clarinets, bass clarinet, 2 bassoons, contrabassoon, 4 horns, 3 trumpets, 3 trombones, tuba, timpani, percussion (triangle, marimba, suspended cymbal, glockenspiel, vibraphone, bass drum, snare drum, xylophone, tam-tam, gong, tambourine), harp, piano, celesta, organ, violin I, violin II, viola, violoncello, double bass, optional brass band (3 trumpets, 3 trombones).
Commissioned by: Ford Lacy and Cece Smith.
Call no.: **2002/113**

1539. Lieberson, Peter, 1946– Ashoka's dream. New York, NY: Associated Music Publisher's [sic], 1997.
1 score (2 v. [504 p.]); 44 cm.
English words by Douglas Penick.
Opera in 2 acts.
Composed for: 3 sopranos, 2 mezzo-sopranos, contralto, 2 tenors, 3 baritones, 2 basses, SATB chorus, 3 flutes (2nd–3rd also piccolo), 2 oboes (2nd also English horn), 2 clarinets (2nd also clarinets in E♭ in A), bass clarinet (also contrabass clarinet), 2 bassoons (2nd also contrabassoon), 4 horns, 3 trumpets, 3 trombones, tuba, timpani, percussion (glockenspiel, bass drum, tuned gong, marimba, tam-tams, snare drum, 3 suspended cymbals, 2 bongos, vibraphone, maracas, claves, small ratchet, xylophone, tom-toms, gong, high cowbell, 2 drums, sizzle cymbal, small cymbal, high woodblocks, crotales), harp, celesta (also piano), violin I, violin II, viola, violoncello, double bass.
Commissioned by: Santa Fe Opera.
Call no.: **1998/091**
Re-entered as: **2000/103**
Also available:
Call no.: **2000/103 libretto**

1540. Lieberson, Peter, 1946– Drala: 1986. New York, NY: G. Schirmer, 1986.
1 score (85 p.); 36 cm.
For orchestra.
Reproduced from holograph.
Composed for: 3 flutes (all also piccolo, 2nd also alto flute), 2 oboes, English horn, 3 clarinets (3rd also clarinet in E♭), 2 bassoons, contrabassoon, 4 horns, 3

trumpets, 2 trombones, bass trombone, tuba, timpani, percussion (vibraphone, crotales, crash cymbals, sleigh bells, 3 tam-tams, glockenspiel, 3 drums, snare drum, triangle, 3 suspended cymbals, 2 woodblocks, tubular bells, 3 roto-toms, tambourine, cuíca, whip, bass drum, xylophone, 3 temple blocks), 2 harps, piano, violin I, violin II, viola, violoncello, double bass.
Commissioned by: Boston Symphony Orchestra.
Call no.: **1987/046**
Re-entered as: **1990/074**

1541. Lieberson, Peter, 1946– King Gesar: (1991–92). New York, NY: Associated Music, 1992.
1 miniature score (165 p.); 28 cm.
English words by Douglas Penick.
Composed for: narrator, flute (also piccolo), clarinet (also bass clarinet), horn, trombone, percussion (glockenspiel, xylophone, triangle, 4 drums, 2 suspended cymbals, crash cymbals, tam-tam), violoncello, 2 pianos.
Commissioned by: City of Munich.
Call no.: **1993/083**
Re-entered as: **1994/083**, **1995/064**, and **1997/087**

1542. Lieberson, Peter, 1946– King Gesar: (1991–92). New York, NY: Associated Music, 1992.
1 score (165 p.); 36 cm.
English words by Douglas Penick.
Composed for: narrator, flute (also piccolo), clarinet (also bass clarinet), horn, trombone, percussion (glockenspiel, xylophone, triangle, 4 drums, 2 suspended cymbals, crash cymbals, tam-tam), violoncello, 2 pianos.
Commissioned by: City of Munich.
Call no.: **1996/090**

1543. Lieberson, Peter, 1946– Piano concerto. N.p.: n.p., 1983.
1 score (203 p.); 36 cm.
Reproduced from holograph.
Composed for: piano, 3 flutes (2nd–3rd also piccolo), 2 oboes, English horn, 2 clarinets, contrabass clarinet, 2 bassoons, contrabassoon, 4 horns, 3 trumpets, 2 trombones, bass trombone, tuba, timpani, percussion (bass drum, snare drum, 2 bongos, 4 tom-toms, xylophone, claves, 2 woodblocks, 2 temple blocks, tambourine, vibraphone, glockenspiel, crotales, 3 suspended cymbals, 2 crash cymbals, triangle, tam-tam), celesta, violin I, violin II, viola, violoncello, double bass.
Commissioned by: Seiji Ozawa and Boston Symphony Orchestra.
Call no.: **1988/068**

1544. Lieberson, Peter, 1946– Piano concerto no. 3: for piano and orchestra. Full score. New York, NY: Associated Music, 2003.
1 score (117 p.); 36 cm.
Composed for: piano, 3 flutes (also piccolo), 2 oboes, English horn, 3 clarinets (also clarinet in E♭ and bass clarinet), 2 bassoons, contrabassoon, 4 horns, 3 trumpets, 2 trombones, bass trombone, tuba, timpani, percussion, harp, violin I, violin II, viola, violoncello, double bass.
Commissioned by: Minnesota Orchestra.
Call no.: **2005/087**

1545. Lieberson, Peter, 1946– Red garuda: (1999). Chester, NY: Schirmer Rental Library, 1999.
1 score (109 p.); 44 cm.
For piano and orchestra.
Composed for: piano, piccolo, 2 flutes, 2 oboes, English horn, clarinet in E♭, 2 clarinets, bass clarinet (also contrabass clarinet), 2 bassoons (also contrabassoon), 4 horns, 3 trumpets, 2 trombones, bass trombone, tuba, timpani, percussion (tubular bells, snare drum, suspended cymbal, wind machine, glockenspiel, tam-tam, vibraphone, crotales, bass drum, Chinese cymbal, whip), celesta, harp, violin I, violin II, viola, violoncello, double bass.
Commissioned by: Boston Symphony Orchestra.
Call no.: **2001/093**

1546. Lieberson, Peter, 1946– Red garuda: for piano and orchestra. New York, NY: Associated Music Publishers, 1999.
1 score (109 p.); 36 cm.
Duration: ca. 24:00.
Composed for: piano, piccolo, 2 flutes, 2 oboes, English horn, clarinet in E♭, 2 clarinets, bass clarinet (also contrabass clarinet), 2 bassoons (also contrabassoon), 4 horns, 3 trumpets, 2 trombones, bass trombone, tuba, timpani, percussion (tubular bells, snare drum, suspended cymbal, wind machine, glockenspiel, tam-tam, vibraphone, crotales, bass drum, Chinese cymbal, whip), celesta, harp, violin I, violin II, viola, violoncello, double bass.
Commissioned by: Boston Symphony Orchestra.
Call no.: **2002/114**
Re-entered as: **2003/074**

1547. Lieberson, Peter, 1946– Rilke songs: for mezzo-soprano and piano. New York, NY: Associated Music Publishers, 2002 (1/22/03 printing).
1 score (39 p.); 26 x 30 cm.
German words by R. M. Rilke.
"Revised 9/2002"—p. 1.
Reproduced from holograph.
Duration: ca. 17:00.

Contents: O ihr Zärtlichen—Atmen, du unsichtbares Gedicht—Wolle die Wandlung—Blummenmuskel . . . [sic]—Stiller Freund.
Composed for: soprano, piano.
Commissioned by: Santa Fe Chamber Music Festival.
Call no.: **2004/073**

1548. Ligeti, György, 1923– Etudes pour piano. Mainz: B. Schott's Söhne, 1985.
37 p. of music; 42 cm.
Reproduced from manuscript.
Contents: Désordre—Cordes vides—Touches bloquées—Fanfares—Arc-en-ciel—Automne à Varsovie.
Lacks Etude Nr. 1.
1986 Grawemeyer Award winning work.
Composed for: piano.
Commissioned by: Bayerische Vereinsbank.
Call no.: **1986/068**

1549. Light, Patricia Parsons, 1933– Mama's mirror: going once. Score. Millfield, OH: Patricia P. Light, 1987.
1 score (various pagings); 22 x 30 cm.
English words.
Opera.
Composed for: soprano, alto, tenor, bass, flute, clarinet, viola, violoncello, acoustic guitar, piano.
Call no.: **1993/084**
Also available:
Call no.: **1993/084 libretto**

1550. Lim, Liza, 1966– Machine for contacting the dead: for 27 musicians (1999–2000). Partitura. Milan: Ricordi, 2000.
1 score (124 p.); 42 cm.
"Provisional perusal score"—cover.
Reproduced from holograph.
Duration: ca. 40:00.
Composed for: bass flute (also piccolo), flute (also piccolo), 2 oboes (2nd also English horn), 2 clarinets, bass clarinet (also contrabass clarinet), bassoon, contrabassoon, horn, 2 trumpets, alto trombone, tenor tuba, percussion (2 maracas, 2 iron ball bells, flexatone, 2 Chinese opera gongs, vibraphone, 2 temple blocks, bongos, 2 tom-toms, bass drum, thundersheet, vibraslap, rain stick, kwengkwari, 2 timpani, geophone, 2 pebbles, 3 Thai gongs, Chinese tam-tam, tawak ibu, roto-tom), harp, piano, 2 violins, 2 violas, 2 violoncellos, double bass.
Commissioned by: Ensemble Intercontemporain.
Call no.: **2003/075**

1551. Lim, Liza, 1966– The oresteia: memory theatre (opera) in 7 parts based on Aeschylus' drama. Partitura. Milano: Ricordi, 1992.
1 score (a–m, 200 p.); 41 cm.
English and Greek words; also printed as text with English translation.
Libretto by Liza Lim and Barrie Kosky; drawn from Aeschylus, Sappho, and Tony Harrison.
Reproduced from holograph.
Duration: 1:15:00.
Composed for: soprano, 2 mezzo-sopranos, countertenor, tenor, baritone, alto flute (also piccolo), clarinet (also bass clarinet), oboe (also English horn), trumpet (also piccolo trumpet), trombone, Turkish baglama saz, percussion (triangle, cowbell, sistrum, small splash cymbal, medium ride cymbal, hi-hat, small Chinese opera gong, Thai nipple gong, steel drum, guiro, vibraslap, flexatone, ratchet, timpani, woodblock, 2 roto-toms, bass drum), electric guitar, viola (also viola d'amore), violoncello, double bass.
Commissioned by: Elision and Treason of Images.
Call no.: **1994/084**

1552. Lin, Minyi, 1950– Beauty and the beast. N.p.: n.p., 199-?.
1 score (142 p.); 28 cm.
Ballet.
Composed for: flute (also piccolo), oboe (also English horn), clarinet (also bass clarinet), bassoon, horn, marimba, vibraphone, celesta, harp, guitar, violin I, violin II, viola, violoncello, double bass.
Commissioned by: Provisional Regional Council.
Call no.: **2001/086**

1553. Lindberg, Magnus, 1958– Aura: in memoriam Witold Lutosławski. London: Chester Music, 1994.
1 score (121 p.); 42 cm.
For orchestra.
Composed for: piccolo, 2 flutes, 2 oboes, English horn, 3 clarinets (3rd also clarinet in E♭), bass clarinet, 2 bassoons, contrabassoon, 4 horns, 3 trumpets (3rd also trumpet in E♭), 3 trombones (3rd also bass trombone), tuba, timpani, percussion (vibraphone, mark tree, claves, bongos, bass drum, opera gong, marimba, woodblocks, snare drum, crotales, glockenspiel, triangle, 3 temple bells, 2 suspended cymbals, 2 tam-tams, 4 tom-toms), harp, celesta (also piano), violin I, violin II, viola, violoncello, double bass.
Commissioned by: Suntory Limited.
Call no.: **1995/065**
Re-entered as: **1997/088** and **2000/104**

1554. Lindberg, Magnus, 1958– Cantigas: (1998–99). Full score. London: Boosey & Hawkes, 1999.
1 score (97 p.); 42 cm.

For orchestra.
Composed for: 3 flutes (3rd also piccolo), 2 oboes, English horn, 3 clarinets (3rd also clarinet in E♭), bass clarinet (also contrabass clarinet), 2 bassoons, contrabassoon, 4 horns, 4 trumpets, 3 trombones, tuba, timpani, percussion (vibraphone, triangle, bell tree, Chinese cymbal, suspended cymbals, bongos, bass drum, marimba, spring coil, mark tree, tam-tam, tom-toms, crotales, tubular bells, tenor drum, maracas, temple blocks, Thai gongs), piano (also celesta), harp, violin I, violin II, viola, violoncello, double bass.
Commissioned by: Cleveland Orchestra.
Call no.: **2001/094**

1555. Lindberg, Magnus, 1958– Feria: (1995–97). Full score. London: Boosey & Hawkes, 1997.
1 score (62 p.); 30 cm.
For orchestra.
"Revised"—cover.
Composed for: piccolo, 2 flutes, 2 oboes, English horn, 3 clarinets, bass clarinet, 2 bassoons, contrabassoon, 4 horns, 3 trumpets, 3 trombones, tuba, timpani, percussion (vibraphone, medium Chinese cymbal, 2 suspended cymbals, bongos, bass drum, bell tree, triangle, medium tam-tam, marimba, large tam-tam, crotales, mark tree, spring coil, large Chinese cymbal, 4 tom-toms), harp, piano (also celesta), violin I, violin II, viola, violoncello, double bass.
Commissioned by: Finnish Broadcasting Company (YLE).
Call no.: **1998/092**

1556. Lindberg, Magnus, 1958– Fresco: for orchestra. London: Boosey & Hawkes, 1999.
1 score (4, 107 p.); 30 cm.
Composer's note in English, French, and German.
Duration: 22:00.
Composed for: piccolo (also alto flute), 2 flutes, 2 oboes, English horn, 3 clarinets (3rd also clarinet in E♭), bass clarinet, 2 bassoons, contrabassoon, 4 horns, 4 trumpets, 4 trombones, tuba, percussion (glockenspiel, vibraphone, bell tree, metal plates, 4 bongos, snare drum, sizzle cymbal, tam-tam, marimba, triangle, spring coil, bass drum, Chinese cymbal, 2 gongs, crotales, tubular bells, mark tree, 4 temple blocks, 4 tom-toms, very small cymbal, 2 suspended cymbals, Thai gongs), piano (also celesta), harp, violin I, violin II, viola, violoncello, double bass.
Commissioned by: Los Angeles Philharmonic.
Call no.: **2002/115**

1557. Lindberg, Magnus, 1958– Piano concerto no. 1. Score. Copenhagen: Edition Wilhelm Hansen, 1991.
1 score (171 p.); 43 cm.
Composed for: piano, 2 flutes (2nd also piccolo), oboe, English horn, 2 clarinets, bass clarinet, 2 bassoons (2nd also contrabassoon), 2 horns, trumpet, trombone, tuba, percussion (glockenspiel, temple bells, vibraphone, mark tree, 2 suspended cymbals, tam-tam, bongos, temple blocks, woodblock, sleigh bells, crotales), harp, violin I, violin II, viola, violoncello, double bass.
Commissioned by: Helsinki Festival.
Call no.: **1992/078**

1558. Liptak, David, 1949– Ancient songs: baritone and chamber ensemble (1992). Score. Saint Louis, MO: Norruth Music, 1992.
1 score (42 p.); 46 cm.
English words; texts include translations of traditional Passamaquoddy, Papago, and Gabon Pygmy poetry, an English nursery rhyme, and a poem by James Wright.
Duration: 22:00.
Reproduced from holograph.
Composed for: baritone, flute (also piccolo), clarinet (also bass clarinet), violin, violoncello, percussion (marimba, vibraphone, tubular bells, crotales, tom-tom, claves, bass drum, tam-tam, 2 suspended triangles, vibraslap, ratchet, woodblock, maracas, guiro, suspended cymbal), piano.
Call no.: **1993/085**

1559. Liptak, David, 1949– Concerto for trumpet and orchestra. Score. N.p.: n.p., 1996.
1 score (93 p.); 40 cm.
Duration: 25:00.
Composed for: trumpet, 2 flutes (2nd also piccolo), 2 oboes, 2 clarinets, 2 bassoons, 4 horns, 2 trumpets, 3 trombones, tuba, timpani, harp, percussion (triangle, suspended cymbal, tam-tam, woodblock, xylophone, glockenspiel, guiro, vibraslap, ratchet), violin I, violin II, viola, violoncello, double bass.
Commissioned by: Rochester Philharmonic Orchestra and Fromm Music Foundation.
Call no.: **1997/089**

1560. Liptak, David, 1949– Concerto for trumpet and orchestra (1996). Score. St. Louis, MO: MMB Music, 1996.
1 score (93 p.); 46 cm.
Duration: 25:00.
Composed for: trumpet, 2 flutes (2nd also piccolo), 2 oboes, 2 clarinets, 2 bassoons, 4 horns, 2 trumpets, 3 trombones, tuba, timpani, harp, percussion (triangle, suspended cymbal, tam-tam, woodblock, xylophone, glockenspiel, guiro, vibraslap, ratchet), violin I, violin II, viola, violoncello, double bass.

Commissioned by: Rochester Philharmonic Orchestra and Fromm Music Foundation.
Call no.: **2002/116**

1561. Liu, Changyuan, 1932– "Burying blossoms": for soprano, violin, cello, piano and percussions. N.p.: n.p., 199-?.
1 score (18 p.); 37 cm.
Composed for: soprano, violin, violoncello, piano, percussion.
Commissioned by: Beijing Trio Ensemble.
Call no.: **2002/117**

1562. Liu, Changyuan, 1932– The first symphony. N.p.: n.p., 198-?.
1 score (various pagings); 27 cm.
Reproduced from manuscript.
Composed for: flute (also piccolo), clarinet, 2 horns, timpani, percussion (xylophone, cymbals, tambourine, tam-tam, drum), piano, celesta, violin I, violin II, viola, violoncello, double bass.
Call no.: **1990/075**

1563. Lloyd, George, 1913–1998. A symphonic mass: for chorus and orchestra. Carnforth, Lancs, England: George Lloyd Music Library: Albany Records, 199-?.
1 score (171 p.); 43 cm.
Reproduced from holograph.
At end: "London, 18th Nov.,'91."
Composed for: SATB chorus, 3 flutes (3rd also piccolo), 2 oboes, English horn, clarinet in E♭, 2 clarinets (both also clarinet in A), 3 bassoons (3rd also contrabassoon), 4 horns, 4 trumpets, 3 trombones, euphonium, tuba, timpani, percussion (glockenspiel, tubular bells, xylophone, marimba, sleigh bells, woodblock, 2 snare drums, tenor drum, bass drum, cymbals, tam-tam), harp, organ, celesta, violin I, violin II, viola, violoncello, double bass.
Call no.: **1998/093**

1564. Lloyd, George, 1913–1998. Symphony no 11. N. p.: n.p., 1985.
1 score (263 p.); 42 cm.
Reproduced from holograph.
Composed for: 3 flutes (3rd also piccolo), 2 oboes, English horn, clarinet in E♭, 2 clarinets, bass clarinet, 3 bassoons, contrabassoon, 4 horns, trumpet in E♭, 2 trumpets, flugelhorn, 2 trombones, bass trombone, euphonium, tuba, timpani, percussion (glockenspiel, xylophone, vibraphone, bells, side drum, 2 tenor drums, 3 bongos, whip, antique cymbals, cymbals, bass drum, triangle, tam-tam, woodblock), harp, celesta, violin I, violin II, viola, violoncello, double bass.
Commissioned by: Albany Symphony Orchestra.
Call no.: **1987/047**

1565. Lloyd, Jonathan, 1948– 2nd symphony.
Call no.: **1990/076**
No materials available.

1566. Lloyd, Jonathan, 1948– Violin concerto. Full score. London: Boosey & Hawkes, 1995.
1 score (69 p.); 42 cm.
Reproduced from holograph.
Composed for: violin, 2 flutes (1st also alto flute, 2nd also piccolo), 2 oboes (2nd also English horn), soprano saxophone, 2 clarinets (2nd also bass clarinet), 2 bassoons (2nd also contrabassoon), 2 horns, trumpet (also bass trumpet and cornet), trombone, percussion (2 marimbas, vibraphone, tam-tam, bell tree, suspended cymbal, 12 tuned gongs, 12 handbells, 8 crotales, timpani), 2 harps, 2 guitars, piano (celesta), harpsichord (also electric organ), violin I, violin II, viola, violoncello, double bass.
Commissioned by: Aldeburgh Foundation.
Call no.: **2000/105**

1567. Lo Presti, Ronald, 1933– Concerto: for bassoonist and chamber players. N.p.: n.p., 1983.
1 score (91 p.); 37 cm.
Reproduced from manuscript.
Composed for: bassoon, flute, oboe, clarinet, soprano saxophone, horn, trumpet, trombone, tuba, timpani, percussion (suspended bass drum, snare drum, suspended cymbal, vibraphone, chimes, orchestra bells), violin I, violin II, viola, violoncello, double bass.
Call no.: **1985/116a**

1568. Locklair, Dan, 1949– A DuBose Heyward triptych: for SATB chorus (divisi) & soloists, a cappella. N.p.: Subito Music, 2001.
1 score (46 p.); 27 cm.
Piano accompaniment for rehearsal only.
English words; also printed as text.
Text by DuBose Heyward.
Duration: 16:00.
Composer's note in English.
Contents: Silences—Landbound—Dusk.
Commissioned by: Carolina Chamber Chorale, Dr. George Taylor, and Marilyn Taylor.
Call no.: **2003/076**

1569. Locklair, Dan, 1949– Reynolda reflections: a trio in five movements for flute, cello & piano (2000). N.p.: Subito Music, 2000.
1 score (58 p.); 31 cm.

"Each of the movements of this twenty-six minute chamber work was inspired by a specific American painting from the collection of the Reynolda House, Museum of American Art, in Winston-Salem, North Carolina"—p. 2.
Duration: ca. 26:00.
Program notes in English.
Contents: Fantasy in the woods—Grounded in machines—Arias to a flower—Dances before the barn—Sons to the wind.
Composed for: flute, violoncello, piano.
Call no.: **2004/074**

1570. Locklair, Dan, 1949– Since dawn: a tone poem for narrator, chorus and orchestra. N.p.: Ricordi, 1995.
1 score (88 p.); 36 cm.
English words.
Based on Maya Angelou's On the pulse of morning.
Composed for: narrator, SATB chorus, 2 flutes (2nd also piccolo), 2 oboes (2nd also English horn), 2 clarinets, 2 bassoons, 4 horns, 2 trumpets, 2 trombones, bass trombone, tuba, timpani, percussion (large suspended cymbal, bell tree, 5 temple blocks, large tam-tam, chimes, crash cymbals, crotales, xylophone, vibraphone, marimba, 3 tom-toms, bass drum, glockenspiel), piano, violin I, violin II, viola, violoncello, double bass.
Call no.: **1997/090**
Re-entered as: **1998/094** and **2001/095**

1571. Loevendie, Theo, 1930– Concerto for piano and orchestra (1995/1996). New York, NY: Peer Music, 1996.
1 score (108 p.); 42 cm.
Reproduced from manuscript.
Duration: ca. 20:00.
Composed for: piano, 2 flutes (2nd also piccolo), 2 oboes (2nd also English horn), 2 clarinets (2nd also clarinet in E♭), bassoon, contrabassoon, 2 horns, trumpet, trombone, percussion (triangle, antique cymbals, tambourine, suspended cymbal, 2 tam-tams, 2 woodblocks, 3 tom-toms, snare drum, bongos, glockenspiel, cowbell, guiro), violin I, violin II, viola, violoncello, double bass.
Commissioned by: Koninklijk Concertgebouw Orkest.
Call no.: **1997/091**

1572. Loevendie, Theo, 1930– Cycles: for violin, clarinet, violoncello and piano (1992). Score. Hamburg; New York, NY: Peer, 1992.
1 score (27 p.); 35 cm.
Composed for: piano, clarinet, violin, violoncello.
Commissioned by: Dutch Ministry of Culture.
Call no.: **1993/086**

1573. Loevendie, Theo, 1930– Esmée: opera in 2 acts, 1987–1994. Hamburg: Peer Musikverlag, 1994.
1 score (2 v. [543 p.]); 42 cm.
Dutch words by Jan Blokker.
Duration: ca. 01:45:00.
Composed for: soprano, mezzo-soprano, 2 tenors, baritone, 2 bass-baritones, SATB chorus, 2 flutes (2nd also piccolo), 2 oboes, English horn, 2 clarinets (1st also clarinet in E♭, 2nd also bass clarinet), 2 bassoons, contrabassoon, 4 horns, 3 trumpets, 2 trombones, bass trombone, tuba, percussion (timpani, anvil, triangle, chocalho, crescent, vibraphone, 2 tam-tams, tambourine, sleigh bells, log drum, 2 tubular bells, whip, glockenspiel, tenor drum, 3 suspended cymbals, guiro, bass drum, marimba, crash cymbals, rattle, crotales, snare drum, claves, vibraslap, tom-toms, 2 woodblocks), harp, piano (also celesta), violin I, violin II, viola, violoncello, double bass, onstage band (clarinet in E♭, violin, piano).
Commissioned by: Holland Festival.
Call no.: **1996/091**

1574. Loevendie, Theo, 1930– Gassir, the hero: chamber opera in seven scenes (1990). Hamburg; New York, NY: Peer, 1990.
1 score (177 p.); 42 cm.
English words.
Reproduced from manuscript.
Duration: 35:00.
Composed for: soprano, countertenor, tenor, baritone, bass-baritone, bass, flute (also piccolo and alto flute), clarinet (also clarinet in E♭), bassoon (also contrabassoon), horn, trumpet, trombone, percussion (triangle, cabasa, 4 cowbells, quad crasher, Chinese cymbal, Turkish cymbal, gong, tam-tam, 2 woodblocks, 4 log drum, 2 temple blocks, vibraslap, djembe, tenor drum, bass drum, crotales, glockenspiel, kalimba, marimba), harp, violin, violoncello, double bass.
Call no.: **1992/079**

1575. Loevendie, Theo, 1930– Naima: (1985): an opera in three acts. Amsterdam: Donemus, 1985.
1 score (3 v. [436 p.]); 42 cm.
Latin, English, and Italian words by Lodewijk de Boer.
Duration: 1:45:00.
Composed for: soprano, 2 mezzo-sopranos, 3 tenors, bass-baritone, SATB chorus, onstage ensemble (3 trombones, bass trombone, piccolo [also flute and bass flute], alto saxophone [also soprano saxophone], bass clarinet [also contrabass clarinet], percussion [marimba, tambourine, 2 finger cymbals, 4 tom-toms, triangle, 4 cowbells, hi-hat]), 3 flutes (3rd also piccolo), 3 oboes (3rd also English horn), 3 clarinets

(3rd also bass clarinet), 2 bassoons, contrabassoon, 4 horns, piccolo trumpet, trumpet in D, 2 trumpets, tuba, timpani, percussion (tenor drum, tambourine, triangle, sistrum, cymbals, tam-tam, whip, glockenspiel, vibraphone, snare drum, bongos, 2 tom-toms, anvil, sleigh bells, sizzle cymbal, tubular bells, xylorimba, guiro, 3 bell plates, bass drum, 4 crotales), harp, piano (also celesta), violin I, violin II, viola, violoncello, double bass.
Commissioned by: Fonds voor de Scheppende Toonkunst.
Call no.: **1986/069**

1576. Loevendie, Theo, 1930– Violin concerto: vanishing dances = Verwehende Tänze. Partitur. New York, NY: Peermusic, 1999.
1 score (102 p.); 42 cm.
Reproduced from manuscript.
Duration: 23:00.
Composed for: violin, 2 flutes (2nd also piccolo), 2 oboes (2nd also English horn), 2 clarinets (2nd also bass clarinet), bassoon, contrabassoon, 2 horns, trumpet, trombone, tuba, percussion (tambourine, triangle, cymbals, snare drum, tam-tam, bass drum, marimba, cowbell), celesta, harp, violin I, violin II, viola, violoncello, double bass.
Call no.: **2001/096**

1577. Lohr, Tom L., 1955– Biblical songs: nine Psalms from the Old Testament: a cycle of quartets and solos for four voices. N.p.: n.p., 1999.
1 score (64 p.); 28 cm.
English words.
Composed for: soprano, mezzo-soprano, tenor, baritone, piano.
Call no.: **2005/088**

1578. Lombardi, Luca, 1945– Due ritratti: per orchestra, 1987/88. Partitura. Milano: G. Ricordi, 1988.
1 score (55 p.); 59 cm.
Reproduced from manuscript.
Composed for: 2 flutes (1st also piccolo, 2nd also alto flute), 2 oboes (2nd also English horn), heckelphone, 2 clarinets (2nd also bass clarinet), 2 bassoons (2nd also contrabassoon), 4 horns, 2 trumpets, bass trombone, tuba, timpani, percussion (3 suspended cymbals, 2 tam-tams, bass drum, 4 tom-toms, xylorimba, triangle, temple blocks, glockenspiel), harp, piano (also celesta), violin I, violin II, viola, violoncello, double bass.
Commissioned by: RTSI (Radio-televisione della suizzeva italiana) Lugano.
Call no.: **1990/077**

1579. Lombardi, Luca, 1945– Faust, un travestimento: in tre tempi e dodici scene, 1986/90. Milano: Ricordi, 1990.
1 score (560 p.); 42 cm.
Italian words by Edoardo Sanguineti, adapted by Luca Lombardi.
Opera.
Reproduced from holograph.
Composed for: 3 sopranos, 3 contraltos, 3 tenors, 2 baritones, bass-baritone, bass, SATB chorus, onstage ensemble (2 violins, viola, violoncello, piano), 2 flutes (1st also piccolo, 2nd also alto flute), 2 oboes (1st also oboe d'amore, 2nd also English horn), heckelphone, 3 clarinets (1st also clarinet in E♭, 2nd–3rd also bass clarinet), soprano saxophone (also alto and baritone saxophones), 2 bassoons (2nd also contrabassoon), 4 horns, 3 trumpets, 3 trombones, contrabass tuba, percussion (11 tom-toms, temple blocks, 2 bass drums, xylorimba, tenor drum, timpani, 3 suspended cymbals, lion's roar, 2 maracas, guiro, tam-tam, chimes, xylophone, castanets, vibraphone, military drum, whip, ratchet, wind machine, glockenspiel, trap set, tubular bells, large triangle, bongos, hi-hat, sleigh bells, whistle, friction drum, hammer, African log drum, jingling jonnie, steel drum, woodblocks, 2 string drums, metallophone, 2 cymbals, dobaci, Jew's harp, harmonica, claves, gong, metal rattle, water gong, vetrophono, glass wind chimes, alarm bell, reco-reco, 2 thundersheets, hyoshigi), harp, piano (also celesta), electric guitar, electric bass guitar, 3–5 keyboards, ondes martenot, tape, violin I, violin II, viola, violoncello, double bass.
Commissioned by: Theater Basel.
Call no.: **1993/087**
Also available:
Call no.: **1993/087 libretto**

1580. Lombardi, Luca, 1945– Terza sinfonia: per soprano, baritono, coro e orchestra, 1992/93. Partitura. Milano: Ricordi, 1994.
1 score (91 p.); 42 cm.
German, Russian, and Italian words; also printed as text.
Texts by A. Blok, B. Brecht, S. Esenin, S. Quasimodo, R. M. Rilke, and G. Ungaretti.
Reproduced from holograph.
Composed for: soprano, baritone, SATB chorus, 4 flutes (all also piccolo and alto flute), 4 oboes (4th also English horn), 4 clarinets (1st also clarinet in E♭, 4th also bass clarinet), 4 bassoons (4th also contrabassoon), 8 horns, 4 trumpets (1st also piccolo trumpet), 4 trombones, contrabass tuba, percussion (xylophone, glockenspiel, 2 tam-tams, bass drum, wood wind chimes, jawbone, 16 tom-toms, small suspended cym-

bal, whip, 4 woodblocks, 2 bongos, triangle, temple blocks, military drum, antique cymbal, vibraphone, anvil, log drum, slit drum, guiro, 2 sirens, timpani, claves, ratchet, whistle, tin drums, bell plate, tubo, martellone), harp, piano, celesta, guitar, violin I, violin II, viola, violoncello, double bass.
Commissioned by: Dieter Rexroth.
Call no.: **1995/066**
Re-entered as: **1996/092**

1581. Lombardi, Luca, 1945– Vanitas?: per soprano, contralto, tenore, basso e orchestra (1999). Partitura. Milano: Ricordi, 1999.
1 score (58 p.); 41 cm.
Latin, Hebrew, German, and Italian words; also printed as text.
Text from Ecclesiastes, translated by Orazio, anonymous, and Lombardi.
Reproduced from manuscript.
Composed for: soprano, contralto, tenor, bass, 4 flutes (all also piccolo), 4 oboes, 4 clarinets (3rd also bass clarinet), 2 bassoons, 2 contrabassoons, 6 horns, 4 trumpets, 3 trombones, tuba, 2 harps, piano (also celesta), percussion (anvil, sleigh bells, triangle, vibraphone, slapstick, temple blocks, xylorimba, bass drum, 4 tom-toms, timpani, crash cymbals, 2 suspended cymbals, tam-tam, glockenspiel, Trinidad steel drum, fissure drum, snare drum), violin I, violin II, viola, violoncello, double bass.
Commissioned by: Essener Philharmonie.
Call no.: **2002/118**

1582. Lombardo, Robert, 1932– Musaic: string quartet III. N.p.: Robert Lombardo, 2000.
1 score (25 p.); 30 cm.
Composed for: 2 violins, viola, violoncello.
Call no.: **2004/075**

1583. Lombardo, Robert, 1932– Orpheus and the Maenads: concerto for mandolin & string orchestra. N.p.: n.p., 1994.
1 score (35 p.); 44 cm.
Composed for: mandolin, violin I, violin II, viola, violoncello, double bass.
Commissioned by: WNIB Radio.
Call no.: **2000/106**

1584. Longtin, Michel, 1946– Quaternions: pour orchestre symphonique. N.p.: Canadian Music Centre, 1997.
1 score (204 p.); 32 cm. + text (21 p.: ill.; 32 cm.)
Accompanying text in French.
Composed for: 3 flutes (also piccolo), 3 oboes, 3 clarinets, 3 bassoons, 4 horns, 3 trumpets (also piccolo trumpet in D), 3 trombones (also bass trombone), tuba, timpani, percussion (glockenspiel, crotales, marimba, vibraphone, xylophone, 4 bongos, suspended cymbals, tarol, side drum, lokole, Balinese gong, coil spring, anvil, musical saw, waterphone, Chinese bell tree, mark tree, metal chimes, glass chimes, whip, Japanese bowl, tubular bells, bass drum, 4 log drums, 4 tom-toms, 2 roto-toms, tam-tam, waterphone, maracas, sandpaper, flexatone, large gong, cymbal on average timpani, wood chimes), harp, violin I, violin II, viola, violoncello, double bass.
Call no.: **2005/089**

1585. Looten, Christophe, 1958– Bonner Messe = Messe de Bonn: Opus 58: für Soli, Chor, und Orchester. Bonn: n.p., 2003.
1 score (various pagings); 42 cm.
Latin words.
Reproduced from manuscript.
Composed for: soprano, mezzo-soprano, tenor, bass, SATB chorus, 2 flutes, 2 oboe, 2 clarinets, 2 bassoons, 4 horns, 2 trumpets, 3 trombones, timpani, organ, violin I, violin II, viola, violoncello, double bass.
Commissioned by: Internationale Beethovenfeste Bonn.
Call no.: **2005/090**

1586. Lopez, George, 1955– Strada degli eroi: for orchestra, organ, and conductor. Partitur. Kassel; New York, NY: Bärenreiter, 1999.
1 score (101 p.); 59 cm.
Reproduced from manuscript.
Duration: ca. 50:00.
Performance instructions in English.
"Uraufführungspartitur"—cover.
Composed for: 4 flutes (1st–2nd also piccolo; 3rd–4th also alto flute), sopranino saxophone (also tenor saxophone), soprano saxophone (also alto and baritone saxophones), alto saxophone (also bass saxophone), 2 clarinets (1st also clarinets in E♭ and A, 2nd also basset horn), bass clarinet, contrabass clarinet, 3 bassoons (all also contrabassoon), contrabassoon, 6 horns (1st, 3rd, and 5th also tenor tuba, 2nd, 4th, and 6th also bass tuba), 3 trumpets (1st also piccolo trumpet), 4 trombones (4th also bass trumpet), contrabass tuba, percussion (tubular bells, bongos, 2 muffled gongs, timpani, tam-tam, triangle, horizontally suspended sheet metal plate, bass drum, drum set [pedal bass drum, hi-hat, snare drums, tom-toms, bongos, suspended cymbals, woodblocks, anvils], tom-tom, cabasa, low tom-tom, tenor drum), harp, piano, mandolin, organ, violin I, violin II, offstage violin III, viola, violoncello, double bass, 4 offstage

oboes, distant percussion (tenor drums, tom-toms, tambourines, bass drum).
Commissioned by: Wiener Konzerthausgesellschaft.
Call no.: **2002/120**

1587. López, José Manuel, 1956– Concerto: per violino e orchestra. Partitura. Milano: Ricordi, 1995.
1 score (88 p.); 74 x 30 cm.
Reproduced from holograph.
Composed for: violin, 4 flutes (1st also piccolo, 4th also alto flute), 3 oboes, English horn, 3 clarinets, bass clarinet, 3 bassoons, contrabassoon, 4 horns, 3 trumpets, 3 trombones, tuba, timpani, percussion (2 tam-tams, tubular bells, suspended cymbals, vibraphone, glockenspiel, bass drum, marimba, tuned crotales, bell plates, 2 Thai gongs), 2 harps, piano, violin I, violin II, viola, violoncello, double bass.
Commissioned by: O.C.N.E. (Spanish National Orchestra).
Call no.: **2000/107**

1588. Lorentzen, Bent, 1935– 2 Enzensberger songs. Copenhagen: Edition Wilhelm Hansen, 1989.
1 score (34 p.); 30 cm.
German words; also printed as text.
Text by Hans Magnus Enzensberger.
Reproduced from manuscript.
Contents: Pozession: für gemischten Chor—Mund: für gemischten Chor.
Composed for: SATB chorus.
Call no.: **1992/080**

1589. Lorentzen, Bent, 1935– Concerto for cello and orchestra, 1984. Score. København: W. Hansen, 1984.
1 score (102 p.); 35 cm.
Duration: 25:00.
Reproduced from manuscript.
Contents: Con dolcezza; Agitato—Misterioso; Macabre—Grottesco—Magico; Agitato.
Composed for: violoncello, alto flute, English horn, clarinet (also basset horn and bass clarinet), bassoon, horn, timpani, percussion (glockenspiel, 3 triangles, suspended cymbal, suspended tambourine, fastened cymbal, tam-tam, claves, 2 tom-toms, samba tritone whistle, crotales, tubular bells, cymbals, 2 bullhorns, bass drum), harp, violin I, violin II, violin III, violin IV, viola I, viola II, violoncello I, violoncello II, double bass I, double bass II.
Call no.: **1987/048**

1590. Lorentzen, Bent, 1935– Genesis: for soprano, tenor and bass soloists, mixed chorus and symphony orchestra, 1992. Copenhagen: Samfundet til udgivelse af dansk musik, 1992.
1 score (154 p.); 42 cm.
Latin words.
Text from Genesis.
Reproduced from holograph.
Duration: 67:00.
Composed for: soprano, tenor, bass, SATB chorus, piccolo, 2 flutes, 2 oboes, English horn, 2 clarinets, bass clarinet, 2 bassoons, contrabassoon, 4 horns, 3 trumpets (3rd also bass trumpet), 4 trombones, tuba, timpani, percussion (cast bell, crotales, 2 cymbals, 2 gongs, 3 tom-toms, skylark effect, dove call, cuckoo whistle, double woodblocks, 2 log drums, 2 wood toms, glockenspiel, 2 tam-tams, nightingale whistle, guiro, tubular bells, bass drum, lion's roar, whip, 4 suspended cymbals, claves), harp, violins I, violin II, viola, violoncello, double bass.
Call no.: **1995/067**

1591. Lorentzen, Bent, 1935– Jupiter: from The planets: suite of seven pieces for organ. Copenhagen: W. Hansen, 1998.
5 p. of music; 25 x 36 cm.
Edited by organist Jens E. Christensen.
Duration: 8:00.
Composed for: organ.
Call no.: **2000/108 no.5**

1592. Lorentzen, Bent, 1935– Luna: from The planets: suite of seven pieces for organ. Copenhagen: W. Hansen, 1998.
2 p. of music; 25 x 36 cm.
Edited by organist Jens E. Christensen.
Duration: 10:00.
Composed for: organ.
Call no.: **2000/108 no.2**

1593. Lorentzen, Bent, 1935– Mars: from The planets: suite of seven pieces for organ. Wilhelm Hansen Ed. Copenhagen: W. Hansen, 1998.
17 p. of music; 25 x 36 cm.
Edited by organist Jens E. Christensen.
Duration: 12:00.
Includes composer's note.
Composed for: organ.
Call no.: **2000/108 no.3**

1594. Lorentzen, Bent, 1935– Mercurius: from The planets: suite of seven pieces for organ. Copenhagen: W. Hansen, 1998.
7 p. of music; 25 x 36 cm.
Edited by organist Jens E. Christensen.
Duration: 4:00.

Composed for: organ.
Call no.: **2000/108 no.4**

1595. Lorentzen, Bent, 1935– Paradiesvogel: for 7 instruments (1983). Score. Copenhagen: Edition Wilhelm Hansen, 1984.
1 score (30 p.); 35 cm.
Reproduced from manuscript.
Duration: 12:30.
Composed for: flute (also piccolo), clarinet, violin, violoncello, guitar, piano, percussion (glockenspiel, tubular bells, 2 suspended cymbals, sizzle cymbal, 2 cymbals, 4 gongs, tam-tam, xylophone, suspended tambourine, 4 tom-toms, pedal bass drum, whistle, nightingale call, slide whistle).
Call no.: **1985/117**

1596. Lorentzen, Bent, 1935– Regenbogen: for solo B♭ trumpet and symphony orchestra: (1991). Score. Copenhagen: Samfundet til udgivelse af dansk musik, 1991.
1 score (56 p.); 42 cm.
Duration: 26:00.
Composed for: trumpet, 3 flutes, 3 oboes, 2 clarinets, bass clarinet, 2 bassoons, contrabassoon, 4 horns, 3 trumpets, 3 trombones, tuba, percussion (glockenspiel, water bell, vibraphone, tubular bells, 4 gongs, water gong), harp, violin I, violin II, viola, violoncello, double bass.
Call no.: **1993/088**

1597. Lorentzen, Bent, 1935– Saturnus: from The planets: suite of seven pieces for organ. Copenhagen: W. Hansen, 1998.
7 p. of music; 25 x 36 cm.
Edited by Jens E. Christensen.
Composed for: organ.
Call no.: **2000/108 no.7**

1598. Lorentzen, Bent, 1935– Saxophone concerto for winds and percussion (1986). Score. København: Edition W. Hansen, 1986.
1 score (70 p.); 42cm.
Duration: 23:00.
Composed for: saxophone, 2 flutes (both also piccolo), 2 oboes, 2 clarinets (1st also sopranino clarinet, 2nd also bass clarinet), 2 bassoons, 2 horns, 2 trumpets, trombone, bass trombone, tuba, timpani, piano, percussion (glockenspiel, 2 triangles, bell tree, tambourine, 2 woodblocks, crash cymbals, 2 tin cans, cowbell, crotales, 2 wooden tom-toms, 4 tom-toms, suspended cymbals, chocalho, tubular bells, log drum, sizzle cymbal, tam-tam, bass drum, maracas).
Call no.: **1989/076**

1599. Lorentzen, Bent, 1935– Sol: from The planets: suite of seven pieces for organ. Copenhagen: W. Hansen, 1998.
13 p. of music; 25 x 36 cm.
Edited by organist Jens E. Christensen.
Duration: 10:00.
Composed for: organ.
Call no.: **2000/108 no.1**

1600. Lorentzen, Bent, 1935– Venus: from The planets: suite of seven pieces for organ. Copenhagen: W. Hansen, 1998.
3 p. of music; 25 x 36 cm.
Edited by Jens E. Christensen.
Composed for: organ.
Call no.: **2000/108 no.6**

1601. Lorentzen, Bent, 1935– Violin concerto: for violin and symphony orchestra, 2001. Copenhagen: Edition Wilhelm Hansen, 2001.
1 score (86 p.); 35 cm.
Reproduced from manuscript.
Duration: 21:00.
Composed for: violin, 2 flutes (2nd also piccolo), 2 oboes, 2 clarinets, 2 bassoons, 2 horns, 2 trumpets, 2 trombones, tuba, percussion (headless tambourine, hi-hat, 2 log drums, 2 suspended cymbals, tam-tam, 4 tom-toms, glockenspiel, slide whistle, bass drum), timpani, violin I, violin II, viola, violoncello, double bass, dance band (trumpet, trombone, percussion [tambourine, hi-hat, 2 log drums], electric bass).
Call no.: **2004/076**

1602. Lorentzen, Bent, 1935– Wunderblumen.
Call no.: **1986/070**
No materials available.

1603. Lorge, John S., 1956– String quartet no. 1: the Equinox, 1985. N.p.: n.p., 1985.
1 score (16 p.); 33 cm.
Reproduced from manuscript.
Composed for: 2 violins, viola, violoncello.
Call no.: **1990/078**

1604. Louie, Alexina, 1949– Music for heaven and earth: for large orchestra. N.p.: Alexina Louie, 1990.
1 score (88 p.); 44 cm.
Reproduced from holograph.
Contents: Procession of celestial deities—Thunder dragon—The void—Earthrise—River of stars.
Composed for: 3 flutes (3rd also piccolo and alto flute), 3 oboes (3rd also English horn), 3 clarinets (3rd also bass clarinet), 3 bassoons (3rd also contrabassoon), 4

horns, 3 trumpets, 2 trombones, bass trombone, tuba, timpani (also large suspended cymbal, 2 elephant bells, brass wind chimes), percussion (kabuki blocks, Chinese gong, 3 suspended cymbals, sizzle cymbal, lion's roar, vibraphone, bass drum, 2 bender gongs, waterphone, claves, 2 elephant bells, 5 temple blocks, glockenspiel, 4 Japanese temple bowls, crash cymbals, 3 tam-tams, Chinese hand cymbals), harp, violin I, violin II, viola, violoncello, double bass.
Commissioned by: Toronto Symphony.
Call no.: **1994/085**

1605. Louie, Alexina, 1949– The scarlet princess. N.p.: n.p., 2001.
1 score (2 v. [575 p.]); 43 cm.
English words by David Henry Hwang.
Reproduced from holograph.
Composed for: 2 flutes (1st also alto flute, 2nd also piccolo), 2 oboes (2nd also English horn), 2 clarinets (2nd also bass clarinet), 2 bassoons (2nd also contrabassoon), 4 horns, 2 trumpets, 2 trombones, bass trombone, tuba, harp, piano (also celesta), percussion, violin I, violin II, viola, violoncello, double bass.
Call no.: **2004/077**

1606. Lowe, Wesley Hoyle, 1950– Songs of Euridice: the way of the moon: three songs for soprano and chamber orchestra. N.p.: Ethos Publishing, 1989.
1 score (74 p.); 29 cm.
English words by Georgia Cowart.
Contents: Lament—Solstice—Nocturne.
Composed for: soprano, flute, oboe, clarinet, horn, bassoon, percussion (triangle, bell tree, wind chimes, tam-tam), piano, violin I, violin II, viola, violoncello, double bass.
Call no.: **1993/089**

1607. Lu, Pei, 1959– Four fantasies for solo violin (1999): (on Chinese folk tunes). N.p.: Lu Pei, 1999.
17 p. of music; 46 cm.
Contents: Sunset-flute-drum—Jasmine—Drama-Beijing Opera—Moon over the spring.
Composed for: violin.
Call no.: **2005/108**

1608. Lu, Pei, 1959– Symphony no. 1: Zhao (1988). N.p.: n.p., 1988.
1 score (77 p.); 29 cm.
For orchestra.
Reproduced from holograph.
Composed for: piccolo, 2 flutes, 2 oboes, English horn, 2 clarinets, bass clarinet, 2 bassoons, contrabassoon, 4 horns, 3 trumpets, 3 trombones, tuba, percussion (timpani, tam-tam, snare drum, vibraphone, cymbals, castanets, tambourine, bass drum, glockenspiel, xylophone, celesta, triangle), harp, piano, violin I, violin II, viola, violoncello, double bass.
Call no.: **1994/086**

1609. Lu, Pei, 1959– Symphony no. 2 (1994): gao yuan fong: music for symphonic band. U.S.A.: Lu Pei, 1994.
1 score (84 p.); 28 cm.
Duration: ca. 27:00.
Contents: Gao yuan fong = Wind from plateau—Ji = The ritual—Shen sheng zi wu = Dance of sacrament.
Composed for: piccolo, 2 flutes, 2 oboes, clarinet in E♭, 3 clarinets, alto clarinet, bass clarinet, bassoon, contrabassoon, alto saxophone, tenor saxophone, baritone saxophone, horn, 3 trumpets, 3 trombones, baritone, tuba, timpani, percussion (xylophone, orchestra bells, chimes, triangle, small gong, large tam-tam, bass drum).
Commissioned by: Iota Mu Chapter of Phi Mu Alpha Sinfonia.
Call no.: **1996/093**

1610. Luby, Timothy, 1946– In the shadow of the rainbow: a requiem. Orchestral score. N.p.: Timothy Luby, 1995.
1 score (161 p.); 28 cm.
Latin words from the medieval Missa pro defunctoris, with additional texts from various sources.
Reproduced from holograph.
Composer notes.
"New master version"—cover.
Composed for: soprano, SATB chorus, flute, oboe, horn, percussion (antique cymbals, gong, large bass drum, large suspended cymbal, sistrum, temple blocks, timpani, 2 tom-toms, tubular bells, vibraphone, 6 sets of wind chimes, xylophone), harp, organ, piano, violin I, violin II, viola, violoncello, double bass.
Commissioned by: Dr. Rudy Nydegger.
Call no.: **2000/109**

1611. Ludtke, William G., 1941– Suite for handbells & orchestra, opus 102. N.p.: W.G. Ludtke, 1993.
1 score (37 p.); 28 x 44 cm.
Reproduced from manuscript.
Composed for: handbells, 2 flutes, 2 oboes, 2 clarinets, 2 bassoons, 2 horns, timpani, percussion (slapstick, tam-tam, claves, suspended cymbal, woodblock, bass drum, triangle, small cymbal, snare drum), violin I, violin II, viola, violoncello, double bass.
Commissioned by: Oakland East Bay Symphony.
Call no.: **1995/068**

1612. Ludtke, William G., 1941– Symphony III. N.p.: n.p., 1996.
1 score (87 p.); 44 cm.
Reproduced from manuscript.
"Pseudonym 7-5-1-3-2."
Composed for: 3 flutes (1st also piccolo, 2nd–3rd also bass and alto flutes), 2 oboes (2nd also English horn), 2 clarinets (1st also bass clarinet, 2nd also contrabass clarinet), 2 bassoons (both also contrabassoon), 4 horns, 2 trumpets, 2 trombones, bass trombone, tuba, percussion (suspended cymbal, handbells, large tam-tam, vibraphone, bass marimba, woodblock, bass drum, temple blocks, wind chimes, tubular chimes, xylophone, tambourine, snare drum, whip, timpani), violin I, violin II, viola, violoncello, double bass.
Call no.: **1998/095**

1613. Ludwig, Thomas, 1952– Violin concerto no. 1. N.p.: n.p., 1993.
1 score (312 p.); 44 cm.
Reproduced from holograph.
Duration: 40:04.
Composed for: violin, piccolo, 2 flutes, 2 oboes, English horn, 2 clarinets, bass clarinet, 2 bassoons, contrabassoon, 4 horns, 3 trumpets, 2 trombones, bass trombone, tuba, timpani, percussion (xylophone, vibraphone, crash cymbals, triangle, snare drum, bass drum, glockenspiel, large tam-tam, suspended cymbal, 5 tom-toms, woodblock, tambourine, crotales), harp, piano (also celesta), violin I, violin II, viola, violoncello, double bass.
Call no.: **1996/094**

1614. Luedeke, Raymond, 1944– Tales of the Netsilik = Contes et légendes Netsilik: for narrator and orchestra. N.p.: Raymond Luedeke, 1988.
1 score (165 p.); 44 cm.
English or French words; also printed as text (p. 160–164).
Words collected by Knud Rasmussen; English version by Edward Field; French translation by Hélène Filion.
Duration: ca. 41:00.
Contents: Prelude—Songs my mother taught me—The earth and the people—Magic words—Day and night: how they came to be—The things in the sky—Sun and moon—Thunder and lightning (1)—Thunder and lightning (2)—How we know about the animals—Hunger—Heaven and Hell (1)—Heaven and Hell (2).
Composed for: 3 flutes (2nd also piccolo), 2 oboes (2nd also English horn), 2 clarinets (2nd also bass clarinet), 2 bassoons (2nd also contrabassoon), 4 horns, 2 trumpets, 3 trombones, tuba, timpani, percussion (bongos, 5 tom-toms, bass drum, crash cymbals, 2 suspended cymbals, xylophone, marimba, bells, 3 tam-tams, vibraphone, snare drum), harp, piano (also celesta), violins I, violin II, viola, violoncello, double bass.
Commissioned by: Toronto Symphony, Montreal Symphony Orchestra, Edmonton Symphony Orchestra, Orchestra London, Orchestre Symphonique de Québec, and Calgary Philharmonic.
Call no.: **1991/073**

1615. Luengen, Ramona Maria, 1960– Stabat mater: for mezzo-soprano solo, women's chorus and orchestra. N.p.: Ramona Luengen, 1995.
1 score (xiv, 308 p.); 37 cm.
Latin, German, French, Russian, and English words; also printed as text with English translation.
Texts by Rainer Maria Rilke, Rina Lasnier, Anna Akhmatova, Gertrud von le Fort, and Edith Sitwell inserted into frame of Stabat mater.
Reproduced from manuscript.
Duration: ca. 1:15:00.
Composed for: mezzo-soprano, women's chorus, 2 flutes, oboe, English horn, 2 clarinets, bassoon, contrabassoon, 2 horns, percussion (bass drum, tom-toms, 2 cymbals, timpani, marimba, vibraphone, tubular bells, glass wind chimes, crotales), piano, violin I, violin II, viola, violoncello, double bass.
Call no.: **1996/095**

1616. Luigi, Flora, 1948– Sea wind. N.p.: n.p., 198-?.
4 parts; 23 cm.
Composed for: treble instrument (C, B♭, or E♭), piano.
Call no.: **1986/039**

1617. Lukáš, Zdeněk, 1928– Requiem: a cappella mixed choir, op. 252. Fish Creek, WI: Alliance Publications, 1995.
1 score (52 p.); 28 cm.
Latin words.
Duration: 25:00.
Composed for: SATB chorus.
Call no.: **1998/096**

1618. Luo, Jing Jing, 1956– An huan: a Chinese requiem: for SATB acappella [sic], 1995. N.p.: Jing Jing Luo, 1996.
1 score (56 p.); 28 cm.
Chinese, Latin, and English words.
"Words are from Li Po's poem Lament of the Frontier Guard, translated by Ezra Pound, and from Tu Fu's poem A restless night in camp, translated by Kenneth Rexroth. Poems rearranged by Stephen Haven"—program note.
Duration: 20:00.

Program note by the composer.
Composed for: SATB chorus.
Commissioned by: Dale Warland Singers.
Call no.: **1997/092**

1619. Lutosławski, Witold, 1913–1994. Symphony no. 3. London: Chester Music, 1984.
1 miniature score (102 p.); 31 cm.
Duration: ca. 28:00.
1985 Grawemeyer Award winning work.
Composed for: 3 flutes (2nd–3rd also piccolo), 3 oboes (3rd also English horn), 3 clarinets (2nd also clarinet in E♭, 3rd also bass clarinet), 3 bassoons (3rd also contrabassoon), 4 horns, 4 trumpets, 4 trombones, tuba, timpani, percussion (xylophone, glockenspiel, marimba, vibraphone, bells, 5 tom-toms, 2 bongos, bass drum, side drum, tenor drum, 3 cymbals, tam-tam, gong, tambourine), 2 harps, piano, celesta, violin I, violin II, viola, violoncello, double bass.
Commissioned by: Chicago Symphony Orchestra.
Call no.: **1985/118**

1620. Lysight, Michel, 1958– Triacle: pour hautbois, clarinette et basson. N.p.: n.p., 1991.
1 score (20 p.); 37 cm.
Reproduced from holograph.
At end of score: "Bruxelles, Le 01.01.1991."
Composed for: oboe, clarinet, bassoon.
Call no.: **1992/081**

1621. Maayani, Ami, 1936– Symphonie de requiem: Hebrew requiem: symphony no. 3. Jerusalem: Israeli Music, 1977.
1 score (121 p.); 52 cm.
Hebrew words.
For mezzo-soprano, chorus, and orchestra.
Poems by Yitzhak Orpaz.
Composed for: mezzo-soprano, SATB chorus, piccolo, 2 flutes, 2 oboes, English horn, clarinet in E♭, 2 clarinets, bass clarinet, 2 bassoons, contrabassoon, 6 horns, 4 trumpets, 3 trombones, tuba, timpani, percussion (woodblock, 3 tambourines, 3 tom-toms, 2 triangles, snare drum, bass drum, 3 bongos, marimba, 2 cymbals, glockenspiel, vibraphone, xylophone, celesta), 2 harps, violin I, violin II, viola, violoncello, double bass.
Call no.: **1993/090**

1622. Maazel, Lorin, 1930– Music for violoncello and orchestra. N.p.: n.p., 1994.
1 score (130 p.); 44 cm.
Reproduced from holograph.
Duration: ca. 31:00.
Composed for: violoncello, 4 flutes (all also piccolo), 3 oboes (3rd also English horn), 2 clarinets (both also clarinet in A), bass clarinet, 3 bassoons (3rd also contrabassoon), contrabassoon, 4 horns, 4 trumpets, 3 trombones, tuba, timpani, percussion (glockenspiel, xylophone, tenor drum, snare drum, suspended cymbal, bongos, crash cymbals, claves, triangle, tom-tom, woodblock, Chinese blocks, Chinese plates, whip, tam-tam, side drum), harp, accordion, piano, harpsichord, celesta, keyboard glockenspiel, violin I, violin II, viola, violoncello, double bass.
Commissioned by: Mstislav Rostropovich.
Call no.: **1997/093**

1623. Mabry, James F., 1933– Concerto: for flute and orchestra. Kenmore, NY: James F. Mabry, 1999.
1 score (80 p.); 28 cm.
Composed for: flute, piccolo, 2 flutes, 2 oboes, English horn, 2 clarinets, bass clarinet, 2 bassoons, contrabassoon, 4 horns, 3 trumpets, 3 trombones, tuba, timpani, percussion (2 snare drums, woodblock, crash cymbals, suspended cymbals, xylophone, temple blocks, bells, claves, bass drum), harp, piano, violin I, violin II, viola, violoncello, double bass.
Call no.: **2004/078**

1624. Macculi, David, 1960– 131 . . . 5141 Aurora: (storia di un dybbuk): per quartetto d'archi. N.p.: n.p., 199-?.
1 score (35 p.); 30 cm.
Reproduced from manuscript.
Composed for: 2 violins, viola, violoncello.
Call no.: **2002/121**

1625. Mâche, François Bernard, 1935– Eridan: quatuor à cordes, op. 57. Paris: Durand, 1986.
1 score (48 p.); 30 cm.
Composed for: 2 violins, viola, violoncello.
Call no.: **1988/069**

1626. Mâche, François Bernard, 1935– L'estuaire du temps. Paris: Durand, 1993.
1 score (76 p.); 42 cm.
For orchestra and piano sampler.
Composed for: 4 flutes (1st also piccolo), 4 oboes, 4 clarinets, 4 bassoons, 4 horns, 4 trumpets, 4 trombones, percussion (maracas, vibraphone, bow, cymbals, crotales, glass chime, woodblock, temple block, snare drum, tenor drum, medium tom-tom, bass drum, side drum, geophone, wood chimes, Chinese block, 4 tom-toms, creole timbales, cabasa, sizzle cymbal, reco-reco, 2 bongos, 2 congas, tambourine, wind machine, wood drum), synthesizer, violin I, violin II, viola, violoncello, double bass.

Commissioned by: Radio-France.
Call no.: **1995/069**

1627. Machover, Tod, 1953– Chansons d'amour: per pianoforte. Paris: Ricordi, 1982.
46 p. of music; 37 cm.
Notes in English and French.
Reproduced from holograph.
Composed for: piano.
Call no.: **1985/119**

1628. Machover, Tod, 1953– Electric etudes: for violoncello and computer generated sounds (1983). N.p.: n.p., 1983.
1 score (29 leaves); 22 x 28 cm.
Reproduced from manuscript.
Includes performance instructions.
Composed for: violoncello, computer.
Call no.: **1985/120**

1629. Machover, Tod, 1953– Resurrection: an opera. Orchestral score. N.p.: Boosey & Hawkes, 1998.
1 score (3 v.); 44 cm.
English words by Laura Harrington, with additional material by Braham Murray.
Based on the novel by Leo Tolstoy.
Composed for: voices, SATB chorus, 2 flutes (2nd piccolo), 2 oboes (2nd also English horn), 2 clarinets (2nd also bass clarinet), 2 bassoons (2nd also contrabassoon), 2 horns, trumpet, trombone, bass trombone, tuba, percussion, 3 hyper-keyboards, violin I, violin II, viola, violoncello, double bass.
Commissioned by: Houston Grand Opera.
Call no.: **2004/079**

1630. Machover, Tod, 1953– Resurrection: an opera. Orchestral score. N.p.: Ricordi, 1999.
1 score (4 v.); 44 cm.
English words by Laura Harrington, with additional material by Braham Murray.
Based on the novel by Leo Tolstoy.
Composed for: voices, SATB chorus, 2 flutes (2nd piccolo), 2 oboes (2nd also English horn), 2 clarinets (2nd also bass clarinet), 2 bassoons (2nd also contrabassoon), 2 horns, trumpet, trombone, bass trombone, tuba, percussion, 3 hyper-keyboards, violin I, violin II, viola, violoncello, double bass.
Commissioned by: Houston Grand Opera.
Call no.: **2001/097**

1631. Machover, Tod, 1953– Valis: an opera (1986/8). N.p.: Ricordi, 1988.
1 miniature score (185 p.); 28 cm.
English words.
Original work by Philip K. Dick.
Reproduced from manuscript.
Composed for: voices, tape, synthesizer, 3 pianos, percussion (claves, cowbells, suspended cymbal, snare drum, tenor drum, bass drum, vibraphone, marimba, xylophone, 3 tam-tams, gong).
Commissioned by: Pompidou Center.
Call no.: **1993/091**

1632. Machuel, Thierry, 1962– In paradisum. N.p.: n.p., 1993.
1 score (20 leaves); 30 cm.
Latin words.
Composed for: soprano, SATB chorus, oboe, 6 violins, 2 violas, 2 violoncellos, double bass.
Call no.: **1994/087**

1633. Mackey, Steven, 1956– Ars moriendi: nine tableaux on the art of dying well, for string quartet. New York, NY: Boosey & Hawkes, 2000.
1 score (77 p.); 28 cm.
Contents: Don't trouble trouble—First lament fragment—Speak like the people, write like the king—Second lament fragment—A peculiar spice—Everything in moderation, including moderation—Third lament—Fibrillation—Londonderry air.
Composed for: 2 violins, viola, violoncello.
Commissioned by: Borromeo String Quartet.
Call no.: **2003/078**

1634. Mackey, Steven, 1956– Banana/dump truck. New York, NY: Hendon Music, 1995.
1 score (88 p.); 33 cm.
For violoncello and orchestra.
Composed for: violoncello, 2 flutes (2nd also piccolo), 2 oboes, 2 clarinets, 2 bassoons, 2 horns, 2 trumpets, 2 trombones, percussion (cowbell, woodblock, marimba, timpani, Chinese tom-toms, talking drum, 2 bass drums, crash cymbals, timbales, medium sizzle cymbal, tuned gong, vibraphone, glockenspiel, congas, claves, egg shaker, large gong, penny whistle, triangle, ratchet, finger cymbals, chimes, bar chimes, lion's roar), harp, piano, violin I, violin II, viola, violoncello, double bass.
Commissioned by: Arts at St. Ann's, Brooklyn, N.Y.
Call no.: **1996/096**

1635. Mackey, Steven, 1956– Deal: for solo electric guitar, solo drum set (optional) and large chamber ensemble (1995). 2nd ed. 7/95. New York, NY: Hendon Music, 1996.
1 score (104 p.); 36 cm.

Composed for: electric guitar, drum set, flute (also piccolo and alto flute), oboe (also English horn), clarinet (also bass clarinet and clarinet in A), bassoon, horn, trumpet, trombone, percussion (marimba, vibraphone, glockenspiel, chimes, sizzle cymbal, large tam-tam, bass drum, woodblock, cowbell, ratchet, 2 suspended cymbals, tuned gong, cowbell, timpani), harp, piano, violin I, violin II, viola, violoncello, double bass.
Commissioned by: Betty Freeman.
Call no.: **1997/094**
Also available:
Call no.: **1997/094 solos**

1636. Mackey, Steven, 1956– Dreamhouse. N.p.: Boosey & Hawkes, 2003.
1 score (181 p.); 36 cm.
English words by Rinde Eckert and Steven Mackey.
For tenor, amplified vocal ensemble, 4 electric guitars, and orchestra.
"5/27/03 1st ed."—p. 1.
Composed for: tenor, SATB amplified vocal quartet, 4 flutes (also piccolo and alto flute), 3 oboes (also English horn), 3 clarinets (also clarinet in E♭ and bass clarinet), 3 bassoons (also contrabassoon), 4 horns, 3 trumpets, 2 trombones, bass trombone, tuba, harp, timpani, percussion (marimba, glockenspiel, xylophone, vibraphone, chimes, log drum, 2 woodblocks, wood plank with hammer, 3 mounted castanets, 2 claves, temple blocks, guiro, drum set [kick bass drum, snare, 2 mounted tom-toms, floor tom-tom, hi-hat, ride cymbal, splash cymbal, crash cymbals, mounted cowbell], 2 Chinese cymbals, 3 suspended cymbals, splash cymbals, sizzle cymbal, crash cymbals, Peking opera gong, water gong, 5 tuned gongs, large tam-tam, 2 anvils, E♭ almglocken, 4 triangles, small triangle, cowbell, 2 agogos, flexatone, bass drum, Chinese tom-tom, djembe, 2 congas, 2 timbales, 2 bongos, 2 mounted tambourines, tambourine, vibraslap, ratchet, egg shaker, mark tree, 2 wine bottles, siren, police whistle, samba whistle, finger cymbals), keyboard synthesizer, 3 electric guitars (with programmable effects units, volume pedals, whammy bar, e-bow, bottleneck slide), electric bass, violin I, violin II, viola, violoncello, double bass.
Commissioned by: Netherlands Programme Service (NPS).
Call no.: **2005/091**

1637. Mackey, Steven, 1956– Pedal tones. 1st ed. 1/27/02 corrected. N.p.: Boosey & Hawkes, 2002.
1 score (101 p.); 36 cm.
For solo organ with orchestra.
Composed for: organ, 4 flutes (2nd also alto flute, 3rd–4th also piccolo), 3 oboes (3rd also English horn), 3 clarinets (2nd also clarinet in E♭, 3rd bass clarinet), bass clarinet (also contrabass clarinet), 3 bassoons (3rd also contrabassoon), 4 horns, 3 trumpets, 2 trombones, bass trombone, tuba, percussion (bass drum, 3 tom-toms, tambourine, 4 triangles, 6 almglocken, nipple gong, large gong, 5 tam-tams, Chinese opera gong, 2 brake drums, wine bottle, 2 roto-toms, 2 timbales, agogo, woodblocks, 3 suspended cymbals, Chinese cymbal, mark tree, 4 Japanese temple bowls, marimba, xylophone, vibraphone, glockenspiel, police whistle, chimes, Chinese tom-tom, log drum, conga, vibraslap, 2 bongos, cowbells, crash cymbals), timpani, harp, violin I, violin II, viola, violoncello, double bass, CD.
Commissioned by: San Francisco Symphony.
Call no.: **2004/080**

1638. Mackey, Steven, 1956– Ravenshead. N.p.: n.p., 1998.
1 score (2 v.); 28 cm.
English words by Rinde Eckert.
Opera.
Composed for: tenor, tape, amplified violin, bassoon (also tenor saxophone), electric guitar, mallet kat, electronic drum set, synthesizer.
Commissioned by: Musical Traditions, Berkeley Repertory Theatre, and Pennsylvania State University's Center for the Performing Arts.
Call no.: **2000/110**

1639. Mackey, Steven, 1956– Ravenshead. N.p.: Hendon Music: Boosey & Hawkes, 2000.
1 score (2 v.); 28 cm.
English words by Rinde Eckert.
Opera.
Composed for: tenor, tape, amplified violin, bassoon (also tenor saxophone), electric guitar, mallet kat, electronic drum set, synthesizer.
Commissioned by: Musical Traditions, Berkeley Repertory Theatre, and Pennsylvania State University's Center for the Performing Arts.
Call no.: **2001/098**

1640. Mackey, Steven, 1956– String quartet. American composers ed. New York, NY: American Composers Alliance, 1983.
1 score (42 p.); 38 cm.
Reproduced from holograph.
Contents: An allegro—Two miniatures—Finale.
Composed for: 2 violins, viola, violoncello.
Call no.: **1985/121**

1641. Mackey, Steven, 1956– Tuck and roll: for electric guitar and orchestra. New York, NY: Hendon Music: Boosey & Hawkes, 2000.

1 score (137 p.); 36 cm.

Composed for: electric guitar, 3 flutes, 3 oboes, 2 clarinets, bass clarinet, 3 bassoons, tenor saxophone, 4 horns, 3 trumpets, 3 trombones, tuba, harp, keyboard synthesizer, percussion (3 triangles, tambourine, large sizzle cymbal, agogo bells, wine bottle, woodblock, 2 timbales, 2 bongos, cowbells, metal pipe, lion's roar, egg shaker, small beaded maraca, Chinese opera cymbal, large concert bass drum, large gong, medium tam-tam, marine band harmonica, glockenspiels, 2 log drums, vibraslap, 2 congas, samba whistle, castanets, bicycle horn, slap happy, 3 temple blocks, guiro, cabasa, claves, tambourine, ratchet, glass wind chimes, medium suspended cymbals, bass bow, tuned nipple gong, crash cymbals, graduated bar chimes, chimes, marimba, vibraphone, pedal bass drum, 3 tom-toms, snare drum, hihat, ride cymbal, Chinese cymbal, crash cymbal, small sizzle cymbal, referee's whistle, slide whistle), timpani, violin I, violin II, viola, violoncello, double bass.

Commissioned by: New World Symphony.

Call no.: **2002/122**

1642. MacKinnon-Andrew, Niki, 1957– Inana. N.p.: n.p., 199-?.

3 leaves of music; 30 cm.

Composed for: piano.

Call no.: **1995/070**

1643. MacMillan, James, 1959– Concerto for cello and orchestra. Full score. London: Boosey & Hawkes, 1996.

1 score (137 p.); 30 cm.

Contents: The mockery—The reproaches—Dearest wood and dearest iron.

Composed for: violoncello, 2 flutes (2nd also piccolo), 2 oboes, 2 clarinets (2nd also clarinet in E♭ and bass clarinet), bassoon, contrabassoon, 4 horns, 3 trumpets, 3 trombones, tuba, timpani, percussion (glockenspiel, metal bar, crash cymbals, suspended cymbal, sizzle cymbal, vibraphone, 2 large plastic jam blocks, bass drum, 2 tam-tams, xylophone, tuned gongs, large plywood cube, large thundersheet, 2 bongos, snare drum), harp, piano, violin I, violin II, viola, violoncello, double bass.

Commissioned by: London Symphony Orchestra.

Call no.: **1998/097**

1644. MacMillan, James, 1959– The confession of Isobel Gowdie. Score. London: Universal Edition, 1990.

1 score (96 p.); 37 cm.

For orchestra.

Preface in English by the composer.

Duration: ca. 20:00.

Reproduced from manuscript.

Composed for: 2 flutes (2nd also piccolo), 2 oboes (2nd also English horn), 2 clarinets (2nd also bass clarinet), 2 bassoons (2nd also contrabassoon), 4 horns, 3 trumpets, 2 trombones, bass trombone, tuba, timpani, percussion (2 congas, 2 timbales, xylophone, 3 tam-tams, anvil, tubular bells, snare drum, vibraphone, bass drum) violin I, violin II, viola, violoncello, double bass.

Commissioned by: BBC.

Call no.: **1992/082**

1645. MacMillan, James, 1959– Parthenogenesis: scena for soprano, baritone, actress and chamber ensemble. Full score. London: Boosey & Hawkes, 2000.

1 score (x, 134 p.); 30 cm.

English words by Michael Symmons Roberts; also printed as text.

Composed for: soprano, baritone, actress, 2 tapes, flute, oboe, clarinet (also bass clarinet), contrabassoon, 2 horns, percussion (glockenspiel, vibraphone, tuned gongs, 2 woodblocks, 5 tom-toms, 2 bongos, snare drum, suspended cymbal, sizzle cymbal, 2 tam-tams), harp, piano, 2 violins, viola, violoncello, double bass.

Call no.: **2003/077**

1646. MacMillan, James, 1959– Quickening: for soloists (counter-tenor, 2 tenors and baritone), children's chorus, mixed chorus and orchestra. Full score. London: Boosey & Hawkes, 1999.

1 score (181 p.); 36 cm.

English words by Michael Symmons Roberts.

Contents: Incarnadine—Midwife—Poppies—Living water.

Composed for: countertenor, 2 tenors, baritone, children's chorus, SATB chorus, piccolo, 2 flutes, 3 oboes (3rd also English horn), 3 clarinets (3rd also bass clarinet), 2 bassoons, contrabassoon, 4 horns, 4 trumpets, 3 trombones, tuba, timpani, percussion (handbells, temple bowl, marimba, triangles, rain stick, woodblocks, congas, temple blocks, brake drums, finger cymbals, glockenspiel, steel drum, snare drum, crash cymbals, suspended cymbals, tam-tam, vibraphone, tuned gongs, cowbells, tom-toms, tubular bells, whip, log drum, bass drum), harp, piano (also celesta), chamber organ, organ (or synthesizer ad lib.), violin I, violin II, viola, violoncello, double bass.

Commissioned by: BBC.

Call no.: **2001/099**

Re-entered as: **2005/092**

1647. MacMillan, James, 1959– Seven last words from the cross. Full score. London: Boosey & Hawkes, 1995.

1 score (89 p.); 36 cm.
Primarily English and Latin words.
Cantata for mixed choir and string orchestra.
Reproduced from manuscript.
Composed for: SATB chorus, violin I, violin II, viola, violoncello, double bass, organ (reduction).
Call no.: **1996/097**

1648. MacMillan, James, 1959– Symphony: "Vigil." Full score. London: Boosey & Hawkes, 1997.
1 score (161 p.); 30 cm.
Composed for: 3 flutes (3rd also piccolo), 2 oboes, English horn, 2 clarinets, bass clarinet, 2 bassoons, contrabassoon, 4 horns, 3 trumpets, 3 trombones, tuba, timpani, percussion (glockenspiel, tubular bells, woodblock, large wooden cube or box, large suspended cymbal, sizzle cymbal, vibraphone, cencerros, tuned gongs, triangle, large piece of metal, large tam-tam, thundersheet, xylophone, 2 congas, 5 temple blocks, 5 tom-toms, 2 timbales, snare drum, bass drum, antique cymbals, suspended cymbal), piano (also celesta), harp, violin I, violin II, viola, violoncello, double bass, off-stage brass quintet (2 trumpets, horn, trombone, tuba).
Commissioned by: London Symphony Orchestra.
Call no.: **2000/111**

1649. MacMillan, James, 1959– Veni, veni, Emmanuel: concerto for percussion and orchestra. Full score. London; New York, NY: Boosey & Hawkes, 1992.
1 score (130 p.); 30 cm.
Reproduced from holograph.
Duration: ca. 25:00.
Composed for: percussion (2 tam-tams, vibraphone, 2 snare drums, 2 congas, 6 tom-toms, 2 timbales, pedal bass drum, 6 Chinese gongs, 6 temple blocks, log drum, 2 woodblocks, 2 cowbells, marimba, mark tree, cymbals, sizzle cymbal, tubular bells), 2 flutes (2nd also piccolo), 2 oboes (2nd also English horn), 2 clarinets (2nd also bass clarinet), 2 bassoons (2nd also contrabassoon), 2 horns, 2 trumpets, trombone, bass trombone, timpani, violin I, violin II, viola, violoncello, double bass.
Commissioned by: Christian Salvesen, PLC.
Call no.: **1993/092**

1650. MacMillan, James, 1959– Visitatio sepulchri. London: Boosey & Hawkes, 1993.
1 score (150 p.); 30 cm.
Latin words.
Sacred opera for 7 singers and chamber orchestra.
Reproduced from manuscript.
Composed for: 7 voices, 2 flutes (2nd also piccolo), 2 oboes (2nd also English horn), clarinet, bass clarinet, bassoon, contrabassoon, 2 horns, 2 trumpets, 2 trombones, bass trombone, timpani, percussion (2 cowbells, woodblocks, 2 bongos, 2 tam-tams, tom-toms, snare drum, glockenspiel, timbales, temple blocks, bass drum, tubular bells, 2 splash cymbals, bell tree, crash cymbals), violin I, violin II, viola, violoncello, double bass.
Call no.: **1994/088**

1651. Macmillan, Scott, 1955– Celtic mass for the sea. N.p.: n.p., 1989.
1 score (various pagings); 36 cm.
Primarily English words by Jenyfer Brickenden.
Reproduced from manuscript.
Composed for: SATB chorus, mandolin, Irish pipes, guitar, fiddle, Irish harp, 2 violins, viola, violoncello, double bass.
Commissioned by: CBC Radio, Halifax.
Call no.: **1995/071**

1652. Mäder, Urban, 1955– Tauber: für Sprecher, Alt, Tenor und Kammerorchester, 1986. Partitur. N.p.: n.p., 1986.
1 score (78 p.); 30 cm.
German words by Heinz Zimmermann.
Reproduced from holograph.
Contents: Meine Haltung ist die—Tafelgebirge—Drinnen/Draussen—Links/Rechts—Die Stadt—Der Tag spitz—Unsichtbares Leben—Rede an meine Kinder—Der Prozess—Leere Perrons—Der Befehl Mittags—Im Bunker—Das Mädchen—Den Boden entfernen—Traum.
Composed for: narrator, alto, tenor, flute, oboe, clarinet, horn, trumpet, trombone, percussion (xylophone, triangle, 2 cymbals, 2 gongs, 3 woodblocks, 3 tom-toms, tenor drum, bass drum), violin I, violin II, viola, violoncello, double bass.
Call no.: **1988/070**

1653. Maggio, Robert, 1964– The wishing tree: four-part chorus, a cappella. Bryn Mawr, PA: Theodore Presser, 1999.
1 score (22 p.); 28 cm.
English words by Seamus Heaney; also printed as text.
Composed for: SATB chorus.
Commissioned by: Choral Arts Society of Philadelphia.
Call no.: **2002/123**

1654. Magnanensi, Giorgio, 1960– Nim: per violino, violoncello e pianoforte. N.p.: n.p., 1988.
1 score (32 p.); 30 x 43 cm.
Reproduced from holograph.
Duration: ca. 13:00.

Composed for: violin, violoncello, piano.
Call no.: **1990/079**

1655. Magnuson, Phillip, 1949– The twelve days of Israel: cantata for narrator, baritone, chorus, and orchestra. N.p.: n.p., 1982.
1 miniature score (110 leaves); 28 cm.
English words.
Reproduced from holograph.
Composed for: narrator, baritone, SATB chorus, flute, oboe, horn, trumpet, percussion (3 finger cymbals, suspended cymbal, tom-tom, timpani), piano, 6 violins, 3 violas, 2 violoncellos, double bass.
Call no.: **1985/122**

1656. Mahelona, Herbert, 1967– Na 'uhane o Hawai'i: an opera in one act. Full score. N.p.: Herbert K. Mahaelona, 1998.
1 score (166 p.); 28 cm.
Principally English with some Hawaiian words edited by Stacey Mailelauli'i.
Glossary of Hawaiian terms and synopsis.
Composed for: voices, piano, flute, 2 violins, violoncello, Hawaiian instruments (kā'eke'eke, kāla'au, ipu).
Commissioned by: Hawai'i Youth Opera Chorus.
Call no.: **2000/112**

1657. Mailman, Martin, 1932–2000. Concerto for violin and orchestra.
Call no.: **1985/123**
No materials available.

1658. Mailman, Martin, 1932–2000. For precious friends hid in death's dateless night: op. 80. Full socre [sic]. Cleveland: Ludwig Music, 1990.
1 score (60 p.); 38 cm.
For band.
Inspired by Shakespeare's sonnets.
Duration: 18:00–20:00.
Contents: Mournful hymns did hush the night—Broken loops of buried memories—Which by and by black night doth take away.
Composed for: piccolo, 2 flutes, 2 oboes, English horn, 2 bassoons, contrabassoon, clarinet in E♭, 3 clarinets, bass clarinet, contrabass clarinet, alto saxophone, tenor saxophone, baritone saxophone, 4 horns, 4 trumpets, 3 trombones, euphonium, tuba, timpani (also suspended cymbal), harp, piano (also celesta), double bass, percussion (glockenspiel, vibraphone, snare drum, xylophone, suspended cymbal, chimes, marimba, bongos, timbales, tambourine, bass marimba, triangle, cymbals, bass drum, gong, tom-toms).
Call no.: **1990/080**

1659. Mailman, Martin, 1932–2000. Love letters from Margaret. N.p.: n.p., 1991.
1 miniature score (89 p.); 28 cm.
English words.
For soprano and orchestra.
Reproduced from manuscript.
Composed for: soprano, 2 flutes (2nd also piccolo), 2 oboes (2nd also English horn), 2 clarinets (2nd also bass clarinet), 2 bassoons, 2 horns, trumpet, trombone, timpani, percussion (vibraphone, glockenspiel, temple blocks, suspended cymbal, triangle, chimes, tam-tam), harp, piano (also celesta), violin I, violin II, viola, violoncello, double bass.
Call no.: **1992/083**
Re-entered as: **1993/093** and **1994/089**

1660. Mailman, Martin, 1932–2000. Symphony no. 3: Fantasies.
Call no.: **1986/071**
No materials available.

1661. Makris, Andreas, 1930–2005. Concerto fantasia: for violin and orchestra. N.p.: n.p., 198-?.
1 score (34); 37 cm.
Reproduced from holograph.
Composed for: violin, 2 flutes, 2 oboes, 2 clarinets, 2 bassoons, 2 horns, 2 trumpets, 2 trombones, tuba, timpani, percussion (snare drum, cymbals, triangle), violin I, violin II, viola, violoncello, double bass.
Call no.: **1990/081**

1662. Makris, Andreas, 1930–2005. A symphony for soprano and strings. N.p.: n.p., 1992.
1 score (125 p.); 29 cm.
English words.
Contents: The passionate shepherd to his love—When I was one and twenty—Longing—When I am dead my dearest—A man's woman—Epitaph in Sirmia.
Composed for: soprano, violin I, violin II, viola, violoncello, double bass.
Call no.: **1994/090**

1663. Maksimović, Rajko, 1935– Pasija: svetoga kneza Lazara: za kazivača, četiri solista, dva hora i orkestar = The St. Prince Lazarus passion: for a narrator, four soloists, two choirs & orchestra. Beograd: Autograph Edition, 1989.
1 score (xxii, 160 p.); 34 cm.
Serbian words (Cyrillic).
Text printed separately in modern Serbian with English, Spanish, French, German, and Russian translations.
Libretto by the composer.
"The work is to be sung and spoke in (ancient) Serbo-

Slavonic language."—title page verso.
Duration: 70:00–75:00.
Composed for: narrator, mezzo-soprano, tenor, baritone, bass, 2 SATB choruses, 2 flutes (1st also alto flute, 2nd also piccolo), 2 oboes (2nd also English horn), 2 bassoons (2nd also contrabassoon), 3 horns, 2 trumpets, timpani (also gong), percussion (3 tom-toms, cymbals, gong, tam-tam, bass drum, xylophone, snare drum, 3 temple blocks, chimes, vibraphone), harp, piano, violin I, violin II, viola, violoncello, double bass.
Call no.: **1991/074**

1664. Maksimović, Rajko, 1935– Testamenat: vladike crnogorskog Petra Petrovića Njegoša: za solo bas, hor i orkestar = Testament: of the Bishop of Montenegro Peter Petrovich Nyegosh: for basso solo, choir & orchestra. Beograd: Autograph Edition, 1987.
1 score (58 p.); 30 cm.
Serbian words with English translation (solo part); also printed as text with English translation.
Text: spiritual part of the bishop's Testament.
Reproduced from holograph.
Duration: 30:00–33:00.
Composed for: bass, SATB chorus, flute, oboe, clarinet, bassoon, horn, trumpet, timpani (also gong), piano, violin I, violin II, viola, violoncello, double bass.
Call no.: **1988/071**

1665. Malec, Ivo, 1925– Exempla: pour grand orchestre (1994). Milano: Ricordi, 1995.
1 score (60 p.); 42 cm.
Reproduced from holograph.
Composed for: piccolo, 3 flutes, 3 oboes, 3 English horns, 3 clarinets, bass clarinet, 2 bassoons, contrabassoon, 6 horns, 4 trumpets, 3 trombones, bass trombone, tuba, timpani, percussion (marimba, 2 congas, snare drum, 4 tom-toms, tambourine, 2 suspended cymbals, triangle, 6 temple blocks, vibraphone, glockenspiel, xylophone, 4 bongos, large tam-tam, 4 cowbells, 2 gongs, 2 woodblocks, claves, 2 maracas, large bass drum, tubular bells), harp, piano, electric organ or synthesizer, violin I, violin II, viola, violoncello, double bass.
Commissioned by: Radio-France.
Call no.: **1998/098**

1666. Malec, Ivo, 1925– Ottava alta: concerto pour violon et orchestre (1995). Partitura. Milano: Ricordi, 1995.
1 score (45 p.); 42 cm.
Reproduced from holograph.
Composed for: violin, 2 flutes, 2 oboes, 2 clarinets, 2 bassoons, 2 horns, 2 trumpets, 2 trombones, piano, timpani (also triangle), percussion (glockenspiel, marimba, 2 bongos, 3 tom-toms, snare drum, 2 congas, tambourine, 6 temple blocks, maracas, vibraphone, woodblock, 3 suspended cymbals, bass drum, tubular bells), violin I, violin II, viola, violoncello, double bass.
Commissioned by: Luxembourg, Ville Européenne de la Culture 1995.
Call no.: **2000/113**

1667. Malec, Ivo, 1925– Ottava bassa: pour contrebasse solo et grand orchestre. Partition d'orchestre. Paris: Editions Salabert, 1983.
1 score (90 p.); 41 cm.
Reproduced from holograph.
Composed for: double bass, piccolo, 3 flutes, 3 oboes, 3 clarinets (3rd also bass clarinet), bass clarinet, 2 bassoons, contrabassoon, 5 horns, 4 trumpets, 3 trombones, bass trombone, tuba, timpani, percussion (marimba, 2 bongos, 2 congas, 3 tom-toms, snare drum, tambourine, pedal bass drum, 3 suspended cymbals, large gong, crash cymbals, sleigh bells, triangle, 5 temple blocks, claves, vibraslap, 2 maracas, vibraphone, glockenspiel, bass drum, xylophone, tam-tam, 2 gongs, 2 woodblocks, hi-hat, tubular bells, 5 cowbells), harp, piano (also celesta), electric organ, violin I, violin II, viola, violoncello, double bass.
Call no.: **1985/124**

1668. Malipiero, Riccardo, 1914–2003. Loneliness: per voce e orchestra: 1987. Partitura. Milano: Edizioni Suvini Zerboni, 1988.
1 score (iv, 62 p.); 42 cm.
English words also printed as text with Italian translation by Riccardo Malipiero.
Duration: ca. 25:00.
Reproduced from holograph.
Contents: Feaver = Febbre / di John Donne—Alone = Solo / di anonimo contemporaneo—Requiescat / di Oscar Wilde.
Composed for: high voice, piccolo, 2 flutes, 2 oboes, English horn, 2 clarinets, bass clarinet, 2 bassoons, contrabassoon, 4 horns, 4 trumpets, 4 trombones, timpani, vibraphone, 2 harps, violin I, violin II, viola, violoncello, double bass.
Call no.: **1993/094**

1669. Mamlok, Ursula, 1928– Constellations: for orchestra. New York, NY: C. F. Peters, 1994.
1 score (61 p.); 36 cm.
Duration: 13:00.
Composed for: 2 flutes (also piccolo), 2 oboes (also English horn), 2 clarinets (2nd also clarinet in E♭), 2 bassoons (2nd also contrabassoon), 3 horns, 2 trumpets,

trombone, tuba, timpani, percussion (glockenspiel, xylophone, vibraphone, ratchet, 3 crotales, 2 chimes, 3 suspended cymbals, tam-tam, triangle, snare drum, 3 woodblocks, 5 temple blocks, 3 bongos, tambourine, maracas, bass drum, marimba, slapstick, 3 gongs, 7 tom-toms), piano, harp, violin I, violin II, viola, violoncello, double bass.
Commissioned by: San Francisco Symphony.
Call no.: **1995/072**

1670. Man, Roderik de, 1941– Chordis canam: for harpsichord and soundtracks, 1989. Amsterdam: Donemus, 1989.
1 score (26 p.); 24 x 32 cm.
Composed for: harpsichord, soundtracks.
Call no.: **1991/028**

1671. Man, Roderik de, 1941– Momentum: for bass-clarinet [sic], harpsichord & tape, 1991. Amsterdam: Donemus, 1991.
1 score (iii, 28 leaves); 21 x 30 cm.
Reproduced from manuscript.
Duration: ca. 8:00.
Composed for: bass clarinet, harpsichord, tape.
Call no.: **1992/031**

1672. Man, Roderik de, 1941– Volatile voices: for ensemble De Volharding & tape (CD), 2000. Amsterdam, Netherlands: NGM (Donemus), 2000.
1 score (56 p.); 30 cm.
Duration: 12:30.
Composed for: tape, flute (also piccolo), 2 clarinets (1st also clarinet in E♭), soprano saxophone, alto saxophone, tenor saxophone (also baritone saxophone), 3 trumpets, horn, 2 trombones, bass trombone, tape, piano, double bass (also electric bass).
Call no.: **2003/030**

1673. Manchado, Marisa, 1956– El cristal de agua fria = Cold water crystal: opera en un acto (preludio, introducción y trece escenas). N.p.: n.p., 1993.
1 score (vi, 149 leaves); 42 cm.
Spanish words by Rosa Montero.
Duration: ca. 1:25:00.
Includes performance instructions.
Composed for: 3 sopranos, 2 countertenors, 3 tenors, baritone, bass, SATB chorus (2 sopranos, 2 mezzo-sopranos, 2 tenors, baritone, bass), piccolo, flute, oboe, clarinet, bass clarinet, bassoon, horn, 2 trumpets, trombone, tuba, percussion (timpani, 3 suspended cymbals, hi-hat, medium crotales, gong, 5 tam-tams, 2 bongos, side drum, tenor drum, bass drum, high cowbells, little bells, 5 temple blocks, 5 woodblocks, maracas, cabasa, 2 sets of chimes, xylophone, vibraphone, glockenspiel, marimba), piano (also celesta), violin I, violin II, viola, violoncello, double bass.
Commissioned by: Spanish Culture Ministry.
Call no.: **1996/098**

1674. Mandanici, Marcella, 1958– Madrigale: per otto voci femminili, attrice, percussioni ed elettronica (1995). N.p.: n.p., 1995.
1 score (63 p.); 42 cm.
Italian words; also printed as text.
Reproduced from holograph.
Composed for: actress, 8 female voices, electronics, percussion (bongos, tom-tom, bass drum, timpani).
Call no.: **1996/099**

1675. Mannino, Franco, 1924– Soltanto il rogo: op. 264. N.p.: n.p., 1987.
1 vocal score (61 p.); 34 cm.
Italian words.
Piano reduction by Francesco La Licata.
Opera.
Reproduced from manuscript.
Composed for: voices, piano (orchestra reduction).
Call no.: **1989/077**

1676. Manookian, Jeff, 1953– Concerto: for two pianos & orchestra. Full score. N.p.: Windsor Editions, 2002.
1 score (120 p.); 44 cm.
Duration: ca. 30:00.
Composed for: 2 pianos, piccolo, 2 flutes, 2 oboes, 2 clarinets, 2 bassoons, 4 horns, 3 trumpets, 3 trombones, tuba, timpani, percussion (triangle, tam-tam, tambourine, suspended cymbal, snare drum, bass drum, castanets, crash cymbals, glockenspiel, xylophone), harp, violin I, violin II, viola, violoncello, double bass.
Call no.: **2004/081**

1677. Manookian, Jeff, 1953– Piano sonata no. 3. N. p.: Windsor Editions, 1990.
66 p. of music; 28 cm.
Composed for: piano.
Call no.: **1992/084**

1678. Manookian, Jeff, 1953– Symphony of tears: for mezzo soprano, boy soprano, choir and orchestra. N.p.: Windsor Editions, 2000.
1 score (169 p.); 34 cm.
Armenian and English words; also printed as text with English translation.
Text by Bradford Nelson and Jeff Manookian with select passages from Armenian liturgy.
Composed for: mezzo-soprano, boy soprano, SATB

chorus, 2 flutes, 2 oboes (2nd also English horn), 2 clarinets (both also bass clarinet), 2 bassoons, 2 horns, 2 trumpets, 2 trombones, timpani, percussion (large gong, finger cymbals, suspended cymbal, triangle, snare drum, tambourine, bass drum, bongos, tubular chimes, crash cymbals, xylophone), harp, piano, violin I, violin II, viola, violoncello, double bass.
Call no.: **2003/079**

1679. Manoury, Philippe, 1952– Sound and fury: pour grand orchestre (1998–99). Paris: Editions Durand, 1999.
1 score (80 p.); 59 cm.
Composed for: 4 flutes (3rd–4th also piccolo), 3 oboes, English horn, 3 clarinets, bass clarinet, 3 bassoons, contrabassoon, 8 horns, 6 trumpets, 6 trombones, tuba, percussion (anvils, triangle, crotales, bell plate, tam-tam, tom-toms, vibraphone, sistrum, suspended cymbals, claves, xylophone, gongs, bongos, cowbells, marimba, tubular bells, glockenspiel, maracas), 2 harps, piano, violin I, violin II, viola, violoncello, double bass.
Commissioned by: Chicago Symphony Orchestra and Cleveland Orchestra.
Call no.: **2001/100**

1680. Mantovani, Bruno, 1974– Le sette chiese: pour ensemble (2002). Paris: H. Lemoine, 2002.
1 score (163 p.); 30 cm.
Includes preface in English and French and performance instructions in French.
Duration: 37:00.
Contents: La piazza Santo Stefano; L'église de Saint Jean-Baptiste; La crypte; La basilique du sépulcre—Basilique des Saints Vital et Agricola; La cour de Pilate; L'église du martyrium; Le cloître; La chapelle du bandeau.
Composed for: flute (also piccolo and alto flute), oboe (also English horn), 2 clarinets (also clarinet in E♭), 2 bassoons, 2 horns, 2 trumpets, 2 trombones, tuba, grand piano, upright piano (also celesta), percussion (bass drum, side drum, 2 mokubios, Chinese cymbal, vibraphone, crotales, wood drum, 5 tom-toms, medium cymbal, 2 congas, marimba, glockenspiel, medium tam-tam, 5 timpani, 7 gongs, 5 temple blocks, splash cymbal, crash cymbals), 2 violins, 2 violas, 2 violoncellos, double bass.
Commissioned by: Festival Musica and Ensemble Intercontemporain.
Call no.: **2005/093**

1681. Manzoni, Giacomo, 1932– Dedica: su testi di Bruno Maderna: per flauto, voce di basso e orchestra sinfonica (con gruppo strumentale da camera e coro ad libitum). Partitura. Milano: Ricordi, 1986.
1 score (58 p.); 69 cm.
Italian and French words; also printed as text.
Performance instructions in Italian.
Duration: ca. 22:00.
Composed for: SATB chorus (ad lib.), flute, bass, piccolo, 3 flutes (3rd also piccolo), 4 oboes, 3 clarinets, bass clarinet, 3 bassoons, contrabassoon, 6 horns, 4 trumpets, 4 trombones, 2 tubas, timpani, percussion (castanets, 3 cowbells, claves, crotales, whip, bass drum, guiro, cymbals, 4 suspended cymbals, 2 snare drums, 2 tam-tams, 4 tom-toms, 2 triangles, glockenspiel, xylophone, 4 woodblocks), 2 harps, piano, celesta, violin I, violin II, viola, violoncello, double bass.
Commissioned by: Orchestra Sinfonica Emilia-Romagna.
Call no.: **1987/049**

1682. Manzoni, Giacomo, 1932– Il deserto cresce: tre metafore da Friedrich Nietzsche: per coro e orchestra (1992). Partitura. Milano: G. Ricordi, 1993.
1 score (vii, 69 p.); 42 cm.
Italian words; also printed as text.
Reproduced from manuscript.
Performance instructions in Italian.
Composed for: SATB chorus, 3 flutes (2nd–3rd also piccolo), 3 oboes, 3 clarinets, bass clarinet, 3 bassoons (3rd also contrabassoon), 4 horns, 3 trumpets, 3 trombones, tuba, timpani, percussion (5 cencerros, small crotales, slide whistle, flexatone, bass drum, crash cymbals, 4 suspended cymbals, tambourine, 2 small drums, 4 tom-toms, small triangle, vibraphone, 4 woodblocks, xylorimba), violin I, violin II, viola, violoncello, double bass.
Commissioned by: Ravenna Festival.
Call no.: **1994/091**

1683. Manzoni, Giacomo, 1932– Doktor Faustus: scene dal romanzo di Thomas Mann. Partitura. Milano: Ricordi, 1988.
1 score (320 p.); 43 cm.
Italian words.
Opera.
Reproduced from holograph.
Composed for: 2 sopranos, mezzo-soprano, 2 tenors, bass-baritone, 2 basses, SATB chorus, women's chorus, men's chorus, children's chorus, 3 flutes (3rd also piccolo), 3 oboes, 3 clarinets, bass clarinet, 2 bassoons, contrabassoon, 4 horns, 4 trumpets, 3 trombones, tuba, timpani, percussion (tubular bells, castanets, 5 cencerros, claves, 3 crotales, whip, bass drum, guiro,

metal plate, maracas, hammer, cymbals, 4 suspended cymbals, ratchet, tambourine, 2 drums, 2 tam-tams, 4 temple blocks, 4 tom-toms, 2 triangles, 4 woodblocks), harp, piano, ondes martenot, celesta, violin I, violin II, viola, violoncello, double bass.
Call no.: **1990/082**
Re-entered as: **1991/075**

1684. Manzoni, Giacomo, 1932– Moi, Antonin A.: per soprano leggero, lettore e orchestra, su testi di Antonin Artaud (1997). Partitura. Milano: Ricordi, 1997.
1 score (75 p.); 42 cm.
French words.
Reproduced from manuscript.
"Provisional perusal score—not to be used for performance."
Duration: ca. 25:00.
Composed for: soprano, 3 flutes (3rd also piccolo), 3 oboes, 3 clarinets, bass clarinet, 3 bassoons (3rd also contrabassoon), 4 horns (3rd also tenor tuba), 3 trumpets, 3 trombones (1st also bass trombone), tuba, timpani, percussion (high bamboo chimes, castanets, 5 cencerros, claves, 3 high crotales, bass drum, 5 suspended cymbals, lion's roar, 2 tambourines, tam-tam, 5 tom-toms, 4 woodblocks, xylorimba), violin I, violin II, viola, violoncello, double bass.
Commissioned by: Maggio Musicale Fiorentino.
Call no.: **1998/099**

1685. Manzoni, Giacomo, 1932– O Europa!: per soprano e orchestra, su testi di Attila József (1999). Partitura. Milano: Ricordi, 2000.
1 score (32 p.); 42 cm.
Italian words; also printed as text with English translation.
Reproduced from holograph.
Duration: ca. 13:00.
Composed for: soprano, 2 flutes (2nd also piccolo), 2 oboes, 2 bassoons, 2 clarinets, 2 horns, 2 trumpets, timpani, percussion (cattle bell, conga, crotales, bass drum, 2 suspended cymbals, string drum, snare drum, 4 tom-toms, woodblock), violin I, violin II, viola, violoncello, double bass.
Call no.: **2004/082**

1686. Manzoni, Giacomo, 1932– Quanto oscura selva trovai: per trombone, coro, processori elettronici e nastro magnetico. Partitura. Milano: Ricordi, 1995.
1 score (2 v.); 29 cm.
Italian words by Dante and others; also printed as text.
Duration: ca. 20:00.
Vol. 1 scored for trombone and mixed choir; vol. 2 contains instructions for live electronics.
Composed for: trombone, SATB chorus, electronic sounds.
Call no.: **1997/095**

1687. Manzoni, Giacomo, 1932– Scene sinfoniche per il Doktor Faustus: con coro ad libitum, 1984. Partitura. Milano: Ricordi, 1984.
1 score (61 p.); 63 cm.
Reproduced from holograph.
Duration: ca. 19:00 (ca. 16:00 without the chorus).
Composed for: SATB chorus (ad lib.), piccolo, 2 flutes, 3 oboes, 3 clarinets, bass clarinet, 2 bassoons, contrabassoon, 4 horns, 4 trumpets, 2 trombones, bass trombone, tuba, timpani, percussion (glockenspiel, xylophone, marimba, castanets, 3 cowbells, claves, 3 crotales, whip, bass drum, guiro, maracas, cymbals, 5 suspended cymbals, ratchet, tambourine, 2 drums, tam-tam, 3 temple blocks, 4 tom-toms, triangle, 4 woodblocks), harp, piano, celesta, organ, ondes martenot, violin I, violin II, viola, violoncello, double bass.
Call no.: **1986/071a**

1688. Maragno, Virtú, 1928– Fantasia: sobre las notas GFFED E AS. N.p.: n.p., 1985.
1 score (12 p.); 34 cm.
Reproduced from holograph.
Composed for: oboe, harp, viola, violoncello.
Call no.: **1986/072**

1689. Marcel, Luc, 1962– Wind. N.p.: n.p., 1996.
1 score (163 p.); 28 cm.
For saxophone quartet.
Reproduced from holograph.
Contents: Sculpture eolienne—Le cube—Salle de bal avec un big-band—Slap—Mouvement d'un objet—Carrousel—Souffle chaud—Le nuge du dragon—Smog—Vents solaires.
Composed for: soprano saxophone, alto saxophone, tenor saxophone, baritone saxophone.
Commissioned by: Dance Umbrella organization.
Call no.: **2000/114**

1690. Marco, Tomás, 1942– Espacio sagrado: concierto coral no. 2. N.p.: n.p., 1984.
1 score (67 p.); 54 cm.
For piano, 2 choruses, and orchestra.
Reproduced from manuscript.
Composed for: piano, 2 choruses, 2 flutes, 2 oboes, 2 clarinets, 2 bassoons, 2 horns, 2 trumpets, 2 trombones, timpani, percussion (suspended cymbal, tam-tam, bass drum, triangle, flexatone, 2 cymbals, crotales, 3 temple blocks, 3 woodblocks, 2 congas, sleigh bells, chimes),

harp, violin I, violin II, viola, violoncello, double bass.
Call no.: **1985/125**

1691. Marcus, Ada Belle, 1929– Brevities: for orchestra. N.p.: n.p., 1989.
1 score (34 p.); 37 cm.
Reproduced from manuscript.
Composed for: 2 flutes, 2 oboes, 2 clarinets, 2 bassoons, 2 horns, 2 trumpets, trombone, timpani, piano, celesta, violin I, violin II, viola, violoncello, double bass.
Call no.: **1990/083**

1692. Marcus, Ada Belle, 1929– Textures: for chamber orchestra. Des Plaines, IA: Ada Belle Marcus, 198-?.
1 score (81 p.); 31 cm.
In 4 movements.
Reproduced from manuscript.
Composed for: flute, piano, violin I, violin II, viola, violoncello, double bass.
Call no.: **1985/126**

1693. Marcus, Bunita, 1952– Adam and Eve. N.p.: n.p., 1989.
1 score (26 p.); 28 cm.
Reproduced from holograph.
"Revised 1989"—p. 1
At end: 6/25/87.
Composed for: flute, violin, violoncello, piano, percussion (2 glockenspiels, 2 vibraphones, 2 marimbas).
Commissioned by: Middelburg Festival.
Call no.: **1991/076**

1694. Marek, Josef, 1948– Cantus tristis: requiem pro orchestr = Requiem for orchestra. N.p.: n.p., 1995.
1 score (107 p.); 39 cm.
Latin words; also printed as text.
For orchestra with soprano (last movement).
Reproduced from manuscript.
Contents: Vize = Vision—Realita = Reality—Člověk = Man—Údel = Destiny—Smíření = Reconciliation.
Composed for: soprano, 2 flutes, 2 oboes, 2 clarinets, 2 bassoons, 3 horns, 2 trumpets, 2 trombones, timpani, percussion (bell, large suspended cymbal, large tam-tam), piano, violin I, violin II, viola, violoncello, double bass, tape.
Call no.: **1997/096**

1695. Marez Oyens, Tera de, 1932–1996. Sinfonía testimonial: for choir, orchestra and tape, 1987. Amsterdam: Donemus, 1987.
1 score (101 p.); 42 cm.
Spanish words by Ariel Dorfman and Rosario Castellanos; printed also as text.
Reproduced from manuscript.
Duration: ca. 40:00.
Composed for: SATB chorus, 3 flutes (3rd also piccolo), 3 oboes (3rd also English horn), 3 clarinets (3rd also bass clarinet), 3 bassoons, 4 horns, 3 trumpets, 3 trombones, tuba, timpani, percussion (triangle, 3 suspended cymbals, cymbals, tam-tam, gong, vibraphone, glockenspiel, xylophone, tubular bells, celesta, 3 woodblocks, 3 temple blocks, tambourine, snare drum, 3 tom-toms, bass drum, bongos), harp, piano, violin I, violin II, viola, violoncello, double bass, tape.
Commissioned by: AVRO-Radio.
Call no.: **1988/072**
Re-entered as: **1989/078**

1696. Mařík, Anthony F., 1921– Destiny = Menschens-Schicksal = Osud člověka: (orchestra with recite). 4. version. N.p.: n.p., 1997.
1 manuscript score (29 p.); 34 cm.
English words.
"Russian text, M. Šolochov; text in Czech, A.F. Mařík; text deutsch, English, K. Mařík."
Holograph.
In ink.
Duration: 6:45.
Composed for: narrator, piccolo, 2 flutes, 2 oboes, 2 clarinets, 2 bassoons, 4 horns, trumpet, trombone, percussion (2 timpani, triangle, snare drum, cymbals, bass drum), violin I, violin II, viola, violoncello, double bass.
Call no.: **2002/124**
Also available:
Call no.: **2002/124 vocal score**

1697. Mařík, Anthony F., 1921– Treasure = Der Schatz = Poklad. N.p.: n.p., 1997.
1 manuscript score (27 p.); 34 cm.
Czech words by A. F. Mařík with English translation by Karel Mařík.
For narrator and orchestra.
In ink.
Duration: 7:10.
Composed for: narrator, 2 flutes (1st also piccolo), 2 oboes, 2 clarinets, 2 bassoons, horn, timpani (also triangle), violin I, violin II, viola, violoncello, double bass.
Call no.: **1998/100**
Also available:
Call no.: **1998/100 vocal score**

1698. Mařík, Anthony F., 1921– Vodník I: melodram = Wassermann I: Melodrama = Water sprite I: recite with musical accompaniment. N.p.: n.p., 1997.

1 manuscript score (60 p.); 34 cm.
Czech words by Karel Jaromir Erben with English and German translations.
Holograph.
In ink.
"First version; text is shorten[ed]."
Duration: ca. 20:00.
Program notes in Czech follow score.
Composed for: narrator, piccolo, 2 flutes, 2 oboes, 2 clarinets, 2 bassoons, 2 horns, trumpet, trombone, percussion (cymbals, small tambourine, triangle, bass drum), violin I, violin II, viola, violoncello, double bass.
Call no.: **2000/115**

1699. Marischal, Louis, 1928– Pluterdag: muzikaal verzinsel, opus 37. N.p.: Louis Marischal, 1985.
1 score (330 p.); 29 cm.
Dutch words by Paul van Herck.
Opera.
Reproduced from manuscript.
Composed for: soprano, 9 tenors, 5 baritones, bass, chorus of tenors, TBB men's chorus, SATB chorus, big band (2 alto saxophones, 2 tenor saxophones, baritone saxophone, 4 trumpets, 3 trombones, guitar, piano, trap set, double bass), 4 flutes (3rd–4th also piccolo), 3 oboes (3rd also English horn), 4 clarinets (4th also bass clarinet), 4 bassoons (4th also contrabassoon), 4 horns, 4 trumpets, 2 trombones, bass trombone, tuba, timpani, percussion (snare drum, cymbals, bass drum, suspended cymbal, triangle, tambourine, xylophone, celesta, glockenspiel, large bells, 2 woodblocks, castanets), harp, piano, celesta, harpsichord, violin I, violin II, viola, violoncello, double bass.
Commissioned by: Belgische Televisie.
Call no.: **1988/073**
Re-entered as: **1989/079**
Also available:
Call no.: **1989/079 libretto**

1700. Maroney, Denman, 1949– Music for words perhaps: ten songs for voice and piano. N.p.: Denman Maroney, 1999.
1 score (1 v.); 28 cm.
English words by W. B. Yeats.
Includes: Hyperpiano: extended piano performance techniques / by Denman F. Maroney.
Contents: The song of the happy shepherd—The second coming—The crazed moon—The song of wandering Aengus—A drinking song—A drunken man's praise of sobriety—The cap and bells—Three songs to the one burden—The two trees—The lamentation of the old pensioner.
Composed for: voice, piano.
Call no.: **2001/101**

1701. Maros, Miklós, 1943– Concerto: for alto saxophone and orchestra. N.p.: n.p., 1990.
1 score (80 p.); 30 cm.
Duration: ca. 22:00.
Composed for: alto saxophone, 2 flutes, 2 oboes, 2 clarinets, 2 bassoons, 2 horns, 2 trumpets, 2 trombones, tuba, percussion (timpani, tam-tam, orchestra bells), harmonium, violin I, violin II, viola, violoncello, double bass.
Commissioned by: Swedish Broadcasting Corporation.
Call no.: **1992/085**

1702. Marshall, Ingram, 1942– Kingdom come: orchestra and tape. N.p.: Ibu Music, 1997.
1 score (23 p.); 28 cm.
Reproduced from manuscript.
Composed for: piccolo, 2 flutes, 2 oboes, English horn, 2 clarinets, bass clarinet, 2 bassoons, contrabassoon, 4 horns, 3 trumpets, 2 trombones, bass trombone, tuba, timpani, percussion (2 marimbas, vibraphone, bass drum), piano, violin I, violin II, viola, violoncello, double bass, tape.
Commissioned by: American Composers Orchestra.
Call no.: **1998/101**
Re-entered as: **2000/116** and **2003/080**

1703. Marson, John, 1932– Sonata: for bassoon & piano. N.p.: n.p., 1986.
1 score (41 p.); 31 cm.
Reproduced from manuscript.
Duration: ca. 23:00.
Composed for: bassoon, piano.
Call no.: **1987/050**

1704. Martín, Jorge, 1959– The glass hammer: scenes from childhood kept against forgetting: a song cycle for baritone and piano. N.p.: JMB Publishing, 1996.
1 score (91 p.); 28 cm.
English words by Andrew Hudgins.
Duration: ca. 1:05:00.
Composed for: baritone, piano.
Call no.: **2002/125**

1705. Martino, Donald, 1931– Concerto: for violin and orchestra. Newton, MA: Dantalian, 1996.
1 score (104 p.); 43 cm.
Dantalian signature edition; no. 108
Includes performance notes.
Composed for: violin, 2 flutes (both also piccolo, 2nd also alto flute), 2 oboes (2nd also English horn), 2 clarinets,

bass clarinet, 3 bassoons (3rd also contrabassoon), 4 horns, 3 trumpets (1st also piccolo trumpet), 2 trombones, bass trombone, percussion (5 temple blocks, 2 woodblocks, snare drum, 2 bongo drums, 2 timbales, 2 tom-toms, 2 suspended cymbals, glockenspiel, marimba, tam-tams, vibraphone, bass drum, triangle), harp, piano, celesta, violin I, violin II, viola, violoncello, double bass.
Commissioned by: National Endowment for the Arts.
Call no.: **1998/102**
Re-entered as: **2000/117** and **2001/102**

1706. Martino, Donald, 1931– String quartet.
Composed for: 2 violins, viola, violoncello.
Commissioned by: Elizabeth Sprague Coolidge Foundation.
Call no.: **1985/127**
No materials available.

1707. Martino, Donald, 1931– The white island: for mixed chorus and chamber orchestra. Newton, MA: Dantalian, 1986.
1 miniature score (84 p.); 27 cm.
Dantalian signature edition; no. 303a.
Words by Robert Herrick; also printed as text.
Reproduced from holograph.
Duration: 22:00.
Contents: The bell-man—Upon time—His letanie, to the Holy Spirit—The goodnesse of his God—The white island, or, place of the blest.
Composed for: SATB chorus, flute (also piccolo), oboe (also English horn), clarinet in A, bass clarinet (also contrabass clarinet), bassoon (also contrabassoon), horn, trumpet (also flugelhorn), trombone, bass trombone, percussion (5 temple blocks, bass drum, 2 tom-toms, 2 timbales, 2 bongos, military drum, snare drum, 2 tam-tams, 2 cymbals, timpani, 6 roto-toms, marimba, 4 tubular chimes, tuned gong, vibraphone, glockenspiel, 2 antique cymbals), piano, celesta, violin I, violin II, viola, violoncello, double bass.
Commissioned by: Boston Symphony Orchestra.
Call no.: **1988/074**
Re-entered as: **1989/080**, **1991/077**, and **1992/086**

1708. Martins, Maria de Lourdes, 1926– Concerto para piano (1990). N.p.: n.p., 1990.
1 score (56 leaves); 30 cm.
Duration: ca. 25:00.
Composed for: piano, 2 flutes, 2 oboes, 2 clarinets, 2 bassoons, 2 horns, 2 trumpets, timpani, percussion (Chinese drum, tenor drum, 3 bongos, 5 temple blocks, bombo, cymbals), violin I, violin II, viola, violoncello, double bass.
Call no.: **1992/087**

1709. Martland, Steve, 1958– Babi Yar: music for large ensemble in 3 groups (1983). N.p.: n.p., 1983.
1 score (89 p.); 60 cm.
Reproduced from holograph.
Composed for: group 1: 2 piccolos, flute, oboe, clarinet in E♭, clarinet, alto saxophone, 3 trumpets, electric guitar, percussion (xylophone, 3 temple blocks, log drum, 2 bongos, vibraslap, 4 tuned gongs, snare drum, 2 crotales on timpani); group 2: 32 violins, 8 violas, 10 violoncellos, 8 double basses, 4 horns, synthesizer, piano, percussion (vibraphone, crotales, tubular bells); group 3: English horn, tenor saxophone, bass clarinet, 2 bassoons, 3 trombones, tuba, bass guitar, percussion (marimba, 2 bongos, log drum, snare drum, metal bar, 3 Korean temple blocks, 4 tuned gongs, 2 crotales on timpani).
Call no.: **1986/073**

1710. Márton, Eugen-Mihai, 1946– Orchesterstück: für 22 Instrumentalisten. Lüneburg: n.p., 1983.
1 score (17 leaves); 43 cm.
Reproduced from manuscript.
Duration: ca. 10:00.
Composed for: 2 flutes (1st also piccolo, 2nd also alto flute), bass flute, oboe (also English horn), 2 clarinets (1st also clarinet in E♭, 2nd also bass clarinet), contrabass clarinet, bassoon (also contrabassoon), cornet, bass trumpet, flugelhorn, trombone, tuba, percussion (timpani, marimba, orchestra bells, tuned bottles, musical saw, 3 congas, triangle, iron chains, snare drum, 2 Chinese tom-toms, 2 timbales, 3 tam-tams, sarténes, tuned glasses, bamboo wind chimes, friction drum, xylophone, cymbals, gongs, cowbells, 2 bongos, o-daiko, suspended Chinese cymbals, whip, maracas, vibraphone, lujon, lithophone, chimes, slide whistle, large derabucca, medium woodblock, 3 temple blocks, sistrum, shell chimes), harp, piano, celesta (also harpsichord), electric organ, double bass.
Call no.: **1985/128**

1711. Marvin, John, 1931– Music from the night: in four movements and three interludes: for 2 oboes and English horn. Score. San Francisco, CA: Fish Creek Music, 2001.
1 score (39 p.); 28 cm.
Composed for: 2 oboes, English horn.
Commissioned by: Julie Ann Giacobassi and Zach Hall.
Call no.: **2005/094**

1712. Mason, Benedict, 1954– Concerto for the viola section. London: Chester Music, 1991.
1 miniature score (83 p.); 30 cm.
Reproduced from manuscript.

Composed for: 3 flutes (all also piccolo), 2 oboes (2nd–3rd also English horn), 3 clarinets (2nd–3rd also bass clarinet, 2nd also clarinet in E♭), soprano (pretending to play clarinet), 3 bassoons (2nd–3rd also contrabassoon), 4 horns (1st–2nd also hand horns, 3rd–4th also Wagner tubas), 3 trumpets (3rd also flugelhorn), 3 trombones (1st also alto trombone), bass (pretending to play trombone), tuba (also euphonium), timpani, percussion (2 marimbas, xylophone, vibraphone, glockenspiel, crotales, tubular bells, cowbells, 6 steel drums, 4 temple blocks, 3 tom-toms, 2 timbales, 2 bongos, 2 congas, log drum, tam-tam, 2 plate bells, 7 pitched gongs, 6 slide whistles, 6 acme sirens, 2 vibraslaps, 3 flexatones, fishing reel, triangle, anvil, bass drum, side drum, suspended cymbal, 2 plate cymbals, sizzle cymbal, Chinese cymbal, cabasa, 2 maracas, tambourines, castanets, sleigh bells, ratchet, whip, chocalho, referee's whistle, electric siren, 6 corrugated plastic tubes, woodblock), 2 harps, 2 pianos (1st also celesta, 2nd also synthesizer), violin I, violin II, viola (also viola d'amore), violoncello, double bass.
Commissioned by: BBC Symphony Orchestra.
Call no.: **1993/095**

1713. Mason, Charles Norman, 1955– Hradĉanska: for full orchestra. Conductor score. Birmingham, AL: Charles Norman Mason, 1997.
1 score (35 p.); 36 cm.
Composed for: piccolo, 2 flutes, 2 oboes, 2 clarinets, 2 bassoons, contrabassoon, 2 horns, 2 trumpets, 2 trombones, tuba, marimba (also xylophone), timpani, violin I, violin II, viola, violoncello, double bass.
Call no.: **2001/103**

1714. Mastrogiovanni, Antonio, 1936– Sol de América: para recitante, coro y orquesta. N.p.: n.p., 1982.
1 score (81 p.); 49 cm.
Spanish words, also printed as text.
Reproduced from manuscript.
Text from Manuel Felipe Rugeles's El bolivar de Alejandro Colina.
Duration: 26:30.
Composed for: narrator, SATB chorus, 3 flutes (3rd also piccolo), 3 oboes (3rd also English horn), 3 clarinets (2nd also bass clarinet, 3rd also clarinet in E♭), 3 bassoons (3rd also contrabassoon), 4 horns, 3 trumpets, 3 trombones, tuba, timpani, percussion (glockenspiel, 4 woodblocks, guiro, bass drum, xylophone, castanets, whip, tam-tam, 4 bongos, vibraphone, 4 temple blocks, 4 tom-toms, xylorimba, 4 cowbells, 4 drums, maracas), harp, piano (also celesta and harpsichord), violin I, violin II, viola, violoncello, double bass.
Call no.: **1985/129**

1715. Matějka, Ladislav, 1938– Broučci: opera in 3 acts for small and big children. Partitura. Ostrava: n.p., 1995.
1 score (3 v. [636 p.]); 30 cm.
Czech words by Miloslav Nekvasil.
Based on Fireflies by Jan Karafiát.
Includes summary in English.
Composed for: voices, 2 flutes, oboe (also English horn), 2 clarinets (2nd also bass clarinet), bassoon, 2 horns, 2 trumpets, 2 trombones, percussion (xylophone, bass drum, crash cymbals, triangle, timpani, temple blocks), harp, piano, celesta, violin I, violin II, viola, violoncello, double bass.
Call no.: **1998/103**

1716. Matějů, Zbyněk, 1958– Golem: for symphony orchestra. N.p.: n.p., 200-?.
1 score (134 p.); 30 cm.
Composed for: 2 flutes (both also piccolo), 2 oboes, 2 clarinets, 2 bassoons, 4 horns, 2 trumpets, 2 trombones, tuba, shofar (from tape, not obligatory), percussion (timpani, crotales, vibraphone, xylophone, chimes, cowbells, flexatone, 2 suspended cymbals, tam-tam, bass drum, guiro, claves, temple blocks, 4 tom-tom, piccolo snare drum), celesta, harp, violin I, violin II, viola, violoncello, double bass.
Commissioned by: Prague Chamber Ballet.
Call no.: **2003/081**

1717. Mathias, William, 1934–1992. Symphony no. 2: summer music: op. 90. London: Oxford University Press, 1983.
1 score (130 p.); 30 cm.
Reproduced from holograph.
Composed for: 3 flutes (3rd also piccolo), 2 oboes, 2 clarinets, 2 bassoons, contrabassoon, 4 horns, 3 trumpets, 3 trombones, tuba, timpani, percussion (bass drum, 2 tam-tams, bell tree, suspended cymbal, 2 snare drums, claves, bell, glockenspiel, tambourine, vibraphone, tenor drum, crash cymbals, crotales, 3 jazz cymbals, triangle, woodblock), harp, piano, celesta, violin I, violin II, viola, violoncello, double bass.
Commissioned by: Royal Liverpool Philharmonic Society and Welsh Arts Council.
Call no.: **1985/132**

1718. Mathias, William, 1934–1992. Symphony no. 3. Study score. New York, NY: Oxford University Press, 1991.
1 score (181 p.); 30 cm.
Reproduced from holograph.
Composed for: 3 flutes (3rd also piccolo), 3 oboes (3rd also English horn), 3 clarinets (3rd also bass clarinet),

2 bassoons, contrabassoon, 4 horns, 3 trumpets, 3 trombones, tuba, timpani, percussion (snare drum, triangle, tambourine, woodblock, cymbals, tam-tam, vibraphone, xylophone, bass drum, bells, glockenspiel, crotales, bongo), harp, piano, celesta, violin I, violin II, viola, violoncello, double bass.
Commissioned by: BBC.
Call no.: **1992/088**

1719. Matthews, Colin, 1946– Broken symmetry. Full score. London: Faber Music, 1992.
1 score (187 p.); 42 cm.
For large orchestra.
Reproduced from holograph.
Composed for: 2 flutes (both also piccolo), alto flute, 2 oboes, English horn, clarinet in E♭, 2 clarinets, bass clarinet, contrabass clarinet, 2 bassoons, contrabassoon, 6 horns, 4 trumpets, 3 trombones, tuba, timpani, percussion (vibraslap, log drums, tam-tams, lujon, bass drums, tom-toms, tubular bells, fishing rod reel, maracas, ratchet, sleigh bells, guiro, sizzle cymbal, 2 hi-hats, crotales, suspended cymbal, tenor drums, 2 vibraphones, bell tree, 4 cowbells, tambourine, anvils, brake drums, crotales, glockenspiel, 4 temple blocks), harp, piano, violin I, violin II, viola, violoncello, double bass.
Commissioned by: BBC.
Call no.: **1996/100**

1720. Matthews, Colin, 1946– Continuum: for mezzo soprano and 23 players (2000). Full score. London: Faber Music, 2000.
1 score (157 p.); 30 cm.
French, Italian, and English words by Rainer Maria Rilke and Eugenio Montale; also printed as text with English translation.
"September 2000"—caption.
Duration: ca. 40:00.
Composed for: mezzo-soprano, flute, alto flute, English horn, clarinet, 2 bass clarinets, bassoon (also contrabassoon), 2 horns, trumpet, trombone, percussion (vibraphone, glockenspiel, crotales, 2 tuned gongs, 2 triangles, suspended cymbal, sizzle cymbal, 2 metal bars, 2 tam-tams), harp, piano, 2 violins, 3 violas, 2 violoncellos, double bass.
Commissioned by: Birmingham Contemporary Music Group.
Call no.: **2002/126**

1721. Matthews, Colin, 1946– Continuum: for mezzo soprano and 23 players (2000). Full score. London: Faber Music, 2001.
1 score (157 p.); 30 cm.
French, Italian, and English words by Rainer Maria Rilke and Eugenio Montale; also printed as text with English translation.
"May 2001"—caption.
Duration: ca. 40:00.
Composed for: mezzo-soprano, flute, alto flute, English horn, clarinet, 2 bass clarinets, bassoon (also contrabassoon), 2 horns, trumpet, trombone, percussion (vibraphone, glockenspiel, crotales, 2 tuned gongs, 2 triangles, suspended cymbal, sizzle cymbal, 2 metal bars, 2 tam-tams), harp, piano, 2 violins, 3 violas, 2 violoncellos, double bass.
Commissioned by: Birmingham Contemporary Music Group.
Call no.: **2004/083**

1722. Matthews, Colin, 1946– Landscape: Sonata no 5 op 17 (1977/81) for orchestra. London: Faber Music; New York, NY: G. Schirmer, 1984.
1 score (114 p.); 38 cm.
Reproduced from holograph.
Duration: ca. 30:00.
Composed for: 3 flutes (2nd–3rd also piccolo), 2 oboes, English horn, 3 clarinets (3rd also bass clarinet), contrabass clarinet, 3 bassoons, 4 horns, 3 trumpets, 3 trombones, tuba, timpani, percussion (2 bongos, 5 tom-toms, slapstick, 3 temple blocks, suspended cymbal, glockenspiel, military drum, 2 tenor drums, gong, castanet, claves, jazz cowbell, 2 bass drums, hi-hat, crash cymbals, triangle, vibraphone, 3 tom-toms, 2 tam-tams, maracas, slapstick, crotales), 2 harps, violin I, violin II, viola, violoncello, double bass.
Call no.: **1985/130**

1723. Matthews, Colin, 1946– Memorial: for large orchestra (1992–93). London: Faber Music, 1993.
1 score (55 p.); 42 cm.
Reproduced from manuscript.
Duration: ca. 20:00.
Composed for: piccolo, 2 flutes, 2 oboes, English horn, clarinet, clarinet in E♭, bass clarinet, 2 bassoons, contrabassoon, 4 horns, 3 trumpets, 3 trombones, tuba, timpani, percussion (crotales, 4 tuned gongs, metal chimes, lujon, glockenspiel, bell tree, sleigh bells, 2 sizzle cymbals, handbells, spring coils, 2 brake drums, vibraphone, suspended cymbal, bell plates, mark tree, brass bells, 3 tam-tams, tubular bells), harp, piano, violin I, violin II, viola, violoncello, double bass.
Commissioned by: London Symphony Orchestra.
Call no.: **1994/092**

1724. Matthews, Colin, 1946– Renewal: for chorus & orchestra. London: Faber Music, 1996.

1 score (25, 20, 187, 45 p.); 43 cm.
Latin words.
Text from Ovid's Metamorphoses book XV.
Reproduced from manuscript.
Contents: Intrada—Threnody—Broken symmetry—Metamorphosis.
Composed for: SATB chorus, piccolo (also flute), flute (also piccolo), alto flute, 2 oboes, English horn, clarinet in E♭, 2 clarinets, bass clarinet, contrabass clarinet, 2 bassoons, contrabassoon, 6 horns, 4 trumpets, 3 trombones, tuba, timpani, percussion, harp, piano (also celesta), violin I, violin II, viola, violoncello, double bass.
Commissioned by: BBC.
Call no.: **1998/104**

1725. Matthews, David, 1943– Violin concerto, op. 31. Full score. London: Faber Music, 1982.
1 score (88 p.); 42 cm.
Reproduced from holograph.
Duration: ca. 24:00.
Composed for: violin, 2 flutes (2nd also piccolo), 2 oboes (2nd also English horn), 2 clarinets (1st also clarinet in A, 2nd also clarinet in E♭), baritone saxophone (also bass clarinet), 2 bassoons (2nd also contrabassoon), 4 horns, 2 trumpets, 2 trombones, tuba, timpani, percussion (jazz kit [bass drum, 2 tom-toms, side drum, 2 cymbals], bass drum, tam-tam, tambourine, triangle, Chinese cymbal, bell tree, glockenspiel, vibraphone, xylophone, marimba, crotales), harp, piano (also celesta), violin I, violin II, viola, violoncello, double bass.
Call no.: **1985/131**

1726. Matthus, Siegfried, 1934– Manhattan concerto: for orchestra. Partitur. Leipzig: Deutscher Verlag für Musik, 1994.
1 score (129 p.); 39 cm.
Reproduced from holograph.
Composed for: piccolo, 2 flutes, 2 oboes, English horn, 2 clarinets, bass clarinet, 3 bassoons, 4 horns, 3 trumpets, 3 trombones, tuba, timpani, percussion (triangle, crotales, glockenspiel, wind chimes, wood wind chimes, claves, 4 temple blocks, tambourine, maracas, 4 suspended cymbals, hi-hat, auto brake drum, anvil, chain, xylophone, metallophone, marimba, tubular bells, 4 gongs, tam-tam, metal foil, slit drum, 5 bongos, 5 tom-toms, 2 snare drums, bass drum, 2 bird whistles, flexatone), harp, celesta, violin I, violin II, viola, violoncello, double bass.
Commissioned by: Manhattan School of Music.
Call no.: **1995/073**

1727. Matthys, Marc, 1956– Reflections: for jazz trio and symphony orch. N.p.: n.p., 1992.
1 score (39 p.); 42 cm.
Reproduced from holograph.
Duration: ca. 17:00.
Contents: Waves—Siciliano.
Composed for: jazz trio (piano, electric bass, drum set), 2 flutes, 2 oboes, 2 clarinets, bass clarinet, 2 bassoons, 4 horns, 3 trumpets, 3 trombones, bass trombone, timpani (also congas), violin I, violin II, viola, violoncello, double bass.
Call no.: **1997/097**

1728. Maves, David W., 1937– Concerto for two pianos and orchestra.
Call no.: **1985/133**
No materials available.

1729. Maw, Nicholas, 1935– Concerto for violin (1993). Full score. London: Faber Music, 1993.
1 score (various pagings); 30 cm.
Duration: ca. 40:00.
Composed for: violin, 2 flutes (2nd also piccolo), 2 oboes (2nd also English horn), 2 clarinets (2nd also clarinet in E♭), 2 bassoons (2nd also contrabassoon), 4 horns, 2 trumpets, tuba, timpani, percussion (side drum, suspended cymbal, crash cymbals, glockenspiel, vibraphone, tambourine, tenor drum), harp, violin I, violin II, viola, violoncello, double bass.
Commissioned by: Roger Norrington and Orchestra of St. Luke's New York and Philharmonia Orchestra, London.
Call no.: **1994/093**

1730. Maw, Nicholas, 1935– Odyssey. London: Faber Music, 1987.
1 score (2 v.); 30 cm.
For orchestra.
Reproduced from manuscript.
Duration: ca. 1:40:00.
Composed for: 3 flutes (2nd also alto flute, 3rd also piccolo), 3 oboes (3rd also English horn), 3 clarinets (all also clarinet in A, 2nd also clarinet in E♭, 3rd bass clarinet), 3 bassoons (3rd also contrabassoon), 8 horns, 4 trumpets (3rd–4th also trumpet in D), 2 trombones, bass trombone, tuba, timpani, percussion (vibraphone, tubular bells, 2 glockenspiels, 2 bongos, 3 tom-toms, side drum, tenor drum, bass drum, 3 suspended cymbals, 3 tam-tams, crash cymbals, gong, triangle, tambourine, maracas, claves), harp, celesta, violin I, violin II, viola, violoncello, double bass.
Commissioned by: LSO and BBC.
Call no.: **1991/078**
Re-entered as: **1992/089**

1731. Maw, Nicholas, 1935– Piano trio: for violin, cello, and piano: (1990–91). London: Faber Music, 1995.
1 score (70 p.) + 2 parts; 31 cm.
At end: "Washington D.C., 30th January 1991."
Duration: ca. 32:00.
Composed for: violin, violoncello, piano.
Commissioned by: Serge Koussevitzky Foundation in the Library of Congress.
Call no.: **1996/101**

1732. Maw, Nicholas, 1935– The world in the evening: for orchestra. Full score. London: Faber Music, 1988.
1 score (111 p.); 43 cm.
Reproduced from holograph.
At end of score: "Washington, D.C. August 19th, 1988."
Composed for: 2 flutes (2nd also piccolo), 2 oboes (2nd also English horn), 2 clarinets (both also clarinet in A), 2 bassoons (2nd also contrabassoon), 4 horns, 3 trumpets, 3 trombones, timpani, percussion (tenor drum, bass drum, crash cymbals, suspended cymbal, tam-tam, whip, triangle, bells), harp, violin I, violin II, viola, violoncello, double bass.
Commissioned by: Royal Opera House.
Call no.: **1993/096**

1733. Maxwell, Michael, 1952– Suite for orchestra, 1989/90. N.p.: n.p., 1990.
1 score (133 p.); 31 cm.
Reproduced from manuscript.
Composed for: 3 flutes (3rd also piccolo), 2 oboes, 4 clarinets (4th also bass clarinet), 3 bassoons (3rd also contrabassoon), 5 horns, 3 trumpets, 3 trombones, bass trombone, 2 tubas, timpani, percussion (triangle, tam-tam, tambourine, tubular bells, snare drum, crash cymbals, bell tree, xylophone, glockenspiel, cabasa, suspended cymbal, bass drum), 2 harps, piano, celesta, violin I, violin II, viola, violoncello, double bass.
Commissioned by: Kerry Stratton and North York Symphony with David Miller and Oakville Symphony.
Call no.: **1991/079**

1734. Mayer, William, 1925– A death in the family.
Call no.: **1985/134**
No materials available.

1735. McAllister, Scott, 1969– Screaming azaleas. N.p.: L.Y.D., 1996.
1 score (34 p.); 36 cm.
English words by the composer; also printed as text.
Composed for: soprano, flute, clarinet, piano, harp, percussion (crotales, vibraphone, tom-toms, crash cymbals), violin, violoncello.
Commissioned by: Elizabeth Buck.
Call no.: **1997/098**

1736. McCabe, John, 1939– Concerto for orchestra (1982). Full score. London; Glen Cove, NY: Novello, 1984.
1 score (135 p.); 49 cm.
"Corrected 11/84."
Reproduced from manuscript.
Duration: ca. 24:00.
Composed for: 3 flutes (3rd also piccolo), 3 oboes, 3 clarinets, 3 bassoons, 4 horns, 3 trumpets, 2 trombones, bass trombone, tuba, timpani, percussion (side drum, bass drum, crash cymbals, suspended cymbal, tambourine, claves, castanets, woodblock, glockenspiel, tubular bells), harp, piano (also celesta), violin I, violin II, viola, violoncello, double bass.
Commissioned by: London Philharmonic Orchestra.
Call no.: **1985/135**

1737. McCabe, John, 1939– Edward II: a ballet in two acts. Full score. London: Novello, 1995.
1 score (2 v.); 30 cm.
Includes synopsis.
Composed for: 3 flutes (3rd also piccolo), 3 oboes (3rd also English horn), 2 clarinets (2nd also clarinet in E♭), bass clarinet, 2 bassoons, contrabassoon, 4 horns, 3 trumpets, 2 trombones, bass trombone, tuba, timpani, percussion (xylophone, vibraphone, bass drum, side drum, tenor drum, tambourine, clash cymbals, tubular bells, glockenspiel, tam-tam, suspended cymbal, anvil, cowbell, whip, 3 bongos, 3 tom-toms, woodblock, jingle bells, 2 large tabors), harp, piano, celesta, electric guitar, violin I, violin II, viola, violoncello, double bass.
Commissioned by: Stuttgart Ballett.
Call no.: **1996/102**

1738. McCabe, John, 1939– Fire at Durilgai: (1988): for orchestra. Full score. London: Novello, 1988.
1 score (99 p.); 39 cm.
Reproduced from holograph.
Duration: ca. 20:00.
Composed for: piccolo, 2 flutes, 3 oboes, 3 clarinets, 3 bassoons, 4 horns, 3 trumpets, 2 trombones, bass trombone, tuba, timpani, percussion (snare drum, bass drum, 3 bongos, 3 tom-toms, tambourine, guiro, whip, glockenspiel, vibraphone, xylophone, suspended cymbal, sizzle cymbal, tam-tam, anvil, tubular bells, 5 mounted crotales), harp, violin I, violin II, viola, violoncello, double bass.
Commissioned by: British Broadcasting Company.
Call no.: **1990/084**

1739. McCarthy, Daniel William, 1955– All the west was moving: string quartet and bassoon. N.p.: American Composers Edition, 1998.
1 score (29 p.); 28 cm.
Duration: 10:00.
Includes program notes.
Composed for: bassoon, 2 violins, viola, violoncello.
Call no.: **2001/104**

1740. McCarthy, Daniel William, 1955– Chamber symphony no. 2 for bassoon and winds. Greensboro, NC: C. Alan Publications, 2002.
1 score (84 p.); 22 x 28 cm.
Duration: ca. 15:00.
Contents: Stomp and buc dance—Interlude—Mechanique—Interlude: Creep—Static—Fire, dance, and wahbekanetta.
Composed for: bassoon, flute, oboe, soprano saxophone, clarinet, bass clarinet, bassoon, horn, percussion, double bass.
Commissioned by: Michigan State University Bands.
Call no.: **2003/082**

1741. McCarthy, Daniel William, 1955– Concerto for marimba, percussion and synthesizers. Greensboro, NC: C. Alan Productions, 1992.
1 score (82 p.); 29 cm.
Contents: Melismatic—Inamst—Rokit!
Composed for: marimba, synthesizers, percussion (marimba, bass marimba, vibraphone, timpani, temple blocks, afuche, 5 log drums, 5 boobams, suspended cymbals, tam-tam, gong, water gong, castanets, woodblock, snare drum, slapstick, bass drum, bongos, bamboo tree, bell tree, 2 timbales, congas, rain tree).
Commissioned by: John Raush.
Call no.: **1994/094**

1742. McCauley, Robert, 1958– …¬,˜˜,˛Pa°°′^˙˙sa≈≈˜˜ca… ,,li˛˘˘ a…: for brass ensemble. N.p.: n.p., 199-?.
1 score (139 p.); 28 cm.
Composed for: 4 trumpets (2nd also piccolo trumpet), 4 horns, 3 trombones, euphonium, tuba, offstage synthesizer.
Call no.: **1998/105**

1743. McCauley, Robert, 1958– …¬ ,˜˜,˛Pa°°′^˙˙sa≈≈˜˜ca…,,li˛˘˘ a…: for brass ensemble. Houston, TX: Circa Now Music Press, 1997.
1 score (127 p.); 28 cm.
Composed for: 4 trumpets (2nd also piccolo trumpet), 4 horns, 3 trombones, euphonium, tuba, offstage synthesizer.
Call no.: **2000/118**

1744. McDougall, Ian, 1938– Concerto: for bass trombone and orchestra. N.p.: n.p., 1993.
1 score (various pagings); 36 cm.
Composed for: bass trombone, 2 flutes (2nd also piccolo), 2 oboes, 2 clarinets (2nd also bass clarinet), 2 bassoons, 4 horns, 3 trumpets, 2 trombones, bass trombone, tuba, timpani, percussion (vibraphone, glockenspiel, xylophone, roto-toms, shaker, triangle, tam-tam, cymbals), violin I, violin II, viola, violoncello, double bass.
Commissioned by: Murray Crewe and Toronto Symphony.
Call no.: **1994/095**

1745. McDougall, Ian, 1938– Concerto for clarinet and string orchestra. N.p.: n.p., 1983.
1 score (64 leaves); 46 cm.
Reproduced from holograph.
Composed for: clarinet, violin I, violin II, viola, violoncello, double bass.
Call no.: **1986/074**

1746. McDougall, Ian, 1938– Ojistoh: for soprano voice & chamber orchestra (may be sung by mezzo-sop. also): a setting of the poem by E. Pauline Johnson (Tekahionwake). Toronto: Canadian Music Centre, 1986.
1 score (96 p.); 43 cm.
Cayuga and English words.
Reproduction of holograph.
Composed for: soprano, 2 flutes (2nd also piccolo), 2 oboes, 2 clarinets (2nd also bass clarinet), 2 bassoons, 2 horns, 2 trumpets, trombone, timpani, violin I, violin II, viola, violoncello, double bass.
Commissioned by: Canadian Broadcasting Corporation.
Call no.: **1987/051**

1747. McFatter, Larry, 1948– Hymn of the earth: for choir, soloists and orchestra. N.p.: Larry McFatter, 1993.
1 score (98 p.); 36 cm.
Latin words.
Contents: Acclaim the Lord—The prayer of Job—The earth is the Lord's.
Composed for: voices, SATB chorus, 2 flutes (1st also piccolo), 2 oboes, 2 clarinets, 2 bassoons, 4 horns, 3 trumpets, 2 trombones, tuba, timpani, percussion (snare drum, medium suspended cymbal, crash cymbal, small suspended triangle, mounted tambourine, mounted crotales, chimes, 4 tom-toms, xylophone, glockenspiel), violin I, violin II, viola, violoncello, double bass.
Call no.: **2002/127**

1748. McGuire, Edward, 1948– Songs of new beginnings: for female voice and wind quintet. N.p.: E. McGuire, 1984.
1 score (39 p.); 30 cm.
English words, also printed as text.
"Setting of Poems of new beginnings by Marianne Carey."
Reproduced from manuscript.
Duration: ca 17:00.
Composed for: female voice, flute (also piccolo and alto flute), oboe (also English horn), clarinet, horn, bassoon.
Commissioned by: David Davies.
Call no.: **1985/136**

1749. McKelvey, Lori, 1959– Iphigenia. N.p.: n.p., 1991.
1 score (322 p.); 32 cm.
English words.
Opera.
Reproduced from holograph.
At end of score: "January 15, 1991 Greenwich, CT."
Composed for: soprano, mezzo-soprano, tenor, baritone, SATB chorus (also wind chimes), 2 flutes (2nd also piccolo), 2 oboes (2nd also English horn), 2 clarinets (2nd also bass clarinet), 2 bassoons (2nd also contrabassoon), 2 horns, 2 trumpets, 2 trombones, percussion (timpani, tubular bells, snare drum, woodblock, triangle, gong, marimba, glockenspiel, crotales, vibraphone, xylophone, temple blocks, crash cymbals, tambourine, castanets, bass drum, thundersheet), harp, piano (also celesta), violin I, violin II, viola, violoncello, double bass.
Call no.: **1992/090**

1750. McKinley, William Thomas, 1938– 9 shades of lament: for clarinet and orchestra. N.p.: n.p., 2000.
1 score (88 p.); 43 cm.
Reproduced from manuscript.
Contents: Lamento cantilena—Lamento parodico—Lamento furioso—Lamento triste—Lamento angelica—Lamento gloriosa—Lamento ironico—Lamento fugace.
Composed for: clarinet, 3 flutes (3rd also piccolo), 3 oboes (3rd also English horn), 2 clarinets, bass clarinet, 3 bassoons (3rd also contrabassoon), 4 horns, 3 trumpets, 3 trombones (all also bass trombone), tuba, timpani, percussion (snare drum, 5 tuned tom-toms, bass drum, timbales, 5 suspended cowbells, 5 suspended woodblocks, temple blocks, marimba, xylophone, vibraphone, glockenspiel, tubular chimes, crash cymbals, 3 suspended cymbals, whip, tam-tam, 2 gongs, sleigh bells, tuned crotales, metal chimes, tambourine, 2 pairs of claves, pair of bongos, maracas, guiro, castanets), celesta, piano, harp, violin I, violin II, viola, violoncello, double bass.
Call no.: **2003/083**

1751. McKinley, William Thomas, 1938– . . . and the presidents said. Orchestral score. N.p.: MMC Publications, 2001.
1 score (26, 73 p.); 43 cm.
English words.
For narrator and orchestra.
Composed for: narrator, piccolo, 2 flutes, 2 oboes, English horn, 2 clarinets, bass clarinet, 2 bassoons, contrabassoon, 4 horns, 2 trumpets, 3 trombones, 2 tubas, timpani, percussion (snare drum, whip, bass drum, anvil, cowbell, suspended cymbal, chimes, xylophone, marimba), piano, violin I, violin II, viola, violoncello, double bass.
Call no.: **2005/095**

1752. McKinley, William Thomas, 1938– Concerto for flute and string orchestra: (1986). N.p.: n.p., 1986.
1 score (51 p.); 48 cm.
Reproduced from holograph.
Duration: 26:30.
Composed for: flute, violin I, violin II, viola, violoncello, double bass.
Commissioned by: Robert Stallman.
Call no.: **1987/052**

1753. McKinley, William Thomas, 1938– Concerto for orchestra no. 2. N.p.: MMC Publications, 1993.
1 score (186 p.); 44 cm.
Reproduced from manuscript.
Composed for: 3 flutes (3rd also piccolo), 2 oboes, English horn, 2 clarinets, bass clarinet, 2 bassoons, contrabassoon, 4 horns, 3 trumpets, 3 trombones, tuba, timpani, percussion (5 tuned tom-toms, suspended cymbal, bass drum, snare drum, large tam-tam, marimba, xylophone, tambourine, tubular bells, vibraphone, 5 suspended cowbells, 2 bongos, castanets, timbales, glass chimes, glockenspiel, triangle, celesta, large woodblock, 5 suspended woodblocks), piano, harp, violin I, violin II, viola, violoncello, double bass.
Commissioned by: Seattle Symphony.
Call no.: **1995/074**

1754. McKinley, William Thomas, 1938– Concerto no. 2: for piano and orchestra (the O'Leary). N.p.: n.p., 1987?
1 score (102 p.); 51 cm.
Reproduced from manuscript.

Composed for: piano, 2 flutes (2nd also piccolo), 2 oboes, 2 clarinets, 2 bassoons (2nd also contrabassoon), 4 horns, 2 trumpets, 2 trombones, tuba, percussion (timpani, xylophone, tubular chimes, marimba, glockenspiel, celesta, 5 suspended gongs, whip, crotales, temple blocks, tambourine, tam-tam, 3 suspended triangles, 2 claves, suspended cymbal, crash cymbals, castanets, snare drum, finger cymbals, 2 bass drums), harp, violin I, violin II, viola, violoncello, double bass.
Call no.: **1989/081**

1755. McKinley, William Thomas, 1938– Concerto no. 2: for viola and orchestra. N.p.: n.p., 198-?.
1 score (122 p.); 49 cm.
Reproduced from manuscript.
Composed for: viola, 2 flutes (2nd also piccolo), 2 oboes (2nd also English horn), 2 clarinets, 2 bassoons (2nd also contrabassoon), 2 horns, 2 trumpets, harp, piano, percussion (claves, snare drum, timpani, small bongos, tubular chimes, tambourine, marimba, vibraphone, xylophone), violin I, violin II, viola, violoncello, double bass.
Commissioned by: Massachusetts Council for the Arts.
Call no.: **1988/075**

1756. McKinley, William Thomas, 1938– Concerto no. 2 for B♭ clarinet and orchestra: 1990. Reading, MA: MMC Publications, 1990.
1 score (155 p.); 36 cm.
Reproduced from holograph.
Composed for: clarinet, 2 flutes (both also piccolo), 2 oboes, 2 clarinets, 2 bassoons, 2 horns, 2 trumpets, 2 trombones, tuba, timpani, percussion (snare drum, bongos, woodblocks, temple blocks, crash cymbals, 2 suspended cymbal, castanets, tam-tam, chimes, glockenspiel, triangle, tubular chimes, xylophone, marimba, celesta, whip, bass drum), harp, piano, violin I, violin II, viola, violoncello, double bass.
Commissioned by: National Endowment for the Arts.
Call no.: **1992/091**
Re-entered as: **1994/096**

1757. McKinley, William Thomas, 1938– Concerto no. 3 for clarinet and orchestra: ("The alchemical"), 1994. N.p.: MMC Publications, 1994.
1 score (132 p.); 44 cm.
Reproduced from manuscript.
Composed for: clarinet, 2 flutes (both also piccolo), 2 oboes, English horn, 2 clarinets, bass clarinet, 2 bassoons, 4 horns, 2 trumpets, 2 trombones, tuba, timpani, percussion (2 bongos, tubular chimes, small claves, 2 cymbals, 2 suspended cymbals, bass drum, snare drum, 3 gongs, marimba, tambourine, temple blocks, small triangle, vibraphone, 5 suspended woodblocks, xylophone), harp, piano, violin I, violin II, viola, violoncello, double bass.
Commissioned by: Gail Coffler.
Call no.: **2000/119**

1758. McKinley, William Thomas, 1938– Movements: for vln (or flute) + string orchestra. N.p.: n.p., 1998.
1 score (69 p.); 36 cm.
Reproduced from holograph.
Composed for: violin (or flute), violin I, violin II, viola, violoncello, double bass.
Call no.: **2001/105**

1759. McKinley, William Thomas, 1938– Seasons of Prague: a concerto for violin and orchestra. N.p.: MMC Publications, 1995.
1 score (195 p.); 44 cm.
Reproduced from manuscript.
Contents: Winter—Spring—Summer—Fall.
Composed for: violin, 3 flutes (3rd also piccolo), 2 oboes, English horn, 2 clarinets, bass clarinet (also clarinet in E♭), 2 bassoons, contrabassoon, 4 horns, 2 trumpets, 2 trombones, tuba, timpani, percussion (5 woodblocks, castanets, snare drum, xylophone, vibraphone, suspended cymbal, tambourine, tubular bells, glockenspiel, anvil, crash cymbals, bass drum, triangle, tam-tam, marimba, bongos, temple blocks, 5 tuned tom-toms, claves, maracas, glass chimes, sleigh bells, metal chimes, guiro, finger cymbals, 6 cowbells, 5 woodblocks, whip, castanets, tambourine), piano, harp, violin I, violin II, viola, violoncello, double bass.
Call no.: **2002/128**

1760. McKinley, William Thomas, 1938– Summer dances. N.p.: n.p., 198-?.
1 score (137 p.); 44 cm.
For violin and chamber orchestra.
Reproduced from holograph.
Duration: ca. 10:30.
Contents: Bolero—Valse—Jig.
Composed for: violin, flute (also piccolo), oboe, clarinet (also clarinet in E♭), bassoon, horn, trumpet, trombone, percussion (snare drum, castanets, tubular chimes, celesta, timpani, tam-tam, tuned tom-toms, tambourine, sleigh bells, bass drum, small triangle), harp, piano, violin, viola, violoncello, double bass.
Call no.: **1986/075**

1761. McKinley, William Thomas, 1938– Symphony #5 (the "Irish"). Reading, MA: MMC, 1989.

1 miniature score (96 p.); 36 cm.
For orchestra.
Reproduced from holograph.
Duration: 19:00.
Composed for: 3 flutes (3rd also piccolo), 2 oboes, English horn, 2 clarinets, bass clarinet, 4 bassoons (4th also contrabassoon), 4 horns, 3 trumpets, 2 trombones, bass trombone, tuba, timpani, percussion (crash cymbals, xylophone, vibraphone, tubular chimes, suspended cymbal, marimba, military drum, 5 suspended temple blocks, bongos, snare drum, triangle, glockenspiel, sleigh bells, tam-tam, 3 suspended gongs), harp, piano, violin I, violin II, viola, violoncello, double bass.
Commissioned by: Pasadena Symphony.
Call no.: **1990/085**

1762. McKinley, William Thomas, 1938– Symphony no. 6, 1990. Reading, MA: MMC Publications, 1990.
1 score (37, 113, 45 p.); 44 cm.
Reproduced from holograph.
Composed for: 3 flutes (3rd also piccolo), 2 oboes, English horn, 2 clarinets, bass clarinet, 3 bassoons, contrabassoon, 4 horns, 3 trumpets, 3 trombones, tuba, timpani, percussion (snare drum, bongos, woodblocks, maracas, finger cymbals, claves, cowbell, tambourine, crotales, crash cymbals, 3 suspended cymbals, castanets, tam-tam, glockenspiel, triangle, tubular chimes, vibraphone, xylophone, marimba, bass drum), harp, piano, celesta, violin I, violin II, viola, violoncello, double bass.
Commissioned by: Queensland Youth Symphony.
Call no.: **1991/080**

1763. McKinley, William Thomas, 1938– Totentanz: a chamber cantata, 1991. N.p.: MMC Publications, 1991.
1 score (229 p.); 36 cm.
German words by Hans-Jörg Modlmayr.
For soprano, alto, baritone, saxophone quartet, string quartet, and percussion.
Text inspired by Franz Möser's graphic cycle Totentanz.
Reproduced from holograph.
Duration: ca. 43:00.
Composed for: SATBar saxophone quartet (all also sopranino, alto, tenor, and baritone saxophones), percussion (10 suspended cowbells, 10 temple blocks, glass chimes, 2 maracas, tubular chimes, bongos, vibraphone, marimba, finger cymbals, 5 tuned tom-toms, bass drum, 3 suspended cymbals, castanets, tambourine, 2 snare drums, sleigh bells, 5 suspended gongs, tam-tam, whip, glockenspiel, timpani, small triangle, keyboard crotales), 2 violins, viola, violoncello.
Commissioned by: Town of Emsdetten, Germany.
Call no.: **1993/097**

1764. McKinley, William Thomas, 1938– Viola concerto no. 3. N.p.: MMC, 1992.
1 score (116 p.); 44 cm.
Reproduced from manuscript.
Duration: ca. 21:55.
Composed for: viola, 2 flutes, 2 oboes, 2 clarinets, 2 bassoons, 4 horns, 2 trumpets, 2 trombones, tuba, timpani, percussion (snare drum, bass drum, bongos, timbales, 5 tuned tom-toms, cowbells, temple blocks, woodblocks, maracas, claves, triangle, finger cymbals, tam-tam, crash cymbals, 2 suspended cymbals, glass chimes, tambourine, xylophone, marimba, vibraphone, tubular chimes, celesta), harp, violin I, violin II, viola, violoncello, double bass.
Commissioned by: Karen Dreyfus.
Call no.: **1997/099**

1765. McLeod, John, 1934– Percussion concerto. N.p.: John McLeod, 1987.
1 score (101 p.); 30 cm.
Reproduced from manuscript.
Duration: 26:10.
Composed for: percussion (timpani, side drum, suspended cymbal, marimba, 5 temple blocks, 5 tom-toms, 3 cowbells, mark tree, 3 Chinese cymbals, vibraphone, crotales, 3 gongs), piccolo, 2 flutes, 2 oboes, English horn, 2 clarinets, bass clarinet, 2 bassoons, contrabassoon, 4 horns, 4 trumpets, 3 trombones, tuba, percussion (whip, tubular bells, side drum, flexatone, bass drum, cymbals, triangle, xylophone, glockenspiel, 3 tom-toms, tam-tam, bell tree, woodblock, maracas, timpani), 2 harps, celesta, violin I, violin II, viola, violoncello, double bass.
Commissioned by: National Youth Orchestra of Scotland.
Call no.: **1989/082**

1766. McLeod, John, 1934– Symphonies of stone and water. Edinburgh, UK: Griffin Music, 2000.
1 score (87 p.); 37 cm.
Program note by the composer.
Contents: Awakening—Body stone—Soul stone—Reflective pools—Mind and body stones—Winding streams—Arching stone—Reclining stone—Tranquility.
Composed for: piano, 3 saxophones, 2 trumpets, 3 trombones, percussion (vibraphone, suspended cymbal, cymbal slash, 5 floor cymbals, large Burmese nipple gong, 5 Chinese gongs, temple bells, chime bar, bell tree, car spring, wind chimes, 6 daiko drums, bass drum, 5 temple blocks, guiro, claves, stones).

Commissioned by: Edinburgh Contemporary Arts Trust.
Call no.: **2003/084**

1767. McMichael, Catherine, 1954– The seven saints and sinners. Saginaw, MI: Camellia Music, 1998.
1 score (59 p.); 35 cm.
Latin and English words.
For six part double choir (SSATBB), soprano solo, tenor solo, woodwind quintet, and piano.
"Lyrics from the Mass Ordinary, Psalm 68, Catherine McMichael and Marshall Fredericks."
Contents: The pious monk—The evil influence—The warrior saint (revised 10-1 F '97; 5-19-98)—Mother and child (revised 3-24-98)—Temptation (revised 5-19-98)—Eve, or the knowledge of good and evil—The good influence (revision 11-1-97).
Composed for: soprano, tenor, SSAATTBB chorus, flute, oboe, clarinet in A, horn, bassoon, piano.
Commissioned by: Marshall M. Fredericks Sculpture Gallery.
Call no.: **2000/120**

1768. McNabb, Michael, 1952– Invisible cities. N.p.: M.McNabb, 1985.
1 score (55 leaves); 28 cm.
Reproduced from holograph.
"Due to the electronic nature of the work, no traditional score yet exists for the third and fourth movements"—leaf 33.
Contents: 1. City of no resistance—2. City of wind—5. City of reflection.
Composed for: saxophone, piano, tape.
Call no.: **1986/076**

1769. McPhee, Jonathan, 1954– Nightingale: ballet in one act: based on the story by Hans Christian Anderson [sic]. N.p.: Jonathan McPhee, 1995.
1 score (111 p.); 28 cm.
"Original choreography by Lucinda Hughey."
Duration: 25:00.
Composed for: 2 flutes, 2 oboes, 2 clarinets, 2 bassoons, 4 horns, 2 trumpets, 3 trombones, tuba, harp, piano, percussion (snare drum, bass drum, suspended cymbals, 2 cymbals, maracas, triangle, high woodblock, tambourine, antique cymbals, tam-tam), timpani, violin I, violin II, viola, violoncello, double bass.
Commissioned by: Boston Ballet.
Call no.: **2000/121**

1770. McTee, Cindy, 1953– Symphony no. 1: ballet for orchestra, 2002. N.p.: n.p., 2002.
1 score (99 p.); 36 cm.
Duration: 27:00.
Program notes in English by the composer.
Contents: Introduction: on with the dance—Adagio: till a silence fell—Waltz: light fantastic—Finale: where time plays the fiddle.
Composed for: piccolo, 2 flutes, 3 oboes, clarinet in E♭, 2 clarinets, 2 bassoons, contrabassoon, 4 horns, 3 trumpets, 2 trombones, bass trombone, tuba, timpani, percussion (3 suspended cymbals, triangle, ratchet, cowbell, flexatone, snare drum, hi-hat, bass drum, tambourine, cabasa, vibraslap, 4 tom-toms, cuíca), piano, harp, violin I, violin II, viola, violoncello, double bass.
Commissioned by: National Symphony Orchestra.
Call no.: **2004/084**

1771. Meachem, Margaret, 1922– Divergencies: for string quartet. N.p.: n.p., 1984.
1 manuscript score (8 leaves); 37 cm.
Reproduced from holograph.
Duration: 10:00.
Composed for: 2 violins, viola, violoncello.
Call no.: **1987/053**

1772. Meachem, Margaret, 1922– In wildness is the preservation of the earth. N.p.: n.p., 1991.
1 score (62 leaves); 35 cm.
English words from texts by Henry David Thoreau, Emily Dickinson, Robert Bridges, and Barbara Krasnoff.
Reproduced from manuscript.
Composed for: soprano, tape, flute (also piccolo and alto flute), clarinet, oboe, horn, percussion (marimba, suspended cymbal, xylophone, glockenspiel, timpani, roto-toms, temple blocks, snare drum, wind chimes), piano, violin I, violin II, viola, violoncello, double bass.
Commissioned by: Atlantic Sinfonietta.
Call no.: **1993/098**

1773. Meij, Johan de, 1953– Casanova: (for solo cello and wind orchestra). Amsterdam: Amstel Music; Milwaukee, WI: Hal Leonard, 2000.
1 score (121 p.) port.; 44 cm.
Notes on composition and performance in English, Dutch, French, and German.
Composed for: violoncello, 3 flutes (3rd also piccolo), 2 oboes, English horn, 2 bassoons, contrabassoon, clarinet in E♭, 3 clarinets, alto clarinet, bass clarinet, 2 alto saxophones, tenor saxophone, baritone saxophone, 4 horns, 4 trumpets, 3 trombones, euphonium, 2 tubas, double bass, timpani, percussion (snare drum, bass drum, suspended cymbal, crash cymbals, triangle, temple block, tam-tam, gong, 2 dobachi, finger cymbals, lion's roar, thundersheet, conga, whip, tom-tom,

tambourine, bells, vibraphone, marimba, xylophone, tubular bells), piano (also celesta), harp.
Commissioned by: Fonds voor de Scheppende Tonkunst.
Call no.: **2002/038**

1774. Meijering, Chiel, 1954– P.W. and his skillet lickers: for solo violoncello, string orchestra, and percussion, 1996. Amsterdam: Donemus, 1996.
1 score (39 p.); 37 cm.
Duration: ca. 12:27.
Composed for: violoncello, percussion (cimbalom, 2 bass drums), violin I, violin II, viola, violoncello, double bass.
Commissioned by: Fonds voor de Scheppende Toonkunst.
Call no.: **1998/106**

1775. Meijering, Chiel, 1954– St. Louis blues: opera in 4 akten: 1994. Partituur in C. Amsterdam: Donemus, 1995.
1 score (2 v.); 38 cm.
Dutch words by Paul Binnerts.
Duration: ca. 115:00.
Composed for: 3 sopranos, 4 tenors, 2 flutes (both also 2 antique cymbals, 1st also tam-tam, 2nd also 2 triangles), clarinet (also bass clarinet and 2 antique cymbals), soprano saxophone (also baritone saxophone, 2 antique cymbals, cabasa), alto saxophone (also 2 antique cymbals and sandpaper blocks), horn (also synthesizer, 5 slit drums, cowbell), trumpet (also talking drum), 2 trombones, tuba, piano, electric guitar, electric bass, percussion (drums, marimba, bass drum, woodblock, antique cymbals, small guiro, glockenspiel, claves, small egg shakers, temple block, 2 bongos, congas, 5 tuned bottles).
Call no.: **1996/104**

1776. Meister, Scott R., 1950– Feles galactica: for winds, percussion, and piano. N.p.: n.p., 198-?.
1 score (36 p.); 28 cm.
Reproduced from manuscript.
Composed for: 2 flutes (both also piccolo), 2 oboes, 3 clarinets, bass clarinet, 2 alto saxophones, tenor saxophone, baritone saxophone, 2 bassoons, 4 horns, 3 trumpets, 2 trombones, bass trombone, baritone, tuba, piano, percussion (xylophone, marimba, triangle, bongos, tom-toms, maracas, tambourine, tam-tam, chimes, suspended cymbal, snare drum, key chimes, 2 glass crystals, orchestra bells, crotales, bass drum, 2 brake drums, small bell, vibraphone, steel drum, large bell, shaker, finger cymbals, timpani, sound effects).
Commissioned by: Appalachian State University Department of Music.
Call no.: **1985/137**

1777. Melby, John, 1941– Concerto for piano and computer-synthesized tape (1985). American Composers ed., Composers facsim. ed. New York, NY: American Composers Alliance, 1985.
1 score (32 p.); 38 cm.
Reproduced from manuscript.
Duration: ca. 17:00.
Includes performance instructions.
Composed for: piano, tape.
Call no.: **1990/086**

1778. Melby, John, 1941– Symphony no. 1: for large orchestra (1991–93). Bryn Mawr, PA: Merion Music, 1994.
1 score (ii, 182 p.); 44 cm.
Reproduced from holograph.
Duration: ca. 40:35.
Includes performance instructions.
Composed for: piccolo (also alto flute), 2 flutes, 2 oboes, English horn, clarinet in E♭, 2 clarinets, (3rd also clarinet in A and contrabass clarinet), bass clarinet, 2 bassoons, contrabassoon, 4 horns (all also Wagner tubas), 3 trumpets, 2 tenor trombones, bass trombone, tuba, timpani, percussion (tambourine, roto-toms, crash cymbals, triangle, ratchet, tam-tams, 5 temple blocks, snare drum, maracas, 3 suspended cymbals, xylophone, celesta, marimba, tubular bells, vibraphone), 2 harps, violin I, violin II, viola, violoncello, double bass.
Call no.: **1995/075**

1779. Melillo, Stephen, 1957– S-matrix. N.p.: Stephen Melillo, 1988.
1 score (various pagings); 36 cm.
For orchestra.
Duration: 19:57.
Contents: Slowstorm—Mindstorm—Uncertainty—S-matrix.
Composed for: 2 piccolos, 2 flutes, 2 oboes, 3 clarinets, 2 bassoons, contrabassoon, 4 horns, 3 trumpets, 3 trombones, tuba, timpani, glockenspiel, percussion (marimba, bass marimba, chimes, vibraphone, 9 tuned cymbals, congas, tambourine, shaker, cowbell, claves, bass drum, crash cymbal, cabasa, timbales, finger cymbals, gong, snare drum, quijada, tom-toms, anvil, tam-tam, triangle), 2 harps, piano (also celesta and synthesizer), violin I, violin II, viola, violoncello, double bass.
Call no.: **1994/097**

1780. Menin, Geoffrey, 1953– Ich lebe mein Leben: a

song cycle. N.p.: Geoffrey Menin, 1993.
1 score (64 p.); 28 cm.
German words by Rainer Maria Rilke; also printed as text with English translation.
Contents: Der Auszug des verlorenen Sohnes—Du im Voraus—Da dich das geflügelte Entzücken—Ausgesetzt auf den Bergen des Herzens—Abend—Klage—Buddha in der Glorie—Jetzt wär es Zeit—Ich lebe mein Leben.
Composed for: voice, piano.
Call no.: **1994/098**

1781. Mercurio, Steven, 1956– For lost loved ones: for large orchestra. N.p.: n.p., 1984.
1 score (175 p.); 36 cm.
Reproduced from manuscript.
Composed for: 2 piccolos, 3 flutes, 3 oboes, English horn, clarinet in E♭, 3 clarinets, bass clarinet, 3 bassoons, contrabassoon, 8 horns, 4 trumpets, 3 trombones, bass trombone, tuba, timpani, percussion (2 triangles, 2 tam-tams, hi-hat, tambourine, crash cymbals, 2 suspended cymbals, snare drum, 2 tenor drums, 2 bass drums, ratchet, 2 whips, 2 temple blocks, 2 cowbells, referee whistle, wooden baseball bat, glockenspiel, xylophone, marimba, vibraphone, chimes, glass wind chimes, 2 crotales), 2 harps, celesta, violin I, violin II, viola, violoncello, double bass.
Call no.: **1992/092**

1782. Mérész, Ignác, 1943– Concertino: marimbára és zenekarra. N.p.: n.p., 199-?.
1 score (91 p.); 42 cm.
Reproduced from holograph.
Composed for: marimba, 2 flutes (2nd also piccolo), 2 oboes, 2 clarinets, 2 bassoons, 2 horns, 2 trumpets, 2 trombones, timpani, percussion, violin I, violin II, viola, violoncello, double bass.
Call no.: **2003/085**

1783. Mérész, Ignác, 1943– Szimfonia. N.p.: n.p., 199-?.
1 score (171 p.); 36 cm.
Reproduced from manuscript.
Composed for: piccolo, 2 flutes, 2 oboes, English horn, 2 clarinets, bass clarinet, 2 bassoons, 4 horns, 3 trumpets, 3 trombones, tuba, timpani, percussion (triangle, cymbals, snare drum, bass drum, 3 temple blocks, 3 tom-toms, xylophone, tubular bells), harp, piano, celesta, violin I, violin II, viola, violoncello, double bass.
Call no.: **1998/107**

1784. Metcalf, John, 1946– Tornrak. Full orchestral. N.p.: n.p., 1990.
1 score (2 v.); 37 cm.
English words.
Opera in two acts.
"As of January 1990."
Composed for: voices, men's chorus, 2 flutes (both also piccolo), oboe (also English horn), 2 clarinets (both also clarinet in E♭), bassoon (also contrabassoon), 2 horns, trumpet, trombone, tuba, percussion (vibraphone, bell tree, tuned water glasses, flexatone, snare drum, maracas, triangle, tambourine, bass drum, sizzle cymbal, tam-tam, thundersheet, tenor drum, sleigh bells, tuned crotales, water gong, small gong, wind machine), piano, violin I, violin II, viola, violoncello, double bass.
Call no.: **1993/099**

1785. Mettraux, Laurent, 1970– Concerto no 3: pour violon et orchestre, M.607 (1999). Courtaman: Editions Laurent Mettraux, 1999.
1 score (51 p.); 30 cm.
Duration: ca. 20:00.
Composed for: violin, piccolo, 2 flutes (2nd also alto flute), 2 oboes, English horn, 3 clarinets (3rd also bass clarinet), 2 bassoons, contrabassoon, 4 horns, 3 trumpets, 3 trombones, contrabass tuba, tam-tam, violin I, violin II, viola, violoncello, double bass.
Commissioned by: Radio Suisse Romande-Espace 2.
Call no.: **2003/086**

1786. Meyer, Aubrey, 1947– Choros: a one-act ballet.
Call no.: **1985/138**
No materials available.

1787. Meyer, Krzysztof, 1943– Konzert Nr. 2 für Violoncello und Orchester = Concerto no. 2 for violoncello and orchestra, opus 85. Hamburg: Musikverlag Hans Sikorski, 1995.
1 score (116 p.); 42 cm.
Duration: ca. 25:00.
Composed for: violoncello, 2 flutes, clarinet in A, 2 bassoons (2nd also contrabassoon), percussion (timpani, tenor drum, bass drum, tubular bells, suspended cymbal, 4 temple blocks, vibraphone, gong, ratchet, 4 tom-toms, crotales, marimba, 4 bongos, snare drum, tambourine, glockenspiel, tam-tam, xylophone), harp, piano, celesta, violin I, violin II, viola, violoncello, double bass.
Commissioned by: Düsseldorfer Symphoniker.
Call no.: **1998/108**

1788. Meyer, Krzysztof, 1943– Kwintet: na dwoje skrzypiec, altówka, wíolouczela i fortepian, op. 76 (1990–91). N.p.: n.p., 1991.
1 score (63 p.); 30 cm.

Reproduced from manuscript.
Duration: ca. 33:00.
Composed for: 2 violins, viola, violoncello, piano.
Commissioned by: KölnMusik GmbH.
Call no.: **1996/103**

1789. Middleton, Owen, 1941– Decoration day. N.p.: Luckenbach Editions, 1997.
27 p. of music; 31 cm.
Contents: Remembering—Seeking—Biding—Marching—Reveling-reconciling.
Composed for: piano.
Call no.: **2005/096**

1790. Miereanu, Costin, 1943– Voyage d'hiver II. Paris: Editions Salabert, 1985.
1 score (40 p.); 36 cm.
For wind instruments and percussion.
Reproduced from manuscript.
Composed for: 4 flutes (3rd–4th also piccolo), 3 oboes (3rd also English horn), 4 clarinets (1st also clarinet in E♭, 3rd also bass clarinet, 4th also contrabass clarinet), 3 bassoons (3rd also contrabassoon), 4 horns, 3 trumpets, 3 trombones, tuba, percussion (chimes, timpani, vibraphone, crotales, glockenspiel, temple blocks, suspended cymbals, cowbells, triangle, celesta, gong, bell plates, marimba, sleigh bells).
Commissioned by: Radio France.
Call no.: **1986/077**

1791. Mihalič, Alexander, 1963– Skladba pre klavír a mg pás = Composition for piano and tape. Klavírny part. N.p.: n.p., 1987.
17 leaves of music; 25 cm.
Reproduced from manuscript.
Includes performance instructions in Slovak and English.
Composed for: piano, tape.
Call no.: **1988/118**

1792. Milburn, Ellsworth, 1938– Chiaroscuro: 1984. St. Louis, MO, USA: Magnamusic-Baton, 1984.
1 score (69 p.); 28 cm.
For orchestra.
Reproduced from holograph.
Composed for: flute (also piccolo), 2 oboes, 2 clarinets, bassoon, 2 horns, trumpet, timpani (also 4 chimes, suspended cymbal), percussion (xylophone, vibraphone, wind chimes, glockenspiel, 4 tom-toms), harp, piano (also celesta), violin I, violin II, viola, violoncello, double bass.
Commissioned by: Houston Symphony Orchestra.
Call no.: **1985/139**

1793. Milburn, Ellsworth, 1938– Entre nous: for violin, cello, and piano. N.p.: Ellsworth Milburn, 2002.
1 score (27 p.); 28 cm.
Composed for: violin, violoncello, piano.
Commissioned by: Pennsylvania Music Teacher's Association.
Call no.: **2005/097**

1794. Miller, Donald Bruce, 1937– Finger Lakes suite. N.p.: Donald Miller, 1989.
1 score (105 p.); 36 cm.
For orchestra.
Duration: ca. 14:00.
Contents: Lake County images—A distant dream—A celebration of the earth's bounty.
Composed for: 2 flutes, 2 oboes, 2 clarinets, bassoon, 4 horns, 3 trumpets, 2 trombones, bass trombone, tuba, percussion (cymbals, snare drum, bass drum, drum set, crotales, chimes, glockenspiel, tuned wine glasses, goat bells, timpani), piano, violin I, violin II, viola, violoncello, double bass.
Call no.: **1991/081**

1795. Minchev, Georgi, 1939– Contrasts: music for orchestra, 2002. N.p.: n.p., 2002.
1 score (59 p.); 30 cm.
Reproduced from manuscript.
Composed for: 2 flutes (also piccolo and alto flute), 2 oboes (also English horn), 3 clarinets (also bass clarinet), 2 bassoons, 4 horns, 3 trumpets, 3 trombones, tuba, percussion (xylophone, vibraphone, tubular bells, suspended cymbals, cymbals, military drum, hi-hat, bongos, maracas, guiro, flexatone, tam-tam, bass drum, timpani), violin I, violin II, viola, violoncello, double bass.
Commissioned by: Heidelberg Philharmonie Orchester.
Call no.: **2005/098**

1796. Mindel, Me'ir, 1946– A Maya prophecy: for mixed choir a cappella (1985). Tel Aviv, Israel: Israel Music Institute, 1986.
1 score (15 p.); 35 cm.
Transliterated Hebrew words; original Hebrew and English translation printed as text.
Includes preface in English and Hebrew.
Duration: ca. 11:00.
Composed for: SATB chorus.
Call no.: **1987/054**

1797. Mindel, Me'ir, 1946– Tamar: for flute, horn and piano (1987). Tel Aviv: Israel Music Institute, 1988.
1 score (19 p.); 30 cm.
Reproduced from manuscript.
Duration: ca. 17:00.

Composed for: flute, horn, piano.
Call no.: **1990/087**

1798. Miranda, Ronaldo, 1948– Dom Casmurro: ópera. N.p.: n.p., 1992.
1 score (3 v.); 33 cm.
Portuguese words by Orlando Codá.
Original work by Machado de Assis.
In 3 acts.
Reproduced from holograph.
Composed for: 3 sopranos, mezzo-soprano, 4 tenors, 2 baritones, bass-baritone, SATB chorus, piccolo, 2 flutes, 2 oboes, 2 clarinets, 2 bassoons, 4 horns, 2 trumpets, 2 trombones, bass trombone, tuba, timpani, percussion (whips, glockenspiel, xylophone, vibraphone), harp, piano, celesta, violin I, violin II, viola, violoncello, double bass.
Call no.: **1993/100**
Also available:
Call no.: **1993/100 libretto**

1799. Miranda, Ronaldo, 1948– Sinfonia 2000. Partitura de orquestra. Rio de Janeiro: Academia Brasileira de Música, 2000.
1 score (108 p.); 42 cm.
For orchestra.
Composed for: piccolo, 2 flutes, 2 oboes, 2 clarinets, 2 bassoons, 4 horns, 3 trumpets, 2 trombones, bass trombone, tuba, timpani, percussion (xylophone, vibraphone, glockenspiel, tubular chimes, crash cymbals, bass drum, tam-tam, woodblocks, temple blocks, cowbells, whip), violin I, violin II, viola, violoncello, double bass.
Commissioned by: Ministry of Culture of Brazil.
Call no.: **2003/087**

1800. Mirenzi, Franco Antonio, 1959– Studio V sul "Vater unser": corale. N.p.: n.p., 1992.
1 score (4 leaves); 30 cm.
German words.
Composed for: SATB chorus.
Call no.: **1994/099**

1801. Miroglio, Francis, 1924– Habeas corpus: pour ensemble vocal. Paris: Editions Salabert, 1984.
1 score (21 p.); 37 cm.
Latin words.
Reproduced from holograph.
Composed for: SATB chorus.
Commissioned by: Radio France.
Call no.: **1986/078**

1802. Miroglio, Francis, 1924– Magnétiques: violon solo, [ou] avec piano, [ou] avec ensemble, [ou] avec orchestre. Paris: Salabert, 198-?.
1 score (iv, 55 p.); 47 cm.
Reproduced from manuscript.
Includes performance instructions in French and English.
Contents: Attractions—Affinités—Cadences—Etreintes.
Composed for: violin, piano, or instrumental ensemble (piano, clarinet [also bass clarinet], bassoon, trumpet, trombone, percussion [high cymbal, pedal bass drum, tam-tam, 3 bronze sheets, 3 cowbells, triangle, side drum, 2 bongos, xylorimba, glockenspiel, woodblock, maracas, claves, mounted guiro, wind chimes], double bass), or orchestra (piccolo, flute, alto flute, 2 oboes, English horn, clarinet in E♭, 2 clarinets [1st also bass clarinet], 2 bassoons, contrabassoon, 4 horns, 3 trumpets, 2 trombones, bass trombone, contrabass tuba, timpani, percussion [cymbals, pedal bass drum, tam-tam, 3 bronze sheets, 3 cowbells, triangle, side drum, 2 bongos, xylorimba, glockenspiel, woodblock, maracas, claves, mounted guiro, wind chimes, gong, tom-tom, vibraphone, glass chimes, sizzle cymbal, steel plate, tam-tam, bass drum, tubular bells, crash cymbals], 2 harps, piano, violin I, violin II, viola, violoncello, double bass).
Call no.: **1985/140**

1803. Mirzoev, Elmir, 1970– Sacrificium intellectus. N.p.: n.p., 1992.
1 score (92 p.); 30 cm.
Reproduced from holograph.
Composer's note in English.
Composed for: oboe, clarinet, horn, organ (electric organ), piano, oriental plucked instrument, violin, viola, violoncello.
Call no.: **1994/100**

1804. Misurell-Mitchell, Janice, 1946– Sermon of the middle-aged revolutionary spider. N.p.: n.p., 1997.
1 score (85 p.); 28 cm.
English words; also printed as text.
For tenor and chamber ensemble, with optional gospel choir.
Duration: 30:00.
Composed for: tenor, optional SATB chorus, clarinet, alto saxophone, trumpet, tenor trombone, percussion (2 congas, 2 tom-toms, drum set, 2 cymbals, 2 cowbells, 4 woodblocks, tambourine, marimba), synthesizer (or organ), violin, violoncello, double bass.
Call no.: **1998/109**
Re-entered as: **2003/088**

1805. Mitchell, Lee, 1948– The holy child is born: a Christmas oratorio: for soli (soprano, contralto, tenor

and baritone), mixed chorus, boy choir, organ and chamber orchestra. Full score. N.p.: Lee Mitchell, 1987.
1 score (256 p.); 36 cm.
English and Latin words.
Words from St. Matthew and St. Luke; original text by the composer.
Reproduced from manuscript.
Composed for: soprano, contralto, tenor, baritone, SATB chorus, boys' chorus, organ, flute, oboe, clarinet, bassoon, violin I, violin II, viola, violoncello, double bass.
Commissioned by: St. David's Church, Baltimore.
Call no.: **1990/088**

1806. Mobberley, James, 1954– Arena: a ballet. Kansas City, MO: Cautious Music, 1996.
1 score (117 p.); 44 cm.
Duration: 22:00.
Composed for: 2 flutes (2nd also piccolo), 2 oboes, 2 clarinets (2nd also bass clarinet), 2 bassoons, 4 horns, 2 trumpets, 2 trombones, bass trombone, tuba, timpani, percussion (vibraphone, 4 tom-toms, cowbell, ride cymbal, low woodblock, bass drum, small and large tam-tams, marimba, triangle, snare drum, woodblock, shaker, suspended cymbal), harp, piano, violin I, violin II, viola, violoncello, double bass.
Commissioned by: Meet the Composer.
Call no.: **2002/129**

1807. Mobberley, James, 1954– Ascension: for wind ensemble and electronic tape. N.p.: n.p., 1988.
1 score (45 p.); 28 cm.
Reproduced from holograph.
Dedicated to the memory of Kenneth Wayne Hill.
Duration: 7:40.
Composed for: 2 flutes (1st also piccolo, 2nd also alto flute), 2 oboes, 2 clarinets, bass clarinet, 2 bassoons, 4 horns, 3 trumpets, 2 trombones, bass trombone, tuba, piano, percussion (crotales, bass drum, marimba, temple blocks, vibraphone, 5 tom-toms, snare drum, crash cymbals, suspended cymbal, timpani), 2-channel tape.
Call no.: **1990/089**

1808. Mobberley, James, 1954– Concerto for piano and orchestra. Kansas City, MO: Cautious Music, 1994.
1 score (98 p.); 44 cm.
Duration: ca. 21:00.
Composed for: piano, 3 flutes (3rd also piccolo), 2 oboes, English horn, 3 clarinets (3rd also bass clarinet), 2 bassoons, 4 horns, 3 trumpets, 3 trombones, tuba, percussion (timpani, triangle, jaw bone, glockenspiel, xylophone, 5 tom-toms, small bass drum, 3 woodblocks, 3 suspended cymbals, 2 tam-tams, police whistle, whip, vibraphone, 2 bongos, 2 congas, flexatone, 5 temple blocks, 2 cowbells, marimba, crotales, tubular chimes, snare drum, large bass drum), harp, violin I, violin II, viola, violoncello, double bass.
Commissioned by: Barlow Endowment for Music Composition at Brigham Young University.
Call no.: **2000/122**

1809. Moerk, Alice A., 1936– Alianor: an operatic monologue for mezzo soprano, vocoder and instruments (optional synthesizers). N.p.: AAM, 1997.
1 vocal score (63 p.); 28 cm.
English words by the composer.
Text includes selections from medieval writers.
Includes program notes.
Contents: Castille, Spain, c. 1200 (Alianor at age 80)—The land (Alianor in her youth)—Love (Alianor in middle age)—The Church (Alianor in middle age)—Lament (Alianor at age eighty).
Composed for: mezzo-soprano, keyboard.
Call no.: **2000/123**

1810. Moerk, Alice A., 1936– Don Quix: a semi-dramatic comedy: for mezzo-soprano or baritone, clarinet, cello and guitar (or keyboard). Fairmont, WV: Moerkworks, 1999.
1 score (16 leaves); 28 cm.
English words.
Original work by Miguel Cervantes.
Composed for: mezzo-soprano, baritone, clarinet, violoncello, guitar (or keyboard).
Call no.: **2001/106**

1811. Moerk, Alice A., 1936– Tina's songs. Anna Maria, FL.: MW MoerkWorks, 2000.
21 p. of music; 29 cm.
English words by Tina M. Paolucci.
Composed for: voice, piano.
Call no.: **2003/089**

1812. Moerschel, Blanche, 1915– Sonata for 'cello and piano in G minor, 1984. N.p.: n.p., 1984.
1 score (10, 5, 12 p.) + 1 part (8 p.); 31 cm.
Reproduced from manuscript.
Composed for: violoncello, piano.
Call no.: **1986/079**

1813. Mollicone, Henry, 1946– Coyote tales: an opera in two acts. Boston, MA: Ione Press, 1997.
1 score (2 v. [621 p]); 44 cm.
English words by Sheldon Harnick.
Composed for: 2 flutes (2nd also piccolo), 2 oboes (2nd

also English horn), 2 clarinets (2nd also bass clarinet), 2 bassoons, 3 horns, 2 trumpets, 2 trombones, percussion (tom-toms, timpani, tambourine, woodblock, small cymbal, gong, finger cymbal, wind chimes, shaker, vibraphone, tam-tams, small triangle, 3 cymbals, marimba, snare drum, glockenspiel, chimes, mark tree, crotales, bass drum, bongos, crash cymbals, wind chimes, roto-toms, hi-hat, bell tree, small woodblock, slapstick, ratchet, trap set, gourd, floor tom-tom, anvil), harp, piano (also celesta), violin I, violin II, viola, violoncello, double bass.
Commissioned by: Lyric Opera of Kansas City.
Call no.: **2000/124**

1814. Monk, Meredith, 1942– A celebration service. N.p.: n.p., 199-?.
1 score (64 leaves); 28 cm.
Text consists of nonsense syllables.
For voices, keyboard (4 hands), and melodica.
Composed for: voices, bass drum, keyboard, melodica.
Call no.: **2000/125**

1815. Monk, Meredith, 1942– New York requiem: (1993). N.p.: Meredith Monk Music, 1993.
1 score (11 leaves); 28 cm.
Wordless.
Composed for: voice, piano.
Call no.: **1997/100**

1816. Montague, Stephen, 1943– Concerto for piano & orchestra (1997). London: United Music, 1997.
1 score (157 p.); 30 cm.
Biographical information and program note in English.
Composed for: piano, 2 flutes (2nd also piccolo), 2 oboes, 2 clarinets (2nd also clarinet in E♭), 2 bassoons, 2 horns, 2 trumpets, bass trombone, percussion (xylophone, crotales, plastic musical tube, 3 triangles, 3 tambourines, large metal cabasa, 4 cymbals, tam-tam, 2 bongos, 3 tom-toms, large cuíca, snare drum, bass drum, 2 woodblocks, 2 sets of maracas), violin I, violin II, viola, violoncello, double bass.
Commissioned by: BBC and Arts Council of England.
Call no.: **1998/110**

1817. Montori, Sergio, 1916– Four vibrations: quartetto per archi. N.p.: Beat Records Co. (SIAE), 198-?.
1 score (10 leaves) + 4 parts; 30 cm.
Reproduced from manuscript.
Composed for: 2 violins, viola, violoncello.
Call no.: **1987/055**

1818. Montori, Sergio, 1916– Metamorfosi di un'immagine. N.p.: Pentaflowers, 1980.
21 leaves of music; 42 cm.
Composed for: piano.
Call no.: **1993/101**

1819. Morel, François, 1926– Aux couleurs du ciel: 7 études pour bois, cuivres, harpes, piano-célesta, timbales et percussions. Québec: Centre de musique canadienne, 1987.
1 score (129 p.); 44 cm.
For band.
Reproduced from manuscript.
Composed for: 4 flutes (1st–3rd also alto flute, 3rd–4th also piccolo), 3 oboes, English horn, clarinet in E♭, 2 clarinets, bass clarinet, 3 bassoons, contrabassoon, 6 horns, 3 trumpets, 3 trombones (3rd also bass trombone), tuba, timpani, 2 harps, piano (also celesta), percussion (vibraphone, xylophone, Turkish suspended cymbal, crotales, 2 bongos, snare drum, 3 Javanese gongs, 2 Balinese gongs, tam-tam, triangle, glockenspiel, Chinese bell tree, 3 tom-toms, bass drum, 2 Chinese suspended cymbals, tubular bells, Chinese cymbal, woodblock, 2 anvils).
Commissioned by: Orchestre Symphonique de Montréal.
Call no.: **1989/083**

1820. Morel, François, 1926– Aux couleurs du ciel: pour bois, cuivres, harpes, piano-célesta, timbales et percussions. Québec: n.p., 1987.
1 score (129 p.); 39 cm.
For band.
Reproduced from manuscript.
Composed for: 4 flutes (1st–3rd also alto flute, 3rd–4th also piccolo), 3 oboes, English horn, clarinet in E♭, 2 clarinets, bass clarinet, 3 bassoons, contrabassoon, 6 horns, 3 trumpets, 3 trombones (3rd also bass trombone), tuba, timpani, 2 harps, piano (also celesta), percussion (vibraphone, xylophone, Turkish suspended cymbal, crotales, 2 bongos, snare drum, 3 Javanese gongs, 2 Balinese gongs, tam-tam, triangle, glockenspiel, Chinese bell tree, 3 tom-toms, bass drum, 2 Chinese suspended cymbals, tubular bells, Chinese cymbal, woodblock, 2 anvils).
Commissioned by: Orchestre Symphonique de Montréal.
Call no.: **1990/090**

1821. Morleo, Luigi, 1970– Verty. N.p.: n.p., 1992.
1 score (6 leaves); 30 cm.
Composed for: soprano saxophone, piano.
Call no.: **1994/101**

1822. Mors, Rudolf, 1920–1988. Der Kreidekreis: Oper in 4 Akten. Partitur. Heidelberg: K. Neufert, 1982.

1 score (610 p.); 30 cm.
German words by Klabund.
Reproduced from holograph.
Composed for: 5 sopranos, mezzo-soprano, 2 altos, 4 tenors, 3 baritones, bass-baritone, SATB chorus, 2 flutes (2nd also piccolo), oboe, 2 clarinets (2nd also bass clarinet), bassoon, 2 horns, trumpet, trombone, timpani, percussion (2 gongs, 2 cymbals, triangle, bass drum, tam-tam, glockenspiel, whip, marimba, snare drum, tubular bells, tambourine, ratchet, tenor drum, flexatone, iron rod, nutshells), harp, violin I, violin II, viola, violoncello, double bass.
Call no.: **1985/141**

1823. Mostel, Raphael, 1948– The travels of Babar. New York, NY: Raphael Mostel, 2000.
1 score (121 p.); 22 x 36 cm.
In English and French.
Original work by Jean de Brunhoff.
For narrator with instrumental ensemble.
Duration: ca. 1:05:00.
Composed for: narrator, viola, violoncello, piano (also celesta), clarinet (also bass clarinet), bassoon, cornet, trombone (also bass trombone), percussion (large marimba, bass drum, bongos, conga, 5 tom-toms, woodblock, slapstick, ratchet, triangle, bell tree, cowbell, ship bell, sleigh bells, police whistle, klaxon, large cymbals, suspended cymbal, thundersheet, rain sticks, lion's roar, whirlies, carnival whistles, bags of marbles).
Commissioned by: Sebastian Tomoji Semba and Toshiba/ EMI.
Call no.: **2004/085**

1824. Mostel, Raphael, 1948– The travels of Babar: an adventure in scales. New York, NY: Raphael Mostel, 2000.
1 score (121 p.); 28 x 44 cm.
In English and French.
English translation by Phyllis Rose.
Original work by Jean de Brunhoff.
For narrator and instrumental ensemble.
"Full presentation of this work includes digital slide show (CD-ROM), stage design and light plot."
Composed for: narrator, viola, violoncello, piano (also celesta), clarinet (also bass clarinet), bassoon, cornet, trombone (also bass trombone), percussion (large marimba, bass drum, bongos, conga, 5 tom-toms, woodblock, slapstick, ratchet, triangle, belltree, cowbell, ship bell, sleigh bells, police whistle, klaxon, large cymbals, suspended cymbal, thundersheet, rain sticks, lion's roar, whirlies, carnival whistles, bags of marbles).
Commissioned by: Sebastian Tomoji Semba and Toshiba/ EMI.
Call no.: **2002/130**
Re-entered as: **2003/090**

1825. Mueller, Robert, 1958– Deep earth passing: for large orchestra. N.p.: R. Mueller, 1988.
1 score (53 p.); 28 cm.
Reproduced from holograph.
Duration: ca. 15:00.
Composed for: 2 flutes (2nd also alto flute), 2 oboes, English horn, 2 clarinets, bass clarinet, 2 bassoons, 4 horns, 3 trumpets, 3 trombones, tuba, timpani, percussion (chimes, marimba, snare drum, tenor drum, bass drum, 2 tuned gongs, glockenspiel, vibraphone, 3 suspended cymbals, 5 tom-toms, triangle, 2 tam-tams, 4 timbales, crotales), harp, piano (also celesta), violin I, violin II, viola, violoncello, double bass.
Call no.: **1990/091**

1826. Muldowney, Dominic, 1952– Piano concerto. Score. London: Universal Edition, 1983.
1 miniature score (68 p.); 28 cm.
Duration: ca. 25:00.
Composed for: piano, 2 flutes (both also piccolo), 2 oboes, 2 clarinets (2nd also clarinet in A), bass clarinet, alto saxophone, 2 bassoons, contrabassoon, 4 horns, 3 trumpets, 3 trombones, tuba, percussion (vibraphone, tam-tam, side drum, bass drum, cymbals, 3 woodblocks, 3 tuned gongs), violin I, violin II, viola, violoncello, double bass.
Commissioned by: British Broadcasting Corporation.
Call no.: **1985/142**

1827. Müller-Siemens, Detlev, 1957– Maïastra: für Orchester (1995/96). Partitur. Mainz: Ars Viva, 1997.
1 score (44 p.); 59 cm.
Duration: 15:00.
Composed for: 3 flutes (3rd also piccolo), 2 oboes, 3 clarinets (3rd also bass clarinet), 3 bassoons, 2 horns, 2 trumpets, 2 trombones, violin I, violin II, viola, violoncello, double bass.
Commissioned by: Philharmonie Hamburg.
Call no.: **1998/111**

1828. Müller-Siemens, Detlev, 1957– Die Menschen: Oper in zwei Akten nach dem gleichnamigen Schauspiel von Walter Hasenclever. Partitur. Mainz: Ars Viva Verlag, 1990.
1 score (203 p.); 54 cm.
German words.
Composed for: 6 sopranos, alto, 3 tenors, 2 baritones, bass-baritone, SATB chorus, bar trio (clarinet, double

bass, piano), 3 flutes (3rd also piccolo), 3 oboes (3rd also English horn), 3 clarinets (3rd also bass clarinet), 3 bassoons (2nd–3rd also contrabassoon), 4 horns, 2 trumpets, 3 trombones, tuba, percussion (timpani, maracas, 4 temple blocks, large cymbals, low tam-tam, bell plate, glockenspiel, xylophone, slide whistle, 3 tom-toms, chimes, claves, woodblock, 3 bongos, bass drum, medium cymbals, 2 congas, snare drum, vibraphone), violin I, violin II, viola, violoncello, double bass.
Commissioned by: Nationaltheater Mannheim.
Call no.: **1994/102**

1829. Müller-Siemens, Detlev, 1957– Phoenix 2: für 13 Instrumentalisten (1993/94). Mainz: Ars Viva, 1994.
1 score (60 p.); 30 x 41 cm.
Reproduced from manuscript.
Duration: 16:00.
Composed for: flute, oboe, clarinet, bassoon, horn, trumpet, trombone (also bass trombone), piano, 2 violins, viola, violoncello, double bass.
Commissioned by: Festival Archipel.
Call no.: **1996/106**

1830. Mumford, Jeffrey, 1955– In forests of evaporating dawns: string quartet. N.p.: n.p., 1996.
1 score (30 p.); 28 cm.
Duration: ca. 18:00.
Program note by the composer.
Composed for: 2 violins, viola, violoncello.
Call no.: **1998/112**

1831. Mumford, Jeffrey, 1955– The promise of the far horizon: string quartet. King of Prussia, PA: Theodore Presser Co., 2002.
1 score (36 p.); 28 cm.
Duration: ca. 16:00.
Program notes by the composer.
Composed for: 2 violins, viola, violoncello.
Commissioned by: Nancy Ruyle Dodge Trust.
Call no.: **2005/099**

1832. Mumford, Jeffrey, 1955– A window of resonant light: for 'cello, piano & percussion. N.p.: n.p., 1997.
1 score (33 p.); 28 cm.
Duration: ca. 14:00.
Contents: That which remains—Blythe—The walls of my Saturday room—Suspended brightness—The radiance of evening's interior—Within a window of resonant light . . . — . . . The glimmering air becomes—That which remains.
Composed for: violoncello, piano, percussion (bell plate, vibraphone, marimba, bongos).
Commissioned by: CORE Ensemble, Duncan Theater at Palm Beach Community College, Mid America Center for Contemporary Music at Bowling Green State University, and Boston Conservatory of Music.
Call no.: **2000/126**

1833. Mundry, Isabel, 1963– Panorama ciego: für Klavier und Orchester. Wiesbaden: Breitkopf & Härtel, 2001.
1 score (35 p.); 42 cm.
Reproduced from manuscript.
"Rev. 8/01"—p. 1 of cover.
Composed for: piano, 2 flutes (both also piccolo), 2 oboes, 2 clarinets (2nd also bass clarinet), 2 bassoons, 2 horns, 2 trumpets, timpani, 4 violins, 2 violas, 2 violoncellos, 2 double basses.
Call no.: **2003/091**

1834. Murray, Diedre, 1951– Running man. N.p.: n.p., 1999.
1 score (various pagings); 28 cm.
English words by Cornelius Eady.
Jazz opera.
Composed for: 2 sopranos, mezzo-soprano, tenor, baritone, violin, violoncello, double bass, guitar, accordion, percussion.
Call no.: **2002/131**

1835. Musgrave, Thea, 1928– Harriet, the woman called Moses: an opera in two acts, 1984. London: Novello, 1985.
1 score (4 v. [iv, 621 p.]); 40 cm.
English words by the composer.
"Corrected Jan 20 1985."
Reproduced from manuscript.
Composed for: soprano, mezzo-soprano, 3 tenors, 3 baritones, bass-baritone, bass, SATB chorus, 2 flutes (2nd also piccolo), 2 oboes (2nd also English horn), 2 clarinets, 2 bassoons (2nd also contrabassoon), 3 horns, 3 trumpets, 2 trombones, bass trombone, timpani, percussion (vibraphone, tambourine, bongos, tenor drum, side drum, bass drum, suspended cymbal, tam-tam, woodblocks, tom-toms, temple blocks, sleigh bells, tubular bells), harp, piano, violin I, violin II, viola, violoncello, double bass.
Commissioned by: Virginia Opera Association and Royal Opera House, Covent Garden.
Call no.: **1988/076**
Re-entered as: **1989/084**

1836. Musgrave, Thea, 1928– Harriet Tubman, the woman called Moses. Norfolk, VA: Virginia Opera, 1985.
1 score (2 v. [621 leaves]); 29 cm.

English words by the composer.
Opera in 2 acts.
"Full score of first performance"—cover.
Reproduced from manuscript.
Composed for: soprano, mezzo-soprano, 3 tenors, 3 baritones, bass-baritone, bass, SATB chorus, 2 flutes (2nd also piccolo), 2 oboes (2nd also English horn), 2 clarinets, 2 bassoons (2nd also contrabassoon), 3 horns, 3 trumpets, 2 trombones, bass trombone, timpani, percussion (vibraphone, tambourine, bongos, tenor drum, side drum, bass drum, suspended cymbal, tam-tam, woodblocks, tom-toms, temple blocks, sleigh bells, tubular bells), harp, piano, violin I, violin II, viola, violoncello, double bass.
Commissioned by: Virginia Opera Association and Royal Opera House, Covent Garden.
Call no.: **1986/080**
Also available:
Call no.: **1986/080 suppl.**

1837. Musgrave, Thea, 1928– Helios: a concerto for oboe & orchestra. Full score. London: Novello, 1994.
1 score (82 p.); 30 cm.
"Perusal score."
Reproduced from manuscript.
Duration: ca. 17:00.
Program and performance notes.
Composed for: oboe, 2 flutes, oboe, English horn, 2 clarinets (2nd also bass clarinet), 2 bassoons, 2 horns, trumpet, violin I, violin II, viola, violoncello, double bass.
Commissioned by: St. Magnus Festival, Orkney.
Call no.: **1997/101**
Re-entered as: **1998/113**

1838. Musgrave, Thea, 1928– Phoenix rising: for orchestra (1997). Full score. London: Novello, 1997.
1 score (83 p.); 30 cm.
Reproduced from manuscript.
Duration: ca. 23:00.
Composed for: piccolo, 2 flutes, 2 oboes, English horn, 2 clarinets, bass clarinet, 2 bassoons, contrabassoon, 4 horns, 3 trumpets, 3 trombones, tuba, timpani, percussion (3 tam-tams, 3 suspended cymbals, vibraphone, snare drum, 4 bongos, 2 Chinese bell trees, xylophone, tenor drum, crotales, 2 bass drums, glockenspiel, tubular bells, marimba, 4 tom-toms, metal wind chimes), 2 harps, violin I, violin II, viola, violoncello, double bass.
Commissioned by: British Broadcasting Corporation.
Call no.: **2000/127**

1839. Naidoo, Shaun, 1962– Move your shadow. N.p.: Shaun Naidoo, 2001.
1 score (107 p.); 36 cm.
Duration: ca. 40:00.
Contents: Burning the future—Holy woman—Move your shadow.
Composed for: clarinet (also bass clarinet), violin, violoncello, piano, 3 synthesizers.
Call no.: **2004/086**

1840. Nakagawa, Norio, 1969– Enjin. N.p.: n.p., 199-?.
1 score (5 p.); 42 cm.
Japanese words.
Composed for: voice, biwa.
Call no.: **1995/076**

1841. Nancarrow, Conlon, 1912–1997. Piece no. 2 for small orchestra: 1986. Baltimore, MD: Smith Publications, 1988.
1 score (85 p.); 28 cm.
Composed for: oboe, clarinet, bassoon, horn, trumpet, 2 pianos, violin I, violin II, viola, violoncello, double bass.
Commissioned by: Betty Freeman.
Call no.: **1989/085**

1842. Nancarrow, Conlon, 1912–1997. Studies for player piano, 1986. N.p.: n.p., 1986.
156 p. of music; 36 cm.
Reproduced from manuscript.
Contents: Introduction: tempo fantasy—Interlude: three improvisations—Finale: three canons with tempo-relations 4/5/6.
Composed for: player piano.
Call no.: **1987/056**

1843. Nanes, Richard, 1938– Rhapsodie pathetique: for violin and orchestra. Livingston, NJ: Delfon Recording Society, 1995.
1 score (80 p.); 28 cm.
Duration: 23:55.
Composed for: violin, 3 flutes (3rd also piccolo), 3 oboes (3rd also English horn), 3 clarinets (3rd also bass clarinet), 2 bassoons (2nd also contrabassoon), contrabassoon, 4 horns, 3 trumpets (all also trumpet in D), 2 trombones, bass trombone, 2 contrabass tubas, timpani, violin I, violin II, viola, violoncello, double bass.
Call no.: **2001/107**

1844. Nanes, Richard, 1938– Rhapsody pathetique: for violin & orchestra. Newark, N.J.: Delfon Recording and Publ. Society, 1985.
1 score (82 p.); 28 cm.
Duration: 23:55.

Composed for: violin, 3 flutes (3rd also piccolo), 3 oboes (3rd also English horn), 3 clarinets (3rd also bass clarinet), 2 bassoons (2nd also contrabassoon), contrabassoon, 4 horns, 3 trumpets (all also trumpet in D), 2 trombones, bass trombone, 2 contrabass tubas, timpani, violin I, violin II, viola, violoncello, double bass.
Call no.: **1991/082**
Re-entered as: **1997/102**
Also available:
Call no.: **1991/082 violin solo**

1845. Nanes, Richard, 1938– Symphony no. 2: in B-major. Newark, NJ: Delfon Recording and Publishing Society, 1986.
1 score (178 p.); 32 cm.
Reproduced from manuscript.
Duration: ca. 28:55.
Composed for: piccolo, 3 flutes (2nd–3rd also piccolo), 2 oboes, English horn, 2 clarinets (2nd also clarinet in E♭), bass clarinet (also clarinet in E♭), 2 bassoons, contrabassoon, 4 horns, 2 trumpets in D, 3 trumpets, 2 trombones, bass trombone, 2 tubas, timpani, percussion (bass drum, triangle, suspended cymbal, crash cymbals, tam-tam), 2 harps, organ, violin I, violin II, viola, violoncello, double bass.
Call no.: **1988/077**

1846. Nanes, Richard, 1938– Symphony no. 3. Livingston, NJ: Delfon Recording Society, 199-?.
1 score (100 p.); 33 cm.
Duration: 23:42.
Composed for: 4 flutes (2nd–4th also piccolo), 3 oboes (3rd also English horn), 3 clarinets (1st also clarinet in E♭, 3rd also bass clarinet), 2 bassoons, contrabassoon, 4 horns, 3 trumpets (all also trumpet in D and piccolo trumpet), 2 trombones, bass trombone, tuba, 2 sets of timpani, percussion (suspended cymbal, tam-tam, bass drum, orchestra chimes, triangle), harp, violin I, violin II, viola, violoncello, double bass.
Call no.: **1998/114**
Re-entered as: **2000/128**

1847. Nanes, Richard, 1938– Symphony no. 4. Newark, NJ: Delfon Recording and Pub. Society, 1988.
1 miniature score (213 p.); 28 cm.
Duration: 38:20.
Composed for: 4 flutes (2nd–4th also piccolo), 3 oboes (3rd also English horn), 3 clarinets (1st also clarinet in E♭, 3rd also bass clarinet), 2 bassoons, contrabassoon, 4 horns, 3 trumpets (all also trumpet in D and piccolo trumpet), 2 trombones, bass trombone, tuba, 2 sets of timpani, percussion (suspended cymbal, tam-tam, bass drum, orchestra chimes, triangle), harp, violin I, violin II, viola, violoncello, double bass.
Call no.: **1992/093**

1848. Nanes, Richard, 1938– Trihedral symphonic suite.
Call no.: **1986/081**
No materials available.

1849. Nečasová, Jindra, 1960– Ballet: pictures of Salvador Dalí: a symphonic triptych. N.p.: n.p., 1998.
1 score (134 p.) port. (some col.); 42 cm.
Reproduced from manuscript.
Duration: ca. 24:00.
Contents: The discovery of America by Christopher Columbus—Archeological reminiscence of Millet's Angelus—The hallucinogenic toreador.
Composed for: piccolo, 2 flutes, 2 oboes, English horn, 2 clarinets, bass clarinet, 2 bassoons, contrabassoon, 4 horns, 3 trumpets, 2 trombones, bass trombone, timpani, percussion (piccolo snare drum, triangle, suspended cymbal, bass drum, woodblocks, whip, gong, claves, tam-tam, chimes, orchestra bells, xylophone, celesta, vibraphone), harp, piano, organ, violin I, violin II, viola, violoncello, double bass.
Call no.: **2001/108**

1850. Neikrug, Marc, 1946– Concerto #2 for violin and orchestra: departures and remembrances. Bryn Mawr, PA: Theodore Presser, 1998.
1 score (60 p.); 44 cm.
Composed for: violin, 2 flutes, 2 oboes, 2 clarinets, 2 bassoons, 4 horns, 2 trumpets, tuba, percussion (vibraphone, suspended cymbals, tam-tam, snare drum, tom-tom, bass drum, tambourine, castanets, maracas, timpani), piano, harp, violin I, violin II, viola, violoncello, double bass.
Commissioned by: Pittsburgh Symphonic Society.
Call no.: **2001/109**

1851. Neikrug, Marc, 1946– Concerto for violin and orchestra. København: Edition W. Hansen, 1982.
1 score (51 p.); 42 cm.
Composed for: violin, 3 flutes (3rd also piccolo), 3 oboes, 3 clarinets (3rd also clarinet in E♭), 3 bassoons, 4 horns, 3 trumpets, 3 trombones, tuba, percussion (vibraphone, glockenspiel, 3 gongs, maracas, crotales, whip, triangle, bass drum, woodblock, mounted castanets, 3 suspended cymbals, xylophone, hi-hat, sleigh bells, cymbals, side drum, tambourine, tom-toms, wind chimes, mark tree, timpani, bells), harp, piano (also celesta), violin I, violin II, viola, violoncello, double bass.

Commissioned by: Houston Symphony Orchestra.
Call no.: **1985/143**

1852. Nelson, Paul, 1929– Cantata psalmorum: choro mixto, superio solo, et orchestrae. N.p.: n.p., 1989.
1 score (106 p.); 44 cm.
Latin words; also printed as text.
Reproduced from manuscript.
At end: 1. VI. 89.
Duration: ca. 32:00.
Contents: Psalmus 95—Psalmus 150—Alleluia.
Composed for: soprano, SATB chorus, 2 flutes, 2 oboes, 2 clarinets, 2 bassoons, 4 horns, 3 trumpets, 3 trombones, timpani, percussion (military drum, triangle, cymbals, 2 suspended cymbals, bass drum, tambourine, tam-tam, chimes), violin I, violin II, viola, violoncello, double bass.
Call no.: **1991/083**

1853. Nelson, Ron, 1929– Passacaglia: homage on B-A-C-H: for band. Full score. Cleveland, OH: Ludwig Music, 1993.
1 score (42 p.); 39 cm.
"An American Bandmasters Association/Ostwald and National Band Association prize winner."
Duration: 10:37.
Biographical and program notes.
Composed for: piccolo, 3 flutes (3rd also alto flute), 2 oboes, English horn, 12 clarinet, 2 bassoons, contrabassoon, 2 alto saxophones, tenor saxophone, baritone saxophone, 6 trumpets, horns, 4 trombones, euphonium, tuba, double bass, timpani, piano, synthesizer, percussion (chimes, glockenspiel, marimba, xylophone, crotales, 2 suspended cymbals, vibraphone, snare drum, tenor drum, bongos, gong, bass drum, tom-tom, slapstick, temple block).
Commissioned by: Eta-Omicron Chapter of Phi Mu Alpha Sinfonia, United States Air Force Band, and University of Cincinnati College Conservatory of Music.
Call no.: **1994/103**

1854. Neuhoff, Judy Austin, 1942– The passion of our Lord Jesus Christ according to John. N.p.: n.p., 1985.
1 score (88 p.); 28 cm.
English words.
For SATB chorus, baritone solo, narrator, organ, harp, cello, and percussion.
Text: Gospel of St. John.
"Revised"—title page.
Duration: ca. 25:00.
Composed for: narrator, baritone, SATB chorus, organ, harp, violoncello, percussion (tam-tam, tenor drum, wind chimes, finger cymbals, timpani, orchestra bells, triangle, suspended cymbal, tambourine, slapstick).
Call no.: **1990/092**

1855. Neuwirth, Olga, 1968– Clinamen/Nodus: für Streichorchester, Schlagzeug und Celesta. München: Ricordi, 1999.
1 score (48 p.); 42 cm.
Reproduced from manuscript.
Duration: 15:00.
Composed for: celesta, percussion (slide whistle, crotales, bass drums, timpani, sirens, vibraphone, triangles, 2 woodblocks, tam-tams, 6 gongs, cymbals, energy chime, 2 bongos, snare drum, lion's roar, bells, anvil, suspended cowbells, bell plate, suspended cymbal, Bavarian zither, whip, small drum, guiro, glockenspiel, Chinese cymbal, mounted ratchet, Chinese opera gong, steel guitar, e-bow, metal slide, pick, 2 tom-toms, military drum, tubular chimes, mounted cowbell, marimba), violin I, violin II (tuned a quarter tone lower), viola, violoncello, double bass.
Commissioned by: London Symphony Orchestra, Konzerthaus Wien, Kölner Philharmonie, Carnegie Hall, Société Philharmonique de Bruxelles 2000, Salzburger Festspiele, Musikfestwochen Luzern and Edinburgh International Festival.
Call no.: **2002/132**

1856. Neuwirth, Olga, 1968– Lost highway. N.p.: Boosey & Hawkes, 2003.
1 score (253 p.); 42 cm.
German and English words by Elfriede Jelinek and Olga Neuwirth.
Original work by David Lynch and Barry Gifford.
Music theater.
Reproduced from holograph.
Composed for: 6 actors, soprano, 2 countertenors, baritone, soprano saxophone (also tenor and baritone saxophones), clarinet (also bass and contrabass clarinets), trombone (also alto and bass trombones), electric guitar (also ukelele), accordion, electric piano (also synthesizer), 2 flutes (also piccolo and harmonica), oboe (also harmonica), 2 clarinets (also clarinet in E♭ and harmonica), bassoon (also contrabassoon and harmonica), 2 trumpets (also piccolo trumpet), horn, trombone, tuba, percussion (glockenspiel, small snare drum, cymbals, metal spring, 2 gongs, 2 cowbells, large sand block, timpani, woodblock, bass drum, tom-tom, triangle, thundersheet, wineglass with pickup, beer bottle, large tam-tam, drum pad, stereo microphone, vibraphone, jingle bells, medium tam-tam, tubular bells), violin I, violin II, viola, violoncello I, violoncello II, double bass,

sampler, 3 offstage microphones, live electronics, tape/CD player.
Call no.: **2005/100**

1857. Newell, Robert M., 1940– Of visions and dreams fulfilled: for mixed chorus and symphony orchestra. N.p.: Robert M. Newell, 1987.
1 score (73 p.); 36 cm.
English words; also printed as text.
Text by the composer (parts 1–2) and H. W. Longfellow (part 3).
Reproduced from manuscript.
Duration: ca. 15:30.
Contents: Visionary—Dreams and qualms of youth—Legacy.
Composed for: SATB chorus, 2 flutes, 2 oboes, 2 clarinets, 2 bassoons, contrabassoon, 4 horns, 4 trumpets, 3 trombones, tuba, percussion (timpani, cymbals, vibraphone, suspended cymbal, bongos, 2 tom-toms, marimba, tam-tam, woodblocks, temple blocks, chimes, crash cymbals, bass drum, glockenspiel, crotales), violin I, violin II, viola, violoncello, double bass.
Commissioned by: Ohio University.
Call no.: **1988/078**
Re-entered as: **1989/086**
Also available:
Call no.: **1989/086 vocal score**

1858. Newsome, Padma, 1961– These walls thy heaven: for tenor and chamber orchestra. N.p.: Padma Newsome, 2000.
1 score (27 p.); 28 x 44 cm.
English words by John Donne.
Duration: ca. 14:30.
Composed for: tenor, flute (also alto flute), oboe (also English horn), clarinet, bass clarinet, bassoon, contrabassoon, 2 horns, piano, percussion (vibraphone, crotales, tubular bells, 2 bass drums, 2 brake drums, 2 woodblocks, 4 suspended cymbals, triangle), violin I, violin II, viola, violoncello, double bass.
Call no.: **2005/101**

1859. Newson, George, 1932– Songs for the turning year: (1992). N.p.: n.p., 1993.
1 score (111 p.); 42 cm.
English words.
For soprano and baritone with orchestra.
Text based on poems by Shakespeare, Fred Ball, George Macbeth, John Wain, George Mackay Brown, Peter Porter, Peter Redgrove, Penelope Shuttle, Edwin Morgan, Leonard Smith, and Patric Dickinson.
Reproduced from manuscript.
Composed for: soprano, baritone, 4 flutes (2nd and 4th also piccolo), 2 oboes, 2 English horns, soprano saxophone, 3 clarinets (3rd also bass clarinet), 4 bassoons (4th also contrabassoon), 6 horns, 5 trumpets (1st–2nd also flugelhorn), 4 trombones, tuba, percussion (timpani, 2 suspended cymbals, large triangle, tubular bells, large coil, sleigh bells, systrum, castanets, metal sheet, glockenspiel, tambourine, snare drum, maracas, 4 Chinese blocks, stones, sizzle cymbals, bongos, 2 congas, crotales, medium tam-tam, 4 tom-toms, bass drum, small triangle, small coil, hi-hat, large tam-tam, marimba), 2 harps, violin I, violin II, viola, violoncello, double bass.
Commissioned by: BBC.
Call no.: **1994/104**

1860. Newson, George, 1932– Songs in exchange. N.p.: Newson, 1996.
1 score (136 p.); 30 cm.
English words.
Contents: The hour of magic / W.H. Davies—Inscription on the tomb of Henri Rousseau / Apollinaire—Pistachio tree at Ch□teau Noir / Frank O'Hara—The clock of the years I / Thomas Hardy—The clock of the years II / William Carlos Williams—Clouds; Heaven / Rupert Brooke—The drunkard & the pig / anon.—A glass of beer / James Stevens—One day I wrote her name upon the strand / Edmund Spenser—Tall nettles / Edward Thomas—The trees / Philip Larkin—Old yew / Tennyson—Bird woman / Neil Astley—Nuer love song / from Two Nuer evocations—The end of the owls / Hans Magnus Ensensberger—Walking song / Marie Scott—The funeral song of Duc Jean Floressas des Esseintes / George Newson after Hysmans—Cantus troili / Chaucer—Serenades / Seamus Heaney—Akrotiri / Michael Langley—Ode to a nightingale / John Keats—Richard Jefferies, his invocation / Newson after Jefferies.
Composed for: soprano, piano.
Call no.: **2002/133**

1861. Newson, George, 1932– String quartet no. 2: (il lirico). Stone-In-Oxney, Kent, England: George Newson, 1990.
1 score (16 p.); 28 cm.
Reproduced from holograph.
Composed for: 2 violins, viola, violoncello.
Call no.: **1993/102**

1862. Nguyễn, Thiên Đạo, 1940– Blessure/soleil. Paris: Editions Salabert, 1983.
1 score (34 p.); 36 cm.
Reproduced from holograph.
Duration: 25:00.

Composed for: 2 flutes, 2 oboes, 2 horns, percussion (tubular bells, 5 Thai gongs, 2 tam-tams, 5 metal plates, 2 woodblocks, 5 temple blocks, log drum, 2 galets, cowbell, timpani, snare drum, 3 contrabass tom-toms, bass drum, Chinese drum, 5 boards, 3 Japanese bowls), 7 violins, 2 violas, 2 violoncellos, double bass.
Call no.: **1985/047**

1863. Nichifor, Şerban, 1954– Simfonia II: via lucis. N.p.: n.p., 198-?.
1 score (112 p.); 37 cm.
"Calea luminii"—Caption.
Reproduced from manuscript.
Composed for: 3 flutes (3rd also piccolo), 3 oboes (3rd also English horn), 3 clarinets, 2 bassoons, contrabassoon, 4 horns, 3 trumpets, 3 trombones, bass trombone, tuba, percussion (timpani, triangle, sleigh bells, suspended sleigh bells, 4 cymbals, xylophone, vibraphone, tam-tam, crash cymbals, 3 tom-toms, chimes, bass drum, glockenspiel, 2 bongos), harp, organ, celesta, violin I, violin II, viola, violoncello, double bass.
Call no.: **1986/082**

1864. Nicholson, George, 1949– Cello concerto, 1990. N.p.: n.p., 1990.
1 score (92 p.); 30 cm.
Duration: ca. 30:00.
Composed for: violoncello, 3 flutes (2nd also alto flute, 3rd also piccolo), 3 oboes (3rd also English horn), 3 clarinets (3rd also bass clarinet), 3 bassoons (3rd also contrabassoon), 4 horns, 3 trumpets, 3 trombones, tuba, timpani, percussion (vibraphone, xylophone, marimba, 2 cymbals, sizzle cymbal, hi-hat, bongos, tambourine, side drum, bass drum, tam-tam, maracas, guiro, rattle, whip, anvil, Chinese bell tree), harp, piano (also celesta), violin I, violin II, viola, violoncello, double bass.
Commissioned by: BBC.
Call no.: **1994/105**

1865. Nicholson, George, 1949– Flute concerto, 1993. N.p.: George Nicholson, 1993.
1 score (149 p.); 30 cm.
Reproduced from holograph.
Composed for: flute, 3 flutes (2nd also piccolo, 3rd also alto flute), 3 oboes (3rd also English horn), clarinet in A (also clarinet in E♭), 2 clarinets (2nd also bass clarinet), 3 bassoons (3rd also contrabassoon), 4 horns, 3 trumpets, 3 trombones, tuba, timpani, percussion (xylophone, vibraphone, tubular bells, snare drum, glockenspiel, marimba, bass drum, 4 tom-toms, woodblock, tambourine), harp, violin I, violin II, viola, violoncello, double bass.
Commissioned by: James Galway and Zürich Tonhalle Orchestra.
Call no.: **1996/108**

1866. Nielsen, Erik, 1950– A fleeting animal: an opera from Judevine. N.p.: Middle Branch Music, 2001.
1 score (2 v.); 28 cm.
English words by David Budbill.
Reproduced from manuscript.
Duration: ca. 1:50:00.
Composed for: 3 sopranos, 2 tenors, 2 baritones, bass-baritone, SATB chorus, clarinet (also bass clarinet), 2 violins, viola, violoncello, percussion (trap set, vibraphone), piano.
Commissioned by: Vermont Opera Theater.
Call no.: **2004/087**

1867. Nielson, Kenneth, 1953– Cantata on four saints. N.p.: n.p., 1990.
1 score (82 p.); 30 x 45 cm.
English words by Jeremey Driscoll.
"For orchestra, chorus, and four soloists (saintly, if possible)."
"Rev. 3/90."
Reproduced from manuscript.
Composed for: soprano, alto, tenor, bass, 2 flutes, 2 oboes, bassoon, horn, 3 trumpets, timpani (also tambourine), harp, organ, violin I, violin II, viola, violoncello, double bass.
Call no.: **1992/094**

1868. Nikiprowetzky, Tolia, 1916–1997. Ode funebre: pour soprano, baryton, choeur et orchestre. N.p.: n.p., 1985.
1 score (136 p.); 38 cm.
French words by André Gaillard.
Reproduced from holograph.
Duration: 47:00.
Composed for: soprano, baritone, SATB chorus, 3 flutes (3rd also piccolo), 2 oboes, English horn, 2 clarinets, bass clarinet, 2 bassoons, contrabassoon, 4 horns, 3 trumpets, 2 trombones, bass trombone, tuba, percussion (timpani, celesta, vibraphone, xylophone, suspended cymbal, snare drum, tambourine, tam-tam, bells), 2 harps, violin I, violin II, viola, violoncello, double bass.
Commissioned by: Radio France.
Call no.: **1989/087**

1869. Nishimura, Akira, 1953– Avatara for piano = Vishunu no keshin. Tokyo: Zen-On Music Co., 2002.
115 p. of music; 31 cm.

Preface in English and Japanese.
Contents: Matsay, the fish—Kūrma, the tortoise—Varāha, the boar—Mrshimha—Vāmana—Kalkin.
Composed for: piano.
Commissioned by: Music from Japan.
Call no.: **2004/088**

1870. Nobre, Marlos, 1939– Cantata do Chimborazo: para tenor, baritono, coro e orquestra, opus 56. N.p.: Marlos Nobre, 1982.
1 score (65 p.); 34 cm.
Spanish words by Simon Bolivar; also printed as text.
Reproduced from manuscript.
Duration: 23:30.
Contents: El manto de Iris—El tiempo—El delirio.
Composed for: tenor, baritone, SATB chorus, piccolo, 2 flutes, 2 oboes, 2 clarinets, 2 bassoons, 4 horns, 3 trumpets, 2 trombones, bass trombone, tuba, timpani, percussion (chimes, xylophone, vibraphone, glockenspiel, triangle, snare drum, 3 suspended cymbals, 2 tam-tams, bass drum, 3 woodblocks), harp, celesta, violin I, violin II, viola, violoncello, double bass.
Call no.: **1986/083**

1871. Nobre, Marlos, 1939– Concertantes do imaginário: para piano e orquestra de cordas, opus 74. Rio de Janeiro: Marlos Nobre, 1989.
1 score (37 p.); 28 cm.
Reproduced from manuscript.
Contents: Desenho = Sketch—Motivo = Motif—Retrato = Protrait.
Composed for: piano, violin I, violin II, viola, violoncello, double bass.
Call no.: **1991/084**

1872. Nobre, Marlos, 1939– Concerto duplo: para dois violõnes e orquestra, opus 82. Rio de Janeiro: Editora Musica Nova do Brasil, 1995.
1 score (156 p.); 43 cm.
For 2 guitars and orchestra.
Duration: 28:45.
Composed for: 2 guitars, timpani, percussion (xylophone, glockenspiel, vibraphone, 3 temple blocks, 3 conga drums, marimba, large woodblock, small bass drum), violin I, violin II, viola, violoncello, double bass.
Commissioned by: GHA Records Belgium.
Call no.: **2000/129**

1873. Nobre, Marlos, 1939– Concerto II: für Streichorchester; op. 53. Partitur. N.p.: n.p., 1986.
1 score (38 p.); 38 cm.
Reproduced from manuscript.
Duration: 19:56.
Composed for: violin I, violin II, viola, violoncello, double bass.
Call no.: **1987/057**

1874. Nobre, Marlos, 1939– Saga Marista: passacaglia para orquestra, opus 84. Rio de Janeiro, Brasil: Editora Musica Nova do Brasil, 1997.
1 score (52 p.); 30 cm.
Reproduced from manuscript.
Duration: 12:50.
Composed for: piccolo, 2 flutes, 2 oboes, English horn, 2 clarinets, bass clarinet, 2 bassoons, contrabassoon, 4 horns, 4 trumpets, 3 trombones, tuba, timpani, percussion (bass drum, 2 tam-tams, snare drum, tenor drum, low drum, 3 tom-toms, glockenspiel, 3 woodblocks, 2 triangles, 3 temple blocks, 3 congas, high suspended cymbal, guiro, xylorimba, tambourine), 2 harps, piano, violin I, violin II, viola, violoncello, double bass.
Call no.: **1998/115**

1875. Nobre, Marlos, 1939– Sonancias III: para 2 pianos e 2 percussions, op. 49. Second, 1991. N.p.: Marlos Nobre, 1992.
1 score (50 p.); 34 cm.
Composed for: 2 pianos, percussion (3 tom-toms, 3 congas, 2 xylophones, 2 vibraphones, timpani).
Call no.: **1993/103**

1876. Nobre, Marlos, 1939– Yanománi: para coro misto, tenor-solo e guitarra, opus 47 (1980). Full score. N.p.: n.p., 1980.
1 score (76 p.); 38 cm.
Yanomamo words; also printed as text.
"Text was organized by the composer, using sounds and words from the language of Brazilian Indians"—title page verso.
Reproduced from manuscript.
Duration: ca. 12:00.
Historical notes in English and performance notes in Portuguese with English translation.
Composed for: tenor, SATB chorus, guitar.
Call no.: **1990/093**

1877. Nocerino, Francesco, 1960– Missa Deus meus: per soprano, coro a quattro voci miste, organo, arpa e percussioni. Napoli: n.p., 1989.
1 score (58 p.); 30 cm.
Italian words; also printed as text.
Reproduced from holograph.
Composed for: soprano, SATB chorus, organ, harp, percussion (tam-tam, triangle, timpani, Chinese blocks, bass drum, crash cymbals).
Call no.: **1993/104**

1878. Norbet, Gregory, 1940– Morning prayer, evening prayer: with chants, songs & prayers. Guitar/choral songbook. Portland, OR.: OCP Publications, 1996.
31 p. of music; 27 cm.
English and Latin words.
Instrumental parts: p. 22–31.
Composed for: SATB chorus, flute, oboe (also English horn), guitar, violoncello.
Call no.: **1997/103**
Also available:
Call no.: **1997/103 meditation book**

1879. Norden, Maarten van, 1955– Square roots: concerto for piano, saxophone and orchestra, 2000. Amsterdam: Donemus, 2000.
1 score (81 p.); 42 cm.
Duration: ca. 28:00.
Composed for: piano, soprano saxophone (also tenor saxophone), piccolo, 2 flutes, 2 oboes, English horn, 2 clarinets, bass clarinet, 2 bassoons, contrabassoon, 4 horns, 3 trumpets, 3 trombones, tuba, timpani (also bass drum), percussion (marimba, xylophone, vibraphone, Thai gong, high gong, crash cymbal, small cymbal, snare drum, bass drum, triangle, woodblock, tubular bells, bell tree, thundersheet, shaker, guiro, timbales, cowbell), piano, violin I, violin II, viola, violoncello, double bass.
Commissioned by: Fonds voor de Scheppende Toonkunst.
Call no.: **2004/141**

1880. Nordheim, Arne, 1931– Aurora: for four singers with crotali and tape. Copenhagen: W. Hansen, 1983.
1 score (21 p.); 21 x 30 cm.
Latin, Italian, and Hebrew words; also printed as text with partial English translation.
Words from Psalm 139 and Dante's Paradiso, canto XXXIII.
Reproduced from holograph.
Composed for: soprano, alto, tenor, bass, crotales, tape.
Call no.: **1985/144**

1881. Nordheim, Arne, 1931– Boomerang: concerto for oboe and chamber orchestra. Score. Copenhagen: Edition W. Hansen; New York, NY: Edition W. Hansen/Chester Music, 1986.
1 score (49 p.); 30 cm.
Duration: ca. 17:00.
Composed for: oboe, 2 horns, harpsichord, violin I, violin II, viola, violoncello, double bass.
Commissioned by: Norwegian Chamber Orchestra.
Call no.: **1986/084**
Re-entered as: **1990/094**

1882. Nordheim, Arne, 1931– Five stages: string quartet 2001. Copenhagen: Edition Wilhelm Hansen, 2001.
1 score (16 p.); 30 cm.
Duration: ca. 16:00.
Contents: Split—Tranquil—Exchange—Basis—Assembling.
Composed for: 2 violins, viola, violoncello.
Commissioned by: Olso String Quartet.
Call no.: **2004/089**

1883. Nordheim, Arne, 1931– Magma: for orchestra. N.p.: n.p., 1988.
1 score (75 p.); 42 cm.
Reproduced from manuscript.
Duration: ca. 23:00.
Composed for: 4 piccolos, 4 oboes, clarinet in E♭, clarinet, 2 bass clarinets, 2 bassoons, 2 contrabassoons, 4 horns, 4 trumpets, 4 trombones, tuba, timpani, percussion (vibraphone, crotales, tubular bells, glockenspiel, tam-tam, 3 tuned Javanese gongs, crash cymbals, suspended cymbal), harp, piano, celesta, organ, violin I, violin II, viola, violoncello, double bass.
Commissioned by: Amsterdam Concertgebouworkest.
Call no.: **1989/088**

1884. Nordheim, Arne, 1931– Magma: for orchestra. Score. Copenhagen: W. Hansen, 1989.
1 score (78 p.); 42 cm.
Duration: ca. 25:00.
Composed for: 4 piccolos, 4 oboes, clarinet in E♭, clarinet, 2 bass clarinets, 2 bassoons, 2 contrabassoons, 4 horns, 4 trumpets, 4 trombones, tuba, timpani, percussion (vibraphone, crotales, tubular bells, glockenspiel, tam-tam, 3 tuned Javanese gongs, crash cymbals, suspended cymbal), harp, piano, celesta, organ, violin I, violin II, viola, violoncello, double bass.
Commissioned by: Amsterdam Concertgebouworkest.
Call no.: **1991/085**

1885. Nordheim, Arne, 1931– Monolith: for orchestra. Copenhagen: Edition Wilhelm Hansen, 1991.
1 score (62 p.); 42 cm.
Reproduced from manuscript.
Duration ca. 16:00.
Composed for: 3 piccolos, 3 oboes, clarinet in E♭, clarinet, bass clarinet, contrabass clarinet, 2 bassoons, contrabassoon, 4 horns, 4 trumpets, 3 trombones, tuba, timpani, percussion (whip, flexatone, crotales, tubular bells, marimba, vibraphone, orchestra bells, tam-tam, bass drum), harp, piano, celesta, violin I, violin II, viola, violoncello, double bass.

Commissioned by: International Program for Music Compositions.
Call no.: **1992/095**

1886. Nordheim, Arne, 1931– Violin concerto. Full score. Copenhagen: Edition W. Hansen, 1996.
1 score (75 p.); 42 cm.
"Proof copy."
Duration: ca. 25:00.
Composed for: violin, 3 flutes (all also piccolo), 3 oboes (3rd also English horn), 2 clarinets (1st also clarinet in E♭, 2nd also bass clarinet), contrabass clarinet, 3 bassoons (3rd also contrabassoon), 4 horns, 3 trumpets, 2 trombones, bass trombone, tuba, percussion (tubular bells, Javanese gongs, vibraphone, medium tam-tam, crotales, 5 Chinese blocks, whip, large tam-tam, glockenspiel, very large tam-tam, bass drum, flexatone), harp, piano, celesta, violin I, violin II, viola, violoncello, double bass.
Commissioned by: Oslo Philharmonic Orchestra.
Call no.: **1998/116**

1887. Nordheim, Arne, 1931– Violin concerto: 1996. Full score. Copenhagen: Edition W. Hansen, 1999.
1 score (76 p.); 43 cm.
Cadenza by and solo part edited by Arve Tellefsen in collaboration with the composer.
Duration: ca. 30:00.
Composed for: violin, 3 flutes (all also piccolo), 3 oboes (3rd also English horn), 2 clarinets (1st also clarinet in E♭, 2nd also bass clarinet), contrabass clarinet, 3 bassoons (3rd also contrabassoon), 4 horns, 3 trumpets, 2 trombones, bass trombone, tuba, percussion (tubular bells, Javanese gongs, vibraphone, medium tam-tam, crotales, 5 Chinese blocks, whip, large tam-tam, glockenspiel, very large tam-tam, bass drum, flexatone), harp, piano, celesta, violin I, violin II, viola, violoncello, double bass.
Commissioned by: Oslo Philharmonic Orchestra.
Call no.: **2001/110**

1888. Nordheim, Arne, 1931– Wirklicher Wald: for soprano and cello solo, chorus, and orchestra. Copenhagen: W. Hansen; New York, NY: Edition Wilhelm Hansen/Chester Music, 1984.
1 score (55 p.); 42 cm.
German or Hebrew words by Rainer Maria Rilke and from the Book of Job.
Duration: 28:00.
Composed for: soprano, violoncello, SATB chorus, 2 piccolos, oboe, English horn, clarinet (also clarinet in E♭), bass clarinet, bassoon, contrabassoon, 2 horns, 2 trumpets, trombone, tuba, timpani, percussion (vibraphone, Javanese gong, 2 bongos, tam-tam, tubular bells, orchestra bells, 2 timbales, crotales, 3 Chinese blocks, 2 congas), harp, electric piano, celesta, violin I, violin II, viola, violoncello, double bass.
Commissioned by: Music Conservatory Oslo.
Call no.: **1985/145**

1889. Nørgård, Per, 1932– "Bach to the future": concerto in 3 movements based on preludes by J.S. Bach: for percussion-duo and orchestra (1997). Copenhagen: Edition Wilhelm Hansen, 1998.
1 score (iii, 92 p.); 43 cm.
"Rettet okt 97; corr. 21/8-98."
Reproduced from holograph.
Duration: ca. 23:00.
Program notes by the composer in English.
Composed for: percussion (vibraphone, marimba, 4 tom-toms, 6 roto-toms, 4 natural skin toms, crotales, 2 steel drums, tubular bells), 2 flutes (1st also alto flute, 2nd also piccolo), 2 oboes (2nd also English horn), 2 clarinets (2nd also bass clarinet), 2 bassoons (2nd also contrabassoon), 2 horns, 2 trumpets, 2 trombones, harp, viola, violoncello, double bass.
Commissioned by: Safri-Duo.
Call no.: **2000/130**

1890. Nørgård, Per, 1932– The divine Tivoli.
Call no.: **1985/148**
No materials available.

1891. Nørgård, Per, 1932– For a change: for percussion and orchestra.
Call no.: **1985/147**
No materials available.

1892. Nørgård, Per, 1932– In between: three movements for cello and orchestra.
Call no.: **1986/085**
No materials available.

1893. Nørgård, Per, 1932– Piano concerto: concerto in due tempi for piano and orchestra. Full score. Copenhagen: Edition Wilhelm Hansen, 1996.
1 score (104 p.); 42 cm.
"Corrections of 12/4 & 22/4 1996."
Reproduced from holograph.
Duration: ca. 30:00.
Performance instructions in Danish follow score.
Composed for: piano, 2 flutes (2nd also piccolo), 2 oboes (2nd also English horn), clarinet (also clarinet in E♭), bass clarinet, bassoon, contrabassoon, 4 horns, 3 trumpets (1st also trumpet in D), 2 trombones, bass

trombone, tuba, timpani, percussion (woodblocks, glockenspiel, crotales, maracas, metal plate, water bell, cymbals, castanets, flexatone, metal wind chimes, 2 wooden metronomes, 5 roto-toms, 5 bongos, military drum, xylophone, vibraphone, marimba, bass drum, tam-tam, Balinese gong), harp, celesta, violin I, violin II, viola, violoncello, double bass.
Commissioned by: Léonie Sonnings Musikfond, Copenhagen.
Call no.: **1997/104**

1894. Nørgård, Per, 1932– Remembering child: two movements for viola and chamber-orchestra. Copenhagen: Edition Wilhelm Hansen, 1986.
1 score (40 p.); 43 cm.
Reproduced from holograph.
Duration: ca. 23:00.
Composed for: viola, flute (also piccolo and alto flute), 2 oboes (2nd also English horn), clarinet (also clarinet in E♭ and bass clarinet), 2 bassoons (2nd also contrabassoon), 2 horns, trumpet (also piccolo trumpet), percussion (crotales, handbells, vibraphone, xylophone, 5 cowbells, flexatone, tambourine, guiro, Peking gong, glass and metal chimes, lion's roar, maracas, woodblock, Chinese blocks, 4 tom-toms, tam-tam, bass drum), piano, violin I, violin II, viola, violoncello, double bass.
Commissioned by: St. Paul Chamber Orchestra.
Call no.: **1987/058**

1895. Nørgård, Per, 1932– Siddharta: opera-ballet in three acts.
Call no.: **1985/146**
No materials available.

1896. Nørgård, Per, 1932– Symfoni nr. 5: for orkester = Symphony no. 5: for orchestra (1986–90). Copenhagen: Edition Wilhelm Hansen, 1990.
1 score (157 p.); 43 cm.
Reproduced from manuscript.
Composed for: 3 flutes (all also piccolo), 2 oboes, English horn, 2 clarinets (2nd also clarinet in E♭), bass clarinet, 2 bassoons, contrabassoon, 4 horns, 3 trumpets (1st also piccolo trumpet and cornet), 3 trombones, tuba, percussion (castanets, 4 Chinese tom-toms, celesta, chimes, 4 cowbells, coins, crotales, 2 congas, 3 suspended cymbals, flexatone, bass drum, 7 gongs, glockenspiel, lion's roar, 2 metal pieces, mouth siren, 2 Peking opera blocks, 2 Peking opera gongs, 2 sleigh bells, snare drum, steel drum, slit drum, 2 Swanee flutes, triangle, tambourine, 5 tom-toms, 2 tam-tams, timpani, xylophone, whip, 4 woodblocks, metal chimes, marimba, vibraphone, 2 Chinese blocks), harp, piano, violin I, violin II, viola, violoncello, double bass.
Commissioned by: Danish Radio.
Call no.: **1991/086**

1897. Nørgård, Per, 1932– Symphony no. 6: at the end of the day. Full score. Copenhagen: Edition Wilhelm Hansen, 2002.
1 score (179 p.); 42 cm.
Duration: ca. 34:00.
Composed for: 4 flutes (all also piccolo, alto and bass flutes), 3 oboes (also English horn), English horn, 3 clarinets (also bass clarinet and clarinet in E♭), bass clarinet, 3 bassoons (also contrabassoon), contrabassoon, 6 horns, 3 trumpets (also piccolo trumpet), bass trumpet, 2 trombones, bass trombone, double bass trombone, double bass tuba, 5 timpani, percussion (metal wind chimes, flexatone, marimba, 5 tom-toms, 2 small tam-tams, 3 suspended cymbals, snare drum, small tambourine, crotales, glockenspiel, vibraphone, 2 congas, Chinese blocks, woodblocks, xylophone, 2 large drums, 4 roto-toms, sleigh bells, 5 log drums, bass drum, drumlins [frame drums with jingles]), harp, piano, violin I, violin II, viola, violoncello, double bass.
Commissioned by: Danish National Radio Symphony Orchestra, Gothenburg Symphony Orchestra, and Oslo Philharmonic Orchestra.
Call no.: **2005/102**

1898. Nørgård, Per, 1932– Tidsrum = Spaces of time (1991): for orchestra with piano. Copenhagen: Edition Wilhelm Hansen, 1991.
1 score (v, 74 p.); 42 cm.
Reproduced from holograph.
"Corrected 16/8 1991."
Includes program note by the composer in English.
Duration: ca. 20:00.
Composed for: piano, 3 flutes (1st also alto flute, 3rd also piccolo), 2 oboes, English horn, 2 clarinets (2nd also clarinet in E♭), bass clarinet, 2 bassoons, contrabassoon, 4 horns, 3 trumpets (1st also trumpet in D), 2 trombones, bass trombone, tuba, timpani, percussion (maracas, sandpaper blocks, lion's roar, woodblock, marimba, crotales, waterphone, whip, gong, metal piece with plastic plate, claves, steel drum, 4 Chinese blocks, cowbell, guiro, snare drum, tam-tam, cabasa, Japanese block, vibraphone, glockenspiel, 2 tom-toms, roto-tom), violin I, violin II, viola, violoncello, double bass.
Commissioned by: Suntory.
Call no.: **1992/096**

1899. Norman, Andrew, 1979– Poem for orchestra. N.p.: A. Norman, 1998.

1 score (30 p.); 28 cm.
Composed for: 2 flutes, 2 oboes, English horn, 2 clarinets, 2 bassoons, 4 horns, 3 trumpets, 3 trombones, tuba, timpani, percussion (bass drum, cymbals), harp, violin I, violin II, viola, violoncello, double bass.
Commissioned by: Modesto Symphony.
Call no.: **2000/131**

1900. Nuernberger, Louis Dean, 1924– The homecoming: an autumn gathering. N.p.: n.p., 1984.
1 score (45 p.); 29 cm.
English and German words by E. A. Robinson and Walther von der Vogelweide; also printed as text with English translation.
For tenor, baritone, early instrumental group, percussion, brass quintet, and string quartet.
Reproduced from manuscript.
At end of score: "Summer, 1984 Oberlin, Ohio."
Composed for: tenor, baritone, glockenspiel, rackbells, Renaissance flute, portative organ with hand bellows, cittern, psaltery, Gothic harp, vielle, finger cymbals, percussion (tam-tam, suspended cymbal, chromatic harp), 2 trumpets, horn, trombone, tuba, 2 violins, viola, violoncello, tape.
Call no.: **1987/059**

1901. Núñez Montes, Francisco, 1945– Aromas de lluvia: 1994. N.p.: n.p., 1994.
1 score (24 leaves); 35 cm.
For piano and chamber orchestra.
Reproduced from holograph.
Composed for: piano, flute, oboe, clarinet, vibraphone, violin I, violin II, viola, violoncello, double bass.
Commissioned by: Orquesta CUICANI de St. Paul, Minnesota.
Call no.: **1997/105**

1902. Núñez Montes, Francisco, 1945– El sacrificio de acteal. N.p.: n.p., 2003.
1 score (21 leaves); 45 cm.
At end of score: Revision 2003.
Reproduced from holograph.
Composed for: clarinet, timpani, percussion, violin I, violin II, viola, violoncello, double bass.
Call no.: **2005/103**

1903. Nyman, Michael, 1944– Concerto for trombone and orchestra (1995). London: Chester Music, 1995.
1 score (73 p.); 30 cm.
Reproduced from manuscript.
Composed for: trombone, piccolo, 3 flutes, 3 oboes, English horn, 3 clarinets, bass clarinet, 4 bassoons, contrabassoon, 2 horns, 2 trumpets, 2 trombones, tuba, percussion (vibraphone, crotales, steel drums, tubular bells, glockenspiel, cowbells, 4 suspended cymbals, hi-hat, cowbell, brake drums, gongs, medium tam-tam, 3 metal sheets, biscuit tin filled with pebbles, 10 suspended saucepans), piano, violin I, violin II, viola, violoncello, double bass.
Commissioned by: BBC.
Call no.: **1996/109**

1904. Nyman, Michael, 1944– Facing Goya: an opera in four acts (2000, revised 2002). London: Chester Music, 2002.
1 score (2 v. [xxxii, 696 p.]); 42 cm.
English words by Victoria Hardie; also printed as text.
"Version for Badisches Staatstheater, Karlsruhe, Germany (20/08/02)."
Duration: ca. 2:30:00.
Composed for: 2 sopranos, contralto, tenor, baritone, flute (also piccolo and alto flute), 2 soprano saxophones (both also alto saxophone), baritone saxophone, horn (also Wagner tuba), trumpet (also flugelhorn), bass trombone (also tuba and bass drum), guitar, piano, violin I, violin II, viola, violoncello, double bass, bass guitar.
Commissioned by: Editorial Paraiso Music S.L.
Call no.: **2004/090**

1905. Nyman, Michael, 1944– MGV. London: Chester Music, 1993.
1 score (129 p.); 30 cm.
For orchestra.
Reproduced from holograph.
Composed for: 4 flutes (also piccolo), 4 oboes, 4 clarinets (3rd–4th also bass clarinets), 4 bassoons, 4 horns, 4 trumpets, 4 trombones, tuba, timpani, harp, piano, celesta, violin I, violin II, viola, violoncello, double bass, 2 violins, violoncello, 2 soprano saxophones, alto saxophone, baritone saxophone, piccolo, bass trombone, bass guitar, piano.
Commissioned by: 1993 Festival de Lille.
Call no.: **1995/077**

1906. Nyrimov, Tchary, 1941– String quartet no. 2: "To memory of Indira Gandhi." N.p.: n.p., 1985.
1 score (18 p.); 40 cm.
Reproduced from manuscript.
Composed for: 2 violins, viola, violoncello.
Call no.: **1986/086**

1907. Nytch, Jeffrey, 1964– Epilogue: in memoriam Yitzhak Rabin: for string orchestra, 1995. Houston: Jeffrey Nytch, 1996.
1 score (14 p.); 28 cm.

Composed for: violin I, violin II, violin III, viola I, viola II, viola III, violoncello I, violoncello II, violoncello III, double bass.
Call no.: **1997/106**

1908. O'Neill, Paul, 1951– Hearts of oak. N.p.: n.p., 1990.
1 score (various pagings); 30 cm.
English words.
Songs.
Contents: The Mayflower: an Englishmans [sic] view of the founding of the new world—The captain is mad: a press ganged sailor's story—England expects: Lord Nelson explains to Lady Hamilton—Drakes [sic] drum: a canzonett [sic]—Echo's/the fish: life under the sea—Submarine: even grown up's [sic] play Hide and seek—Lifeboatmen: a tribute to those unpaid hero's—The loss of the Birkenhead: a true story of British soldiers—Slave trader: a slaves [sic] story—Hang him from the yard iron: based on an actual occurence [sic] at an English slave scale in the eighteenth century—The widows [sic] lament: a song for one of those left behind—The mysteries of the sea.
Composed for: voice, 3 descant recorders, treble recorder, flageolet, percussion (xylophone, marimba, vibraphone, trap set, timpani, finger cymbals), melodion, piano, 2 synthesizers, 3 guitars, electric guitar, electric bass guitar, 2 violins, violoncello.
Call no.: **1991/087**

1909. Oak, Kil-Sung, 1945– Sonata for piano. N.p.: n.p., 199-?.
50 p. of music; 30 cm.
Composed for: piano.
Call no.: **1998/117**

1910. Oak, Kil-Sung, 1945– Sonata for piano. N.p.: Ye-Dang Publishing, 1998.
49 p. of music; 30 cm.
Composed for: piano.
Call no.: **2002/134**

1911. Oak, Kil-Sung, 1945– Symphony: (synthetics 3). N.p.: n.p., 199-?.
1 score (95 p.); 36 cm.
Reproduced from manuscript.
Duration: 19:42.
Composed for: 2 flutes (1st also piccolo, 2nd also alto flute), 2 oboes, English horn, 2 clarinets, 2 bassoons, 4 horns, 2 trumpets, 3 trombones, tuba, timpani, percussion (xylophone, suspended cymbal, glockenspiel, slapstick, tam-tam, bass drum, snare drum, gong, chimes, anvil, rattle, 5 bongos, whistle, vibraphone, triangle, 5 temple blocks), harp, piano, celesta, violin I, violin II, viola, violoncello, double bass.
Call no.: **1996/110**

1912. Obst, Michael, 1955– Miroirs: für sechs Vokalisten: nach mittel- und spätmittelalterlicher Lyrik Nordfrankreichs, 1989. Wiesbaden: Breitkopf & Härtel, 1989.
1 score (14 p.); 30 x 39 cm.
Old and Middle French words.
Texts by Jacques de Cysoing, Adam de la Halle, Rutebeuf, Christine de Pisan, and Charles d'Orléans.
Reproduced from holograph.
Composed for: 2 sopranos, mezzo-soprano, tenor, baritone, bass.
Commissioned by: Südwestfunk Baden-Baden.
Call no.: **1991/088**
Also available:
Call no.: **1991/088 text**

1913. Ofenbauer, Christian, 1961– "Bruchstück VI" (1996): für grosses Orchester. Partitur. Wien: Doblinger, 1996.
1 score (27 p.); 42 cm.
Reproduced from manuscript.
Duration: ca. 12:00.
Composed for: piccolo, 2 flutes, 2 oboes, clarinet in E♭, 2 clarinets, bass clarinet, contrabass clarinet, 2 bassoons, contrabassoon, 4 horns, 2 trumpets, trombone, bass trombone, contrabass tuba, percussion (timpani, antique cymbals, crotales, 2 triangles, xylophone, bass drum, 2 tam-tams, vibraphone, marimba, large suspended cymbals, 2 metal plates, glockenspiel, 3 bongos, 5 tom-toms, 4 woodblocks, tenor drum, 5 temple blocks, snare drum), harp, piano, celesta, violin I, violin II, viola, violoncello, double bass.
Commissioned by: ORF.
Call no.: **1998/118**

1914. Ogilvy, Susan, 1949– Flight from Bosnia: a programmatic work in five movements for digital piano and digital keyboard orchestra. N.p.: Ogilvy Music, 1996.
1 score (ca. 44 p.); 28 cm.
Contents: The mission—The jungle chase—Eating ants and grass—Introspection—The rescue.
Composed for: digital piano, digital keyboard.
Call no.: **1998/119**

1915. Ohta, Tutsuya, 1920– Pastrale. N.p.: n.p., 1987.
1 score (66 p.); 35 cm.
For orchestra.
Reproduced from manuscript.

Composed for: piccolo, 2 flutes, 2 oboes, 2 clarinets, bass clarinet, bassoon, 4 horns, 3 trumpets, 2 trombones, bass trombone, timpani, percussion (suspended cymbal, timpani), violin I, violin II, viola, violoncello, double bass.
Call no.: **1988/079**

1916. Oliverio, James, 1956– Timpani concerto #1 (1987). World premiere ed. 1.1. N.p.: Collected Editions, 1990.
1 score (94 p.); 36 cm.
Performance and composer's program notes.
Composed for: timpani, piccolo, 2 flutes, 2 oboes, English horn, 2 clarinets, bass clarinet, 2 bassoons, contrabassoon, 4 horns, 3 trumpets, 2 trombones, bass trombone, tuba, percussion (marimba, xylophone, woodblock, bass drum, snare drum, glockenspiel, temple bowls, tubular bells, cowbell, lead pipe, suspended cymbal, crash cymbals), harp, violin I, violin II, viola, violoncello, double bass.
Commissioned by: National Endowment for the Arts.
Call no.: **1991/089**

1917. Oliverio, James, 1956– Timpani concerto #1 (1987). World premiere ed. 2.0. N.p.: Collected Editions, 1990.
1 score (96 p.); 43 cm.
Program notes by the composer.
Composed for: timpani, piccolo, 2 flutes, 2 oboes, English horn, 2 clarinets, bass clarinet, 2 bassoons, contrabassoon, 4 horns, 3 trumpets, 2 trombones, bass trombone, tuba, percussion (marimba, xylophone, woodblock, bass drum, snare drum, glockenspiel, temple bowls, tubular bells, cowbell, lead pipe, suspended cymbal, crash cymbals), harp, violin I, violin II, viola, violoncello, double bass.
Commissioned by: National Endowment for the Arts.
Call no.: **1992/097**

1918. Olivero, Betty, 1954– Bakashòt. Partitura. Milano: Casa Ricordi, 1996.
1 score (80 p.); 63 cm.
Hebrew words; also printed as text.
For chorus, clarinet, and orchestra.
Reproduced from manuscript.
Duration: ca. 30:00.
Composed for: clarinet, SATB chorus, 3 flutes (all also piccolo, 2nd–3rd also alto flute), 3 oboes (3rd also English horn), 3 clarinets (2nd–3rd also clarinet in E♭, 3rd also bass clarinet), 3 bassoons (3rd also contrabassoon), 4 horns, 3 trumpets, 3 trombones, tuba, timpani, percussion (2 marimbas, 2 xylophones, glockenspiel, vibraphone, tubular bells, 5 gongs, crotales, 2 sets of roto-toms, 3 large suspended cymbals, tam-tam, bells, tom-toms, bongos, congas, bass drum, tambourine), harp, piano (also celesta), violin I, violin II, viola, violoncello, double bass.
Commissioned by: Norddeutscher Rundfunk.
Call no.: **1997/107**

1919. Olivero, Betty, 1954– Merkavot: per orchestra (1999). Partitura. Italy: Ricordi, 1999.
1 score (71 p.); 42 cm.
Reproduced from manuscript.
Duration: ca. 23:00.
Composed for: 4 flutes (also piccolo and alto flute), 4 oboes (also English horn), 4 clarinets (also clarinet in E♭ and bass clarinet), 3 bassoons (also contrabassoon), 4 horns, 3 trumpets, 3 trombones, tuba, harp, piano (also celesta), percussion (medium suspended cymbal, tam-tam, crotales, xylorimba, large suspended cymbals, gongs, xylophone, bass drum, chimes, vibraphone, glockenspiel), violin I, violin II, viola, violoncello, double bass.
Commissioned by: Jerusalem Symphony Orchestra.
Call no.: **2005/104**

1920. Orbón, Julián, 1925– Partitea no. 4: symphonic movement for piano and orchestra. N.p.: n.p., 198-?.
1 score (135 p.); 30 cm.
Reproduced from manuscript.
Composed for: piano, 2 flutes, 2 oboes, 2 clarinets, 2 bassoons, 4 horns, 3 trumpets, 2 trombones, bass trombone, timpani, percussion (snare drum, medium gong, suspended cymbals, xylophone, bongos, claves, triangle), violin I, violin II, viola, violoncello, double bass.
Commissioned by: Dallas Symphony Orchestra.
Call no.: **1989/089**
Re-entered as: **1990/095**

1921. Orlandi, Amedeo, 1969– A snowy day: ballad. N.p.: n.p., 1992.
1 score (5 leaves); 31 cm.
Melody with chordal accompaniment and chord symbols.
Composed for: unspecified.
Call no.: **1996/111**

1922. Orrego Salas, Juan, 1919– Concierto no. 2, para piano y orquesta, opus 93. N.p.: n.p., 1985.
1 score (90 p.); 33 cm.
Reproduced from manuscript.
Composed for: piano, piccolo, 2 flutes, 2 oboes, English horn, 2 clarinets, bass clarinet, 2 bassoons, 4 horns, 3 trumpets, trombones, tuba, timpani, percussion (vibra-

phone, glockenspiel, suspended cymbal, tom-toms, 2 woodblocks, tambourine, snare drum, cymbals, xylophone, whip, temple blocks, bongos, bass drum), harp, violin I, violin II, viola, violoncello, double bass.
Call no.: **1988/080**

1923. Orrego Salas, Juan, 1919– Concierto para violin y orquesta (1983). N.p.: n.p., 1983.
1 score (30 p.); 33 cm.
Reproduced from holograph.
Composed for: violin, piccolo, 2 flutes, 2 oboes, English horn, 2 clarinets, bass clarinet, 2 bassoons, 4 horns, 2 trumpets, 3 trombones, tuba, timpani, percussion (temple blocks, 2 suspended cymbals, cowbell, triangle, bongos, bass drum, tambourine, snare drum, tom-tom, antique cymbals, woodblock, gong, xylophone, glockenspiel, vibraphone), harp, celesta, violin I, violin II, viola, violoncello, double bass.
Call no.: **1985/149**

1924. Ortega, Sergio, 1938–2003. L'anniversaire de l'infante: conte musical ecrit d'aprés le recit d'Oscar Wilde. N.p.: n.p., 1985.
1 score (90 leaves); 30 x 42 cm.
French words by the composer and Sophie Geoffroy-Dechaume.
Reproduced from manuscript.
Composed for: soprano, 6 children's choruses, flute, clarinet, trumpet, percussion (gongs, bass drum, temple blocks, xylophone, marimba, tam-tam, flexatone, timpani, snare drum, bells, 3 suspended cymbals, guiro, siren, tambourine, whip, castanets, congas, tom-toms, military drum, glockenspiel, vibraphone, bamboo chimes), lute (also guitar), violin I, violin II, viola, violoncello, double bass.
Call no.: **1990/096**
Also available:
Call no.: **1990/096 libretto**

1925. Ortega, Sergio, 1938–2003. Fulgor y muerte de Joaquím Murieta: opera: sur un texte de Pablo Neruda. Boulogne-Billancourt, France: Barcarolle, 1998.
1 score (2 v.); 42 cm.
Spanish words.
Composed for: 12 sopranos, 6 mezzo-sopranos, alto, 8 tenors, 6 baritones, bass-baritone, 6 basses, children's chorus, SATB chorus, women's chorus, 2 flutes (2nd also piccolo), 2 oboes (2nd also English horn), 2 clarinets (2nd also bass clarinet), 2 bassoons, 2 horns, 3 trumpets, 3 trombones, percussion (tam-tam, 2 rain sticks, xylophone, crotales, chimes, marimba, bass drum, vibraphone, gong, maracas, guiro, timbales, bells, flexatone, cencerros, conga, bongo, glockenspiel, espuelas de plata, spring coil, suspended cymbals, snare drum, whip, tambourine, metal sheet, timpani, tom-toms, Thai gong, rattle, temple block, triangle, siren), harp, violin I, violin II, viola, violoncello, double bass.
Call no.: **2000/132**
Also available:
Call no.: **2000/132 libretto**

1926. Ortega, Sergio, 1938–2003. Harcelement et mort d'un homme = Acoso y muerte de un hombre = Harassing and death of a man: sept mouvements pour quatuor à cordes = seven movements for string quartet. Paris: Editions Salabert, 1990.
1 score (29 p.); 42 cm.
Reproduced from manuscript.
Composed for: 2 violins, viola, violoncello.
Call no.: **1992/098**

1927. Ortíz, Gabriela, 1964– Altar de piedra: concerto for orchestra, timpani and three percussion players, 2002. Santoyo, Mexico: Chapela Mendoza, 2003.
1 score (104 p.); 45 cm.
Notes on the composer in Spanish with English translation.
Contents: Un ángel maraquero—Rítmo genésico—Torrente.
Composed for: piccolo, 2 flutes, 2 oboes, 2 clarinets, bass clarinet, 2 bassoons, contrabassoon, 4 horns, 4 trumpets, 2 trombones, bass trombone, tuba, timpani, percussion (large suspended cymbal, tam-tams, 2 Chinese opera gongs, slapstick, maracas, wood chimes, 4 woodblocks, Peruvian box, glockenspiel, crotales, tuned cowbells, marimba, piccolo drum, 4 Chinese tom-toms, snare drum, tenor drum, pedal bass drum, gong, guiro, quijada/jaw bone, 2 teponaztlis, water drum, vibraphone, xylophone, tubular bells, piccolo drum, bongos, congas, triangle, suspended Chinese cymbal, 2 cowbells, 3 Thai gongs, 2 caxixis/African shakers, 5-octave marimba, tom-toms, bass drum), harp, celesta, piano, violin I, violin II, viola, violoncello, double bass.
Commissioned by: Los Angeles Philharmonic.
Call no.: **2005/105**

1928. Ortíz, Gabriela, 1964– Concierto candela: for solo percussion and orchestra (1993). Full score. N.p.: n.p., 1993.
1 score (121 p.); 36 cm.
Duration: ca. 24:00.
Composed for: percussion (marimba, 2 teponaztlis, tuned cowbells, 4 tuned iron pipes, 3 Chinese cymbals, 2 bongos, 4 congas, 2 tom-toms, pedal bass drum, 2

Chinese opera gongs), piccolo, 2 flutes, 2 oboes, 2 clarinets, bass clarinet, 2 bassoons, 4 horns, 3 trumpets, 2 trombones, bass trombone, tuba, timpani, percussion (glockenspiel, bass drum, guiro, 2 crotales, xylophone, claves, woodblock, tambourine, triangle, 5 temple blocks, 3 cowbells, medium suspended cymbal, vibraphone, snare drum, wind chimes, medium tam-tam, tubular bells, large suspended cymbal, large tam-tam, 4 tom-toms), harp, piano, violin I, violin II, viola, violoncello, double bass.
Commissioned by: Ricardo Gallardo.
Call no.: **1997/108**

1929. Osborne, Nigel, 1948– The electrification of the Soviet Union. Full score. London: Universal Edition, 1987.
1 score (2 v.); 37 cm.
English words by Craig Raine from Boris Pasternak's novella The last summer and from his poem Spectorsky.
Opera.
Reproduced from manuscript.
Composed for: 3 sopranos, mezzo-soprano, 3 baritones, bass, 2 flutes (2nd also alto flute), 2 oboes (2nd also English horn), 2 clarinets (2nd also bass clarinet), 2 bassoons (2nd also contrabassoon), 3 horns, 2 trumpets, 2 trombones, tuba, timpani, percussion (5 cymbals, 3 tam-tams, tubular bells, vibraphone, crotales, antique cymbals, triangle, 2 snare drums, bass drum, sizzle cymbal, wind machine, timbales, 2 hi-hats, 3 gongs, marimba, celesta, flexatone, xylorimba), harp, piano, violin I, violin II, viola, violoncello, double bass.
Commissioned by: BBC.
Call no.: **1989/090**

1930. Ott, David, 1947– Concerto for three brass. N.p.: n.p., 1991.
1 score (96 p.); 43 cm.
Reproduced from holograph.
At end: Grayton Beach, Fla. Dec. 19, 1990.
Composed for: horn, trumpet, trombone, piccolo, 2 flutes, 2 oboes, 2 clarinets, 2 bassoons, 3 horns, 2 trumpets, 2 trombones, tuba, timpani, percussion (glockenspiel, crash cymbals, bass drum, snare drum, suspended cymbal, xylophone, tam-tam, tenor drum, crotales, woodblock), harp, violin I, violin II, viola, violoncello, double bass.
Commissioned by: National Symphony Orchestra.
Call no.: **1992/099**

1931. Ott, David, 1947– Concerto for two cellos. N.p.: n.p., 1987.
1 score (90 p.); 36 cm.
Reproduced from holograph.
Duration: 23:00.
Composed for: 2 violoncellos, piccolo, 2 flutes (2nd also alto flute), 2 oboes, 2 clarinets, 2 bassoons, contrabassoon, 4 horns, 3 trumpets, 3 trombones, tuba, timpani, percussion (vibraphone, xylophone, snare drum, tambourine, suspended cymbal, crash cymbals, tubular bells, tam-tam, triangle, bass drum, tenor drum), harp, violin I, violin II, viola, violoncello, double bass.
Commissioned by: National Symphony Orchestra.
Call no.: **1989/091**

1932. Owen, Jerry, 1944– Concerto: for piano and orchestra. N.p.: n.p., 1990.
1 score (130 p.); 36 cm.
Duration: 24:00.
Contents: Salutations—Monologues and dialogues—Confluence.
Composed for: piano, 2 flutes (2nd also piccolo), 2 oboes, 2 clarinets, 2 bassoons, 4 horns, 2 trumpets, 2 trombones, bass trombone, tuba, timpani, percussion (snare drum, orchestra bells, bass drum, triangle, wind chimes, xylophone, suspended cymbal, crash cymbals, splash cymbal), violin I, violin II, viola, violoncello, double bass.
Call no.: **1993/105**

1933. Owen, Jerry, 1944– The mystic trumpeter: a cantata for string orchestra, mixed chorus and soprano, alto, tenor, and baritone solists [sic]. Cedar Rapids, IA: Jerry M. Owen, 1988.
1 score (129 p.); 30 cm.
English words.
Based on the poem by Walt Whitman.
Composed for: soprano, alto, tenor, baritone, SATB chorus, violin I, violin II, viola, violoncello, double bass.
Commissioned by: Beta Kappa Chapter of Phi Mu Alpha Sinfonia.
Call no.: **1989/092**

1934. Owen, Richard, 1922– Abigail Adams: opera in two acts. N.p.: Richard Owen, 1987.
1 score (132 p.); 36 cm.
English words by the composer.
Reproduced from manuscript.
Composed for: voices, flute, trumpet, horn, piano, violin, violoncello, percussion (timpani, snare drum).
Call no.: **1988/081**

1935. Paccione, Paul, 1952– Three medieval English songs. Hanover, NH: Frog Peak Music, 1992.
1 score (49 p.); 28 cm.
Middle English words; also printed as text.

For choir (SATB) and orchestra.
Texts from Chaucer (mvts. 1 & 3).
Includes historical information in English.
Contents: Merciless beauty—I sing of a maiden—Welcome, summer.
Composed for: SATB chorus, 2 flutes, oboe, 2 clarinets, bassoon, 2 horns, violin I, violin II, viola, violoncello, double bass.
Commissioned by: Western Illinois University's College of Fine Arts.
Call no.: **1994/106**

1936. Palermo, Vincenzo, 1967– Concerto per pianoforte e orchestra (1992). N.p.: n.p., 1992.
1 score (224 p.); 30 cm.
"Prima revisione."
Duration: ca. 24:00.
Composed for: piano, piccolo, 2 flutes, 2 oboes, English horn, 2 clarinets, 2 bassoons, contrabassoon, 4 horns, 2 trumpets, 3 trombones, tuba, timpani, percussion (cymbals, triangle), violin I, violin II, viola, violoncello, double bass.
Call no.: **1993/106**

1937. Páll P. Pálsson, 1928– Symphony "Northern lights" = Sinfonie Nordlicht, 1998. Partitur. N.p.: n.p., 1998.
1 score (93 p.); 30 cm.
Reproduced from manuscript.
Duration: ca. 30:00.
Composed for: 2 flutes (2nd also piccolo), 2 oboes, 2 clarinets, 2 bassoons, 3 horns, 3 trumpets, 2 trombones, bass trombone, tuba, timpani, percussion (glockenspiel, vibraphone, marimba, cymbals, tam-tam, bongos, tom-toms, snare drum, field drum, bass drum), violin I, violin II, viola, violoncello, double bass.
Call no.: **2001/111**

1938. Palmer, John, 1959– Koan: for shakuhachi & chamber ensemble. N.p.: n.p., 1999.
1 score (vi, 60 p.); 30 x 42 cm.
Reproduced from manuscript.
Duration: ca. 18:00.
Performance instructions in English.
Composed for: shakuhachi, flute (also alto flute), oboe (also English horn), clarinet (also bass clarinet), percussion (marimba, vibraphone, maracas, bamboo chimes, 5 temple blocks, large suspended cymbal, 3 tam-tams [large, medium, small], 7 roto-toms, handbell [middle range], 2 crystal glasses, 2 congas, cimbalom), piano (without lid), violin, viola, violoncello.
Call no.: **2004/091**

1939. Panufnik, Andrzej, 1914–1991. Arbor cosmica.
Call no.: **1985/150**
No materials available.

1940. Panufnik, Andrzej, 1914–1991. Concerto for bassoon and small orchestra. N.p.: n.p., 1985.
1 score (43 leaves); 42 cm.
Reproduced from holograph, with corrections from the premiere performance, 19 May 1986.
Composed for: bassoon, flute, 2 clarinets, violin I, violin II, viola, violoncello, double bass.
Commissioned by: University of Wisconsin at Milwaukee and Polanki (Polish Women's Cultural Club of Milwaukee).
Call no.: **1987/060**

1941. Panufnik, Andrzej, 1914–1991. Symphony no. 10. Full score. N.p.: n.p., 1990.
1 score (57 p.); 31 cm.
Duration: ca 19:00.
"Revised, June 1990."
Reproduced from holograph.
Composed for: 3 flutes, 2 oboes, English horn, 3 clarinets (3rd also bass clarinet), 2 bassoons, contrabassoon, 6 horns, 3 trumpets, 3 trombones, tuba, percussion (snare drum, tenor drum, bass drum, cymbals, gong, tam-tam), harp, piano, violin I, violin II, viola, violoncello, double bass.
Commissioned by: Chicago Symphony Orchestra.
Call no.: **1991/090**

1942. Parać, Frano, 1948– Simfonija. Croatia: Pliva, 1992.
1 score (64 p.); 39 cm.
Duration: ca. 17:00.
Composed for: 2 flutes (2nd also piccolo), 2 oboes, 2 clarinets, 2 bassoons, 4 horns, 2 trumpets, 3 trombones, tuba, timpani, percussion (tam-tam, suspended cymbal, military drum, triangle, xylophone, bell), harp, violin I, violin II, viola, violoncello, double bass.
Call no.: **1994/107**

1943. Parella, Marc, 1963– Sex. for strings. N.p.: n.p., 199-?.
1 score (39 p.); 28 cm.
Composed for: 2 violins, 2 violas, violoncello, double bass.
Call no.: **1992/100**

1944. Parker, Alice, 1925– Songs from the dragon quilt. N.p.: A. Parker, 1984.
1 score (150 p.); 44 cm.

English words by Sheila Nickerson; also printed as text.
For narrator, soprano solo, chorus, and chamber orchestra.
Reproduced from holograph.
Contents: Basket of scraps—Sunshine and shadow—Black velvet raven—Dragon cloud—Alpenglow—Storm at sea—Tree everlasting—Hands all around—Variable star.
Composed for: narrator, soprano, SATB chorus, flute, alto flute, bassoon, horn, trumpet, trombone, timpani, percussion (triangle, woodblock, drum, tam-tam, orchestra bells, xylophone, rattle, shells), harp, violin I, violin II, viola, violoncello, double bass.
Commissioned by: Juneau (Alaska) Oratorio Choir.
Call no.: **1985/151**

1945. Parmentier, F. Gordon, 1921– The lost dauphin: opera in 3 acts. N.p.: F.G. Parmentier, 1999.
1 score (366 p.); 28 cm.
Principally English words.
Includes "Bayshore Opera translations" from Oneida into English.
Reproduced from manuscript.
Annotated for performance.
Composed for: 3 sopranos, 3 altos, contralto, 3 tenors, baritone, bass-baritone, bass, SATB chorus, children's chorus, 2 flutes (1st also piccolo), 2 oboes, English horn, 2 clarinets, bass clarinet, 2 bassoons, contrabassoon, 4 horns, 3 trumpets, 3 trombones, tuba, timpani, percussion (bells, snare drum, tom-tom, rattle, glockenspiel, cymbals, tambourine, woodblock, bass drum), harp, piano, harpsichord, banjo, violin I, violin II, viola, violoncello, double bass.
Call no.: **2002/135**
Re-entered as: **2005/106**
Also available:
Call no.: **2005/106 libretto**
Call no.: **2005/106 vocal score**

1946. Parmentier, F. Gordon, 1921– Odyssey: Voyage to the inland seas.
Call no.: **1986/087**
No materials available.

1947. Parmentier, F. Gordon, 1921– Two gothic loves. N.p.: n.p., 1989.
1 score (52 p.); 34 cm.
English words by the composer.
Reproduced from manuscript.
Composed for: soprano, alto, tenor, baritone, SATB chorus, clarinet, piano, percussion (small bells, tenor drum, cymbals), 15–25 violins, 8–12 violoncellos.
Call no.: **1991/091**

1948. Parris, Robert, 1924– Chamber music for orchestra: (1984). N.p.: n.p., 1985.
1 score (85 leaves); 51 cm.
Reproduced from manuscript.
Contents: Nocturne—Burlesque—Variations.
Composed for: piccolo, 2 flutes, 2 oboes, clarinet in E♭, 2 clarinets, bass clarinet, 2 bassoons, contrabassoon, 4 horns, 3 trumpets (1st also trumpet in D), 2 trombones, bass trombone, tuba, percussion (vibraphone, bells, timpani, bass drum, suspended cymbals, crash cymbals, tam-tam, xylophone, marimba, wind machine, drum set [pedal bass drum, floor tom-tom, timbales, 2 bongos, side drum, cowbell, hi-hat, triangle, 5 temple blocks, cymbals]), harp, celesta, violin I, violin II, viola, violoncello, double bass.
Call no.: **1986/088**

1949. Parris, Robert, 1924– Symphonic variations: for orchestra. N.p.: n.p., 1987.
1 score (96 leaves); 44 cm.
Reproduced from manuscript.
Composed for: 3 flutes (3rd also piccolo), 2 oboes, clarinet in E♭, 2 clarinets, bass clarinet, 2 bassoons, contrabassoon, soprano saxophone, alto saxophone, tenor saxophone, 4 horns, 4 trumpets (1st–3rd also piccolo trumpet), 3 trombones (1st–2nd also euphonium), tuba, timpani, percussion (trap set, bass drum, 3 tom-toms, side drum, cymbals, hi-hat, tam-tam, bells, vibraphone, suspended cymbal, crash cymbals), harp, piano, celesta, violin I, violin II, viola, violoncello, double bass.
Commissioned by: National Symphony Orchestra.
Call no.: **1989/093**

1950. Pärt, Arvo, 1935– Cecilia, vergine romana: für Chor (SATB) und Orchester (2000, rev.2002). Studienpartitur. Wien: Universal Edition, 2002.
1 miniature score (50 p.); 30 cm.
Italian words; also printed as text with English translation.
Text: Breviario Romano, 22 novembre, terza lettura.
Duration: ca. 17:00–19:00.
Composed for: SATB chorus, 2 flutes, 2 oboes (2nd also piccolo), 2 clarinets, 2 bassoons (2nd also contrabassoon), 4 horns, 2 trumpets, 2 trombones, tuba, percussion (glockenspiel, chimes, triangle, snare drum, bass drum), harp, violin I, violin II, viola, violoncello, double bass.
Commissioned by: Agenzia Romana.
Call no.: **2003/092**

1951. Pärt, Arvo, 1935– Como anhela la cierva: für Sopran und Orchester (1998, rev. 1999). Studienpartitur. Wien: Universal Edition, 1999.

1 score (vii, 96 p.); 30 cm.
For soprano solo and orchestra.
Spanish words from Psalms 42–43 (41–42); also printed as text with English and German translations.
"Ausgabe 08.09.1999."
Duration: ca. 30:00.
Composed for: soprano, piccolo, 2 flutes (2nd also alto flute), 2 oboes, English horn, 2 clarinets, bass clarinet, 2 bassoons, contrabassoon, 4 horns, 2 trumpets, 3 trombones, percussion (xylophone, glockenspiel, tubular bells, timpani, castanets, temple block, triangle, cymbals, tambourine, piccolo snare drum, tam-tam, bass drum), harp, violin I, violin II, viola, violoncello, double bass.
Commissioned by: 15° Festival de Musica de Canarias.
Call no.: **2001/112**

1952. Pärt, Arvo, 1935– Kanon pokajanen: für Chor (SATB) a cappella (1997). Studienpartitur. Wien: Universal Edition, 1998.
1 miniature score (xvi, 163 p.); 30 cm.
Church Slavonic words (Cyrillic and romanized); also printed as text (Cyrillic) with German and English translations.
Based on the Canon of repentance attributed to Saint Andrew of Crete.
"Provisorische Ausgabe, 04.01.1998."
Composed for: SATB chorus.
Commissioned by: Kölnmusik GmbH.
Call no.: **2000/133**

1953. Pärt, Arvo, 1935– Lamentate: homage to Anish Kapoor and his sculpture "Marsyas": for piano and orchestra (2002). Studienpartitur. Wien: Universal Edition, 2003.
1 score (69 p.); 30 cm.
"Ausgabe 26.09.2003."
Duration: ca. 35:00–40:00.
Composed for: piano, piccolo, 2 flutes (also alto flute), 2 oboes (also English horn), 2 clarinets in A, 2 bassoons, 4 horns, 2 trumpets, 2 trombones, 5 timpani, percussion (tubular bells, 3 suspended cymbals, tambourine, military drum, large marimba, vibraphone, tam-tam, glockenspiel, triangle, 2 cymbals, 2 tom-toms, bass drum), violin I, violin II, viola, violoncello, double bass.
Commissioned by: Tate and Egg Live.
Call no.: **2005/163**

1954. Pärt, Arvo, 1935– Litany: prayers of St. John Chrysostom for each hour of the day and night: per soli (A[Ct]TTB), coro (SATB) ed orchestra (1994). Partitura. Wien: Universal Edition, 1994.
1 score (88 p.); 37 cm.
English words; also printed as text.
"Korr. 4.5.1994/j.s.d."
"Autori töö partituur, 28 VIII 94."
Reproduced from manuscript.
Duration: 30:00.
Composed for: alto (or countertenor), 2 tenors, bass, SATB chorus, 2 flutes (both also piccolo), 2 oboes, 2 clarinets in A, 2 bassoons, 2 horns, trumpet, trombone, percussion (tubular bells, timpani, triangle, tam-tam, bass drum), violin I, violin II, viola, violoncello, double bass.
Commissioned by: Oregon Bach Festival.
Call no.: **1995/078**

1955. Pärt, Arvo, 1935– Litany: prayers of St. John Chrysostom for each hour of the day and night: per soli (A[Ct]TTB), coro (SATB) ed orchestra (1994). Partitura. Wien: Universal Edition, 1995.
1 score (89 p.); 38 cm.
English words, also printed as text.
"Korr. 4.5.1994/j.s.d. + ua-korr. 28.8.1994/a.p."
"2/95"—p. 1 of cover.
Reproduced from manuscript.
Duration: ca. 30:00.
Composed for: alto (or countertenor), 2 tenors, bass, SATB chorus, 2 flutes (both also piccolo), 2 oboes, 2 clarinets in A, 2 bassoons, 2 horns, trumpet, trombone, percussion (tubular bells, timpani, triangle, tam-tam, bass drum), violin I, violin II, viola, violoncello, double bass.
Commissioned by: Oregon Bach Festival.
Call no.: **1996/112**

1956. Pärt, Arvo, 1935– Stabat Mater. Partitur. Wien: Universal Edition, 1985.
1 score (40 p.); 24 x 31 cm.
For SAT soloists and string trio.
Duration: ca. 20:00–25:00.
Composed for: soprano, alto, tenor, violin, viola, violoncello.
Call no.: **1990/097**

1957. Pasquotti, Corrado, 1954– Quartetto i "Riflessi." Partitura. Milano: Ricordi, 1983.
1 score (15 p.); 62 cm.
Reproduced from holograph.
Composed for: 2 violins, viola, violoncello.
Commissioned by: Festival di Musica Contemporanea di Bolzano.
Call no.: **1985/152**

1958. Patterson, Andy J., 1929– Oratorio: prayers, prophecies, and praises. N.p.: n.p., 1989.

1 score (ca. 300 p.); 44 cm.
English words.
Reproduced from manuscript.
Composed for: clarinet, SATB chorus, 2 flutes, 2 oboes, 2 clarinets, 2 bassoons, 3 horns, 2 trumpets, 2 trombones, tuba, timpani, percussion (triangle, cymbals, orchestra bells, snare drum, tambourine, suspended cymbal, tubular chimes), harp, violin I, violin II, viola, violoncello, double bass.
Commissioned by: Hardin-Simmons University Centennial Committee.
Call no.: **1992/101**

1959. Paulus, Stephen, 1949– The age of American passions: for orchestra. N.p.: n.p., 1999.
1 score (87 p.); 44 cm.
Duration: ca. 23:00.
Composed for: 2 flutes, 2 oboes, 2 clarinets, 2 bassoons, 4 horns, 2 trumpets, 2 trombones, bass trombone, tuba, timpani, percussion (snare drum, bass drum, tom-toms, chimes, crash cymbals, hi-hat, xylophone, ratchet, brake drum, woodblocks, large tam-tam, temple blocks, large suspended cymbal), violin I, violin II, viola, violoncello, double bass.
Commissioned by: Louisiana Symphony Association.
Call no.: **2000/134**

1960. Paulus, Stephen, 1949– Concerto for string quartet and orchestra: (three places of enlightenment). N.p.: n.p., 1994.
1 score (92 p.); 44 cm.
Contents: From within—From afar—From all around and radiating ever outward.
Composed for: 2 violins, viola, violoncello, 3 flutes (3rd also piccolo), 3 oboes, 3 clarinets, 3 bassoons, 4 horns, 3 trumpets, 3 trombones, tuba, timpani, percussion (brake drum, tom-toms, bass drum, xylophone, large suspended cymbal, hi-hat, temple blocks, crash cymbals, large tam-tam, chimes, snare drum), harp, piano, violin I, violin II, viola, violoncello, double bass.
Commissioned by: Richard J. Bogomolny and Patricia M. Kozerefsky.
Call no.: **1997/109**

1961. Paulus, Stephen, 1949– Concerto for violin, 'cello and orchestra: (the veil of illusion). N.p.: European American Music, 1994.
1 score (102 p.); 44 cm.
Duration: ca. 25:00.
Composed for: violin, violoncello, 3 flutes (also piccolo), 3 oboes, 3 clarinets, 3 bassoons, 4 horns, 3 trumpets, 3 trombones, tuba, timpani, percussion (large suspended cymbal, tom-toms, bass drum, marimba, chimes, maracas, woodblocks (low, high), xylophone, guiro, slapstick, vibraphone, snare drum, tambourine, bell tree, hi-hat, temple blocks, brake drum, large tam-tam, handbells, crash cymbals), harp, violin I, violin II, viola, violoncello, double bass.
Commissioned by: New York Philharmonic and Atlanta Symphony Orchestra.
Call no.: **1995/079**

1962. Paulus, Stephen, 1949– Mass: for mixed chorus, timpani, percussion, harp, organ and strings. Full score. N.p.: n.p., 1999.
1 score (114 p.); 28 cm.
Latin words.
Duration: 25:00.
Composed for: SATB chorus, timpani, percussion (chimes, suspended cymbal, hi-hat, tom-toms, snare drum, bass drum, tam-tam, crash cymbals, bell tree, glockenspiel), harp, organ, violin I, violin II, viola, violoncello, double bass.
Commissioned by: New Choral Society of Central Westchester.
Call no.: **2001/113**
Also available:
Call no.: **2001/113 vocal score**

1963. Paulus, Stephen, 1949– Voices: for chorus and orchestra. N.p.: European American Music, 1988.
1 score (249 p.); 28 cm.
English words; also printed as text.
Text from English translations of poems by Rainer Maria Rilke.
Reproduced from holograph.
Duration: 35:00.
Contents: Opening—Song of the beggar—Song of the drunkard—Song of the suicide—Song of the leper—I am, o anxious one—As once the winged energy of delight—Voices.
Composed for: SATB chorus, 3 flutes (3rd also piccolo), 3 oboes, 3 clarinets, 3 bassoons, 4 horns, 3 trumpets, 3 trombones, tuba, timpani, percussion (crash cymbals, tom-toms, 2 bass drums, snare drum, hi-hat, xylophone, tam-tam, suspended cymbal, vibraphone, crotales, ratchet, slapstick, castanets, 2 woodblocks, chimes), harp, piano (also celesta), violin I, violin II, viola, violoncello, double bass.
Commissioned by: Association for Clinical Pastoral Education and Minnesota Orchestral Association.
Call no.: **1989/094**

1964. Pavlov, Filip, 1949– Sinfonische Ouvertüre: für Streichorchester. N.p.: n.p., 1995.
1 score (27 p.); 30 cm.

Reproduced from holograph.
Composed for: violin I, violin II, viola, violoncello, double bass.
Call no.: **1996/113**

1965. Payne, Anthony, 1936– Time's arrow. London: Chester Music, 1990.
1 score (142 p.); 30 cm.
For orchestra.
Reproduced from manuscript.
Composed for: 3 flutes, 2 oboes, English horn, 3 clarinets, 2 bassoons, contrabassoon, 6 horns, 4 trumpets, 3 trombones, tuba, timpani, percussion (bass drum, gong, suspended cymbals, glockenspiel, tom-toms, tubular bells, crotales), harp, violin I, violin II, viola, violoncello, double bass.
Commissioned by: BBC.
Call no.: **1991/092**

1966. Pécou, Thierry, 1965– Symphonie du jaguar: pour cinq voix de femmes, solistes et orchestre. Paris: Editions musicales européennes, 2002.
1 score (128 p.); 42 cm.
Mayan and French words.
Texts from the Chilam Balam, freely translated by the composer.
Note by the composer and pronunciation guide in French.
Composed for: 3 sopranos, mezzo-soprano, contralto, clarinet, trombone, violin, violoncello, 3 flutes (also piccolo), 3 oboes, 3 clarinets, 2 bassoons, contrabassoon, 4 horns, piccolo trumpet, 3 trumpets, 3 trombones, tuba, percussion, timpani, violin I, violin II, viola, violoncello, double bass.
Commissioned by: Radio France.
Call no.: **2005/107**

1967. Peel, John, 1946– Concerto for violin and orchestra. N.p.: n.p., 2000.
1 score (198 p.); 44 cm.
Composed for: violin, 2 flutes (2nd also piccolo and alto flute), 2 oboes (2nd also English horn), 2 clarinets (2nd also bass clarinet), 2 bassoons (2nd also contrabassoon), 4 horns, 2 trumpets, trombone, bass trombone, percussion (bass drum, crotales, glockenspiel, snare drum, suspended cymbal, triangle, tam-tam, tambourine, xylophone), timpani, celesta, harp, violin I, violin II, viola, violoncello, double bass.
Call no.: **2003/093**

1968. Peel, John, 1947– Voces vergiliannae: opera-oratorio in four scenes. N.p.: n.p., 1998.
1 score (3 v. [273 p.]); 44 cm.
Latin words by M.D. Usher after Virgil.
Composed for: female voice, male voice, SATB chorus, 2 flutes (1st–2nd also piccolo, 2nd and alto flute), 2 oboes (2nd also English horn), 2 clarinets (1st–2nd also clarinet in A, 1st also clarinet in E♭), bass clarinet, 2 bassoons (2nd also contrabassoon), 4 horns, 2 off-stage horns, 2 trumpets, 2 trombones, bass trombone, timpani, celesta, percussion, harp, violin I, violin II, viola, violoncello, double bass.
Commissioned by: Williamette University.
Call no.: **2001/114**

1969. Penderecki, Krzysztof, 1933– Adagio: für Orchester (1989). Partitur. Mainz; New York, NY: Schott, 1989.
1 score (80 p.); 39 cm.
Duration: ca. 33:00.
1992 Grawemeyer Award winning work.
Composed for: piccolo, 2 flutes, 2 oboes, English horn, clarinet in E♭, 2 clarinets, bass clarinet, 2 bassoons, contrabassoon, 5 horns, 3 trumpets, 4 trombones, tuba, timpani, percussion (triangle, cymbals, tam-tam, military drum, roto-toms, tambourine, jingling jonnie, chimes, xylophone, mounted triangle, mounted crotales), harp, piano, celesta, violin I, violin II, viola, violoncello, double bass.
Call no.: **1992/102**

1970. Penderecki, Krzysztof, 1933– Polish requiem.
Call no.: **1985/153**
No materials available.

1971. Penderecki, Krzysztof, 1933– Die schwarze Maske: Oper in einem Akt nach dem gleichnamigen Schauspiel von Gerhart Hauptmann (1985/86). Partitur. Mainz: Schott, 1986.
1 score (281 p.); 59 cm.
Words by Harry Kupfer and Krzysztof Penderecki.
Reproduced from holograph.
Composed for: 3 sopranos, mezzo-soprano, alto, 4 tenors, baritone, bass-baritone, 4 basses, SATB chorus, stage band (2 piccolos, 2 clarinets in E♭, 3 trumpets, 3 trombones, 3 recorders, percussion [snare drum, tenor drum, 2 military drums, 2 ratchets, castanets, sleigh bells, timbales, tambourine], harpsichord, violoncello), 3 flutes (3rd also piccolo), 2 oboes, English horn, 3 clarinets (3rd also clarinet in E♭), bass clarinet, soprano saxophone, 2 alto saxophones, 2 bassoons, contrabassoon, 4 horns, 3 trumpets, 3 trombones, tuba, timpani, percussion (bass drum, military drum, tenor drum, tambourine, 6 timbales, roto-toms, 6 tom-toms, 6 suspended cymbals, glockenspiel, chimes, 3 tam-tams, 2 gongs, xylophone, vibraphone, marimba,

guiro, flexatone, slide whistle, castanets, crotales, sleigh bells, whip, vibraslap, church bells, bell tree, suspended triangle), organ, celesta, violin I, violin II, viola, violoncello, double bass.
Commissioned by: Salzburger Festspiele.
Call no.: **1987/061**

1972. Penhorwood, Edwin, 1939– Too many sopranos: a comic opera in two acts. Bloomington, IN: T.I.S. Music, 2000.
1 score (275 p.); 44 cm.
English words by Miki L. Thompson.
Composed for: voices, 2 flutes (2nd also piccolo), 2 oboes, 2 clarinets, 2 bassoons, 2 horns, 2 trumpets, bass trombone, piano, celesta, harp, timpani, percussion (bass drum, cymbals, snare drum, triangle, bongos, claves), violin I, violin II, viola, violoncello, double bass.
Call no.: **2002/136**

1973. Pennisi, Francesco, 1934–2000. Tristan: studio per una azione musicale sul "Play modelled [sic] on the Noh" di Ezra Pound (1995). Partitura. Milano: G. Ricordi, 1995.
1 score (136 p.); 42 cm.
English words; also printed as text with Italian translation.
Reproduced from holograph.
Composed for: 2 sopranos, tenor, baritone, 2 flutes (2nd also piccolo), oboe, clarinet, bass clarinet, bassoon, horn, percussion (glockenspiel, triangle, bell plates, gong, 3 large tom-toms, 3 woodblocks, marimba, 2 suspended cymbals, shell wind chimes, guiro, timpani, vibraphone), harp, piano (also celesta), violin I, violin II, viola, violoncello, double bass.
Commissioned by: Teatro Comunale di Bolonga.
Call no.: **1997/110**

1974. Pépin, Clermont, 1926– Implosion: symphonie no. 5 (1983). N.p.: n.p., 1983.
1 score (120 p.); 41 cm.
Reproduced from holograph.
Composed for: 3 flutes (3rd also piccolo), 2 oboes, English horn, 3 clarinets, 3 bassoons, 5 horns, 3 trumpets, 2 trombones, bass trombone, tuba, timpani, percussion (crotales, 6 suspended cymbals, 3 woodblocks, 3 African tree drums, log drum, slit drum, xylophone, 7 small gongs, 2 brake drums, 5 steel plates, vibraphone, 5 Balinese gongs, 5 tom-toms, 5 tam-tams, military drum, field drum, marimba), harp, violin I, violin II, viola, violoncello, double bass.
Commissioned by: Orchestre Symphonique de Montréal.
Call no.: **1985/154**

1975. Pérez, Juan Carlos, 1958– String quartet, n. 1. N.p.: n.p., 199-?.
1 score (ca. 81 p.); 30 cm.
Reproduced from holograph.
Composed for: 2 violins, viola, violoncello.
Call no.: **1998/120**

1976. Perle, George, 1915– Brief encounters: 14 movements for string quartet. Boston, MA: Galaxy Music, 1999.
1 score (69 p.); 31 cm.
Duration: 26:00.
Composed for: 2 violins, viola, violoncello.
Commissioned by: Rosemary Schnell.
Call no.: **2001/115**

1977. Perle, George, 1915– Concerto for piano and orchestra. Boston, MA: Galaxy Music: E.C. Schirmer, 1990.
1 score (104 p.); 36 cm.
Duration: ca. 25:00.
Composed for: piano, 4 flutes (4th also piccolo), 3 oboes, English horn, 4 clarinets (4th also bass clarinet), 4 bassoons (4th also contrabassoon), 4 horns, 4 trumpets, 3 trombones, tuba, timpani, percussion (xylophone, marimba, tam-tam, 2 triangles, crash cymbals, suspended cymbals, snare drum, celesta, chimes), harp, violin I, violin II, viola, violoncello, double bass.
Commissioned by: San Francisco Symphony.
Call no.: **1992/103**

1978. Perle, George, 1915– Concerto no. 2 for piano and orchestra. Full score. Boston, MA: ECS Pub., 1992.
1 score (75 p.); 31 cm.
Duration: ca. 18:00.
Composed for: piano, piccolo, flute, 2 oboes, 2 clarinets, 2 bassoons, 4 horns, 2 trumpets, timpani, percussion (glockenspiel, snare drum, whip, vibraphone), violin I, violin II, viola, violoncello, double bass.
Commissioned by: Serge Koussevitzky Music Foundation in the Library of Congress, Utah Symphony, Columbus Symphony, Orchestra of St. Luke's, Fairfield Orchestra, and Richmond Symphony.
Call no.: **1994/108**

1979. Perle, George, 1915– Critical moments 2: (in nine movements). Boston, MA: ECS Pub., 2002.
1 score (41 p.); 31 cm.
Duration: 11:00.
Composed for: flute (also alto flute), clarinet (also bass clarinet), violin, violoncello, piano, percussion (triangle, temple blocks, suspended cymbals, 3 tom-toms, bongos, woodblock, snare drum, gong, xylophone, vibraphone).

Commissioned by: Walter W. Naumburg Foundation.
Call no.: **2004/092**

1980. Perle, George, 1915– Serenade no. 3: for piano and chamber orchestra.
Commissioned by: Frank Taplin.
Call no.: **1985/155**
No materials available.

1981. Permont, Haim, 1950– Dear son of mine: chamber opera in 6 scenes (1995/99). Tel Aviv: Israel Music Institute, 2000.
1 score (253 p.); 42 cm.
Hebrew words (romanized) by Talma Alyagon-Ros.
Duration: ca. 1:30:00.
Composed for: soprano, alto, tenor, bass-baritone, flute (also piccolo), oboe (also English horn), clarinet, bassoon, horn, trumpet, trombone, percussion (glockenspiel, vibraphone, tambourine, darbuka, tom-tom, 2 congas, timpani), violin I, violin II, viola, violoncello, double bass.
Commissioned by: New Israeli Opera, Jehoshua Rabinovitz Foundation for the Arts, and Israel Music Institute.
Call no.: **2002/137**
Also available:
Call no.: **2002/137 libretto**

1982. Permont, Haim, 1950– Like the leaden sky before it rains: for alto, choir, piano and orchestra. N.p.: n.p., 1994.
1 score (64 p.); 42 cm.
Hebrew words; also printed as text.
Reproduced from manuscript.
"To text by an anonymous boy at the Terezenstadt Ghetto."
Translated by Lea Goldberg.
Composed for: alto, SATB chorus, piano, 2 flutes (1st also piccolo), 2 oboes, 2 clarinets, 2 bassoons, 2 horns, 2 trumpets, timpani, violin I, violin II, viola, violoncello, double bass.
Call no.: **1996/114**

1983. Pernes, Thomas, 1956– Rückblende. Studienpartitur. Wien: Universal Edition, 1985.
1 score (iii, 65 p.); 42 cm.
Latin words; also printed as text.
For tenor, baritone, piano, improvised percussion, tape, mixed chorus, and orchestra.
Text: prologue of Gospel of St. John.
Reproduced from manuscript.
Duration: ca. 45:00.
Composed for: tenor, baritone, piano, tape, SATB chorus, 3 flutes (3rd also piccolo), 3 oboes (3rd also English horn), 3 clarinets (3rd also bass clarinet), 3 bassoons (3rd also contrabassoon), 6 horns, 4 trumpets, 4 trombones, tuba, percussion (timpani, 3 tom-toms, 4 bell plates, whip, 5 steel plates, hammer, antique cymbals, bass drum, suspended cymbal, 2 tam-tams, 2 suspended cymbals), violin I, violin II, viola, violoncello, double bass.
Commissioned by: Liva.
Call no.: **1988/082**

1984. Peterson, Wayne, 1927– And the winds shall blow: a fantasy for saxophone quartet, winds and percussion. N.p.: n.p., 1994.
1 score (137 p.); 44 cm.
Reproduced from manuscript.
Composed for: soprano saxophone, alto saxophone, tenor saxophone, bass saxophone, 3 flutes (3rd also piccolo), 2 oboes, English horn, 2 clarinets, bass clarinet, 2 bassoons, 4 horns, 3 trumpets, 2 trombones, bass trombone, tuba, timpani, harp, piano (also celesta), percussion (suspended cymbal, tambourine, 5 temple blocks, 2 woodblocks, vibraphone, glockenspiel, triangle, tam-tam, marimba, 2 bongos, 2 timbales, 2 tom-toms, snare drum, vibraslap).
Commissioned by: Philharmonic Orchestra of Freiburg.
Call no.: **1996/115**

1985. Peterson, Wayne, 1927– The face of the night, the heart of the dark: for orchestra. New York, NY: Henmar Press, 1992.
1 score (123 p.); 44 cm.
Reproduced from manuscript.
Composed for: 3 flutes (3rd also piccolo and alto flute), 2 oboes, English horn, 2 clarinets, bass clarinet, 2 bassoons, contrabassoon, 4 horns, 3 trumpets, 3 bass trombones, tuba, timpani, percussion (2 cymbals, tambourine, triangle, claves, glockenspiel, vibraphone, finger cymbals, 2 woodblocks, castanets, 5 temple blocks, 2 cowbells, vibraslap, snare drum, bass drum, tam-tams, crotales, whip, tenor drum, 2 bongos, 2 timbales, 2 tom-toms, marimba, xylophone), harp, piano (also celesta), violin I, violin II, viola, violoncello, double bass.
Commissioned by: San Francisco Symphony.
Call no.: **1993/107**

1986. Peterson, Wayne, 1927– String quartet # 2. N.p.: Wayne Peterson, 1991.
1 score (50 p.); 22 x 28 cm.
Contents: Apparitions—Jazz play.
Composed for: 2 violins, viola, violoncello.
Commissioned by: Composers, Inc.
Call no.: **1994/109**

1987. Peterson, Wayne, 1927– Vicissitudes: for chamber ensemble. N.p.: n.p., 1995.
1 score (80 p.); 28 cm.
Composed for: flute (also piccolo and alto flute), clarinet (also bass clarinet), percussion (3 cymbals, tambourine, triangle, 3 cowbells, brass bar, medium tam-tam, vibraslap, 5 temple blocks, snare drum, 2 bongos, 2 timbales, 2 tom-toms, crotales, vibraphone, marimba), piano, violin, violoncello.
Commissioned by: Fromm Music Foundation.
Call no.: **2002/138**

1988. Peterson, Wayne, 1927– Vicissitudes: for chamber ensemble. N.p.: n.p., 1997.
1 score (80 p.); 36 cm.
Composed for: flute (also piccolo and alto flute), clarinet (also bass clarinet), percussion (3 cymbals, tambourine, triangle, 3 cowbells, brass bar, medium tam-tam, vibraslap, 5 temple blocks, snare drum, 2 bongos, 2 timbales, 2 tom-toms, crotales, vibraphone, marimba), piano, violin, violoncello.
Commissioned by: Fromm Music Foundation.
Call no.: **1997/111**
Re-entered as: **1998/121**

1989. Petrosyan, Aram, 1972– Narek: symphony-cantata n1: for baritone with full symphony orchestra, mixed and discant's choruses, 1998. Score. N.p.: n.p., 2000.
1 score (106 p.); 42 cm.
Armenian words.
Chiefly reproduced from holograph.
Duration: ca. 40:00.
Composed for: baritone, SATB chorus, descant chorus, piccolo, 3 flutes, 3 oboes, 3 clarinets, 3 bassoons, contrabassoon, 3 trumpets, 6 horns, 3 trombones, tuba, percussion (timpani, triangle, log drums, claves, burvar, snare drum, tenor drum, temple block, bongos, 3 tom-toms, thundersheet, slapstick, flexatone, ratchet, crash cymbals, suspended cymbals, drum, tam-tam, antique cymbals, glockenspiel, xylophone, vibraphone, tubular bells), cembalo, harp, 2 pianos, organ, phonogram, violin I, violin II, viola, violoncello, double bass.
Commissioned by: Wiener Konzerthaus-Gesellschaft.
Call no.: **2002/139**

1990. Phillips, Harvey, 1929– Amanda Miranda's amazing birthday. N.p.: n.p., 1986.
1 score (208 p.); 28 cm.
English words by Sara Wattenbarger.
Reproduced from holograph.
Composed for: 2 flutes (2nd also piccolo), 2 oboes (2nd also English horn), 2 clarinets (2nd also clarinet in E♭), bass clarinet, 2 bassoons (2nd also contrabassoon), 4 horns, 3 trumpets, 2 trombones, bass trombone, tuba, timpani, percussion (snare drum, bass drum, cymbals, orchestra bells, chimes, triangle, xylophone, tam-tam), harp, piano, celesta, violin I, violin II, viola, violoncello, double bass.
Commissioned by: Huntsville Symphony Orchestra.
Call no.: **1988/083**

1991. Picker, Tobias, 1954– Emmeline: an opera. Complete orchestral score. N.p.: Helicon Music, 1997.
1 score (2 v.); 44 cm.
English words by J. D. McClatchy.
Original work by Judith Rossner.
"Revised January 1997"—caption.
Duration: 2:00:00.
Composed for: 5 sopranos, mezzo-soprano, 2 tenors, 2 baritones, 2 basses, women's chorus, onstage violin, 2 flutes (2nd also piccolo), 2 oboes, English horn, 2 clarinets, bass clarinet, 2 bassoons, 4 horns, 2 trumpets, 2 trombones, bass trombone, timpani, harp, piano, harmonica, violin I, violin II, viola, violoncello, double bass.
Commissioned by: Santa Fe Opera.
Call no.: **1997/112**

1992. Picker, Tobias, 1954– Keys to the city.
Commissioned by: City of New York.
Call no.: **1985/156**
No materials available.

1993. Picker, Tobias, 1954– New memories: for string quartet. N.p.: Helicon Music Corp., 1987.
1 score (52 p.); 28 cm.
Composed for: 2 violins, viola, violoncello.
Commissioned by: Santa Fe Chamber Music Festival.
Call no.: **1992/104**

1994. Pierson, Tom, 1948– Antiphony: for organ, soprano sax., piano, 17 horns + 4 trumpets. N.p.: n.p., 1988.
1 score (52 p.); 36 cm.
Reproduced from manuscript.
Composed for: organ, soprano saxophone, piano, 17 horns, 4 trumpets.
Call no.: **1990/098**

1995. Pierson, Tom, 1948– In memory: Benigno S. Aquino. N.p.: n.p., 1983.
1 miniature score (36 p.); 36 cm.
Reproduced from holograph.
Composed for: 3 flutes (3rd also piccolo), 3 oboes (2nd

also English horn), 3 clarinets (3rd also bass clarinet), 2 bassoons, 4 horns, 3 trumpets, 2 trombones, bass trombone, tuba, harp, piano, violin I, violin II, viola, violoncello, double bass.
Commissioned by: Corpus Christi Symphony.
Call no.: **1985/157**

1996. Pierson, Tom, 1948– Piano sonata (1985). N.p.: n.p., 1985.
15 leaves of music; 36 cm.
Reproduced from manuscript.
Composed for: piano.
Call no.: **1988/084**

1997. Pigovat, B., 1953– Requiem "The holocaust": for viola & symphony orchestra. Tel Aviv: Israeli Music Center, 1995.
1 score (130 p.); 37 cm.
Contents: Requiem aeternam—Dies irae—Lacrimosa—Lux aeterna.
Composed for: viola, 3 flutes (3rd also piccolo), 2 oboes, 3 clarinets (3rd also bass clarinet), 2 bassoons, contrabassoon, 4 horns, 3 trumpets, 3 trombones, tuba, percussion (5 timpani, 3 log drums, tambourine, snare drum, tenor drum, 4 tom-toms, whip, suspended cymbals, crash cymbals, bass drum, tam-tam, glockenspiel, tubular bells, xylophone, vibraphone, marimba) celesta, piano, harp, violin I, violin II, viola, violoncello, double bass.
Call no.: **2004/093**
Re-entered as: **2005/109**

1998. Pilon, Daniel, 1957– Transparences: pièce pour quatuor de saxophones (SATB). N.p.: n.p., 1985.
1 score (18 p.); 47 cm.
Reproduced from holograph.
Composed for: soprano saxophone, alto saxophone, tenor saxophone, bass saxophone.
Call no.: **1986/089**

1999. Pintscher, Matthias, 1971– Hérodiade-Fragmente: dramatische Szene für Sopran und Orchester, 1999. Partitur. Kassel; New York, NY: Bärenreiter, 1999.
1 score (56 p.); 59 cm.
French words; also printed as text.
Text excerpted from Hérodiade by Stéphane Mallarmé.
Reproduced from manuscript.
Duration: ca. 20:00.
Performance instructions in German and Italian.
Composed for: soprano, 3 flutes (2nd–3rd also piccolo, 3rd also bass flute), 2 oboes, 3 clarinets (2nd also clarinet in E♭, 3rd also bass clarinet), 2 bassoons, contrabassoon, 4 horns, 3 trumpets, 3 trombones, contrabass tuba, harp, piano, celesta, percussion (vibraphone, crotales, tam-tam, 4 bongos, 3 cowbells, lion's roar, 2 steel discs, tubular bells, xylophone, timpani, 2 suspended cymbals, 3 triangles, flexatone, slapstick, ratchet, metal disc, marimba, bass drum, log drum, paper chimes, glockenspiel, 3 gongs, sizzle cymbal, anvil, vibraslap, castanets, metal chimes, crash cymbals, 2 guiros, 2 temple blocks, switch), violin I, violin II, viola, violoncello, double bass.
Commissioned by: Berliner Philharmonisches Orchester.
Call no.: **2002/140**

2000. Pintscher, Matthias, 1971– Thomas Chatterton: Oper in zwei Teilen nach Hans Henny Jahnn: 1994–1998. Partitur. Kassel; New York, NY: Bärenreiter, 1998.
1 score (336 p.); 42 cm.
German words by Claus H. Henneberg and the composer.
Reproduced from composer's manuscript.
Performance instructions in German.
Composed for: 3 sopranos, mezzo-soprano, 3 tenors, 3 baritones, bass-baritone, bass, 3 flutes (1st–2nd also piccolo, 3rd also alto flute), 2 oboes (2nd also heckelphone), English horn, 2 clarinets (2nd also clarinet in E♭), bass clarinet, contrabass clarinet, 2 bassoons, contrabassoon, 4 horns, 4 trumpets, 3 trombones, contrabass tuba, timpani, percussion (vibraphone, 2 tam-tams, 3 suspended cymbals, 5 bongos, snare drum, 3 triangles, tambourine, ratchet, tenor drum, bells, sistrum, log drum, vibraslap, maracas, large bell, wind machine, marimba, crotales, bass drum, 3 woodblocks, 4 temple blocks, whip, large castanets, lion's roar, gong, cowbells, xylophone, 4 tom-toms, crash cymbals, flexatone, glass chimes), harp, piano (also cembalo), celesta (also harmonium), violin I, violin II, viola, violoncello, double bass, 2 tenor recorders, 4 soprano voices.
Commissioned by: Sächsische Staatsoper Dresden (Semperoper).
Call no.: **2000/135**

2001. Pinzón Urrea, Jesús, 1928– Goé—Payari: canto después de la muerte: basado en un ritual de los indios tucanos. N.p.: n.p., 198-?.
1 score (61 p.); 44 cm. + 1 booklet (6 leaves)
Tucano words; also printed as text with Spanish translation.
For mixed choir and orchestra.
Includes historical information and performance instructions in Spanish.
Booklet contains separate English translation of text,

historical information, and performance instructions.
Contents: Mundo sebrático—Siriri payari: canto a la muerte—Goeri: retorno al universo.
Composed for: SATB chorus, 2 piccolos, 2 flutes, 2 oboes, English horn, clarinet in E♭, 2 clarinets, bass clarinet, 2 bassoons, contrabassoon, 4 horns, 3 trumpets, 3 trombones, tuba, percussion (timpani, tenor drum, drum, cabasa, 2 jingles, bongo, bass drum, woodblock, xylophone, suspended cymbal, triangle, 3 tom-toms, ratchet, tubular bells, 2 sets of sonajas, snare drum, guiro, flexatone, jingle, 2 tam-tams, 2 wood drums, keyboard glockenspiel), piano, violin I, violin II, viola, violoncello, double bass.
Call no.: **1989/095**

2002. Pinzón Urrea, Jesús, 1928– Ritmologia: para un percusionista, 1988. N.p.: n.p., 1988.
14 p. of music; 34 cm.
Reproduced from holograph.
Composed for: marimba, Japanese temple bells, tam-tam, crotales, 2 bongos, 2 bass drums, 2 cymbals, glass chimes, wood chimes, 5 temple blocks, 2 cowbells.
Call no.: **1991/093**

2003. Pinzón Urrea, Jesús, 1928– Las voces silenciosas de los muertos: voz soprano y percusión, 1996. N.p.: n.p., 1996.
1 score (62 p.); 22 x 29 cm.
Spanish words; English translation printed as text.
Poem by José Asunción Silva.
Reproduced from manuscript.
Composed for: soprano, percussion (xylophone, guiro, high suspended cymbal, vibraslap, 2 medium tom-toms, marimba, large sistrum, 2 high metal bells, high tam-tam, large suspended cymbal, 2 large tom-toms, bass drum, high sistrum, 2 cencerros, temple block, drum box, small tubular bells, bongo, 2 congas, cabasa, 2 Chinese woodblocks, tam-tam, cuíca, large drum, 2 timbales).
Call no.: **1998/122**

2004. Pirula, Luka J., 1937– Alla turca. N.p.: n.p., 198-?.
1 score (93 leaves); 35 cm.
After a theme by W. A. Mozart.
Reproduced from manuscript.
Composed for: 2 flutes, 2 oboes, 2 clarinets, alto saxophone, tenor saxophone, 2 bassoons, 2 horns, 3 trumpets, 3 trombones, timpani, percussion (2 tambourines, cymbals, xylophone), violin I, violin II, viola, violoncello, double bass.
Call no.: **1988/085**

2005. Pisati, Maurizio, 1959– -70 mV: per orchestra. Partitura. Milano: Ricordi, 1989.
1 score (viii, 48 p.); 61 cm.
Reproduced from holograph.
Includes performance instructions in Italian.
Composed for: piccolo, 2 flutes, 2 oboes, English horn, 2 clarinets, bass clarinet, 2 bassoons, 2 horns, trumpet, 3 trombones, tuba, percussion (xylophone, 2 woodblocks, 2 flexatones, whip, tubular bells, suspended cymbal, roto-toms, bass drum), harp, celesta, violin I, violin II, viola, violoncello, double bass.
Call no.: **1990/099**

2006. Pishny-Floyd, Monte Keene, 1941– "Aller Anfang ist schwer": notes from the fringes of Beethoven's sketchbooks. N.p.: n.p., 1986.
1 score (85 p.); 36 cm.
English words by the composer.
For chamber orchestra, narrator, and mimes.
Reproduced from holograph.
Duration: 32:00.
Composed for: narrator, flute, oboe, clarinet, horn, bassoon, 2 violins, viola, violoncello, double bass, tape, mimes.
Commissioned by: Saskatoon Symphony Players.
Call no.: **1987/062**

2007. Pishny-Floyd, Monte Keene, 1941– Four movements for bassoon and string trio. N.p.: Monte Keene Pishny-Floyd, 1983.
1 score (36 p.); 36 cm. + 4 parts; 31 cm.
Reproduced from manuscript.
Duration: ca. 10:00.
Composed for: bassoon, violin, viola, violoncello.
Call no.: **1990/100**

2008. Pishny-Floyd, Monte Keene, 1941– The lost children of Dunblande: for narrator, 2 B♭ clarinets, piano, & percussion. N.p.: M.K. Pishny-Floyd, 2001.
1 score (45 p.); 28 x 44 cm.
Principally English, Latin, and German words by the composer.
"Rev. 2001."
Reproduced from manuscript.
Composed for: narrator, 2 clarinets, piano, percussion.
Call no.: **2004/094**

2009. Pishny-Floyd, Monte Keene, 1941– Sonata for double bass and piano. N.p.: n.p., 1992.
1 score (45 p.); 28 cm.
Reproduced from manuscript.
Composed for: double bass, piano.
Call no.: **1994/110**

2010. Pishny-Floyd, Monte Keene, 1941– Suite from "Aller Anfang ist schwer . . . ." N.p.: n.p., 1999.
1 score (64 p.); 36 cm.
Principally English and some German words by the composer.
For narrator and chamber orchestra.
Reproduced from manuscript.
Composed for: narrator, flute, oboe, clarinet, bassoon, horn, violin I, violin II, viola, violoncello, double bass.
Commissioned by: Saskatoon Symphony Society.
Call no.: **2001/116**

2011. Plate, Anton, 1950– "At the river": für grosses Orchester. Köln: Eichen Musikvelag, 2003.
1 score (43 p.); 42 cm.
Composed for: 3 piccolos (also flute), flute, 4 oboes, 4 clarinets (also clarinet in A), 3 bassoons, contrabassoon, 4 horns, 4 trumpets, 4 trombones, tuba, harp, piano, timpani, percussion (2 cymbals, piccolo snare drum, bass drum, metal chimes, crash cymbals, triangle, tam-tam, wind machine), violin I, violin II, viola, violoncello, double bass.
Call no.: **2005/110**

2012. Platz, Robert H. P., 1951– Schreyahn: Zeitinstallation für Violoncello und Instrumentalgruppen. Wiesbaden: Breitkopf & Härtel, 1990.
1 score (various pagings); 29 x 36 cm.
Reproduced from holograph.
Composed for: violoncello, flute, English horn, clarinet, tenor saxophone, bassoon, 2 horns, trumpet, 2 trombones, 2 tubas, 2 pianos.
Commissioned by: Rencontre International de Musique Contemporaine Metz.
Call no.: **1991/094**

2013. Plog, Anthony, 1947– Concerto no. 2: for trumpet and orchestra (1994/95). Bulle: Editions Bim, 1995.
1 score (161 p.); 42 cm.
Reproduced from manuscript.
Duration: ca. 27:00.
Composed for: trumpet, piccolo, 2 flutes, 2 oboes, English horn, 2 clarinets, bass clarinet, 2 bassoons, 4 horns, 2 trumpets, 3 trombones, tuba, percussion (woodblock, glockenspiel, snare drum, triangle, xylophone), piano (also celesta), violin I, violin II, viola, violoncello, double bass.
Commissioned by: Utah Symphony.
Call no.: **2003/095**

2014. Polansky, Larry, 1954– Lonesome road: (the Crawford variations): 51 variations for piano. Pencil draft. N.p.: n.p., 1991.
122 p. of music; 28 cm.
Reproduced from holograph.
"Variations on Ruth Crawford's harmonization of the folk song of the same name"—title page verso.
"First draft"—p. 1.
At end: First draft completed 8/19/90 Mendocino, CA. Revised, Hanover, NH 3/91.
Composed for: piano.
Call no.: **1995/080**

2015. Polifrone, Jon, 1937– Requiem: for those we love. N.p.: New Harmony Press, 1992.
1 score (149 p.); 38 cm.
English words by Helen McGaughey interspersed with the Latin requiem.
Composed for: mezzo-soprano, baritone, child's voice, SATB chorus, flute, oboe, clarinet, bassoon, 2 horns, 2 trumpets, 2 trombones, piano, orchestra bells, violin I, violin II, viola, violoncello, double bass.
Call no.: **1994/111**

2016. Pollock, Robert, 1946– Metaphor V. Ship Bottom, NJ: Association for the Promotion of New Music, 1986.
1 score (44 p.); 42 cm.
For string quartet.
Reproduced from holograph.
At end: April 29, 1986 Ship Bottom.
Duration: ca. 22:00.
Composed for: 2 violins, viola, violoncello.
Commissioned by: Trustees of Noyes Museum, New Jersey.
Call no.: **1987/063**

2017. Poné, Gundaris, 1932–1994. American portraits: for orchestra. N.p.: n.p., 198-?.
1 score (103 p.); 51 cm.
Reproduced from manuscript.
Composed for: 2 flutes (2nd also piccolo), 2 oboes, 2 clarinets, 2 bassoons, 2 horns, 2 trumpets, 2 trombones, percussion (tubular chimes, vibraphone, glockenspiel, tambourine, hi-hat, 3 suspended cymbals, crash cymbals, 3 cowbells, anvil, 2 nipple gongs, 2 tam-tams, guiro, claves, maracas, 5 temple blocks, tenor drum, bass drum, timpani, drum set (snare drum, bass drum, cymbals, cowbell, hi-hat, 3 tom-toms), coconut shells), piano (also electronic keyboard), violin I, violin II, viola, violoncello, double bass.
Call no.: **1987/064**

2018. Poné, Gundaris, 1932–1994. Concerto for violin and orchestra.
Call no.: **1986/090**
No materials available.

2019. Poné, Gundaris, 1932–1994. Titzarin: per grande orchestra. New York, NY: American Composers Alliance, 1985.
1 score (135 p.); 37 cm.
Reproduced from holograph.
Duration: ca. 21:00.
Includes program note in Italian and English by the composer.
Composed for: 3 flutes (3rd also piccolo), 2 oboes, English horn, 2 clarinets, bass clarinet, 2 bassoons, contrabassoon, 4 horns, 3 trumpets, 2 trombones, bass trombone, tuba, timpani, percussion (chimes, vibraphone, marimba, triangle, 3 suspended cymbals, crash cymbals, 2 Javanese gongs, 3 cowbells, 2 tam-tams, woodblock, temple blocks, 2 tambourines, 3 tom-toms, 2 timbales, bass drum, maracas), piano, celesta, violin I, violin II, viola, violoncello, double bass.
Call no.: **1991/095**

2020. Popp, William, 1950– Concerto for accordion and string orchestra. N.p.: n.p., 2002.
1 score (50 p.); 35 cm.
Reproduced from holograph.
Composed for: accordion, violin I, violin II, viola, violoncello, double bass.
Call no.: **2004/095**

2021. Pospíchal, Jiří, 1961– Fünf Reliefs. N.p.: n.p., 1986.
1 score (24 p.); 35 cm.
Reproduced from manuscript.
Duration: ca. 9:20.
Composed for: 2 trumpets, horn, 2 trombones, 2 violoncellos, double bass, timpani, bell.
Call no.: **1987/065**

2022. Potes, Alba Lucia, 1954– Entre arrullos y madrigales = Between madrigals and lullabies: for soprano, flute, clarinet/bass clarinet, cello, piano and percussion. N.p.: Sala Luis Angel Arango, 2002.
1 score (27 p.); 28 x 43 cm.
Spanish words by Aurelio Arturo; also printed as text with English translation.
Reproduced from manuscript.
Contents: Remota luz = Remote light—Morada al Sur (V) = Southern stay (V)—Arrullo = Lullaby—Madrigales = Madrigals.
Composed for: soprano, flute, clarinet (also bass clarinet), violoncello, piano, percussion (gong, glissando gong, bass drum, tenor drum, log drums, rain stick, snare drum, 2 suspended crash cymbals, suspended finger cymbal, triangle, bamboo wind chimes, metal wind chimes, glass wind chimes, crotales, vibraphone, marimba, metal shaker made of aluminum foil).
Commissioned by: Sala Luis Arango/Banco de la Republica de Colombia.
Call no.: **2005/111**

2023. Potes, César Iván, 1957– Taking forms to give forms, unmaking things to make things. N.p.: n.p., 199-?.
1 score (1 v.); 22 x 36 cm.
Chinese words; also printed as text with English translation.
Text by Wai-lim Yip.
Composed for: soprano, flute (also crotales), violoncello, piano, bass drum, tape.
Call no.: **2000/136**

2024. Pott, Francis, 1957– Christus: passion symphony for large organ (1990). London: United Music, 1992.
116 p. of music; 42 cm.
Reproduced from holograph.
At end: "Hand-copied by the composer. London, 16: iii:1991."
Composed for: organ.
Call no.: **1992/105**

2025. Pott, Francis, 1957– Sonata: for 'cello and piano (1995). N.p.: n.p., 1995.
1 score (132 p.); 30 cm.
Composed for: violoncello, piano.
Call no.: **1998/123**

2026. Pott, Francis, 1957– A song on the end of the world: oratorio in seven movements for soli, chorus and orchestra. N.p.: n.p., 1999.
1 score (v, 255 p.); 43 cm.
English and Latin words; also printed as text.
Text from Psalms 22, 130, and 139, and by George Mackay Brown, William Blake, Czeslaw Milosz, Isaac Rosenberg, Thomas Merton, Randall Jarrell, Mervyn Peake, Dylan Thomas, and Charles Causley.
Composed for: voices, SATB chorus, 2 flutes, 2 oboes (2nd also English horn), 2 clarinets, 2 bassoons, 4 horns, 2 trumpets, 2 trombones, bass trombone, tuba, timpani, harp, violin I, violin II, viola, violoncello, double bass.
Commissioned by: Three Choirs Festival, Worcester Cathedral, 1999.
Call no.: **2001/117**

2027. Poulsen, James Viggo, 1958– Five poems of Edgar Allan Poe. Conductor score. N.p.: James V. Poulsen, 1999.
1 score (64 p.); 36 cm.

English words.
For tenor and orchestra.
Contents: Alone—Evening star—Hymn—A dream—To one in paradise.
Composed for: tenor, flute, oboe, clarinet, bassoon, contrabassoon, 2 horns, trumpet, 2 trombones, tuba, timpani, percussion, celesta, violin I, violin II, viola, violoncello, double bass.
Commissioned by: Jack and Dawn Taylor.
Call no.: **2004/096**

2028. Powell, Mel, 1923–1998. Duplicates: a concerto for two pianos and orchestra. N.p.: G. Schirmer, 1990.
1 score (107 p.); 63 cm.
Reproduced from holograph.
Composed for: 2 pianos, piccolo, 2 flutes (1st also alto flute), 2 oboes, English horn, clarinet in E♭, 2 clarinets, bass clarinet, 2 bassoons, contrabassoon, 4 horns, 3 trumpets, 3 trombones, tuba, timpani, percussion (glockenspiel, xylophone, vibraphone, marimba, crotales, chimes, triangle, finger cymbals, 2 suspended cymbals, sizzle cymbal, Chinese cymbal, 2 tam-tams, zing tree, cluster of small bells, elephant bells, bell plate, 6 cowbells, 4 brake drums, tambourine, 2 bongos, 2 timbales, snare drum, parade drum, 2 tom-toms, tenor drum, 2 bass drums, chocalho, guiro, jawbone, castanets, claves, temple blocks), 2 harps, violin I, violin II, viola, violoncello, double bass.
Commissioned by: Betty Freeman.
Call no.: **1991/096**

2029. Powers, Anthony, 1953– Chamber concerto: for fourteen players. Oxford, Oxfordshire; New York, NY: Oxford University Press, 1985.
1 score (95 p.); 30 cm.
Reproduced from holograph.
Duration: 23:00.
Composed for: flute (also alto flute), oboe (also English horn), clarinet (also bass clarinet), bassoon, trumpet, horn, trombone, piano, marimba (also vibraphone), 2 violins, viola, violoncello, double bass.
Call no.: **1986/091**

2030. Powers, Daniel, 1960– Concerto for piano and orchestra: "Reliquary." N.p.: D. Powers, 1997.
1 score (61 p.); 28 cm.
Duration: ca. 20:00.
Includes program notes.
Composed for: piano, piccolo, 2 flutes, 2 oboes, 2 clarinets in A, 2 bassoons, 4 horns, 3 trumpets, 3 trombones, timpani, percussion (chimes, cymbals, 2 suspended cymbals, triangle, snare drum, 4 tom-toms, bass drum, brake drum, flexatone, ratchet), violin I, violin II, viola, violoncello, double bass.
Commissioned by: Terre Haute Symphony Orchestra.
Call no.: **2000/137**

2031. Prater, Jeffrey, 1947– Veni creator spiritus: for solo flute, solo soprano, mixed chorus (SSAATTBB) and symphony orchestra: (2000). Ames, IA: J. Prater, 2000.
1 score (168 p.); 44 cm.
Latin words; also printed as text with English translation.
Composed for: soprano, flute, SATB chorus, 2 flutes, 2 oboes, 2 clarinets, 2 bassoons (2nd also contrabassoon), 4 horns, 3 trumpets, 3 trombones, tuba, timpani, percussion (tubular chimes, xylophone, orchestra bells, snare drum, woodblocks, medium suspended cymbals, temple blocks, small triangle, tom-toms, bass drum, crash cymbals), violin I, violin II, viola, violoncello, double bass.
Call no.: **2004/097**

2032. Premru, Raymond Eugene, 1934–1998. Concerto for tuba and orchestra. N.p.: Raymond Premru, 1992.
1 score (68 p.); 43 cm.
Duration: ca. 23:00.
Composed for: tuba, 3 flutes, 3 oboes, 3 clarinets (3rd also bass clarinet), 3 bassoons (3rd also contrabassoon), 4 horns, 3 trumpets, 3 trombones, timpani, percussion (small Chinese bell, sizzle cymbal, suspended cymbal, glockenspiel, small triangle, crash cymbals, bass drum, snare drum, whip), harp, piano, violin I, violin II, viola, violoncello, double bass.
Commissioned by: T.U.B.A. (Tubist Universal Brotherhood Association).
Call no.: **1994/112**

2033. Premru, Raymond Eugene, 1934–1998. Symphony no. 2. Score. N.p.: n.p., 1988.
1 score (79 p.); 44 cm.
Reproduced from holograph.
Composed for: 3 flutes (1st–2nd also alto flute, 3rd also piccolo), 3 oboes (3rd also English horn), 3 clarinets (3rd also bass clarinet), 3 bassoons (3rd also contrabassoon), 4 horns, 3 trumpets, 3 trombones, tuba, timpani, percussion (suspended cymbals, crash cymbals, bass drum, glockenspiel, woodblock, triangle, 3 tenor drums, sizzle cymbal, ratchet), harp, piano (also celesta and electric piano), violin I, violin II, viola, violoncello, double bass.
Call no.: **1991/097**

2034. Previn, André, 1929– A streetcar named Desire: based on the play by Tennessee Williams. New York, NY: G. Schirmer, 1998.
1 score (3 v. [684 p.]); 44 cm.
English words by Philip Littell.
Opera.
Duration: ca. 2:30:00.
Composed for: 2 sopranos, 2 mezzo-sopranos, 2 tenors, 2 baritones, 3 flutes (2nd–3rd also piccolo and alto flute), 2 oboes (2nd also English horn), 3 clarinets (1st–2nd also clarinet in E♭, 2nd alto saxophone, 3rd also bass clarinet), 2 bassoons (2nd also contrabassoon), 4 horns, 3 trumpets, 2 trombones, bass trombone, tuba, timpani (also bass drum), percussion (suspended cymbals, vibraphone, bells, snare drum, xylophone, bass drum, trap set, claves, tam-tam, small gongs, whip, tom-tom, small snare drum, castanets, large bass drum), harp, celesta, violin I, violin II, viola, violoncello, double bass.
Commissioned by: San Francisco Opera.
Call no.: **2000/138**
Also available:
Call no.: **2000/138 vocal score**

2035. Previn, André, 1929– A streetcar named Desire: based on the play by Tennessee Williams. New York, NY: G. Schirmer, 1999.
1 score (3 v. [675 p.]); 36 cm.
English words by Philip Littell.
Opera.
"Corrected 8/99"—p. 1.
Duration: ca. 2:50:00.
Composed for: 2 sopranos, 2 mezzo-sopranos, 2 tenors, 2 baritones, 3 flutes (2nd–3rd also piccolo and alto flute), 2 oboes (2nd also English horn), 3 clarinets (1st–2nd also clarinet in E♭, 2nd alto saxophone, 3rd also bass clarinet), 2 bassoons (2nd also contrabassoon), 4 horns, 3 trumpets, 2 trombones, bass trombone, tuba, timpani (also bass drum), percussion (suspended cymbals, vibraphone, bells, snare drum, xylophone, bass drum, trap set, claves, tam-tam, small gongs, whip, tom-tom, small snare drum, castanets, large bass drum), harp, celesta, violin I, violin II, viola, violoncello, double bass.
Commissioned by: San Francisco Opera.
Call no.: **2002/141**

2036. Previn, André, 1929– A streetcar named Desire: based on the play by Tennessee Williams. New York, NY: G. Schirmer, 2001.
1 score (3 v. [675 p.]); 36 cm.
English words by Philip Littell.
Opera.
"Corrected 7/01"—p. 1.
Duration: ca. 2:50:00.
Composed for: 2 sopranos, 2 mezzo-sopranos, 2 tenors, 2 baritones, 3 flutes (2nd–3rd also piccolo and alto flute), 2 oboes (2nd also English horn), 3 clarinets (1st also clarinet in E♭, 2nd also clarinet in E♭ and alto saxophone, 3rd also bass clarinet), 2 bassoons (2nd also contrabassoon), 4 horns, 3 trumpets, 2 trombones, bass trombone, tuba, timpani (also bass drum), percussion (suspended cymbals, vibraphone, bells, snare drum, xylophone, bass drum, trap set, claves, tam-tam, small gongs, whip, tom-tom, small snare drum, castanets, large bass drum), harp, celesta, violin I, violin II, viola, violoncello, double bass.
Commissioned by: San Francisco Opera.
Call no.: **2003/096**

2037. Previn, André, 1929– Violin concerto. New York, NY: G. Schirmer, 2002 (1/22/03 printing).
1 score (175 p.); 36 cm.
"Corrected 4/02"—p. 1.
Duration: ca. 39:00.
Composed for: violin, 3 flutes (3rd also piccolo), 2 oboes, English horn, 2 clarinets, bass clarinet, 2 bassoons, contrabassoon, 4 horns, 3 trumpets, 3 trombones, timpani, percussion, celesta, harp, violin I, violin II, viola, violoncello, double bass.
Commissioned by: Boston Symphony Orchestra.
Call no.: **2004/098**

2038. Previn, André, 1929– Violin concerto. New York, NY: G. Schirmer, 2002 (3/11/02 printing).
1 score (175 p.); 36 cm.
"Corrected 3/02"—p. 1.
Duration: ca. 38:00.
Composed for: violin, 3 flutes (3rd also piccolo), 2 oboes, English horn, 2 clarinets, bass clarinet, 2 bassoons, contrabassoon, 4 horns, 3 trumpets, 3 trombones, timpani, percussion, celesta, harp, violin I, violin II, viola, violoncello, double bass.
Commissioned by: Boston Symphony Orchestra.
Call no.: **2005/112**

2039. Primosch, James, 1956– The cloud of unknowing: a cantata for female voice and chamber orchestra: 1987. Newton Centre, MA: Margun Music, 1989.
1 miniature score (104 p.); 28 cm.
English words; also printed as text
Based on texts by Gerard Manley Hopkins, 14th century anonymous, John Donne, Brother Antoninus, and Thomas Merton.
Duration: 37:00.
Composed for: soprano, flute (also piccolo), oboe, clari-

net (also bass clarinet), bassoon (also contrabassoon), horn, trumpet, trombone, percussion (vibraphone, tubular bells, tam-tam, 5 temple blocks, 3 cowbells, ratchet, glass wind chimes, 2 bongos, snare drum, marimba, glockenspiel, finger cymbals, 3 woodblocks, 3 tom-toms, bass drum, crotales, timpani, 2 suspended cymbals, sizzle cymbal, 3 triangles, 3 mounted glass bottles, castanets, vibraslap, 3 brake drums, log drum, claves, guiro), piano (also celesta), violin I, violin II, viola, violoncello, double bass.
Call no.: **1992/106**

2040. Primosch, James, 1956– Fire-memory/river-memory. N.p.: J. Primosch, 1998.
1 score (67 p.); 44 cm.
English words; also printed as text.
For chorus (SATB) and orchestra.
Text by Denise Levertov.
At the end of score: 12/8/97.
Composed for: SATB chorus, 2 flutes (2nd also piccolo), 2 oboes, 2 clarinets (2nd also bass clarinet), 2 bassoons, 4 horns, 2 trumpets, 2 trombones (2nd also bass trombone), timpani, percussion (vibraphone, bass drum, marimba, tubular bells, crotales, medium suspended cymbal, gong, tam-tam), harp, violin I, violin II, viola, violoncello, double bass.
Commissioned by: Mendelssohn Club of Philadelphia.
Call no.: **2000/139**

2041. Primosch, James, 1956– From a book of hours. N.p.: James Primosch, 2001.
1 score (77 p.); 44 cm.
German words; also printed as text with English translation.
Song cycle for soprano with orchestra.
Words from Rilke's Das Stundenbuch.
Contents: Du, Nachbar Gott—Mein Leben—Lösch mir die Augen aus—Ich lese es heraus.
Composed for: soprano, 3 flutes (2nd also alto flute, 3rd also piccolo), 3 oboes (3rd also English horn), 3 clarinets (3rd also bass clarinet), 3 bassoons, 4 horns, 3 trumpets, 3 trombones (3rd bass trombone), tuba, timpani, percussion (vibraphone, suspended cymbal, glockenspiel, marimba, tubular bells, 2 tom-toms, crotales, bass drum, metal wind chimes, triangle, large tam-tam), harp, celesta, violin I, violin II, viola, violoncello, double bass.
Call no.: **2004/099**
Re-entered as: **2005/113**

2042. Primosch, James, 1956– Holy the firm. N.p.: James Primosch, 1999.
1 score (39 p.); 28 cm.
English words; also printed as text.
Song cycle for soprano and piano.
At the end of score: 1/26/99.
Includes program note by the composer in English.
Contents: ". . . That passeth all understanding" / Denise Levertov—Every day is a God / Annie Dillard—The ladder of divine ascent / John Climacus—Cinder / Susan Stewart—Deathbeds / Annie Dillard.
Composed for: soprano, piano.
Commissioned by: Barlow Endowment for Music Composition at Brigham Young University.
Call no.: **2002/142**

2043. Primosch, James, 1956– Holy the firm. King of Prussia, PA: Merion Music: T. Presser, 2002.
1 score (39 p.); 28 cm.
English words.
Texts by Denise Levertov, Annie Dillard, John Climacus, and Susan Stewart.
Song cycle for soprano and piano.
At the end of score: 1/26/99.
Includes program note by the composer in English.
Contents: ". . . That passeth all understanding" / Denise Levertov—Every day is a god / Annie Dillard—The ladder of divine ascent / John Climacus—Cinder / Susan Stewart—Deathbeds / Annie Dillard.
Composed for: soprano, piano.
Commissioned by: Barlow Endowment for Music Composition at Brigham Young University.
Call no.: **2003/097**

2044. Primosch, James, 1956– String quartet no. 3. Bryn Mawr, PA: Theodore Presser, 1999.
1 score (43 p.); 28 cm.
Composed for: 2 violins, viola, violoncello.
Commissioned by: Philadelphia Chamber Music Society.
Call no.: **2001/118**

2045. Proctor, Simon, 1959– Serpent concerto. N.p.: Simon Proctor, 1987.
1 score (92 p.); 30 cm.
Reproduced from holograph.
Composed for: serpent, 2 flutes, 2 oboes, 2 clarinets, 2 bassoons, 2 horns, percussion, violin I, violin II, viola, violoncello, double bass.
Call no.: **2001/119**

2046. Proctor, Simon, 1959– Trombone concerto. N.p.: Simon Proctor, 1997.
1 score (96 p.); 30 cm.
Reproduced from manuscript.
Composed for: trombone, piccolo, 2 flutes, 2 oboes,

English horn, 2 clarinets, bass clarinet, 2 bassoons, contrabassoon, 4 horns, 3 trumpets, 2 trombones, bass trombone, tuba, timpani, percussion (woodblock, triangle, snare drum, glockenspiel, xylophone, marimba, tambourine, tam-tam, cymbals, bass drum, tubular bells, skulls, suspended cymbal, vibraphone), harp, violin I, violin II, viola, violoncello, double bass.
Commissioned by: Kent County Youth Orchestra.
Call no.: **2000/140**

2047. Proto, Frank, 1941– Can this be man: a music drama for violin and orchestra [sic]. Cincinnati, OH: Liben Music, 1998.
1 score (89 p.); 44 cm.
Composed for: violin, 3 flutes (all also piccolo), 2 oboes, English horn, 2 clarinets, bass clarinet, 2 bassoons, 4 horns, 3 trumpets, 2 trombones, tuba, percussion (snare drum, crash cymbals, xylophone, glockenspiel, suspended cymbals, 4 tom-toms, marimba, vibraphone, chimes, maracas, bass drum, field drum, large tam-tam, claves, tambourine, timpani; offstage: low bell in C, snare drum, 5 tom-toms), violin I, violin II, viola, violoncello, double bass.
Call no.: **2000/141**

2048. Proto, Frank, 1941– Can this be man?: a music drama for violin and orchestra [sic]. Cincinnati, OH: Liben Music, 1998.
1 score (88 p.); 32 cm.
Program notes follow score.
Composed for: violin, 3 flutes (all also piccolo), 2 oboes, English horn, 2 clarinets, bass clarinet, 2 bassoons, 4 horns, 3 trumpets, 2 trombones, tuba, percussion (snare drum, crash cymbals, xylophone, glockenspiel, suspended cymbals, 4 tom-toms, marimba, vibraphone, chimes, maracas, bass drum, field drum, large tam-tam, claves, tambourine, timpani; offstage: low bell in C, snare drum, 5 tom-toms), violin I, violin II, viola, violoncello, double bass.
Call no.: **2004/100**

2049. Proto, Frank, 1941– Ghost in machine: an American music drama for vocalist, narrator and orchestra. Cincinnati, OH: Liben Music, 1995.
1 score (178 p.); 44 cm.
English words by John Chenault.
Includes program notes and biographical information (p. 173–178).
Composed for: voice, narrator, piccolo (also alto flute), 2 flutes, 2 oboes, English horn, 4 clarinets (4th also bass clarinet), 3 bassoons (3rd also contrabassoon), soprano saxophone (also tenor saxophone), 4 horns, 4 trumpets, 4 trombones (3rd also bass trombone), tuba, timpani, percussion (bass drum, cowbell, crash cymbals, 2 drum sets, 2 glockenspiels, guiro, African drums, large tam-tam, maracas, marimba, sleigh bells, small metal can, snare drum, suspended cymbals, tambourine, tenor drum, triangle, tom-toms, 2 vibraphones, xylophone), harp, piano, celesta, organ, banjo, amplified acoustic bass (also electric bass), violin I, violin II, viola, violoncello, double bass.
Commissioned by: Cincinnati Symphony Orchestra.
Call no.: **1998/124**

2050. Proto, Frank, 1941– My name is Citizen Soldier: for narrator and orchestra. Cincinnati, OH: Liben Music Publishers, 2000.
1 score (101 p.); 43 cm.
English words by John Chenault.
Composed for: narrator, piccolo (also alto flute), 2 flutes (all also piccolo), 2 oboes, English horn, 2 clarinets (2nd also clarinet in E♭), bass clarinet, 2 bassoons, contrabassoon, alto saxophone, 4 horns, 3 trumpets, 3 trombones, tuba, piano, harp, tape, percussion (timpani, bass drum, triangle, glockenspiel, suspended cymbal, 2 snare drums, tenor drum, bass large bell, vibraphone, xylophone, gong, tam-tam, crash cymbals, 4 bongos, tambourine, marimba, drum set, sizzle cymbal), violin I, violin II, viola, violoncello, double bass.
Commissioned by: American Composers Form.
Call no.: **2002/143**

2051. Proto, Frank, 1941– The profanation of Hubert J. Fort: an allegory in four scences [i.e., scenes]: for voice, clarinet/tenor saxophone and double bass. Cincinnati, OH: Liben Music Publishers, 2003.
1 score (47 p.); 28 cm.
English words.
"Working score V. 40 (June 1, 2003)"—p. 2.
Contents: Crime—Arrest—Trial—Aga montuna.
Composed for: voice, clarinet (also tenor saxophone), double bass.
Call no.: **2005/114**

2052. Prudencio, Cergio, 1955– Cantos de Piedra. N.p.: n.p., 1989.
1 score (35 leaves); 33 cm.
For ethnic Bolivian instruments in 10 groups.
Composed for: group 1: tarkas kurawaras, sicus maltas, pinquillos koikos; group 2: tarkas salinas, sicus maltas, alma pinquillos; group 3: tarkas ullaras, 5 pairs of maltas de italaques, sicus maltas, pifanos; group 4: tarkas kurawaras, 5 pairs of maltas de italaques, sicus maltas, quenas; group 5: tarkas salinas, 5 pairs of maltas de italaques, sicus sankas, pinquillos koikos; group 6: tarkas ullaras, 5 pairs of maltas de italaques,

sicus sankas, quenas mollo; group 7: tarkas kurawaras, 5 pairs of maltas de italaques, sicus toyos, alma pinquillos; group 8: tarkas salinas, quenas pusipias, 5 pairs of maltas de italaques, sicus toyos; group 9: 3 amplified guitars; group 10: marimba, cuíca, ocarina, guiro, afuche, hi-hat, claves, 2 wancaras, bombo de italaque.
Call no.: **1992/107**

2053. Psathas, John, 1966– View from Olympus: double concerto for percussion, piano & orchestra. Wellington, New Zealand: Promethean Editions, 2003.
1 score (125 p.); 31 cm.
Includes program and biographical notes.
Contents: The furies—To yelasto paithi (the smiling child)—Dance of the Maenads.
Composed for: piano, percussion (vibraphone, marimba, simtak, dulcimer/santouri, bass steel drums, wind chimes, bell tree, mark tree, triangle, finger cymbals, drum station [4 octobans, 4 tom-toms, cymbals, hi-hat cymbals]), piccolo, 2 flutes (also piccolo), 2 oboes, 2 clarinets (also clarinet in E♭), 2 bassoons, 4 horns, 3 trumpets, 2 trombones, bass trombone, tuba, timpani, percussion (triangle, snare drum, mark tree, glockenspiel, tubular bells, marimba, cowbell, vibraphone, cymbals, bass drum, tambourine, 3 high tom-toms, large tam-tam, finger cymbals, vibraphone), harp, violin I, violin II, viola, violoncello, double bass.
Commissioned by: Evelyn Glennie.
Call no.: **2005/115**

2054. Pstrokońska-Nawratil, Grażyna, 1947– Éternel: for soprano, boy's [sic] and mixed choirs and large symphony orchestra. N.p.: n.p., 1987.
1 score (133 p.); 30 cm.
French words, also printed as text with English translation.
Text: Psalm 8.
Reproduced from holograph.
Duration: ca. 35:00.
Contents: Chorale of the sea = Choral morza—Psalm at daybreak = Psalm o wschodzie storica—Passacaglia of raindrops = Passacaglia wielkiego deszczu—Psalm at twilight = Psalm o zachodrie—Chorale of the sea = Choral morza.
Composed for: soprano, boys' chorus, SATB chorus, piccolo, 4 flutes, 4 oboes, 4 clarinets, 4 bassoons, contrabassoon, 6 horns, 4 trumpets, 3 trombones, tuba, percussion (xylophone, timpani, 2 bass drums, cymbals, 2 tambourines, tam-tam, celesta, glockenspiel, 2 triangles, 2 bongos, 2 tom-toms, 2 gongs, 2 military drums, chimes), harp, piano, violin I, violin II, viola, violoncello, double bass.
Commissioned by: International Festival Wratislavia Cantans.
Call no.: **1991/098**

2055. Pstrokońska-Nawratil, Grażyna, 1947– Uru anna: for lyric tenor, large-mixed choir and large-symphony orchestra, 1998/99. N.p.: n.p., 1999.
1 score (112 p.); 42 cm.
Latin words; also printed as text.
Texts from Genesis 1.16–17, Psalms 39–40, and Matthew 4.16.
Reproduced from holograph.
Duration: ca. 45:00.
Includes performance instructions.
Contents: Luminaria magna/achaico/—Lux caelestium/cosmico/—Lumen Christi/quotidiano/.
Composed for: tenor, SATB chorus, 4 flutes (4th also piccolo), 3 oboes, 3 clarinets (3rd also bass clarinet), 3 bassoons, contrabassoon, 4 trumpets, 6 horns, 4 trombones, tuba, 2 harps, piano, percussion (timpani, xylophone, vibraphone, marimba, tubular bells, orchestra bells, crotales, gongs, cymbals, tam-tams, steel drum, celesta, triangles, cowbells, flexatone, siren, military snare drum, tambourine, bongos, tom-toms, bass drums, finger bells, cabasa, guiro, temple blocks, maracas, sleigh bells, thundersheets, anvils, slapstick, claves, ratchet, castanets, wind machine, glass chimes, metal chimes, wood chimes), violin I, violin II, viola, violoncello, double bass.
Commissioned by: Polish Radio.
Call no.: **2001/120**

2056. Ptaszyńska, Marta, 1943– Holocaust memorial cantata: 1991–1992. Full orchestra score. Bryn Mawr, PA: Theodore Presser, 1992.
1 score (64 p.); 44 cm.
Primarily English words; also printed as text with partial Hebrew and Yiddish translations.
For 3 soloists (STBar), mixed choir, and orchestra.
Text from Leslie Woolf Hedley's poem Chant for all the people on Earth, incorporating additional text by Yehudi Menuhin.
Reproduced from holograph.
Duration: ca. 40:00.
Composed for: soprano, tenor, baritone, SATB chorus, 2 flutes, 2 oboes, 2 clarinets, 2 bassoons, 2 horns, 2 trumpets, 2 trombones, tuba, percussion (glockenspiel, marimba, chimes, bass drum, gong, 3 suspended cymbals, snare drum, 4 tom-toms, tambourine, tam-tam, whip), violin I, violin II, viola, violoncello, double bass.
Commissioned by: Lira Singers of Chicago.
Call no.: **1994/113**

Re-entered as: **1998/125**
Also available:
Call no.: **1998/125 miniature score**

2057. Pulido, Luis, 1958– Crepitaciones: 1985. N.p.: n.p., 1986.
1 score (62 p.); 35 cm.
Reproduced from manuscript.
Composed for: piccolo, 2 flutes, 2 oboes, 2 clarinets, 2 bassoons, 4 horns, 3 trumpets, 3 trombones, tuba, timpani, percussion (suspended cymbal, xylophone, 3 tom-toms, guacharaca, temple block, tam-tam, cowbell, timpani, bass drum), violin I, violin II, viola, violoncello, double bass.
Call no.: **1987/033**

2058. Pura, William, 1948– Suite for two pianos, 1983. N.p.: n.p., 1984.
1 score (79 leaves); 34 cm.
At end of score: "Revised February 1984, W. Pura."
Reproduced from holograph.
Composed for: 2 pianos.
Call no.: **1985/159**

2059. Pursell, William, 1926– Symphony no. 2: "The heritage": in four movements for full symphony orchestra. N.p.: William Pursell, 1989.
1 score (various pagings); 51 cm.
Reproduced from manuscript.
Duration: ca. 28:30.
Contents: United Electric Railway; 1890: Allegro energico—Centenniel; 1897: Waltz—Aftermath; December 18, 1964: Adagio grave—The Ryman: allegro vivace.
Composed for: piccolo, 2 flutes, 2 oboes, English horn, 2 clarinets, bass clarinet, 2 bassoons, contrabassoon, 4 horns, 3 trumpets, 3 trombones, tuba, percussion (xylophone, bell tree, glockenspiel, roto-toms, suspended cymbal, crash cymbals, field drum, chimes, cabasa, marimba, snare drum, sand blocks, 2 triangles, tam-tam, tambourine, bass drum, cymbals), harp, piano (also celesta), violin I, violin II, viola, violoncello, double bass.
Commissioned by: Aladdin Industries.
Call no.: **1991/099**

2060. Qin, Daping, 1957– Timber of time.
Call no.: **2002/144**
No materials available.

2061. Quartieri, Leo, 1958– Concerto-danza. N.p.: n.p., 198-?.
1 score (19 leaves); 30 x 43 cm.
For instrumental ensemble.
Reproduced from manuscript.
Composed for: trumpet, alto saxophone, organ, guitar, double bass, percussion.
Call no.: **1989/096**

2062. Quate, Amy, 1953– Hymns to Inanna. N.p.: n.p., 1986.
1 score (xxvi, 123 leaves); 28 cm.
English words based on a translation of Sumerian text.
Includes analysis and discussion by the composer.
Composed for: SATB chorus, 4 flutes (1st also piccolo), harp, tape, percussion (timpani, bass drum, cymbals, 2 gongs, suspended cymbal, triangle, crotales, tambourine, glockenspiel, chimes, snare drum, tom-tom, sistrum, bell tree, vibraphone, wind chimes, tam-tam, wind machine).
Call no.: **1987/066**

2063. Quate, Amy, 1953– The other side of the mirror: for solo tuba and taped computer music. Denton, TX: Amy Quate, 1987.
1 score (13 p.); 36 cm.
Reproduced from manuscript.
Composed for: tuba, tape.
Commissioned by: Don Little.
Call no.: **1988/086**

2064. Quell, Michael, 1960– Anamorphosis II: (Polymorphia): for flute (bass flute), oboe, clarinet (bass clarinet), percussion, piano, violin, viola and violoncello (2002/2003). N.p.: n.p., 2002.
1 score (69 leaves); 30 x 42 cm.
Composed for: flute (also bass flute), oboe, clarinet (also bass clarinet), percussion (vibraphone, marimba, 2 tam-tams, 3 plate bells, 2 woodblocks, guiro, claves, bamboo chimes, 3 tom-toms, bass drum), piano, violin, viola, violoncello.
Call no.: **2005/116**

2065. Quilling, Howard, 1935– Concerto for organ & orchestra. N.p.: n.p., 1986.
1 score; 36 cm.
Reproduced from holograph.
Composed for: organ, horn, 2 trumpets, trombone, bass trombone, percussion (glockenspiel, snare drum, timpani), violin I, violin II, viola, violoncello, double bass.
Call no.: **1987/067**

2066. Raaff, Robin de, 1968– Der Einsame im Herbst: for large ensemble, 1998. Amsterdam: Donemus, 1998.

1 score (79 p.); 42 cm.
Duration: ca. 16:00.
Reproduced from holograph.
Composed for: piccolo, flute (also alto flute and piccolo), oboe, English horn, clarinet in E♭, clarinet, bass clarinet, bassoon, contrabassoon, 2 horns, trumpet, trombone, percussion (vibraphone, glockenspiel, crotales, marimba, xylophone, 2 triangles, 5 tam-tams, 7 temple blocks, bass drum, 6 woodblocks, 7 roto-toms, small bongo, 3 congas, large Chinese cymbal, large gong, mark tree, claves), 2 pianos, violin I, violin II, viola, violoncello, double bass.
Commissioned by: Rotterdam Philharmonic.
Call no.: **2002/039**

2067. Rabe, Folke, 1935– To love. Stockholm: Edition Reimers, 1984.
1 score (23 leaves); 37 cm.
English words.
Reproduced from manuscript.
Composed for: SATB chorus.
Call no.: **1985/160**

2068. Raboy, Asher, 1957– Orchestral dances. N.p.: n.p., 2000.
1 score (48 p.); 36 cm.
Composed for: 3 flutes (3rd also piccolo), 2 oboes, 3 clarinets (1st also clarinet in E♭, 3rd also bass clarinet), 2 bassoons, 4 horns, 3 trumpets, 3 trombones, tuba, timpani, percussion (cymbals, snare drum, xylophone, tambourine, bass drum, triangle), piano, harp, violin I, violin II, viola, violoncello, double bass.
Call no.: **2003/098**

2069. Rackley, Lawrence, 1932– The chambered nautilus: episodes for orchestra. N.p.: Lawrence R. Smith, 1991.
1 score (70 p.); 43 cm.
Duration: ca. 11:30.
Composed for: 2 flutes, 2 oboes, 2 clarinets, bass clarinet, 2 bassoons, 4 horns, 2 trumpets, 3 trombones, tuba, timpani, percussion (finger cymbals, triangle, suspended cymbal, snare drum, field drum, bass drum), harp, piano, celesta, violin I, violin II, viola, violoncello, double bass.
Call no.: **1995/081**

2070. Radovanović, Vladan, 1932– Constellations. Score. Beograd: Clio, 1997.
1 score (66 p.); 29 cm.
For 12 singers/walkers/players, 12 sounding-shining spheres, computer music, body motion (staging), video projection of cosmic scenes, slide projection of the score, slide projection of markers of constellations and of directions of moving.
Includes instructions for performance, biography of composer and interview with composer in Serbian and English.
Composed for: 59 synthesized sounds.
Call no.: **2001/121**

2071. Radovanović, Vladan, 1932– The eternal lake. Beograd: ART Jugoslovaska radio-televizija Radio Beograd, 1984.
1 score (ii, 46 p.); 42 cm.
English words.
"A musical-poetic work which exists only in radiophonic form. The sound material consists of vocal and instrumental, electronic and environmental sounds, intelligible speech and non-verbally treated voice"—p. ii.
Reproduced from manuscript.
Duration: ca. 24:05.
Program notes and performance instructions in English.
Call no.: **1988/087**

2072. Radulescu, Horatiu, 1942– Das Andere: for cello solo, opus 49. Versailles, France: Lucero Print, 1985.
1 score (xiii, 18 leaves); 30 x 42 cm.
For a string instrument tuned in perfect fifths.
Performance instructions in German with French and English translations.
Composed for: violoncello.
Commissioned by: Gulbekian Foundation.
Call no.: **1986/092**

2073. Radulescu, Horatiu, 1942– Angolo divino: large orchestra, opus 87, 1994. Stuttgart: Lucero Print, 1994.
1 score (iv, 67 p.); 30 cm.
Reproduced from manuscript.
Duration: ca. 35:00.
Composed for: 4 flutes (1st and 4th also piccolo, 2nd–3rd also alto flute), 4 oboes (2nd and 4th also English horn), 4 clarinets (2nd also clarinet in E♭, 4th also bass clarinet), 4 bassoons (2nd and 4th also contrabassoon), 6 horns, 4 trumpets (1st also piccolo trumpet), 4 trombones (1st also alto trombone, 3rd also bass trombone), tuba, timpani, percussion (timpani, bass drum, 2 tam-tams, 4 bronze sheets, 6 Thai gongs, vibraphone, glockenspiel, crotales, tubular bells), 2 harps, piano (also celesta), violin I, violin II, viola, violoncello, double bass.
Call no.: **1996/116**

2074. Radulescu, Horatiu, 1942– Christe eleison: for organ, opus 69. London: Lucero Print, 1986.

6 p. of music; 42 cm.
Reproduced from manuscript.
Duration: ca. 15:00.
Composed for: organ.
Commissioned by: Internationale Musik Tage "Dom zu Speyer."
Call no.: **1987/068**

2075. Radulescu, Horatiu, 1942– Infinite to be cannot be infinite, infinite anti-be could be infinite: opus 33 (1976–1987). Versailles, France: Lucero Print, 1987.
2 scores; 21–31 cm.
"For 9 string quartets; 8 pre-recorded & 1 (the 9th one) live"—cover.
Score 1 for 9th live string quartet; score 2 for 8 string quartets (live or taped) in nontraditional notation.
Duration: 49:00.
Includes explanations and performance instructions in English (6 leaves).
Composed for: string quartet (2 violins, viola, violoncello), 8 string quartets (live or prerecorded).
Commissioned by: Ministère de la Culture Française.
Call no.: **1988/088**
Re-entered as: **1989/097**

2076. Radulescu, Horatiu, 1942– Inner time II: for 7 clarinets in B♭: opus 42β. London: Lucero Print, 1993.
1 score (xiii, 112 leaves); 22 x 30 cm.
Duration: 56:00.
Includes performance instructions.
Composed for: 7 clarinets.
Commissioned by: Gulbenkian Foundation.
Call no.: **1997/113**

2077. Radulescu, Horatiu, 1942– The quest: concerto for piano and large orchestra, opus 90, 1996. London: Lucero Print, 1996.
1 score (118 p.); 30 cm.
Composed for: piano, 4 flutes (1st–2nd also piccolo, 3rd–4th also alto flute), 3 oboes, English horn, 3 clarinets, bass clarinet, 3 bassoons, contrabassoon, 6 horns, 4 trumpets, 2 trombones (1st also alto trombone), 2 bass trombones, tuba, timpani, percussion (bass drum, 6 Thai gongs, 4 very large bronze plates, glockenspiel, large tam-tam, vibraphone, very large tam-tam, 25 bells, 25 antique crotales), 2 harps, piano (also celesta), violin I, violin II, viola, violoncello, double bass.
Commissioned by: Frankfurt Radio and Baden-Württemberg Ministry for Science and the Arts.
Call no.: **2000/142**

2078. Radulescu, Horatiu, 1942– You will endure forever: third piano sonata, opus 86: 1992–1999. London: Lucero Print, 1999.
78 p. of music; 30 cm.
Title from an English Lao-tzu's Dao te ching.
Contents: If you stay in the center—And embrace death with your heart—Doïna—Dance of the eternal—You will endure forever.
Composed for: piano.
Commissioned by: Baden-Württemberg Ministry for Science and the Arts.
Call no.: **2004/101**

2079. Radzynski, Jan, 1950– Serenade for strings. Tel Aviv: Keshet Music Publications, 2000.
1 score (various pagings); 28 cm.
Contents: Preludio—Minuetto—Sarabanda—Tarantella.
Composed for: 4 violins, 2 violas, 2 violoncellos, double bass.
Commissioned by: Concertante Chamber Players.
Call no.: **2002/145**

2080. Rajna, Thomas, 1928– Amarantha: opera in seven scenes. Claremont: n.p., 1995.
1 score (446 p.); 30 cm.
English words.
"Libretto based on the story 'How beautiful with shoes' by Daniel Wilbur Steele and adapted by the composer."
Reproduced from holograph.
At end of score: "Froggy Pond, Simon's Town–Claremont, Cape Town 1 July 1991 – 18 February 1995."
Duration: ca. 01:21:30.
Composed for: 2 flutes, 2 oboes, 2 clarinets, 2 bassoons, 3 horns, 2 trumpets, 2 trombones, tuba, harp, celesta, timpani, percussion, violin I, violin II, viola, violoncello, double bass.
Call no.: **2003/099**

2081. Rajna, Thomas, 1928– Concerto for harp and orchestra (1990). Study score. Cape Town: Amanuensis Quality Editions, 1990.
1score (93 p.); 30 cm.
Duration: ca. 24:22.
Composed for: harp, 2 flutes (2nd also alto flute), 2 oboes (2nd also English horn), 2 clarinets (2nd also bass clarinet), bassoon, 2 horns, timpani, percussion (triangle, woodblock, whip, Chinese bell tree, tambourine, castanets, crash cymbals, suspended cymbal, glockenspiel, snare drum, tam-tam), violin I, violin II, viola, violoncello, double bass.
Commissioned by: Total SA.
Call no.: **1997/114**

2082. Rajna, Thomas, 1928– Piano concerto no II. N.p.: n.p., 1984.
1 score (189 p.); 31 cm.
Reproduced from manuscript.
Duration: ca. 35:05.
Composed for: piano, piccolo, 2 flutes, 2 oboes (2nd also English horn), 2 clarinets, 2 bassoons, 4 horns, 3 trumpets, 3 trombones, tuba, timpani, percussion (side drum, bass drum, crash cymbals, suspended cymbal, triangle, tambourine, gong, celesta), violin I, violin II, viola, violoncello, double bass.
Commissioned by: Oude Libertas.
Call no.: **1989/098**

2083. Rajna, Thomas, 1928– Suite for violin and harp, 1998. Chicago, IL: Lyon & Healy Harps, 1998.
1 score (33 p.); 32 cm.
Composed for: violin, harp.
Commissioned by: Lyon and Healy Harps of Chicago.
Call no.: **2001/122**

2084. Rakowski, David, 1958– Cerberus: concerto for B♭ clarinet (doubling bass clarinet) and chamber orchestra, 1991–92. N.p.: n.p., 1992.
1 score (141 p.); 38 cm.
Reproduced from manuscript.
Duration: ca. 20:00.
Composed for: clarinet (also bass clarinet), flute (also piccolo), oboe, clarinet, bass clarinet, horn, trumpet, percussion (marimba, vibraphone, 3 suspended cymbals, snare drum, tam-tam), piano, violin I, violin II, viola, violoncello, double bass.
Call no.: **1993/108**

2085. Rakowski, David, 1958– Concerto: for violin and chamber orchestra, 1983. N.p.: David Rakowski, 1983.
1 score (133 p.); 49 cm.
Reproduced from holograph.
Duration: ca. 27:00.
Composed for: violin, flute (also alto flute), oboe (also English horn), clarinet (also bass clarinet), bassoon, horn, trumpet, trombone, percussion (vibraphone, marimba, glockenspiel, 2 suspended cymbals, 5 tom-toms, timpani, snare drum, 2 tubular bells, tam-tam), piano, violin I, violin II, viola, violoncello, double bass.
Call no.: **1991/100**

2086. Rakowski, David, 1958– Persistent memory: for chamber orchestra. New York, NY: C. F. Peters, 1998.
1 score (66 p.); 42 cm.
Duration: ca. 21:00.
Contents: Elegy—Variations, scherzo, and variations.
Composed for: 2 flutes (2nd also piccolo), 2 oboes, 2 clarinets (2nd also bass clarinet), 2 bassoons, 2 horns, violin I, violin II, viola, violoncello, double bass.
Commissioned by: Orpheus Chamber Orchestra.
Call no.: **2000/143**
Re-entered as: **2002/146**

2087. Rakowski, David, 1958– Ten of a kind: symphony no. 2: for clarinet section and wind ensemble. N.p.: David Rakowski, 2000.
1 score (114 p.); 42 cm.
Duration: ca. 28:00.
Composed for: piccolo, 3 flutes (2nd also alto flute), 2 oboes, English horn, clarinet in E♭, 6 clarinets, alto clarinet, bass clarinet, contrabass clarinet, 2 bassoons, contrabassoon, 4 horns, 4 trumpets, 4 trombones, 2 euphoniums, tuba, percussion (timpani, party whistle, tambourine, crotales, 4 temple blocks, ratchet, bass drum, vibraphone, 4 tom-toms, snare drum, glockenspiel, cymbals, 2 suspended cymbals, marimba, triangle).
Commissioned by: "The President's Own" United States Marine Band.
Call no.: **2004/102**

2088. Raminsh, Imant, 1943– Sonnets to Orpheus: for baritone solo, large choir (SATB) and orchestra. N.p.: Imant Raminsh, 1998.
1 score (247 p.); 37 cm.
English words.
Poems by Rainer Maria Rilke; translated by Stephen Mitchell.
Reproduced from holograph.
Composed for: baritone, SATB chorus, 2 flutes, 2 oboes, 2 clarinets, 2 bassoons, 2 horns, 2 trumpets, trombone, timpani, percussion, harp, violin I, violin II, viola, violoncello, double bass.
Commissioned by: Orpheus Choir of Toronto.
Call no.: **2001/123**

2089. Raminsh, Imant, 1943– Symphony of psalms: for soprano and mezzosoprano [sic] soli, treble choir and orchestra. N.p.: by Imant Raminsh, 2001.
1 score (various pagings); 28 cm.
Latin, German, Spanish, Old Church Slavonic, Hebrew, French, Latvian, English, or Latin words.
Reproduced from holograph.
Contents: Jubilate Deo, omnis terra (Ps. 100)—Aus der Tiefe ruf' ich, Herr, zu Dir (Ps. 130)—Piedad de mí, Señor (Salmo 51)—Blagoslavi dushe moya Gospoda (Ps. 104)—Adonai roī, lo eḥsar (Ps. 23)—Seigneur, tu sais tout de moi (Psaume 139)—Redzi, cik jauki (Ps. 133)—The earth is the Lord's (Ps. 24)—Laudate Dominum (Ps. 150).

Composed for: soprano, mezzo-soprano, treble chorus, 2 flutes, 2 oboes, 2 clarinets, 2 bassoons, 2 horns, 2 trumpets, 3 trombones, timpani, percussion, harp, violin I, violin II, viola, violoncello, double bass.
Commissioned by: Lourdes Singers.
Call no.: **2004/103**

2090. Ran, Shulamit, 1949– Between two worlds. N.p.: S. Ran, 1997.
1 score (604 p.); 44 cm.
English words.
Opera in 2 acts.
Libretto by Charles Kondek after S. Ansky.
Composed for: 2 flutes (both also piccolo, 1st also alto flute), oboe (also English horn and oboe d'amore), clarinet (also clarinet in E♭), clarinet in A (also bass clarinet), bassoon (also contrabassoon), horn, 2 trumpets, 2 trombones, percussion, harp, keyboard, violin I, violin II, violin III, violin IV, viola I, viola II, violoncello I, violoncello II, double bass.
Call no.: **1998/126**

2091. Ran, Shulamit, 1949– Concerto for orchestra (1986). Bryn Mawr, PA: Theodore Presser, 1986.
1 score (98 p.); 56 cm.
Reproduced from manuscript.
Composed for: 2 flutes (1st also piccolo, 2nd also alto flute), 2 oboes (2nd also English horn), 3 clarinets (1st also clarinet in E♭, 3rd also bass clarinet), 3 bassoons (3rd also contrabassoon), 4 horns, 3 trumpets, 2 trombones, bass trombone, tuba, timpani, percussion (bass drum, gong, snare drum, xylophone, tambourine, 6 tom-toms, 4 suspended cymbals, triangle, sizzle cymbal, tam-tam, crotales, 5 temple blocks, woodblock, crash cymbals, chimes), piano, violin I, violin II, viola, violoncello, double bass.
Commissioned by: American Composers Orchestra.
Call no.: **1989/099**

2092. Ran, Shulamit, 1949– Legends: in two movements, 1992–1993. Bryn Mawr, PA: Theodore Presser, 1993.
1 score (102 p.); 44 cm.
Includes performance notes.
Composed for: 3 flutes (3rd also piccolo, 2nd also alto flute), 2 oboes (2nd also English horn), 3 clarinets (2nd also clarinet in E♭, 2nd–3rd also bass clarinet), 3 bassoons (3rd also contrabassoon), 4 horns, 3 trumpets, 2 trombones, bass trombone, 2 tubas, timpani, percussion (marimba, xylophone, vibraphone, glockenspiel, chimes, crotales, bass drum, tenor drum, snare drum, 5 tom-toms, temple blocks, 2 woodblocks, 2 tambourines, whip, maracas, crash cymbals, 3 suspended cymbals, sizzle cymbal, bell tree, 2 tam-tams, 2 triangles, gong, glass wind chimes), harp, piano, celesta, violin I, violin II, viola, violoncello, double bass.
Commissioned by: AT&T Foundation and Meet the Composer Orchestra Residencies Program.
Call no.: **1994/114**
Re-entered as: **1995/082**

2093. Ran, Shulamit, 1949– Symphony. N.p.: Shulamit Ran, 1990.
1 score (120 p.); 44 cm.
Reproduced from manuscript.
Composed for: 2 flutes (2nd also piccolo), 2 oboes (2nd also English horn), 2 clarinets (2nd also clarinet in E♭), bass clarinet (also clarinet in A), 3 bassoons (3rd also contrabassoon), 6 horns, 4 trumpets, 2 trombones, bass trombone, tuba, timpani, percussion (chimes, snare drum, tam-tam, tom-toms, 4 cymbals, maracas, vibraphone, bass drum, tambourine, woodblocks, xylophone, roto-toms, whip, temple blocks, triangle, boobams, 2 bongos, 2 timbales, orchestra bells, sizzle cymbal, crash cymbals), violin I, violin II, viola, violoncello, double bass.
Commissioned by: Philadelphia Orchestra.
Call no.: **1991/101**

2094. Randalls, Jeremy S., 1959– Scène de naufrage: (1993). N.p.: Jeremy S. Randalls, 1993.
1 score (41 p.); 30 cm.
For orchestra.
"A montage in music based on the painting Le radeau de la Mèduse by Theodore Gèricault"—title page verso.
Reproduced from holograph.
Duration: ca. 17:00.
Composed for: piccolo, 2 flutes, 2 oboes, English horn, 2 clarinets (2nd also clarinet in E♭), bass clarinet, 2 bassoons, contrabassoon, 4 horns, 3 trumpets, 3 trombones (3rd also bass trombone), tuba, timpani, percussion (glockenspiel, snare drum, gong, timbrels, triangle, bass drum, woodblocks, crotales, tubular bells, sandpaper block, xylophone, crash cymbals, large suspended cymbal, castanets, bell tree, bamboos, anvil), harp, piano (also celesta), violin I, violin II, viola, violoncello, double bass.
Call no.: **1997/115**

2095. Rands, Bernard, 1934– Apókryphos: for solo soprano, chorus and orchestra. N.p.: Bernard Rands, 2002.
1 score (131 p.); 43 cm.
German and English words; also printed as text with English translation.
Texts based on the Apocrypha and on poems by Hein-

rich Heine, Else Lasker-Schüller, Franz Werfel, Nelly Sachs, and Paul Celan.
Duration: 35:00.
Composed for: soprano, large SATB chorus, 3 flutes, piccolo, 2 oboes, English horn, 3 clarinets, bass clarinet, 3 bassoons (also contrabassoon), 4 horns, 3 trumpets, 3 trombones, bass trombone, tuba, 2 harps, celesta, piano, percussion (vibraphone, marimba, claves, cowbells, cencerros, triangle, tam-tams, bass drum, tubular bells, button gong, 2 triangles, snare drum, 2 bongos, 3 tom-toms, glockenspiel, sizzle cymbal, xylophone, 5 temple blocks, maracas, tambourine), 5 timpani, violin I, violin II, viola, violoncello, double bass.
Commissioned by: Chicago Symphony Orchestra and Chorus.
Call no.: **2005/117**

2096. Rands, Bernard, 1934– Belladonna: an opera in two acts. N.p.: n.p., 1999.
1 score (2 v. [vi, 309 p.]); 43 cm.
English words by Leslie Dunton-Downer.
Duration: 1:23:00.
Composed for: 2 sopranos, boy soprano, mezzo-soprano, contralto, countertenor, 2 tenors, baritone, 2 bass-baritones, 2 small SATB choruses, flute (also alto flute), oboe, clarinet (also bass clarinet), alto saxophone, bassoon, horn, trumpet, trombone, harp, piano, percussion (vibraphone, glockenspiel, woodblocks, bongos, suspended cymbal, button gong, bass drum, marimba, tubular bells, claves, snare drum, triangle, button gong, tam-tam), violin I, violin II, viola, violoncello, double bass.
Commissioned by: Susan and Ford Schumann.
Call no.: **2001/124**

2097. Rands, Bernard, 1934– Bells. Full score. London: Universal Edition, 1989.
1 score (59 p.); 51 cm.
English words; also printed as text.
For SATB chorus and orchestra.
Texts from Edgar Allan Poe, E. E. Cummings, and Mark van Doren.
Reproduced from manuscript.
Composed for: SATB chorus, piccolo, 2 flutes, 2 oboes, English horn, 2 clarinets, bass clarinet, 2 bassoons, contrabassoon, 4 horns, 3 trumpets, 2 trombones, bass trombone, tuba, timpani, percussion (2 vibraphones, 2 triangles, bell tree, 2 sets of tubular bells, 4 bongos, marimba, cowbells, 3 tam-tams, bass drum, snare drum, 3 gongs, 3 tom-toms, claves, tambourine, xylophone, 3 sizzle cymbals, maracas), 2 harps, piano, celesta, violin I, violin II, viola, violoncello, double bass.
Call no.: **1990/101**

2098. Rands, Bernard, 1934– Canti d'amor: for S.A.T.B. chorus, a cappella. N.p.: n.p., 1991.
1 score (40 p.); 28 cm.
Text from Chamber music by James Joyce.
Duration: 21:30.
Composed for: SATB chorus.
Call no.: **1993/109**

2099. Rands, Bernard, 1934– Canti dell'eclissi: for orchestra and bass soloist, 1992. N.p.: Bernard Rands, 1993.
1 score (112 p.); 44 cm.
Italian, English, French, and German words; also printed as text.
Song cycle.
Texts by San Francesco, Pindar, René Daumal, John Milton, Torquato Tasso, Al-Ghassani, Salvatore Quasimodo, Emily Dickinson, René Char, James DePreist, Octavio Paz, Paul Celan, and Henry Vaughan.
Composed for: bass, 3 flutes (3rd also alto flute), 2 oboes, English horn, 4 clarinets (3rd also bass clarinet, 4th also contrabass clarinet), 3 bassoons (3rd also contrabassoon), 4 horns, 3 trumpets, 3 trombones, bass trombone, tuba, timpani, percussion (vibraphone, marimba, tambourine, 3 woodblocks, tubular bells, tom-toms, bongos, snare drum, claves, 2 triangles, suspended cymbal, bass drum, 2 tam-tams, glockenspiel, xylophone, 5 temple blocks), 2 harps, piano, celesta, electric organ, violin I, violin II, viola, violoncello, double bass.
Commissioned by: Philadelphia Orchestra and Meet the Composer Orchestra Residencies Program.
Call no.: **1994/115**

2100. Rands, Bernard, 1934– Canzoni per orchestra. Full score. N.p.: Berard Rands, 1995.
1 score (77 p.); 44 cm.
Musical narrative based upon poems from "Chamber music" by James Joyce.
Duration: 32:00.
Composed for: 2 flutes, alto flute, 2 oboes, English horn, 3 clarinets (3rd also clarinet in A), bass clarinet, 2 bassoons, 4 horns, 3 trumpets, 3 trombones, tuba, timpani, percussion (vibraphone, tubular bells, 2 triangles, bongos, tambourine, snare drum, tam-tam, bass drum), 2 harps, violin I, violin II, viola, violoncello, double bass.
Commissioned by: Philadelphia Orchestra.
Call no.: **1996/117**

2101. Rands, Bernard, 1934– Canzoni per orchestra. Full score. Valley Forge, PA: Helicon Music: European American Music, 1995.
1 score (77 p.); 43 cm.

Musical narrative based upon poems from "Chamber music" by James Joyce.
Duration: 32:00.
Composed for: 2 flutes, alto flute, 2 oboes, English horn, 3 clarinets (3rd also clarinet in A), bass clarinet, 2 bassoons, 4 horns, 3 trumpets, 3 trombones, tuba, timpani, percussion (vibraphone, tubular bells, 2 triangles, bongos, tambourine, snare drum, tam-tam, bass drum), 2 harps, violin I, violin II, viola, violoncello, double bass.
Commissioned by: Philadelphia Orchestra.
Call no.: **1997/116**

2102. Rands, Bernard, 1934– Ceremonial 3. London: Universal Edition, 1991.
1 score (58 p.); 36 cm.
For orchestra.
"Proof copy"—p. 1 of cover.
Composed for: 3 flutes (2nd–3rd also alto flute), 2 oboes, English horn, 3 clarinets (3rd also clarinet in A), bass clarinet, 2 bassoons, contrabassoon, 4 horns, 3 trumpets, 2 trombones, bass trombone, tuba, timpani, percussion (bass drum, 2 tam-tams, vibraphone, snare drum, tubular bells, tom-toms, marimba, bongos, triangle), 2 harps, piano, celesta, electric organ, violin I, violin II, viola, violoncello, double bass.
Call no.: **1992/108**

2103. Rands, Bernard, 1934– Concertino. Full score. Miami, FL: Helicon, 2001.
1 score (45 p.); 37 cm.
Duration: ca. 16:00.
Composed for: oboe, flute, clarinet, violin I, violin II, viola, violoncello.
Commissioned by: Network for New Music.
Call no.: **2003/100**

2104. Rands, Bernard, 1934– Concerto #1: for 'cello and orchestra. N.p.: European American Music, 1997.
1 score (89 p.); 45 cm.
Duration: ca. 27:00.
Composed for: violoncello, 3 flutes (2nd–3rd also alto flute, 3rd also piccolo), 2 oboes, English horn, 2 clarinets, bass clarinet (also clarinet), 2 bassoons, contrabassoon, 4 horns, 3 trumpets, 3 trombones, tuba, timpani, percussion (vibraphone, xylophone, glockenspiel, tubular bells, 2 bongos, medium triangle, medium tam-tam, bass drum, large tam-tam, cowbells, bass drum, marimba), 2 harps, piano, violin I, violin II, viola, violoncello, double bass.
Commissioned by: Boston Symphony Orchestra.
Call no.: **1998/127**
Re-entered as: **2000/144**

2105. Rands, Bernard, 1934– Symphony, 1994. Full score. N.p.: Bernard Rands, 1994.
1 score (119 p.); 44 cm.
Composed for: 3 flutes (2nd also alto flute, 3rd also piccolo), 2 oboes, English horn, 3 clarinets (3rd also bass clarinet), 3 bassoons (3rd also contrabassoon), 4 horns, 3 trumpets, 3 trombones, tuba, timpani, percussion (marimba, vibraphone, tubular bells, tam-tam, 3 triangles (small, medium, large), bongos, tom-toms, temple blocks, snare drum, bass drum, claves), 2 harps, piano, celesta, violin I, violin II, viola, violoncello, double bass.
Commissioned by: Los Angeles Philharmonic.
Call no.: **1995/083**

2106. Rands, Bernard, 1934– Le tambourin: suites 1 & 2. Score. London: Universal Edition, 1986.
1 score (40 p.); 59 cm.
Reproduced from holograph.
Composed for: 4 flutes, 2 oboes, English horn, clarinet in E♭, 2 clarinets, bass clarinet, 2 bassoons, contrabassoon, 4 horns, 3 trumpets, 2 trombones, bass trombone, tuba, timpani, percussion (marimba, 2 vibraphones, tom-toms, bass drum, cymbals, bongos, snare drum, 2 sets of tubular bells, temple blocks, 2 tambourines, 3 sizzle cymbals, cowbells, 2 triangles, finger cymbals, 2 tam-tams, claves, woodblocks, xylophone), 2 harps, piano, celesta, electric organ, violin I, violin II, viola, violoncello, double bass.
Call no.: **1985/161**
Re-entered as: **1988/089** and **1989/100**

2107. Ranjbaran, Behzad, 1955– The blood of Seyavash. New York, NY: Harmonisch Music, 1994.
1 score (267 p.); 44 cm.
For orchestra.
Duration: 40:00.
Composed for: piccolo, 2 flutes, 2 oboes, English horn, 2 clarinets, bass clarinet, 2 bassoons, contrabassoon, 4 horns, 3 trumpets, 3 trombones, tuba, timpani, percussion (wind chimes, triangle, cymbals, tambourine, tam-tam, xylophone, vibraphone, marimba, snare drum, bass drum), harp, celesta, violin I, violin II, viola, violoncello, double bass.
Commissioned by: Nashville Ballet.
Call no.: **1995/084**

2108. Ranjbaran, Behzad, 1955– Concerto for violoncello and orchestra. Bryn Mawr, PA: Theodore Presser, 1998.
1 score (164 p.); 36 cm.
Reproduced from manuscript.
Duration: 27:00.

Composed for: violoncello, 2 flutes (2nd also piccolo), 2 oboes (2nd also English horn), 2 clarinets, 2 bassoons, 4 horns, 3 trumpets, 2 trombones, bass trombone, tuba, timpani, percussion (triangle, cymbals, tambourine, tam-tam, xylophone, snare drum, bass drum), harp, violin I, violin II, viola, violoncello, double bass.
Commissioned by: New Heritage Music.
Call no.: **2003/101**

2109. Ranjbaran, Behzad, 1955– Open secret: for chorus and chamber orchestra. N.p.: Behzad Ranjbaran, 1999.
1 score (45 p.); 36 cm.
English words.
Poems by Rumi; translated by Coleman Barks.
Reproduced from manuscript.
Duration: 13:00.
Composed for: SATB chorus, flute, oboe, clarinet, percussion (vibraphone, cymbals, bass drum, tam-tam), harp, violin, viola, violoncello.
Commissioned by: New Amsterdam Singers.
Call no.: **2001/125**

2110. Ranjbaran, Behzad, 1955– Seemorgh. New York: Harmonisch Music, 1991.
1 score (118 p.); 28 cm.
For orchestra.
Reproduced from manuscript.
Duration: 20:00.
Composed for: piccolo, 2 flutes, 2 oboes, English horn, clarinet in E♭, clarinet, bass clarinet, 2 bassoons, contrabassoon, 4 horns, 3 trumpets, 2 trombones, bass trombone, tuba, timpani, percussion (wind chimes, triangle, cymbals, tambourine, tam-tam, xylophone, vibraphone, marimba, snare drum, bass drum), harp, celesta, violin I, violin II, viola, violoncello, double bass.
Commissioned by: Long Beach Symphony.
Call no.: **1994/116**

2111. Ranjbaran, Behzad, 1955– Seven passages: for orchestra. Bryn Mawr, PA: Theodore Presser, 2000.
1 score (82 p.); 36 cm.
Reproduced from manuscript.
Composed for: piccolo, 2 flutes, 2 oboes, English horn, 2 clarinets, bass clarinet, 2 bassoons, contrabassoon, 4 horns, 3 trumpets, 2 trombones, bass trombone, tuba, timpani, percussion (vibraphone, xylophone, glockenspiel, marimba, wind chimes, triangle, cymbals, tambourine, tubular bells, ratchet, cabasa, slapstick, wind machine, tam-tam, bass drum, snare drum, temple blocks), celesta, harp, violin I, violin II, viola, violoncello, double bass.
Commissioned by: Long Beach Symphony Orchestra.
Call no.: **2002/147**

2112. Ranjbaran, Behzad, 1955– Songs of eternity: for soprano and orchestra. King of Prussia, PA: Theodore Presser, 2002.
1 score (66 p.); 36 cm.
English words; also printed as text.
Text from an English translation of Rubā'īyāt by Omar Khayyam.
Duration: 17:00.
Composed for: soprano, 2 flutes, 2 oboes (2nd also English horn), 2 clarinets, 2 bassoons, 2 horns, 2 trumpets, trombone, tuba, timpani, percussion (triangle, cymbals, tambourine, tubular bells, glockenspiel, tam-tam, bass drum), harp, violin I, violin II, viola, violoncello, double bass.
Call no.: **2004/104**

2113. Ranjbaran, Behzad, 1955– Thomas Jefferson: for narrator, cello and orchestra. Bryn Mawr, PA: Theodore Presser Co., 1998.
1 score (88 p.); 36 cm.
English words.
Reproduced from manuscript.
Duration: 16:00.
Composed for: narrator, violoncello, 2 flutes (2nd also piccolo), 2 oboes (2nd also English horn), 2 clarinets, 2 bassoons, 4 horns, 3 trumpets, 2 trombones, bass trombone, tuba, timpani, percussion (triangle, tam-tam, cymbals, tambourine, xylophone, snare drum, bass drum), harp, violin I, violin II, viola, violoncello, double bass.
Commissioned by: New Heritage Music Foundation.
Call no.: **2000/145**

2114. Rapchak, Lawrence, 1951– The life work of Juan Diaz. N.p.: L.R., 1990.
1 score (a–d leaves, 255 p.); 28 cm.
English words.
"Story and screenplay by Ray Bradbury; adapted as a libretto by Carl Ratner."
Chamber opera.
Reproduced from manuscript.
Duration: ca. 1:25:00.
Composed for: 2 sopranos, boy soprano, alto, tenor, baritone, bass-baritone, 2 oboes (also English horn), bassoon, harp, percussion (timpani, 3 timbales, bass drum, tam-tam, Chinese cymbal, hand cymbal, small hand cymbal, stone, claves, gato drum, kokiriki, suspended resonant metal instrument, cup bells, dish of water, cricket, rain stick, wooden clackers, 2 snare drums, low chimes), celesta (also organ and synthesizer),

acoustic guitar , violin I, violin II, viola, violoncello, double bass.
Call no.: **1995/085**

2115. Rapchak, Lawrence, 1951– Sinfonia antiqua: for orchestra. N.p.: n.p., 1990.
1 score (62 p.); 28 cm.
Reproduced from holograph.
At end: 10/28/89, 2/15/90.
Duration: 11:00.
Composed for: piccolo, 2 flutes, 3 oboes, English horn, clarinet in A, 2 bass clarinets, 3 bassoons, contrabassoon, 4 offstage horns, 3 trumpets, 3 trombones, tuba, timpani, percussion (marimba, hand cymbal, Chinese cymbal, glockenspiel, 2 cymbals, 3 bongos, triangle, chimes, vibraphone, tambourine, tam-tam, bass drum), harp, celesta, violin I, violin II, viola, violoncello, double bass.
Call no.: **1992/109**

2116. Rasgado, Víctor, 1959– Anacleto Morones: opera en un acto (1990–91). Partitura. Milano: Ricordi, 1994.
1 score (345 p.); 42 cm.
Spanish words from "Anacleto Morones" by Juan Rulfo.
Reproduced from manuscript.
Composed for: mezzo-soprano, contralto, tenor, baritone, women's chorus, flute (also piccolo), oboe, clarinet, bassoon, horn, trumpet, trombone, tuba, percussion (tam-tam, cymbals, 2 suspended cymbals, guiro, 2 gongs, metal chimes, 4 roto-toms, glass chimes, vibraphone, 4 cowbells, bass drum, tubular bells, whip, 2 bongos, 2 congas, marimba, 4 woodblocks, 2 timbales, 4 cencerros), tape, violin I, violin II, viola, violoncello, double bass.
Call no.: **1998/128**
Also available:
Call no.: **1998/128 vocal score**

2117. Rasgado, Víctor, 1959– El conejo y el coyote: opera de cámara en un acto: para orquesta de cámara, soprano, barítono, tenor y narrador infantil (1998–1999). México: n.p., 1999.
1 score (131 leaves); 28 cm.
Spanish words.
"Narración de leyendas populares zapotecas adaptao por Gloria de la Cruz y Víctor de la Cruz; libreto en idioma animal imaginario de Víctor Rasgado."
Reproduced from holograph.
Composed for: soprano, baritone, tenor, narrator, piccolo, flute, oboe, clarinet, bassoon, soprano saxophone, alto saxophone, baritone saxophone, 2 horns, trumpet, trombone, tuba, celesta, percussion (tam-tam, gong, suspended cymbal, tubular bells, 4 roto-toms, 4 temple blocks, whip, 2 timpani, bows, vibraphone, metal chimes, marimba, 2 bongos, 2 congas, 4 cowbells, maracas, glockenspiel, 3 suspended crotales or cymbals, 4 tom-toms, 4 woodblocks, bass drum, slide whistle, guiro, military drum, triangle), violin I, violin II, viola, violoncello, double bass.
Commissioned by: Coordinacion Nacional de Musica y Opera.
Call no.: **2005/118**

2118. Ratiu, Horia, 1951– Homéomorphismes: pour piano, 1993–1994. N.p.: n.p., 1994.
20 p. of music; 36 cm.
Reproduced from manuscript.
Duration: ca. 12:00.
Composed for: piano.
Call no.: **1997/117**

2119. Ratiu, Horia, 1951– Horizons: pour orchestre de chambre. N.p.: n.p., 1990.
1 score (80 p.); 35 cm.
Duration: ca. 20:00.
Reproduced from manuscript.
Composed for: 2 flutes (both also piccolo), oboe, clarinet (also bass clarinet), contrabassoon, horn, trumpet, bass trombone, percussion (glockenspiel, tubular bells, timpani, suspended cymbal, 2 woodblocks, 2 bongos, maracas, sleigh bells, 2 tom-toms, bass drum, tam-tam, triangle, vibraphone, xylophone), piano, guitar, 2 violins, viola, violoncello, double bass.
Commissioned by: Futurs Musiques—A. D. I. A. M. du Val de Marne.
Call no.: **1992/110**

2120. Rattenbach, Augusto Benjamín, 1927– Edipo en San Telmo: opera de cámara en 1 acto, 1985. N. p.: n.p., 1985.
1 score (164 p.); 36 cm.
Spanish words by Helena García de la Mata with German translation.
Reproduced from manuscript.
Composed for: soprano, 2 mezzo-sopranos, tenor, 2 baritones, flute (also piccolo), oboe (also English horn), clarinet, bassoon, horn, percussion (bass drum, triangle, tam-tam, tenor drum), piano, violin I, violin II, viola, violoncello, double bass.
Call no.: **1991/102**

2121. Rattenbach, Augusto Benjamín, 1927– Variaciones "Buenos Aires": para orquesta. N.p.: n.p., 1982.
1 score (76 p.); 36 cm.
Reproduced from manuscript.

Composed for: piccolo, 2 flutes, 2 oboes, English horn, 2 clarinets, 2 bassoons, 4 horns, 3 trumpets, 3 trombones, tuba, timpani, percussion (triangle, bass drum, cymbals, tam-tam, military drum), harp, piano, violin I, violin II, viola, violoncello, double bass.
Call no.: **1986/093**

2122. Rautavaara, Einojuhani, 1928– On the last frontier. Espoo, Finland: Edition Fazer, 1997.
1 score (120 p.); 36 cm.
English words by the composer, based on Edgar Allan Poe; also printed as text with Finnish translation.
Fantasy for chorus and orchestra.
Duration: ca. 26:00.
Composed for: SATB chorus, piccolo, 2 flutes, 2 oboes, English horn, 2 clarinets, bass clarinet, 2 bassoons, contrabassoon, 4 horns, 3 trumpets, 3 trombones, tuba, timpani, percussion (cymbals, vibraphone, glockenspiel, xylophone, flexatone, tom-tom, tam-tam), harp, violin I, violin II, viola, violoncello, double bass.
Commissioned by: Helsinki Philharmonic Orchestra.
Call no.: **2000/146**

2123. Rautavaara, Einojuhani, 1928– Symphony no. 8: "The journey." Score. Finland: Warner/Chappell Music, 1999.
1 score (114 p.); 30 cm.
Duration: ca. 27:00.
Composer's note in English.
Composed for: piccolo, 2 flutes, 2 oboes, English horn, 2 clarinets, bass clarinet, 2 bassoons, contrabassoon, 4 horns, 4 trumpets, 3 trombones, tuba, percussion (timpani, vibraphone, xylophone, glockenspiel, tubular bells, 4 tom-toms, cymbals, gong, 3 tam-tams), 2 harps, violin I, violin II, viola, violoncello, double bass.
Commissioned by: Philadelphia Orchestra.
Call no.: **2002/148**

2124. Rautavaara, Einojuhani, 1928– Symphony no. 8: "The journey." Finland: Warner/Chappell Music, 2000.
1 miniature score (114 p.); 25 cm.
Duration: 29:00.
Composed for: piccolo, 2 flutes, 2 oboes, English horn, 2 clarinets, bass clarinet, 2 bassoons, contrabassoon, 4 horns, 4 trumpets, 3 trombones, tuba, percussion (timpani, vibraphone, xylophone, glockenspiel, tubular bells, 4 tom-toms, cymbals, gong, 3 tam-tams), 2 harps, violin I, violin II, viola, violoncello, double bass.
Commissioned by: Philadelphia Orchestra.
Call no.: **2003/102**

2125. Reale, Paul, 1943– Columbus concerto. N.p.: n.p., 1991.
1 score (80 p.); 44 cm.
For organ and band.
Composed for: organ, 6 flutes, 2 alto saxophones, tenor saxophone, baritone saxophone, 6 trumpets, 4 horns, 3 trombones, euphonium, 2 tubas, percussion (glockenspiel, 2 vibraphones, marimba, tubular bells, 2 suspended cymbals, timpani, triangle, 2 bass drums, tam-tam, tom-tom, snare drum, 2 crash cymbals, 2 gongs, crotales, glass wind chimes, finger cymbals, trap set, mark tree, Chinese blocks, xylophone).
Commissioned by: Ahmanson Organ Programming Endowment and National Endowment for the Arts.
Call no.: **1994/117**

2126. Reale, Paul, 1943– Inferno: for wind ensemble with antiphonal percussion. N.p.: n.p., 2003.
1 score (63 p.); 36 cm.
"Revised, November 2003"—caption.
Composed for: 2 flutes (also piccolo), 2 oboes, 3 clarinets, 2 bassoons, 2 alto saxophones (also soprano saxophone), tenor saxophone, baritone saxophone, 4 horns, 6 trumpets, 3 trombones, euphonium, tuba, piano (also celesta), percussion (tom-toms, vibraphone with bass bow, low gong, suspended cymbal, high tambourine, crash cymbal, snare drum, bass drum, tubular bells, xylophone, marimba, bamboo wind chimes, glockenspiel, triangle, high gong, flexatone, cowbell, 4 brake drums, glass wind chimes, 5 Chinese blocks, tam-tam, high siren, timpani).
Call no.: **2005/119**

2127. Reale, Paul, 1943– Piano concerto no. 2: "Matisse-jazz." N.p.: n.p., 1996.
1 score (62 p.); 49 cm.
Reproduced from manuscript.
Composed for: piano, 2 flutes (both also piccolo), 2 oboes, clarinet, 2 bassoons, 2 horns, trumpet, 2 trombones, percussion (timpani, 2 tubular bells, suspended cymbal, 2 glockenspiels, triangle, marimba, high gong, xylophone, timbales, vibraphone, snare drum, tambourine, tam-tam, finger cymbals, mark tree, bass drum, hi-hat, tom-toms), violin I, violin II, viola, violoncello, double bass.
Call no.: **1998/129**

2128. Redel, Martin Christoph, 1947– Bruckner-essay: op. 31.
Call no.: **1985/162**
No materials available.

2129. Reed, Alfred, 1921– Third symphony: for concert band/wind ensemble, 1987. N.p.: n.p., 1988.

1 manuscript score (106 leaves); 49 cm.
In pencil with some ink markings.
Composed for: piccolo, 3 flutes, 2 oboes, English horn, 2 bassoons, contrabassoon, clarinet in E♭, alto clarinet, 3 clarinets, bass clarinet, contrabass clarinet, 2 alto saxophones, tenor saxophone, baritone saxophone, 4 horns, 4 trumpets, 2 cornets, 3 trombones, bass trombone, treble baritone, bass baritone, tuba, timpani, double bass, harp, percussion (snare drum, bass drum, crash cymbals, suspended cymbals, gong, bells, vibraphone, xylophone, chimes).
Call no.: **1989/101**

2130. Reich, Steve, 1936– The cave. London: Hendon Music; Boosey & Hawkes, 1993.
1 score (3 v.); 35 cm.
Composed for: 2 flutes, oboe, English horn, clarinet, bass clarinet, percussion (prerecorded click track, typewriter, 2 bass drums, 2 vibraphones, 2 claves), 2 synthesizers, 2 pianos, violin I, violin II, viola, violoncello.
Call no.: **1994/118**

2131. Reich, Steve, 1936– City life. 2nd ed., April 1995. N.p.: Hendon Music; New York, NY: Boosey & Hawkes, 1995.
1 score (251 p.); 36 cm.
"Unrevised score; for promotional use only. This score is not to be used for performance."—p. 1 of cover.
Composed for: 2 flutes, 2 oboes, 2 clarinets, percussion (2 bass drums, snare drum, suspended cymbal, 2 vibraphones), 2 pianos, 2 violins, viola, violoncello, 2 Akai S-3000 samplers.
Commissioned by: Ensemble Modern, London Sinfonietta, and Ensemble InterContemporain.
Call no.: **1996/118**

2132. Reich, Steve, 1936– City life. 5th ed., 7/96. N.p.: Hendon Music: Boosey & Hawkes, 1996.
1 score (247 p.); 36 cm.
Composed for: 2 flutes, 2 oboes, 2 clarinets, percussion (2 bass drums, snare drum, suspended cymbal, 2 vibraphones), 2 pianos, 2 violins, viola, violoncello, double bass, 2 Akai S-3000 samplers.
Commissioned by: Ensemble Modern, London Sinfonietta, and Ensemble InterContemporain.
Call no.: **1998/130**

2133. Reich, Steve, 1936– The desert music.
Call no.: **1985/163**
No materials available.

2134. Reich, Steve, 1936– Different trains.
Composed for: tape (includes samples and 3 string quartets: 6 violins, 3 violas, 3 violoncellos), live string quartet (2 violins, viola, violoncello).
Commissioned by: Betty Freeman.
Call no.: **1989/102**
No materials available.

2135. Reich, Steve, 1936– Proverb. Third ed. 7/96. N. p.: Boosey & Hawkes: Hendon Music, 1996.
1 score (56 p.); 36 cm.
English words; text from Ludwig Wittgenstein's Culture and value.
Composed for: 3 sopranos, 2 tenors, 2 vibraphones, 4 synthesizers.
Commissioned by: BBC Proms and Early Music Festival of Utrecht.
Call no.: **1997/118**

2136. Reich, Steve, 1936– Proverb. Fourth ed. 2/97. N. p.: Boosey & Hawkes: Hendon Music, 1997.
1 score (iii, 56 p.); 36 cm.
English words; text from Ludwig Wittgenstein's Culture and value.
Includes program note by the composer.
Composed for: 3 sopranos, 2 tenors, 2 vibraphones, 4 synthesizers.
Commissioned by: BBC Proms and Early Music Festival of Utrecht.
Call no.: **2000/147**

2137. Reich, Steve, 1936– Three movements for orchestra. New York, NY: Hendon Music: Boosey & Hawkes, 1986.
1 score (68 p.); 36 cm.
Reproduced from holograph.
Composed for: 2 piccolos, 2 flutes, 3 oboes (3rd also English horn), 3 clarinets, 3 bassoons (3rd also contrabassoon), contrabassoon, 4 horns, 3 trumpets (1st also piccolo trumpet), 2 trombones, bass trombone, tuba, percussion (2 marimbas, 2 vibraphones, bass drum), 2 pianos, violin I, violin II, viola, violoncello, double bass.
Call no.: **1987/069**

2138. Reich, Steve, 1936– Three tales. New York, NY: Hendon Music/Boosey & Hawkes, 2002.
1 score (429 p.); 28 cm.
English words.
Video opera.
Contents: Hindenburg—Bikini—Dolly.
Composed for: 2 sopranos, 3 tenors, percussion (2 vibraphones, 2 snare drums, 2 kick drums, 2 suspended cymbals), 2 keyboards, 2 violins, viola, violoncello, prerecorded tape.

Commissioned by: Vienna Festival, BITE:02 Barbican Centre–London, FestivaldAutomne a Paris/Cite de la Musique, Hebbel Theater-Berlin, Holland Festival, Settembre Musica–Torino City Council, Centre Belem-Lisbon, Brooklyn Academy of Music Next Wave Festival, Spoleto Festival–USA, and Musica in Strasbourg.
Call no.: **2005/120**

2139. Reich, Steve, 1936– Triple quartet. 2nd ed. New York, NY: Hendon Music: Boosey & Hawkes, 1999.
1 score (152 p.); 28 cm.
"Quartets 2 and 3 are prerecorded or may be played by small string ensemble or string orchestra"—p. 1.
"2nd edition 9/99"—p. 2.
Composed for: 3 string quartets (6 violins, 3 violas, 3 violoncellos).
Commissioned by: National Endowment for the Arts.
Call no.: **2001/126**
Re-entered as: **2002/149**

2140. Reimann, Aribert, 1936– Ein apokalyptisches Fragment: für Mezzosopran, Klavier und Orchester, 1987. Partitur. Mainz; New York, NY: B. Schott's Söhne, 1987.
1 score (ii, 56 p.); 59 cm.
German words by Karoline von Günderrode.
Reproduced from manuscript.
Duration: 25:00.
Composed for: mezzo-soprano, piano, flute, alto flute (also piccolo), oboe, English horn, heckelphone, clarinet in A, basset horn, bass clarinet, bassoon, contrabassoon, 2 horns, timpani, percussion (suspended cymbal, 2 tam-tams), harp, violin I, violin II, viola, violoncello, double bass.
Commissioned by: City of Berlin.
Call no.: **1988/090**

2141. Reimann, Aribert, 1936– Bernarda Albas Haus: Oper in drei Akten (1998–2000). Partitur. Mainz; New York, NY: Schott, 2000.
1 score (292 p.); 42 cm.
German words by Frederico García Lorca, translated by the composer.
Original work by Enrique Beck.
Composed for: 5 sopranos, 2 mezzo-sopranos, alto, men's chorus, piccolo, flute, alto flute, bass flute, clarinet in E♭, clarinet, basset horn, bass clarinet, 3 trumpets, 3 trombones, tuba, 4 pianos, 12 violoncellos.
Commissioned by: Bayerische Staatsoper München.
Call no.: **2003/103**

2142. Reimann, Aribert, 1936– Finite infinity: poems by Emily Dickinson: for sopran[o] and orchestra = für Sopran und Orchester: (1994/95). Partitur. Mainz; New York, NY: Schott, 1996.
1 score (102 p.); 42 cm.
English words; also printed as text.
Composed for: soprano, piccolo, flute, alto flute, oboe, English horn, clarinet in E♭, clarinet, bass clarinet, bassoon, contrabassoon, 3 trumpets, 2 trombones, bass trombone, harp, violin I, violin II, viola, violoncello, double bass.
Commissioned by: Tonhalle-Gesellschaft Zürich.
Call no.: **1997/119**

2143. Reimann, Aribert, 1936– Konzert für Violine und Orchester, 1995/96. Partitur. Mainz; New York, NY: Schott, 1997.
1 score (89 p.); 42 cm.
Composed for: violin, piccolo, flute, alto flute, bass flute, oboe, English horn, heckelphone, clarinet in E♭, clarinet, bass clarinet, bassoon, 2 contrabassoons, 4 horns, 2 trumpets, trumpet, 2 trombones, tuba, timpani, percussion (4 tam-tams, suspended bronze plate, tubular bells), 2 harps, viola, double bass.
Commissioned by: Chicago Symphony Orchestra.
Call no.: **1998/131**

2144. Reimann, Aribert, 1936– Konzert für Violine, Violoncello und Orchester (1988/89). Partitur. Mainz; New York, NY: Schott, 1989.
1 score (60 p.); 59 cm.
Duration: ca. 25:00.
Composed for: violin, violoncello, piccolo, flute, alto flute, oboe, English horn, heckelphone, clarinet in E♭, clarinet, bass clarinet, 2 bassoons, contrabassoon, 4 horns, 3 trumpets, 2 trombones, tuba, timpani, percussion (suspended cymbals, 5 tam-tams, 5 bongos, 5 tom-toms), 2 harps, 6 double basses.
Commissioned by: Niedersächsisches Staatstheater Hannover.
Call no.: **1992/111**

2145. Reimann, Aribert, 1936– Kumi ori: für Bariton und Orchester: drei Gedichte von Paul Celan und Zeilen aus den Psalmen 74, 79, 122. Partitur. Mainz; New York: Schott, 1999.
1 score (35 p.); 42 cm.
Words in German and Hebrew.
Composed for: baritone, piccolo, flute (also piccolo), alto flute, oboe, oboe d'amore, heckelphone, bassoon, 2 contrabassoon, 2 trumpets in C (1st also trumpet in F), trumpet in B♭, bass trumpet, 2 trombones, bass trombone, tuba, percussion (9 gongs, 2 tam-tams), harp, violin I, violin II, viola, double bass.
Commissioned by: NDR Hamburg.
Call no.: **2004/105**

2146. Reimann, Aribert, 1936– Neun Stücke für Orchester (1993). Mainz; New York, NY: Schott, 1994.
1 score (54 p.); 42 cm.
Duration: 23:00.
Composed for: piccolo, flute, alto flute, oboe, English horn, clarinet in E♭, clarinet, bass clarinet, bassoon, contrabassoon, 4 horns, 3 trumpets, 2 trombones, tuba, timpani, percussion (3 tam-tams, bronze gongs, tubular bells), harp, piano, violin I, violin II, viola, violoncello, double bass.
Commissioned by: Houston Symphony.
Call no.: **1995/086**

2147. Reimann, Aribert, 1936– Das Schloss: nach dem Roman von Franz Kafka und der Dramatisierung von Max Brod: 1989–1991. Partitur. Mainz; New York, NY: Schott, 1992.
1 score (x, 491 p.); 42 cm.
Opera.
Reproduced from manuscript.
Composed for: voices, piccolo, flute, alto flute, oboe, English horn, heckelphone, clarinet in E♭, clarinet, bass clarinet, 2 bassoons, 2 contrabassoons, 4 horns, 2 trumpets, 2 trumpets, 3 trombones, tuba, percussion (chimes, glockenspiel, vibraphone, xylophone, timpani, military drum, snare drum, tenor drum, bass drum, tom-toms), 2 harps, piano, violin I, violin II, viola, violoncello, double bass.
Commissioned by: Deutsche Oper Berlin.
Call no.: **1993/110**

2148. Reimann, Aribert, 1936– Troades: nach den "Troerinnen" des Euripides von Franz Werfel: 1984–85. Partitur. Mainz; New York, NY: Schott, 1986.
1 score (301 p.); 59 cm.
German words by Gerd Albrecht and the composer.
Opera.
Reproduced from holograph.
Composed for: 2 sopranos, mezzo-soprano, alto, tenor, baritone, women's chorus, 2 flutes (both also piccolo), alto flute, bass flute, oboe, oboe d'amore, English horn, heckelphone, clarinet in E♭, clarinet (also clarinet in A), basset horn, bass clarinet, contrabass clarinet, 2 bassoons (2nd also contrabassoon), contrabassoon, 6 horns, 4 trumpets (1st–2nd also trumpet in D), 4 trombones (1st also bass trumpet), tuba, timpani, percussion (3 cymbals, 6 tam-tams, 3 suspended bronze plates, thundersheet, hi-hat, bass drum), 2 harps, organ, 12 violins, 10 violoncellos, 8 double basses.
Commissioned by: Bayerische Staatsoper München.
Call no.: **1987/070**

2149. Reise, Jay, 1950– Rasputin: opera in two acts. N.p.: Jay Reise, 1988.
1 miniature score (2 v.); 28 cm.
English words by the composer.
"Libretto: New York City Opera premiere version."
Reproduced from manuscript.
Duration: ca. 2:00:00.
Composed for: soprano, contralto, 5 tenors, baritone, bass-baritone, bass, SATB chorus, 3 flutes (1st and 3rd also piccolo, 2nd also alto flute), 3 oboes (3rd also English horn), 2 clarinets (1st also clarinet in E♭, 2nd also alto saxophone), bass clarinet, 2 bassoons, contrabassoon, 4 horns, 3 trumpets, 2 trombones, bass trombone, tuba, timpani, percussion (crotales, tam-tams, chimes, gongs, vibraphone, bass drum, slapstick, suspended cymbals, snare drum, side drum, bell tree, amplified church bells, tenor drum, Chinese temple blocks, cowbells, Chinese cymbal, wind machine, triangle, sizzle cymbal, marimba, maracas), harp, piano, upright piano, celesta, violin I, violin II, viola, violoncello, double bass.
Commissioned by: New York City Opera.
Call no.: **1991/103**
Also available:
Call no.: **1991/103 libretto**

2150. Reise, Jay, 1950– The selfish giant: choreographic tone-poem in six scenes based on the fairy tale by Oscar Wilde. N.p.: Jay Reise, 1997.
1 score (101 p.); 44 cm.
For orchestra.
Duration: ca. 26:00.
Includes synopsis program note and biographical information.
Contents: The children's romp in the giant's garden—Revel of the wind, hail, and snow in the unending winter—The children's carol—The giant and his friend—The death of the giant—The giant rises in a blaze of light.
Composed for: 2 flutes (2nd also piccolo), 2 oboes, 2 clarinets, 2 bassoons, contrabassoon, 4 horns, 3 trumpets, 2 trombones, bass trombone, tuba, timpani, percussion (very deep tam-tam, high gong, chimes, crash cymbals, xylophone, snare drum, crotales, suspended cymbal, bass drum, 5 temple blocks, 3 tom-toms), optional organ, violin I, violin II, viola, violoncello, double bass.
Commissioned by: Djong Victorin Yu and Philharmonia Orchestra.
Call no.: **2000/148**

2151. Reise, Jay, 1950– The selfish giant: choreographic tone-poem in six scenes, based on the fairy tale by Oscar Wilde. Study score. N.p.: Jay Reise, 1997.

1 score (101 p.); 36 cm.
For orchestra.
Duration: ca. 26:00.
Includes synopsis of the action.
Contents: The children's romp in the giant's garden—Revel of the wind, hail, and snow in the unending winter—The children's carol—The giant and his friend—The death of the giant—The giant rises in a blaze of light.
Composed for: 2 flutes (2nd also piccolo), 2 oboes, 2 clarinets, 2 bassoons, contrabassoon, 4 horns, 3 trumpets, 2 trombones, bass trombone, tuba, timpani, percussion (very deep tam-tam, high gong, chimes, crash cymbals, xylophone, snare drum, crotales, suspended cymbal, bass drum, 5 temple blocks, 3 tom-toms), optional organ, violin I, violin II, viola, violoncello, double bass.
Commissioned by: Djong Victorin Yu and Philharmonia Orchestra.
Call no.: **2001/127**

2152. Reiter, Herwig, 1941– Konzert für Violoncello und Orchester. N.p.: n.p., 2001.
1 score (11, 101 p.); 30 cm.
Reproduced from manuscript.
Composer's note and performance instructions in German.
Duration: ca. 29:30.
Composed for: violoncello, 3 flutes (all also piccolo ad lib.), 3 oboes, 3 clarinets (2nd–3rd also bass clarinet), 3 bassoons (3rd also contrabassoon), 3 horns, 3 trumpets, 4 trombones, percussion (2 rattles, chimes, timpani, 6 tom-toms, woodblock, 4 bongos, 3 congas, snare drum, bass drum, tambourine, 5 temple blocks, glockenspiel, gong, slapstick, guiro), harp, harpsichord, 2 keyboards, violin I, violin II, viola, violoncello, double bass.
Commissioned by: Wiener Jeunesse Orchester.
Call no.: **2003/104**

2153. Rekašius, A., 1928– Simfonija no. 7: in memoriam. Partitura. N.p.: n.p., 1987.
1 manuscript score (113 p.); 39 cm.
Holograph.
In ink.
Composed for: 4 flutes (1st also piccolo), 4 oboes, 4 bassoons (4th also contrabassoon), 4 horns, 4 trumpets, 4 trombones (4th also tuba), timpani, percussion (orchestra bells, tom-toms, snare drum, cymbals, claves, bass drum, vibraphone, woodblocks, chimes, gong, trap set, cowbells, triangle), harp, piano, violin I, violin II, viola, violoncello, double bass.
Call no.: **1990/102**

2154. Rendón G, Guillermo, 1935– Pentamorfosis en marron y argenta: marimba e clarinetto basso. N.p.: n.p., 1986.
1 score (25 p.); 23 x 34 cm.
Reproduced from holograph.
Duration: 28:00.
Contents: Penta-trimo—Pentafonia—Pentamorfosis.
Program notes and performance instructions in English and Spanish.
Composed for: bass clarinet, marimba.
Commissioned by: Duo Contemporain.
Call no.: **1989/103**

2155. Reynolds, Roger, 1934– Ariadne's thread: string quartet and computer synthesized sound. New York, NY: C. F. Peters, 1994.
1 score (39 p.); 28 x 43 cm.
Reproduced from holograph.
Duration: ca. 16:00.
Program note by the composer; includes performance instructions.
Contents: Finding the path—Pressing inwards—Animated line—Extremity—Exuberant line—Desperate line—Line of desire.
Composed for: 2 violins, viola, violoncello, electronics.
Commissioned by: Radio France, Florence Gould Foundation, and Ateliers UPIC.
Call no.: **1997/120**

2156. Reynolds, Roger, 1934– Dreaming: [for] orchestra. New York, NY: Edition Peters, 1992.
1 score (57 p.); 44 cm.
Composed for: piccolo, 2 flutes, 3 oboes, clarinet in E♭, clarinet, bass clarinet, 2 bassoons, contrabassoon, 3 horns, 3 trumpets, 2 trombones, bass trombone, tuba, timpani, percussion (3 triangles, crotales, tam-tam, vibraphone, marimba, xylophone, celesta, low gong, 3 suspended cymbals), harp, piano, violin I, violin II, viola, violoncello, double bass, tape.
Call no.: **1994/119**
Re-entered as: **1995/087** and **1996/119**

2157. Reynolds, Roger, 1934– Justice: for actress, soprano, percussionist, multichannel computer sound, real-time surround sound, and staging. New York, NY: C. F. Peters, 1999.
1 score (40 p.); 28 x 44 cm.
English words; also printed as text.
"A musical/dramatic presentation of Clytemnestra's primary scenes from [Reynold's] text: The red act (itself drawn from plays of Euripides and Aeschylus"—preface.
Reproduced from manuscript.

Contents: Sacrifice—Absence—Nightmare and judgment.
Composed for: soprano, computer, percussion (maracas, seed-pod rattle, Turkish tambourine, large Brazilian scraper, castanets, whip, tam-tam, bass drum, wind gong, wood snare drum, large Tibetan cymbals, vibraphone, crotales).
Commissioned by: Library of Congress.
Call no.: **2002/150**

2158. Reynolds, Roger, 1934– The red act arias. New York, NY: C. F. Peters Corp., 1997.
1 score (84 p.); 44 cm.
English words.
For orchestra, chorus, and computer sound.
Text by the composer, based on Aeschylus and Euripides.
Composed for: SATB chorus, computer, 4 flutes (3rd–4th also piccolo), 3 oboes, English horn, 3 clarinets (3rd also clarinet in E♭), bass clarinet, 3 bassoons, contrabassoon, 4 horns, 4 trumpets, 4 trombones (3rd–4th also bass trombone), tuba, percussion (xylophone, 3 Tibetan cymbals, high gong, vibraphone, crotales, medium gong, low tam-tam, high bass drum, marimba, 3 triangles, low gong, medium tam-tam, low bass drum, celesta, 3 woodblocks, 2 bongos, 2 tom-toms, medium bass drum), harp, piano, violin I, violin II, viola, violoncello, double bass.
Commissioned by: BBC.
Call no.: **1998/132**
Re-entered as: **2000/149** and **2001/128**

2159. Reynolds, Roger, 1934– Symphony (myths). New York, NY: C. F. Peters, 1990.
1 score (44 p.); 44 cm.
For orchestra.
Includes performance instructions.
Duration: ca. 25:00.
Contents: Futami ga Ura—Intermezzo—Kyaneai Symplegades.
Composed for: 4 flutes (3rd–4th also piccolo), 3 oboes, English horn, clarinet in E♭, 2 clarinets, bass clarinet, 3 bassoons, contrabassoon, 4 horns, 4 trumpets, 3 trombones, bass trombone, tuba, timpani, percussion (3 suspended cymbals, sizzle cymbal, 2 gongs, tam-tam, glockenspiel, xylophone, marimba, vibraphone, celesta, crotales, cowbells, 3 tom-toms, 2 bass drums), harp, piano, violin I, violin II, viola, violoncello, double bass.
Commissioned by: Suntory.
Call no.: **1991/104**
Re-entered as: **1992/112** and **1993/111**

2160. Rhodes, Phillip, 1940– Reels and reveries: variations for orchestra, 1990–91. N.p.: n.p., 1991.
1 score (83 p.); 36 cm.
Composed for: 3 flutes (3rd also piccolo), 2 oboes (2nd also English horn), clarinet in A, clarinet, 2 bassoons, 4 horns, 2 trumpets, 2 trombones, bass trombone, timpani, percussion (glockenspiel, vibraphone, xylophone, marimba, suspended cymbal, finger cymbals, tambourine, triangle, crash cymbals), harp, violin I, violin II, viola, violoncello, double bass.
Commissioned by: Yeager Charitable Trust.
Call no.: **1994/120**

2161. Ricketts, Ted, 1952– Drum taps: for choir, baritone solo, and orchestra. Full score. N.p.: Ted Ricketts, 2000.
1 score (17, 7, 17 p.); 28 cm.
English words.
Contents: Drum taps; Reconciliation / lyrics by Walt Whitman—War is kind / lyrics by Stephen Crane.
Composed for: baritone, SATB chorus, 2 flutes (1st also piccolo), 2 oboes (2nd also English horn), 2 clarinets, 2 bassoons, 4 horns, 3 trumpets, 2 trombones, bass trombone, tuba, timpani, percussion (snare drum, bass drum, suspended cymbals, gong, chimes, tubular bells, xylophone, marimba, crashed cymbals, vibraphone, vibraslap), harp, violin I, violin II, viola, violoncello, double bass.
Commissioned by: Bach Festival Choir.
Call no.: **2002/151**

2162. Rickli, Fritz, 1942– Soli deo gloria: Kanon für gemischten Chor und Brass Band, nach einer alten Kanonmelodie. Zuchwil, Switzerland: Musikverlag Frank, 2000.
1 score (18 p.); 30 cm.
Latin words.
Composed for: trumpet, horn, SATB chorus, piccolo trumpet, 3 trumpets, flugelhorn, 3 horns, 2 baritones, 2 trombones, bass trombone, euphonium, 2 tubas, drums, timpani.
Call no.: **2002/152**

2163. Riesco, Carlos, 1925– Mortal mantenimiento: para voz y orquesta. N.p.: n.p., 1980.
1 score (56 p.); 37 cm.
Spanish words by Roque Esteban Scarpa.
Reproduced from manuscript.
Composed for: soprano, piccolo, 2 flutes, 2 oboes, English horn, 2 clarinets, bass clarinet, 2 bassoons, contrabassoon, 4 horns, 2 trumpets, 2 trombones, tuba, timpani, percussion (military drum, tambourine, suspended cymbal, 2 tam-tams, bongos, tenor drum, claves, woodblock, triangle, temple blocks), harp, piano, celesta, violin I, violin II, viola, violoncello, double bass.
Call no.: **1993/112**

2164. Riesco, Carlos, 1925– Sinfonia no. 1: "De profundis." N.p.: n.p., 1984.
1 score (59 p.); 39 cm.
Latin words.
Composed for: 3 flutes (3rd also piccolo), 2 oboes, English horn, 3 clarinets (3rd also bass clarinet), 2 bassoons, contrabassoon, 4 horns, 3 trumpets, 3 trombones, tuba, timpani, percussion (bass drum, vibraphone, triangle, bongos, tenor drum, military drum, chimes, suspended cymbal, tam-tam, crash cymbals), violin I, violin II, viola, violoncello, double bass.
Call no.: **1986/094**

2165. Rihm, Wolfgang, 1952– Andere Schatten: musikalische Szene. Partitur. Wien: Universal Edition, 1985.
1 score (69 p.); 34 cm.
German words.
Based on Jean Paul's "Rede des toten Christus vom Weltgebäude herab, dass kein Gott sei."
For narrator, soprano, mezzo-soprano, baritone, mixed choir, and orchestra.
Reproduced from holograph.
Composed for: soprano, mezzo-soprano, baritone, SATB chorus, 2 flutes (2nd also piccolo), oboe, English horn, 2 clarinets (1st also clarinet in E♭), bass clarinet, bassoon, contrabassoon, 2 horns, trumpet, trombone, percussion (bass drum, 2 tom-toms, snare drum, woodblock, steel plate, 3 suspended cymbals, tam-tam, crash cymbals, anvil, chimes, slit drum, thundersheet, steel plate, bell plates), harp, piano, 2 violins, viola, 2 violoncellos, double bass.
Commissioned by: Alte Oper Frankfurt.
Call no.: **1986/095**

2166. Rihm, Wolfgang, 1952– Bildlos/weglos: Orchesterkomposition mit sieben Frauenstimmen, 1990/91. Partitur. Wien: Universal Edition, 1991.
1 score (20 p.); 42 cm.
Without words.
"Die Komposition kann mit dem Dopplelstrich nach Takt 161 enden—als reines Orchesterstück ohne Frauenstimmen"—p. iii.
Duration: ca. 14:00.
Composed for: 7 sopranos; group I: piccolo, 2 violins, percussion (2 antique cymbals, 2 bongos, snare drum); group II: harp, piano, 2 horns, flute, bass clarinet, contrabass tuba, percussion (2 antique cymbals, 4 domed gongs, 2 woodblocks, snare drum), viola, violoncello, double bass; group III: clarinet in A, 4 trumpets, 4 trombones, timpani, percussion (2 antique cymbals, whip, snare drum, bass drum), 6 violoncellos, 6 double basses.
Call no.: **1992/113**

2167. Rihm, Wolfgang, 1952– Deus passus: Passions-Stücke nach Lukas für Soli, Chor und Orchester (1999/2000). Studienpartitur. Vienna; New York, NY: Universal Edition, 2000.
1 miniature score (160 p.); 30 cm.
German or Latin words.
Reproduced from holograph.
Composed for: soprano, mezzo-soprano, alto, tenor, baritone, SATB chorus, 2 flutes (both also alto flute), 2 oboes, English horn, baritone oboe, bassoon, contrabassoon, 4 trombones, percussion (hyoshigi, tam-tam, snare drum, bass drum, 4 chimes, 2 domed gongs, 3 woodblocks, hammer), harp, organ, violin I, violin II, viola, violoncello, double bass.
Commissioned by: Internationale Bach-Akademie Stuttgart.
Call no.: **2002/153**

2168. Rihm, Wolfgang, 1952– Ernster Gesang: für Orchester (1996). Partitur. Wien: Universal Edition, 1997.
1 score (28 p.); 30 cm.
Duration: ca. 13:00.
Program note by the composer in German and English.
Composed for: English horn, 4 clarinets in A, 2 bassoons, contrabassoon, 4 horns, 3 trombones, bass tuba, 4 timpani, viola, violoncello, double bass.
Commissioned by: Philadelphia Orchestra Association.
Call no.: **1998/133**

2169. Rihm, Wolfgang, 1952– Die Eroberung von Mexico: Musik-Theater (1987–1991). Partitur. Wien: Universal Edition, 1991.
1 score (vii, 233 p.); 30 cm.
German words.
"Korr. 12.XI.1991."
Libretto by the composer based on texts by Antonin Artaud, Octavio Paz, and anonymous poems, "cantares mexicanos."
Includes selected source texts in German.
Reproduced from manuscript.
Composed for: soprano, baritone, SATB chorus, 3 flutes (all also piccolo), 3 oboes, English horn, 3 clarinets in A, bass clarinet, contrabassoon, 3 horns, 3 trumpets, 3 trombones, contrabass tuba, timpani, percussion (antique cymbals, 2 triangles, claves, 3 bongos, snare drums, flexatone, 3 chimes, 5 domed gongs, xylophone, 4 woodblocks, 3 guiros, 3 Alpine cowbells, bass drum, 3 tom-toms, vibraphone), harp, piano, electric organ, electric bass guitar, violin I, violin II, viola, violoncello, double bass.
Commissioned by: Hamburgische Staatsoper.
Call no.: **1993/113**

2170. Rihm, Wolfgang, 1952– Europa nach dem letzten Regen: elf Gedichte von Durs Grünbein: für Sopran, Alt, Tenor und Orchester (2003). Studienpartitur. Wien: Universal Edition, 2003.
1 score (160 p.); 31 cm.
German words; also printed as text.
"Korr. IX/2003"—p. 1.
Duration: ca. 50:00.
Reproduced from manuscript.
Composed for: soprano, alto, tenor, 2 flutes, piccolo, oboe, English horn, 2 clarinets in A, bass clarinet, 2 bassoons, contrabassoon, 4 horns, 2 trumpets, 3 trombones, tuba, timpani, percussion (antique cymbals, 2 gongs, 3 woodblocks, 3 suspended cymbals, piccolo snare drums, tom-tom, bass bow, large tam tam), harp, piano, violin I, violin II, viola, violoncello, double bass.
Commissioned by: Sächsische Staatsoper Dresden.
Call no.: **2005/121**

2171. Rihm, Wolfgang, 1952– Geheime Blöcke: 1988/89. Wien: Universal Edition, 1989.
1 score (15, 51, 33 p.); 32 cm.
French or German words; also printed as text.
For mixed chorus, speaking chorus (minimum 20 voices), 22 instruments; movement 2 for 4 voices, chorus, orchestra; movement 3 for soprano, orchestra with soprano.
Reproduced from manuscript.
Contents: Départ / text by Arthur Rimbaud—Geheimer Block: für Stimmen und Orchester (1988/89)—Frau/ Stimme für Sopran und Orchester mit Sopran / words from Heiner Müller's Der Auftrag.
Composed for: soprano, SATB chorus, speaking chorus, piccolo, 2 clarinets in E♭, 2 trumpets, 2 trombones, percussion (3 chimes, xylophone, 2 woodblocks, tam-tam, glockenspiel, snare drum, bass drum, 3 domed gongs, antique cymbals, slit drum, vibraphone, claves, guiro, tom-tom, 3 bongos), organ, 2 harps, 2 piano (1st also electric organ, 2nd also celesta), 2 violoncellos, 2 double basses.
Commissioned by: Wien Modern and Claudio Abbado.
Call no.: **1990/103**

2172. Rihm, Wolfgang, 1952– Gejagte Form: für Orchester (1995/96). Partitur. Wien: Universal Edition, 1997.
1 score (32 p.); 33 x 41 cm.
Reproduced from holograph.
Composed for: 2 flutes, English horn, 2 clarinets in A (1st also bass clarinet, 2nd also contrabass clarinet), contrabassoon, 2 horns, 2 trumpets, 2 trombones, bass tuba, percussion (3 woodblocks, snare drum, bass drum, 3 bongos, 3 tom-toms, 2 suspended cymbals, 3 tuned gongs, crash cymbals, marimba, conga), harp, piano, celesta, violin I, violin II, viola, violoncello, double bass.
Commissioned by: Ensemble Modern.
Call no.: **1997/121**

2173. Rihm, Wolfgang, 1952– Gesungene Zeit: Musik für Violine und Orchester (1991/92). Partitur. Wien: Universal Edition, 1993.
1 score (21 p.); 41 cm.
Reproduced from holograph.
Duration: ca. 25:00.
Composed for: violin, piccolo (also flute), flute, 2 oboes, clarinet in A, bass clarinet, bassoon, contrabassoon, horn, 2 trumpets, trombone, percussion (crotales, 2 bongos, large tam-tam, 2 tubular bells, small drum, 2 tom-toms, bow), harp, 2 violins, 4 violas, 4 violoncellos, 2 double basses.
Call no.: **1994/121**
Re-entered as: **1995/088**

2174. Rihm, Wolfgang, 1952– Ins Offene . . . : für Orchester (1990). Partitur. Wien: Universal Edition, 1990.
1 score (52 p.); 30 cm.
Reproduced from manuscript.
Duration: ca. 22:00.
Composed for: 3 piccolos, 3 clarinets in A, bass clarinet, contrabassoon, 3 horns, 3 trumpets, 3 trombones, contrabass tuba, percussion (antique cymbals, 3 bongos, snare drum, xylophone, 3 tom-toms, bass drum, vibraphone, 4 woodblocks, 2 triangles, 2 domed gongs, tam-tam), harp, piano, 2 violins, 2 violas, 6 violoncellos, 4 double basses.
Commissioned by: Scottish National Orchestra, Glasgow.
Call no.: **1991/105**

2175. Rihm, Wolfgang, 1952– Ins Offene . . . : für Orchester (2. Fassung, 1990/92). Partitur. Wien: Universal Edition, 1995.
1 score (iv, 56 p.); 42 cm.
"Die 1. Fassung dieser Komposition ist weiterhin gültig, allerdings nur in der überarbeiteten Form von 1992 (UA: Bologna 4.6.92); die im September 1990 in Glasgow uraufgeführte 'Urfassung' is ungültig"—p. iv.
Reproduced from holograph.
Duration: ca. 27:00.
Composed for: 3 piccolos, 3 clarinets in A, bass clarinet, contrabassoon, 3 horns, 3 trumpets, 3 trombones, contrabass tuba, percussion (2 antique cymbals, 4 bongos, snare drum, guiro, xylophone, 3 tom-toms, bass drum,

vibraphone, 4 woodblocks, 2 triangles, 4 button gongs, large tam-tam), harp, piano, 2 violins, 2 violas, 6 violoncellos, 4 double basses.
Commissioned by: Scottish National Orchestra, Glasgow.
Call no.: **1996/120**

2176. Rihm, Wolfgang, 1952– Jagden und Formen: für Orchester (1995/2001). Studienpartitur. Wien: Universal Edition, 2001.
1 miniature score (169 p.); 30 cm.
Principally reproduced from manuscript.
Duration: 55:00.
Composed for: 2 flutes, English horn, 2 clarinets (1st–2nd also bass clarinet, 2nd also contrabass clarinet), bassoon (also contrabassoon), 2 horns, 2 trumpets, 2 trombones, tuba (also bass tuba), percussion (antique cymbals, vibraphone, chimes, 4 woodblocks, suspended cymbal, 2 tam-tams, bass drums, marimba, 2 timpani, 3 bongos, 3 tom-toms, 6 domed gongs, conga), guitar, harp, piano, violin I, violin II, viola, violoncello, double bass.
Call no.: **2003/105**

2177. Rihm, Wolfgang, 1952– Klangbeschreibung I: (Fassung V/1988). Partitur. Wien: Universal Edition, 1988.
1 score (43 p.); 46 cm.
For 3 orchestral groups.
Reproduced from manuscript.
Composed for: group 1: piccolo, clarinet in E♭ (also bass clarinet), contrabass clarinet, 2 harps, piano, 2 violins, percussion (chimes, bass drum, bongo); group 2: 4 clarinets in A, contrabassoon, 4 horns, 2 trombones, contrabass tuba, 4 violoncellos, 4 double basses, percussion (snare drum, bass drum, African slit drum, 3 tom-toms, 3 woodblocks, xylophone, triangle, 2 metal plates, cowbells, antique cymbals, 5 chimes, bell plates, 3 button gongs, pistol shot, tam-tam); group 3: 5 flutes (also 2 piccolos), 3 oboes, 5 trumpets (also 2 piccolo trumpets), 2 trombones, piano, percussion (3 tam-tams, 3 snare drums, 3 woodblocks, 3 chimes).
Call no.: **1989/104 no. 1**

2178. Rihm, Wolfgang, 1952– Klangbeschreibung II: innere Grenze, 1987. Partitur. Wien: Universal Edition, 1987.
1 score (24 p.); 35 x 46 cm.
German words from a poem by Friedrich Nietzsche.
Reproduced from manuscript.
Composed for: 3 sopranos, mezzo-soprano, 2 trumpets, horn, trombone, contrabass trombone, percussion (3 bell plates, 8 antique cymbals, woodblock, hammer, 4 suspended cymbals, chimes, button gong, xylophone, hyoshigi, lion's roar, 3 tom-toms, bass drum, thundersheet, 2 bongos).
Call no.: **1989/104 no. 2**

2179. Rihm, Wolfgang, 1952– Klangbeschreibung III, 1984–1987. Partitur. Wien: Universal Edition, 1987.
1 score (103 p.); 46 cm.
For orchestra.
Reproduced from manuscript.
Composed for: 2 piccolos, 3 flutes, 3 oboes (3rd also English horn), clarinet in E♭ (also clarinet in A), 3 clarinets in A (1st–2nd also clarinet in E♭, 2nd–3rd bass clarinet), bass clarinet, 2 bassoons, contrabassoon, 4 horns, 4 trumpets (4th also piccolo trumpet), 4 trombones (4th also bass trombone), tuba, percussion (3 chimes, 10 bell plates, 4 button gongs, 8 metal plates, cowbells, 5 bongos, snare drum, 2 tom-toms, 16 woodblocks, African slit drum, hyoshigi, suspended cymbal, 5 crash cymbals, 6 tam-tams, 4 bass drums, triangle), 2 harps, piano, electric organ (also celesta), violin I, violin II, viola, violoncello, double bass.
Call no.: **1989/104 no. 3**

2180. Rihm, Wolfgang, 1952– Sotto voce: Notturno für Klavier und kleines Orchester (1999). Partitur. Wien: Universal Edition, 1999.
1 score (45 p.); 30 cm.
Duration: ca. 14:00.
Composed for: piano, piccolo, flute, oboe, English horn, clarinet, bassoon, 2 horns, timpani, harp, violin I, violin II, viola, violoncello, double bass.
Commissioned by: Berliner Philharmoniker and Chicago Symphony Orchestra.
Call no.: **2001/129**

2181. Rihm, Wolfgang, 1952– Unbenannt: Orchesterkomposition, 1986. Partitur. Wien: Universal Edition, 1986.
1 score (34 p.); 36 cm.
Reproduced from manuscript.
Composed for: 2 piccolos, 3 flutes (all also piccolo), 3 oboes, 2 English horns, 3 clarinets in A, 2 bass clarinets, 3 bassoons, 2 contrabassoons, 6 horns, 4 trumpets (2nd also piccolo trumpet), 4 trombones, 2 contrabass tubas, timpani, percussion (2 woodblocks, 2 tom-toms, slit drum, 3 tam-tams, antique cymbals, bongo, 3 bass drums, chimes, bell plates, metal plate, button gong, snare drum, hyoshigi, slapstick), 2 harps, large organ, harpsichord, violin I, violin II, viola, violoncello, double bass.
Commissioned by: Münchner Philharmoniker.
Call no.: **1987/071**

2182. Rihm, Wolfgang, 1952– Vers une symphonie fleuve IV: Orchesterkomposition (1997/1998). Partitur. Wien: Universal Edition, 1998.
1 miniature score (122 p.); 30 cm.
Duration: ca. 30:00.
At end: 3. März 1998, Wissenschaftskolleg zu Berlin.
Composed for: 4 flutes (4th also piccolo), 2 oboes, 2 English horns, 4 clarinets in A, 2 bass clarinets, 2 bassoons, 2 contrabassoons, 4 horns, 2 piccolo trumpets, 4 trumpets, 4 trombones, 2 tubas, timpani, percussion (2 woodblocks, 2 bongos, high woodblock, large tam-tam, low tom-tom, tubular bells, 3 suspended cymbals, snare drum), violin I, violin II, viola, violoncello, double bass.
Commissioned by: Sächsische Staatskapelle Dresden.
Call no.: **2000/150**

2183. Riley, Terry, 1935– Salome dances for peace. N.p.: Terry Riley, 1986.
1 score (5 v.); 22–28 cm.
For string quartet.
Reproduced from manuscript.
Duration: ca. 1:32:00.
Contents: Anthem of the Great Spirit—The gift—Conquest of the war demons—Good medicine—The ecstasy.
Composed for: 2 violins, viola, violoncello.
Call no.: **1991/106**

2184. Riley, Terry, 1935– Sun rings: for string quartet, chorus and pre-recorded spacescapes. N.p.: Terry Riley, 2001.
1 score (various pagings); 22 x 37 cm.
English words.
Text based on prayers.
Duration: ca. 1:30:00.
Contents: Sun rings overture—Hero danger—BeeBopteriso—Planet Elf Sindoori—Earth whistlers—Earth Jupiter kiss—Electron cyclotron frequency parlour—Prayer central—Audio interlude—Prayer central (part II)—Venus upstream—One earth, one people, one love.
Composed for: 2 violins, viola, violoncello, 80-voice SATB chorus, 20-voice women's chorus.
Commissioned by: NASA Art Program and National Endowment for the Arts.
Call no.: **2005/122**

2185. Rimkevicius, Gediminas, 1964– Energy, streams and directions. N.p.: n.p., 1993.
1 score (27 p.); 30 x 43 cm.
For instrumental ensemble.
Reproduced from manuscript.
Duration: ca. 11:15.
Composed for: flute, piccolo, oboe, clarinet, bassoon, bass clarinet, horn, trumpet, trombone, percussion, piano, 2 violins, viola, violoncello, double bass.
Call no.: **1995/089**

2186. Rimmer, John, 1939– Europa: concerto for brass band and orchestra. N.p.: John Rimmer, 2002.
1 score (79 p.); 35 cm. + 1 brass band rehearsal score (39 p.; 21 cm x 30 cm).
Duration: ca. 25:00.
Composed for: piccolo, 2 flutes, 2 oboes, 2 clarinets, bass clarinet, 2 bassoons, contrabassoon, 4 horns, 3 trumpets, 2 trombones, bass trombone, tuba, timpani, percussion (suspended cymbals [small, large], tam-tam, glockenspiel, vibraphone, xylophone, tubular bells, snare drum, 2 bongos, 3 tom-toms, bass drum), harp, brass band (soprano cornet, 10 cornets, flugelhorn, 3 tenor horns, 2 baritone horns, 2 trombones, bass trombone, 2 euphoniums, 2 E♭ basses, 2 B♭ basses), violin I, violin II, viola, violoncello, double bass.
Commissioned by: Aukland Philharmonia.
Call no.: **2005/123**

2187. Rimmer, John, 1939– Symphony: the feeling of sound, 1989. N.p.: John Rimmer, 1989.
1 score (115 p.); 37 cm.
Duration: ca. 25:00.
Program notes by the composer.
Composed for: 2 flutes (2nd also piccolo), 2 oboes, 2 clarinets (2nd also bass clarinet), 2 bassoons, 4 horns, 2 trumpets, 2 trombones, bass trombone, tuba, timpani, percussion (claves, glockenspiel, marimba, 3 temple blocks, snare drum, suspended cymbal, 2 gongs, bongos, 3 tom-toms, vibraphone, timpani, xylophone, tam-tam, triangle), harp, violin I, violin II, viola, violoncello, double bass.
Commissioned by: Auckland Philharmonia Orchestra.
Call no.: **1990/104**

2188. Rindfleisch, Andrew, 1963– The light fantastic: for wind ensemble (2001). N.p.: n.p., 2001.
1 score (143 p.); 31 cm.
Composed for: 3 flutes (all also piccolo), 2 oboes, 2 clarinets, bass clarinet, 2 bassoons, 2 horns, 2 trumpets, 2 trombones, tuba.
Commissioned by: Serge Koussevitsky Foundation and Library of Congress.
Call no.: **2003/106**

2189. Ritchie, Anthony, 1960– Symphony: "Boum." N.p.: Anthony Ritchie, 1993.
1 score (190 p.); 30 cm.
Reproduced from manuscript.

Duration: ca. 32:00.
Composed for: piccolo, 2 flutes, 2 oboes, 2 clarinets, bass clarinet, alto saxophone, 2 bassoons, 4 horns, 3 trumpets, 3 trombones, tuba, percussion (timpani, 2 tom-toms, tam-tam, log drum, xylophone, tubular bells, glockenspiel, bass drum, triangle), violin I, violin II, viola, violoncello, double bass.
Commissioned by: Dunedin Sinfonia.
Call no.: **1996/121**

2190. Robbins, Scott, 1964– The heart's trapeze: for orchestra. Tallahassee, FL: Scott Robbins, 1994.
1 score (59 p.); 28 cm.
Duration: ca. 13:00.
Composed for: piccolo, 2 flutes, 2 oboes, English horn, 2 clarinets, bass clarinet, 2 bassoons, contrabassoon, 4 horns, 3 trumpets, 2 trombones, bass trombone, tuba, timpani, percussion (finger cymbals, small suspended cymbal, crash cymbals, crotales, glockenspiel, tubular chimes, sandpaper blocks, 5 temple blocks, small triangle, large suspended cymbal, large tam-tam, vibraphone, marimba, tenor drum, 2 tom-toms, bell tree, 5 bowl gongs, castanets, bass drum), harp, celesta, violin I, violin II, viola, violoncello, double bass.
Call no.: **2000/151**

2191. Rochberg, George, 1918–2005. Circles of fire: for two pianos (1996–1997). Bryn Mawr, PA: T. Presser, 1998.
1 score (157 p.); 37 cm.
Duration: ca. 70:00–75:00.
Includes appendix, The symmetry of Contrapunctus XII and Contrapunctus XIII, J. S. Bach, the Art of fugue (relating to movement 13, Fuga a sei voci), and program note by the composer.
Contents: Solemn refrain (I)—Chiaroscuro—Canonic variations—Gioco del fuoco—Solemn refrain (II)—Gargoyles—Nebulae—Solemn refrain (III)—Sognando—The infinite ricercare—Solemn refrain (IV)—Caprichos—Fuga a sei voci—Chiaroscuro (II)—Solemn refrain (V).
Composed for: 2 pianos.
Commissioned by: Hopkins Center at Dartmouth College, Grammage Auditorium Series at Arizona State University, George Bishop Lane Artist Series at University of Vermont, Duke University Department of Music series Encounters With the Music of Our Time, and Penn Contemporary Music at University of Pennsylvania Department of Music.
Call no.: **2000/152**

2192. Rochberg, George, 1918–2005. Concerto for clarinet and orchestra (1994–1995). Bryn Mawr, PA: Theodore Presser, 1995.
1 score (108 p.); 44 cm.
Reproduced from manuscript.
Duration: ca. 26:00.
Composed for: clarinet, 3 flutes (3rd also piccolo), 2 oboes, English horn, 2 bassoons, contrabassoon, 4 horns, 3 trumpets, 3 trombones, tuba, timpani, percussion (large suspended cymbal, small cymbal, crash cymbals, tam-tam, bass drum, tubular bells), harp, celesta, violin I, violin II, viola, violoncello, double bass.
Commissioned by: Philadelphia Orchestra.
Call no.: **1998/134**

2193. Rochberg, George, 1918–2005. Symphony no. 5 for large orchestra, 1984. Bryn Mawr, PA: T. Presser, 1986.
1 score (151 p.); 49 cm.
Reproduced from holograph.
Duration: ca. 23:00.
Composed for: 3 flutes (3rd also piccolo), 2 oboes, English horn, 2 clarinets, bass clarinet, 2 bassoons, contrabassoon, 4 horns, 4 trumpets, 2 trombones, bass trombone, tuba, timpani, harp, piano, celesta, vibraphone, violin I, violin II, viola, violoncello, double bass.
Call no.: **1987/072**

2194. Rochberg, George, 1918–2005. Symphony no. 6 (1986–1987). Bryn Mawr, PA: T. Presser, 1987.
1 score (203 p.); 51 cm.
For orchestra.
Reproduced from manuscript.
Duration: ca. 33:00.
Composed for: piccolo, 3 flutes, 3 oboes, English horn, clarinet in E♭, 3 clarinets, bass clarinet, 3 bassoons, contrabassoon, 4 horns, 4 trumpets, 2 trombones, bass trombone, tuba, timpani, percussion (xylophone, vibraphone, tubular bells, triangle, 2 suspended cymbals, crash cymbals, tam-tam, whip, guiro, snare drum, tenor drum, bass drum), 2 harps, celesta, violin I, violin II, viola, violoncello, double bass.
Commissioned by: Pittsburgh Symphony Society.
Call no.: **1988/091**
Re-entered as: **1989/105** and **1991/107**

2195. Rodriguez, Robert Xavier, 1946– Bachanale: concertino for orchestra (1999). New York, NY: G. Schirmer, 1999.
1 score (129 p.); 43 cm.
Contents: Die Brücke über dem Bach—Die Brücke geschmückt—Noch einmal über die Brücke—Ecco l'eco—Samba da gamba.
Composed for: piccolo, 2 flutes, 2 oboes, English horn,

2 clarinets, bass clarinet, 2 bassoons, contrabassoon, 4 horns, 3 trumpets, 2 trombones, bass trombone, tuba, percussion (crotales, suspended cymbal, marimba, chimes, conga, sandpaper blocks, cuíca, cabasa, tom-tom, vibraslap, vibraphone, gong, timpani, finger cymbals, shaker, claves, wind chimes, cowbells, Chinese cymbal, tambourine, temple blocks, glockenspiel, triangle, whip, snare drum, crash cymbals, agogo bells, bongos, police whistle), 2 keyboards, harp, violin I, violin II, viola, violoncello, double bass.
Commissioned by: San Antonio Symphony.
Call no.: **2001/130**

2196. Rodriguez, Robert Xavier, 1946– Bachanale: concertino for orchestra, 1999. New York, NY: G. Schirmer, 1999.
1 miniature score (129 p.); 36 cm.
Contents: Die Brücke über dem Bach—Die Brücke geschmückt—Noch einmal über die Brücke—Ecco l'eco—Samba da gamba.
Composed for: piccolo, 2 flutes, 2 oboes, English horn, 2 clarinets, bass clarinet, 2 bassoons, contrabassoon, 4 horns, 3 trumpets, 2 trombones, bass trombone, tuba, percussion (crotales, suspended cymbal, marimba, chimes, conga, sandpaper blocks, cuíca, cabasa, tom-tom, vibraslap, vibraphone, gong, timpani, finger cymbals, shaker, claves, wind chimes, cowbells, Chinese cymbal, guiro, tambourine, temple blocks, glockenspiel, triangle, whip, snare drum, crash cymbals, agogo bells, bongos, police whistle), 2 keyboards, harp, violin I, violin II, viola, violoncello, double bass.
Commissioned by: San Antonio Symphony.
Call no.: **2003/107**

2197. Rodriguez, Robert Xavier, 1946– A colorful symphony. New York, NY: Galaxy Music, 1988.
1 score (47 p.); 51 cm.
English words by Norton Juster from his book The phantom tollbooth.
For narrator and orchestra.
Duration: ca. 20:00.
Composed for: narrator, piccolo, 2 flutes, 2 oboes, 2 clarinets, 2 bassoons, 4 horns, 2 trumpets, 2 trombones, bass trombone, tuba, timpani, percussion (glockenspiel, triangle, glass wind chimes, tambourine, gong, vibraphone, tenor drum, suspended cymbal, finger cymbals, snare drum, crotales, chimes, xylophone, bass drum, cymbals), harp, piano, violin I, violin II, viola, violoncello, double bass.
Commissioned by: Indianapolis Symphony Orchestra.
Call no.: **1990/105**

2198. Rodriguez, Robert Xavier, 1946– Forbidden fire: cantata for the next millennium for bass-baritone, double chorus and orchestra (1998). New York, NY: G. Schirmer, 1998.
1 score (90 p.); 44 cm.
English and German words.
"Text adapted by the composer from Aeschylus . . . [et al.]."
Duration: 22:00.
Composed for: bass-baritone, SATB chorus, piccolo, 2 flutes, 2 oboes, 2 clarinets in A, 2 bassoons, 4 horns, 3 trumpets, 2 trombones, bass trombone, tuba, timpani, percussion (vibraphone, brass wind chimes, bass drum, chimes, gong, crotales, triangle, suspended cymbal, glockenspiel, marimba, cymbals), harp, piano, violin I, violin II, viola, violoncello, double bass.
Commissioned by: Abraham Frost Commission Series at University of Miami School of Music.
Call no.: **2000/153**

2199. Rodriguez, Robert Xavier, 1946– Forbidden fire: cantata for the next millennium for bass-baritone, double chorus, and orchestra (1998). New York, NY: G. Schirmer, 1998.
1 miniature score (90 p.); 36 cm.
English and German words.
"Text adapted by the composer from Aeschylus . . . [et al.]."
Duration: 22:00.
Composed for: bass-baritone, SATB chorus, piccolo, 2 flutes, 2 oboes, 2 clarinets in A, 2 bassoons, 4 horns, 3 trumpets, 2 trombones, bass trombone, tuba, timpani, percussion (vibraphone, brass wind chimes, bass drum, chimes, gong, crotales, triangle, suspended cymbal, glockenspiel, marimba, cymbals), harp, piano, violin I, violin II, viola, violoncello, double bass.
Commissioned by: Abraham Frost Commission Series at University of Miami School of Music.
Call no.: **2004/106**

2200. Rodriguez, Robert Xavier, 1946– Frida: the story of Frida Kahlo. Full score. N.p.: n.p., 1991.
1 score (2 v.); 36 cm.
English words by Hilary Blecher and Migdalia Cruz.
Opera in two acts.
Composed for: voices, clarinet in A (also alto saxophone), trumpet (also flugelhorn), bass trombone, percussion (bass drum, 2 tambourines, marimba, castanets, wind chimes, woodblocks, ratchet, maracas, sizzle cymbal, chimes, timpani, glockenspiel, suspended cymbals, triangle, snare drum, gong, bell tree, tenor drum, gunshot), guitar, accordion, piano, keyboards, violin I, violin II, viola, violoncello, double bass.
Call no.: **1994/122**

2201. Rodriguez, Robert Xavier, 1946– Máscaras: for violoncello and orchestra (1993). N.p.: n.p., 199-?.
1 score (153 p.); 28 cm.
"For performance either as a concert piece or as a ballet"—program notes.
Program notes in English.
Contents: Evocación—El murciélago—La sirena—Compañeros de la oscuridad—El angel—El tigre.
Composed for: violoncello, 2 flutes (2nd also piccolo), 2 oboes (2nd also English horn), 2 clarinets (2nd also clarinet in E♭, bass clarinet), 2 bassoons, 2 horns, 2 trumpets, tenor trombone (also bass trombone), 4 timpani (also tambourine, triangle, suspended cymbals), percussion (marimba, crotales, large tom-tom, chimes, crash cymbal, sleigh bells, bell tree, whip, ratchet, guiro, cabasa, castanets, slide whistle, vibraphone, snare drum, bass drum, lion's roar, gong, temple blocks, jawbone of an ass, brass wind chimes, maracas, cowbell, tambourine), harp, piano, violin I, violin II, viola, violoncello, double bass.
Commissioned by: Carlos Prieto.
Call no.: **1997/122**

2202. Rodriguez, Robert Xavier, 1946– Meta 4: for string quartet (1993). New York, NY: G. Schirmer, 1993.
1 score (31 p.); 31 cm.
Duration: 17:00.
Composed for: 2 violins, viola, violoncello.
Call no.: **1996/122**

2203. Rodriguez, Robert Xavier, 1946– Sinfonía à la mariachi: (1997). New York, NY: G. Schirmer, 1998.
1 score (111 p.); 36 cm.
For 2 orchestral groups.
Duration: 20:00.
Contents: Mariage—Calaveras—Las barricadas misteriosas—Plaza de los mariachis.
Composed for: orchestra I: piccolo, 2 flutes (2nd also piccolo), 2 oboes (2nd also English horn), 2 clarinets (2nd also clarinet in E♭), 2 bassoons, 4 horns, 2 trumpets, 2 trombones, bass trombone, timpani, percussion (3 additional timpani, woodblock, maracas, vibraphone, brass wind chimes, temple blocks, ratchet, triangle, tubular bells, suspended cymbals, gong, tubo, vibraslap, tambourine, glass wind chimes, guiro, claves), piano (also synthesizer), violin I, violin II, viola, violoncello, double bass; orchestra II: 2 trumpets, percussion (marimba, crotales), accordion, harp, guitar, violin I, violin II, viola, violoncello, double bass; additional optional instruments: 2 trumpets, violins, guitars, bass guitar.
Commissioned by: San Antonio Symphony Orchestra.
Call no.: **2002/154**

2204. Rodriguez, Robert Xavier, 1946– Suor Isabella.
Call no.: **1985/164**
No materials available.

2205. Rogillio, Kathy J., 1950– Pange lingua. N.p.: n.p., 198-?.
1 score (26 p.); 29 cm.
English words.
Reproduced from manuscript.
Duration: ca. 7:00.
Composed for: SATB chorus, organ.
Call no.: **1986/096**

2206. Rohde, Kurt, 1966– Double trouble: chamber concerto for two violas and small ensemble (2002). N.p.: Kurt Rohde, 2002.
1 score (19, 11, 16 p.); 36 cm.
Duration: 17:00.
Program notes in English.
Contents: Obsessive compulsive—Double—Spazoid.
Composed for: 2 violas, flute (doubling piccolo), clarinet in A (doubling bass clarinet), piano, violin, violoncello.
Call no.: **2004/107**

2207. Rohlig, Harald, 1926– Sonatina for violin and piano. Tuscaloosa, AL: Alderpoint Press, 1994.
1 score (20 p.) + 1 part (7 p.); 28 cm.
Composed for: violin, piano.
Call no.: **2000/154**

2208. Rohlig, Harald, 1926– Symphony 1993. Birmingham, AL: Alderpoint Press, 1993.
1 score (284 p.); 30 cm.
Composed for: 2 flutes, 2 oboes, 2 clarinets, 2 bassoons, contrabassoon, 4 horns, 2 trumpets, 3 trombones, tuba, timpani, violin I, violin II, viola, violoncello, double bass.
Call no.: **1996/123**

2209. Roig-Francolí, Miguel A., 1953– Cantata: on Dante's Vita nuova: for baritone, mixed chorus and orchestra. N.p.: n.p., 1984.
1 score (111 p.); 33 cm.
Italian words; also printed as text.
Reproduced from holograph.
Duration: ca. 37:00.
Composed for: baritone, SATB chorus, 3 flutes (3rd also piccolo), 3 oboes (3rd also English horn), 3 clarinets, 3 bassoons (3rd also contrabassoon), 4 horns, 2 trumpets, 3 trombones, tuba, timpani, percussion (xylophone, glockenspiel, triangle, tambourine, snare drum, jingles, suspended cymbal, tam-tam, cymbals, bass

drum), 2 harps, piano, celesta, mandolin, violin I, violin II, viola, violoncello, double bass.
Commissioned by: National Orchestra and Choir of Spain.
Call no.: **1985/165**

2210. Rokeach, Martin, 1953– Quartet for piano and strings (1996). Martinez, CA: M. Rokeach, 1996.
1 score (57 p.); 28 cm.
Duration: 16:00.
Includes program notes by the composer.
Contents: Haunted: theme and nine brief variations—Island of calm—Facing the storm: fugue.
Composed for: violin, viola, violoncello, piano.
Call no.: **2001/131**

2211. Rokeach, Martin, 1953– Sonata for violoncello and piano.
Composed for: violoncello, piano.
Call no.: **1985/166**
No materials available.

2212. Rollin, Robert, 1947– Dreamtime images: for orchestra. N.p.: Seesaw Music, 1995.
1 score (65 p.); 28 cm.
Based on Aboriginal legends as embodied in the paintings of Ainslee Roberts.
Duration: ca. 18:00.
Composed for: piccolo, 2 flutes, 2 oboes, 2 clarinets, 2 bassoons, 4 horns, 3 trumpets, 2 trombones, bass trombone, tuba, timpani, percussion (chimes, glockenspiel, bass drum, tenor drum, 2 temple blocks, claves, woodblock, xylophone, vibraphone, snare drum, marimba, sizzle cymbal, tam-tam, 3 triangles, tambourine, hand cymbals, suspended cymbal), harp, violin I, violin II, viola, violoncello, double bass.
Commissioned by: Cleveland Philharmonic.
Call no.: **1996/124**

2213. Roosenschoon, Hans, 1952– Iconography. N.p.: n.p., 1983.
1 score (49 leaves); 42 cm.
For orchestra.
Reproduced from holograph.
Contents: Skadubeeld = Silhouette—Ilusie = Illusion—Kinetika = Kinetics.
Composed for: 3 flutes, 2 oboes, English horn, 3 clarinets (3rd also bass clarinet), 3 bassoons (3rd also contrabassoon), 4 horns, 3 trumpets, 2 trombones, bass trombone, tuba, percussion (sleigh bells, crotales, 2 cowbells, 4 suspended cymbals, 2 gongs, tam-tam, woodblock, 4 Chinese temple blocks, tubular bells, vibraphone, xylophone, 2 bongos, 4 tom-toms, timpani), piano, violin, viola, violoncello, double bass.
Commissioned by: Southern African Music Rights Organization (SAMRO).
Call no.: **1991/108**

2214. Roosenschoon, Hans, 1952– The magic marimba. N.p.: n.p., 1991.
1 miniature score (99 p.); 30 cm.
For orchestra.
Reproduced from holograph.
Composed for: piccolo, 2 flutes, 2 oboes, English horn, clarinet in E♭, 2 clarinets, bass clarinet, alto saxophone, 2 bassoons, contrabassoon, 4 horns, 3 trumpets, 2 trombones, bass trombone, tuba, percussion (marimba, crotales, gong, maracas, xylophone, 2 suspended cymbals, claves, 2 bongos, 4 tom-toms, 3 cowbells, 5 Chinese temple blocks, tambourine, guiro, glockenspiel, tubular bells, triangle, bell tree, tam-tam, bass drum), timpani, piano (4 hands), organ, violin I, violin II, viola, violoncello, double bass.
Commissioned by: Stigting vir die Skeppende Kunste.
Call no.: **1992/114**

2215. Roosenschoon, Hans, 1952– Mantis: ballet in five tableaux. Cape Town: Amanuensis Quality Editions, 1992.
1 score (125 p.); 30 cm.
For orchestra.
Duration: ca. 30:00.
Contents: Introduction—A dream dreaming us—The first fire—Death and honey—Metamorphosis—The son of mantis.
Composed for: flute (also piccolo), oboe (also English horn), clarinet (also bass clarinet), bassoon, horn, trumpet, trombone, percussion (glockenspiel, vibraphone, chimes, marimba, 4 Chinese blocks, maracas, bass drum, tam-tam, 2 bongos, 4 tom-toms, 2 cymbals, claves, guiro), piano, violin I, violin II, viola, violoncello, double bass.
Commissioned by: Total SA.
Call no.: **1993/114**

2216. Roosenschoon, Hans, 1952– Timbila: for chopi xylophone orchestra and symphony orchestra. N.p.: n.p., 1985.
1 score (28 leaves); 42 cm.
Reproduced from holograph.
Includes description of music required from chopi (5 leaves; 22 cm).
Composed for: xylophone orchestra (sanje, dibhinda, chinzumana xylophones, njele rattles), 3 flutes, 2 oboes, English horn, 2 clarinets, bass clarinet, 2 bassoons, contrabassoon, 4 horns, 3 trumpets, 2 trom-

bones, bass trombone, tuba, violin I, violin II, viola, violoncello, double bass.
Commissioned by: Oude Meester Foundation for the Performing Arts.
Call no.: **1988/092**

2217. Roqué Alsina, Carlos, 1941– Concerto: pour piano et orchestre. Milano: Suvini Zerboni, 1985.
1 score (46 p.); 54 cm.
Reproduced from manuscript.
Composed for: piano, 3 flutes (3rd also piccolo), 3 oboes, English horn, 3 clarinets (3rd also clarinet in E♭, 2nd also bass clarinet), 3 bassoons (3rd also contrabassoon), 5 horns, 3 trumpets, 3 trombones, tuba, timpani, percussion (2 cymbals, triangle, marimba, bass drum, tam-tam, tubular bells, wood chimes, crash cymbals, tambourine, 5 temple blocks), harp, violin I, violin II, viola, violoncello, double bass.
Call no.: **1986/004**

2218. Roqué Alsina, Carlos, 1941– Prima sinfonia: per tre solisti e orchestra. Milano: Edizioni Suvini Zerboni, 1983.
1 score (63 p.); 55 cm.
German words in 3rd movement.
For soprano, flute, violoncello, and orchestra.
Reproduced from holograph.
Composed for: 3 flutes (2nd–3rd also piccolo), 3 oboes (3rd also English horn), 3 clarinets (2nd also clarinet in E♭, 3rd also bass clarinet), 3 bassoons (3rd also contrabassoon), 4 horns, 3 trumpets, 3 trombones, tuba, percussion (3 tom-toms, snare drum, 5 temple blocks, crash cymbals, hyoshige, sleigh bells, maracas, castanets, triangle, timpani, tambourine, 2 cymbals, tam-tam, whip, bass drum), violin I, violin II, viola, violoncello, double bass.
Commissioned by: International Festival for Contemporary Music of Metz.
Call no.: **1985/003**

2219. Rorem, Ned, 1923– Aftermath: for medium voice, violin, cello, and piano. New York, NY: Boosey & Hawkes, 2002.
1 score (48 p.); 31 cm.
English words; also printed as text.
Texts by John Scott of Amwell, Richard Eberhart, John Hollander, Shakespeare, Walter Savage Landour, Elizabeth Barrett Browning, Jorge Luis Borges, Randall Jarrell, and Muriel Rukeyser.
Composer's note in English.
Contents: The drum—Tygers of wrath—The fury of the aerial bombardment—The park—Sonnet LXIV—On his seventy-fifth birthday—Grief—Remorse for any death—Losses—Then.
Composed for: voice, violin, violoncello, piano.
Commissioned by: Ravinia Festival, Highland Park, IL.
Call no.: **2005/124**

2220. Rorem, Ned, 1923– Concerto for English horn and orchestra. New York, NY: Boosey & Hawkes, 1992.
1 score (59 p.); 36 cm.
Duration: ca. 24:00.
Composed for: English horn, 2 flutes (2nd also piccolo), 2 oboes, 2 clarinets, 2 bassoons, 2 horns, 2 trumpets, timpani, percussion (xylophone, snare drum, glockenspiel, tenor drum, bass drum, triangle, 3 bongos, large cymbal, castanets, tambourine, slapstick, metal plate), harp, piano (also celesta), violin I, violin II, viola, violoncello, double bass.
Commissioned by: Philharmonic-Symphony Society of New York.
Call no.: **1996/125**

2221. Rorem, Ned, 1923– Evidence of things not seen: 36 songs for 4 singers. N.p.: Boosey & Hawkes, 1997.
1 score (xvi, 165 p.); 28 cm.
Song cycle.
English words; also printed as text.
Texts by various authors.
Composed for: soprano, alto, tenor, baritone, piano.
Commissioned by: New York Festival of Song and Leonore and Ira Gershwin Trust.
Call no.: **2000/155**

2222. Rorem, Ned, 1923– Evidence of things not seen: thirty-six songs for four solo voices and piano. N.p.: Boosey & Hawkes, 1999.
1 score (xiv, 165 p.); 31 cm.
Song cycle.
For 1–4 voices (SATB, in various combinations).
Words by various authors; also printed as text.
Duration: ca. 1:40:00.
Composed for: soprano, alto, tenor, baritone, piano.
Commissioned by: New York Festival of Song and Leonore and Ira Gershwin Trust.
Call no.: **2001/132**
Re-entered as: **2002/155**

2223. Rorem, Ned, 1923– Goodbye my fancy: an oratorio for mixed chorus and orchestra with alto and baritone soloists. New York, NY: Boosey & Hawkes, 1990.
1 miniature score (184 p.); 28 cm.
English words based on the verse and prose of Walt Whitman.

Reproduced from manuscript.
Composed for: alto, baritone, SATB chorus, 3 flutes (3rd also piccolo), 3 oboes (3rd also English horn), 3 clarinets, 2 bassoons, 4 horns, 3 trumpets, 3 trombones, tuba, timpani, percussion (triangle, glockenspiel, snare drum, bass drum, xylophone, vibraphone, tom-toms, tenor drum, woodblock, tambourine, 2 suspended cymbals, gong, metal plate), harp, piano (also celesta), violin I, violin II, viola, violoncello, double bass.
Commissioned by: Chicago Symphony.
Call no.: **1991/109**

2224. Rorem, Ned, 1923– Organ concerto. New York, NY: Boosey & Hawkes, 1985.
1 score (138 p.); 28 cm.
Duration: 30:00.
Composed for: organ, 2 horns, trumpet, trombone, timpani, violin I, violin II, viola, violoncello, double bass.
Call no.: **1990/106**

2225. Rorem, Ned, 1923– Piano concerto for left hand and orchestra. Full score. New York, NY: Boosey & Hawkes, 1993.
1 score (209 p.); 36 cm.
Duration: 34:00.
Composed for: piano, 2 flutes (2nd also piccolo), 2 oboes, 2 clarinets, 2 bassoons, 2 horns, 2 trumpets, 2 trombones, timpani, percussion (bass drum, snare drum, tenor drum, tom-toms, bongos, triangle, gong, glockenspiel, anvil, metal plate, marimba, cymbals, chimes, slapstick, vibraphone), harp, celesta, violin I, violin II, viola, violoncello, double bass.
Commissioned by: Curtis Institute of Music.
Call no.: **1994/123**
Re-entered as: **1997/123**

2226. Rorem, Ned, 1923– Pilgrim strangers.
Call no.: **1985/167**
No materials available.

2227. Rorem, Ned, 1923– String symphony, 1985. New York, NY: Boosey & Hawkes, 1986.
1 score (59 p.); 36 cm.
"Score corrected 1/8/86 (R.W.)."
Duration: ca. 23:00.
Composed for: violin I, violin II, viola, violoncello, double bass.
Commissioned by: Atlanta Symphony Orchestra.
Call no.: **1986/097**

2228. Rorem, Ned, 1923– Swords and plowshares. New York, NY: Boosey & Hawkes, 1991.
1 score (175 p.); 44 cm.
English words by Arthur Rimbaud, Lord Byron, W. H. Auden, W. B. Yeats, Archibald MacLeish, E. A. Robinson, Emily Dickinson, Walt Whitman, Denise Levertov, and from Psalm 133.
For solo voices (SATB) and orchestra.
Reproduced from holograph.
Contents: Asleep in the valley—I had a dream—O what is the sound . . . —An Irish airman foresees his death—The silent slain—The dark hills—Success is counted sweetest—Death of a Wisconsin officer—Making peace—The Lake Isle of Innisfree—To make a prairie it takes . . . —So we'll go no more a-roving—I dreamed in a dream—Behold how good and how pleasant.
Composed for: soprano, alto, tenor, bass, 3 flutes (3rd also piccolo), 3 oboes (3rd also English horn), 3 clarinets, 2 bassoons, 4 horns, 3 trumpets, 3 trombones, tuba, timpani, percussion (snare drum, tenor drum, xylophone, cymbals, gong, anvil, metal plate, slapstick, vibraphone, triangle, glockenspiel, woodblock, 2 tom-toms, bass drum, tam-tam, castanets, chimes), harp, piano (also celesta), violin I, violin II, viola, violoncello, double bass.
Commissioned by: WCRB 102.5 FM Classical Radio Station Boston.
Call no.: **1992/115**

2229. Rorem, Ned, 1923– Swords and plowshares. New York, NY: Boosey & Hawkes, 1992.
1 score (175 p.); 36 cm.
English words by Arthur Rimbaud, Lord Byron, W. H. Auden, W. B. Yeats, Archibald MacLeish, E. A. Robinson, Emily Dickinson, Walt Whitman, Denise Levertov, and from Psalm 133.
For 4 solo voices (SATB) and orchestra.
"Corrected 1/10/92"—p. 3.
Reproduced from manuscript.
Duration: ca. 45:00.
Contents: Asleep in the valley—I had a dream—O what is the sound . . . —An Irish airman foresees his death—The silent slain—The dark hills—Success is counted sweetest—Death of a Wisconsin officer—Making peace—The Lake Isle of Innisfree—To make a prairie it takes . . . —So we'll go no more a-roving—I dreamed in a dream—Behold how good and how pleasant.
Composed for: soprano, alto, tenor, bass, 3 flutes (3rd also piccolo), 3 oboes (3rd also English horn), 3 clarinets, 2 bassoons, 4 horns, 3 trumpets, 3 trombones, tuba, timpani, percussion (snare drum, tenor drum, xylophone, cymbals, gong, anvil, metal plate, slapstick, vibraphone, triangle, glockenspiel, woodblock, 2 tom-toms, bass drum, tam-tam, castanets, chimes), harp, piano (also celesta), violin I, violin II, viola, vio-

loncello, double bass.
Commissioned by: WCRB 102.5 FM Classical Radio Station Boston.
Call no.: **1993/115**

2230. Rose, Griffith, 1936– Louis le magnifique: en deux mouvements (1987–1988). N.p.: n.p., 1988.
1 score (126 p.); 30 cm.
For orchestra.
Reproduced from holograph.
Duration: 27:00.
Contents: L'homme—L'oeuvre.
Composed for: flute (also piccolo, alto flute), oboe (also English horn), clarinet (also bass clarinet), bassoon, horn, trumpet, trombone, piano, violin I, violin II, viola, violoncello, double bass.
Call no.: **1992/116**

2231. Rose, Griffith, 1936– Piano concerto: for Riccardo Licata (1990). N.p.: n.p., 1990.
1 score (94 p.); 36 cm.
Reproduced from manuscript.
Composed for: piano, flute (also piccolo), oboe, clarinet, horn, trumpet, trombone, harp, violin, viola, violoncello, double bass.
Commissioned by: Festival of Kiev.
Call no.: **1993/116**

2232. Rosenblum, Mathew, 1954– Nü kuan tzu. N.p.: n.p., 1996.
1 score (vii, 193 p.); 34 cm.
French or English words; also printed as text.
Performance instructions in English.
Contents: Le départ / Apollinaire—Automne malade / Apollinaire—Jade censer / Wen—She is graceful / Wen—Stars are few / Wen—Voyelles / Rimbaud—Fleurs / Rimbaud—Being beauteous / Rimbaud—Adieu / Rimbaud.
Composed for: soprano, mezzo-soprano, flute (also piccolo), clarinet, horn, bass trombone, percussion (vibraphone, marimba, glockenspiel, small bass drum, orchestral bass drum, 3 tom-toms, snare drum, 2 cowbells, hi-hat, 5 suspended cymbals, tuned gong, medium tam-tam, Peking gong), piano (also digital sampling keyboard), violin, viola, violoncello, double bass.
Commissioned by: National Endowment for the Arts.
Call no.: **2000/156**
Re-entered as: **2001/133**

2233. Rosenhaus, Steve, 1952– Symphony for band. N.p.: Steven L. Rosenhaus, 2003.
1 score (97 p.); 44 cm.
Composed for: clarinet, piccolo, 2 flutes, 2 oboes, clarinet in E♭, 2 clarinets, bass clarinet, 2 bassoons, 2 alto saxophones, tenor saxophone, baritone saxophone, 3 trumpets, 4 horns, 3 trombones, bass trombone, euphonium, tuba, double bass, timpani, percussion (glockenspiel, snare drum, bass drum, cymbals).
Call no.: **2005/125**

2234. Rosenhaus, Steve, 1952– Violin concerto: 1994. Forest Hills, NY: Music-Print Publishers, 1994.
1 score (28 p.); 36 cm.
Composed for: violin, 2 flutes (2nd also piccolo), 2 oboes, 2 clarinets, 2 bassoons, 2 horns, timpani, violin I, violin II, viola, violoncello, double bass.
Call no.: **2004/108**

2235. Rosenman, Leonard, 1924– Concerto no. 2: for violin and large orchestra. New York, NY: Peermusic, 199-?.
1 score (165 p.); 36 cm.
Duration: ca. 29:00.
Composed for: violin, piccolo, 2 flutes, 2 oboes, English horn, 2 clarinets, bass clarinet, 2 bassoons, contrabassoon, 4 horns, 3 trumpets, 3 trombones, tuba, timpani, percussion (triangle, cymbals, gong, tam-tam, woodblock, temple block, glockenspiel, xylophone, marimba, chimes, 5 bongos, snare drum, tom-tom, bass drum), harp, piano (also celesta), 4 female voices, violin I, violin II, viola, violoncello, double bass.
Commissioned by: National Symphony Orchestra.
Call no.: **1998/135**

2236. Rosenzweig, Michael, 1951– Symphony in one movement.
Call no.: **1988/093**
No materials available.

2237. Rosenzweig, Morris, 1952– Quartet (1997). N.p.: Morris Rosenzweig, 1997.
1 score (47 p.); 28 cm.
Duration: 18:00.
Composed for: 2 violins, viola, violoncello.
Commissioned by: Abramyan String Quartet.
Call no.: **2002/156**

2238. Ross, Robert A. M., 1955– Psalm 51: for SATB div. and 11 solo strings (or string orchestra) (2001–02). Full score. N.p.: Ralamar Sparks Enterprises, 2002.
1 score (41 p.); 36 cm.
Hebrew words; also printed as text with English translation.
Program notes by the composer in English.

Composed for: SATB chorus, 6 violins, 2 violas, 2 violoncellos, double bass.
Commissioned by: Choir Cantinovum.
Call no.: **2004/109**

2239. Rossi, Mick, 1956– Periphery: solo marimba with percussion ensemble. N.p.: n.p., 1986.
1 score (19 leaves); 29 x 43 cm.
Reproduced from holograph.
Composed for: marimba, 2 vibraphones, tam-tam, timpani, glockenspiel, celesta, chimes, triangle, suspended cymbal, claves, snare drum, hand cymbal, finger cymbals, bass drum, field drum, bell tree, bongos.
Commissioned by: Glassboro State College Percussion Ensemble.
Call no.: **1988/094**

2240. Rostomyan, Stepan, 1956– Fo[u]rth symphony. N.p.: n.p., 1997.
1 score (66 p.); 41 cm.
Reproduced from holograph.
Duration: ca. 30:00.
Composed for: SATB chorus, flute (also piccolo), oboe, clarinet (also clarinet in E♭), bassoon, horn, trumpet, trombone, timpani, percussion (tambourine, snare drum, tam-tam, tubular bells, vibraphone, campane cleocen), piano, 2 synthesizers, violin I, violin II, viola, violoncello, double bass.
Commissioned by: Paragon Ensemble Scotland.
Call no.: **2000/157**

2241. Roth, Alec, 1948– Arion and the dolphin. Full score. N.p.: Alec Roth and Vikram Seth, 1994.
1 score (404 p.); 30 cm.
English words by Vikram Seth.
Opera in nine scenes.
Duration: ca. 1:45:00.
Composed for: mezzo-soprano, tenor, baritone, bass-baritone, SATB chorus (also male chorus, female chorus, dancers), children's chorus, flute (also piccolo and alto flute), 2 clarinets (2nd also bass clarinet), 2 horns, trumpet, percussion (large bass drum, timpani, snare drum, 3 tam-tams, cymbals, roto-tom, small drum, ching or antique cymbal, tambourine, suspended cymbal, tom-toms, hi-hat, vibraphone, marimba, 3 nipple gongs, woodblocks, flexatone, guiro, cowbell, triangle), harp, keyboard, violin I, violin II, viola, violoncello, double bass, stage band (1 or more guitars, mandolin, double bass).
Commissioned by: English National Opera.
Call no.: **2000/158**

2242. Rotondi, Umberto, 1937– Osservando i disegni di Marzia: per chitarra. Milano: Edizioni Suvini Zerboni, 1981.
3 p. of music; 25 x 35 cm.
Composed for: guitar.
Call no.: **1985/193**

2243. Rouse, Christopher, 1949– Flute concerto. New York, NY: Boosey & Hawkes: Hendon Music, 1994.
1 score (162 p.); 28 cm.
Duration: ca. 23:00.
Contents: Àmhran—Alla marcia—Elegia—Scherzo—Àmhran.
Composed for: flute, 3 flutes, 2 oboes, 2 clarinets, 2 bassoons (2nd also contrabassoon), 4 horns, 2 trumpets, 3 trombones, tuba, timpani, percussion (glockenspiel, xylophone, suspended cymbal, crash cymbals, slapstick, large tam-tam, chimes, snare drum, tenor drum, tambourine, bass drum, vibraphone, sandpaper blocks, rute), harp, violin I, violin II, viola, violoncello, double bass.
Commissioned by: Carol Wincenc and Detroit Symphony Hall.
Call no.: **1997/124**

2244. Rouse, Christopher, 1949– Kabir padavali: for soprano and orchestra. N.p.: Boosey & Hawkes; Hendon Music, 1998.
1 score (v, 147 p.); 36 cm.
Hindi words (romanized); English translation printed as text.
Poems by Kabir.
"4th proof, 11/11/98"—p. 1.
Duration: ca. 28:00.
Composed for: soprano, 2 flutes (2nd also piccolo), 2 oboes, 2 clarinets, 2 bassoons, 4 horns, 2 trumpets, 3 trombones, tuba, timpani, percussion (bass drum, claves, slapstick, glockenspiel, suspended cymbal, Chinese cymbal, Chinese opera gong, maracas, chimes, tam-tam, xylophone, antique cymbals), harp, accordion, celesta, violin I, violin II, viola, violoncello, double bass.
Commissioned by: Minnesota Orchestra.
Call no.: **2001/134**

2245. Rouse, Christopher, 1949– Kabir padavali: for soprano and orchestra. 1st ed. N.p.: Boosey & Hawkes; Hendon Music, 2000, c1998.
1 score (v, 147 p.); 36 cm.
Hindi words (romanized); English translation printed as text.
Poems by Kabir.
"1st edition, corr 5/23/00"—p. 1.
Duration: ca. 28:00.

Composed for: soprano, 2 flutes (2nd also piccolo), 2 oboes, 2 clarinets, 2 bassoons, 4 horns, 2 trumpets, 3 trombones, tuba, timpani, percussion (bass drum, claves, slapstick, glockenspiel, suspended cymbal, Chinese cymbal, Chinese opera gong, maracas, chimes, tam-tam, xylophone, antique cymbals), harp, accordion, celesta, violin I, violin II, viola, violoncello, double bass.
Commissioned by: Minnesota Orchestra.
Call no.: **2004/110**

2246. Rouse, Christopher, 1949– Karolju: for chorus and orchestra. N.p.: Helicon Music, 1992.
1 score (118 p.); 28 cm.
Latin, Swedish, French, Spanish, Russian, Czech, German, or Italian words.
"Corrected 1/92"—p. 1.
Reproduced from manuscript.
Duration: ca. 25:00.
Program notes in English by the composer.
Composed for: SATB chorus, 2 flutes (2nd also piccolo), 2 oboes, 2 clarinets, 2 bassoons, 4 horns, 3 trumpets, 3 trombones, tuba, timpani, percussion (glockenspiel, tambourine, snare drum, triangle, crash cymbals, bass drum, chimes, sleigh bells, maracas, guiro), harp, violin I, violin II, viola, violoncello, double bass.
Commissioned by: Baltimore Symphony Orchestra.
Call no.: **1992/117**

2247. Rouse, Christopher, 1949– Rapture: for orchestra. New York, NY: Hendon Music: Boosey & Hawkes, 2000.
1 miniature score (87 p.); 36 cm.
Duration: ca. 11:00.
Composed for: 3 flutes, 3 oboes, 3 clarinets, 3 bassoons, 4 horns, 4 trumpets, 4 trombones, tuba, harp, timpani, percussion (bass drum, 2 triangles, antique cymbals, tam-tam, glockenspiel, Chinese cymbal, suspended cymbal), violin I, violin II, viola, violoncello, double bass.
Commissioned by: Pittsburgh Symphony Orchestra.
Call no.: **2002/157**

2248. Rouse, Christopher, 1949– Seeing. New York, NY: Boosey & Hawkes: Hendon Music, 1999.
1 score (113 p.); 36 cm.
For piano and orchestra.
"Study score"—cover.
Composed for: piano, 3 flutes, 3 oboes (3rd also English horn), 2 clarinets, clarinet in A (also bass clarinet), 3 bassoons (3rd also contrabassoon), 4 horns, 3 trumpets, 3 trombones, tuba, percussion (suspended cymbal, 2 brake drums, sandpaper blocks, large cabasa, 2 woodblocks, triangle, timpani, hammer, bongos, tenor drum, bass drum, rute, maracas, cowbell, tam-tam, Chinese cymbal, slapstick, snare drum, guiro, claves), celesta, violin I, violin II, viola, violoncello, double bass.
Commissioned by: Lillian and Maurice Barbash.
Call no.: **2003/108**

2249. Rouse, Christopher, 1949– Symphony no. 1. Rev. ed. N.p.: Helicon Music Corp., 1986.
1 score (40 p.); 36 cm.
Duration: ca. 24:00.
Composed for: 4 flutes (all also piccolo, 1st–2nd also alto flute), 4 oboes (3rd–4th also English horn), 2 clarinets, 2 clarinets in A, soprano saxophone, 4 bassoons (4th also contrabassoon), 6 horns, 4 trumpets, 4 trombones, tuba, timpani, percussion (glockenspiel, xylophone, crotales, tubular bells, tambourine, suspended cymbal, 2 Chinese gongs, tam-tam, Japanese woodblock, snare drum, metal wind chimes, vibraphone, Basler drum, 2 tuned bell plates, flexatone, bass drum, 2 Balinese gongs), harp, piano, keyboard, synthesizer, violin I, violin II, viola, violoncello, double bass.
Commissioned by: Meet the Composer Orchestra Residencies Program.
Call no.: **1989/106**
Re-entered as: **1991/110**

2250. Rouse, Christopher, 1949– Symphony no. 2: for orchestra. New York, NY: Hendon Music, 1995.
1 score (168 p.); 33 cm.
"Corrected 4/95"—p. 1.
Duration: ca. 25:00.
Composed for: piccolo, 2 flutes, 2 oboes, English horn, 2 clarinets, bass clarinet, 3 bassoons, 4 horns, 3 trumpets, 3 trombones, tuba, timpani, percussion (cymbals, xylophone, glockenspiel, bongo, snare drum, tam-tam, bass drum, suspended cymbal, field drum, Chinese cymbal, tenor drum, tambourine), harp, violin I, violin II, viola, violoncello, double bass.
Commissioned by: Houston Symphony.
Call no.: **1996/126**

2251. Rouse, Christopher, 1949– Symphony no. 2: for orchestra. New York, NY: Hendon Music, 1995.
1 score (168 p.); 36 cm.
"Corrected 4/95"—p. 1.
Duration: ca. 25:00.
Composed for: piccolo, 2 flutes, 2 oboes, English horn, 2 clarinets, bass clarinet, 3 bassoons, 4 horns, 3 trumpets, 3 trombones, tuba, timpani, percussion (cymbals, xylophone, glockenspiel, bongo, snare drum, tam-tam, bass drum, suspended cymbal, field drum, Chinese cymbal, tenor drum, tambourine), harp, violin I, violin

II, viola, violoncello, double bass.
Commissioned by: Houston Symphony.
Call no.: **1998/136**
Re-entered as: **2000/159**

2252. Rouse, Christopher, 1949– Trombone concerto. Study score. N.p.: Helicon Music; Valley Forge, PA: European American Music Distributors, 1993.
1 score (78 p.); 31 cm.
Duration: ca. 27:00.
Composed for: trombone, 3 bassoons (3rd also contrabassoon), 4 horns, 3 trumpets, 3 trombones, tuba, timpani, percussion (xylophone, snare drum, suspended cymbal, glockenspiel, cymbals, tenor drum, hammer, marimba, 4 tom-toms, bass drum, chimes, 2 bongos, 2 tam-tams), harp, violin I, violin II, violas, violoncello, double bass.
Commissioned by: Philharmonic Symphonic Society of New York.
Call no.: **1994/124**

2253. Rouse, Christopher, 1949– Violin concerto. N.p.: n.p., 1991.
1 score (122 p.); 36 cm.
Reproduced from manuscript.
Duration: ca. 20:00.
Composed for: violin, 2 flutes (2nd also piccolo), 2 oboes (2nd also English horn), 2 clarinets (2nd also bass clarinet), 2 bassoons (2nd also contrabassoon), 4 horns, 2 trumpets, 3 trombones, tuba, timpani, percussion (chimes, snare drum, Chinese cymbal, suspended cymbal, bass drum, high bongo, tambourine, woodblock, triangle, glockenspiel, tam-tam, tenor drum, field drum), harp, celesta, violin I, violin II, viola, violoncello, double bass.
Commissioned by: Aspen Music Festival.
Call no.: **1993/117**

2254. Rouse, Christopher, 1949– Violoncello concerto. New York, NY: Boosey & Hawkes, 1993.
1 score (105 p.); 28 cm.
Reproduced from holograph.
At end: Deo Gratias, January 7, 1993.
Duration: ca. 23:00.
Composed for: violoncello, 2 flutes (also piccolo), 2 oboes (also English horn), 2 clarinets (also bass clarinet), 2 bassoons, 4 horns, 3 trumpets, 3 trombones, tuba, timpani, percussion (3 woodblocks, piccolo woodblock, sandpaper blocks, castanets, bongo, suspended cymbal, guiro, vibraslap, snare drum, tambourine, hammer, metal plate, switch, glockenspiel, 5 temple blocks, ratchet, triangle, bass drum, xylophone, maracas, claves, slapstick, tenor drum, Chinese cymbal, tam-tam, 2 water gongs), harp, violin I, violin II, viola, violoncello, double bass.
Call no.: **1995/090**

2255. Rouse, Mikel, 1957– Dennis Cleveland. N.p.: Club Soda Music, 1996.
1 score (2 v.); 28 cm.
English words.
Opera.
Set on a television talk show in the late 20th century.
Composed for: voices, electronics.
Call no.: **2000/160**
Also available:
Call no.: **2000/160 libretto**

2256. Routh, Francis, 1927– Poème fantastique: [op. 48]. Full score. London: Redcliffe Edition, 1988.
1 score (190 p.); 36 cm.
For piano and orchestra.
Reproduced from manuscript.
Duration: ca. 30:00.
Composed for: piano, 2 flutes, 2 oboes (2nd also English horn), 2 clarinets, 2 bassoons (2nd also contrabassoon), 4 horns, 3 trumpets, 2 trombones, bass trombone, tuba, timpani, percussion (side drum, tenor drum, bass drum, cymbals, triangle, tam-tam), harp, violin I, violin II, viola, violoncello, double bass.
Call no.: **1990/107**

2257. Rovics, Howard, 1936– St. Jakob's Church in Rothenburg: a cantata for mixed chorus, soloists (soprano, alto, tenor & bass), narrator, organ & chamber orchestra. N.p.: Howard Rovics, 1996.
1 score (92 p.); 43 cm.
English words by Rivka Kasthan; also printed as text.
Reproduced from holograph.
Duration: 35:00.
Composed for: narrator, soprano, alto, tenor, bass, SATB chorus, oboe (also English horn), trumpet, percussion (timpani, suspended cymbals, snare drum, timbales, 4 tom-toms, bass drum, 2 gongs, marimba, chimes), organ, violin I, violin II, viola, violoncello, double bass.
Call no.: **2000/161**

2258. Roxburgh, Edwin, 1937– Concerto for clarinet and orchestra. London: Ricordi, 1996.
1 score (168 p.); 42 cm.
Reproduced from holograph.
Duration: 30:00.
Composed for: clarinet, piccolo, 2 flutes, 2 oboes, English horn, clarinet, clarinet in A, bass clarinet, 2 bassoons, contrabassoon, 4 horns, 2 trumpets, 3 trombones, tuba, timpani, percussion (vibraphone,

whip, bongos, 2 tom-toms, log drums, marimba, small tam-tam, claves, crotales, xylophone, 2 maracas, bell tree, tambourine, suspended cymbal, bass drum, large woodblock, high gong), harp, violin I, violin II, viola, violoncello, double bass.
Commissioned by: Donald Hunt.
Call no.: **2000/162**

2259. Rozbicki, Kazimierz, 1932– Missa festiva: for solo voices, mixed choir and symphony orchestra. N.p.: n.p., 2000.
1 score (156 p.); 42 cm.
Latin words.
Reproduced from holograph.
Duration: ca. 1:05:00.
Composed for: soprano, mezzo-soprano, SATB chorus, 2 flutes, oboe, clarinet, bassoon, 2 piccolo trumpets, 2 horns, timpani, violin I, violin II, viola, violoncello, double bass.
Call no.: **2002/158**

2260. Rubens, Jo, 1924– Jazz-rhapsody. N.p.: J. Rubens, 1995.
1 score (56 p.); 30 x 42 cm.
Concert piece in 5 movements for jazz band.
Reproduced from manuscript.
Composed for: clarinet, 2 flugelhorns, 2 trumpets, alto horn, tenor horn, euphonium, trombone, tuba, bass tuba, contrabass tuba, percussion (timbales, snare drum, bass drum, cymbals, tom-toms, tambourine, triangle).
Call no.: **1997/125**

2261. Ruders, Poul, 1949– Concerto in pieces: Purcell variations for orchestra, 1994–95. Score. Copenhagen: W. Hansen, 1995.
1 score (70 p.); 45 cm.
For orchestra with spoken commentary.
Duration: ca. 17:00.
Includes program note by the composer.
Composed for: narrator, 3 flutes (3rd also piccolo), 3 oboes (3rd also English horn), 3 clarinets (3rd also clarinet in E♭ and clarinet in A), bass clarinet, alto saxophone, 3 bassoons (3rd also contrabassoon), 4 horns, 3 trumpets, 3 trombones, tuba, timpani, percussion (bass drum, water chimes (tubular bells in water), crotales, water gong (tuned gong in water), Basler drum, vibraphone, metal wind chimes, 5 roto-toms, snare drum, tubular bells, glockenspiel, tam-tam, Java gong, 7 tuned gongs), harp, piano (also celesta, synthesizer), violin I, violin II, viola, violoncello, double bass.
Commissioned by: BBC Symphony Orchestra.
Call no.: **1996/127**
Re-entered as: **2000/163**

2262. Ruders, Poul, 1949– Corpus cum figuris. Copenhagen: W. Hansen, 1986.
1 miniature score (67 p.); 30 cm.
For chamber orchestra.
Reproduced from manuscript.
Duration: ca. 20:00.
Composed for: flute (also piccolo), oboe (also English horn), 2 clarinets (both also bass clarinet), 2 bassoons (2nd also contrabassoon), horn, trumpet in D, bass trombone, percussion (timpani, vibraphone, crotales, cowbell, 5 temple blocks, marimba, glockenspiel, tubular bells, 4 bongos, tam-tam, bass drum), harp, piano, 2 violins, 2 violas, 2 violoncellos, double bass.
Commissioned by: Danmarks Radio.
Call no.: **1989/107**

2263. Ruders, Poul, 1949– The handmaid's tale = Tjenerindens fortælling: an opera in a prologue, a prelude, two acts and an epilogue. Ur-text. Copenhagen: Edition Wilhelm Hansen, 1998.
1 score (2 v.); 43 cm.
English and Danish words by Paul Bentley after Margaret Atwood's novel.
Reproduced from holograph.
Duration: ca. 2:20:00.
Composed for: 3 sopranos, 5 mezzo-sopranos, 3 altos, 5 tenors, baritone, SATB chorus, 3 flutes (1st–2nd also alto flute, 3rd also piccolo), 3 oboes (3rd also English horn), 3 clarinets (3rd also bass clarinet), 3 bassoons (3rd also contrabassoon), 4 horns, 3 trumpets, 3 trombones, tuba, timpani, percussion (bass drum, woodblock, glockenspiel, crotales, thundersheet, anvil, tubular bells, vibraphone, snare drum, brake drum, Bali gong, xylophone, mark tree, empty roto-tom frame, metal plate, whip, triangle, champagne cork pump, flexatone, tam-tam, coil or metal chain, tambourine, Chinese cymbal, crash cymbals, guiro, hi-hat, Basler drum, offstage bass drum), Akai S-3000 sampler and keyboard, harp, offstage organ, digital piano, violin I, violin II, viola, violoncello, double bass.
Call no.: **2002/159**
Also available:
Call no.: **2002/159 libretto**

2264. Ruders, Poul, 1949– Paganini variations: guitar concerto no. 2: for guitar solo and orchestra: 1999–2000. Copenhagen: Wilhelm Hansen, 2001.
1 score (87 p.); 42 cm.
Variations on the theme from Paganini's Caprice no. 24.
Duration: ca. 18:00.

Includes composer's note in English and Danish.
Composed for: guitar, 2 flutes (also piccolo), 2 oboes, 2 clarinets (also clarinet in A), 2 bassoons, 2 horns, 2 trumpets, percussion (tubular bells, vibraphone, glockenspiel, sandpaper, large tam tam, mark tree, triangle, crotales, guiro, whip, tambourine), harp, digital piano, violin, I, violin II, viola, violoncello, double bass.
Commissioned by: David Starobin and Odense Symphony Orchestra.
Call no.: **2005/126**

2265. Ruders, Poul, 1949– Psalmodies: for guitar solo and nine instruments: 1989. Copenhagen: Edition W. Hansen, 1992.
1 score (38 p.); 38 cm.
Duration: ca. 30:00.
Preface in English.
Contents: Entrance for one—Solo for two—Six in the air—A fanfare for all—With passion for all—A chorale and a song—Cadenza for one—Cadenza for all—A march of light and darkness—A prayer with halo—Exit for one.
Composed for: guitar, oboe (also metal wind chimes), clarinet (also bass clarinet), bassoon (also contrabassoon), horn, 2 violins, viola, violoncello, double bass.
Commissioned by: Albert Augustine Ltd.
Call no.: **1993/118**

2266. Ruders, Poul, 1949– The solar trilogy: for symphony orchestra. Copenhagen: Edition Wilhelm Hansen, 1995.
1 score (A–D, 231 p.); 42 cm.
Reproduced from holograph.
Duration: ca. 1:10:00.
Program notes in English by the composer.
Contents: Gong—Zenith—Corona.
Composed for: 3 flutes (all also piccolo), 3 oboes (3rd also English horn), 3 clarinets (3rd also bass clarinet), bassoons, contrabassoon, 4 horns, 3 trumpets, 3 trombones (3rd also euphonium), tuba, percussion (large bass drum, suspended cymbal, piccolo triangles, water gong, water chimes, small Chinese cymbal, sizzle cymbals, 4 empty roto-tom frame, thundersheet, vibraphone, tubular bells, anvil, Basler drum, medium tam-tam, small Bali gong, metal wind chimes, water roto-tom, medium Chinese cymbal, small woodblock, maracas, crotales, large tam-tam, large Bali gong, small metal plate, brake drum, large bronze plate, large Chinese cymbal, metal shaker, 2 timpani, Akai S-1000 sampler), piano, digital piano, violin I, violin II, viola, violoncello, double bass.
Commissioned by: Danish National Radio Symphony Orchestra ("Gong"), Tivoli Symphony Orchestra ("Zenith"), and Odense Symphony Orchestra ("Corona").
Call no.: **1998/137**

2267. Ruders, Poul, 1949– The solar trilogy: for symphony orchestra. Copenhagen: Edition Wilhelm Hansen, 1996.
1 miniature score (A–D, 230 p.); 29 cm.
Reproduced from holograph.
Duration: ca. 1:10:00.
Program notes in English by the composer.
Contents: Gong—Zenith—Corona.
Composed for: 3 flutes (all also piccolo), 3 oboes (3rd also English horn), 3 clarinets (3rd also bass clarinet), bassoons, contrabassoon, 4 horns, 3 trumpets, 3 trombones (3rd also euphonium), tuba, percussion (large bass drum, suspended cymbal, piccolo triangles, water gong, water chimes, small Chinese cymbal, sizzle cymbals, 4 empty roto-tom frames, thundersheet, vibraphone, tubular bells, anvil, Basler drum, medium tam-tam, small Bali gong, metal wind chimes, water roto-tom, medium Chinese cymbal, small woodblock, maracas, crotales, large tam-tam, large Bali gong, small metal plate, brake drum, large bronze plate, large Chinese cymbal, metal shaker, 2 timpani, Akai S-1000 sampler), piano, digital piano, violin I, violin II, viola, violoncello, double bass.
Commissioned by: Danish National Radio Symphony Orchestra ("Gong"), Tivoli Symphony Orchestra ("Zenith"), and Odense Symphony Orchestra ("Corona").
Call no.: **1997/126**

2268. Ruders, Poul, 1949– Symphony: "Himmelhoch jauchzend—zum Tode betrübt": for large orchestra (1989). Partitur. Kobenhavn: Edition W. Hansen, 1989.
1 score (124 p.); 43 cm.
Reproduced from manuscript.
Duration: ca. 35:00.
Composed for: 4 flutes (all also piccolo, 1st–2nd also alto flute), 4 oboes (3rd–4th also English horn), 2 clarinets, 2 clarinets in A, soprano saxophone, 4 bassoons (4th also contrabassoon), 6 horns, 4 trumpets, 4 trombones, tuba, timpani, percussion (glockenspiel, xylophone, crotales, tubular bells, tambourine, suspended cymbal, 2 Chinese gongs, large tam-tam, Japanese woodblock, snare drum, metal wind chimes, vibraphone, Basler drum, flexatone, 2 bell plates, large bass drum, 2 Bali gongs), harp, piano, digital piano, synthesizer, violin I, violin II, viola, violoncello, double bass.
Commissioned by: BBC Symphony Orchestra.
Call no.: **1991/111**

2269. Ruders, Poul, 1949– Symphony: "Himmelhoch jauchzend—zum Tode betrübt": for large orchestra,

1989. Score. Copenhagen: Wilhelm Hansen, 1993.
1 score (133 p.); 42 cm.
Includes preface by Anthony Burton.
Duration: ca. 35:00.
Composed for: 4 flutes (all also piccolo, 1st–2nd also alto flute), 4 oboes (3rd–4th also English horn), 2 clarinets, 2 clarinets in A, soprano saxophone, 4 bassoons (4th also contrabassoon), 6 horns, 4 trumpets, 4 trombones, tuba, timpani, percussion (glockenspiel, xylophone, crotales, tubular bells, tambourine, suspended cymbal, 2 Chinese gongs, large tam-tam, Japanese woodblock, snare drum, metal wind chimes, vibraphone, Basler drum, flexatone, 2 bell plates, large bass drum, 2 Bali gongs), harp, piano, digital piano, synthesizer, violin I, violin II, viola, violoncello, double bass.
Commissioned by: BBC Symphony Orchestra.
Call no.: **1994/125**

2270. Ruders, Poul, 1949– Violin concerto, no. 2, for violin solo and orchestra. Copenhagen: Wilhem Hansen, 1994.
1 score (76 p.); 38 cm.
Program notes in English by the composer.
Composed for: violin, 2 flutes (both also piccolo), 2 oboes (2nd also English horn), clarinet (also clarinet in E♭), clarinet in A (also bass clarinet), 2 bassoons (also contrabassoon), 4 horns, 2 trumpets, 2 trombones, percussionist (tam-tam, bass drum, suspended cymbal, sizzle cymbal, crotales, tubular bells, vibraphone), harp, violin I, violin II, viola, violoncello, double bass.
Commissioned by: Scandinavian Tobacco Company.
Call no.: **1995/091**

2271. Rulon, C. Bryan, 1954– " . . . I'm Yolanda Vega! . . . " N.p.: n.p., 1997.
1 score (63 p.) and 6 parts; 22 x 28 cm.
English words from Jean Baudrillard's The transparency of evil; also printed as text.
Performance and program notes.
Composed for: flute (also 2 music boxes), clarinet (also bass clarinet and 2 music boxes), piano (optional), percussion (marimba, vibraphone, nipple gong, 3 suspended cymbals, pedal bass drum, 3 cowbells, 2 woodblocks, slapstick, chime, snare drum, 3 tom-toms, bell mark, ratchet), violin (also small wind chime), violoncello (also small wind chime).
Commissioned by: New Millennium Ensemble.
Call no.: **2002/160**

2272. Saariaho, Kaija, 1952– . . . à la fumée: (1990). Copenhagen: Edition Wilhelm Hansen, 1990.
1 score (a–d, 63 p.); 42 cm.
Reproduced from holograph.
Includes performance instructions.
Notation is a mixture of traditional and special symbols; key to special symbols included with performance instructions.
Composed for: flute, violoncello, 4 flutes (all also piccolo, alto flute), 3 oboes, 3 clarinets (3rd also clarinet in E♭), bass clarinet, 2 bassoons, alto saxophone, 4 horns, 3 trumpets, 3 trombones, tuba, percussion (crotales, xylophone, triangle, bamboo wind chimes, lion's roar, gong, bass drum, glockenspiel, claves, cabasa, sandpaper blocks, 2 suspended cymbals, vibraphone, maracas, tom-tom, metal plate, tam-tam, marimba, wooden wind chimes, timpani), harp, piano, synthesizer, violin I, violin II, viola, violoncello, double bass.
Commissioned by: Finnish Broadcasting Company.
Call no.: **1992/118**

2273. Saariaho, Kaija, 1952– L'amour de loin: opera in five acts. Full score. London: Chester Music; Bury St. Edmonds: Music Sales Ltd, 2000.
1 score (2 v.); 42 cm.
French words by Amin Maalouf.
Opera.
"Perusal score."
"Version 2; complete: May 2000."
Duration: ca. 2:00:00.
Includes remarks on scoring and notation in English and synopsis in French and English.
2003 Grawemeyer Award winning work.
Composed for: soprano, mezzo-soprano, baritone, men's chorus, women's chorus, 4 flutes (2nd and 4th also alto flute, 3rd–4th also piccolo), 3 oboes (3rd also English horn), 3 clarinets (3rd also bass clarinet), 3 bassoons (3rd also contrabassoon), 4 horns, 2 trumpets, 3 trombones, tuba, percussion (crotales, triangle, glockenspiel, vibraphone, 2 temple blocks, 2 tom-toms, tambourine, xylophone, odaiko, shell chimes, 4 suspended cymbals, large tam-tam, marimba, large bass drum, glass chimes, frame drum, small finger cymbals, guiro, timpani), 2 harps, piano, violin I, violin II, viola, violoncello, double bass.
Commissioned by: Salzburg Festival and Theatre du Chatelet, Paris.
Call no.: **2002/161**
Re-entered as: **2003/109**
Also available:
Call no.: **2003/109 libretto (English)**
Call no.: **2003/109 libretto (French & German)**

2274. Saariaho, Kaija, 1952– Château de l'âme: five songs for solo soprano, eight female voices and or-

chestra. London: Chester Music, 1996.
1 score (110 p.); 42 cm.
French words; also printed as text.
Words from ancient Hindu and Egyptian poetry.
Preface and performance instructions in English.
Contents: La liane—A la terre—La liane—Pour repousser l'esprit—Les formules.
Composed for: soprano, 4 sopranos, 4 mezzo-sopranos, 2 flutes (both also piccolo), 2 oboes, 2 clarinets, 2 bassoons, 4 horns, 2 trumpets, 2 trombones, tuba, percussion (crotales, xylophone, marimba, triangle, large suspended cymbal, frame drum, maracas, vibraphone, guiro, 2 tam-tams, tom-tom, Chinese tom-tom, bass drum, timpani), harp, piano, violin I, violin II, viola, violoncello, double bass.
Commissioned by: Betty Freeman.
Call no.: **1998/138**

2275. Saariaho, Kaija, 1952– Nymphea: for string quartet and live electronics, 1987. København: Edition Wilhelm Hansen, 1987.
1 score (62 p.); 21 x 30 cm.
English words.
Reproduced from holograph.
Composed for: 2 violins, viola, violoncello, electronics.
Commissioned by: Lincoln Center and Doris and Myron Beigler.
Call no.: **1989/108**

2276. Saariaho, Kaija, 1952– Oltra mar: seven preludes for the new millennium: for orchestra and choir (1998–99). London: Chester Music, 1999.
1 score (66 p.); 30 cm.
French words.
"Rev. 7/99"—p. 1.
"Perusal score."
Duration: ca. 15:00.
Contents: Départ—Amour—Vagues—Temps—Souvenir de vagues—Mort—Arrivée.
Composed for: SATB chorus, 4 flutes (3rd also alto flute, 4th also piccolo), 4 oboes, 4 clarinets, 4 bassoons, 4 horns, 4 trumpets, 4 trombones, tuba, percussion (crotales, triangle, temple blocks, log drum, vibraphone, bells, bass drum, tom-tom, suspended cymbals, timpani), violin I, violin II, viola, violoncello, double bass.
Commissioned by: New York Philharmonic.
Call no.: **2001/135**

2277. Sacco, Peter, 1928– Violin concerto: no. 1. N.p.: n.p., [between 1974 and 1996].
1 score (69 p.); 37 cm.
"Thanksgiving Day, 1969; revision—Thanksgiving Day, 1974"—caption.
Reproduced from manuscript.
Composed for: violin, 3 flutes (3rd also piccolo), 3 oboes (3rd also English horn), 3 clarinets, 3 bassoons, 4 horns, 3 trumpets, 3 trombones, tuba, timpani, percussion (bass drum, crash cymbals, suspended cymbals, 2 bongos, 2 congas, snare drum, tambourine), piano, violin I, violin II, viola, violoncello, double bass.
Commissioned by: Frank Hauser.
Call no.: **1997/127**

2278. Sacco, Steven Christopher, 1965– Fantasy for cello. Cliffside Park, NJ: Ex Mente Sacchi Edition, 1999.
13 p. of music; 28 cm.
Composed for: violoncello.
Commissioned by: Arts and Letters Foundation.
Call no.: **2004/111**

2279. Sahbaï, Iradj, 1945– Nâghouss. N.p.: n.p., 1990.
1 score (62 leaves); 25 cm.
Language undetermined.
For voice and percussion ensemble.
Reproduced from manuscript.
Composed for: voice, percussion (2 marimbas, vibraphone, Thai gongs, Bali gong, 3 snare drums, timbales, bass drum, 2 tam-tams, glockenspiel, roto-toms, tubular bells).
Call no.: **1994/126**

2280. Saïdaminova, Dilorom, 1943– Afrasiab's frescos: (piano cycle). N.p.: n.p., 1996.
30 p. of music; 34 cm.
Reproduced from manuscript.
Composed for: piano.
Call no.: **2000/164**

2281. Saïdaminova, Dilorom, 1943– By the sound of Francesca. N.p.: n.p., 1996.
1 score (8 p.); 42 cm.
Primarily wordless; some Italian words.
For soprano and instrumental ensemble.
Composed for: soprano, flute, violin, violoncello, piano, percussion (jingle bells, bamboo tubes, bar chimes, vibraslap).
Call no.: **1998/139**

2282. Saïdaminova, Dilorom, 1943– The garden of my childhood: for 2 pianofortes and full orchestra. Moscow: n.p., 2002.
1 score (158 p.); 30 cm.
Composed for: 2 pianos, piccolo, 2 flutes, 2 oboes, English horn, 2 clarinets, bass clarinet, 2 bassoons,

contrabassoon, 4 horns, 3 trumpets, 3 trombones, tuba, percussion (timpani, xylophone, vibraphone, marimba, snare drum, 5 bongos, chimes, tam-tam, crotales, temple blocks, triangle, glockenspiel, 2 maracas, tambourine, 4 cymbals, flexatone, cowbell, woodblock), harp, violin I, violin II, viola, violoncello, double bass.
Call no.: **2004/112**

2283. Saĭdaminova, Dilorom, 1943– In memory of my friends. Moscow: n.p., 2000.
1 score (30 p.); 42 cm.
For orchestra.
Composed for: 3 flutes (3rd also piccolo), 3 oboes (3rd also English horn), 3 clarinets (3rd also bass clarinet), 3 bassoons (3rd also contrabassoon), 4 horns, 3 trumpets, 3 trombones, tuba, percussion (timpani, bass drum, tam-tam, bells, snare drum, 4 tom-toms, 4 bongos, crash cymbals, suspended cymbals, xylophone, vibraphone, glockenspiel, maracas), harp, violin I, violin II, viola, violoncello, double bass.
Call no.: **2002/162**

2284. Saĭdaminova, Dilorom, 1943– Sextet: for two violin[s], viola, violoncello, c-bass, piano: "Lost in the eternity." Moscow: n.p., 1998.
1 score (30 p.); 32 cm.
Reproduced from manuscript.
Composed for: 2 violins, viola, violoncello, double bass, piano.
Call no.: **2001/136**

2285. Sallinen, Aulis, 1935– Kullervo. London: Novello, 1988.
1 miniature score (608); 30 cm.
Finnish words by the composer, derived from the epic Kalevala and from a play by Aleksis Kivi.
Opera in two acts.
Reproduced from manuscript.
Duration: ca. 2:25:00.
Composed for: 2 sopranos, mezzo-soprano, contralto, 3 tenors, 3 baritones, bass-baritone, bass, SATB chorus, 3 flutes (3rd also piccolo), 3 oboes (3rd also English horn), 3 clarinets (2nd also clarinet in E♭, 3rd also bass clarinet), 3 bassoons (3rd also contrabassoon), 4 horns, 3 trumpets, 3 trombones, tuba, timpani, percussion (3 tom-toms, 3 woodblocks, 3 bongos, marimba, vibraphone, glockenspiel, tubular bells, crotales, military snare drum, piccolo snare drum, tenor drum, bass drum, castanets, claves, triangle, cymbals, 3 suspended cymbals, large tam-tam), harp, synthesizer, violin I, violin II, viola, violoncello, double bass.
Commissioned by: Finnish National Opera.
Call no.: **1993/121**

2286. Sallinen, Aulis, 1935– Kullervo. London: Novello, 1988.
1 score (2 v.); 42 cm.
Finnish words by the composer, derived from the epic Kalevala and from a play by Aleksis Kivi.
Opera in two acts.
Reproduced from manuscript.
Duration: ca. 2:25:00.
Composed for: 2 sopranos, mezzo-soprano, contralto, 3 tenors, 3 baritones, bass-baritone, bass, SATB chorus, 3 flutes (3rd also piccolo), 3 oboes (3rd also English horn), 3 clarinets (2nd also clarinet in E♭, 3rd also bass clarinet), 3 bassoons (3rd also contrabassoon), 4 horns, 3 trumpets, 3 trombones, tuba, timpani, percussion (3 tom-toms, 3 woodblocks, 3 bongos, marimba, vibraphone, glockenspiel, tubular bells, crotales, military snare drum, piccolo snare drum, tenor drum, bass drum, castanets, claves, triangle, cymbals, 3 suspended cymbals, large tam-tam), harp, synthesizer, violin I, violin II, viola, violoncello, double bass.
Commissioned by: Finnish National Opera.
Call no.: **1994/127**

2287. Sallinen, Aulis, 1935– Symphony no 7, opus 71: (the dreams of Gandalf). London: Novello, 1996.
1 score (108 p.); 42 cm.
Reproduced from holograph.
"Perusal score."
Duration: ca. 25:00.
Composed for: 3 flutes (3rd also piccolo), 3 oboes, 3 clarinets (3rd also bass clarinet), 3 bassoons (3rd also contrabassoon), 4 horns, 4 trumpets, 3 trombones, tuba, timpani, percussion (small tambourine, snare drum, 3 tom-toms, bass drum, triangle, cymbals, tam-tam, glockenspiel, vibraphone, marimba), harp, celesta, violin I, violin II, viola, violoncello, double bass.
Commissioned by: Göteborgs Symfoniker.
Call no.: **1998/140**

2288. Salonen, Esa-Pekka, 1958– Gambit: for orchestra (1998). London: Chester Music, 1998.
1 score (34 p.); 43 cm.
"Revised 7/98"—p. 1.
"Perusal score."
Composed for: piccolo, 2 flutes, 3 oboes, 2 clarinets (2nd also clarinet in E♭), bass clarinet, contrabass clarinet, 2 bassoons, contrabassoon, 4 horns, 3 trumpets, 3 trombones, tuba, timpani, percussion (vibraphone, 4 woodblocks, bass drum, marimba, 4 temple blocks, 4 log drums, crash cymbals, 2 congas, large claves, large tam-tam, glockenspiel), harp, piano, violin I, violin II, viola, violoncello, double bass.
Call no.: **2000/165**

2289. Salonen, Esa-Pekka, 1958– LA variations. London: Chester Music, 1996.
1 score (96 p.); 42 cm.
For orchestra.
Composed for: piccolo, 2 flutes (2nd also alto flute), 2 oboes, English horn, 2 clarinets, bass clarinet, contrabass clarinet, 2 bassoons, contrabassoon, 4 horns, 3 trumpets, 3 trombones, tuba, timpani, percussion (3 tam-tams, marimba, vibraphone, tubular bells, 2 congas, 4 tuned gongs, glockenspiel, crotales, roto-toms, log drums, mark tree, bongos, tom-toms, bass drum), harp, celesta, synthesizer, violin I, violin II, viola, violoncello, double bass.
Commissioned by: Los Angeles Philharmonic.
Call no.: **1998/141**

2290. Sampaoli, Luciano, 1955– Exemplum: Il martirio di San Guniforto. N.p.: n.p., 1986.
1 score (a–e, 50 leaves); 30 cm.
Italian words; also printed as text.
Oratorio.
Reproduced from holograph.
Composed for: 2 sopranos, 3 mezzo-sopranos, alto, 3 tenors, 3 baritones, bass-baritone, bass, flute, oboe, clarinet, bassoon, horn, timpani, piano, violin I, violin II, viola, violoncello, double bass, prerecorded tape.
Call no.: **1987/073**

2291. Sánchez Navarro, Alejandro, 1960– Arrecife de Alacranes = Scorpion's reef (1987–1997). N.p.: n.p., 1997.
1 score (108 p.); 29 cm.
Partially reproduced from manuscript.
Contents: Obertura—Varicion I—Varicion II—Varicion III—Varicion IV—Conclusion: Oceánica.
Composed for: piccolo, 2 flutes, 2 oboes, English horn, 2 clarinets, bass clarinet, 2 bassoons, contrabassoon, 4 horns, 2 trumpets, 2 trombones, bass trombone, tuba, percussion (guiro, timbales, triangle, congas, bells, timpani), piano, guitar, violin I, violin II, viola, violoncello, double bass.
Call no.: **2000/166**

2292. Sandresky, Margaret Vardell, 1921– Sonata for viola and piano. N.p.: Margaret Vardell Sandresky, 1996.
1 score (44 leaves) + 1 part (11 p.); 28 cm.
Composed for: viola, piano.
Call no.: **2000/167**

2293. Sanina, Nina, 1937– A song of a dead bird: cantata-elegy: for woman's voice and ensemble of instruments (flute, violoncello and piano obligato). N.p.: n.p., 1989.
1 manuscript score (70 p.); 31 cm.
Russian (Cyrillic) words with English translation.
Poems by modern Greek poets P. Antheos and N. Vrettakos.
In ink.
Includes performance instructions in English.
Composed for: female voice, flute, violoncello, piano.
Call no.: **1994/128**

2294. Sansar, Sangidorj, 1969– Pieces for piano. N.p.: n.p., 1999.
1 v. (various pagings) of music; 31 cm.
Contents: Pantomima oreintal = Oreint pantomime—Las tres cuentos . . . = Three tales about my teacher. Beginning . . . ; Continuing . . . ; Ending—Escalera interminable = Endless stairways—Adios al pasado 11:11 = Farewell to the past 11:11—El invitado del "Diavolo" = Staying with the devil.
Composed for: piano.
Call no.: **2005/127**

2295. Sapieyevski, Jerzy, 1945– Mazurka: variations for string quartet. Score. Bryn Mawr, PA: Mercury: T. Presser, 1986.
1 score (16 p.); 31 cm.
Duration: ca. 9:00.
Composed for: 2 violins, viola, violoncello.
Commissioned by: Kindler Foundation of the Library of Congress.
Call no.: **1989/109**

2296. Sargon, Simon A., 1938– Elul: midnight: for baritone solo, mixed choir, brass quintet (2 trumpets, French horn, trombone, bass trombone), timpani and organ. N.p.: n.p., 1983.
1 score (82 p.); 36 cm.
English words.
At end of score: "Revised scoring—Dallas, TX 5/12/83."
Reproduced from manuscript.
Composed for: baritone, SATB chorus, 2 trumpets, horn, trombone, bass trombone, timpani, organ.
Call no.: **1985/168**

2297. Sargon, Simon A., 1938– Tapestries: four scenes from Saul, King of Israel. Dallas, TX: Simon A. Sargon, 1997.
1 score (104 p.); 44 cm.
For orchestra.
Duration: ca. 22:00.
Contents: Saul among the prophets—Sanctuary—The oath—The supreme command.

Composed for: 3 flutes (3rd also piccolo, alto flute), 3 oboes (3rd also English horn), 3 clarinets (2nd also clarinet in E♭, 3rd also bass clarinet), 2 bassoons, contrabassoon, 4 horns, 3 trumpets, 2 trombones, bass trombone, tuba, timpani, percussion (bass drum, triangle, finger cymbals, suspended cymbal, tam-tam, snare drums, 2 tom-toms, ratchet, tambourine, vibraphone, whip, xylophone, bells), harp, piano (also celesta), violin I, violin II, viola, violoncello, double bass.
Call no.: **2000/168**

2298. Sarmientos, Jorge Alvaro, 1931– Bolivar: coro poema-sinfónico: cantata lírica poetica para orquesta, coros y declamador. N.p.: n.p., 1986.
1 score (53 p.); 43 cm.
Spanish words by Miguel Angel Asturias.
Reproduced from manuscript.
Composed for: narrator, SATB chorus, 3 flutes (3rd also piccolo), 3 oboes (3rd also English horn), 3 clarinets (3rd also bass clarinet), 3 bassoons (3rd also contrabassoon), 4 horns, 4 trumpets, 3 trombones, tuba, timpani, percussion (suspended cymbals, bass drum, gong, tam-tam, xylophone, bongos, snare drum, vibraphone, tom-toms, coconut shells, bombo, crotales, tambourine, triangle, temple blocks), piano, celesta, violin I, violin II, viola, violoncello, double bass.
Commissioned by: Orquesta Sinfonica Nacional.
Call no.: **1987/074**

2299. Sarmientos, Jorge Alvaro, 1931– Diferencias: para violoncello y orquesta (concerto), 1967. N.p.: n.p., 1985.
1 score (49 p.); 37 cm.
Reproduced from manuscript.
Composed for: violoncello, piccolo, 2 flutes, 2 oboes, English horn, 2 clarinets, bass clarinet, 2 bassoons, contrabassoon, 4 horns, 4 trumpets, 4 trombones, tuba, timpani, percussion (bombo, military drum, cymbals, woodblock, triangle, bongos, cocos, 2 drums), piano, celesta, violin I, violin II, viola, violoncello, double bass.
Call no.: **1986/098**

2300. Sartor, David P., 1956– Polygon: for brass quintet, 1987. N.p.: David P. Sartor, 1987.
1 score (55 p.); 28 cm.
Reproduced from manuscript.
Composed for: 2 trumpets, horn, trombone, tuba.
Call no.: **1989/110**

2301. Sato, Kimi, 1949– Genso-Teien: for grand orchestra. N.p.: n.p., 1987.
1 score (23 p.); 49 cm.
Reproduced from manuscript.
Composed for: 3 flutes (3rd also piccolo), 3 oboes, 3 clarinets, 2 bassoons, 2 horns, 2 trumpets, 2 trombones, percussion (vibraphone, tubular bells, temple blocks), harp, piano, celesta, violin I, violin II, viola, violoncello, double bass.
Commissioned by: Berkeley Symphony Orchestra.
Call no.: **1988/095**

2302. Satoh, Somei, 1947– Kisetsu. N.p.: Zen-On Music, 2002.
1 score (23 p.); 36 cm.
For orchestra.
Reproduced from holograph.
Duration: ca. 15:00.
Composed for: 2 flutes, 2 oboes, 2 clarinets, 2 bassoons, 2 horns, percussion (vibraphone, Tibet crotales, tubular bells, chromatic gongs, 5 cowbells), harp, violin I, violin II, viola, violoncello, double bass.
Commissioned by: New York Philharmonic Orchestra.
Call no.: **2004/113**

2303. Saul, Walter, 1954– Five Biblical songs. Portland, OR: Tarsus Music, 1986.
1 score (46 p.); 29 cm.
Contents: In the beginning—O Lord, how long shall I cry?—Hast thou not known?—Who shall separate us from the love of Christ?—Psalm 121.
Composed for: high voice, piano.
Commissioned by: North Carolina Music Teachers Association.
Call no.: **1989/111**

2304. Sawer, David, 1961– From morning to midnight: an opera in seven scenes (1998–2001). Full score. London: Universal Edition, 2001.
1 score (2 v.); 43 cm.
English words by the composer after the play Von morgens bis mitternachts by Georg Kaiser.
Composed for: 3 sopranos, mezzo-soprano, contralto, 3 tenors, 2 baritones, bass, SATB chorus, 3 flutes (all also alto flute, 2nd–3rd also piccolo), 2 oboes (2nd also English horn), 4 clarinets (2nd also bass clarinet and clarinet in A, 3rd also clarinet in E♭), 2 bassoons (2nd also contrabassoon), 4 horns, 4 trumpets, 3 trombones, euphonium, 2 tubas, timpani, percussion (2 bongos, small tom-tom, bass drum, cowbell, spring coil, small maraca, castanets, small ratchet, rute, glockenspiel, crotales, large triangle, pair of agogos, finger cymbals, 3 Chinese temple blocks, whip, vibraslap, lion's roar, large metal saucepan, washboard, police whistle, claves, 2 woodblocks, log drum, medium triangle, hi-hat, crash cymbals, tambourine, sistrum, antique

cymbal, small metal chain, large metal baking tray, xylophone, vibraphone, tubular bells, small triangle, sizzle cymbal, suspended cymbal, metal cabasa, tam-tam, guiro, large ratchet, large set of bamboo wood chimes, 2 very large metal saucepan lids, flexatone, small side drums, wind machine, small pair of crash cymbals attached to small bass drum), harp, keyboard (sampler with piano, electric piano, celesta, electric organ, chamber organ, bicycle bells), violin I, violin II, viola, violoncello, double bass.
Commissioned by: English National Opera.
Call no.: **2003/110**

2305. Sawer, David, 1961– The greatest happiness principle: for orchestra (1997). London: Universal Edition, 1997.
1 score (72 p.); 42 cm.
Composed for: 3 flutes (2nd–3rd also piccolo, 3rd also alto flute), 2 oboes (2nd also English horn), 3 clarinets (2nd also clarinet in E♭, 3rd also bass clarinet), 2 bassoons, contrabassoon, 4 horns, 3 trumpets, 4 trombones, tuba, percussion (tambourine, metal cabasa, 2 triangles, sleigh bells, sistrum, tam-tam, hi-hat, glockenspiel, xylophone, 2 wooden shakers, crash cymbals, 2 woodblocks, sizzle cymbal, crotales, small suspended cymbal, conga, 2 bongos, timpani, bass drum, 2 log drums, flexatone, ratchet, guiro, chains), harp, violin I, violin II, viola, violoncello, double bass.
Commissioned by: BBC National Orchestra of Wales.
Call no.: **1998/142**

2306. Saxton, Robert, 1953– Caritas: an opera in two acts, without an interval. London: Chester Music, 1991.
1 score (383 p.); 30 cm.
English words by Arnold Wesker, based on his play of the same name.
Duration: ca: 1:20:00.
Composed for: soprano, 2 mezzo-sopranos, 3 tenors, 2 bass-baritones, bass, 3 trebles, flute (also piccolo), oboe (also English horn), clarinet (also bass clarinet), bassoon, horn, trumpet, timpani, percussion (tam-tam, suspended cymbal, 5 tom-toms, bass drum, snare drum, crotales, vibraphone, glockenspiel), string quintet (2 violins, viola, violoncello, double bass).
Commissioned by: Opera North.
Call no.: **1992/119**
Re-entered as: **1993/122**

2307. Scearce, J. Mark, 1960– Canto IX: waiting for the key to the city of Dis: for concert band. Boca Raton, FL: J Ballerbach Music, 1993.
1 score (65 p.); 43 cm.
Reproduced from holograph.
Duration: 12:00.
Composed for: piccolo, 2 flutes, oboe, bassoon, clarinet in E♭, 3 clarinets, alto clarinet, bass clarinet, 2 alto saxophones, tenor saxophone, baritone saxophone, 3 trumpets, 4 horns, 3 trombones, baritone, tuba, timpani, percussion (3 suspended cymbals, crash cymbal, sizzle cymbal, glockenspiel, chimes, brake drum, triangle, vibraslap, broken glass with baseball bat, xylophone, 3 gongs, very large tam-tam, bell tree, 2 slit drums, maracas, marimba, tambourine, 2 handbells, cowbell, claves, lion's roar, vibraphone, 5 temple blocks, metal wind chimes, slapstick, ratchet, snare drum, tenor drum, bongos, woodblock, 5 tom-toms, bass drum).
Commissioned by: Music Department of North Carolina State University.
Call no.: **2000/169**

2308. Scearce, J. Mark, 1960– The shade of Orpheus: for soprano and chamber ensemble. N.p.: J. Mark Scearce, 1995.
1 score (81 p.); 22 x 29 cm.
English words by Allen Mandelbaum; also printed as text.
Duration: 19:00.
Composed for: soprano, flute (also piccolo), clarinet (also bass clarinet), viola, double bass, harp, percussion (triangle, suspended cymbal, sizzle cymbal, chimes, glockenspiel, vibraphone, 5 temple blocks, marimba, snare drum, 4 tom-toms, bongos, bass drum, timpani).
Call no.: **1996/128**

2309. Scearce, J. Mark, 1960– String quartet 1º: (Y2K). N.p.: BMI?, 2000.
1 score (87 p.); 22 x 28 cm.
Duration: 20:00.
Composed for: 2 violins, viola, violoncello.
Commissioned by: Meet the Composer.
Call no.: **2002/163**
Re-entered as: **2004/114**

2310. Scearce, J. Mark, 1960– Urban primitive: for orchestra. N.p.: J.M. Scearce, 1996.
1 score (55 p.); 44 cm.
Duration: 8:00.
Composed for: 3 flutes (3rd also piccolo), 2 oboes, 2 clarinets, bass clarinet, 2 bassoons, contrabassoon, 4 horns, 3 trumpets, 2 trombones, bass trombone, tuba, timpani, percussion (metal wind chimes, 4 triangles, 2 suspended cymbals, glockenspiels, marimba, bongos, conga, snare drum, bass drums, police whistle, vibraslap, tam-tam, 5 temple blocks, xylophone, vi-

braphone, chimes, 5 tom-toms, sizzle cymbal, hi-hat, 2 brake drums, maracas), harp, piano (also celesta), violin I, violin II, viola, violoncello, double bass.
Call no.: **1997/128**
Re-entered as: **2001/137**

2311. Schafer, R. Murray, 1933– Concerto for flute and orchestra. N.p.: n.p., 1984.
1 score (91 p.); 36 cm.
Reproduced from holograph.
Includes performance instructions.
Composed for: flute, 2 piccolos, 2 oboes, 2 clarinets, 2 bassoons, 4 horns, 2 trumpets, 2 trombones, tuba, percussion (temple blocks, 4 temple bowls, 2 bongos, tubular chimes, 2 cowbells, 2 tom-toms, crotales, tam-tam, anvil, gong, marimba, 4 cowbells, triangle, glockenspiel, vibraphone, log drum, woodblock, suspended cymbal, bass drum, snare drum), harp, piano, celesta, violin I, violin II, viola, violoncello, double bass.
Commissioned by: Ontario Arts Council and Canada Council.
Call no.: **1985/169**

2312. Schafer, R. Murray, 1933– Guitar concerto: (1989). Indian River, ON: Arcana Editions, 1989.
1 score (70 p.); 29 cm.
Reproduced from manuscript.
Includes performance instructions.
Composed for: guitar, 2 flutes (1st also alto flute, 2nd also piccolo), oboe, 2 clarinets, bassoon, trumpet, percussion (xylophone, glockenspiel, 4 congas, 2 maracas, triangle, 5 temple blocks, 4 bongos, 2 cowbells, calabash, suspended cymbal, tom-tom, crotales, musical saw, 2 woodblocks, sandpaper blocks, agogo bells, darbuka), violins I, violin II, viola, violoncello, double bass.
Commissioned by: Toronto Symphony Orchestra.
Call no.: **1991/112**

2313. Schat, Peter, 1935–2003. Symposion: opera in twee akten, opus 33, 1982–1989, revisie 1994. Amsterdam: Donemus, 1994.
1 score (4 v. [739 p.]); 35 cm.
Dutch words by Gerrit Komrij.
"Peter Iljitsj Tsjaikofsky" is a lead role in the opera.
Reproduced from holograph.
Composed for: 2 sopranos, mezzo-soprano, 3 tenors, 2 baritone, 2 basses, SATB chorus, 3 flutes (all also piccolo, 3rd also alto flute), 3 oboes (3rd also English horn), 3 clarinets, 3 alto saxophones (1st–2nd also soprano saxophone, 3rd also baritone saxophone), 3 bassoons, contrabassoon, 4 horns, 3 trumpets, 3 trombones, 2 tubas, 2 harps, 2 marimbas, bass marimba, percussion (bass drum, suspended cymbals, tam-tam, cymbals, sound of escaping steam, whip, 4 tom-toms, celesta, wind machine, 2 snare drums, congas, maracas, woodblock, vibraphone, 2 kempul gongs, 2 gongs ageng, gong suwukan), violin I, violin II, viola, violoncello, double bass.
Commissioned by: Gerard Mortier and National Opera of Brussels.
Call no.: **1998/143**

2314. Scherr, Hans-Jörg, 1935– Der letzte Tag Jesu: ein musikalisches Drama in einem Vorspiel, neun Bildern und einem Nachspiel: für Sprecher, Soli, Chor, Orgel und grosses Orchester. Partitur. Karnberg, Österreich: Ikarus Verlag, 1987.
1 score (170 p); 40 cm.
German words.
Reproduced from manuscript.
Composed for: narrator, 2 sopranos, alto, tenor, 2 baritones, bass-baritone, bass, SATB chorus, women's chorus, men's chorus, 2 flutes (2nd also piccolo), 2 oboes (both also English horn), 2 clarinets (both also clarinet in A, 2nd also bass clarinet), 2 bassoons, 4 horns, 3 trumpets, 3 trombones, bass trombone, contrabass tuba, timpani, percussion (bass drum, snare drum, tenor drum, 3 bongos, woodblock, 3 temple blocks, 3 tom-toms, cymbals, 2 suspended cymbals, 2 tam-tams, whip, ratchet, cowbell, guiro, triangle, castanets, glockenspiel, xylophone, vibraphone, chimes), organ, piano, violin I, violin II, viola, violoncello, double bass.
Call no.: **1991/113**
Also available:
Call no.: **1991/113 libretto**

2315. Schiavone, John, 1947– Mary's tryptich: an oratorio in three parts: for soprano and baritone soli, SATB choir, chamber orchestra, and organ. N.p.: John Schiavone, 1999.
1 score (125 p.); 44 cm.
Principally Latin or English words by the composer.
Text based on passages from the New Testament.
Contents: Mary's joy—Mary's sorrow—Mary's glory.
Composed for: soprano, baritone, SATB chorus, flute, oboe, bassoon, 2 horns, 2 trumpets, trombone, percussion (suspended cymbal, triangle, snare drum, bass drum), violin I, violin II, viola, violoncello, double bass.
Call no.: **2004/115**

2316. Schickele, Peter, 1935– Concerto: for bassoon and orchestra. Bryn Mawr, PA: Elkan Vogel, 1999.
1 score (137 p.); 39 cm.

"Revised June, 1999"—caption.
Duration: ca. 23:00.
Contents: Blues—Intermezzo—Scherzo—Song—Romp.
Composed for: bassoon, 2 flutes (2nd also piccolo), 2 oboes, 2 clarinets, bassoon, 2 horns, 2 trumpets, percussion (vibraphone, timpani, bells, claves, suspended cymbal, bongos, marimba, crash cymbals, triangle, woodblock, hi-hat), piano, violin I, violin II, viola, violoncello, double bass.
Commissioned by: ProMusica Chamber Orchestra of Columbus, OH.
Call no.: **2001/138**

2317. Schickele, Peter, 1935– Concerto for cello and orchestra: "In memoriam F.D.R." Bryn Mawr, PA: Elkan-Vogel, 1999.
1 score (126 p.); 37 cm.
Duration: ca. 22:00.
Contents: Invocation—Intermezzo—Song set—Eulogy and cortège.
Composed for: violoncello, 2 flutes (2nd also piccolo), 2 oboes, 2 clarinets (2nd also bass clarinet), 2 bassoons, 2 horns, 3 trumpets, timpani, percussion (vibraphone, castanets, 2 temple blocks, pair of bongos, chimes, xylophone, small triangle, claves, glass wind chimes, 2 suspended cymbals, bass drum, 2 tom-toms, orchestra bells, marimba, glockenspiel, medium triangle, bass drum), piano, violin I, violin II, viola, violoncello, double bass.
Commissioned by: New Heritage Music Foundation.
Call no.: **2002/164**

2318. Schickele, Peter, 1935– Concerto for piano and chorus: The twelve months: for S.A.T.B. chorus and piano. Bryn Mawr, PA: Elkan-Vogel, 1990.
1 score (5 v.); 27 cm.
Duration: ca. 28:00.
Contents: Prologue (August)—Fall: Thirty days hath (September); Now lay up thy barley land (October); Now Neptune's sullen month appears (November)—Winter: Wondrous news the angel brings (December); Plaint (January); Now winter nights enlarge (February)—Spring: Cadenza (March); Interlude (April); Before my lady's window gay (May)—Summer: Celebration with bells (June); Epilogue (July).
Composed for: SATB chorus, piano.
Call no.: **1991/114**

2319. Schickele, Peter, 1935– Symphony no. 1: "Songlines." Bryn Mawr, PA: Elkan-Vogel, 1995.
1 score (156 p.); 44 cm.
Duration: ca. 27:00.
Contents: Journey—Refrains—Dance music.
Composed for: 3 flutes (3rd also piccolo), 3 oboes (3rd also English horn), 3 clarinets (2nd also clarinet in E♭, 3rd also bass clarinet), 3 bassoons (3rd also contrabassoon), 4 horns, 3 trumpets, 2 trombones, bass trombone, tuba, timpani, percussion (xylophone, vibraphone, chimes, bass drums, beanbag, snare drum, woodblock, orchestra bells, 2 mounted bongos, medium cowbell, 2 maracas, marimba, medium suspended cymbal, large cowbell, 3 tom-toms), harp, piano, celesta, violin I, violin II, viola, violoncello, double bass.
Commissioned by: National Symphony Orchestra of Washington, DC.
Call no.: **1997/129**

2320. Schiffman, Harold, 1928– Concerto. N.p.: H. Schiffman, 1982.
1 score (52 p.); 38 cm.
For piano and orchestra.
Reproduced from holograph.
Duration: ca. 22:00.
Composed for: piano, 2 flutes, 2 oboes, 2 clarinets (2nd also bass clarinet), 2 bassoons (2nd also contrabassoon), 4 horns, 2 trumpets, 2 trombones, bass trombone, tuba, timpani, violin I, violin II, viola, violoncello, double bass.
Call no.: **1985/170**

2321. Schipizky, Frederick, 1952– Symphony no. 1.
Call no.: **1986/099**
No materials available.

2322. Schmidt, William, 1926– Concerto of the winds. Los Angeles, CA: Avant Music, 1986.
1 score (160 p.); 37 cm.
Composed for: piccolo, 4 flutes, 2 oboes, clarinet in E♭, 3 clarinets, alto clarinet, bass clarinet, contrabass clarinet, 2 bassoons, soprano saxophone, alto saxophone, tenor saxophone, baritone saxophone, 4 horns, 2 trumpets in D, 2 trumpets, 6 trumpets, 4 trombones, 2 baritones, 2 tubas, timpani, harp, piano, percussion (bass drum, bells, chimes, marimba, xylophone, 4 tom-toms, suspended cymbal, tam-tam, 4 temple blocks, 4 woodblocks, vibraphone, ride cymbal, snare drum, piccolo snare drum, field drum, bells).
Commissioned by: Tau Beta Sigma and Kappa Kappa Psi.
Call no.: **1986/100**

2323. Schmidt-Binge, Walter, 1931– New York report: für Sprecher, zwei Chöre u. zwei Orchester. N.p.: n.p., 198-?.
1 score (212 p.); 44 cm.

German words.
Text by Alexander Rentsch.
Reproduced from manuscript.
Composed for: narrator, SATB chorus, band: alto saxophone, tenor saxophone, baritone saxophone, 3 trumpets, 2 trombones, piano, guitar, tom-toms; orchestra: 3 flutes (3rd also piccolo), 2 oboes, English horn, 2 clarinets (2nd also bass clarinet), 2 bassoons (2nd also contrabassoon), 4 horns, 3 trumpets, 3 trombones, percussion (glockenspiel, xylophone, vibraphone, chimes, glass harp, auto horn, pea whistle, bicycle bell, sleigh bells, 2 triangles, whip, temple blocks, siren, flexatone, pandeiro, cabasa, bongos, tumba, cymbals, bass drum, anvil), harp, violin I, violin II, viola, violoncello, double bass.
Call no.: **1987/075**
Also available:
Call no.: **1987/075 chorus scores**
Call no.: **1987/075 orchestral parts**
Call no.: **1987/075 text**

2324. Schnebel, Dieter, 1930– Hymnus: Konzert für Klavier und Orchester, aus: Sinfonie X, 1989–92. Partitur. Mainz; New York, NY: Schott, 1994.
1 score (101 p.); 42 cm.
Duration: 20:00.
Composed for: piano, 3 flutes (1st also piccolo, 3rd also alto flute), 3 oboes, 3 clarinets, 3 bassoons, 4 horns, 3 trumpets, 3 trombones, tuba, timpani, percussion (triangle, 2 tam-tams, 2 cymbals, 4 tom-toms, crotales, glockenspiel, xylophone, tubular bells, bell plates, 2 gongs, metal chimes, cowbells, thundersheet, 2 maracas, anvil, sistrum, flexatone, jingle bells, church bells, ship's bell, hyoshige, knife with whetstone), harp, accordion, ondes martenot, violin I, violin II, viola, violoncello, double bass.
Call no.: **1996/129**

2325. Schnebel, Dieter, 1930– Monotonien: für Klavier und live Elektronik, 1987–89. N.p.: n.p., 1989.
1 score (73 p.); 34 cm.
Reproduced from manuscript.
Duration: ca. 1:00:00.
Composed for: piano, electronics.
Commissioned by: Südwestfunk (Christof Bitter, Joef Hansler).
Call no.: **1995/092**

2326. Schnebel, Dieter, 1930– Sinfonie X: für grosses Orchester, Altstimme, und Tonband (1987–1992). Mainz; New York, NY: Schott, 1992.
1 score (184 p.); 57 cm.
Vocal part is wordless.
Reproduced from manuscript.
Duration: 2:30:00.
Composed for: alto, tape, group I: bass clarinet (also clarinet in E♭, clarinet, bird call), 2 violins, 2 violas (both also maracas), harp, percussion (tam-tam, 2 cymbals, 3 bongos, tom-tom, friction drum, guiro, sandpaper block, metal box with stones, 2 thundersheets, ratchet, scythe with whetstone, wildlocker, metal plate, porcelain plate, bird whistle, large stone, slapstick, temple block, taiko, cowbell, stone, bell plate, whistle, lion's roar, shaker, tambourine, rain stick); group II: horn (also wildlocker and Wagner tuba), 2 violoncellos, percussion (cymbals, tam-tam, tom-tom, 3 bongos, guiro, maracas, slapstsick, balloons, friction drum, sandpaper block, ratchet, metal box with stones, scythe with whetstone, water gong, metal plate, wildlocker, large stone, temple block, ship's horn, cowbells, 2 thundersheets, whistle, lion's roar, shaker, tambourine); group III: trumpet, 2 double basses, percussion (vibraphone, tam-tam, tom-tom, cymbals, 3 bongos, guiro, sandpaper block, metal box with stones, friction drum, ratchet, scythe with whetstone, glass chimes, sistrum, balloons, different foils, large stone, temple block, 2 thundersheets, porcelain plate, anvil, whistle, lion's roar, shaker, tambourine, rain stick, slapstick, steel drum); group IV: English horn (also oboe), 2 violins, 2 violas, percussion (marimba, 2 cymbals, tom-tom, 3 bongos, balloons, friction drum, guiro, sandpaper block, metal box with stones, ratchet, scythe with whetstone, cowbells, tambourine, maracas, paper sheets, plastic, glass pieces, wildlocker, metal plate, porcelain plate, stone, woodblock, temple block, 2 thundersheets, whistle, lion's roar, shaker, tambourine, slapstick); large orchestra: 3 flutes (1st–2nd also piccolo, 3rd also alto flute), 3 oboes, 3 clarinets (1st also clarinet in E♭), 3 bassoons (3rd also contrabassoon), saxophone, 4 horns (2nd and 4th also Wagner tubas), 3 trumpets (all also piccolo trumpet), 3 trombones, tuba, percussion (triangle, tam-tam, 2 cymbals, crotales, 4 tom-toms, bongo, taiko, snare drum, bass drum, tambourine, steel drum, timpani, glockenspiel, xylophone, vibraphone, flexatone, chimes, bell plates, church bells, ship's bell, 2 gongs, ondes martenot, thundersheet, 2 maracas, 2 guiros, friction drum, ratchet, hyoshigi, woodblock, temple block, sandpaper block, anvil, wind machine, slapstick, bird whistle, wildlocker, balloons, stone, metal box with stones, siren, sistrum, castanets, claves, tambourine, bull roarer, whip, police whistle, stick, knife with whetstone, wood with knife, paper, water, bottle, taxi horn, switch, chains), piano, accordion, violin I, violin II, viola, violoncello, double bass.
Commissioned by: SWF Baden-Baden.
Call no.: **1993/123**

2327. Schnittke, Alfred, 1934–1998. 4. Concerto grosso, 5. Sinfonie. Hamburg: Musikverlag H. Sikorski, 1988.
1 score (80 p.); 42 cm.
Reproduced from manuscript.
Composed for: 3 flutes (all also piccolo), 3 oboes (3rd also English horn), 3 clarinets (1st also clarinet in E♭, 3rd also bass clarinet), 3 bassoons (3rd also contrabassoon), 4 horns, 4 trumpets, 4 trombones, tuba, timpani, percussion (triangle, flexatone, whip, military drum, 3 bongos, 2 tom-toms, cymbals, tam-tam, bass drum, tubular bells, glockenspiel, crotales, xylophone, vibraphone, marimba), harp, piano, celesta, cembalo, violin I, violin II, viola, violoncello, double bass.
Call no.: **1991/115**

2328. Schnittke, Alfred, 1934–1998. Kont͡sert dli͡a al′ta s orkestrom. N.p.: n.p., 1985.
1 score (50 p.); 40 cm.
Reproduced from holograph.
Composed for: viola, 3 flutes (2nd also piccolo, 3rd also alto flute), 3 oboes (3rd also English horn), 3 clarinets (2nd also clarinet in E♭, 3rd also bass clarinet), 3 bassoons (3rd also contrabassoon), 4 horns, 4 trumpets, 4 trombones, tuba, timpani, percussion (2 cymbals, 2 bass drums, 2 tam-tams, flexatone, xylophone, vibraphone, chimes, triangle), harp, piano, celesta, harpsichord, viola, violoncello, double bass.
Call no.: **1988/096**

2329. Schnittke, Alfred, 1934–1998. Kont͡sert dli͡a smeshannogo khora. N.p.: n.p., 198-?.
1 score (60 p.); 31 cm.
Russian words (Cyrillic) by Grigora Nareka͡tsi (951–1003).
Reproduced from manuscript.
"Posvi͡a shchae͡tsia Kamernomu Khoru SSSP i ego rukoviditeli͡u Valerii͡u Kuz′michu Poli͡anskomu."
Composed for: chorus.
Call no.: **1989/112**

2330. Schnyder, Daniel, 1961– Concerto for bass trombone and orchestra. Roswell, GA: E. Williams Music, 1999.
1 score (146 p.); 36 cm.
Composed for: bass trombone, flute (also piccolo), oboe, English horn, clarinet, bass clarinet, bassoon, contrabassoon, horn, trumpet, trombone, percussion (crash cymbals, suspended cymbal, woodblock, tom-tom, flexatone, cowbell, snare drum, hi-hat, crotales, Arab drum, tambourine, conga, marimba), piano, violin I, violin II, viola, violoncello, double bass.
Commissioned by: Absolute Ensemble, Elwood Williams, and David Taylor.
Call no.: **2002/165**

2331. Schöllhorn, Johannes, 1962– "Liu-yi/Wasser": pour orchestre. Paris: Editions Musicales Européennes, 2002.
1 score (23 p.); 60 cm.
Composed for: 2 flutes (also piccolo), 2 oboe, clarinet, bass clarinet, 2 bassoons, 2 horns, 3 trumpets, 3 trombones, percussion (bass drum, 2 large cymbals, large tam-tam, woodblock, log drum, 3 crotales, large Japanese rin, 2 timpani), violin I, violin II, viola, violoncello, double bass.
Commissioned by: Westdeutscher Rundfunk.
Call no.: **2005/129**

2332. Schonthal, Ruth, 1924– Evening music and nocturnal fantasy with ocean waves: for orchestra. N.p.: Ruth Schonthal, 1992.
1 score (44 leaves); 45 cm.
Composed for: piccolo, 2 flutes, 2 oboes, 2 clarinets (2nd also bass clarinet), 2 bassoons, contrabassoon, 4 horns, 3 trumpets, 3 trombones, tuba, timpani, percussion (bells, vibraphone, triangle, suspended cymbal, tam-tam, tambourine), harp, piano, tape, violin I, violin II, viola, violoncello, double bass.
Call no.: **1993/124**

2333. Schroeter, Guilherme, 1960– 29 prelúdios: para piano: Em tonalidade, op. 1. N.p.: Guira Produç̃es, 199-?.
1 v. of music; 28 cm.
"Rev. pelo autor."
Composed for: piano.
Call no.: **2005/128**

2334. Schuller, Gunther, 1925– An arc ascending. New York, NY: Associated Music Publishers, 1996.
1 score (41 p.); 36 cm.
For orchestra.
Reproduced from manuscript.
Duration: 10:00.
Composed for: piccolo, 3 flutes (2nd also alto flute, 3rd also bass flute), 2 oboes (2nd also oboe d'amore), English horn, heckelphone, 3 clarinets (2nd–3rd also bass clarinet), contrabass clarinet, 3 bassoons (3rd also contrabassoon), 4 horns, 3 trumpets, 3 trombones, tuba, timpani, percussion (bass drum, bell tree, claves, glockenspiel, gong, crash cymbals, marimba, 4 suspended cymbals, 2 tam-tams, 3 tom-toms, 3 triangles, vibraphone, wind machine), piano (also celesta), harp, violin I, violin II, viola, violoncello, double bass.
Commissioned by: American Symphony Orchestra

League and Cincinnati Symphony.
Call no.: **2002/166**

2335. Schuller, Gunther, 1925– The black warrior: an oratorio. N.p.: n.p., 1998.
1 score (83 p.); 43 cm.
Words by Martin Luther King.
For narrator, soprano, baritone, SATB chorus, vocal quartet seated within the orchestra, and orchestra.
At end: Oct. 24, 1998.
Reproduced from holograph.
Composed for: soprano, baritone, vocal quartet (soprano, alto, tenor, bass), SATB chorus, 2 piccolos, 2 flutes, 2 oboes, English horn, clarinet in E♭, 2 clarinets, bass clarinet, 2 bassoons, contrabassoon, 4 horns, 4 trumpets, 4 trombones, tuba, timpani, percussion (metal plate, 2 tam-tams, glockenspiel, vibraphone, chimes, bass drum, suspended cymbals, vibraphone, slapstick, small gong, snare drum, 2 triangles, marimba), harp, piano, celesta, organ, violin I, violin II, viola, violoncello, double bass.
Call no.: **2001/139**
Re-entered as: **2004/116**

2336. Schuller, Gunther, 1925– Concerto for flute (and piccolo) and orchestra. Corrected 9/88. New York, NY: Associated Music Publishers, 1988.
1 score (80 p.); 46 cm.
Reproduced from holograph.
Composed for: flute (also piccolo), 2 flutes (both also piccolo, 2nd also alto flute), 2 oboes, English horn, 2 clarinets (2nd also clarinet in E♭, bass clarinet), bass clarinet, 3 bassoons (3rd also contrabassoon), 4 horns, 3 trumpets, 3 trombones, tuba, timpani, percussion (glockenspiel, vibraphone, xylophone, marimba, 5 suspended cymbals, small choke cymbal, 2 tam-tams, triangle, snare drum, woodblock, maracas, 2 crash cymbals, tom-tom, flexatone, tambourine, whip, sleigh bells), harp, electric piano (also celesta), violin I, violin II, viola, violoncello, double bass.
Commissioned by: students and colleagues of Walfrid Kujala.
Call no.: **1989/113**

2337. Schuller, Gunther, 1925– Concerto for piano three hands: (two pianos & chamber orchestra). Full score. N.p.: Associated Music, 1990.
1 score (59 p.); 36 cm.
Reproduced from manuscript.
Composed for: 2 pianos, 2 flutes (2nd also piccolo), 2 oboes (2nd also English horn), 2 clarinets (2nd also clarinet in E♭ and bass clarinet), 2 bassoons (1st also contrabassoon), 2 horns, 2 trumpets, trombone, timpani, percussion (glockenspiel, 5 temple blocks, 5 suspended cymbals, woodblock, 2 tam-tams, claves, 3 tom-toms, triangle, tenor drum, glass chimes, bass drum, guiro, small cymbal, chimes, vibraphone, crotales, maracas, marimba, tambourine), harp, violin I, violin II, viola, violoncello, double bass.
Call no.: **1993/125**

2338. Schuller, Gunther, 1925– Concerto no. 2: for violin and orchestra (1991). New York, NY: Associated Music, 1991.
1 score (89 p.); 36 cm.
Duration: ca. 26:00.
Reproduced from manuscript.
Composed for: violin, 3 flutes (3rd also piccolo), 3 oboes (3rd also English horn), 3 clarinets (3rd also bass clarinet), 3 bassoons (3rd also contrabassoon), 4 horns, 3 trumpets, 3 trombones, tuba, timpani, percussion (marimba, suspended cymbals, choke cymbal, snare drum, bass drum, triangle, hi-hat, glockenspiel, woodblocks, vibraphone), harp, piano (also celesta), violin I, violin II, viola, violoncello, double bass.
Call no.: **1992/120**

2339. Schuller, Gunther, 1925– Concerto quaternio: for violin, flute, oboe, trumpet and orchestra. N.p.: n.p., 1984.
1 score (63 p.); 62 cm.
For 4 solo instruments and 4 orchestral groups.
Reproduced from holograph.
Composed for: violin, flute, oboe, trumpet, piccolo, flute, alto flute, 2 oboes, English horn, clarinet in E♭, 2 clarinets, bass clarinet, 3 bassoons, 4 horns, 3 trumpets, 3 trombones, tuba, timpani, percussion (2 triangles, glass chimes, glockenspiel, 3 suspended cymbals, gourd, 2 sets of wood chimes, marimba, temple blocks, 2 vibraphones, roto-toms, sleigh bells, 2 tom-toms, bass drum, tam-tam, tambourine, xylophone, gong, cymbals, sizzle cymbal, 4 woodblocks, ratchet), harp, harpsichord, celesta, violin I, violin II, viola, violoncello, double bass, voices.
Commissioned by: Philharmonic Symphony Society of New York.
Call no.: **1985/171**
Re-entered as: **1988/097**

2340. Schuller, Gunther, 1925– Farbenspiel: Konzert für Orchester, 1985. Pennsauken, NJ: G. Schirmer/Associated Music Publishers, 1985.
1 score (82 p.); 51 cm.
Reproduced from manuscript.
Contents: Chorisch—Solistisch—Orchestral.
Composed for: 2 piccolos, 2 flutes (2nd also alto flute),

3 oboes, 2 English horns, 2 clarinets (2nd also bass clarinet), alto clarinet, 4 bassoons, contrabassoon, 4 horns, 4 trumpets, 4 trombones, tuba, percussion (2 suspended cymbals, tambourine, bass drum, marimba, 4 tom-toms, tam-tam, vibraphone, 3 triangles, 2 glockenspiels, xylophone, timpani, antique cymbal, choke cymbal, maracas, 2 bongos, claves, snare drum, 3 temple blocks, chimes, sandpaper blocks), harp, celesta, violin I, violin II, viola, violoncello, double bass.
Commissioned by: Glimmerglass Opera.
Call no.: **1986/101**
Re-entered as: **1990/108**

2341. Schuller, Gunther, 1925– Impromptus and cadenzas: for oboe, clarinet, bassoon, horn, violin and cello (1990). New York, NY: Associated Music Publishers, 1990.
1 score (43 p.); 28 cm.
Reproduced from manuscript.
Composed for: oboe, clarinet, bassoon, horn, violin, violoncello.
Commissioned by: Chamber Music Society.
Call no.: **1991/116**

2342. Schuller, Gunther, 1925– Of reminiscences and reflections. New York, NY: Associated Music Publishers, 1993.
1 score (48 p.); 36 cm.
For orchestra.
Reproduced from holograph.
Composed for: 4 flutes (2nd and 4th also alto flute, 3rd–4th also piccolo), 4 oboes (3rd–4th also English horn), clarinet in E♭ (also bass clarinet), 2 clarinets (2nd also clarinet in A), bass clarinet, 4 bassoons (4th also contrabassoon), 6 horns, 4 trumpets, 4 trombones, tuba, timpani, percussion (tambourine, claves, 3 tom-toms, tam-tam, 2 snare drums, 6 suspended cymbals, whip, bass drum, xylophone, vibraphone, glockenspiel, marimba, triangle, timpani), harp, piano (also celesta), violin I, violin II, viola, violoncello, double bass.
Commissioned by: Louisville Orchestra.
Call no.: **1994/129**

2343. Schuller, Gunther, 1925– Of reminiscences and reflections. New York, NY: Associated Music Publishers, 1995.
1 miniature score (68 p.); 36 cm.
For orchestra.
"Revised 7/95"—p. 1.
Composed for: 4 flutes (2nd and 4th also alto flute, 3rd–4th also piccolo), 4 oboes (3rd–4th also English horn), clarinet in E♭ (also bass clarinet), 2 clarinets (2nd also clarinet in A), bass clarinet, 4 bassoons (4th also contrabassoon), 6 horns, 4 trumpets, 4 trombones, tuba, timpani, percussion (tambourine, claves, 3 tom-toms, tam-tam, 2 snare drums, 6 suspended cymbals, whip, bass drum, xylophone, vibraphone, glockenspiel, marimba, triangle, timpani), harp, piano (also celesta), violin I, violin II, viola, violoncello, double bass.
Commissioned by: Louisville Orchestra.
Call no.: **1996/130**
Re-entered as: **1997/130**

2344. Schuller, Gunther, 1925– Of reminiscences and reflections. New York, NY: Associated Music Publishers, 1995.
1 (68 p.); 44 cm.
For orchestra.
"Revised 7/95"—p. 1.
Composed for: 4 flutes (2nd and 4th also alto flute, 3rd–4th also piccolo), 4 oboes (3rd–4th also English horn), clarinet in E♭ (also bass clarinet), 2 clarinets (2nd also clarinet in A), bass clarinet, 4 bassoons (4th also contrabassoon), 6 horns, 4 trumpets, 4 trombones, tuba, timpani, percussion (tambourine, claves, 3 tom-toms, tam-tam, 2 snare drums, 6 suspended cymbals, whip, bass drum, xylophone, vibraphone, glockenspiel, marimba, triangle, timpani), harp, piano (also celesta), violin I, violin II, viola, violoncello, double bass.
Commissioned by: Louisville Orchestra.
Call no.: **1998/144**

2345. Schuller, Gunther, 1925– The past is in the present. New York, NY: Associated Music Publishers, 1994.
1 score (53 p.); 36 cm.
For orchestra.
Composed for: 4 flutes (2nd also alto flute, 3rd–4th also piccolo), 3 oboes (3rd–4th also English horn), English horn, 3 clarinets (all also clarinet in A), bass clarinet, 4 bassoons (4th also contrabassoon), 5 horns, 4 trumpets, 4 trombones, tuba, timpani, percussion (3 triangles, bass drum, chimes, crash cymbals, flexatone, glockenspiel, marimba, snare drum, suspended cymbals, tambourine, tam-tam, tenor drum, vibraphone, woodblocks, xylophone), 2 harps, piano (also celesta), violin I, violin II, viola, violoncello, double bass.
Commissioned by: Cincinnati Symphony.
Call no.: **1995/093**

2346. Schuller, Gunther, 1925– String quartet no. 3. Newton Centre, MA: Margun Music, 1986.
1 score (41 p.); 31 cm.
Reproduced from manuscript.
Composed for: 2 violins, viola, violoncello.

Commissioned by: Syracuse Friends of Chamber Music.
Call no.: **1987/076**

2347. Schuman, William, 1910–1992. On freedom's ground: an American cantata: for baritone, chorus, and orchestra. Bryn Mawr, PA: Merion Music: Theodore Presser, 1986.
1 score (147 p.); 44 cm.
English words by Richard Wilbur; also printed as text.
Duration: ca. 40:00.
Contents: Back then—Our risen states—Like a great statue—Come dance—Immigrants still.
Commissioned by: New York Philharmonic.
Call no.: **1987/077**
Also available:
Call no.: **1987/077 chorus score**

2348. Schuman, William, 1910–1992. A question of taste: opera in one act. Bryn Mawr, PA: Merion Music, 1989.
1 score (2 v.); 31 cm.
English words by J. D. McClatchy, based on a story by Roald Dahl.
Composed for: soprano, 2 mezzo-sopranos, tenor, baritone, bass-baritone, 2 flutes (both also piccolo), 2 oboes, 2 clarinets, 2 bassoons, 2 horns, 2 trumpets, 2 trombones, percussion (crash cymbals, snare drum, bass drum, glockenspiel, xylophone, tambourine, triangle, suspended cymbal, tubular bells), celesta, violin I, violin II, viola, violoncello, double bass.
Commissioned by: Eugene V. and Clare Thaw Charitable Trust.
Call no.: **1990/109**

2349. Schurmann, Gerard, 1928– Concerto for orchestra. London: Novello, 1996.
1 score (128 p.); 42 cm.
Program note by the composer.
Contents: Summa ferri—Moonbird—A spirit in mourning—Aubade—Le grand concert.
Duration: 32:00.
Composed for: 3 flutes (3rd also piccolo), 3 oboes (3rd also English horn), clarinet in E♭, 3 clarinets (3rd also bass clarinet), 2 bassoons, contrabassoon, 4 horns, 4 trumpets, 3 trombones, tuba, timpani, percussion (bass drum, xylophone, vibraphone, marimba, snare drum, suspended cymbal, crotales, glockenspiel, large gong, tenor drum, tubular bells, tom-toms, large tam-tam, tambourine, whip, triangle, 3 bongos, 3 woodblocks), harp, piano (also celesta), violin I, violin II, viola, violoncello, double bass.
Commissioned by: Pittsburgh Symphony.
Call no.: **1997/131**

2350. Schurmann, Gerard, 1928– The gardens of exile: concerto for cello and orchestra. London: Novello, 1991.
1 score (85 p.); 42 cm.
Includes composer's note.
Duration: ca. 30:00.
Composed for: violoncello, 3 flutes (3rd also piccolo), 2 oboes, English horn, 2 clarinets, bass clarinet, 2 bassoons, contrabassoon, 4 horns, 3 trumpets, 2 trombones, bass trombone, tuba, timpani, percussion (xylophone, marimba, vibraphone, glockenspiel, tubular bells, crotales, 2 suspended cymbals, side drum, tenor drum, bass drum, claves, tambourine), harp, piano (also celesta), violin I, violin II, viola, violoncello, double bass.
Commissioned by: Western Orchestral Society.
Call no.: **1992/121**

2351. Schurmann, Gerard, 1928– Quartet: for piano and strings. London: Novello, 1986.
1 score (41 p.); 40 cm.
Reproduced from manuscript.
Duration: ca. 22:00.
Composed for: violin, viola, violoncello, piano.
Commissioned by: US National Endowment for the Arts.
Call no.: **1987/078**

2352. Schwantner, Joseph C., 1943– Concerto for percussion + orchestra, 1994. N.p.: n.p., 1994.
1 score (124 p.); 44 cm.
Reproduced from manuscript.
Composed for: percussion (amplified marimba, xylophone, crotales, tom-toms, bass drum, timbales, bongos, vibraphone, 2 triangles, tenor drum, water gong, suspended cymbals, 9 pitched cowbells, rute, shekere), piccolo, 2 flutes, 2 oboes, English horn, 2 clarinets, bass clarinet, 2 bassoons, contrabassoon, 4 horns, 3 trumpets, 3 trombones, tuba, timpani, percussion (glockenspiel, marimba, timbales, 2 triangles, mark tree, small suspended cymbal, claves, brake drum, vibraphone, 3 tom-toms, bell tree, medium suspended cymbal, maracas, tubular bells, xylophone, bass drum, Japanese wind chimes, large suspended cymbal, tam-tam, anvil), harp, amplified piano, violin I, violin II, viola, violoncello, double bass.
Commissioned by: New York Philharmonic.
Call no.: **1996/131b**

2353. Schwantner, Joseph C., 1943– Concerto for percussion and orchestra. N.p.: Helicon Music, 1994.
1 score (73 p.); 44 cm.
Composed for: percussion (amplified marimba, xylo-

phone, crotales, tom-toms, bass drum, timbales, bongos, vibraphone, 2 triangles, tenor drum, water gong, suspended cymbals, 9 pitched cowbells, rute, shekere), piccolo, 2 flutes, 2 oboes, English horn, 2 clarinets, bass clarinet, 2 bassoons, contrabassoon, 4 horns, 3 trumpets, 3 trombones, tuba, timpani, percussion (glockenspiel, marimba, timbales, 2 triangles, mark tree, small suspended cymbal, claves, vibraphone, 3 tom-toms, bell tree, medium suspended cymbal, maracas, brake drum, tubular bells, xylophone, bass drum, Japanese wind chimes, large suspended cymbal, tam-tam, anvil), harp, amplified piano, violin I, violin II, viola, violoncello, double bass.
Commissioned by: New York Philharmonic.
Call no.: **1996/131a**

2354. Schwantner, Joseph C., 1943– Concerto for percussion and orchestra. N.p.: Helicon Music Corp.; Valley Forge, PA: European American Music Distributors Corp., 1994.
1 score (73 p.); 44 cm.
Composed for: percussion (amplified marimba, xylophone, crotales, tom-toms, bass drum, timbales, bongos, vibraphone, 2 triangles, tenor drum, water gong, suspended cymbals, 9 pitched cowbells, rute, shekere), piccolo, 2 flutes, 2 oboes, English horn, 2 clarinets, bass clarinet, 2 bassoons, contrabassoon, 4 horns, 3 trumpets, 3 trombones, tuba, timpani, percussion (glockenspiel, marimba, timbales, 2 triangles, mark tree, small suspended cymbal, claves, vibraphone, 3 tom-toms, bell tree, medium suspended cymbal, maracas, brake drum, tubular bells, xylophone, bass drum, Japanese wind chimes, large suspended cymbal, tam-tam, anvil), harp, amplified piano, violin I, violin II, viola, violoncello, double bass.
Commissioned by: New York Philharmonic.
Call no.: **1998/145**

2355. Schwantner, Joseph C., 1943– Concerto for percussion and orchestra. Rev. and corr. ed. N.p.: Helicon Music Corp; Valley Forge, PA: European American Music Distributors Corp., 1999.
1 score (73 p.); 43 cm.
Composed for: percussion (amplified marimba, xylophone, crotales, tom-toms, bass drum, timbales, bongos, vibraphone, 2 triangles, tenor drum, water gong, suspended cymbals, 9 pitched cowbells, rute, shekere), piccolo, 2 flutes, 2 oboes, English horn, 2 clarinets, bass clarinet, 2 bassoons, contrabassoon, 4 horns, 3 trumpets, 3 trombones, tuba, timpani, percussion (glockenspiel, marimba, timbales, 2 triangles, mark tree, small suspended cymbal, claves, vibraphone, 3 tom-toms, bell tree, medium suspended cymbal, maracas, brake drum, tubular bells, xylophone, bass drum, Japanese wind chimes, large suspended cymbal, tam-tam, anvil), harp, amplified piano, violin I, violin II, viola, violoncello, double bass.
Commissioned by: Philharmonic-Symphony Society of New York.
Call no.: **2001/140**

2356. Schwantner, Joseph C., 1943– Concerto for piano and orchestra. N.p.: Helicon Music, 1988.
1 score (160 p.); 45 cm.
Reproduced from manuscript.
Contents: "Distant runes and incantations"—Soliloquy "Veiled autumn" (Kindertodeslied)—"The unbroken circle of the moon's dark halo."
Composed for: piano, 2 flutes (2nd also piccolo), 2 oboes (2nd also English horn), 2 clarinets (2nd also bass clarinet), 2 bassoons, 2 horns, 2 trumpets, 2 trombones, tuba, percussion (vibraphone, glockenspiel, marimba, xylophone, 2 suspended triangles, bass drum, 2 timbales, 2 bongos, tam-tam, suspended cymbal, water gong, 3 tom-toms, bell tree, crotales, tubular bells, timpani), celesta, violin I, violin II, viola, violoncello, double bass.
Commissioned by: Chase Manhattan Bank.
Call no.: **1989/114**

2357. Schwantner, Joseph C., 1943– Concerto for piano and orchestra. N.p.: Helicon Music, 1988.
1 score (160 p.); 28 cm.
Reproduced from manuscript.
Contents: "Distant runes and incantations"—Soliloquy "Veiled autumn" (Kindertodeslied)—"The unbroken circle of the moon's dark halo."
Composed for: piano, 2 flutes (2nd also piccolo), 2 oboes (2nd also English horn), 2 clarinets (2nd also bass clarinet), 2 bassoons, 2 horns, 2 trumpets, 2 trombones, tuba, percussion (vibraphone, glockenspiel, marimba, xylophone, 2 suspended triangles, bass drum, 2 timbales, 2 bongos, tam-tam, suspended cymbal, water gong, 3 tom-toms, bell tree, crotales, tubular bells, timpani), celesta, violin I, violin II, viola, violoncello, double bass.
Commissioned by: Chase Manhattan Bank.
Call no.: **1990/110**

2358. Schwantner, Joseph C., 1943– Concerto for piano and orchestra. Study score. N.p.: Helicon Music; Valley Forge, PA: European American Music Distributors Corp., 1988 (1990 printing).
1 score (160 p.); 28 cm.
Reproduced from manuscript.
Duration: 29:00.

Contents: "Distant runes and incantations"—Soliloquy "Veiled autumn" (Kindertodeslied)—"The unbroken circle of the moon's dark halo."
Composed for: piano, 2 flutes (2nd also piccolo), 2 oboes (2nd also English horn), 2 clarinets (2nd also bass clarinet), 2 bassoons, 2 horns, 2 trumpets, 2 trombones, tuba, percussion (vibraphone, glockenspiel, marimba, xylophone, 2 suspended triangles, bass drum, 2 timbales, 2 bongos, tam-tam, suspended cymbal, water gong, 3 tom-toms, bell tree, crotales, tubular bells, timpani), celesta, violin I, violin II, viola, violoncello, double bass.
Commissioned by: Chase Manhattan Bank.
Call no.: **1991/117**

2359. Schwantner, Joseph C., 1943– Evening land: symphony for orchestra with soprano solo. N.p.: Helicon Music; Valley Forge, PA: European American Music Distributors, 1995.
1 miniature score (63 p.); 44 cm.
"Poems by Pär Lagerkvist from Evening land; translated by W. H. Auden"; also printed as text.
Duration: ca. 28:00.
Composed for: soprano, 3 flutes (3rd also piccolo), 3 oboes (3rd also English horn), 3 clarinets (3rd also bass clarinet), 2 bassoons, contrabassoon, 4 horns, 3 trumpets, 2 trombones, bass trombone, tuba, timpani, percussion (large bass drum, suspended cymbal, timbales, tam-tam, small suspended cymbal, tom-toms, 3 triangles, crotales), harp, amplified piano (also harpsichord), violin I, violin II, viola, violoncello, double bass.
Commissioned by: Barlow Endowment for Music Composition at Brigham Young University and Saint Louis Symphony Orchestra.
Call no.: **1997/132**
Re-entered as: **2000/170**

2360. Schwantner, Joseph C., 1943– Magabunda: four poems of Agueda Pizarro.
Call no.: **1985/172**
No materials available.

2361. Schwantner, Joseph C., 1943– A sudden rainbow: for orchestra. Pali, PA: Helicon Music Corp.; Valley Forge, PA: European American Music, 1985.
1 score (vi, 66 p.); 34 cm.
Reproduced from manuscript.
Duration: ca. 15:00.
Composed for: 3 flutes (3rd also piccolo), 3 oboes (3rd also English horn), 3 clarinets (3rd also bass clarinet), 3 bassoons (3rd also contrabassoon), 4 horns, 3 trumpets, 3 trombones, tuba, timpani, percussion (vibraphone, xylophone, suspended triangle, suspended cymbal, timbales, tam-tam, glockenspiel, marimba, 3 tom-toms, bass drum, crotales, tubular bells, 2 button gongs), harp, piano (also celesta), violin I, violin II, viola, violoncello, double bass.
Commissioned by: Exxon Corporation, Rockefeller Foundation, and National Endowment for the Arts.
Call no.: **1987/079**

2362. Schwartz, Elliott, 1936– Dream music with variations: for violin, viola, cello & piano. Bryn Mawr, PA: Theodore Presser, 1983.
1 score (A–B, 34 p.); 28 cm.
Reproduced from holograph.
Duration: 19:00.
Includes performance instructions and program notes.
Composed for: violin, viola, violoncello, piano.
Call no.: **1985/173**

2363. Schwartz, Elliott, 1936– Equinox: concerto for orchestra. Newton Centre, MA: Margun Music, 1994.
1 score (82 p.); 36 cm.
Duration: 21:00.
Includes performance instructions.
Composed for: 2 flutes (2nd also piccolo), 2 oboes (2nd also English horn), 2 clarinets (2nd also bass clarinet), 2 bassoons (2nd also contrabassoon), 4 horns, 2 trumpets, 2 trombones, bass trombone, tuba, timpani, percussion (marimba, 4 tom-toms, snare drum, vibraphone, bass drum, 3 woodblocks, tubular chimes, suspended cymbal, glockenspiel, tambourine, flexatone, tam-tam), harp, piano (also celesta), harmonica, violin I, violin II, viola, violoncello, double bass.
Commissioned by: Portland Symphony Orchestra.
Call no.: **1997/133**

2364. Schwartz, Elliott, 1936– Mehitabel's serenade: concerto for alto saxophone and orchestra. N.p.: n.p., 2000.
1 score (40 p.); 36 cm.
Duration: ca. 16:00.
Composed for: alto saxophone, 2 flutes (2nd also piccolo), 2 oboes (2nd also English horn), 2 clarinets (2nd also bass clarinet), 2 bassoons (2nd also contrabassoon), 4 horns, 2 trumpets, 2 trombones, bass trombone, tuba, timpani, percussion (xylophone, 5 woodblocks, tubular chimes, roto-toms, tam-tam, vibraphone, suspended cymbals, snare drum, tambourine, tom-toms, bass drum, triangle, glockenspiel), harp, piano, violin I, violin II, viola, violoncello, double bass.
Call no.: **2003/111**

2365. Schwendinger, Laura, 1962– Celestial city: for B♭ clarinet, violin, viola, cello and piano. N.p.: Laura Elise Schwendinger, 2002.

1 score (49 p.); 28 x 44 cm.
Duration: 17:60.
Composed for: clarinet, violin, viola, violoncello, piano.
Call no.: **2005/130**

2366. Schwendinger, Laura, 1962– Chamber concerto: for piano and mixed ensemble. N.p.: Laura Elise Schwendinger, 1995.
1 score (134 p.); 36 cm.
Composed for: piano, flute (also piccolo, alto flute), oboe (also English horn), clarinet (also bass clarinet), bassoon, horn, trumpet, trombone, percussion (vibraphone, glockenspiel, suspended cymbal, chimes, 2 tam-tams, bell tree, snare drum, 5 tom-toms, bass drum), 2 violins, viola, violoncello, double bass.
Call no.: **1996/132**

2367. Schwendinger, Laura, 1962– Songs of heaven and earth: four settings from Ts'ai Yen's epic work 18 verses to a Tatar reed whistle. N.p.: L.E. Schwendinger, 1997.
1 score (41, 21, 19, 39 p.); 28 x 44 cm.
English words; translations by Kenneth Rexroth and Ling Chung, also printed as texts.
Contents: I was born in a time of peace—A Ta-tar chief . . . —The sun sets . . . —I never believed . . .
Composed for: mezzo-soprano, flute (also alto flute), clarinet (also bass clarinet), violin, violoncello, piano, harp, percussion (3 tam-tams, 2 gongs, Chinese cymbal, sizzle cymbal, vibraphone, glockenspiel, crotales, bell tree, wind chimes, tubular bells, snare drum, tom-toms, bass drum).
Call no.: **2000/171**
Re-entered as: **2002/167**

2368. Schwertsik, Kurt, 1935– Sinfonia-sinfonietta: five movements for orchestra: opus 73. London: Boosey & Hawkes, 1997.
1 miniature score (99 p.); 19 cm.
Includes composer's description of each movement in German with English and French translations.
Duration: 21:00.
Composed for: piccolo, 2 flutes, 2 oboes, 2 clarinets, 2 bassoons, 4 horns, 2 trumpets, 3 trombones, tuba, timpani, percussion (temple block, snare drum, bass drum, crash cymbals, suspended cymbal, tam-tam, anvil), violin I, violin II, viola, violoncello, double bass.
Commissioned by: Gesellschaft der Musikfreunde in Wien.
Call no.: **1998/146**

2369. Sciarrino, Salvatore, 1947– L'opera per flauto. Milano: Ricordi, 1990.
37 p. of music; 47 cm.
Contents: All'aure in una lontananza—Hermes—Come vengono prodotti gli incantesimi?—Canzona di ringraziamento—Venere che le grazie la fioriscono—L'orizzonte luminoso di aton—Fra i testi dedicati alle nubi.
Composed for: flute.
Call no.: **1993/126**

2370. Sciortino, Edouard, 1893–1979. Ibère; berbère: pour piano: op. 8. Paris: L. Philippo, 1961.
19 p. of music; 32 cm.
Ibère: op. 8, no. 1; Berbère: op. 8, no. 2.
Composed for: piano.
Call no.: **1988/098**

2371. Sclater, James, 1943– Witness to matters human and divine: for narrator, soprano solo, SATB chorus, and orchestra. N.p.: James Sclater, 1993.
1 score (vii, 204 p.); 36 cm.
English words by James Agee.
Reproduced from manuscript.
Program notes in English.
Composed for: narrator, soprano, SATB chorus, piccolo, 2 flutes, 2 oboes, 2 clarinets, 2 bassoons, 4 horns, 2 trumpets, 3 trombones, tuba, timpani, percussion (triangle, bells, xylophone, mark tree, rain stick, chimes, guiro, woodblock, ratchet, maracas, whip, bass drum, gong, bell chimes), harp (or piano), violin I, violin II, viola, violoncello, double bass.
Call no.: **1997/134**

2372. Scogna, Flavio E., 1956– Anton: opera in 1 atto. Partitura. N.p.: RCA Edizioni Musicali, 1985.
1 score (182 leaves); 42 cm.
Italian words by Claudio Casini and the composer.
Composed for: male voice, mezzo-soprano, flute (also piccolo), oboe (also English horn), clarinet (also bass clarinet), percussion (tam-tam, 2 suspended cymbals, 2 triangles, chains, sleigh bells, chimes, 2 tubular bells, thundersheet, tambourine, woodblock, temple blocks, tenor drum, 2 tom-toms, crotales), piano, violin I, violin II, viola, violoncello.
Call no.: **1986/102**

2373. Scott, David R., 1962– Arras: a garden of cinema: for mezzo-soprano, string orchestra, string quartet, harp and three percussionists. N.p.: Gravity Press Editions, 1992.
1 miniature score (72 p.); 28 cm.
English words by P. K. Page; also printed as text.
Duration: ca. 20:00.
Composed for: mezzo-soprano, percussion (2 brake drums, castanets, tambourine, jawbone, 4 tom-toms,

bass drum, timpani, tubular bells, crotales, vibraphone, 2 medium suspended cymbals, metal wind chimes, 2 tam-tams, wooden wind chimes, claves, marimba, cymbals, 2 woodblocks, 5 temple blocks), harp, string quartet (2 violins, viola, violoncello), violin I, violin II, viola, violoncello, double bass.
Call no.: **1994/130**

2374. Scott, Stephen, 1944– The tears of Niobe: a composition for bowed piano, ten players. N.p.: Adigital Music BMI, 1986.
14 p. of music; 28 cm.
Reproduced from manuscript.
Composed for: prepared piano.
Call no.: **1991/118**

2375. Scott, Stephen, 1944– Vikings of the sunrise: fantasy on the Polynesian star path navigators. Colorado Springs, CO: Adigital Music BMI, 1995.
1 score (27 p.); 28 x 44 cm.
"For bowed piano on themes of navigation, exploration and discovery in the Pacific from ancient times until the present era"—program notes.
Composed for: prepared piano.
Call no.: **1998/147**

2376. Sculthorpe, Peter, 1929– Piano concerto. Full score. London: Faber Music, 1982.
1 score (90 p.); 43 cm.
Reproduced from manuscript.
Duration: ca. 23:00.
Includes performance instructions and note by the composer.
Composed for: piano, 2 oboes, 2 bassoons, contrabassoon, 2 horns, 2 trumpets, 2 trombones, bass trombone, tuba, percussion (tam-tam, suspended cymbal, crotales, glockenspiel, bongos, congas, tom-toms, bass drum), violin I, violin II, viola, violoncello, double bass.
Commissioned by: Australian Broadcasting Commission.
Call no.: **1985/174**

2377. Sculthorpe, Peter, 1929– String quartet no. 11: jabiru dreaming. London: Faber Music, 1990.
1 score (25 leaves); 36 cm.
Duration: ca. 14:00.
Composed for: 2 violins, viola, violoncello.
Commissioned by: Musica Viva Australia.
Call no.: **1992/122**

2378. Sedícias, Dímas Segundo, 1930– Banzo maracatu. N.p.: n.p., 198-?.
1 score (4 leaves); 33 cm.
Portuguese words.
Reproduced from manuscript.
Composed for: SATB chorus.
Call no.: **1985/175**

2379. Seltzer, Dov, 1932– Lament to Yitzhak: requiem to a leader: for symphonic orchestra, mixed choir, children['s] choir, soloists (1997). N.p.: Acum Israel, 1997.
1 score (208 p.); 42 cm.
Hebrew words.
Traditional texts selected and edited by Shalom Razabi; original texts by J. H. Brener, Sh. Razabi, and T. Harpaz.
Composed for: SATB chorus (also soloists), children's chorus, piccolo, 2 flutes, 2 oboes, English horn, 2 clarinets, bass clarinet, 2 bassoons, contrabassoon, 4 horns, 4 trumpets, 3 trombones, tuba, timpani, percussion (bass drum, cymbals, tam-tam, vibraphone, glockenspiel, snare drum, gong, marimba, timbales, crash cymbal, tubular bells, 4 shofars, roto-toms, triangle, xylophone, ploter, 2 tom-toms, sleigh bells, jingle bells, wind chimes, darbuka), harp, piano (also celesta), violin I, violin II, viola, violoncello, double bass.
Commissioned by: Friends of Yitzhak Rabin Center for Israel Studies.
Call no.: **2000/172**

2380. Seltzer, Dov, 1932– Stempeniu: a symphonic legend. N.p.: n.p., 1985.
1 score (183 p.); 36 cm. + 1 text (3 leaves; 30 cm.)
Hebrew words; English translation printed as text.
Based on Stempeniu by Sholem Aleichem; text adapated by Dov Seltzer; English translation by Jerry Hyman.
For symphony orchestra with narrator and violin obligato.
Composed for: narrator, violin, piccolo, 2 flutes, 2 oboes (2nd also English horn), 2 clarinets (1st also bass clarinet), 2 bassoons, 4 horns, 3 trumpets, 3 trombones, tuba, timpani, percussion (3 bass drums, tambourine, snare drum, triangle, glockenspiel, xylophone, crotales, roto-toms, temple blocks, 2 tom-toms, crash cymbals, bell plates, noise maker, jingle bells, gong, finger cymbals, timbales, 2 cymbals, 2 woodblocks, flexatone, vibraslap, floor-tom, orchestra bells), harp, piano (also celesta), violin I, violin II, viola, violoncello, double bass.
Commissioned by: Israel Philharmonic Orchestra and Zubin Mehta.
Call no.: **1990/111**

2381. Senator, Ronald, 1926– Requiem: Kaddish for Terezin. Full score. South Croydon, Surrey: Alfred Lengnick & Co., 1986.

1 score (80 p.); 42 cm.
Principally English with some German and Hebrew (romanized) words.
For children's and adult choirs, narrator, high baritone, solo soprano, and orchestra.
Reproduced from manuscript.
Composed for: soprano, SATB chorus, children's chorus, 2 flutes (1st also piccolo), 2 oboes, 2 clarinets, 2 bassoons, shofar, 4 horns, 2 trumpets, 2 trombones, tuba, percussion (3 timpani, glockenspiel, xylophone, marimba, bass drum, side drum, cymbals, tambourine, gong, triangle, woodblocks, guiro, whistle, whip, tubular bells), harp, celesta, violin I, violin II, viola, violoncello, double bass.
Call no.: **1987/080**
Re-entered as: **1990/112**

2382. Senju, Akira, 1960– Henri's sky: [for] shinobue, shakuhachi & computer. N.p.: n.p., 1991.
1 score (19 leaves); 22 x 30 cm.
Reproduced from manuscript.
Duration: 8:25.
Composed for: shinobue, shakuhachi, computer.
Call no.: **1992/123**

2383. Senju, Akira, 1960– Shun Kou for shakuhachi, synthesizer and computer (1987). N.p.: n.p., 1987.
1 score (10 p.); 26 x 37 cm.
"Tape music in category of electroacoustic music."
Reproduced from manuscript.
Duration: 8:10.
Composed for: shakuhachi, synthesizer, computer.
Call no.: **1990/113**

2384. Serebrier, José, 1938– Violin concerto: "Winter." Conductor's score. Boca Raton, FL: Edwin F. Kalmus, 1993.
1 score (112 p.); 33 cm.
Reprint. Originally published: Peer International, c1993.
Duration: 16:00.
At end: Miami, Bloomington, Avignon, London, New York. January/June 1992.
Composed for: violin, 2 flutes (2nd also piccolo), 2 oboes (2nd also optional English horn), 2 clarinets (2nd also bass clarinet, 2 bassoons, 4 horns, 2 trumpets, 2 trombones, bass trombone, tuba, timpani, percussion (3 suspended cymbals, crash cymbals, tam-tam, large bass drum, snare drum, small snare drum, 3 tuned drums, trap set, whip, xylophone, vibraphone, tubular bells), violin I, violin II, viola, violoncello, double bass.
Call no.: **1998/149**

2385. Serei, Zsolt, 1954– One minuit [i.e. minute] stories: five scenic movements based on the One minute stories of István Örkény. N.p.: n.p., 1999.
1 score (126 p.); 30 cm.
Hungarian words.
Chamber opera.
Reproduced from manuscript.
Composed for: voices, flute (also piccolo), oboe, clarinet, bassoon, horn, trumpet, trombone, harp, piano, percussion (bass drum, 3 tom-toms, 3 cymbals, vibraphone, gong, tam-tam), violin I, violin II, viola, violoncello, double bass.
Commissioned by: Budapesti Kamara Opera.
Call no.: **2002/168**

2386. Shaffer, Sherwood, 1934– Catherine wheels: for orchestra. N.p.: Sherwood Shaffer, 1990.
1 score (129 p.); 36 cm.
Duration: ca. 10:00.
Includes program notes and biographical information in English.
Composed for: piccolo, 2 flutes, 2 oboes, English horn, 2 clarinets, bass clarinet, 2 bassoons, contrabassoon, 4 horns, 2 trumpets, 2 trombones, bass trombone, tuba, timpani (also slapstick), percussion (xylophone, snare drum, chimes, Chinese temple blocks, crash cymbals, suspended cymbal, ratchet, sandpaper blocks, 3 suspended triangles, bell tree, orchestra bells), harp, violin I, violin II, viola, violoncello, double bass.
Commissioned by: Greensboro Symphony Orchestra.
Call no.: **1992/124**

2387. Shahidi, Tolib, 1946– Konzert n. 3: for piano and orchestra. N.p.: n.p., 1993.
1 manuscript score (113 p.); 40 cm.
In ink.
Composed for: piano, piccolo, flute, oboe, bassoon, 2 horns, timpani, percussion (tom-tom, triangle, tambourine, woodblocks), violin I, violin II, viola, violoncello, double bass.
Call no.: **1994/131**

2388. Shapey, Ralph, 1921–2002. Concerto: for cello-piano & string orchestra. N.p.: n.p., 1986.
1 score (95 p.); 36 cm.
Reproduced from holograph.
"4/12/86–11/29/86."
Composed for: violoncello, piano, violin I, violin II, viola, violoncello, double bass.
Call no.: **1990/114**

2389. Shapey, Ralph, 1921–2002. Concerto fantastique: for symphony orchestra, 1/10/88–9/8/89. Bryn Mawr, PA: Theodore Presser, 1990.

1 score (121 p.); 46 cm.
Duration: ca. 53:38.
Composed for: piccolo, 2 flutes (both also piccolo), 2 oboes, English horn, 2 clarinets (all also clarinet in E♭), bass clarinet, 2 bassoons, contrabassoon, 4 horns, piccolo trumpet, 3 trumpets, alto trombone, 3 trombones, bass trombone, tuba, percussion (timpani, xylophone, glockenspiel, marimba, vibraphone, chimes, crotales, 5 temple blocks, 3 irons, 3 woodblocks, 3 cymbals, tam-tam, 3 tom-toms, bass drum, piano, celesta), violin I, violin II, viola, violoncello, double bass.
Commissioned by: Chicago Symphony Orchestra.
Call no.: **1992/125**

2390. Shapey, Ralph, 1921–2002. Gamper Festival concerto: for flute, clarinet, violin, cello, piano and chamber orchestra. Bryn Mawr, PA: Theodore Presser, 1999.
1 score (48 p.); 28 cm.
Composed for: flute, clarinet, violin, violoncello, piano, oboe, bassoon, horn, percussion (vibraphone, marimba, 5 woodblocks, timpani, glockenspiel, 5 tom-toms, 4 cymbals, temple blocks), violin I, violin II, viola, violoncello, double bass.
Commissioned by: Harold Newman.
Call no.: **2001/141**

2391. Shapey, Ralph, 1921–2002. Symphonie concertante: for symphony orchestra, 1985. Full score. Bryn Mawr, PA: T. Presser Co., 1985.
1 score (82 p.); 75 cm.
Reproduced from manuscript.
Duration: ca. 30:00.
Composed for: ensemble: flute (also piccolo), oboe (also English horn), clarinet (also clarinet in E♭, bass clarinet), bassoon (also contrabassoon), horn, piccolo trumpet, trombone, violin, viola, violoncello, double bass; orchestra: piccolo, 2 flutes (both also piccolo), 3 oboes (3rd also English horn), 2 clarinets (both also clarinet in E♭), bass clarinet, 3 bassoons (3rd also contrabassoon), 3 horns, 3 trumpets, 3 trombones, bass trombone, tuba, percussion (timpani, 3 iron pipes, 3 woodblocks, 5 temple blocks, 3 tom-toms, bass drum, 3 suspended cymbals, tam-tam, xylophone, glockenspiel, crotales, chimes), piano, celesta, violin I, violin II, viola, violoncello, double bass.
Commissioned by: Philadelphia Orchestra.
Call no.: **1988/099**
Re-entered as: **1989/115**

2392. Sharkey, Jack, 1931– The picture of Dorian Gray.
Call no.: **1985/176**
No materials available.

2393. Sharman, Rodney, 1958– Elsewhereless: a chamber opera, 1998. N.p.: Rodney Sharman, 1998.
1 score (124 p.); 28 x 44 cm.
English words by Atom Egoyan.
Reproduced from manuscript.
Composed for: mezzo-soprano, tenor, 2 baritones, bass, 2 flutes (1st also alto flute, 2nd also bass flute), 2 bass clarinets, mandolin, guitar, harp, percussion (chimes, vibraphone, gongs, 2 tam-tams, Chinese opera gong, 3 triangles, log drum, bass drum, woodblock, suspended cymbal, crash cymbals, cuíca), violin, double bass.
Commissioned by: Vancouver New Music.
Call no.: **2000/173**

2394. Sharman, Rodney, 1958– Love, beauty, desire. N.p.: Rodney Sharman, 2002.
1 score (72 p.); 28 cm.
English and German words.
Texts by Atom Egoyan, Gerard Reve, and George Sandys.
For soprano solo, baritone solo, SATB choir, and orchestra.
Reproduced from manuscript.
Composed for: soprano, baritone, SATB chorus, 2 flutes, 2 oboes (2nd also English horn), 2 clarinets, 2 bassoons, 2 horns, 2 trumpets, percussion (crotales, vibraphone, chimes, tuned gongs, triangle, suspended cymbal, tam-tam, bass drum), timpani, harp, violin I, violin II, viola, violoncello, double bass.
Call no.: **2004/118**

2395. Sharp, Elliott, 1951– Calling. N.p.: Zoar Music, 2002.
1 miniature score (89 p.); 28 cm.
For orchestra.
Composed for: piccolo, alto flute, oboe, 2 bass clarinets, bassoon, horn, 2 trumpets, 2 trombones, tuba, violin I, violin II, viola, violoncello, double bass, piano, percussion (timpani, bass drums with wood and metal rattles, medium toms, bongos, sizzle cymbal, dome cymbals).
Call no.: **2005/131**

2396. Shatin, Judith, 1949– Coal. N.p.: J. Shatin, 1994.
1 score (84 p.); 44 cm.
English words.
For mixed choir, Appalachian ensemble, and electronics.
Performance instructions by the composer.
Composed for: SATB chorus, banjo, fiddle, guitar, hammered dulcimer, synthesizer, DAT.
Commissioned by: Shepherd College.
Call no.: **1995/094**

2397. Shattenkirk, Ray, 1954– American icons: for five solo voices, treble chorus, SATB chorus and orchestra. New York, NY: Peermusic Classical, 2001.
1 score (163 p.); 36 cm.
English and Latin words; also printed as text.
Duration: ca. 1:05:00.
Composed for: 5 voices, treble chorus, SATB chorus, piccolo, 2 flutes, 3 oboes (3rd also English horn), 3 clarinets (1st also clarinet in E♭, 3rd also bass clarinet), 2 bassoons, contrabassoon, 4 horns, 2 trumpets, 3 trombones, tuba, timpani, percussion (snare drum, glockenspiel, crotales, chimes, finger cymbals, sizzle cymbal, mark tree, triangle, gong, slapstick, tam-tam, tambourine, 3 brake drums, vibraphone, tenor drum, suspended cymbal, crash cymbals, xylophone, 2 Alpine herd bells, marimba, whip, metal chimes, bass drum, bongos), harp, piano, organ, violin I, violin II, viola, violoncello, double bass.
Commissioned by: Grand Rapids Symphony.
Call no.: **2003/112**

2398. Shchedrin, Rodion Konstantinovich, 1932– Concerto cantabile: für Violine und Streichorchester (1997). Partitur. Mainz; New York, NY: Schott, 1998.
1 score (24 p.); 42 cm.
Composed for: violin, violin I, violin II, viola, violoncello, double bass.
Call no.: **2000/174**

2399. Shchedrin, Rodion Konstantinovich, 1932– Dama s sobachkoĭ: balet v odnom deĭstvii po motivam rasskaza A.P. Chekhova = A lady with a little dog: one-act ballet after Anton P. Chekhov's short story. N.p.: n.p., 1985.
1 score (63 p.); 41 cm.
For orchestra.
Reproduced from holograph.
Composed for: 2 oboes (2nd also English horn), 2 horns, celesta, violin I, violin II, viola, violoncello, double bass.
Call no.: **1986/103**

2400. Shchedrin, Rodion Konstantinovich, 1932– Konzert für Violoncello und Orchester: "sotto voce concerto" (1994). Partitur. Mainz; New York, NY: Schott, 1994.
1 score (58 p.); 42 cm.
Duration: ca. 33:00.
Composed for: violoncello, 3 flutes (2nd also piccolo, 3rd also alto flute), alto or tenor recorder, 2 oboes, English horn, 2 clarinets in A, 2 bassoons, contrabassoon, 4 horns, 2 trumpets, 3 trombones, tuba, timpani, percussion (cowbells, snare drum, bass drum, tubular bells, chocalho, small stones, glass chimes), harp, violin I, violin II, viola, violoncello, double bass.
Commissioned by: London Symphony Orchestra.
Call no.: **1996/133**

2401. Shchedrin, Rodion Konstantinovich, 1932– Starinnai͡a muzyka rossiĭskikh provint͡sial'nykh t͡sirkov: dli͡a bol'shogo simfonicheskogo orkestra = Old Russian circus musik [sic]: for full symphony orchestra = Vergangene russische Circusmusik. N.p.: n.p., 1988.
1 score (103 p.); 44 cm.
Concerto for orchestra.
Reproduced from holograph.
Duration: ca. 20:00.
Composed for: 4 flutes (3rd–4th also piccolo), 2 oboes, English horn, 4 clarinets in A, 2 bassoons, contrabassoon, 4 horns, 3 trumpets, 3 trombones, tuba, timpani, percussion (jamburo, suspended crotales, chocalho, cup gong, guiro, claves, whistle, hi-hat, bell plate, sleigh bells, 4 temple blocks, maracas, flexatone, glockenspiel, cymbals, glass chimes, 4 bongos, bird whistle, drum, 4 tom-toms, suspended cymbal, whip, tam-tam), piano (also celesta), violin I, violin II, viola, violoncello, double bass.
Commissioned by: Chicago Symphony Orchestra.
Call no.: **1991/119**

2402. Shchedrin, Rodion Konstantinovich, 1932– Der verzauberte Pilger: Parabel für Violoncello-Solo, mit Streichorchester und Pauken = The enchanted pilgrim: parable for violoncello solo with string orchestra and timpani (2001). Partitur. Mainz; New York, NY: Schott, 2001.
1 score (18 p.); 42 cm.
Duration: ca. 15:00.
Composed for: violoncello, timpani, violin I, violin II, viola, violoncello, double bass.
Commissioned by: Kronberg Academy.
Call no.: **2003/113**

2403. Sheinfeld, David, 1906–2002. "E=MC²": a symphony for orchestra and string quartet. N.p.: David Sheinfeld, 1998.
1 score (83 p.); 36 cm.
Composed for: string quartet (2 violins, viola, violoncello), 3 flutes (all also piccolo), 2 oboes, English horn, 3 clarinets (3rd also clarinet in E♭), bass clarinet, 3 bassoons (3rd also contrabassoon), 4 horns, 3 trumpets, 3 trombones (3rd also bass trombone), tuba, percussion (xylophone, crotales, 2 triangles, high gong, sizzle cymbal, crash cymbals, bongos, tambourine, vibraphone, glockenspiel, medium cymbal, snare drum, tenor drum, claves, bamboo chimes, guiro, 3

tam-tams, woodblocks, timbales, cowbells, tom-toms, large cymbal, bass drum, suspended cymbals, bamboo chimes, large ratchet), harp, piano, celesta, violin I, violin II, viola, violoncello, double bass.
Commissioned by: Berkeley Symphony.
Call no.: **2000/175**

2404. Sheinfeld, David, 1906–2002. The earth is a sounding board. N.p.: n.p., 1978.
1 score (ii, 65 p.); 56 cm.
English words.
For small mixed choir and orchestra.
Reproduced from manuscript.
"Revised and corrected 12/"—p. ii.
Composed for: SATB chorus, 4 flutes (all also piccolo), 3 oboes, English horn, 2 clarinets, alto clarinet, bass clarinet, 2 bassoons, contrabassoon, 4 horns, 3 trumpets, 3 trombones, tuba, timpani, percussion (vibraphone, xylophone, glockenspiel, tubular bells, 2 snare drums, 2 timbales, 2 bongos, 2 Japanese wood bells, 2 Chinese gongs, claves, small tam-tam, conga, 3 woodblocks, bean gourd, tenor drum, drum kit, 3 tam-tams, bass drum, 3 cowbells, 2 maracas, bamboo chimes, 3 suspended cymbals, 3 crotales, steel sheet, wood plate drum, tambourine, large tam-tam), harp, piano, electric violin, violin I, violin II, viola, violoncello, double bass.
Call no.: **1994/132**
Re-entered as: **1995/095**

2405. Shenderov, Anatoliĭ, 1945– Concerto in Do: for cello and symphony orchestra (2002). N.p.: n.p., 2002.
1 score (85 p.); 42 cm.
Reproduced from manuscript.
Composed for: violoncello, 2 flutes, 2 oboes, 2 clarinets, 2 bassoons, 4 horns, 2 trumpets, 3 trombones, tuba, percussion (chimes, tam-tam, snare drums, 2 temple blocks, 3 tom-toms, crotales, bass drum, vibraphone, 2 handbells, wind chimes), celesta (also piano), violin I, violin II, viola, violoncello, double bass.
Commissioned by: young.euro.classic.
Call no.: **2004/117**

2406. Shenderov, Anatoliĭ, 1945– Simeni kahotam al libeha . . . = Prispauski prie širdies mane kaip antspauda . . . = Set me as a seal on your heart . . . Partitūra = Score. N.p.: n.p., 1992.
1 score (148 p.); 42 cm.
Hebrew words.
For soprano, bass, percussion solo, and symphony orchestra.
Text from "Song of songs" (Old Testament).
Reproduced from manuscript.
Composed for: soprano, bass, percussion (oriental bells, antique cymbals, Tibetan cymbals, gong, Chinese cymbals, bongos, marimba), 3 flutes (1st and 3rd also piccolo, 1st–2nd also recorder, 2nd alto flute), 2 oboes, English horn, 2 clarinets in A, bass clarinet, 2 bassoons, contrabassoon, 4 horns, 3 trumpets, 3 trombones, tuba, 4 timpani, percussion (triangle, tambourine, castanets, maracas, 3 temple blocks, 3 bongos, cymbals, wind chimes, tam-tam, chimes, vibraphone, marimba), harp, piano, celesta, cembalo, violin I, violin II, viola, violoncello, double bass.
Call no.: **1994/133**

2407. Shenderov, Anatoliĭ, 1945– Šma Israel: (klausyk, O Izraeli): vyrų ir berniukų chorams, kantoriui ir simfoniniam orkestrui = Hear, O Israel: for cantor, men's and boys' choirs and symphony orchestra. N.p.: n.p., 1997.
1 score (183 p.); 30 cm.
Hebrew words; English translation printed as text.
Reproduced from holograph.
Composed for: boys' chorus, men's chorus, 2 flutes (1st also piccolo), clarinet, contrabassoon, horn, 3 trumpets, 3 trombones, tuba, harp, piano (also celesta), percussion (timpani, tubular bells, vibraphone, 2 suspended cymbals, Chinese cymbal, crash cymbals, hi-hat, 3 tom-toms, 4 temple blocks, 2 gongs, crotales, tambourine, guiro, bamboo tubes, 3 wind chimes, vibraslap, bells, tam-tam), jazz set, tape, shofar, violin I, violin II, viola, violoncello, double bass.
Call no.: **1998/148**

2408. Sheng, Bright, 1955– China dreams. New York, NY: G. Schirmer, 1995.
1 score (119 p.); 44 cm.
Suite for orchestra.
Contents: Prelude for orchestra—Fanfare—The stream flows—Finale.
Composed for: piccolo, 2 flutes (2nd also piccolo), 2 oboes, English horn, 3 clarinets (2nd also clarinet in E♭, 3rd also clarinet in A and bass clarinet), 3 bassoons (3rd also contrabassoon), 4 horns, 3 trumpets (1st also trumpet in D, piccolo trumpet), 2 trombones, bass trombone, tuba, percussion (glockenspiel, chimes, large bass drum, 2 suspended cymbals, bongos, woodblocks, large tambourine, small Peking opera gong, bell tree, triangle, xylophone, large tam-tam, crotales, slapstick), harp, piano (also celesta), violin I, violin II, viola, violoncello, double bass.
Commissioned by: Cristoph Eschenbach and Houston Symphony (movement I) and New York Philharmonic (movement II).
Call no.: **1996/134**

2409. Sheng, Bright, 1955– China dreams. New York, NY: G. Schirmer, 1996.
1 score (112 p.); 28 cm.
Suite for orchestra.
"I & II revised 11/95; III & IV revised 6/96"—p. 1.
Contents: Prelude—Fanfare—The stream flows—Finale: the three gorges of the Long River.
Composed for: piccolo, 2 flutes (2nd also piccolo), 2 oboes, English horn, 3 clarinets (2nd also clarinet in E♭, 3rd also clarinet in A and bass clarinet), 3 bassoons (3rd also contrabassoon), 4 horns, 3 trumpets (1st also trumpet in D, piccolo trumpet), 2 trombones, bass trombone, tuba, percussion (glockenspiel, chimes, large bass drum, 2 suspended cymbals, bongos, woodblocks, large tambourine, small Peking opera gong, bell tree, triangle, xylophone, large tam-tam, crotales, slapstick), harp, piano (also celesta), violin I, violin II, viola, violoncello, double bass.
Commissioned by: Cristoph Eschenbach and Houston Symphony (movement I) and New York Philharmonic (movement II).
Call no.: **1997/135**

2410. Sheng, Bright, 1955– Flute moon. New York, NY: G. Schirmer, 1999.
1 score (78 p.); 28 cm.
For solo piccolo/flute, harp, piano, percussion, and strings.
"Corr. 4/00"—p. 1.
Duration: ca. 10:00.
Contents: Chi Lin's dance—Flute moon.
Composed for: flute (also piccolo), timpani, percussion (xylophone, marimba, large bass drum, small ratchet, slapstick, bell tree, 2 sets of chimes, wind gong, cowbells, large crash cymbals, low tam-tam, brake drum, glockenspiel), harp, piano, violins I, violin II, viola, violoncello, double bass.
Commissioned by: Houston Symphony.
Call no.: **2001/142**

2411. Sheng, Bright, 1955– H'un = (Lacerations): in memoriam. Full score. New York, NY: G. Schirmer, 1988.
1 score (49 [i.e. 51 p.); 44 cm.
For orchestra.
Reproduced from manuscript.
At end: 1988 in NY.
Duration: ca. 22:00.
Includes performance instructions in English.
Composed for: 2 flutes (both also piccolo, 2nd also alto flute), 2 oboes, 2 clarinets (both also bass clarinet), 2 bassoons (2nd also contrabassoon), 4 horns, 2 trumpets (1st also trumpet in D), 2 trombones, percussion (timpani, 4 Chinese tom-toms, Peking opera gong, tambourine, marimba, temple block, suspended cymbal, guiro, Japanese woodblock, slapstick, tam-tam, Chinese bass drum), harp, piano, violin I, violin II, viola, violoncello, double bass.
Commissioned by: 92nd Street Y.
Call no.: **1992/126**

2412. Sheng, Bright, 1955– H'un = (Lacerations): in memoriam. New York, NY: G. Schirmer, 1988.
1 score (49 p.); 36 cm.
Reproduced from holograph.
At end: 1988 in NY.
Performance note by the composer.
Composed for: 2 flutes (both also piccolo, 2nd also alto flute), 2 oboes, 2 clarinets (both also bass clarinet), 2 bassoons (2nd also contrabassoon), 4 horns, 2 trumpets (1st also trumpet in D), 2 trombones, percussion (timpani, 4 Chinese tom-toms, Peking opera gong, tambourine, marimba, temple block, suspended cymbal, guiro, Japanese woodblock, slapstick, tam-tam, Chinese bass drum), harp, piano, violin I, violin II, viola, violoncello, double bass.
Commissioned by: 92nd Street Y.
Call no.: **1993/127**

2413. Sheng, Bright, 1955– H'un = (Lacerations): in memoriam 1966–1976: for orchestra, 1987. N.p.: n.p., 1988.
1 score (49 [i.e., 51] p.); 44 cm.
Reproduced from manuscript.
At end: 12-31-87 New York.
Includes program note in English.
Composed for: 2 flutes (both also piccolo, 2nd also alto flute), 2 oboes, 2 clarinets (both also bass clarinet), 2 bassoons (2nd also contrabassoon), 4 horns, 2 trumpets (1st also trumpet in D), 2 trombones, percussion (timpani, 4 Chinese tom-toms, Peking opera gong, tambourine, marimba, temple block, suspended cymbal, guiro, Japanese woodblock, slapstick, tam-tam, Chinese bass drum), harp, piano, violin I, violin II, viola, violoncello, double bass.
Commissioned by: 92nd Street Y.
Call no.: **1990/115**
Re-entered as: **1991/120**

2414. Sheng, Bright, 1955– Madame Mao: opera in two acts. Full score. New York: G. Schirmer, 2003.
1 score (2 v. [514 p.]); 44 cm.
English words by Colin Graham.
"Corrected 05/05/03"—p. 1.
Program note by the composer in English.
Composed for: 3 sopranos, 2 mezzo-sopranos, 3 tenors,

3 baritones, 2 basses, 2 flutes (also piccolo), 2 oboes (also English horn), 2 clarinets (also clarinet in E♭ and bass clarinet), 2 bassoons (also contrabassoon), 4 horns, 3 trumpets, 2 trombones, bass trombone, tuba, timpani, percussion, harp, violin I, violin II, viola, violoncello, and double bass.
Commissioned by: Santa Fe Opera.
Call no.: **2005/132**
Also available:
Call no.: **2005/132 vocal score**

2415. Sheng, Bright, 1955– Nanking! Nanking! a threnody for orchestra and pipa (1999). New York, NY: G. Schirmer, 2000.
1 score (94 p.); 36 cm.
"Corrected 10/2000"—p. 1.
Duration: 26:00.
Program note in English by the composer.
Composed for: pipa, 3 flutes (2nd–3rd also piccolo), 3 oboes (3rd also English horn), 3 clarinets (2nd also clarinet in E♭, 3rd also bass clarinet), 3 bassoons (3rd also contrabassoon), 4 horns, 3 trumpets, 3 trombones, tuba, timpani, percussion (ratchet, slapstick, lion's roar, bass drum, temple block, tam-tam, Chinese opera gong, Chinese opera cymbal, wind gong, woodblock, guiro, cowbells, brake drum, 4 bongos, xylophone), harp, piano, violin I, violin II, viola, violoncello, double bass.
Commissioned by: Norddeutscher Rundfunk and Marshall Cloyd.
Call no.: **2002/169**

2416. Sheng, Bright, 1955– Nanking! Nanking! a threnody for orchestra and pipa (1999). New York, NY: G. Schirmer, 2000 (1/22/02 printing).
1 score (94 p.); 36 cm.
"Corrected 11/2001"—p. 1.
Duration: 26:00.
Program note in English by the composer.
Composed for: pipa, 3 flutes (2nd–3rd also piccolo), 3 oboes (3rd also English horn), 3 clarinets (2nd also clarinet in E♭, 3rd also bass clarinet), 3 bassoons (3rd also contrabassoon), 4 horns, 3 trumpets, 3 trombones, tuba, timpani, percussion (ratchet, slapstick, lion's roar, bass drum, temple block, tam-tam, Chinese opera gong, Chinese opera cymbal, wind gong, woodblock, guiro, cowbells, brake drum, 4 bongos, xylophone), harp, piano, violin I, violin II, viola, violoncello, double bass.
Commissioned by: Norddeutscher Rundfunk and Marshall Cloyd.
Call no.: **2003/114**

2417. Sheng, Bright, 1955– Nanking! Nanking! a threnody for orchestra and pipa (1999) / Bright Sheng. New York, NY: G. Schirmer, 2000 (1/22/03 printing).
1 score (94 p.); 36 cm.
"Corrected 11/2001"—p. 1.
Duration: 26:00.
Program note in English by the composer.
Composed for: pipa, 3 flutes (2nd–3rd also piccolo), 3 oboes (3rd also English horn), 3 clarinets (2nd also clarinet in E♭, 3rd also bass clarinet), 3 bassoons (3rd also contrabassoon), 4 horns, 3 trumpets, 3 trombones, tuba, timpani, percussion (ratchet, slapstick, lion's roar, bass drum, temple block, tam-tam, Chinese opera gong, Chinese opera cymbal, wind gong, woodblock, guiro, cowbells, brake drum, 4 bongos, xylophone), harp, piano, violin I, violin II, viola, violoncello, double bass.
Commissioned by: Norddeutscher Rundfunk and Marshall Cloyd.
Call no.: **2004/119**

2418. Sheng, Bright, 1955– Postcards. New York, NY: G. Schirmer, 1998.
1 score (62 p.); 44 cm.
For orchestra.
"Revised 10/12/98"—p. 1.
Duration: ca. 15:00.
Contents: From the mountains—From the river valley—From the savage land—Wish you were here.
Composed for: flute (also piccolo), 2 oboes (2nd also English horn), clarinet (also clarinet in E♭ and bass clarinet), 2 bassoons, 2 horns, trumpet, piano (also celesta), percussion (glockenspiel, small tam-tam, chimes, marimba, timpani, 2 tambourines, bass drum, guiro, low brake drum, bongos, small suspended cymbal, crotales, wind gong), violin I, violin II, viola, violoncello, double bass.
Commissioned by: Ruth and John Huss.
Call no.: **2000/176**

2419. Sheng, Bright, 1955– The song of Majnun: an opera of lyric tragedy in one act. New York, NY: G. Schirmer, 1993.
1 score (275 p.); 36 cm.
Words by Andrew Porter.
"Corrected 1/14/93"—p. 1.
Reproduced from holograph.
Composed for: soprano, 3 mezzo-sopranos, tenor, 2 baritones, bass, SATB chorus, 2 flutes (both also piccolo), oboe (also English horn), clarinet (also bass clarinet), bassoon (also contrabassoon), 2 horns, trumpet (also piccolo trumpet), percussion (4 woodblocks, sizzle cymbal, 2 suspended cymbals (small, large), large anvil, 2 tam-tams (small, large), bell tree, crotales, guiro,

xylophone, marimba, vibraphone, 4 bongos, 3 timpani, large bass drum), harp, piano, violin I, violin II, viola, violoncello, double bass.
Commissioned by: Lyric Opera of Chicago Composer-in-Residence program.
Call no.: **1994/134**

2420. Sheng, Bright, 1955– The song of Majnun: an opera of lyric tragedy in one act. New York, NY: G. Schirmer, 1994.
1 score (275 p.); 36 cm.
Words by Andrew Porter.
"Corrected 5/9/94"—p. 1.
Reproduced from holograph.
Composed for: soprano, 3 mezzo-sopranos, tenor, 2 baritones, bass, SATB chorus, 2 flutes (both also piccolo), oboe (also English horn), clarinet (also bass clarinet), bassoon (also contrabassoon), 2 horns, trumpet (also piccolo trumpet), percussion (4 woodblocks, sizzle cymbal, 2 suspended cymbals (small, large), large anvil, 2 tam-tams (small, large), bell tree, crotales, guiro, xylophone, marimba, vibraphone, 4 bongos, 3 timpani, large bass drum), harp, piano, violin I, violin II, viola, violoncello, double bass.
Commissioned by: Lyric Opera of Chicago Composer-in-Residence program.
Call no.: **1995/096**

2421. Sheng, Bright, 1955– Spring dreams: for violoncello and Chinese traditional orchestra. New York, NY: G. Schirmer, 1997.
1 score (99 p.); 44 cm.
"Corrected 6/97"—p. 1.
Program note by the composer.
Contents: Midnight bells—Spring opera.
Composed for: violoncello, 3 di, 3 sheng, 3 suona, di guan, liu qin, pipa, 2 ran, yang qin, zheng, percussion, 3 hu, violoncello, double bass.
Commissioned by: Carnegie Hall.
Call no.: **1998/150**

2422. Sheriff, Noam, 1935– "La follia" variations: for symphony orchestra (1984). Tel Aviv, Israel: Israel Music Institute, 1985.
1 score (82 p.); 35 cm.
Reproduced from holograph.
Composed for: piccolo, 2 flutes, 2 oboes, English horn, 2 clarinets, bass clarinet, 2 bassoons, contrabassoon, 4 horns, 3 trumpets, 3 trombones, tuba, timpani, percussion (vibraphone, xylorimba, antique cymbal, maracas, guiro, triangle, tambourine, tam-tam, 3 suspended cymbals, 2 tom-toms, timbales, glockenspiel, tubular bells, bongos, snare drum, bass drum), harp, violin I, violin II, viola, violoncello, double bass.
Call no.: **1986/104**

2423. Sheriff, Noam, 1935– Mehaye hametim = Wiederbelebung der Toten = Revival of the dead: symphony for tenor, baritone, boys' choir, men's choir & orchestra (1985). Partitur. Frankfurt; New York, NY: C. F. Peters/H. Litolff's Verlag, 1987.
1 score (180 p.); 47 cm.
Reproduced from manuscript.
Composed for: tenor, baritone, boys' chorus, men's chorus, piccolo, 2 flutes, 2 oboes, English horn, 2 clarinets, bass clarinet, 2 bassoons, contrabassoon, 4 horns, 3 trumpets, 3 trombones, tuba, timpani, percussion (xylophone, xylorimba, maracas, glockenspiel, tubular bells, vibraphone, snare drum, woodblock, triangle, crash cymbals, suspended cymbal, 3 temple blocks, tambourine, bongos, 3 tom-toms, 2 tam-tams, guiro, bass drum), harp, violin I, violin II, viola, violoncello, double bass.
Commissioned by: Bernard Bronkhorst, Amsterdam.
Call no.: **1989/116**

2424. Shields, Alice, 1943– Dust: computer piece for dance. Port Chester, NY: Jilmar Music, 2003.
1 score (7 p.); 22 x 28 cm.
"With rhythmic sequences from Bharata natyam (South Indian dance drama) and pitch material from two North Indian ragas."
Duration: 30:39.
Composed for: computer.
Commissioned by: Dance Alloy of Pittsburgh.
Call no.: **2004/120**

2425. Shih, 1950– Vatermord: Gewalt und Autonomie in neun Episoden. N.p.: n.p., 1993.
1 score (176 p.); 31 x 43 cm.
German words by Cornelia Krauss.
Original work by Arnolt Bronnen.
Chamber music theater.
Reproduced from manuscript.
Composed for: mezzo-soprano, countertenor, baritone, bass, flute, alto flute, piccolo, oboe, English horn, clarinet in E♭, clarinet, basset horn, bass clarinet, horn, Wagner tuba, timpani, percussion (bass drum, tenor drum, piccolo drum, 4 bongos, 4 temple blocks, cymbals, tam-tam, marimba, vibraphone, whip, maracas, castanets, glass wind chimes, wind machine), violin I, violin II, viola, violoncello, double bass.
Commissioned by: Pocket Opera Company Nürnberg.
Call no.: **1995/097**

2426. Shinohara, Makoto, 1931– Cooperation: for 8 Japanese and 8 Western instrumentalists (1990). N.p.:

n.p., 1991.
1 score (24 p.); 42 cm.
Duration: ca. 20:00.
Reproduced from holograph.
At end: (Rev. Apr. 91), 6.91.
Composed for: Japanese ensemble: nōkan (also shinobue, hirazuri-daiko), 2 shakuhachis (also hyōshigi), hichiriki (also orugōru), shō (also 5 mokugyos, koto (also ō-tsuzumi, 2 mame-daikos), shamisen (also atarigane), biwa (also 2 doras), kokyū (also 2 mokushos); Western ensemble: English horn (also oboe, bass oboe, bongo with beans), clarinet (also bass clarinet, 4 cowbells), trumpet (also tom-toms, chains), bass trombone (also tam-tam, chains), glockenspiel (also vibraphone, marimba, shime-daiko, odaiko, tom-tom, tam-tam), piano (also maracas, bongo, tom-tom), violin (also antique cymbal), violoncello (also shell chimes).
Commissioned by: Serge Koussevitzky Music Foundation.
Call no.: **1992/127**

2427. Shinohara, Makoto, 1931– Tabiyuki.
Commissioned by: Société de musique contemporaine du Québec.
Call no.: **1986/105**
No materials available.

2428. Shinohara, Makoto, 1931– Yumeji: for orchestra of Japanese and western instruments and mixed chorus. N.p.: n.p., 1992.
1 score (32 p.); 42 cm.
Duration: ca. 15:00.
Reproduced from manuscript.
Composed for: SATB chorus, 2 fues (both on ryuteki, nokan, shinobues), 2 shakuhachis, 2 hichirikis, 2 shos, koto, jushichigen, shamisen, biwa, 2 kokyus, 2 clarinets (both also clarinet in E♭, 2nd also bass clarinet), 2 bassoons (both also contrabassoon), 4 horns, 2 trumpets (both also trumpet in D), bass trombone, tuba, percussion (vibraphone, 2 kinshos, 6 cowbells, 2 tam-tams, maracas, xylophone, 2 mokushos, 2 woodblocks, 3 bongos, 3 tom-toms, hirazuri-daiko, glass chimes, otsuzumi, daibyoshi, odaiko, 6 mokugyos, takezutsu, 4 orugoru, shoko, kin, 4 atariganes, dora, ishi, tsukegi, hyoshigi), violin I, violin II, viola, violoncello, double bass.
Commissioned by: Min-on Concert Association, Inc. (Japan).
Call no.: **1994/135**

2429. Shrude, Marilyn, 1946– Psalms of David: [for] orchestra. Score. N.p.: Marilyn Shrude, 1983.
1 score (42 p.); 52 cm.
Reproduced from manuscript.
Includes instructions for performance.
Composed for: 3 flutes (1st also alto flute, 3rd also piccolo), 2 oboes, 3 clarinets, 2 bassoons, contrabassoon, 4 horns, 3 trumpets, 3 trombones, tuba, timpani, percussion (vibraphone, bass drum, tam-tam, 2 suspended cymbals, xylophone, glockenspiel, 5 temple blocks, crash cymbals, crotales, chimes, snare drum, field drum, 5 tom-toms, triangle), harp, piano, celesta, violin I, violin II, viola, violoncello, double bass.
Commissioned by: Yuval Zaliouk and Toledo Symphony Orchestra.
Call no.: **1985/177**

2430. Sica, Salvatore, 1966– La stazione. N.p.: n.p., 199-?.
1 score (17 leaves); 43 cm.
Wordless.
Film music.
Reproduced from holograph.
Composed for: soprano, flute (also recorder), oboe (also English horn or soprano saxophone), 2 horns, guitar, timpani, harp, synthesizer, harpsichord, violin I, violin II, viola, violoncello, double bass.
Call no.: **1998/151**

2431. Sichel, John, 1959– Concerto mystico II: for piano and small orchestra. N.p.: John Sichel, 1996.
1 score (118 p.); 44 cm.
Reproduced from holograph.
Duration: ca. 25:00.
Composed for: piano, 2 flutes (also piccolo), oboe, English horn, 2 clarinets in A (also bass clarinet), 2 bassoons (also contrabassoon), 2 horns, 2 trumpets, trombone, percussion (tam-tam, bass drum, suspended cymbal, crash cymbals, hi-hat, 3 timpani/timpani-cymbal, 3 tom-toms, glockenspiel, vibraphone, slide-whistle, 2 large pebbles), violin I, violin II, viola, violoncello, double bass.
Call no.: **2005/133**

2432. Sicilianos, Yorgos, 1922– Kassandra: tragikē kantata = Cassandra: a tragic cantata = Cassandre: cantate tragique. Athēna: n.p., 1983.
1 score (138 p.); 38 cm.
Greek words (Greek characters and romanized); also printed as text (Greek characters) with English translation.
On the original text from Aeschylus's tragedy Agamemnon.
For mezzo-soprano, bass, mixed choir, and orchestra.
Reproduced from holograph.
Duration: ca. 55:00.

Composed for: mezzo-soprano, bass, SATB chorus, 3 flutes (3rd also piccolo), 4 oboes (3rd also English horn), 4 clarinets (3rd also clarinet in E♭, 4th also bass clarinet), 3 bassoons, contrabassoon, 6 horns, 4 trumpets, 2 trombones, bass trombone, tuba, timpani, percussion (glockenspiel, xylophone, vibraphone, antique cymbal, cymbals, tam-tam, 2 cowbells, triangle, snare drum, bass drum), harp, violin I, violin II, viola, violoncello, double bass.
Call no.: **1991/121**

2433. Sidel′nikov, Nikolaĭ Nikolaevich, 1930– Duėli: kont͡sertnaia simfonii͡a dli͡a violoncheli, kontrabasa, dvukh fortepiano i udarnykh = Duels: concert symphony for cello, double bass, two pianos and percussion. Partitura = Score. Moskva: Sovetskiĭ kompozitor, 1976.
1 score (94 p.); 29 cm.
Contents: Sootnoshenie neopredelennosteĭ = Correlation of vaguenesses—Bor′ba garmonii i khaosa = Struggle between harmony and chaos—Poedinok zakonomernosti i sluchai͡a = Duel between law and chance.
Composed for: violoncello, double bass, 2 pianos, percussion (crotales, orchestra bells, vibraphone, chimes, triangle, 5 temple blocks, ratchet, timpani, 5 bongos, drum, 4 suspended cymbals, 2 gongs, tam-tam).
Call no.: **1992/128**

2434. Siegel, Stephen, 1943– Fire & fleete & candlelighte: for solo violin. N.p.: Stephen Siegel, 2001.
13 p. of music; 34 cm.
Composed for: violin.
Call no.: **2004/121**

2435. Sierra, Roberto, 1953– Concerto for saxophones & orchestra. Study score. N.p.: Subito Music, 2002.
1 miniature score (92 p.); 31 cm.
Composed for: saxophone (tenor and soprano saxophones), piccolo, 2 flutes, 2 oboes, 2 clarinets, bass clarinet, 2 bassoons, 4 horns, 3 trumpets, 3 trombones, timpani, harp, piano drum set, percussion (marimba, vibraphone, suspended cymbal, tam-tam, cabasa, gong, bass drum, triangle, tambourine, woodblock), violin I, violin II, viola, violoncello, double bass.
Commissioned by: Detroit Symphony.
Call no.: **2004/122**

2436. Sierra, Roberto, 1953– Concierto para orquesta = Concerto for orchestrta [sic] (2001). N.p.: Subito Music, 2000.
1 score (108 p.); 28 cm.
Contents: Dibujos—Atardecer—Danzas imaginarias.
Composed for: piccolo, 2 flutes, 2 oboes, English horn, 2 clarinets, bass clarinet, 2 bassoons, contrabassoon, 4 horns, 3 trumpets, 3 trombones, tuba, timpani, percussion (suspended cymbals, vibraphone, marimba, temple blocks, maracas, bongos, congas, guiro, xylophone, tom-toms, bass drum, woodblocks, glockenspiel, tam tam, triangle, crotales, ratchet, snare drum, gong, sizzle cymbal, crash cymbals, mark tree, whip, cencerro, chimes, almglocken, tambourine, claves, cabasa), harp, piano (also celesta), violin I, violin II, viola, violoncello, double bass.
Call no.: **2005/134**

2437. Sierra, Roberto, 1953– Cuentos. Verona, NJ: Subito Music, 1997.
1 score (89 p.); 41 cm.
For chamber orchestra.
Contents: Lenguas desconocidas—Lo que pasóen las nubes—Batata-coco (Mambo?).
Composed for: flute, oboe, clarinet, bassoon, alto saxophone, horn, trumpet (also piccolo trumpet), trombone, percussion (4 bongos, congas, vibraphone, cymbals, cencerros, marimba, xylophone, maracas, bass drums, brake drums, glockenspiel, whip, temple blocks, cabasa, guiro, vibraslap, ratchet, Chinese gong, tam-tam, suspended cymbals, 3 triangles, tom-toms, 3 woodblocks), piano, violin I, violin II, viola, violoncello, double bass.
Commissioned by: Camerata de las Américas.
Call no.: **1998/152**

2438. Sierra, Roberto, 1953– Evocaciones: concierto para violín y orquesta: 1994. Long Island City, NY: Subito Music Pub., 1994.
1 score (113 p.); 33 cm.
Duration: ca. 20:00.
Contents: Rapsódico—Profundo—Caprichoso.
Composed for: violin, 2 flutes, 2 oboes, 2 clarinets, 2 bassoons, 2 horns, 3 trumpets, 3 trombones, tuba, timpani, percussion (xylophone, vibraphone, triangle, claves, cencerros, guiro, maracas, cabasa, woodblock, cymbals, tubular bells, snare drum, glockenspiel, marimba, tam-tam, suspended cymbals, bass drum), piano (also celesta), violin I, violin II, viola, violoncello, double bass.
Commissioned by: Pittsburgh Symphony Society.
Call no.: **1996/135**

2439. Sierra, Roberto, 1953– Imágenes: for violin, guitar and orchestra. Long Island City, NY: Subito Music Pub., 1993.
1 score (183 p.); 29 cm.
Composed for: violin, guitar, 2 flutes, oboe, English horn, clarinet, bass clarinet, 2 bassoons, 2 horns, trumpet,

percussion (bongos, maracas, marimba, glockenspiel, vibraphone, claves, triangle, snare drum, tambourine, bass drum, suspended cymbal, castanets, tam-tam), violin I, violin II, viola, violoncello, double bass.
Commissioned by: Saarländischer-Rundfunk.
Call no.: **1994/136**

2440. Sierra, Roberto, 1953– Piezas imaginarias = [Imaginary pieces]: for piano (1994–1995). Verona, NJ: Subito Music; King of Prussia, PA: T. Presser, 2000.
30 p. of music; 31 cm.
Composed for: piano.
Call no.: **2002/170**

2441. Sierra, Roberto, 1953– Tropicalia: for large orchestra. N.p.: n.p., 1991.
1 score (118 p.); 31 cm.
Duration: ca. 23:00.
Contents: Foliage—Nocturne—Celebration.
Composed for: piccolo, 2 flutes, 2 oboes, English horn, 2 clarinets, bass clarinet, 2 bassoons, contrabassoon, 4 horns, 3 trumpets, 3 trombones, tuba, timpani, percussion (antique cymbals, glockenspiel, vibraphone, xylophone, marimba, claves, maracas, guiro, bongos, congas, triangle, suspended cymbals, tambourine, snare drum, bass drum, tam-tam), harp, piano (also celesta), violin I, violin II, viola, violoncello, double bass.
Commissioned by: Milwaukee Symphony Orchestra.
Call no.: **1992/129**

2442. Silver, Sheila, 1946– Concerto for piano and orchestra, 1996. Saint Louis, MO: MMB Music, 1997.
1 score (189 p.); 36 cm.
Reproduced from holograph.
"11/8/96, rev. 11/97"—p. 189.
Composed for: piano, 3 flutes (3rd also piccolo), 2 oboes (2nd also English horn), 2 clarinets (1st also clarinet in E♭, 2nd also bass clarinet), 2 bassoons (2nd also contrabassoon), 4 horns, 2 trumpets, 2 trombones (2nd also bass trombone), tuba, timpani, percussion (3 tam-tams, suspended cymbal, triangle, 3 tuned gongs, snare drum, 3 tom-toms, tambourine, vibraphone, glockenspiel, xylophone, chimes, crash cymbals, high cowbell, claves, crotales, bass drum, small crash cymbal, marimba, celesta), violin I, violin II, viola, violoncello, double bass.
Commissioned by: American Composers Orchestra, Richmond Symphony, Illinois Symphony, and Annapolis Symphony.
Call no.: **2003/115**

2443. Silver, Sheila, 1946– To the spirit unconquered: violin, violoncello and piano (1992). St. Louis, MO: MMB Music, 1992.
1 score (45 p.); 32 cm.
Composed for: violin, violoncello, piano.
Commissioned by: Chamber Music America.
Call no.: **1996/136**

2444. Simonacci, Giancarlo, 1948– Fase quinta: per archi. Roma: Edipan, 1992.
1 score (17 p.); 35 cm.
For string orchestra.
Reproduced from manuscript.
Duration: ca. 13:00.
Composed for: violin I, violin II, violin III, violin IV, violin V, violin VI, violin VII, viola I, viola II, violoncello I, violoncello II, double bass.
Call no.: **1993/128**

2445. Sims, Ezra, 1928– Concert piece: for viola with flute, clarinet, violoncello, and small orchestra, 1990. N.p.: n.p., 1990.
1 score (83 p.); 36 cm.
Microtonal music.
Reproduced from holograph.
At end: 25 March 90 Cambridge, Provincetown, Woodside.
Composed for: viola, flute, oboe, clarinet, 2 bassoons, 2 horns, 3 trumpets, 2 trombones, computer, violoncello, double bass.
Commissioned by: Anne Black and Pro Arte.
Call no.: **1993/129**

2446. Singleton, Alvin, 1940– 56 blows (Quis custodiet custodies?): for orchestra. Study score. Valley Forge, PA: European American Music Corp., 1993.
1 score (18 p.); 28 cm.
Duration: ca. 12:00.
Composed for: 2 flutes, 2 oboes, 2 clarinets, 2 bassoons, 4 horns, 2 trumpets, 2 trombones, bass trombone, tuba, percussion (snare drum, field drum, timbales, 3 tom-toms), harp, violin I, violin II, viola, violoncello, double bass.
Commissioned by: Philadelphia Orchestra Association.
Call no.: **1998/153**

2447. Singleton, Alvin, 1940– Blueskonzert: for piano and orchestra. United States: European American Music, 1995.
1 score (38 p.); 33 cm.
Duration: ca. 17:00.
Composed for: piano, 2 flutes, 2 oboes, 2 clarinets, 2 bassoons, 2 horns, 2 trumpets, 2 trombones, violin I, violin II, viola, violoncello, double bass.

Commissioned by: Houston Symphony, Detroit Symphony Orchestra, and Kansas City Symphony.
Call no.: **1996/137**

2448. Singleton, Alvin, 1940– Cara mia Gwen: for orchestra, 1993. N.p.: n.p., 1993.
1 score (21 p.); 44 cm.
Duration: ca. 15:00.
Composed for: 2 flutes, 2 oboes, 2 clarinets (2nd also clarinet in E♭), 2 bassoons, 4 horns, 2 trumpets, 2 trombones, violin I, violin II, viola, violoncello, double bass.
Commissioned by: Florida Orchestra.
Call no.: **1994/137**

2449. Singleton, Alvin, 1940– Even tomorrow: 1991. N. p.: Alvin Singleton, 1991.
1 score (36 p.); 44 cm.
For orchestra.
Duration: ca. 15:00.
Composed for: 3 flutes (2nd–3rd also piccolo), 3 oboes, 3 clarinets (2nd also clarinet in E♭), 3 bassoons (3rd also contrabassoon), 4 horns, 3 trumpets, 3 trombones, tuba, timpani, percussion (vibraphone, xylophone, 5 roto-toms, marimba, crotales, bongos, glockenspiel, 4 cowbells, timbales, tubular bells, 2 brake drums, bass drum), harp, piano (also celesta), violin I, violin II, viola, violoncello, double bass.
Commissioned by: Northwest Indiana Symphony Orchestra and Alabama Symphony Orchestra.
Call no.: **1992/130**

2450. Singleton, Alvin, 1940– Praisemaker: for SATB chorus and orchestra. Miami, FL: European American Music, 1998.
1 score (33 p.); 44 cm.
English words by Susan Kouguell.
Duration: ca. 20:00.
Composed for: SATB chorus, 2 flutes, 2 oboes, English horn, 2 clarinets, bass clarinet, 2 bassoons, contrabassoon, 4 horns, 2 trumpets, 3 trombones, tuba, percussion (crotales, tubular bells, vibraphone), harp, violin I, violin II, viola, violoncello, double bass.
Commissioned by: Cincinnati May Festival.
Call no.: **2000/177**
Re-entered as: **2004/123**

2451. Singleton, Alvin, 1940– Umoja—each one of us counts: for narrator and orchestra. N.p.: European American Music, 1996.
1 score (64 p.); 33 cm.
English words by Rita Dove.
Duration: ca. 23:00.
Composed for: narrator, piccolo, 2 flutes (2nd also alto flute), 2 oboes, English horn, 2 clarinets, bass clarinet, 2 bassoons, contrabassoon, 4 horns, 3 trumpets, 3 trombones, tuba, timpani, percussion (medium suspended cymbal, medium brake drum, snare drum, marimba, large suspended cymbal, tenor drum, medium tam-tam, vibraphone, hi-hat, timbales, small tam-tam, large triangle), harp, violin I, violin II, viola, violoncello, double bass.
Commissioned by: Atlanta Committee of the Olympic Games Cultural Oympiad.
Call no.: **1997/136**

2452. Sirota, Eric B., 1959– Day of wrath: a musical drama. N.p.: n.p., 1990.
1 vocal score (343 p.); 28 cm.
English words; also printed as text.
Text by the composer and Sharon Sudol; based on Frankenstein by Mary W. Shelley.
Composed for: unspecified.
Call no.: **1992/131**
Also available:
Call no.: **1992/131 libretto**

2453. Situ, Gang, 1954– Concerto: for violin, erhu and strings (1997). San Francisco, CA: Gang Situ, 1997.
1 score (19, 21 p.); 29 cm.
Contents: Largo—Allegro.
Composed for: violin, erhu, violin I, violin II, viola, violoncello, double bass.
Call no.: **2001/143**

2454. Situ, Gang, 1954– Double concerto: for violin and erhu. San Francisco, CA: Gang Situ, 1995.
1 score (50, 44, 52 p.); 29 cm.
Contents: Largo—Andante—Allegro.
Composed for: violin, erhu, piccolo, 2 flutes, 2 oboes, 2 clarinets, 2 bassoons, 4 horns, 2 trumpets, 3 trombones, timpani, percussion (tamburo, gong), violin I, violin II, viola, violoncello, double bass.
Call no.: **1996/138**

2455. Situ, Gang, 1954– Double concerto: for violin and erhu. N.p.: Gang Situ, 1996.
1 score (50, 42 p.); 29 cm.
Contents: Largo—Allegro.
Composed for: violin, erhu, piccolo, 2 flutes, 2 oboes, 2 clarinets, 2 bassoons, 4 horns, 2 trumpets, 3 trombones, timpani, percussion (tamburo, gong), violin I, violin II, viola, violoncello, double bass.
Call no.: **1997/137**

2456. Situ, Gang, 1954– Strings calligraphy. N.p.: n.p., 2000.

1 score (10, 10, 13, 10, 16 leaves); 29 cm.
Suite.
Composed for: erhu, 2 violins, viola, violoncello, double bass.
Commissioned by: San Francisco Arts Commission.
Call no.: **2002/171**

2457. Skrowaczewski, Stanisław, 1923– Concerto for orchestra. Rev. ed. (1998). N.p.: n.p., 1998.
1 score (69 p.); 34 cm.
Reproduced from holograph.
Composed for: 3 flutes (2nd also alto flute, 3rd also piccolo), 3 oboes, 3 clarinets (2nd also clarinet in A, 3rd also bass clarinet), 3 bassoons (3rd also contrabassoon), 4 horns, 4 trumpets, 2 trombones, bass trombone, tuba, 5 timpani, percussion (3 gongs, 5 bongos, 5 temple blocks, cymbals, 2 tam-tams, glockenspiel, boobams, chimes, vibraphone, marimba), harp, piano, violin I, violin II, viola, violoncello, double bass.
Commissioned by: Minnesota Orchestra.
Call no.: **2003/116**

2458. Skrowaczewski, Stanisław, 1923– Concerto for orchestra (1985). Rev., 1998. N.p.: n.p., 1998.
1 score (63 p.); 39 cm.
Duration: ca. 28:00.
Composed for: 3 flutes (2nd also alto flute, 3rd also piccolo), 3 oboes, 3 clarinets (2nd also clarinet in A, 3rd also bass clarinet), 3 bassoons (3rd also contrabassoon), 4 horns, 4 trumpets, 2 trombones, bass trombone, tuba, 5 timpani, percussion (3 gongs, 5 bongos, 5 temple blocks, cymbals, 2 tam-tams, glockenspiel, boobams, chimes, vibraphone, marimba), harp, piano, violin I, violin II, viola, violoncello, double bass.
Commissioned by: Minnesota Orchestra.
Call no.: **2000/178**

2459. Skrowaczewski, Stanisław, 1923– Passacaglia immaginaria, 1995. N.p.: n.p., 1996.
1 miniature score (58 p.); 28 cm.
For orchestra.
Reproduced from manuscript.
Duration: ca. 28:00.
Composed for: 3 flutes (3rd also piccolo), 3 oboes, 3 clarinets (all also clarinet in A, 3rd also bass clarinet), 3 bassoons (3rd also contrabassoon), 4 horns, 4 trumpets, 3 trombones, tuba, percussion (5 temple blocks, 4 tom-toms, 4 bongos, marimba, vibraphone, tam-tam, cymbals, tubular bells, glockenspiel), timpani, harp, piano (also celesta), violin I, violin II, viola, violoncello, double bass.
Commissioned by: Minnesota Orchestral Association.
Call no.: **1997/138**

2460. Skrowaczewski, Stanisław, 1923– Passacaglia immaginaria: for full orchestra. N.p.: S. Skrowaczewski, 1996.
1 score (45 p.); 44 cm.
Composed for: 3 flutes (3rd also piccolo), 3 oboes, 3 clarinets (all also clarinet in A, 3rd also bass clarinet), 3 bassoons (3rd also contrabassoon), 4 horns, 4 trumpets, 3 trombones, tuba, percussion (5 temple blocks, 4 tom-toms, 4 bongos, marimba, vibraphone, tam-tam, cymbals, tubular bells, glockenspiel), timpani, harp, piano (also celesta), violin I, violin II, viola, violoncello, double bass.
Commissioned by: Minnesota Orchestral Association.
Call no.: **2002/172**

2461. Skrzypczak, Bettina, 1962– Decision: für Bläseroktett und Kontrabass. N.p.: n.p., 1994.
1 score (33 leaves); 30 cm.
Duration: ca. 10:00.
Composed for: 2 oboes, clarinet, bass clarinet, 2 horns, 2 bassoons, contrabassoon, double bass.
Commissioned by: Ensemble Octomania.
Call no.: **1995/098**

2462. Skrzypczak, Bettina, 1962– Konzert für Klavier und Orchester: 1997/98. Partitur. N.p.: Ricordi, 1998.
1 score (71 p.); 42 cm.
Reproduced from manuscript.
Duration: 14:00.
Composed for: piano, 3 flutes, 3 oboes, 2 clarinets, bass clarinet, 3 bassoons, 4 horns, 3 trumpets, 3 trombones, percussion (bongo, temple block, tam-tam, tom-tom, snare drum, xylophone, cymbals, glass chimes, vibraphone, conga, drums, timpani), violin I, violin II, viola, violoncello, double bass.
Commissioned by: Migros Kulturprozent.
Call no.: **2002/173**

2463. Skrzypczak, Bettina, 1962– Kwartet smyczkowy = Streichquartett. N.p.: n.p., 1991.
1 score (51 p.); 37 cm.
Duration: ca. 20:00.
Composed for: 2 violins, viola, violoncello.
Commissioned by: Swiss Broadcast Corporation (Radio DRS) and Pro Helvetia.
Call no.: **1993/130**

2464. Skrzypczak, Bettina, 1962– Verba: for symphony orchestra. N.p.: n.p., 1988.
1 score (56 p.); 42 cm.
Reproduced from manuscript.
Duration: ca. 13:00.
Composed for: 3 flutes, 3 oboes, 2 clarinets, bass clari-

net, 3 bassoons (3rd also contrabassoon), 4 horns, 3 trumpets, 3 trombones, percussion (cymbals, 4 temple blocks, snare drum, 2 bongos, 4 tom-toms, vibraphone, glass chimes, shell chimes, wood wind chimes, 3 suspended cymbals, tam-tam, timpani, maracas, bass drum, xylophone), piano, violin I, violin II, viola, violoncello, double bass.
Call no.: **1991/122**

2465. Slavický, Milan, 1947– Dvě kapitoly z apokalypsy: pro velký orchestr = Two chapters from the Revelation: for large orchestra (1995). N.p.: Milan Slavický, 1995.
1 score (57 p.); 42 cm.
Reproduced from manuscript.
Duration: ca. 21:00.
Contents: Ohnivé jezero = The lake of fire—Nový Jeruzelém = New Jerusalem.
Composed for: 3 flutes (2nd–3rd also piccolo), 3 oboes (3rd also English horn), 3 clarinets (2nd also clarinet in E♭, 3rd also bass clarinet), 3 bassoons (3rd also contrabassoon), 4 horns, 3 trumpets, 2 trombones, bass trombone, tuba, percussion (snare drum, 4 bongos, 3 tom-toms, tenor drum, timpani, bass drum, 4 suspended cymbals, 4 gongs, 2 tam-tams, 3 triangles, metal chimes, vibraphone, tubular bells, glockenspiel), celesta, violin I, violin II, viola, violoncello, double bass.
Call no.: **1996/139**

2466. Slavický, Milan, 1947– Ich dien': a meditation for chamber orchestra, 1995. Praha: M. Slavický, 1995.
1 score (4 leaves); 30 cm.
Duration: ca. 13:00.
Composed for: 2 flutes, 2 oboes, 2 clarinets, 2 bassoons, 2 horns, 2 trumpets, timpani, percussion (tubular bells, snare drum), violin I, violin II, viola, violoncello, double bass.
Commissioned by: Solistes Européens, Luxembourg.
Call no.: **1997/139**

2467. Sleeper, Thomas M., 1956– Concerto for horn and orchestra. N.p.: n.p., 1999.
1 score (108 p.); 28 cm.
Composed for: horn, 2 flutes, 2 oboes, 2 clarinets, 2 bassoons, 4 horns, 2 trumpets, 2 trombones, bass trombone, tuba, timpani, percussion, harp, violin I, violin II, viola, violoncello, double bass.
Call no.: **2004/124**

2468. Small, Haskell, 1948– Symphony for solo piano, 1995–1998. N.p.: n.p., 1998.
70 p. of music; 28 cm.
Reproduced from manuscript.
Composed for: piano.
Call no.: **2001/144**
Re-entered as: **2003/117** and **2004/125**

2469. Small, Haskell, 1948– Symphony for solo piano, 1995–1998. N.p.: n.p., 1998.
70 p. of music; 33 cm.
Reproduced from manuscript.
Composed for: piano.
Call no.: **2002/174**

2470. Smalley, Denis, 1946– Piano nets: piano with electro-acoustic sounds, 1990. N.p.: n.p., 1990.
1 score (ii, 16 leaves); 22 x 31 cm.
Reproduced from manuscript.
Composed for: piano, electro-acoustic sounds.
Commissioned by: Sonic Arts Network.
Call no.: **1993/131**

2471. Smirnov, Dmitriĭ Nikolaevich, 1948– A song of liberty: an oratorio for 4 singers, mixed chorus and orchestra, op. 59, 1991. New (1993). Moscow: n.p., 1993.
1 score (118 p.); 26 cm.
English words by William Blake; also printed as text.
Reproduced from manuscript.
Composed for: soprano, alto, tenor, bass, SATB chorus, piccolo, flute, 2 oboes, clarinet, bass clarinet, bassoon, contrabassoon, 2 horns, 2 trumpets, 3 trombones, percussion (timpani, triangle, cymbals, snare drum, drum, bells), harp, organ, violin I, violin II, viola, violoncello, double bass.
Commissioned by: Leeds Festival Chorus.
Call no.: **1996/140**

2472. Smith, G. Wiley, 1946– Whisper on the land: flute/piano. Lemars, IA: Medici Music Press, 1988.
1 score (8 p.) + 1 part (3 p.); 28 cm.
"Grade 4"—cover.
Composed for: flute, piano.
Call no.: **1989/117**

2473. Smith, Gregg, 1931– Earth requiem. N.p.: n.p., 1996.
1 score (133 p.); 44 cm.
English and Latin words.
Texts from the Latin Mass and a paraphrase of Isaiah 55, from writings by Chief Plenty-Coups (Crow), Walt Whitman, Nancy Murphy, Kim Rich, Gerard Manley Hopkins, and E. E. Cummings, and from Iroquois and Navajo prayers.
Composed for: soprano, alto, tenor, bass, SATB chorus,

children's chorus, 2 flutes (2nd also piccolo), 2 oboes, 2 clarinets, alto saxophone, 2 bassoons, 2 horns, 2 trumpets, 3 trombones, tuba, timpani, harp, 2 organs, violin I, violin II, viola, violoncello, double bass.
Call no.: **1998/154**

2474. Snell, David, 1936– Requiem. London: David Snell, 1995.
1 score (230 p.); 30 cm.
Latin words.
Composed for: SATB chorus, piano, violin I, violin II, viola, violoncello, double bass.
Commissioned by: Susan Farrow and Dulwich Choral Society.
Call no.: **1997/140**

2475. Snopek, Sigmund, 1950– Love poems of the woman d'Esté: for soprano and ensemble. N.p.: Couth Youth, 1992.
1 score (2 v.); 22 x 28 cm.
English words by Cynthia D'Este.
Song cycle.
Composed for: soprano, flute, clarinet (also bass clarinet, alto saxophone), percussion (vibraphone, glockenspiel, crotales, Chinese bell tree, triangle, suspended cymbal, snare drum, trap set), piano, violin, viola, violoncello, double bass, didgeridoo.
Call no.: **1997/141**

2476. Snopek, Sigmund, 1950– Sirens fugue. N.p.: n.p., 1991.
1 score (49 p.); 36 cm.
English words taken from James Joyce.
"Based on research by Margaret Rogers on the sirens chapter of Ulysses by James Joyce."
For vocal quartet, string quartet, hand bells, accordion, flute and penny whistles.
Composed for: SATB vocal quartet, flute, 2 tin whistles, handbells, accordion, 2 violins, viola, violoncello.
Call no.: **1993/132**

2477. Søderlind, Ragnar, 1945– Av hav der du komen: symfonisk diktning: for 4 talrøyster, solofiolin, kvinnekor og orkester. N.p.: n.p., 1985.
1 score (165 p.); 42 cm.
Norwegian, English, or French words by Åse-Marie Nesse.
For 4 narrators, solo violin, women's choir, and orchestra.
Reproduced from manuscript.
Duration: ca. 50:00.
Composed for: 4 narrators, violin, women's chorus, 3 flutes (3rd also piccolo), oboe, English horn, 2 clarinets, bass clarinet, bassoon, contrabassoon, 4 horns, 3 trumpets, 3 trombones, tuba, timpani, percussion (vibraphone, 2 suspended cymbals, tam-tam, snare drum, bass drum, small bell, 2 glockenspiels, bongos, glass wind chimes, cymbals), harp, piano (also celesta, electric organ), violin I, violin II, viola, violoncello, double bass.
Call no.: **1986/106**

2478. Soenen, Willy, 1937– Concerto: for clarinet and orchestra. N.p.: n.p., 2000.
1 score (95 p.); 30 cm.
Composed for: clarinet, piccolo, 2 flutes, 2 oboes, 2 clarinets, 2 bassoons, alto saxophone, tenor saxophone, baritone saxophone, 4 horns, 2 trumpets, 2 trombones, bass trombone, contrabass trombone, tuba, timpani, percussion (vibraphone, bells, glockenspiel, marimba, 2 side drums, bass drums, suspended cymbal, 2 cymbals, tam-tam, 2 bongos, 3 tom-toms, ride cymbal, crash cymbal), violin I, violin II, viola, violoncello, double bass.
Commissioned by: Ostend (Belgian seaside resort).
Call no.: **2001/145**

2479. Soenen, Willy, 1937– Quartetto per archi: "La vita." N.p.: n.p., 199-?.
1 score (28 p.); 42 cm.
Reproduced from manuscript.
Composed for: 2 violins, viola, violoncello.
Call no.: **1996/141**

2480. Sohal, Naresh, 1939– Lila. N.p.: Music Production Co., 1996.
1 score (109 p.); 43 cm.
Wordless.
For soprano and orchestra.
Duration: 48:00.
Composed for: soprano, 3 flutes (1st–2nd also piccolo, 3rd also alto flute), 3 oboes (3rd also English horn), 3 clarinets (2nd also alto saxophone, 3rd also bass clarinet), 3 bassoons (3rd also contrabassoon), 4 horns, 4 trumpets, 3 trombones, tuba, timpani, percussion (timpani, roto-toms, vibraphone, xylophone, 5 suspended cymbals, tubular bells, 5 tam-tams, 2 thundersheets, marimba, bell plates, 4 tom-toms, bass drum, boobams, glockenspiel, 5 anvils, wind machine, antique cymbals), 2 harps, piano (also celesta), violin I, violin II, viola, violoncello, double bass.
Commissioned by: BBC Symphony Orchestra.
Call no.: **2000/179**

2481. Sohal, Naresh, 1939– Madness lit by lightning. N.p.: Music Production Co., 1989.

1 score (227 p.); 30 cm.
English words by Trevor Preston.
Chamber opera.
Duration: 50:00.
Composed for: soprano, mezzo-soprano, tenor, baritone, bass, flute (also piccolo), clarinet (also bass clarinet), bassoon (also contrabassoon), horn, trumpet, percussion (3 tam-tams, vibraphone, xylophone, 3 suspended cymbals, 4 tom-toms, bass drum, glockenspiel, vibraslap, side drum, whip, small metal sheet), piano, violin, violoncello, double bass.
Commissioned by: Paragon Ensemble.
Call no.: **1994/138**

2482. Sohal, Naresh, 1939– Songs of the five rivers. London: Music Production Co., 2002.
1 score (42 p.); 42 cm.
Punjabi words by Bullay Sha and Waras Shah; also printed as text with English translation.
For soprano and orchestra.
Duration: ca. 25:00.
Composed for: soprano, 2 flutes (also piccolo), 2 oboes (also English horn), 2 clarinets (also bass clarinet), 2 bassoons (also contrabassoon), 2 horns, 2 trumpets, 2 trombones, tuba, timpani, percussion (marimbaphone, bass drum, 4 tom-toms, glockenspiel, 3 suspended cymbals, 3 thundersheets, 3 tam-tams, tabla, dholak), harp, sampler/synthesizer, violin I, violin II, viola, violoncello, double bass.
Commissioned by: Roger Wright, controller, BBC Radio 3.
Call no.: **2005/135**

2483. Solbiati, Alessandro, 1956– Di luce: concerto per violino e orchestra (1982). Copia dal manoscritto. Milano: Edizioni Suvini Zerboni, 1982.
1 score (48 p.); 42 cm.
Reproduced from manuscript.
Duration: ca. 16:00.
Composed for: violin, 4 flutes, 2 oboes, 2 bassoons, 4 horns, bass drum, harp, guitar, violin I, violin II, viola, violoncello, double bass.
Call no.: **1985/178**

2484. Soler, Josep, 1935– Edipo y yocasta: opera in two acts. N.p.: n.p., 1970.
1 score (275 p.); 42 cm.
Latin words.
Text from plays by Seneca and Sophocles.
Reproduced from manuscript.
Composed for: soprano, 5 baritones, SATB chorus, piccolo, 2 flutes, 2 oboes, English horn, 2 clarinets, bass clarinet, alto saxophone, 2 bassoons, contrabassoon, 6 horns, 3 trumpets, 3 trombones, contrabass trombone, tuba, timpani, percussion (wind machine, castanets, 2 rattles, lithophone, flexatone, 2 cymbals, chains, anvil, 2 bass drums, woodblock), 2 harps, piano, celesta, organ, Hawaiian guitar, violin I, violin II, viola, violoncello, double bass.
Call no.: **1987/081**

2485. Sommer, Silvia, 1944– Vastatio: für Orchester. N.p.: Ex-Silva-Edition, 1991.
1 score (72 p.); 30 cm.
Duration: 13:00.
Composed for: 2 flutes (also piccolo), 2 oboes, 2 clarinets, 2 bassoons, 4 horns, 2 trumpets, 3 trombones, tuba, timpani, percussion (crash cymbals, snare drum, bass drum), harp, violin I, violin II, viola, violoncello, double bass.
Commissioned by: Niederösterreichische Gesellschaft für Kunst und Kultur.
Call no.: **1995/099**

2486. Soong, Fu Yuan, 1940– Poems for string quartet. N.p.: n.p., 199-?.
1 score (71 p.); 29 cm.
Contents: Childhood memories—Thoughts on an ancient battlefield—Moonlight before my bed—The morning and evening stars—Song of war and conscription—By a quiet pond—From a Chinese opera theme—War and sobbing of ghosts—By the little river—Nostalgia on a summer day.
Composed for: 2 violins, viola, violoncello.
Call no.: **1996/142**

2487. Sotelo, Mauricio, 1961– Si después de morir . . . : für Stimme (Cantaor oder Alt), Flöte, Tonträger und Orchester (1999–2000). Partitur. Vienna; New York, NY: Universal Edition, 2002.
1 score (iv, 43 p.); 49 cm.
Spanish words; also printed as text with French translation.
"Ausgabe 31.10.2002."
After by poem the Elegía: Fragmento (1994) by José Ángel Valente.
Composed for: alto (or cantaor), flute, 2 flutes (1st also alto flute, 2nd also bass flute), 2 oboes, 2 clarinets, 2 bassoons, 4 horns, 2 trumpets, 3 trombones, tuba, percussion (xylophone, marimba, vibraphone, 3 Chinese cymbals [small, medium, large], wind machine, bass drum, crotales, glockenspiel, tubular bells, gong, lastra, tubular bells, timpani, large tam-tam, 4 tom-toms), tape (or speaker), violin I, violin II, viola, violoncello, double bass.
Call no.: **2004/126**

2488. Soto Millán, Eduardo, 1956– Corazón sur: cuarteto de percusiones. N.p.: n.p., 1994.
1 score (6 leaves); 22 x 34 cm.
Reproduced from manuscript.
Duration: ca. 20:00.
Composed for: percussion (tenor djembe, teponaztlis, high claves, 4 cowbells, 2 cymbals, crotales, medium claves, turtle shell, low claves, bass djembe, maracas).
Commissioned by: XXII Festival Internacional Cervantíno.
Call no.: **1996/105**

2489. SpaenC, Bo, 1958– Goya. N.p.: n.p., 1995.
1 score (2 v.); 34 cm.
Dance production (music composed for instrumental ensemble); choreographed by Jochen Ulrich.
Composed for: tape, flute (also piccolo), oboe (also English horn), 2 clarinets, 2 soprano saxophones (both also alto, tenor, and baritone saxophones), trumpet (also piccolo trumpet), trombone, piano, percussion (gongs, wind chimes, bells).
Call no.: **1996/143**

2490. Spratlan, Lewis, 1940– In memoriam. N.p.: L. Spratan, 1993.
1 score (199 p.); 39 cm.
English words.
For 5 soloists, double chorus, and orchestra.
"In the year of the Columbus anniversary, In memoriam honors the victims of the conquest. It focuses primarily in the Mayans and their kin, and their successors among the peoples of Latin America"—p. 2 of cover.
Contents: Prologue and prophecy—The hero—Death and lives of a revolutionary—Mexican serenade and prayer to the sun.
Composed for: 2 sopranos, tenor, 2 baritones, 2 SATB choruses, piccolo, 2 flutes (1st also alto flute), 2 oboes, 2 clarinets, 2 bassoons, 4 horns, 2 trumpets (1st also piccolo trumpet), 3 trombones, tuba, percussion (timpani, tubular bells, crotales, vibraphone, suspended cymbal, maracas, guiro, tambourine, glockenspiel, bongos, triangle, timbales, snare drum, bass drum, xylophone, temple blocks, 2 anvils, crash cymbals, castanets, ratchet, 2 woodblocks, slapstick), harp, celesta, mandolin, guitar, violin I, violin II, viola, violoncello, double bass.
Call no.: **1994/139**

2491. Spring, Glenn, 1939– Dona nobis pacem: for baritone and chamber orchestra. N.p.: G. Spring, 1984.
1 score (vi, 49 p.); 36 cm.
English or Latin words, also printed as text.
"Text by Wilfred Owen, Francis of Assisi, and the composer, with excerpts from the Latin Mass."
Reproduced from manuscript.
Composed for: baritone, 2 flutes, 2 oboes, 2 clarinets, 2 bassoons, 2 horns, 2 trumpets, 2 trombones, percussion (timpani, bass drum, triangle, snare drum, xylophone, suspended cymbal, gong), violin I, violin II, viola, violoncello, double bass.
Call no.: **1987/082**

2492. Spyratos, Panos, 1950– Fantasy. N.p.: n.p., 1988.
19 p. of music; 37 cm.
For piano.
Reproduced from holograph.
Composed for: piano.
Call no.: **1991/123**

2493. Staar, René, 1951– Just an accident?: requiem for Anton Webern and other victims of the absurd: melodram [sic] for narrator, soprano and full orchestra: op. 9, version 1985. Partitur. Wien: Edition Contemp-Art, 1985.
1 score (60 p.); 42 cm.
English words by Alan Levy.
Reproduced from holograph.
Duration: ca. 22:00.
Composed for: 3 flutes (2nd also piccolo), 2 oboes, English horn, 2 clarinets, bass clarinet, alto saxophone, 2 bassoons, contrabassoon, 4 horns, 3 trumpets, cornet, 3 trombones, percussion (timpani, tam-tam, pistol, 3 side drums, triangle, suspended cymbal, bass drum, glockenspiel, vibraphone, celesta, crash cymbals, castanets, marimba, woodblock, tambourine, claves, maracas, thundersheet, metal whip, wood rattle, chimes, siren, church bell), tuba, harp, piano, violin I, violin II, viola, violoncello, double bass.
Commissioned by: Second Annual Fesival of New Music in Wiener Neustadt, Austria.
Call no.: **1991/124**

2494. Staar, René, 1951– Bagatellen auf den Namen György Ligeti: op. 14 Nr. 3a: für Klavier. Wien: Edition Contemp Art, 1999.
xxxii, 61 p. of music; 31 cm.
Performance instructions in English and German.
Schematic diagrams precede music.
Partially reproduced from manuscript.
Composed for: piano.
Call no.: **2002/175**

2495. Stagnitta, Frank, 1948– Four songs, opus 13: mezzo-soprano and piano. N.p.: n.p., 1984.

1 score (22 leaves); 30 cm.
English words.
Reproduced from holograph.
Contents: Will / Ella Wheeler Wilcox—Good fortune / Heinrich Heine—January / Weldon Kees—Words for the wind / Theodore Roethke.
Composed for: mezzo-soprano, piano.
Call no.: **1989/118**

2496. Stallcop, Glenn, 1950– Millennial opening: for orchestra. N.p.: n.p., 1999.
1 score (57 p.); 36 cm.
Duration: ca. 17:00.
Program notes in English.
Composed for: 3 flutes (3rd also piccolo), 2 oboes, 2 clarinets, bass clarinet (also clarinet in E♭), 2 bassoons, 4 horns, 3 trumpets, 2 trombones, bass trombone, tuba, timpani, percussion (marimba, chimes, tenor drum, 2 suspended cymbals, crash cymbals, tambourine, 2 gliss gongs, woodblock, cowbell, 2 tom-toms, bass drum, large tubular wind chimes, snare drum, triangle), celesta, harp, violin I, violin II, viola, violoncello, double bass.
Call no.: **2004/127**

2497. Stamatelos, Katerina, 1951– Songs and prayers of the Abyss: for mezzo soprano, brass quintet and nine percussion players. N.p.: n.p., 2000.
1 score (80 p.); 44 cm.
Greek words by Katerina Stamatelos; also printed as text with English translation.
Reproduced from manuscript.
Composed for: mezzo-soprano, 2 trumpets, horn, trombone, tuba, percussion (claves, ratchets, 2 tambourines, 3 snare drums, 2 metal maracas, 3 suspended cymbals, crotales, 5 temple blocks, 5 timpani, 4 tom-toms, 3 tam-tams, bass drum).
Call no.: **2001/146**

2498. Standford, Patric, 1939– Symphony no. 5. N.p.: Redcliffe Edition, 1985.
1 score (175 p.); 30 cm.
For soprano and orchestra.
Latin words, from anonymous poems in Carmina Burana; also printed as text with English translation.
Composed for: soprano, 3 flutes (2nd–3rd also piccolo), 3 oboes (2nd–3rd also English horn), 3 clarinets (2nd–3rd also bass clarinet), 2 bassoons, contrabassoon, 4 horns, 3 trumpets, 2 trombones, bass trombone, tuba, timpani, percussion (tam-tam, vibraphone, 3 suspended cymbals, glockenspiel, snare drum, triangle, bass drum, marimba, crash cymbals, xylophone, tambourine, tom-toms, sizzle cymbal, woodblock, gong, tenor drum, jingle bells, 3 crotales), harp, violin I, violin II, viola, violoncello, double bass.
Call no.: **1987/083**

2499. Stanley, Bryan, 1972– The cask of Amontillado: a one-act opera adapted from the tale of Edgar Allen Poe. N.p.: n.p., 1996.
1 score (153 p.); 34 cm.
English words by Patrick Buckley and the composer.
Duration: ca. 35:00.
Composed for: baritone, bass-baritone, SATB chorus, flute (also piccolo), clarinet, bassoon, 2 horns, percussion (woodblock, glockenspiel, suspended cymbal, snare drum, chimes), violin I, violin II, viola, violoncello, double bass.
Call no.: **1998/155**

2500. Starer, Robert, 1924–2001. Duo for violin and piano (1988). New York, NY: MCA Music Pub., 1988.
1 score (24 p.) + 1 part (8 p.); 31 cm.
Composed for: violin, piano.
Commissioned by: McKim Fund of Library of Congress.
Call no.: **1991/125**

2501. Starer, Robert, 1924–2001. To think of time. Full score. St. Louis, MO: MMB Music, 1986.
1 score (29 p.); 35 cm.
English words by Walt Whitman.
Songs for soprano and string quartet.
Duration: ca. 14:00.
Contents: To think of time—After the dazzle of day—Yet, yet, ye downcast hours—Darest thou now o soul.
Composed for: soprano, 2 violins, viola, violoncello.
Commissioned by: Horizon Concerts.
Call no.: **1987/084**

2502. Stark, Anthony, 1944– 3d sonata: "portrait" (in one movement): for solo piano. 3d draft. N.p.: n.p., 1996.
17 p. of music; 36 cm.
"Second draft score 3/13–14/96; third draft score 5/5–7/96."
Reproduced from holograph.
Duration: 20:30.
Program note by the composer.
Composed for: piano.
Commissioned by: Ernest Ragogini.
Call no.: **1997/142**

2503. Stark, Anthony, 1944– The Milkweed chronicles: an American cycle, 1982–1984. N.p.: Anthony Stark, 1984.

1 score (various pagings); 37 cm.
English words; also printed as text.
For high voice and mixed chamber ensemble.
Reproduced from holograph.
Includes performance instructions and program note in English.
Duration: 52:20.
Composed for: high voice, flute (also piccolo, alto, and bass flutes), clarinet (also clarinet in E♭ and bass clarinet), percussion (vibraphone, glockenspiel, crotales, small triangle, 2 cowbells, suspended cymbal, large tam-tam, snare drum, large tom-tom, bass drum, glass wind chimes), piano, violin, violoncello.
Commissioned by: Contemporary Music Forum of Washington, DC, San Francisco Contemporary Music Players, and Speculum Musicae of New York City.
Call no.: **1993/133**

2504. Stark, Anthony, 1944– The Milkweed chronicles: the songs (1983). 2nd draft score. N.p.: Anthony Stark, 1984.
1 score (v, 41 p.); 28 cm.
English words, also printed as text.
For high voice and chamber ensemble.
"Rev. 2–3/84"—p. 1.
Reproduced from holograph.
Includes performance instructions and program note in English.
Duration: 24:00.
Contents: The flock of birds—Frost—If my silence deceives you—Spring morning Minnesota—The metamorphosis of stone—Blue flame—Waking in a field.
Composed for: high voice, flute (also piccolo, alto, and bass flutes), clarinet (also clarinet in E♭ and bass clarinet), percussion (vibraphone, glockenspiel, crotales, small triangle, 2 cowbells, suspended cymbal, large tam-tam, snare drum, large tom-tom, bass drum, glass wind chimes), piano, violin, violoncello.
Commissioned by: Contemporary Music Forum of Washington, DC, San Francisco Contemporary Music Players, and Speculum Musicae of New York City.
Call no.: **1985/179**

2505. Staron, Michael, 1956– W. N.p.: n.p., 1999.
1 score (26 leaves); 28 x 44 cm.
For orchestra.
Reproduced from holograph.
At end of score: "Fine 5/1/99 Mike Staron."
Composed for: flute, oboe, clarinet, soprano saxophone, alto saxophone, tenor saxophone, bassoon, 2 trombones, tuba, percussion (snare drum, claves, glockenspiel, timpani, trap set, xylophone, chimes), piano (also celesta), violin I, violin II, violoncello, double bass.
Call no.: **2001/147**

2506. Staud, Johannes Maria, 1974– Polygon: Musik für Klavier und Orchester (2002). Studienpartitur. Wien: Universal Edition, 2002.
1 score (48 p.); 42 cm.
Reproduced from manuscript.
Duration: ca. 12:00.
Composed for: piano, 3 flutes (1st–2nd also piccolo, 3rd also bass flute), 2 oboes, 2 clarinets, soprano saxophone (also baritone saxophone), alto saxophone (also baritone saxophone), 3 bassoons (3rd also contrabassoon), 3 Wagner tubas (1st–2nd also tenor tubas in B♭, 3rd also bass tuba in F), 3 trumpets (1st–2nd also piccolo trumpet), 2 trombones, contrabass tuba, percussion (timpani, 2 splash cymbals, crash cymbals, ride cymbal, hi-hat, tam-tam, 3 bongos, snare drum, military drum, tenor drum, field drum, bass drum, glockenspiel, vibraphone, 5 gongs, Chinese cymbal, 4 temple blocks, vibraslap, xylorimba, 2 triangles, 2 congas, 4 tom-toms), accordion, harp, page turner, violin I, violin II, viola, violoncello, double bass.
Commissioned by: RSO Wien.
Call no.: **2004/128**

2507. Steinke, Greg A., 1942– Native American notes: the bitter roots of peace (Image music VI): for string quartet. N.p.: n.p., 1990.
1 score (44 p.); 28 cm.
Based upon poems by K'os Naahaabii in his Notes from the center of the earth and Songs of the fire circles.
Composed for: 2 violins, viola, violoncello.
Commissioned by: Lark String Quartet of NYC.
Call no.: **1995/100**

2508. Stern, David, 1949– We stand for freedom: in memoriam, Sept. 11, 2001: for orchestra. Muncie, IN: David Stern, 2002.
1 score (32 p.); 36 cm.
Composed for: 2 flutes, 2 oboes, 2 clarinets, 2 bassoons, 4 horns, 3 trumpets, 3 trombones, tuba, timpani, percussion (crash cymbals, glockenspiel, suspended cymbal, triangle), harp, violin I, violin II, viola, violoncello, double bass.
Call no.: **2004/129**

2509. Stern, Max, 1947– Haazinu: cantata for double bass and orchestra. N.p.: n.p., 1988.
1 score (151 p.); 37 cm.
Duration: ca. 30:00.
Composed for: double bass, piccolo, flute, oboe, English horn, clarinet, bass clarinet, bassoon, contrabassoon,

2 horns, 2 trumpets, timpani, percussion (snare drum, tenor drum, bass drum, triangle, suspended cymbals, crash cymbals, tambourine, sandpaper blocks, large tam-tam, bells), harp, violin I, violin II, viola, violoncello, double bass.
Commissioned by: Gary Karr.
Call no.: **1994/140**

2510. Stevens, James, 1923– Celebration for the dead: a Buddhist requiem: for large orchestra or synthesiser, voices & soprano. Essex, England: B. Ramsey, 1984.
1 score (74 p.); 42 cm.
Based on texts by Giambatista Cinthio Giraldi, Marcus Aurelius, and Virgil.
Reproduced from manuscript.
Composed for: soprano, voices (predominantly male), 4 flutes (4th also piccolo), 4 oboes, 4 clarinets (4th also bass clarinet), 4 bassoons (4th also contrabassoon), 4 horns, 4 trumpets, 3 trombones, bass trombone, tuba, percussion (tubular bells, timpani, glockenspiel, 2 gongs, celesta, 2 cymbals, vibraphone, bass drum, xylophone, woodblock, snare drum), harp, violin I, violin II, viola, violoncello, double bass.
Call no.: **1988/100**
Re-entered as: **1989/119**

2511. Stevenson, Ronald, 1928– Violin concerto. N.p.: R. Stevenson, 1992.
1 score (212 p.); 31 cm.
Reproduced from holograph.
Composed for: violin, 2 flutes (2nd also piccolo), 2 oboes (2nd also English horn), 2 clarinets in A, 2 bassoons (2nd also contrabassoon), 2 horns, 4 timpani, percussion (celesta, triangle, tambourine, snare drum, bass drum, xylophone, tubular bells, vibraphone, cymbals), harp, piano, cimbalom, violin I, violin II, viola, violoncello, double bass.
Commissioned by: Yehudi Menuhin.
Call no.: **1997/143**

2512. Stewart, Richard N., 1942– Benedictus qui venit. N.p.: n.p., 1985.
1 score (88 p.); 44 cm.
English words.
For tenor solo, chorus (SATB), children's voices, wind and percussion ensemble, and tape.
Reproduced from holograph.
Composed for: tenor, SATB chorus, children's chorus, 2 flutes, 2 oboes, 2 clarinets, 2 bassoons, 4 horns, 2 trumpets, 2 trombones, bass trombone, timpani, percussion (tubular chimes, bells, cymbals), violin I, violin II, viola, violoncello, double bass.
Call no.: **1986/107**

2513. Stewart, Richard N., 1942– Psalm 102/Kyrie: a cantata for chorus, baritone solo and orchestra. N.p.: n.p., 1995.
1 score (111 p.); 44 cm.
English words.
Reproduced from manuscript.
Composed for: baritone, SATB chorus, 2 flutes, 2 oboes (2nd also English horn), 2 clarinets, 2 bassoons, 4 horns, 2 trumpets, 3 trombones, tuba, timpani, harp, violin I, violin II, viola, violoncello, double bass.
Call no.: **1998/156**

2514. Stewart, Richard N., 1942– Te Deum. N.p.: n.p., 1999.
1 score (87 p.); 44 cm.
English words.
For SATB, orchestra, and organ.
Composed for: SATB chorus, 2 flutes, 2 oboes, 2 clarinets, 2 bassoons, 4 horns, 2 trumpets, 3 trombones, timpani, violin I, violin II, viola, violoncello, double bass, organ.
Call no.: **2002/176**

2515. Stiles, Frank, 1924– Quartet no. 3. N.p.: Frank Stiles, 1984.
1 score (50 p.); 31 cm.
Reproduced from manuscript.
Composed for: 2 violins, viola, violoncello.
Call no.: **1985/180**

2516. Stimpson, Michael, 1948– Concerto for oboe. N.p.: n.p., 1999 or 2000.
1 score (154 p.); 30 cm.
Composed for: oboe, 2 flutes, 2 clarinets, 2 bassoons, 2 horns, trumpet, tuba, percussion (timpani, bass drum, cymbals, gong, snare drum), violin I, violin II, viola, violoncello, double bass.
Call no.: **2001/148**

2517. Stimpson, Michael, 1948– String quartet no. 1: Robben Island. N.p.: n.p., 2000.
1 score (41 p.); 30 cm.
Contents: Chorale 1—Agitated and violent—Lilting, but with edge: restless, quasi-dance—With some panic: from afar—Majestically: joyous—Chorale 2.
Composed for: 2 violins, viola, violoncello.
Call no.: **2004/130**

2518. Stock, David, 1939– Second symphony. St. Louis, MO: MMB Music, 1996.
1 score (76, 32, 53 p.); 44 cm.
Composed for: 3 flutes (3rd also piccolo), 3 oboes (3rd also English horn), 2 clarinets, bass clarinet, 2 bas-

soons, contrabassoon, 4 horns, 4 trumpets, 3 trombones, tuba, harp, timpani, percussion (xylophone, glockenspiel, crotales, chimes, snare drum, field drum, 4 tom-toms, 2 bongos, 2 timbales, 2 bass drums, crash cymbals, heavy finger cymbals, splash cymbals, 2 suspended cymbals, triangle, cowbell, medium gong, woodblock, log drum, vibraslap, tambourine), violin I, violin II, viola, violoncello, double bass.
Commissioned by: Seattle Symphony.
Call no.: **2004/131**

2519. Stock, David, 1939– Violin concerto (1995). Saint Louis, MO: MMB Music, 1995.
1 score (159 p.); 43 cm.
Composed for: violin, piccolo, 2 flutes (2nd also piccolo and alto flute), 2 oboes, English horn, 2 clarinets (2nd also clarinet in E♭), bass clarinet, 2 bassoons, contrabassoon, 4 horns, 3 trumpets, 3 trombones, tuba, timpani, percussion (vibraphone, snare drum, glockenspiel, suspended cymbal, xylophone, chimes, field drum, marimba, low tom-tom, bass drum, woodblock, tambourine, 2 cowbells), harp, violin I, violin II, viola, violoncello, double bass.
Commissioned by: Pittsburgh Symphony.
Call no.: **1997/144**
Re-entered as: **1998/157**

2520. Stockhausen, Karlheinz, 1928– Evas Zauber: für Bassetthorn, Altflöte und Piccolo, gemischten Chor, Kinderchor, 3 x 2 Synthesizer, einen Schlagzeuger und Tonband, 1986. Partitur. Germany: K. Stockhausen, 1986.
1 score (60 leaves); 38 cm. + 1 booklet (12 p.; 30 cm.)
German words.
The 3rd act of the opera Montag, from the cycle Licht; may be performed by itself, either staged or in a quasi concert version.
Reproduced from manuscript.
Booklet contains historical commentary on the composition, a biography of the composer, and a bibliography.
Contents: Evas Spiegel—Nachricht—Susani—Ave—Der Kinderfänger—Entführung.
Composed for: basset horn, alto flute (also piccolo), SATB chorus, children's chorus, 3 synthesizers, percussion (bell plates, antique cymbals), tape.
Call no.: **1987/085**

2521. Stockhausen, Karlheinz, 1928– Luzifers Tanz: (vom Samstag aus Licht): für Bass-Stimme (oder Posaune oder Euphonium), Piccolo-Trompete, Piccolo-Flöte/Harmonie-Orchester oder Sinfonie-Orchester (und Stelzentänzer, Tänzer, Ballett oder Mimen bei szenischen Aufführungen): 1983: Werk Nr. 53. First ed. Kürten, West Germany: Stockhausen-Verlag, 1987.
1 score (xi, 133 p.); 42 cm.
German words by the composer.
Scene 3 of the opera Samstag from the cycle Licht.
Reproduced from manuscript.
Duration: ca. 50:00.
Prefatory material and performance instructions in German.
Composed for: trombone or euphonium, piccolo trumpet, piccolo, wind orchestra in 10 groups: group I: kettle bell, 6 flutes, 3 basset horns; group II: glockenspiel, 6 clarinets, bass clarinet; group III: 2 alarm bells, 2 soprano saxophones, 2 alto saxophones, tenor saxophone, baritone saxophone, bass saxophone; group IV: 3 rin, 2 oboes, 2 English horns, 2 bassoons, contrabassoon; group V: 2 tubular bells, 6 trumpets, 3 trombones; group VI: 2 Javanese gongs, 6 trumpets, 3 trombones; group VII: percussion (hi-hat, 2 cymbals, 2 Thai gongs, Chinese opera gong, bell plate, snare drum, tom-tom, bass drum); group VIII: percussion (vibraphone, 2 cinelli), 8 horns; group IX: percussion (antique cymbal, 2 tam-tams), 4 euphoniums; group X: percussion (bronze bowl bell, tam-tam), 2 alto trombones, 2 baritones, 4 bass tubas; symphony orchestra in 10 groups: group I: kettle bell, 4 flutes, basset horn; group II: glockenspiel, 2 clarinets, bass clarinet; group III: 2 alarm bells, 6 violins, 4 violas, 4 violoncellos, 2 double basses; group IV: 3 rin, 2 oboes, 2 English horns, 2 bassoons, contrabassoon; group V: 2 tubular bells, 3 trumpets, 2 trombones; group VI: 2 Javanese gongs, 2 trumpets, 2 trombones; group VII: percussion (hi-hat, 2 cymbals, 2 Thai gongs, Chinese opera gong, bell plate, snare drum, tom-tom, bass drum); group VIII: percussion (vibraphone, 2 cinelli), 4 horns; group IX: percussion (antique cymbal, 2 tam-tams), 2 euphoniums; group X: percussion (bronze bowl bell, tam-tam), synthesizer, 2 tubas.
Commissioned by: University of Michigan Symphony Band.
Call no.: **1988/101**

2522. Stockhausen, Karlheinz, 1928– Luzifers Tanz: (vom Samstag aus Licht): für Bass-Stimme (oder Posaune oder Euphonium), Piccolo-Trompete, Piccolo-Flöte/Harmonie-Orchester oder Sinfonie-Orchester (und Stelzentänzer, Tänzer, Ballett oder Mimen bei szenischen Aufführungen): Werk Nr. 53. First ed. Kürten, West Germany: Stockhausen-Verlag, 1991.
1 score (x, 133 leaves); 42 cm.
German words by the composer.
Scene 3 of the opera Samstag from the cycle Licht.
Reproduced from manuscript.

Prefatory material and performance instructions in German.

Composed for: trombone or euphonium, piccolo trumpet, piccolo, wind orchestra in 10 groups: group I: kettle bell, 6 flutes, 3 basset horns; group II: glockenspiel, 6 clarinets, bass clarinet; group III: 2 alarm bells, 2 soprano saxophones, 2 alto saxophones, tenor saxophone, baritone saxophone, bass saxophone; group IV: 3 rin, 2 oboes, 2 English horns, 2 bassoons, contrabassoon; group V: 2 tubular bells, 6 trumpets, 3 trombones; group VI: 2 Javanese gongs, 6 trumpets, 3 trombones; group VII: percussion (hi-hat, 2 cymbals, 2 Thai gongs, Chinese opera gong, bell plate, snare drum, tom-tom, bass drum); group VIII: percussion (vibraphone, 2 cinelli), 8 horns; group IX: percussion (antique cymbal, 2 tam-tams), 4 euphoniums; group X: percussion (bronze bowl bell, tam-tam), 2 alto trombones, 2 baritones, 4 bass tubas; symphony orchestra in 10 groups: group I: kettle bell, 4 flutes, basset horn; group II: glockenspiel, 2 clarinets, bass clarinet; group III: 2 alarm bells, 6 violins, 4 violas, 4 violoncellos, 2 double basses; group IV: 3 rin, 2 oboes, 2 English horns, 2 bassoons, contrabassoon; group V: 2 tubular bells, 3 trumpets, 2 trombones; group VI: 2 Javanese gongs, 2 trumpets, 2 trombones; group VII: percussion (hi-hat, 2 cymbals, 2 Thai gongs, Chinese opera gong, bell plate, snare drum, tom-tom, bass drum); group VIII: percussion (vibraphone, 2 cinelli), 4 horns; group IX: percussion (antique cymbal, 2 tam-tams), 2 euphoniums; group X: percussion (bronze bowl bell, tam-tam), synthesizer, 2 tubas.

Commissioned by: University of Michigan Symphony Band.

Call no.: **1991/126**

2523. Stockhausen, Karlheinz, 1928– Montag aus Licht: Oper in drei Akten für 21 musikalische Darsteller (14 Solo-Stimmen, 6 Solo-Instrumentalisten, 1 Akteur), Chor, Kindeschor, modernes Orchester. First ed. Kürten: Stockhausen-Verlag, 1988.

1 score (3 v.); 42 cm.

German words.

Reproduced from holograph.

Contents: I. Akt: Evas Erstgeburt (ca. 1:25:00)—II. Akt: Evas Zweitgeburt (ca. 1:05:00)—III. Akt: Evas Zauber (ca. 55:00).

Composed for: 3 sopranos, 3 tenors, bass, SATB chorus, children's chorus, 4 basset horns, flute (also piccolo and alto flute), piano, 9 electric keyboards, percussion (tam-tam, parade drum, ratchet, mouth siren, auto horn, small whip, bass drum, hi-hat, bronze bell, metal cabasa, pea whistle, slide whistle, 5 antique cymbals, bamboo sticks, friction drum, child's lyre, woodblock, flexatone, 2 cowbells, 2 round saw blades, rin, child's slot machine, wind instrument for duck call, bicycle bell, jumping jack, violin string, claves, cabasa, tambourine, triangle, child's laser gun, guiro, snare drum, Indian bells, maracas, Thai gong, cymbals, darbuka, toy piano, Chinese cymbals, 2 Turkish cymbals, 2 crash cymbals, Thai gamelan, temple block, nightingale call, Balinese gong, keisu, punch puppet with 2 finger cymbals, clown puppet with steel drum, sheet of paper, steel coil, gan-sa-dahn, brass plate, iron grill, paper coil, caxixi), tape.

Call no.: **1989/120**

2524. Stockhausen, Karlheinz, 1928– Solisten Version von Michaels Reise vom Donnerstag aus Licht: für einen Trompeter, 9 Mitspieler und Klangregisseur, Werk Nr. 48 2/3. N.p.: n.p., 198-?.

1 score (vii, 67 leaves); 42 cm.

Duration: 48:00.

Includes performance instructions in German.

Composed for: trumpet, basset horn, alto flute, clarinet, clarinet (also basset horn and bass clarinet), trombone (also euphonium), synthesizer, electric organ, percussion (2 antique cymbals, geisha bell, 2 Thai gongs, tam-tam, bongo, vibraphone, rin, keisu, cymbals, 3 tom-toms, 2 con).

Call no.: **1990/116**

2525. Stockhausen, Karlheinz, 1928– Welt-Parlament: für Chor a cappella: vom Mittwoch aus Licht: 1995, Werk Nr.: 66. 1st ed. Kürten, Germany: Stockhausen-Verlag, 1996.

1 score (xxx, 81 p.); 28 x 38 cm.

Introduction and performance instructions.

Duration: ca. 38:00.

Composed for: SATB chorus.

Commissioned by: Süddeutscher Rundfunks Stuttgart.

Call no.: **2000/180**

2526. Stokes, Harvey J., 1957– Concerto no. 2 for oboe and strings. New York, NY: Seesaw Music Corp., 2000.

1 score (47 p.); 28 cm.

Duration: ca. 15:30.

Composed for: oboe, violin I, violin II, viola, violoncello, double bass.

Call no.: **2003/118**

2527. Strahan, Derek, 1935– China spring: for cello and piano. N.p.: Australian Music Centre, 1989.

1 score (30 p.); 30 cm.

Reproduced from holograph.

Includes poem The malignant dwarf of Beijing.

Composed for: violoncello, piano.
Commissioned by: Georg Pedersen.
Call no.: **1994/141**

2528. Strahan, Derek, 1935– Rose of the bay. N.p.: n.p., 1987.
1 score (135 p.); 30 cm.
English words; also printed as text.
Song cycle about Sydney for voice, clarinet, and piano.
Duration: 51:51.
Contents: Sydney—Before—After—Threads—Meeting places—Notes—Rose of the bay—Indecision—Immortal beloved.
Composed for: voice, clarinet (also clarinet in E♭), piano.
Commissioned by: Lauris Elms.
Call no.: **1992/132**

2529. Stroppa, Marco, 1959– Hiranyaloka: (1993–94). Partitura. Milano: Ricordi, 1994.
1 score (74 p.); 55 cm.
For orchestra.
Composed for: 4 flutes (3rd–4th also piccolo, 4th also alto flute), 2 oboes, English horn, 3 clarinets (2nd also clarinet in E♭, 3rd also bass clarinet), alto saxophone, tenor saxophone, 2 bassoons, contrabassoon, 4 horns, 4 trumpets, 2 trombones, bass trombone, contrabass tuba, 4 timpani, percussion (crotales, vibraphone, cowbell, pellet bells, small suspended cymbal, triangle, whip, 2 woodblocks, 2 snare drums, 2 bongos, tambourine, large suspended cymbal, harmonica, 2 tom-toms, 2 congas, Chinese cymbal, 2 crystal goblets, large gong, 2 tam-tams, thundersheet, bass drum), harp, violin I, violin II, viola, violoncello, double bass.
Commissioned by: Südwestfunk Baden-Baden.
Call no.: **1997/145**

2530. Stroppa, Marco, 1959– Upon a blade of grass: a concerto for piano and large orchestra (1995–96). Partitura. Italy: Ricordi, 1996.
1 score (90 p.); 42 cm.
Reproduced from holograph.
Composed for: piano, 4 flutes (3rd also bass flute, 3rd–4th also piccolo), 3 oboes, English horn, 2 clarinets in A, 2 clarinets (1st also clarinet in E♭, 2nd also bass clarinet), 4 bassoons (4th also contrabassoon), 6 horns, 4 trumpets (4th also bass trumpet), 3 trombones (all also bass trombones), contrabass tuba, 4 timpani, percussion (vibraphone, crotales, 2 suspended cymbals, medium tam-tam, gong, small triangle, metal chimes, 2 triangles, medium suspended sizzle cymbal, large tam-tam, medium sleigh bells, large bell tree, large suspended sizzle cymbal, very large tam-tam, large sleigh bells, large triangle), 2 harps, violin I, violin II, viola, violoncello, double bass.
Call no.: **2001/149**

2531. Strouse, Charles, 1928– Concerto: for piano and orchestra. N.p.: n.p., 1994.
1 score (185 p.); 36cm.
Reproduced from manuscript.
Duration: 20:45.
Composed for: piano, 2 flutes (2nd also piccolo), 2 oboes, 2 clarinets, 2 bassoons, 4 horns, 2 trumpets, 3 trombones, tuba, percussion (glockenspiel, anvil, bass drum, xylophone, snare drum, timpani, tenor drum, vibraphone, triangle, chimes, woodblocks, claves, slapstick, suspended cymbal, crash cymbals, tam-tam), harp, violin I, violin II, viola, violoncello, double bass.
Call no.: **1996/144**

2532. Strouse, Charles, 1928– Concerto America. N.p.: Charles Strouse Publications, 2002.
1 score (116 p.); 43 cm.
For solo piano with orchestra.
Composed for: piano, flute, oboe, clarinet, soprano saxophone, tenor saxophone, bassoons, 2 horns, 2 trumpets, trombone, bass trombone, tuba, percussion (vibraphone, glockenspiel, marimba, xylophone, timpani, woodblocks, castanets, tambourine, triangle, conga drums, timbales, tam-tam, bass drum, drum set), banjo, harp, violin I, violin II, viola, violoncello, double bass.
Commissioned by: South Florida Council, Chopin Foundation of the United States, Carol Carnes, and Isa and Marvin Leibowitz.
Call no.: **2004/132**

2533. Stucky, Steven, 1949– American muse: for baritone and orchestra. Bryn Mawr, PA: Merion Music: T. Presser, 1999.
1 score (104 p.); 36 cm.
English words; also printed as text.
Contents: American lights, seen from off abroad / John Berryman—Buffalo Bill's / E.E. Cummings—Delaware Water Gap / A.R. Ammons—I hear America singing / Walt Whitman.
Composed for: baritone, 2 flutes (2nd also piccolo), 2 oboes (2nd also English horn), 2 clarinets (all also clarinet in A, 2nd also bass clarinet), 2 bassoons, 2 horns, 2 trumpets, trombone, tuba, timpani, percussion (glockenspiel, chimes, xylophone, hi-hat, bongos, China dishes, celesta, snare drum, 4 tom-toms, woodblocks, 2 cowbells, 3 suspended cymbals, marimba,

police whistle, corrugated cardboard, bass drum, tam-tam, vibraphone), harp, violin I, violin II, viola, violoncello, double bass.
Commissioned by: Robert and Linda Attiyeh.
Call no.: **2001/150**

2534. Stucky, Steven, 1949– Angelus. N.p.: Steven Stucky, 1990.
1 score (57 p.); 44 cm.
For orchestra.
Reproduced from manuscript.
Duration: 12:00.
Composed for: piccolo, 3 flutes (2nd also piccolo, 3rd also alto flute), 3 oboes, English horn, 3 clarinets (3rd also clarinet in E♭), 3 bassoons, contrabassoon, 4 horns, 4 trumpets, 2 trombones, bass trombone, tuba, timpani, percussion (chimes, vibraphone, marimba, bass drum, glockenspiel, tam-tam, 5 suspended cymbals, 3 tuned gongs, 2 crotales, 8 handbells), harp, piano (also celesta), violin I, violin II, viola, violoncello, double bass.
Commissioned by: Carnegie Hall and Los Angeles Philharmonic Association.
Call no.: **1991/127**

2535. Stucky, Steven, 1949– Concerto for orchestra. Bryn Mawr, PA: T. Presser Co., 1988.
1 score (104 p.); 59 cm.
Duration: 27:00–28:00.
Composed for: 3 flutes (2nd also alto flute, 2nd–3rd also piccolo), 3 oboes (3rd also English horn), 3 clarinets (3rd also bass clarinet), 3 bassoons (3rd also contrabassoon), 4 horns, 4 trumpets, 3 trombones, tuba, timpani, percussion (vibraphone, 3 woodblocks, 4 tom-toms, bass drum, log drum, marimba, xylophone, claves, 5 temple blocks, 3 roto-toms, crotales, chimes, glockenspiel, bongos, whip, automobile spring coil, 3 suspended cymbals, 3 gongs, tam-tam), harp, piano (also celesta), violin I, violin II, viola, violoncello, double bass.
Commissioned by: Philadelphia Orchestra.
Call no.: **1989/121**

2536. Stucky, Steven, 1949– Concerto for two flutes and orchestra. Bryn Mawr, PA: Merion Music: Theodore Presser, 1995.
1 score (76 p.); 44 cm.
Duration: 17:00.
Contents: Elegy—Games—Hymn.
Composed for: 2 flutes, 2 oboes (2nd also English horn), 2 clarinets (1st also clarinet in E♭, 2nd also bass clarinet), 2 bassoons, 2 horns, 2 trumpets, trombone, timpani, percussion (tam-tam, xylophone, vibraphone, marimba, chimes, 3 suspended cymbals, bass drum, snare drum, 3 woodblocks, 3 temple blocks, glockenspiel, triangle, 3 tom-toms, claves, crash cymbals, maracas, whip, cowbell), harp, piano (also celesta), violin I, violin II, viola, violoncello, double bass.
Commissioned by: Meet the Composer.
Call no.: **1996/145**

2537. Stucky, Steven, 1949– Dreamwaltzes. New York, NY: American Composers Edition, 1986.
1 score (78 p.); 28 cm.
For orchestra.
Reproduced from manuscript.
Duration: ca. 15:00.
Composed for: 3 flutes (2nd–3rd also piccolo), 3 oboes (3rd also English horn), 3 clarinets (3rd also bass clarinet), 2 bassoons, contrabassoon, 4 horns, 4 trumpets, 3 trombones, tuba, timpani, percussion (vibraphone, tam-tam, 3 woodblocks, 5 temple blocks, Chinese cymbal, marimba, glockenspiel, xylophone, tambourine, chimes, 3 suspended cymbals, crotales, triangle, 4 tom-toms, bass drum), harp, piano (also celesta), violin I, violin II, viola, violoncello, double bass.
Commissioned by: Minnesota Orchestral Association.
Call no.: **1990/117**

2538. Stucky, Steven, 1949– Impromptus for orchestra. N.p.: Merion Music; Bryn Mawr, PA: T. Presser Co., 1991.
1 score (66 p.); 49 cm.
Duration: ca. 18:00.
Composed for: 3 flutes (3rd also piccolo), 2 oboes, English horn, 3 clarinets, bass clarinet, 3 bassoons (3rd also contrabassoon), 4 horns, 4 trumpets, 2 trombones, bass trombone, tuba, timpani, percussion (vibraphone, marimba, tam-tam, chimes, glockenspiel, 3 suspended cymbals, Chinese cymbal, 4 tom-toms, bass drum, tuned gong, crotales, claves), harp, piano, violin I, violin II, viola, violoncello, double bass.
Commissioned by: Saint Louis Symphony Orchestra.
Call no.: **1992/133**

2539. Stucky, Steven, 1949– Nell'ombra, nella luce: for string quartet. PA: Merion Music: T. Presser, 2000.
1 score (29 p.); 36 cm.
Composed for: 2 violins, viola, violoncello.
Commissioned by: Institute of American Music at Eastman School of Music.
Call no.: **2002/177**

2540. Stucky, Steven, 1949– Pinturas de Tamayo = (Paintings of Tamayo): for orchestra. Bryn Mawr, PA: Merion Music: Theodore Presser, 1996.

1 score (71 p.); 44 cm.
Duration: ca. 21:00.
Contents: Amigas de los pájaros = Friends of the birds—Anochecer = Sunset—Mujeres alcanzando la luna = Women reaching for the moon—Músicas dormidas = Sleeping musicians—La gran galaxia = The great galaxy.
Composed for: 3 flutes (2nd–3rd also piccolo), 3 oboes (3rd also English horn), 3 clarinets (2nd also clarinet in E♭, 3rd also bass clarinet), 3 bassoons (3rd also contrabassoon), 4 horns, 3 trumpets (1st also piccolo trumpet), 2 trombones, bass trombone, tuba, percussion (xylophone, vibraphone, marimba, bass drum, 2 triangles, chimes, glockenspiel, claves, maracas, tam-tam, 2 suspended cymbals, tambourines, 2 woodblocks, Chinese cymbal), harp, piano, violin I, violin II, viola, violoncello, double bass.
Commissioned by: Chicago Symphony Orchestra.
Call no.: **1997/146**

2541. Subotnick, Morton, 1933– A desert flowers: for chamber orchestra and computer (1988–89). N.p.: European American Music Corporation, 1989.
1 score (145 p.); 28 cm.
Composed for: computer, flute, clarinet, bassoon, horn, trumpet, trombone, tuba, percussion (marimba, rototom), piano, violin I, violin II, viola, violoncello, double bass.
Commissioned by: Cleveland Chamber Symphony.
Call no.: **1990/118**

2542. Subotnick, Morton, 1933– Echoes from the silent call of Girona: for string quartet and CDROM (Oct 1998). Paoli, PA: European American Music, 1998.
1 score (39 p.); 33 cm.
Composed for: 2 violins, viola, violoncello, CD-ROM.
Commissioned by: Meet the Composer.
Call no.: **2000/181**

2543. Subotnick, Morton, 1933– Jacob's room. N.p.: n.p., 1994.
1 score (138 p.); 28 cm.
English words.
Multimedia opera.
Composed for: voices, violoncello, computer-generated sounds.
Call no.: **1994/142**

2544. Suderburg, Robert, 1936– Concerto: for solo harp and orchestra. N.p.: n.p., 1989.
1 score (113 p.); 49 cm.
Duration: ca. 26:00.
"Revised '89."
Contents: Cadenza; Dark pageant; Lyric—Cadenza; Night presto; Meditation.
Composed for: harp, piccolo, 3 flutes, 2 oboes, English horn, 2 clarinets, bass clarinet, 2 bassoons, contrabassoon, 4 horns, 3 trumpets, 3 trombones, tuba, timpani, percussion (crotales, snare drum, tenor drum, dulcitone, vibraphone, 3 suspended cymbals, tambourine, bass drum, 3 tom-toms, crash cymbals, tam-tam, chimes, tambourine, 2 triangles, sleigh bells, maracas), glass harmonica, violin I, violin II, viola, violoncello, double bass.
Commissioned by: Marilyn Costello.
Call no.: **1990/119**

2545. Sullivan, Timothy, 1954– Dream play. N.p.: n.p., 1988.
1 score (185 p.); 29 cm.
English words by the composer; adapted from August Strindberg.
Opera.
Reproduced from manuscript.
Duration: 1:10:00.
Composed for: 2 sopranos, mezzo-soprano, tenor, baritone, bass, flute, clarinet, violin, violoncello, piano (also synthesizer).
Commissioned by: Canadian Opera Company.
Call no.: **1989/122**

2546. Sulzberger, Hermann, 1957– Concertino: für Violoncello und Orchester, op. 6. N.p.: n.p., 1986.
1 score (50 leaves); 35 cm.
Reproduced from manuscript.
Composed for: violoncello, 2 flutes, 2 oboes, 2 clarinets, 2 bassoons, 2 horns, 2 trumpets, trombone, violin I, violin II, viola, violoncello, double bass.
Call no.: **1989/123**

2547. Summer, Joseph, 1956– Hippolytus.
Call no.: **1985/181**
No materials available.

2548. Sung, Stella, 1959– Constellations: for orchestra. N.p.: Sonic Star Music Productions, 2002.
1 miniature score (76 p.); 36 cm.
Composed for: piccolo, 2 flutes, 2 oboes, 2 clarinets, bass clarinet, 2 bassoons, 4 horns, 3 trumpets, 2 trombones, bass trombone, tuba, timpani, percussion (suspended cymbal, tom-toms, triangles (small, medium), crotales, chimes, glockenspiel, snare drum, crash cymbal, bass drum, marimba), piano, 2 harps, violin I, violin II, viola, violoncello, double bass.
Call no.: **2005/136**

2549. Sur, Donald, 1935– Slavery documents: for soloists, chorus, and orchestra. N.p.: n.p., 1989.
1 score (147 p.); 43 cm.
English words.
Text partially based on Cotton Mather's The negro christianized.
Reproduced from manuscript.
Composed for: voices, SATB chorus, 3 flutes (3rd also piccolo), 3 oboes (3rd also English horn), 3 clarinets (3rd also bass clarinet), 3 bassoons (3rd also contrabassoon), 4 horns, 3 trumpets, 3 trombones, tuba, percussion (tambourine, timpani, tam-tam, claves, suspended cymbal, xylophone, tubular bells, cymbals, bass drum, side drum, timbales, cowbell), organ, harp, piano, celesta, banjo, violin I, violin II, viola, violoncello, double bass.
Commissioned by: Cantata Singers and Ensemble.
Call no.: **1991/128**

2550. Suslin, Viktor, 1942– Sonata: per violoncello e percussione (1983). Hamburg: Musikverlag Hans Sikorski, 1983.
1 score (17 p.); 35 cm.
Reproduced from holograph.
Percussion requires 2 players.
Duration: ca. 12:00.
Includes performance instructions in German.
Composed for: violoncello, percussion (timpani, 2 tomtoms, 2 suspended cymbals, 2 gongs, tam-tam, bass drum, 2 plucked string instruments, vibraphone, marimba, tubular bells).
Call no.: **1985/182**

2551. Svoboda, Milan, 1951– Mowgli: the ballet based on The jungle book by Rudyard Kipling: for symphony orchestra, jazz orchestra and mezzosoprano [sic]. Full score. N.p.: n.p., 1996.
1 score (353 p.); 34 cm.
Czech words.
Reproduced from holograph.
Composed for: mezzo-soprano, flute (also alto flute), oboe (also English horn), clarinet (also bass clarinet), bassoon, 2 horns, 3 trumpets, 2 trombones, tuba, percussion (cabasa, marimba, timpani, cymbals, vibraphone, xylophone, triangle, chimes, trap set, cymbals, congas, claves, bongos, temple blocks, snare drum, tabla, hi-hat, tambourine, military drum), guitar, bass guitar, piano (also organ and electric piano), violin I, violin II, viola, violoncello, double bass.
Call no.: **1997/147**

2552. Svoboda, Tomas, 1939– Concerto for marimba and orchestra: op. 148. Portland, OR: Thomas C. Stangland, 1995.
1 score (98 p.); 31 cm.
Composed for: marimba, piccolo, 2 flutes, 2 oboes, 2 clarinets, bass clarinet, 2 bassoons, 4 horns, 3 trumpets, 3 trombones, tuba, percussion (timpani, orchestra bells, crotales, suspended cymbal, bass drum, crash cymbals), harp, piano, celesta, violin I, violin II, viola, violoncello, double bass.
Commissioned by: Oregon Symphony Orchestra.
Call no.: **1996/146**

2553. Svoboda, Tomas, 1939– Concerto no. 2: for piano and orchestra, op. 134. Portland, OR: T.C. Stangland, 1989.
1 score (177 p.); 31 cm.
Duration: 41:00.
Composed for: piano, piccolo, 2 flutes, 2 oboes, 2 clarinets, bass clarinet, 2 bassoons, 4 horns, 3 trumpets, 3 trombones, tuba, timpani, percussion (crash cymbals, suspended cymbal, woodblock, bass drum, snare drum, chimes, orchestra bells), violin I, violin II, viola, violoncello, double bass.
Commissioned by: West Virginia Symphony.
Call no.: **1991/129**
Re-entered as: **1993/134**

2554. Svoboda, Tomas, 1939– Duo concerto for trumpet and organ, op. 152. Portland, OR: T.C. Stangland Co., 2002.
1 score (30 p.); 31 cm. + 2 parts; 28 cm.
Originally titled Duo concerto, was subsequently orchestrated and re-titled as Remembrance, op. 152a.
Composed for: trumpet, organ.
Call no.: **2003/119**

2555. Svoboda, Tomas, 1939– Sonata: for clarinet and piano, op. 167. Portland, OR: Thomas C. Stangland Co., 2002.
1 score (43 p.); 28 cm.
Composed for: clarinet, piano.
Call no.: **2005/137**

2556. Svoboda, Tomas, 1939– Theme and variations for flute, clarinet and piano, op. 142. Portland, OR: T.C. Stangland, 1993.
1 score (46 p.) + 2 parts; 31 cm.
Composed for: flute, clarinet, piano.
Call no.: **1998/158**

2557. Svoboda, Tomas, 1939– Trio for violin, cello and piano: op. 116.
Commissioned by: Florestan Trio.
Call no.: **1986/108**
No materials available.

2558. Swayne, Giles, 1946– The silent land: for solo cello and 40-part choir (1996). London: Novello, 1996.
1 score (53 p.); 42 cm.
English or Latin words; also printed as text.
Words from Latin requiem mass and poems by Christina Rossetti and Dylan Thomas.
"Perusal score."
Includes program notes and performance instructions in English.
Composed for: violoncello, 8 5-part choruses.
Commissioned by: Phyllis Lee.
Call no.: **2000/182**

2559. Swerts, Piet, 1960– Symphony no. 2: "Morgenrot": for soprano, choir and orchestra. N.p.: n.p., 2000.
1 score (203 p.); 30 cm.
Latin or German words; also printed as text.
German text from poems by R. M. Rilke.
Duration: ca. 01:10:00.
Contents: Introitus—Kyrie—Dies irae—An die Musik
Composed for: soprano, SATB chorus, piccolo, 2 flutes, 2 oboes, English horn, 2 clarinets, bass clarinet, 2 bassoons, contrabassoon, 4 horns, 3 trumpets, 3 trombones, tuba, harp, percussion (timpani, side drum, bass drum, cymbals, crotales, xylophone, glockenspiel, tam-tam, gong, tubular bells, 5 tom-toms), violin I, violin II, viola, violoncello, double bass.
Call no.: **2003/094**

2560. Syler, James, 1961– Symphony no. 1 "Blue": for wind ensemble, chorus and soprano. Boca Raton, FL: Ballerbach, 1999.
1 score (83 p.); 36 cm.
English words; also printed as text.
Text by the composer.
Duration: 35:00.
Composed for: soprano, SATB chorus, 2 flutes (1st also piccolo), 2 oboes, 3 clarinets, bass clarinet, 2 bassoons, 2 alto saxophones, tenor saxophone, baritone saxophone, 3 trumpets, 4 horns, 3 trombones, baritone, 2 tubas, harp, timpani, percussion.
Commissioned by: Baylor University, Bowling Green State University, Brigham Young University, Butler University, California State University, Concorida University, Georgia State University, Illinois State University, Kansas State University, McNeese State University, Miami University, Michigan State University, Mississippi State University, Murray State University, Northern Illinois University, Old Dominion University, Peabody Conservatory of Music, Salisbury State University, Southwest Texas State University, State University of West Georgia, Stephen F. Austin State University, Texas A&M University at Commerce, Texas Christian University, College of New Jersey, University of Georgia, University of Illinois, University of Kentucky, University of Massachusetts, University of Miami, University of Nebraska, University of Nevada at Reno, University of North Texas, University of Oregon, University of Texas at Arlington, University of Texas at El Paso, University of Washington, University of Wisconsin at Milwaukee, University of Wisconsin at Stevens Point, Valparaiso University, and Virginia Commonwealth University.
Call no.: **2004/133**

2561. Syswerda, Todd Elton, 1968– Symphony no. 1. N.p.: n.p., 2002.
1 score (141 p.); 44 cm.
English or Latin words; also printed as text.
For orchestra and choir.
Text by the composer.
Composed for: SATB chorus, 2 flutes, 2 oboes, 2 clarinets, 2 bassoons, 4 horns, 3 trumpets, 3 trombones, tuba, percussion (timpani, vibraphone, xylophone, chimes, 4 tom-toms, suspended cymbal, triangle, gong, snare drum, tambourine, and bass drum), harp, violin I, violin II, viola, violoncello, double bass.
Call no.: **2005/138**

2562. Szőllősy, András, 1921– Miserere. N.p.: n.p., 1984.
1 score (28 p.); 30 cm.
Latin words; also printed as text.
Text from Psalm 50.
Composed for: 6 male voices.
Call no.: **1986/109**

2563. Szőllősy, András, 1921– Quartetto per archi. N.p.: n.p., 1988.
1 score (17 p.); 42 cm.
Reproduced from holograph.
Composed for: 2 violins, viola, violoncello.
Call no.: **1990/120**

2564. Szőllősy, András, 1921– Tristia. Budapest: Editio Musica, 1983.
1 score (8 p.); 42 cm.
For string orchestra.
Duration: ca. 10:00.
Composed for: violin I, violin II, viola, violoncello, double bass.
Call no.: **1985/183**

2565. Tabakov, Emil, 1947– Symphony n 5 = [Simfonii͡a n 5]. Score. Sofia: Musica Publishing House, 2002.

1 score (252 p.); 30 cm.
Composed for: piccolo, 3 flutes (3rd also piccolo 2), 4 oboes, 2 clarinets in E♭, 2 clarinets, 3 bassoons, contrabassoon, 6 horns, 4 trumpets, 4 trombones, tuba, percussion (2 sets of timpani, snare drum, tenor drum, Bulgarian drum, crash cymbals, hi-hat, bass drum, tam-tam, chimes, gongs, vibraphone, marimba), synthesizer (or organ), violin I, violin II, viola, violoncello, double bass.
Commissioned by: Bulgarian National Radio.
Call no.: **2004/134**

2566. Taggart, Mark Alan, 1956– September, 1999: for string quartet. N.p.: n.p., 2001.
1 score (77 p.); 28 cm.
Contents: September 5—Lacrimare—September 16.
Composed for: 2 violins, viola, violoncello.
Call no.: **2005/139**

2567. Takano, Kicho, 1924– Silence; reminiscence. Tokyo: Japan Music Friends Association, 198-?.
11, 6 p. of music; 30 cm.
Includes notes in English.
Includes original Japanese notation.
Composed for: shamisen.
Call no.: **1985/099**

2568. Takemitsu, Tōru, 1930–1996. And then I knew 'twas wind: for flute, viola and harp. Mainz; New York, NY: Schott, 1992.
1 score (21 p.) + 3 parts; 31 cm.
Duration: 13:00.
Composed for: flute, viola, harp.
Commissioned by: Mr. Akira Obi, the Million Concert Co. Ltd.
Call no.: **1993/135**

2569. Takemitsu, Torū, 1930–1996. Dream/window: for orchestra. N.p.: Schott Japan, 1985.
1 miniature score (26 p.); 43 cm.
Reproduced from manuscript.
Composed for: 3 flutes (2nd–3rd also piccolo, 3rd also alto flute), 3 oboes (3rd also English horn), 3 clarinets (3rd also bass clarinet), 3 bassoons (3rd also contrabassoon), 4 horns, 3 trumpets, 3 trombones, percussion (antique cymbals, glockenspiel, vibraphone, tubular bells, 2 suspended cymbals, Chinese cymbal, 3 triangles, 3 gongs, 3 tam-tams, bass drum, timpani), 2 harps, guitar, celesta, violin I, violin II, viola, violoncello, double bass.
Call no.: **1988/102**

2570. Takemitsu, Tōru, 1930–1996. Fantasma/cantos: for clarinet and orchestra. N.p.: Schott Japan, 1991.
1 score (29 p.); 52 cm.
Composed for: clarinet, 3 flutes (2nd also piccolo, 3rd also alto flute), 3 oboes (2nd also oboe d'amore, 3rd also English horn), 3 clarinets (2nd also clarinet in E♭, 3rd also bass clarinet), 2 bassoons, contrabassoon, 4 horns, 3 trumpets, 3 trombones, percussion (vibraphone, glockenspiel, antique cymbals, tubular bells, 3 suspended cymbals, 2 inverted cymbals on timpani skin, 3 tam-tams, 2 gongs), harp, celesta, violin I, violin II, viola, violoncello, double bass.
Commissioned by: BBC.
Call no.: **1992/134**

2571. Takemitsu, Tōru, 1930–1996. Fantasma/cantos: for clarinet and orchestra. Mainz; New York, NY: Schott, 1993.
1 score (40 p.); 37 cm.
Duration: 20:00.
1994 Grawemeyer Award winning work.
Composed for: clarinet, 3 flutes (2nd also piccolo, 3rd also alto flute), 3 oboes (2nd also oboe d'amore, 3rd also English horn), 3 clarinets (2nd also clarinet in E♭, 3rd also bass clarinet), 2 bassoons, contrabassoon, 4 horns, 3 trumpets, 3 trombones, percussion (vibraphone, glockenspiel, antique cymbals, tubular bells, 3 suspended cymbals, 2 inverted cymbals on timpani skin, 3 tam-tams, 2 gongs), harp, celesta, violin I, violin II, viola, violoncello, double bass.
Commissioned by: BBC.
Call no.: **1994/143**

2572. Takemitsu, Tōru, 1930–1996. Gemeaux. Japan: Schott Japan, 1986.
1 miniature score (64 p.); 42 cm.
For solo oboe, solo trombone, 2 orchestras, and 2 conductors.
Reproduced from manuscript.
Duration: ca. 36:00.
Contents: Strophe—Genesis—Traces—Antistrophe.
Composed for: oboe, trombone; orchestra I: 2 flutes (2nd also piccolo, alto flute), oboe (also English horn), 2 clarinets (1st also clarinet in E♭ and bass clarinet, 2nd also contrabass clarinet), 2 bassoons (2nd also contrabassoon), 3 horns, 2 trumpets, 2 trombones, percussion (glockenspiel, vibraphone, marimba, tubular bells, 2 gongs, 3 tam-tams, 2 cowbells, 4 Japanese prayer bells on timpani, maracas, bass drum, 3 suspended cymbals, 4 antique cymbals), harp, celesta, mandolin, 12 violins, 6 violas, 5 violoncellos, 4 double basses; orchestra II: 2 flutes (2nd also piccolo, alto flute), oboe (also English horn), 2 clarinets (1st also clarinet in E♭, 2nd also bass clarinet), 2 bassoons (2nd also contra-

bassoon), 3 horns, 2 trumpets, 2 trombones, percussion (glockenspiel, vibraphone, marimba, tubular bells, 3 gongs, 3 tam-tams, 2 cowbells, 4 Japanese prayer bells on timpani, maracas, 3 suspended cymbals, 2 antique cymbals), harp, piano, guitar, 12 violins, 6 violas, 5 violoncellos, 4 double basses.
Commissioned by: Suntory.
Call no.: **1987/086**

2573. Takemitsu, Tōru, 1930–1996. Nostalghia: in memory of Andrei Tarkovskij for violin and string orchestra = Vaiorin to gengaku ōkesutora no tame no nosutarujia: Andorei Tarukofusukī no tsuioku ni. Mainz; New York, NY: Schott, 1988.
1 score (25 p.); 31 cm.
Duration: 11:00.
Composed for: violin, violin I, violin II, viola, violoncello, double bass.
Commissioned by: Scottish Post Office.
Call no.: **1989/124**

2574. Takemitsu, Tōru, 1930–1996. A string around autumn = Un fil autour de l'automne: for viola and orchestra. N.p.: Schott Japan, 1989.
1 score (31 p.); 52 cm.
Duration: 20:00.
Composed for: viola, 3 flutes (1st–2nd also piccolo, 3rd also alto flute), 3 oboes (2nd also oboe d'amore, 3rd also English horn), 3 clarinets, contrabass clarinet, 3 bassoons (3rd also contrabassoon), 4 horns, 3 trumpets, 3 trombones, percussion (vibraphone, glockenspiel, 3 suspended cymbals, 2 crash cymbals, timpani, 3 gongs, tubular bells, 3 tam-tams), 2 harps, piano (also celesta), violin I, violin II, viola, violoncello, double bass.
Commissioned by: Festival d'Automne à Paris.
Call no.: **1990/121**

2575. Takemitsu, Tōru, 1930–1996. Visions: for orchestra. N.p.: Schott Japan Co., 1989.
1 score (23 p.); 56 cm.
Reproduced from manuscript.
Contents: Mystère—Les yeux clos.
Composed for: 4 flutes (2nd–3rd also piccolo, 3rd also alto flute, 4th also bass flute), 3 oboes (2nd also oboe d'amore, 3rd also English horn), 3 clarinets (2nd also clarinet in E♭, 3rd also bass clarinet), contrabass clarinet, 3 bassoons (3rd also contrabassoon), 4 horns, 3 trumpets, bass trumpet, 3 trombones, percussion (vibraphone, antique cymbal, glockenspiel, tubular bells, 3 suspended cymbals, 2 Chinese cymbals, 2 cymbals, timpani, 3 tam-tams), 2 harps, piano, celesta, violin I, violin II, viola, violoncello, double bass.
Commissioned by: Chicago Symphony Orchestra.
Call no.: **1991/130**

2576. Tal, Josef, 1910– Symphony no. 5: for symphony orchestra (1991). Score. Tel Aviv: Israeli Music Publication, 1991.
1 score (80 p.); 30 cm.
Duration: ca. 21:00.
Composed for: piccolo (also alto flute), 2 flutes, 2 oboes, English horn, clarinet in E♭ (also bass clarinet), 2 clarinets, alto saxophone, 2 bassoons, 4 horns, 3 trumpets, 3 trombones, tuba, timpani, percussion (tubular bells, marimba, suspended cymbal, crash cymbals, 4 bongos, 2 snare drums, bass drum, tam-tam), 2 harps, violin I, violin II, viola, violoncello, double bass.
Commissioned by: Berlin Philharmonic Orchestra.
Call no.: **1993/136**

2577. Talma-Sutt, Michał, 1969– Avalon's gates: for flute and computer. N.p.: n.p., 1997.
1 score (19 p.); 30 cm.
Reproduced from manuscript.
Composed for: flute, computer.
Commissioned by: Warsaw Autumn Festival.
Call no.: **2001/151**

2578. Tan, Dun, 1957– Death and fire: dialogue with Paul Klee (1992). New York, NY: G. Schirmer, 1993.
1 score (67 p.); 36 cm.
For orchestra.
"Corrected 4/93"—p. 1.
Reproduced from manuscript.
Duration: ca. 26:30.
Includes performance instructions in English.
Composed for: piccolo (also alto flute), 2 flutes (both also piccolo), 2 oboes, 2 clarinets, bass clarinet, 2 bassoons, contrabassoon, 4 horns, 3 trumpets, 3 trombones, tuba, percussion (timpani, 2 cymbals, marimba, 2 Chinese cymbals, pair of stones, whistle, sleigh bells, tubular chimes, 5 roto-toms, 4 woodblocks, xylophone, suspended cymbal, maracas, large bass drum, guiro, 5 Chinese tom-toms, tam-tam, ratchet, 3 cowbells, vibraphone, whip), harp, violin I, violin II, viola, violoncello, double bass.
Call no.: **1994/144**

2579. Tan, Dun, 1957– Marco Polo. New York, NY: G. Schirmer, 1996.
1 score (247 p.); 44 cm.
English words by Paul Griffiths.
Opera.
Reproduced from holograph.
"Corr. 10/96"—p. 1.
Duration: 1:40:00.
1998 Grawemeyer Award winning work.
Composed for: 2 sopranos, mezzo-soprano, 2 tenors,

bass-baritone, bass, SATB chorus, flute (also piccolo, recorder), oboe (also English horn), clarinet (also bass clarinet), bassoon (also contrabassoon), 2 horns, 2 trumpets (both also optional Tibetan horns), 2 trombones, percussion (tabla drums, water gong, tambourine, bass drum, medium crash cymbals, cowbells, Chinese cymbals, snare drum, triangle, flexatone, tubular chimes, tam-tam, 2 bongos, slapstick, large crash cymbals, small Peking opera gong, timpani, xylophone, small Chinese drum, large Peking opera gong; additional percussion: 6 Tibetan singing bowls, 16 pairs of Tibetan bells), harp, prepared piano, optional sitar, optional pipa, violin I, violin II, viola, violoncello, double bass.
Commissioned by: Edinburgh International Festival.
Call no.: **1997/148**
Re-entered as: **1998/159**

2580. Tan, Dun, 1957– Nine songs. N.p.: n.p., 1989.
1 score (31 leaves); 44 cm.
Opera.
Accompanying ensemble comprised of Western and Chinese string-wind-percussion instruments.
Chinese or English words based on poems by Ch'ü Yüan.
Performance instructions in English.
Composed for: voices, conductor (also sings), Chinese fiddle, 3 suona, 2 contrabassoons, sheng, 6 bamboo pan-pipes, zheng, pipa, moon zither, gu-ching, percussion (4 Chinese drums, Peking opera drum, 5 tom-toms, roto-toms, 8 pottery jars, 8 pottery pipes, shueng, 2 sets of pots, set of moons, set of platters, set of pottery sticks, 5 pairs of wood sticks, marimba, set of bamboo pieces, 5 pairs of Chinese cymbals, 6 pairs of metal pipes, tam-tam, large gong, 3 Peking gongs, 2 small gongs, vibraphone).
Call no.: **1990/122**

2581. Tan, Dun, 1957– On Taoism. N.p.: n.p., 198-?.
1 score (27 leaves); 28 cm.
For orchestra with wordless voice.
Reproduced from manuscript.
Composed for: voice, 3 flutes (3rd also piccolo), oboe, clarinet, bassoon, 2 horns, trumpet, 3 trombones, percussion (orchestra bells, tam-tam, Peking gong, 4 woodblocks, Chinese tom-tom, Chinese gong, Chinese bass drum, small gong), harp, piano, violin I, violin II, viola, violoncello, double bass.
Call no.: **1989/031**

2582. Tan, Dun, 1957– Orchestral theatre I: Xun. New York, NY: G. Schirmer, 1990.
1 score (46 p.); 28 cm.
Reproduced from holograph.
For 2 solo xuns (Chinese vessel flutes) and orchestra; woodwind players also double on xun.
Performance instructions in English.
Composed for: 2 xuns, piccolo (also xun), 2 flutes (both also xun), 2 oboes (both also xun), 2 clarinets (both also xun), bass clarinet (also xun), 2 bassoons (both also xun), contrabassoon, 4 horns, 3 trumpets, 3 trombones, tuba, percussion (timpani, 3 woodblocks, crash cymbals, suspended cymbal, vibraphone, bass drum, tubular bells, marimba, triangle, tam-tam, 5 roto-toms, whip, snare drum, 2 Chinese cymbals, Chinese gong, 5 tom-toms), harp, piano, celesta, violin I, violin II, viola, violoncello, double bass.
Commissioned by: BBC.
Call no.: **1993/035**

2583. Tan, Dun, 1957– Orchestral theatre I: Xun. New York, NY: G. Schirmer, 1990.
1 score (46 p.); 36 cm.
Reproduced from holograph.
For 2 solo xuns (Chinese vessel flute) and orchestra; woodwind players also double on xun.
Performance instructions in English.
Composed for: 2 xuns, piccolo (also xun), 2 flutes (both also xun), 2 oboes (both also xun), 2 clarinets (both also xun), bass clarinet (also xun), 2 bassoons (both also xun), contrabassoon, 4 horns, 3 trumpets, 3 trombones, tuba, percussion (timpani, 3 woodblocks, crash cymbals, suspended cymbal, vibraphone, bass drum, tubular bells, marimba, triangle, tam-tam, 5 roto-toms, marimba, whip, snare drum, 2 Chinese cymbals, Chinese gong, 5 tom-toms), harp, piano, celesta, violin I, violin II, viola, violoncello, double bass.
Commissioned by: BBC.
Call no.: **1995/101**

2584. Tan, Dun, 1957– Orchestral theatre II: Re: for divided orchestra, bass voice and audience with two conductors. New York, NY: G. Schirmer, 1993.
1 score (42 p.); 36 cm.
Text consists principally of arbitrary syllables, some in English.
Duration: 22:00.
Composed for: bass, 3 piccolos, 2 oboes, English horn, 2 clarinets, bass clarinet, 2 bassoons, 4 horns, 3 trumpets in D, 3 trombones, tuba, percussion (water gong, water triangle, bottle, flexatones, 2 cowbells, suspended cymbal, pair of stones, timpani, tam-tam, crash cymbals, 2 bongos, small triangle, bass drum, tubular chimes, slapstick), harp, piano, violin I, violin II, viola, violoncello, double bass.
Commissioned by: Suntory.
Call no.: **1996/147**

2585. Tanenbaum, Elias, 1924– Columbus. New York, NY: American Composers Alliance, 1992.
1 score (97 p.); 44 cm.
For orchestra.
"Revised."
Reproduced from manuscript.
Duration: ca. 27:00.
Composed for: 3 flutes (all also piccolo, 1st also alto flute), 3 oboes (3rd also English horn), 3 clarinets (3rd also bass clarinet), 3 bassoons (3rd also contrabassoon), 4 horns, 3 trumpets, 3 trombones, tuba, timpani, percussion (guiro, marimba, vibraphone, glockenspiel, crotales, snare drum, bass drum, cymbals, claves, suspended cymbal, gong, tambourine, 4 tom-toms, 4 temple blocks, bongos, conga, whip, triangle), harp, tape, violin I, violin II, viola, violoncello, double bass.
Call no.: **1993/137**

2586. Tanenbaum, Elias, 1924– First Bass Man: for contrabass and orchestra (1996). New York, NY: American Composers Alliance, 1996.
1 score (67 p.); 43 cm.
Duration: ca. 26:00.
Composed for: double bass, 3 flutes (1st also piccolo), 2 oboes, English horn, 2 clarinets, bass clarinet, 2 bassoons, contrabassoon, 4 horns, 3 trumpets, 3 trombones, tuba, timpani, percussion (vibraphone, snare drum, conga drum, marimba, cymbals, tubular chimes, 4 tom-toms, suspended cymbal, triangle, 2 woodblocks, trap set, 4 temple blocks, glockenspiel, claves, bass drums, bongos, large tam-tam), harp, violin I, violin II, viola, violoncello, double bass.
Call no.: **2001/152**

2587. Tanenbaum, Elias, 1924– Last letters from Stalingrad. New York, NY: American Composers Alliance, 1981.
1 score (43 p.); 29 x 37 cm.
Composed for: baritone, viola (also percussion), guitar (also piano, percussion), percussion (military drum, snare drum, bass drum, crotales, tubular chimes, 2 thundersheets, cricket sticks, guiro, 3 suspended cymbals, marimba, vibraphone, maracas, 4 temple blocks, gong, 2 woodblocks, bongos, 5 tom-toms, glockenspiel).
Call no.: **1985/184**

2588. Tarp, Svend Erik, 1908–1994. Symfoni nr. 8: opus 88. Partitur. Copenhagen: Samfundet til Udgivelse af Dansk Musik, 1990.
1 score (94 p.); 30 cm.
Duration: ca. 55:00.
Composed for: 3 flutes, 2 oboes, English horn, 2 clarinets, 2 bassoons, 4 horns, 3 trumpets, 3 trombones, timpani, percussion (bells, cymbals, gong, marimba, snare drum, bass drum, small bell), harp, piano, celesta, violin I, violin II, viola, violoncello, double bass.
Call no.: **1993/138**

2589. Tashjian, Charmian, 1950– Coalescences: for full orchestra. N.p.: Charmian Tashjian, 1993.
1 score (17 p.); 44 cm.
"1984, revised 1993"—caption.
Reproduced from manuscript.
Duration: ca. 15:00.
Composed for: 4 flutes (2 also piccolo), 3 oboes (also English Horn), 3 clarinets (also bass clarinet), 3 bassoons (also contrabassoon), 3 trumpets (also piccolo trumpet), 4 horns, 3 trombones, tuba, percussion (xylophone, vibraphone, glockenspiel, chimes, crotales, 2 suspended cymbals, 2 tam-tams, snare drum, tuned tom-toms, bass drum, 4 timpani), celesta (also harpsichord), 2 harps, violin I, violin II, viola, violoncello, double bass.
Call no.: **1995/102**

2590. Tassone, Pasquale, 1949– Laudate Dominum. N.p.: Migida Musica, 1999.
1 score (30 p.); 29 cm.
Latin words.
For SATB chorus and orchestra.
Text: Psalm 150.
Duration: ca. 10:30.
Composed for: SATB chorus, 2 flutes (piccolo), 2 oboes, 2 clarinets, 2 bassoons, 2 horns, 2 trumpets, 2 trombones, tuba, timpani, percussion (chimes, suspended cymbal, bass drum, crash cymbals, antique cymbal), violin I, violin II, viola, violoncello, double bass.
Call no.: **2002/178**

2591. Taub, Bruce J., 1948– ". . . The limit of the flame . . .": (piano quartet). N.p.: Bruce J. Taub, 1997.
1 score (54 p.); 36 cm.
Composed for: violin, viola, violoncello, piano.
Commissioned by: Ross Bauer and Empyrean Ensemble.
Call no.: **2000/183**

2592. Taub, Bruce J., 1948– An often fatal malady. N.p.: n.p., 1990.
1 score (106 p.); 36 cm.
Reproduced from holograph.
At end: (thanks to Bill Holab!) New York city 5-5-90.
Duration: ca. 15:00.
"This piece is a sequel to 'Of the wing of madness.'"
Composed for: flute, oboe, clarinet, bassoon, horn, trum-

pet, trombone, percussion (timpani, 2 timbales, 2 bongos, 4 tom-toms, bass drum, vibraphone), piano, violin I, violin II, viola, violoncello, double bass.
Commissioned by: Cleveland Chamber Symphony.
Call no.: **1992/135**
Re-entered as: **1993/139**

2593. Taub, Bruce J., 1948– Preludes. N.p.: n.p., 198-?.
44 p. of music; 36 cm.
Composed for: piano.
Call no.: **1990/123**

2594. Taub, Bruce J., 1948– Preludes, piano solo. New York, NY: C. F. Peters, 1990.
44 p. of music; 31 cm.
Duration: ca. 40:00.
Composed for: piano.
Call no.: **1991/131**

2595. Tavener, John, 1944– Akhmatova songs: for soprano and cello. London: Chester Music, 1993.
1 score (13 p.); 30 cm.
Russian (Cyrillic and romanized) words; also printed as text with English translations by Mother Thekla.
Composer's note in English.
Contents: Dante—Pushkin and Lermontov—Boris Pasternak—Dvustishie = Couplet—Muza = The muse—Smert′ = Death.
Composed for: soprano, violoncello.
Commissioned by: Cricklade Music Festival.
Call no.: **1997/149**

2596. Tavener, John, 1944– The apocalypse: ikons of the Revelation. Bury St. Edmunds, Suffolk: Chester Music, 1994.
1 score (a–d, 304 p.); 42 cm.
Principally English words; adapted from The apocalypse of St. John by Mother Thekla.
For solo voices, choruses, and orchestra.
Reproduced from manuscript.
Composed for: high gallery: soprano, bass, 10 trumpets (1st–2nd also trumpet in E♭, 3rd–8th also piccolo trumpet), 4 trombones, 2 contrabass trombones, 2 sets of timpani, percussion (gongs, tam-tam); medium gallery: treble chorus (80 voices), 7 countertenors, 5 recorders; ground level: tenor, alto, treble voices, male chorus (4 basses, 3 tenors), soprano saxophone (also alto saxophone), handbells, organ, string quartet (2 violins, viola, violoncello), violin (section), double bass (section).
Commissioned by: BBC.
Call no.: **1995/103**
Re-entered as: **1996/148**

2597. Tavener, John, 1944– Fall and resurrection. Special order ed. Full score. London: Chester Music, 1999.
1 score (ii, 97 p.); 42 cm.
Primarily English and Biblical Greek words.
"Text compiled by Mother Tekla"—p. ii.
Sacred cantata for soloists, mixed chorus, and orchestra.
Composer's note and performance instructions.
Composed for: soprano, countertenor, psaltis (tenor), bass-baritone, SATB chorus, 2 piccolos, 2 kavals, 4 recorders, 2 oboes, soprano saxophone (also baritone saxophone), alto saxophone (also baritone saxophone), 2 bassoons (both also contrabassoon), rams horn trumpet, 2 horns, 2 piccolo trumpets, 2 trombones, 2 bass trombones, 2 sets of timpani, percussion (5 tom-toms, 2 Tibetan temple blocks, very large tam-tam), guitar, synthesizer, organ, 8 violins, 2 violoncellos, 6 double basses.
Commissioned by: Judith and Nicholas Goodison.
Call no.: **2002/179**

2598. Tavener, John, 1944– Ikon of eros: for solo violin, orchestra and chorus. London: Chester Music, 2002.
1 score (87 p.); 30 cm.
Greek or Sanskrit words.
Text by St. Gregory of Nyssa, St. John Climacus, Isaac of Nineveh, and from a Sanskrit invocation.
"Perusal score."
Duration: ca. 45:00.
Composed for: violin, SATB chorus, 2 flutes, 2 oboes, 2 clarinets, 2 bassoons, 4 horns, 4 trumpets, 3 trombones, bass trombone, percussion (small Tibetan temple bowl, large tam-tam, dholak, large Tibetan temple bowl, medium Tibetan temple bowl), violin I, violin II, viola, violoncello, double bass.
Commissioned by: Minnesota Orchestra.
Call no.: **2004/135**

2599. Tavener, John, 1944– The protecting veil: for cello and string orchestra. London: Chester Music; Bury St. Edmunds, Suffolk: Music Sales Ltd., 1993.
1 score (75 p.); 30 cm.
Duration: ca. 42:00.
Composer's note and biographical information in English.
Composed for: violoncello, violin I, violin II, viola, violoncello, double bass.
Commissioned by: BBC.
Call no.: **1994/145**

2600. Tavener, John, 1944– The protecting veil: for cello and strings. London: Chester Music, 1988.
1 score (114 p.); 30 cm.

"Perusal score."
Reproduced from manuscript.
Composed for: violoncello, violin I, violin II, viola, violoncello, double bass.
Commissioned by: BBC.
Call no.: **1990/124**
Re-entered as: **1991/132**

2601. Tavener, John, 1944– Total eclipse: for treble, countertenor, tenor and saxophone soloists, and orchestra. London: Chester Music, 2000.
1 score (59 p.); 30 cm.
Greek (Cyrillic) and English words; also printed as text with English translation.
Duration: ca. 40:00.
Composer's note in English.
Composed for: treble, countertenor, tenor, Baroque oboe, soprano saxophone, Baroque trumpet, Baroque trombone, 2 sets of chromatic timpani, handbells, Tibetan temple bowl, very large tam-tam, Baroque violin I, Baroque violin II, Baroque viola, Baroque violoncello, Baroque double bass.
Commissioned by: Keating Chambers.
Call no.: **2003/120**

2602. Tavener, John, 1944– The veil of the temple. London: Chester Music, 2002.
1 score (4 v. [viii, 801 p.]); 30 cm.
English, Greek, Church Slavonic, Sanskrit, and Aramaic words.
For solo soprano, mixed choir, and instrumental ensemble.
Text from various sources.
Duration: ca. 8:00:00.
Composed for: soprano, SATB chorus, duduk, Tibetan temple horn, 3 horns, 2 trumpets, trombone, bass trombone, timpani, percussion (3 Tibetan temple bowls, very large tam-tam, tubular bells, handbells, simantron), organ, synthesizer, Indian harmonium, optional strings (violin I, violin II, viola, violoncello, double bass).
Commissioned by: Temple Music Trust.
Call no.: **2005/140**

2603. Tavener, John, 1944– The vigil service of the Orthodox Church: for mixed choir and hand bells. London: Chester Music, 1984.
1 score (vi, 194 p.); 31 cm.
English, Greek, and Church Slavonic words.
"This setting of the Vigil should be celebrated between Easter and Ascension Day"—p. ii.
Reproduced from manuscript.
Introductory note by the composer, and notes on the Vigil service by Archpriest Michael Fortounatto.
Composed for: SATB chorus, handbells.
Commissioned by: Francis Grier.
Call no.: **1989/125**

2604. Taxin, Ira, 1950– Concerto for brass quintet and orchestra.
Call no.: **1985/185**
No materials available.

2605. Taylor, Rowan S., 1927– Clarinet concerto no. 3. Full score. N.p.: n.p., 1994.
1 score (163 p.); 28 cm.
For clarinet and band.
Reproduced from manuscript.
Composed for: clarinet, piccolo, 2 flutes, 2 oboes, clarinet in E♭, 3 clarinets, alto clarinet, bass clarinet, 2 alto saxophones, tenor saxophone, baritone saxophone, 2 bassoons, 4 horns, 3 trumpets, 2 trombones, bass trombone, baritone, tuba, percussion (suspended cymbal, bass drum, snare drum, timpani, cymbals, triangle, finger cymbals, gong).
Call no.: **1996/149**

2606. Taylor, Rowan S., 1927– Horn concerto no. 2. Full score. N.p.: n.p., 1998.
1 score (84 p.); 28 cm.
For horn and band.
Reproduced from manuscript.
Composed for: horn, piccolo, 2 flutes, 2 oboes, clarinet in E♭, 3 clarinets, alto clarinet, bass clarinet, 2 alto saxophones, tenor saxophone, baritone saxophone, 2 bassoons, 4 horns, 3 trumpets, 3 trombones, baritone, tuba, percussion (cymbals, bass drum, finger cymbals, gong, xylophone, snare drum, timpani, celesta).
Call no.: **2001/153**

2607. Tcherepnin, Ivan, 1943–1998. And so it came to pass. N.p.: n.p., 1991.
1 score (90 p.); 44 cm.
English words.
Oratorio for soprano, tenor, chorus (SATB), and orchestra.
Reproduced from manuscript.
Contents: . . . and so it came to pass—Vanitas—Koheleth—Dulce lumen.
Composed for: soprano, tenor, SATB chorus, piccolo, 2 flutes, 2 oboes, English horn, clarinet in E♭, 2 clarinets, bass clarinet, 2 bassoons, contrabassoon, 4 horns, 3 trumpets, 3 trombones, tuba, timpani, percussion (bass drum, side drum, snare drum, wood chimes, jawbone, glockenspiel, tubular bells, tam-tam, suspended cymbal, crash cymbals, glockenspiel, triangle, tambourine), harp, xylorimba, celesta, violin I, violin II, viola, violoncello, double bass.
Call no.: **1992/136**

2608. Tcherepnin, Ivan, 1943–1998. Double concerto: for violin, violoncello and orchestra (1995). N.p.: n.p., 1995.
1 score (64 p.); 44 cm.
Reproduced from holograph.
1996 Grawemeyer Award winning work.
Composed for: violin, violoncello, 3 flutes (3rd also piccolo), 2 oboes, English horn, 2 clarinets, bass clarinet, 2 bassoons, contrabassoon, 4 horns, 3 trumpets, 2 trombones, bass trombone, tuba, timpani, percussion (tambourine, sleigh bells, clapper, 3 tom-toms, snare drum, hi-hat, triangle, tam-tam, glockenspiel, 2 woodblocks, crash cymbals, 2 suspended cymbals, bass drum, tubular bells), marimba (also xylophone), harp, violin I, violin II, viola, violoncello, double bass.
Commissioned by: Greater Boston Youth Symphony Orchestra and M.P. Beliaeff Editions.
Call no.: **1996/150**
Also available:
Call no.: **1996/150 short score**

2609. Temmingh, Roelof, 1946– Drie sonnette = Three sonnets. N.p.: n.p., 1988.
1 score (18 p.); 30 cm.
For strings.
Reproduced from manuscript.
Composed for: violin I, violin II, viola, violoncello, double bass.
Commissioned by: University of Stellenbosch String Ensemble.
Call no.: **1993/140**

2610. Teodorescu-Ciocănea, Livia, 1959– "Le rouge et le noir": ballet in 3 acts. Orchestral score. N.p.: n.p., 2000.
1 score (381 p.); 30 cm.
Words by the composer after Stendhal.
Reproduced from manuscript.
Duration: 1:33:00.
Composed for: soprano, countertenor, men's chorus, 3 flutes (2nd also alto flute, 3rd also piccolo), 2 oboes, English horn, 2 clarinets (2nd also clarinet in E♭), bass clarinet, 2 bassoons, contrabassoon, 4 horns, 3 trumpets, 3 trombones, tuba, timpani, percussion, harp, synthesizer (harp, celesta, harpsichord, organ, piano, French accordion), violin I, violin II, viola, violoncello, double bass.
Call no.: **2003/121**

2611. Testoni, Giampaolo, 1957– Sinfonia: per orchestra (op. 15), 1982–83. Partitura. Milano: Ricordi, 1983.
1 score (102 p.); 49 cm.
Reproduced from holograph.
Composed for: 3 flutes (3rd also piccolo), 2 oboes (2nd also English horn), 2 clarinets, bass clarinet, 2 bassoons, contrabassoon, 4 horns, 3 trumpets, 2 trombones, bass trombone, bass tuba, timpani, percussion (glockenspiel, crash cymbals, bass drum, tambourine, triangle), harp, piano, celesta, violin I, violin II, viola, violoncello, double bass.
Commissioned by: RAI-Radiotelevisione Italiana.
Call no.: **1986/110**

2612. Testoni, Giampaolo, 1957– Wonderland variations: per orchestra (1984). Partitura. Milano: Ricordi, 1984.
1 score (36 p.); 47 cm.
Reproduced from holograph.
Composed for: 2 flutes, 2 oboes, 2 clarinets, 2 bassoons, 2 horns, 2 trumpets, bass trombone, percussion (timpani, bass drum, crash cymbals, glockenspiel, military drum, tambourine), harp, piano (also celesta), violin I, violin II, viola, violoncello, double bass.
Commissioned by: Orchestra A. Scarlatti Rai Napoli.
Call no.: **1985/186**

2613. Thayer, Fred, 1941– Gloria. N.p.: n.p., 198-?.
1 score (67 p.); 36 cm.
Latin words.
For solo vocal quartet, SATB chorus, and orchestra.
Reproduced from manuscript.
Contents: Gloria in excelsis—Laudamus te—Domine deus—Qui tollis peccata mundi—Quoniam tu solus sanctus—Cum sancto spiritu.
Composed for: soprano, mezzo-soprano, tenor, bass, SATB chorus, flute, oboe, clarinet, bassoon, horn, trumpet, trombone, harp, violin I, violin II, viola, violoncello, double bass.
Call no.: **1985/187**

2614. Theofanidis, Chris, 1967– O vis aeternitatis: for piano quintet (1999). N.p.: n.p., 1999.
1 score (21 p.); 28 cm.
Reproduced from manuscript.
At end of score: "5 May 1999 Rome."
Composed for: 2 violins, viola, violoncello, piano.
Commissioned by: Norfolk Music Festival, Speculum Musicae, Kosciuszko Foundation, and Settlement Music School.
Call no.: **2001/154**

2615. Thomas, Andrew, 1939– The heroic triad: for guitar, percussion, & string orchestra. N.p.: n.p., 2000.
1 score (53 p.); 45 cm.
"Inspired by the book The heroic triad by Tom Horgan."

"Scenario by Howard L. Kessler."
Composed for: acoustic guitar, percussion (slapstick, suspended cymbal, tam-tam, snare drum, 3 tom-toms, 5 roto-toms, pedal bass drum, concert bass drum, marimba, vibraphone), violin I, violin II, viola, violoncello, double bass.
Commissioned by: 20th Century Unlimited.
Call no.: **2004/136**

2616. Thomas, Augusta Read, 1964– 5 Haiku: for piano and orchestra: 1995. Full score. Bryn Mawr, PA: Presser, 1995.
1 score (84 p.); 44 cm.
Duration: 17:00–18:00.
Contents: Mirage—Dune—Boulder garden—Winds—Twilight.
Composed for: piano, piccolo, flute (also alto flute), oboe, English horn, clarinet, bass clarinet, 2 horns, 2 trumpets (1st also piccolo trumpet), 2 trombones, percussion (glockenspiel, crotales, tubular chimes, suspended cymbal, medium tam-tam, large bass drum, 2 triangles, large tam-tam, 5 tom-toms), harp, violin I, violin II, viola, violoncello, double bass.
Commissioned by: Brown University.
Call no.: **1996/151**

2617. Thomas, Augusta Read, 1964– Glass moon: 1988. N.p.: n.p., 1988.
1 score (49 p.); 44 cm.
For large orchestra.
Reproduced from manuscript.
Duration: 11:00.
Composed for: piccolo, 2 flutes, 2 oboes, 2 clarinets, bass clarinet, 2 bassoons, 4 horns, 3 trumpets, 3 trombones, tuba, timpani, percussion (triangle, suspended cymbal, crotales, orchestra bells, crash cymbals, cabasa, bass drum, tambourine, woodblock, temple blocks, xylophone, chimes, 2 bongos, sizzle cymbal, marimba, snare drum, 2 tam-tams, vibraphone, 5 tom-toms), harp, piano, violin I, violin II, viola, violoncello, double bass.
Call no.: **1992/137**

2618. Thomas, Augusta Read, 1964– In my sky at twilight: songs of passion and love. New York, NY: G. Schirmer, 2002 (1/22/03 printing).
1 miniature score (77 p.); 36 cm.
English words; also printed as text.
Texts from various sources.
For solo soprano and chamber orchestra.
Duration: ca. 20:00–22:00.
Contents: Deeper than all roses—Lament.
Composed for: soprano, piccolo, flute, oboe, 2 clarinets, 2 horns, piccolo trumpet, trumpet, percussion (vibraphone, xylophone, 3 crotales, large woodblock, large bass drum, suspended cymbal, triangles (small, large), maracas, cowbells, tubular chimes, glockenspiel, bongos, large tam-tam, graduated metal wind chimes), 2 pianos (2nd also celesta), harp, violin I, violin II, viola, violoncello, double bass.
Commissioned by: Family of Marilyn M. Simpson.
Call no.: **2004/137**

2619. Thomas, Augusta Read, 1964– In my sky at twilight: songs of passion and love. New York, NY: G. Schirmer, 2002 (9/17/02 printing).
1 miniature score (77 p.); 36 cm.
English words; also printed as text.
Texts from various sources.
For solo soprano and chamber orchestra.
Duration: ca. 20:00–22:00.
Contents: Deeper than all roses—Lament.
Composed for: soprano, piccolo, flute, oboe, 2 clarinets, 2 horns, piccolo trumpet, trumpet, percussion (vibraphone, xylophone, 3 crotales, large woodblock, large bass drum, suspended cymbal, triangles (small, large), maracas, cowbells, tubular chimes, glockenspiel, bongos, large tam-tam, graduated metal wind chimes), 2 pianos (2nd also celesta), harp, violin I, violin II, viola, violoncello, double bass.
Commissioned by: Family of Marilyn M. Simpson.
Call no.: **2005/141**

2620. Thomas, Augusta Read, 1964– Orbital beacons: concerto for orchestra, 1998. N.p.: Augusta Read Thomas, 1998.
1 score (122 leaves); 65 cm.
Duration: 25:00.
Contents: Aquila—Lyra—Eridanus—Cygnus—Coma Berenices—Andromeda.
Composed for: piccolo, 3 flutes, 4 oboes, 3 clarinets (2nd also bass clarinet), 2 bassoons, contrabassoon, 5 horns, piccolo trumpet, 3 trumpets, 2 trombones, bass trombone, tuba, percussion (xylophone, vibraphone, suspended cymbal, 5 tom-toms, triangles, claves, 2 button gongs, bass marimba, glockenspiel, tubular chimes, 2 woodblocks, medium tam-tam, crotales, 2 bongos, sizzle cymbal, large tam-tam, marimba, 2 timbales, bass drum, 6 cowbells), 2 harps, piano, celesta, violin I, violin II, viola, violoncello, double bass.
Commissioned by: Louise Durham Mead New Music Fund.
Call no.: **2001/155**

2621. Thomas, Augusta Read, 1964– Song in sorrow. Full score. New York, NY: G. Schirmer, 2000 (2001 printing).

1 score (67 p.); 36 cm.
Words by Percy Bysshe Shelley.
For solo soprano, 6 solo voices (SSSSAA), large chorus (SATB) and orchestra.
Duration: 22:00.
"April 2000, final edition"—p. 67.
Contents: Sing again—Black despair: (confessions of war)—When soft voices die.
Composed for: 5 sopranos, 2 altos, SATB chorus, piccolo, 3 flutes, 3 oboes, 3 clarinets, bassoon, 4 horns, 3 trumpets (3rd also piccolo trumpet), trombone, percussion (vibraphone, triangles, glockenspiel, suspended cymbal, 2 congas, large tam-tam, marimba, crotales, 2 bongos, woodblock, large bass drum), harp, violin I, violin II, viola, violoncello, double bass.
Commissioned by: Kent State University and Cleveland Orchestra.
Call no.: **2002/180**

2622. Thomas, Augusta Read, 1964– Song in sorrow. Full score. New York, NY: G. Schirmer, 2000 (1/23/02 printing).
1 score (67 p.); 44 cm.
Words by Percy Bysshe Shelley.
For solo soprano, 6 solo voices (SSSSAA), large chorus (SATB) and orchestra.
Duration: 22:00.
"April 2000, final edition"—p. 67.
Contents: Sing again—Black despair: (confessions of war)—When soft voices die.
Composed for: 5 sopranos, 2 altos, SATB chorus, piccolo, 3 flutes, 3 oboes, 3 clarinets, bassoon, 4 horns, 3 trumpets (3rd also piccolo trumpet), trombone, percussion (vibraphone, triangles, glockenspiel, suspended cymbal, 2 congas, large tam-tam, marimba, crotales, 2 bongos, woodblock, large bass drum), harp, violin I, violin II, viola, violoncello, double bass.
Commissioned by: Kent State University and Cleveland Orchestra.
Call no.: **2003/122**

2623. Thomas, Augusta Read, 1964– Triple concerto: night's midsummer blaze: for flute, viola, harp and orchestra. Bryn Mawr, PA: Theodore Presser, 1991.
1 score (75 p.); 44 cm.
Reproduced from manuscript.
Duration: 20:00.
Composed for: flute, viola, harp, 3 flutes (3rd also piccolo), 2 oboes, English horn, 2 clarinets, bass clarinet, 2 bassoons, contrabassoon, 4 horns, 3 trumpets, 3 trombones, tuba, timpani, percussion (bell tree, suspended cymbal, 3 tam-tams (small, medium, large), tubular chimes, crotales, 5 tom-toms, sizzle cymbal, large bass drum, glockenspiel, 5 temple blocks, vibraphone, claves, marimba), piano, violin I, violin II, viola, violoncello, double bass.
Commissioned by: Debussy Trio Music Foundation.
Call no.: **1994/147**

2624. Thomas, Augusta Read, 1964– Wind dance, 1989. N.p.: n.p., 1989.
1 score (42 p.); 59 cm.
For orchestra.
Reproduced from manuscript.
Duration: 16:00.
Composed for: 3 flutes (3rd also piccolo), 2 oboes, English horn, 2 clarinets, bass clarinet, 2 bassoons, contrabassoon, 4 horns, 3 trumpets, 3 trombones (2nd also alto trombone), tuba, timpani, percussion (finger cymbals, 5 temple blocks, tubular chimes, xylophone, triangle, suspended cymbal, sizzle cymbal, bell tree, vibraphone, glockenspiel, crotales, tambourine, tam-tam, 2 timbales, 5 tom-toms, marimba, 3 button gongs), 2 harps, piano (also celesta), violin I, violin II, viola, violoncello, double bass.
Call no.: **1991/133**

2625. Thomas, Augusta Read, 1964– Words of the sea. N.p.: A.R. Thomas, 1996.
1 score (77 p.); 44 cm.
For orchestra.
Duration: 17:00.
Contents: . . . words of the sea . . . — . . . the ever-hooded, tragic-gestured sea . . . — . . . beyond the genius of the sea . . . — . . . mountainous atmospheres of sky and sea . . .
Composed for: piccolo, 3 flutes, 2 oboes, English horn, 3 clarinets (3rd also contrabass clarinet), bass clarinet, 2 bassoons, contrabassoon, 4 horns, 2 trumpets, piccolo trumpet, 2 trombones, bass trombone, tuba, 5 timpani, percussion (vibraphone, crotales, 2 button gongs, suspended cymbal, large bass drum, marimba, 2 bongos, 3 congas, 2 tam-tams [medium, large], glockenspiel, 5 roto-toms, claves, tubular chimes, xylophone, 2 triangles, sizzle cymbal), harp, piano, violin I, violin II, viola, violoncello, double bass.
Commissioned by: Chicago Symphony Orchestra.
Call no.: **2000/184**

2626. Thomas, Augusta Read, 1964– Words of the sea: for orchestra, 1996. Full score. N.p.: Augusta Read Thomas, 1996.
1 score (77 leaves); 44 cm.
Duration: 17:00.
Contents: . . . words of the sea . . . — . . . the ever-hooded, tragic-gestured sea . . . — . . . beyond the genius of the

sea . . . — . . . mountainous atmospheres of sky and sea . . . : homage to Debussy.
Composed for: piccolo, 3 flutes, 2 oboes, English horn, 3 clarinets (3rd also contrabass clarinet), bass clarinet, 2 bassoons, contrabassoon, 4 horns, 2 trumpets, piccolo trumpet, 2 trombones, bass trombone, tuba, 5 timpani, percussion (vibraphone, crotales, 2 button gongs, suspended cymbal, large bass drum, marimba, 2 bongos, 3 congas, 2 tam-tams [medium, large], glockenspiel, 5 roto-toms, claves, tubular chimes, xylophone, 2 triangles, sizzle cymbal), harp, piano, violin I, violin II, viola, violoncello, double bass.
Commissioned by: Chicago Symphony Orchestra.
Call no.: **1997/150**

2627. Thomas, Augusta Read, 1964– Words of the sea: for orchestra, 1996. Full score. Rochester, NY: A.R.T. Musings, 1996.
1 score (77 p.); 44 cm.
Duration: 17:00.
Contents: . . . words of the sea . . . — . . . the ever-hooded, tragic-gestured sea . . . — . . . beyond the genius of the sea . . . — . . . mountainous atmospheres of sky and sea . . . : homage to Debussy.
Composed for: piccolo, 3 flutes, 2 oboes, English horn, 3 clarinets (3rd also contrabass clarinet), bass clarinet, 2 bassoons, contrabassoon, 4 horns, 2 trumpets, piccolo trumpet, 2 trombones, bass trombone, tuba, 5 timpani, percussion (vibraphone, crotales, 2 button gongs, suspended cymbal, large bass drum, marimba, 2 bongos, 3 congas, 2 tam-tams [medium, large], glockenspiel, 5 roto-toms, claves, tubular chimes, xylophone, 2 triangles, sizzle cymbal), harp, piano, violin I, violin II, viola, violoncello, double bass.
Commissioned by: Chicago Symphony Orchestra.
Call no.: **1998/161**

2628. Thomas, Michael Tilson, 1944– From the diary of Anne Frank. N.p.: Kongcha Music, 1990.
1 score (140 p.); 36 cm.
Words by Anne Frank.
For narrator and orchestra.
Composed for: narrator, 3 flutes (3rd also piccolo), 2 oboes, English horn, 2 clarinets, bass clarinet, 2 bassoons, contrabassoon, 4 horns, 3 trumpets, 2 trombones, bass trombone, tuba, timpani, percussion (vibraphone, crotales, glockenspiel, marimba, xylophone, gong, tam-tam, suspended cymbal, crash cymbals, snare drum, field drum, 2 bass drums, chimes, triangle, tambourine, 2 tom-toms, bongos, woodblock, small metal pipe, metal plate), harp, piano, violin I, violin II, violas, violoncello, double bass.
Commissioned by: UNICEF.
Call no.: **1994/148**

2629. Thome, Diane, 1942– Masks of eternity.
Composed for: tape.
Commissioned by: Washington State Chapter of Music Teachers National Association.
Call no.: **1996/152**
No materials available.

2630. Thome, Diane, 1942– The ruins of the heart: for soprano, orchestra and tape. Seattle, WA: n.p., 1990.
1 score (36 p.); 36 cm.
Text from a poem by 13th-century poet Jelaluddin Rumi, translated by Edmund Helminski.
Composed for: soprano, tape, piccolo, 2 flutes, 2 oboes, English horn, 2 clarinets, 2 bassoons, 2 horns, 2 trumpets, 2 trombones, percussion (xylophone, vibraphone, glockenspiel, chimes, triangle, timpani), harp, piano, violin I, violin II, viola, violoncello, double bass.
Commissioned by: Peter Erös and University Symphony.
Call no.: **1993/141**

2631. Thoresen, Lasse, 1949– Symphonic concerto: for violin and orchestra: 1984. Oslo: Norsk Musikkinformasjon, 1984.
1 score (157 p.); 37 cm.
Includes performance instructions.
Duration: ca. 42:00.
Composed for: violin, 3 flutes (1st also alto flute, 3rd also piccolo), 2 oboes, English horn, 2 clarinets, bass clarinet, 3 bassoons (3rd also contrabassoon), 4 horns, 3 trumpets, 2 trombones (2nd also bass trombone), bass trombone, tuba, timpani, percussion (marimba, glockenspiel, bass drum, slapstick, woodblock, temple blocks, 2 suspended cymbals, sizzle cymbal, vibraphone, 2 timbales, crash cymbals, tubular bells, tam-tam,), harp, piano (also celesta), violin I, violin II, viola, violoncello, double bass, tape.
Commissioned by: Norwegian Section of ISCM.
Call no.: **1986/111**

2632. Thorne, Francis, 1922– Cello concerto no. 2, 1995. Bryn Mawr, PA: T. Presser, 1996.
1 score (65 p.); 44 cm.
Duration: 23:00.
Composed for: violoncello, 2 flutes (2nd also piccolo), 2 oboes, 2 clarinets, 2 bassoons, 2 horns, 3 trumpets, 2 trombones, timpani, percussion (xylophone, vibraphone, 2 triangles (small, large), 2 woodblocks (small, large), 2 cowbells (small, large), snare drum, large suspended cymbal, tenor drum, glockenspiel, crash

cymbals, medium tam-tam, bass drum), harp, piano, violin I, violin II, viola, violoncello, double bass.
Commissioned by: American Composers Orchestra.
Call no.: **1997/151**

2633. Thorne, Francis, 1922– Clarinet concerto (1996–97). Bryn Mawr, PA: Merion Music: T. Presser, 1997.
1 score (67 p.); 44 cm.
Composed for: clarinet, 2 flutes, 2 oboes, 2 clarinets, 2 bassoons, 2 horns, 2 trumpets, timpani, percussion (xylophone, glockenspiel, snare drum, tambourine, large crash cymbals, suspended cymbals, medium tam-tam, medium, triangle, cowbell, woodblock), harp, violin I, violin II, viola, violoncello, double bass.
Commissioned by: Paul Underwood.
Call no.: **2001/156**

2634. Thorne, Francis, 1922– Concerto for orchestra (2000–2001). King of Prussia, PA: Merion Music: Theodore Presser Co., 2001.
1 score (69 p.); 44 cm.
Reproduced from manuscript.
Duration: ca. 23:00.
Composed for: 2 flutes, piccolo, 2 oboes, English horn, 2 clarinets, bass clarinet, 2 bassoons, contrabassoon, 4 horns, 3 trumpets, 2 trombones, bass trombone, tuba, timpani, percussion (glockenspiel, suspended cymbals (small, large), cowbells (small, large), snare drum, vibraphone, triangles (small, large), tenor drum, woodblocks (small, large), crash cymbals, tambourine, xylophone, large tam-tam, bass drum, castanets, chimes), piano, harp, violin I, violin II, viola, violoncello, double bass.
Call no.: **2005/142**

2635. Thorne, Francis, 1922– Mario and the magician: opera in a prologue and one act. Piano/vocal score. Bryn Mawr, PA: Merion Music: Theodore Presser, 1993.
1 vocal score (113 p.); 39 cm.
English words by J. D. McClatchy; after the story by Thomas Mann.
Reproduced from manuscript.
Duration: 1:05:00.
Composed for: 2 sopranos, mezzo-soprano, 3 tenors, baritone, bass-baritone, 2 basses, SATB chorus, flute (also piccolo), oboe, clarinet, bassoon, horn, trumpet, trombone, bass trombone, tuba, percussion, guitar (also electric guitar), piano (also harpsichord), violin I, violin II, viola, violoncello, double bass.
Call no.: **1995/104**

2636. Thorne, Francis, 1922– Piano concerto no. 3: in three movements (1989). Bryn Mawr, PA: Theodore Presser, 1989.
1 score (79 p.); 44 cm.
Reproduced from manuscript.
Duration: 23:30.
Composed for: piano, 2 flutes (2nd also piccolo), 2 oboes, 2 clarinets, 2 bassoons, 4 horns, 2 trumpets, 2 trombones, bass trombone, tuba, timpani, percussion (vibraphone, xylophone, whip, triangle, suspended cymbal, snare drum, 3 cowbells, 2 woodblocks, claves, glockenspiel, chimes, crash cymbals, bass drum, 2 bongos, tam-tam), harp, violin I, violin II, viola, violoncello, double bass.
Commissioned by: Albany Symphony Orchestra.
Call no.: **1991/134**

2637. Thorne, Francis, 1922– Symphony no. 5: in five movements. New York, NY: American Composer Alliance; Pennsauken, NJ: G. Schirmer/Associated Music Publishers, 1985.
1 score (82 p.); 53 cm.
"Revised 1985"—cover.
Lacks 4th movement (p. 54–59).
Duration: ca. 20:00.
Composed for: piccolo, 2 flutes, 2 oboes, English horn, 2 clarinets, bass clarinet, 2 bassoons, contrabassoon, 4 horns, 3 trumpets, 2 trombones, bass trombone, tuba, timpani, percussion (xylophone, glockenspiel, tubular bells, bass drum, tenor drum, snare drum, tam-tam, crash cymbals, 2 triangles, vibraphone, 2 cowbells, 2 woodblocks, 2 suspended cymbals, conga, castanets, tambourine, slapstick, 2 bongos, 5 temple blocks, claves), harp, piano, violin I, violin II, viola, violoncello, double bass.
Commissioned by: Albany Symphony Orchestra.
Call no.: **1986/112**

2638. Threatte, Charles, 1940– Voyage. N.p.: n.p., 1984.
1 score (66 p.); 44 cm.
For orchestra.
Reproduced from holograph.
At end of score: "Winter Park, Florida; Dec. 20 1983."
Composed for: 3 flutes (3rd also piccolo), 2 oboes, English horn, 2 clarinets, 2 bassoons, 4 horns, 4 trumpets, 2 trombones, bass trombone, tuba, timpani, percussion (chimes, suspended cymbal, glockenspiel, tam-tam, bass drum, snare drum), harp, violin I, violin II, viola, violoncello, double bass.
Call no.: **1985/188**

2639. Ticheli, Frank, 1958– An American dream: a symphony of songs: for soprano and orchestra. Full score. Pasadena, CA: F. Ticheli, 1998.

1 score (135 p.); 28 cm.
English words by Philip Littell; also printed as text.
Reproduced from manuscript.
Duration: 38:00.
Composed for: soprano, piccolo, 2 flutes (both also alto flute), 2 oboes, English horn, 2 clarinets (both also clarinet in A), bass clarinet, 2 bassoons, 4 horns, 3 trumpets, 2 trombones, bass trombone, tuba, timpani (also suspended cymbal, crotales), percussion (vibraphone, hi-hat, suspended cymbals, triangles [small, medium], large slapstick, 4 tom-toms, 2 bass drums [small, large], small rain stick, glockenspiel, crotales, suspended ride cymbal, tambourine, vibraslap, 2 woodblocks, large tam-tam, marimba, snare drum, medium Chinese cymbal, 2 pairs of maracas, ratchet), harp, piano, violin I, violin II, viola, violoncello, double bass.
Commissioned by: Pacific Symphony Orchestra.
Call no.: **2000/185**
Re-entered as: **2003/123**

2640. Ticheli, Frank, 1958– Radiant voices: a fantasy for orchestra. N.p.: n.p., 1993.
1 score (111 p.); 28 cm.
Reproduced from holograph.
At end: January 6, 1993, Pasadena.
Duration: 20:00.
Composed for: piccolo, 2 flutes, 2 oboes, English horn, 2 clarinets, 2 bassoons, contrabassoon, 4 horns, 3 trumpets, 3 trombones, tuba, timpani (also cymbals), percussion (vibraphone, suspended cymbals [small, medium], triangles [small, medium], temple blocks, 4 timbales, bass drum, cabasa, tambourine, glockenspiel, crotales, crash cymbal, ratchet, 2 woodblocks, 2 bongos, police whistle, xylophone, tam-tam, slapstick, snare drum, 4 tom-toms, vibraslap, flexatone), harp, violin I, violin II, viola, violoncello, double bass.
Commissioned by: Pacific Symphony Orchestra.
Call no.: **1994/149**

2641. Tiensuu, Jukka, 1948– Musica ambigua: for recorder or flute, violin, viola da gamba and harpsichord. N.p.: n.p., 1998.
1 score (27 p.); 30 cm.
Performance instructions in English.
Contents: Yksin?: for viola da gamba and optional harpsichord—Möbius: for alto recorder or (Baroque) flute and (Baroque) violin—Sleepwalk: for sopranino recorder, violin, viola da gamba and harpsichord—La fervente: for alto recorder or (Baroque) flute, (Baroque) violin, viola da gamba and harpsichord—Kitkat: for recorder, violin, viola da gamba and harpsichord—Veto: for recorder or flute, and/or violin, and/or viola da gamba, and/or harpsichord.
Composed for: flute (or recorder), violin, viola da gamba, harpsichord.
Commissioned by: Markku Luolajan-Mikkola and Warsaw Autumn Festival.
Call no.: **2003/124**

2642. Timofeyew, Adelina, 1915– Wind on the mesa. N.p.: n.p., 1985.
1 score (i, 40 leaves); 29 cm.
English words; also printed as text.
Reproduced from manuscript.
Composed for: soprano, 2 violins, violoncello, piano.
Call no.: **1986/113**

2643. Tippett, Michael, 1905–1998. Byzantium: for soprano and orchestra. London; New York, NY: Schott, 1991.
1 score (105 p.); 30 cm.
English words by W. B. Yeats; also printed as text.
Music of our time = Musik unserer Zeit.
Duration: 25:00.
Program note by the composer and performance instructions in English.
Composed for: soprano, 3 flutes (all also piccolo), 2 oboes, English horn, 3 clarinets (1st also clarinet in E♭, 3rd also bass clarinet), 2 bassoons, contrabassoon, 4 horns, 2 trumpets, 3 trombones, tuba, percussion (glockenspiel, vibraphone, bells, snare drum, tenor drum, bass drum, 2 woodblocks, crash cymbal, suspended cymbal, triangle, castanets, claves, 3 anvils, crotales, tuned gongs, roto-toms), 2 harps, electric organ, celesta, violin I, violin II, viola, violoncello, double bass.
Commissioned by: Chicago Symphony Orchestra and Carnegie Hall.
Call no.: **1992/138**

2644. Tippett, Michael, 1905–1998. The mask of time. London: Schott, 1984.
1 score (2 v.); 59 cm.
English words.
For soloists, chorus, and orchestra.
Reproduced from manuscript.
Includes performance notes in English.
Composed for: soprano, mezzo-soprano, tenor, baritone, SATB chorus, 3 flutes (all also piccolo), 2 oboes, English horn, 2 clarinets, bass clarinet, 2 bassoons, contrabassoon, soprano saxophone, alto saxophone, 6 horns, 3 trumpets, 3 trombones, tuba, timpani, percussion (xylophone, marimba, vibraphone, glockenspiel, tubular bells, claves, castanets, bamboo chimes, suspended cymbal, crash cymbals, triangle, thundersheet,

snare drum, tenor drum, 3 tom-toms, boobams, bass drum, 3 woodblocks, 2 anvils, tambourine, tam-tam, 2 gongs, 4 tuned gongs, 2 cymbals, maracas), harp, piano, electronic organ, violin I, violin II, viola, violoncello, double bass.
Commissioned by: Boston Symphony Orchestra.
Call no.: **1988/103**
Also available:
Call no.: **1988/103 vocal score**

2645. Tippett, Michael, 1905–1998. New Year. N.p.: n.p., 1988.
1 score (3 v.); 37 cm.
English words.
Opera in 3 acts.
Reproduced from manuscript.
Composed for: voices, 3 flutes (all also piccolo), 2 oboes, English horn, clarinet, bass clarinet, alto saxophone, tenor saxophone, baritone saxophone, bassoon, contrabassoon, 4 horns, 2 trumpets, 2 trombones, bass trombone, tuba, percussion (glockenspiel, xylophone, tubular bells, side drum, bass drum, 2 gongs, jazz kit [snare drum, tom-tom, bass drum, suspended cymbal, woodblock], tambourine, tenor drum, vibraphone, police whistle, hi-hat, 5 tom-toms, guiro, claves, 2 woodblocks, castanets, electric bell, crash cymbals, metal bar, maracas, 2 tam-tams, bells, brake drum, rattle, 2 suspended cymbals, 2 triangles, crash cymbals, whip, slit drum, 2 steel drums, 2 cowbells, 2 temple blocks, hi-hat, electric bell), harp, electric guitar, electric bass guitar, violin I, violin II, viola, violoncello, double bass.
Commissioned by: Houston Grand Opera, Glyndebourne, and BBC.
Call no.: **1991/135**

2646. Tippett, Michael, 1905–1998. The rose lake: a song without words for orchestra (1991–93). Study score. London; New York, NY: Schott, 1994.
1 score (84 p.); 31 cm.
Music of our time = Musik unserer Zeit.
Duration: ca. 25:00.
Composed for: 3 flutes (all also piccolo), 2 oboes, English horn, 2 clarinets, bass clarinet, 2 bassoons, contrabassoon, 6 horns, 3 trumpets, 3 trombones, tuba, percussion (snare drum, bass drum, 2 suspended cymbals, castanets, 2 tam-tams, xylophone, marimba, vibraphone, glockenspiel, roto-toms, tubular bells, large pitched gong), 2 harps, violin I, violin II, viola, violoncello, double bass.
Commissioned by: London Symphony Orchestra, Boston Symphony Orchestra, and Toronto Symphony Orchestra.
Call no.: **1997/152**

2647. Tjeknavorian, Loris, 1937– Othello: symphonic suite for orchestra, [op. 31]. N.p.: Loris Tjeknavorian, 1984.
1 miniature score (246 p.); 30 cm.
Reproduced from manuscript.
Composed for: piccolo, 2 flutes, 2 oboes, 2 clarinets, 2 bassoons, 4 horns, 4 trumpets, 3 trombones, tuba, timpani, percussion (suspended cymbals, tam-tam, bass drum, xylophone, glockenspiel, bongos, crotales, tambourine, Chinese wind chimes, finger cymbals, crash cymbals, wind machine, triangle, snare drum, 4 tom-toms, woodblock, tubular bells), harp, celesta, violin I, violin II, viola, violoncello, double bass.
Call no.: **1985/189**

2648. Toews, Theodore, 1929– Magnificat: scored for chorus, soloists and orchestra. N.p.: n.p., 1997.
1 score (63 p.); 36 cm.
Latin words.
Based on verses 46–55 of chapter 1 of the Gospel according to St. Luke and the Gloria Patri.
Composed for: flute, 2 oboes, clarinet, bassoon, 2 horns, 2 trumpets, violin I, violin II, viola, violoncello, double bass.
Commissioned by: Schola Cantorum.
Call no.: **2003/125**

2649. Toledo, Josefino, 1959– Kantus: Tagabawa: for orchestra, 1999. Quezon City, Philippines: J. Toldeo, 1999.
1 score (39 p.); 42 cm.
Reproduced from holograph.
Composed for: 2 flutes, 2 oboes, 2 clarinets, 2 bassoons, 4 horns, 2 trumpets, 2 trombones, bass trombone, percussion, violin I, violin II, viola, violoncello, double bass.
Commissioned by: 1999 Hong Kong Musicarama.
Call no.: **2003/126**

2650. Tomaro, Robert, 1951– Tribe: a ballet in one act for chamber orchestra. N.p.: n.p., 1987.
1 score (99 p.); 22 x 36 cm.
Composed for: flute, oboe, bassoon, horn, percussion (bass drum, bells, shaker, tom-toms, suspended cymbals, snare drum, glockenspiel, clapper, triangle, cabasa, rattles, woodblock, duck call, gong, bell tree), violin I, violin II, viola, violoncello, double bass.
Commissioned by: Imago Dance Co. of New York.
Call no.: **1987/087**

2651. Torke, Michael, 1961– Book of Proverbs: for chorus and orchestra, with solo soprano and solo baritone. N.p.: Adjustable Music, 1996.

1 score (166 p.); 33 cm.
English words; also printed as text.
Composed for: soprano, baritone, SATB chorus, 3 flutes, 2 oboes, English horn, 2 clarinets (all also clarinet in A, 3rd also bass clarinet), 2 bassoons, soprano saxophone, alto saxophone, tenor saxophone, baritone saxophone, 4 horns, 3 trumpets, 3 trombones, tuba, timpani, percussion (glockenspiel, xylophone, vibraphone, triangle, suspended cymbal, tam-tam, snare drum, tambourine, jingle bells, slapstick, bass drum, bongo), violin I, violin II, viola, violoncello, double bass.
Commissioned by: Netherlands Radio Philharmonic.
Call no.: **1997/153**
Re-entered as: **2000/186**

2652. Torke, Michael, 1961– Four seasons: for soprano, mezzo-soprano, tenor, and baritone soloists, adult and children's choirs, and orchestra. 4th ed. Full score. N.p.: Adjustable Music: Wonderland Music, 1999.
1 score (282 p.); 36 cm.
Words by Philip Littell.
Composed for: soprano, mezzo-soprano, tenor, baritone, SATB chorus, children's chorus, 4 flutes (3rd–4th also piccolo), 3 oboes, English horn, 2 clarinets, 2 bass clarinets (2nd also clarinet in E♭), soprano saxophone, 2 alto saxophones, 2 tenor saxophones, baritone saxophone, 3 bassoons, contrabassoon, 6 horns, 4 trumpets, 3 trombones, bass trombone, tuba, timpani, percussion (bass drum, 2 snare drums, 4 tom-toms, 2 bongos, 2 woodblocks, tam-tam, triangle, 4 temple blocks, suspended cymbal, 2 brake drums, tambourine, claves, sandpaper blocks, maracas, glockenspiel, xylophone, 2 vibraphones, 2 marimbas), harp, piano, violin I, violin II, viola, violoncello, double bass.
Commissioned by: Disney Company.
Call no.: **2002/181**

2653. Torke, Michael, 1961– Rapture: concerto for percussion and orchestra. 2nd ed., Jan. 21, 2001. N.p.: Adjustable Music, 2001.
1 score (169 p.); 36 cm.
Duration: 27:00.
Composed for: percussion, piccolo, 2 flutes, 2 oboes, English horn, 2 clarinets, bass clarinet, soprano saxophone, tenor saxophone, 3 bassoons, 6 horns, 2 trumpets, 2 trombones, bass trombone, tuba, timpani, harp, piano (also celesta), percussion (6 tom-toms, bass drum, triangle, glockenspiel, tubular bells, crotales, suspended cymbal), violin I, violin II, viola, violoncello, double bass.
Commissioned by: Royal Scottish National Orchestra.
Call no.: **2003/127**

2654. Torke, Michael, 1961– Strawberry fields: an opera in one act (1999). 3rd ed. Full score. N.p.: Adjustable Music, 1999.
1 score (168 p.); 28 cm.
English words by A. R. Gurney.
"3rd edition, June 1999"—caption.
Duration: 36:00.
Composed for: 2 sopranos, mezzo-soprano, contralto, 2 tenors, 3 baritones, SATB chorus, 2 flutes, oboe, English horn, 2 clarinets (all also clarinet in A, 2nd also bass clarinet), 2 bassoons, 4 horns, 2 trumpets, 2 trombones, bass trombone, timpani, percussion (glockenspiel, vibraphone, marimba, triangle, claves, tom-tom, suspended cymbal, tambourine), harp, piano (also celesta), violin I, violin II, viola, violoncello, double bass.
Commissioned by: Glimmerglass Opera, New York City Opera, and "Great Performances."
Call no.: **2001/157**
Also available:
Call no.: **2001/157 vocal score**

2655. Torke, Michael, 1961– Verdant music. N.p.: Hendon Music; New York, NY: Boosey & Hawkes, 1986.
1 score (74 p.); 34 cm.
For orchestra.
Reproduced from holograph.
Duration: 16:00.
Composed for: 3 flutes (3rd also piccolo), 2 oboes, English horn, 2 clarinets, bass clarinet, 2 bassoons, 4 horns, 3 trumpets, 3 trombones, tuba, timpani, percussion (xylophone, marimba, vibraphone, glockenspiel, crotales, triangle, 3 bongos, crash cymbals, suspended cymbal, tom-tom, slapstick), piano, violin I, violin II, viola, violoncello, double bass.
Commissioned by: Robert E. Gard Foundation.
Call no.: **1987/088**

2656. Tosar Errecart, Héctor Alberto, 1923– 5 piezas concertantes: para violin y orquesta. N.p.: n.p., 198-?.
1 score (61 p.); 32 cm.
Reproduced from manuscript.
Duration: ca. 23:00.
Contents: Scherzando—Ad libitum—Misterioso—Moto perpetuo—Elegiaco.
Composed for: violin, 3 flutes (3rd also piccolo), 2 oboes, English horn, 2 clarinets, bass clarinet, 3 bassoons (3rd also contrabassoon), 4 horns, 3 trumpets, 2 trombones, bass trombone, tuba, percussion (triangle, 2 suspended cymbals, crash cymbals, 2 woodblocks, castanets, maracas, guiro, 2 bongos, tambourine, tenor drum, bass drum, bombo, glockenspiel, vibraphone, timpani), harp, violin I, violin II, viola, violoncello, double bass.
Call no.: **1989/126**

2657. Toussaint, Eugenio, 1954– Días de los Muertos = Days of the Dead. N.p.: n.p., 1997.
1 score (2 v. in various pagings); 22 x 29 cm.
Ballet in 2 acts.
Composed for: flute (also piccolo), oboe, clarinet, bass clarinet, saxophone, bassoon, horn, 2 trumpets, trombone, tuba, percussion (crash cymbals, glockenspiel, piccolo snare drum, bass drum, bongos, hi-hat, woodblocks, xylophone, cabasa, 2 congas), harp, violin I, violin II, viola, violoncello, double bass.
Commissioned by: Ballet Arizona.
Call no.: **2001/158**

2658. Tower, Joan, 1938– Piano concerto, 1985. New York, NY: Associated Music Publishers, 1986.
1 score (77 p.); 28 cm.
Duration: 21:00.
Composed for: piano, 2 flutes (2nd also piccolo), oboe, 2 clarinets (2nd also bass clarinet), bassoon, 2 horns, trumpet, bass trombone, percussion (vibraphone, 3 cymbals, woodblock, 4 temple blocks, glockenspiel, xylophone, chimes, 3 tom-toms, 2 cymbals), violin I, violin II, viola, violoncello, double bass.
Commissioned by: National Endowment for the Arts.
Call no.: **1987/089**

2659. Tower, Joan, 1938– Silver ladders: for orchestra, 1986. New York, NY: Associated Music Publishers, 1986.
1 score (166 p.); 36 cm.
Reproduced from holograph.
Duration: ca. 21:00.
1990 Grawemeyer Award winning work.
Composed for: piccolo, 2 flutes, 2 oboes, English horn, 2 clarinets, bass clarinet, 2 bassoons, contrabassoon, 4 horns, 3 trumpets, 2 trombones, bass trombone, tuba, timpani, percussion (tam-tam, tom-tom, bass drum, xylophone, crotales, glockenspiel, woodblock, tenor drums, snare drum, triangle, 3 tuned tom-toms, vibraphone, 3 cymbals, 4 temple blocks, chimes, marimba), harp, piano (also celesta), violin I, violin II, viola, violoncello, double bass.
Commissioned by: Saint Louis Symphony Orchestra and Meet the Composer.
Call no.: **1988/104**
Re-entered as: **1989/127** and **1990/125**

2660. Trajković, Vlastimir, 1947– Concerto: for viola and orchestra, in G minor, op. 23. Belgrade: SAKOJ, 1993.
1 score (87 p.); 32 cm.
Reproduced from manuscript.
Composed for: viola, 2 flutes (1st also piccolo, 2nd also alto flute), 2 oboes (2nd also English horn), 2 clarinets (2nd also bass clarinet), 2 bassoons, contrabassoon, 2 horns, 2 trumpets, 2 trombones (2nd also bass trombone), tuba, percussion (timpani, 2 suspended cymbals, bass drum, tambourine, tenor drum, triangle, whip, woodblock, 2 pairs of crash cymbals, flexatone, snare drum, tam-tam), harp, piano (also celesta), violin I, violin II, viola, violoncello, double bass.
Commissioned by: BEMUS–Belgrade Music Festival.
Call no.: **2000/187**

2661. Traversi, Francesco, 1969– Adrift: a symphonic poem on water in seven zones and a planctus: for soprano and orchestra, 2003. N.p.: Francesco Traversi, 2003.
1 score (174 p.); 42 cm.
Italian words (last mvt.); also printed as text with English translation.
Contents: Zona #1. Bere quando si ha sete di fronte a un vulcano = To drink when thirsty before a volcano—Zona #2. Sudare freddo = To be in a cold sweat—Zona #3. Essere la pioggia (perenne) = To be the rain (unending)—Zona #4. Intuire il proprio navigare dentro l'utero materno = To sense your own floating in to mother's womb—Zona #5. Guardare le onde del mare, di notte = To watch the waves of the sea, at night—Zona #6. Annagare = To drown—Zona #7. Toccare il seme dell'amato = To touch the seed of the beloved—Planctus.
Composed for: soprano, 2 flutes, 2 oboes, 2 clarinets, 2 bassoons, 4 horns, 2 trumpets, 2 trombones, timpani, percussion (snare drum, bass drum, 3 tom-toms, cymbals, triangle), harp, violin I, violin II, viola, violoncello, double bass.
Call no.: **2005/143**

2662. Tremblay, Gilles, 1932– Avec: wampum symphonique: pour chœur mixte, solistes (soprano, basse, récitant), et grand orchestre. Montréal: Gilles Tremblay, 1992.
1 score (135 p.); 44 cm.
French words.
Reproduced from holograph.
Duration: 45:00.
Performance notes by the composer in French.
Composed for: soprano, bass, SATB chorus, 3 flutes (1st also piccolo), 3 oboes, 3 clarinets (1st also clarinet in E♭, 3rd also bass clarinet), 2 bassoons, 4 horns, 3 trumpets, 2 trombones, bass trombone, 2 tubas, percussion (vibraphone, xylophone, glockenspiel, wood chimes, snare drum, claves, tchien-tchiens, 2 congas, ratchet, 5 temple blocks, maracas, tubular bells, 3 gongs, 3 woodblocks, large cymbal, guiro, chocalho,

2 large gongs, 3 Turkish cymbals, 3 Chinese temple gongs, Chinese theater gong, Thai gong, 2 crotales, flexatone, 3 tam-tams, bass drum, 2 bongos, 2 cymbals), piano, violin I, violin II, viola, violoncello, double bass.
Commissioned by: Radio-Canada.
Call no.: **1994/150**

2663. Trigg, Ted, 1962– Four distractions. N.p.: n.p., 198-?.
28 leaves of manuscript music; 32 cm.
In ink.
Contents: This is how my life's been lately—Sitting in a dark room contemplating a single lit candle—Circus: minuet and trio "homage to Frederic Chopin"—Tocatta.
Composed for: piano.
Call no.: **1989/128**

2664. Trigos, Juan, 1965– Danza concertante no. 1: para piccolo y orquesta (1992). N.p.: n.p., 1992.
1 score (42 leaves); 44 cm.
Reproduced from manuscript.
Composed for: piccolo, trombone (also bass trombone), tuba, percussion (2 Indian drums, suspended cymbal, 2 cencerros, Latin timbales, huehuetl, log drum, very small temple block, large woodblock, large guiro, 3 congas), violin I, violin II, viola, violoncello, double bass.
Call no.: **1997/154**

2665. Trigos, Juan, 1965– DeCachetitoRaspado: opera de hemoficción para 4 cantantes y ensamble de cámara (1999), rev. 2000. N.p.: n.p., 2000.
1 score (210 p.); 44 cm.
Spanish words.
Reproduced from manuscript.
Composed for: voices, flute (also piccolo, bass flute), clarinet, baritone saxophone (also soprano and alto saxophones), trombone, percussion (triangle, cowbell, metal chimes, guiro, maracas, rattle, temple blocks, tambourine, 4 tom-toms, 2 congas, pedal bass drum, tam-tam, tubular chimes, marimba, 2 suspended cymbals, claves, Indian drum, 2 bongos, timbales, vibraphone), guitar, harp, piano.
Call no.: **2003/128**

2666. Trinkley, Bruce, 1945– Mountain laurels. N.p.: Bruce Trinkley, 1996.
1 score (18 v.); 22–36 cm.
English words.
"A choral symphony celebrating the Centennial of State College, Pennsylvania, with texts drawn from the works of Central Pennsylvania poets"—v. 1, p. 1.
Contents: Prologue—Seasons: for SSAA chorus, harp and strings—Mountain airs: for chamber choir unaccompanied—Journeys: for men's chorus, brass quintet and timpani—Mother Nature: seven songs for young voices and piano—Images and elegies: for mixed choir, piano and percussion—Frothiana: for barbershop chorus—The grooves of academe: four revolutionary folk songs for men's voices and piano—The descant of man: three evolutionary love songs for women's chorus and piano—Willow songs: an old college medley—Four toccatas: for SATB chorus and piano or chamber orchestra—Summer evenings: for voice(s) and chamber ensembles—Frothy encores: for barbershop chorus or quartet—The willow: for chorus and wind ensemble—Dandelions in march: for wind band—The campus: for chorus and wind ensemble—The willow (reprise): for chorus and wind ensemble—Keystones: five choral songs with orchestra.
Composed for: SATB chorus (and soloists), piano trio (violin, violoncello, piano), string quartet (2 violins, viola, violoncello), woodwind quintet (alto flute, English horn, bass clarinet, horn, contrabassoon), brass quintet (2 trumpets, horn, trombone, tuba), piano, harp, timpani, orchestra (2 flutes, 2 oboes, 2 clarinets, 2 bassoons, 4 horns, 6 trumpets, 3 trombones, tuba, timpani, percussion, harp, piano, violin I, violin II, viola, violoncello, double bass), wind ensemble (piccolo, 2 flutes, 2 oboes, 2 bassoons, 3 clarinets, bass clarinet, 2 alto saxophones, tenor saxophone, baritone saxophone, 4 trumpets, 4 horns, 3 trombones, 2 baritones, tuba, double bass, timpani, percussion).
Commissioned by: Borough of State College.
Call no.: **1997/155**

2667. Trinkley, Bruce, 1945– York: the voice of freedom: music drama in two acts. N.p.: Bruce Trinkley, 2002.
1 score (2 v.); 36 cm.
English words by J. Jason Charnesky.
Includes synopsis in English.
Composed for: mezzo-soprano, 3 baritones, SATB chorus, flute (also piccolo), oboe (also English horn), clarinet (also clarinet in A, bass clarinet), bassoon (also contrabassoon), 2 horns, trumpet, trombone, percussion (orchestra bells, chimes, xylophone, vibraphone, snare drum, side drum, tenor drum, tom-toms, bass drum, triangle, suspended cymbal, wind gong, tam-tam, rain stick, tambourine, woodblock, hi-hat, ratchet, 4 timpani), harp, violin I, violin II, viola, violoncello, double bass.
Call no.: **2004/138**

2668. Trojahn, Manfred, 1949– Was ihr wollt: Oper von Claus H. Henneberg nach William Shakespeares "Twelfth night." Partitur. Basel; New York, NY: Bärenreiter, 1998.
1 score (367 p.); 42 cm.
Reproduced from holograph.
Composed for: 3 sopranos, 4 tenors, 5 baritones, 2 basses, 3 flutes (3rd also piccolo), 2 oboes, English horn, 2 clarinets (both also clarinet in E♭), bass clarinet, 3 bassoons (3rd also contrabassoon), 4 horns, 3 trumpets, 3 trombones, bass trombone, timpani, percussion (snare drum, bass drum, tenor drum, cymbals, 2 tam-tams, wind machine, whip, ratchet, thundersheet), harp, violin I, violin II, viola, violoncello, double bass.
Commissioned by: Bayerische Staatsoper München.
Call no.: **2000/188**

2669. Tsontakis, George, 1951– The dove descending: (1995). Bryn Mawr, PA: Merion Music: Theodore Presser, 1995.
1 score (49 p.); 43 cm.
Reproduced from manuscript.
Duration: ca. 13:00.
Composed for: 3 flutes (3rd also piccolo), 2 oboes, English horn, 2 clarinets, bass clarinet, 2 bassoons, contrabassoon, 4 horns, 3 trumpets, 3 trombones, tuba, timpani, percussion (sandpaper block, vibraphone, 2 suspended cymbals, bass drum, large tam-tam, marimba), harp, piano, violin I, violin II, viola, violoncello, double bass.
Commissioned by: Pasadena Symphony.
Call no.: **1997/156**

2670. Tsontakis, George, 1951– Dust: trio for horn, violin, and piano. Bryn Mawr, PA: Merion Music., 2000.
1 score (60 p.); 28 cm.
Composed for: horn, violin, piano.
Commissioned by: Fontana Concert Society.
Call no.: **2001/159**

2671. Tsontakis, George, 1951– Eclipse: 1995. Bryn Mawr, PA: Merion Music: Theodore Presser, 1995.
1 score (47 p.); 28 x 39 cm.
Reproduced from manuscript.
Composed for: clarinet, violin, violoncello, piano.
Commissioned by: Music in the Mountains Festival.
Call no.: **1996/153**

2672. Tsontakis, George, 1951– Ghost variations: for piano. Bryn Mawr, PA: Merion Music: T. Presser, 1998.
64 p. of music; 31 cm.
Duration: ca. 31:00.
Includes program notes by Stephen Hough in English.
Composed for: piano.
Commissioned by: Fromm Foundation.
Call no.: **2000/189**

2673. Tsontakis, George, 1951– Meditations at perigee: [for] piano, clarinet, horn, violin, viola, cello, bass (1997). Bryn Mawr, PA: Merion Music, 1997.
1 score (46 p.); 34 cm.
Reproduced from manuscript.
Composed for: piano, clarinet, horn, violin, viola, violoncello, double bass.
Commissioned by: Da Camera of Houston, Reader's Digest, Meet the Composer, and five other groups (not specified by composer).
Call no.: **1998/162**

2674. Tsontakis, George, 1951– October (2001). N.p.: Merion Music; King of Prussia, PA: T. Presser, 2001.
1 score (88? p.); 44 cm.
For orchestra.
Composed for: 3 flutes (1st also alto flute, 3rd also piccolo), 2 oboes, English horn, 2 clarinets, bass clarinet, 2 bassoons, contrabassoon, 4 horns, 3 trumpets, 2 trombones, bass trombone, tuba, percussion (vibraphone, crotales, chimes, xylophone, Chinese cymbal, medium tom-tom, brake drum, tam-tam, sandpaper, snare drum, 2 bass drums, siren, 3 bell plates, splash cymbal, suspended cymbal, small woodblock), harp, piano (also celesta), violin I, violin II, viola, violoncello, double bass.
Commissioned by: Baltimore Symphony Orchestra.
Call no.: **2003/129**

2675. Tsontakis, George, 1951– Perpetual angelus: (1992). Bryn Mawr, PA: Theodore Presser, 1992.
1 miniature score (73 p.); 36 cm.
"Perpetual angelus was the first work composed in what will be an orchestral cycle of several parts, to bear the title Four quartets"—program note.
Title derived from the 3rd part of T. S. Eliot's poetical cycle, Four quartets.
Duration: 15:00.
Reproduced from manuscript.
Composed for: 2 flutes (2nd also piccolo), 2 oboes, 2 clarinets, 2 bassoons, 4 horns, 2 trumpets, trombone, timpani, percussion (vibraphone, marimba, tuned gong, gong, chimes, Trinidad steel drum, flexatone, cowbell, bass drum), harp, violin I, violin II, viola, violoncello, double bass.
Commissioned by: Tuscaloosa Symphony.
Call no.: **1994/151**

2676. Tsontakis, George, 1951– String quartet no. 4:

Beneath thy tenderness of heart (1988). N.p.: n.p., 1988.
1 score (55 p.); 28 cm.
Reproduced from holograph.
Contents: Introduction: chorale and meditations—Scherzo—Postlude: the Madonna weeps.
Composed for: 2 violins, viola, violoncello.
Commissioned by: Chamber Music America.
Call no.: **1990/126**

2677. Tsontakis, George, 1951– Violin concerto no. 1. King of Prussia, PA: Merion Music: Theodore Presser Co., 1998.
1 score (131 p.); 36 cm.
Composed for: violin, 3 flutes (3rd also piccolo), 2 oboes, English horn, 2 clarinets, bass clarinet, 2 bassoons, contrabassoon, 4 horns, 3 trumpets, 3 trombones, tuba, timpani, percussion, harp, piano, violin I, violin II, viola, violoncello, double bass.
Call no.: **2004/139**

2678. Tsontakis, George, 1951– Violin concerto no. 2. King of Prussia, PA: Merion Music: Theodore Presser Co., 2003.
1 score (92 p.); 28 cm.
For violin with chamber orchestra.
2005 Grawemeyer Award winning work.
Composed for: violin, flute (also piccolo), oboe, clarinet (also bass clarinet), bassoon, horn, trumpet, trombone, percussion, harp, piano (also celesta), violin I, violin II, viola, violoncello, double bass.
Call no.: **2005/144**

2679. Tsontakis, George, 1951– Winter lightning, (1993). Bryn Mawr, PA: Merion Music: Theodore Presser Co., 1993.
1 score (70 p.); 44 cm.
For orchestra.
Reproduced from manuscript.
Composed for: 2 flutes (also piccolo), 2 oboes, English horn, 2 clarinets, bass clarinet, 2 bassoons, contrabassoon, 4 horns, 3 trumpets, 3 trombones, tuba, timpani, percussion (chimes, medium tam-tam, large maracas, vibraphone, bass drum, marimba, cowbell, sandpaper, metal bar, roto-tom, crotales, suspended cymbal, wind machine, bow), harp, piano, violin I, violin II, viola, violoncello, double bass.
Commissioned by: Koussevitzky Foundation.
Call no.: **1995/105**

2680. Tucker, Dan, 1925– Many moons: an opera in two acts. N.p.: Dan Tucker, 1984.
1 score (223 leaves); 37 cm.
English words.
"Based on a story by James Thurber."
Reproduced from manuscript.
Composed for: voices, piccolo, 2 flutes, oboe, clarinet, bassoon, 2 horns, trumpet, trombone, bass trombone, tuba, percussion (bass drum, cymbals, suspended cymbal, snare drum, temple blocks, tambourine, triangle), violin I, violin II, viola, violoncello, double bass.
Call no.: **1985/191**

2681. Tull, Fisher, 1934–1994. Dialogues: for multiple percussion soloist and orchestra, 1988. N.p.: Boosey & Hawkes, 1988.
1 score (64 p.); 42 cm.
Duration: ca. 15:00.
Composed for: percussion (vibraphone, gongs, crotales, timpani, slapstick, hi-hat, whip, flexatone, trap set, temple blocks, cowbells), 2 flutes (2nd also piccolo), 2 oboes, 2 clarinets, 2 bassoons, 4 horns, 3 trumpets, 2 trombones, bass trombone, tuba, piano, violin I, violin II, viola, violoncello, double bass.
Commissioned by: Steve Houghton.
Call no.: **1990/127**

2682. Tull, Fisher, 1934–1994. Missa brevis: for mixed chorus & percussion. N.p.: n.p., 198-?.
1 score (28 p.); 28 cm.
Latin words.
Composed for: SATB chorus, percussion (2 sets of chimes, ratchet, woodblocks, tenor drum, tom-toms, snare drum, tambourine, maracas).
Call no.: **1988/105**
Re-entered as: **1989/129**

2683. Turnage, Mark-Anthony, 1960– Blood on the floor: for three jazz soloists and large ensemble (1993–96). London: Schott, 1996.
1 score (256 p.); 30 cm.
Music of our time = Musik unserer Zeit.
Duration: ca. 1:10:00.
Contents: Blood on the floor—Junior addict—Shout—Sweet and decay—Needles—Elegy for Andy—Cut up—Crackdown—Dispelling the fears.
Reproduced from manuscript.
Composed for: electric guitar, drum set (hi-hat, bass drum, low tom-tom, snare drum, piccolo snare drum, ride cymbal, crash cymbals, sizzle cymbal, mounted cowbell, metal bar, tambourine), soprano saxophone (also alto saxophone, bass clarinet), 2 flutes (both also alto flute, scaffolding), 2 oboes (both also English horn), 2 clarinets (1st also scaffolding, both also bass clarinet), 2 soprano saxophones (both also alto saxophone), 2 bassoons (both also contrabassoon),

2 horns, 2 trumpets, 2 trombones, euphonium, tuba, percussion (2 large bass drums, 2 bongos, tabla, bodhran, small splash cymbal, large piece of wood and hammer, 2 tambourines, mounted sleigh bell, large tam-tam, 4 low gongs, Japanese temple bells, tuned cowbells, log drum, marimba, vibraphone, glockenspiel, crotales, tubular bells, tuned bell plates, maracas, claves, large lion's roar, djembe, large saucepan), harp, piano (also celesta, electric piano), electric guitar, bass guitar (also fretless bass, double bass), violin I, violin II, viola, violoncello, double bass.
Commissioned by: Ensemble Modern, SBC, Kölner Philharmonie, and Konzerthaus Wien.
Call no.: **2000/190**

2684. Turnage, Mark-Anthony, 1960– Dark crossing: for chamber orchestra (2000). Study score. Mainz: Schott, 2002.
1 miniature score (77 p.); 30 cm.
Music of our time = Musik unserer Zeit.
Duration: ca. 20:00.
Composed for: 2 flutes (1st also piccolo, 2nd also alto flute), oboe (also English horn), clarinet (also bass clarinet), bass clarinet (also contrabass clarinet), bassoon (also contrabassoon), soprano saxophone (also alto saxophone), 2 horns, trumpet (also flugelhorn), trombone (also euphonium, bass trombone), percussion (timpani, large bass drum, woodblock, claves, large tambourine, marimba, vibraphone, crotales, 2 tuned gongs), piano (also celesta), harp, 3 violins, 2 violas, 2 violoncellos, 2 double basses.
Commissioned by: Europäischer Musikmonat and London Sinfonietta.
Call no.: **2003/130**

2685. Turnage, Mark-Anthony, 1960– The silver tassie: opera in four acts (1997–99). 1st ed. London: Schott, 1999.
1 score (2 v.); 30 cm.
English words by Amanda Holden based on the play by Sean O'Casey.
Synopsis in English.
Duration: ca. 2:00:00.
Composed for: voices, 3 flutes (2nd–3rd also piccolo, 3rd also alto flute), 3 oboes (3rd also English horn), 2 clarinets (2nd also bass clarinet, clarinet in A), bass clarinet (also clarinet), 3 bassoons (3rd also contrabassoon), soprano saxophone (also alto saxophone), 4 horns, 3 trumpets, 3 trombones (3rd also euphonium), tuba, percussion (timpani, snare drum, tenor drum, large bass drum, pedal bass drum, 2 tom-toms, suspended cymbals [small, large], splash cymbal, sizzle cymbal, woodblock, 4 temple blocks, tambourine, whip, triangle, large tam-tam, 7 tuned gongs, Japanese temple bell, 4 large cowbells, log drum, brake drum, marimba, vibraphone, crotales, tubular bells, large metal bar, castanets, lion's roar, harmonica), harp, piano (also celesta), upright piano, violin I, violin II, viola, violoncello, double bass.
Commissioned by: English National Opera and Dallas Opera.
Call no.: **2002/182**

2686. Turrin, Joseph, 1947– Hemispheres: for woodwinds, brass, harp, piano, celesta & percussion. Greensboro, NC: C. Alan Publications, 2002.
1 score (86 p.); 36 cm.
Notes by the composer in English.
Contents: Genesis—Earth canto—Rajas.
Composed for: piccolo, 3 flutes, 3 oboes, English horn, clarinet in E♭, 2 clarinets, bass clarinet, 3 bassoons, contrabassoon, 5 horns, 4 trumpets, 3 trombones, bass trombone, tuba, harp, piano (also celesta), timpani, percussion.
Commissioned by: New York Philharmonic.
Call no.: **2004/140**

2687. Tuserkani, Djahan, 1936– Fragen nach Tschernobyl: Tragiphonie nach einem Gedicht von Erich Fried. N.p.: n.p., 1994.
1 score (44 p.); 57 cm.
German words; also printed as text.
For mezzo-soprano, actors, tape, and chamber orchestra.
Reproduced from manuscript.
Commentary by the composer.
Composed for: mezzo-soprano, tape, 2 flutes (both also alto flute, piccolo), 2 oboes, 2 bassoons, 2 horns, 2 trumpets, trombone, percussion (2 bongos, thundersheet, triangles [small, large], large anvil, friction drums [small, large], whistles, Russian dolls [small, large], tenor drums, medium guiro, bin-sasara, tubular bells, 4 woodblocks, large bones, 2 cymbals, pedal bass drum, large guiro, 2 maracas, siren, shell chimes, xylophone, geophone, 2 slit drums, 2 tam-tams, thundersheet, 2 tom-toms), piano, guitar, violin I, violin II, viola, violoncello, double bass.
Commissioned by: 1. Frauenkammerorchester von Österreich.
Call no.: **1997/157**

2688. Tutino, Marco, 1954– La foresta incantata: per grande orchestra. Milano: Edizioni Suvini Zerboni, 1982.
1 score (69 p.); 43 cm.
Duration: ca. 15:00.

Composed for: 3 flutes (3rd also piccolo), 2 oboes, 4 clarinets (3rd also clarinet in E♭, 4th also bass clarinet), 2 bassoons, 4 horns, 3 trumpets, 3 trombones, tuba, timpani, bass drum, harp, piano, celesta, violin I, violin II, viola, violoncello, double bass.
Call no.: **1985/192**

2689. Ul'ïanich, Viktor, 1956– Christ is risen from the dead: sviatozvony for large symphony orchestra. N.p.: n.p., 1993.
1 score (168 p.); 39 cm.
Reproduced from manuscript.
Duration: 21:00.
Contents: Death—Resurrection.
Composed for: piccolo, 2 flutes, 2 oboes, English horn, 2 clarinets, bass clarinet, 3 bassoons, 4 horns, 3 trumpets, 3 trombones, tuba, percussion (orchestra bells, xylophone, vibraphone, marimba, triangle, 4 suspended cymbals, crotales, 2 tam-tams, 4 gongs, woodblocks, 7 tom-toms, temple blocks, bass drum, timpani, crash cymbals, chimes), 2 harps, piano, celesta, violin I, violin II, violin III, violin IV, violin V, violin VI, viola I, violin II, violoncello I, violoncello II, double bass I, double bass II.
Call no.: **1994/152**

2690. Ul'ïanich, Viktor, 1956– Play of the light: musical meditations for harp quartet in four movements. Moscow: Victor Ulianich, 1987.
1 score (77 p.); 40 cm.
Reproduced from manuscript.
Contents: Glimmering of stars—The wandering flames—The patches on the water—The moon aureole.
Composed for: 4 harps.
Call no.: **1991/136**

2691. Ung, Chinary, 1942– Inner voices: for full orchestra. New York, NY: C. F. Peters, 1986.
1 score (72 p.); 49 cm.
Duration: 19:00.
1989 Grawemeyer Award winning work.
Composed for: 3 flutes (3rd also piccolo), alto flute, 2 oboes, English horn, clarinet in E♭, 2 clarinets, bass clarinet, 2 bassoons, contrabassoon, 4 horns, 2 trumpets, 2 trombones, bass trombone, tuba, timpani, percussion (vibraphone, 3 cowbells, crotales, 4 mounted bongos, bass drum, claves, tambourine, log drum, suspended sleigh bells, suspended glass chimes, 2 timbales, 3 woodblocks, 2 congas, 4 suspended cymbals, Javanese gong, 5 temple blocks, tam-tam, marimba, 4 tom-toms, bell tree, gong, 2 crotales, glockenspiel, suspended sizzle cymbal, tubular bells, crash cymbal), 2 harps, piano, celesta, violin I, violin II, viola, violoncello, double bass.
Commissioned by: Philadelphia Orchestra.
Call no.: **1989/130**

2692. Urbaitis, Mindaugas, 1952– Bachvariationen: keturiem smuikams arba smuikui ir magnetofono juostai = for four violins or for violin and pre-recorded tape, 1985–1988. N.p.: n.p., 1988.
1 score (40 leaves); 30 cm.
Reproduced from manuscript.
Composed for: 4 violins (or violin and prerecorded tape).
Call no.: **1990/128**

2693. Urbanner, Erich, 1936– Concerto xiii: für Saxophonquartett und 9 Spieler (1989/90). Partitur. Wien: Edition Contemp-Art, 1990.
1 score (61 p.) + 13 parts; 30 cm.
Duration: ca. 18:00.
Composed for: soprano saxophone, alto saxophone, tenor saxophone, baritone saxophone, harp, piano (also celesta), violin, viola, violoncello, double bass, percussion (hi-hat, snare drum, pedal drum, 2 tom-toms, suspended cymbals, 2 cowbells, triangle, conga, 2 bongos, glockenspiel, 2 woodblocks, tam-tam, marimba, castanets, chimes, tambourine).
Call no.: **1991/137**

2694. Urbanner, Erich, 1936– Multiphonie: für grosses Orchester (1998/99). Partitur. Wien: Doblinger, 1999.
1 score (92 p.); 42 cm.
Reproduced from manuscript.
Duration: ca. 20:00.
Composed for: 3 flutes (3rd also piccolo), 2 oboes, English horn, 3 clarinets (3rd also bass clarinet), 3 bassoons (3rd also contrabassoon), 4 horns, 3 trumpets, 3 trombones, bass tuba, percussion (vibraphone, marimba, snare drum, bass drum, tambourine, cymbals, timpani), harp, violin I, violin II, viola, violoncello, double bass.
Call no.: **2001/160**

2695. Uzor, Charles, 1961– Notre vie: for voices and large ensemble, on a poem by Paul Éluard: written 1997–98. N.p.: n.p., 1998.
1 score (67 leaves); 42 cm.
French words; also printed as text.
Reproduced from manuscript.
Duration: ca. 20:00.
Composer's note and performance instructions in English.
Composed for: 2 sopranos, 2 altos, tenor, bass-baritone, trombone, percussion (marimba, vibraphone, glockenspiel, crotales, 7 gongs, 2 tam-tams, triangle, wood-

block, maracas, tenor drum, bass drum, 3 timpani), piano, 2 harps, 3 violins, 2 violas, 2 violoncellos, 2 double basses.
Call no.: **2003/131**

2696. Vacchi, Fabio, 1949– Concerto per pianoforte e orchestra. Partitura. Milano: Ricordi, 1983.
1 score (75 p.); 49 cm.
Reproduced from holograph.
Composed for: piano, 2 flutes (2nd also piccolo), 2 oboes, clarinet, bass clarinet, bassoon, contrabassoon, 2 horns, 2 trumpets, percussion (vibraphone, bass drum, 2 bongos, tubular bells, 5 suspended cymbals, tam-tam, timpani, xylorimba, triangle, glockenspiel), violin I, violin II, viola, violoncello, double bass.
Call no.: **1985/194**

2697. Vacchi, Fabio, 1949– Prima dell'alba: per orchestra. Partitura. Milano: G. Ricordi, 1992.
1 score (86 p.); 51 cm.
Reproduced from manuscript.
Duration: ca. 25:00.
Composed for: 2 flutes (2nd also piccolo), 2 oboes (2nd also English horn), 2 clarinets in A (2nd also clarinet in E♭), bass clarinet, 2 bassoons (2nd also contrabassoon), 2 horns, 2 trumpets, trombone, percussion (timpani, chimes, glockenspiel, thundersheet, xylorimba, finger cymbals, vibraphone, large tam-tam, bass drum, crotales, 5 suspended cymbals, 2 tam-tams, 4 tom-toms), harp, celesta, violin I, violin II, viola, violoncello, double bass.
Commissioned by: Rai-Radiotelevisione italiana.
Call no.: **1994/153**

2698. Vacchi, Fabio, 1949– La station thermale: dramma giocoso in tre atti. Milano: Ricordi, 1993.
1 score (406 p.); 42 cm.
French words by Myriam Tanant.
Based on Bagni d'Abano by Carlo Goldoni.
Reproduced from holograph.
Composed for: 5 sopranos, mezzo-soprano, contralto, 5 baritones, bass-baritone, bass flute (also alto flute, piccolo), oboe (also English horn), clarinet in A (also clarinet in E♭, bass clarinet), bassoon (also contrabassoon), horn, percussion (xylorimba, vibraphone, 5 suspended cymbals, timpani, glockenspiel, tubular bells, bass drum, military drum, cymbals, 3 tam-tams, hi-hat, triangle, 2 bongos, temple blocks, whip), harp, piano (also celesta), violin I, violin II, viola, violoncello, double bass, offstage ensemble (clarinet in E♭, 2 trumpets, trombone, harpsichord).
Call no.: **1997/158**

2699. Vacchi, Fabio, 1949– Il viaggio. Partitura. Milano: G. Ricordi, 1989.
1 score (221 p.); 50 cm.
Italian words by Tonino Guerra.
Opera.
Composed for: mezzo-soprano, tenor, 2 baritones, SATB chorus, 2 flutes (2nd also piccolo), 2 oboes, 2 clarinets in A (2nd also clarinet in E♭), bass clarinet, 2 bassoons (2nd also contrabassoon), 2 horns, 2 trumpets, trombone, percussion (timpani, xylorimba, vibraphone, 5 suspended cymbals, 3 tam-tams, bass drum, tubular bells, tuned gongs, glockenspiel, large bell, 3 tom-toms, bongos, military drum, crotales, triangle, crash cymbals, thundersheet, 2 Chinese gongs, ice bells), harp, piano (also celesta), violin I, violin II, viola, violoncello, double bass.
Call no.: **1991/138**

2700. Vajda, János, 1949– Mario and the magician: opera in 1 act. N.p.: n.p., between 1985 and 1991.
1 miniature score (209 p.); 29 cm.
Hungarian words by Gábor Bókkon after Thomas Mann's short story.
Reproduced from manuscript.
Composed for: voices, SATB chorus, 2 flutes (2nd also piccolo), 2 oboes, 2 clarinets, 2 bassoons, 4 horns, 2 trumpets, 3 trombones, tuba, timpani, percussion (snare drum, suspended cymbal, bass drum, crash cymbals, tam-tam, tambourine, 5 tom-toms, claves, whip, vibraphone, marimba, temple blocks, triangle, drums), harp, celesta, piano, violin I, violin II, viola, violoncello, double bass.
Call no.: **1992/139**

2701. Valdambrini, Francesco, 1933– Sonanza infinita: ritrovato tricordale per pianoforte, in un unico risuono di 50 minuti. N.p.: n.p., between 1990 and 1992.
82 p. of music; 29 x 35 cm.
Composed for: piano.
Call no.: **1993/142**

2702. Valverde, Gabriel, 1957– Overstrung. N.p.: n.p., 1985.
1 score (11, 20 leaves); 23 x 32 cm.
Reproduced from manuscript.
Duration: ca. 14:40.
Performance instructions in Spanish.
Composed for: flute, trombone, violin, violoncello, synthesizer, percussion (vibraphone, xylophone, timpani, 2 tom-toms, 3 suspended cymbals, tam-tam, crotales, 3 woodblocks, 3 temple blocks, sleigh bells, metal chimes, tubular bells).
Call no.: **1989/131**

2703. Van Appledorn, Mary Jeanne, 1927– Les hommes vidés: un penny pour le vieux guy: SATB. Bryn Mawr, PA: Hildegard Pub. Co., 1997.
1 score (26 p.); 28 cm.
French words, translated from T. S. Eliot's The hollow men by Pierre Leyris; English translation printed as text.
Includes piano accompaniment for rehearsal only.
Preface in English.
Composed for: SATB chorus.
Call no.: **1998/163**

2704. Van Appledorn, Mary Jeanne, 1927– A Liszt fantasie: for piano (1984). N.p.: n.p., 1984.
10 leaves of music; 39 cm.
Reproduced from manuscript.
Includes tune index.
Composed for: piano.
Call no.: **1986/114**

2705. Van Appledorn, Mary Jeanne, 1927– Rhapsody: for violin and orchestra. N.p.: n.p., 1996.
1 score (37 p.); 44 cm.
Reproduced from manuscript.
Composed for: violin, piccolo, flute, 2 oboes, 2 clarinets, bassoon, contrabassoon, 2 horns, trumpet, trombone, timpani, percussion (suspended cymbal, vibraphone, castanets, tambourine, roto-toms, bell tree, snare drum, triangle, crash cymbal, tenor drum, marimba, tam-tam), harp, violin I, violin II, viola, violoncello, double bass.
Call no.: **2002/183**

2706. Van Appledorn, Mary Jeanne, 1927– Terrestrial music: a double concerto for solo violin, solo piano and string orchestra. N.p.: n.p., 199-?.
1 score (45 p.); 28 x 43 cm.
Reproduced from holograph.
Includes program notes.
Composed for: violin, piano, violin I, violin II, viola, violoncello, double bass.
Commissioned by: Kazuko Inoue.
Call no.: **1993/143**

2707. Van de Vate, Nancy, 1930– All quiet on the western front: 1999. Vienna: Vienna Masterworks, 1999.
1 score (293 p.); 30 cm.
English words by the composer, based on the novel by Erich Maria Remarque.
Opera in 3 acts.
Composed for: 2 sopranos, contralto, 3 tenors, 4 baritones, bass-baritone, 2 flutes (also piccolo), 2 oboes (also English horn), 2 clarinets (also bass clarinet), 2 horns, 2 trumpets, trombone, bass trombone, percussion (timpani, side drum, tenor drum, bass drum, 4 tom-toms, tambourine, crash cymbal, suspended cymbals (medium, large), large tam-tam, low bell, 5 temple blocks, 3 woodblocks, vibraslap, flexatone, whip, cabasa, glockenspiel, xylophone, chimes), harp, piano, violin I, violin II, viola, violoncello, double bass.
Call no.: **2005/145**

2708. Van de Vate, Nancy, 1930– Concerto for viola and orchestra, 1990. Vienna: Vienna Masterworks (BMI), 1990.
1 score (37 p.); 42 cm.
Duration: 16:00.
Composed for: viola, piccolo, 3 flutes, 3 oboes, English horn, 3 clarinets, bass clarinet, 3 bassoons, contrabassoon, 4 horns, 3 trumpets, 3 trombones, tuba, timpani, percussion (glockenspiel, xylophone, snare drum, bass drum, tam-tam, marimba, chimes, temple blocks, whip, crash cymbals, vibraphone, tenor drum, suspended cymbals (medium, large), tambourine, 5 tom-toms), harp, piano, celesta, violin I, violin II, viola, violoncello, double bass.
Call no.: **1995/107**

2709. Van de Vate, Nancy, 1930– Distant worlds: for violin and orchestra, 1985. New York, NY: American Composers Alliance, 1985.
1 score (46 p.); 43 cm.
Reproduced from manuscript.
Duration: 16:00.
Composed for: violin, piccolo, 2 flutes, 2 oboes, 2 clarinets, 2 bassoons, 4 horns, 3 trumpets, 3 trombones, tuba, timpani, percussion (vibraphone, marimba, xylophone, chimes, glockenspiel, 2 suspended cymbals, tam-tam, 5 tom-toms, snare drum, bass drum, tenor drum, temple blocks, 3 woodblocks, castanets, maracas), harp, piano, celesta, violin I, violin II, viola, violoncello, double bass.
Call no.: **1988/106**
Re-entered as: **1989/132**

2710. Van de Vate, Nancy, 1930– Journeys: 1984. New York, NY: American Composers Alliance, 1984.
1 score (47 p.); 45 cm.
For orchestra.
Reproduced from holograph.
Duration: 15:00.
Composed for: piccolo, 2 flutes, 2 oboes, 2 clarinets, 2 bassoons, 4 horns, 3 trumpets, 3 trombones, tuba, timpani, percussion (chimes, xylophone, glockenspiel, temple blocks, 3 woodblocks, 2 suspended cymbals, bass drum, snare drum, 2 triangles, cabasa, vibraphone,

6 tom-toms, tam-tam, tambourine), harp, piano, celesta, violin I, violin II, viola, violoncello, double bass.
Call no.: **1986/116**

2711. Van de Vate, Nancy, 1930– Katyń. N.p.: Nancy Van de Vate, 1989.
1 score (44 p.); 30 cm.
Latin or Polish words.
For mixed chorus and orchestra.
Composed for: SATB chorus, piccolo, 2 flutes, 2 oboes, English horn, 3 clarinets, 3 bassoons, 4 horns, 3 trumpets, 3 trombones, tuba, timpani, percussion (tam-tam, tenor drum, bass drum, 2 suspended cymbals, whip, flexatone, vibraphone, triangle, xylophone, bongos, congas, marimba, chimes, 5 tom-toms, snare drum, woodblock, glockenspiel, bell), harp, piano, violin I, violin II, viola, violoncello, double bass.
Call no.: **1993/144**

2712. Van de Vate, Nancy, 1930– Katyn: for orchestra and chorus. Vienna, Austria: Vienna Masterworks, 1989.
1 score (44 p.); 38 cm.
Latin or Polish words.
Composed for: SATB chorus, piccolo, 2 flutes, 2 oboes, English horn, 3 clarinets, 3 bassoons, 4 horns, 3 trumpets, 3 trombones, tuba, timpani, percussion (tam-tam, tenor drum, bass drum, 2 suspended cymbals, whip, flexatone, vibraphone, triangle, xylophone, bongos, congas, marimba, chimes, 5 tom-toms, snare drum, woodblock, glockenspiel, bell), harp, piano, violin I, violin II, viola, violoncello, double bass.
Call no.: **1990/129**

2713. Vanaver, Bill, 1943– P'nai el = The face of God: a tone poem on Jacob's struggle with the angel: for orchestra and Balkan style alto. Orchestral score. Rosendale, NY: Vanaver Caravan, 1996.
1 score (109 p.); 33 cm.
Hebrew words; English translation printed as text.
Text from Genesis 32.
Composed for: alto, piccolo, 2 flutes, oboe, English horn, 2 clarinets, bass clarinet, bassoon, contrabassoon, 4 horns, 3 trumpets, 2 trombones (also conch, shofar), bass trombone, tuba, timpani, percussion (xylophone, glockenspiel, 2 triangles, suspended cymbal, crash cymbals, gong, sizzle cymbal, tambourine, snare drum, field drum, bass drum), harp, violin I, violin II, viola, violoncello, double bass.
Call no.: **1997/159**

2714. Várkonyi, Mátyás, 1950– Rock odüsszeia. N.p.: n.p., 1984.
1 score (75 p.); 30 cm.
Hungarian words.
"Odyssey now"—cover.
Composed for: high voice, SATB chorus, saxophone, 3 electric keyboards, guitar, electric bass, drums, percussion.
Call no.: **1995/108**

2715. Varotsis, Constantinos, 1963– Schillern: Kammermusik für 15 Instrumentalisten = Iridescence (Iridismoi): chamber music for 15 instrumentalists. N.p.: n.p., 198-?.
1 score (43 leaves); 30 cm.
Reproduced from manuscript.
Composed for: flute (also piccolo, alto flute), oboe (also English horn), clarinet (also bass clarinet), bassoon (also contrabassoon), trumpet, horn, trombone, percussion (timpani, vibraphone, marimba, small cymbals, 7 tuned gongs, chimes, guiro, ratchet, vibraslap, glass and bamboo wind chimes, 2 tablas, 4 temple blocks, triangle, low tam-tam, cymbals, bass drum), piano (also harpsichord), violin, viola, violoncello, double bass.
Call no.: **1989/133**

2716. Vasks, Pēteris, 1946– 2. Symphonie für grosses Orchester (1998/99). Partitur. Mainz; New York, NY: Schott, 1999.
1 score (107 p.); 42 cm.
Composed for: 3 flutes (1st also alto flute, 3rd also piccolo), 3 oboes (3rd also English horn), 3 clarinets (3rd also bass clarinet), 3 bassoons (3rd also contrabassoon), 4 horns, 3 trumpets, 3 trombones, tuba, timpani, percussion (triangle, dinner bell, claves, 2 woodblocks, ratchet, 5 temple blocks, whip, military drum, suspended cymbal, crash cymbals, 4 bongos, 4 tom-toms, bass drum, tam-tam, handbell, xylophone, marimba, flexatone, vibraphone, tubular bells), harp, piano (also celesta), violin I, violin II, viola, violoncello, double bass.
Commissioned by: Bournemouth Orchestras and BBC.
Call no.: **2001/161**

2717. Vasks, Pēteris, 1946– Concerto: per violoncello ed orchestra (1993/94). Partitur. Mainz; New York, NY: Schott, 1994.
1 score (134 p.); 42 cm.
Reproduced from holograph.
Duration: ca. 34:00.
Composed for: violoncello, piccolo, 2 flutes (2nd also alto flute), 2 oboes, 2 clarinets, 2 bassoons, 4 horns, 3 trumpets, 3 trombones, tuba, timpani, percussion (suspended cymbals, crash cymbals, tam-tam, 4 bongos, 4

tom-toms, snare drum, bass drum, tambourine, claves, 2 woodblocks, temple blocks, maracas, guiro, ratchet, flexatone, tubular bells, glockenspiel, xylophone, vibraphone, marimba), harp, piano, celesta, violin I, violin II, viola, violoncello, double bass.
Commissioned by: Sender Freies Berlin.
Call no.: **1996/155**

2718. Vasks, Pēteris, 1946– Koncerts vijolei un stīgu orķestrim: "Tālā gaisma" = Konzert für Violine und Streichorchester: "Fernes Licht," 1997. Partitur. Mainz: Schott, 1997.
1 score (56 p.); 37 cm.
Reproduced from holograph.
Duration: ca. 23:00.
Composed for: violin, violin I, violin II, viola, violoncello, double bass.
Commissioned by: Salzburger Festspiele.
Call no.: **1998/165**

2719. Vaughn, Jonathan Roderick, 1965– Wings. N.p.: n.p., 1991.
1 score (64 p.); 28 cm.
For instrumental ensemble.
Composed for: piccolo, flute, oboe, violin, violoncello, piano.
Commissioned by: H.R.H. Prince Bandar, Saudi Arabian Ambassador to the United States.
Call no.: **1992/140**

2720. Vayo, David, 1957– Music for violin. N.p.: n.p., 1997.
10 p. of music; 36 cm.
Composed for: violin.
Call no.: **2004/142**

2721. Vera, Santiago, 1950– Apocaliptika III: "Love is the beginning and the end": work for orchestra, piano, organ and mixed choir (Oviedo, Spain, 1990–1991). Santiago, Chile: SVR Producciones, 2002.
1 score (43 p.); 44 cm.
Latin words; also printed as text with English translation.
Text: Hymn to Saint John the Baptist by Paolo Diacono.
Composed for: SATB chorus, piccolo, 3 flutes, 3 oboes, English horn, 3 clarinets, bass clarinet, 3 bassoons, contrabassoon, 6 horns, 4 trumpets, 4 trombones, tuba, percussion (tubular bells, timpani, triangle, cymbals, tam-tam, maracas, snare drum, bass drum), organ, piano, violin I, violin II, viola, violoncello, double bass.
Call no.: **2004/143**

2722. Vera, Santiago, 1950– Silogistika II: para contralto, clarinete si♭, violin, violoncello y piano. Santiago, Chile: SVR-Producciones, 1992.
1 score (44 p.); 28 cm.
Language undetermined.
Duration: 10:03.
Composed for: alto, clarinet, violin, violoncello, piano.
Call no.: **1994/154**

2723. Verhaalen, Marion, 1930– On children: three songs. N.p.: S. Marion Verhaalen, 1994.
1 score (21 p.); 22 x 28 cm.
English words.
Song cycle for soprano and piano, string quartet, string bass, flute, and bassoon.
Contents: On children / Kahlil Gibran—On the seashore of endless worlds / Rabindranath Tagore—Children's laughter / Iris M. Amend.
Composed for: soprano, flute, bassoon, piano, 2 violins, viola, violoncello, double bass.
Call no.: **1997/160**

2724. Vermeersch, Hans, 1957– Kacheri: concerto for bass clarinet and orchestra. N.p.: n.p., 1994.
1 score (106 leaves); 22 x 30 cm.
Reproduced from manuscript.
Composed for: bass clarinet, bamboo flute, tarshehnai (Indian bowed instrument), karnatic violin, violin I, violin II, viola, violoncello, double bass, keyboard, Indian tanpura, Indian percussion (ghatam, mridangam, khanjani).
Call no.: **1996/156**

2725. Veteška, Lubomír, 1934– Rebel: musical. N.p.: n.p., 1992.
1 vocal score (231 p.); 30 cm.
Czech words by Eva Pospšilová with some English translations.
Reproduced from manuscript.
Composed for: flute (also piccolo), horn, 2 trumpets, trombone, synthesizer, guitar, bass guitar, timpani, percussion (glockenspiel, tubular bells, triangle), violin I, violin II, viola, violoncello.
Call no.: **1997/161**
Also available:
Call no.: **1997/161 libretto**

2726. Viana, Hélio Bacelar, 1954– Urubu-rei: for 14 performers. N.p.: n.p., 1996.
1 score (62 p.); 30 cm.
Composed for: piccolo, flute, alto flute, oboe, clarinet, bassoon, percussion (agogo bells, tom-tom, suspended cymbal, crash cymbals, crotales, ratchet, snare drum, timpani), piano, 2 violins, viola, violoncello, double bass.
Call no.: **2000/009**

2727. Viera, Julio Martín, 1943– Divertimento III: for one percussion player and tape (1992). Buenos Aires: Ricordi Americana, 1992.
1 score (32 p.); 22 x 35 cm.
Reproduced from manuscript.
Duration: ca. 11:30.
Composed for: percussion (bongos, congas, snare drum, 2 low tom-toms, 2 high log drums, 2 low crash cymbals, hi-hat, 3 Latin cowbells, 3 cowbells, bell tree, spring coil, gong, tam-tam), tape.
Commissioned by: Fromm Foundation at Harvard University.
Call no.: **1997/162**

2728. Vieru, Anatol, 1926–1998. Simfonia VI: (1988–1989). N.p.: n.p., 199-?.
1 score (177 p.); 30 cm.
Reproduced from manuscript.
Contents: Tangochaconna—Exodus—San Antoia de la Florida—Pale sun.
Composed for: 3 flutes, 2 oboes, English horn, 2 clarinets, 2 bassoons, contrabassoon, 4 horns, 3 trumpets, 3 trombones, tuba, percussion (snare drum, glockenspiel, bass drum, cymbals, tambourine, 3 Chinese woodblocks, vibraphone, 3 tom-toms, suspended cymbal, high simantra, maracas, tam-tam, marimba, tubular bells, gong, low woodblock, timpani, triangle, guiro, 3 ratchets, wind machine, 4 bongos, anvil, low simantra, bird whistle), accordion, violin I, violin II, viola, violoncello, double bass.
Call no.: **1998/166**

2729. Viñao, Alejandro, 1951– Algebra (on) fire. N.p.: Alejandro Viñao, 1991.
1 score (158 p.); 42 cm.
For orchestra.
Duration: ca. 22:00.
Composed for: flute (also alto flute), oboe, 2 clarinets (2nd also bass clarinet), 2 horns, trumpet, trombone, percussion (marimba, glockenspiel, timpani, rototom), piano, computer, violin I, violin II, viola, violoncello, double bass.
Commissioned by: Ircam.
Call no.: **1994/155**

2730. Viñao, Alejandro, 1951– Epitafios: for choir and computer, 1999. N.p.: Alejandro Viñao, 1999.
1 score (81 p.); 30 cm.
Spanish words; also printed as text with English translation.
Texts by the composer, Santa Teresa de Avila, Francisco de Quevedo, and Antonio Machado.
Duration: 26:30.
Contents: Epitafio para Teresa—Epitafio para Quevedo—Epitafio para Borges—Epitafio para Machado.
Composed for: SATB chorus, computer.
Commissioned by: Ircam and New London Chamber Choir.
Call no.: **2001/162**

2731. Viñao, Alejandro, 1951– Marimba concerto (1993). Partitura. London: Crew Studio, 1993.
1 score (iii, 169 p.); 30 cm.
For 5-octave marimba and chamber orchestra.
Duration: ca. 19:00.
Composed for: marimba, flute (also alto flute), oboe (also English horn), 2 clarinets (1st also clarinet in E♭, 2nd also bass clarinet), 2 horns, trumpet, trombone, timpani, piano, violin I, violin II, viola, violoncello, double bass.
Commissioned by: Antwerpen Festival 1993 and Arts Council of Great Britain.
Call no.: **1996/157**

2732. Viñao, Alejandro, 1951– Phrase & fiction: for string quartet and computer (1995). London: Crew Studios, 1995.
1 score (92 p.); 30 cm.
Duration: 19:00.
Composed for: 2 violins, viola, violoncello, computer.
Commissioned by: Swedish Radio, Malmö.
Call no.: **1998/168**

2733. Viñao, Alejandro, 1951– Trilogy for soprano & computer. London: Crew Studios, 1992.
1 score (3 v.); 22 cm.
Italian, French, or Spanish words (pt. 1); Latin words (pt. 2); and Turkish words (pt. 3).
Duration: 41:30.
Performance instructions in English by the composer.
Contents: Chant d'ailleurs—Hildegard's dream—Borges y el espejo.
Commissioned by: État français (part 1), Group de Recherche musicales and Frances Lynch (part 2), and Groupe de musique experimentale de Bourges (part 3).
Call no.: **1995/109**

2734. Viñao, Ezequiel, 1960– 6 études: piano solo. New York, NY: TLON, 1993.
58 p. of music; 28 cm.
Contents: In polyrhythms—In repeated notes—In trills—In octaves—In endurance—In finger independence.
Composed for: piano.
Call no.: **1996/158**

2735. Viñao, Ezequiel, 1960– Arcanum: for voice & chamber ensemble (1996). New York, NY: TLØN Editions, 1996.

1 score (v, 106 p.); 29 cm.
Latin, Greek, or German words.
Texts from the Old and the New Testaments of the Bible and by Virgil, Parmenides, Plotinus, Scotus Erigena, Plutarch, Augustine, and Angelus Silesius.
Duration: ca. 1:10:00.
Commentary on the text in English.
Composed for: voice, oboe (also English horn), trombone, percussion (gong, tam-tam, tabla, bass drum, bells, 2 sets of timpani, 4 roto-toms, triangle, antique cymbal, crash cymbals, suspended cymbal), violin I, violin II, viola, violoncello, double bass.
Call no.: **1998/169**

2736. Viñao, Ezequiel, 1960– Saga: for violin, piano and chamber ensemble (2002). New York, NY: TLØN Editions, 2002.
1 score (235 p.); 28 cm.
Duration: ca. 1:02:00.
Composed for: violin, piano, flute (also piccolo, oboe (also English horn), 2 clarinets (also clarinet in E♭, bass clarinet), bassoon, 2 horns, 2 trumpets (also piccolo trumpet), trombone, percussion (triangles, 2 crotales, tambourine, 10 roto-toms, timbales, 4 tom-toms, snare drum, bass drum, 3 pitched gongs, large tam tam, tubular bells, glockenspiel, vibraphone, xylophone, marimba, crash cymbals, 3 suspended cymbals), 2 violas, violoncello, double bass with extension.
Commissioned by: Absolute Ensemble.
Call no.: **2005/146**

2737. Viñao, Ezequiel, 1960– Viviane of Avalon: for soprano and orchestra (1988). Full score. New York, NY: TLØN Editions, 1998.
1 score (94 p.); 44 cm.
Consists of excerpts from the 1st scene of Merlin, an opera in three acts.
Words by Caleb Carr; also printed as text.
Duration: ca. 26:00.
Composed for: soprano, piccolo, 2 flutes, alto flute, 3 oboes, English horn, clarinet in E♭, 2 clarinets, bass clarinet, 3 bassoons, contrabassoon, 8 horns, piccolo trumpet, 3 trumpets, bass trumpet, 3 trombones, bass trombone, contrabass tuba, timpani, percussion (bells, large gong, bass drum, large tam-tam, 2 triangles, glockenspiel, snare drum, castanets, marimba, 3 suspended cymbals, vibraphone, crotales, triangle, crash cymbals, xylophone), 4 harps, celesta, violin I, violin II, viola, violoncello, double bass.
Call no.: **2001/163**

2738. Vine, Carl, 1954– Piano concerto. London: Faber Music, 1997.
1 score (103 p.); 37 cm.
"First draft."
Duration: ca. 24:00.
Composed for: piano, piccolo, flute (also piccolo), 2 oboes (2nd also English horn), 2 clarinets (2nd also bass clarinet), bassoon, contrabassoon, 4 horns, 2 trumpets, 2 trombones, tuba, timpani, percussion (tam-tam, glockenspiel, 2 bongos, crash cymbals, bass drum, 2 low tom-toms, xylophone), harp, violin I, violin II, viola, violoncello, double bass.
Commissioned by: Sydney Symphony Orchestra.
Call no.: **1998/167**

2739. Vine, Carl, 1954– Symphony no. 3. London: Chester Music, 1990.
1 score (86 p.); 43 cm.
Duration: ca. 25:00.
Composed for: piccolo, 3 flutes (1st–2nd also alto flute), 3 oboes, English horn, 3 clarinets, bass clarinet, 3 bassoons, contrabassoon, 6 horns, 4 trumpets, 3 trombones, bass trombone, tuba, timpani, percussion (vibraphone, tubular bells, 2 tom-toms, crash cymbals, maracas, bass drum, bell tree, glockenspiel, tam-tam), 2 harps, celesta, violin I, violin II, viola, violoncello, double bass.
Commissioned by: Elder Conservatorium of Music at University of Adelaide.
Call no.: **1992/141**

2740. Violette, Andrew, 1953– Piano sonata 7. N.p.: n.p., 2001.
92 leaves of music; 30 cm.
Reproduced from manuscript.
Composed for: piano.
Call no.: **2005/147**

2741. Vir, Param, 1952– Ion: opera in four scenes with prologue. London: Novello, 2003.
1 score (2 v. [609 p.]); 30 cm.
English words by David Lan, after Euripides.
"Perusal score."
Duration: ca. 2:15:00.
Synopsis in English.
Composed for: 4 sopranos, 3 mezzo-sopranos, contralto, tenor, 3 baritones, bass, flute (also piccolo, alto flute, bass flute, swanee whistle), oboe (also English horn), 2 clarinets (also clarinet in E♭, bass clarinet, contrabass clarinet), bassoon (also whip, ratchet, rain stick), 2 horns, 2 trumpets (also piccolo trumpet in B♭, finger cymbals, large axatse), percussion (timpani, 4 hand drums, side drum, 2 boobams, bass drum, pedal bass drum, large roto-tom, xylophone, Chinese woodblock, maracas, 5 temple blocks, whip, woodblocks, vibraslap, crotales with bow, glockenspiel, tubular bells, large

steel spring, mark tree, cabasa, suspended cymbal, triangle, hi-hat cymbal, tam-tam), harp (also 2 xylophone bars), piano (also bass drum, cabasa, tam-tam), violin I, violin II, viola, violoncello, double bass.
Commissioned by: Almeida Opera, Music Theatre Wales, Opera National du Rhin, and Berlin Festival.
Call no.: **2005/148**

2742. Vir, Param, 1952– Snatched by the gods: a chamber opera. London: Novello, 1991.
1 score (252 p.); 30 cm.
Words by William Radice, based on a poem by Rabindranath Tagore.
Duration: ca. 50:00.
Reproduced from manuscript.
Composed for: soprano, mezzo-soprano, 2 contraltos, tenor, 2 baritones, 2 basses, flute (also piccolo, alto flute), oboe (also English horn), clarinet (also clarinet in E♭), bassoon, 2 horns, trumpet (also tubular bell), bass trombone, percussion (4 tom-toms, tuned roto-toms, bass drum, claves, whip, 2 woodblocks, 5 temple blocks, 2 ratchets, xylophone, crotales, tubular bells, 2 suspended cymbals, tam-tam, finger cymbals, side drum, 4 roto-toms, timpani, castanets, vibraphone, tubular bells, 4 gongs, cowbell, hi-hat, anvil, cabasa, 2 Chinese cymbals), harp, violin I, violin II, viola, violoncello, double bass.
Commissioned by: Landeshauptstadt München.
Call no.: **1993/146**

2743. Visser, Dick, 1926– Array: for solo guitar and guitar ensembles. N.p.: n.p., 1994.
1 score (93 p.); 30 cm.
"Min. 5 (quintet) up to 13 guitars (max.)"
Reproduced from manuscript.
Composed for: guitar, 5–13 guitars.
Call no.: **1996/159**

2744. Vogt, Hans, 1911–1992. Sinfonie in einem Satz: "Dona nobis pacem": 1984. Partitur. Berlin: Bote & Bock, 1986.
1 score (43 p.); 31 cm.
Duration: 15:00–16:00.
Reproduced from holograph.
Composed for: 3 flutes (2nd–3rd also piccolo, alto and bass flutes), 2 oboes, English horn, 2 clarinets (1st also clarinet in A), bass clarinet, alto saxophone, 2 bassoons, contrabassoon, 3 horns, 3 trumpets, 3 trombones, tuba, timpani, percussion (xylophone, marimba, glockenspiel, chimes, suspended cymbals, snare drum, bass drum, 4 tom-toms, 4 pairs of bongos, 4 temple blocks, tambourine, triangle, tam-tam), harp, piano (also celesta), violin I, violin II, viola, violoncello, double bass.
Call no.: **1987/090**

2745. Volans, Kevin, 1949– Cello concerto (1997, revised 1998). London: Chester Music, 1998.
1 score (76 p.); 30 cm.
"Perusal score."
Duration: ca. 22:00.
Composed for: violoncello, 2 flutes (1st also piccolo), 2 oboes (2nd also English horn), 2 clarinets (1st also clarinet in E♭), 2 bassoons (2nd also contrabassoon), 4 horns, 2 trumpets, 2 trombones, harp, violin I, violin II, viola, violoncello, double bass.
Commissioned by: Musica Viva.
Call no.: **2000/191**

2746. Volans, Kevin, 1949– Concerto for piano and wind instruments. London: Chester Music, 1996.
1 score (94 p.); 30 cm.
Composed for: piano, 3 flutes (1st–2nd also piccolo), 3 oboes, 3 clarinets (1st also clarinet in E♭), 2 bassoons, contrabassoon, 4 horns, 2 trumpets, 3 trombones, tuba, percussion (xylophone, tubular bells, vibraphone, marimba), 3 double basses.
Commissioned by: BBC.
Call no.: **1998/170**

2747. Vores, Andy, 1956– Actaeon: for solo cello, two horns and strings. N.p.: n.p., 1997.
1 score (54 p.); 28 cm.
Contents: The chase—The sacred grove—Metamorphosis—The hunt—The death of Actaeon.
Composed for: violoncello, 2 horns, 10 violins, 4 violas, 4 violoncellos, 2 double basses.
Commissioned by: Metamorphosen.
Call no.: **1998/171**

2748. Vores, Andy, 1956– Sh'ma: for tenor solo, chorus, obligato piano, and orchestra. N.p.: A. Vores, 1995.
1 score (134 p.); 28 cm.
Principally English with some Hebrew words (final chorus); also printed as text.
Text from poems by Dunash Ben Labrat, Primo Levi, Yizhak Katzenelson, Uri Zvi Greenberg, and Lena Allen-Shore.
"In memory of those whose lives were consumed in the Holocaust and dedicated to those who survived."
Composed for: tenor, SATB chorus, piano, 2 flutes (1st also piccolo), 2 clarinets, tuba, timpani (also gong), piano, electric keyboard, violin I, violin II, viola, violoncello, double bass.
Commissioned by: Brookline Chorus.
Call no.: **1997/163**

2749. Voronina, Tat'i͡ana, 1933– Russian suite: mini-ballet. N.p.: n.p., 2000.
1 score (20 p.) + 1 part (8 p.); 30 cm.
Composed for: violin, piano.
Call no.: **2002/184**

2750. Vriend, Jan, 1938– Hymn to Ra: for mixed choir, soprano and baritone solo, symphony orchestra, 2002. Nederland, Amsterdam: Donemus: Muziekgroep Nederland, 2003.
1 score (94 p.); 42 cm.
Egyptian, German, English, or Sanskrit words; also printed as text with English translations.
Text fragments from: Akhenaten's great hymn to the Aten, Also sprach Zarathustra by Friedrich Nietzsche, Guide to the sun by Kenneth Phillips, and The gayatri.
Duration: ca. 30:00.
Composed for: soprano, baritone, SATB chorus, piccolo, 2 flutes (also alto flute), 2 oboes, English horn, 2 clarinets (also clarinet in A), bass clarinet, 2 bassoons, contrabassoon, 4 horns, 2 trumpets, 2 trombones, bass trombone, percussion (xylophone, crotales, 3 suspended cymbals, crash cymbal, tam-tam, bronze chimes, 4 congas, bass drum, timpani), keyboard, violin I, violin II, viola, violoncello, double bass.
Commissioned by: Dutch Broadcasting Organisation KRO and Music Sacra.
Call no.: **2005/149**

2751. Vriend, Jan, 1938– In paradisum: for ensemble, 1999–2000. Amsterdam: Donemus, 2001.
1 score (96 p.); 36 cm.
Duration: ca. 22:00.
Introduction by the composer in English.
Composed for: flute (also piccolo, alto flute), oboe (also English horn), clarinet, 2 horns, trumpet, trombone, bassoon, contrabassoon, contrabass clarinet, double bass, percussion (tam-tam, bell plate, tubular bells, field drum, snare drum, log drum, bass drum, crotales, 3 temple blocks, 4 congas, sleigh bells, 2 woodblocks, triangle, whip, gongs, 6 tom-toms, 5 suspended cymbals, guiro), piano, harp, violin I, violin II, 2 violas, 2 violoncellos.
Commissioned by: Asko Ensemble.
Call no.: **2003/132**

2752. Vriend, Jan, 1938– Jets d'orgue: for organ, 1991. Amsterdam: Donemus, 1991.
3 v. of music; 26–37 cm.
Reproduced from manuscript.
Duration: ca. 45:00.
Composed for: organ.
Commissioned by: Amserdams Fonds voor de Kunst (number I only).
Call no.: **2000/192**

2753. Wagner, Heribert, 1952– Gaia: a story for jazzgroup and symphonic orchestra, 1990. Amsterdam: Donemus, 1992.
1 score (108 p.); 30 x 42 cm.
Duration: 35:00.
Composed for: jazz group (violin, vibraphone, double bass, drum set), 3 flutes (2nd also piccolo), 2 oboes 2 clarinets, 2 bassoons, 4 horns, 3 trumpets, 3 trombones, tuba, percussion (glockenspiel, timpani, steel drum, suspended cymbal, tam-tam, 3 tom-toms, snare drum, bass drum, triangle, cabasa, harp, tambourine, xylophone), violin I, violin II, viola, violoncello, double bass.
Call no.: **1995/111**

2754. Wagner, Melinda, 1957– Concerto for flute, strings and percussion. Bryn Mawr, PA: Theodore Presser, 1998.
1 score (136 p.); 36 cm.
"Corrected 7/11 1998"—p. 1.
Reproduced from holograph.
Composed for: flute, percussion (glockenspiel, crotales, xylophone, small triangle, finger cymbal, castanets, vibraphone, chimes, tam-tam, high bongo, 5 tom-toms, temple blocks, small suspended cymbal, sizzle cymbal, marimba, tambourine, bell tree, bass drum, snare drum), timpani, piano (also celesta), violin I, violin II, viola, violoncello, double bass.
Commissioned by: Westchester Philharmonic.
Call no.: **2000/193**

2755. Wagner, Melinda, 1957– Falling angels: poem for orchestra. Bryn Mawr, PA: T. Presser, 1992.
1 score (75 p.); 44 cm.
Reproduced from holograph.
Composed for: piccolo, 2 flutes, 2 oboes, English horn, 2 clarinets, bass clarinet, 2 bassoons, contrabassoon, 4 horns, 3 trumpets, 3 trombones, tuba, timpani, percussion (crotales, glockenspiel, xylophone, vibraphone, marimba, chimes, triangle, bell tree, sizzle cymbal, crash cymbals, 3 suspended cymbals, tam-tam, tambourine, sleigh bells, 3 temple blocks, 2 woodblocks, 2 bamboo chimes, vibraslap, slapstick, slide whistle, snare drum, 2 bongos, 4 tom-toms, bass drum), harp, piano, celesta, violin I, violin II, viola, violoncello, double bass.
Commissioned by: Ernst and Young Emerging Composers Fund.
Call no.: **1994/156**

2756. Wagner, Melinda, 1957– Wick. Bryn Mawr, PA: Theodore Presser, 2000.
1 score (56 p.); 43 cm.
For small orchestra.
Composed for: flute (also piccolo, alto flute), clarinet (also bass clarinet), violin, violoncello, piano, percussion (vibraphone, marimba, glockenspiel, crotales, chimes, 2 gongs, deep tam-tam, suspended cymbal, finger cymbal, wind chimes, jingle bells, agogo bells, metal Africa clave, cowbell, brake drum, woodblock, small triangle, bongos).
Commissioned by: New York New Music Ensemble.
Call no.: **2002/185**

2757. Wagner, Wolfram, 1962– Hiob: Oratorium für Sopran, Tenor, Bariton Sprecher, gemischten Chor, Orchester und Orgel. N.p.: n.p., 1989.
1 score (90 p.); 30 cm.
German or Latin words from the New Testament and by Werner Kraft and Karl Wolfskehl.
Reproduced from manuscript.
Composed for: soprano, tenor, baritone, SATB chorus, organ, 2 flutes (2nd also piccolo), 2 oboes, 2 clarinets, 2 bassoons, 2 horns, 2 trumpets, 2 trombones, bass trombone, percussion (timpani, small drum, bass drum, 3 tom-toms, suspended cymbals, hi-hat, tambourine, jingle bells, claves, xylophone, tam-tam, tubular bells ad lib.), violin I, violin II, viola, violoncello, double bass.
Call no.: **1995/110**

2758. Wagner, Wolfram, 1962– Secundum scripturas: für gemischten Chor a cappella, 1995. Wien: Doblinger, 1996.
1 score (39 p.); 28 cm.
German words by Herbert Vogg; also printed as text.
Duration: ca. 12:00.
Composed for: SATB chorus.
Call no.: **1998/172**

2759. Wagner, Wolfram, 1962– Wenn der Teufel tanzt . . . : komische Oper von Ernst A. Ekker. Partitur. Wien: Doblinger, 1996.
1 score (3 v. [385 p.]); 35 cm.
German words.
Reproduced from manuscript.
Commentary by the composer.
Composed for: narrator, soprano, mezzo-soprano, alto, 2 tenors, 2 baritones, bass-baritone, SATB chorus, flute (also piccolo), oboe, clarinet (also clarinet in E♭), bassoon, horn, trumpet, trombone, percussion (triangle, tubular bells, snare drum, bass drum, tambourine, tam-tams, claves, bongos, glockenspiel), harpsichord, violin I, violin II, viola, violoncello, double bass.
Call no.: **1997/164**

2760. Waignein, André, 1942– Cantate aux etoiles. N.p.: n.p., 1990.
1 score (185 p.); 42 cm.
French words by Monique Cardon.
For mixed choir, children's choir, soprano and tenor solo, reciter, and orchestra.
Reproduced from manuscript.
Composed for: narrator, soprano, tenor, SATB chorus, children's chorus, piccolo, 2 flutes, 2 oboes, English horn, 2 clarinets, bass clarinet, 2 bassoons, contrabassoon, 4 horns, 3 trumpets, 3 trombones, tuba, timpani, percussion (bass drum, xylophone, snare drum, gong, bells, glockenspiel, vibraphone, bongos, whip, chimes, tom-toms, tambourine, metal rods, cymbals, temple blocks, suspended cymbal, tam-tam, triangle, woodblock), piano, violin I, violin II, viola, violoncello, double bass.
Call no.: **1992/143**

2761. Waignein, André, 1942– Mir vu bausse gekuckt: (impressions luxembourgeoises). N.p.: n.p., 1999.
1 score (109 p.); 42 cm.
For band.
Reproduced from manuscript.
Contents: Clervaux—Wiltz—Diekirch—Vianden—Capellen—Mersch—Redange—Echternach—Grevenmacher—Remich—Esch sur Alzelte—Luxembourg.
Composed for: flute (also piccolo), oboe, English horn, bassoon, clarinet in E♭, 3 clarinets, alto clarinet, bass clarinet, 2 alto saxophones, tenor saxophone, baritone saxophone, 3 trumpets, 3 horns, 3 trombones, baritone, 2 tubas, timpani, percussion (chimes, snare drum, bass drum, xylophone, tam-tam, temple blocks, vibraphone, bell tree, tambourine, congas, triangle, bells).
Call no.: **2002/186**

2762. Walden, Stanley, 1932– Invisible cities: variations for wind orchestra, harps, percussion & keyboards: 1986. Bryn Mawr, PA: T. Presser, 1987.
1 score (86 p.); 58 cm.
Duration: 22:00–23:00.
Composed for: 4 flutes (3rd–4th also piccolo, 4th also alto flute), 4 oboes (2nd also heckelphone, 4th also English horn), 4 clarinets (1st–2nd also clarinet in A, 3rd also clarinet in E♭ and contrabass clarinet, 4th also bass clarinet), 4 bassoons (4th also contrabassoon), 6 horns, 4 trumpets (1st also piccolo trumpet), 3 trombones, bass trombone, tuba, timpani, 2 harps, piano (also celesta, harpsichord), percussion (xylophone, crotales, timpani, temple blocks, 2

triangles, 2 timbales, snare drum, tam-tam, mounted tambourine, finger cymbals, 3 suspended cymbals, marimba, suspended spring coil, tubular bells, 3 Chinese gongs, Chinese opera gong, 2 congas, vibraslap, mounted bongos, glockenspiel, claves, 4 roto-toms, bass drum, 2 mounted Moroccan clay drums, hi-hat, crash cymbals, cowbell, guiro, maracas, vibraphone, 2 tom-toms, field drum, agogo bells, 3 cup gongs, sizzle cymbal, 2 tambourines).
Commissioned by: Philadelphia Orchestra.
Call no.: **1989/134**

2763. Walker, George, 1922– Canvas: wind ensemble, voices, and chorus (2000 rev. 2001). Saint Louis, MO: MMB Music, 2001.
1 score (89 p.); 36 cm.
English words by the composer and from Psalm 121; also printed as text (mvt. 2 only).
Contents: Extract I: Landscape—Extract II: Commentary—Extract III: Psalm.
Composed for: voices, SATB chorus, piccolo, 3 flutes, alto flute, 2 oboes, English horn, clarinet in E♭, 2 clarinets, bass clarinet, alto saxophone, 2 bassoons, contrabassoon, 4 horns, 4 trumpets, 2 trombones, bass trombone, tuba, timpani, celesta, harp, double bass, percussion (glockenspiel, xylophone, vibraphone, marimba, chimes, triangle, woodblocks, temple blocks, claves, maracas, castanets, tambourine, suspended cymbal, anvil, timbales, snare drum, bass drum, roto-toms, tam-tam, glass wind chimes).
Commissioned by: College Band Directors National Association.
Call no.: **2003/133**

2764. Walker, George, 1922– Pageant and proclamation. Saint Louis, MO: MMB Music, 1997.
1 score (40 p.); 44 cm.
Composed for: piccolo, 2 flutes, 2 oboes, English horn, 2 clarinets, bass clarinet, 2 bassoons, contrabassoon, 4 horns, 4 trumpets, 2 trombones, bass trombone, tuba, timpani, percussion (xylophone, vibraphone, chimes, triangle, snare drum, 4 tom-toms, bass drum, suspended cymbal, gong, claves, tambourine, temple block, glockenspiel, marimba, woodblock, glass chimes), harp, piano (also celesta), violin I, violin II, viola, violoncello, double bass.
Commissioned by: AT&T Foundation.
Call no.: **1998/173**

2765. Walker, George, 1922– Poem for soprano and chamber ensemble.
Call no.: **1989/135**
No materials available.

2766. Walker, George, 1922– Poème: violin and orchestra (1991). Rev. 6/91. Score. Saint Louis, MO: MMB Music, 1991.
1 score (84 p.); 36 cm.
Composed for: violin, piccolo, flute, 2 oboes, clarinet, bass clarinet, bassoon, contrabassoon, 2 horns, trumpet, trombone, tuba, timpani, percussion (xylophone, vibraphone, triangle, chimes, snare drum, tambourine, maracas, claves, glockenspiel, suspended cymbals), harp, piano, violin I, violin II, viola, violoncello, double bass.
Call no.: **1996/160**

2767. Wallace, Stewart, 1960– Gorilla in a cage: concerto for percussion and orchestra. New York, NY: Sidmar Music, 1998.
1 score (83 p.); 44 cm.
Composed for: percussion (bell cymbal, splash cymbal, Chinese splash cymbal, handmade cymbal, handmade cymbal with sizzles, large suspended crash cymbal, 9 temple blocks, 4 timbales, agogo bells, medium cowbell, snare drum, 5 tom-toms, kick drum, frogmouth cowbells, batonka, marimba, OM chimes, bass chimes), 2 flutes (2nd also piccolo), 2 oboes (2nd also English horn), 2 clarinets, bass clarinet, 2 bassoons (2nd also contrabassoon), 4 horns, 2 trumpets, trombone, bass trombone, timpani, percussion (tam-tam, xylophone, chimes, glockenspiel, dulcimer), piano, violin I, violin II, viola, violoncello, double bass.
Commissioned by: Bochum Symphony.
Call no.: **2001/164**

2768. Wallace, Stewart, 1960– Harvey Milk. N.p.: Sid-Mar Music, 1995.
1 score (3 v.); 36 cm.
Words by Michael Korie.
Opera.
Contents: The closet: act one—The castro: act two—City hall: act three.
Composed for: soprano, girl soprano, male soprano, mezzo-soprano, 2 tenors, boy tenor, 2 baritones, bass, SATB chorus, 2 flutes (both also piccolo), 2 oboes (2nd also English horn), 3 clarinets (2nd also clarinet in E♭, 3rd also bass clarinet), 2 bassoons (2nd also contrabassoon), 4 horns, 3 trumpets, 3 trombones, 2 tubas, timpani, percussion (cimbalom, chimes, glockenspiel, marimba, tam-tam, bass drum, crash cymbals, triangle, vibraphone, woodblock, snare drum, suspended cymbal, hi-hat, siren, xylophone, low tom-tom, anvil, police whistle, agogo bells, temple blocks, timbales, samba whistle, cowbell, 4 tom-toms), keyboard, violin I, violin II, viola, violoncello, double bass.
Commissioned by: Houston Grand Opera, New York

City Opera, and San Francisco Opera.
Call no.: **1997/165**

2769. Wallace, William, 1933– Concerto no. 2: for piano and orchestra. N.p.: William Wallace, 1998.
1 score (130 p.); 43 cm.
Composed for: piano, 2 flutes (also piccolo), 2 oboes, 2 clarinets, 2 bassoons, 4 horns, 2 trumpets, timpani, percussion (snare drum, suspended cymbal, xylophone), violin I, violin II, viola, violoncello, double bass.
Call no.: **2002/187**

2770. Wallach, Joelle, 1950– In memory the heart still sings: a rhapsody: for basset (or A) clarinet and chamber orchestra. Dec. 1998 ed. Boston, MA: Highgate Press, 2002.
1 score (15 p.); 36 cm.
Duration: 10:30.
Composed for: clarinet in A, 2 flutes (1st also piccolo), 2 bassoons, horn, percussion (timpani, glockenspiel, finger cymbals, suspended cymbals), violin I, violin II, viola, violoncello, double bass.
Call no.: **2004/144**

2771. Wallach, Joelle, 1950– La musica, los muertos y las estrellas: (1988). N.p.: n.p., 1988.
1 score (13 p.); 28 cm.
Spanish words by Juan Ramón Jiménez; also printed as text with English translation.
Contents: Por doquiera que mi alma—Esta desilusión—Esta música que tocan.
Composed for: SATB chorus (or SATB vocal quartet).
Call no.: **1992/144**

2772. Wallach, Joelle, 1950– String quartet, 1995. N.p.: J. Wallach, 1995.
1 score (17 p.); 28 cm.
Composed for: 2 violins, viola, violoncello.
Call no.: **1997/166**
Re-entered as: **2002/188**

2773. Wallach, Joelle, 1950– Three Spanish songs. N.p.: Joelle Wallach, 1985.
1 score (23 p.); 28 cm.
Spanish words; also printed as texts with English translation.
Texts from Federico Garcia-Lorca (1st song), Graciela Perez Trevisan (2nd song), and Antonio Machado (3rd song).
Contents: Gemido de la guitarra—Soñando sueños de tango—Los ojos.
Composed for: voice, piano.
Call no.: **1990/130**

2774. Wallmann, Johannes, 1952– Glocken Requiem Dresden. N.p.: n.p., 1995.
1 score (4 v.); 30 cm.
Seven-part work composed of 47 individual pieces for peals of bells of Dresden churches.
Dedication, texts, and performance notes, in German and English, precede music in each volume.
Reproduced from holograph.
Composed for: church bells of Dresden.
Call no.: **1996/161**

2775. Wallmann, Johannes, 1952– Innenklang: Musik im Raum für vier Orchestergruppen und Soprane. Berlin: Johannes Wallmann, 1997.
1 score (4 v., [232 p.]); 42 cm.
Texts consist of vowel sounds.
Reproduced from holograph.
Contents: Sinfonia: Zusammenklang—Pastorale: aus Leabenden sein—Phonas/aria: Gegensatz Energie—Resonanz: in Klang, in Stille.
Composed for: 5 sopranos; orchestra I: 2 flutes, clarinet, bass clarinet, bassoon, 6 trumpets, percussion (bass drum, 2 congas, temple blocks, ratchet, 4 large tam-tams, marimba, xylorimba, tubular bells), violin I, violin II, viola, violoncello, double bass; orchestra II: 2 oboes (2nd also English horn), clarinet, bassoon (also contrabassoon), 4 horns, percussion (bass drum, 3 tam-tams, 3 gongs, 2 bongos, temple blocks, vibraphone), violin I, violin II, viola, violoncello, double bass; orchestra III: 2 flutes, clarinet (also bass clarinet), bassoon, 6 trombones, tuba, percussion (bass drum, 2 congas, temple blocks, 3 tam-tams), celesta, violin I, violin II, viola, violoncello, double bass; orchestra IV: 2 oboes (2nd also English horn), clarinet, bassoon (also contrabassoon), 4 horns, percussion (bass drum, 2 bongos, temple blocks, 3 tam-tams, 3 gongs, vibraphone), violin I, violin II, viola, violoncello, double bass.
Call no.: **2000/194**

2776. Wang, Peng Jia, 1961– C major: tone poem for piano. N.p.: n.p., 2000.
14 p. of music; 39 cm.
Reproduced from manuscript.
Composed for: piano.
Call no.: **2003/134**

2777. Wang, Xilin, 1936– Symphony no. 4: for grand orchestra (1999–2000). N.p.: Xilin Wang, 2000.
1 score (103 p.); 37 cm.
Duration: ca. 38:00.
Program note in English.
Composed for: 3 flutes (2nd–3rd also piccolo), 3 oboes,

3 clarinets, 3 bassoons, contrabassoon, 4 trumpets, 4 horns, 3 trombones, tuba, 4 timpani, percussion (Chinese cymbals, crash cymbals, suspended cymbals, drum, 5 tom-toms, slapstick, bass drum, tam-tam, glockenspiel, celesta, xylophone, vibraphone), piano, violin I, violin II, viola, violoncello, double bass.
Call no.: **2003/135**

2778. Wangerin, Mark, 1964– Prelude and fanfare: for symphonic band. Full score. N.p.: n.p., 1992.
1 score (27 p.); 44 cm.
Composed for: piccolo, 4 flutes, 2 oboes, 3 clarinets, bassoon, alto saxophone, tenor saxophone, baritone saxophone, 2 horns, 4 trumpets, 3 trombones, euphonium, tuba, timpani, percussion (bells, xylophone, snare drum, bass drum, crash cymbals).
Call no.: **1993/147**

2779. Ward, David, 1941– Beyond the far haaf: symphonic cantata for mezzo soprano, baritone [and] orchestra. Isle of Lewis, Scotland: Vanderbeek & Imbrie, 1989.
1 score (iv, 166 p.); 43 cm.
English words by Robert Alan Jamieson, with occasional phrases in Shetlandic.
Reproduced from holograph.
Duration: ca. 55:00.
Composer's note.
Composed for: mezzo-soprano, baritone, 2 flutes (2nd also piccolo), 2 oboes (2nd also English horn), 2 clarinets, bass clarinet, 2 bassoons, contrabassoon, 4 horns, 3 trumpets, 2 trombones, bass trombone, timpani, percussion (bass drum, tam-tam), harp, violin I, violin II, viola, violoncello, double bass.
Commissioned by: Shetlands Arts Trust.
Call no.: **1997/167**

2780. Ward, Robert, 1917– Roman fever: opera in one act after the story by Edith Wharton. Full score. Boston, MA: Vireo Press: ECS Pub., 1993.
1 score (310 p.); 28 cm.
English words by Roger Brunyate.
Includes synopsis.
Duration: ca. 01:00:00.
Composed for: 2 sopranos, 2 mezzo-sopranos, baritone, flute, oboe, clarinet, bassoon, horn, trumpet, percussion (timpani, snare drum, glockenspiel, tubular bells, trap set), synthesizer, violin I, violin II, viola, violoncello, double bass.
Call no.: **1997/168**

2781. Ware, Peter, 1951– Kusawa: for orchestra. Toronto, ON: Acoma, 1987.
1 score (28 p.); 36 cm.
Reproduced from holograph.
Composed for: piccolo, 2 flutes, 2 oboes, English horn, 2 clarinets, bass clarinet, 2 bassoons, 4 horns, 2 trumpets, 2 trombones, bass trombone, tuba, timpani, percussion (cymbals, medium suspended cymbal, large suspended cymbal, nipple gong, large tam-tam, bass drum), harp, violin I, violin II, viola, violoncello, double bass.
Call no.: **1988/107**

2782. Warren, Betsy, 1921– Gift of the Magi: a chamber opera from the story by O'Henry [sic]. Orchestral score. London; Wiscasset, ME: Wiscasset Music Pub. Co., 1985.
1 score (59 p.); 31 cm.
Words by David McCord.
Reproduced from holograph.
Duration: 18:00.
Composed for: soprano, mezzo-soprano, baritone, oboe, bassoon, 2 horns, violin I, violin II, viola, violoncello, double bass.
Call no.: **1992/145**
Also available:
Call no.: **1992/145 vocal score**

2783. Warshauer, Maxine M., 1949– Shacharit: an interpretation of the Sabbath morning service for full orchestra, mixed chorus, soprano and tenor soloists. N.p.: n.p., 1989.
1 score (162 p.); 36 cm.
Hebrew and English words.
Text from prayer books of the Ashkenaz tradition; translations adapted by the composer.
Reproduced from manuscript.
Composed for: soprano, tenor, SATB chorus, 3 flutes (3rd also piccolo), 2 oboes, 2 clarinets, 2 bassoons, 4 horns, 2 trumpets, 3 trombones, tuba, timpani, percussion (triangle, suspended cymbal, tambourine, vibraslap, claves, guiro, xylophone, vibraphone, marimba, mark tree, glockenspiel, crash cymbals, tam-tam, 2 woodblocks, snare drum, 3 tom-toms, bass drum, crotales, chimes), harp, violin I, violin II, viola, violoncello, double bass.
Call no.: **1991/140**

2784. Waters, Joseph, 1952– Desert island pieces: ruminations on a troubled planet: a work in four movements for violin, cello & piano with auxiliary electronics. N.p.: Voice House Publishing, 2003.
1 score (159 p.); 28 cm.
Includes performance instructions.
Contents: The loneliness of the sun—Aloiloi, pakuikui: the fast shallows—Ghosts of the evening tides—The roaring of the moon.

Composed for: violin, violoncello, piano, electronics.
Commissioned by: Bakken Trio and Donors.
Call no.: **2005/150**

2785. Weber, Margaret A., 1917– Three holy sonnets of John Donne. N.p.: Margaret A. Weber, 1986.
1 score (36 leaves); 35 cm.
English words.
Reproduced from manuscript.
Contents: At the round earth's imagin'd corners—If poysonous mineralls—Death be not proud.
Composed for: SATB, chorus, flute, horn, viola, violoncello.
Call no.: **1989/136**

2786. Weddington, Maurice, 1941– Fire in the lake: a concerto for symphony orchestra. N.p.: n.p., 1989.
1 score (58 p.); 81cm.
Duration: 40:00.
Composed for: 4 flutes (2nd and 4th also alto flute), 4 oboes (all also English horn), 4 clarinets (1st–2nd also clarinet in E♭, 3rd–4th also bass clarinet), 4 bassoons (1st–2nd also crotales, 3rd–4th also contrabassoon), alto saxophone, tenor saxophone, baritone saxophone, bass saxophone, 6 horns, 2 trumpets in D (both also piccolo trumpet), 2 trumpets (both also trumpet in D), 3 trombones, 2 tubas, percussion (2 guiros, 2 temple blocks, 2 woodblocks, 2 bongos, 2 timbales, tom-tom, 2 bass drums, 4 large tam-tams, 2 vibraphones, 2 triangles, 4 cymbals, 2 claves, tenor drum, chimes, orchestra bells, 2 crotales), violin I, violin II, viola, violoncello, double bass.
Call no.: **1993/148**

2787. Weed, Kevin, 1962– Concerto: for Highland bagpipe and orchestra. N.p.: Kevin Weed, 1989.
1 score (35 p.); 36 x 45 cm.
Reproduced from manuscript.
Composed for: bagpipes, piccolo, 2 flutes, 2 oboes, 2 clarinets, 2 bassoons, 4 horns, 2 trumpets, 3 trombones, percussion (suspended cymbal, crash cymbals, timpani), violin I, violin II, viola, violoncello, double bass.
Commissioned by: Celtic Society of CSUF.
Call no.: **1993/149**

2788. Wegren, Thomas J., 1946– Songs of gitanjali: for tenor & piano and cassette tape. N.p.: T. Wegren, 1993.
1 score (63 p.); 36 cm.
Words by Rabindranath Tagore.
Reproduced from manuscript.
Contents: Silent amazement—Rhythms in time—Flower of simplicity—The ultimate offering—The carefree spirits—Veiled progress—Humanity's freedom—Infant's secret—Butterfly sails.
Composed for: tenor, piano, tape.
Call no.: **1994/157**

2789. Weidenaar, Reynold, 1945– Night flame ritual.
Call no.: **1985/195**
No materials available.

2790. Weir, Judith, 1954– Moon and star: (1995). London: Chester Music, 1995.
1 score (52 p.); 42 cm.
For mixed voices (SSAATTBB) and orchestra.
Words by Emily Dickinson, also printed as text.
Reproduced from manuscript.
Duration: ca. 15:00.
Composed for: SSAATTBB chorus, 3 flutes (all also piccolo), 2 oboes, English horn, 3 clarinets, 3 bassoons, 4 horns, trumpet in D, 3 trumpets, 3 trombones, tuba, percussion (crotales, vibraphone, tubular bells, 3 glockenspiels, marimba), piano, violin I, violin II, viola, violoncello, double bass.
Commissioned by: BBC.
Call no.: **1998/174**

2791. Weir, Judith, 1954– Natural history: for soprano and orchestra. London: Chester Music, 1999.
1 score (89 p.); 30 cm.
English words; also printed as text.
Texts from The inner chapters of Chuang Tzu.
"Revised 3/99"—p. 1.
Reproduced from holograph.
Duration: ca. 17:00.
Composed for: soprano, 3 flutes (3rd also piccolo, alto flute), 3 oboes, 3 clarinets, 3 bassoons (3rd also contrabassoon), 4 horns, 3 trumpets, tuba, timpani, percussion (cymbals, tubular bells, suspended cymbal, glockenspiel, snare drum, tam-tam, xylophone, bamboo chimes, metal wind chimes, gong), harp, violin I, violin II, viola, violoncello, double bass.
Call no.: **2001/165**

2792. Weir, Judith, 1954– Piano concerto (1996/7). London: Chester Music, 1997.
1 score (65 p.); 30 cm.
Originally written for piano and an ensemble of 9 solo strings, but it may be performed by a string orchestra, with several instruments to each part.
Reproduced from manuscript.
"Perusal score."
Duration: ca. 15:00.
Composed for: piano, 4 violins, 2 violas, 2 violoncellos, double bass.

Commissioned by: Dr. and Mrs. Anthony Henfrey.
Call no.: **2000/195**

2793. Weir, Judith, 1954– The vanishing bridegroom. London: Chester Music; Bury St. Edmunds, Suffolk: Music Sales, 1990.
1 score (394 p.); 30 cm.
English words.
Text taken from Popular tales of the West Highlands, Carmina Gadelica, and other Celtic sources.
Opera in three acts.
Includes synopsis.
Composed for: soprano, mezzo-soprano, tenor, 2 baritones, SATB chorus, TTBB men's chorus, SSAA women's chorus, 2 flutes (2nd also piccolo), 2 oboes (2nd also English horn), 2 clarinets (2nd also bass clarinet), 2 bassoons, 4 horns, 2 trumpets (both also trumpet in D), 3 trombones, timpani, percussion (xylophone, glockenspiel, side drum, cymbals), violin I, violin II, viola, violoncello, double bass.
Commissioned by: Glasgow District Council.
Call no.: **1991/141**

2794. Weir, Judith, 1954– We are shadows: for mixed chorus, children's choir and symphony orchestra (1999). London: Chester Music, 1999.
1 score (91 p.); 42 cm.
English words; also printed as text.
Text from a poem by Emily Dickinson, Scottish gravestones, and a translation of Chuang Tzu.
Reproduced from holograph.
Duration: ca. 24:00.
Contents: Preface—Inscription I—The changer—The frontier guardsman's daughter—Inscription II—We are shadows.
Composed for: SATB chorus, children's chorus, 3 flutes (3rd also piccolo), 2 oboes, 3 clarinets, 2 bassoons, contrabassoon, 4 horns, 3 trumpets, 2 trombones, bass trombone, tuba, percussion (xylophone, glockenspiel, tuned cowbells, metal chimes, 3 roto-toms, crash cymbals, side drum, tubular bells, thundersheet, bass drum, pair of bongos, metal chain, triangle, tam-tam, bamboo chimes), timpani, harp, violin I, violin II, viola, violoncello, double bass.
Call no.: **2003/136**

2795. Weir, Judith, 1954– The welcome arrival of rain. London: Chester Music, 2002.
1 score (95 p.); 37 cm.
Reproduced from manuscript.
Duration: 16:00.
Composed for: 3 flutes (also piccolo), 2 oboes, English horn, 3 clarinets, 3 bassoons, 4 horns, 4 trumpets, percussion (glockenspiel, roto-toms, tom-toms), timpani, harp, violin I, violin II, viola, violoncello, double bass.
Commissioned by: Minnesota Orchestra.
Call no.: **2005/151**

2796. Weir, Judith, 1954– Woman.life.song. London: Chester Music, 2000.
1 score (174 p.); 30 cm.
For solo soprano and instrumental ensemble.
English words; also printed as text.
"Revised June 2000"—p. 1.
Reproduced from manuscript.
Includes biographical notes.
Duration: ca. 45:00.
Contents: On youth / Maya Angelou—Breasts! Song of the innocent wild-child / Clarissa Pinkola Estés—Edge; Eve remembering / Toni Morrison—The mothership, when a good mother sails from this world; The mothership, stave two / Clarissa Pinkola Estés—On maturity / Maya Angelou.
Composed for: soprano, 3 flutes (3rd also alto flute, piccolo), 3 clarinets (3rd also bass clarinet), percussion (vibraphone, marimba, xylophone, glockenspiel, tubular bells, bass drum, 2 congas, pair of bongos, tam-tam, suspended cymbals, triangle, tambourine, guiro), guitar, harp, piano, 2 violins, 2 violas, 2 violoncellos, double bass.
Commissioned by: Carnegie Hall.
Call no.: **2002/189**

2797. Weisgall, Hugo, 1912–1997. Esther: opera in three acts. Full score. Bryn Mawr, PA: Theodore Presser, 1993.
1 score (3 v.); 28 cm.
English words by Charles Kondek.
Composed for: soprano, mezzo-soprano, contralto, 4 tenors, 2 baritones, bass-baritone, bass, SATB chorus, children's chorus, 3 flutes (3rd also piccolo, alto flute), 2 oboes (2nd also English horn), 2 clarinets (2nd also bass clarinet), 2 bassoons, 4 horns, 3 trumpets, 3 trombones, tuba, timpani, percussion (cymbals, xylophone, snare drum, glockenspiel, ratchet, tom-toms, crash cymbals, suspended cymbals, crotales, triangle, tenor drum, vibraphone, bass drum, marimba, woodblock, tambourine, bell tree, castanets, tam-tam, slapstick, finger cymbals, claves, sizzle cymbal, brake drums, guiro, medium gong), harp, violin I, violin II, viola, violoncello, double bass.
Commissioned by: San Francisco Opera Association and New York City Opera Company.
Call no.: **1994/158**

2798. Weisgall, Hugo, 1912–1997. Evening liturgies. N.p.: n.p., 1996.

1 score (iii, 98 p.); 28 cm.
Hebrew words.
"Texts are from the traditional Friday evening service"—p. iii.
Contents: Ma tovu I—Ma tovu II—Borchu I—Borchu II—Sh'ma Yisroel—V'ohavto—Mi chomocho—Hashkivenu—V'shomru I—V'shomru II—Yi'hyu l'rotzon—Verses from Yigdal.
Composed for: SATB chorus, organ.
Commissioned by: Florilegium Musicum.
Call no.: **1997/169**

2799. Welcher, Dan, 1948– Bright wings: valediction for large orchestra. Full score. Bryn Mawr, PA: Theodore Presser, 1997.
1 score (59 p.); 44 cm.
Composed for: piccolo, 2 flutes (2nd also piccolo), 3 oboes (3rd also English horn), 3 clarinets (3rd also bass clarinet), 2 bassoons, contrabassoon, 4 horns, 4 trumpets, 3 trombones, tuba, timpani, percussion (xylophone, snare drum, tambourine, glockenspiel, marimba, vibraphone, tom-toms, chimes, 4 cowbells, bongos, triangle, crotales, 3 brake drums, 3 suspended cymbals, 2 woodblocks, tam-tam, bass drum, sizzle cymbal, castanets, temple blocks, glass wind chimes), harp, piano (also celesta), violin I, violin II, viola, violoncello, double bass.
Commissioned by: Dallas Symphony Orchestra.
Call no.: **1998/175**

2800. Welcher, Dan, 1948– Concerto for piano and orchestra: Shiva's drum (1993–94). Full score. Bryn Mawr, PA: Elkan-Vogel, 1994.
1 score (183 p.); 44 cm.
Composed for: piano, piccolo, 2 flutes, 2 oboes, 2 clarinets, 2 bassoons, contrabassoon, 4 horns, 3 trumpets, 3 trombones, tuba, timpani, percussion (xylophone, marimba, crotales, whip, bass drum, suspended cymbal, cowbells, tom-toms, tambourine, snare drum, bongos, 2 triangles, finger cymbals, glockenspiel, whip, sizzle cymbal, 3 high woodblocks, 3 temple blocks, tam-tam, 3 river stones, castanets), harp, piano, violin I, violin II, viola, violoncello, double bass.
Commissioned by: James Dick and Festival Institute at Round Top, Texas.
Call no.: **1995/112**

2801. Welcher, Dan, 1948– Haleakalā: how Maui snared the sun: for narrator and full orchestra. N.p.: D. Welcher, 1991.
1 score (107 p.); 44 cm.
Words by Ann McCutchan.
Reproduced from holograph.
Composed for: narrator, piccolo, 2 flutes (2nd also piccolo), 2 oboes, English horn, 2 clarinets, bass clarinet, 2 bassoons, contrabassoon, 4 horns (1st also conch shell), 3 trumpets, 3 trombones, tuba, timpani, percussion (2 pahus, marimba, tam-tam, 3 gongs, bamboo wind chimes, vibraphone, mark tree, uliuli, bass drum, suspended cymbal, triangle, crotales, tom-toms, glockenspiel, vibraslap, sizzle cymbal, snare drum, xylophone, 4 woodblocks, bass marimba, temple blocks, glass wind chimes, bongos, flexatone, 3 puniu, kala'au, 'ili'ili), harp, piano (also celesta), violin I, violin II, viola, violoncello, double bass.
Commissioned by: Honolulu Symphony Orchestra and Meet the Composer.
Call no.: **1992/146**

2802. Welcher, Dan, 1948– JFK: the voice of peace. Full score. Bryn Mawr, PA: Elkan-Vogel, 1999.
1 score (v, 216 p.); 28 cm.
English words; also printed as text.
Texts selected by Ann McCutchan.
"Narrator's readings excerpted from the speeches of President John F. Kennedy"—p. ii.
Oratorio for chorus, orchestra, narrator, and solo violoncello.
Composed for: narrator, violoncello, SATB chorus, 2 flutes (all also piccolo), 2 oboes, 2 clarinets, 2 bassoons, 2 horns, 2 trumpets, timpani, percussion (suspended cymbal, sizzle cymbal, bass drum, tubular bells, crotales, 4 tom-toms, castanets, triangle, 2 bongos, marimba, glockenspiel, snare drum, vibraphone, tam-tam, woodblocks, cowbells, brake drums, temple blocks), harp, piano, violin I, violin II, viola, violoncello, double bass.
Commissioned by: New Heritage Music.
Call no.: **2001/166**

2803. Welcher, Dan, 1948– JFK: the voice of peace. Full score. N.p.: Dan Welcher, 1998.
1 score (v, 216 p.); 43 cm.
English words; also printed as text.
Texts selected by Ann McCutchan from speeches of J. F. Kennedy and various poems.
Oratorio for chorus, orchestra, narrator, and solo violoncello.
Composed for: narrator, violoncello, SATB chorus, 2 flutes (all also piccolo), 2 oboes, 2 clarinets, 2 bassoons, 2 horns, 2 trumpets, timpani, percussion (suspended cymbal, sizzle cymbal, bass drum, tubular bells, crotales, 4 tom-toms, castanets, triangle, 2 bongos, marimba, glockenspiel, snare drum, vibraphone, tam-tam, woodblocks, cowbells, brake drums, temple blocks), harp, piano, violin I, violin II, viola, violoncello, double bass.

Commissioned by: New Heritage Music Foundation.
Call no.: **2005/152**

2804. Welcher, Dan, 1948– Night watchers: symphony #2 for large orchestra (1994). Bryn Mawr, PA: Theodore Presser, 1994.
1 score (124 p.); 36 cm.
Composed for: 3 flutes (3rd also piccolo), 3 oboes (3rd also English horn), 3 clarinets (1st also clarinet in E♭, 3rd also bass clarinet), 3 bassoons (3rd also contrabassoon), 4 horns, 3 trumpets, 3 trombones, tuba, timpani, percussion (bass drum, tam-tams, suspended cymbals, tom-toms, sizzle cymbal, vibraphone, temple blocks, bongos, 2 triangles, seed-pod rattle, marimba, xylophone, castanets, glockenspiel, cymbals, marimba, tambourine, snare drum, triangle, cowbells, woodblocks, small hand drum), harp, piano (also celesta), violin I, violin II, viola, violoncello, double bass.
Commissioned by: Transition Foundation.
Call no.: **1996/162**

2805. Welcher, Dan, 1948– Symphony #1: (1992). Bryn Mawr, PA: Elkan-Vogel, 1992.
1 score (189 p.); 44 cm.
Duration: 38:00.
Composed for: 3 flutes (3rd also piccolo), 3 oboes (3rd also English horn), 3 clarinets (2nd also clarinet in E♭, 3rd also bass clarinet), 3 bassoons (3rd also contrabassoon), 4 horns, 4 trumpets, 2 trombones, bass trombone, tuba, timpani (also timbales, roto-tom), percussion (crotales, glockenspiel, xylophone, vibraphone, marimba, woodblock, tambourine, 2 bongos, 5 tom-toms, triangle, 2 suspended cymbals, crash cymbals, snare drum, bass drum, tam-tam, temple blocks, pahu drum, genguari drum, wind chimes), harp, piano, violin I, violin II, viola, violoncello, double bass.
Commissioned by: Organizing Committee.
Call no.: **1994/159**

2806. Wen, Loong-Hsing, 1944– Mus slur of the two poles: for orch. & piano. N.p.: n.p., 1993.
1 score (35 p.); 36 cm.
Reproduced from holograph.
Composed for: piano, piccolo (also alto flute), 2 flutes, 2 oboes, English horn, 2 clarinets, bass clarinet, 2 bassoons, contrabassoon, 4 horns, 3 trumpets, 2 trombones, bass trombone, tuba, timpani, percussion (bell tree, suspended cymbal, snare drum, triangle, small tambourine, tam-tam, tubular bells, 5 temple blocks, glockenspiel, marimba, vibraphone, medium tambourine, xylophone), violin I, violin II, viola, violoncello, double bass.
Call no.: **1996/163**

2807. Wernick, Richard, 1934– Musica da camerata. Bryn Mawr, PA: Theodore Presser, 1999.
1 score (70 p.); 36 cm.
For orchestra.
Composed for: flute, 2 oboes, 2 bassoons, 2 horns, violin I, violin II, viola, violoncello, double bass.
Call no.: **2002/190**

2808. Wernick, Richard, 1934– Piano concerto, 1989–90. Bryn Mawr, PA: Theodore Presser, 1990.
1 score (98 p.); 58 cm.
Reproduced from manuscript.
Composed for: piano, piccolo, 2 flutes, 2 oboes, English horn, 3 clarinets in A (2nd also clarinet in E♭, 3rd also bass clarinet), 3 bassoons, contrabassoon, 4 horns, 3 trumpets (1st also trumpet in D), 3 trombones, tuba, timpani, percussion (bass drum, vibraphone, bass drum, bongo, tambourine, chimes, tam-tam, suspended cymbal, marimba, crotales, glockenspiel, xylophone, tom-tom, snare drum, 4 button gongs, rute), harp, violin I, violin II, viola, violoncello, double bass.
Commissioned by: National Symphony Orchestra.
Call no.: **1992/147**

2809. Wernick, Richard, 1934– Quintet for horn and string quartet. King of Prussia, PA: Theodore Presser, 2002.
1 score (32 p.); 28 cm.
Composed for: horn, 2 violins, viola, violoncello.
Commissioned by: Library of Congress.
Call no.: **2005/153**

2810. Wernick, Richard, 1934– Sonata for piano: reflections of a dark light. Bryn Mawr, PA: T. Presser Co., 1984.
30 p. of music; 31 cm.
Duration: ca. 35:00.
Contents: Reflections of a dark light—Fragments of things remembered—". . . in the forehead of the morning sky."
Composed for: piano.
Commissioned by: Lambert Orkis.
Call no.: **1988/108**
Re-entered as: **1989/137**

2811. Wernick, Richard, 1934– String quartet no. 5, with soprano. Score and parts. Bryn Mawr, PA: T. Presser, 1998.
1 score (49 p.) + 4 parts; 28 cm.
English words by Hannah Senesh; also printed as text.
Poems translated from the Hebrew by Ziva Shapiro (1st movement) and Marie Syrkin (4th movement).
Duration: ca. 21:00.

At end: Wolcott, VT; Media, PA; 10/14/95.
Contents: At the crossroads—Scherzo I—Scherzo II—Blessed is the match.
Composed for: soprano, 2 violins, viola, violoncello.
Commissioned by: Philadelphia Chamber Music Society.
Call no.: **1998/176**

2812. Wernick, Richard, 1934– Symphony no. 2: for orchestra and soprano. Bryn Mawr, PA: Theodore Presser, 1993.
1 score (91 p.); 44 cm.
English or Italian words; also printed as text.
Texts by Hannah Senesh (Her life and diary) and Dante (Paradiso).
Composed for: soprano, piccolo, 2 flutes, 2 oboes, English horn, 2 clarinets in A, bass clarinet, contrabass clarinet, 2 bassoons, contrabassoon, 4 horns, 3 trumpets, 3 trombones, tuba, timpani, percussion (glockenspiel, xylophone, vibraphone, tambourine, rute, chimes, suspended cymbal, marimba, crotales, 4 tomtoms, temple bells, low tam-tam, bass drum, bell tree, triangle), harp, piano (also celesta), violin I, violin II, viola, violoncello, double bass.
Commissioned by: Philadelphia Orchestra.
Call no.: **1996/164**

2813. Wesley-Smith, Martin, 1945– Quito. Lilyfield, Sydney, Australia: Purple Ink, 1997.
1 score (100 p.); 30 cm.
English words by the composer and Peter Wesley-Smith.
Audiovisual music theater.
Composed for: SATB chorus, tape.
Call no.: **1998/177**

2814. Westbrook, Mike, 1936– London Bridge is broken down: a composition for voice, jazz orchestra and chamber orchestra. Paris: Metisse Music, 1987.
1 score (2 v.); 39 cm.
"Texts written and selected by Kate Westbrook."
Reproduced from holograph.
Contents: Book II. Vienna—Picardie.
Composed for: voice; jazz orchestra: 3 clarinets, 3 soprano saxophones, 2 alto saxophones, tenor saxophone, baritone saxophone, trumpet (also flugelhorn), trombone, tuba, guitar, bass guitar, piano, drums; chamber orchestra: flute, oboe, clarinet, bassoon, violin I, violin II, viola, violoncello, double bass.
Call no.: **1992/148**

2815. Westendorf, Lynette, 1951– Dreams of the internal animals. N.p.: Lynette Westendorf, 1996.
1 score (35 p.); 22 x 36 cm.
Duration: 1:10:00.
Contents: Some kind of Kansas—The last grove of forest anywhere—Skeleton of an angel—A circle of bears—Fountains and lions, rivers and wolves.
Composed for: trumpet, alto saxophone (also flute and piccolo), tenor saxophone (also soprano saxophone), piano, double bass, percussion.
Commissioned by: Seattle Arts Commission.
Call no.: **1997/170**

2816. Westergaard, Peter, 1931– The tempest: opera in three acts after Shakespeare, 1990. N.p.: Peter Westergaard, 1992.
1 score (3 v. [819 p.]); 44 cm.
English words, by the composer.
Performance instructions by the composer.
Composed for: 8 sopranos, 6 tenors, 5 baritones, 2 bass-baritones, 4 basses, SATB chorus, flute (also piccolo, alto flute), oboe (also English horn), clarinet in A (also clarinet in E♭), bass clarinet (also clarinet, clarinet in A), bassoon, 2 horns, trumpet, bass trombone, harp, percussion (2 agogo bells, anvil, bass drum, castanets, caxixi, cuíca, guiro, maracas, ratchet, snare drum, suspended cymbal, tambourine, tam-tam, temple blocks, triangles, vibraphone, woodblock, xylophone, bell lyra, steel drum, tubular bells, glockenspiel, roto-toms, timpani, bongos, conga), celesta (also synthesizer), violin I, violin II, viola, violoncello, double bass.
Call no.: **2000/196**

2817. Wheeler, Kenny, 1930– The one more time suite for the Maritime Jazz Orchestra. N.p.: K. Wheeler, 1999.
1 score (187 p.); 44 cm.
Wordless.
For solo voice and jazz orchestra.
Reproduced from manuscript.
Composed for: voice, flugelhorn, 2 alto saxophones (1st also soprano saxophone), 2 tenor saxophones, baritone saxophone, 4 flugelhorns, 4 trombones, piano, guitar, double bass, drums.
Call no.: **2003/137**

2818. Wheeler, Scott, 1952– The angle of the sun: cantata for chorus and orchestra with mezzo soprano and baritone soloists. N.p.: Davidge Publishing, 1994.
1 score (172 p.); 28 cm.
English or Latin words.
Texts include poems by Mark Van Doren and Paul Goodman.
Composed for: mezzo-soprano, baritone, SATB chorus, horn, trombone, percussion (marimba, vibraphone,

timpani, bass drum, bongos, tom-toms, claves, cowbell, suspended cymbals, snare drum, slapstick, maracas, anvil), harp, piano (also harpsichord), violin I, violin II, viola, violoncello, double bass.
Commissioned by: Boston Cecilia.
Call no.: **1997/171**

2819. Wheeler, Scott, 1952– Before sleeping. North Reading, MA: Scott Wheeler Music, 1990.
1 score (79 p.); 28 cm.
For orchestra.
Reproduced from manuscript.
Composed for: 2 flutes (2nd also piccolo), 2 oboes, 2 clarinets (2nd also bass clarinet), 2 bassoons, 2 horns, trumpet, trombone, violin I, violin II, viola, violoncello, double bass.
Commissioned by: Virgil Thomson Foundation.
Call no.: **1992/149**

2820. Wheeler, Scott, 1952– Concerto for violin and orchestra. North Reading, MA: Scott Wheeler Music, 2001.
1 score (140 p.); 36 cm.
Composed for: violin, 2 alto recorders, 2 oboes, 2 clarinets, 2 bassoons, 2 horns, 2 trumpets, trombone, percussion (log drum, marimba, vibraphone, 2 bongos, 2 tom-toms, 2 suspended cymbals, 2 woodblocks, maracas, bass drum, timpani, snare drum, anvil, triangle, tam-tam), mandolin, harpsichord, violin I, violin II, viola, violoncello, double bass.
Commissioned by: Toledo Symphony and Sharan Leventhal.
Call no.: **2003/138**

2821. Wheeler, Scott, 1952– The construction of Boston: a dramatic cantata for chorus, soloists, and chamber ensemble. N.p.: n.p., 198-?.
1 score (408 p.); 28 cm.
Words by Kenneth Koch.
Composed for: soprano, alto, 2 tenors, 2 basses, SATB chorus, flute (also piccolo), oboe, clarinet (also bass clarinet), bassoon, horn, trumpet, trombone, percussion (marimba, tam-tam, slapstick, bass drum, tom-toms, woodblock, bongos, timpani, 3 suspended cymbals, snare drum, bass drum, tambourine, claves, hi-hat, maracas, glockenspiel, anvil, triangle, woodblock), banjo, harpsichord (also piano), violin I, violin II, viola, violoncello, double bass.
Commissioned by: John Oliver Chorale.
Call no.: **1990/132**

2822. Whettam, Graham, 1927– Andromeda: for percussion quartet. Full score. Ingatestone, Essex, England: Meriden Music, 1993.
1 score (19 p.); 30 cm.
Duration: 20:00.
Composed for: percussion (glockenspiel, marimba, vibraphone, 4 bongos, 3 congas, 4 cymbals, 4 tom-toms, 2 snare drums, tam-tam).
Commissioned by: Kalengo Ensemble.
Call no.: **1995/113**

2823. Whettam, Graham, 1927– Concerto drammatico: for violoncello & orchestra. Full score. Woolaston, Gloucestershire: Meriden Music; Bryn Mawr, PA: T. Presser, 1998.
1 score (133 p.); 37 cm.
Duration: ca. 30:00.
Contents: Scena—Danza vigorosa—Scena ultima.
Composed for: violoncello, 3 flutes (3rd also piccolo), oboe, English horn, 2 clarinets (2nd also bass clarinet), 2 bassoon, 4 horns, 2 trumpets, tuba, 5 timpani, percussion (snare drum, tenor drum, bass drum, tam-tam, tambourine, triangle, cymbals, glockenspiel, vibraphone, xylophone), celesta, harp, violin I, violin II, viola, violoncello, double bass.
Call no.: **2002/191**
Re-entered as: **2003/139**

2824. Whettam, Graham, 1927– Hymnos quartet. Lydney, Gloucestershire: Meriden Music; Bryn Mawr, PA: Theodore Presser, 1997.
1 score (39 p.); 30 cm.
Duration: ca. 28:00.
Composed for: 2 violins, viola, violoncello.
Commissioned by: Dore Abbey Festival.
Call no.: **1998/178**

2825. Whettam, Graham, 1927– Marimba sonata. N. Lydney, Gloucestershire, England: Meriden Music; Bryn Mawr, PA: T. Presser, 1998.
30 p. of music; 30 cm.
Includes composer's note.
Duration: ca. 24:00.
Composed for: marimba.
Call no.: **2000/197**

2826. Whettam, Graham, 1927– Percussion partita: for six players (1985). Ingatestone, Essex: Meriden Music, 1985.
1 score (30 p.); 32 cm.
Reproduced from manuscript.
Duration: ca. 19:00.
Contents: Ritual—Incantation—Scherzo—Finale.
Composed for: percussion (glockenspiel, crotales, 2 xylophones, 2 marimbas, 2 vibraphones, 2 tubular bells,

2 side drums, tenor drum, log drum, bass drum, bongos, 2 temple blocks, 8 tom-toms, timpani, triangle, 4 suspended cymbals, crash cymbals, 3 tam-tams, 4 tuned gongs).
Commissioned by: Percussion Ensemble of Royal Northern College of Music.
Call no.: **1986/118**

2827. Whettam, Graham, 1927– Solo violin sonata no. 3. Gloucestershire, England: Meriden Music, 1990.
19 p. of music; 30 cm.
Duration: ca. 28:00.
Composed for: violin.
Call no.: **1992/150**

2828. Whettam, Graham, 1927– Symphony no. 5. Full score. Woolaston, Gloucestershire, England: Meriden Music; King of Prussia, PA: T. Presser, 2001.
1 score (156 p.); 36 cm.
Duration: ca. 28:00.
Composed for: 2 flutes (2nd also piccolo), oboe, English horn, 2 clarinets in A (2nd also bass clarinet), 2 bassoons, 2 horns, trumpet, timpani, percussion (marimba, glockenspiel, 6 Korean woodblocks, 3 congas, tam-tam, snare drum, tenor drum, tambourine, crash cymbals, suspended cymbal, bass drum, triangle), violin I, violin II, viola, violoncello, double bass.
Call no.: **2004/145**

2829. Whiffin, Lawrence, 1930– Murchitt: a daydream. N.p.: n.p., 1999.
1 score (132 p.); 34 cm.
English words by William Henderson.
"Tragi-comic prose-poem."
"Revised January 1999"—p. 132.
Composed for: narrator, soprano, tenor, SATB chorus, flute (also piccolo), clarinet (also clarinet in E♭), bass clarinet, trumpet, percussion (ratchet, 3 woodblocks, bongos, suspended cymbal, tambourine, vibraphone, xylophone, trap set, 2 kazoos, tubular bells, large tam-tam), piano, synthesizer, violin, violoncello.
Call no.: **2000/198**

2830. Whitlow, Charles G., 1954– Seven songs on New York City. N.p.: n.p., 198-?.
1 score (15 leaves); 28 cm.
English words by the composer.
Reproduced from manuscript.
Contents: Coney Island—3 stops—Clones—Stock exchange—Columbus Avenue—The park—The pier.
Composed for: voice, piano.
Call no.: **1989/138**

2831. Wiernik, Adam, 1916– Pezzo levantico: for cello solo with double wind quintet. Stockholm: Gehrmans Musikförlag, 1994.
1 score (28 p.); 31 cm.
Cello part and cadenza in collaboration with Ola Karlsson.
Duration: 12:00.
Composed for: violoncello, 2 flutes, 2 oboes, 2 clarinets, 2 bassoons, 2 horns.
Call no.: **1996/165**
Also available:
Call no.: **1996/165 piano accompaniment**

2832. Wiggins, Christopher, 1956– Concerto: for four horns and orchestra, opus 93. N.p.: C.D. Wiggins, 1993.
1 score (86 p.); 28 cm.
Reproduced from manuscript.
Duration: 17:50.
Composed for: 4 horns, piccolo, 2 flutes, 2 oboes, 2 clarinets, 2 bassoons, 2 horns, 2 trumpets, 3 trombones, tuba, timpani, violin I, violin II, viola, violoncello, double bass.
Commissioned by: James Emerson of Denver, CO.
Call no.: **1994/160**

2833. Wild, Earl, 1915– Variations on an American theme: "Doo-dah" variations: piano and orchestra. N.p.: M.R. Davis Productions, 1992.
1 score (136 p.); 44 cm.
"Orchestrated by Michael Ruszczynski."
Based on the song Camptown races by Stephen Foster.
Duration: ca. 25:00.
Composed for: piano, 3 flutes (3rd also piccolo), 3 oboes, 3 clarinets, 3 bassoons, 4 horns, 3 trumpets, 3 trombones, tuba, timpani, percussion (hand cymbals, hi-hat, triangle, tom-tom, snare drum, glockenspiel, marimba, bass drum, chimes, ratchet), harp, violin I, violin II, viola, violoncello, double bass.
Call no.: **1993/150**

2834. Wild, Earl, 1915– Variations on a theme of Stephen Foster: "Doo-dah" variations. Revised score. N.p.: M.R. Davis Productions, 1993.
1 score (135 p.); 44 cm.
For piano and orchestra.
Based on the song Camptown races by Stephen Foster.
Duration: ca. 26:00.
Composed for: piano, 3 flutes (3rd also piccolo), 3 oboes, 3 clarinets, 3 bassoons, 4 horns, 3 trumpets, 3 trombones, tuba, timpani, percussion (hand cymbals, hi-hat, triangle, tom-tom, snare drum, glockenspiel, marimba, bass drum, chimes, ratchet), harp, violin I,

violin II, viola, violoncello, double bass.
Call no.: **1996/166**

2835. Wilhour, Brian E., 1969– Symphony no. 2. N.p.: B. Wilhour, 2002.
1 score (41, 45, 22, 45 p.); 28 cm.
Composed for: 2 flutes, 2 oboes, 2 clarinets, 2 bassoons, 2 horns, 2 trumpets, 2 trombones, tuba, timpani, percussion, violin I, violin II, viola, violoncello.
Commissioned by: Betty Brockett of Idaho Falls, ID.
Call no.: **2004/146**

2836. Wilkins, Margaret Lucy, 1939– Kanal 1. N.p.: n.p., 1990.
1 score (v, 22 p.); 30 x 42 cm.
English words.
"Multi-media environmental experience"—p. i.
For choir (SATB), actors, dancers, brass instruments, percussion, and electronic tapes.
Composed for: 1st location: 6–12 actors, SATB chorus, trumpet, 2 horns, conductor; 2nd location: narrator, 8 trumpets (also cornets, flugelhorns), 4 horns (also baritones, euphoniums), 3 trombones, 2 tubas, conductor; 3rd location: actors, tape; 4th location: tenor drum, 3 tambourines, tape, dancers.
Call no.: **1993/151**

2837. Wilkins, Margaret Lucy, 1939– Revelations of the seven angels. N.p.: Margaret Lucy Wilkins, 1988.
1 score (103 p.); 42 cm.
English words.
For solo soprano, string quartet, cathedral choir (boys SA; men TB), and orchestra.
Reproduced from manuscript.
Duration: ca. 46:00.
Contents: Alpha: the beginning—The angel of universality—Station I: The firmament—The angel of love—Station 2: Seraphim—The angel of visions—Station 3: The stars—The angel of security—Station 4: Earth mother—The angel of compassion—Station 5: The Lamb of God—The angel of wickedness—Station 6: Gargoyles—The angel of innocence—Station 7: Cherubim (49 alleluias)—Omega: Eternity.
Composed for: soprano, SATB chorus (boys and men only), strings quartet (2 violins, viola, violoncello), 2 flutes, oboe, 3 clarinets, bassoon, 4 horns, 2 trumpets, 3 trombones, tuba, harp (also guitar, celesta harpsichord), 2 descant recorders, percussion (2 vibraphones, glockenspiel, tubular bells, crotales, triangles, cymbals, tam-tam, metal sheets, glass chimes, tuned gongs), violin I, violin II, viola, violoncello, double bass.
Call no.: **2002/192**

2838. Willi, Herbert, 1956– Begegnung: für Orchester (1997/98). Partitur. Mainz; New York, NY: Schott, 1998.
1 score (58 p.); 42 cm.
Duration: ca. 16:00.
Composed for: 3 flutes (2nd also alto flute, 3rd also piccolo), oboe, English horn, 2 clarinets, bass clarinet, 2 bassoons (2nd also contrabassoon), 4 horns, 3 trumpets, 2 trombones, tuba, timpani, percussion (crotales, high triangle, high bongo, military drum, crash cymbals, glockenspiel, woodblock, suspended cymbals, metal plate, chimes), harp, violin I, violin II, viola, violoncello, double bass.
Commissioned by: Wiener Philhamoniker.
Call no.: **2001/167**

2839. Willi, Herbert, 1956– Eirene: Konzert: für Trompete und Orchester (2001): aus dem Zyklus "Montafon." Partitur. Mainz; New York, NY: Schott, 2002.
1 score (39 p.); 42 cm.
Duration: ca. 15:00.
Composed for: trumpet, piccolo, flute, oboe, English horn, clarinet, bass clarinet, soprano saxophone, alto saxophone, 2 bassoons, 2 horns, 2 trumpets, 2 trombones, tuba, timpani, percussion (triangle, 3 suspended cymbals, 2 pairs of crash cymbals, splash cymbals, 3 bongos, snare drum, bass drum, slapstick, crotales, chimes, glockenspiel), harp, piano, violin I, violin II, viola, violoncello, double bass.
Commissioned by: Gesellschaft der Musikfreunde, Wien.
Call no.: **2004/147**

2840. Willi, Herbert, 1956– Flötenkonzert: (1993). Partitur. Mainz; New York, NY: Schott, 1993.
1 score (38 p.); 60 cm.
Duration: ca. 15:00.
Composed for: flute, 2 flutes (1st also alto flute, 2nd also piccolo), 2 oboes (2nd also English horn), 2 clarinets (2nd also bass clarinet), 2 bassoons, 2 horns, 2 trumpets, bass trombone, timpani, percussion (2 triangles, crotales, military drum, woodblock, glockenspiel), harp, violin I, violin II, viola, violoncello, double bass.
Commissioned by: Bayerische Staatsoper München.
Call no.: **1994/161**

2841. Willi, Herbert, 1956– Flötenkonzert (1993). Partitur. Mainz; New York, NY: Schott, 1993.
1 score (38 p.); 42 cm.
Duration: ca. 12:00.
Composed for: flute, 2 flutes (1st also alto flute, 2nd also piccolo), 2 oboes (2nd also English horn), 2 clarinets

(2nd also bass clarinet), 2 bassoons, 2 horns, 2 trumpets, bass trombone, timpani, percussion (2 triangles, crotales, military drum, woodblock, glockenspiel), harp, violin I, violin II, viola, violoncello, double bass.
Commissioned by: Bayerische Staatsoper.
Call no.: **1996/167**

2842. Willi, Herbert, 1956– Der Froschmäusekrieg: 1989. Wien: Verlag Doblinger, 1989.
1 miniature score (58 p.); 42 cm.
German words.
Text based on the ancient Greek Batrachomyomachie.
For solo voice (Sprechgesang), three orchestral groups and tape.
Reproduced from manuscript.
Composed for: voice, tape; 1st group: flute (also piccolo), clarinet, bass clarinet, bassoon, 2 violins, viola, violoncello, double bass, harp; 2nd group: oboe, English horn, 2 horns, 2 trumpets, trombone, bass trombone, tuba, 3–8 violoncellos, 2–5 double basses; 3rd group: flute, soprano saxophone, 3 violins, 2 violas, 2 violoncellos, piano, timpani, percussion (marimba, steel drum, suspended cymbal, 5 gongs, tam-tam, 2 bongos, snare drum).
Commissioned by: Österreichische Gesellschaft für Musik.
Call no.: **1990/133**

2843. Willi, Herbert, 1956– Konzert für Orchester, 1991/92. Partitur. Mainz; New York, NY: Schott, 1992.
1 score (40 p.); 61 cm.
Reproduced from manuscript.
Duration: ca. 10:00.
Composed for: 3 flutes (all also piccolo), 3 oboes (3rd also English horn), 2 clarinets, bass clarinet, soprano saxophone, 3 bassoons (3rd also contrabassoon), 4 horns, 3 trumpets, 2 trombones, bass trombone, tuba, timpani, percussion (sizzle cymbal, snare drum, glockenspiel, vibraphone, cabasa, 2 bongos, crotales, xylophone, 2 suspended cymbals, woodblocks, small tambourine, mounted tambourine, marimba), harp, violin I, violin II, viola, violoncello, double bass.
Commissioned by: Salzburger Festspiele and Cleveland Orchestra.
Call no.: **1993/152**

2844. Willi, Herbert, 1956– Rondino: für Orchester (1999/2000): nach der Oper "Schlafes Bruder." Partitur. Mainz; New York, NY: Schott, 2000.
1 score (57 p.); 42 cm.
Duration: ca. 16:00.
Composed for: 3 flutes (2nd also alto flute, 3rd also piccolo), oboe, English horn, 2 clarinets, bass clarinet, 2 bassoons, 4 horns, 4 trumpets, 2 trombones, bass trombone, tuba, timpani, percussion (woodblock, 2 bongos, 5 roto-toms, 5 tom-toms, military drum), harp, piano, violin I, violin II, viola, violoncello, double bass.
Commissioned by: Land Vorarlberg.
Call no.: **2003/140**

2845. Willi, Herbert, 1956– Schlafes Bruder: 1994/95. Partitur. Mainz; New York, NY: Schott, 1996.
1 score (267 p.); 42 cm.
Words by Robert Schneider in cooperation with the composer.
Composed for: 4 sopranos, alto, countertenor, 3 tenors, 2 baritones, 3 basses, SATB chorus, 3 flutes (1st also alto flute, 2nd–3rd also piccolo), oboe, English horn, clarinet, bass clarinet, soprano saxophone, 2 bassoons, 2 horns, 2 trumpets, trombone, bass trombone, tuba, timpani, percussion (military drum, glockenspiel, xylophone, triangle, woodblock, 2 bongos, crotales, vibraphone, marimba), harp, piano (also celesta), violin I, violin II, viola, violoncello, double bass.
Commissioned by: Opernhaus Zürich.
Call no.: **1997/172**

2846. Willi, Herbert, 1956– Streichquartett 1986. Wien: Doblinger, 1987.
1 score (41 p.); 30 cm.
Reproduced from manuscript.
Duration: ca. 10:00.
Composed for: 2 violins, viola, violoncello.
Call no.: **1988/109**

2847. Willi, Herbert, 1956– Trio für Violine, Horn und Klavier, 1992 = for violin, horn and piano. Mainz; New York, NY: Schott, 1992.
1 score (28 p.) + 2 parts; 31 cm.
Duration: ca. 8:00.
Composed for: violin, horn, piano.
Call no.: **1995/114**

2848. Williams, Zika, 1949– "Journey": a symphony. N.p.: n.p., 1997.
1 score (103 p.); 36 cm.
Wordless.
For chorus and orchestra.
Contents: Dignity—Tumult—Peace—Prayer—Triumph.
Composed for: SATB chorus, piccolo, 2 flutes, 2 oboes, 2 clarinets, 2 bassoons, 4 horns, 3 trumpets, 3 trombones, tuba, percussion (timpani, bells, triangle, snare drum, bass drum, suspended cymbal, anvil, tambourine, floor

tom-tom, crash cymbal, finger cymbals), piano, violin I, violin II, viola, violoncello, double bass.
Call no.: **1998/179**

2849. Williamson, Malcolm, 1931–2003. The dawn is at hand: choral symphony for soprano, contralto, tenor, and baritone soli, chorus and orchestra. Full score. Sandon, Buntingford, Hertfordshire, England: Campion Press, 1991.
1 score (236 p.); 42 cm.
English words by Oodgeroo of the tribe Noonuccal, custodian of the land Minjerribah (Kath Walker); also printed as text.
Reproduced from manuscript.
Composed for: soprano, contralto, tenor, baritone SATB chorus, 3 flutes (2nd–3rd also piccolo, 3rd also alto flute), 3 oboes (3rd also English horn), 3 clarinets (1st–2nd also clarinet in A, 3rd also bass clarinet), 3 bassoons (3rd also contrabassoon), 4 horns, 4 trumpets (4th also trumpet in D), 2 trombones, bass trombone, tuba, timpani, percussion (click sticks, tam-tam, triangle, 2 gongs, glockenspiel, tubular bells, tenor drum, 3 cymbals, 4 woodblocks, snare drum, 2 bongos, vibraphone, xylophone, tom-toms, bass drum, crotales, whip, anvil, thundersheet, suspended cymbal, Chinese bell tree), harp, piano, violin I, violin II, viola, violoncello, double bass.
Commissioned by: Queensland State and Municipal Choir.
Call no.: **1992/151**

2850. Wilson, Curtis W., 1941– Concerto for trumpet and chamber orchestra. N.p.: n.p., 1990.
1 score (131 p.); 43 cm.
Reproduced from manuscript.
Duration: ca. 19:00.
Composed for: trumpet, 2 flutes (2nd also piccolo), 2 oboes, 2 clarinets, 2 bassoons, 2 horns, 2 trumpets (both also piccolo trumpet), percussion (timpani, xylophone, orchestra bells, snare drum, timbales, triangle, mark tree), violin I, violin II, viola, violoncello, double bass.
Commissioned by: Fort Worth Chamber Orchestra and John Giordano.
Call no.: **1992/152**

2851. Wilson, Curtis W., 1941– Concerto for trumpet and wind ensemble. N.p.: n.p., 2001.
1 score (various pagings); 36 cm.
Contents: Pesante/moderato—Slowly (tranquil)—Spirited.
Composed for: trumpet, piccolo, 2 flutes, 2 oboes, clarinet in E♭, 3 clarinets, bass clarinet, contrabass clarinet, 2 bassoons, 2 alto saxophones, tenor saxophone, baritone saxophone, 3 trumpets, 4 horns, 3 trombones, euphonium, tuba, xylophone, contrabass, timpani, percussion.
Call no.: **2005/154**

2852. Wilson, Ian, 1964– Messenger: concerto no. 1 for violin and orchestra. London: Universal Edition, 2000.
1 score (44 p.); 30 x 42 cm.
Composed for: violin, 2 flutes (2nd also piccolo), 2 oboes (2nd also English horn), 2 clarinets (2nd also clarinet in E♭), 2 bassoons, 4 horns, 2 trumpets, 2 trombones, bass trombone, tuba, harp, violin I, violin II, viola, violoncello, double bass.
Commissioned by: RTÉ.
Call no.: **2003/141**

2853. Wilson, Mick, 1943– New games from other worlds. N.p.: n.p., 1983.
1 score (38 p.); 42 cm.
English words.
Reproduced from holograph.
Duration: 25:00.
Contents: The blind men—Queen of the wake—Scherzo for tourists—P.K.—War games.
Composed for: contralto (also tam-tam, handbell, tambourine), 2 electric violins (both also African drum), electric viola (also gong ageng), electric violoncello (also shaker), bass guitar, drum kit (2 tom-toms, snare drum, floor tom-tom, bass drum, ride cymbal, crash cymbals, 2 hi-hats).
Call no.: **1985/196**

2854. Wilson, Olly, 1937– Hold on: symphony no. 3 (1998). N.p.: n.p., 1998.
1 score (147 p.); 44 cm.
Composed for: piccolo, 3 flutes (3rd also alto flute), 2 oboes, English horn, 2 clarinets, bass clarinet, 2 bassoons, 4 horns, 3 trumpets (all also piccolo trumpet), 3 trombones, tuba, timpani, percussion (3 suspended cymbals, 3 suspended sizzle cymbals, antique cymbals, 3 triangles, metal wind chimes, medium Chinese gong, 2 gongs, 2 cowbells, steel drum, tubular chimes, vibraphone, marimba, xylophone, 4 timbales, bass drum), harp, piano, violin I, violin II, viola, violoncello, double bass.
Commissioned by: Edward F. Schmidt Family Commissioning Fund.
Call no.: **2001/168**

2855. Wilson, Richard, 1941– Æthelred the Unready: opera in 7 scenes. New York, NY: Peermusic Classical, 2001.

1 score (various pagings); 28 cm.
English words.
Accompaniment for chamber ensemble.
Libretto by the composer.
"Opera in fourteen scenes"—cover.
Composed for: voices, clarinet (also clarinet in A), violin, violoncello, percussion, piano.
Call no.: **2003/142**
Also available:
Call no.: **2003/142 libretto**

2856. Wilson, Richard, 1941– Pamietam: for mezzo-soprano and orchestra. New York, NY: Southern Music, 1995.
1 score (iii, 123 p.); 36 cm.
English words; also printed as text.
Poems by Leopold Staff and Mieczysław Jastrun translated into English by Czeslaw Milosz.
Reproduced from manuscript.
Duration: ca. 18:00.
Commentary by the composer.
Contents: Foundations—The bridge—Three towns—Beyond time.
Composed for: mezzo-soprano, 2 flutes (2nd also alto flute, piccolo), 2 oboes (2nd also English horn), 2 clarinets (2nd also bass clarinet), 2 bassoons (2nd also contrabassoon), 2 horns, 2 trumpets, timpani, percussion (5 tuned drums, vibraphone, crotales, xylophone, guiro, 3 suspended cymbals, marimba, glockenspiel, gong), violin I, violin II, viola, violoncello, double bass.
Call no.: **1997/173**

2857. Wilson, Richard, 1941– String quartet no. 4 (1997). New York, NY: Peermusic, 1997.
1 score (61 p.); 28 cm.
Composed for: 2 violins, viola, violoncello.
Commissioned by: Chicago Chamber Musicians.
Call no.: **2000/199**

2858. Wilson, Richard, 1941– Triple concerto: for horn, bass clarinet, marimba and orchestra (1998). New York, NY: Peermusic, 1998.
1 score (229 p.); 36 cm.
Duration: ca. 27:00.
Contents: Gatherings—Linkages—Pathways.
Composed for: horn, bass clarinet, marimba, 3 flutes (3rd also piccolo), 3 oboes (3rd also English horn), 3 clarinets (3rd also clarinet in E♭, clarinet in A), 3 bassoons (3rd also contrabassoon), 4 horns, 3 trumpets, 3 trombones, tuba, timpani, percussion (glockenspiel, vibraphone, xylophone, crotales, sizzle cymbal, tam-tam, 3 suspended cymbals, claves, slapstick, snare drum, 5 temple blocks, 5 tom-toms, bass drum), harp, piano (also celesta), violin I, violin II, viola, violoncello, double bass.
Commissioned by: Serge Koussevitzky Music Foundation in the Library of Congress, Koussevitzky Music Foundation, and American Symphony Orchestra.
Call no.: **2001/169**

2859. Wilson, Thomas, 1927–2001. Piano concerto (1984). Glasgow: Queensgate Music, 1985.
1 score (124 p.); 37 cm.
Reproduced from holograph.
Duration: ca. 30:00.
Composed for: piano, 3 flutes (3rd also piccolo, alto flute), 3 oboes (3rd also English horn), 3 clarinets (3rd also bass clarinet), 3 bassoons (3rd also contrabassoon), 4 horns, 3 trumpets, 2 trombones, bass trombone, tuba, timpani, percussion (side drum, 2 suspended cymbals, marimba, vibraphone, bass drum, tam-tam, tom-toms, 4 bongos, triangle, glockenspiel, tubular bells, tambourine, xylophone), harp, celesta, violin I, violin II, viola, violoncello, double bass.
Commissioned by: Bryden Thomson.
Call no.: **1989/139**

2860. Wilson, Thomas, 1927–2001. Saint Kentigern suite: 1986. Glasgow: Queensgate Music, 1986.
1 score (36 p.); 30 cm.
For string ensemble.
Reproduced from holograph.
Contents: Bird: Kentigern the aspirant—Fish: the Christian activist—Ring: the contemplative—Bell: the proclaimer of the word—Tree: Kentigern's legacy.
Composed for: violin I, violin II, viola, violoncello, double bass.
Commissioned by: Friends of Glasgow Cathedral.
Call no.: **1990/134**

2861. Wilson, Thomas, 1927–2001. Viola concerto (1987). Glasgow: Queensgate Music, 1987.
1 score (114 p.); 30 cm.
Reproduced from holograph.
Composed for: viola, 2 flutes, 2 oboes (2nd also English horn), 2 clarinets, 2 bassoons, 4 horns, 3 trumpets, 2 trombones, bass trombone, tuba, timpani, percussion (marimba, suspended cymbals, vibraphone, snare drum, bongos, glockenspiel, maracas, bass drum, tam-tam, tubular bells, 2 gongs, triangle), harp, piano (also celesta), violin I, violin II, viola, violoncello, double bass.
Commissioned by: James Durrant.
Call no.: **1988/110**

2862. Winstin, Robert Ian, 1959– Piano concerto #2. Chicago, IL: E.R.M., 1994.
1 score (104 p.); 28 cm.
Composed for: piano, 2 flutes (1st also piccolo), 2 oboes, 2 clarinets, 2 alto saxophones, 2 tenor saxophones, 2 bassoons, 2 horns, 2 trumpets, trombone, timpani, cymbals, violin I, violin II, viola, violoncello, double bass.
Call no.: **1997/174**

2863. Winteregg, Steven, 1952– An American Cinderella. N.p.: n.p., 1996.
1 score (1 v.); 28 cm.
Ballet.
"The music can be performed by an entirely acoustic orchestra with a few MIDI-generated and taped pieces, or a combination of MIDI and acoustic instruments, or entirely as a MIDI-generated and taped performance"—prefatory notes.
Composed for: flute (also piccolo), oboe (also English horn), clarinet, bassoon, 2 alto saxophones, tenor saxophone, baritone saxophone, trumpet, trombone, tuba, percussion (trap set, suspended cymbal, glockenspiel, 2 marimbas, tambourine, castanets, bongos, shakers, log drums, gong, timpani, tom-tom, crash cymbals, whistle, vibraslap, woodblock, 2 drums, small cymbals, temple blocks, 2 gamelans, hi-hat, 2 sets of bells, 2 hollow drums, congas, tam-tam, church bell, chimes), banjo, optional harmonica, harp, piano (also celesta), harpsichord, synthesizer, violin I, violin II, viola, violoncello, double bass.
Call no.: **1998/180**

2864. Winteregg, Steven, 1952– Christmas carol: the ballet. N.p.: n.p., 1999.
1 score (396 p.); 28 cm.
Composed for: optional soprano, 2 flutes (2nd also piccolo), 2 oboes (2nd also English horn), 2 clarinets (2nd also bass clarinet), 2 bassoons, 2 horns, 2 trumpets, 2 trombones, tuba, timpani, percussion (jingle bells, suspended cymbals, tambourine, tam-tam, triangle, chimes, woodblocks, bass drum, temple blocks, gong, crash cymbals, castanets, snare drum, glockenspiel, finger cymbals, tam-tam, xylophone, hi-hat), optional guitar, piano (also synthesizer), celesta (also synthesizer), violins I, violin II, viola, violoncello, double bass.
Call no.: **2001/170**

2865. Winteregg, Steven, 1952– Mystic edges: a concerto for English horn. Full score. N.p.: n.p., 1993.
1 score (92 p.); 28 cm.
Contents: Night rondo—A brief romantic interlude—Flashback.
Composed for: English horn, flute, clarinet, bassoon, trumpet, horn, bass trombone, percussion (vibraphone, marimba, glockenspiel, tubular bells, snare drum, bass drum, log drums, suspended cymbal, triangle, small gong), harpsichord, violin I, violin II, viola, violoncello, double bass.
Call no.: **1995/115**

2866. Winther, Jens, 1960– The 4 elements. N.p.: n.p., 1996.
1 score (3 v.); 50 cm.
Wordless; includes recitation in English.
For singers and instrumental ensemble.
Reproduced from holograph.
Contents: Spirit—Fire—Air—Water—Earth.
Composed for: female voices, 2 alto saxophones, 2 tenor saxophones, baritone saxophone, 7 trumpets (also flugelhorns), 3 trombones, 2 bass trombones, 2 keyboards (2nd also piano), guitar, electric bass, percussion (vibraphone, 2 gongs, bass drums, Latin percussion).
Call no.: **1997/175**

2867. Winther, Jens, 1960– Alien cult. N.p.: Jens Winther, 1990.
1 score (17 p.); 39 cm.
For jazz band.
Reproduced from manuscript.
Composed for: 2 alto saxophones (both also flute), 2 tenor saxophones (1st also clarinet, 2nd also bass clarinet), baritone saxophone (also bass clarinet), 5 trumpets (4th–5th also flugelhorn), 5 trombones, percussion (gongs, bass drum, snare drum, cymbals, bells, mallet percussion, chimes, hi-hat), guitar, piano, double bass.
Call no.: **1992/153**

2868. Winther, Jens, 1960– Angels. N.p.: n.p., 1998.
1 score (116 p.); 42 cm.
Latin words.
For mixed choir and jazz band.
Reproduced from manuscript.
Duration: ca. 43:00.
Composed for: SATB chorus, clarinet (or flute or alto saxophone), flute (or soprano saxophone), clarinet (or tenor saxophone), flute (or piccolo or bass clarinet or tenor saxophone), flute (or clarinet or bass clarinet or baritone saxophone), 5 trumpets (all also flugelhorns), 5 trombones (4th–5th also bass trombone), rhythm section (piano [also keyboard], guitar [also glockenspiel], double bass [also electric bass and keyboard]), drum section (drums, timpani, wind chimes, bass drum, triangle), percussion (3 tam-tams, triangle, bass drum,

wind chimes, chimes, glockenspiel, bongos, various Latin percussion instruments).
Commissioned by: Danish Radio Jazz Orchestra and Danish Radio Choir.
Call no.: **2000/200**

2869. Winther, Jens, 1960– Den grå dame = The grey lady. N.p.: Jens Winther, 1993.
1 score (32 p.); 34 x 42 cm.
For big band.
Reproduced from manuscript.
Composed for: 2 alto saxophones, 2 tenor saxophones, baritone saxophone, 5 trumpets, 5 trombones, guitar, piano, double bass, percussion (trap set, gongs, chimes, Latin percussion instruments).
Call no.: **1994/162**

2870. Winther, Jens, 1960– Koncert for trompet og orkester. N.p.: n.p., 1994.
1 score (53 p.); 41 cm.
Reproduced from manuscript.
Composed for: trumpet, 3 flutes, 3 oboes, 2 clarinets, bass clarinet, 3 bassoons, 4 horns, 3 trumpets, 3 trombones, tuba, percussion (triangle, tam-tam, snare drum), timpani, harp, violin I, violin II, viola, violoncello, double bass.
Call no.: **1995/116**

2871. Witt, Greg, 1965– Pearl Harbor: a musical tribute: for concert band with chorus & synchronized video. Midland, TX: Greg Witt, 2002.
1 score (various pagings); 44 cm.
English words.
Duration: ca. 16:08.
Composed for: SATB chorus, piccolo, flute, oboe, bassoon, 3 clarinets, bass clarinet, 2 alto saxophones, tenor saxophone, baritone saxophone, 2 trumpets, 2 horns, 3 trombones, baritone, tuba, electric bass, timpani, percussion (glockenspiel, bass drum, snare drum, cymbals, chimes, drum kit).
Call no.: **2004/148**

2872. Wittinger, Róbert, 1945– Concerto per trio d'archi e orchestra, op. 58 (1997). Bühl/Baden: Antes Edition, 1997.
1 score (84 p.); 30 cm.
Reproduced from manuscript.
Duration: 21:00.
Composed for: violin, viola, violoncello, 3 flutes (3rd also piccolo), 3 oboes, 3 clarinets, 2 bassoons, contrabassoon, 4 horns, 3 trumpets, 3 trombones, tuba, timpani, percussion (tam-tams, 3 suspended cymbals, tambourine, bells, bass drum, 4 tom-toms, large whip, 4 bongos), harp, violin I, violin II, viola, violoncello, double bass.
Commissioned by: Ministerium für Bildung und Kultur Rheinland-Pfalz.
Call no.: **1998/181**

2873. Wittinger, Róbert, 1945– Concerto per violino solo e orchestra op. 43 (1986): Riflessioni I. Studienpartitur. Celle: Moeck, 1987.
1 miniature score (74 p.); 30 cm.
Reproduced from holograph.
Composed for: violin, 4 flutes (4th also piccolo), 4 oboes, 3 clarinets, bass clarinet, 3 bassoons, contrabassoon, 6 horns, 4 trumpets, 3 trombones, bass trombone, tuba, timpani, percussion (marimba, vibraphone, tubular bells, bass chimes, snare drum, triangle, whip, bass drum, 4 tom-toms, 4 suspended cymbals, 4 tam-tams), harp, piano (also celesta and harpsichord), violin I, violin II, viola, violoncello, double bass.
Commissioned by: Südwestfunk Baden-Baden.
Call no.: **1988/111**

2874. Wittinger, Róbert, 1945– Concerto per violoncello solo e orchestra, op. 44 (1987): Riflessioni II. Studienpartitur. Celle: Moeck, 1987.
1 miniature score (75 p.); 30 cm.
Reproduced from holograph.
Composed for: violoncello, 4 flutes, 4 oboes, 3 clarinets, bass clarinet, 3 bassoons, contrabassoon, 6 horns, 4 trumpets, 3 trombones, bass trombone, tuba, timpani, percussion (marimba, vibraphone, tubular bells, whip, bass drum, 4 tom-toms, 4 suspended cymbals, 4 tam-tams), harp, piano (also harpsichord), violin I, violin II, viola, violoncello, double bass.
Commissioned by: Land Rheinland-Pfalz.
Call no.: **1989/140**

2875. Wittinger, Róbert, 1945– Maldoror: spettacolo in quattro atti con 13 immagini, op. 47 (1978–88): per 4 solisti, coro misto, narratore, balletto, orchestra da camera, grande orchestra. Studienpartitur. Celle: Moeck, 1989.
1 miniature score (665 p.); 30 cm.
German or Latin words by Lautréamont, Martin Grzimek, and Róbert Wittinger.
Commentary in German, composer's biography in German and English.
Composed for: narrator, soprano, alto, tenor, baritone (or bass), SATB chorus, stage band (flute, oboe, clarinet, violoncello, double bass, harp, harpsichord), 4 flutes (2nd and 4th also piccolo), 4 oboes (4th also English horn), 4 clarinets (4th also bass clarinet), 4 bassoons (4th also contrabassoon), 6 horns, 4 trumpets, 4 trom-

bones, tuba, timpani, percussion (tam-tams, suspended cymbals, whip, marimba, bass drum, snare drum, bongos, tom-toms, vibraphone, triangle, chimes, crash cymbals), harp, piano, celesta, violin I, violin II, violin III, violin IV, viola I, viola II, violoncello I, violoncello II, double bass I, double bass II.
Call no.: **1990/135**

2876. Wittinger, Róbert, 1945– Maldoror-Requiem: per coro misto, narratore e grande orchestra, op. 42 (1984–1986). Studienpartitur. Celle: Moeck, 1986.
1 score (178 p.); 30 cm.
German or Latin words by Martin Grzimek after Lautréamont (Isidore-Ducasse).
Composed for: narrator, SATB chorus, 4 flutes (4th also piccolo), 4 oboes, 3 clarinets, bass clarinet, 3 bassoons, contrabassoon, 6 horns, 4 trumpets, 3 trombones, bass trombone, tuba, timpani, percussion (marimba, vibraphone, tubular bells, bass bell, snare drum, triangle, whip, bass drum, 4 tom-toms, 4 suspended cymbals, 4 tam-tams), harp, piano (also celesta and harpsichord), violin I, violin II, viola, violoncello, double bass.
Commissioned by: Süddeutscher Rundfunk.
Call no.: **1987/091**

2877. Wittinger, Róbert, 1945– Sinfonia: no. 3, op. 37a, per grande orchestra. Studienpartitur. Celle: Moeck, 1985.
1 score (151 p.); 32 cm.
Duration: ca. 38:00.
Reproduced from holograph.
Composed for: 4 flutes (4th also piccolo), 4 oboes (4th also English horn), 3 clarinets, bass clarinet, 3 bassoons, contrabassoon, 6 horns, 4 trumpets, 3 trombones, bass trombone, tuba, timpani, percussion (xylophone, marimba, vibraphone, tubular bells, 3 bass chimes, 4 tom-toms, 4 suspended cymbals, 4 tam-tams, whip, triangle, bass drum, 4 bongos, piccolo snare drum), harp, piano (also celesta), violin I, violin II, viola, violoncello, double bass.
Call no.: **1986/119**

2878. Wittinger, Róbert, 1945– Sinfonia no. 5 per grande orchestra, op. 54 (1994–95). Bühl: Antes, 1995.
1 score (iv, 119 p.); 30 cm.
Reproduced from holograph.
Duration: ca. 30:00.
Composed for: 4 flutes (4th also piccolo), 4 oboes, 4 clarinets, 4 bassoons (4th also contrabassoon), 6 horns, 4 trumpets, 3 trombones, bass trombone, tuba, timpani, percussion (tubular bells, large tam-tam, 2 suspended cymbals, bass drum, large tom-tom, bongos), harp, violin I, violin II, viola, violoncello, double bass.
Commissioned by: Ministerium für Bildung and Kultur Rheinland-Pfalz.
Call no.: **1997/176**

2879. Wittinger, Róbert, 1945– Sinfonietta per piccola orchestra sinfonica, op. 53 (1994). Bühl: Antes, 1995.
1 score (iv, 108 p.); 30 cm.
Reproduced from holograph.
Duration: ca. 17:00.
Composed for: flute, oboe, clarinet, bassoon, 2 horns, trumpet, trombone, harp, piano, timpani, percussion (tubular bells, bass drum, large bongo, 4 tom-toms, 4 suspended cymbals, 2 tam-tams, 2 whips), violin I, violin II, viola, violoncello, double bass.
Commissioned by: Badisches Staatstheater.
Call no.: **2000/201**

2880. Wolking, Henry, 1948– Forever yesterday = El ayer, siempre: a ballet in 3 acts. Salt Lake City, UT: Wolking Music, 1992.
1 score (174 p.); 28–44 cm.
Reproduced from manuscript.
Duration: 30:00.
Composed for: 2 flutes (1st also Sioux or cedar flute, 2nd also piccolo), oboe (also English horn), clarinet, bass clarinet (also clarinet in E♭), bassoon, horn, trumpet (also flugelhorn), trombone, timpani, percussion (claves, triangle, marimba, tom-tom, suspended cymbals, wine glass, snare drum, glockenspiel, bell sticks, bell tree, rain stick), Native American percussion (2 elk skin Indian drums, rattles, rasp, gourd, hardwood tone drum), piano, violin I, violin II, viola, violoncello, double bass.
Commissioned by: Barlow Endowment for Music Composition at Brigham Young University.
Call no.: **1996/168**

2881. Wolking, Henry, 1948– Trombone tales: a concerto for trombone and orchestra in six movements. Salt Lake City, UT: Wolking Music Publications, 1994.
1 score (115 p.); 44 cm.
Reproduced from manuscript.
Duration: 28:00.
Contents: Fanfare—Bluebell variations—Bourree—Circus scherzo: a three ring circus—Jazz: child of Saturn/ Dan's tune—Salsa and finale.
Composed for: trombone, piccolo, 2 flutes, alto flute, 2 oboes, English horn, 2 clarinets, bass clarinet, 2 bassoons, contrabassoon, 4 horns, 3 trumpets (also flugelhorn), 3 trombones, tuba, timpani, percussion (jazz drum set, marimba, xylophone, glockenspiel, temple

blocks, suspended cymbal, concert crash cymbals, small splash cymbal, Chinese cymbal, snare drum, bass drum, brake drum, anvil, gong, tam-tam, 2 triangles, tubular bells, maracas, bell stick, tenor drums, whip, agogo bells, congas, timbales, bongos, police whistle, cabasa, guiro, woodblock, claves, cowbell), harp, piano, electric bass guitar, violin I, violin II, viola, violoncello, double bass.
Call no.: **1995/117**

2882. Wolman, Amnon, 1955– Concerto for piano, pianos and orchestra: for MIDI grand piano, six MIDI controlled pianos, and orchestra. N.p.: n.p., 1990.
1 score (99 p.); 36 cm.
Duration: ca. 23:00.
Composed for: piano, MIDI pianos, 2 flutes (2nd also piccolo), 2 oboes, 2 clarinets, 2 tenor saxophones, 2 bassoons, 3 horns, percussion (marimba, vibraphone, chimes, xylophone, sizzle cymbal, bass drum, tenor drum, claves, tambourine, maracas, 3 cowbells, triangle, gong, crotales, guiro, hi-hat, temple blocks, suspended cymbal, congas, timpani, snare drum, cymbals, guiro), violin I, violin II, viola, violoncello, double bass.
Commissioned by: Banff Centre, Rockefeller Foundation/Villa Bellaggio, and Djerassi Foundation.
Call no.: **1991/142**

2883. Wolpe, Michael, 1960– Concerto: for recorders' player and chamber orchestra, 1995. N.p.: n.p., 1995.
1 score (80 p.); 30 x 42 cm.
Composed for: recorder, 2 flutes (1st also piccolo), oboe (also English horn), 2 clarinets, horn (or alto saxophone), bassoon, percussion (wind chimes, tambourine, timpani, triangle, vibraphone, darbuka), violin I, violin II, viola, violoncello, double bass.
Call no.: **1997/177**

2884. Wong, Jeffrey, 1938– Wonders of the sky: modern Chinese symphony. United States: Spotlight Design & Printing, 2000.
1 score (113 p.); 28 cm.
For orchestra of Chinese instruments.
Composed for: 2 di, suona, sheng, gu zheng, yang qin, pi pa, zhong ruan, timpani, side drum, triangle, tambourine, woodblock, crash cymbals, pai drum, gao hu, 2 er hus, zhong hu, violoncello, double bass.
Call no.: **2003/143**

2885. Wood, Hugh, 1932– Piano concerto, op. 32 [i.e., 31]. London: Chester Music, 1991.
1 score (150 p.); 30 cm.
Composed for: piano, 2 flutes (2nd also piccolo), 2 oboes (2nd also English horn), clarinet in E♭, 2 clarinets in A (2nd also bass clarinet), 2 bassoons (2nd also contrabassoon), 2 horns, 2 trumpets, trombone, tuba, timpani, percussion (xylophone, tambourine, crash cymbals, whip, triangle, 4 bongos, 5 tom-toms, bass drum, tam-tam, side drum, 3 suspended cymbals, woodblock), harp, celesta, violin I, violin II, viola, violoncello, double bass.
Commissioned by: BBC.
Call no.: **1992/154**

2886. Wood, Hugh, 1932– String quartet no. 4. London: Chester Music, 1993.
1 score (33 p.); 21 x 30 cm.
Reproduced from holograph.
Composed for: 2 violins, viola, violoncello.
Commissioned by: BBC.
Call no.: **1994/163**

2887. Wood, Hugh, 1932– String quartet no. 5, op. 45. London: Chester Music, 2001.
1 score (39 p.); 30 cm.
"Perusal score."
Composed for: 2 violins, viola, violoncello.
Commissioned by: Yorkshire ArtSpace and Music in the Round.
Call no.: **2003/144**

2888. Wood, Hugh, 1932– Variations: for orchestra. London: Chester Music, 1998.
1 score (65 p.); 42 cm.
"Rev. 1998"—p. 1.
Reproduced from manuscript.
Duration: ca. 12:00.
Composed for: 3 flutes (3rd also piccolo), 3 oboes (3rd also English horn), 3 clarinets in A (3rd also bass clarinet), 3 bassoons (3rd also contrabassoon), 4 horns, 3 trumpets, 3 trombones, tuba, timpani, percussion (snare drum, tenor drum, bass drum, suspended cymbal, crash cymbals, large tam-tam, castanets, triangle, tambourine), harp, piano, violin I, violin II, viola, violoncello, double bass.
Call no.: **2000/202**

2889. Wood, Jeffrey, 1954– Lamentationes Ieremiæ prophetæ: for chorus (SATB), vocal soloists and string orchestra. N.p.: Jeffrey Wood, 1998.
1 score (79 p.); 28 cm.
Principally Latin or English with some German words; also printed as text with English translation.
Texts from the Lamentations of Jeremiah and the poetry of Paul Celan, Nelly Sachs, and Dan Pagis.
Note by the composer.

Contents: Introduction—O the night of the weeping children—Death fugue—Tenebræ—Epilogue.
Composed for: soprano, mezzo-soprano, SATB chorus, violin I, violin II, viola, violoncello, double bass.
Commissioned by: Center for the Creative Arts at Austin Peay State University.
Call no.: **2002/193**

2890. Woods, Mike, 1952– Brother: man?. N.p.: n.p., 1992.
1 score (45 leaves); 22 x 29 cm.
Jazz/rock tone poem for chamber orchestra.
For orchestra.
Reproduced from holograph.
Composed for: 2 flutes (both also piccolo), 2 oboes, 2 clarinets, 2 bassoons, 4 horns, 3 trumpets, 2 trombones, tuba, timpani, percussion (vibraphone, trap set, chimes, marimba, temple blocks, crash cymbals, timpani, woodblock, tambourine, tubular bells), violin I, violin II, viola, violoncello, double bass.
Call no.: **1994/164**

2891. Woolf, Randall, 1959– Where the wild things are: a ballet, for chamber orchestra. N.p.: n.p., 1997.
1 score (various pagings); 28 cm.
Based on the book by Maurice Sendak.
Duration: 40:00.
Composed for: flute, piccolo, clarinet, bass clarinet, trumpet, trombone, violin, electric violin, electric bass, double bass, 2 electric keyboards, drum set, marimba.
Call no.: **2002/194**

2892. Wright, George, 1970– The fall of Paris: (a composer finds himself in the shadow of an insurance tower): a string quartet. N.p.: George Wright, 1996.
1 score (55 p.); 28 cm.
Contents: The battle of New Orleans (Poulenc)—The battle of Boston (Messaien [sic])—Tennessee victory rondo (Ives).
Composed for: 2 violins, viola, violoncello.
Call no.: **2000/203**

2893. Wright, Maurice, 1949– Taylor series: for alto saxophone, piano, synthesized sounds and images. Glendale, PA: Maurice Wright, 1997.
1 score (57 p.); 28 cm.
Duration: 30:00.
Composed for: alto saxophone, piano, synthesizer.
Commissioned by: Annie Baker.
Call no.: **2003/145**

2894. Wuorinen, Charles, 1938– Concerto for saxophone quartet and orchestra. New York, NY: C. F. Peters, 1993.
1 score (146 p.); 33 cm.
Duration: 25:00.
Composed for: soprano saxophone, alto saxophone, tenor saxophone, bass saxophone, 3 flutes (3rd also piccolo), 3 oboes, 3 clarinets (3rd also bass clarinet), 3 bassoons (3rd also contrabassoon), 4 horns, 3 trumpets, 3 trombones, tuba, timpani, percussion (xylophone, marimba, vibraphone, glockenspiel, crotales, 4 tom-toms, bass drum, tam-tam), harp, piano, violin I, violin II, viola, violoncello, double bass.
Commissioned by: Beethovenhalle Orchester, Bonn.
Call no.: **1995/118**

2895. Wuorinen, Charles, 1938– Five. New York, NY: C. F. Peters, 1988.
1 score (126 p.); 36 cm.
For amplified violoncello solo and orchestra.
Composed for: amplified violoncello, 2 flutes (2nd also piccolo), 2 oboes, 2 clarinets (2nd also bass clarinet), 2 bassoons (2nd also contrabassoon), 4 horns, 2 trumpets, 2 trombones, bass trombone, tuba, timpani, percussion (bass drum, marimba, woodblocks, vibraphone, xylophone, glockenspiel, tenor drum), harp, violin I, violin II, viola, violoncello, double bass.
Commissioned by: New York City Ballet.
Call no.: **1991/143**

2896. Wuorinen, Charles, 1938– Genesis: for chorus and orchestra (1989). New York, NY: C. F. Peters, 1989.
1 miniature score (180 p.); 33 cm.
Latin words.
Oratorio.
Duration: ca. 35:00.
Composed for: SATB chorus, 3 flutes (3rd also piccolo), 3 oboes, 3 clarinets in A (3rd also bass clarinet), 3 bassoons (3rd also contrabassoon), 4 horns, 3 trumpets, 2 trombones, bass trombone, tuba, timpani, percussion (glockenspiel, vibraphone, marimba, xylophone, tam-tam, 4 tom-toms, bass drum), harp, piano, violin I, violin II, viola, violoncello, violoncello.
Commissioned by: Orchestras of Honolulu, Minnesota, and San Francisco.
Call no.: **1992/155**

2897. Wuorinen, Charles, 1938– Genesis: for chorus and orchestra (1989). New York, NY: C. F. Peters, 1990.
1 score (180 p.); 44 cm.
Latin words.
Oratorio.
Duration: ca. 35:00.

Composed for: SATB chorus, 3 flutes (3rd also piccolo), 3 oboes, 3 clarinets in A (3rd also bass clarinet), 3 bassoons (3rd also contrabassoon), 4 horns, 3 trumpets, 2 trombones, bass trombone, tuba, timpani, percussion (glockenspiel, vibraphone, marimba, xylophone, tam-tam, 4 tom-toms, bass drum), harp, piano, violin I, violin II, viola, violoncello, violoncello.
Commissioned by: Orchestras of Honolulu, Minnesota, and San Francisco.
Call no.: **1993/153**

2898. Wuorinen, Charles, 1938– The golden dance, 1985/6. New York, NY: C. F. Peters, 1986.
1 score (170 p.); 33 cm.
For orchestra.
Reproduced from holograph.
Duration: ca. 21:00.
Composed for: 3 flutes (3rd also piccolo), 3 oboes (3rd also English horn), 3 clarinets in A (3rd also bass clarinet), 3 bassoons (3rd also contrabassoon), 4 horns, 3 trumpets, 3 trombones, tuba, timpani, percussion (antique cymbals, glockenspiel, xylophone, marimba, vibraphone, chimes, triangle, 2 suspended cymbals, tam-tam, snare drum, tom-toms, bass drum), harp, piano (also celesta), violin I, violin II, viola, violoncello, double bass.
Commissioned by: San Francisco Symphony and Meet the Composer Orchestra Residencies Program.
Call no.: **1987/092**

2899. Wuorinen, Charles, 1938– The great procession: for six players. New York, NY: C. F. Peters Co., 1995.
1 score (102 p.); 36 cm.
Duration: 25:00.
Contents: The seven lights—The elders—The chariot—The griffin—The seven virtues—The departure—The unveiling.
Composed for: flute (also piccolo), clarinet (also bass clarinet), violin, violoncello, piano, percussion (marimba, vibraphone, crotales, timpani, bass drum).
Commissioned by: Christian Humann Foundation and New York City Ballet.
Call no.: **1996/169**

2900. Wuorinen, Charles, 1938– The great procession: for six players. New York, NY: C. F. Peters Co., 1995.
1 score (102 p.); 44 cm.
For flute (piccolo), violin, clarinet (bass clarinet), violoncello, percussion (marimba, vibraphone, crotales, timpani, bass drum), and piano.
Duration: 25:00.
Contents: The seven lights—The elders—The chariot—The griffin—The seven virtues—The departure—The unveiling.
Composed for: flute (also piccolo), clarinet (also bass clarinet), violin, violoncello, piano, percussion (marimba, vibraphone, crotales, timpani, bass drum).
Commissioned by: Christian Humann Foundation and New York City Ballet.
Call no.: **2000/204**

2901. Wuorinen, Charles, 1938– The Haroun songbook: for soprano, alto, tenor, bass and piano. New York, NY: C. F. Peters, 2002.
1 score (154 p.); 28 cm.
English words by James Fenton.
"Excerpts, with a newly composed piano accompaniment, from the opera Haroun and the sea of stories"—p. 1.
Duration: ca. 48:00.
Contents: I. Zembla, Zenda, Xanadu; My father noticed none of this; Oh, I am the ocean of notions; Excuse me if I mention; If I could catch those words; Tell us a story; Well, what's the use? I'm empowered; We are two men; My fault again; Get on the bus; Soldiers everywhere; All the people will vote for me; The moody land; Now means now; A person may choose; I wish; An outlandish knight; On the far side of the moon; Now the lagoon is blue—II. It's a princess rescue story; What a chattering, clattering quarelling [sic] crew; Heart shadow; Hush for a moment; To the South Pole; O brave machine; Spies/You can't chop me; I wish; War! Batcheat's song; It's a princess rescue story; It's a party! Back home.
Composed for: soprano, alto, tenor, bass, piano.
Call no.: **2004/149**
Re-entered as: **2005/155**

2902. Wuorinen, Charles, 1938– Piano concerto no. 3.
Call no.: **1985/197**
No materials available.

2903. Wuorinen, Charles, 1938– Piano quintet: (1993–1994). New York, NY: C. F. Peters, 1994.
1 score (75 p.); 37 cm.
Duration: ca. 22:00.
Composed for: 2 violins, viola, violoncello, piano.
Commissioned by: Lincoln Center Productions.
Call no.: **1997/178**

2904. Wuorinen, Charles, 1938– The river of light: for string orchestra with percussion (1995–1996). New York, NY: C. F. Peters, 1996.
1 score (115 p.); 44 cm.
Duration: ca. 17:00.
Composed for: percussion (antique cymbals, chimes, 2 vibraphones, glockenspiel, marimba, cowbell, bass drum, 4 tom-toms, tam-tam, timpani), harp, piano,

celesta, violin I, violin II, viola, violoncello, double bass.
Commissioned by: New York City Ballet.
Call no.: **1998/182**

2905. Wuorinen, Charles, 1938– Sonata for violin and piano (1988). New York, NY: C. F. Peters, 1988.
1 score (57 p.) + 1 part (20 p.); 28 cm.
Duration: ca. 20:00.
Composed for: violin, piano.
Commissioned by: Library of Congress McKim Fund.
Call no.: **1989/141**

2906. Wuorinen, Charles, 1938– String sextet (1988/89). New York, NY: C. F. Peters, 1989.
1 score (74 p.); 28 cm.
Composed for: 2 violins, 2 violas, 2 violoncellos.
Call no.: **1990/136**

2907. Wuorinen, Charles, 1938– Symphony seven: (1996–1997). New York, NY: C. F. Peters, 1997.
1 score (167 p.); 36 cm.
Duration: ca. 30:00.
Composed for: 3 flutes (3rd also piccolo), 3 oboes, 3 clarinets (3rd also bass clarinet), 3 bassoons, 4 horns, 3 trumpets, 2 trombones, bass trombone, tuba, timpani, violin I, violin II, viola, violoncello, double bass.
Commissioned by: Orchestras of Milwaukee, Toledo, Berkeley, and New Hampshire, Meet the Composer, and Koussevitzky Music Foundation in the Library of Congress.
Call no.: **2001/171**
Re-entered as: **2002/195**

2908. Wuorinen, Charles, 1938– Third string quartet: (1986/87). New York, NY: C. F. Peters, 1987.
1 score (28 p.); 36 cm.
Duration: 25:30.
Composed for: 2 violins, viola, violoncello.
Commissioned by: Dartmouth College.
Call no.: **1988/112**

2909. Wuorinen, Charles, 1938– A winter's tale: for soprano and six instruments: a setting of Dylan Thomas' poem, (1992). New York, NY: C. F. Peters, 1992.
1 score (85 p.); 36 cm.
English words by Dylan Thomas.
Duration: ca. 25:00.
Composed for: soprano, clarinet in A, horn, violin, viola, violoncello, piano.
Commissioned by: Brown Foundation of Houston.
Call no.: **1994/165**

2910. Wygant, Shawn, 1965– Piano concerto no. 1. N. p.: A.M.I., 1992.
1 score (25 leaves); 28 x 44 cm.
Reproduced from holograph.
Composed for: piano, 2 flutes, 2 oboes, English horn, bassoon, 4 horns, 2 trumpets, 3 trombones, timpani, violin I, violin II, viola, violoncello, double bass.
Call no.: **1993/154**

2911. Wyner, Yehudi, 1929– Lyric harmony: 1995 (revised 1996). N.p.: Yehudi Wyner, 1996.
1 score (105 p.); 36 cm.
For orchestra.
Composed for: 2 flutes (2nd also piccolo), 2 oboes (2nd also English horn), 2 clarinets (both also clarinet in A, 2nd also bass clarinet), 2 bassoons, contrabassoon, 4 horns, 2 trumpets, 2 trombones, bass trombone, tuba, timpani, percussion (4 tom-toms, 2 pairs of bongos, 5 temple blocks, snare drum, 3 suspended cymbals, bass drum), harp, violin I, violin II, viola, violoncello, double bass.
Commissioned by: Carnegie Hall Corporation.
Call no.: **1998/183**

2912. Wyner, Yehudi, 1929– Prologue and narrative: for cello and orchestra, 1994. New York, NY: American Composers Alliance, 1994.
1 score (124 p.); 44 cm.
Publisher and series from p. 1 of cover.
Composed for: violoncello, piccolo, 2 flutes, alto flute, 2 oboes, English horn, 2 clarinets, bass clarinet, 2 bassoons, contrabassoon, 4 horns, 3 trumpets, 3 trombones, tuba, violin I, violin II, viola, violoncello, double bass.
Commissioned by: RNCM and Peter Biddulph.
Call no.: **1995/119**

2913. Xenakis, Iannis, 1922–2001. Alax.
Call no.: **1986/120**
No materials available.

2914. Xenakis, Iannis, 1922–2001. Keqrops: pour piano et orchestre. Paris: Editions Salabert, 1986.
1 score (36 p.); 40 cm.
Duration: ca. 17:00.
Composed for: piano, 4 flutes, 4 oboes, 4 clarinets (4th also bass clarinet), 4 bassoons (4th also contrabassoon), 4 horns, 4 trumpets, 4 trombones, tuba, timpani, percussion (2 bongos, 3 tom-toms, bass drum), harp, piano, violin I, violin II, viola, violoncello, double bass.
Commissioned by: Phynea and Peter Paroulakis of Australia.
Call no.: **1987/093**

2915. Xenakis, Iannis, 1922–2001. Keqrops: pour piano et orchestre. Paris: Editions Salabert, 1987.
1 score (36 p.); 35 cm.
Duration: ca. 17:00.
Composed for: piano, 4 flutes, 4 oboes, 4 clarinets (4th also bass clarinet), 4 bassoons (4th also contrabassoon), 4 horns, 4 trumpets, 4 trombones, tuba, timpani, percussion (2 bongos, 3 tom-toms, bass drum), harp, piano, violin I, violin II, viola, violoncello, double bass.
Commissioned by: Phynea and Peter Paroulakis of Australia.
Call no.: **1988/113**

2916. Xing, Liu, 1962– First concerto for zhong ruan. N.p.: n.p., 1987.
1 score (133 p.); 38 cm.
Reproduced from manuscript.
Composed for: ruan, 5 dis, 6 shengs, 6 suonas, 2 liuye qins, 4 pipas, 2 ruans, 2 bass ruans, 8 gaohus, 10 er hus, percussion (Chinese cymbals, timpani, bass drum), 6 violoncellos, 4 double basses.
Call no.: **1991/144**

2917. Xu, Shuya, 1959– Symphony no. 1: "Curves" (1986). N.p.: n.p., 1986.
1 score (78 p.); 36 cm.
Reproduced from manuscript.
Duration: ca. 25:00.
Composed for: 3 flutes (all also piccolo, 1st also alto flute), 3 oboes (3rd also English horn), 3 clarinets (3rd also bass clarinet), 3 bassoons (3rd also contrabassoon), 4 horns, 4 trumpets, 3 trombones, tuba, percussion (timpani, glockenspiel, tambourine, bass drums, 5 Chinese tom-toms, xylophone, triangle, maracas, side drum, vibraphone, cymbals, tubular bells, 3 Chinese gongs, 5 woodblocks, 2 tam-tams), harp, piano (also celesta), violin I, violin II, viola, violoncello, double bass.
Call no.: **1988/114**

2918. Yang, Yong, 1955– River songs: for erhu and orchestra. N.p.: Yang Yong, 2002.
1 score (39 p.); 28 cm.
Contents: The river spirit—Da shosho—To the west frontier—a farewell song.
Composed for: erhu, flute (also piccolo), oboe, clarinet, bassoon, horn, trumpet, trombone, percussion (4 temple blocks, small cymbal, ban, triangle, danpi drum, tam-tam, small Chinese bell, whip, 4 tom-toms, small gong, suspended cymbal, wind chimes, Tibetan singing bowl, bass drum, large Chinese gong), violin I, violin II, viola, violoncello, double bass.
Call no.: **2004/150**

2919. Yang, Yong, 1955– Valley spirit: for konghou (Chinese harp) and large orchestra. N.p.: Yang Yong, 1998.
1 score (124 p.); 28 cm.
Duration: 30:00.
Composed for: konghou, piccolo, 2 flutes, 2 oboes, English horn, 2 clarinets, bass clarinet, 2 bassoons, contrabassoon, 4 horns, 3 trumpets, 2 trombones, bass trombone, tuba, 4 timpani, percussion (xylophone, glockenspiel, temple blocks, triangle, tambourine, crash cymbals, vibraphone, suspended cymbal, whip, Chinese drum, 3 tom-toms, hand gong, 2 gongs, marimba, wind chimes, tenor drum, bass drum), violin I, violin II, viola, violoncello, double bass.
Call no.: **2002/197**

2920. Yannatos, James, 1929– Concerto: for string quartet and orchestra. N.p.: James Yannatos, 1996.
1 score (115 p.); 40 cm.
Duration: 22:00.
Program notes by the composer.
Composed for: 2 violins, viola, violoncello, 2 flutes, 2 oboes, 2 clarinets, 2 bassoons, 2 horns, 2 trumpets, 2 trombones, percussion (snare drum, bass drum, bells, suspended cymbal, 3 temple blocks, woodblock, 3 bongos, tambourine, triangle, guiro), violin I, violin II, viola, violoncello, double bass.
Call no.: **1998/184**

2921. Yannatos, James, 1929– Symphonies sacred and secular: prais'd be the fathomless universe (symphony 7). N.p.: James Yannatos, 2002.
1 score (186 p.); 43 cm.
German, Latin, Dutch, Hebrew, English, or Spanish words.
Contents: Prais'd be the fathomless universe. O virtus sapiente; Creation sings its own song; Prais'd be the fathomless universe; Let your heart dance; Prais'd be (Version II); Creation sings its own song—Out of the earth I sing. Out of the earth I sing; I saw creation; In beauty it is finished; My river runs to thee; Sing a joyous song; Out of the earth (reprise)—Strings in the earth and air. Make a joyful noise; Strings in the earth and air; Sans la musique; Make a joyful noise; Asi es mi vida; Instrumental interlude; The family of mankind; Instrumental interlude; A little wave; The family of mankind (reprise); The setting sun.
Composed for: soprano, bass-baritone, 3 flutes (also piccolo), 2 oboes, 2 clarinets, 2 bassoons, 4 horns, 3 trumpets, 3 trombones, tuba, percussion (bells, marimba, xylophone, chimes, 2 Indian bells, wind chimes, 2 suspended cymbals, tam-tam, triangle, maracas, claves, guave, 3 temple blocks, wind chimes (shell), 3

tom-toms, snare drum, tenor drum, bass drum), SATB chorus, harp, violin I, violin II, viola, violoncello, double bass.
Call no.: **2005/156**

2922. Yannatos, James, 1929– Tiananmem [sic] square: symphony no. 4. Cambridge, MA: Sonory, 1992.
1 score (138 p.); 40 cm.
Reproduced from manuscript.
Includes program note by the composer.
Composed for: 2 piccolos, 3 flutes (3rd also piccolo), 2 oboes, 2 clarinets, 2 bassoons, 4 horns, 3 trumpets, 3 trombones, tuba, percussion (bells, xylophone, triangle, suspended cymbal, 2 gongs, maracas, tambourine, timpani, snare drum, tenor drum, bass drum, woodblock), harp, piano, violin I, violin II, viola, violoncello, double bass.
Call no.: **1994/167**
Re-entered as: **1997/179**

2923. Yim, Jay Alan, 1958– Rough magic: for large orchestra. N.p.: Shinkyoku Edition, 2000.
1 score (73 p.); 42 cm.
Duration: ca. 14:00.
Composed for: 3 flutes (all three also piccolo), 3 oboes (1st also oboes d'amore, 3rd also English horn), 3 clarinets, (3rd also bass clarinet), 2 bassoons, contrabassoon, 4 horns, 3 trumpets (all also optional piccolo trumpet), 2 trombones, bass trombone, 2 tubas, 2 harps, 3 keyboard players (piano [4 hands], synthesizer), percussion (brake drum, glockenspiel, xylophone, wood drum, vibraphone, congas, electronic drum trigger-pad, marimba, Chinese dish gong, snare drum, woodblock, bass drum, triangle, woodblock, metal claves, slapstick, 3 roto-toms, Latin cowbells, crotales, tuned anvils, chimes), violin I, violin II, viola, violoncello, double bass.
Commissioned by: Chicago Symphony Orchestra.
Call no.: **2002/196**

2924. Young, La Monte, 1935– The well-tuned piano. 92 I 20 edition. N.p.: DBA Just Eternal Music, 1992.
1 v. of music; 36 cm.
"A compilation of program notes, master theme list, frequency and tuning charts, transcriptions and notation of themes and chordal areas, and timed score of the May 10th, 1987 version"—cover.
Duration: ca. 6:25:00.
Composed for: piano.
Commissioned by: MELA Foundation.
Call no.: **1992/156**

2925. Yttrehus, Rolv, 1926– Symphony number one: for orchestra. New York, NY: APNM, 1997.
1 score (vi, 106 p.); 44 cm.
Duration: ca. 20:00.
Includes structural notes with musical examples.
Composed for: 3 flutes (3rd also piccolo), 3 oboes (3rd also English horn), 3 clarinets in A (3rd also bass clarinet), 3 bassoons (3rd also contrabassoon), 4 horns, 3 trumpets, 2 trombones, bass trombone, tuba, timpani, percussion (xylophone, vibraphone, bass drum, snare drum, 3 tom-toms, 3 tam-tams, 3 suspended cymbals), harp, piano, violin I, violin II, viola, violoncello, double bass.
Call no.: **2000/206**
Re-entered as: **2004/151**

2926. Yttrehus, Rolv, 1926– Symphony number one: for orchestra. Rev. and corr. (Dec. 1998). New York, NY: APNM, 1998.
1 score (vi, 106 p.); 44 cm.
Duration: ca. 24:00.
Includes structural notes with musical examples.
Composed for: 3 flutes (3rd also piccolo), 3 oboes (3rd also English horn), 3 clarinets in A (3rd also bass clarinet), 3 bassoons (3rd also contrabassoon), 4 horns, 3 trumpets, 2 trombones, bass trombone, tuba, timpani, percussion (xylophone, vibraphone, bass drum, snare drum, 3 tom-toms, 3 tam-tams, 3 suspended cymbals), harp, piano, violin I, violin II, viola, violoncello, double bass.
Call no.: **2002/198**
Re-entered as: **2003/147**

2927. Yu, Julian, 1957– Hsiang-wen = Filigree clouds: for orchestra, opus 23. London: Universal Edition, 1993.
1 score (68 p.); 37 cm.
Reproduced from holograph.
Duration: ca. 21:00.
Composed for: 2 piccolos, 2 flutes, 2 oboes, English horn, 3 clarinets, 2 bassoons (2nd also contrabassoon), 4 horns, 2 trumpets, 2 trombones, bass trombone, tuba, percussion (timpani, tam-tam, 3 triangles, 4 temple blocks, glockenspiel, xylophone, high woodblocks, suspended cymbal, small Chinese gong, vibraphone, metal wind chimes, cymbals), harp, piano, violin I, violin II, viola, violoncello, double bass.
Call no.: **1998/185**

2928. Yu, Julian, 1957– Hsiang-wen = Filigree clouds: for orchestra, opus 23. N.p.: Universal Edition, 1995.
1 score (68 p.); 42 cm.
Reproduced from holograph.
Duration: ca. 12:00.
Composed for: 2 piccolos, 2 flutes, 2 oboes, English

horn, 3 clarinets, 2 bassoons (2nd also contrabassoon), 4 horns, 2 trumpets, 2 trombones, bass trombone, tuba, percussion (timpani, tam-tam, 3 triangles, 4 temple blocks, glockenspiel, xylophone, high woodblocks, suspended cymbal, small Chinese gong, vibraphone, metal wind chimes, cymbals), harp, piano, violin I, violin II, viola, violoncello, double bass.
Call no.: **1996/170**

2929. Yu, Julian, 1957– The white snake: opera for marionettes & musical instruments, 1989. London: Universal Edition, 1989.
1 score (133 p.); 30 cm.
Reproduced from manuscript.
Duration: ca. 41:00.
Composed for: clarinet (also clarinet in E♭, bass clarinet, tam-tam, tambourine, fruit tin, 2 temple blocks, drinking glass), trumpet (also woodblock, triangle, crash cymbals, 4 temple blocks, drinking glass, fruit tin, metal wind chimes), trombone (also pengling pair, xiao-tang-gu, crotales, 3 suspended cymbals, xiao-luo, medium gong, drinking glass, 3 triangles), percussion (4 woodblocks, tam-tam, 3 suspended cymbals, vibraphone, xiao-luo, 4 temple blocks, 3 triangles, gong, glockenspiel, marimba, bass drum, metal wind chimes, xiao-bo, xylophone, glass wind chimes, timpani, 3 tom-toms), piano (also celesta), violin (also viola, medium gong, xiao-bo, drinking glass, fruit tin, siren whistle), double bass (also xiao-tang-gu, woodblock, xiao-lu, drinking glass, fruit tin).
Commissioned by: Hans Werner Henze and Münchener Biennale.
Call no.: **1992/157**

2930. Yu, Julian, 1957– Wu-yu: for orchestra. N.p.: Universal Edition, 1990.
1 miniature score (34 p.); 31 cm.
Duration: ca. 10:00.
Reproduced from holograph.
Composed for: 3 flutes (1st also piccolo), 2 oboes, 3 clarinets, 2 bassoons, 4 horns, 2 trumpets, 2 trombones, bass trombone, tuba, percussion (vibraphone, glockenspiel, tam-tam, triangle, suspended cymbal, xylophone, timpani), harp, piano, violin I, violin II, viola, violoncello, double bass.
Call no.: **1991/145**

2931. Yuasa, Jōji, 1929– Chronoplastic III for orchestra (2001): between stasis and kinesis: in memory of Iannis Xenakis. N.p.: n.p., 2001.
1 score (22 p.); 40 cm.
Reproduced from manuscript.
Duration: ca. 13:00.
Composed for: 3 flutes (also piccolo and alto flute), 3 oboes (also English horn), 3 clarinets (also clarinet in E♭ and bass clarinet), 4 horns, 3 trumpets, 3 trombones (also bass trombone), tuba, percussion (vibraphone, suspended cymbal, 2 woodblocks, marimba, tubular bells, tom-tom, mokusho, xylophone, steel drum, bass drum, glockenspiel, cowbells, chromatic gong, crotales, timpani), 2 harps, piano, celesta, violin I, violin II, viola, violoncello, double bass.
Commissioned by: NHK Symphony Orchestra.
Call no.: **2005/158**

2932. Yuasa, Jōji, 1929– Nine levels by Ze-Ami: for quadraphonic computer-generated tape and chamber ensemble. N.p.: Schott Japan Company, 1988.
1 score (57 p.); 37 cm.
Reproduced from manuscript.
Includes English translation by Yasunari Takahashi.
Composed for: tape, 2 flutes (1st also piccolo and alto flute, 2nd also piccolo and bass flute), oboe (also English horn), 2 clarinets (1st also clarinet in E♭, 2nd also bass clarinet), horn, trumpet, trombone (also bass trombone), percussion (vibraphone, wood plate drum, slit drum, 5 woodblocks, bongos, congas, gamelan gong, 2 tam-tams, suspended cymbals, timpani, tubular bells, marimba, xylophone, 5 tom-toms, 5 temple blocks, crotales, Chinese tam-tam, antique cymbal, claves, 4 temple gongs), piano, celesta (also electric piano), 2 violins, viola, violoncello, double bass.
Commissioned by: Ircam.
Call no.: **1991/146**

2933. Yuasa, Jōji, 1929– Revealed time: for viola and orchestra. Tokyo: Schott Japan, 1986.
1 score (42 p.); 42 cm.
Reproduced from manuscript.
Duration: 16:00.
Composed for: viola, 3 flutes (all also piccolo), 2 oboes (2nd also English horn), 3 clarinets (3rd also clarinet in E♭, bass clarinet), 2 bassoons (2nd also contrabassoon), 4 horns, 3 trumpets, 3 trombones, percussion (vibraphone, xylophone, side drum, woodblock, marimba, glockenspiel, celesta, tubular bells, suspended cymbals, bongo, timpani, antique cymbals, crotales), harp, piano (also celesta), violin I, violin II, viola, violoncello, double bass.
Commissioned by: Suntory Foundation.
Call no.: **1988/115**

2934. Yun, Isang, 1917–1995. Symphonie III: in einem Satz, 1985. Partitur. Berlin: Bote & Bock, 1985.
1 score (40 p.); 38 cm.
Reproduced from holograph.

Duration: ca. 24:00.
Composed for: 2 flutes (both also piccolo), 2 oboes, 2 clarinets (2nd also bass clarinet), 2 bassoons (2nd also contrabassoon), 4 horns, 3 trumpets, 2 trombones, tuba, timpani, percussion (guiro, 5 tom-toms, celesta, xylophone, 5 gongs, sleigh bells, glockenspiel, snare drum, bass drum, 2 triangles, 5 temple blocks, 2 tam-tams, 5 cymbals), harp, violin I, violin II, viola, violoncello, double bass.
Commissioned by: 35. Berliner Festwochen.
Call no.: **1986/121**

2935. Zaidel-Rudolph, Jeanne, 1948– At the end of the rainbow. N.p.: n.p., 1988.
1 score (63 p.); 43 cm.
Symphonic poem.
Reproduced from manuscript.
Commentary by the composer.
Composed for: piccolo, 2 flutes, 2 oboes, 2 clarinets, 2 bassoons, contrabassoon, 4 horns, 3 trumpets, 2 trombones, tuba, percussion (timpani, bass drum, hi-hat, crash cymbals, claves, 3 tom-toms, snare drum, 5 temple blocks, tubular bells, tam-tam, woodblock, vibraslap, xylophone, glockenspiel, vibraphone, suspended cymbal, whip, tambourine), harp, violin I, violin II, viola, violoncello, double bass.
Call no.: **1992/158**

2936. Zaidel-Rudolph, Jeanne, 1948– Lifecycle: for choir and chamber ensemble. N.p.: n.p., 2002.
1 score (79 p.); 30 cm.
Wordless.
Composed for: women's chorus with 1 male (also uhadi bows, mouth bows, friction bow, friction drum, double-sided drum), flute, oboe, clarinet (also bass clarinet), bassoon, horn, marimba, percussion (djembe, cabasa, baby rattle, maracas, woodblock, snare drum, 5 temple blocks, cowbell), 2 violins, violoncello, double bass.
Call no.: **2005/159**

2937. Zaimont, Judith Lang, 1945– . . . 3: 4, 5 . . . : oboe, clarinet, violin, viola, bass. Minneapolis, MN: Jeanné, 1997.
1 score (45 p.); 28 cm.
Duration: 18:00.
Composed for: oboe, clarinet, violin, viola, double bass.
Commissioned by: Jeanné, Inc.
Call no.: **2002/199**
Re-entered as: **2003/148**

2938. Zaimont, Judith Lang, 1945– Lamentation.
Composed for: mezzo-soprano, baritone, double SATB chorus, piano, percussion.
Commissioned by: Gregg Smith Singers, Philadelphia Singers, Dale Warland Singers, and I Cantori.
Call no.: **1986/122**
No materials available.

2939. Zaimont, Judith Lang, 1945– The magic world: ritual music for three: bass-baritone, piano, percussion. N.p.: n.p., 1979.
1 score (v, 43 p.); 37 cm.
English words; also printed as text.
Song cycle in 6 movements, based on American Indian texts.
Reproduced from manuscript.
Composed for: bass-baritone (also Indian drum), piano (also finger cymbals), percussion (suspended cymbals, glockenspiel, finger cymbals, jingle bells, tambourine, triangle, 2 woodblocks, 2 cowbells, claves, chimes, Chinese bell tree).
Commissioned by: Duncan Bockus.
Call no.: **1985/198**

2940. Zaimont, Judith Lang, 1945– Sonata: for piano solo. N.p.: n.p., 1999.
52 p. of music; 36 cm.
Program note by the composer.
Contents: Ricerca—Canto—Impronta digitale.
Composed for: piano.
Call no.: **2004/152**
Re-entered as: **2005/160**

2941. Zaimont, Judith Lang, 1945– Symphony no. 1, 1994. N.p.: n.p., 1994.
1 score (123 p.); 43 cm.
Composed for: piccolo, 2 flutes, 2 oboes, English horn, 2 clarinets, bass clarinet, 2 bassoons, contrabassoon, 4 horns, 3 trumpets, 3 trombones, tuba, harp, piano (also celesta), percussion (timpani, vibraphone, glockenspiel, snare drum, 2 tom-toms, tenor drum, bass drum, 2 triangles, tambourine, crash cymbals, suspended cymbal, tam-tam, tubular bells, whip), violin I, violin II, viola, violoncello, double bass.
Commissioned by: Central Wisconsin Symphony Orchestra.
Call no.: **1995/120**
Re-entered as: **1996/171** and **2000/207**

2942. Zeidman, Eyal, 1959– Passacaglia for violin solo: [op. 1]. N.p.: n.p., 1989.
23 leaves of music; 37 cm.
Reproduced from holograph.
Duration: ca. 18:00.
Composed for: violin.
Call no.: **1990/137**

2943. Zeidman, Eyal, 1959– Violin concerto. N.p.: n.p., 199-?.
1 score (55 p.); 30 x 43 cm.
Reproduced from manuscript.
Duration: 28:00.
Composed for: violin, 2 flutes (1st also piccolo), 2 oboes, 2 clarinets, bass clarinet, 2 bassoons, 2 horns, 2 trumpets, 2 trombones, bass trombone, tuba, percussion (timpani, 2 snare drums, 2 cymbals, whip, bass drum, tam-tam), violin I, violin II, viola, violoncello, double bass.
Call no.: **1991/147**

2944. Zhang, Zhao, 1964– First string quartet: op. 20. N.p.: n.p., 1998.
1 score (16 p.); 37 cm.
Reproduced from manuscript.
Performance notes in Chinese and English.
Composed for: 2 violins, viola, violoncello.
Call no.: **2003/149**

2945. Zhou, Long, 1953– Poems from Tang = Tang shi si shou: for string quartet and orchestra. Bryn Mawr, PA: Theodore Presser Co., 1996.
1 score (141 p.); 44 cm.
Composed for: 2 violins, viola, violoncello, 3 flutes (3rd also piccolo), 3 oboes (3rd also English horn), 3 clarinets (3rd also bass clarinet), 2 bassoons, contrabassoon, 4 horns, 3 trumpets, 3 trombones, tuba, timpani (also crotales, Chinese cymbal, cymbals), percussion (xylophone, glockenspiel, striking bells, Chinese cymbals, suspended cymbal, tam-tam, triangle, sharp block, bamboo chimes, vibraphone, temple blocks, crash cymbals, wind chimes, nipple gong, marimba, crotales, hand gong, large tom-tom, tubular chimes, wind gong, 2 bongos, 2 timbales, 2 congas, Chinese bass drum, claves), harp, violin I, violin II, viola, violoncello, double bass.
Commissioned by: Brooklyn Philharmonic Orchestra.
Call no.: **1996/172**

2946. Zhou, Long, 1953– Rites of chimes: for winds, percussion, pipa, zheng, erhu, and violoncello. Study score. New York, NY: Oxford University Press, 2000.
1 miniature score (151 p.); 28 cm.
Third movement not included.
Duration: ca. 1:15:00.
Program notes and biographical notes on composer.
Contents: Spirit of chimes—Secluded orchid—Impression of wintersweet: movement pending—Tipsy improvisation—Tang court music—Dunhuang pipa—Tales from the cave.
Composed for: violoncello, dadi (also qudi, bangdi, xiao, xun), sheng (also guanzi), percussion (bronze bells, nao, clink bells, glockenspiel, Chinese cymbals, hand gongs, suspended cymbal, tam-tam, wind gong, high block, Chinese bass drum, 3 Chinese tom-toms, claves, chime stones, 5 temple blocks, mark tree, clappers, tom-tom, yangqin, yunlou, deep gong), pipa, zheng (also clink bells and claves), erhu.
Call no.: **2002/119**
Also available:
Call no.: **2002/119 mvt 3**

2947. Zhou, Long, 1953– Tian ling = Nature and spirit: for pipa and 14 players. New York, NY: Zhou Long, 1992.
1 score (68 p.); 28 cm.
Duration: 15:00.
Composed for: pipa, flute (also alto flute), oboe (also English horn), clarinet (also bass clarinet), bassoon, trumpet, horn, trombone, percussion (vibraphone, 5 temple blocks, high suspended cymbal, marimba, glockenspiel, tubular bell, pitched drums, 2 bongos, 5 woodblocks, small striking bells, 2 gongs, tam-tam, mark tree, low suspended cymbal, bass drum), piano, violin, viola, violoncello, double bass.
Commissioned by: Music lives.
Call no.: **1995/121**

2948. Zhu, Jianer, 1922– Ecstasy of nature: concerto for so-na and orchestra, op. 30. N.p.: n.p., 1989.
1 score (48 p.); 32 cm.
Reproduced from manuscript.
Composed for: so-na, piccolo, 2 flutes, 2 oboes, 2 clarinets, 4 horns, 2 trumpets, 2 trombones, timpani, percussion (crash cymbals, suspended cymbals, tambourine, tam-tam, triangle, xylophone, chimes, snare drum), harp, piano, violin I, violin II, viola, violoncello, double bass.
Call no.: **1990/138**

2949. Zhu, Jianer, 1922– Harmonious: quintet for Chinese ethnic instruments (di, cheng, er-hu, bass-hu, percussion). N.p.: n.p., 1992.
1 score (8 p.); 28 cm.
Composed for: di, cheng, er-hu, bass-hu, percussion.
Call no.: **1996/173**

2950. Zhu, Jianer, 1922– Symphony no. 1: op. 27. N. p.: n.p., 1986.
1 score (136 p.); 36 cm.
Reproduced from manuscript.
Duration: ca 46:00.
Composed for: 3 flutes (all also piccolo), 3 oboes (3rd also English horn), 2 clarinets, clarinet in E♭ (also

bass clarinet), 2 bassoons, contrabassoon, 6 horns, 4 trumpets, 3 trombones, tuba, percussion (timpani, triangle, castanets, maracas, whip, 2 tambourines, cymbals, suspended cymbals, bass drum, tam-tam, 4 tom-toms, woodblock, temple block, bangu, tanggu, mang-lo, bell, xylophone, vibraphone), 2 harps, piano, violin I, violin II, viola, violoncello, double bass.
Call no.: **1988/116**
Re-entered as: **1989/142**

2951. Zhu, Jianer, 1922– Symphony no. 4: 6.4.2-1, op. 31. N.p.: n.p., 1990.
1 score (38 p.); 33 cm.
"Chamber symphony for bamboo flute and 22 strings"—caption.
Reproduced from manuscript.
Composed for: bamboo flute, 12 violins, 4 violas, 4 violoncellos, 2 double basses.
Call no.: **1995/122**

2952. Zhu, Jianer, 1922– Symphony no. 6: "3 Y." N.p.: n.p., 1994.
1 score (75 p.); 28 cm.
For orchestra and tape.
Reproduced from manuscript.
Duration: ca 46:00.
Composed for: tape, piccolo, flute, alto flute, 2 oboes, English horn, 2 clarinets, bass clarinet, 2 bassoons, contrabassoon, 4 horns, 4 trumpets, 3 trombones, tuba, timpani, percussion (dabo, daluo, crash cymbals, suspended cymbal, bar chimes, tom-tom, tambourine, whip, vibraphone, medium clapper bell, ciao-bo, paigu, temple blocks, cymbals, maracas, low clapper bell, ratchet, thundersheet, tam-tam, bass drum, xylophone, triangle, tambourine, bozhong), harp, violin I, violin II, viola, violoncello, double bass.
Call no.: **1997/180**
Re-entered as: **1998/186** and **2000/208**

2953. Zhu, Jianer, 1922– Symphony no. 10: "Fishing in snow": for tape (recital and quin) and orchestra). N.p.: n.p., 1998.
1 score (45 p.); 30 cm.
Chinese words; also printed as text with English translation.
Poem by Liu Zon-yuan.
Reproduced from manuscript.
Composed for: tape, 3 flutes (3rd also piccolo), 3 oboes, 3 clarinets (3rd also bass clarinet), 2 bassoons, contrabassoon, 4 horns, 3 trumpets, 3 trombones, tuba, timpani, percussion (bass drum, vibraslap, 5 tom-toms, whip, cymbals, snare drum, xylophone, suspended cymbal, maracas, tam-tam, crotales, 2 temple blocks, sandpaper blocks, ratchet, vibraphone, piano), violin I, violin II, viola, violoncello, double bass.
Commissioned by: Fromm Music Foundation, Harvard University.
Call no.: **2002/200**

2954. Zhu, Jianer, 1922– Symphony no. 10: "The snowbound river": for tape (recital and quin) and orchestra). N.p.: n.p., 1998.
1 score (43 p.); 29 cm.
Chinese words by Liu Zon-yuan; also printed as text with English translation.
Reproduced from manuscript.
Composed for: tape, 3 flutes (3rd also piccolo), 3 oboes, 3 clarinets (3rd also bass clarinet), 2 bassoons, contrabassoon, 4 horns, 3 trumpets, 3 trombones, tuba, timpani, percussion (bass drum, vibraslap, 5 tom-toms, whip, cymbals, snare drum, xylophone, suspended cymbal, maracas, tam-tam, crotales, 2 temple blocks, sandpaper blocks, ratchet, vibraphone, piano), violin I, violin II, viola, violoncello, double bass.
Commissioned by: Fromm Music Foundation, Harvard University.
Call no.: **2001/172**

2955. Zhuo, Rui-Shi, 1956– Dao ban: for pi-pa and chamber ensemble. Vancouver: Zhuo Rui-Shi, 1993.
1 score (22 p.); 29 cm.
Reproduced from holograph.
Composed for: pipa, flute, clarinet, horn, trumpet, piano, percussion (xylophone, small Chinese tam-tam, temple block, Chinese cymbals, na bong zi, Chinese drum), violin, 2 violoncellos, 2 double basses.
Commissioned by: Vancouver New Music Society and Vancouver Symphony Orchestra.
Call no.: **1995/123**
Re-entered as: **2000/209**

2956. Zhuo, Rui-Shi, 1956– Go for me to China: opera in concert format. Vancouver: Canadian Conservatory of Music, 2001.
1 miniature score (various pagings); 28 cm.
English words by Elizabeth Hlookoff.
Composed for: 2 flutes (2nd also piccolo), 2 oboes, 2 clarinets, 2 bassoons, 3 horns, 2 trumpets, trombone, bass trombone, timpani, percussion (snare drum, xylophone, bass drum, glockenspiel, cymbals, suspended cymbal, triangle), harp, piano, violin I, violin II, viola, violoncello, double bass.
Commissioned by: Far East Broadcasting Associate of Canada.
Call no.: **2003/150**

2957. Zhuo, Rui-Shi, 1956– Prelude for pi-pa and sino-west percussions. N.p.: n.p., 1991.
1 score (16 leaves); 28 cm.
Reproduced from holograph.
Composed for: pipa, percussion (timpani, piano, vibraphone, orchestra bells, xylophone, marimba, claves, Chinese blocks, temple blocks, woodblocks, 2 Chinese tam-tams, Chinese cymbals, Chinese tom-tom, metal chimes, guiro, suspended cymbal, sizzle cymbal).
Call no.: **1993/119**

2958. Ziffrin, Marilyn J., 1926– Orchestra piece. N.p.: n.p., 198-?.
1 score (39 p.); 40 cm.
Reproduced from manuscript.
Duration: ca. 8:30.
Composed for: 2 flutes, 2 oboes, 2 clarinets, 2 bassoons, 2 horns, 2 trumpets, 2 trombones, timpani, percussion (snare drum, suspended cymbal, crash cymbals), violin I, violin II, viola, violoncello, double bass.
Call no.: **1985/199**

2959. Zimmermann, Heinz Werner, 1930– The Hebrew chillen's hallelu. N.p.: n.p., 198-?.
1 score (125 p.); 42 cm.
English words.
Cantata for soloists, chorus, and orchestra.
Texts from 8 American spirituals.
Reproduced from manuscript.
Duration: ca. 40:00.
Contents: He's got the whole world in His hands—My God is a rock in a weary land—Give me that old-time religion—Go down, Moses—Joshua fit the Battle of Jericho—Little David, play on your harp—Job (I'm on my way)—We shall overcome.
Composed for: soprano, contralto, tenor, bass, boys' chorus, SATB chorus, 3 flutes (3rd also piccolo), 2 oboes, 2 clarinets, 2 bassoons, contrabassoon, 4 horns, 3 trumpets, 3 trombones, tuba, timpani, percussion (trap set, celesta, vibraphone, woodblock, suspended cymbal, 7 tom-toms, tam-tam, bass drum, tambourine), harp, violin I, violin II, viola, violoncello, double bass.
Commissioned by: Philharmonischer Chor Berlin.
Call no.: **1987/094**

2960. Zimmermann, Walter, 1949– Vom Nutzen des Lassens.
Call no.: **1985/200**
No materials available.

2961. Zinkus, Giedrius, 1969– Kontrastinė simfonija: 1993. N.p.: G. Zinkus, 1993.
1 score (56 p.); 30 cm.
For orchestra.
Composed for: 3 flutes (1st also piccolo), 3 oboes (3rd also English horn), 3 clarinets (1st also clarinet in E♭, 3rd also bass clarinet), 3 bassoons (3rd also contrabassoon), 4 horns, 3 trumpets, 3 trombones, tuba, percussion (timpani, tam-tam, bass drum, vibraphone, triangle, snare drum, ratchet, glockenspiel, 5 cowbells, xylophone, tambourine, cymbals, elephant bell, 5 tom-toms, hi-hat), harp, piano, harpsichord, celesta, violin I, violin II, viola, violoncello, double bass.
Call no.: **1995/124**

2962. Zohn-Muldoon, Ricardo, 1962– Candelabra III. N.p.: n.p., 2002.
1 score (75 p.); 28 cm.
Reproduced from manuscript.
Performance notes in English and program note in English and Spanish.
Composed for: percussion, piano, bass clarinet, violin I, violin II, viola, violoncello, double bass.
Call no.: **2005/161**

2963. Zonn, Paul Martin, 1938– The clarinet in my mind. N.p.: n.p., 1988.
1 score (48 p.); 22 x 36 cm.
Reproduced from manuscript.
Contents: Mirror and reflections—Old dances—And nothing more—A five minute stillness in September—Like the spider-spin of the imagination—New dances—From a forgotten dream.
Composed for: clarinet, bassoon, horn, trumpet, trombone, violin, double bass, percussion (bamboo wind chimes, snare drum, tambourine, xylophone, tom-toms, bass drum, cowbells, cymbals, maracas, metal wind chimes, triangle).
Commissioned by: John Bruce Yeh and Chicago Pro Musica.
Call no.: **1989/143**

2964. Zorn, John, 1953– Contes de fées. Full score. N.p.: Carl Fischer, 2000.
1 score (65 p.); 43 cm.
For violin and orchestra.
Duration: ca. 12:00.
Composed for: violin, flute, alto flute, oboe, English horn, clarinet in E♭ (also bass clarinet), clarinet (also bass clarinet), bassoon, contrabassoon, horn, trombone, tuba, percussion (glockenspiel, 5 tom-toms, bass drum, 2 suspended cymbals, gong, 5 Burmese gongs, wind machine, metal, castanets, high claves, slapsticks, 6 temple blocks, crotales, vibraphone, shaker, snare drum, small triangle, tam-tam, small prayer bell, guiro, low claves, 2 maracas, very small prayer bell, 4

timpani, tubular bells, bongos, 5 triangles, crash cymbals, 5 woodblocks), keyboard (piano, organ, celesta, harpsichord), violin I, violin II, viola, violoncello, double bass.
Call no.: **2002/201**

2965. Zorzi, Juan Carlos, 1935– Antígona Vélez: tragedia lirica en 3 actos y 5 cuadros. N.p.: n.p., 1991.
1 score (3 v.); 36 cm.
Spanish words by Javier Collazo, after Leopoldo Marechal.
Composed for: voices, SATB chorus, 3 flutes (3rd also piccolo), 3 oboes (3rd also English horn), 3 clarinets (3rd also bass clarinet), 3 bassoons (3rd also contrabassoon), 4 horns, 3 trumpets, 3 trombones, tuba, timpani, percussion (vibraphone, xylophone, glockenspiel, 3 cymbals, large tam-tam, bass drum, bombo, orchestra bells, timbre, jingles, slapstick, woodblock, triangle, guiro), harp, 2 pianos (2nd also celesta), 2 amplified guitars, violin I, violin II, viola, violoncello, double bass.
Call no.: **1992/159**
Re-entered as: **1993/155**
Also available:
Call no.: **1993/155 libretto**

2966. Zorzi, Juan Carlos, 1935– Epopeya. N.p.: n.p., 1986.
1 score (72 p.); 36 cm.
For orchestra.
Reproduced from manuscript.
Composed for: 3 flutes (3rd also piccolo), 3 oboes, 3 clarinets, 3 bassoons, 4 horns, 3 trumpets, trumpet in A, 3 trombones, tuba, timpani, percussion (vibraphone, glockenspiel, 2 suspended cymbals, crash cymbals, bass drum, snare drum), 2 harps, piano (also celesta), violin I, violin II, viola, violoncello, double bass.
Call no.: **1990/139**

2967. Zupko, Ramon, 1932– Where the mountain crosses: for mezzo soprano and piano, 1982. N.p.: n.p., 1982.
1 score (45 p.); 28 cm.
English words, also printed as text.
Song cycle, based on lyrics of American Indian tribes.
Reproduced from manuscript.
Duration: ca. 25:00.
Contents: Dream song (Chippewa)—Twelfth song of the thunder (Navajo)—The rock (Omaha)—Dream song (Wintun)—The wind blows from the sea (Papago)—Love song (Otomi)—Lullaby (Hopi)—Fire-fly song (Ojibwa)—Mountain chant (Navajo)—Dream song (Papago).
Composed for: mezzo-soprano, piano.
Call no.: **1985/201**

2968. Zwilich, Ellen Taaffe, 1939– Clarinet concerto. King of Prussia, PA: Merion Music: T. Presser, 2002.
1 score (43 p.); 44 cm.
Composed for: clarinet, flute, oboe, bassoon, 2 horns, cornet, percussion, violin I, violin II, viola, violoncello, double bass.
Commissioned by: Arlene and Dr. Milton D. Berkman Philanthropic Fund.
Call no.: **2004/153**

2969. Zwilich, Ellen Taaffe, 1939– Concerto: for piano, violin, cello and orchestra. Bryn Mawr, PA: Merion Music: Theodore Presser, 1995.
1 score (101 p.); 36 cm.
Duration: ca. 24:00.
Composed for: piano, violin, violoncello, flute, 2 oboes, 2 clarinets, 2 bassoons, 2 horns, 2 trumpets, timpani, violin I, violin II, viola, violoncello, double bass.
Commissioned by: Minnesota Orchestra.
Call no.: **1997/181**

2970. Zwilich, Ellen Taaffe, 1939– Concerto for flute and orchestra. Full score. N.p.: Merion Music, 1989.
1 score (107 p.); 44 cm.
Reproduced from holograph.
Composed for: flute, oboe, English horn, 2 clarinets, 2 bassoons, 2 cornets, 2 trombones, bass trombone, timpani, percussion (4 suspended cymbals, triangle, tambourine, conga, crotales), harp, violin I, violin II, viola, violoncello, double bass.
Commissioned by: Boston Symphony Orchestra.
Call no.: **1991/148**

2971. Zwilich, Ellen Taaffe, 1939– Concerto for oboe and orchestra, 1990. Full score. Bryn Mawr, PA: T. Presser, 1990.
1 score (63 p.); 38 cm.
Reproduced from holograph.
Composed for: oboe, piccolo, flute, oboe, oboe d'amore, English horn, 2 clarinets, bassoon, contrabassoon, 4 horns, 2 cornets, timpani, percussion (crotales, glockenspiel, xylophone, 2 suspended cymbals, sizzle cymbal, 4 roto-toms), violin I, violin II, viola, violoncello, double bass.
Commissioned by: Musical Arts Association and friends of John Mack.
Call no.: **1992/160**

2972. Zwilich, Ellen Taaffe, 1939– Concerto for piano and orchestra (1986). Bryn Mawr, PA: T. Presser Co., 1986.

1 score (155 p.); 46 cm.
Reproduced from holograph.
Duration: ca. 22:00.
Composed for: piano, piccolo, 2 flutes, 2 oboes, English horn, 2 clarinets (2nd also clarinet in E♭), bass clarinet, 2 bassoons, contrabassoon, 4 horns, 3 trumpets, 3 trombones, tuba, timpani, percussion (vibraphone, marimba, glockenspiel, piccolo snare drum, tenor drum, bass drum, 2 suspended cymbals, gong), violin I, violin II, viola, violoncello, double bass.
Commissioned by: Carnegie Hall, Detroit Symphony Orchestra, and American Symphony Orchestra League.
Call no.: **1987/095**
Also available:
Call no.: **1987/095 study score**

2973. Zwilich, Ellen Taaffe, 1939– Concerto for piano and orchestra (1986). Bryn Mawr, PA: T. Presser Co., 1986.
1 score (155 p.); 46 cm.
Reproduced from holograph.
Duration: ca. 24:00.
Correction in pencil on p. 155.
Composed for: piano, piccolo, 2 flutes, 2 oboes, English horn, 2 clarinets (2nd also clarinet in E♭), bass clarinet, 2 bassoons, contrabassoon, 4 horns, 3 trumpets, 3 trombones, tuba, timpani, percussion (vibraphone, marimba, glockenspiel, piccolo snare drum, tenor drum, bass drum, 2 suspended cymbals, gong), violin I, violin II, viola, violoncello, double bass.
Commissioned by: Carnegie Hall, Detroit Symphony Orchestra, and American Symphony Orchestra League.
Call no.: **1989/144**

2974. Zwilich, Ellen Taaffe, 1939– Concerto for trombone and orchestra (1988). N.p.: Ellen Taaffe Zwilich, 1990.
1 score (87 p.); 58 cm.
Reproduced from manuscript.
Composed for: trombone, piccolo, 2 flutes, 2 oboes, English horn, 2 clarinets, bass clarinet, 2 bassoons, contrabassoon, 6 horns, 3 trumpets, 2 trombones, bass trombone, tuba, timpani, percussion (vibraphone, glockenspiel, sizzle cymbal, suspended cymbal, gong, tom-toms, snare drum, bass drum), piano, violin I, violin II, viola, violoncello, double bass.
Commissioned by: Chicago Symphony Orchestra.
Call no.: **1990/140**

2975. Zwilich, Ellen Taaffe, 1939– Concerto for violin and orchestra (1997). Full score. King of Prussia, PA: Merion Music: Theodore Presser, 1998.
1 score (123 p.); 43 cm.
Duration: ca. 26:00.
Composed for: violin, piccolo, flute, oboe, English horn, clarinet, bass clarinet, bassoon, contrabassoon, 2 horns, 2 trumpets, timpani, harp, violin I, violin II, viola, violoncello, double bass.
Commissioned by: Carnegie Hall Corporation.
Call no.: **2000/210**
Re-entered as: **2003/151**

2976. Zwilich, Ellen Taaffe, 1939– Concerto for violin, violoncello, and orchestra. Bryn Mawr, PA: Merion Music: T. Presser, 1992.
1 score (98 p.); 31 cm.
Reproduced from holograph.
Duration: ca. 18:00.
Composed for: violin, violoncello, 2 flutes, oboe, English horn, 2 clarinets, 2 bassoons, 2 horns, 2 trumpets, timpani, violin I, violin II, viola, violoncello, double bass.
Commissioned by: Louisville Orchestra.
Call no.: **1993/156**

2977. Zwilich, Ellen Taaffe, 1939– Double quartet.
Composed for: 4 violins, 2 violas, 2 violoncellos.
Commissioned by: Chamber Music Society of Lincoln Center.
Call no.: **1985/202**
No materials available.

2978. Zwilich, Ellen Taaffe, 1939– Symphony no. 2 for orchestra: 'cello symphony. Bryn Mawr, PA: Merion Music; T. Presser Co., 1987.
1 score (116 p.); 31 cm.
Reproduced from holograph.
Duration: ca. 24:00.
Composed for: violoncello, piccolo, 2 flutes, 2 oboes, English horn, 2 clarinets (2nd also clarinet in E♭), bass clarinet, 2 bassoons, contrabassoon, 4 horns, 3 trumpets, 2 trombones, bass trombone, tuba, timpani, percussion (snare drum, bass drum, 2 suspended cymbals, suspended sizzle cymbal, gong, slapstick, crotales), piano, violin I, violin II, viola, violoncello, double bass.
Commissioned by: Dr. and Mrs. Ralph I. Dorfman.
Call no.: **1986/123**
Re-entered as: **1988/117**

2979. Zwilich, Ellen Taaffe, 1939– Symphony no. 3. Bryn Mawr, PA: Merion Music: Theodore Presser, 1993.
1 score (79 p.); 44 cm.
Reproduced from holograph.
Duration: ca. 22:00.

Composed for: piccolo, 2 flutes, alto flute, 2 oboes, English horn, 2 clarinets, bass clarinet, 2 bassoons, contrabassoon, 4 horns, 3 trumpets, 3 trombones, tuba, timpani, percussion (xylophone, vibraphone, tambourine, 3 cymbals, hi-hat, 2 pedal bass drums, 2 orchestra cymbals, 2 tam-tams, 2 sizzle cymbals, 2 bass drums), violin I, violin II, viola, violoncello, double bass.
Commissioned by: Philharmonic-Symphonic Society of New York.
Call no.: **1995/125**

2980. Zwilich, Ellen Taaffe, 1939– Symphony no. 3 (1992). Full score. Bryn Mawr, PA: Merion Music: T. Presser Co., 1992.
1 score (79 p.); 44 cm.
Reproduced from holograph.
Duration: ca. 22:00.
Composed for: piccolo, 2 flutes, alto flute, 2 oboes, English horn, 2 clarinets, bass clarinet, 2 bassoons, contrabassoon, 4 horns, 3 trumpets, 3 trombones, tuba, timpani, percussion (xylophone, vibraphone, tambourine, 3 cymbals, hi-hat, 2 pedal bass drums, 2 orchestra cymbals, 2 tam-tams, 2 sizzle cymbals, 2 bass drums), violin I, violin II, viola, violoncello, double bass.
Commissioned by: Philharmonic-Symphonic Society of New York.
Call no.: **1994/168**

2981. Zwilich, Ellen Taaffe, 1939– Symphony no. 4: "The gardens": for orchestra, with mixed chorus and children's chorus. Bryn Mawr, PA: Merion Music: T. Presser Co., 2000.
1 score (95 p.); 31 cm.
English or Latin words.
Duration: ca. 28:00.
Contents: Litany of endangered plants—Meditation on living fossils—A pastoral journey—The children's promise.
Composed for: SATB chorus, children's chorus, piccolo, 2 flutes, 2 oboes, English horn, 2 clarinets, bass clarinet, 2 bassoons, contrabassoon, 4 horns, 3 trumpets, 2 trombones, bass trombone, tuba, timpani, percussion (vibraphone, glockenspiel, tubular bells, hi-hat cymbals, suspended cymbals, tam-tams, large bass drum), violin I, violin II, viola, violoncello, double bass.
Commissioned by: Michigan State University.
Call no.: **2002/202**
Re-entered as: **2005/162**

Appendix A

Winning Entries by Competition Year

The following is a chronologic list of the winners of the Grawemeyer Award for Music Composition.

1985: Witold Lutosławski, *Symphony no. 3*
1986: György Ligeti, *Etudes for piano*
1987: Harrison Birtwistle, *The mask of Orpheus*
1988: No award
1989: Chinary Ung, *Inner voices*
1990: Joan Tower, *Silver ladders*
1991: John Corigliano, *Symphony no. 1*
1992: Krzysztof Penderecki, *Adagio for large orchestra*
1993: Karel Husa, *Concerto for violoncello and orchestra*
1994: Tōru Takemitsu, *Fantasma/cantos for clarinet and orchestra*
1995: John Adams, *Violin concerto*
1996: Ivan Tcherepnin, *Double concerto for violin, violoncello, and orchestra*
1997: Simon Bainbridge, *Ad ora incerta–four orchestral songs from Primo Levi*
1998: Tan Dun, *Marco Polo*
1999: No competition
2000: Thomas Adès, *Asyla*
2001: Pierre Boulez, *Sur incises*
2002: Aaron Jay Kernis, *Colored field*
2003: Kaija Saariaho, *L'amour de loin*
2004: Unsuk Chin, *Concerto for violin and orchestra*
2005: George Tsontakis, *Violin concerto no. 2*

Appendix B

Entries by Competition Year

The following is an alphabetic list of the composers who submitted entries to the Grawemeyer Award for Music Composition by competition year. Winners in each year appear in bold.

1985

Adams, John Luther
Ain, Noa
Applebaum, Edward
Argento, Dominick
Armer, Elinor
Bach, Jan
Balassa, Sándor
Balliana, Franco
Bates, Augusta Cecconi
Beaser, Robert
Berkeley, Michael
Biggs, John
Bilucaglia, Claudio
Birtwistle, Harrison
Bisceglia, Stefano
Blake, David
Body, Jack
Bokser, Zelman
Bolcom, William
Borwick, Doug
Boykan, Martin
Brant, Henry
Bresnick, Martin
Brody, Jeffrey
Bryant, Curtis
Burgstahler, Elton
Campana, Jose Luis
Campbell, Ramón
Carr, Edwin
Carter, Elliott
Chan, Ka Nin
Chiaramello, Giancarlo
Cikker, Ján
Cohan, John Alan
Colgrass, Michael
Consoli, Marc-Antonio
Constant, Marius
Constantinides, Dinos
Conyngham, Barry
Cooney, Cheryl
Cooper, Paul
Coral, Giampaolo
Cresswell, Lyell
Daniels, M. L.
Del Tredici, David
Delz, Christoph
Depraz, Raymond
Dillon, James
Dinescu, Violeta
Donatoni, Franco
Downey, John W.
Druckman, Jacob
Durkó, Zsolt
Dusapin, Pascal
Earnest, John David
Einaudi, Ludovico
Eliasson, Anders
Faith, Richard
Farquhar, David
Fermani, Simone
Ferris, William
Flagello, Nicolas
Francesconi, Luca
Freund, Don
Gaburo, Kenneth
Garuti, Mario
Garwood, Margaret
Gentile, Ada
Gerber, Steven. R.
Goldstaub, Paul R.
Gould, Morton
Halffter, Cristóbal
Hall, Charles J.
Hanger, Howard
Hanson, Geoffrey
Harbison, John
Harper, William
Harris, Ross
Harrison, Lou
Heisinger, Brent
Hespos, Hans-Joachim
Hill, Jackson
Hoffman, Joel
Hopkins, James
Hovhaness, Alan
Howard, Dean C.
Hutcheson, Jere T.
Ichiba, Kōsuke
Ichikawa, Toshiharu
Ivey, Jean Eichelberger
Jankowski, Loretta
Jevtic, Ivan
Kantušer, Božidar
Kaufmann, Dieter
Kikuchi, Masaharu
Knussen, Oliver
Kobialka, Daniel
Koc, Marcelo
Kraft, William
Kramer, Jonathan D
Kvam, Oddvar S.
La Montaine, John
Laderman, Ezra

Láng, István
Lee, Thomas Oboe
Lees, Benjamin
Lo Presti, Ronald
Lorentzen, Bent
Lutosławski, Witold
Machover, Tod
Mackey, Steven
Magnuson, Phillip
Mailman, Martin
Malec, Ivo
Marco, Tomás
Marcus, Ada Belle
Martino, Donald
Márton, Eugen-Mihai
Mastrogiovanni, Antonio
Mathias, William
Matthews, Colin
Matthews, David
Maves, David W
Mayer, William
McCabe, John
McGuire, Edward
Meister, Scott R.
Meyer, Aubrey
Milburn, Ellsworth
Miroglio, Francis
Mors, Rudolf
Muldowney, Dominic
Neikrug, Marc
Nguyên, Thiên Đạo
Nordheim, Arne
Nørgård, Per
Orrego Salas, Juan
Panufnik, Andrzej
Parker, Alice
Pasquotti, Corrado
Penderecki, Krzysztof
Pépin, Clermont
Perle, George
Picker, Tobias
Pierson, Tom
Pura, William
Rabe, Folke
Rands, Bernard
Redel, Martin Christoph
Reich, Steve
Rodriguez, Robert Xavier
Roig-Francolí, Miguel A.
Rokeach, Martin
Roqué Alsina, Carlos
Rorem, Ned
Rotondi, Umberto
Sargon, Simon A
Schafer, R. Murray
Schiffman, Harold
Schuller, Gunther
Schwantner, Joseph C.
Schwartz, Elliott
Sculthorpe, Peter
Sedícias, Dímas Segundo
Sharkey, Jack
Shrude, Marilyn
Solbiati, Alessandro
Stark, Anthony
Stiles, Frank
Summer, Joseph
Suslin, Viktor
Szőllősy, András
Takano, Kicho
Tanenbaum, Elias
Taxin, Ira
Testoni, Giampaolo
Thayer, Fred
Threatte, Charles
Tjeknavorian, Loris
Tucker, Dan
Tutino, Marco
Vacchi, Fabio
Weidenaar, Reynold
Wilson, Mick
Wuorinen, Charles
Zaimont, Judith Lang
Ziffrin, Marilyn J.
Zimmermann, Walter
Zupko, Ramon
Zwilich, Ellen Taaffe

1986

Adams, John
Adler, Samuel
Albert, Stephen
Arcà, Paolo
Archer, Violet
Argento, Dominick
Atehortuá, Blas Emilio
Berkeley, Michael
Biggin, Tony
Biggs, John
Binkerd, Gordon
Bo, Sonia
Bond, Victoria
Bose, Hans-Jürgen von
Brief, Todd
Brizzi, Aldo
Bruce, Neely
Buhr, Glenn
Buller, John
Buren, John van
Bussotti, Sylvano
Butsch, John Austin
Carter, Elliott
Charpentier, Jacques
Cohan, John Alan
Cohen, Shimon
Coleman, Randolph
Colgrass, Michael
Cooper, Rose Marie
Cotel, Morris Moshe
Dan, Ikuma
Davies, Peter Maxwell
Dembski, Stephen
Diaconoff, Ted
Diamond, David
Dinescu, Violeta
Eaton, John
Erb, Donald
Ferneyhough, Brian
Flagello, Nicolas
Flynn, George
Friedman, Stan
Gaburo, Kenneth
Goehr, Alexander
Gonzalez, Luis Jorge
Gould, Morton
Grisey, Gérard
Halffter, Cristóbal
Harper, Edward
Harrison, Lou
Haubenstock-Ramati, Roman
Hazon, Roberto
Healey, Derek
Henze, Hans Werner
Hespos, Hans-Joachim
Holliger, Heinz
Holmboe, Vagn
Howard, Robert Charles
Hsu, Wen-ying
Huber, Nicolaus A.
Ichikawa, Toshiharu
Kandov, Alexander
Kirchner, Leon
Kolb, Barbara
Kramer, Jonathan D.

Landowski, Marcel
Lee, Thomas Oboe
Lees, Benjamin
Ligeti, György
Loevendie, Theo
Lorentzen, Bent
Luigi, Flora
Mailman, Martin
Manzoni, Giacomo
Maragno, Virtú
Martland, Steve
McDougall, Ian
McKinley, William Thomas
McNabb, Michael
Miereanu, Costin
Miroglio, Francis
Moerschel, Blanche
Musgrave, Thea
Nanes, Richard
Nichifor, Şerban
Nobre, Marlos
Nordheim, Arne
Nørgård, Per
Nyrimov, Tchary
Parmentier, F. Gordon
Parris, Robert
Pilon, Daniel
Poné, Gundaris
Powers, Anthony
Radulescu, Horatiu
Rattenbach, Augusto B.
Riesco, Carlos
Rihm, Wolfgang
Rogillio, Kathy J.
Roqué Alsina, Carlos
Rorem, Ned
Sarmientos, Jorge A.
Schipizky, Frederick
Schmidt, William
Schuller, Gunther
Scogna, Flavio E.
Shchedrin, Rodion Konstantinovich
Sheriff, Noam
Shinohara, Makoto
Søderlind, Ragnar
Stewart, Richard N.
Svoboda, Tomas
Szőllősy, András
Testoni, Giampaolo
Thoresen, Lasse
Thorne, Francis
Timofeyew, Adelina
Van Appledorn, Mary Jeanne
Van de Vate, Nancy
Whettam, Graham
Wittinger, Róbert
Xenakis, Iannis
Yun, Isang
Zaimont, Judith Lang
Zwilich, Ellen Taaffe

1987

Albert, Stephen
Alexander, Josef
Antoniou, Theodore
Babbitt, Milton
Barati, George
Bawden, Rupert
Bellucci, Giacomo
Biggs, John
Birtwistle, Harrison
Bryant, Curtis
Bush, Alan Dudley
Calabro, Louis
Callahan, James P.
Calo, Paolo Ferdinando
Carter, Elliott
Cooper, Rose Marie
Corigliano, John
Correggia, Enrico
Crivelli, Carlo
Eaton, John
Estévez, Milton
Faulconer, Bruce
Ferneyhough, Brian
Ferrero, Lorenzo
Foss, Lukas
Gellman, Steven
Gould, Morton
Gubaĭdulina, Sof͡ia Asgatovna
Halffter, Cristóbal
Hankinson, Ann S.
Harvey, Jonathan
Henze, Hans Werner
Husa, Karel
Imbrie, Andrew
Kagel, Mauricio
Keuris, Tristan
Khachaturi͡an, Karėn
Kievman, Carson
Killmayer, Wilhelm
Kinsey, Richard
Lachenmann, Helmut
Laderman, Ezra
Lauber, Anne
Lee, Thomas Oboe
Lieberson, Peter
Lloyd, George
Lorentzen, Bent
Manzoni, Giacomo
Marson, John
McDougall, Ian
McKinley, William Thomas
Meachem, Margaret
Mindel, Me'ir
Montori, Sergio
Nancarrow, Conlon
Nobre, Marlos
Nørgård, Per
Nuernberger, Louis Dean
Panufnik, Andrzej
Penderecki, Krzysztof
Pishny-Floyd, Monte Keene
Pollock, Robert
Poné, Gundaris
Pospíchal, Jiří
Pulido, Luis
Quate, Amy
Quilling, Howard
Radulescu, Horatiu
Reich, Steve
Reimann, Aribert
Rihm, Wolfgang
Rochberg, George
Sampaoli, Luciano
Sarmientos, Jorge A.
Schmidt-Binge, Walter
Schuller, Gunther
Schuman, William
Schurmann, Gerard
Schwantner, Joseph C.
Senator, Ronald
Soler, Josep
Spring, Glenn
Standford, Patric
Starer, Robert
Stockhausen, Karlheinz
Takemitsu, Tōru
Tomaro, Robert
Torke, Michael
Tower, Joan
Vogt, Hans
Wittinger, Róbert
Wuorinen, Charles

Xenakis, Iannis
Zimmermann, Heinz Werner
Zwilich, Ellen Taaffe

1988

Albert, Stephen
Allanbrook, Douglas
Andriessen, Louis
Armer, Elinor
Austin, Dorothea
Bacon, Ernst
Ballif, Claude
Baumgartner, Roland
Beadell, Robert
Bernstein, Charles Harold
Blaha, Joseph Leon
Blechinger, Alexander
Bolcom, William
Bussotti, Sylvano
Cassils, Craig
Chance, Nancy Laird
Charpentier De Castro, Eduardo
Chesne, Steven
Chiarappa, Richard
Colgrass, Michael
Cordero, Roque
Corghi, Azio
Davis, Anthony
DeGaetano, Robert
Dillon, James
Dinescu, Violeta
Downes, Andrew
Downey, John W.
Dreznin, Sergei
Druckman, Jacob
Dubrovay, László
Dutilleux, Henri
Ebenhöh, Horst
Ekizian, Michelle
Erb, Donald
Estévez, Milton
Ferneyhough, Brian
Fink, Myron
Foss, Lukas
Furman, James
Gellman, Steven
Gielen, Michael
Glass, Paul
Gorelli, Olga
Gubaĭdulina, Sof'i͡a Asgatovna
Guyard, Christophe
Harbison, John
Havelka, Svatopluk
He, Xuntian
Henze, Hans Werner
Hespos, Hans-Joachim
Husa, Karel
Imbrie, Andrew
Jin, Xiang
Kagel, Mauricio
Kernis, Aaron Jay
Keuris, Tristan
Killmayer, Wilhelm
Klein, Immanuel
Kraft, William
Krenek, Ernst
Kuerti, Anton
Kurtág, György
Laderman, Ezra
Lee, Thomas Oboe
Lees, Benjamin
Levinson, Gerald
Lieberson, Peter
Mâche, François Bernard
Mäder, Urban
Maksimović, Rajko
Marez Oyens, Tera de
Marischal, Louis
Martino, Donald
McKinley, William Thomas
Mihalič, Alexander
Musgrave, Thea
Nanes, Richard
Newell, Robert M.
Ohta, Tutsuya
Orrego Salas, Juan
Owen, Richard
Pernes, Thomas
Phillips, Harvey
Pierson, Tom
Pirula, Luka J.
Quate, Amy
Radovanović, Vladan
Radulescu, Horatiu
Rands, Bernard
Reimann, Aribert
Rochberg, George
Roosenschoon, Hans
Rosenzweig, Michael
Rossi, Mick
Sato, Kimi
Schnittke, Alfred
Schuller, Gunther
Sciortino, Edouard
Shapey, Ralph
Stevens, James
Stockhausen, Karlheinz
Takemitsu, Torū
Tippett, Michael
Tower, Joan
Tull, Fisher
Van de Vate, Nancy
Ware, Peter
Wernick, Richard
Willi, Herbert
Wilson, Thomas
Wittinger, Róbert
Wuorinen, Charles
Xenakis, Iannis
Xu, Shuya
Yuasa, Jōji
Zhu, Jianer
Zwilich, Ellen Taaffe

1989

Albert, Stephen
Ambrosi, Angela
Angius, Fulvio
Asch, Glenn
Asia, Daniel
Bailey, Keith McDonald
Ballif, Claude
Baratello, Marino
Berio, Luciano
Bernstein, Charles Harold
Blake, Christopher
Brief, Todd
Brizzi, Aldo
Buhr, Glenn
Carter, Elliott
Cassils, Craig
Castiglioni, Niccolo
Chance, Nancy Laird
Clarke, Rosemary
Coleman, Randolph
Colgrass, Michael
Cooper, Rose Marie
Copley, Evan
Corozine, Vince
Crouser, Jennifer Jean
Cummings, Robert
Davis, Anthony
Dembski, Stephen
Distler, Jed
Dubedout, Bertrand

Eaton, John
Ebenhöh, Horst
Eder, Helmut
Erb, Donald
Ėshpaĭ, Andreĭ I͡Akovlevich
Fanticini, Fabrizio
Flagello, Nicolas
Freund, Don
Gaburo, Kenneth
Galli, Hervé
Gates, Crawford
Gellman, Steven
Ghosn, Rita
Glass, Paul
Glick, Andrew J.
Gould, Morton
Grisey, Gérard
Halffter, Cristóbal
Harbison, John
Hartke, Stephen Paul
Haubenstock-Ramati, Roman
He, Xuntian
Henze, Hans Werner
Hétu, Jacques
Hölszky, Adriana
Holt, Simon
Hundemer, Thomas
Husa, Karel
Imbrie, Andrew
Jin, Xiang
Johnston, Ben
Kagel, Mauricio
Kaipainen, Jouni
Kechley, David
Kempf, Davorin
Kolb, Barbara
Kraft, William
Krenek, Ernst
Kupferman, Meyer
Kurtág, György
Laderman, Ezra
Lanza, Alcides
Levinson, Gerald
Levy, Marvin David
Lorentzen, Bent
Mannino, Franco
Marez Oyens, Tera de
Marischal, Louis
Martino, Donald
McKinley, William Thomas
McLeod, John
Morel, François
Musgrave, Thea
Nancarrow, Conlon
Newell, Robert M.
Nikiprowetzky, Tolia
Nordheim, Arne
Orbón, Julián
Osborne, Nigel
Ott, David
Owen, Jerry
Parris, Robert
Paulus, Stephen
Pinzón Urrea, Jesús
Quartieri, Leo
Radulescu, Horatiu
Rajna, Thomas
Ran, Shulamit
Rands, Bernard
Reed, Alfred
Reich, Steve
Rendón G., Guillermo
Rihm, Wolfgang
Rochberg, George
Rouse, Christopher
Ruders, Poul
Saariaho, Kaija
Sapieyevski, Jerzy
Sartor, David P.
Saul, Walter
Schnittke, Alfred
Schuller, Gunther
Schwantner, Joseph C.
Shapey, Ralph
Sheriff, Noam
Smith, G. Wiley
Stagnitta, Frank
Stevens, James
Stockhausen, Karlheinz
Stucky, Steven
Sullivan, Timothy
Sulzberger, Hermann
Takemitsu, Tōru
Tan, Dun
Tavener, John
Tosar Errecart, Héctor A.
Tower, Joan
Trigg, Ted
Tull, Fisher
Ung, Chinary
Valverde, Gabriel
Van de Vate, Nancy
Varotsis, Constantinos
Walden, Stanley
Walker, George
Weber, Margaret A.
Wernick, Richard
Whitlow, Charles G.
Wilson, Thomas
Wittinger, Róbert
Wuorinen, Charles
Zhu, Jianer
Zonn, Paul Martin
Zwilich, Ellen Taaffe

1990

Albert, Stephen
Armer, Elinor
Artemov, V.
Asia, Daniel
Bach, Jan
Balakauskas, Osvaldas
Ballif, Claude
Blake, Christopher
Brief, Todd
Brizzi, Aldo
Bussotti, Sylvano
Caggiano, Felice
Charloff, Aaron
Child, Peter
Chou, Wên-chung
Clayton, Laura
Cooper, Rose Marie
Cotel, Morris Moshe
Cresswell, Lyell
Curran, Alvin S.
Danielpour, Richard
Davis, Anthony
Davis, William Mac
Dembski, Stephen
Dench, Chris
Dillon, James
Doherty, Sue
Donatoni, Franco
Ekizian, Michelle
Elias, Brian
Eötvös, Peter
Ermirio, Federico
Eyerly, Scott
Fanticini, Fabrizio
Ferneyhough, Brian
Foss, Lukas
Franzén, Olov
Glinsky, Albert
Goode, Daniel
Gorelli, Olga
Gubaĭdulina, Sof'i͡a Asgatovna

Guinjoan, Joan
Haines, Margaret E.
Hanson, Geoffrey
Harrison, Lou
Henze, Hans Werner
Hespos, Hans-Joachim
Hétu, Jacques
Hody, Jean
Holab, William
Holewa, Hans
Höller, York
Holsinger, David R.
Hosokawa, Toshio
Hundemer, Thomas
Jones, Robert W.
Kaczynski, Adam
Kernis, Aaron Jay
Kinsella, John
Kirchner, Leon
Kohler, Leonard R.
Kraft, William
Kramer, Jonathan D.
Krouse, Ian
Kuerti, Anton
Kurtág, György
Lachenmann, Helmut
Laderman, Ezra
Langenhuysen, Niko
Lauricella, Massimo
Lauricella, Sergio
Lerdahl, Fred
Letelier Llona, Alfonso
Lieberson, Peter
Liu, Changyuan
Lloyd, Jonathan
Lombardi, Luca
Lorge, John S.
Magnanensi, Giorgio
Mailman, Martin
Makris, Andreas
Manzoni, Giacomo
Marcus, Ada Belle
McCabe, John
McKinley, William Thomas
Melby, John
Mindel, Me'ir
Mitchell, Lee
Mobberley, James
Morel, François
Mueller, Robert
Neuhoff, Judy Austin
Nobre, Marlos
Nordheim, Arne
Orbón, Julián
Ortega, Sergio
Pärt, Arvo
Pierson, Tom
Pisati, Maurizio
Pishny-Floyd, Monte Keene
Rands, Bernard
Rekašius, A.
Rihm, Wolfgang
Rimmer, John
Rodriguez, Robert Xavier
Rorem, Ned
Routh, Francis
Schuller, Gunther
Schuman, William
Schwantner, Joseph C.
Seltzer, Dov
Senator, Ronald
Senju, Akira
Shapey, Ralph
Sheng, Bright
Stockhausen, Karlheinz
Stucky, Steven
Subotnick, Morton
Suderburg, Robert
Szőllősy, András
Takemitsu, Tōru
Tan, Dun
Taub, Bruce J.
Tavener, John
Tower, Joan
Tsontakis, George
Tull, Fisher
Urbaitis, Mindaugas
Van de Vate, Nancy
Wallach, Joelle
Wheeler, Scott
Willi, Herbert
Wilson, Thomas
Wittinger, Róbert
Wuorinen, Charles
Zeidman, Eyal
Zhu, Jianer
Zorzi, Juan Carlos
Zwilich, Ellen Taaffe

1991

Albert, Stephen
Albright, William
Arrigo, Girolamo
Asia, Daniel
Baker, Claude
Bank, Jacques
Bianchi, Frederick W.
Blake, Christopher
Blum, Yaakov
Boer, Ed de
Bolcom, William
Bond, Victoria
Brief, Todd
Broadstock, Brenton
Callaway, Ann
Camps, Pompeyo
Carter, Elliott
Charloff, Aaron
Clausen, René
Colgrass, Michael
Cooper, Paul
Corghi, Azio
Corigliano, John
Cotel, Morris Moshe
Danielpour, Richard
Davidovsky, Mario
Davye, John J.
De Sutter, Rudy
Del Tredici, David
Deutsch, Herbert A.
Dick, Robert
Diemer, Emma Lou
Donatoni, Franco
Downey, John W.
Einem, Gottfried von
Ekizian, Michelle
Elias, Brian
Erb, Donald
Eröd, Iván
Ferneyhough, Brian
Gamberini, Leopoldo
Glass, Paul
Goode, Daniel
Grantham, Donald
Grisey, Gérard
Halffter, Cristóbal
Hall, Juliana
Hallberg, Bengt
Hannay, Roger
Harbison, John
He, Xuntian
Heller, Duane
Henze, Hans Werner
Hirt, James A.
Holloway, Robin
Huang, Tian
Husa, Karel

Iannaccone, Anthony
Jacobs, Kenneth Allan
Kapsomenos, Dimitris
Kassyanik, Uri
Kernis, Aaron Jay
Keuris, Tristan
Kohler, Leonard R.
Korndorf, N.
Kuehl, William F.
Laderman, Ezra
Lanford, John Carrol
Lazarof, Henri
Lee, Thomas Oboe
Levinson, Gerald
Lewis, Robert Hall
Luedeke, Raymond
Maksimović, Rajko
Man, Roderik de
Manzoni, Giacomo
Marcus, Bunita
Martino, Donald
Maw, Nicholas
Maxwell, Michael
McKinley, William Thomas
Miller, Donald Bruce
Nanes, Richard
Nelson, Paul
Nobre, Marlos
Nordheim, Arne
Nørgård, Per
Obst, Michael
Oliverio, James
O'Neill, Paul
Panufnik, Andrzej
Parmentier, F. Gordon
Payne, Anthony
Pinzón Urrea, Jesús
Platz, Robert H. P.
Poné, Gundaris
Powell, Mel
Premru, Raymond Eugene
Pstrokońska-Nawratil, Grażyna
Pursell, William
Rakowski, David
Ran, Shulamit
Rattenbach, Augusto B.
Reise, Jay
Reynolds, Roger
Rihm, Wolfgang
Riley, Terry
Rochberg, George
Roosenschoon, Hans
Rorem, Ned
Rouse, Christopher
Ruders, Poul
Schafer, R. Murray
Scherr, Hans-Jörg
Schickele, Peter
Schnittke, Alfred
Schuller, Gunther
Schwantner, Joseph C.
Scott, Stephen
Shchedrin, Rodion Konstantinovich
Sheng, Bright
Sicilianos, Yorgos
Skrzypczak, Bettina
Spyratos, Panos
Staar, René
Starer, Robert
Stockhausen, Karlheinz
Stucky, Steven
Sur, Donald
Svoboda, Tomas
Takemitsu, Tōru
Taub, Bruce J.
Tavener, John
Thomas, Augusta Read
Thorne, Francis
Tippett, Michael
Ul'i͡anich, Viktor
Urbanner, Erich
Vacchi, Fabio
Warshauer, Maxine M.
Weir, Judith
Wolman, Amnon
Wuorinen, Charles
Xing, Liu
Yu, Julian
Yuasa, Jōji
Zeidman, Eyal
Zwilich, Ellen Taaffe

1992

Albert, Stephen
Andriessen, Louis
Artemov, Vi͡acheslar
Asia, Daniel
Baiocchi, Regina A. Harris
Balada, Leonardo
Barnes, Milton
Bauman, Jon W.
Beaser, Robert
Bell, Elizabeth
Bernstein, Charles Harold
Bianchi Alarcon, Vicente
Blake, Christopher
Blechinger, Alexander
Bond, Victoria
Bose, Hans-Jürgen von
Boudreau, Walter
Breznikar, Joseph
Brief, Todd
Broadstock, Brenton
Cacioppo, Curt
Cecconi, Monic
Cerha, Friedrich
Challulau, Tristan Patrice
Colgrass, Michael
Conyngham, Barry
Cox, Alan
Danielpour, Richard
Davies, Peter Maxwell
Dawson, Sarah
Deak, John
Dench, Chris
Downes, Andrew
Drew, James
Druckman, Jacob
Du, Mingxin
Dutton, Brent
Edwards, Ross
Ekizian, Michelle
Esbrí, Alejandro
Faulconer, Bruce
Forsyth, Malcolm
Gagneux, Renaud
García, Orlando Jacinto
Gentile, Ada
Gerber, Steven R.
Gillingham, David
Gordon, Jerold James
Górecki, Henryk Mikołaj
Greenberg, Robert M.
Grisey, Gérard
Gruber, Heinz Karl
Guy, Barry
Haigh, Howard
Harbison, John
Hartke, Stephen Paul
Hobbs, Allen
Hodkinson, Sydney
Hoffmann, Tom
Höller, York
Holloway, Robin
Horvath, Josef Maria
Husa, Karel
Ivey, Jean Eichelberger

Jacobs, Lawrence A.
Jin, Xiang
Kechley, David
Kernis, Aaron Jay
Kittelsen, Guttorm
Kreutz, Robert
Kulenty, Hanna
Laderman, Ezra
Lee, Thomas Oboe
Lewis, Robert Hall
Lewkovitch, Bernhard
Li, Heping
Liebermann, Lowell
Lindberg, Magnus
Loevendie, Theo
Lorentzen, Bent
Lysight, Michel
MacMillan, James
Mailman, Martin
Man, Roderik de
Manookian, Jeff
Maros, Miklós
Martino, Donald
Martins, Maria de Lourdes
Mathias, William
Maw, Nicholas
McKelvey, Lori
McKinley, William Thomas
Mercurio, Steven
Nanes, Richard
Nielson, Kenneth
Nordheim, Arne
Nørgård, Per
Oliverio, James
Ortega, Sergio
Ott, David
Parella, Marc
Patterson, Andy J.
Penderecki, Krzysztof
Perle, George
Picker, Tobias
Pott, Francis
Primosch, James
Prudencio, Cergio
Rands, Bernard
Rapchak, Lawrence
Ratiu, Horia
Reimann, Aribert
Reynolds, Roger
Rihm, Wolfgang
Roosenschoon, Hans
Rorem, Ned
Rose, Griffith
Rouse, Christopher
Saariaho, Kaija
Saxton, Robert
Schuller, Gunther
Schurmann, Gerard
Sculthorpe, Peter
Senju, Akira
Shaffer, Sherwood
Shapey, Ralph
Sheng, Bright
Shinohara, Makoto
Sidel'nikov, Nikolaĭ Nikolaevich
Sierra, Roberto
Singleton, Alvin
Sirota, Eric B.
Strahan, Derek
Stucky, Steven
Takemitsu, Tōru
Taub, Bruce J.
Tcherepnin, Ivan
Thomas, Augusta Read
Tippett, Michael
Vajda, János
Vaughn, Jonathan Roderick
Vine, Carl
Waignein, André
Wallach, Joelle
Warren, Betsy
Welcher, Dan
Wernick, Richard
Westbrook, Mike
Wheeler, Scott
Whettam, Graham
Williamson, Malcolm
Wilson, Curtis W.
Winther, Jens
Wood, Hugh
Wuorinen, Charles
Young, La Monte
Yu, Julian
Zaidel-Rudolph, Jeanne
Zorzi, Juan Carlos
Zwilich, Ellen Taaffe

1993

Albright, William
Ancarola, Francesca
Antoniou, Theodore
Asia, Daniel
Bach, Jan
Bassett, Leslie
Bentoiu, Pascal
Berio, Luciano
Bimstein, Phillip Kent
Bjerno, Erling D.
Blackwood, Easley
Blaha, Joseph Leon
Bo, Sonia
Bolcom, William
Brant, Henry
Brief, Todd
Broadstock, Brenton
Buller, John
Burrs, Leslie Savoy
Butt, James
Cacioppo, Curt
Carter, Elliott
Clay, Carleton
Coates, Gloria
Cohen, Howard A.
Colgrass, Michael
Constant, Marius
Corghi, Azio
Dalbavie, Marc-André
Danielpour, Richard
Davis, Anthony
Deutsch, Herbert A.
DiDomenica, Robert
Dijk, Rudi Martinus van
Downes, Andrew
Druckman, Jacob
Eaton, John
Ekizian, Michelle
Erb, Donald
Escot, Pozzi
Foss, Lukas
Funk, Eric
Fussell, Charles
Gerber, Steven R.
Gomez, Alice
Gonzalez, Luis Jorge
Gordon, Jerold James
Greenbaum, Matthew
Guy, Barry
Halffter, Cristóbal
Hamilton, Iain
Hammerth, Johan
Harrison, Charles A.
Haubenstock-Ramati, Roman
Holloway, Robin
Hölszky, Adriana
Horvath-Thomas, Istvan
Hundemer, Thomas
Husa, Karel

Jager, Robert E.
Kagel, Mauricio
Kaminski, Stephen
Kanding, Ejnar
Kechley, David
Kernis, Aaron Jay
Keuris, Tristan
Kimmel, Corliss
Kirchner, Leon
Klatzow, Peter
Kolb, Barbara
Kopytman, Mark Ruvimovich
Laderman, Ezra
Lauricella, Massimo
Lazarof, Henri
Lee, Thomas Oboe
Lees, Benjamin
Lendvay, Kamilló
Leprai, Andrea
Levines, Thomas Allen
Levinson, Gerald
Lewkovitch, Bernhard
Licata, Charles
Liebermann, Lowell
Lieberson, Peter
Light, Patricia Parsons
Liptak, David
Loevendie, Theo
Lombardi, Luca
Lorentzen, Bent
Lowe, Wesley Hoyle
Maayani, Ami
Machover, Tod
MacMillan, James
Mailman, Martin
Malipiero, Riccardo
Mason, Benedict
Maw, Nicholas
McKinley, William Thomas
Meachem, Margaret
Metcalf, John
Miranda, Ronaldo
Montori, Sergio
Newson, George
Nobre, Marlos
Nocerino, Francesco
Owen, Jerry
Palermo, Vincenzo
Peterson, Wayne
Rakowski, David
Rands, Bernard
Reimann, Aribert
Reynolds, Roger
Riesco, Carlos
Rihm, Wolfgang
Roosenschoon, Hans
Rorem, Ned
Rose, Griffith
Rouse, Christopher
Ruders, Poul
Sallinen, Aulis
Saxton, Robert
Schnebel, Dieter
Schonthal, Ruth
Schuller, Gunther
Sciarrino, Salvatore
Sheng, Bright
Simonacci, Giancarlo
Sims, Ezra
Skrzypczak, Bettina
Smalley, Denis
Snopek, Sigmund
Stark, Anthony
Svoboda, Tomas
Takemitsu, Tōru
Tal, Josef
Tan, Dun
Tanenbaum, Elias
Tarp, Svend Erik
Taub, Bruce J.
Temmingh, Roelof
Thome, Diane
Valdambrini, Francesco
Van Appledorn, Mary Jeanne
Van de Vate, Nancy
Vir, Param
Wangerin, Mark
Weddington, Maurice
Weed, Kevin
Wild, Earl
Wilkins, Margaret Lucy
Willi, Herbert
Wuorinen, Charles
Wygant, Shawn
Zhuo, Rui-Shi
Zorzi, Juan Carlos
Zwilich, Ellen Taaffe

1994

Adams, John
Aĭzenshtadt, A. M.
Andersson, Magnus F.
Andriessen, Louis
Antunes, Jorge
Asia, Daniel
Atehortúa, Blas Emilio
Baiocchi, Regina A. Harris
Bajoras, Feliksas Romualdas
Baker, Claude
Balada, Leonardo
Ballard, Louis W.
Barnes, Milton
Bellisario, Angelo
Bello, Joakin
Berio, Luciano
Bibalo, Antonio
Blechinger, Alexander
Brant, Henry
Brief, Todd
Carnota, Raul
Cerha, Friedrich
Chaĭkovskiĭ, Aleksandr
Challulau, Tristan Patrice
Chambers, Wendy Mae
Chandler, Stephan
Chasalow, Eric
Chernishev, Igor
Clay, Carleton
Colgrass, Michael
Corghi, Azio
Cox, Alan
Curtis-Smith, Curtis
Danielpour, Richard
Dapelo, Riccardo
Davidovsky, Mario
Davis, Anthony
Downes, Andrew
Drew, James
Englund, Einar
Erb, Donald
Ėshpaĭ, Andreĭ I͡Akovlevich
Festinger, Richard
Flynn, George
Foss, Lukas
Funk, Eric
Gabeli, Katia
Gates, Crawford
Gerber, Steven R.
Glass, Philip
Glickman, Sylvia
Globokar, Vinko
Górecki, Henryk Mikołaj
Gould, Morton
Gubaĭdulina, Sofʹi͡a Asgatovna
Guy, Barry
Halffter, Cristóbal
Harbison, John

Harvey, Jonathan
Helms, Marjan
Hendricks, W. Newell
Höller, York
Holt, Simon
Huang, Joan
Iannaccone, Anthony
Ichikawa, Toshiharu
Ivey, Jean Eichelberger
Jones, Samuel
Kalmanoff, Martin
Kechley, David
Kernis, Aaron Jay
Kingman, Daniel
Kirchner, Leon
Kirchner, Volker David
Koo, Chat-Po
Koprowski, Peter Paul
Kraft, William
Krivit͡skiĭ, David Isaakovich
Laderman, Ezra
Lanza, Alcides
Lee, Ilse-Mari
Lennon, John Anthony
Leviev, Milcho
Liebermann, Lowell
Lieberson, Peter
Lim, Liza
Louie, Alexina
Lu, Pei
Machuel, Thierry
MacMillan, James
Mailman, Martin
Makris, Andreas
Manzoni, Giacomo
Matthews, Colin
Maw, Nicholas
McCarthy, Daniel William
McDougall, Ian
McKinley, William Thomas
Melillo, Stephen
Menin, Geoffrey
Mirenzi, Franco Antonio
Mirzoev, Elmir
Morleo, Luigi
Müller-Siemens, Detlev
Nelson, Ron
Newson, George
Nicholson, George
Paccione, Paul
Parać, Frano
Perle, George
Peterson, Wayne
Pishny-Floyd, Monte Keene
Polifrone, Jon
Premru, Raymond Eugene
Ptaszyńska, Marta
Ran, Shulamit
Rands, Bernard
Ranjbaran, Behzad
Reale, Paul
Reich, Steve
Reynolds, Roger
Rhodes, Phillip
Rihm, Wolfgang
Rodriguez, Robert Xavier
Rorem, Ned
Rouse, Christopher
Ruders, Poul
Sahbaï, Iradj
Sallinen, Aulis
Sanina, Nina
Schuller, Gunther
Scott, David R.
Shahidi, Tolib
Sheinfeld, David
Shenderov, Anatoliĭ
Sheng, Bright
Shinohara, Makoto
Sierra, Roberto
Singleton, Alvin
Sohal, Naresh
Spratlan, Lewis
Stern, Max
Strahan, Derek
Subotnick, Morton
Takemitsu, Tōru
Tan, Dun
Tavener, John
Thomas, Augusta Read
Thomas, Michael Tilson
Ticheli, Frank
Tremblay, Gilles
Tsontakis, George
Ulʹ͡ianich, Viktor
Vacchi, Fabio
Vera, Santiago
Viñao, Alejandro
Wagner, Melinda
Wegren, Thomas J.
Weisgall, Hugo
Welcher, Dan
Wiggins, Christopher
Willi, Herbert
Winther, Jens
Wood, Hugh
Woods, Mike
Wuorinen, Charles
Yannatos, James
Zwilich, Ellen Taaffe

1995

Adams, John
Arnold, Malcolm
Asia, Daniel
Baksa, Andreas
Batik, Roland
Beerman, Burton
Berio, Luciano
Bernstein, Charles Harold
Bird, Hubert
Bon, André
Carter, Elliott
Cerha, Friedrich
Charloff, Aaron
Chen, Yi
Correggia, Enrico
Curtis-Smith, Curtis
Cyr, Gordon
Danielpour, Richard
Davis, Anthony
Dillon, James
Downes, Andrew
Druckman, Jacob
Dubrovay, László
Duckworth, William
Eaton, John
Ekizian, Michelle
Erb, Donald
Escot, Pozzi
Ėshpaĭ, Andreĭ Ī͡Akovlevich
Falik, Ī͡Uriĭ Aleksandrovich
Felder, David
Fennelly, Brian
Finsterer, Mary
Foss, Lukas
García, Orlando Jacinto
Gerber, Steven R.
Gould, Morton
Guy, Barry
Halffter, Cristóbal
Harbison, John
He, Xuntian
Hennig, Michael
Hirabe, Yayoi
Ivey, Jean Eichelberger
Jirásek, Jan

Jong, Hans de
Kelemen, Milko
Kernis, Aaron Jay
Keulen, Geert van
Keuris, Tristan
Kirchner, Leon
Kirchner, Volker David
Kocsák, Tibor
Kolb, Barbara
Koprowski, Peter Paul
Kramer, Jonathan D.
Kulesha, Gary
Laderman, Ezra
Lake, Tim
Lauricella, Massimo
Lazarof, Henri
León, Tania
Levitch, Leon
Lewkovitch, Bernhard
Lieberson, Peter
Lindberg, Magnus
Lombardi, Luca
Lorentzen, Bent
Ludtke, William G.
Mâche, François Bernard
MacKinnon-Andrew, Niki
Macmillan, Scott
Mamlok, Ursula
Matthus, Siegfried
McKinley, William Thomas
Melby, John
Nakagawa, Norio
Nyman, Michael
Pärt, Arvo
Paulus, Stephen
Polansky, Larry
Rackley, Lawrence
Ran, Shulamit
Rands, Bernard
Ranjbaran, Behzad
Rapchak, Lawrence
Reimann, Aribert
Reynolds, Roger
Rihm, Wolfgang
Rimkevicius, Gediminas
Rouse, Christopher
Ruders, Poul
Schnebel, Dieter
Schuller, Gunther
Shatin, Judith
Sheinfeld, David
Sheng, Bright
Shih
Skrzypczak, Bettina
Sommer, Silvia
Steinke, Greg A.
Tan, Dun
Tashjian, Charmian
Tavener, John
Thorne, Francis
Tsontakis, George
Van de Vate, Nancy
Várkonyi, Mátyás
Viñao, Alejandro
Wagner, Heribert
Wagner, Wolfram
Welcher, Dan
Whettam, Graham
Willi, Herbert
Winteregg, Steven
Winther, Jens
Wolking, Henry
Wuorinen, Charles
Wyner, Yehudi
Zaimont, Judith Lang
Zhou, Long
Zhu, Jianer
Zhuo, Rui-Shi
Zinkus, Giedrius
Zwilich, Ellen Taaffe

1996

Albright, William
Agudelo, Graciela
Aguila, Miguel del
Androsch, Peter
Anichini, Antonio
Armer, Elinor
Asia, Daniel
Bainbridge, Simon
Baker, Claude
Beamish, Sally
Berio, Luciano
Berkeley, Michael
Bingham, Judith
Blockeel, Dirk
Bolcom, William
Bond, Victoria
Brant, Henry
Bröder, Alois
Brody, Jeffrey
Cacioppo, Curt
Caltabiano, Ronald
Canepa, Louise P.
Cantón, Edgardo
Carter, Elliott
Challulau, Tristan Patrice
Chen, Yi
Coenen, Carl
Coleman, Linda Robbins
Colgrass, Michael
Cordero, Roque
Corghi, Azio
Cotel, Morris Moshe
Curtis-Smith, Curtis
Cyr, Gordon
Danielpour, Richard
Davis, Anthony
Decker, Pamela
Dobrowolny, Miro
Donatoni, Franco
Downes, Andrew
Druckman, Jacob
Ekizian, Michelle
Escobar, Roberto
Fedele, Ivan
Firsova, Elena
Fišer, Luboš
Fleischer, Tsippi
Floyd, Carlisle
Freidlin, Jan
Funk, Eric
García, Orlando Jacinto
Gerber, Steven R.
Globokar, Vinko
Goleminov, Marin
Gould, Morton
Greenberg, Robert M.
Greenleaf, Robert B.
Gustafson, Dwight
Hanuš, Jan
Heinrichs, William
Höller, York
Holsinger, David R.
Hutcheson, Jere T.
Jenkins, Joseph Willcox
Jones, Samuel
Kasteelen, Ilse van de
Kechley, David
Keig, Betty
Kelemen, Milko
Kernis, Aaron Jay
Keuris, Tristan
Kievman, Carson
Kirchner, Leon
Koch, Frederick
Kolb, Barbara

Koprowski, Peter Paul
Krivit͡skiĭ, David Isaakovich
Kuerti, Anton
La Montaine, John
Laderman, Ezra
Lang, David
Lanza, Alcides
Lee, Thomas Oboe
Leek, Stephen
Lees, Benjamin
LeFanu, Nicola
Leprai, Andrea
Levinson, Gerald
Levitch, Leon
Lewis, Peter Scott
Lewkovitch, Bernhard
Lieberson, Peter
Loevendie, Theo
Lombardi, Luca
Lu, Pei
Ludwig, Thomas
Luengen, Ramona Maria
Mackey, Steven
MacMillan, James
Manchado, Marisa
Mandanici, Marcella
Matthews, Colin
Maw, Nicholas
McCabe, John
Meijering, Chiel
Meyer, Krzysztof
Müller-Siemens, Detlev
Nicholson, George
Nyman, Michael
Oak, Kil-Sung
Orlandi, Amedeo
Pärt, Arvo
Pavlov, Filip
Permont, Haim
Peterson, Wayne
Radulescu, Horatiu
Rands, Bernard
Reich, Steve
Reynolds, Roger
Rihm, Wolfgang
Ritchie, Anthony
Rodriguez, Robert Xavier
Rohlig, Harald
Rollin, Robert
Rorem, Ned
Rouse, Christopher
Ruders, Poul
Scearce, J. Mark
Schnebel, Dieter
Schuller, Gunther
Schwantner, Joseph C.
Schwendinger, Laura
Shchedrin, Rodion Konstantinovich
Sheng, Bright
Sierra, Roberto
Silver, Sheila
Singleton, Alvin
Situ, Gang
Slavický, Milan
Smirnov, Dmitriĭ
Soenen, Willy
Soong, Fu Yuan
Soto Millán, Eduardo
SpaenC, Bo
Strouse, Charles
Stucky, Steven
Svoboda, Tomas
Tan, Dun
Tavener, John
Taylor, Rowan S.
Tcherepnin, Ivan
Thomas, Augusta Read
Thome, Diane
Tsontakis, George
Vasks, Pēteris
Vermeersch, Hans
Viñao, Alejandro
Viñao, Ezequiel
Visser, Dick
Walker, George
Wallmann, Johannes
Welcher, Dan
Wen, Loong-Hsing
Wernick, Richard
Wiernik, Adam
Wild, Earl
Willi, Herbert
Wolking, Henry
Wuorinen, Charles
Yu, Julian
Zaimont, Judith Lang
Zhou, Long
Zhu, Jianer

1997

Adès, Thomas
Adler, Samuel
Aĭzenshtadt, A. M.
Albright, William
Antunes, Jorge
Argento, Dominick
Aviram, Eilon
Bach, Jan
Bainbridge, Simon
Bajoras, Feliksas Romualdas
Balada, Leonardo
Bank, Jacques
Battistelli, Giorgio
Bauer, Ross
Beerman, Burton
Bjerno, Erling D.
Blumenfeld, Harold
Bolcom, William
Bradić, Srećko
Brouwer, Margaret
Carlson, David
Carter, Elliott
Cerha, Friedrich
Challulau, Tristan Patrice
Chambers, Wendy Mae
Chen, Yi
Child, Peter
Childs, William
Cleary, David
Cogan, Robert
Coleman, Linda Robbins
Colgrass, Michael
Corghi, Azio
Curtis-Smith, Curtis
Dănceanu, Liviu
Danielpour, Richard
Davis, Anthony
Downes, Andrew
Downey, John W.
Drummond, Dean
Dzubay, David
Eaton, John
Eben, Petr
Escot, Pozzi
Ėshpaĭ, Andreĭ I͡Akovlevich
Feld, Jindřich
Felder, David
Flammer, Ernst Helmuth
Foison, Tristan
Freund, Don
Friedman, Stan
Furrer, Beat
Gerber, Steven R.
Gomez, Alice
Grisey, Gérard
Grové, Stefans
Guy, Barry

Haas, Georg Friedrich
Henshall, Dalwyn
Hillborg, Anders
Ho, Fred Wei-han
Holloway, Robin
Hopkins, James
Hush, David
Isopp, Werner
Jaffe, Stephen
Jarrell, Michael
Kagel, Mauricio
Karmanov, Pavel
Kaulkin, Michael
Kelemen, Milko
Kernis, Aaron Jay
Kirchner, Leon
Knussen, Oliver
Koc, Marcelo
Koch, Frederick
Kolb, Barbara
Koprowski, Peter Paul
Kox, Hans
Laderman, Ezra
Larsen, Libby
Lauricella, Massimo
Lavista, Mario
Lees, Benjamin
Levowitz, Adam B.
Liebermann, Lowell
Lieberson, Peter
Lindberg, Magnus
Liptak, David
Locklair, Dan
Loevendie, Theo
Luo, Jing Jing
Maazel, Lorin
Mackey, Steven
Manzoni, Giacomo
Marek, Josef
Matthys, Marc
McAllister, Scott
McKinley, William Thomas
Monk, Meredith
Musgrave, Thea
Nanes, Richard
Norbet, Gregory
Nørgård, Per
Núñez Montes, Francisco
Nytch, Jeffrey
Olivero, Betty
Ortíz, Gabriela
Paulus, Stephen
Pennisi, Francesco
Peterson, Wayne
Picker, Tobias
Radulescu, Horatiu
Rajna, Thomas
Randalls, Jeremy S.
Rands, Bernard
Ratiu, Horia
Reich, Steve
Reimann, Aribert
Reynolds, Roger
Rihm, Wolfgang
Rodriguez, Robert Xavier
Rorem, Ned
Rouse, Christopher
Rubens, Jo
Ruders, Poul
Sacco, Peter
Scearce, J. Mark
Schickele, Peter
Schuller, Gunther
Schurmann, Gerard
Schwantner, Joseph C.
Schwartz, Elliott
Sclater, James
Sheng, Bright
Singleton, Alvin
Situ, Gang
Skrowaczewski, Stanisław
Slavický, Milan
Snell, David
Snopek, Sigmund
Stark, Anthony
Stevenson, Ronald
Stock, David
Stroppa, Marco
Stucky, Steven
Svoboda, Milan
Tan, Dun
Tavener, John
Thomas, Augusta Read
Thorne, Francis
Tippett, Michael
Torke, Michael
Trigos, Juan
Trinkley, Bruce
Tsontakis, George
Tuserkani, Djahan
Vacchi, Fabio
Vanaver, Bill
Verhaalen, Marion
Veteška, Lubomír
Viera, Julio M.
Vores, Andy
Wagner, Wolfram
Wallace, Stewart
Wallach, Joelle
Ward, David
Ward, Robert
Weisgall, Hugo
Westendorf, Lynette
Wheeler, Scott
Willi, Herbert
Wilson, Richard
Winstin, Robert Ian
Winther, Jens
Wittinger, Róbert
Wolpe, Michael
Wuorinen, Charles
Yannatos, James
Zhu, Jianer
Zwilich, Ellen Taaffe

1998

Abbado, Marcello
Adams, John Luther
Adès, Thomas
Adler, James
Albright, William
Amram, David
Andriessen, Louis
Anichini, Antonio
Argento, Dominick
Asia, Daniel
Barab, Seymour
Barrett, Richard
Bartholomée, Pierre
Benzecry, Esteban
Berger, Jonathan
Berio, Luciano
Bernstein, Seymour
Blake, Christopher
Blauvelt, Peter
Blumenfeld, Harold
Bradić, Srećko
Brant, Henry
Brizzi, Aldo
Brody, Jeffrey
Burghardt, Benedikt
Burrell, Diana
Cacioppo, Curt
Carter, Elliott
Cerha, Friedrich
Chalaev, Shirvani
Charloff, Aaron

Chen, Yi
Childs, William
Cleary, David
Colgrass, Michael
Constant, Marius
Corghi, Azio
Correggia, Enrico
Crumb, George
Danielpour, Richard
Davis, Anthony
Derfler, Carl
Di Vittorio, Salvatore
Donatoni, Franco
Downes, Andrew
Dubrovay, László
Eben, Petr
Eliasson, Anders
Felder, David
Forsyth, Malcolm
Foss, Lukas
Frank, Lawrence E.
Friedman, David
Gabay Vigil, Marcos
Gandy, G. Patrick
Gardner, Maurice
Gerber, Steven R.
Glickman, Sylvia
Glise, Anthony
Grisey, Gérard
Gruhn, Oliver
Gubaĭdulina, Sof'i͡a Asgatovna
Guy, Barry
Haflidi, Hallgrimsson
Halffter, Cristóbal
Holland, Anthony G.
Höller, York
Hove, Luc van
Hus, Walter
Hush, David
Hutcheson, Jere T.
Igoa, Enrique
Ince, Kamran
Joseph, David
Kagel, Mauricio
Kelemen, Milko
Kernis, Aaron Jay
Kessner, Daniel
Killmayer, Wilhelm
Kirchner, Leon
Kirchner, Volker David
Ko, Fang-Long
Kopelent, Marek
Krajči, Mirko
Krček, Jaroslav
Krouse, Ian
Kuerti, Anton
Kupferman, Meyer
Lauermann, Herbert
Lendvay, Kamilló
León, Tania
Lesemann, Frederick
Liebermann, Lowell
Lieberson, Peter
Lindberg, Magnus
Lloyd, George
Locklair, Dan
Ludtke, William G.
Lukáš, Zdeněk
MacMillan, James
Malec, Ivo
Manzoni, Giacomo
Mařík, Anthony, F.
Marshall, Ingram
Martino, Donald
Matějka, Ladislav
Matthews, Colin
McCauley, Robert
Meijering, Chiel
Mérész, Ignác
Meyer, Krzysztof
Misurell-Mitchell, Janice
Montague, Stephen
Müller-Siemens, Detlev
Mumford, Jeffrey
Musgrave, Thea
Nanes, Richard
Nobre, Marlos
Nordheim, Arne
Oak, Kil-Sung
Ofenbauer, Christian
Ogilvy, Susan
Pérez, Juan Carlos
Peterson, Wayne
Pinzón Urrea, Jesús
Pott, Francis
Proto, Frank
Ptaszyńska, Marta
Ran, Shulamit
Rands, Bernard
Rasgado, Víctor
Reale, Paul
Reich, Steve
Reimann, Aribert
Reynolds, Roger
Rihm, Wolfgang
Rochberg, George
Rosenman, Leonard
Rouse, Christopher
Ruders, Poul
Saariaho, Kaija
Saĭdaminova, Dilorom
Sallinen, Aulis
Salonen, Esa-Pekka
Sawer, David
Schat, Peter
Schuller, Gunther
Schwantner, Joseph C.
Schwertsik, Kurt
Scott, Stephen
Serebrier, José
Shenderov, A.
Sheng, Bright
Sica, Salvatore
Sierra, Roberto
Singleton, Alvin
Smith, Gregg
Stanley, Bryan
Stewart, Richard N.
Stock, David
Svoboda, Tomas
Tan, Dun
Thomas, Augusta Read
Tsontakis, George
Van Appledorn, Mary Jeanne
Vasks, Pēteris
Vieru, Anatol
Viñao, Alejandro
Viñao, Ezequiel
Vine, Carl
Volans, Kevin
Vores, Andy
Wagner, Wolfram
Walker, George
Weir, Judith
Welcher, Dan
Wernick, Richard
Wesley-Smith, Martin
Whettam, Graham
Williams, Zika
Winteregg, Steven
Wittinger, Róbert
Wuorinen, Charles
Wyner, Yehudi
Yannatos, James
Yu, Julian
Zhu, Jianer

2000

Adès, Thomas
Adler, Samuel

Agudelo, Graciela
Antoniou, Theodore
Antunes, Jorge
Applebaum, Edward
Argersinger, Charles
Asia, Daniel
Badian, Maya
Baldissera, Marino
Barnett, Carol
Bauer, Ross
Beall, John
Beck, Jeremy
Bolcom, William
Bon, André
Boykan, Martin
Brady, Tim
Brant, Henry
Breznikar, Joseph
Brisman, Heskel
Brody, Jeffrey
Buelow, W. L.
Bulow, Harry
Bussotti, Sylvano
Cacioppo, Curt
Carter, Elliott
Cerha, Friedrich
Challulau, Tristan Patrice
Chambers, Wendy Mae
Chen, Yi
Chin, Unsuk
Chung, Sundo
Cleary, David
Coleman, Linda Robbins
Colgrass, Michael
Dalbavie, Marc-André
D'Alessio, Greg
Danielpour, Richard
Davidson, Tina
Davis, Anthony
Del Tredici, David
Dillon, James
Dillon, Lawrence
Downes, Andrew
Dubrovay, László
Eaton, John
Ekizian, Michelle
Elias, Brian
Erb, Donald
Ėshpaĭ, Andreĭ I͡Akovlevich
Falik, I͡Uriĭ Aleksandrovich
Ferneyhough, Brian
Fields, Matthew H.
Fleischer, Tsippi
Foss, Lukas
Fouad, Ashraf
Frazelle, Kenneth
Funicelli, Stanley A.
Gaslini, Giorgio
Gerber, Steven R.
Gillingham, David
Glise, Anthony
Golijov, Osvaldo
Gubaĭdulina, Sof'i͡a Asgatovna
Guy, Barry
Gwiazda, Henry
Haas, Georg Friedrich
Hatzis, Christos
Herrmann, Peter
Holloway, Robin
Holt, Simon
Hoover, Katherine
Hosokawa, Toshio
Hummel, Bertold
Hus, Walter
Ince, Kamran
Jarrett, Jack M.
Johnson, Tom
Joseph, David
Kang, Sukhi
Käser, Mischa
Kechley, David
Kelemen, Milko
Kernis, Aaron Jay
Kirchner, Leon
Koc, Marcelo
Koch, Frederick
Krieger, Edino
Kupferman, Meyer
Laderman, Ezra
Lang, David
LaPoint, Crystal
Larsen, Libby
Lasoń, Aleksander
Lateef, Yusef
Lazarof, Henri
Leef, Yinam
Lees, Benjamin
Levinson, Gerald
Levy, Marvin David
Liebermann, Lowell
Lieberson, Peter
Lindberg, Magnus
Lloyd, Jonathan
Lombardo, Robert
López, José Manuel
Lorentzen, Bent
Luby, Timothy
Mackey, Steven
MacMillan, James
Mahelona, Herbert
Malec, Ivo
Marcel, Luc
Mařík, Anthony, F.
Marshall, Ingram
Martino, Donald
McCauley, Robert
McKinley, William Thomas
McMichael, Catherine
McPhee, Jonathan
Mobberley, James
Moerk, Alice A.
Mollicone, Henry
Monk, Meredith
Mumford, Jeffrey
Musgrave, Thea
Nanes, Richard
Nobre, Marlos
Nørgård, Per
Norman, Andrew
Ortega, Sergio
Pärt, Arvo
Paulus, Stephen
Pintscher, Matthias
Potes, César Iván
Powers, Daniel
Previn, André
Primosch, James
Proctor, Simon
Proto, Frank
Radulescu, Horatiu
Rakowski, David
Rands, Bernard
Ranjbaran, Behzad
Rautavaara, Einojuhani
Reich, Steve
Reise, Jay
Reynolds, Roger
Rihm, Wolfgang
Robbins, Scott
Rochberg, George
Rodriguez, Robert Xavier
Rohlig, Harald
Rorem, Ned
Rosenblum, Mathew
Rostomyan, Stepan
Roth, Alec
Rouse, Christopher
Rouse, Mikel
Rovics, Howard
Roxburgh, Edwin
Ruders, Poul
Saĭdaminova, Dilorom

Salonen, Esa-Pekka
Sánchez Navarro, Alejandro
Sandresky, Margaret Vardell
Sargon, Simon A
Scearce, J. Mark
Schwantner, Joseph C.
Schwendinger, Laura
Seltzer, Dov
Sharman, Rodney
Shchedrin, Rodion Konstantinovich
Sheinfeld, David
Sheng, Bright
Singleton, Alvin
Skrowaczewski, Stanisław
Sohal, Naresh
Stockhausen, Karlheinz
Subotnick, Morton
Swayne, Giles
Taub, Bruce J.
Thomas, Augusta Read
Ticheli, Frank
Torke, Michael
Trajković, Vlastimir
Trojahn, Manfred
Tsontakis, George
Turnage, Mark-Anthony
Viana, Hélio Bacelar
Volans, Kevin
Vriend, Jan
Wagner, Melinda
Wallmann, Johannes
Weir, Judith
Westergaard, Peter
Whettam, Graham
Whiffin, Lawrence
Wilson, Richard
Winther, Jens
Wittinger, Róbert
Wood, Hugh
Wright, George
Wuorinen, Charles
Yttrehus, Rolv
Zaimont, Judith Lang
Zhu, Jianer
Zhuo, Rui-Shi
Zwilich, Ellen Taaffe

2001

Aaronson, Peter
Adams, John Luther
Adler, Samuel
Aigmüller, Andreas
Aitken, Hugh
Allanbrook, Douglas
Andriessen, Louis
Antoniou, Theodore
Antunes, Jorge
Arad, Atar
Auerbach, Lera
Austin, Elizabeth R.
Avni, Tzvi
Bajoras, Feliksas Romualdas
Barrett, Richard
Barroso, Sergio
Beamish, Sally
Beaser, Robert
Beck, Jeremy
Berio, Luciano
Berkeley, Michael
Biggs, John
Biriotti, León
Bischof, Rainer
Blauvelt, Peter
Bodorová, Sylvie
Bolle, James
Bond, Victoria
Boulez, Pierre
Bryant, Curtis
Burghardt, Daryl
Burrs, Leslie Savoy
Buss, Howard J.
Caltabiano, Ronald
Capanna, Robert
Carter, Elliott
Charloff, Aaron
Chihara, Paul
Childs, William
Cleary, David
Cohen, Shimon
Cohn, James
Curtis-Smith, Curtis
Czarnecki, Sławomir Stanisław
Dalbavie, Marc-André
Deane, Raymond
Del Tredici, David
Dillon, Lawrence
Drummond, Dean
Eaton, John
Ekizian, Michelle
Erić, Zoran
Escot, Pozzi
Farago, Pierre
Feldmann, Francine Greshler
Ferko, Frank
Fink, Myron
Foss, Lukas
Gerber, Steven R.
Godfrey, Daniel
Gruber, Heinz Karl
Gubaĭdulina, Sof′i͡a Asgatovna
Guy, Barry
Guyot, Vincent
Hakim, Naji
Halffter, Cristóbal
Hanks, N. Lincoln
Harbison, John
Harvey, Jonathan
Hatzis, Christos
Herrmann, Peter
Heucke, Stefan
Hodkinson, Sydney
Holloway, Robin
Hopkins, James
Ikramova, A.
Johnson, Tom
Kaplan, Amelia S.
Karchin, Louis
Kelemen, Milko
Kernis, Aaron Jay
Kirchner, Leon
Kritz, Robert
Kupferman, Meyer
Laderman, Ezra
Lees, Benjamin
Lenchantín, Ana Lía
León, Tania
Lewis, Clovice A.
Lewis, Peter Scott
Liebermann, Lowell
Lieberson, Peter
Lin, Minyi
Lindberg, Magnus
Locklair, Dan
Loevendie, Theo
Machover, Tod
Mackey, Steven
MacMillan, James
Manoury, Philippe
Maroney, Denman
Martino, Donald
Mason, Charles Norman
McCarthy, Daniel William
McKinley, William Thomas
Moerk, Alice A.
Nanes, Richard
Nečasová, Jindra
Neikrug, Marc

Nordheim, Arne
Páll P. Pálsson
Pärt, Arvo
Paulus, Stephen
Peel, John
Perle, George
Pishny-Floyd, Monte Keene
Pott, Francis
Primosch, James
Proctor, Simon
Pstrokońska-Nawratil, Grażyna
Radovanović, Vladan
Rajna, Thomas
Raminsh, Imant
Rands, Bernard
Ranjbaran, Behzad
Reich, Steve
Reise, Jay
Reynolds, Roger
Rihm, Wolfgang
Rodriguez, Robert Xavier
Rokeach, Martin
Rorem, Ned
Rosenblum, Mathew
Rouse, Christopher
Saariaho, Kaija
Saĭdaminova, Dilorom
Scearce, J. Mark
Schickele, Peter
Schuller, Gunther
Schwantner, Joseph C.
Shapey, Ralph
Sheng, Bright
Situ, Gang
Small, Haskell
Soenen, Willy
Stamatelos, Katerina
Staron, Michael
Stimpson, Michael
Stroppa, Marco
Stucky, Steven
Talma-Sutt, Michał
Tanenbaum, Elias
Taylor, Rowan S.
Theofanidis, Chris
Thomas, Augusta Read
Thorne, Francis
Torke, Michael
Toussaint, Eugenio
Tsontakis, George
Urbanner, Erich
Vasks, Pēteris
Viñao, Alejandro
Viñao, Ezequiel
Wallace, Stewart
Weir, Judith
Welcher, Dan
Willi, Herbert
Wilson, Olly
Wilson, Richard
Winteregg, Steven
Wuorinen, Charles
Zhu, Jianer

2002

Adler, Samuel
Aho, Kalevi
Aĭzenshtadt, A. M.
Anderson, Beth
Antunes, Jorge
Asia, Daniel
Austin, Elizabeth R.
Bank, Jacques
Barsom, Paul
Bassett, Leslie
Bauer, Ross
Baur, John
Beamish, Sally
Beaser, Robert
Beckel, Jim
Bell, Larry
Biggs, Hayes
Biggs, John
Blank, William
Blauvelt, Peter
Borkowski, Marian
Brant, Henry
Broadstock, Brenton
Bruce, Neely
Bukowski, Mirosław
Capister, Loris
Carter, Elliott
Catán, Daniel
Chen, Yi
Chou, Wen-Chung
Clearfield, Andrea
Cleary, David
Coelho de Souza, Rodolfo Nogueira
Cunningham, Karen
Curtis-Smith, Curtis
Czernowin, Chaya
Dalbavie, Marc-André
Danielpour, Richard
Dayer, Xavier
Dean, Brett
Del Tredici, David
Deussen, Nancy Bloomer
Deutsch, Bernd Richard
Diamond, David
Dillon, James
Dillon, Lawrence
Dobbins, Lori
Dolden, Paul
Dzubay, David
Eder, Helmut
Elias, Brian
Eliasson, Anders
Eötvös, Peter
Errázuriz, Sebastián
Escot, Pozzi
Felder, David
Floyd, Carlisle
Freedman, Harry
Furrer, Beat
Gamstorp, Göran
Garton, Graham
Gerber, Steven R.
Giannotti, Stefano
Gillingham, David
Glise, Anthony
Ġlonti, P'elik's
Golijov, Osvaldo
Grové, Stefans
Gubaĭdulina, Sof'i͡a Asgatovna
Guy, Barry
Gyulai-Gaál, János
Haas, Georg Friedrich
Haflidi, Hallgrimsson
Hakim, Naji
Hannah, Ronald
Harbison, John
Heggie, Jake
Hellawell, Piers
Herrmann, Peter
Hertig, Godi.
Higdon, Jennifer
Hill, William R.
Holland, Anthony G.
Holloway, Robin
Holt, Simon
Hosokawa, Toshio
Hyla, Lee
Iannaccone, Anthony
Jaffe, Stephen
Jeney, Zoltán
Kagel, Mauricio
Kaplan, Aaron

Karchin, Louis
Karnecki, Zbigniew
Kechley, David
Kernis, Aaron Jay
Kessner, Daniel
Kilstofte, Mark
Kirchner, Leon
Kittelsen, Guttorm
Korneitchouk, Igor
Kramer, Jonathan D.
Laderman, Ezra
Laitman, Lori
Lazarof, Henri
LeBaron, Anne
Lee, Thomas Oboe
Lees, Benjamin
Lentz, Georges
Levinson, Gerald
Liebermann, Lowell
Lieberson, Peter
Lindberg, Magnus
Liptak, David
Liu, Changyuan
Lombardi, Luca
Lopez, George
Macculi, David
Mackey, Steven
Maggio, Robert
Mařík, Anthony F.
Martín, Jorge
Matthews, Colin
McFatter, Larry
McKinley, William Thomas
Meij, Johan de
Mobberley, James
Mostel, Raphael
Murray, Diedre
Neuwirth, Olga
Newson, George
Oak, Kil-Sung
Parmentier, F. Gordon
Penhorwood, Edwin
Permont, Haim
Peterson, Wayne
Petrosyan, Aram
Pintscher, Matthias
Previn, André
Primosch, James
Proto, Frank
Qin, Daping
Raaff, Robin de
Radzynski, Jan
Rakowski, David
Ranjbaran, Behzad
Rautavaara, Einojuhani
Reich, Steve
Reynolds, Roger
Ricketts, Ted
Rickli, Fritz
Rihm, Wolfgang
Rodriguez, Robert Xavier
Rorem, Ned
Rosenzweig, Morris
Rouse, Christopher
Rozbicki, Kazimierz
Ruders, Poul
Rulon, C. Bryan
Saariaho, Kaija
Saĭdaminova, Dilorom
Scearce, J. Mark
Schickele, Peter
Schnyder, Daniel
Schuller, Gunther
Schwendinger, Laura
Serei, Zsolt
Sheng, Bright
Sierra, Roberto
Situ, Gang
Skrowaczewski, Stanisław
Skrzypczak, Bettina
Small, Haskell
Staar, René
Stewart, Richard N.
Stucky, Steven
Tassone, Pasquale
Tavener, John
Thomas, Augusta Read
Torke, Michael
Turnage, Mark-Anthony
Van Appledorn, Mary Jeanne
Voronina, Tat′i͡ana
Wagner, Melinda
Waignein, André
Wallace, William
Wallach, Joelle
Weir, Judith
Wernick, Richard
Whettam, Graham
Wilkins, Margaret Lucy
Wood, Jeffrey
Woolf, Randall
Wuorinen, Charles
Yang, Yong
Yim, Jay Alan
Yttrehus, Rolv
Zaimont, Judith Lang
Zhou, Long
Zhu, Jianer
Zorn, John
Zwilich, Ellen Taaffe

2003

Adamo, Mark
Albert, Thomas
Arad, Atar
Auerbach, Lera
Bach, Jan
Bajoras, Feliksas Romualdas
Balada, Leonardo
Barrett, Richard
Beamish, Sally
Bell, Elizabeth
Bingham, Judith
Biscarini, Marco
Blackford, Richard
Bolcom, William
Börtz, Daniel
Botti, Susan
Brophy, Gerard
Brouwer, Margaret
Butterley, Nigel
Carter, Elliott
Cerha, Friedrich
Chasalow, Eric
Chen, Yi
Chin, Unsuk
Collier, Graham
Crumb, David
Curtis-Smith, Curtis
Danielpour, Richard
Daugherty, Michael
Dawson, Sarah
Dean, Brett
Del Tredici, David
Demos, Nick
Denev, Ljubomir
Dillon, Lawrence
Dran, Tatiana Grecic
Dubrovay, László
Eberhard, Dennis
Escot, Pozzi
Estrada, Julio
Felciano, Richard
Ferreyra, Beatriz
Foss, Lukas
García, Orlando Jacinto
Gerber, Steven R.

Gerulewicz, Gerardo Américo
Grové, Stefans
Guy, Barry
Hagen, Daron
Harbison, John
Harman, Chris Paul
Harmon, John
Harrison, Lou
Hartke, Stephen Paul
Hatzis, Christos
Henze, Hans Werner
Holland, Anthony G.
Howrani, Waleed
Kechley, David
Kimper, Paula M.
Kirchner, Leon
Kiszko, Martin
Knight, Edward
Koc, Marcelo
Kohler, Leonard R.
Komarova, Tatiana
Kyburz, Hanspeter
Laderman, Ezra
Lang, David
Lee, Thomas Oboe
Lewis, Peter Scott
Licata, Charles
Liebermann, Lowell
Lieberson, Peter
Lim, Liza
Locklair, Dan
Mackey, Steven
MacMillan, James
Man, Roderik de
Manookian, Jeff
Marshall, Ingram
Matějů, Zbyněk
McCarthy, Daniel William
McKinley, William Thomas
McLeod, John
Mérész, Ignác
Mettraux, Laurent
Miranda, Ronaldo
Misurell-Mitchell, Janice
Moerk, Alice A.
Mostel, Raphael
Mundry, Isabel
Pärt, Arvo
Peel, John
Plog, Anthony
Previn, André
Primosch, James
Raboy, Asher
Rajna, Thomas
Rands, Bernard
Ranjbaran, Behzad
Rautavaara, Einojuhani
Reimann, Aribert
Reiter, Herwig
Rihm, Wolfgang
Rindfleisch, Andrew
Rodriguez, Robert Xavier
Rouse, Christopher
Saariaho, Kaija
Sawer, David
Schwartz, Elliott
Shattenkirk, Ray
Shchedrin, Rodion Konstantinovich
Sheng, Bright
Silver, Sheila
Skrowaczewski, Stanisław
Small, Haskell
Stokes, Harvey J.
Svoboda, Tomas
Swerts, Piet
Tavener, John
Teodorescu-Ciocănea, Livia
Thomas, Augusta Read
Ticheli, Frank
Tiensuu, Jukka
Toews, Theodore
Toledo, Josefino
Torke, Michael
Trigos, Juan
Tsontakis, George
Turnage, Mark-Anthony
Uzor, Charles
Vriend, Jan
Walker, George
Wang, Peng Jia
Wang, Xilin
Weir, Judith
Wheeler, Kenny
Wheeler, Scott
Whettam, Graham
Willi, Herbert
Wilson, Ian
Wilson, Richard
Wong, Jeffrey
Wood, Hugh
Wright, Maurice
Yttrehus, Rolv
Zaimont, Judith Lang
Zhang, Zhao
Zhuo, Rui-Shi
Zwilich, Ellen Taaffe

2004

Abrams, Arthur
Adamo, Mark
Aikman, James
Aitken, Hugh
Alvear, Maria de
Amram, David
Asia, Daniel
Baltakas, Vykintas
Barry, Gerald
Beamish, Sally
Bermel, Derek
Borzova, Alla
Bradić, Srećko
Brant, Henry
Butler, Martin
Bužarovski, Dimitrije
Cacioppo, Curt
Causton, Richard
Cavanna, Bernard
Charloff, Aaron
Chin, Unsuk
Clarke, James
Cleary, David
Cogan, Robert
Cohen, Allen
Colgrass, Michael
Cotton, Jeffery
Crumb, George
Curtis-Smith, Curtis
Danielpour, Richard
Davies, Peter Maxwell
De Rossi Re, Fabrizio
Del Tredici, David
Dosaj, Dev
Dzubay, David
Eaton, John
Escot, Pozzi
Faiman, Jonathan
Feld, Jindřich
Ferber, Sharon
Ferko, Frank
Foley, John B.
Foss, Lukas
Funk, Eric
Gerber, Steven R.
Godfrey, Daniel
Golijov, Osvaldo
Grantham, Donald
Guy, Barry
Haflidi, Hallgrimsson
Harbison, John

Herrmann, Peter
Higdon, Jennifer
Hofmeyr, Hendrik
Holland, Anthony G.
Hoover, Jeffrey
Kagel, Mauricio
Katz, Darrell
Kechley, David
Kiurkchiĭski, Krasimir
Knapik, Eugeniusz
Knussen, Oliver
Kohoutek, Ctirad
Kritz, Robert
Kubo, Mayako
Laderman, Ezra
Lee, Ilse-Mari
Lees, Benjamin
Lentz, Daniel
León, Tania
Liderman, Jorge
Liebermann, Lowell
Lieberson, Peter
Locklair, Dan
Lombardo, Robert
Lorentzen, Bent
Louie, Alexina
Mabry, James F.
Machover, Tod
Mackey, Steven
Manookian, Jeff
Manzoni, Giacomo
Matthews, Colin
McTee, Cindy
Mostel, Raphael
Naidoo, Shaun
Nielsen, Erik
Nishimura, Akira
Norden, Maarten van
Nordheim, Arne
Nyman, Michael
Palmer, John
Perle, George
Pigovat, B.
Pishny-Floyd, Monte Keene
Popp, William
Poulsen, James Viggo
Prater, Jeffrey
Previn, André
Primosch, James
Proto, Frank
Radulescu, Horatiu
Rakowski, David
Raminsh, Imant
Ranjbaran, Behzad
Reimann, Aribert
Rodriguez, Robert Xavier
Rohde, Kurt
Rosenhaus, Steve
Ross, Robert A. M.
Rouse, Christopher
Sacco, Steven Christopher
Saĭdaminova, Dilorom
Satoh, Somei
Scearce, J. Mark
Schiavone, John
Schuller, Gunther
Sharman, Rodney
Shenderov, Anatoliĭ
Sheng, Bright
Shields, Alice
Siegel, Stephen
Sierra, Roberto
Singleton, Alvin
Sleeper, Thomas M.
Small, Haskell
Sotelo, Mauricio
Stallcop, Glenn
Staud, Johannes Maria
Stern, David
Stimpson, Michael
Stock, David
Strouse, Charles
Syler, James
Tabakov, Emil
Tavener, John
Thomas, Andrew
Thomas, Augusta Read
Trinkley, Bruce
Tsontakis, George
Turrin, Joseph
Vayo, David
Vera, Santiago
Wallach, Joelle
Whettam, Graham
Wilhour, Brian E.
Willi, Herbert
Witt, Greg
Wuorinen, Charles
Yang, Yong
Yttrehus, Rolv
Zaimont, Judith Lang
Zwilich, Ellen Taaffe

2005

Anderson, Julian
Andriessen, Louis
Austin, Elizabeth R.
Azevedo, Sérgio
Babcock, David
Bäcker, Horst-Hans
Bartholomée, Pierre
Beall, John
Beamish, Sally
Benjamin, George
Beveridge, Thomas
Biggs, John
Bond, Victoria
Bonneau, Paul G.
Bouliane, Denys
Boyce, Cary
Brauns, Martins
Bresnick, Martin
Bruce, Neely
Burghardt, Benedikt
Carpenter, Gary
Carrabré, Thomas P.
Carter, Elliott
Cerha, Friedrich
Chasalow, Eric
Chen, Qigang
Chen, Yi
Clay, Carleton
Coble, William
Colgrass, Michael
Correggia, Enrico
Cotton, Jeffery
Cowie, Edward
Crumb, George
Cumming, Richard
Curran, Alvin S.
Custer, Beth
Dal Porto, Mark
Dalbavie, Marc-André
Damnianovitch, Alexandre
Danielpour, Richard
Dean, Brett
Dick, Robert
Dong, Kui
Dorman, Avner
Downes, Andrew
Eaton, John
Escot, Pozzi
Estacio, John
Fikejz, Daniel
Foss, Lukas
Francesconi, Luca
Frazelle, Kenneth
Gerber, Steven R.
Gołembiowski, Jarosław
Gondai, Atsuhiko

Grové, Stefans
Gruber, Heinz Karl
Gubaĭdulina, Sofi͡a Asgatovna
Guy, Barry
Haas, Georg Friedrich
Haflidi, Hallgrimsson
Hakola, Kimmo
Harbison, John
Hartke, Stephen Paul
Harvey, Jonathan
Henze, Hans Werner
Herrmann, Peter
Hersch, Michael Nathaniel
Higdon, Jennifer
Hosokawa, Toshio
Hyla, Lee
Jaffe, Stephen
Kagel, Mauricio
Kanding, Ejnar
Kazandzhiev, Vasil
Kechley, David
Kiefer, John
Kirchner, Leon
Kraft, William
Krček, Jaroslav
Kulenty, Hanna
Kyr, Robert
Laderman, Ezra
Lauten, Elodie
Lee, Thomas Oboe
Levinson, Gerald
Lieberson, Peter
Lohr, Tom L.
Longtin, Michel
Looten, Christophe
Lu, Pei
Mackey, Steven
MacMillan, James
Mantovani, Bruno
Marvin, John
McKinley, William Thomas
Middleton, Owen
Milburn, Ellsworth
Minchev, Georgi
Mumford, Jeffrey
Neuwirth, Olga
Newsome, Padma
Nørgård, Per
Núñez Montes, Francisco
Olivero, Betty
Ortíz, Gabriela
Parmentier, F. Gordon
Pärt, Arvo
Pécou, Thierry
Pigovat, B.
Plate, Anton
Potes, Alba Lucia
Previn, André
Primosch, James
Proto, Frank
Psathas, John
Quell, Michael
Rands, Bernard
Rasgado, Víctor
Reale, Paul
Reich, Steve
Rihm, Wolfgang
Riley, Terry
Rimmer, John
Rorem, Ned
Rosenhaus, Steve
Ruders, Poul
Sansar, Sangidorj
Schöllhorn, Johannes
Schroeter, Guilherme
Schwendinger, Laura
Sharp, Elliott
Sheng, Bright
Sichel, John
Sierra, Roberto
Sohal, Naresh
Sung, Stella
Svoboda, Tomas
Syswerda, Todd Elton
Taggart, Mark Alan
Tavener, John
Thomas, Augusta Read
Thorne, Francis
Traversi, Francesco
Tsontakis, George
Van de Vate, Nancy
Viñao, Ezequiel
Violette, Andrew
Vir, Param
Vriend, Jan
Waters, Joseph
Weir, Judith
Welcher, Dan
Wernick, Richard
Wilson, Curtis W.
Wuorinen, Charles
Yannatos, James
Yuasa, Jōji
Zaidel-Rudolph, Jeanne
Zaimont, Judith Lang
Zohn-Muldoon, Ricardo
Zwilich, Ellen Taaffe

Index

Numbers following each entry are catalog entry numbers used in the main body of this catalog. Names appear in the index in their official, authorized form, which may differ slightly from those in the catalog entry. Names of composers found alphabetically in the main body of the catalog are excluded from this index.

About the Authors

Julia Graepel is technical services librarian at the International University Bremen in Bremen, Germany. Prior to this position, she was assistant director of the Dwight Anderson Music Library at the University of Louisville in Louisville, Kentucky. Graepel holds a B.M.Ed. from Morehead State University in Morehead, Kentucky, an M.M. in flute performance from the University of Louisville, Louisville, Kentucky, and an M.L.S. with an emphasis in music librarianship from the University at Buffalo, the State University of New York in Buffalo, New York.

Karen Little is director of the Dwight Anderson Music Library at the University of Louisville in Louisville, Kentucky. Previous positions include assistant director of the Anderson Music Library and assistant music librarian at the University of Virginia in Charlottesville, Virginia. Little holds a B.A. in music and mathematics from Oberlin College–Conservatory of Music, Oberlin, Ohio, and an M.A. in music history and literature and an M.L.S. with an emphasis in music librarianship, both from Indiana University. Previous publications include *Frank Bridge: A Bio-bibliography* and *NOTES: An Index to Volumes 1–50.*